P9-DGL-977

◄ 96TH ANNUAL EDITION ►

WRITER'S MARKET

2017

Robert Lee Brewer, Editor

WRITER'S DIGEST
BOOKS

WritersDigest.com
Cincinnati, Ohio

Writer's Market 2017. Copyright © 2016 F + W Media, Inc. Published by Writer's Digest Books, an imprint of F+W Media, Inc., 10151 Carver Road, Suite 200, Blue Ash, Ohio 45242. Printed and bound in the United States of America.

Publisher: Phil Sexton

Writer's Market website: www.writersmarket.com
Writer's Digest website: www.writersdigest.com

Distributed in Canada by Fraser Direct
100 Armstrong Avenue
Georgetown, Ontario, Canada L7G 5S4
Tel: (905) 877-4411

Distributed in the U.K. and Europe by F&W Media International
Brunel House, Newton Abbot, Devon, TQ12 4PU, England
Tel: (+44) 1626-323200, Fax: (+44) 1626-323319
E-mail: postmaster@davidandcharles.co.uk

Library of Congress Catalog Number 31-20772
ISSN: 0084-2729
ISBN-13: 978-1-44034-773-3
ISBN-13: 978-1-44034-774-0 (Writer's Market Deluxe Edition)
ISBN-10: 1-44034-773-5
ISBN-10: 1-44034-774-3 (Writer's Market Deluxe Edition)

Attention Booksellers: This is an annual directory of F + W Media, Inc. Return deadline for this edition is December 31, 2017.

Edited by: Robert Lee Brewer
Designed by: Alexis Estoye
Production coordinated by: Debbie Thomas

CONTENTS

TRADE JOURNALS 628

FROM
THE EDITOR

What's the most important secret to freelance success? That's the question I ask myself each year as I assign articles for *Writer's Market*, and I've found that the answer can't be pinned down to one quality or trait. Each successful writer cuts their own path to success.

For some writers, it might be an effective approach to queries, which is why this book includes the article "Write Better Queries and Sell More Articles." For other writers, their success flows through owning the conference experience: See "Tips for a Great Conference Experience."

Still other writers know "How to Develop an Effective Author Brand" or find success with "Promotions, PR, and Publicity." Heck, some writers are super at "Connecting With Book Clubs."

At the end of the day, I know we're here to provide options, instruction, and inspiration for you to follow a path that has worked for another writer or to cut your own. Read all the articles, use the listings, and start making success happen for you.

Also, be sure to take advantage of a specially recorded webinar for *Writer's Market* readers. Learn more at www.writersmarket.com/wm17-webinar.

Until next we meet, keep writing and marketing what you write.

Robert Lee Brewer
Senior Content Editor
Writer's Market and WritersMarket.com

http://writersdigest.com/editor-blogs/poetic-asides
http://blog.writersmarket.com
http://twitter.com/robertleebrewer

HOW TO USE WRITER'S MARKET

///

Writer's Market is here to help you decide where and how to submit your writing to appropriate markets. Each listing contains information about the editorial focus of the market, how it prefers material to be submitted, payment information, and other helpful tips.

WHAT'S INSIDE?

Since 1921, *Writer's Market* has been giving you the information you need to knowledgeably approach a market. We've continued to develop improvements to help you access that information more efficiently.

NAVIGATIONAL TOOLS. We've designed the pages of *Writer's Market* with you, the writer, in mind. Within the pages you will find **readable market listings** and **accessible charts and graphs**. One such chart can be found in the ever-popular "How Much Should I Charge?" article.

We've taken all of the updated information in this feature and put it into an easy-to-read-and-navigate chart, making it convenient for you to find the rates that accompany the freelance jobs you're seeking.

ICONS. There are a variety of icons that appear before each listing. A complete Key to Icons & Abbreviations appears on the right. Icons let you know whether a book publisher accepts only agented writers (**Ⓐ**), comparative pay rates for a magazine (**$-$$$$**), and more.

CONTACT NAMES, ROYALTY RATES AND ADVANCES. In every section, we identify key contact people with the boldface word **Contact** to help you get your manuscript to the right person.

EDITORS, PAY RATES, ROYALTIES, ADVANCES, AND PERCENTAGE OF MATERIAL WRITTEN BY FREELANCE WRITERS. For Book Publishers, royalty rates and advances are highlighted in boldface, as is other important information on the percentage of first-time writers and unagented writers the company publishes, the number of books published, and the number of manuscripts received each year. In the Consumer Magazines and Trade Journals sections, we identify the amount (percentage) of material accepted from freelance writers, and the pay rates for features, columns and departments, and fillers in boldface to help you quickly identify the information you need to know when considering whether to submit your work.

QUERY FORMATS. We asked editors how they prefer to receive queries and have indicated in the listings whether they prefer them by mail, e-mail, fax or phone. Be sure to check an editor's individual preference before sending your query.

ARTICLES. Writers who want to improve their submission techniques should read the articles in the **Finding Work** section. The **Managing Work** section is geared more toward post-acceptance topics, such as contract negotiation, organization, and self-promotion.

IF THIS BOOK IS NEW TO YOU . . .

Look at the **Contents** pages to familiarize you with the arrangement of *Writer's Market*. The three largest sections of the book are the market listings of Book Publishers; Consumer Magazines; and Trade Journals. You will also find other sections of market listings for Literary Agents and Contests & Awards. More opportunities can be found on the WritersMarket.com website.

KEY TO ICONS & ABBREVIATIONS

(A)	market accepts agented submissions only
(⊘)	market does not accept unsolicited submissions
(⌖)	Canadian market
(🌐)	market located outside of the U.S. and Canada
($)	market pays 0-9¢/word or $0-$150/article
($$)	market pays 10-49¢/word or $151-$750/article
($$$)	market pays 50-99¢/word or $751-$1,500/article
($$$$)	market pays $1/word or over $1,500/article
(💬)	comment from the editor of Writer's Market
(🔑)	tips to break into a specific market
MS, MSS	manuscript(s)
B&W	black & white (photo)
SASE	self-addressed, stamped envelope
SAE	self-addressed envelope
IRC	International Reply Coupon, for use when mailing to countries other than your own

3

IMPORTANT LISTING INFORMATION

1. Listings are based on editorial questionnaires and interviews. They are not advertisements; publishers do not pay for their listings. The markets are not endorsed by *Writer's Market* editors. Writer's Digest Books and its employees go to great effort to ascertain the validity of information in this book. However, transactions between users of the information and individuals and/or companies are strictly between those parties.

2. All listings have been verified before publication of this book. If a listing has not changed from last year, then the editor said the market's needs have not changed and the previous listing continues to accurately reflect its policies.

3. *Writer's Market* reserves the right to exclude any listing.

4. When looking for a specific market, check the index. A market may not be listed for one of these reasons:
   - It doesn't solicit freelance material.
   - It doesn't pay for material.
   - It has gone out of business.
   - It has failed to verify or update its listing for this edition.
   - It hasn't answered *Writer's Market* inquiries satisfactorily.

Narrowing your search

After you've identified the market categories that interest you, you can begin researching specific markets within each section.

Consumer Magazines and Trade Journals are categorized by subject within their respective sections to make it easier for you to identify markets for your work.

There is a subject index available for Book Publishers in the back of the book. It is broken into fiction and nonfiction categories and subcategories.

Contests & Awards are categorized by genre of writing. If you want to find journalism contests, you would search the Journalism category; if you have an unpublished novel, check the Fiction category.

Interpreting the markets

Once you've identified companies or publications that cover the subjects in which you're interested, you can begin evaluating specific listings to pinpoint the markets most receptive to your work and most beneficial to you.

In evaluating individual listings, check the location of the company, the types of material it is interested in seeing, submission requirements, and rights and payment policies. Depending on your personal concerns, any of these items could be a deciding factor as you determine which markets you plan to approach. Many listings also include a reporting time.

Whenever possible, obtain submission guidelines before submitting material. You can usually obtain guidelines by sending a SASE to the address in the listing or by checking online. Many of the listings contain instructions on how to obtain sample copies, catalogs or market lists. The more research you do upfront, the better your chances of acceptance, publication and payment.

BEFORE YOUR FIRST SALE

Everything in life has to start somewhere and that somewhere is always at the beginning. Stephen King, Stephenie Meyer, Jeff Kinney, Nora Roberts—they all had to start at the beginning. It would be great to say becoming a writer is as easy as waving a magic wand over your manuscript and "Poof!" you're published, but that's not how it happens. While there's no one true "key" to becoming successful, a long, well-paid writing career *can* happen when you combine four elements:

- Good writing
- Knowledge of writing markets
- Professionalism
- Persistence

Good writing is useless if you don't know which markets will buy your work or how to pitch and sell your writing. If you aren't professional and persistent in your contact with editors, your writing is just that—your writing. But if you are a writer who embraces the above four elements, you have a good chance at becoming a paid, published writer who will reap the benefits of a long and successful career.

As you become more involved with writing, you may read articles or talk to editors and authors with conflicting opinions about the right way to submit your work. The truth is, there are many different routes a writer can follow to get published, but no matter which route you choose, the end is always the same—becoming a published writer.

The following advice on submissions has worked for many writers, but it is by no means the be-all-end-all of proper submission guidelines. It's very easy to get wrapped up in the specifics of submitting (Should I put my last name on every page of my manuscript?) and ignore the more important issues (Will this idea on ice fishing in Alaska be appropriate for a regional magazine in Seattle?). Don't allow yourself to become so blinded by submission procedures that you forget common sense. If you use your common sense and develop professional, courteous relations with editors, you will eventually find your own submission style.

DEVELOP YOUR IDEAS, THEN TARGET THE MARKETS

Writers often think of an interesting story, complete the manuscript, and then begin the search for a suitable publisher or magazine. While this approach is common for fiction, poetry and screenwriting, it reduces your chances of success in many nonfiction writing areas. Instead, choose categories that interest you and study those sections in *Writer's Market*. Select several listings you consider good prospects for your type of writing. Sometimes the individual listings will even help you generate ideas.

Next, make a list of the potential markets for each idea. Make the initial contact with markets using the method stated in the market listings. If you exhaust your list of possibilities, don't give up. Instead, reevaluate the idea or try another angle. Continue developing ideas and approaching markets. Identify and rank potential markets for an idea and continue the process.

As you submit to the various publications listed in *Writer's Market*, it's important to remember that every magazine is published with a particular audience and slant in mind. Probably the number one complaint we receive from editors is the submissions they receive are completely wrong for their magazines or book line. The first mark of professionalism is to know your market well. Gaining that knowledge starts with *Writer's Market*, but you should also do your own detective work. Search out back issues of the magazines you wish to write for, pick up recent issues at your local newsstand, or visit magazines' websites—anything that will help you figure out what subjects specific magazines publish. This research is also helpful in learning what topics have been covered ad nauseum—the topics you should stay away from or approach in a fresh way. Magazines' websites are invaluable as most post the current issue of the magazine, as well as back issues, and most offer writer's guidelines.

The same advice is true for submitting to book publishers. Research publisher websites for their submission guidelines, recently published titles and their backlist. You can use this information to target your book proposal in a way that fits with a publisher's other titles while not directly competing for sales.

Prepare for rejection and the sometimes lengthy wait. When a submission is returned, check your file folder of potential markets for that idea. Cross off the market that rejected the idea. If the editor has given you suggestions or reasons why the manuscript was not accepted, you might want to incorporate these suggestions when revising your manuscript.

After revising your manuscript mail it to the next market on your list.

Take rejection with a grain of salt

Rejection is a way of life in the publishing world. It's inevitable in a business that deals with such an overwhelming number of applicants for such a limited number of positions.

Anyone who has published has lived through many rejections, and writers with thin skin are at a distinct disadvantage. A rejection letter is not a personal attack. It simply indicates your submission is not appropriate for that market. Writers who let rejection dissuade them from pursuing their dream or who react to an editor's "No" with indignation or fury do themselves a disservice. Writers who let rejection stop them do not get published. Resign yourself to facing rejection now. You will live through it, and you'll eventually overcome it.

QUERY AND COVER LETTERS

A query letter is a brief, one-page letter used as a tool to hook an editor and get him interested in your idea. When you send a query letter to a magazine, you are trying to get an editor to buy your idea or article. When you query a book publisher, you are attempting to get an editor interested enough in your idea to request your book proposal or your entire manuscript. (Note: Some book editors prefer to receive book proposals on first contact. Check individual listings for which method editors prefer.)

Here are some basic guidelines to help you create a query that's polished and well-organized. For more tips see "Query Letter Clinic" article.

- **LIMIT IT TO ONE PAGE, SINGLE-SPACED,** and address the editor by name (Mr. or Ms. and the surname). *Note*: Do not assume that a person is a Mr. or Ms. unless it is obvious from the name listed. For example, if you are contacting a D.J. Smith, do not assume that D.J. should be preceded by Mr. or Ms. Instead, address the letter to D.J. Smith.
- **GRAB THE EDITOR'S ATTENTION WITH A STRONG OPENING.** Some magazine queries, for example, begin with a paragraph meant to approximate the lead of the intended article.
- **INDICATE HOW YOU INTEND TO DEVELOP THE ARTICLE OR BOOK.** Give the editor some idea of the work's structure and content.
- **LET THE EDITOR KNOW IF YOU HAVE PHOTOS** or illustrations available to accompany your magazine article.
- **MENTION ANY EXPERTISE OR TRAINING THAT QUALIFIES YOU** to write the article or book. If you've been published before, mention it; if not, don't.
- **END WITH A DIRECT REQUEST TO WRITE THE ARTICLE.** Or, if you're pitching a book, ask for the go-ahead to send in a full proposal or the entire manuscript. Give the editor an idea of the expected length and delivery date of your manuscript.

A common question that arises is: If I don't hear from an editor in the reported response time, how do I know when I can safely send the query to another market? Many writers find it helpful to indicate in their queries that if they don't receive a response from the editor (slightly after the listed reporting time), they will assume the editor is not interested. It's best to take this approach, particularly if your topic is timely.

A brief, single-spaced cover letter is helpful when sending a manuscript as it helps personalize the submission. However, if you have previously queried the editor, use the cover letter to politely and briefly remind the editor of that query—when it was sent, what it contained, etc. "Here is the piece on low-fat cooking that I queried you about on December 12. I look forward to hearing from you at your earliest convenience." Do not use the cover letter as a sales pitch.

If you are submitting to a market that accepts unsolicited manuscripts, a cover letter is useful because it personalizes your submission. You can, and should, include information about the manuscript, yourself, your publishing history, and your qualifications.

In addition to tips on writing queries, the "Query Letter Clinic" article offers eight example query letters, some that work and some that don't, as well as comments on why the letters were either successful or failed to garner an assignment or contract.

Querying for fiction

Fiction is sometimes queried, but more often editors prefer receiving material. Many fiction editors won't decide on a submission until they have seen the complete manuscript. When submitting a fiction book idea, most editors prefer to see at least a synopsis and sample chapters (usually the first three). For fiction published in magazines, most editors want to see the complete short story manuscript. If an editor does request a query for fiction, it should include a description of the main theme and story line, including the conflict and resolution. Take a look at individual listings to see what editors prefer to receive.

THE SYNOPSIS

Most fiction books are sold by a complete manuscript, but most editors and agents don't have the time to read a complete manuscript of every wannabe writer. As a result, publishing decision-makers use the synopsis and sample chapters to help the screening process of fiction. The synopsis, on its most basic level, communicates what the book is about.

The length and depth of a synopsis can change from agent to agent or publisher to publisher. Some will want a synopsis that is one to two single-spaced pages; others will want a synopsis that can run up to 25 double-spaced pages. Checking your listings in *Writer's Market*, as well as double-checking with the listing's website, will help guide you in this respect.

The content should cover all the essential points of the novel from beginning to end and in the correct order. The essential points include main characters, main plot points, and, yes, the ending. Of course, your essential points will vary from the editor who wants a one-page synopsis to the editor who wants a 25-page synopsis.

NONFICTION PROPOSALS

Most nonfiction books are sold by a book proposal—a package of materials that details what your book is about, who its intended audience is, and how you intend to write the book. It includes some combination of a cover or query letter, an overview, an outline, author's information sheet, and sample chapters. Editors also want to see information about the audience for your book and about titles that compete with your proposed book.

Submitting nonfiction proposals

A proposal package should include the following items:

- **A COVER OR QUERY LETTER.** This letter should be a short introduction to the material you include in the proposal.
- **AN OVERVIEW.** This is a brief summary of your book. It should detail your book's subject and give an idea of how that subject will be developed.
- **AN OUTLINE.** The outline covers your book chapter by chapter and should include all major points covered in each chapter. Some outlines are done in traditional outline form, but most are written in paragraph form.
- **AN AUTHOR'S INFORMATION SHEET.** This information should acquaint the editor with your writing background and convince him of your qualifications regarding the subject of your book.
- **SAMPLE CHAPTERS.** Many editors like to see sample chapters, especially for a first book. Sample chapters show the editor how you write and develop ideas from your outline.
- **MARKETING INFORMATION.** Facts about how and to whom your book can be successfully marketed are now expected to accompany every book proposal. If you can provide information about the audience for your book and suggest ways the book publisher can reach those people, you will increase your chances of acceptance.
- **COMPETITIVE TITLE ANALYSIS.** Check the *Subject Guide to Books in Print* for other titles on your topic. Write a one- or two-sentence synopsis of each. Point out how your book differs and improves upon existing topics.

For more information on nonfiction book proposals, read Michael Larsen's *How to Write a Book Proposal* (Writer's Digest Books).

A WORD ABOUT AGENTS

An agent represents a writer's work to publishers, negotiates contracts, follows up to see that contracts are fulfilled, and generally handles a writer's business affairs, leaving the writer free to write. Effective agents are valued for their contacts in the publishing industry, their knowledge about who to approach with certain ideas, their ability to guide an author's career, and their business sense.

While most book publishers listed in *Writer's Market* publish books by unagented writers, some of the larger houses are reluctant to consider submissions that have not reached them through a literary agent. Companies with such a policy are noted by an (**Ⓐ**) icon at the beginning of the listing, as well as in the submission information within the listing.

Writer's Market includes a list of literary agents who are all members of the Association of Authors' Representatives and who are also actively seeking new and established writers.

MANUSCRIPT FORMAT

You can increase your chances of publication by following a few standard guidelines regarding the physical format of your manuscript. It should be your goal to make your manuscript readable. Follow these suggestions as you would any other suggestions: Use what works for you and discard what doesn't.

In general, when submitting a manuscript, you should use white, 8½×11, 20 lb. paper, and you should also choose a legible, professional looking font (i.e., Times New Roman)—no all-italic or artsy fonts. Your entire manuscript should be double-spaced with a 1½-inch margin on all sides of the page. Once you are ready to print your manuscript, you should print either on a laser printer or an ink-jet printer.

ESTIMATING WORD COUNT

All computers provide you with a word count of your manuscript. Your editor will count again after editing the manuscript. Although your computer is counting characters, an editor or production editor is more concerned about the amount of space the text will occupy on a page. Several small headlines or subheads, for instance, will be counted the same by your computer as any other word of text. However, headlines and subheads usually employ a different font size than the body text, so an editor may count them differently to be sure enough space has been estimated for larger type.

For short manuscripts, it's often quickest to count each word on a representative page and multiply by the number of pages. You can get a very rough count by multiplying the

MANUSCRIPT FORMATTING SAMPLE

1 Your Name   50,000 Words **3**
Your Street Address
City State ZIP Code
Day and Evening Phone Numbers
E-mail Address

Website (if applicable)
2

1 Type your real name (even if you use a pseudonym) and contact information **2** Double-space twice **3** Estimated word count **4** Type your title in capital letters, double-space and type "by," double-space again, and type your name (or pseudonym if you're using one) **5** Double-space twice, then indent first paragraph and start text of your manuscript **6** On subsequent pages, type your name, a dash, and the page number in the upper left or right corner

TITLE

by

4 Your Name

5 You can increase your chances of publication by following a few standard guidelines regarding the physical format of your article or manuscript. It should be your goal to make your manuscript readable. Use these suggestions as you would any other suggestions: Use what works for you and discard what doesn't.

In general, when submitting a manuscript, you should use white, 8½×11, 20-lb. bond paper, and you should also choose a legible, professional-looking font (i.e., Times New Roman)—no all-italic or artsy fonts. Your entire manuscript should be double-spaced with a 1½-inch margin on all sides of the page. Once you are ready to print your article or manuscript, you should print either on a laser printer or an ink-jet printer.

Remember, articles should be written after you send a one-page query letter to an editor, and the editor then asks you to write the article. If, however, you are sending an article "on spec" to an editor, you should send both a query letter and the complete article.

Fiction and poetry is a little different from nonfiction articles, in that it is rarely queried. More often than not, poetry and fiction editors want to review the complete manuscript before making a final decision.

number of pages in your manuscript by 250 (the average number of words on a double-spaced typewritten page).

PHOTOGRAPHS AND SLIDES

In some cases, the availability of photographs and slides can be the deciding factor as to whether an editor will accept your submission. This is especially true when querying a publication that relies heavily on photographs, illustrations or artwork to enhance the article (e.g., craft magazines, hobby magazines, etc.). In some instances, the publication may offer additional payment for photographs or illustrations.

Check the individual listings to find out which magazines review photographs and what their submission guidelines are. Most publications prefer you do not send photographs with your submission. However, if photographs or illustrations are available, you should indicate that in your query. As with manuscripts, never send the originals of your photographs or illustrations. Instead, send digital images, which is what most magazine and book publishers prefer to use.

SEND PHOTOCOPIES

If there is one hard-and-fast rule in publishing, it's this: *Never* send the original (or only) copy of your manuscript. Most editors cringe when they find out a writer has sent the only copy of their manuscript. You should always send copies of your manuscript.

Some writers choose to send a self-addressed, stamped postcard with a photocopied submission. In their cover letter they suggest if the editor is not interested in their manuscript, it may be tossed out and a reply sent on the postcard. This method is particularly helpful when sending your submissions to international markets.

MAILING SUBMISSIONS

No matter what size manuscript you're mailing, always include a self-addressed, stamped envelope (SASE) with sufficient return postage. The website for the U.S. Postal Service (www.usps.com) and the website for the Canadian Post (www.canadapost.ca) both have postage calculators if you are unsure how much postage to affix.

A book manuscript should be mailed in a sturdy, well-wrapped box. Enclose a self-addressed mailing label and paper clip your return postage to the label. However, be aware that some book publishers do not return unsolicited manuscripts, so make sure you know the practice of the publisher before sending any unsolicited material.

Types of mail service

There are many different mailing service options available to you whether you are sending a query letter or a complete manuscript. You can work with the U.S. Postal Service, United

Parcel Service, Federal Express, or any number of private mailing companies. The following are the five most common types of mailing services offered by the U.S. Postal Service.

- **FIRST CLASS** is a fairly expensive way to mail a manuscript, but many writers prefer it. First-Class mail generally receives better handling and is delivered more quickly than Standard mail.
- **PRIORITY MAIL** reaches its destination within two or three days.
- **STANDARD MAIL** rates are available for packages, but be sure to pack your materials carefully because they will be handled roughly. To make sure your package will be returned to you if it is undeliverable, print "Return Postage Guaranteed" under your address.
- **CERTIFIED MAIL** must be signed for when it reaches its destination.
- **REGISTERED MAIL** is a high-security method of mailing where the contents are insured. The package is signed in and out of every office it passes through, and a receipt is returned to the sender when the package reaches its destination.

MAILING MANUSCRIPTS

- Fold manuscripts under five pages into thirds, and send in a #10 SASE.
- Mail manuscripts five pages or more unfolded in a 9×12 or 10×13 SASE.
- For return envelope, fold the envelope in half, address it to yourself, and add a stamp, or, if going to Canada or another international destination, International Reply Coupons (available at most post office branches).
- Don't send by Certified Mail—this is a sign of an amateur.

QUERY LETTE

CLINIC

Many great writers ask year after year, "Why is it so hard to get published?" In many cases, these writers have spent years developing their craft. They submit to the appropriate markets, yet rejection is always the end result. The culprit? A weak query letter.

The query letter is often the most important piece of the publishing puzzle. In many cases, it determines whether editors or agents will even read your manuscript. A good query makes a good first impression; a bad query earns a swift rejection.

ELEMENTS OF A QUERY

A query letter should sell editors or agents on your idea or convince them to request your finished manuscript. The most effective query letters get into the specifics from the very first line. It's important to remember that the query is a call to action, not a listing of features and benefits.

In addition to selling your idea or manuscript, a query can include information on the availability of photographs or artwork. You can include a working title and projected word count. Depending on the piece, you might also mention whether a sidebar might be appropriate and the type of research you plan to conduct. If appropriate, include a tentative deadline and indicate whether the query is being simultaneously submitted.

Biographical information should be included as well, but don't overdo it unless your background actually helps sell the article or proves that you're the only person who could write your proposed piece.

THINGS TO AVOID IN QUERY

The query is not a place to discuss pay rates. This step comes after an editor has agreed to take on your article or book. Besides making an unprofessional impression, it can so work to your disadvantage in negotiating your fee. If you ask too much, an editor may not even contact you to see if a lower rate works. If you ask for too little, you may start an editorial relationship where you make less than the normal rate.

You should also avoid rookie mistakes, such as mentioning your work is copyrighted or including the copyright symbol on your work. While you want to make it clear that you've researched the market, avoid using flattery as a technique for selling your work. It often has the opposite effect of what you intend. In addition, don't hint that you can rewrite the piece, as this only leads the editor to think there will be a lot of work involved in shaping up your writing.

Also, never admit several other editors or agents have rejected the query. Always treat your new audience as if they are the first place on your list.

HOW TO FORMAT A QUERY

It's OK to break writing rules in a short story or article, but you should follow the rules when it comes to crafting an effective query. Here are guidelines for query writing.

- Use a normal font and typeface, such as Courier and 10- or 12-point type.
- Include your name, address, phone number, e-mail address and website.
- Use one-inch margin on paper queries.
- Address a specific editor or agent. (Note: It's wise to double-check contact names online or by calling.)
- Limit query to one single-spaced page.
- Include self-addressed, stamped envelope or postcard for response with post submissions.

HOW TO FOLLOW UP

Accidents do happen. Queries may not reach your intended reader. Staff changes or interoffice mail snafus may end up with your query letter thrown away. Or the editor may have set your query off to the side for further consideration and forgotten it. Whatever the case may be, there are some basic guidelines you should use for your follow-up communication.

Most importantly, wait until the reported response time, as indicated in *Writer's Market* or their submission guidelines, has elapsed before contacting an editor or agent. Then, you should send a short and polite e-mail describing the original query sent, the date it was sent, and asking if they received it or made a decision regarding its fate.

The importance of remaining polite and businesslike when following up cannot be stressed enough. Making a bad impression on an editor can often have a ripple effect—as that editor may share his or her bad experience with other editors at the magazine or publishing company. Also, don't call.

HOW THE CLINIC WORKS

As mentioned earlier, the query letter is the most important weapon for getting an assignment or a request for your full manuscript. Published writers know how to craft a well-written, hard-hitting query. What follows are eight queries: four are strong; four are not. Detailed comments show what worked and what did not. As you'll see, there is no cut-and-dried "good" query format; every strong query works on its own merit.

GOOD NONFICTION MAGAZINE QUERY

Jimmy Boaz, editor
American Organic Farmer's Digest
8336 Old Dirt Road
Macon GA 00000

Dear Mr. Boaz, **1**

There are 87 varieties of organic crops grown in the United States, but there's only one farm producing 12 of these—Morganic Corporation. **2**

Located in the heart of Arkansas, this company spent the past decade providing great organic crops at a competitive price helping them grow into the ninth leading organic farming operation in the country. Along the way, they developed the most unique organic offering in North America.

As a seasoned writer with access to Richard Banks, the founder and president of Morganic, I propose writing a profile piece on Banks for your Organic Shakers department. After years of reading this riveting column, I believe the time has come to cover Morganic's rise in the organic farming industry. **3**

This piece would run in the normal 800-1,200 word range with photographs available of Banks and Morganic's operation.

I've been published in *Arkansas Farmer's Deluxe, Organic Farming Today* and in several newspapers. **4**

Thank you for your consideration of this article. I hope to hear from you soon.

Sincerely,

Jackie Service
34 Good St.
Little Rock AR 00000
jackie.service9867@email.com

1 My name is only available on our magazine's website and on the masthead. This writer has done her research. **2** Here's a story that hasn't been pitched before. I didn't know Morganic was so unique in the market. I want to know more. **3** The writer has access to her interview subject, and she displays knowledge of the magazine by pointing out the correct section in which her piece would run. **4** While I probably would've assigned this article based on the idea alone, her past credits do help solidify my decision.

BAD NONFICTION MAGAZINE QUERY

Dear Gentlemen, **1**

I'd like to write the next great article you'll ever publish. My writing credits include amazing pieces I've done for local and community newspapers and for my college English classes. I've been writing for years and years. **2**

Your magazine may not be a big one like *Rolling Stone* or *Sports Illustrated*, but I'm willing to write an interview for you anyway. I know you need material, and I need money. (Don't worry. I won't charge you too much.) **3**

Just give me some people to interview, and I'll do the best job you've ever read. It will be amazing, and I can re-write the piece for you if you don't agree. I'm willing to re-write 20 times if needed. **4**

You better hurry up and assign me an article though, because I've sent out letters to lots of other magazines, and I'm sure to be filled up to capacity very soon. **5**

Later gents,

Carl Bighead
76 Bad Query Lane
Big City NY 00000

1 This is sexist, and it doesn't address any contact specifically. **2** An over-the-top claim by a writer who does not impress me with his publishing background. **3** Insults the magazine and then reassures me he won't charge too much? **4** While I do assign material from time to time, I prefer writers pitch me their own ideas after studying the magazine. **5** I'm sure people aren't going to be knocking down his door anytime soon.

GOOD FICTION MAGAZINE QUERY

Marcus West
88 Piano Drive
Lexington KY 00000

August 8, 2011 **1**

Jeanette Curic, editor
Wonder Stories
45 Noodle Street
Portland OR 00000

Dear Ms. Curic,

Please consider the following 1,200-word story, "Turning to the Melon," a quirky coming-of-age story with a little magical realism thrown in the mix. **2**

After reading *Wonder Stories* for years, I think I've finally written something that would fit with your audience. My previous short story credits include *Stunned Fiction Quarterly* and *Faulty Mindbomb*. **3**

Thank you in advance for considering "Turning to Melon."

Sincerely,

Marcus West
(123) 456-7890
marcusw87452@email.com

Encl: Manuscript and SASE **4**

1 Follows the format we established in our guidelines. Being able to follow directions is more important than many writers realize. **2** Story is in our word count, and the description sounds like the type of story we would consider publishing. It's flattering to know he reads our magazine. While it won't guarantee publication, it does make me a little more hopeful that the story I'm reading will be a good fit. Also, good to know he's been published before. **4** I can figure it out, but it's nice to know what other materials were included in the envelope. This letter is not flashy, but it gives me the basics and puts me in the right frame of mind to read the actual story.

BAD FICTION MAGAZINE QUERY

To: curic@wonderstories808.com **1**
Subject: A Towering Epic Fantasy

Hello there. **2**

I've written a great fantasy epic novel short story of about 25,000 words that may be included in your magazine if you so desire. **3**

More than 20 years, I've spent chained to my desk in a basement writing out the greatest story of our modern time. And it can be yours if you so desire to have it. **4**

Just say the word, and I'll ship it over to you. We can talk money and movie rights after your acceptance. I have big plans for this story, and you can be part of that success. **5**

Yours forever (if you so desire), **6**

Harold
(or Harry for friends)

1 We do not consider e-mail queries or submissions. **2** This is a little too informal. **3** First off, what did he write? An epic novel or short story? Second, 25,000 words is way over our 1,500-word max. **4** I'm lost for words. **5** Money and movie rights? We pay moderate rates and definitely don't get involved in movies. **6** I'm sure the writer was just trying to be nice, but this is a little bizarre and kind of creepy. I do not so desire more contact with "Harry."

GOOD NONFICTION BOOK QUERY

To: corey@bigbookspublishing.com
Subject: Query: Become a Better Parent in 30 Days **1**

Dear Mr. Corey,

2 As a parent of six and a high school teacher for more than 20 years, I know first hand that being a parent is difficult work. Even harder is being a good parent. My proposed title, **3** *Taking Care of Yourself and Your Kids: A 30-day Program to Become a Better Parent While Still Living Your Life*, would show how to handle real-life situations and still be a good parent.

This book has been years in the making, as it follows the outline I've used successfully in my summer seminars I give on the topic to thousands of parents every year. It really works, because past participants contact me constantly to let me know what a difference my classes have made in their lives. **4**

In addition to marketing and selling *Taking Care of Yourself and Your Kids* at my summer seminars, I would also be able to sell it through my website and promote it through my weekly e-newsletter with over 25,000 subscribers. Of course, it would also make a very nice trade title that I think would sell well in bookstores and possibly retail outlets, such as Wal-Mart and Target. **5**

Please contact me for a copy of my full book proposal today. **6**

Thank you for your consideration.

Marilyn Parent
8647 Query St.
Norman OK 00000
mparent8647@email.com
www.marilynsbetterparents.com

1 Effective subject line. Lets me know exactly what to expect when I open the e-mail. **2** Good lead. Six kids and teaches high school. I already trust her as an expert. **3** Nice title that would fit well with others we currently offer. **4** Her platform as a speaker definitely gets my attention. **5** 25,000 e-mail subscribers? She must have a very good voice to gather that many readers. **6** I was interested after the first paragraph, but every paragraph after made it impossible to not request her proposal.

BAD NONFICTION BOOK QUERY

To: info@bigbookspublishing.com
Subject: a question for you (1)

I really liked this book by Mega Book Publishers called *Build Better Trains in Your Own Backyard*. It was a great book that covered all the basics of model train building. My father and I would read from it together and assemble all the pieces, and it was magical like Christmas all through the year. Why wouldn't you want to publish such a book? (2)

Well, here it is. I've already copyrighted the material for 2006 and can help you promote it if you want to send me on a worldwide book tour. As you can see from my attached digital photo, I'm not the prettiest person, but I am passionate. (3)

There are at least 1,000 model train builders in the United States alone, and there might be even more than that. I haven't done enough research yet, because I don't know if this is an idea that appeals to you. If you give me maybe $500, I could do that research in a day and get back to you on it. (4)

Anyway, this idea is a good one that brings back lots of memories for me.

Jacob (5)

(1) The subject line is so vague I almost deleted this e-mail as spam without even opening it. (2) The reason we don't publish such a book is easy—we don't do hobby titles. (3) I'm not going to open an attachment from an unknown sender via e-mail. Also, copyrighting your work years before pitching is the sign of an amateur. (4) 1,000 possible buyers is a small market, and I'm not going to pay a writer to do research on a proposal. (5) Not even a last name? Or contact information? At least I won't feel guilty for not responding.

GOOD FICTION BOOK QUERY

Jeremy Mansfield, editor
Novels R Us Publishing
8787 Big Time Street
New York NY 00000

Dear Mr. Mansfield,

My 62,000-word novel, *The Cat Walk,* is a psychologically complex thriller in the same mold as James Patterson's Alex Cross novels, but with a touch of the supernatural a la Stephenie Meyer. **1**

Rebecca Frank is at the top of the modeling world, posing for magazines in exotic locales all over the world and living life to its fullest. Despite all her success, she feels something is missing in her life. Then she runs into Marcus Hunt, a wealthy bachelor with cold blue eyes and an ambiguous past.

Within 24 hours of meeting Marcus, Rebecca's understanding of the world turns upside down, and she finds herself fighting for her life and the love of a man who may not have the ability to return her the favor.

Filled with demons, serial killers, trolls, maniacal clowns and more, *The Cat Walk* follows Rebecca through a gauntlet of trouble and turmoil, leading up to a final climactic realization that may lead to her own unraveling. **2**

The Cat Walk should fit in well with your other titles, such as *Bone Dead* and *Carry Me Home*, though it is a unique story. Your website mentioned supernatural suspense as a current interest, so I hope this is a good match. **3**

My short fiction has appeared in many mystery magazines, including a prize-winning story in *The Mysterious Oregon Quarterly*. This novel is the first in a series that I'm working on (already half-way through the second). **4**

As stated in your guidelines, I've included the first 30 pages. Thank you for considering *The Cat Walk*.

Sincerely,

Merry Plentiful
54 Willow Road
East Lansing MI 00000
merry865423@email.com

1 Novel is correct length and has the suspense and supernatural elements we're seeking. **2** The quick summary sounds like something we would write on the back cover of our paperbacks. That's a good thing, because it identifies the triggers that draw a response out of our readers. **3** She mentions similar titles we've done and that she's done research on our website. She's not afraid to put in a little extra effort. **4** At the moment, I'm not terribly concerned that this book could become a series, but it is something good to file away in the back of my mind for future use.

BAD FICTION BOOK QUERY

Jeremy Mansfield
Novels R Us Publishing
8787 Big Time Street
New York NY 00000

Dear Editor,

My novel has an amazing twist ending that could make it a worldwide phenomenon overnight while you are sleeping. It has spectacular special effects that will probably lead to a multi-million dollar movie deal that will also spawn action figures, lunch boxes, and several other crazy subsidiary rights. I mean, we're talking big-time money here. **1**

I'm not going to share the twist until I have a signed contract that authorizes me to a big bank account, because I don't want to have my idea stolen and used to promote whatever new initiative "The Man" has in mind for media nowadays. Let it be known that you will be rewarded handsomely for taking a chance on me. **2**

Did you know that George Lucas once took a chance on an actor named Harrison Ford by casting him as Han Solo in Star Wars? Look at how that panned out. Ford went on to become a big actor in the Indiana Jones series, *The Fugitive, Blade Runner*, and more. It's obvious that you taking a risk on me could play out in the same dramatic way. **3**

I realize that you've got to make money, and guess what? I want to make money too. So we're on the same page, you and I. We both want to make money, and we'll stop at nothing to do so.

If you want me to start work on this amazing novel with an incredible twist ending, just send a one-page contract agreeing to pay me a lot of money if we hit it big. No other obligations will apply. If it's a bust, I won't sue you for millions. **4**

Sincerely,

Kenzel Pain
92 Bad Writer Road
Austin TX 00000

1 While I love to hear enthusiasm from a writer about his or her work, this kind of unchecked excitement is worrisome for an editor. **2** I need to know the twist to make a decision on whether to accept the manuscript. Plus, I'm troubled by the paranoia and emphasis on making a lot of money. **3** I'm confused. Does he think he's Harrison Ford? **4** So that's the twist: He hasn't even written the novel yet. There's no way I'm going to offer a contract for a novel that hasn't been written by someone with no experience or idea of how the publishing industry works.

WRITE BETTER QUERIES AND SELL MORE ARTICLES

....

by Krissy Brady

The steps to scoring a byline in your favorite publication are straightforward enough: Come up with a mind-blowing article idea for your target market. Write an attention-grabbing query letter. Submit it to the appropriate editor. Rinse. Repeat. But there's one aspect of the pitching process new writers tend to ignore that could spell disaster for them down the line.

Once you've got the nuts-and-bolts of query writing on lockdown, your primary goal as a writer needs to shift from learning how to write quality pitches to learning how to write them more efficiently. As assignments start rolling in (and they will), you'll inevitably have less time to dedicate to pitches—and the last thing you want is your income stream slowing to a trickle.

By making the following tiny changes now, you'll not only avoid the whole assignments vs. pitches tug-of-war as your portfolio grows, but churn out top notch query letters in a fraction of the time. (This is not a drill.)

1. ESTABLISH YOUR EXACT MISSION

Make sure the focus of your primary writing goal is laser sharp. Don't just decide the category of magazine you want to write for: Pinpoint your exact target demographic within that category, the exact magazines that cater to that demographic, and the exact section you want to break into. Focus your attention on the bullseye, not the entire dartboard. It will make the process of breaking in much less overwhelming—and once you've built a solid relationship with the editor of one department, you'll have an automatic referral once you're ready to branch out into others.

2. KEEP TABS ON YOUR MARKETS

Know your markets better than you know yourself. Keep files on each market you'd like to write for, and track everything you learn about them along the way. Include submission guidelines (which you score by signing up for a Mediabistro.com premium membership), the name of the section you want to break into, as well as the name and e-mail address of the editor who runs that department. If they also accept pitches for their website, add their web editor's info to your roster as well.

For unlimited access to your target markets (not to mention years worth of back issues!), sign up for a Texture.com account. Keep track of the articles that are being published in your section: List each headline and sub-headline in your file, along with a brief description of how each article was packaged (feature with sidebars, list post, as told to, etc.). As each new issue launches, update your file. Finally, visit their website on a daily or weekly basis and track what they're publishing online.

Sure, it's a little cyber-stalkerish, but studying your markets on a regular basis takes the guesswork out of what to pitch, who to pitch to, and how to package your ideas, putting you miles ahead of the competition. Over time, your files will become a treasure trove of information that other writers would hand over a kidney for.

3. FIND THE DIAMONDS IN THE ROUGH

While it's important to subscribe to sites like ScienceDaily and EurekAlert! for the latest news on studies and scientific breakthroughs, they're not the best places for new writers to find interesting stories—especially if you don't already have a relationship with the editor you're pitching the story to. More often than not, a staff writer or regular contributor will have written the story before you've so much as decided on a lede.

Instead, visit sites like Google Scholar (scholar.google.com), PubMed (www.ncbi.nlm.nih.gov/pubmed), and ScienceDirect (www.sciencedirect.com). Search for interesting studies that haven't hit the mainstream using keywords that best describe the topics you're most interested in writing about. Best of all, all three sites let you create alerts based on your fave keywords, so you can have the latest studies sent directly to your inbox on a daily or weekly basis. Not sure if a study is worth writing about? Grab a copy of *Basics for Evaluating Medical Research Studies: A Simplified Approach*, by Sheri Ann Strite and Michael E. Stuart, M.D. (Delfini Group, 2013) to help you wade through the medical jargon.

4. LET THE INFORMATION COME TO YOU

Set up an e-mail address specifically for subscribing to scholarly journals, press release websites, and newsletters by the top experts in your field. Each time you read a new article in your niche, look into the studies that were mentioned, where they were published, and subscribe to notifications from those journals. Add the experts that were quoted to your contact list for future reference, and follow them on social media. If applicable, introduce yourself to the PR people who represent these experts and let them know you'd like to be kept in the loop on interesting developments. Use digital doodads like Flipboard (flipboard.com) and Nuzzel (nuzzel.com) to streamline your news hunting experience. Instead of scouring the Internet for new material (which almost always leads to hours of unnecessary Facebook and IMDB creeping), all you'll have to do is check your e-mail and voila—so many ideas, so little time.

5. PITCH LESS

No, but seriously. Focus on the quality of your pitches, not on how fast you can send them out. Once the process of building a solid query is second nature to you, the speed at which you write them will increase naturally. In the meantime, think each of your ideas through from head(line) to toe, and thoughtfully decide which markets you're going to submit them to. I now send one-quarter of the pitches that I used to, but receive (way) more acceptances than rejections—which is the only statistic that matters.

6. BE A PERSONAL PROFESSIONAL

Ditch the business speak and write your pitches like you're writing an e-mail to a friend. Allow the editor to hear your voice as they read your words. I've built an entire writing career using my emotional baggage as bait, and you can too. Define what makes you quirky, and run with it.

7. HONE YOUR PACKAGING SKILLS

Once you've worked with the same editor a few times, you don't have to be as formal with your query letters since they already know you've got the goods. But your pitches still need to pack a punch, and this is where the art of packaging comes in handy. Each time you come up with a new idea, search articles that have been written on the topic in the past and brainstorm ways to package your idea to make it stand out. Consistently putting this habit into practice means the next time a breaking story hits your radar, you'll be able to send your editor an insta-packaged idea that just might lead to an insta-assignment.

8. DON'T LET ANYTHING SLIP THROUGH THE CRACKS

Eventually, you're not only going to have multiple assignments on the go at various stages of completion, but multiple pitches circulating that will need to be followed up on at specific times. Use a program or app like Story Tracker (andrewnicolle.com) to remind yourself of when to touch base with an editor—and when to send your pitch elsewhere.

9. DEVELOP BACKUP ANGLES AND PITCHES

Like you, I was told the odds are slim-to-none that two editors will show interest in the same pitch. And then it happened. Twice. In a row. Naturally, I wasn't prepared, and didn't know whether to do a happy dance or throw up. Save yourself the panic attack by developing 1-2 backup angles for each pitch that can be offered to the second editor if they work for a non-competing market, and a backup pitch that's of equal or higher value if they work for a direct competitor.

10. CREATE YOUR OWN LEARNING EXPERIENCE

Typically, editors only respond to the ideas they're interested in publishing, which means it's on you to determine why your rejected queries were... well, rejected. We've all sent out pitches that were slightly off or "almost" worthy of a sale, and it's important to take stock of what went wrong to refine your process. Compare them to pitches you've nailed in the past, and you'll find the answers are right in front of you: Maybe your intro wasn't catchy enough or your angle was too vague. Maybe your headline was a snore or you sent the pitch from a place of impatience instead of finality. You don't need an editor to write back and confirm your suspicions, because deep down you already know what you need to improve on.

11. PITCH FOR THE RIGHT REASONS

Pitch stories you're drawn to and have a legit interest in covering; don't just pitch an idea because you think it'll sell. If you come across a study that'd make an excellent front-of-book piece for your target market du jour, but you find the subject matter blasé, your query will reflect that. Editors can tell the difference between your heart calling the shots—and your empty wallet.

Krissy Brady is so out of shape, it's like she has the innards of an 80-year-old—so naturally, she became a women's health + wellness writer. Since turning her emotional baggage into a writing career, she's been published in magazines like *Cosmopolitan* and *Women's Health*, as well as on websites like Prevention.com and Shape.com. You can follow her shenanigans at writtenbykrissy.com (you know, if you want).

LANDING THE SIX-FIGURE DEAL

What Makes Your Proposal Hot

....

by SJ Hodges

It's the question every first-time author wants to ask:

"If I sell my book, will the advance even cover my rent?"

Authors, I am happy to tell you that, yes, the six-figure book deal for a newbie still exists—even if you're not a celebrity with your own television show! As a ghostwriter, I work with numerous authors and personalities to develop both nonfiction and fiction proposals, and I've seen unknown first-timers land life-changing deals even in a down economy. Is platform the ultimate key to their success? You better believe it's a huge consideration for publishers, but here's the good news: Having a killer platform is only one element that transforms a "nice deal" into a "major deal."

You still have to ensure the eight additional elements of your proposal qualify as major attractions. Daniela Rapp, editor at St. Martin's Press explains, "In addition to platform, authors need to have a fantastic, original idea. They have to truly be an expert in their field and they must be able to write." So how do you craft a proposal that conveys your brilliance, your credentials, your talent and puts a couple extra zeroes on your check?

ONE: NARRATIVE OVERVIEW

Before you've even written word one of your manuscript, you are expected to, miraculously, summarize the entirety of your book in such a compelling and visceral way that a publisher or agent will feel as if they are reading *The New York Times* review. Sound impossible? That's because it is.

That's why I'm going to offer two unorthodox suggestions. First, consider writing the first draft of your overview after you've created your table of contents and your chapter outlines. You'll know much more about the content and scope of your material even if you're not 100 percent certain about the voice and tone. That's why you'll take another pass after you complete your sample chapters. Because then you'll be better acquaint-

ed with the voice of your book which brings me to unorthodox suggestion number two…
treat your overview as literature.

I believe every proposal component needs to be written "in voice" especially because
your overview is the first page the editor sees after the title page. By establishing your
voice on the page immediately, your proposal becomes less of a sales document and more
of a page-turner. Remember, not everyone deciding your fate works in marketing and
sales. Editors still have some buying power and they are readers, first and foremost.

TWO: TABLE OF CONTENTS AND CHAPTER OUTLINES

Television writers call this "breaking" a script. This is where you break your book or it
breaks you. This is where you discover if what you plan to share with the world actually
merits 80,000 words and international distribution.

Regardless of whether you're writing fiction or nonfiction, this element of your proposal must take your buyer on a journey (especially if it's nonfiction) and once more, I'm
a big fan of approaching this component with creativity particularly if you're exploring a
specific historical time period, plan to write using a regional dialect, rely heavily on "slan-
guage," and especially if the material is highly technical and dry.

This means you'll need to style your chapter summaries and your chapter titles as a form
of dramatic writing. Think about the arc of the chapters, illuminating the escalating conflict,
the progression towards a resolution, in a cinematic fashion. Each chapter summary should
end with an "emotional bumper," a statement that simultaneously summarizes and entices
in the same way a television show punches you in the gut before they cut to a commercial.

Is it risky to commit to a more creative approach? Absolutely. Will it be perfect the
first time you write it? No. The fifth time you write it? No. The tenth time? Maybe. But the
contents and chapter summary portion of your proposal is where you really get a chance
to show off your skills as an architect of plot and structure and how you make an editor's job much, much easier. According to Lara Asher, acquisitions editor at Globe Pequot
Press, it is the single most important component of your proposal. "If I can't easily understand what a book is trying to achieve then I can't present it to my colleagues," Asher says.
"It won't make it through the acquisitions process."

THREE: YOUR AUTHOR BIO

Your author bio page must prove that you are more than just a pro, that you are recognized by the world at large as "the definitive expert" on your topic, that you have first-
hand experience tackling the problems and implementing your solutions, and that you've
seen positive results not only in your personal life but in the lives of others. You have to
have walked the walk and talked the talk. You come equipped with a built-in audience,

mass media attention, and a strong social network. Your bio assures your buyer that you are the right writer exploring the right topic at the right time.

FOUR: YOUR PLATFORM

Platform, platform, platform. Sit through any writing conference, query any agent, lunch with any editor and you'll hear the "P" word over and over again. What you won't hear is hard-and-fast numbers about just how large this platform has to be in order to secure a serious offer. Is there an audience-to-dollar-amount ratio that seems to be in play? Are publishers paying per head?

"I haven't found this to be the case," says Julia Pastore, former editor for Random House. "It's easier to compel someone to 'Like' you on Facebook or follow you on Twitter than it is to compel them to plunk down money to buy your book. Audience engagement is more important than the sheer number of social media followers."

With that said, if you're shooting for six-figures, publishers expect you'll have big numbers and big plans. Your platform will need to include:

Cross-promotional partnerships

These are organizations or individuals that already support you, are already promoting your brand, your products or your persona. If you host a show on HGTV or Nike designed a tennis racket in your honor, they definitely qualify. If, however, you're not rolling like an A-lister just yet, you need to brainstorm any and every possible connection you have to organizations with reach in the 20,000+ range. Maybe your home church is only 200 people but the larger association serves 40,000 and you often write for their newsletter. Think big. Then think bigger.

Specific, verifiable numbers proving the loyalty of your audience

"Publishers want to see that you have direct contact with a loyal audience," says Maura Teitelbaum, an agent at Folio Literary Management. This means having a calendar full of face-to-face speaking engagements, a personal mailing list, extensive database and verifiable traffic to your author website.

But how much traffic does there need to be? How many public appearances? How many e-mails in your Constant Contact newsletter? Publishers are loathe to quote concrete numbers for "Likes" and "Followers" so I'll stick my neck out and do it instead. At a minimum, to land a basic book deal, meaning a low five-figure sum, you'll need to prove that you've got 15,000-20,000 fans willing to follow you into hell and through high water.

For a big six-figure deal, you'll need a solid base of 100,000 rabid fans plus access to hundreds of thousands more. If not millions. Depressed yet? Don't be. Because we live in a time when things as trivial as Angry Oranges or as important as scientific TED talks can go viral and propel a writer out of obscurity in a matter of seconds. It is only your job to become part of the conversation. And once your foot is in the door, you'll be able to gather...

Considerable media exposure

Publishers are risk averse. They want to see that you're a media darling achieving pundit status. Organize and present all your clips, put together a DVD demo reel of your on-air appearances and be able to quote subscriber numbers and demographics about the publications running your articles or features about you.

Advance praise from people who matter

Will blurbs really make a difference in the size of your check? "I would include as many in a proposal as possible," says Teitelbaum. "Especially if those people are willing to write letters of commitment saying they will promote the book via their platform. That shows your efforts will grow exponentially."

FIVE: PROMOTIONAL PLANS

So what is the difference between your platform and your promotional plan? Your promotional plan must demonstrate specifically how you will activate your current platform and the expected sales results of that activation. These are projections starting three to six months before your book release date and continuing for one year after its hardcover publication. They want your guarantee to sell 15,000 books within that first year.

In addition, your promotional plan also issues promises about the commitments you are willing to make in order to promote the book to an even wider market. This is your expansion plan. How will you broaden your reach and who will help you do it? Publishers want to see that your goals are ambitious but doable.

Think about it this way. If you own a nail salon and you apply for a loan to shoot a movie, you're likely to be rejected. But ask for a loan to open your second salon and your odds get much better. In other words, keep your promotional plans in your wheelhouse while still managing to include:

- Television and radio appearances
- Access to print media
- A massive social media campaign
- Direct e-mail solicitations
- E-commerce and back-of-room merchandising
- New joint partnerships
- Your upcoming touring and speaking schedule with expected audience

You'll notice that I did not include hiring a book publicist as a requirement. Gone are the days when an advance-sucking, three-month contract with a book publicist makes any difference. For a six-figure author, publishers expect there is a team in place: a powerful agent, a herd of assistants and a more generalized media publicist already managing the day-to-day affairs of building your brand, growing your audience. Hiring a book publicist at the last minute is useless.

SIX: YOUR MARKET ANALYSIS

It would seem the odds against a first-time author hitting the jackpot are slim but that's where market analysis provides a glimmer of hope. There are actually markets considered more desirable to publishers. "Broader is generally better for us," says Rapp. "Niche generally implies small. Not something we [St. Martin's Press] can afford to do these days. Current affairs books, if they are explosive and timely, can work. Neuroscience is hot. Animal books (not so much animal memoirs) still work. Military books sell."

"The health and diet category will always be huge," says Asher. "But in a category like parenting which is so crowded, we look for an author tackling a niche topic that hasn't yet been covered."

Niche or broad, your market analysis must position your book within a larger context, addressing the needs of the publishing industry, the relevant cultural conversations happening in the zeitgeist, your potential audience and their buying power, and the potential for both domestic and international sales.

SEVEN: YOUR C.T.A.

Choose the books for your Competitive Title Analysis not only for their topical similarities but also because the author has a comparable profile and platform to your own. Says Pastore, "It can be editorially helpful to compare your book to *Unbroken* by Hillenbrand, but unless your previous book was also a bestseller, this comparison won't be helpful to our sales force."

Limit your C.T.A. to five or six solid offerings then get on BookScan and make sure none of the books sold fewer than 10,000 copies. "Higher sales are preferable," says Rapp. "And you should leave it to the publisher to decide if the market can hold one more title or not. We always do our own research anyway, so just because the book is not mentioned in your line-up doesn't mean we won't know about it."

EIGHT: SAMPLE CHAPTERS

Finally, you have to/get to prove you can … write. Oh yeah, that!

This is the fun part, the pages of your proposal where you really get to shine. It is of upmost importance that these chapters, in harmony with your overview and chapter summaries, allow the beauty, wisdom and/or quirkiness of your voice to be heard. Loud and clear.

"Writing absolutely matters and strong sample chapters are crucial." Pastore explains, "An author must be able to turn their brilliant idea into engaging prose on the page."

Approach the presentation of these chapters creatively. Consider including excerpts from several different chapters and not just offering the standard Introduction, Chapter One and Two. Consider the inclusion of photographs to support the narrative, helping your editor put faces to names. Consider using sidebars or box quotes from the narrative throughout your proposal to build anticipation for the actual read.

NINE: YOUR ONE-PAGER

Lastly, you'll need a one-pager, which is a relatively new addition to the book proposal format. Publishers now expect an author to squeeze a 50- or 60-page proposal down to a one-page summary they can hand to their marketing and sales teams. In its brevity, the one-pager must provide your buyer with "a clear vision of what the book is, why it's unique, why you are the best person to write it, and how we can reach the audience," says Pastore. And it must do that in fewer than 1,000 words. There is no room to be anything but impressive.

And if you're shooting for that six-figure deal, impressive is what each component of your book proposal must be. Easy? No. But still possible? Yes.

SJ HODGES is an 11-time published playwright, ghostwriter and editor. Her most recent book, a memoir co-authored with Animal Planet's "Pit Boss" Shorty Rossi was purchased by Random House/Crown, hit #36 on the Amazon bestseller list and went into its 3rd printing less than six weeks after its release date. As a developmental editor, SJ has worked on books published by Vanguard Press, Perseus Book Group and St. Martin's Press. SJ is a tireless advocate for artists offering a free listing for jobs, grants and fellowships at her Facebook page: facebook.com/constantcreator. She can be reached through her website: sjhodges.com.

HOW TO FIND SUCCESS IN THE MAGAZINE WORLD

by Kerrie Flanagan

Contrary to popular belief, magazines are still going strong. According to the latest study by the Magazine Publishers of America there are more than 20,000 magazines in print. This is good news if you are looking to write for magazines. But before you jump in, there are a few things you should know that will increase your chances of getting an acceptance letter.

KNOW THE READER

Every magazine has a certain readership; teenage girl, mother of young children, budget traveler and so on. It is imperative you know as much about that reader as you can before submitting a query to the editor, because the more you know about who reads the magazine, the more you can tailor your query, article, or essay to best reach that audience.

Geoff Van Dyke, deputy editor of the Denver magazine *5280* says, "I wish people would truly read the magazine, like cover to cover, and understand our readership and voice and mission before sending queries. Sometimes—more often than not—writers submit queries that make it clear that they don't really understand *5280*, don't understand our readers or our mission, and, thus, the query is a bad fit. If they just spend a little more time on the front end, it would make all the difference."

So how can you find out who is the target audience for a specific magazine? The key is in the advertising. Companies spend thousands of dollars getting their messages out to their consumers. They are only going to invest their money in a magazine directed at their target market. By paying attention to the ads in a publication (and this goes for on-line too) you can learn a lot about the reader. What are the ages of the people in the ads? Are they families? Singles? What types of products are highlighted? Expensive clothes? Organic foods? Luxury cars and world travel or family cars and domestic travel?

Another way to find out the demographics of the reader is to locate the media kit on the magazine's website. This is a document intended to provide information to potential advertisers about their readership, but is a gold mine for freelance writers. The media kit provides information like the average age, income, gender, hobbies, home ownership, education and marital status.

This becomes invaluable when looking at ideas and topics to pitch to a magazine. For instance, in the media kit for *5280* magazine, 71 percent of the readers are married, 93 percent own their own home and 78 percent have lived in Colorado for more than 10 years or are natives of the state. With this little bit of information, pitching an article on where to find the best deals on apartments in Denver, is definitely not a good fit since most of their readers own their own home. An article on the best bars in Denver to meet other singles is also not a good idea for this publication, but one on the most romantic weekend getaways in Colorado to take your spouse is a possibility. It is also clear that, when writing the article, time does not have to be spent explaining to the reader things about Colorado that people who live in the state already know since 78 percent of the readers have been there for more than a decade.

KNOW THE MAGAZINE

Once you understand the reader, then you need to familiarize yourself with the actual magazine. Take the time to explore who are the writers, the length of the articles and the departments.

Tom Hess, editor with *Encompass Magazine*, wishes more writers would take the time to know his magazine, in all its forms, before querying. "Too few writers make the effort, and those who do, get my immediate attention."

One way to do this with print magazines is to literally take apart the magazine. To see who writes for the magazine, find the masthead, the page in the front of the magazine that lists the editors and contributing writers. Tear it out so you have it as a reference. Now, go through the magazine, page by page and make a note by each article with a byline to find out who wrote the piece. Was it an editor? A contributing editor? If you can't find their names on the masthead, then they are typically freelance writers. A contributing editor is usually not on staff, but writes frequently for the magazine.

Now go through and pay attention to the length of articles and the various departments. How many feature stories are there? Is there a back page essay? Are there short department pieces in the front?

By knowing all of this information, you can better direct your query to the areas of the magazine that are more open to freelance writers and tailor your idea to better fit the type of articles they publish.

KNOW THE STYLE

Each magazine has its own style and tone. It's what makes the difference between *The New Yorker* and *Time*. Some magazines are very literary, others are more informational, so it is important to study the magazines to have a good understanding of their style.

Below are two travel writing examples portraying Ketchikan, Alaska, but with very different styles. As you read over each selection, pay attention to the style by looking at the use of quotes, the point of view (first person, third person…), the descriptions and the overall tone of the article.

EXAMPLE 1

In Ketchikan, there are many great things to see and do. The roots of the three Native Alaskan tribes, the Tlingit, Haida, and Tsimshian run deep on this island where you can find the world's largest collection of totem poles. In a beautiful cove, eight miles north of downtown is Totem Bight State Park where 14 historic totems are found along with a native clanhouse. Totems can also be viewed at the Totem Heritage Center and the Southest Discovery Center. At the Saxman Tribal house and at the Metlakatla Long House, skilled groups bring Native dance to life with regular performances.

EXAMPLE 2

The rest of the world disappeared when I entered this lush, green rainforest. Stillness and peace embraced me while I strolled on the wooden walkway, in awe of the surrounding beauty: moss hung from trees, foliage so dense it provided shelter from the rain and beautiful rivers flowed, in search of the ocean. Ketchikan, Alaska, is in the heart of the Tongass National Forest, and an unlikely place to find the Earth's largest remaining temperate rainforest.

The first article provides information and facts about traveling to Ketchikan to see the totem poles. This article would be a good fit for a magazine like *Family Motor Coaching*. The second article definitely has a different style; one that is more poetic and descriptive and more likely to be found in *National Geographic Traveler*.

Both pieces are good but are unique in their style and tone. By understanding this aspect of a magazine, your query or article can better reflect the voice of the publication and increase your chances of an assignment and well-received article.

KNOW THE GUIDELINES

Most magazines put together submission guidelines, spelling out exactly what they are looking for with articles and how to submit your idea to them.

"I wish writers would understand exactly what kind of material we are looking for," says Russ Lumpkin, managing editor of *Gray's Sporting Journal*, "and that they would adhere strictly to our submission guidelines. We publish fly fishing and hunting stories and accept only digital submissions via e-mail. A poem about watching butterflies submitted through the mail creates work that falls out of my ordinary work flow. And that's aggravating."

The submission guidelines are usually found in the "About Us" or "Contact Us" section on a magazine's website as well as in resources like *Writer's Market*. Read the guidelines carefully and follow them when submitting your query or article.

KNOW HOW TO WRITE AN EFFECTIVE QUERY LETTER

Once you have done all your upfront research and have found a magazine that is a good fit for your idea, it is time to write a good query letter. The letter should be professional and written in a style and tone similar to the article you are pitching.

Robbin Gould, editor of *Family Motor Coaching*, believes a writer needs to submit as comprehensive a query as possible and be fully aware of the magazine's focus, particularly when dealing with a niche publication. "A writer who misuses terms or makes erroneous statements about the subject he or she proposes to cover indicates a lack of knowledge to the editor," says Gould. "Or a query that simply states, 'Would you be interested in an article about XXX?' with minimal explanation wastes everyone's time and suggests the writer is looking for any publication to take the article. If the writer doesn't show much attention to detail up front, the editor probably won't spend much time considering the idea."

There are basic components that should be included in every query letter.

- **SALUTATION (DEAR MR. SMITH).** Find out who the correct editor is to direct your query. You should be able to find this information online. If not make a quick phone call to the publishing company and ask, "Who would I direct a travel query to?" Ask for spelling and the editor's e-mail. Unless you know the editor, use a formal salutation with Mr., Mrs., or Ms. If you are not sure if the editor is a man or woman, put their full name.
- **GOOD HOOK.** You have about 10 seconds to catch the attention of an editor. The opening should be about one to three sentences in length and needs to lure the editor in right away.
- **ARTICLE CONTENT.** This is the bulk of your query and should be about one paragraph. It will focus on the main points of the article and the topics you plan to cover.
- **SPECIFICS.** Here you will include the specifics of the article: word count, department where you think it will fit, possible experts you are going to interview and other information pertinent to the piece.
- **PURPOSE.** In one sentence, share the purpose of your article. Will your article inform, educate, inspire, or entertain?

- **QUALIFICATIONS.** This is not the place to be shy. You need to convince the editor that you are the perfect person to write this article. If you do not have any published clips, then really expand more on your experiences that relate to your article. If you are pitching a parenting article and you have six kids, mention that. It clearly positions you as an expert in the parenting field.
- **SENDING.** Most magazines accept and want queries by e-mail. When sending a query via e-mail, include your information in the body of the message, not in an attachment. Make sure your contact information is at the bottom of the e-mail. Put something noticeable in the subject line. For example: "QUERY: The Benefits of Chocolate and the Creative Process."

By following all the steps in this article you will be ready set off on a magazine-writing journey equipped with the necessary tools and confidence to get your queries noticed, and, in the end, see your articles in print.

KERRIE FLANAGAN has 130+ published articles and essays to her credit. In addition she is the director of Northern Colorado Writers, a group she founded in 2007 that supports and encourages writers of all levels and genres through classes, networking events, retreats and an annual writer's conference. Kerrie is also available for writing coaching. Visit her website for more information about her and NCW. www.KerrieFlanagan.com.

EARN A FULL-TIME INCOME FROM BLOGGING

by Carol Tice

It sounds like a dream: Instead of sending query letters and relying on editors to give you paying assignments, you start your own blog and turn it into a money-maker. No matter where in the world you want to live, you're able to earn a good living.

For a growing number of writers, it's not a dream. I'm among the writers who now earn more from their own blogs than they do from freelance assignments.

But it's not easy, by any means. The vast majority of blogs never find an audience and their authors never earn a dime. It's hard to stand out—at the end of 2011, pollster Nielsen reported there were over 181 million blogs, up from 36 million in 2006.

In this vast sea of blogs, how can you write one that stands out and becomes the basis for a money-earning business? It begins with setting up the blog to attract a loyal readership. Once you build an audience, there are a limited number of ways you can earn income from your blog audience—I spotlight five of the most popular methods below.

SETTING IT UP TO EARN

Many blogs don't attract readers because they lack basic elements of design and usability that make blogs appealing, says Seattle WordPress trainer Bob Dunn (www.bobwp.com). Dunn's own blog is the platform on which he's built his business.

How do you create an attractive blog?

USE A PROFESSIONAL PLATFORM

Free blog platforms such as Blogger and Moveable Type have limitations that make it hard to look professional (and some free platforms prohibit commerce). If you're serious about blogging, pay for a host and use WordPress—it's now the dominant blogging platform, Technorati reports.

OFFER CONTACT INFORMATION

Many bloggers cultivate an air of mystery, using a pen name and providing no contact info. But readers want to know who you are and be able to e-mail you questions, says Dunn.

HAVE AN "ABOUT" PAGE

With a million scams on the Internet, the About page has become a vital blog component— it's usually the most-visited page after the Home page, Dunn says. This is the place where readers get to know you and learn why you write your blog.

"I can't tell you how many times I go on a blog and there's no About page," says, Dunn. "It should be more than a résumé, too—tell a story."

CLEAN UP THE DESIGN

No matter how wonderful your writing is, if your blog is a clutter of tiny type, dark back-grounds, multiple sidebars, and flashing ads, readers will leave, Dunn says. Begin with a simple, graphical header, title, and tagline that quickly communicate what your blog is about. You have just a few seconds in which to convey what you write about before read-ers leave, so be clear.

MAKE NAVIGATION SIMPLE

Many bloggers end up with multiple rows of tabs or long drop-down menus. Try to sim-plify—for every additional click you require, you will lose some readers, Dunn says.

PICK A NICHE TOPIC

While most blogs ramble about whatever the author feels like discussing that day, busi-ness-focused blogs stick to a subject or a few related topics, notes Dunn. This allows you to attract and keep readers interested in your subject.

CREATE USEFUL CONTENT

Write with your readers' needs in mind, rather than about your own interests, says Mexi-co-based Jon Morrow. His year-old blog Boost Blog Traffic (boostblogtraffic.com) earned $500,000 in 2012. If you don't know what readers want, Morrow says, take polls and ask questions to find out.

WRITE STRONG HEADLINES

If you want readers to find your posts online, your headlines need key words and phrases that relate to your topic, to help them rank well in Google searches for your topic. You can do keyword research free using Google's tool (https://adwords.google.com/o/Keyword-Tool). Headlines also need to be lively and interesting to draw readers—Morrow offers a Headline Hacks report on his blog that dissects effective headline styles.

USE BLOG STYLE

Blog posts are different from magazine articles because of how people read—make that skim—online, says Dunn. Good blog-post paragraphs are short, often just one or two sentences. Posts with bold subheads or bulleted or numbered lists are easy to scan and often enjoy higher readership.

MAKE SHARING EASY

To grow your audience, you'll need readers to spread the word, says Dunn. Make that easy with one-click sharing buttons for Twitter, Facebook and other popular social-media platforms. You should be active in these platforms, too, building relationships with influential people who might send you readers.

START GUEST-POSTING

One of the fastest ways to build your blog audience is by guest-posting on popular blogs with lots of traffic. Your guest post will give you a link back to your own blog and allow new readers to find you. This is usually not paid work, but think of it as a marketing cost for your blog-based business. Many top blogs do accept guest posts—look for writer's guidelines on their sites.

"The big secret to making money from blogging is to get serious about marketing," Morrow says.

BUILD AN E-MAIL LIST

The best way to stay in touch with readers is via an e-mail list visitors are encouraged to join, says Dunn. Subscribers who sign up through real simple syndication, or RSS, don't reveal their e-mail address, so it's hard to sell them anything.

START EARNING

Once your blog is set up to entice readers, you're ready to experiment with ways to generate income off your blog. Among the common approaches:

1. Freelance Gigs

Add a "Hire Me" tab to your site to begin attracting freelance blogging gigs from online businesses and publications. That's the approach U.K.-based writer Tom Ewer took when he quit his job and launched his blog Leaving Work Behind (www.leavingworkbehind.com) in 2011.

A brand-new writer at the time, Ewer quickly got a couple of freelance blogging clients by applying to online job ads. More clients approached him after seeing his guest posts on big blogs and finding his blog from there. Ewer was soon blogging for pay about topics including WordPress and government contracting. By late 2012, he was earning $4,000 a month as a paid blogger at $100 a post and up, working part-time hours.

A similar strategy worked for Nigerian blogger Bamidele Onibalusi, who began his online-earning themed blog YoungPrePro (www.youngprepro.com) in 2010, when he was just 16. By 2012, he was making $50,000 a year writing for blog owners who learned of him from his dozens of guest posts on top blogs including DailyBlogTips and ProBlogger.

He's blogged for paying clients in the United States, United Kingdom, Greece, and elsewhere about real estate, accounting, and weight loss, among other topics. Onibalusi says he impresses prospects with long, highly useful posts with strong keywords that attract an ongoing stream of readers.

"Google has sent me most of my business," he says.

2. Books & E-books

Build a major following on your blog, and you can earn good money writing and selling your own books and e-books. That strategy has been successful for Jeff Goins of the writing and social-change blog GoinsWriter (goinswriter.com), who has two Kindle e-books and a traditionally published print book under his belt.

Launched in 2010 and now boasting 25,000 subscribers, GoinsWriter has loyal fans who help drive more than $3,500 a month in sales of his two low-priced e-books, including his co-authored *You Are a Writer (So Start Acting Like One)*, which goes for just $2.99.

Goins first creates excitement around his e-books by blogging about the upcoming release first. Then, as the publication date nears, he gives more than 100 die-hard fans a free PDF of the e-book in exchange for Amazon reviews. When he officially publishes a few days later on Amazon and elsewhere, the glowing reviews help encourage thousands of purchases. The reviews and frequent downloads keep his e-books ranking highly for the writing category, which drives more sales. Links in the e-book also help bring more blog readers.

E-book sales also kicked off the blog-earning career of Pat Flynn, a southern Californian who first had modest blog-monetizing success with an e-book he wrote on how to pass an architectural exam. He started the Smart Passive Income (www.smartpassiveincome.com) blog in 2008 to dissect that success. This second blog went on to greatly surpass the original project, bringing in over $200,000 its first year alone.

3. Affiliate Sales

Flynn earns primarily through affiliate sales, a strategy in which a blogger receives a commission for selling someone else's product or service. It's an approach that works best with a large audience—Smart Passive Income has 57,000 subscribers and gets 100,000 visitors a month.

His audience includes many bloggers who need to set up their websites, so many of his affiliate products are tools or services that enable bloggers. Flynn's top-selling affiliate product in 2012 was website host Bluehost, from which he now typically earns $20,000 or more monthly. He receives a commission every time someone signs up for website hosting through his unique affiliate links.

"I find products that help them get from A to Z," he says. "They're recommended products I've actually used. You want to be sort of an expert in it."

Flynn builds loyalty by creating free blog posts that offer "high value content that would usually require payment." Rather than slapping up ads that might annoy readers, he simply states that site links earn him a commission. Fans are happy to click, and even send him thank-you notes about the products he sells.

Like many top-earning bloggers, Flynn uses videos and podcasts to help promote his blogs. Flynn's Smart Passive Income Podcast has brought many new readers—it's one of the top business-related podcasts on iTunes and has seen more than 2 million downloads.

4. Courses & Coaching

When you've built your reputation through delivering useful blog posts, you can sell your fans more advanced information on your topic. Courses and coaching are the main earners for Boost Blog Traffic's Morrow, who teaches a guest-blogging class and takes just 10 students at a time in his $10,000-a-head, five-month coaching course. The secret sauce in the guest-blogging class includes personal introductions by Morrow to top blog editors.

Build your authority enough, and customers pay just for the opportunity to learn from someone they respect, says Morrow.

"I'm not really selling products," he says. "I'm selling me."

Morrow attributes part of his earning success to hard work to improve the marketing campaigns for his paid programs. He says he's spent hundreds of hours testing and tinkering with marketing e-mails and promotional videos that help sell the courses. Now that he's refined his process, he says he needs to spend only five hours a week on his guest-blogging course. Affiliates do much of the selling of his blogging course for him.

An extension of this teaching niche is public speaking, for which top presenters can earn tens of thousands of dollars per appearance. Morrow recently presented at the New Media Expo (formerly known as BlogWorld), for instance.

5. Membership Community

Once they're publishing, teaching, speaking, and creating audio and video materials on a topic, bloggers can leverage all that content to earn even more through a paid membership community. Inside the community, members can access large amounts of training materials and their favorite expert's advice via chat forums for one low monthly rate, instead of paying for it piecemeal. The community model allows bloggers to earn more as additional members join without having to do much more work, as members mostly access existing content.

Large communities can be major money generators—for instance, A-List Blogger Club (www.alistbloggingbootcamps.com/alist-blogger-club-join), a blog-building training community started by top blogger Leo Babauta of Zen Habits that I used to learn how to build my own blog, had roughly 900 members in 2012 paying $20 apiece per month. The blog Write to Done (writetodone.com) serves as the main platform that introduces writers to the club.

Blogging is not for every writer. It's a lot of work coming up with post ideas and writing several posts a month or even a week. It can be many months until a blog starts to earn money, and there are no guarantees it will ever catch on. But for writers with the drive to stick with it and a willingness to learn about blog marketing, the rewards can be rich.

CAROL TICE writes the Make a Living Writing (www.makealivingwriting.com) blog and runs the writers learning community Freelance Writers Den (freelancewritersden.com). She has written two nonfiction business books and co-authored the Kindle e-book *13 Ways to Get the Writing Done Faster* (www.amazon.com/Ways-Writing-Done-Faster-ebook/dp/B009XM03SK).

FUNDS FOR WRITERS 101

Find Money You Didn't Know Existed

....

by C. Hope Clark

When I completed writing my novel over a decade ago, I imagined the next step was simply to find a publisher and watch the book sell. Like most writers, my goal was to earn a living doing what I loved so I could walk away from the day job. No such luck. Between rejection and newfound knowledge that a novel can take years to sell enough for a single house payment, I opened my mind to other writing avenues. I learned that there's no *one* way to find funds to support your writing; instead there are *many*. So many, in fact, that I felt the need to share the volume of knowledge I collected, and I called it FundsforWriters.com.

Funds are money. But obtaining those funds isn't necessarily a linear process, or a one-dimensional path. As a serious writer, you study all options at your fingertips, entertaining financial resources that initially don't make sense as well as the obvious.

GRANTS

Grants come from government agencies, nonprofits, businesses and even generous individuals. They do not have to be repaid, as long as you use the grant as intended. No two are alike. Therefore, you must do your homework to find the right match between your grant need and the grant provider's mission. Grantors like being successful at their mission just as you like excelling at yours. So they screen applicants, ensuring they fit the rules and show promise to follow through.

Don't fear grants. Sure, you're judged by a panel, and rejection is part of the game, but you already know that as a writer. Gigi Rosenberg, author of *The Artist's Guide to Grant Writing*, states, "If one funder doesn't want to invest in your project, find another who does. And if nobody does, then begin it any way you can. Once you've started, that momentum will help your project find its audience and its financial support."

TYPES OF GRANTS

Grants can send you to retreats, handle emergencies, provide mentors, pay for conferences, or cover travel. They also can be called awards, fellowships, residencies, or scholarships. But like any aspect of your writing journey, define how any tool, even a grant, fits into your plans. Your mission must parallel a grantor's mission.

The cream-of-the-crop grants have no strings attached. Winning recipients are based upon portfolios and an application that defines a work-in-progress. You don't have to be a Pulitzer winner, but you must prove your establishment as a writer.

You find most of these opportunities in state arts commissions. Find them at www.nasaa-arts.org or as a partner listed at the National Endowment for the Arts website, www.nea.gov. Not only does your state's arts commission provide funding, but the players can direct you to other grant opportunities, as well as to artists who've gone before you. Speaking to grant winners gives you a wealth of information and a leg up in designing the best application.

Foundations and nonprofits fund the majority of grants. Most writers' organizations are nonprofits. Both the Mystery Writers of America (www.mysterywriters.org) and Society of Children's Book Writers and Illustrators (www.scbwi.org) offer scholarships and grants.

Many retreats are nonprofits. Journalist and freelancer Alexis Grant, (http://alexisgrant.com/) tries to attend a retreat a year. Some ask her to pay, usually on a sliding scale based upon income, and others provide scholarships. Each time, she applies with a clear definition of what she hopes to gain from the two to five-week trips. "It's a great way to get away from the noise of everyday responsibilities, focus on writing well and meet other people who prioritize writing. I always return home with a new perspective." One resource to find writing retreats is the Alliance of Artists Communities (www.artistcommunities.org/).

Laura Lee Perkins won four artist-in-residence slots with the National Park Service (www.nps.gov). The federal agency has 43 locations throughout the United States where writers and artists live for two to four weeks. From Acadia National Park in Maine to Sleeping Bear Dunes National Lakeshore in Michigan, Perkins spoke to tourists about her goals to write a book about Native American music. "Memories of the US National Parks' beauty and profound serenity will continue to enrich my work. Writers find unparalleled inspiration, quietude, housing, interesting staff, and a feeling of being in the root of your artistic desires."

Don't forget writers' conferences. While they may not advertise financial aid, many have funds available in times of need. Always ask as to the availability of a scholarship or work-share program that might enable your attendance.

Grants come in all sizes. FundsforWriters posts emergency grants on its grants page (www.fundsforwriters.com) as well as new grant opportunities such as the Sustainable Arts Foundation (www.sustainableartsfoundation.org) that offers grants to writers and artists with children under the age of 18, or the Awesome Foundation (www.awecomefoundation.org), which gives $1,000 grants to creative projects.

Novelist Joan Dempsey won an Elizabeth George Foundation grant (http://www.elizabethgeorgeonline.com/foundation/index.htm) in early 2012. "I applied to the Foundation for a research grant that included three trips to places relevant to my novel-in-progress, trips I otherwise could not have afforded. Not only does the grant provide travel funds, but it also provides validation that I'm a serious writer worthy of investment, which is great for my psyche and my résumé."

FISCAL SPONSORSHIP

Nonprofits have access to an incredibly large number of grants that individuals do not, and have the ability to offer their tax-exempt status to groups and individuals involved in activities related to their mission. By allowing a nonprofit to serve as your grant overseer, you may acquire funds for your project.

Deborah Marshall is President of the Missouri Writers Guild (www.missouriwritersguild.org) and founder of the Missouri Warrior Writers Project, with ample experience with grants in the arts. "Although grant dollars are available for individual writers, writing the grant proposal becomes difficult without significant publication credits. Partnering with a nonprofit organization, whether it is a writing group, service, community organization, or any 501(c)3, can fill in those gaps to make a grant application competitive. Partnering not only helps a writer's name become known, but it also assists in building that all-important platform."

Two excellent groups that offer fiscal sponsorship for writers are The Fractured Atlas (www.fracturedatlas.org) and Artspire (www.artspire.org) sponsored by the New York Foundation for the Arts and open to all US citizens. Visit The Foundation Center (www.foundationcenter.org) for an excellent tutorial guide to fiscal sponsorship.

CROWD SOURCING

Crowd sourcing is a co-op arrangement where people support artists directly, much like the agricultural co-op movement where individuals fund farming operations in exchange for fresh food. Kickstarter (www.kickstarter.com) has made this funding method successful in the arts.

Basically, the writer proposes his project, and for a financial endorsement as low as $1, donors receive some token in return, like an autographed book, artwork, or bookmark. The higher the donation, the bigger the *wow* factor in the gift. Donors do not receive ownership in the project.

Meagan Adele Lopez (www.ladywholunches.net) presented her debut self-published book *Three Questions* to Kickstarter readers, requesting $4,400 to take her book on tour, create a book trailer, pre-order books, and redesign the cover. Eighty-eight backers pledged a total of $5,202. She was able to hire an editor and a company that designed film trailers. For every $750 she received over her plan, she added a new city to her book tour.

Other up-and-coming crowd sourcing companies include Culture 360 (www.culture360.org) that serves Asia and Europe, and Indiegogo (www.indiegogo.com), as well as Rocket Hub (www.rockethub.com). And nothing stops you from simply asking those you know to support your project. The concept is elementary.

CONTESTS

Contests offer financial opportunity, too. Of course you must win, place or show, but many writers overlook the importance that contests have on a career. These days, contests not only open doors to publishing, name recognition, and money, but listing such achievements in a query letter might make an agent or publisher take a second glance. Noting your wins on a magazine pitch might land a feature assignment. Mentioning your accolades to potential clients could clinch a freelance deal.

I used contests as a barometer when fleshing out my first mystery novel, *A Lowcountry Bribe* (Bell Bridge Books). After I placed in several contests, earned a total of $750, and reached the semi-finals of the Amazon Breakthrough Novel Award (www.createspace.com/abna), my confidence grew strong enough to pitch agents. My current agent admits that the contest wins drew her in.

Contests can assist in sales of existing books, not only aiding sales but also enticing more deals for future books . . . or the rest of your writing profession.

Whether writing short stories, poetry, novels, or nonfiction, contests abound. As with any call for submission, study the rules. Double checking with entities that screen, like FundsforWriters.com and WinningWriters.com, will help alleviate concerns when selecting where to enter.

FREELANCING

A thick collection of freelancing clips can make an editor sit up and take notice. You've been vetted and accepted by others in the business, and possibly established a following. The more well known the publications, the brighter your aura.

Sooner or later in your career, you'll write an article. In the beginning, articles are a great way to gain your footing. As your career develops, you become more of an expert, and are expected to enlighten and educate about your journey and the knowledge you've acquired. Articles are, arguably, one of the best means to income and branding for writers.

Trade magazines, national periodicals, literary journals, newsletters, newspapers and blogs all offer you a chance to present yourself, earn money, and gain readers for a platform. Do not discount them as income earners.

Linda Formichelli, of Renegade Writer fame (www.therenegadewriter.com) leaped into freelance magazine writing because she simply loved to write, and that love turned her into an expert. "I never loved working to line someone else's pockets." A full-time freelancer since 1997, with credits like *Family Circle*, *Redbook*, and *Writer's Digest*, she also writes articles, books, e-courses, and e-books about her profession as a magazine writer.

JOBS

Part-time, full-time, temporary or permanent, writing jobs hone your skills, pad your resume, and present avenues to movers and shakers you wouldn't necessarily meet on your own. Government and corporate managers hire writers under all sorts of guises like Social Media Specialist and Communications Specialist, as well as the expected Reporter and Copywriter.

Alexis Grant considers her prior jobs as catapults. "Working at a newspaper (*Houston Chronicle*) and a news magazine (*US News & World Report*) for six years provided the foundation for what I'm doing now as a freelancer. Producing stories regularly on tight deadlines will always make you a better writer."

Joan Dempsey chose to return to full-time work and write her novel on the side, removing worries about her livelihood. "My creative writing was suffering trying to freelance. So, I have a day job that supports me now." She still maintains her Facebook presence to continue building her platform for her pending novel.

DIVERSIFICATION

Most importantly, however, is learning how to collect all your funding options and incorporate them into your plan. The successful writer doesn't perform in one arena. Instead, he thrives in more of a three-ring circus.

Grant states it well: "For a long while I thought of myself as only a journalist, but there are so many other ways to use my skills. Today my income comes from three streams: helping small companies with social media and blogging (the biggest source), writing and selling e-guides and courses (my favorite), and taking freelance writing or editing assignments."

Formichelli is proud of being flexible. "When I've had it with magazine writing, I put more energy into my e-courses, and vice versa. Heck, I'm even a certified personal trainer, so if I get really sick of writing I can work out. But a definite side benefit to diversifying is that I'm more protected from the feast-or-famine nature of writing."

Sometimes pursuing the more common sense or lucrative income opportunity can open doors for the dream. When my novel didn't sell, I began writing freelance articles. Then I established FundsforWriters, using all the grant, contest, publisher and market research I did for myself. A decade later, once the site thrived with over 45,000 readers, I used the very research I'd gleaned for my readers to find an agent and sign a publishing contract . . . for the original novel started so long ago.

You can fight to fund one project or study all resources and fund a career. Opportunity is there. Just don't get so wrapped up in one angle that you miss the chance to invest more fully in your future.

C. HOPE CLARK manages FundsForWriters.com and is the author of several books, including *Lowcountry Bribe* and *Palmetto Poison*. Learn more at http://chopeclark.com.

WRITING FROM THE ROAD

....

by Tom Bentley

Topping the small hill in the almost hallucinatory heat and seeing the dizzying number of centuries-old pagodas small and large, the sacred shrines polished and crumbling, the diverse animal and spirit statuary—and yet more and more of all, up and up into the higher hills above, I had a feeling I've had just a few times before: This is unbelievable. Unbelievable on a couple of levels: first, that I was traveling through vivid, mysterious, ancient Myanmar, a country whose borders were basically closed to tourists just a few years before. Second, that I hadn't paid a dime for the long flights, the extravagant hotels, nor the meals and tours that structured the trip.

Why? Well, words. In the Myanmar case, I'd exchanged just the promise of words to come for an all-expenses paid press trip in late 2015, hosted by an international immersive-travel company. This was only the fourth press trip I'd been on, but one that had by far the most writers in tow, 17 in all. That unbelievable feeling? I'd also had it only three months before the Myanmar trip, coming out of the water from a snorkeling session on Hawaii's Big Island, at a cove so dazzlingly beautiful, with its wind-whipped palms and gleaming waves, that it gave me chills, despite the warm water. That wasn't the only time I was bedazzled on that trip, because I stayed with my girlfriend on the Big Island rent-free for five weeks.

Why? Again, words.

Let me explain: In the past few years, I've spent a couple of months in the Bahamas, seven weeks in Panama, seven weeks in Mexico and the time in Hawaii. I stayed in an incredible penthouse in Vegas for five days, and went on a jolly six-day trip through the Florida Keys. I've had a few comped rooms at great California B&Bs. All because I was either directly writing about the trip for a PR agency or the like, or because I was being rewarded for a prior published piece about a place, or because I was house-sitting with my girlfriend in a place from which we could both do our work. Writing work.

THIS IS NOT MY BEAUTIFUL HOUSE.
(BUT IT'S MINE FOR NOW)

Let's talk about the house-sitting first. First of all, for it to be doable, you have to have the kind of work that allows you to leave your house for relatively long stretches of time. It's clear that the Internet and its communication efficiencies have opened the floodgates for "solopreneurs" who can sell services or goods from their own homes—or, in my girl-friend's and my case, even from other people's homes. I've been freelancing for many years from my home office as a marketing writer, magazine and newspaper writer, essay-ist and fiction writer. My girlfriend, Alice, works within a narrower range as a marketing writer, but again, she's worked from home for years.

Alice had heard about an online service called Caretakers Gazette that listed hous-esitting opportunities all over the world. With that service and subsequent ones we en-gaged, the basics are the same: you pay a small subscription fee, put up a profile of your interests, skills and experience, and then you can see listings from homeowners. The listings run a remarkable gamut, and they are truly international: there are listings to be the head butler of extended households at imposing castles, to maintaining what ap-pears to be a lean-to on a tiny island. There are opportunities from staying at a compact flat in Central London to helping build a dream house in a remote part of the Costa Ri-can jungle.

That "build a dream house" part is where things can get sticky. Some homeown-ers might simply want you to take care of a couple of cats, bring in the mail and keep the house up, as we did for a period in lovely San Miguel de Allende, Mexico. Other ones might want you to care for unusual animals, like the parrots, toucans and deer we attend-ed to, among other beasts, in Panama. (And the deer being one that we were encouraged to "walk"!) Or the four dogs, all with varying medical needs (and one definitely in need of a psychoanalyst) that we cared for in the Bahamas.

PREREQUISITES AND PITFALLS

If you need to work close to regular 8-hour days, then being part of a homeowner's plans for you to manage their three Airbnbs and help build a horse stable while they are gone aren't realistic. We did Skype with the homeowners of the Bahamas house, but because that was one of our first housesitting experiences, we didn't ask enough questions. We could have found out more details about the irregular Internet, how much attention the dogs actually needed, and how the owner, who we originally thought would be gone for two full months, would be popping back in for a week at a time, with disconcerting results.

Back in your native land, you have to make sure your own mortgage/rent is set up to be paid, as well as your other bills, so online payments are your friend. We have had house-sitters stay in our house several times while we've gone gallivanting about the world, so you either need to register with the same kind of online service, or have reliable friends or trusted acquaintances. And we have a cat to care for, but thank god, unlike the deer, she doesn't need to be walked.

But you know how things work in your own country; be prepared for things not to work in quite the same way in another. Language and cultural barriers can be perplexing, but operating in a patient spirit of adventure and openness to the exotic or simply weird is helpful. (Though I don't recommend the adventure of crashing the host's car, as I did. It worked out OK, but some lessons are less worth learning.)

But mostly, these excursions are worth it. Travel takes you out of yourself, out of the coffin of your conventional thinking, out of one-day-follows-another, endlessly, until your own end. The housesitting service we use now, MindMyHouse.com, sends regular listings that we mull—and sometimes pine—over. We thought maybe, just maybe, we could do the Moroccan oasis one, but had to drop out. No fears though—there are always new ones to come. Housesitting isn't always easy and the unexpected can happen. But who wants the expected? Dublin in the spring, anyone?

TRAVEL WRITING FOR FUN AND (NOT SO MUCH) PROFIT

You can see that being a writer in general sets the stage for the house-sitting trips. An additional advantage is being a travel writer too, because you can then write about the house-sitting locales for newspapers and magazines. I mentioned staying in Hawaii: I wrote a piece on fun coffee tours there for the *San Jose Mercury News*, have another on a famous Big Island architectural wonder coming for the Hana Hou in-flight mag, and another in the offing on a fun kava bar for the *Los Angeles Times*.

Now those are straight pitch/approval/submission pieces, where I approached an editor and landed an assignment. Always keep an eye out (and a notebook handy) when you're traveling because there's double-duty potential there: You can trek around interesting places, and get paid later for writing about it. I've gotten advance assignments from editors for places I knew I'd be traveling, and also gotten them later after I returned.

Get competent with a camera too. Today's more image-conscious publications are sometimes sold on the photos alone, with the text a complement. The newest smartphones can take quality images if you are careful, though I still carry a digital camera. And some pubs (like the *Los Angeles Times*) pay for photos separately, though sadly in my experience, travel articles in general pay less than they did years ago.

The money (or lack of it) brings up another issue: many publications will not accept any articles that derive from media or press trips, even if only part of the trip (say, the flight) was comped. Considering that it's tough to make a living as a writer, and a travel writer in particular, and with travel expenses never cheap, this feels punitive. My stories for the publications mentioned above were all on my own dime, since we paid for the Hawaii flights and other expenses, just not rent for our lodging.

PRESS TRIPS CAN IMPRESS

However, there are some publications that are looser about press-trip stories, or that are the intermediaries for publishing them. For instance, that Myanmar trip mentioned at the beginning? The reason I was given that trip was because I'd won second place in a travel-writing contest for Dave's Travel Corner in 2013 (and a third-place win in 2014). I'd written about the Florida Keys for his site before, so when a Keys PR agency contacted him with the offer of a media trip for a writer, Dave turned the trip over to me. (Do submit to writing contests—you never know what the outcome—and the lingering aftermath—might be.)

PR agencies and media-relations organizations for destinations often engage connected travel writers to write about sights, excursions and restaurants for their clients. If you have a relationship with a highly trafficked venue like Dave's (huge volume of site traffic, and he tweets your articles to his list of nearly 270,000 Twitter followers), you're in good stead to be offered fully paid media trips, like the ones I took through him to Myanmar, the Keys and Las Vegas (and he offered others I couldn't go on).

Now, for none of these trips did I receive any cash for writing about them later. And media trips are typically so venue-filled, morning into night, that you are a cross-eyed dishrag at day's end, so you can't do any of your other writing. But damn, to go to an exotic place like Myanmar (and in their own ways, exotic places like the Keys and Vegas), and venture to the peculiar and always colorful venues in those places, without paying a cent? Sign me up.

Another potential perk that can come from writing straightforward articles on places where you've paid expenses is that they might later offer free stays, like I received from two beautiful bed and breakfasts, one outside Pinnacles National Park and one outside Placerville, CA. Those were both unexpected treats.

TRAVEL IS A TONIC

You might feel an unstated yet tangible pressure to only write about the good on such journeys. After all, they are underwritten by companies that have a stake in the game. But I never had any of the entities behind the trips push a slant or writing agenda. I was intrigued to be offered such trips, and they all exceeded my expectations, so it was easy to write with appreciation. However, I didn't write about some of the less thrilling aspects of travel for any of those trips (like the stomach bacteria I returned with from Myanmar)—

it didn't seem integral to the tales I told. But I did feel fully open to writing about some of the oddities and weirdnesses I encountered.

Travel, particularly to faraway places, can be irritating, stressful, and take you far from your comfort zones. But your comfort zones aren't the places that expand your thinking, deepen your sense of self, make you say "wow!" Traveling as a writer can pack extra satisfaction, because you can reflect upon your journey, and put it on the page. Putting a trek into words can itself be a form of travel: you move through your mind, made more elastic by the new electricity you've brought to it by seeing novel sights.

Your writing will take you places. Literally.

....

TOM BENTLEY is a business writer and editor, an essayist, and a fiction writer. (He does not play banjo.) He's published hundreds of freelance pieces—ranging from first-person essays to travel pieces to more journalistic subjects—in newspapers, magazines, and online. His small-press short story collection, *Flowering and Other Stories*, was published in the spring of 2012. His self-published book on finding and cultivating your writer's voice, *Think Like a Writer: How to Write the Stories You See* was published in June of 2015. He would like you to pour him a Manhattan right at five.

....

TIPS FOR A GREAT CONFERENCE EXPERIENCE

by Kerrie Flanagan

When I was new to writing 17 years ago, I wanted to soak in all I could about the publishing industry and the craft of writing. What transported me into this world at light speed was my first writing conference.

I felt like Captain Kirk landing the Spaceship Enterprise on some alien planet. I was uncomfortable, I didn't speak the language and at times I wanted Scotty to beam me up. But, once I completed my mission, I realized all my doubts and apprehensions about whether or not I belonged were self-inflicted. No one cared that I hadn't published anything yet. It was clear we were all there for the same reasons; because we were passionate about writing and because we wanted to continue to hone our craft.

Over the years, I have attended many conferences, presented at some and even hosted one for 10 years. During this time it has become quite clear that regardless of where you are in your writing journey, conferences are the perfect way to connect with industry professions, and continue to learn more about the craft, the business and what is happening in the publishing world.

PICKING THE RIGHT CONFERENCE

There are many great ones across the country. They vary in size, specialty and cost. It is important to find the ones that fit your needs and your budget. Some are very genre specific like a mystery or romance writer's conference and others are more general, providing sessions on a variety of writing related topics like writing dialogue and character development as well as the business of writing.

Where to find conferences

The Shaw Guides (writing.shawguides.com) is a great online resource. You can search based on location or specific month. It provides all the basic information you require about each event and a link to that conference's website. Writing magazines and resource books, like the *Guide to Literary Agents* are also great sources.

What is included?

When looking for a conference, don't let the first price you see influence your decision. Delve deeper to see what is included at that price. Are meals included? Do agent/editor pitch session come with the registration fee? How about critiques or special workshops? Sometimes the price looks almost too good to be true and when you look closer, it is.

For instance, Conference A is only $150 for two days, but then each of the four meals is an extra $20, there is a $15 fee to get a pitch session with an agent, and the 2-hour workshop with your favorite author is another $35. So if you take advantage of the full conference your total cost is $280. Sure, you can bring your own lunch or go somewhere else (which will cost you as well), but you will miss out on some great opportunities to talk with other writers, the presenters, agents and editors. On the flip side, Conference B is also a two-day conference with the same amount of workshops and pitch sessions and it is $290, but everything is included.

By researching further, you find they are both comparable in price. Now, examine the offerings of each and decide which best meets your needs.

Selection of workshops

Workshops make up the bulk of any writers' conference, so you want to make sure there are a wide variety of choices for you to pick from. Think about what you want to get out of it. Do you want to focus on the craft of writing, the business side of it or explore new genres? Look at the topics to see if they fit with your plan. Then be sure to research the presenters to learn more about their writing and their level of expertise. Finding workshops in your genre is important, but it is good to expand your writing horizons and consider attending some in different genres.

Access to industry professionals

Having a chance to talk with professionals in the industry and ask them questions is a definite perk. Find out what opportunities are available like cocktail hours or ask if presenters are assigned to tables at meal times. These are ideal times to start up casual conversations with the agents, editors or presenters and make a connection (this is not a time to pitch your book idea though, unless asked).

Pitch sessions

Many offer opportunities to pitch your book idea to an agent or editor face to face. This can be a definite plus if you have a completed manuscript or book proposal and are seeking representation. Research each editor or agent to make sure there is at least one who represents your genre before deciding if this is the right conference for you.

Keynote speakers

A big-name author can be a huge draw, but I caution you not to base your decision on this factor alone. Many times, the keynote speaker comes in, does her talk and then leaves after a book signing. This is only about one hour out of the whole event, so make sure the rest of the it lives up to the hype of the one speaker.

MAKING THE MOST OUT OF THE CONFERENCE

A conference is an investment in yourself and your writing. Once you have found one you are interested in, you want to be prepared so you can get the most out of your experience.

Network

Many writers hear this word and want to find the nearest wormhole to hide in. After all, our writing time is spent by ourselves with only our characters to keep us company. Mingling with strangers can be downright intimidating. With a little preparation it doesn't have to be scary. Make time for a little cyber research. Google the presenters. Visit their websites and find out more about who they are and their writing. Follow them on social media and if you are on those platforms, begin by interacting with them that way. Then when you have the chance to visit with them during a cocktail hour or meal, you will have some topics you can talk about. Another tip for easing the discomfort of networking is to have a few standard questions ready to go. People generally like to talk about themselves, so ask about their family, their job, and what they like to do for fun when they are not writing. One great phrase to use is, "Tell me about..." This way you don't have to ask questions that seem intrusive like, "Are you married?" Instead you can say, "Tell me about your family."

Be Professional

Whether we like it or not, publishing is a business and needs to be treated like one. First and foremost, dress the part. When you are at home writing you may love your big comfy sweat pants and warm flannel shirt, but home is where they should stay. For the conference, plan to dress professionally. It isn't necessary to wear a business suit, but you should wear something nice and something you will be comfortable in all day. Also, maintain your poise when you are interacting with agents and editors. There are always designated times when you can discuss your manuscript with them. Don't corner them and pitch your book during a cocktail hour and don't slide your manuscript under a bathroom stall door. You will be remembered, but not for the right reasons.

Participate

Once you are there, you need to, "give her all she's got, Captain." Take advantage of everything that is being offered and participate in as much as you can. After all, you paid for it so you might as well get your money's worth. If you are in a session that is not meeting your expectations, it is okay to quietly slip out and find another one. Toward the end of the event, you are going to be tired and your brain will be full, but I encourage you to turn on the thrusters and stay until the very end.

Keep an open mind

It's easy to stay the course and focus only on your genre. But why not challenge yourself and go boldly where you have not gone before? Explore different worlds and expand your writing horizons. If you write children's books, attend a short story workshop or attend a screenwriting session. By keeping an open mind, you can always learn something new that you can apply to your own writing.

FOLLOWING UP

Once the conference is over and you are back at home base, there is still some work to be done. It is easy to skip this part, but you will make a lasting impression if you put effort into making one final connection.

Thank you notes

Take an afternoon to write handwritten thank you notes to the agents, editors, presenters and the conference organizers you met. Thank them for their time and if there was something they said during a presentation or during a conversation that resonated with you or something they did, mention that as well. They all put a lot of time into the event and a short note from you can go a long way.

Send any requested manuscripts in a timely fashion

If after a pitch session, an agent or editor requested a partial or full manuscript, then be sure to send it within a couple of weeks. If it needs some extra polishing before sending, then make time to work on the edits so you can get it out quickly. The longer you wait, the longer you risk them not remembering you and the easier it is for you to not do it.

Set Goals

Now it is time to think about what you want to accomplish with your newfound knowledge and your regenerated energy. Do you want to finish the first draft of a novel? Find an agent? Publish short stories or articles? Pick a couple and write those down. Give yourself a deadline as to when you want them completed. Then write the action steps needed to achieve those goals. For instance, if you want to have your novel completed in six months, then one action step may be to set aside four hours a week to write. Now, decide how you will reward yourself once you complete your task; go shopping, go to a movie, have a spa day. By creating big goals and the steps needed to complete them, you provide yourself with a path that, if followed, will lead to success.

Writing conferences are a worthwhile investment in you and your writing. Take the voyage to explore different genres, to seek out new information and new connections, and to boldly go where others have gone before.

KERRIE FLANAGAN is an accomplished freelance writer, author and publisher from Colorado. Her books include: *Write Away; A Year of Musings and Motivations for Writers, and Planes, Trains* and *Chuck & Eddie*. Her publishing company, Hot Chocolate Press, creates books to warm your heart, nourish your soul and spark your sense of adventure. http://HotChocolatePress.com

CREATE CONTENT TO GROW YOUR AUDIENCE

by Sage Cohen

Writers today have access to a wide range of technology platforms that give us instant access to readers. The key to reaching them effectively and keeping them engaged is consistently delivering great content (meaning information and experiences) that provides real value in the area of our expertise. When we join the conversation and make a meaningful contribution, we can grow our audience, fortify our platform, and sustain our own interest in our work for the long term. Following are some strategies that can help you deliver content that connects—and converts one-time readers into long-term believers.

GIVE YOUR AUDIENCE WHAT YOU PROMISED THEM

We build credibility and connection with our audience/s by having the conversations they have come to us to have. Because many of us have multiple contexts in which we write, live, and serve, we must be intentional about which of our tribes we are speaking to when we share content.

When I am posting in my Radical Divorce blog, for example, I don't share my thoughts about the craft of poetry. And when I'm writing a post on Path of Possibility, my blog for writers, I'm not likely to discuss the challenges and opportunities of co-parenting. I have separate Facebook pages for each topic. And I generally hashtag my tweets with #radicaldivorce, #lifepoetic or #productivewriter (my three literary platforms) to make it easier for people to see at a glance if the info I'm sharing is meant for them. On LinkedIn, I share only info related to my marketing communications consulting firm. And when I want to share with my personal network, I tweet without a hashtag, post on my main Facebook page, or upload to a private Vimeo page.

Not sure what kind of content you should be offering, to whom? These questions can help you clarify your approach. If you have multiple platforms, you can run through this list for each one.

- **WHAT IS YOUR TOPIC OR GENRE? AND WHAT IS YOUR UNIQUE ANGLE OR POINT OF VIEW IN THIS AREA?** For example, in my Radical Divorce blog, my topic is doing divorce differently. My unique angle is: I see the breakdown of divorce as a once-in-a-lifetime opportunity for breakthrough—to greater happiness, healing, and wholeness for everyone in the family.
- **WHAT IS YOUR MISSION?** I want to help divorcing parents rewrite their story, reboot their heart, and revise their divorce—so everyone in the family can thrive.
- **WHO IS YOUR AUDIENCE?** I serve divorcing parents with my Radical Divorce blog and digital products. You may not be sure who your readers are (or will be) yet, and that is fine. Start with a clear picture of who you intend your readers to be—and write for them. (I wrote for my friend Sebastian for years, and I believe that helped me eventually attract other readers like her.) As you go, you'll learn more about the people drawn to your work, how it adds value to their lives, and how this influences (or not) the direction you take in your writing.
- **WHO IS YOUR COMMUNITY?** My Radical Divorce community consists of single parents and their support network: coaches, therapists, authors, lawyers, and entrepreneurs. Again, you may not know who your community is yet, and that is fine. As you go deeper into your topic or your genre, you will learn more about your peers and your role models from the content you read, the conversations that your content generates, and the places where your content is shared. Think of content as your trail of crumbs that you scatter to find your way to a new kind of belonging.

With clarity about who your audience is and the value you bring to them comes the opportunity to be in conversation with them, learn with and from them, and relentlessly help and satisfy them.

MAKE IT IRRESISTIBLE

Reader loyalty is established one piece of irresistible content at a time. To discover how you and your readers define irresistible content, consume as much content as you can, from the sources and people you admire in your field. Tune into your favorite podcasts, notice which tweets get you to click on the link to read more, which e-mails you stop everything to read when they arrive in your inbox, which posts on Facebook you share with your community. Through the constellation of content you consume, you can better understand your own passions and preferences—and see what gets you and others to respond.

15 ways to engage

Not sure how to begin, or sustain, a content creation practice? Following are a range of ideas for writing and sharing content that can help grow your audience over time.

1. **REBLOGGING.** This is one of the simplest and most common ways to share content. You can excerpt a provocative quote from a piece of writing you admire, share a link to the full piece, and describe why you think it is valuable.

2. **GUEST-POSTING.** Offer to write a guest post for a blog in your field, or invite a writer you admire to share their work on your blog. This gives both of you greater visibility to each other's audience.

3. **INTERVIEWS.** Interviewing experts in your field or a related field can provide a great service to your audience and bring that expert's audience to you.

4. **CONTESTS, CHALLENGES AND GIVEAWAYS.** Create an exciting opportunity to get something free, try something new, or compete in good company, and people are often inspired to join in—and spread the word.

5. **ENDORSEMENTS.** Share weekly or monthly link lists to the content that you think best serves your audience. This gives them something incredibly useful, while helping the authors of that content increase their traction.

6. **HOW-TO.** Share what you know—from quick tips to step-by-step instructions. This is a great way to become invaluable to readers, and keep them coming back for more.

7. **GENRE-SPECIFIC.** Share insights and make recommendations about the craft of your genre, as well as the related news, products, and services.

8. **SERIALIZATION.** Share small amounts of your writing over time. This is a strategy fiction writers sometimes use to get readers hooked on a story or book.

9. **LITERARY CITIZENSHIP.** Comment on literary news, events, authors, or the publishing industry.

10. **THOUGHT LEADERSHIP.** Whether it's a book, a class or lecture, or a downloadable PDF, give your audience a deep dive into your topic and help them discover something of great importance to their lives or work.

11. **RESPOND TO THE ZEITGEIST.** Reflect on news related to your field of expertise in ways that shed light and share your unique perspective.

12. **PERSONAL VIGNETTES.** Share stories about how you've dealt with or are dealing with a topic in your own life that your readers are also interested in addressing.

13. **INSPIRATION.** Offer quotes, poems, art, wisdom, and insights designed to motivate and inspire.

14. **REVIEWS.** Share a detailed analysis of books, tools, technologies, or other resources that could be valuable to your readers.

15. **PROMPTS.** Offer prompts and provocations to help your audience find new ways forward.

SHARE STRATEGICALLY

What is a writer to do with this range of compelling content? Where and how should you distribute it? First, it's important to understand the ways in which content travels:

- You write/create and share
- Other people or companies or media channels write/create, and you share—adding your own commentary or perspective (I call this "curating" content)
- You write/create and other people share

Next, consider the most common digital channels through which writers today share content. I've described the advantages of each and ways to maximize each share.

CHANNEL	ADVANTAGES
BLOG POSTS	Share content of any length, at the intervals you choose, on your chosen topic. Use any of the 15 content strategies above.
E-MAIL	Arrive in the inbox of people who have opted in to hear from you. Use the content you share to inspire and invite people to join your e-mail list, where you can continue to serve them well.
FACEBOOK	Easily excerpt and share your blog content and others' content. Create specific pages for community engagement related to your platform.
TWITTER	Tweet a compelling excerpt or insight, and link readers directly to the content you are sharing. Use hashtags to make it instantly clear what your content is about and whom it is for.
LINKEDIN	Offer targeted content such as blog posts or reblogging targeted to your colleagues and professional network.
INSTAGRAM	Share the photos and videos that deliver your message.
PINTEREST	Offer visual inspiration that people will want to pin and display.
PERISCOPE	Take them someplace and show them around with live video, if this is meaningful to what you offer.
YOUTUBE	Tell your story in video.

PODCASTS	Are you more of a talker than a writer? Then this could be a powerful channel for you. Share content of any length, at the intervals you choose, on your chosen topic, by audio.

Plus, there are newsletters, billboards, matchbook covers, thank you notes, and endless other channels through which to reach your readers in interesting and compelling ways. I propose that you start with one or two that appeal to you most, then diversify from there over time.

MAKE AN EDITORIAL PLAN, AND STICK TO IT

Creating and sharing fresh content regularly takes discipline, creativity, and stamina. I find it far easier to face the blank page with an editorial calendar in hand that reflects my premeditated goals for reaching my audience. My plan reflects both the content I intend to create and the channels where I intend to share it.

For example, if the main place your tribe gathers is in a Facebook community, you may want your editorial plan to reflect a daily post there. If blogging is your main channel of communication, your plan should reflect how all of your social media revolves around that. If you plan to use Twitter as a channel, you can determine tweet volume and frequency goals. Eventually, when you are generating a great deal of content in multiple channels on a regular basis, you can use social media tools like Buffer or Hootsuite to organize, schedule, and automate the content you share.

Here's an example of how you might plan to generate, share, and promote a weekly blog post.

DAY	CHANNEL	CONTENT TYPE	TOPICS
Mondays	* Blog: Write / publish post * E-mail: Send post by email to blog subscribers * Twitter: Tweet 3X, each featuring unique quotes and linking to blog post with topic hashtag * Facebook: Post an excerpt in FB community page and link to blog post * LinkedIn: Share a different excerpt and link to blog post	* First Mondays: expert interviews * Second Mondays: reblogging * Third Mondays: how-to articles * Fourth Mondays: book reviews	[Here you'd map out every Monday throughout the year with the experts you will interview, the how-to topics you will cover, and the books you will review.]

As you see, you can even weave some of the 15 types of content into your plan, so you have a blueprint for keeping it interesting for readers. In Evernote, I have a notebook for each of my editorial categories for each of my platforms. I use these to log content ideas and save great links. Then, when it's time to write, I usually have a long list of ideas to choose from. This makes it much easier for me to get started—and sustain my momentum.

SERVING YOUR AUDIENCE GROWS YOUR AUDIENCE

Creating and curating content is a practice. I invite you to start small, experiment, and have fun. Over time, you will find the right rhythm for you and your readers. The more you write, read, and share content, the clearer you will be about your platform and what your audience wants and needs from you. As your confidence and expertise grow, a constellation of readers, colleagues, and collaborators will grow with you. Content can be the rich tapestry that weaves you all together in shared purpose, passion, and possibility.

SAGE COHEN is the author of the nonfiction books *Writing the Life Poetic*; *The Productive Writer*; and *Fierce on the Page* (forthcoming) all from Writer's Digest Books and the poetry collection *Like the Heart, the World* from Queen of Wands Press. Her essays, fiction, poems and how-to articles have appeared in a wide range of publications, including: *Rattle*; Hip Mama; The Night, and the Rain, and the River; The Truth of Memoir; Cup of Comfort for Writers, and *Writer's Digest* magazine. Sage holds an MFA from New York University and a BA from Brown University. She offers strategies and support for writers at pathofpossibility.com and for divorcing parents at radicaldivorce.com.

HOW TO DEVELOP AN EFFECTIVE AUTHOR BRAND

by Leslie Lee Sanders

An author's brand isn't just the specific colors of your website, a catchy tagline, or a recognizable face. Branding is delivering on a promise after setting an expectation. Determining how you want to be perceived and what sets you apart is essential when organizing an author's image, but that is only the tip of the iceberg when it comes to branding. Diving deeper when creating an author brand is a must.

Following is an in-depth look at how to build a successful author brand and become a fierce competitor in the publishing business.

ESTABLISH AN IMAGE

When establishing your image, think beyond color scheme and website layout. Humans are unique for their feeling capabilities, and the way we feel about something usually stays with us longer than any color or image. If applied properly, certain phrases, images, and colors trigger emotions, and this is your main goal when establishing your image. However, you must recognize the emotion you want to convey and how it links people to your brand.

For example, you might want to convey love, calm, excitement, wonder, intrigue, nostalgia, or even hilarity, but deep down the feeling should be universal enough to be relatable.

This is how branding works. A brand effectively engages emotion. Remember the Geico commercial where the massive camel awkwardly strolls through a busy office during the middle of the day asking the workers what day it is? Sure, it is a funny ad, but what is that commercial doing on a deeper level? The commercial is selling a service using a situation most people relate to by making you laugh. Actually, Geico's history of running funny ads have become their brand, from the gecko, the cavemen, Maxwell the Pig, and now the "Hump Day" camel.

Most people relate to the situation of working a demanding nine-to-five and counting the days until the weekend. Most people are probably familiar with a co-worker who, much like the camel, points out the middle of the week in the same tedious way, prompting tired sighs and eye rolls. The commercial triggers something most people "get" and therefore it sticks with them. This is what your brand should do too.

What you do for your readers through your website, blogs, videos, and podcasts is your "service." The books and stories you sell is your "product." How you manage it is your "business." Connect to your audience using emotion to form your reputation and establish your image.

What feelings do you want to trigger?

List the emotions you want others to feel when visiting your website or when reading your books. An easy way to accomplish this is by asking yourself what words you want to associate with your image. Take the third party route, step outside of yourself, and look at what you offer through an objective view. If someone were to describe you and your brand, what words or emotion would you like them to use? Trigger those emotions by using specific words in your content, books, blog posts, and author bio. Use images and colors on your website and book covers to convey your overall message.

What emotion or message do you want to resonate?

Triggering feelings and having them resonate are two different things. The former is what sucks you into the brand. The latter is what you take from it, what you're left with, or what stays with you. What would you like readers to take away from your book after reading it? After visiting your website, what message will they remember you by? Make your mission clear in your work.

What promises do you want to communicate?

By communicating a promise, and most importantly, delivering on that promise, you establish trust that produces satisfied readers, which not only translates into repeat service from avid fans, but generates new readers through word-of-mouth marketing. People will seek you out because you've become the go-to person for your particular service and product. Think Starbucks and coffee. When you've become the go-to person, you have successfully built a brand. Your brand's promise is what your audience comes to expect from your business.

To further expand or maintain your brand requires consistency.

CREATE CONSISTENCY

Being consistent falls under the tier of delivering on your promises. There's a cycle when building a brand; make a promise, deliver, build trust, and repeat. By performing this cycle, you are practicing consistency, which is the reason people come to you instead of your competitor. Take away one of the components and you break the cycle. Break the cycle and your brand might suffer.

You might think to get ahead or to produce sales requires you to beat your competitors, and to be on top means to flaunt what makes you unique. Today, in the writing business, this kind of thinking is retroactive because with so many books and authors flooding the market, being unique is a one in a million chance. The truth is, establishing a brand, building an audience, and keeping your audience satisfied is the trick to success in most businesses. Do this and in return your readers will help you expand your audience by advertising your products and services through recommendations (i.e., word of mouth, social media sharing, and book reviews). This is the tried-and-true formula of every successful brand.

How do you satisfy your audience? Consistency.

Consistency with book releases, series, and the production and design of content

Whatever your service, provide it regularly. Readers expect a new book from you once a year? Meet or exceed that expectation and release a new book every year or sooner. If your newsletter subscribers expect a monthly newsletter and your YouTube videos to highlight important writing techniques for novelist, continue giving them what they come for or give them what they want and more.

Establishing your place within your genre

Sure, you write in a specific genre with no plans of crossing genres anytime soon. Still there are other ways to stay consistent. Do your novels end with happily ever after? Don't try experimenting with the latest story now. You may lose some readers if they're convinced their favorite author or series is becoming something other than what they've grown to love.

Cultivating an overall tone and a distinct voice

Your voice and style, the words you use, and the way you piece them together in your writing is unique to you and your personality. Your audience will grow familiar with your writing mechanics and may even recognize your style in your speaking voice. Keep it consistent. You may have read a book by an author whose writing style reminded you of another author. For example, you may believe the book you are currently hooked on reads like a Stephen King or J.K. Rowling novel. If you're consistent, your style can become recognizable and be a distinctive part of your brand too.

BUILD TRUST

Establishing your image, being consistent, and building trust are some of what it takes to build an effective brand. Let's talk coffee. When mentioning coffee, which establishment do you think of first, Starbucks or McDonalds? Most would say Starbucks. Why? Because Starbucks successfully built their coffeehouse brand.

Starbucks is one of the largest and most successful coffeehouses for many reasons, but one reason is they are consistent with their products, using the same ingredients and measurements to make each coffee the same as the one before. You know exactly how your favorite latte should taste, and they meet that expectation each time. Your brand should build a similar kind of trust with your audience.

Image familiarity, logos, and other insignia

When mentioning branding your business, the next thought might be logos. Your logo is not your brand but the visual symbol of your brand. Your logo is a way to identify your brand in its simplest form, a visual representation of your business.

Here are the best ways to use your logo to maximize your brand's exposure:

- **BOOK SERIES COVER.** A perfect way to use a logo is on the cover of your books in a particular series. It's a recognizable insignia that communicates the promise and trust exchange between you and your readers. When they see that logo on the cover they know each book contains your familiar voice and writing style, and they will know what to expect of the books in that series.
- **STATIONARY, BUSINESS CARDS, BOOKMARKS, LETTERHEAD, ETC.** Office supplies are probably the most obvious place to add your logo. Also make sure your logo appears on business forms like invoices, packing slips, and receipts.
- **ONLINE USE.** Use your logo in place of your profile picture on Twitter and Facebook. Add it to your website header and favicon. Use it in your e-mail signature, in your guest posts, or in your Gravitar (Globally Recognized Avatar) in conjunction with guest posting to get your logo in front of new audiences when commenting on other people's blogs.
- **CUSTOM GOODS.** Add your logo to custom-made apparel, mugs, water bottles, chocolates, pens, totes, etc. Make sure the logo is large enough to be discernable at a distance, and use colors and fonts that can be easily read.

REPUTATION

Overall, your brand, brand identity, logo, content, message, storytelling, and reader experience is your reputation. Your reputation is built from the general feelings, opinions, and beliefs of the majority of people who encounter your brand. And to be just as successful in your niche as Starbucks is to coffee, remember these steps to building your author brand:

1. Establish your image by creating a specific emotion to trigger; message to resonate; and promise to communicate.

2. The following should stay consistent in your brand: identity; voice and style; and roduction.

3. Build trust by staying consistent; delivering on promises; and creating a visual representation of your business.

LESLIE LEE SANDERS is a published author with over ten years of fiction writing and book publishing experience. She teaches the art and craft of blogging, writing, and publishing on her blog at leslieleesanders.com. Her work has been included in the following Writer's Market books: 2016 Writer's Market, 2016 Novel and Short Story Writer's Market, the 2014 and 2015 editions of Guide to Self-Publishing. She's currently writing the fifth installment of her post-apocalyptic and dystopian book series, Refuge Inc.

PROMOTIONS, PR, AND PUBLICITY:

How to Make Them Work for You

by Janice Hussein

Book marketing is the process of planning and executing the conception, pricing, promotion, and distribution of a book, and then creating exchanges that satisfy readers. An important part of any marketing strategy in the book business is creating what is called word-of-mouth "buzz." How can you get that word-of-mouth buzz started and moving among your readership or potential readers?

DEVELOP A MARKETING PLAN

First, develop a Marketing Plan, starting at least nine months before a book launch, especially a first book launch. You'll need to establish a website, blog, and set up accounts with social media profiles, such as Twitter and Facebook, and with reader communities like Goodreads.

To develop that Marketing Plan, let's open the marketing toolkit and review the 5 major tools: selling, advertising, and the three P's: promotions, public relations, and publicity. First, briefly, how do these terms differ?

Selling

In publishing, personal selling happens anywhere authors and readers would personally connect—book signings, reader retreats, readers conferences like the Romantic Times Booklover's Convention, and national and regional book festivals, such as Book Expo America (BEA), the fall book festival in Seattle, WA, or Wordstock in Portland, OR.

Advertising

Advertising, a term that seems all-inclusive, refers to activities that are paid for. And the advertiser controls the content—what product to advertise, what to say about it, where to advertise, and when and how it will appear. The TV commercial is the perfect example of this.

Publicity

Publicity is free and usually appears in the form of news coverage. Publicity tools are news releases, news conferences, editorials, or product announcements. Think reviews. No one paid the media outlet or reviewer (usually) to do the interview or to mention the author or book. If it's not paid for, then it's publicity, though there are indirect costs with publicity. And with publicity—unlike advertising—there is little control over what is said.

Promotions

Promotions, like publicity, can be free. Examples are in-store displays, giveaways, and contests. Other examples are coupons, short-term price reductions, samples—the book is offered for free or as a trial size (sample chapters, prequel novellas, or short stories)—and Point-of-Purchase displays, the items we see near cash registers in bookstores.

Public Relations

Public relations, on the other hand, creates an image in the public's mind, one that is attached to the book or author. Examples of authors who do this are Brenda Novak and her campaign against diabetes or David Baldacci's Wish You Well Foundation to combat illiteracy in America.

MAKING PUBLICITY WORK

How can you make publicity work for you? Your publicity tools would be pitch letters, press releases, press kits, media alerts, articles (unless they're paid), interviews, and reviews.

Pitch letters are a single-page letter with a hook and a call to action, targeted to specific journalists at magazines that cover books, such as *The New York Times* and *Publisher's Weekly*, and to radio and television stations.

A press release is a one-page announcement of a newsworthy event. For authors, the first Press Release announces your book launch. Subsequent releases should offer some new or useful information in a way that sells your book—how the book helps readers overcome a problem or satisfies a need—or the book or one of its themes ties into a current event or holiday. Consider your audience when you write these, and target their interests—don't just sell your book. And if your focus is a bookstore buyer, then use a longer-term angle.

The press kit, which should be available in print and online as a PDF or Zip file, is directed at journalists, and usually includes the press release. Maintain an up-to-date press kit. Traditionally, a press kit contains a cover letter, sell sheet, professional author photo and the book cover, blurbs, bio, interviews, reviews, advertisements, a list of past and present events, and excerpts of novels, like booklets and sample chapters. Send these press kits to booksellers, book reviewers, newspapers, television stations, radio stations, libraries, and so on. You have a much better chance of a response from them if the materials are at hand.

Consider writing articles to gain attention for your book(s) and for yourself as a writer, either paid or unpaid (publicity). This can mean big sales for your book. Having written and published a novel, you would be considered a good source of information on the topic of writing. Other ideas are to focus on a theme within the book, to use a large section of the book and make it into an article, or to write something unrelated to your book but which will reach your target market of readers. Remember your audience—the article should address the needs of the magazine's readership. And magazine editors often need filler articles, so offering them a free article saves them money and gives you free publicity. However, request enough space after the article for a very short bio, the book title, and info on how people can order your book.

There are at least two types of reviews: a review by someone else, and an objective ready-made book review—the mock review written by the author—one that a busy editor can just insert into the publication. A book has a better chance of appearing in a publication when accompanied by a press kit and mock review, one that could be used as-is or excerpted. But check submissions guidelines for the publication, as many of them assign articles months ahead of their publication dates. For the mock review, include all the book's details: title, author, ISBN, publisher, price, and where readers could find it, either online or at a bookstore. In the last paragraph, also include a very short bio, with the author's credentials or expertise listed.

Good reviews not only increase your discoverability for readers but they also add a stamp of approval and interest, especially those that are paid, such as *Kirkus Reviews* and *Romantic Times (RT) Review Source*. Lead time for *RT Book Review Magazine* is four months before publication date, and if submitted after publication date, then about four to six weeks for *RT Review Source*. Lead time for *Kirkus* is seven to nine weeks before publication. If you missed the publication date, you can purchase a review through their Indie program, even if you're not self-published. About six to nine months before your launch, familiarize yourself with the blog sites and reviewers that authors of similar books have used for reviews and blog tours, and then approach those blogs and reviewers yourself.

MAKING PROMOTION WORK

How do you make promotions work for you? As previously stated, promotions include giveaways, contests, coupons, short-term price reductions, and samples.

Giveaways and contests have become an important element in any marketing plan, especially for authors who self-publish. These can be done on an author's website and through blog tours, Facebook, and Goodreads. Keep them relatively short in duration, a maximum of three weeks long. Start approaching blog owners several months ahead of your release date, as dates fill up quickly. Also, about a month before your release date—but ending before the launch—run a pre-launch contest, giving away something like a gift card, and then a signed copy of the book when it comes out.

By having a newsletter and developing a list of readers to send it to, you can announce your upcoming releases and book launch, including a short-term price reduction or coupon for those readers. This also helps to develop your relationship with your readers, both by staying in touch and by offering them price reductions. Set up an account with an e-mail marketing service like MailChimp, and start building your list about six to nine months ahead of your launch date, or as soon as you can. On your launch day, send out an e-mail newsletter with a link to buy the book.

Authors often have a year in between book releases, but could offer a free or trial size sample chapter or prequel or short story—related to the current book or to a series or not related. This could promote a new series or a much-awaited conclusion to a series or just keep you in the readers' mind. Some authors offer coupons to their established readership or to those who attend the book launch or book signings.

MAKING PUBLIC RELATIONS WORK

How can you make public relations work for you? Public relations is usually associated with a charity or other worthy cause—literacy, animal rescue, or fund-raising for cures for such diseases as cancer or diabetes.

And authors can become involved with public relations through speaking engagements, a Public Relations tool. Speaking engagements remain one of the bedrocks of any well-constructed PR program, even for authors, positioning the author as an expert or leader. It is excellent for generating extensive media and/or industry exposure.

PUTTING IT ALL TOGETHER

How can the three P's work together? Here's an example of that, using a "fictitious" novel about a rescue dog or the Humane Society. To market the novel, the author starts a contest—using press releases (publicity) to promote the contest and drive participation—asking readers to write letters about adopting a dog, with the most touching and unusual stories winning a prize and attendance at a free luncheon and/or fundraiser with the author. That contest is a promotion. The author could also sell tickets to the fundraiser. Again, press releases and a press kit can promote the event. Then newspapers, television, and radio are pitched to interview you about the contest, your book, and/or the fundraiser. The interviews are publicity. You can also advertise the contest in the local newspaper and in book industry magazines, such as *Writer's Digest*, or *Romantic Times Book Review Maga-*

zine. When you pick the winners and runners-up, hold a dinner for them, while also including the local animal shelter and rescue organizations—the Humane Society, Shelter Pet projects, etc. The dinner is public relations. Invite the media to cover the dinner, and that is publicity.

Marketing pays off when it's done consistently and over time. Building "buzz" usually starts with local media, moves to regional, and then national. Continue your focused marketing efforts up to three months after your launch, seeking reviews, holding contests, and posting regularly to your social media sites. And after the initial campaign is over, stay in contact with readers by blogging and posting to social media. And to anyone who helped to promote your book—reviewers, interviewers, television and radio hosts, the bookstores that carried your book, and the one that hosted your launch party—always send thank-you notes. This helps build relationships for future book releases over the course of your writing career.

JANICE HUSSEIN is a freelance writer, with 5 years of experience. She is also a freelance editor with 12 years of experience and a Master's degree in Writing. She edits short stories and novels, and offers classes and workshops at conferences and elsewhere, to writers at all levels. Hussein is a member of NW Independent Editors Guild, the National Writers Union, RWA, and the Oregon Writers Colony, and I network on Twitter, Facebook, LinkedIn, and Google+. Her articles have been previously published in F+W Media's *2016 Writer's Market*, the *2015 Guide to Self-Publishing*, and *The Novel & Short Story Writer's Market*, for the years 2010, 2011, 2013 (2), and 2014. "The Unsympathetic Protagonist," appeared in the 2010 edition; a tearsheet is available. Her work has also been published with RWR, including "The Espresso Book Machine."

CONNECTING WITH BOOK CLUBS

To Enhance Author Success

....

by Rekaya Gibson

Several sources estimate the U.S. has about five million book club members. This figure doesn't even include online groups. Book clubs are an ideal market for book sales; however, very few authors are tapping into this great resource. Bestselling author Brian W. Smith meets with an average of 20 book clubs per year. One of his self-published books became so successful that he sold it to Strebor/Simon and Schuster. He is relentless in stressing the importance of book clubs, both large and small. Though author experiences may vary, collaborating with book clubs can contribute greatly to author success. Smith and others in the industry readily testify about the benefits of connecting with book clubs, finding and approaching them, preparing for book club meetings, engaging readers at meetings, and maintaining long-lasting relationships.

THE BENEFITS OF CONNECTING WITH BOOK CLUBS

Connecting with book clubs not only offers authors great feedback, but it also comes with other perks. Authors consider it one of the best vehicles to move multiple books at one time. Membership specifics may vary, but sales potential could be great. Also keep in mind, book club members share their feelings about books with family, friends, other book clubs and groups on social media and by word-of-mouth, which could have a residual effect. Additionally, book clubs become repeat customers and supporters. Smith has seen firsthand the benefits of partnering with book clubs by quickly establishing a fan base while receiving multiple book reviews.

Book clubs get the opportunity to meet the author and engage in a book discussion. Authors, in turn, receive priceless feedback on their masterpieces. This often spawns long-term relationships that other authors can only dream about in their careers. "Book clubs want to be a part of the history," explains Ella Curry, chief executive officer of a marketing, branding and promotions firm for EDC-Creations Media Group—a firm that inter-acts with more than 40 book clubs a year.

HOW TO FIND AND APPROACH BOOK CLUBS

When Smith started seeking book clubs about 10 years ago, Facebook wasn't the craze it is today. He, like many other authors, relied on the Internet to search for proximal book clubs. The Internet is still one of best methods to find book clubs, and many well-orga-nized clubs have websites. Search engines such as Google and Bing provide countless list-ings worldwide by typing in the keywords *book club*. Libraries and bookstores sometimes list them on their websites. For example, Barnes & Noble posts public book club meetings on its events page for each store. Tamika Newhouse, Founder and President of African-Americans on the Move Book Club (AAMBC) and Literary Awards—a virtual book club with more than 900 members—warns authors not to overlook book clubs on Meetup.com. This can be helpful, especially when visiting other cities. Of course, most social media sites make it easy to find book clubs by using the search feature.

The old-fashion way works as well: attending events and meeting book clubs face-to-face. TaNisha Webb, president of KC Girlfriends Book Club and publisher and editor of *Book Club 101 Magazine*, recommends attending literary and book club-sponsored events. The last few book choices her club selected were from authors the book club members had chosen from functions such as the annual National Book Club Conference.

Once an author has identified potential book clubs, it is then time to approach the book club president or its member(s). This can be done multiple ways. Author Terrie L. Branch likes to introduce herself to members at soirees. She loves meeting people, so en-gaging audiences comes natural to her. Introverts may struggle with this part. Branch shares, "Force yourself to interact with people and imagine yourself having a conversa-tion with a friend." Book clubs want to get to know and assist new authors.

Some book clubs prefer interested authors to fill out the contact form on their web-site, or by e-mailing them directly. When using e-mail, keep it short—two or three para-graphs. Author Ni'cola C. Mitchell likes to send a brief press release to introduce herself. Some book clubs use Facebook exclusively for correspondence. Do not leave comments or book images on their pages; rather, send them a private message expressing interest. Tamika Newhouse looks for the five W's (who, what, where, when and why) when some-one sends a query to her book club.

HOW TO PREPARE FOR A BOOK CLUB MEETING

It works in the author's favor to be ready and flexible for meetings. When making ar-rangements with a book club, find out the specifics for the day such as who will be attending, when it will be held, the timeframe, where the meeting will be held, parking, attire and format. Curry tells her clients to ask upfront whether the book club will be providing a stipend, transportation, and hotel accommodations, especially for gatherings out of the area. Otherwise, the author should expect to incur the costs, so plan accordingly. If you agree to be there, Curry says, "Keep your word and be on time."

Of course, plan to bring books to sell. Members will also be likely to purchase newer/older novels, too, so include them as well. Order the novels at least two to four weeks ahead of time to ensure delivery. Don't forget to take Sharpies, working pens and paper in order to autograph books and collect e-mail addresses. It's a good idea to generate a list of questions about your book. This may require you to revisit the book. Whatever you do, make sure you are prepared for a book discussion. Sometimes an author can anticipate questions and write them down ahead of time. They may also want to ask the reader about certain characters or situations. Ask questions about the club members and offer some fun facts about yourself. Members want to get to know the author and you should want to engage the book clubs you want to patronize you in the future.

Authors can also find cool giveaways to share with members such as audiobooks, bookmarks and candy. When Mitchell prepares for a meeting, she brings ice breaker games and activities along. She searches and finds them online.

Some other things to consider: promote the upcoming event on social media and other mediums, especially if it's open to the public. Book clubs and libraries will sometimes sponsor gatherings. The library will promote it on Facebook and pass along the information to local news outlets. The book club will develop and pass out flyers in the community. When preparing for a book club meeting, Curry sums it up best: "Plan to be social and have a good time."

HOW TO KEEP READERS ENGAGED DURING A BOOK CLUB MEETING

The author's prepared questions will help keep readers engaged during a book club meeting. Some of my favorite questions are: What did you like/dislike about the book characters? What did you think about the ending? How would you describe the book in one word? Sometimes the discussion will lead to other questions to ask the readers. It's okay to go with the flow. The conversation can lead down different paths that will bring out the best of the book club members.

Another helpful tool to keep the crowd engaged is LitVersations, a Book Conversation Game. This card game provides 70 open-ended questions to start and keep the LitVersations going about a book. Though this interactive game comes with two ways to play, use the cards in a way that fits that particular audience. The book club meeting should be lively with all those questions. If that doesn't work, "Do a giveaway to get people excited,"

Mitchell says. Quick games, ice breakers, and do-you-knows about the author and the book itself can help as well.

HOW TO MAINTAIN A LONG-LASTING RELATIONSHIP AFTER THE BOOK CLUB MEETING

When the meeting ends, the second phase begins: maintaining the relationship. Though expressing thanks at a meeting is nice, take time to follow-up again after you leave. Use the club's preferred method of correspondence to contact them. Terrie Branch actually sends thank-you cards via snail mail. Some authors distribute electronic newsletters to keep readers abreast of book releases, events (past and future), and contests. Feature the book clubs in your newsletter by highlighting your visit. Authors also send invitations to members about upcoming events. Mitchell always includes them, and they show up to support her. Follow members on social media and interact with them.

Sending copies of new books to club presidents is a good method that keeps book clubs in the loop. Curry suggests posting pictures and recaps of the time spent with the book club. Brian Smith asks readers to join his street team, a group of people who buy and actively get the word out about authors and their products. His experience demonstrates the importance of maintaining lasting relationships. Smith celebrated a 10-year anniversary with the first book club he met with to discuss his book. Recently, the club honored him along with the mayor of Daytona Beach, FL, with a key to the city.

Successfully nurturing and sustaining relationships with multiple book clubs is a great method of obtaining sales and relevance as an author. Simply put, take time to become familiar with book club members like you would anyone else. Maintaining polite communication and being thoughtful goes a long way. After all, you're selling yourself, not the book. In return, book clubs will spread the love—a key ingredient to becoming a successful author.

REKAYA GIBSON has written articles for Amtrak, *Cuisine Noir Magazine* and various lifestyle magazines. In addition, she has penned six books. She maintains a food blog based on my first fiction novel, The Food Temptress. She enjoys completing word searches while traveling the country by train and dancing freely. Follow her on Twitter @RekayaGibson

CONTRACTS 101

by Cindy Ferraino

After you do a victory dance about getting the book deal you always dreamed about or your article hitting the top of the content list of a popular magazine, the celebration quickly comes to a halt when you realize you are not at the finish line yet. Your heart begins to beat faster because you know the next possible hurdle is just around the corner—the contract. For many, the idea of reviewing a contract is like being back in first grade. You know you have to listen to the teacher when you could be playing outside. You know you have to read this contract but why because there are terms in there that look like an excerpt from a foreign language syllabus.

Before I changed my status to self-employed writer, I was working as a grants and contracts administrator at a large medical university in Philadelphia. I helped shepherd the M.D. and Ph.D. researchers through the channels of grants and contracts administration. While the researchers provided the technical and scientific pieces that could potentially be the next cure for diabetes, heart disease, or cancer, I was there to make sure they did their magic within the confines of a budget and imposed contractual regulations. The budget process was easy but when it came to contract regulations—oh well, that was a different story. I became familiar with the terms such as indemnifications, property and intellectual rights, and conditions of payments. I was an integral part of reviewing and negotiating a grant or contract that had the best interests for every party involved.

After my son was born, I left the university and my contracts background went on a brief hiatus. Once my son went off to school, I began freelance writing. After a few writing gigs sprinkled with a few too many rejection slips, I landed an assignment for *Dog Fancy* magazine. I was thrilled and eagerly anticipated the arrival of a contract in my inbox. As I opened the document, the hiatus had lifted. I read through the contract and was able to send it back within a few hours.

For many new freelancers or writers who have been around the block, contract administration is not something that they can list as a perk on their resume. Instead of searching through the Yellow Pages for a contract lawyer or trying to call in a special favor to a writer friend, there are some easy ways for a newbie writer or even a seasoned writer to review a contract before putting a smiley face next to the dotted line.

TAKE A DEEP BREATH, THEN READ ON

Remember breaking those seals on test booklets and the voice in the background telling you, "Please read the directions slowly." As you tried to drown out the voice because your stomach was in knots, little did you know that those imparting words of wisdom would come in handy as you perspired profusely over the legal jargon that unfolded before your eyes. The same words go for contracts.

Many writers, including myself, are anxious to get an assignment underway, but the contract carrot continues to loom over our creative minds. "I'm surprised by writers who just skim a contract and then sign it without understanding what it means," says Kelly James-Enger, author of books including *Six Figure Freelancing: The Writer's Guide to Making More* (Random House) and the blog Dollarsanddeadlines.blogspot.com. "Most of the language in magazine contracts isn't that complicated, but it can be confusing when you're new to the business."

When I receive a contract from a new publisher or editor, I make a second copy. My children call it "my sloppy copy." I take out a highlighter and begin to mark up the key points of the contract: beginning and end date, conditions of payment, how my relationship is defined by the publisher, and what the outline of the article should look like.

The beginning and end date of a contract is crucial. After I recently negotiated a contract, the editor changed the due date of the article in an e-mail. I made sure the contract was changed to reflect the new due date. The conditions of the payments are important because it will describe when the writer will be paid and by what method. Most publishers have turned to incremental payment schedules or payments to be made online like PayPal. How the publisher considers your contractor status is important. If you're a freelance contract writer, the contract should reflect that as well as identify you as an independent contractor for IRS tax purposes. Finally, the contract will highlight an outline of what your article or proposal should look like.

As you slowly digest the terms you are about to agree to for your assignment or book project, you gain a better understanding of what an editor or publisher expects from you and when.

CUTTING TO THE LEGAL CHASE

Once you have had a chance to review a contract, you may be scratching your head and saying, "Okay, now what does this all mean to me as a writer?" James-Enger describes three key areas where writers should keep sharp on when it comes to contracts—indemnification, pay and exclusivity provisions.

INDEMNIFICATION is a publisher's way of saying if something goes wrong, we are not responsible. If a claim is brought against another writer's work, a publisher does not want to be responsible for the legal aftermath but you could be the one receiving a notice in the mail. James-Enger warns writers to be on the lookout for indemnification clauses. "In the U.S., anyone can sue anyone over just about anything," she says; "I'm okay with agreeing to indemnification clauses that specify breaches of contract because I know I'm not going to plagiarize, libel or misquote anyone. But I can't promise that the publication will never be sued by anyone whether or not I actually breached the contract."

PAY is where you want the publisher "to show you the money." Writers need to be aware of how publishers will discuss the terms of payment in the contract. James-Enger advises to have "payment on acceptance." This means you will be paid when the editor agrees to accept your manuscript or article. If there is "no payment on acceptance," some publishers will pay when the article is published. "Push for payment whenever you can," she says.

PAYMENT TYPES

There are any number of different arrangements for publishers to pay writers. However, here are three of the most common and what they mean.

- Pays on acceptance. This means a publisher pays (or cuts a check) for the writer upon acceptance of the manuscript. This is usually the best deal a writer can hope to receive.

- Pays on publication. In these cases, a publisher pays (or cuts a check) for the writer by the publication date of the manuscript. For magazines, this could mean several months after the manuscript was accepted and approved. For books, this could mean more than a year.

- Pays after publication. Sometimes contracts will specify exactly how long after publication. Be wary of contracts that leave it open-ended.

EXCLUSIVITY PROVISIONS are where a particular publisher will not allow the writer to publish an article or manuscript that is "about the same or similar subject" during the time the publisher runs the piece. Because of the nature of the writing business, James-Enger feels writers need to negotiate this part of the contract. "I specialize in health, fitness and nutrition, and I'm always writing about a similar subject," she says.

CONTRACT TIPS

Even seasoned freelancers can find themselves intimidated by contracts. Here are a few things to consider with your contract:

- **KEEP COPY ON RECORD.** If the contract is sent via e-mail, keep a digital copy, but also print up a hard copy and keep it in an easy-to-find file folder.
- **CHECK FOR RIGHTS.** It's almost never a good idea to sell all rights. But you should also pay attention to whether you're selling any subsidiary or reprint rights. The more rights you release the more payment you should expect (and demand).
- **WHEN PAYMENT.** Make sure you understand when you are to be paid and have it specified in your contract. You may think that payment will come when the article is accepted or published, but different publishers have different policies. Get it in writing.
- **HOW MUCH PAYMENT.** The contract should specify exactly how much you are going to be paid. If there is no payment listed on the contract, the publisher could use your work for free.
- **TURN IN CONTRACT BEFORE ASSIGNMENT.** Don't start working until the contract is signed, and everything is official. As a freelancer, time is as important as money. Don't waste any of your time and effort on any project that is not yet contracted.

WHEN TO HEAD TO THE BARGAINING TABLE

Recently, I became an independent contractor for the American Composites Manufacturing Association (ACMA). When I reviewed the terms of the contract, I was concerned how my independent contractor status was identified. Although I am not an ACMA employee, I wanted to know if I could include my ACMA publications on my resume. Before I signed the contract, I questioned this issue with my editor. My editor told me I may use this opportunity to put on my resume. I signed the contract and finished my assignment.

Writers should be able to talk to an editor or a publisher if there is a question about a term or clause in a contract. "Don't be afraid to talk to the editor about the changes you'd like to make to a contract," James-Enger says; "You don't know what you'll get or if an editor is willing to negotiate it, until you ask."

When writers have to approach an editor for changes to a contract, James-Enger advises writers to act professionally when it comes to the negotiations. "I start out with saying—I am really excited to be working with you on this story and I appreciate the assignment, but I have a couple of issues with the contract that I'd like to talk to you about," she says. "Sure I want a better contract but I also want to maintain a good working relationship with my editor. A scorched-earth policy doesn't benefit any freelancer in the long run."

Negotiating payment terms is a tricky subject for some writers. Writers want to get the most bang for their buck but they don't want to lose a great writing assignment. Do your research first before you decide to ask an editor for more money to complete the assignment. Double check the publisher's website or look to see if the pay scale is equivalent to other publishers in the particular industry. Some publishers have a set publishing fee whereas others may have a little more wiggle room depending on the type of the assignment given. In today's economy, writers are a little more reluctant to ask for a higher rate for an article. If the publisher seems to be open to discussion about the pay scale, just make sure you approach the situation in a professional manner so as to not turn the publisher away from giving you another assignment.

WHO OWNS YOUR WRITING?

Besides payment terms, another area that writers may find themselves on the other end of the negotiation table is with ownership rights. We all want to take credit for the work that we have poured our heart and soul into. Unfortunately, the business of publishing has different ways of saying how a writer can classify their work. Ownership rights vary, but the biggest one that writers have a hard time trying to build up a good case against is "all rights." "All rights" is exactly what it means: *hope you are not in love with what you have just written because you will not be able to use it again.*

In recent months, I have written for two publications that I had given "all rights" to the company. My rationale is that I knew I would never need to use those articles again but I did make sure I was able to include those articles for my byline to show that I have publishing experience.

If you feel that you want to reuse or recycle an article that you had written a few years ago, you might want to consider negotiating an "all rights" clause or maybe going to another publisher. "We don't take all rights so there is no reason for authors to request we change the rights clause," says Angela Hoy, author and owner of WritersWeekly.com and Booklocker.com. "Our contracts were rated 'Outstanding' by Mark Levine (author of *The Fine Print of Self-Publishing*) and has also been called the clearest and fairest in the industry."

James-Enger is also an advocate of negotiating against contracts with an "all rights" clause. "I hate 'all rights' contracts, and try to avoid signing them as they preclude me from ever reselling the piece as a reprint to other markets," she says. "I explain that to editors, and I have been able to get editors to agree to let me retain nonexclusive reprint rights even when they buy all rights—which still lets me market the piece as a reprint." James-Enger also advises that "if the publisher demands all rights, then negotiate if the payment is sub-standard."

So if you are just receiving a contract in the mail for the first time or you are working with a new publisher, you should not be afraid of the legal lingo that blankets the message "we want to work with you." Contracts are meant to protect both the interests of the publishers and writers. Publishers want the commitment from writers that he or she will provide their best work and writers want to be recognized for their best work. But between those contracts lines, the legal lingo can cause writers to feel they need a law degree to review the contract. No, just sit back and relax and enjoy the prose that will take your writing to the next level.

RIGHTS AND WHAT THEY MEAN

A creative work can be used in many different ways. As the author of the work, you hold all rights to the work in question. When you agree to have your work published, you are granting a publisher the right to use your work in any number of ways. Whether that right is to publish the manuscript for the first time in a publication, or to publish it as many times and in as many ways as a publisher wishes, is up to you—it all depends on the agreed-upon terms. As a general rule, the more rights you license away, the less control you have over your work and the money you're paid. You should strive to keep as many rights to your work as you can.

Writers and editors sometimes define rights in a number of different ways. Below you will find a classification of terms as they relate to rights.

- **FIRST SERIAL RIGHTS.** Rights that the writer offers a newspaper or magazine to publish the manuscript for the first time in any periodical. All other rights remain with the writer. Sometimes the qualifier "North American" is added to these rights to specify a geographical limitation to the license. When content is excerpted from a book scheduled to be published, and it appears in a magazine or newspaper prior to book publication, this is also called first serial rights.
- **ONE-TIME RIGHTS.** Nonexclusive rights (rights that can be licensed to more than one market) purchased by a periodical to publish the work once (also known as simultaneous rights). That is, there is nothing to stop the author from selling the work to other publications at the same time.
- **SECOND SERIAL (REPRINT) RIGHTS.** Nonexclusive rights given to a newspaper or magazine to publish a manuscript after it has already appeared in another newspaper or magazine.
- **ALL RIGHTS.** This is exactly what it sounds like. "All rights" means an author is selling every right he has to a work. If you license all rights to your work, you forfeit the right to ever use the work again. If you think you may want to use the article again, you should avoid submitting to such markets or refuse payment and withdraw your material.
- **ELECTRONIC RIGHTS.** Rights that cover a broad range of electronic media, including websites, CD/DVDs, video games, smart phone apps, and more. The contract should specify if—and which—electronic rights are included. The presumption is unspecified rights remain with the writer.
- **SUBSIDIARY RIGHTS.** Rights, other than book publication rights, that should be covered in a book contract. These may include various serial rights; movie, TV, audio,

and other electronic rights; translation rights, etc. The book contract should specify who controls the rights (author or publisher) and what percentage of sales from the licensing of these rights goes to the author.

- **DRAMATIC, TV, AND MOTION PICTURE RIGHTS.** Rights for use of material on the stage, on TV, or in the movies. Often a one-year option to buy such rights is offered (generally for 10 percent of the total price). The party interested in the rights then tries to sell the idea to other people—actors, directors, studios, or TV networks. Some properties are optioned numerous times, but most fail to become full productions. In those cases, the writer can sell the rights again and again.

Sometimes editors don't take the time to specify the rights they are buying. If you sense that an editor is interested in getting stories, but doesn't seem to know what his and the writer's responsibilities are, be wary. In such a case, you'll want to explain what rights you're offering (preferably one-time or first serial rights only) and that you expect additional payment for subsequent use of your work.

The Copyright Law that went into effect January 1, 1978, states writers are primarily selling one-time rights to their work unless they—and the publisher—agree otherwise in writing. Book rights are covered fully by contract between the writer and the book publisher.

CINDY FERRAINO has been blessed with a variety of assignments, including newspaper articles, magazine articles, ghost-written articles, stories for books, and most recently authoring a book on accounting and bookkeeping terminology, *The Complete Dictionary of Accounting & Bookkeeping Terms Explained Simply* (Atlantic Publishing Group).

MAKING THE MOST OF THE MONEY YOU EARN

by Sage Cohen

Writers who manage money well can establish a prosperous writing life that meets their short-term needs and long-term goals. This article will introduce the key financial systems, strategies, attitudes, and practices that will help you cultivate a writing life that makes the most of your resources and sustains you over time.

DIVIDING BUSINESS AND PERSONAL EXPENSES

If you are reporting your writing business to the IRS, it is important that you keep the money that flows from this source entirely separate from your personal finances. Here's what you'll need to accomplish this:

- **BUSINESS CHECKING ACCOUNT:** Only two types of money go into this account: money you have been paid for your writing and/or "capital investments" you make by depositing your own money to invest in the business. And only two types of payments are made from this account: business-related expenses (such as: subscriptions, marketing and advertisement, professional development, fax or phone service, postage, computer software and supplies), and "capital draws" which you make to pay yourself.
- **BUSINESS SAVINGS ACCOUNT OR MONEY MARKET ACCOUNT:** This account is the holding pen where your quarterly tax payments will accumulate and earn interest. Money put aside for your retirement account(s) can also be held here.
- **BUSINESS CREDIT CARD:** It's a good idea to have a credit card for your business as a means of emergency preparedness. Pay off the card responsibly every month and this will help you establish a good business credit record, which can be useful down the line should you need a loan for any reason.

When establishing your business banking and credit, shop around for the best deals, such as highest interest rates, lowest (or no) monthly service fees, and free checking. Mint.com is a good source for researching your options.

EXPENSE TRACKING AND RECONCILING

Once your bank accounts are set up, it's time to start tracking and categorizing what you earn and spend. This will ensure that you can accurately report your income and itemize your deductions when tax time rolls around every quarter. Whether you intend to prepare your taxes yourself or have an accountant help you, immaculate financial records will be the key to speed and success in filing your taxes.

For the most effective and consistent expense tracking, I highly recommend that you use a computer program such as QuickBooks. While it may seem simpler to do accounting by hand, I assure you that it isn't. Even a luddite such as I, who can't comprehend the most basic principles of accounting, can use QuickBooks with great aplomb to plug in the proper categories for income and expenses, easily reconcile bank statements, and with a few clicks prepare all of the requisite reports that make it easy to prepare taxes.

PAYING BILLS ONLINE

While it's certainly not imperative, you might want to check out your bank's online bill pay option if you're not using this already. Once you've set up the payee list, you can make payments in a few seconds every month or set up auto payments for expenses that are recurring. Having a digital history of bills paid can also come in handy with your accounting.

MANAGING TAXES

Self-employed people need to pay quarterly taxes. A quick, online search will reveal a variety of tax calculators and other online tools that can help you estimate what your payments should be. Programs such as TurboTax are popular and useful tools for automating and guiding you step-by-step through tax preparation. An accountant can also be helpful in understanding your unique tax picture, identifying and saving the right amount for taxes each quarter, and even determining SEP IRA contribution amounts (described later in this article). The more complex your finances (or antediluvian your accounting skills), the more likely that you'll benefit from this kind of personalized expertise.

Once you have forecasted your taxes either with the help of a specialized, tax-planning program or an accountant, you can establish a plan toward saving the right amount for quarterly payments. For example, once I figured out what my tax bracket was and the approximate percentage of income that needed to be set aside as taxes, I would immediately transfer a percentage of every deposit to my savings account, where it would sit and grow a little interest until quarterly tax time came around. When I could afford to do so, I would also set aside the appropriate percentage of SEP IRA contribution from each deposit so that I'd be ready at end-of-year to deposit as much as I possibly could for retirement.

THE PRINCIPLE TO COMMIT TO IS THIS: Get that tax-earmarked cash out of your hot little hands (i.e., checking account) as soon as you can, and create whatever deterrents you need to leave the money in savings so you'll have it when you need it.

INTELLIGENT INVESTING FOR YOUR CAREER

Your writing business will require not only the investment of your time but also the investment of money. When deciding what to spend and how, consider your values and your budget in the three, key areas in the chart below: education, marketing and promotion, and keeping the wheels turning.

This is not an absolute formula for spending—just a snapshot of the types of expenses you may be considering and negotiating over time. My general rule would be: start small and modest with the one or two most urgent and/or inexpensive items in each list, and grow slowly over time as your income grows.

The good news is that these legitimate business expenses may all be deducted from your income—making your net income and tax burden less. Please keep in mind that the IRS allows losses as long as you make a profit for at least three of the first five years you are in business. Otherwise, the IRS will consider your writing a non-deductible hobby.

EDUCATION	MARKETING AND PROMOTION	KEEPING THE WHEELS TURNING
Subscriptions to publications in your field	URL registration and hosting for blogs and websites	Technology and application purchase, servicing and back-up
Memberships to organizations in your field	Contact database subscription (such as Constant Contact) for communicating with your audiences	Office supplies and furniture
Books: on topics you want to learn, or in genres you are cultivating	Business cards and stationery	Insurance for you and/or your business
Conferences and seminars	Print promotions (such as direct mail), giveaways and schwag	Travel, gas, parking
Classes and workshops	Online or print ad placement costs	Phone, fax and e-mail

PREPARATION AND PROTECTION FOR THE FUTURE

As a self-employed writer, in many ways your future is in your hands. Following are some of the health and financial investments that I'd recommend you consider as you build and nurture The Enterprise of You. Please understand that these are a layperson's suggestions. I am by no means an accountant, tax advisor, or financial planning guru. I am simply a person who has educated herself on these topics for the sake of her own writing business, made the choices I am recommending, and benefited from them. I'd like you to benefit from them, too.

SEP IRAS

Individual Retirement Accounts (IRAs) are investment accounts designed to help individuals save for retirement. But I do recommend that you educate yourself about the Simplified Employee Pension Individual Retirement Account (SEP IRA) and consider opening one if you don't have one already.

A SEP IRA is a special type of IRA that is particularly beneficial to self-employed people. Whereas a Roth IRA has a contribution cap of $5,000 or $6,000, depending on your age, the contribution limit for self-employed people in 2011 is approximately 20% of adjusted earned income, with a maximum contribution of $49,000. Contributions for a SEP IRA are generally 100% tax deductible and investments grow tax deferred. Let's say your adjusted earned income this year is $50,000. This means you'd be able to contribute $10,000 to your retirement account. I encourage you to do some research online or ask your accountant if a SEP IRA makes sense for you.

CREATING A 9-MONTH SAVINGS BUFFER

When you're living month-to-month, you are extremely vulnerable to fluctuation in the economy, client budget changes, life emergencies and every other wrench that could turn a good working groove into a frightening financial rut. The best way to prepare for the unexpected is to start (or continue) developing a savings buffer. The experts these days are suggesting that we accumulate nine months of living expenses to help us navigate transition in a way that we feel empowered rather than scared and desperate to take the next thing that comes along.

I started creating my savings buffer by opening the highest-interest money market account I could find and setting up a modest, monthly automatic transfer from my checking account. Then, when I paid off my car after five years of monthly payments, I added my car payment amount to the monthly transfer. (I'd been paying that amount for five years, so I was pretty sure I could continue to pay it to myself.) When I paid off one of my credit cards in full, I added that monthly payment to the monthly savings transfer. Within a year, I had a hefty sum going to savings every month before I had time to think about it, all based on expenses I was accustomed to paying, with money that had never been anticipated in the monthly cash flow.

What can you do today—and tomorrow—to put your money to work for your life, and start being as creative with your savings as you are with language?

DISABILITY INSURANCE

If writing is your livelihood, what happens if you become unable to write? I have writing friends who have become incapacitated and unable to work due to injuries to their brains, backs, hands and eyes. Disability insurance is one way to protect against such emergencies and ensure that you have an income in the unlikely event that you're not physically able to earn one yourself.

Depending on your health, age, and budget, monthly disability insurance payments may or may not be within your means or priorities. But you won't know until you learn more about your coverage options. I encourage you to investigate this possibility with several highly rated insurance companies to get the lay of the land for your unique, personal profile and make an informed decision.

HEALTH INSURANCE

Self-employed writers face tough decisions about health insurance. If you're lucky, there's someone in your family with health coverage also available to you. Without the benefit of group health insurance, chances are that self-costs are high and coverage is low. As in disability insurance, age and health status are significant variables in costs and availability.

Ideally, of course, you'll have reasonably-priced health insurance that helps make preventive care and health maintenance more accessible and protects you in case of a major medical emergency. The following are a few possibilities to check out that could reduce costs and improve access to health coverage:

- Join a group that aggregates its members for group coverage, such as a Chamber of Commerce or AARP. Ask an insurance agent in your area if there are any other group coverage options available to you.
- Consider a high-deductible health plan paired with a Health Savings Account (HSA). Because the deductible is so high, these plans are generally thought to be most useful for a major medical emergency. But an HSA paired with such a plan allows you to put aside a chunk of pre-tax change every year that can be spent on medical expenses or remain in the account where it can be invested and grow.

Establishing effective financial systems for your writing business will take some time and energy at the front end. I suggest that you pace yourself by taking an achievable step or two each week until you have a baseline of financial management that works for you. Then, you can start moving toward some of your bigger, longer-term goals. Once it's established, your solid financial foundation will pay you in dividends of greater efficiency, insight, and peace of mind for the rest of your writing career.

SAGE COHEN is the author of *The Productive Writer* and *Writing the Life Poetic,* both from Writer's Digest Books. She's been nominated for a Pushcart Prize, won first prize in the Ghost Road Press Poetry contest and published dozens of poems, essays and articles on the writing life. Sage holds an MFA in creative writing from New York University and a BA from Brown University. Since 1997, she has been a freelance writer serving clients including Intuit, Blue Shield, Adobe, and Kaiser Permanente.

HOW MUCH SHOULD I CHARGE?

by Aaron Belz

The first question most aspiring freelance writers ask themselves is, "Where do I find paying gigs?" But once a writer finds that first freelance gig, they often ask, "How much should I charge?"

They ask this question, because often their clients ask them. In the beginning, this can be one of the most stressful parts of the freelancing process: Trying to set rates that don't scare away clients, but that also help put dinner on the table.

Maybe that's why the "How Much Should I Charge?" pay rate chart is one of the most popular and useful pieces of the *Writer's Market*. Freelancers use the rates to justify their worth on the market to potential clients, and clients use the chart as an objective third party authority on what the current market is paying.

Use the following chart to help you get started in figuring out your freelance rates. If you're a beginner, it makes sense to price yourself closer to the lower end of the spectrum, but always use your gut in negotiating rates. The rate on that first assignment often helps set the expectations for future rates.

As you find success in securing work, your rates should naturally increase. If not, consider whether you're building relationships with clients that lead to multiple assignments. Also, take into account whether you're negotiating for higher rates on new assignments with familiar and newer clients.

Remember that smarter freelancers work toward the goal of higher rates, because better rates mean one of two things for writers: Either they're able to earn money, or they're able to earn the same money in less time. For some freelancers, having that extra time is worth more than anything money can buy.

Use the listings in *Writer's Market* to find freelance work for magazines, book publishers, and other traditional publishing markets. But don't restrict your search to the traditional markets if you want to make a serious living as a freelance writer.

As the pay rate chart shows, there are an incredible number of opportunities for writers to make a living doing what they love: writing. Maybe that writing critiques, editing anthologies, blogging, or something else entirely.

While this pay rate chart covers a wide variety of freelance writing gigs, there are some that are just too unique to get a going rate. If you can't find a specific job listed here, try to find something that is similar to use as a guide for figuring out a rate. There are times when you just have to create the going rate yourself.

Thank you, Aaron Belz, for assembling this pay rate chart and sharing your sources in the sidebar below. I know it will help more than one freelance writer negotiate the freelance rates they deserve.

—*Robert Lee Brewer*

PARTICIPATING ORGANIZATIONS

Here are the organizations surveyed to compile the "How Much Should I Charge?" pay rate chart. You can also find Professional Organizations in the Resources.

- American Medical Writers Association (AMWA), www.amwa.org
- American Society of Journalists & Authors (ASJA), www.asja.org
- American Society of Media Photographers (ASMP), www.asmp.org
- American Society of Picture Professionals (ASPP), www.aspp.com
- American Translators Association (ATA), www.atanet.org
- Association of Independents in Radio (AIR), www.airmedia.org
- Educational Freelancers Association (EFA), www.the-efa.org
- Freelance Success (FLX), www.freelancesucess.com
- Investigative Reporters & Editors (IRE), www.ire.org
- Media Communicators Association International (MCA-I), www.mca-i.org
- National Cartoonists Society (NCS), www.reuben.org/main.asp
- National Writers Union (NWU), www.nwu.org
- National Association of Science Writers (NASW), www.nasw.org
- Society of Professional Journalists (SPJ), www.spj.org
- Women in Film (WIF), www.wif.org
- Writer's Guild of America East (WGAE), www.wgaeast.org
- Writer's Guild of America West (WGA), www.wga.org

AARON BELZ is the author of *The Bird Hoverer* (BlazeVOX), *Lovely, Raspberry* (Persea), and *Glitter Bomb* (Persea). A St. Louis native, he now lives and works in Hillsborough, North Carolina. Visit him online at belz.net or follow him on Twitter @aaronbelz.

ADVERTISING & PUBLIC RELATIONS

	PER HOUR			PER PROJECT			OTHER		
	HIGH	LOW	AVG	HIGH	LOW	AVG	HIGH	LOW	AVG
Advertising copywriting	$156	$36	$84	$9,000	$160	$2,760	$3/word	30¢/word	$1.57/word
Advertising editing	$125	$20	$65	n/a	n/a	n/a	$1/word	30¢/word	66¢/word
Advertorials	$182	$51	$93	$1,890	$205	$285	$3/word	85¢/word	$1.58/word
Business public relations	$182	$30	$85	n/a	n/a	n/a	$500/day	$200/day	$356/day
Campaign development or product launch	$156	$36	$100	$8,755	$1,550	$4,545	n/a	n/a	n/a
Catalog copywriting	$156	$25	$71	n/a	n/a	n/a	$350/item	$30/item	$116/item
Corporate spokesperson role	$182	$72	$107	n/a	n/a	n/a	$1,200/day	$500/day	$740/day
Direct-mail copywriting	$156	$36	$85	$8,248	$500	$2,839	$4/word	$1/word	$2.17/word
							$400/page	$200/page	$315/page
Event promotions/publicity	$126	$30	$76	n/a	n/a	n/a	n/a	n/a	$500/day
Press kits	$182	$31	$81	n/a	n/a	n/a	$850/60sec	$120/60sec	$458/60sec
Press/news release	$182	$30	$80	$1,500	$125	$700	$2/word	50¢/word	$1.20/word
							$750/page	$150/page	$348/page

	PER HOUR			PER PROJECT			OTHER		
	HIGH	LOW	AVG	HIGH	LOW	AVG	HIGH	LOW	AVG
Radio commercials	$102	$30	$74	n/a	n/a	n/a	$850/60sec	$120/60sec	$456/60sec
Speech writing/editing for individuals or corporations	$168	$36	$92	$10,000	$2,700	$5,036	$355/minute	$105/minute	$208/minute
BOOK PUBLISHING									
Abstracting and abridging	$125	$30	$74	n/a	n/a	n/a	$2/word	$1/word	$1.48/word
Anthology editing	$80	$23	$51	$7,900	$1,200	$4,588	n/a	n/a	n/a
Book chapter	$100	$35	$60	$2,500	$1,200	$1,758	20¢/word	8¢/word	14¢/word
Book production for clients	$100	$40	$67	n/a	n/a	n/a	$17.50/page	$5/page	$10/page
Book proposal consultation	$125	$25	$66	$1,500	$250	$788	n/a	n/a	n/a
Book publicity for clients	n/a	n/a	n/a	$10,000	$500	$2,000	n/a	n/a	n/a
Book query critique	$100	$50	$72	$500	$75	$202	n/a	n/a	n/a
Children's book writing	$75	$35	$50	n/a	n/a	n/a	$5/word	$1/word	$2.75/word
							$5,000/adv	$450/adv	$2,286/adv
Content editing (scholarly/textbook)	$125	$20	$51	$15,000	$500	$4,477	$20/page	$3/page	$6.89/page

	PER HOUR			PER PROJECT			OTHER		
	HIGH	LOW	AVG	HIGH	LOW	AVG	HIGH	LOW	AVG
Content editing (trade)	$125	$19	$54	$20,000	$1,000	$6,538	$20/page	$3.75/page	$8/page
Copyediting (trade)	$100	$16	$46	$5,500	$2,000	$2,892	$6/page	$1/page	$4.22/page
Encyclopedia articles	n/a	n/a	n/a	n/a	n/a		50¢/word	15¢/word	35¢/word
							$3,000/item	$50/item	$933/item
Fiction book writing (own)	n/a	n/a	n/a	n/a	n/a		$40,000/adv	$525/adv	$14,193/adv
Ghostwriting, as told to	$125	$35	$67	$47,000	$5,500	$22,892	$100/page	$50/page	$87/page
Ghostwriting, no credit	$125	$30	$73	n/a	n/a		$3/word	50¢/word	$1.79/word
							$500/page	$50/page	$206/page
Guidebook writing/editing	n/a	n/a	n/a	n/a	n/a		$14,000/adv	$10,000/adv	$12,000/adv
Indexing	$60	$22	$35	n/a	n/a		$12/page	$2/page	$4.72/page
Manuscript evaluation and critique	$150	$23	$66	$2,000	$150	$663	n/a	n/a	n/a
Manuscript typing	n/a	n/a	$20	n/a	n/a		$3/page	95¢/page	$1.67/page
Movie novelizations	n/a	n/a	n/a	$15,000	$5,000	$9,159	n/a	n/a	n/a

	PER HOUR			PER PROJECT			OTHER		
	HIGH	LOW	AVG	HIGH	LOW	AVG	HIGH	LOW	AVG
Nonfiction book writing (collaborative)	$125	$40	$80	n/a	n/a	n/a	$110/page $75,000/adv	$50/page $1,300/adv	$80/page $22,684/adv
Nonfiction book writing (own)	$125	$40	$72	n/a	n/a	n/a	$110/page $50,000/adv	$50/page $1,300/adv	$80/page $14,057/adv
Novel synopsis (general)	$60	$30	$45	$450	$150	$292	$100/page	$10/page	$37/page
Personal history writing/editing (for clients)	$125	$30	$60	$40,000	$750	$15,038	n/a		n/a
Proofreading	$75	$15	$31	n/a	n/a	n/a	$5/page	$2/page	$3.26/page
Research for writers or book publishers	$150	$15	$52	n/a	n/a	n/a	$600/day	$400/day	$525/day
Rewriting/structural editing	$120	$25	$67	$50,000	$2,500	$13,929	14¢/word	5¢/word	10¢/word
Translation—literary	n/a	n/a	n/a	$95,000	$6,500	$8,000	17¢/target word	4¢/target word	8¢/target word
Translation—nonfiction/technical	n/a	n/a	n/a	n/a	n/a	n/a	30¢/target word	5¢/target word	12¢/target word

BUSINESS

	PER HOUR			PER PROJECT			OTHER		
	HIGH	LOW	AVG	HIGH	LOW	AVG	HIGH	LOW	AVG
Annual reports	$185	$60	$102	$15,000	$500	$5,850	$600	$100	$349
Brochures, booklets, flyers	$150	$45	$91	$15,000	$300	$4,230	$2.50/word	35¢/word	$1.21/word
							$800/page	$50/page	$341/page
Business editing (general)	$155	$40	$80	n/a	n/a	n/a	n/a	n/a	n/a
Business letters	$155	$40	$79	n/a	n/a	n/a	$2/word	$1/word	$1.47/word
Business plan	$155	$40	$87	$15,000	$200	$4,115		n/a	n/a
Business writing seminars	$155	$70	$112	$8,600	$550	$2,919		n/a	n/a
Consultation on communications	$155	$50	$80	n/a	n/a	n/a	$1,300/day	$530/day	$830/day
Copyediting for business	$155	$35	$65	n/a	n/a	n/a	$4/page	$2/page	$3/page
Corporate histories	$155	$45	$91	160,000	$5,000	$54,525	$2/word	$1/word	$1.50/word
Corporate periodicals, editing	$155	$45	$74	n/a	n/a	n/a	$2.50/word	75¢/word	$1.42/word
Corporate periodicals, writing	$155	$45	$83	n/a	n/a	n/a	$3/word	$1/word	$1.71/word
Corporate profiles	$155	$45	$93	n/a	n/a	n/a	$2/word	$1/word	$1.50/word

	PER HOUR			PER PROJECT			OTHER		
	HIGH	LOW	AVG	HIGH	LOW	AVG	HIGH	LOW	AVG
Ghostwriting for business execs	$155	$45	$89	$3,000	$500	$1,400	$2.50/word	50¢/word	$2/word
Ghostwriting for businesses	$155	$45	$114	$3,000	$500	$1,790	n/a	n/a	n/a
Newsletters, desktop publishing/production	$155	$45	$75	$6,600	$1,000	$3,490	$750/page	$150/page	$429/page
Newsletters, editing	$155	$35	$72	n/a	n/a	$3,615	$230/page	$150/page	$185/page
Newsletters, writing	$155	$35	$82	$6,600	$800	$3,581	$5/word; $1,250/page	$1/word; $150/page	$2.31/word; $514/page
Translation services for business use	$80	$45	$57	n/a	n/a	n/a	$35/target word; $1.41/target line	7¢/target word; $1/target line	$2.31/target word; $1.21/target line
Resume writing	$105	$70	$77	$500	$150	$295	n/a	n/a	n/a
COMPUTER, INTERNET & TECHNICAL									
Blogging—paid	$150	$35	$100	$2,000	$500	$1,250	$500/post	$6/post	$49/post
E-mail copywriting	$135	$30	$85	n/a	n/a	$300	$2/word	30¢/word	91¢/word

	PER HOUR			PER PROJECT			OTHER		
	HIGH	LOW	AVG	HIGH	LOW	AVG	HIGH	LOW	AVG
Educational webinars	$500	$0	$195	n/a	n/a	n/a	n/a	n/a	n/a
Hardware/Software help screen writing	$95	$60	$81	$6,000	$1,000	$4,000	n/a	n/a	n/a
Hardware/Software manual writing	$165	$30	$80	$23,500	$5,000	$11,500	n/a	n/a	n/a
Internet research	$95	$25	$55	n/a	n/a	n/a	n/a	n/a	n/a
Keyword descriptions	n/a	n/a	n/a	n/a	n/a	n/a	$200/page	$130/page	$165/page
Online videos for clients	$95	$60	$76	n/a	n/a	n/a	n/a	n/a	n/a
Social media postings for clients	$95	$25	$62	n/a	n/a	$500	n/a	n/a	$10/word
Technical editing	$150	$30	$65	n/a	n/a	n/a	n/a	n/a	n/a
Technical writing	$160	$30	$80	n/a	n/a	n/a	n/a	n/a	n/a
Web editing	$100	$25	$57	n/a	n/a	n/a	$10/page	$4/page	$5.67/page
Webpage design	$150	$25	$80	$4,000	$200	$1,278	n/a	n/a	n/a
Website or blog promotion	n/a	$30	n/a	$650	$195	$335	n/a	n/a	n/a

	PER HOUR			PER PROJECT			OTHER		
	HIGH	LOW	AVG	HIGH	LOW	AVG	HIGH	LOW	AVG
Website reviews	n/a	$30	n/a	$900	$50	$300	n/a	n/a	n/a
Website search engine optimization	$89	$30	$76	$50,000	$8,000	$12,000	n/a	n/a	n/a
White papers	$135	$30	$82	$10,000	$2,500	$4,927	n/a	n/a	n/a
EDITORIAL/DESIGN PACKAGES									
Desktop publishing	$150	$18	$67	n/a	n/a	n/a	$750/page	$30/page	$202/page
Photo brochures	$125	$60	$87	$15,000	$400	$3,869	$65/picture	$30/picture	$48/picture
Photography	$100	$45	$71	$10,500	$50	$2,100	$2,500/day	$500/day	$1,340/day
Photo research	$75	$45	$49	n/a	n/a	n/a	n/a	n/a	n/a
Picture editing	$100	$45	$64	n/a	n/a	n/a	$65/picture	$30/picture	$53/picture
EDUCATIONAL & LITERARY SERVICES									
Author appearances	n/a	n/a	n/a	n/a	n/a	n/a	$500/hour	$100/hour	$285/hour
at national events							$30,000/event	$500/event	$5,000/event

	PER HOUR			PER PROJECT			OTHER		
	HIGH	LOW	AVG	HIGH	LOW	AVG	HIGH	LOW	AVG
Author appearances at regional events	n/a	n/a	n/a	n/a	n/a	n/a	$1,500/event	$50/event	$615/event
Author appearances at local groups	$63	$40	$47	n/a	n/a	n/a	$400/event	$75/event	$219/event
Authors presenting in schools	$125	$25	$78	n/a	n/a	n/a	$350/class	$50/class	$183/class
Educational grant and proposal writing	$100	$35	$67	n/a	n/a	n/a		n/a	n/a
Manuscript evaluation for theses/dissertations	$100	$15	$53	$1,550	$200	$783	n/a	n/a	n/a
Poetry manuscript critique	$100	$25	$62	n/a	n/a	n/a	n/a	n/a	n/a
Private writing instruction	$60	$50	$57	n/a	n/a	n/a	n/a	n/a	n/a
Readings by poets, fiction writers	n/a	n/a	n/a	n/a	n/a	n/a	$3,000/event	$50/event	$225/event
Short story manuscript critique	$150	$30	$75	$175	$50	$112	n/a	n/a	n/a
Teaching adult writing classes	$125	$30	$82	n/a	n/a	n/a	$800/class	$115/class	$450/class
							$5,000/course	$500/course	$2,667/course

	PER HOUR			PER PROJECT			OTHER		
	HIGH	LOW	AVG	HIGH	LOW	AVG	HIGH	LOW	AVG
Writer's workshop panel or class	$220	$30	$92	n/a	n/a	n/a	$5,000/day	$60/day	$1,186/day
Writing for scholarly journals	$100	$40	$63	$450	$100	$285	n/a	n/a	n/a
FILM, VIDEO, TV, RADIO, STAGE									
Book/novel summaries for film producers	n/a	n/a	n/a	n/a	n/a	n/a	$34/page	$15/page	$23/page / $120/book
Business film/video scriptwriting	$150	$50	$97	n/a	n/a	$600	$1,000/run min	$50/run min	$334/run min / $500/day
Comedy writing for entertainers	n/a	n/a	n/a	n/a	n/a	n/a	$150/joke / $500/group	$5/joke / $100/group	$50/joke / $283/group
Copyediting audiovisuals	$90	$22	$53	n/a	n/a	n/a	n/a	n/a	n/a
Educational or training film/video scriptwriting	$125	$35	$81	n/a	n/a	n/a	$500/run min	$100/run min	$245/run min
Feature film options	First 18 months, 10% WGA minimum; 10% minimum each 18-month period thereafter.								
TV options	First 180 days, 5% WGA minimum; 10% minimum each 180-day period thereafter.								

	PER HOUR			PER PROJECT			OTHER		
	HIGH	LOW	AVG	HIGH	LOW	AVG	HIGH	LOW	AVG
Industrial product film/video scriptwriting	$150	$30	$99	n/a	n/a	n/a	$500/run min	$100/run min	$300/run min
Playwriting for the stage	5-10% box office/Broadway, 6-7% box office/off-Broadway, 10% box office/regional theatre.								
Radio editorials	$70	$50	$60	n/a	n/a	n/a	$200/run min / $400/day	$45/run min / $250/day	$124/run min / $325/day
Radio interviews	n/a	n/a	n/a	$1,500	$110	$645	n/a	n/a	n/a
Screenwriting (original screenplay-including treatment)	n/a	n/a	n/a	n/a	n/a	n/a	$118,745	$63,526	$92,153
Script synopsis for agent or film	$2,344/30 min, $4,441/60 min, $6,564/90 min								
Script synopsis for business	$75	$45	$62	n/a	n/a	n/a	n/a	n/a	n/a
TV commercials	$99	$60	$81	n/a	n/a	n/a	$2,500/30 sec	$150/30 sec	$1,204/30 sec
TV news story/feature	$1,550/5 min, $3,000/10 min, $4,200/15 min								
TV scripts (non-theatrical)	Prime Time: $33,700/60 min, $47,500/90 min								
	Not Prime Time: $12,900/30 min, $23,500/60 min, $35,300/90 min								

	PER HOUR			PER PROJECT			OTHER		
	HIGH	LOW	AVG	HIGH	LOW	AVG	HIGH	LOW	AVG
TV scripts (teleplay/MOW)		$70,000/120 min							
MAGAZINES & TRADE JOURNALS									
Article manuscript critique	$130	$25	$69	n/a	n/a	n/a	n/a	n/a	n/a
Arts query critique	$105	$50	$80	n/a	n/a	n/a	n/a	n/a	n/a
Arts reviewing	$100	$65	$84	$335	$95	$194	$1.25/word	12¢/word	63¢/word
Book reviews	n/a	n/a	n/a	$900	$12	$348	$1.50/word	20¢/word	73¢/word
City magazine calendar	n/a	n/a	n/a	$250	$45	$135	$1/word	35¢/word	75¢/word
Comic book/strip writing	$225 original story, $525 existing story, $50 short script.								
Consultation on magazine editorial	$155	$35	$86	n/a	n/a	n/a	n/a	n/a	$100/page
Consumer magazine column	n/a	n/a	n/a	$2,500	$70	$898	$2.50/word	37¢/word	$1.13/word
Consumer front-of-book	n/a	n/a	n/a	$850	$320	$550	n/a	n/a	n/a
Content editing	$130	$30	$62	$6,500	$2,000	$3,700	15¢/word	6¢/word	11¢/word
Contributing editor	n/a	n/a	n/a	n/a	n/a	n/a	$160,000/ contract	$22,000/ contract	$53,000/ contract

	PER HOUR			PER PROJECT			OTHER		
	HIGH	LOW	AVG	HIGH	LOW	AVG	HIGH	LOW	AVG
Copyediting magazines	$105	$18	$55	n/a	n/a	n/a	$10/page	$2.90/page	$5.78/page
Fact checking	$130	$15	$46	n/a	n/a	n/a	n/a	n/a	n/a
Gag writing for cartoonists	$35/gag; 25% sale on spec.								
Ghostwriting articles (general)	$225	$30	$107	$3,500	$1,100	$2,200	$10/word	65¢/word	$2.50/word
Magazine research	$125	$20	$53	n/a	n/a	n/a	$500/item	$100/item	$200/item
Proofreading	$80	$20	$40	n/a	n/a	n/a	n/a	n/a	n/a
Reprint fees	n/a	n/a	n/a	$1,500	$20	$439	$1.50/word	10¢/word	76¢/word
Rewriting	$130	$25	$74	n/a	n/a	n/a	n/a	n/a	$50/page
Trade journal feature article	$128	$45	$80	$4,950	$150	$1,412	$3/word	20¢/word	$1.20/word
Transcribing interviews	$185	$95	$55	n/a	n/a	n/a	$3/min	$1/min	$2/min
MEDICAL/SCIENCE									
Medical/scientific conference coverage	$125	$50	$85	n/a	n/a	n/a	$800/day	$300/day	$600/day
Medical/scientific editing	$96	$15	$33	n/a	n/a	n/a	$12.50/page	$3/page	$4.40/page
							$600/day	$500/day	$550/day

	PER HOUR			PER PROJECT			OTHER		
	HIGH	LOW	AVG	HIGH	LOW	AVG	HIGH	LOW	AVG
Medical/scientific writing	$91	$20	$46	$4,000	$500	$2,500	$2/word	25¢/word	$1.12/word
Medical/scientific multimedia presentations	$100	$50	$75	n/a	n/a	n/a	$100/slide	$50/slide	$77/slide
Medical/scientific proofreading	$80	$18	$50	n/a	n/a	$500	$3/page	$2.50/page	$2.75/page
Pharmaceutical writing	$125	$100	$50	n/a	n/a	n/a	n/a	n/a	n/a
NEWSPAPERS									
Arts reviewing	$69	$30	$53	$200	$15	$101	60¢/word	6¢/word	36¢/word
Book reviews	$69	$45	$58	$350	$15	$140	60¢/word	25¢/word	44¢/word
Column, local	n/a	n/a	n/a	$600	$25	$206	$1/word	38¢/word	50¢/word
Column, self-syndicated	n/a	n/a	n/a	n/a	n/a	n/a	$35/insertion	$4/insertion	$16/insertion
Copyediting	$35	$15	$27	n/a	n/a	n/a	n/a	n/a	n/a
Editing/manuscript evaluation	$75	$25	$35	n/a	n/a	n/a	n/a	n/a	n/a
Feature writing	$79	$40	$63	$1,040	$85	$478	$1.60/word	10¢/word	59¢/word
Investigative reporting	n/a	n/a	n/a	n/a	n/a	n/a	$10,000/grant	$250/grant	$2,250/grant

	PER HOUR			PER PROJECT			OTHER		
	HIGH	LOW	AVG	HIGH	LOW	AVG	HIGH	LOW	AVG
Obituary copy	n/a	n/a	n/a	$225	$35	$124	n/a	n/a	n/a
Proofreading	$45	$15	$23	n/a	n/a	n/a	n/a	n/a	n/a
Stringing	n/a	n/a	n/a	$2,400	$40	$525	n/a	n/a	n/a
NONPROFIT									
Grant writing for nonprofits	$150	$12	$75	$3,000	$400	$1,852	n/a	n/a	n/a
Nonprofit annual reports	$100	$28	$60	n/a	n/a	n/a	n/a	n/a	n/a
Nonprofit writing	$150	$17	$65	$17,600	$100	$4,706	n/a	n/a	n/a
Nonprofit editing	$125	$16	$50	n/a	n/a	n/a	n/a	n/a	n/a
Nonprofit fundraising literature	$110	$35	$74	$3,500	$200	$1,597	$1,000/day	$300/day	$767/day
Nonprofit presentations	$100	$40	$73	n/a	n/a	n/a	n/a	n/a	n/a
Nonprofit public relations	$100	$30	$60	n/a	n/a	n/a	n/a	n/a	n/a
POLITICS/GOVERNMENT									
Government agency writing/editing	$110	$25	$64	n/a	n/a	n/a	$1.25/word	25¢/word	75¢/word

	PER HOUR			PER PROJECT			OTHER		
	HIGH	LOW	AVG	HIGH	LOW	AVG	HIGH	LOW	AVG
Government grant writing/editing	$150	$19	$72	n/a	n/a	n/a	n/a	n/a	n/a
Government-sponsored research	$110	$35	$66	n/a	n/a	n/a	n/a	n/a	$600/day
Public relations for political campaigns	$150	$40	$86	n/a	n/a	n/a	n/a	n/a	n/a
Speechwriting for government officials	$200	$40	$96	$4,550	$1,015	$2,755	$200/run min	$110/run min	$155/run min
Speechwriting for political campaigns	$155	$65	$101	n/a	n/a	n/a	$200/run min	$100/run min	$162/run min

LITERARY AGENTS

///

The literary agencies listed in this section are open to new clients and are members of the Association of Authors' Representatives (AAR), which means they do not charge for reading, critiquing, or editing. Some agents in this section may charge clients for office expenses such as photocopying, foreign postage, long-distance phone calls, or express mail services. Make sure you have a clear understanding of what these expenses are before signing any agency agreement.

FOR MORE...

The *2017 Guide to Literary Agents* (Writer's Digest Books) offers more than 800 literary agents, as well as information on writers' conferences. It also offers a wealth of information on the author/agent relationship and other related topics.

SUBHEADS

Each listing is broken down into subheads to make locating specific information easier. In the first section, you'll find contact information for each agency. Further information is provided which indicates an agency's size, its willingness to work with a new or previously unpublished writer, and its general areas of interest.

ADAMS LITERARY

7845 Colony Rd., C4 #215, Charlotte NC 28226. (704) 542-1440. **Fax:** (704) 542-1450. **E-mail:** info@adamsliterary.com. **Website:** www.adamsliterary.com. **Contact:** Tracey Adams, Josh Adams. Estab. 2004. Member of AAR. Other memberships include SCBWI and WNBA.

MEMBER AGENTS Tracey Adams, Josh Adams, Samantha Bagood (assistant).

REPRESENTS Considers these fiction areas: middle grade, picture books, young adult.

HOW TO CONTACT Submit through online form on website only. Send e-mail if that is not operating correctly. All submissions and queries should first be made through the online form on website. Will not review—and will promptly recycle—any unsolicited submissions or queries received by mail. Before submitting work for consideration, review complete guidelines online, as the agency sometimes shuts off to new submissions. Accepts simultaneous submissions. "While we have an established client list, we do seek new talent—and we accept submissions from both published and aspiring authors and artists."

TERMS Agent receives 15% commission on domestic sales; 20% on foreign sales. Offers written contract.

BETSY AMSTER LITERARY ENTERPRISES

6312 SW Capitol Hwy #503, Portland OR 97239. **E-mail:** b.amster.assistant@gmail.com (for adult titles); b.amster.kidsbooks@gmail.com (for children's and YA). **Website:** www.amsterlit.com. **Contact:** Betsy Amster (adult); Mary Cummings (children's and YA). Estab. 1992. Member of AAR. Represents more than 65 clients.

REPRESENTS Nonfiction, fiction, juvenile books. **Considers these nonfiction areas:** business, cooking, creative nonfiction, decorating, gardening, history, horticulture, interior design, investigative, memoirs, money, multicultural, parenting, popular culture, psychology, self-help, women's issues. **Considers these fiction areas:** crime, detective, juvenile, literary, middle grade, multicultural, mystery, picture books, police, women's, young adult.

HOW TO CONTACT For adult titles: b.amster.assistant@gmail.com. "For fiction or memoirs, please embed the first three pages in the body of your e-mail. For nonfiction, please embed your proposal." For children's and YA: b.amster.kidsbooks@gmail.com. See submission requirements online at website. "For pic-

ture books, please embed the entire text in the body of your e-mail. For novels, please embed the first three pages." Accepts simultaneous submissions. Responds in 1 month to queries; in 2 months to mss. Obtains most new clients through recommendations from others, solicitations, conferences.

TERMS Agent receives 15% commission on domestic sales; 20% commission on foreign sales. Offers written contract, binding for 1 year; three-month notice must be given to terminate contract. Charges for photocopying, postage, messengers, galleys/books used in submissions to foreign and film agents and to magazines for first serial rights. (Please note that it is rare to incur much in the way of expenses now that most submissions are made by e-mail.)

APONTE LITERARY AGENCY

E-mail: agents@aponteliterary.com. **Website:** aponteliterary.com. **Contact:** Natalia Aponte. Member of AAR. Signatory of WGA.

MEMBER AGENTS Natalia Aponte (any genre of mainstream fiction and nonfiction, but she is especially seeking women's novels, historical novels, supernatural and paranormal fiction, fantasy novels, political and science thrillers); Victoria Lea (any category — especially interested in women's fiction, science fiction and speculative fiction).

REPRESENTS Novels. **Considers these fiction areas:** fantasy, historical, paranormal, science fiction, supernatural, thriller, women's.

HOW TO CONTACT E-query. Accepts simultaneous submissions. Responds in 6 weeks if interested.

THE AXELROD AGENCY

55 Main St., P.O. Box 357, Chatham NY 12037. (518)392-2100. **E-mail:** steve@axelrodagency.com. **Website:** www.axelrodagency.com. **Contact:** Steven Axelrod. Member of AAR. Represents 15-20 clients.

REPRESENTS Novels. **Considers these fiction areas:** crime, mystery, new adult, romance, women's.

HOW TO CONTACT Query via e-mail. Accepts simultaneous submissions. Obtains most new clients through recommendations from others.

TERMS Agent receives 15% commission on domestic sales; 20% commission on foreign sales.

AZANTIAN LITERARY AGENCY

E-mail: queries@azantianlitagency.com. **Website:** www.azantianlitagency.com. **Contact:** Jennifer Azantian. Estab. 2014. Member of AAR. Signatory of WGA.

REPRESENTS Novels. **Considers these fiction areas:** fantasy, horror, middle grade, science fiction, young adult.

HOW TO CONTACT To submit, send your query letter, 1-2 page synopsis, and first 10-15 pages all pasted in an e-mail (no attachments) to queries@azantianlitagency.com. Please note in the e-mail subject line if your work was requested at a conference, is an exclusive submission, or if your work was referred by a current client. Accepts simultaneous submissions. Responds within 6 weeks. Check the website before submitting to make sure Jennifer is currently open to queries.

CAROL BANCROFT & FRIENDS

P.O. Box 2030, Danbury CT 06813. (203)730-8270 or (800)720-7020. **Fax:** (203)730-8275. **E-mail:** cbfriends@sbcglobal.net. **Website:** www.carolbancroft.com. **Contact:** Joy Elton Tricarico, owner; Carol Bancroft, founder. Estab. 1972. Member of AAR. Signatory of WGA. Member of Society of Illustrators, Graphic Artists Guild, National Art Education Association, SCBWI.

REPRESENTS Considers these nonfiction areas: juvenile nonfiction. **Considers these fiction areas:** juvenile. **Considers these script areas:** juvenile.

HOW TO CONTACT Mail e-mail 2-3 samples with your contact information/website Accepts simultaneous submissions.

TERMS Rep receives 25% commission. Advertising costs are split: 75% paid by talent; 25% paid by representative.

BARONE LITERARY AGENCY

385 North St., Batavia OH 45103. (513)732-6740. **Fax:** (513)297-7208. **E-mail:** baroneliteraryagency@roadrunner.com. **Website:** www.baroneliteraryagency.com. **Contact:** Denise Barone. Estab. 2010. Member of AAR. Signatory of WGA. RWA Represents 10 clients.

REPRESENTS Fiction, novels. **Considers these nonfiction areas:** memoirs. **Considers these fiction areas:** action, adventure, cartoon, comic books, commercial, confession, contemporary issues, crime, detective, erotica, ethnic, experimental, family saga, fantasy, feminist, frontier, gay, glitz, hi-lo, historical, horror, humor, inspirational, juvenile, lesbian, literary, mainstream, metaphysical, military, multicultural, multimedia, mystery, new adult, New Age, occult, paranormal, plays, police, psychic, regional, religious,

romance, satire, science fiction, sports, supernatural, suspense, thriller, urban fantasy, war, westerns, women's, young adult. **Considers these script areas:** action, adventure, animation, cartoon, comedy, contemporary issues, crime, detective, erotica, ethnic, experimental, family saga, fantasy, feminist, gay, glitz, historical, horror, juvenile, lesbian, mainstream, mystery, police, psychic, religious, romantic comedy, romantic drama, science fiction, sports, supernatural, teen, thriller, western.

HOW TO CONTACT "We are no longer accepting snail mail submissions; send a query letter via e-mail instead. If I like your query letter, I will ask for the first three chapters and a synopsis as attachments." Accepts simultaneous submissions. Obtains new clients by queries/submissions via e-mail only.

TERMS 15% commission on domestic sales, 20% on foreign sales. Offers written contract.

THE BENT AGENCY

E-mail: info@thebentagency.com. **Website:** www.thebentagency.com. **Contact:** Jenny Bent; Susan Hawk; Molly Ker Hawn; Gemma Cooper; Louise Fury; Brooks Sherman; Beth Phelan; Victoria Lowes; Heather Flaherty. Estab. 2009. Member of AAR.

MEMBER AGENTS Jenny Bent (adult fiction including women's fiction, romance and crime/suspense; she particularly likes novels with magical or fantasy elements that fall outside of genre fiction; young adult and middle grade fiction; memoir; humor); Susan Hawk (young adult and middle grade and picture books; within the realm of kids stories, she likes contemporary, mystery, fantasy, science fiction, and historical fiction); Molly Ker Hawn (young adult and middle grade books, including contemporary, historical, fantasy, science fiction, thrillers, mystery); Gemma Cooper (all ages of children's and young adult books, including picture books, likes historical, contemporary, thrillers, mystery, humor, and science fiction); Louise Fury (picture books, literary middle grade, all young adult; speculative fiction, suspense/thriller, commercial fiction, all sub-genres of romance including erotic; nonfiction: cookbooks, pop culture); Brooks Sherman (speculative and literary adult fiction, select narrative nonfiction; all ages of children's and young adult books, including picture books; likes historical, contemporary, thrillers, humor, fantasy, and horror); Beth Phelan (young adult, thrillers, suspense and mystery, romance and women's fiction, literary and general fiction, cookbooks, lifestyle and pets/animals); Victoria Lowes (romance and women's fiction, thrillers and mystery, and young adult); Heather Flaherty (young adult and middle grade fiction: all genres; select adult fiction: upmarket fiction, women's fiction, and female-centric thrillers; select nonfiction: pop-culture, humorous, and social media based projects, as well as teen memoir).

REPRESENTS Nonfiction, fiction, novels, short story collections, juvenile books. **Considers these nonfiction areas:** animals, cooking, creative nonfiction, foods, juvenile nonfiction, popular culture, women's issues, young adult. **Considers these fiction areas:** commercial, crime, erotica, fantasy, feminist, historical, horror, juvenile, literary, mainstream, middle grade, multicultural, mystery, picture books, romance, suspense, thriller, women's, young adult.

HOW TO CONTACT For Jenny Bent, e-mail: queries@thebentagency.com; for Susan Hawk, e-mail: kidsqueries@thebentagency.com; for Molly Ker Hawn, e-mail: hawnqueries@thebentagency.com; for Gemma Cooper, e-mail: cooperqueries@thebentagency.com.; for Louise Fury, e-mail: furyqueries@ thebentagency.com; for Brooks Sherman, e-mail: shermanqueries@thebentagency.com; for Beth Phelan, e-mail: phelanagencies@thebentagency.com; for Victoria Lowes, e-mail: lowesqueries@thebentagency. com; for Heather Flaherty, e-mail flahertyqueries@ thebentagency.com. "Tell us briefly who you are, what your book is, and why you're the one to write it. Then include the first 10 pages of your material in the body of your e-mail. We respond to all queries; please resend your query if you haven't had a response within 4 weeks." Accepts simultaneous submissions.

VICKY BIJUR LITERARY AGENCY

27 West 20th Street, Suite 1003, New York NY 10011. **E-mail:** queries@vickybijuragency.com. **Website:** www.vickybijuragency.com. Estab. 1988. Member of AAR.

MEMBER AGENTS Vicky Bijur; Alexandra Franklin.

REPRESENTS Nonfiction, novels. **Considers these nonfiction areas:** memoirs. **Considers these fiction areas:** commercial, literary, mystery, new adult, thriller, women's, young adult, Campus novels, coming-of-age.

HOW TO CONTACT "Please send a query letter of no more than three paragraphs on what makes your book special and unique, a very brief synopsis, its length and genre, and your biographical information, along with the first ten pages of your manuscript. Please let us know in your query letter if it is a multiple submission, and kindly keep us informed of other agents' interest and offers of representation. If sending electronically, paste the pages in an e-mail as we don't open attachments from unfamiliar senders. If sending by hard copy, please include an SASE for our response. If you want your material returned, include an SASE large enough to contain pages and enough postage to send back to you." Include a cover letter with a proposal and the first ten pages for nonfiction projects. Accepts simultaneous submissions. "We generally respond to all queries within eight weeks of receipt."

DAVID BLACK LITERARY AGENCY

335 Adams St., Suite 2707, Brooklyn NY 11201. (718) 852-5500. **Fax:** (718) 852-5539. **Website:** www.davidblackagency.com. **Contact:** David Black, owner. Member of AAR. Represents 150 clients.

MEMBER AGENTS David Black; Jenny Herrera; Gary Morris; Joy E. Tutela (narrative nonfiction, memoir, history, politics, self-help, investment, business, science, women's issues, GLBT issues, parenting, health and fitness, humor, craft, cooking and wine, lifestyle and entertainment, commercial fiction, literary fiction, MG, YA.); Susan Raihofer (commercial fiction and nonfiction, memoir, pop-culture, music, inspirational, thrillers, literary fiction); Sarah Smith (memoir, biography, food, music, narrative history, social studies, literary fiction).

REPRESENTS Nonfiction, novels. **Considers these nonfiction areas:** biography, business, cooking, crafts, gay/lesbian, health, history, humor, inspirational, memoirs, music, parenting, popular culture, politics, science, self-help, sociology, sports, women's issues. **Considers these fiction areas:** commercial, literary, middle grade, thriller, young adult.

HOW TO CONTACT "To query an individual agent, please follow the specific query guidelines outlined in the agent's profile on our website. Not all agents are currently accepting unsolicited queries. To query the agency, please send a 1-2 page query letter describing your book, and include information about any previously published works, your audience, and your platform." Do not e-mail your query unless an agent specifically asks for an e-mail. Accepts simultaneous submissions. Responds in 2 months to queries.

BOOK CENTS LITERARY AGENCY, LLC

364 Patteson Drive, #228, Morgantown WV 26505.
E-mail: cw@bookcentsliteraryagency.com. **Website:**
www.bookcentsliteraryagency.com. **Contact:** Christine Witthohn. Estab. 2005. Member of AAR. RWA, MWA, SinC, KOD

MEMBER AGENTS Christine Witthohn.

REPRESENTS Considers these nonfiction areas:
cooking, gardening, travel, women's issues. **Considers these fiction areas:** commercial, literary, mainstream, multicultural, mystery, new adult, paranormal, romance, suspense, thriller, urban fantasy, women's, young adult.

HOW TO CONTACT Accepts e-submissions only from agency's website via an online form. Accepts simultaneous submissions.

BOOKENDS LITERARY AGENCY

E-mail: JFSubmissions@bookendsliterary.com;
KLsubmissions@bookendsliterary.com; JAsubmissions@bookendsliterary.com; MFsubmissions@bookendsliterary.com; BCsubmissions@bookendsliterary.com. **Website:** www.bookendsliterary.com. **Contact:**
Jessica Faust, Kim Lionetti, Jessica Alvarez, Moe Ferrara, Beth Campbell. Estab. 1999. Member of AAR. RWA, MWA, SCBWI Represents 50+ clients.

MEMBER AGENTS Jessica Faust, JFsubmissions@bookendsliterary.com (fiction: women's fiction, mysteries, thrillers suspense); Kim Lionetti, KLsubmissions@bookendsliterary.com (only currently considering contemporary romance, women's fiction, cozies, new adult, and contemporary young adult); Jessica Alvarez, JAsubmissions@bookendsliterary.com (romance, women's fiction, erotica, romantic suspense); Beth Campbell, BCsubmissions@bookendsliterary.com (urban fantasy, science fiction, YA, suspense, romantic suspense, and mystery); Moe Ferrara, MFsubmissions@bookendsliterary.com (adult science fiction and fantasy).

REPRESENTS Nonfiction, novels. **Considers these nonfiction areas:** business, creative nonfiction, ethnic, how-to, money, women's issues. **Considers these fiction areas:** crime, detective, erotica, fantasy, gay, lesbian, mainstream, middle grade, multicultural, mystery, police, romance, science fiction, thriller, urban fantasy, women's, young adult.

HOW TO CONTACT Visit bookendsliterary.com/index.php/submissions for the most up-to-date material. Review website for guidelines, as they change.

BookEnds is no longer accepting unsolicited proposal packages or snail mail queries. Send query in the body of e-mail to only 1 agent. No attachments. Accepts simultaneous submissions. "Our response time goals are 6 weeks for queries and 12 weeks on requested partials and fulls."

THE BOOK GROUP

20 W. 20th St., Suite 601, New York NY 10011.
(212)803-3360. **E-mail:** submissions@thebookgroup.com. **Website:** www.thebookgroup.com. Estab. 2015. Member of AAR. Signatory of WGA.

MEMBER AGENTS Julie Barer; Faye Bender; Brettne Bloom (fiction: literary and commercial fiction, select young adult; nonfiction, including cookbooks, lifestyle, investigative journalism, history, biography, memoir, and psychology); Elisabeth Weed (upmarket fiction, especially plot-driven novels with a sense of place); Rebecca Stead (innovative forms, diverse voices, and open-hearted fiction for children, young adults, and adults); Dana Murphy (story-driven fiction with a strong sense of place, narrative nonfiction/essays with a pop-culture lean, and YA with an honest voice).

REPRESENTS Considers these nonfiction areas:
biography, cooking, history, investigative, memoirs, psychology. **Considers these fiction areas:** commercial, literary, mainstream, women's, young adult.

HOW TO CONTACT Send a query letter and 10 sample pages to submissions@thebookgroup.com, with the first and last name of the agent you are querying in the subject line. All material must be in the body of the e-mail, as the agents do not open attachments. "If we are interested in reading more, we will get in touch with you as soon as possible." Accepts simultaneous submissions.

BRADFORD LITERARY AGENCY

5694 Mission Center Rd., #347, San Diego CA 92108.
(619) 521-1201. **E-mail:** queries@bradfordlit.com. **Website:** www.bradfordlit.com. **Contact:** Laura Bradford, Natalie Lakosil, Sarah LaPolla, Monica Odom. Estab. 2001. Member of AAR. RWA, SCBWI, ALA Represents 130 clients.

MEMBER AGENTS Laura Bradford; Natalie Lakosil; Sarah LaPolla; and Monica Odom.

REPRESENTS Nonfiction, fiction, novels, juvenile books. **Considers these nonfiction areas:** biography, business, cooking, creative nonfiction, cultural interests, foods, history, humor, juvenile nonfiction, memoirs, parenting, popular culture, politics, self-help, women's issues, women's studies, young adult. **Considers these fiction areas:** erotica, juvenile, middle grade, multicultural, mystery, new adult, paranormal, picture books, romance, science fiction, thriller, women's, young adult.

HOW TO CONTACT Accepts e-mail queries only; For submissions to Laura Bradford or Natalie Lakosil, send to queries@bradfordlit.com. For submissions to Sarah LaPolla, send to sarah@bradfordlit.com. For submissions to Monica Odom, send to Monica@bradfordlit.com. The entire submission must appear in the body of the e-mail and not as an attachment. The subject line should begin as follows: "QUERY: (the title of the ms or any short message that is important should follow)." For fiction: e-mail a query letter along with the first chapter of ms and a synopsis. Include the genre and word count in your query letter. Nonfiction: e-mail full nonfiction proposal including a query letter and a sample chapter. Accepts simultaneous submissions. Responds in 2-4 weeks to queries. Responds in 10 weeks to mss. Obtains most new clients through queries.

TERMS Agent receives 15% commission on domestic sales; 25% commission on foreign sales. Offers written contract. Charges for extra copies of books for foreign submissions.

BRANDT & HOCHMAN LITERARY AGENTS, INC.

1501 Broadway, Suite 2310, New York NY 10036. (212)840-5760. **Fax:** (212)840-5776. **Website:** brandthochman.com. **Contact:** Gail Hochman. Member of AAR. Represents 200 clients.

MEMBER AGENTS Gail Hochman (works of literary fiction, idea-driven nonfiction, literary memoir and children's books); Marianne Merola (fiction, nonfiction and children's books with strong and unique narrative voices); Bill Contardi (voice-driven young adult and middle grade fiction, commercial thrillers, psychological suspense, quirky mysteries, high fantasy, commercial fiction and memoir); Emily Forland (voice-driven literary fiction and nonfiction, memoir, narrative nonfiction, history, biography, food writing, cultural criticism, graphic novels, and young adult fiction); Emma Patterson (fiction from dark, literary novels to upmarket women's and historical fiction; narrative nonfiction that includes memoir, investi-

gative journalism, and popular history; young adult fiction); Jody Kahn (literary and upmarket fiction; narrative nonfiction, particularly books related to sports, food, history, science and pop-culture—including cookbooks, and literary memoir and journalism); Henry Thayer (nonfiction on a wide variety of subjects and fiction that inclines toward the literary). The e-mail addresses and specific likes of each of these agents is listed on the agency website.

REPRESENTS Nonfiction, novels. **Considers these nonfiction areas:** biography, cooking, current affairs, foods, health, history, memoirs, music, popular culture, science, sports, narrative nonfiction, journalism. **Considers these fiction areas:** fantasy, historical, literary, middle grade, mystery, suspense, thriller, women's, young adult.

HOW TO CONTACT "We accept queries by e-mail and regular mail; however, we cannot guarantee a response to e-mailed queries. For queries via regular mail, be sure to include a self-addressed stamped envelope for our reply. Query letters should be no more than two pages and should include a convincing overview of the book project and information about the author and his or her writing credits. Address queries to the specific Brandt & Hochman agent whom you would like to consider your work. Agent e-mail addresses and query preferences may be found at the end of each agent profile on the 'Agents' page of our website." Accepts simultaneous submissions. Obtains most new clients through recommendations from others.

TERMS Agent receives 15% commission on domestic sales; 20% commission on foreign sales.

THE BRATTLE AGENCY

P.O. Box 380537, Cambridge MA 02238. (617) 721-5375. **E-mail:** christopher.vyce@thebrattleagency.com. **E-mail:** submissions@thebrattleagency.com. **Website:** thebrattleagency.com. **Contact:** Christopher Vyce. Member of AAR. Signatory of WGA.

MEMBER AGENTS Christopher Vyce.

REPRESENTS Nonfiction, fiction. **Considers these nonfiction areas:** art, cultural interests, history, politics, sports, race studies, American studies. **Considers these fiction areas:** literary, graphic novels.

HOW TO CONTACT Query by e-mail. Include cover letter, brief synopsis, brief CV. Accepts simultaneous submissions. Responds to queries in 72 hours. Responds to approved submissions in 6-8 weeks.

BARBARA BRAUN ASSOCIATES, INC.

7 E. 14th St., #19F, New York NY 10003. **Fax:** (212)604-9023. **E-mail:** bbasubmissions@gmail.com. **Website:** www.barbarabraunagency.com. **Contact:** Barbara Braun. Member of AAR. Authors Guild, PEN Center USA

MEMBER AGENTS Barbara Braun.

REPRESENTS Nonfiction, novels. **Considers these nonfiction areas:** architecture, art, biography, design, film, history, photography, politics, psychology, women's issues, social issues, cultural criticism, fashion, narrative nonfiction. **Considers these fiction areas:** commercial, historical, literary, multicultural, mystery, thriller, women's, young adult, Art-related.

HOW TO CONTACT "We no longer accept submissions by regular mail. Please send all queries via e-mail, marked 'Query' in the subject line. Your query should include: a brief summary of your book, word count, genre, any relevant publishing experience, and the first 5 pages of your manuscript pasted into the body of the e-mail. (No attachments—we will not open these.)" Accepts simultaneous submissions.

TERMS Agent receives 15% commission on domestic sales; 20% commission on foreign sales. No reading fees.

CURTIS BROWN, LTD.

10 Astor Place, New York NY 10003-6935. (212)473-5400. **Website:** www.curtisbrown.com. **Contact:** Ginger Knowlton. Member of AAR. Signatory of WGA.

MEMBER AGENTS Noah Ballard (literary debuts, upmarket thrillers and narrative nonfiction, and he is always on the look-out for honest and provocative new writers); Ginger Clark (science fiction, fantasy, paranormal romance, literary horror, and young adult and middle grade fiction); Kerry D'Agostino (a wide range of literary and commercial fiction, as well as narrative nonfiction and memoir); Katherine Fausset (literary fiction, upmarket commercial fiction, journalism, memoir, popular science, and narrative nonfiction); Holly Frederick; Peter Ginsberg, President; Elizabeth Harding, Vice President (represents authors and illustrators of juvenile, middle-grade and young adult fiction); Steve Kasdin (commercial fiction, including mysteries/thrillers, romantic suspense—emphasis on the suspense, and historical fiction; narrative nonfiction, including biography, history and current affairs; and young adult fiction, particularly if it has adult crossover appeal; NOT interested in SF/Fantasy, Memoirs, Vampires and writers trying to capitalize on trends); Ginger Knowlton, Executive Vice President (authors and illustrators of children's books in all genres); Timothy Knowlton, Chief Executive Officer; Jonathan Lyons (biographies, history, science, pop culture, sports, general narrative nonfiction, mysteries, thrillers, science fiction and fantasy, and young adult fiction); Laura Blake Peterson, Vice President (memoir and biography, natural history, literary fiction, mystery, suspense, women's fiction, health and fitness, children's and young adult, faith issues and popular culture); Maureen Walters, Senior Vice President (working primarily in women's fiction and nonfiction projects on subjects as eclectic as parenting & child care, popular psychology, inspirational/motivational volumes as well as a few medical/nutritional books); Mitchell Waters (literary and commercial fiction and nonfiction, including mystery, history, biography, memoir, young adult, cookbooks, self-help and popular culture).

REPRESENTS Nonfiction, novels. **Considers these nonfiction areas:** biography, computers, cooking, current affairs, ethnic, health, history, humor, memoirs, popular culture, psychology, science, self-help, spirituality, sports. **Considers these fiction areas:** fantasy, horror, humor, juvenile, literary, mainstream, middle grade, mystery, paranormal, picture books, religious, romance, spiritual, sports, suspense, thriller, women's, young adult.

HOW TO CONTACT Please refer to the "Agents" page on the website for each agent's submission guidelines. Accepts simultaneous submissions. Responds in 3 weeks to queries; 5 weeks to mss. Obtains most new clients through recommendations from others, solicitations, conferences.

TERMS Agent receives 15% commission on domestic sales; 20% on foreign sales. Offers written contract. 75-day notice must be given to terminate contract. Charges for some postage (overseas, etc.).

BROWNE & MILLER LITERARY ASSOCIATES, LLC

410 South Michigan Ave., Suite 460, Chicago IL 60605. (312) 922-3063. **Fax:** (312)922-1905. **E-mail:** mail@browneandmiller.com. **Website:** www.browneandmiller.com. Estab. 1971. Member of AAR. Signatory of WGA. RWA, MWA

MEMBER AGENTS Danielle Egan-Miller; Abby Saul (runs the gamut from literary newbies and classics, to cozy mysteries, to sappy women's fiction, to dark and twisted thrillers); Joanna MacKenzie (women's fiction, thrillers, new adult, and young adult genres).

REPRESENTS Nonfiction, fiction, novels. **Considers these fiction areas:** commercial, crime, historical, inspirational, literary, romance, women's, young adult, Amish fiction, time-travel.

HOW TO CONTACT E-query. No attachments. Do not send unsolicited manuscripts. Accepts simultaneous submissions.

ANDREA BROWN LITERARY AGENCY, INC.

E-mail: andrea@andreabrownlit.com; caryn@andreabrownlit.com; lauraqueries@gmail.com; jennifer@andreabrownlit.com; kelly@andreabrownlit.com; jennL@andreabrownlit.com; jamie@andreabrownlit.com; jmatt@andreabrownlit.com; kathleen@andreabrownlit.com; lara@andreabrownlit.com; soloway@andreabrownlit.com. **Website:** www.andreabrownlit.com. Member of AAR.

MEMBER AGENTS Andrea Brown (president); Laura Rennert (executive agent); Caryn Wiseman (senior agent); Jennifer Laughran (senior agent); Jennifer Rofé (senior agent); Kelly Sonnack (agent); Jamie Weiss Chilton (agent); Jennifer Mattson (agent); Kathleen Rushall (agent); Lara Perkins (associate agent, digital manager); Jennifer March Soloway (assistant agent).

REPRESENTS Nonfiction, fiction, juvenile books. **Considers these nonfiction areas:** juvenile nonfiction, young adult, narrative. **Considers these fiction areas:** juvenile, picture books, young adult, middle-grade, all juvenile genres..

HOW TO CONTACT For picture books, submit a query letter and complete ms in the body of the e-mail. For fiction, submit a query letter and the first 10 pages in the body of the e-mail. For nonfiction, submit proposal, first 10 pages in the body of the e-mail. Illustrators: submit a query letter and 2-3 illustration samples (in jpeg format), link to online portfolio, and text of picture book, if applicable. "We only accept queries via e-mail. No attachments, with the exception of jpeg illustrations from illustrators." Visit the agents' bios on our website and choose only *one* agent to whom you will submit your e-query. Send a short e-mail query letter to that agent with "QUERY" in the subject field. Accepts simultaneous submissions.

TERMS Agent receives 15% commission on domestic sales; 25% commission on foreign sales. Offers written contract.

SHEREE BYKOFSKY ASSOCIATES, INC.

PO Box 706, Brigantine NJ 08203. **E-mail:** shereebee@aol.com. **E-mail:** submitbee@aol.com. **Website:** www.shereebee.com. **Contact:** Sheree Bykofsky. Estab. 1991. Member of AAR. Memberships include Author's Guild, Atlantic City Chamber of Commerce, PRC Council Represents Over 1000 clients.

MEMBER AGENTS Sheree Bykofsky; Janet Rosen, associate.

REPRESENTS Nonfiction, fiction, novels, scholarly books. **Considers these nonfiction areas:** Americana, animals, anthropology, architecture, art, autobiography, biography, business, child guidance, cooking, crafts, creative nonfiction, cultural interests, current affairs, dance, decorating, diet/nutrition, design, economics, education, environment, ethnic, film, foods, gardening, gay/lesbian, government, health, history, hobbies, how-to, humor, inspirational, language, law, literature, medicine, memoirs, metaphysics, military, money, multicultural, music, New Age, parenting, philosophy, photography, popular culture, politics, psychology, recreation, regional, religious, science, self-help, sex, sociology, software, spirituality, sports, technology, theater, translation, travel, true crime, war, women's issues, creative nonfiction. **Considers these fiction areas:** commercial, contemporary issues, crime, detective, literary, mainstream, mystery, suspense, women's. **Considers these script areas:** , Dramatic rights represented by Joel Gotler.

HOW TO CONTACT "We only accept e-queries now and will only respond to those in which we are interested. E-mail short queries to submitbee@aol.com. Please no attachments, snail mail, or phone calls. One-page query, one-page synopsis, and first page of ms in the body of the e-mail. Nonfiction: One-page query in the body of the e-mail. We cannot open attached Word files or any other types of attached files." Accepts simultaneous submissions. Responds in 1 month to requested mss. Obtains most new clients through recommendations from others.

TERMS Agent receives 15% commission on domestic sales; 15% commission on foreign sales, plus international co-agent receives another 10%. Offers written contract, binding for 1 year. Charges for international postage.

KIMBERLEY CAMERON & ASSOCIATES

1550 Tiburon Blvd., #704, Tiburon CA 94920. (415) 789-9191. **Website:** www.kimberleycameron.com.

Contact: Kimberley Cameron. Member of AAR. Signatory of WGA.

MEMBER AGENTS Kimberley Cameron; Elizabeth Kracht, liz@kimberleycameron.com (literary, commercial, women's, thrillers, mysteries, historical, YA with crossover appeal, health, science, environment, prescriptive, investigative, true crime, memoir, sexuality, spirituality, animal/pet stories); Pooja Menon, pooja@kimberleycameron.com (currently closed to unsolicited submissions); Amy Cloughley, amyc@kimberleycameron.com (literary and upmarket fiction, women's, historical, narrative nonfiction, travel or adventure memoir); Mary C. Moore (currently closed to submissions); Lisa Abellera, lisa@kimberlycameron.com (currently closed to unsolicited submissions); Douglas Lee, douglas@kimberlycameron.com (looking for SFF manuscripts that utilize the craft elements of literary fiction and the best parts of imaginative genre, open to all sub-genres of SFF; has a soft spot for Cyberpunk, Weird Fiction in the flavor of China Mieville, Steampunk and noir influenced voices; welcomes LBTQ manuscripts).

REPRESENTS Considers these nonfiction areas: animals, environment, health, memoirs, science, spirituality, travel, true crime, narrative nonfiction. **Considers these fiction areas:** commercial, fantasy, historical, literary, mystery, romance, science fiction, thriller, women's, young adult, LGBTQ.

HOW TO CONTACT Prefers e-mail queries. Only query one agent at a time. For fiction, fill out the correct submissions form for the individual agent and attach the first 50 pages and a synopsis (if requested) as a Word doc or PDF. For nonfiction, fill out the correct submission form of the individual agent and attach a full book proposal and sample chapters (includes the first chapter and no more than 50 pages) as a Word doc or PDF. Accepts simultaneous submissions. Obtains new clients through recommendations from others, solicitations.

CYNTHIA CANNELL LITERARY AGENCY

54 W. 40th Street, New York NY 10018. (212) 396-9595. **Website:** www.cannellagency.com. **Contact:** Cynthia Cannell. Estab. 1997. Member of AAR. Women's Media Group and the Authors Guild

REPRESENTS Nonfiction, fiction. **Considers these nonfiction areas:** biography, current affairs, memoirs, self-help, spirituality.

HOW TO CONTACT "Please query us with an e-mail or letter. If querying by e-mail, send a brief description of your project with relevant biographical information including publishing credits (if any) to info@cannellagency.com. Do not send attachments. If querying by conventional mail, enclose an SASE." Responds if interested. Accepts simultaneous submissions.

CAPITAL TALENT AGENCY

1330 Connecticut Ave. NW, Suite 271, Washington DC 20036. (202)429-4785. **Fax:** (202) 429-4786. **E-mail:** literary.submissions@capitaltalentagency.com. **Website:** capitaltalentagency.com/html/literary.shtml. **Contact:** Cynthia Kane. Estab. 2014. Member of AAR. Signatory of WGA.

MEMBER AGENTS Cynthia Kane.

REPRESENTS Nonfiction, fiction, movie scripts, stage plays.

HOW TO CONTACT "We accept submissions only by e-mail. We do not accept queries via postal mail or fax. For fiction and nonfiction submissions, send a query letter in the body of your e-mail. Please note that while we consider each query seriously, we are unable to respond to all of them. We endeavor to respond within six weeks to projects that interest us." Accepts simultaneous submissions.

MARIA CARVAINIS AGENCY, INC.

Rockefeller Center, 1270 Avenue of the Americas, Suite 2320, New York NY 10020. (212)245-6365. **Fax:** (212)245-7196. **E-mail:** mca@mariacarvainisagency.com. **Website:** mariacarvainisagency.com. Estab. 1977. Member of AAR. Signatory of WGA. Other memberships include Authors Guild, Women's Media Group, ABA, MWA, RWA. Represents 75 clients.

MEMBER AGENTS Maria Carvainis, President/Literary Agent; Elizabeth Copps, Associate Agent.

REPRESENTS Fiction, novels. **Considers these nonfiction areas:** biography, business, history, memoirs, popular culture, psychology, science. **Considers these fiction areas:** action, adventure, commercial, contemporary issues, crime, historical, horror, humor, juvenile, literary, mainstream, middle grade, multicultural, mystery, romance, suspense, thriller, women's, young adult.

HOW TO CONTACT If you would like to query the agency, please send a query letter, a synopsis of the work, first 5-10 pages, and note of any writing credentials. Please e-mail queries to mca@mariacarvainisagency.com. All attachments must be either Word documents or PDF files. We also accept queries by mail: Maria Carvainis Agency, Inc., Attention: Query Department, 1270 Avenue of the Americas, Suite 2320, New York, NY 10020. If you want the materials returned to you, please enclose a stamped, self-addressed envelope. Otherwise, please be sure to include your e-mail address. We typically respond to queries within one month, if not earlier. The agency does not represent screenplays, children's picture books, science fiction, or poetry. There is no reading fee. Accepts simultaneous submissions. Obtains most new clients through recommendations from others, conferences, query letters.

TERMS Agent receives 15% commission on domestic sales; 20% commission on foreign sales. Offers written contract. Charges clients for foreign postage and bulk copying.

CASTIGLIA LITERARY AGENCY

P.O. Box 1094, Sumerland CA 93067. **E-mail:** castigliaagency-query@yahoo.com. Member of AAR. Other memberships include PEN. Represents 65 clients.

MEMBER AGENTS Julie Castiglia (not accepting queries at this time); Win Golden (fiction: thrillers, mystery, crime, science fiction, YA, commercial/literary fiction; nonfiction: narrative nonfiction, current events, science, journalism).

REPRESENTS Novels. **Considers these nonfiction areas:** creative nonfiction, current affairs, investigative, science. **Considers these fiction areas:** commercial, crime, literary, mystery, science fiction, thriller, young adult.

HOW TO CONTACT Query via e-mail to CastigliaAgency-query@yahoo.com. Send no materials via first contact besides a one-page query. No snail mail submissions accepted. Accepts simultaneous submissions. Obtains most new clients through recommendations from others, solicitations, conferences.

TERMS Agent receives 15% commission on domestic sales; 25% commission on foreign sales. Offers written contract; 6-week notice must be given to terminate contract.

CHALBERG & SUSSMAN

115 West 29th St, Third Floor, New York NY 10001. (917) 261-7550. **Website:** www.chalbergsussman.com. Member of AAR. Signatory of WGA.

MEMBER AGENTS Terra Chalberg; Rachel Sussman (narrative journalism, memoir, psychology, history, humor, pop culture, literary fiction); Nicole James (plot-driven fiction, psychological suspense, uplifting female-driven memoir, upmarket self-help, and lifestyle books); Lana Popovic (young adult, middle grade, contemporary realism, speculative fiction, fantasy, horror, sophisticated erotica, romance, select nonfiction, international stories).

REPRESENTS Nonfiction, fiction, novels. **Considers these nonfiction areas:** history, humor, memoirs, psychology, self-help, narrative journalism, pop culture. **Considers these fiction areas:** erotica, fantasy, horror, literary, middle grade, romance, science fiction, suspense, young adult, Contemporary realism, speculative fiction.

HOW TO CONTACT To query by e-mail, please contact one of the following: terra@chalbergsussman.com, rachel@chalbergsussman.com, nicole@chalbergsussman.com, lana@chalbergsussman.com. To query by regular mail, please address your letter to one agent and include a self-addressed stamped envelope. Accepts simultaneous submissions.

JANE CHELIUS LITERARY AGENCY

548 Second St., Brooklyn NY 11215. (718) 499-0236. **Fax:** (718) 832-7335. **E-mail:** Jane@janechelius.com. **Website:** www.janechelius.com. Member of AAR.

MEMBER AGENTS Jane Chelius, Mark Chelius.

REPRESENTS **Considers these nonfiction areas:** natural history, narrative.

HOW TO CONTACT **Currently closed to submissions** Accepts simultaneous submissions. Responds in 3-4 weeks usually.

WM CLARK ASSOCIATES

186 Fifth Ave., Second Floor, New York NY 10010. (212)675-2784. **E-mail:** general@wmclark.com. **Website:** www.wmclark.com. Estab. 1997. Member of AAR.

REPRESENTS Nonfiction, novels. **Considers these nonfiction areas:** architecture, art, autobiography, biography, cultural interests, current affairs, dance, design, ethnic, film, history, inspirational, memoirs, music, popular culture, politics, religious, science, sociology, technology, theater, translation, travel. **Considers these fiction areas:** contemporary issues, ethnic, historical, literary, mainstream, young adult.

HOW TO CONTACT Accepts queries via online form only. "We will endeavor to respond as soon as possible as to whether or not we'd like to see a proposal or sample chapters from your manuscript." Responds in 1-2 months to queries.

TERMS Agent receives 15% commission on domestic sales; 20% commission on foreign sales. Offers written contract.

FRANCES COLLIN, LITERARY AGENT

P.O. Box 33, Wayne PA 19087-0033. **E-mail:** queries@francescollin.com. **Website:** www.francescollin.com. Member of AAR. Represents 90 clients.

HOW TO CONTACT E-mail queries, no attachments. Snail mail queries must include a SASE. No phone or fax queries. Accepts simultaneous submissions.

DON CONGDON ASSOCIATES INC.

110 William St., Suite 2202, New York NY 10038. (212)645-1229. **Fax:** (212)727-2688. **E-mail:** dca@doncongdon.com. **Website:** doncongdon.com. **Contact:** Michael Congdon, Susan Ramer, Cristina Concepcion, Maura Kye Casella, Katie Kotchman, Katie Grimm. Member of AAR. Represents 100 clients.

MEMBER AGENTS Christina Concepcion (crime fiction, narrative nonfiction, political science, journalism, history, books on cities, classical music, biography, science for a popular audience, philosophy, food and wine, iconoclastic books on health and human relationships, essays and arts criticism); Michael Congdon (commercial and literary fiction, suspense, mystery, thriller, history, military history, biography, memoir, current affairs and narrative nonfiction [adventure, medicine, science, and nature]); Katie Grimm (literary fiction, historical, women's fiction, short story collections, graphic novels, mysteries, YA, MG, memoirs, science, academic); Katie Kotchman (business [all areas], narrative nonfiction [particularly popular science and social/cultural issues], self-help, success, motivation, psychology, pop culture, women's fiction, realistic young adult, literary fiction, and psychological thrillers); Maura Kye-Casella (narrative nonfiction, cookbooks, women's fiction, young adult, self-help and parenting and is seeking literary works, women's fiction, horror, multicultural voices, any well-written novels with quirky characters and/or unique plots and settings, YA, MG, food, cookbooks, pop culture, sports, humor); Susan Ramer (literary fiction, upmarket commercial fiction [contemporary and historical], narrative nonfiction, social history, cultural history, smart pop culture [music, film, food, art], women's issues, psychology and mental health, and memoir).

REPRESENTS Nonfiction, novels, short story collections, graphic novels. **Considers these nonfiction areas:** art, biography, business, cooking, creative nonfiction, cultural interests, current affairs, film, foods, history, humor, medicine, memoirs, military, multicultural, music, parenting, philosophy, popular culture, politics, psychology, science, self-help, sociology, sports, women's issues, journalism, relationships, essays/criticism, nature, adventure, academic, mental health. **Considers these fiction areas:** crime, historical, literary, middle grade, mystery, suspense, thriller, young adult.

HOW TO CONTACT "For queries via e-mail, you must include the word 'Query' and the agent's full name in your subject heading. Please also include your query and sample chapter in the body of the e-mail, as we do not open attachments for security reasons. Please query only one agent within the agency at a time. If you are sending your query via regular mail, please enclose a self-addressed stamped envelope for our reply. If you would like us to return your materials, please make sure your postage will cover their return." Does not accept unsolicited manuscripts. Accepts simultaneous submissions.

CORNERSTONE LITERARY, INC.

4525 Wilshire Blvd., Suite 208, Los Angeles CA 90010. (323)930-6039. **Fax:** (323)930-0407. **E-mail:** info@cornerstoneliterary.com. **Website:** www.cornerstoneliterary.com. **Contact:** Helen Breitwieser. Member of AAR.

REPRESENTS Nonfiction, novels. **Considers these nonfiction areas:** creative nonfiction. **Considers these fiction areas:** commercial, literary.

HOW TO CONTACT "Submissions should consist of a one-page query letter detailing the book as well as the qualifications of the author. For fiction, submissions may also include the first ten pages of the novel pasted in the e-mail or one short story from a collection. We receive hundreds of queries each month, and make every effort to give each one careful consideration. We appreciate your patience in waiting 6-8 weeks for a response before contacting us with a gentle reminder. We cannot guarantee a response to queries submitted electronically due to the volume of queries received." Accepts simultaneous submissions.

CORVISIERO LITERARY AGENCY

275 Madison Ave., at 40th, 14th Floor, New York NY 10016. **E-mail:** query@corvisieroagency.com. **Website:** www.corvisieroagency.com. **Contact:** Marisa A.

Corvisiero, senior agent and literary attorney. Member of AAR. Signatory of WGA.

MEMBER AGENTS Marisa A. Corvisiero, senior agent and literary attorney (contemporary romance, thrillers, adventure, paranormal, urban fantasy, science fiction, MG, YA, picture books, Christmas themes, time travel, space science fiction, nonfiction, self-help, science business); Sarıtza Hernandez, senior agent (all kinds of romance, GLBT, young adult, erotica); Sarah Negovetich (young adult); Doreen McDonald (do not query); Cate Hart (YA, fantasy, magical realism, MG, mystery, fantasy, adventure, historical romance, LGBTQ, erotic, history, biography); Samantha Bremekamp (children's, middle grade, young adult, and new adult—closed to blind queries); Veronica Park (Dark or edgy YA/NA, Commercial Adult, Adult Romance and Romantic Suspense, and funny and/or current/controversial Nonfiction); Vanessa Robins (New Adult, human, YA, thrillers, romance, sci-fi, sports-centric plots, memoirs, cultural/ethnic/sexuality, humor, medical narratives); Kelly Peterson (Middle grade, Fantasy, Paranormal, Sci-fi, YA, Steampunk, Historical, Dystopian, Sword and Sorcery, NA, Romance, Historical Romance, Adult, Fantasy, Romance).

REPRESENTS Nonfiction, fiction, novels. **Considers these nonfiction areas:** biography, business, history, medicine, memoirs, science, self-help, spirituality. **Considers these fiction areas:** adventure, erotica, fantasy, gay, historical, lesbian, middle grade, mystery, paranormal, picture books, romance, science fiction, suspense, thriller, urban fantasy, young adult, Magical realism, steampunk, dystopian, sword and sorcery.

HOW TO CONTACT Accepts submissions via e-mail only. Include 5 pages of complete and polished ms pasted into the body of an e-mail, and a 1-2 page synopsis. For nonfiction, include a proposal instead of the synopsis. Put "Query for [Agent]" in the e-mail subject line. Accepts simultaneous submissions.

CREATIVE MEDIA AGENCY, INC.

1745 Broadway, 17th Floor, New York NY 10019. (212) 812-1494. **E-mail:** paige@cmalit.com. **Website:** www.cmalit.com. **Contact:** Paige Wheeler. Member of AAR. WMG, RWA, MWA, Authors Guild. Represents over 30 clients.

REPRESENTS Nonfiction, fiction. **Considers these nonfiction areas:** biography, business, creative nonfiction, diet/nutrition, health, inspirational, memoirs,

money, parenting, popular culture, self-help, women's issues. **Considers these fiction areas:** commercial, crime, detective, historical, inspirational, mainstream, middle grade, mystery, new adult, police, romance, suspense, thriller, women's, young adult.

HOW TO CONTACT E-query. Write "query" in your e-mail subject line. For fiction, paste in the first 5 pages of the ms after the query. For nonfiction, paste in an extended author bio as well as the marketing section of your book proposal after the query. Accepts simultaneous submissions.

LAURA DAIL LITERARY AGENCY, INC.

350 Seventh Ave., Suite 2003, New York NY 10001. (212)239-7477. **E-mail:** ldail@ldlainc.com. **E-mail:** queries@ldlainc.com. **Website:** www.ldlainc.com. Member of AAR.

MEMBER AGENTS Laura Dail; Tamar Rydzinski.

REPRESENTS Nonfiction, fiction, novels, juvenile books. **Considers these nonfiction areas:** biography, cooking, creative nonfiction, current affairs, government, history, investigative, juvenile nonfiction, memoirs, multicultural, popular culture, politics, psychology, sociology, true crime, war, women's studies, young adult. **Considers these fiction areas:** commercial, crime, detective, fantasy, feminist, historical, juvenile, mainstream, middle grade, multicultural, mystery, thriller, women's, young adult.

HOW TO CONTACT "If you would like, you may include a synopsis and no more than 10 pages. If you are mailing your query, please be sure to include a self-addressed, stamped envelope; without it, you may not hear back from us. To save money, time and trees, we prefer queries by e-mail to queries@ldlainc.com. We get a lot of spam and are wary of computer viruses, so please use the word 'Query' in the subject line and include your detailed materials in the body of your message, not as an attachment." Accepts simultaneous submissions.

DARHANSOFF & VERRILL LITERARY AGENTS

133 West 72nd St., Room 304, New York NY 10023. (917)305-1300. **E-mail:** submissions@dvagency.com. **Website:** www.dvagency.com. Member of AAR.

MEMBER AGENTS Liz Darhansoff; Chuck Verrill; Michele Mortimer; Eric Amling.

REPRESENTS Nonfiction, novels. **Considers these nonfiction areas:** creative nonfiction, juvenile nonfiction, memoirs, young adult. **Considers these fiction areas:** literary, middle grade, suspense, young adult. **HOW TO CONTACT** Send queries via e-mail. Accepts simultaneous submissions.

LIZA DAWSON ASSOCIATES

350 Seventh Ave., Suite 2003, New York NY 10001. (212)465-9071. **Website:** www.lizadawsonassociates. com. **Contact:** Caitie Flum. Member of AAR. Other memberships include MWA, Women's Media Group. Represents 50+ clients.

MEMBER AGENTS Liza Dawson, queryliza@ LizaDawsonAssociates.com (plot-driven literary and popular fiction, historicals, thrillers, suspense, history,psychology [both popular and clinical], politics, narrative nonfiction and memoirs); Caitlin Blasdell, queryCaitlin@LizaDawsonAssociates.com (science fiction, fantasy [both adult and young adult], parenting, business, thrillers and women's fiction; Hannah Bowman, queryHannah@LizaDawsonAssociates.com (commercial fiction — especially science fiction and fantasy, young adult, also nonfiction in the areas of mathematics, science, and spirituality); Jennifer Johnson-Blalock, queryjennifer@LizaDawsonAssociates.com (nonfiction, particularly current events, social sciences, women's issues, law, business, history, the arts and pop culture, lifestyle, sports, and food, and commercial and upmarket fiction, especially thrillers/mysteries, women's fiction, contemporary romance, young adult, and middle grade); Caitie Flum, querycaitie@LizaDawsonAssociates.com (commercial fiction, especially historical, women's fiction, mysteries, young adult, middle grade; MG, YA and crossover fantasy, nonfiction in the areas of theater, memoir, current affairs and pop culture).

REPRESENTS Considers these nonfiction areas: agriculture, Americana, animals, anthropology, archeology, architecture, art, autobiography, biography, business, computers, cooking, creative nonfiction, cultural interests, current affairs, environment, ethnic, film, gardening, gay/lesbian, history, humor, investigative, juvenile nonfiction, memoirs, multicultural, parenting, popular culture, politics, psychology, religious, science, sex, sociology, spirituality, theater, travel, true crime, women's issues, women's studies, young adult. **Considers these fiction areas:** action, adventure, commercial, contemporary issues, crime, detective, ethnic, family saga, fantasy, feminist, gay, historical, horror, humor, juvenile, lesbian, mainstream, middle grade, multicultural, mystery, new adult, police, romance, science fiction, supernatural, suspense, thriller, urban fantasy, women's, young adult.

HOW TO CONTACT Query by e-mail only. No phone calls. Each of these agents has their own specific submission requirements, which you can find online at their website. Accepts simultaneous submissions. Responds in 6 weeks to queries; 8 weeks to mss. Obtains most new clients through recommendations from others, conferences, and queries.

TERMS Agent receives 15% commission on domestic sales; 20% commission on foreign sales. Offers written contract.

DEFIORE & CO. LITERARY MANAGEMENT, INC.

47 E. 19th St., 3rd Floor, New York NY 10003. (212)925-7744. **Fax:** (212)925-9803. **E-mail:** info@ defliterary.com; submissions@defliterary.com. **Website:** www.defliterary.com. Member of AAR. Signatory of WGA.

MEMBER AGENTS Brian DeFiore (popular nonfiction, business, pop culture, parenting, commercial fiction); Laurie Abkemeier (memoir, parenting, business, how-to/self-help, popular science); Matthew Elblonk (young adult, popular culture, narrative nonfiction); Caryn Karmatz-Rudy (popular fiction, self-help, narrative nonfiction); Adam Schear (commercial fiction, humor, YA, smart thrillers, historical fiction, and quirky debut literary novels. For nonfiction: popular science, politics, popular culture, and current events); Meredith Kaffel Simonoff(smart upmarket women's fiction, literary fiction [especially debut] and literary thrillers, narrative nonfiction, nonfiction about science and tech, sophisticated pop culture/humor books); Rebecca Strauss (literary and commercial fiction, women's fiction, urban fantasy, romance, mystery, YA, memoir, pop culture, and select nonfiction); Lisa Gallagher (fiction and nonfiction); Nicole Tourtelot (narrative and prescriptive nonfiction, food, lifestyle, wellness, pop culture, history, humor, and memoir, select young adult and adult fiction); Ashely Collum (women's fiction, kids and teens, psychological thrillers, memoir, politics, photography, cooking, narrative nonfiction, LGBTQ+ issues, feminism, and the occult); Colin Farstad (iterary fiction, upmarket fiction, young adult, narrative nonfiction, graphic novels, SFF); Miriam Altshuler (adult literary and commercial fiction, narrative nonfiction, MG/YA, memoir, narrative nonfiction, and self-help, family sagas, historical novels); Reiko Davis (adult literary and upmarket fiction, narrative nonfiction, YA/MG, memoir).

REPRESENTS Novels, short story collections. **Considers these nonfiction areas:** autobiography, biography, business, child guidance, cooking, economics, foods, how-to, inspirational, money, multicultural, parenting, photography, popular culture, politics, psychology, religious, science, self-help, sports, technology, travel, women's issues, young adult. **Considers these fiction areas:** commercial, ethnic, literary, mainstream, middle grade, mystery, paranormal, picture books, romance, short story collections, suspense, thriller, urban fantasy, women's, young adult.

HOW TO CONTACT Query with SASE or e-mail to submissions@defliterary.com. "Please include the word 'Query' in the subject line. All attachments will be deleted; please insert all text in the body of the e-mail. For more information about our agents, their individual interests, and their query guidelines, please visit our 'About Us' page on our website." Accepts simultaneous submissions. Obtains most new clients through recommendations from others.

TERMS Agent receives 15% commission on domestic sales; 20% commission on foreign sales. Offers written contract; 10-day notice must be given to terminate contract. Charges clients for photocopying and overnight delivery (deducted only after a sale is made).

JOELLE DELBOURGO ASSOCIATES, INC.

101 Park St., Montclair NJ 07042. (973)773-0836. **Fax:** (973)783-6802. **E-mail:** joelle@delbourgo.com. **E-mail:** submissions@delbourgo.com. **Website:** www.delbourgo.com. Member of AAR. Represents more than 500 clients.

MEMBER AGENTS Joelle Delbourgo; Jacqueline Flynn.

REPRESENTS Novels. **Considers these nonfiction areas:** Americana, animals, anthropology, archeology, autobiography, biography, business, child guidance, cooking, creative nonfiction, current affairs, dance, decorating, diet/nutrition, design, economics, education, environment, film, gardening, gay/lesbian, government, health, history, how-to, humor, inspirational, interior design, investigative, juvenile nonfiction, literature, medicine, memoirs, military, money, multicultural, music, parenting, philosophy, popular

culture, politics, psychology, science, self-help, sex, sociology, spirituality, sports, translation, travel, true crime, war, women's issues, women's studies. **Considers these fiction areas:** adventure, commercial, contemporary issues, crime, detective, fantasy, feminist, juvenile, literary, mainstream, middle grade, military, mystery, new adult, New Age, romance, science fiction, thriller, urban fantasy, women's, young adult.

HOW TO CONTACT It's preferable if you submit via e-mail to a specific agent. Query one agent only. No attachments. Put the word "Query" in the subject line. "While we do our best to respond to each query, if you have not received a response in 60 days you may consider that a pass. Please do not send us copies of self-published books unless requested. Let us know if you are sending your query to us exclusively or if this is a multiple submission. For nonfiction, let us know if a proposal and sample chapters are available. If not, you should probably wait to send your query when you have a completed proposal. For fiction and memoir, embed the *first* 10 pages of manuscript into the e-mail after your query letter. Please no attachments. If we like your first pages, we may ask to see your synopsis and more manuscript. Please do not cold call us or make a follow-up call unless we call you." Accepts simultaneous submissions.

TERMS Agent receives 15% commission on domestic sales; 20% commission on foreign sales. Offers written contract. Charges clients for postage and photocopying.

SANDRA DIJKSTRA LITERARY AGENCY

1155 Camino del Mar, PMB 515, Del Mar CA 92014. **E-mail:** elise@dijkstraagency.com. **E-mail:** queries@dijkstraagency.com. **Website:** www.dijkstraagency.com. Member of AAR. Authors Guild, Organization of American Historians, RWA Represents 100+ clients.

MEMBER AGENTS Sandra Dijkstra president (adult only); Acquiring Associate agents: Elise Capron (adult only); Jill Marr (adult only); Thao Le (adult and YA); Roz Foster (adult and YA); Jessica Watterson (subgenres of adult and new adult romance, and women's fiction).

REPRESENTS Nonfiction, fiction, novels, short story collections, juvenile books, scholarly books. **Considers these nonfiction areas:** Americana, anthropology, art, biography, business, creative nonfiction, cultural interests, current affairs, design, economics, environment, ethnic, gardening, government, health, history, juvenile nonfiction, literature, memoirs, multicultural, popular culture, politics, psychology, science, self-help, true crime, young adult, narrative. **Considers these fiction areas:** commercial, horror, literary, middle grade, new adult, romance, science fiction, suspense, thriller, women's, young adult.

HOW TO CONTACT "Please see guidelines on our website, www.dijkstraagency.com. Please note that we only accept e-mail submissions. Due to the large number of unsolicited submissions we receive, we are only able to respond those submissions in which we are interested." Accepts simultaneous submissions. Responds to queries of interest within 6 weeks.

TERMS Works in conjunction with foreign and film agents. Agent receives 15% commission on domestic sales and 20% commission on foreign sales. Offers written contract. No reading fee.

DONADIO & OLSON, INC.

40 West 27th St., 5th Floor, New York NY 10001. (212)691-8077. **Fax:** (212)633-2837. **E-mail:** neil@donadio.com. **E-mail:** mail@donadio.com. **Website:** donadio.com. **Contact:** Neil Olson. Member of AAR.

MEMBER AGENTS Neil Olson (no queries); Edward Hibbert (no queries); Carrie Howland, carrie@donadio.com (adult literary fiction and narrative nonfiction as well as young adult, middle grade, and picture books).

REPRESENTS Nonfiction, novels. **Considers these nonfiction areas:** creative nonfiction. **Considers these fiction areas:** literary, middle grade, picture books, young adult.

HOW TO CONTACT "Please send a query letter and the first three chapters/first 25 pages of the manuscript to mail@donadio.com. Please allow a minimum of one month for a reply. Accepts simultaneous submissions.

JANIS A. DONNAUD & ASSOCIATES, INC.

525 Broadway, Suite 201, New York NY 10012. (212)431-2664. **Fax:** (212)431-2667. **E-mail:** jdonnaud@aol.com; donnaudassociate@aol.com. **Website:** www.publishersmarketplace.com/members/JanisDonnaud/. **Contact:** Janis A. Donnaud. Member of AAR. Signatory of WGA. Represents 40 clients.

REPRESENTS Nonfiction. **Considers these nonfiction areas:** animals, biography, business, cooking, creative nonfiction, cultural interests, current affairs, diet/nutrition, film, foods, health, history,

humor, inspirational, memoirs, money, psychology, self-help.

HOW TO CONTACT Query first, e-mail letter with detailed description of project; send proposal if requested. Obtains most new clients through recommendations from others.

TERMS Agent receives 15% commission on domestic and film sales; 20% commission on foreign sales. Offers written contract; 1-month notice must be given to terminate contract.

DREISBACH LITERARY MANAGEMENT

P.O. Box 5379, El Dorado Hills CA 95762. (916)804-5016. **E-mail:** verna@dreisbachliterary.com. **Website:** www.dreisbachliterary.com. **Contact:** Verna Dreisbach. Estab. 2007. Member of AAR. Signatory of WGA.

REPRESENTS Nonfiction. **Considers these nonfiction areas:** biography, business, economics, health, history, memoirs, multicultural, parenting, science, technology, travel, true crime, women's issues.

HOW TO CONTACT E-mail queries only. No attachments in the query; they will not be opened. No unsolicited mss. *Accepting new nonfiction clients only through a writers conference or a personal referral. Not accepting fiction.* Accepts simultaneous submissions.

DUNHAM LITERARY, INC.

110 William St., Suite 2202, New York NY 10038. (212)929-0994. **E-mail:** query@dunhamlit.com. **Website:** www.dunhamlit.com. **Contact:** Jennie Dunham. Estab. 2000. Member of AAR. SCBWI Represents 50 clients.

MEMBER AGENTS Jennie Dunham, Bridget Smith.

REPRESENTS Nonfiction, fiction, novels, juvenile books. **Considers these nonfiction areas:** anthropology, archeology, biography, creative nonfiction, cultural interests, environment, health, history, language, literature, medicine, memoirs, multicultural, parenting, popular culture, politics, psychology, science, technology, women's issues, women's studies, young adult. **Considers these fiction areas:** fantasy, historical, humor, juvenile, literary, mainstream, middle grade, multicultural, mystery, picture books, science fiction, women's, young adult.

HOW TO CONTACT E-mail queries preferred, with all materials pasted in the body of the e-mail. Attachments will not be opened. Paper queries are also accepted. Please include a SASE for response and return of materials. If submitting to Bridget Smith, please include the first five pages with the query. Accepts simultaneous submissions. Responds in 4 weeks to queries; 2 months to mss. Obtains most new clients through recommendations from others, solicitations.

TERMS Agent receives 15% commission on domestic sales; 20% commission on foreign sales.

DUNOW, CARLSON, & LERNER AGENCY

27 W. 20th St., Suite 1107, New York NY 10011. (212)645-7606. **E-mail:** mail@dclagency.com. **E-mail:** mail@dclagency.com. **Website:** www.dclagency.com. Member of AAR.

MEMBER AGENTS Jennifer Carlson (narrative nonfiction writers and journalists covering current events and ideas and cultural history, as well as literary and upmarket commercial novelists); Henry Dunow (quality fiction – literary, historical, strongly written commercial – and with voice-driven nonfiction across a range of areas – narrative history, biography, memoir, current affairs, cultural trends and criticism, science, sports); Erin Hosier (nonfiction: popular culture, music, sociology and memoir); Betsy Lerner (nonfiction writers in the areas of psychology, history, cultural studies, biography, current events, business; fiction: literary, dark, funny, voice driven); Yishai Seidman (broad range of fiction: literary, postmodern, and thrillers; nonfiction: sports, music, and pop culture); Amy Hughes (nonfiction in the areas of history, cultural studies, memoir, current events, wellness, health, food, pop culture, and biography; also literary fiction); Eleanor Jackson (literary, commercial, memoir, art, food, science and history); Julia Kenny (fiction — adult, middle grade and YA — and is especially interested in dark, literary thrillers and suspense); Edward Necarsulmer IV (strong new voices in teen & middle grade as well as picture books); Stacia Decker; Arielle Datz (fiction—adult, YA, or middle-grade— literary and commercial, nonfiction—essays, unconventional memoir, pop culture, and sociology).

REPRESENTS Nonfiction, fiction, novels, short story collections. **Considers these nonfiction areas:** art, biography, creative nonfiction, cultural interests, current affairs, foods, health, history, memoirs, music, popular culture, psychology, science, sociology, sports. **Considers these fiction areas:** commercial, literary, mainstream, middle grade, mystery, picture books, thriller, young adult.

HOW TO CONTACT Query via snail mail with SASE, or by e-mail. E-mail preferred, paste 10 sample pages below query letter. No attachments. Will respond only if interested. Accepts simultaneous submissions. 4-6 weeks if interested

DYSTEL & GODERICH LITERARY MANAGEMENT

1 Union Square W., Suite 904, New York NY 10003. (212)627-9100. **Fax:** (212)627-9313. **Website:** www.dystel.com. Estab. 1994. Member of AAR. Other membership includes SCBWI. Represents 600+ clients.

MEMBER AGENTS Jane Dystel; Miriam Goderich, miriam@dystel.com (literary and commercial fiction as well as some genre fiction, narrative nonfiction, pop culture, psychology, history, science, art, business books, and biography/memoir); Stacey Kendall Glick, sglick@dystel.com (adult narrative nonfiction including memoir, parenting, cooking and food, psychology, science, health and wellness, lifestyle, current events, pop culture, YA, middle grade, children's nonfiction, and select adult contemporary fiction); Michael Bourret, mbourret@dystel.com (middle grade and young adult fiction, commercial adult fiction, and all sorts of nonfiction, from practical to narrative; he's especially interested in food and cocktail related books, memoir, popular history, politics, religion (though not spirituality), popular science, and current events); Jim McCarthy, jmccarthy@dystel.com (literary women's fiction, underrepresented voices, mysteries, romance, paranormal fiction, narrative nonfiction, memoir, and paranormal nonfiction); Jessica Papin, jpapin@dystel.com (plot-driven literary and smart commercial fiction, and narrative nonfiction across a range of subjects, including history, medicine, science, economics and women's issues); Lauren E. Abramo, labramo@dystel.com (humorous middle grade and contemporary YA on the children's side, and upmarket commercial fiction and well-paced literary fiction on the adult side. She's also interested in adult narrative nonfiction, especially pop culture, psychology, pop science, reportage, media, and contemporary culture. In nonfiction she has a strong preference for interdisciplinary approaches, and in all categories she's especially interested in underrepresented voices); John Rudolph, jrudolph@dystel.com (picture book author/illustrators, middle grade, YA, select commercial fiction, and narrative nonfiction—especially in music, sports, history, popular science, "big think", performing arts, health, business, memoir, military history, and humor); Sharon Pelletier, spelletier@dystel.com (smart commercial fiction, from upmarket women's fiction to domestic suspense to literary thrillers, and strong contemporary romance novels; compelling nonfiction projects, especially feminism and religion); Michael Hoogland, mhoogland@dystel.com (thriller, SFF, YA, upmarket women's fiction, and narrative nonfiction); Erin Young, eyoung@dystel.com (YA/MG, literary and intellectual commercial thrillers, memoirs, biographies, sport and science narratives); Amy Bishop, abishop@dystel.com (commercial and literary women's fiction, fiction from diverse authors, historical fiction, YA, personal narratives, and biographies); Kemi Faderin, kfaderin@dystel.com (smart, plot-driven YA, historical fiction/nonfiction, contemporary women's fiction, and literary fiction); Eric Myers, emyers@dystel.com (YA/MG fiction and adult nonfiction, especially history, biography, psychology, health and wellness, mind/body/spirit, pop culture, thriller, and memoir).

REPRESENTS Considers these nonfiction areas: animals, art, autobiography, biography, business, cooking, cultural interests, current affairs, ethnic, foods, gay/lesbian, health, history, humor, inspirational, investigative, medicine, memoirs, metaphysics, military, New Age, parenting, popular culture, politics, psychology, religious, science, sports, women's issues, women's studies. **Considers these fiction areas:** commercial, ethnic, gay, lesbian, literary, mainstream, middle grade, mystery, paranormal, romance, suspense, thriller, women's, young adult.

HOW TO CONTACT Query via e-mail and put "Query" in the subject line. "Synopses, outlines or sample chapters (say, one chapter or the first 25 pages of your manuscript) should either be included below the cover letter or attached as a separate document. We won't open attachments if they come with a blank e-mail." Accepts simultaneous submissions. Responds in 6 to 8 weeks to queries; within 8 weeks to mss. Obtains most new clients through recommendations from others, solicitations, conferences.

TERMS Agent receives 15% commission on domestic sales; 19% commission on foreign sales. Offers written contract.

EDEN STREET LITERARY

P.O. Box 30, Billings NY 12510. **E-mail:** info@edenstreetlit.com. **E-mail:** submissions@edenstreetlit.

com. **Website:** www.edenstreetlit.com. **Contact:** Liza Voges. Member of AAR. Signatory of WGA. Represents over 40 clients.

REPRESENTS Nonfiction, fiction, novels, juvenile books. **Considers these fiction areas:** juvenile, middle grade, picture books, young adult.

HOW TO CONTACT Check the website before submitting, as the agency will close itself off to submissions sometimes.When open, contact Submissions@edenstreetlit.com. Accepts simultaneous submissions. Responds only to submissions of interest.

EDUCATIONAL DESIGN SERVICES LLC

5750 Bou Ave, Suite 1508, N. Bethesda MD 20852. 301-881-8611. **E-mail:** blinder@educationaldesignservices.com. **Website:** www.educationaldesignservices.com. **Contact:** B. Linder. Estab. 1981. Member of AAR. Signatory of WGA.

REPRESENTS Nonfiction, textbooks, poetry books. **Considers these nonfiction areas:** education.

HOW TO CONTACT Query by e-mail or with SASE or send outline and 1 sample chapter. Considers simultaneous queries and submissions if so indicated. Returns material only with SASE. Prefers e-submissions (MS Word format). Accepts simultaneous submissions. Responds in 6-8 weeks to queries/mss. Obtains clients through recommendations from others, queries/solicitations, or through conferences.

TERMS Agent receives 15% commission on domestic sales; 25% on foreign sales. Offers written contract, binding until any party opts out. Terminate contract through certified letter.

EINSTEIN LITERARY MANAGEMENT

27 West 20th St., No. 1003, New York NY 10011. **E-mail:** submissions@einsteinliterary.com. **Website:** einsteinliterary.com. **Contact:** Susanna Einstein. Estab. 2015. Member of AAR. Signatory of WGA.

MEMBER AGENTS Susanna Einstein.

REPRESENTS Nonfiction, fiction. **Considers these nonfiction areas:** cooking, creative nonfiction, memoirs, blog-to-book projects. **Considers these fiction areas:** commercial, crime, historical, literary, romance, women's.

HOW TO CONTACT Please submit a query letter and the first 10 double-spaced pages of your manuscript in the body of the e-mail (no attachments). Does not respond to mail queries or telephone queries or queries that are no specifically addressed to this agency. Accepts simultaneous submissions. Responds in 6 weeks if interested.

THE LISA EKUS GROUP, LLC

57 North St., Hatfield MA 01038. (413)247-9325. **Fax:** (413)247-9873. **E-mail:** info@lisaekus.com. **Website:** www.lisaekus.com. **Contact:** Lisa Ekus. Member of AAR.

MEMBER AGENTS Lisa Ekus; Sally Ekus.

REPRESENTS Considers these nonfiction areas: cooking, diet/nutrition, foods, occasionally health/well-being and women's issues.

HOW TO CONTACT "For more information about our literary services, visit lisaekus.com/services/literary-agency/. Submit a query via e-mail or through our contact form on the website. You can also submit complete hard copy proposal with title page, proposal contents, concept, bio, marketing, TOC, etc. Include SASE for the return of materials." Accepts simultaneous submissions.

ETHAN ELLENBERG LITERARY AGENCY

155 Suffolk St., No. 2R, New York NY 10002. (212)431-4554. **E-mail:** agent@ethanellenberg.com. **Website:** ethanellenberg.com. **Contact:** Ethan Ellenberg. Estab. 1984. Member of AAR. Science Fiction and Fantasy Writer's of American, SCBWI, RWA, and MWA.

MEMBER AGENTS Ethan Ellenberg, president; Evan Gregory, senior agent; Bibi Lewis, associate agent (YA and women's fiction).

REPRESENTS Nonfiction, fiction. **Considers these nonfiction areas:** biography, cooking, current affairs, health, history, memoirs, New Age, popular culture, psychology, science, spirituality, true crime, adventure. **Considers these fiction areas:** commercial, ethnic, fantasy, literary, middle grade, mystery, picture books, romance, science fiction, thriller, women's, young adult, general.

HOW TO CONTACT Query by e-mail. Paste all of the material in the order listed. Fiction: query letter, synopsis, first 50 pages. Nonfiction: query letter, book proposal. Picture books: query letter, complete ms, 4-5 sample illustrations. Illustrators: query letter, 4-5 sample illustrations, link to online portfolio. Will not respond unless interested. Accepts simultaneous submissions. Responds in 2 weeks.

EMPIRE LITERARY

115 W. 29th St., 3rd Floor, New York NY 10001. (917)213-7082. **E-mail:** abarzvi@empireliterary.com.

Website: www.empireliterary.com. Estab. 2013. Member of AAR. Signatory of WGA.

MEMBER AGENTS Andrea Barzvi.

HOW TO CONTACT Accepts simultaneous submissions.

FELICIA ETH LITERARY REPRESENTATION

555 Bryant St., Suite 350, Palo Alto CA 94301-1700. **E-mail:** feliciaeth.literary@gmail.com. **Website:** eth-literary.com. **Contact:** Felicia Eth. Member of AAR.

REPRESENTS Novels. **Considers these nonfiction areas:** cooking, creative nonfiction, investigative, memoirs, parenting, popular culture, psychology, sociology, travel, women's issues. **Considers these fiction areas:** historical, literary, mainstream, suspense.

HOW TO CONTACT For fiction: Please write a query letter introducing yourself, your book, your writing background. Don't forget to include degrees you may have, publishing credits, awards and endorsements. Please wait for a response before including sample pages. "We only consider material where the manuscript for which you are querying is complete, unless you have previously published." For nonfiction: A query letter is best, introducing idea and what you have written already (proposal, manuscript?). "For writerly nonficiton (narratives, bio, memoir) please let us know if you have a finished manuscript. Also it's important you include information about yourself, your background and expertise, your platform and notoriety, if any. We do not ask for exclusivity in most instances but do ask that you inform us if other agents are considering the same material." Accepts simultaneous submissions.

TERMS Agent receives 15% commission on domestic sales; 20% commission on foreign sales. Agent receives 20% commission on film sales. Charges clients for photocopying and express mail service.

MARY EVANS INC.

242 E. Fifth St., New York NY 10003. (212)979-0880. **Fax:** (212)979-5344. **E-mail:** info@maryevansinc.com. **Website:** maryevansinc.com. Member of AAR.

MEMBER AGENTS Mary Evans (progressive politics, alternative medicine, science and technology, social commentary, American history and culture); Julia Kardon (literary and upmarket fiction, narrative nonfiction, journalism, and history); Mary Gaule (picture books, middle grade, and YA fiction).

REPRESENTS Nonfiction, novels. **Considers these nonfiction areas:** creative nonfiction, cultural interests, history, medicine, politics, science, technology, social commentary, journalism. **Considers these fiction areas:** literary, middle grade, picture books, young adult, upmarket.

HOW TO CONTACT Query by mail or e-mail. If querying by mail, include a SASE. If querying by e-mail, put "Query" in the subject line. For fiction: Include the first few pages, or opening chapter of your novel as a single Word attachment. For nonfiction: Include your book proposal as a single Word attachment. Accepts simultaneous submissions. Responds within 4-8 weeks.

FAIRBANK LITERARY REPRESENTATION

P.O. Box 6, Hudson NY 12534-0006. (617)576-0030. **Fax:** (617)576-0030. **E-mail:** queries@fairbankliterary.com. **Website:** www.fairbankliterary.com. **Contact:** Sorche Fairbank. Member of AAR.

MEMBER AGENTS Sorche Fairbank (narrative nonfiction, commercial and literary fiction, memoir, food and wine); Matthew Frederick, matt@fairbankliterary.com (scout for sports nonfiction, architecture, design).

REPRESENTS Novels, short story collections. **Considers these nonfiction areas:** agriculture, architecture, art, autobiography, biography, cooking, crafts, cultural interests, current affairs, decorating, diet/nutrition, design, environment, ethnic, foods, gay/lesbian, government, hobbies, horticulture, how-to, interior design, investigative, law, memoirs, photography, popular culture, politics, science, sociology, sports, technology, true crime, women's issues, women's studies. **Considers these fiction areas:** action, adventure, feminist, gay, lesbian, literary, mainstream, mystery, sports, suspense, thriller, women's, Southern voices.

HOW TO CONTACT Query with SASE. Submit author bio. Accepts simultaneous submissions. Obtains most new clients through recommendations from others, solicitations, conferences, ideas generated in-house.

TERMS Agent receives 15% commission on domestic sales; 20% commission on foreign sales. Offers written contract, binding for 12 months; 45-day notice must be given to terminate contract.

LEIGH FELDMAN LITERARY

E-mail: query@lfliterary.com. **Website:** www.publishersmarketplace.com/members/leighfeldman.

Contact: Leigh Feldman. Estab. 2014. Member of AAR. Signatory of WGA.

REPRESENTS Nonfiction, fiction, novels, short story collections. **Considers these nonfiction areas:** creative nonfiction, memoirs. **Considers these fiction areas:** contemporary issues, family saga, feminist, gay, historical, lesbian, literary, multicultural, short story collections, women's, young adult.

HOW TO CONTACT E-query. "Please include 'query' in the subject line. Due to large volume of submissions, we regret that we can not respond to all queries individually. Please include the first chapter or the first 10 pages of your manuscript (or proposal) pasted after your query letter. I'd love to know what led you to query me in particular, and please let me know if you are querying other agents as well." Accepts simultaneous submissions.

DIANA FINCH LITERARY AGENCY

116 W. 23rd St., Suite 500, New York NY 10011. (917)544-4470. **E-mail:** diana.finch@verizon.net. **Website:** dianafinchliteraryagency.blogspot.com. **Contact:** Diana Finch. Estab. 2003. Member of AAR. Represents 40 clients.

REPRESENTS Nonfiction, fiction, novels. **Considers these nonfiction areas:** autobiography, biography, business, child guidance, computers, cultural interests, current affairs, dance, economics, environment, ethnic, film, government, health, history, how-to, humor, investigative, juvenile nonfiction, law, medicine, memoirs, military, money, music, parenting, photography, popular culture, politics, psychology, satire, science, self-help, sports, technology, theater, translation, true crime, war, women's issues, women's studies. **Considers these fiction areas:** action, adventure, contemporary issues, crime, detective, ethnic, historical, literary, mainstream, police, sports, thriller, young adult.

HOW TO CONTACT This agency prefers submissions via its online form: https://dianafinchliteraryagency.submittable.com/submit Accepts simultaneous submissions. Obtains most new clients through recommendations from others.

TERMS Agent receives 15% commission on domestic sales; 20% commission on foreign sales. Offers written contract. "I charge for overseas postage, galleys, and books purchased, and try to recoup these costs from earnings received for a client, rather than charging outright."

FINEPRINT LITERARY MANAGEMENT

115 W. 29th, 3rd Floor, New York NY 10001. (212)279-1282. **Website:** www.fineprintlit.com. Member of AAR.

MEMBER AGENTS Peter Rubie, CEO, peter@fineprintlit.com (nonfiction interests include narrative nonfiction, popular science, spirituality, history, biography, pop culture, business, technology, parenting, health, self help, music, and food; fiction interests include literate thrillers, crime fiction, science fiction and fantasy, military fiction and literary fiction, middle grade and boy-oriented YA fiction); Stephany Evans, stephany@fineprintlit.com (nonfiction: health and wellness, spirituality, lifestyle (including home renovating, decorating, food and drink, and sustainability), running and fitness, memoir, and narrative nonfiction; fiction interests include women's fiction, from literary to romance, including mystery, historical, and romantic suspense); Janet Reid, janet@fineprintlit.com (crime fiction and narrative nonfiction); Laura Wood, laura@fineprintlit.com (serious nonfiction, especially in the areas of science and nature, along with substantial titles in business, history, religion, and other areas by academics, experienced professionals, and journalists; select genre fiction only (no poetry, literary fiction or memoir) in the categories of science fiction and fantasy and mystery); June Clark, june@fineprintlit.com (nonfiction projects in the areas of entertainment, self-help, parenting, reference/how-to books, food and wine, style/beauty, and prescriptive business titles); Penny Moore, penny@fineprintlit.com (all genres of middle grade and young adult fiction; adult fiction, specifically upmarket, speculative fiction, sci-fi, fantasy, psychological thrillers, and select romance; nonfiction projects in the realm of pop culture, humor, travel, food, and pets); Jacqueline Murphy, jacqueline@fineprintlit.com.

REPRESENTS Considers these nonfiction areas: biography, business, foods, health, history, how-to, humor, memoirs, music, parenting, popular culture, science, self-help, spirituality, technology, travel, fitness, lifestyle. **Considers these fiction areas:** commercial, crime, fantasy, historical, middle grade, mystery, romance, science fiction, suspense, thriller, women's, young adult.

HOW TO CONTACT E-query. For fiction, send a query, synopsis, bio, and 30 pages pasted into the e-mail. No attachments. For nonfiction, send a query only; proposal requested later if the agent is interested. Accepts simultaneous submissions. Obtains most new clients through recommendations from others, solicitations.

TERMS Agent receives 15% commission on domestic sales; 20% commission on foreign sales.

FLETCHER & COMPANY

E-mail: info@fletcherandco.com. **Website:** www.fletcherandco.com. **Contact:** Christy Fletcher. Estab. 2003. Member of AAR.

MEMBER AGENTS Christy Fletcher (referrals only); Melissa Chinchillo (select list of her own authors); Rebecca Gradinger (literary fiction, up-market commercial fiction, narrative nonfiction, self-help, memoir, Women's studies, humor, and pop culture); Gráinne Fox (literary fiction and quality commercial authors, award-winning journalists and food writers, American voices, international, literary crime, upmarket fiction, narrative nonfiction); Lisa Grubka (fiction — literary, upmarket women's, and young adult; and nonfiction — narrative, food, science, and more); Sylvie Greenberg (literary fiction, business, sports, science, memoir and history); Donald Lamm (history, biography, investigative journalism, politics, current affairs, and business); Todd Sattersten (business books).

REPRESENTS Nonfiction, novels. **Considers these nonfiction areas:** biography, business, creative nonfiction, current affairs, foods, history, humor, investigative, memoirs, popular culture, politics, science, self-help, sports, women's studies. **Considers these fiction areas:** commercial, crime, literary, women's, young adult.

HOW TO CONTACT Send queries to info@fletcherandco.com. Please do not include e-mail attachments with your initial query, as they will be deleted. Address your query to a specific agent. No snail mail queries. Accepts simultaneous submissions.

FOLIO LITERARY MANAGEMENT, LLC

The Film Center Building, 630 Ninth Ave., Suite 1101, New York NY 10036. (212)400-1494. **Fax:** (212)967-0977. **Website:** www.foliolit.com. Member of AAR. Represents 100+ clients.

MEMBER AGENTS Claudia Cross (romance novels, commercial women's fiction, cooking and food writing, serious nonfiction on religious and spiritual topics); Scott Hoffman (literary and commercial fiction, journalistic or academic nonfiction, narrative nonfiction, pop-culture books, business, history, politics, spiritual or religious-themed fiction and nonfiction, sci-fi/fantasy literary fiction, heartbreaking memoirs, humorous nonfiction); Jeff Kleinman (bookclub fiction (not genre commercial, like mysteries or romances), literary fiction, thrillers and suspense novels, narrative nonfiction, memoir); Dado Derviskadic (nonfiction: cultural history, biography, memoir, pop science, motivational self-help, health/nutrition, pop culture, cookbooks; fiction that's gritty, introspective, or serious); Frank Weimann (biography, business/investing/finance, history, religious, mind/body/spirit, health, lifestyle, cookbooks, sports, African-American, science, memoir, special forces/CIA/FBI/mafia, military, prescriptive nonfiction, humor, celebrity; adult and children's fiction); Michael Harriot (commercial nonfiction (both narrative and prescriptive) and fantasy/science fiction); Erin Harris (book club, historical fiction, literary, narrative nonfiction, psychological suspense, young adult), Molly Jaffa (middle grade, YA, select nonfiction), Katherine Latshaw (blogs-to-books, food/cooking, middle grade, narrative and prescriptive nonfiction); Annie Hwang (literary and upmarket fiction with commercial appeal; select nonfiction: popular science, diet/health/fitness, lifestyle, narrative nonfiction, pop culture, and humor); Erin Niumata (fiction: commercial women's fiction, romance, historical fiction, mysteries, psychological thrillers, suspense, humor; nonfiction: self-help, women's issues, pop culture and humor, pet care/pets, memoirs, and anything blogger); Ruth Pomerance (narrative nonfiction and commercial fiction); Marcy Posner (adult: commercial women's fiction, historical fiction, mystery, biography, history, health, and lifestyle, commercial novels, thrillers, narrative nonfiction; children's: contemporary YA and middle-grade novels, mystery series for boys, select historical fiction and fantasy); Jeff Silberman (narrative nonfiction, biography, history, politics, current affairs, health, lifestyle, humor, food/cookbook, memoir, pop culture, sports, science, technology; commercial, literary, and book club fiction); Steve Troha; Emily van Beek (young adult, middle grade, picture books), Melissa White (general nonfiction, literary and commercial fiction, middle grade, YA); John Cusick (middle grade, picture books, YA).

REPRESENTS Nonfiction, novels. **Considers these nonfiction areas:** animals, art, biography, business, cooking, creative nonfiction, economics, environment, foods, health, history, how-to, humor, inspirational, memoirs, military, parenting, popular culture, politics, psychology, religious, satire, science, self-help, technology, war, women's issues, women's studies. **Considers these fiction areas:** commercial, fantasy, horror, literary, middle grade, mystery, picture books, religious, romance, thriller, women's, young adult.

HOW TO CONTACT Query via e-mail only (no attachments). Read agent bios online for specific submission guidelines and e-mail addresses, and to check if someone is closed to queries. "All agents respond to queries as soon as possible, whether interested or not. If you haven't heard back from the individual agent within the time period that they specify on their bio page, it's possible that something has gone wrong, and your query has been lost – in that case, please re-e-mail a follow-up."

JEANNE FREDERICKS LITERARY AGENCY, INC.

221 Benedict Hill Rd., New Canaan CT 06840. (203)972-3011. **Fax:** (203)972-3011. **E-mail:** jeanne.fredericks@gmail.com. **Website:** www.jeannefredericks.com. **Contact:** Jeanne Fredericks. Estab. 1997. Member of AAR. Other memberships include Authors Guild.

REPRESENTS Nonfiction. **Considers these nonfiction areas:** Americana, animals, autobiography, biography, child guidance, cooking, decorating, foods, gardening, health, history, how-to, interior design, medicine, parenting, photography, psychology, self-help, women's issues.

HOW TO CONTACT Query first by e-mail, then send outline/proposal, 1-2 sample chapters, if requested and after you have consulted the submission guidelines on the agency website. If you do send requested submission materials, include the word "Requested" in the subject line. Accepts simultaneous submissions. Responds in 3-5 weeks to queries. Responds in 2-4 months to mss. Obtains most new clients through recommendations from others, solicitations, conferences.

TERMS Agent receives 15% commission on domestic sales; 25% commission on foreign sales with co-agent. Offers written contract, binding for 9 months; 2-month notice must be given to terminate contract.

Charges client for photocopying of whole proposals and mss, overseas postage, priority mail, express mail services.

GRACE FREEDSON'S PUBLISHING NETWORK

7600 Jericho Turnpike, Suite 300, Woodbury NY 11797. (516)931-7757. **Fax:** (516)931-7759. **E-mail:** gfreedson@gmail.com. **Contact:** Grace Freedson. . Estab. 2000. Member of AAR. women's Media Group; Author's Guild; Represents 100 clients.

REPRESENTS Nonfiction, scholarly books. **Considers these nonfiction areas:** animals, business, child guidance, computers, cooking, crafts, creative nonfiction, current affairs, diet/nutrition, economics, education, environment, foods, gardening, health, history, hobbies, horticulture, how-to, humor, inspirational, interior design, juvenile nonfiction, language, law, memoirs, metaphysics, money, multicultural, parenting, philosophy, popular culture, psychology, recreation, regional, satire, science, self-help, sports, technology, true crime, war, women's issues, women's studies. **Considers these script areas:** test preparation.

HOW TO CONTACT Query with SASE. Submit synopsis, SASE. Responds in 2-6 weeks to queries. Obtains most new clients through recommendations from others.

TERMS Agent receives 15% commission on domestic sales. Offers written contract; 30-day notice must be given to terminate contract.

REBECCA FRIEDMAN LITERARY AGENCY

E-mail: Abby@rfliterary.com. **Website:** www.rfliterary.com/. Estab. 2013. Member of AAR. Signatory of WGA.

MEMBER AGENTS Rebecca Friedman, brandie@rfliterary.com (commercial and literary fiction with a focus on literary novels of suspense, women's fiction, contemporary romance, and young adult, as well as journalistic nonfiction and memoir); Kimberly Brower, kimberly@rfliterary.com (commercial and literary fiction, with an emphasis in contemporary romance, women's fiction, mysteries/thrillers and young adult); Rachel Marks, rachel@rfliterary.com (young adult, fantasy, science fiction, new adult and romance).

REPRESENTS Nonfiction, fiction. **Considers these nonfiction areas:** memoirs, journalistic nonfiction. **Considers these fiction areas:** commercial, fantasy, literary, mystery, new adult, romance, science fiction, suspense, women's, young adult.

HOW TO CONTACT Please submit your query letter and first chapter (no more than fifteen pages, double-spaced). If querying Kimberly, paste a full synopsis into the e-mail submission. No attachments. Accepts simultaneous submissions. Tries to respond in 6-8 weeks.

THE FRIEDRICH AGENCY

19 W. 21st St., Suite 201, New York NY 10010. 212-317-8810. **E-mail:** mfriedrich@friedrichagency.com; lcarson@friedrichagency.com; kwolf@friedrichagency.com. **Website:** www.friedrichagency.com. **Contact:** Molly Friedrich; Lucy Carson; Kent D. Wolf. Estab. 2006. Member of AAR. Signatory of WGA. Represents 50+ clients.

MEMBER AGENTS Molly Friedrich, founder and agent (open to queries); Lucy Carson, TV/film rights director and agent (open to queries); Kent D. Wolf, foreign rights director and agent (open to queries).

REPRESENTS Nonfiction, fiction, novels, short story collections. **Considers these nonfiction areas:** creative nonfiction, memoirs. **Considers these fiction areas:** commercial, literary.

HOW TO CONTACT Query by e-mail only. Please query only one agent at this agency. Accepts simultaneous submissions.

FULL CIRCLE LITERARY, LLC

Website: www.fullcircleliterary.com. **Contact:** Stefanie Von Borstel. Estab. 2005. Member of AAR. Society of Children's Books Writers & Illustrators, Authors Guild Represents 100+ clients.

MEMBER AGENTS Stefanie Von Borstel; Adriana Dominguez; Taylor Martindale (multicultural voices); Lilly Ghahremani.

REPRESENTS **Considers these nonfiction areas:** creative nonfiction, how-to, interior design, multicultural, women's issues, young adult. **Considers these fiction areas:** literary, middle grade, multicultural, picture books, women's, young adult.

HOW TO CONTACT Online submissions only via Submissions Form at www.fullcircleliterary.com Please complete the form and submit cover letter, author information and sample writing. For sample writing: fiction please include the first 10 manuscript pages. For nonfiction, include a proposal with one sample chapter. Accepts simultaneous submissions.

"Due to the high volume of submissions, please keep in mind we are no longer able to personally respond to every submission. However, we read every submission with care and often share for a second read within the office. If we are interested, we will contact you by e-mail to request additional materials (such as a complete manuscript or additional manuscripts). Please keep us updated if there is a change in the status of your project, such as an offer of representation or book contract." If you have not heard from us in 6-8 weeks, your project is not right for our agency at the current time and we wish you all the best with your writing. Thank you for considering Full Circle Literary, we look forward to reading! Obtains most new clients through recommendations from others and conferences.

TERMS Agent receives 15% commission on domestic sales; 25% commission on foreign sales. Offers written contract which outlines responsibilities of the author and the agent.

FUSE LITERARY

Website: www.fuseliterary.com. Member of AAR. Signatory of WGA.

MEMBER AGENTS Laurie McLean (only accepting referral inquiries and submissions requested at conferences or online events, with the exception of unsolicited adult and children's science fiction); Gordon Warnock, querygordon@fuseliterary.com (fiction: high-concept commercial fiction, literary fiction (adults through YA), graphic novels (adults through MG); nonfiction: memoir (adult, YA, NA, graphic), cookbooks/food narrative/food studies, illustrated/art/photography (especially graphic nonfiction), political and current events, pop-science, pop-culture (especially punk culture and geek culture), self-help, how-to, humor, pets, business and career); Connor Goldsmith, queryconnor@fuseliterary.com (fiction: sci-fi/fantasy/horror, thrillers, and upmarket commercial fiction with a unique and memorable hook; books by and about people from marginalized perspectives, such as LGBT people and/or racial minorities; nonfiction (from recognized experts with established platforms): history (particularly of the ancient world), theater, cinema, music, television, mass media, popular culture, feminism and gender studies, LGBT issues, race relations, and the sex industry); Sara Sciuto, querysara@fuseliterary.com (middle grade, young adult, standout picture books); Michelle Richter, que-rymichelle@fuseliterary.com (primarily seeking fiction, specifically book club reads, literary fiction, and mystery/suspense/thrillers; for nonfiction, seeking fashion, pop culture, science/medicine, sociology/social trends, and economics); Emily S. Keyes, queryemily@fuseliterary.com (young adult, middle grade, and select commercial fiction, including fantasy & science fiction, women's fiction, new adult fiction, pop culture and humor); Tricia Skinner, querytricia@fuseliterary.com (Romance: science fiction, futuristic, fantasy, military/special ops, medieval historical; brand new relationships; diversity); Jennifer Chen Tran, queryjennifer@fuseliterary.com (literary fiction, commercial fiction, women's fiction, upmarket fiction, contemporary romance, mature Young Adult, New Adult, suspense/thriller, select graphic novels (adult, YA, MG); memoir, narrative nonfiction in the areas of adventure, biography, business, current affairs, medical, history, how-to, pop-culture, psychology, social entrepreneurism, social justice, travel, and lifestyle books (home, design, fashion, food).

HOW TO CONTACT E-query an individual agent. Check the website to see if any individual agent has closed themselves to submissions, as well as each agent's individual submission preferences. Accepts simultaneous submissions.

THE G AGENCY, LLC

P.O. Box 374, Bronx NY 10471. (718)664-4505. **E-mail:** gagencyquery@gmail.com. **Website:** www.publishersmarketplace.com/members/jeffg/. **Contact:** Jeff Gerecke. Estab. 2012. Member of AAR. Signatory of WGA.

MEMBER AGENTS Jeff Gerecke.

REPRESENTS **Considers these nonfiction areas:** biography, business, computers, history, military, money, popular culture, technology. **Considers these fiction areas:** mainstream, mystery.

HOW TO CONTACT E-mail submissions preferred - attach sample chapters or proposal if you wish. Enter "QUERY" along with the title in the subject line of e-mails or on the envelope of snail mail. "I cannot guarantee replies to every submission. If you do not hear from me the first time, you may send me one reminder." Accepts simultaneous submissions.

GELFMAN SCHNEIDER / ICM PARTNERS

850 7th Ave., Suite 903, New York NY 10019. **E-mail:** mail@gelfmanschneider.com. **Website:** www.gelf-

manschneider.com. **Contact:** Jane Gelfman, Deborah Schneider. Member of AAR. Represents 300+ clients.

MEMBER AGENTS Deborah Schneider (all categories of literary and commercial fiction and nonfiction); Jane Gelfman; Victoria Marini, victoria.gsliterary@gmail.com (literary fiction, commercial fiction, pop-culture nonfiction, young adult and middle grade fiction; particular interest in engaging literary fiction and mysteries/suspense, commercial women's fiction [suspense, mystery, thriller, magical realism & fantasy], and Young Adult [contemporary and sci-fi/fantasy]); Heather Mitchell (particularly interested in narrative nonfiction, historical fiction and young debut authors with strong voices); Penelope Burns, penelope.gsliterary@gmail.com (literary and commercial fiction and nonfiction, as well as a variety of young adult and middle grade).

REPRESENTS Nonfiction, fiction, juvenile books. **Considers these nonfiction areas:** creative nonfiction, popular culture. **Considers these fiction areas:** commercial, fantasy, historical, literary, mainstream, middle grade, mystery, science fiction, suspense, women's, young adult.

HOW TO CONTACT Query. Check Submissions page of website to see which agents are open to queries and further instructions. To query Victoria Marini or Penelope Burns, please send a query letter and sample chapters (1-3) (pasted, no attachments) to their individual e-mails. Please include "query" in the subject line. For Victoria, please check victoriamarini.com/submissions for updates and response times as they may vary. Accepts simultaneous submissions.

TERMS Agent receives 15% commission on domestic sales; 20% commission on foreign sales. Agent receives 15% commission on film sales. Offers written contract. Charges clients for photocopying and messengers/couriers.

GHOSH LITERARY

E-mail: submissions@ghoshliterary.com. **Website:** www.ghoshliterary.com. Member of AAR. Signatory of WGA.

REPRESENTS Nonfiction, fiction.

HOW TO CONTACT E-query. Please send an e-mail to submissions@ghoshliterary.com briefly introducing yourself and your work. Although no specific format is required, it is helpful to know the following: your qualifications for writing your book, including any publications and recognition for your work; who

you expect to buy and read your book; similar books and authors. Accepts simultaneous submissions.

GLASS LITERARY MANAGEMENT

138 West 25th St., 10th Floor, New York NY 10001. (646)237-4881. **E-mail:** submissions@glassliterary.com. **Website:** www.glassliterary.com. **Contact:** Alex Glass. Estab. 2014. Member of AAR. Signatory of WGA.

REPRESENTS Nonfiction, novels.

HOW TO CONTACT "Please send your query letter in the body of an e-mail and if we are interested, we will respond and ask for the complete manuscript or proposal. No attachments." Accepts simultaneous submissions.

GLOBAL LION INTELLECTUAL PROPERTY MANAGEMENT

P.O. Box 669238, Pompano Beach FL 33066. **E-mail:** queriesgloballionmgt@gmail.com. **Website:** www.globallionmanagement.com. **Contact:** Peter Miller. Estab. 2013. Member of AAR. Signatory of WGA.

HOW TO CONTACT E-query. Global Lion Intellectual Property Management. Inc. accepts exclusive submissions only. "If your work is under consideration by another agency, please do not submit it to us." Below the query, paste a one page synopsis, a sample of your book (20 pages is fine), a short author bio, and any impressive social media links.

BARRY GOLDBLATT LITERARY LLC

320 Seventh Ave. #266, Brooklyn NY 11215. **E-mail:** query@bgliterary.com. **Website:** www.bgliterary.com/. **Contact:** Barry Goldblatt. Estab. 2000. Member of AAR. Signatory of WGA.

MEMBER AGENTS Barry Goldblatt; Jennifer Udden, query.judden@gmail.com (speculative fiction of all stripes, especially innovative science fiction or fantasy; contemporary/erotic/LGBT/paranormal/historical romance; contemporary or speculative YA; select mysteries, thrillers, and urban fantasies. Please, do not send to Jen: any middle-grade, chapter, or picture books; nonfiction.).

REPRESENTS Fiction. **Considers these fiction areas:** fantasy, middle grade, mystery, romance, science fiction, thriller, young adult.

HOW TO CONTACT "E-mail queries can be sent to query@bgliterary.com and should include the word 'query' in the subject line. To query Jen Udden specifically, e-mail queries can be sent to query.judden@

gmail.com. Please know that we will read and respond to every e-query that we receive, provided it is properly addressed and follows the submission guidelines below. We will not respond to e-queries that are addressed to no one, or to multiple recipients. While we do not require exclusivity, exclusive submissions will receive priority review. If your submission is exclusive to Barry Goldblatt Literary, please indicate so by including the word 'Exclusive' in the subject line of your e-mail. Your e-query should include the following within the body of the e-mail: your query letter, a synopsis of the book, and the first five pages of your manuscript. We will not open or respond to any e-mails that have attachments." Our response time is four weeks on queries, six to eight weeks on full manuscripts. If you haven't heard from us within that time, feel free to check in via e-mail." Accepts simultaneous submissions. Obtains clients through referrals, queries, and conferences.

TERMS Agent receives 15% commission on domestic sales; 20% on foreign and dramatic sales. Offers written contract. 60 days notice must be given to terminate contract.

FRANCES GOLDIN LITERARY AGENCY, INC.

214 W. 29th St., Suite 410, New York NY 10001. (212)777-0047. **Fax:** (212)228-1660. **Website:** www. goldinlit.com. Estab. 1977. Member of AAR.

MEMBER AGENTS Frances Goldin, founder/president; Ellen Geiger, vice president/principal (nonfiction: history, biography, progressive politics, photography, science and medicine, women, religion and serious investigative journalism; fiction: literary thriller, and novels in general that provoke and challenge the status quo, as well as historical and multicultural works. Please no New Age, romance, how-to or rightwing politics); Matt McGowan, agent/rights director, mm@goldinlit.com, (literary fiction, essays, history, memoir, journalism, biography, music, popular culture & science, sports [particularly soccer], narrative nonfiction, cultural studies, as well as literary travel, crime, food, suspense and sci-fi); Sam Stoloff, vice president/principal, (literary fiction, memoir, history, accessible sociology and philosophy, cultural studies, serious journalism, narrative and topical nonfiction with a progressive orientation); Ria Julien, agent/counsel; Nina Cochran, literary assistant.

REPRESENTS Nonfiction, novels. **Considers these nonfiction areas:** biography, creative nonfiction, cultural interests, foods, history, investigative, medicine, memoirs, music, philosophy, photography, popular culture, politics, science, sociology, sports, travel, women's issues, crime. **Considers these fiction areas:** historical, literary, mainstream, multicultural, suspense, thriller.

HOW TO CONTACT There is an online submission process you can find here: www.goldinlit.com/contact.html Responds in 4-6 weeks to queries.

IRENE GOODMAN LITERARY AGENCY

27 W. 24th St., Suite 700B, New York NY 10010. **Website:** www.irenegoodman.com. Member of AAR.

MEMBER AGENTS Irene Goodman, Miriam Kriss, Barbara Poelle, Rachel Ekstrom, Beth Vesel, Kim Perel, Anne Baltazar, Brita Lundberg.

REPRESENTS Nonfiction, novels, juvenile books. **Considers these nonfiction areas:** , parenting, social issues, francophilia, anglophilia, Judaica, lifestyles, cooking, memoir. **Considers these fiction areas:** crime, detective, historical, mystery, romance, thriller, women's, young adult.

HOW TO CONTACT Query. Submit synopsis, first 10 pages pasted into the body of the e-mail. E-mail queries only! See the website submission page. No e-mail attachments. Query one agent only. Accepts simultaneous submissions. Responds in 2 months to queries. Consult website for each agent's submission guidelines.

DOUG GRAD LITERARY AGENCY, INC.

68 Jay St., Suite N3, Brooklyn NY 11201. (718)788-6067. **E-mail:** query@dgliterary.com. **Website:** www. dgliterary.com. **Contact:** Doug Grad. Estab. 2008. Member of AAR. Signatory of WGA.

MEMBER AGENTS Doug Grad (narrative nonfiction, military, sports, celebrity memoir, thrillers, mysteries, historical fiction, music, style, business, home improvement, cookbooks, science and theater).

REPRESENTS Nonfiction, fiction, novels. **Considers these nonfiction areas:** Americana, autobiography, business, cooking, creative nonfiction, current affairs, diet/nutrition, design, film, government, history, humor, military, music, popular culture, politics, science, sports, technology, theater, travel, true crime, war. **Considers these fiction areas:** action, adventure, commercial, crime, detective, historical, horror, literary, mainstream, military, mystery, police, science fiction, suspense, thriller, war, young adult.

HOW TO CONTACT Query by e-mail first at query@dgliterary.com. No sample material unless requested; no printed submissions by mail. Accepts simultaneous submissions.

ASHLEY GRAYSON LITERARY AGENCY

1342 W. 18th St., San Pedro CA 90732. **E-mail:** graysonagent@earthlink.net. **Website:** www.publishersmarketplace.com/members/CGrayson/. Estab. 1976. Member of AAR.

MEMBER AGENTS Ashley Grayson (fantasy, mystery, thrillers, young adult); Carolyn Grayson, carolyngraysonagent@earthlink.net (women's fiction, romance, urban fantasy, paranormal romance, mysteries, thrillers, children's books, nonfiction); Lois Winston, lois.graysonagent@earthlink.net (women's fiction, romance, chick lit, mystery).

REPRESENTS Nonfiction, novels. **Considers these nonfiction areas:** business, parenting, popular culture, science, spirituality, true crime. **Considers these fiction areas:** fantasy, juvenile, middle grade, mystery, romance, thriller, women's, young adult.

HOW TO CONTACT "The agency is temporarily closed to queries from fiction writers who are not previously published at book length (self published or print-on-demand do not count). There are only three exceptions to this policy: (1) Unpublished authors who have received an offer from a reputable publisher, who need an agent before beginning contract negotiations; (2) Authors who are recommended by a published author, editor or agent who has read the work in question; (3) Authors whom we have met at conferences and from whom we have requested submissions. Nonfiction authors who are recognized within their field or area may still query with proposals. Note: We cannot review self-published, subsidy-published, and POD-published works to evaluate moving them to mainstream publishers. If you meet the criteria above, send query letter plus list of your publication credits, including by whom published and year of publication. Ashley Grayson, Carolyn Grayson, and Lois Winston accept queries by e-mail. Do not include attachments to your e-mail unless requested. Do not query more than one agent in our agency, whether by e-mail or post; we will make sure that your query reaches the right person." Accepts simultaneous submissions.

TERMS Agent receives 15% commission on domestic sales; 20% commission on foreign sales.

SANFORD J. GREENBURGER ASSOCIATES, INC.

55 Fifth Ave., New York NY 10003. (212)206-5600. **Fax:** (212)463-8718. **Website:** www.greenburger.com. Member of AAR. Represents 500 clients.

MEMBER AGENTS Matt Bialer, LRibar@sjga.com (fantasy, science fiction, thrillers, and mysteries as well as a select group of literary writers, and also loves smart narrative nonfiction including books about current events, popular culture, biography, history, music, race, and sports); Brenda Bowen, queryBB@sjga.com (literary fiction, writers and illustrators of picture books, chapter books, and middle-grade and teen fiction); Faith Hamlin, fhamlin@sjga.com (receives submissions by referral); Heide Lange, queryHL@sjga.com (receives submissions by referral); Daniel Mandel, querydm@sjga.com (literary and commercial fiction, as well as memoirs and nonfiction about business, art, history, politics, sports, and popular culture); Courtney Miller-Callihan, cmiller@sjga.com (YA, middle grade, women's fiction, romance, and historical novels, as well as nonfiction projects on unusual topics, humor, pop culture, and lifestyle books); Nicholas Ellison, nellison@sjga.com; Chelsea Lindman, clindman@sjga.com (playful literary fiction, upmarket crime fiction, and forward thinking or boundary-pushing nonfiction); Rachael Dillon Fried, rfried@sjga.com (both fiction and nonfiction authors, with a keen interest in unique literary voices, women's fiction, narrative nonfiction, memoir, and comedy); Lindsay Ribar, co-agents with Matt Bialer (young adult and middle grade fiction); Bethany Buck querybbuck@sjga.com (middle-grade fiction and chapter books, teen fiction, and a select list of picture book authors and illustrators); Stephanie Delman sdelman@sjga.com (literary/upmarket contemporary fiction, psychological thrillers/suspense, and atmospheric, near-historical fiction); Ed Maxwell emaxwell@sjga.com (expert and narrative nonfiction authors, novelists and graphic novelists, as well as children's book authors and illustrators).

REPRESENTS Nonfiction, fiction, novels, juvenile books. **Considers these nonfiction areas:** art, biography, business, creative nonfiction, current affairs, ethnic, history, humor, memoirs, music, popular culture, politics, sports. **Considers these fiction areas:** commercial, crime, family saga, fantasy, feminist, historical, literary, middle grade, multicultural, mystery, picture books, romance, science fiction, thriller, women's, young adult.

HOW TO CONTACT E-query. "Please look at each agent's profile page for current information about what each agent is looking for and for the correct e-mail address to use for queries to that agent. Please be sure to use the correct query e-mail address for each agent." Agents may not respond to all queries; will respond within 6-8 weeks if interested. Obtains most new clients through recommendations from others.

TERMS Agent receives 15% commission on domestic sales; 20% commission on foreign sales. Charges for photocopying and books for foreign and subsidiary rights submissions.

THE GREENHOUSE LITERARY AGENCY

E-mail: submissions@greenhouseliterary.com. **Website:** www.greenhouseliterary.com. Member of AAR. Other memberships include SCBWI. Represents 20 clients.

MEMBER AGENTS Sarah Davies, vice president (fiction by North American authors, from middle grade through young adult); Polly Nolan, agent (fiction by UK, Irish, Commonwealth — including Australia, NZ and India – authors, plus European authors writing in English, from picture books (under 1000 words) to young fiction series, through middle grade and young adult).

HOW TO CONTACT Query one agent only. Put the target agent's name in the subject line. Paste the first 5 pages of your story (or your complete picture book) after the query. Accepts simultaneous submissions.

TERMS Agent receives 15% commission on domestic sales; 25% commission on foreign sales. Offers written contract. This agency occasionally charges for submission copies to film agents or foreign publishers.

GREYHAUS LITERARY

3021 20th St., Pl. SW, Puyallup WA 98373. **E-mail:** scott@greyhausagency.com. **E-mail:** submissions@greyhausagency.com. **Website:** www.greyhausagency.com. **Contact:** Scott Eagan, member RWA. Estab. 2003. Member of AAR. Signatory of WGA.

REPRESENTS Novels. **Considers these fiction areas:** romance, women's.

HOW TO CONTACT Submissions to Greyhaus can be done in one of three ways: 1) A standard query letter via e-mail. If using this method, do not attach documents or send anything else other than a query letter. 2) Use the Submission Form found on the website on the Contact page. Or 3) send a query, the first 3 pages and a synopsis of no more than 3-5 pages (and a SASE), using a snail mail submission. Accepts simultaneous submissions.

THE JOY HARRIS LITERARY AGENCY, INC.

1501 Broadway, Suite 2310, New York NY 10036. (212)924-6269. **Fax:** (212)540-5776. **E-mail:** submissions@joyharrisliterary.com. **Website:** joyharrisliterary.com. **Contact:** Joy Harris. Estab. 1990. Member of AAR. Represents More than 100 clients.

MEMBER AGENTS Joy Harris (literary fiction, strongly-written commercial fiction, narrative nonfiction across a broad range of topics, memoir and biography); Adam Reed (literary fiction, science and technology, and pop culture).

REPRESENTS Nonfiction, fiction. **Considers these nonfiction areas:** art, biography, creative nonfiction, memoirs, popular culture, science, technology. **Considers these fiction areas:** commercial, literary.

HOW TO CONTACT Please e-mail all submissions, comprised of a query letter, outline or sample chapter, to submissions@joyharrisliterary.com." Accepts simultaneous submissions. Obtains most new clients through recommendations from clients and editors.

TERMS Agent receives 15% commission on domestic sales; 20% commission on foreign sales. Charges clients for some office expenses.

JOHN HAWKINS & ASSOCIATES, INC.

80 Maiden Lane, Suite 1503, New York NY 10038. (212)807-7040. **E-mail:** jha@jhalit.com. **Website:** www.jhalit.com. **Contact:** Moses Cardona (rights and translations); Liz Free (permissions); William Reiss, literary agent; Warren Frazier, literary agent; Anne Hawkins, literary agent. Member of AAR. Represents 100+ clients.

MEMBER AGENTS William Reiss, reiss@jhalit.com (historical narratives, biography, slightly off-beat fiction and nonfiction, children's books, nature writing); Moses Cardona, moses@jhalit.com (commercial fiction, suspense, business, science, and multicultural fiction); Warren Frazier, frazier@jhalit.com ((fiction; nonfiction, specifically technology, history, world affairs and foreign policy); Anne Hawkins, ahawkins@jhalit.com (thrillers to literary fiction to serious nonfiction; interested in science, history, public policy, medicine and women's issues).

REPRESENTS Novels. **Considers these nonfiction areas:** biography, business, history, medicine, politics, science, technology, women's issues. **Considers these fiction areas:** commercial, historical, literary, multicultural, suspense, thriller.

HOW TO CONTACT Query. Include the word "Query" in the subject line. For fiction, include 1-3 chapters of your book as a single Word attachment. For nonfiction, include your proposal as a single attachment. E-mail a particular agent directly if you are targeting one. Accepts simultaneous submissions. Responds in 1 month to queries. Obtains most new clients through recommendations from others.

TERMS Agent receives 15% commission on domestic sales; 20% commission on foreign sales. Charges clients for photocopying.

RICHARD HENSHAW GROUP

145 W. 28th St., 12th Floor, New York NY 10001. (212)414-1172. **E-mail:** submissions@henshaw.com. **Website:** www.richardhenshawgroup.com. **Contact:** Rich Henshaw. Member of AAR.

REPRESENTS Novels. **Considers these fiction areas:** fantasy, historical, horror, literary, mainstream, mystery, police, romance, science fiction, thriller, young adult.

HOW TO CONTACT "Please feel free to submit a query letter in the form of an e-mail of fewer than 250 words to submissions@henshaw.com address." No snail mail queries. Accepts simultaneous submissions. Obtains most new clients through recommendations from others, solicitations, conferences.

TERMS Agent receives 15% commission on domestic sales; 20% commission on foreign sales. No written contract. Charges clients for photocopying and book orders.

HOLLOWAY LITERARY

Raleigh NC **E-mail:** submissions@hollowayliterary-agency.com. **Website:** hollowayliteraryagency.com. **Contact:** Nikki Terpilowski. Estab. 2011. Member of AAR. Signatory of WGA. International Thriller Writers and Romance Writers of America

MEMBER AGENTS Nikki Terpilowski (romance, women's fiction, Southern fiction, historical fiction, cozy mysteries); Rachel Burkot (young adult contemporary, women's fiction, upmarket/book club fiction, contemporary romance, Southern fiction, urban fiction, literary fiction).

REPRESENTS Fiction. **Considers these fiction areas:** erotica, ethnic, fantasy, glitz, historical, literary, mainstream, middle grade, multicultural, regional, romance, thriller, women's, young adult.

HOW TO CONTACT Send your query and the first 15 pages of your manuscript pasted into the body of your e-mail to submissions@hollowayliteraryagency.com. In the subject header write: Nikki/Title/Genre. You can expect a response in 4-6 weeks. If Nikki is interested, she'll respond with a request for more material. If she's not interested in your query but thinks it will be a good fit for others at the agency, she'll share your submission. Accepts simultaneous submissions.

THE HOLMES AGENCY

1942 Broadway, Suite 314, Boulder CO 80302. (720)443-8550. **E-mail:** kristina@holmesliterary.com. **Website:** www.holmesliterary.com. **Contact:** Kristina A. Holmes. Member of AAR. Signatory of WGA.

MEMBER AGENTS Kristina A. Holmes.

REPRESENTS **Considers these nonfiction areas:** business, cooking, environment, foods, health, memoirs, psychology, science, sex, spirituality, women's issues.

HOW TO CONTACT "To submit your book for consideration, please e-mail your query and full book proposal to submissions@holmesliterary.com. (Please note that this agency does not represent fiction of any kind, true crime, poetry, or children's books.) In your query, please briefly describe your book (content, vision, purpose, and audience), as well as a bit about your background as an author (including notable platform highlights such as national media, a popular blog or website, speaking career, etc)." Accepts simultaneous submissions.

HSG AGENCY

37 West 28th St., 8th Floor, New York NY 10001. **E-mail:** channigan@hsgagency.com; jsalky@hsgagency.com; jgetzler@hsgagency.com; dburby@hsgagency.com; tprasanna@hsgagency.com; leigh@hsgagency.com. **Website:** hsgagency.com. **Contact:** Carrie Hannigan; Jesseca Salky; Josh Getzler; Danielle Burby; Tanusri Prasanna; Leigh Eisenman.. Estab. 2011. Member of AAR. Signatory of WGA.

MEMBER AGENTS Carrie Hannigan; Jesseca Salky (literary and mainstream fiction); Josh Getzler (foreign and historical fiction; both women's fiction, straight-ahead historical fiction, and thrillers and mysteries); Danielle Burby (YA, women's fiction, mysteries, fantasy); Tanusri Prasanna (associate assisting current kidlit agents); Leigh Eisenman (literary and commercial fiction, foodie/cookbooks, health and fitness, lifestyle, and select narrative nonfiction).

REPRESENTS Nonfiction, fiction, novels, juvenile books. **Considers these nonfiction areas:** business, creative nonfiction, current affairs, diet/nutrition, education, environment, foods, memoirs, multicultural, photography, politics, psychology, science, self-help, women's issues, women's studies. **Considers these fiction areas:** adventure, commercial, contemporary issues, crime, detective, ethnic, family saga, historical, juvenile, literary, mainstream, middle grade, multicultural, mystery, picture books, thriller, translation, women's, young adult.

HOW TO CONTACT Electronic submissions only. Send query letter, first 5 pages of ms within e-mail to appropriate agent. Avoid submitting to multiple agents within the agency. Picture books: include entire ms. Accepts simultaneous submissions. Responds in 4-6 weeks.

HUDSON AGENCY

3 Travis Lane, Montrose New York 10548. (914)737-1475. **Website:** www.hudsonagency.net. **Contact:** Sue Giordano. Signatory of WGA. Represents 20+ clients.

MEMBER AGENTS Sue Giordano (partner/agent); Pat Giordano (partner/producer); Leif Giordano (agent/creative consultant).

HOW TO CONTACT Accepts simultaneous submissions.

THE CAROLYN JENKS AGENCY

30 Cambridge Park Dr., #3150, Cambridge MA 02140. (617)354-5099. **E-mail:** queries@carolynjenksagency.com. **Website:** www.carolynjenksagency.com. **Contact:** Carolyn Jenks. Estab. 1987. Member of AAR. Signatory of WGA.

MEMBER AGENTS Carolyn Jenks; Eric Wing. "See agency website for current member preferences" as well as a list of junior agents.

REPRESENTS **Considers these nonfiction areas:** architecture, art, autobiography, biography, business, cultural interests, current affairs, design, education, ethnic, gay/lesbian, government, history, juvenile nonfiction, language, law, literature, memoirs, metaphysics, military, money, music, New Age, religious, science, technology, translation, true crime, women's issues, women's

studies. **Considers these fiction areas:** action, adventure, ethnic, experimental, family saga, fantasy, feminist, frontier, gay, historical, horror, humor, inspirational, juvenile, lesbian, literary, mainstream, mystery, psychic, regional, religious, science fiction, supernatural, thriller, westerns, women's, young adult. **Considers these script areas:** autobiography, biography, contemporary issues, ethnic, experimental, family saga, fantasy, feminist, frontier, gay, historical, horror, inspirational, lesbian, mainstream, mystery, psychic, religious, romantic comedy, romantic drama, science fiction, supernatural, suspense, thriller, western.

HOW TO CONTACT Please submit a one page query including a brief bio via the form on the agency website. "Due to the high volume of queries we receive, we are unable to respond to everyone. Queries are reviewed on a rolling basis, and we will follow up directly with the author if there is interest in a full manuscript. Queries should not be addressed to specific agents. All queries go directly to the director for distribution." Accepts simultaneous submissions. Obtains new clients by recommendations from others, queries/submissions, agency outreach.

TERMS Offers written contract, 1-3 years depending on the project. Requires 60 day notice before terminating contract.

HARVEY KLINGER, INC.

300 W. 55th St., Suite 11V, New York NY 10019. (212)581-7068. **E-mail:** queries@harveyklinger.com. **Website:** www.harveyklinger.com. **Contact:** Harvey Klinger. Member of AAR. Represents 100 clients.

MEMBER AGENTS Harvey Kliinger; David Dunton (popular culture, music-related books, literary fiction, young adult, fiction, and memoirs); Sara Crowe (children's and young adult authors, adult fiction and nonfiction, foreign rights sales); Andrea Somberg (literary fiction, commercial fiction, romance, sci-fi/fantasy, mysteries/thrillers, young adult, middle grade, quality narrative nonfiction, popular culture, how-to, self-help, humor, interior design, cookbooks, health/fitness); Wendy Levinson (literary and commercial fiction, occasional children's YA or MG, wide variety of nonfiction).

REPRESENTS Nonfiction, fiction, novels, juvenile books. **Considers these nonfiction areas:** autobiography, biography, business, child guidance, cooking, crafts, creative nonfiction, cultural interests, current affairs, diet/nutrition, foods, health, history, how-to, investigative, literature, medicine, memoirs, psychology, science, self-help, spirituality, sports, technology, true crime, women's issues, women's studies, young adult. **Considers these fiction areas:** action, adventure, commercial, crime, detective, erotica, family saga, fantasy, gay, glitz, historical, horror, juvenile, lesbian, literary, mainstream, middle grade, mystery, police, suspense, thriller, women's, young adult.

HOW TO CONTACT Use online e-mail submission form on the website, or query with SASE via snail mail. No phone or fax queries. Don't send unsolicited manuscripts or e-mail attachments. Make submission letter to the point and as brief as possible. Accepts simultaneous submissions. Responds in 2-4 weeks to queries, if interested. Obtains most new clients through recommendations from others.

TERMS Agent receives 15% commission on domestic sales; 25% commission on foreign sales. Offers written contract. Charges for photocopying mss and overseas postage for mss.

THE KNIGHT AGENCY

570 East Avenue, Madison GA 30650. **E-mail:** submissions@knightagency.net. **Website:** knightagency.net/. **Contact:** Elaine Spencer. Estab. 1996. Member of AAR. SCWBI, WFA, SFWA, RWA Represents 200+ clients.

MEMBER AGENTS Deidre Knight (romance, women's fiction, erotica, commercial fiction, inspirational, m/m fiction, memoir and nonfiction narrative, personal finance, true crime, business, popular culture, self-help, religion, and health); Pamela Harty (romance, women's fiction, young adult, business, motivational, diet and health, memoir, parenting, pop culture, and true crime); Elaine Spencer (romance (single title and category), women's fiction, commercial "book-club" fiction, cozy mysteries, young adult and middle grade material); Lucienne Diver (fantasy, science fiction, romance, suspense and young adult); Nephele Tempest (literary/commercial fiction, women's fiction, fantasy, science fiction, romantic suspense, paranormal romance, contemporary romance, historical fiction, young adult and middle grade fiction); Melissa Jeglinski (romance [contemporary, category, historical, inspirational], young adult, middle grade, women's fiction and mystery); Kristy Hunter(romance, women's fiction, commercial fiction, young adult and middle grade material), Travis Pennington (young adult, middle grade, mysteries, thrillers, commercial fiction, and romance [nothing paranormal/fantasy in any genre for now]).

REPRESENTS Nonfiction, fiction, novels. **Considers these nonfiction areas:** current affairs, diet/nutrition, design, economics, gay/lesbian, health, juvenile nonfiction, memoirs, politics, self-help, sociology, travel, true crime, women's issues, young adult. **Considers these fiction areas:** commercial, fantasy, middle grade, new adult, romance, science fiction, thriller, women's, young adult.

HOW TO CONTACT E-queries only. "Your submission should include a one page query letter and the first five pages of your manuscript. All text must be contained in the body of your e-mail. Attachments will not be opened nor included in the consideration of your work. Queries must be addressed to a specific agent. Please do not query multiple agents." Accepts simultaneous submissions. Two weeks on queries, six on partials. Yes

TERMS 15% Simple agency agreement with open-ended commitment 15% commission on all domestic sales, 20% on foreign and film

LINDA KONNER LITERARY AGENCY

10 W. 15th St., Suite 1918, New York NY 10011. (212)691-3419. **E-mail:** ldkonner@cs.com. **Website:** www.lindakonnerliteraryagency.com. **Contact:** Linda Konner. Member of AAR. Signatory of WGA. Other memberships include ASJA. Represents 85 clients.

REPRESENTS Nonfiction. **Considers these nonfiction areas:** gay/lesbian, health, medicine, money, parenting, popular culture, psychology, science, self-help, women's issues, biography (celebrity), African American and Latino issues, relationships, popular science.

HOW TO CONTACT Query by e-mail or by mail with SASE, synopsis, author bio, sufficient return postage. Prefers to read materials exclusively for 2 weeks. Accepts simultaneous submissions. Obtains most new clients through recommendations from others, occasional solicitation among established authors/journalists.

TERMS Agent receives 15% commission on domestic sales; 25% commission on foreign sales. Offers written contract. Charges one-time fee for domestic expenses; additional expenses may be incurred for foreign sales.

STUART KRICHEVSKY LITERARY AGENCY, INC.

6 East 39th Street, Suite 500, New York NY 10016. (212)725-5288. **Fax:** (212)725-5275. **Website:** www.skagency.com. Member of AAR.

MEMBER AGENTS Stuart Krichevsky, query@skagency.com (emphasis on narrative nonfiction, literary journalism and literary and commercial fiction); Allison Hunter, AHquery@skagency.com (literary and commercial fiction, memoir, narrative nonfiction, cultural studies and pop culture; she is always looking for funny female writers, great love stories, family epics, and for nonfiction projects that speak to the current cultural climate); Ross Harris, RHquery@skagency.com (voice-driven humor and memoir, books on popular culture and our society, narrative nonfiction and literary fiction); David Patterson, dp@skagency.com (writers of upmarket narrative nonfiction and literary fiction, historians, journalists and thought leaders).

REPRESENTS Novels. **Considers these nonfiction areas:** creative nonfiction, humor, memoirs, popular culture. **Considers these fiction areas:** commercial, contemporary issues, literary.

HOW TO CONTACT Please send a query letter and the first few (up to 10) pages of your manuscript or proposal in the body of an e-mail (not an attachment) to one of the e-mail addresses. No attachments. Responds if interested. Accepts simultaneous submissions. Obtains most new clients through recommendations from others, solicitations.

SARAH LAZIN BOOKS

19 West 21st Street, Suite 501, New York NY 10010. (212)989-5757. **Fax:** (212)989-1393. **E-mail:** julia@lazinbooks.com. **Website:** www.lazinbooks.com. **Contact:** Julia Conrad. Estab. 1984. Member of AAR.
MEMBER AGENTS Sarah Lazin; Julia Conrad (subsidiary rights).

REPRESENTS Nonfiction. **Considers these nonfiction areas:** autobiography, biography, business, current affairs, environment, history, investigative, memoirs, music, parenting, photography, popular culture, politics, women's studies. **Considers these fiction areas:** commercial, literary, short story collections.

HOW TO CONTACT As of 2015: "We accept submissions through referral only." Accepts simultaneous submissions. Only accepts queries on referral.

TERMS Agent receives 15% commission on domestic sales; 20% commission on foreign sales.

THE LESHNE AGENCY

16 W. 23rd St., 4th Floor, New York NY 10010. **E-mail:** info@leshneagency.com. **E-mail:** submissions@leshneagency.com. **Website:** www.leshneagency.com. **Contact:** Lisa Leshne, agent and owner. Member of AAR. Signatory of WGA.

MEMBER AGENTS Lisa Leshne, agent and owner; Sandy Hodgman, director of foreign rights.

REPRESENTS **Considers these nonfiction areas:** business, creative nonfiction, health, memoirs, parenting, politics, sports. **Considers these fiction areas:** commercial, middle grade, young adult.

HOW TO CONTACT "Submit all materials in the body of an e-mail; no attachments. Be sure to include the word 'QUERY' and the title of your ms in the subject line. Include brief synopsis, TOC or chapter outline, 10 sample pages, bio, any previous publications, word count, how much of the ms is complete, and the best way to reach you." Accepts simultaneous submissions.

LEVINE GREENBERG ROSTAN LITERARY AGENCY, INC.

307 Seventh Ave., Suite 2407, New York NY 10001. (212)337-0934. **Fax:** (212)337-0948. **E-mail:** submit@lgrliterary.com. **Website:** www.lgrliterary.com. Member of AAR. Represents 250 clients.

MEMBER AGENTS Jim Levine (nonfiction, including business, science, narrative nonfiction, social and political issues, psychology, health, spirituality, parenting); Stephanie Rostan (adult and YA fiction; nonfiction, including parenting, health & wellness, sports, memoir); Melissa Rowland; Daniel Greenberg (nonfiction: popular culture, narrative nonfiction, memoir, and humor; literary fiction); Victoria Skurnick; Danielle Svetcov (nonfiction); Lindsay Edgecombe (narrative nonfiction, memoir, lifestyle and health, illustrated books, as well as literary fiction); Monika Verma (nonfiction: humor, pop culture, memoir, narrative nonfiction and style and fashion titles; some young adult fiction (paranormal, historical, contemporary)); Kerry Sparks (young adult and middle grade; select adult fiction and occasional nonfiction); Tim Wojcik (nonfiction, including food narratives, humor, pop culture, popular history and science; literary fiction); Arielle Eckstut (no queries).

REPRESENTS Nonfiction, novels. **Considers these nonfiction areas:** business, creative nonfiction, health, history, humor, memoirs, parenting, popular culture, science, spirituality, sports. **Considers these fiction areas:** literary, mainstream, middle grade, young adult.

HOW TO CONTACT E-query to submit@lgrliterary. com, or online submission form. "If you would like to direct your query to one of our agents specifically, please feel free to name them in the online form or in the e-mail you send." Cannot respond to submissions by mail. Do not attach more than 50 pages. "Due to the volume of submissions we receive, we are unable to respond to each individually. If we would like more information about your project, we'll contact you within three weeks (though we do get backed up on occasion!)." Accepts simultaneous submissions. Obtains most new clients through recommendations from others.

TERMS Agent receives 15% commission on domestic sales; 20% commission on foreign sales. Offers written contract. Charges clients for out-of-pocket expenses—telephone, fax, postage, photocopying—directly connected to the project.

LIVING WORD LITERARY AGENCY

P.O. Box 40974, Eugene OR 97414. **E-mail:** livingwordliterary@gmail.com. **Website:** livingwordliterary.wordpress.com. **Contact:** Kimberly Shumate, agent. Estab. 2009. Member of AAR. Signatory of WGA. Member Evangelical Christian Publishers Association

REPRESENTS Considers these nonfiction areas: health, parenting, self-help, relationships. **Considers these fiction areas:** inspirational, adult fiction, Christian living.

HOW TO CONTACT Submit a query with short synopsis and first chapter via Word document. Agency only responds if interested.

LKG AGENCY

465 West End Ave., 2A, New York NY 10024. **E-mail:** query@lkgagency.com. **E-mail:** For MG or YA: mgya@lkgagency.com For nonfiction: nonfiction@lkgagency.com. **Website:** lkgagency.com. **Contact:** Lauren Galit Caitlen Rubino-Bradway. Estab. 2005. Member of AAR. Signatory of WGA.

MEMBER AGENTS Lauren Galit (nonfiction, middle grade, young adult); Caitlen Rubino-Bradway (middle grade and young adult, some nonfiction).

REPRESENTS Nonfiction, juvenile books. **Considers these nonfiction areas:** animals, child guidance, creative nonfiction, diet/nutrition, design, health, how-to, humor, juvenile nonfiction, memoirs, parenting, popular culture, psychology, women's issues, young adult. **Considers these fiction areas:** middle grade, young adult.

HOW TO CONTACT For nonfiction submissions, please send a query letter to nonfiction@lkgagency. com, along with a Table of Contents and two sample chapters. The Table of Contents should be fairly detailed, with a paragraph or two overview of the content of each chapter. Please also make sure to mention any publicity you have at your disposal. For middle grade and young adult submissions, please send a query, synopsis, and the three (3) chapters, and address all submissions to mgya@lkgagency.com. On a side note, while both Lauren and Caitlen consider young adult and middle grade, Lauren tends to look more for middle grade, while Caitlen deals more with young adult fiction. **Please note: due to the high volume of submissions, we are unable to reply to every one. If you do not receive a reply, please consider that a rejection.** Accepts simultaneous submissions.

STERLING LORD LITERISTIC, INC.

65 Bleecker St., New York NY 10012. **Fax:** (212)780-6095. **E-mail:** info@sll.com. **Website:** www.sll.com. Estab. 1987. Member of AAR. Signatory of WGA.

MEMBER AGENTS Philippa Brophy (represents journalists, nonfiction writers and novelists, and is most interested in current events, memoir, science, politics, biography, and women's issues); Laurie Liss (represents authors of commercial and literary fiction and nonfiction whose perspectives are well developed and unique); Sterling Lord; Peter Matson (abiding interest in storytelling, whether in the service of history, fiction, the sciences); Douglas Stewart (primarily fiction for all ages, from the innovatively literary to the unabashedly commercial); Neeti Madan (memoir, journalism, popular culture, lifestyle, women's issues, multicultural books and virtually any intelligent writing on intriguing topics); Robert Guinsler (literary and commercial fiction (including YA), journalism, narrative nonfiction with an emphasis on pop culture, science and current events, memoirs and biographies); Jim Rutman; Celeste Fine (expert, celebrity, and corporate clients with strong national and international platforms, particularly in the health, science, self-help, food, business, and lifestyle fields); Erica Rand Silverman (children's: represents picture books through young adult novels, both fiction and nonfiction; adult: represents nonfiction predominantly in the areas of parenting and humor); Martha

Millard (fiction and nonfiction, including well-written science fiction and young adult); Mary Krienke (literary fiction, memoir, and narrative nonfiction, including psychology, popular science, and cultural commentary); Jenny Stephens (nonfiction: cookbooks, practical lifestyle projects, transportive travel and nature writing, and creative nonfiction; fiction: contemporary literary narratives strongly rooted in place); Alison MacKeen (idea-driven research books: social scientific, scientific, historical, relationships/parenting, learning and education, sexuality, technology, the life-cycle, health, the environment, politics, economics, psychology, geography, and culture; literary fiction, literary nonfiction, memoirs, essays, and travel writing).; John Maas (serious nonfiction, specifically business, personal development, science, self-help, health, fitness, and lifestyle); Sarah Passick (commercial nonfiction in the celebrity, food, blogger, lifestyle, health, diet, fitness and fashion categories).

REPRESENTS Nonfiction, fiction. **Considers these nonfiction areas:** biography, business, cooking, creative nonfiction, current affairs, economics, education, foods, gay/lesbian, history, humor, memoirs, multicultural, parenting, popular culture, politics, psychology, science, technology, travel, women's issues, fitness. **Considers these fiction areas:** commercial, juvenile, literary, middle grade, picture books, science fiction, young adult.

HOW TO CONTACT Query via snail mail. "Please submit a query letter, a synopsis of the work, a brief proposal or the first three chapters of the manuscript, a brief bio or resume, and a stamped self-addressed envelope for reply. Original artwork is not accepted. Enclose sufficient postage if you wish to have your materials returned to you. We do not respond to unsolicited e-mail inquiries." Accepts simultaneous submissions.

TERMS Agent receives 15% commission on domestic sales; 20% commission on foreign sales. Offers written contract.

THE LOTTS AGENCY

303 West 18th St., New York NY 10011. Estab. 2013. Member of AAR. Signatory of WGA.

HOW TO CONTACT Accepts simultaneous submissions.

LOWENSTEIN ASSOCIATES INC.

115 East 23rd St., Floor 4, New York NY 10010. (212)206-1630. **Fax:** (212)727-0280. **E-mail:** assistant@bookhaven.com. **Website:** www.lowensteinassociates.com. **Contact:** Barbara Lowenstein. Member of AAR.

MEMBER AGENTS Barbara Lowenstein, president (nonfiction interests include narrative nonfiction, health, money, finance, travel, multicultural, popular culture, and memoir; fiction interests include literary fiction and women's fiction); Mary South (literary fiction and nonfiction on subjects such as neuroscience, bioengineering, women's rights, design, and digital humanities, as well as investigative journalism, essays, and memoir).

REPRESENTS Novels. **Considers these nonfiction areas:** creative nonfiction, health, memoirs, money, multicultural, popular culture, travel. **Considers these fiction areas:** commercial, fantasy, literary, middle grade, science fiction, women's, young adult.

HOW TO CONTACT "For fiction, please send us a 1-page query letter, along with the first 10 pages pasted in the body of the message by e-mail to assistant@bookhaven.com. If nonfiction, please send a 1-page query letter, a table of contents, and, if available, a proposal pasted into the body of the e-mail. Please put the word 'QUERY' and the title of your project in the subject field of your e-mail and address it to the agent of your choice. Please do not send an attachment as the message will be deleted without being read and no reply will be sent." Accepts simultaneous submissions. Responds in 6 weeks to queries. Obtains most new clients through recommendations from others, solicitations, conferences.

TERMS Agent receives 15% commission on domestic sales; 20% commission on foreign sales. Offers written contract. Charges for large photocopy batches, messenger service, international postage.

GINA MACCOBY LITERARY AGENCY

P.O. Box 60, Chappaqua NY 10514. (914)238-5630. **E-mail:** query@maccobylit.com. **Website:** www.publishersmarketplace.com/members/GinaMaccoby/. **Contact:** Gina Maccoby. Member of AAR. AAR Board of Directors; Royalties and Ethics and Contracts subcommittees; Authors Guild. Represents 25 clients.

MEMBER AGENTS Gina Maccoby.

REPRESENTS Novels. **Considers these nonfiction areas:** autobiography, biography, cultural interests, current affairs, ethnic, history, juvenile nonfiction, popular culture, women's issues, women's studies. **Considers these fiction areas:** juvenile, literary, mainstream, mystery, thriller, young adult.

HOW TO CONTACT Query by e-mail only. Accepts simultaneous submissions. Owing to volume of submissions, may not respond to queries unless interested. Obtains most new clients through recommendations from clients and publishers.

TERMS Agent receives 15% commission on domestic sales; 20-25% commission on foreign sales, which includes subagents commissions. May recover certain costs, such as legal fees or the cost of shipping books by air to Europe or Japan.

CAROL MANN AGENCY

55 Fifth Ave., New York NY 10003. (212)206-5635. **Fax:** (212)675-4809. **E-mail:** submissions@carolmannagency.com. **Website:** www.carolmannagency.com. **Contact:** Isabella Ruggiero. Member of AAR. Represents Roughly 200 clients.

MEMBER AGENTS Carol Mann (health/medical, religion, spirituality, self-help,parenting, narrative nonfiction, current affairs); Laura Yorke; Gareth Esersky; Myrsini Stephanides (nonfiction areas of interest: pop culture and music, humor, narrative nonfiction and memoir, cookbooks; fiction areas of interest: offbeat literary fiction, graphic works, and edgy YA fiction); Joanne Wyckoff (nonfiction areas of interest: memoir, narrative nonfiction,personal narrative, psychology, women's issues, education, health and wellness, parenting, serious self-help, natural history; also accepts fiction); Lydia Shamah (edgy, modern fiction and timely nonfiction in the areas of business, self-improvement, relationship and gift books, particularly interested in female voices and experiences).

REPRESENTS Novels. **Considers these nonfiction areas:** anthropology, archeology, architecture, art, autobiography, biography, business, child guidance, cultural interests, current affairs, design, ethnic, government, health, history, law, medicine, money, music, parenting, popular culture, politics, psychology, self-help, sociology, sports, women's issues, women's studies. **Considers these fiction areas:** commercial, literary, young adult, Graphic works.

HOW TO CONTACT Please see website for submission guidelines. Accepts simultaneous submissions. Responds in 4 weeks to queries.

TERMS Agent receives 15% commission on domestic sales; 20% commission on foreign sales. Offers written contract.

MANSION STREET LITERARY MANAGEMENT

Website: mansionstreet.com. **Contact:** Jean Sagendorph; Michelle Witte. Member of AAR. Signatory of WGA.

MEMBER AGENTS Jean Sagendorph, querymansionstreet@gmail.com (pop culture, gift books, cookbooks, general nonfiction, lifestyle, design, brand extensions), Michelle Witte, querymichelle@mansionstreet.com (young adult, middle grade, early readers, picture books (especially from author-illustrators), juvenile nonfiction).

REPRESENTS Nonfiction, novels. **Considers these nonfiction areas:** cooking, design, popular culture. **Considers these fiction areas:** juvenile, middle grade, young adult.

HOW TO CONTACT Send a query letter and no more than the first 10 pages of your manuscript in the body of an e-mail. Query one specific agent at this agency. No attachments. You must list the genre in the subject line. If the genre is not in the subject line, your query will be deleted. Accepts simultaneous submissions. Responds in up to 6 weeks.

MANUS & ASSOCIATES LITERARY AGENCY, INC.

425 Sherman Ave., Suite 200, Palo Alto CA 94306. (650)470-5151. **Fax:** (650)470-5159. **E-mail:** manuslit@manuslit.com. **Website:** www.manuslit.com. **Contact:** Jillian Manus, Jandy Nelson, Penny Nelson. NYC address: 444 Madison Ave., 29th Floor, New York, NY 10022 Member of AAR.

MEMBER AGENTS Jandy Nelson (currently not taking on new clients). Jillian Manus, jillian@manuslit.com (political, memoirs, self-help, history, sports, women's issues, thrillers); Penny Nelson, penny@manuslit.com (memoirs, self-help, sports, nonfiction).

REPRESENTS Novels. **Considers these nonfiction areas:** cooking, history, inspirational, memoirs, politics, psychology, religious, self-help, sports, women's issues. **Considers these fiction areas:** thriller.

HOW TO CONTACT Snail mail submissions welcome. E-queries also accepted. For nonfiction, send a full proposal via snail mail. For fiction, send a query letter and 30 pages (unbound) if submitting via snail mail. Send only an e-query if submitting fiction via e-mail. If querying by e-mail, submit directly to one of the agents. Accepts simultaneous submissions. Responds in 3 months to queries. Responds in 3 months to mss. Obtains most new clients through recommendations from others, solicitations, conferences.

TERMS Agent receives 15% commission on domestic sales; 20-25% commission on foreign sales. Offers written contract, binding for 2 years; 60-day notice must be given to terminate contract. Charges for photocopying and postage/UPS.

THE DENISE MARCIL LITERARY AGENCY, LLC

483 Westover Road, Stamford CT 06902. (203)327-9970. **E-mail:** dmla@DeniseMarcilAgency.com; AnneMarie@denisemarcilagency.com. **Website:** www.denisemarcilagency.com. **Contact:** Denise Marcil, Anne Marie O'Farrell. Address for Anne Marie O'Farrell: 86 Dennis Street, Manhasset, NY 11030. Member of AAR. Women's Media Group

MEMBER AGENTS Denise Marcil (self-help and popular reference books such as wellness, health, women's issues, self-help, and popular reference); Anne Marie O'Farrell (books that convey and promote innovative, practical and cutting edge information and ideas which help people increase their self-awareness and fulfillment and maximize their potential in whatever area they choose; she is dying to represent a great basketball book).

REPRESENTS Nonfiction. **Considers these nonfiction areas:** business, cooking, diet/nutrition, education, health, how-to, New Age, psychology, self-help, spirituality, women's issues. **Considers these fiction areas:** commercial, suspense, thriller, women's.

HOW TO CONTACT E-query. Accepts simultaneous submissions.

TERMS Agent receives 15% commission on domestic sales; 20% commission on foreign sales. Offers written contract, binding for 2 years.

MARSAL LYON LITERARY AGENCY, LLC

PMB 121, 665 San Rodolfo Dr. 124, Solana Beach CA 92075. **Website:** www.marsallyonliteraryagency.com. **Contact:** Kevan Lyon, Jill Marsal. Member of AAR. Signatory of WGA.

MEMBER AGENTS Kevan Lyon (women's fiction, with an emphasis on commercial women's fiction, young adult fiction and all genres of romance); Jill Marsal (all types of women's fiction and all types of romance; mysteries, cozies, suspense, and thrillers; nonfiction in the areas of current events, business,

health, self-help, relationships, psychology, parenting, history, science, and narrative nonfiction); Patricia Nelson (literary fiction and commercial fiction, all types of women's fiction, contemporary and historical romance, young adult and middle grade fiction, LGBTQ fiction for both YA and adult); Deborah Ritchkin (lifestyle books, specifically in the areas of food, design and entertaining; pop culture; women's issues; biography; and current events; her niche interest is projects about France, including fiction); Shannon Hassan (literary and commercial fiction, young adult and middle grade fiction, and select nonfiction).

REPRESENTS Nonfiction, fiction, novels, juvenile books. **Considers these nonfiction areas:** animals, biography, business, cooking, creative nonfiction, current affairs, diet/nutrition, history, investigative, memoirs, parenting, popular culture, politics, psychology, science, self-help, sports, women's issues, women's studies. **Considers these fiction areas:** commercial, juvenile, literary, mainstream, middle grade, multicultural, mystery, paranormal, romance, suspense, thriller, women's, young adult.

HOW TO CONTACT Query by e-mail. Query only one agent at this agency at a time. "Please visit our website to determine who is best suited for your work. Write 'query' in the subject line of your e-mail. Please allow up to several weeks to hear back on your query." Accepts simultaneous submissions.

THE EVAN MARSHALL AGENCY

Indie Rights Agency, 1 Pacio Court, Roseland NJ 07068-1121. (973)287-6216. **Fax:** (973)488-7910. **E-mail:** evan@evanmarshallagency.com. **Website:** www.evanmarshallagency.com. **Contact:** Evan Marshall. Estab. 1987. Member of AAR. Novelists, Inc. Represents 50+ clients.

MEMBER AGENTS Evan Marshall.

REPRESENTS Fiction, novels. **Considers these fiction areas:** action, adventure, crime, detective, erotica, ethnic, family saga, fantasy, feminist, frontier, gay, glitz, historical, horror, humor, inspirational, lesbian, literary, mainstream, military, multicultural, multimedia, mystery, new adult, New Age, occult, paranormal, police, psychic, regional, religious, romance, satire, science fiction, spiritual, sports, supernatural, suspense, thriller, translation, urban fantasy, war, westerns, women's, young adult, romance (contemporary, gothic, historical, regency).

HOW TO CONTACT Actively seeking new clients. E-mail query letter, synopsis and first three chapters of novel within body of e-mail. Accepts simultaneous submissions. Responds in 1 week to queries. Responds in 1 month to mss. Through queries and through recommendations from editors and current clients.

TERMS Agent receives 15% commission on domestic sales; 20% commission on foreign sales. Offers written contract.

MARGRET MCBRIDE LITERARY AGENCY

P.O. Box 9128, La Jolla CA 92038. (858)454-1550. **Fax:** (858)454-2156. **E-mail:** staff@mcbridelit.com. **Website:** www.mcbrideliterary.com. **Contact:** Michael Daley, submissions manager. Member of AAR. Other memberships include Authors Guild.

MEMBER AGENTS Margret McBride; Faye Atchinson.

REPRESENTS Novels. **Considers these nonfiction areas:** autobiography, biography, business, cooking, cultural interests, current affairs, economics, ethnic, foods, government, health, history, how-to, law, medicine, money, popular culture, politics, psychology, science, self-help, sociology, technology, women's issues, style. **Considers these fiction areas:** action, adventure, crime, detective, historical, humor, literary, mainstream, mystery, police, satire, suspense, thriller.

HOW TO CONTACT Submit a query letter via e-mail (staff@mcbridelit.com). In your letter, provide a brief synopsis of your work, as well as any pertinent information about yourself. There are detailed nonfiction proposal guidelines online. Accepts simultaneous submissions. Responds in 8 weeks to queries. Responds in 6-8 weeks to mss.

TERMS Agent receives 15% commission on domestic sales; 25% commission on foreign sales. Charges for overnight delivery and photocopying.

THE MCCARTHY AGENCY, LLC

456 Ninth St., No. 28, Hoboken NJ 07030. **E-mail:** McCarthylit@aol.com. **Contact:** Shawna McCarthy. Member of AAR.

MEMBER AGENTS Shawna McCarthy.

REPRESENTS Novels. **Considers these fiction areas:** fantasy, middle grade, mystery, new adult, science fiction, women's, young adult.

HOW TO CONTACT E-queries only. Accepts simultaneous submissions.

MCCORMICK LITERARY

37 West 20th St., New York NY 10011. (212)691-9726. **Website:** mccormicklit.com/. Member of AAR. Signatory of WGA.

MEMBER AGENTS David McCormick; Pilar Queen (narrative nonfiction, practical nonfiction, and commercial women's fiction); Bridget McCarthy (literary and commercial fiction, narrative nonfiction, memoir, and cookbooks); Alia Hanna Habib (literary fiction, narrative nonfiction, memoir and cookbooks); Edward Orloff (literary fiction and narrative nonfiction, especially cultural history, politics, biography, and the arts); Daniel Menaker.

HOW TO CONTACT Snail mail queries only. Send an SASE. Accepts simultaneous submissions.

MCINTOSH & OTIS, INC.

353 Lexington Ave., New York NY 10016. (212)687-7400. **Fax:** (212)687-6894. **E-mail:** info@mcintoshandotis.com. **Website:** www.mcintoshandotis.com. **Contact:** Eugene H. Winick, Esq.. Estab. 1927. Member of AAR. Signatory of WGA. SCBWI

MEMBER AGENTS Elizabeth Winick Rubinstein, EWRquery@mcintoshandotis.com (literary fiction, women's fiction, historical fiction, and mystery/suspense, along with narrative nonfiction, spiritual/self-help, history and current affairs); Shira Hoffman, SHquery@mcintoshandotis.com (young adult, MG, mainstream commercial fiction, mystery, literary fiction, women's fiction, romance, urban fantasy, fantasy, science fiction, horror and dystopian); Christa Heschke, CHquery@mcintoshandotis.com (picture books, middle grade, young adult and new adult projects); Adam Muhlig, AMquery@mcintoshandotis.com (music–from jazz to classical to punk–popular culture, natural history, travel and adventure, and sports); Eugene Winick; Shannon Powers, SPquery@mcintoshandotis.com (literary fiction, mystery, horror, popular history, and romance; young adult and middle grade—mysteries and thrillers with high emotional stakes, projects with romantic elements, horror, light sci-fi or fantasy, and contemporary with a unique premise); Amelia Appel, AAquery@mcintoshandotis.com (literary fiction, mystery, thriller, historical fiction, science fiction and fantasy, and horror; some young adult).

REPRESENTS Considers these nonfiction areas: creative nonfiction, current affairs, history, popular culture, self-help, spirituality, sports, travel. **Consid-**

ers these fiction areas: fantasy, historical, horror, literary, middle grade, mystery, new adult, paranormal, picture books, romance, science fiction, suspense, urban fantasy, women's, young adult.

HOW TO CONTACT E-mail submissions only. Each agent has their own e-mail address for subs. For fiction: Please send a query letter, synopsis, author bio, and the first three consecutive chapters (no more than 30 pages) of your novel. For nonfiction: Please send a query letter, proposal, outline, author bio, and three sample chapters (no more than 30 pages) of the manuscript. For children's & young adult: Please send a query letter, synopsis and the first three consecutive chapters (not to exceed 25 pages) of the manuscript. Accepts simultaneous submissions. Obtains clients through recommendations from others, editors, conferences and queries.

TERMS Agent receives 15% commission on domestic sales; 20% on foreign sales.

SALLY HILL MCMILLAN, LLC

429 E. Kingston Ave., Charlotte NC 28203. (704)334-0897. **E-mail:** mcmagency@aol.com. **Website:** www. publishersmarketplace.com/members/McMillanAgency/. **Contact:** Sally Hill McMillan. Member of AAR.

REPRESENTS Considers these nonfiction areas: creative nonfiction, health, history, women's issues, women's studies. **Considers these fiction areas:** commercial, literary, mainstream, mystery.

HOW TO CONTACT "Please query first with SASE and await further instructions. E-mail queries will be read, but not necessarily answered." Accepts simultaneous submissions.

MENDEL MEDIA GROUP, LLC

115 W. 30th St., Suite 800, New York NY 10001. (646)239-9896. **Fax:** (212)685-4717. **E-mail:** scott@ mendelmedia.com. **Website:** www.mendelmedia. com. Member of AAR. Represents 40-60 clients.

REPRESENTS Novels. **Considers these nonfiction areas:** Americana, animals, anthropology, architecture, art, biography, business, child guidance, cooking, current affairs, dance, education, environment, ethnic, foods, gardening, gay/lesbian, government, health, history, how-to, humor, investigative, language, medicine, memoirs, military, money, multicultural, music, parenting, philosophy, popular culture, psychology, recreation, regional, religious, science, self-help, sex, sociology, software, spirituality, sports, true crime, war, women's issues, women's studies, Jewish topics; creative nonfiction. **Considers these fiction areas:** action, adventure, contemporary issues, crime, detective, erotica, ethnic, feminist, gay, glitz, historical, humor, inspirational, juvenile, lesbian, literary, mainstream, mystery, picture books, police, religious, romance, satire, sports, thriller, young adult, Jewish fiction.

HOW TO CONTACT Query with SASE. Do not e-mail or fax queries. For nonfiction, include a complete, fully edited book proposal with sample chapters. For fiction, include a complete synopsis and no more than 20 pages of sample text. Responds in 2 weeks to queries. Responds in 4-6 weeks to mss. Obtains most new clients through recommendations from others.

TERMS Agent receives 15% commission on domestic sales; 20% commission on foreign sales.

ROBIN MIZELL LITERARY REPRESENTATION

1600 Burnside St., Suite 205, Beaufort SC 29902. (614)774-7405. **E-mail:** mail@robinmizell.com. **Website:** www.robinmizell.com. **Contact:** Robin Mizell. Member of AAR. Signatory of WGA.

REPRESENTS Nonfiction, novels. **Considers these nonfiction areas:** popular culture, psychology, sociology. **Considers these fiction areas:** literary, young adult.

HOW TO CONTACT E-query with the first 5 pages of your work pasted below in the e-mail. More specific submission instructions can be found on the agency website. Accepts simultaneous submissions.

HOWARD MORHAIM LITERARY AGENCY

30 Pierrepont St., Brooklyn NY 11201. (718)222-8400. **Fax:** (718)222-5056. **Website:** www.morhaimliterary. com. Member of AAR.

MEMBER AGENTS Howard Morhaim (no unsolicited submissions), Kate McKean, kmckean@ morhaimliterary.com (adult fiction: contemporary romance, contemporary women's fiction, literary fiction, historical fiction set in the 20th Century, high fantasy, magical realism, science fiction, middle grade, young adult; in nonfiction, books by authors with demonstrable platforms in the areas of sports, food writing, humor, design, creativity, and craft [sewing, knitting, etc.], narrative nonfiction by authors with or without an established platform. Some memoir); DongWon Song, dongwon@morhaimliterary.com (science fiction, fantasy; nonfiction: food writing, science, pop culture); Kim-Mei Kirtland, kimmei@morhaimliterary.com (hard science fiction, literary fiction; nonfiction: history, biography, business, economics).

REPRESENTS Considers these nonfiction areas: biography, business, cooking, crafts, creative nonfiction, design, economics, foods, health, humor, memoirs, parenting, self-help, sports. **Considers these fiction areas:** fantasy, historical, literary, middle grade, new adult, romance, science fiction, women's, young adult, LGBTQ young adult, magical realism, fantasy should be high fantasy, historical fiction should be no earlier than the 20th century..

HOW TO CONTACT Query via e-mail with cover letter and three sample chapters. See each agent's listing for specifics. Accepts simultaneous submissions.

MOVEABLE TYPE MANAGEMENT

244 Madison Ave., Suite 334, New York NY 10016. **E-mail:** AChromy@MovableTM.com. **Website:** www.MovableTM.com. **Contact:** Adam Chromy.

MEMBER AGENTS Adam Chromy.

REPRESENTS Nonfiction, fiction, novels. **Considers these nonfiction areas:** Americana, business, creative nonfiction, film, foods, history, how-to, humor, literature, memoirs, money, popular culture, politics, psychology, satire, science, self-help, sex, sports, technology, theater, true crime, war, women's issues, women's studies. **Considers these fiction areas:** commercial, crime, detective, erotica, literary, mainstream, mystery, romance, science fiction, sports, suspense, thriller, women's.

HOW TO CONTACT E-queries only. Responds if interested. For nonfiction: Send a query letter in the body of an e-mail that precisely introduces your topic and approach, and includes a descriptive bio. For journalists and academics, please also feel free to include a CV. Fiction: Send your query letter and the first 10 pages of your novel in the body of an e-mail. Your subject line needs to contain the word "Query" or your message will not reach the agency. No attachments and no snail mail. Accepts simultaneous submissions.

JEAN V. NAGGAR LITERARY AGENCY, INC.

JVNLA, Inc., 216 E. 75th St., Suite 1E, New York NY 10021. (212)794-1082. **E-mail:** www.jvnla.com. **Website:** www.jvnla.com. **Contact:** Jennifer Weltz. Estab. 1978. Member of AAR. Other memberships include Women's Media Group, SCBWI, Pace University's Masters in Publishing Board Member. Represents 450 clients.

MEMBER AGENTS Jennifer Weltz (well researched and original historicals, thrillers with a unique voice, wry dark humor, and magical realism; enthralling narrative nonfiction; voice driven young adult, middle grade); Alice Tasman (literary, commercial, YA, middle grade, and nonfiction in the categories of narrative, biography, music or pop culture); Laura Biagi (literary fiction, magical realism, psychological thrillers, young adult novels, middle grade novels, and picture books).

REPRESENTS Nonfiction, fiction, novels, short story collections, novellas, juvenile books, scholarly books, poetry books.

HOW TO CONTACT "Visit our website www.jvnla.com to send submissions and see what our individual agents are looking for. No Snail Mail submissions please!" Accepts simultaneous submissions. Depends on the agent. No responses for Queries unless the agent is interested.

TERMS Agent receives 15% commission on domestic sales; 20% commission on foreign sales. Offers written contract. Charges for overseas mailing, messenger services, book purchases, photocopying—all deductible from royalties received.

NELSON LITERARY AGENCY

1732 Wazee St., Suite 207, Denver CO 80202. (303)292-2805. **E-mail:** querykristin@nelsonagency.com. **Website:** www.nelsonagency.com. **Contact:** Kristin Nelson, President. Estab. 2002. Member of AAR. RWA, SCBWI, SFWA. Represents 33 clients.

REPRESENTS Fiction, novels, young adult, middle grade, literary commercial, upmarket women's fiction, single title romance, science fiction, fantasy. **Considers these nonfiction areas:** NLA does not represent nonfiction, picture books, screenplays, or memoir. **Considers these fiction areas:** commercial, fantasy, literary, mainstream, middle grade, romance, science fiction, women's, young adult. **Considers these script areas:** NLA does not represent screenwriters.

HOW TO CONTACT "Please visit our website to carefully read our submission guidelines: nelsonagency.com/submission-guidelines/." Kristin does not accept any queries by Facebook or Twitter. Query by e-mail only. Put the word "Query" in the e-mail subject line along with the title of your novel. No attachments but okay to include the first 10 pages of your novel in the body of the e-mail. querykristin@nelsonagency.com Accepts simultaneous submissions. Tries to respond to all queries within 10 business day. Full manuscript requests can take 2 months or more.

TERMS Industry standard.

NEW LEAF LITERARY & MEDIA, INC.

110 W. 40th St., Suite 2201, New York NY 10018. (646)248-7989. **Fax:** (646)861-4654. **E-mail:** query@newleafliterary.com. **Website:** www.newleafliterary.com. Estab. 2012. Member of AAR.

MEMBER AGENTS Joanna Volpe (women's fiction, thriller, horror, speculative fiction, literary fiction and historical fiction, young adult, middle grade, art-focused picture books); Kathleen Ortiz, Director of Subsidiary Rights and literary agent (new voices in YA and animator/illustrator talent); Suzie Townsend (new adult, young adult, middle grade, romance [all subgenres], fantasy [urban fantasy, science fiction, steampunk, epic fantasy] and crime fiction [mysteries, thrillers]); Pouya Shahbazian, Director of Film and Television (no unsolicited queries); Mackenzie Brady (her taste in nonfiction extends beyond science books to memoirs, lost histories, epic sports narratives, true crime and gift/lifestyle books; she represents select adult and YA fiction projects, as well); Peter Knapp (middle grade, young adult, general adult fiction, grounded science fiction, genre-agnostic for all); Jaida Temperly (all fiction: magical realism, historical fiction; literary fiction; stories that are quirky and fantastical; nonfiction: niche, offbeat, a bit strange; middle grade).

REPRESENTS Nonfiction, fiction, novels, novellas, juvenile books, poetry books. **Considers these nonfiction areas:** cooking, crafts, creative nonfiction, science, technology, women's issues, young adult. **Considers these fiction areas:** crime, fantasy, historical, horror, literary, mainstream, middle grade, mystery, new adult, paranormal, picture books, romance, thriller, women's, young adult.

HOW TO CONTACT Send query to query@newleafliterary.com. Please do not query via phone. The word "Query" must be in the subject line, plus the agent's name, i.e. – Subject: Query, Suzie Townsend. You may include up to 5 double-spaced sample pages within the body of the e-mail. NO ATTACHMENTS, unless specifically requested. Include all necessary contact information. You will receive an auto-response confirming receipt of your query. "We only respond if we are interested in seeing your work." Responds only if interested. All queries read within 2 weeks.

DANA NEWMAN LITERARY

9720 Wilshire Blvd., 5th Floor, Beverly Hills CA 90212. **Fax:** (866) 636-7585. **E-mail:** dananewmanliterary@gmail.com. **Website:** dananewman.com. **Contact:** Dana Newman. Estab. 2009. Member of AAR. Represents 28 clients.

MEMBER AGENTS Dana Newman (narrative nonfiction, business, biography, lifestyle, current affairs, parenting, memoir, pop culture, health, literary, and upmarket fiction).

REPRESENTS Nonfiction, fiction, novels, short story collections. **Considers these nonfiction areas:** architecture, art, autobiography, biography, business, child guidance, cooking, creative nonfiction, cultural interests, current affairs, diet/nutrition, design, education, ethnic, film, foods, gay/lesbian, government, health, history, how-to, inspirational, investigative, language, law, literature, medicine, memoirs, money, multicultural, music, parenting, popular culture, politics, psychology, science, self-help, sociology, sports, technology, theater, travel, true crime, women's issues, women's studies. **Considers these fiction areas:** commercial, contemporary issues, family saga, feminist, historical, horror, literary, multicultural, sports, women's.

HOW TO CONTACT E-mail queries only. For both nonfiction and fiction, please submit a query letter including a description of your project and a brief biography. "If we are interested in your project, we will contact you and request a full book proposal (nonfiction) or a synopsis and the first 25 pages (fiction)." Accepts simultaneous submissions. "If we have requested your materials after receiving your query, we usually respond within 2-4 weeks." Obtains new clients through recommendations from others, queries, and submissions.

TERMS Obtains 15% commission on domestic sales; 20% on foreign sales. Offers 1 year written contract. Notice must be given 30 days prior to terminate a contract.

HAROLD OBER ASSOCIATES

425 Madison Ave., New York NY 10017. (212)759-8600. **Fax:** (212)759-9428. **Website:** www.haroldober.

com. **Contact:** Appropriate agent. Member of AAR. Represents 250 clients.

MEMBER AGENTS Phyllis Westberg; Pamela Malpas; Craig Tenney (few new clients, mostly Ober backlist); Jake Elwell (previously with Elwell & Weiser).

HOW TO CONTACT Submit concise query letter addressed to a specific agent with the first 5 pages of the ms or proposal and SASE. No fax or e-mail. Does not handle filmscripts or plays. Responds as promptly as possible. Obtains most new clients through recommendations from others.

TERMS Agent receives 15% commission on domestic sales; 20% commission on foreign sales. Charges clients for express mail/package services.

RUBIN PFEFFER CONTENT

648 Hammond St., Chestnut Hill MA 02467. **E-mail:** info@rpcontent.com. **Website:** www.rpcontent.com. **Contact:** Rubin Pfeffer. Estab. 2014. Member of AAR. Signatory of WGA.

REPRESENTS **Considers these fiction areas:** juvenile, middle grade, picture books, young adult.

HOW TO CONTACT *Note: This agent accepts submissions by referral only. Specify the contact information of your reference when submitting.* Authors/illustrators should send a query and a 1-3 chapter ms via e-mail (no postal submissions). The query, placed in the body of the e-mail, should include a synopsis of the piece, as well as any relevant information regarding previous publications, referrals, websites, and biographies. The ms may be attached as a .doc or a .pdf file. Specifically for illustrators, attach a PDF of the dummy or artwork to the e-mail. Accepts simultaneous submissions. Responds within 6-8 weeks.

AARON M. PRIEST LITERARY AGENCY

200 W. 41st St., 21st Floor, New York NY 10036. (212)818-0344. **Fax:** (212)573-9417. **E-mail:** info@aaronpriest.com. **Website:** www.aaronpriest.com. Estab. 1974. Member of AAR.

MEMBER AGENTS Aaron Priest, querypriest@aaronpriest.com (thrillers, commercial fiction, biographies); Lisa Erbach Vance, queryvance@aaronpriest.com (contemporary fiction, thrillers/suspense, international fiction, narrative nonfiction); Lucy Childs Baker, querychilds@aaronpriest.com (literary and commercial fiction, memoir, edgy women's fiction); Melissa Edwards, queryedwards@aaronpriest.com (middle grade, young adult, women's fiction, thrill-

ers); Mitch Hoffman (thrillers, suspense, crime fiction, and literary fiction, as well as narrative nonfiction, politics, popular science, history, memoir, current events, and pop culture).

REPRESENTS **Considers these nonfiction areas:** biography, current affairs, history, memoirs, popular culture, politics, science. **Considers these fiction areas:** commercial, contemporary issues, crime, literary, middle grade, suspense, thriller, women's, young adult.

HOW TO CONTACT Query one of the agents using the appropriate e-mail listed on the website. "Please do not submit to more than 1 agent at this agency. We urge you to check our website and consider each agent's emphasis before submitting. Your query letter should be about one page long and describe your work as well as your background. You may also paste the first chapter of your work in the body of the e-mail. Do not send attachments." Accepts simultaneous submissions. Responds in 4 weeks, only if interested.

TERMS Agent receives 15% commission on domestic sales.

PROSPECT AGENCY

551 Valley Road, PMB 377, Upper Montclair NJ 07043. (718)788-3217. **Fax:** (718)360-9582. **Website:** www.prospectagency.com. Estab. 2005. Member of AAR. Signatory of WGA.

MEMBER AGENTS Emily Sylvan Kim, esk@prospectagency.com (romance, women's, commercial, young adult, new adult); Rachel Orr, rko@prospectagency.com (picture books, illustrators, middle grade, young adult); Becca Stumpf, becca@prospectagency.com (young adult and middle grade [all genres, including fantasy/SciFi, literary, mystery, contemporary, historical, horror/suspense], especially MG and YA novels featuring diverse protagonists and life circumstances. Adult SciFi and Fantasy novels with broad appeal, upmarket women's fiction, smart, spicy romance novels); Carrie Pestritto, carrie@prospectagency.com (narrative nonfiction, general nonfiction, biography, and memoir; commercial fiction with a literary twist, women's fiction, romance, upmarket, historical fiction, high-concept YA and upper MG); Teresa Kietlinski, tk@prospectagency.com (picture book artists and illustrators); Linda Camacho, linda@prospectagency.com (middle grade, young adult, and adult fiction across all genres, especially women's fiction/romance, horror, fantasy/sci-fi, graphic novels, contemporary; select literary fiction; fiction featuring diverse/marginalized groups); Kirsten Carleton, kcarleton@prospectagency.com (upmarket speculative, thriller, and literary fiction for adult and YA).

REPRESENTS Nonfiction, fiction, novels, novellas, juvenile books. **Considers these nonfiction areas:** biography, memoirs. **Considers these fiction areas:** commercial, contemporary issues, crime, ethnic, family saga, fantasy, feminist, gay, historical, horror, humor, juvenile, lesbian, literary, mainstream, middle grade, multicultural, mystery, new adult, picture books, romance, science fiction, suspense, thriller, urban fantasy, women's, young adult.

HOW TO CONTACT Note that each agent at this agency has a different submission e-mail address and different submission policies. Check the agency website for the latest formal guideline per each agent. Accepts simultaneous submissions. Obtains new clients through conferences, recommendations, queries, and some scouting.

TERMS Agent receives 15% on domestic sales, 20% on foreign sales sold directly and 25% on sales using a subagent. Offers written contract.

THE PURCELL AGENCY

E-mail: TPAqueries@gmail.com. **Website:** www.the-purcellagency.com. **Contact:** Tina P. Schwartz. Estab. 2012. Member of AAR. Signatory of WGA.

MEMBER AGENTS Tina P. Schwartz; Kim Blair McCollum; Mary Buza.

REPRESENTS Nonfiction, novels. **Considers these nonfiction areas:** juvenile nonfiction. **Considers these fiction areas:** juvenile, middle grade, young adult.

HOW TO CONTACT Check the website to see if agency is open to submissions and for submission guidelines.

REES LITERARY AGENCY

14 Beacon St., Suite 710, Boston MA 02108. (617)227-9014. **Website:** reesagency.com. Estab. 1983. Member of AAR. Represents more than 100 clients.

MEMBER AGENTS Ann Collette, agent10702@aol.com (fiction: literary, upscale commercial women's, crime [including mystery, thriller and psychological suspense], upscale western, historical, military and war, and horror; nonfiction: narrative, military and war, books on race and class, works set in Southeast Asia, biography, pop culture, books on film and op-

era, humor, and memoir); Lorin Rees, lorin@reesagency.com (literary fiction, memoirs, business books, self-help, science, history, psychology, and narrative nonfiction); Rebecca Podos, rebecca@reesagency.com (young adult and middle grade fiction, particularly books about complex female relationships, beautifully written contemporary, genre novels with a strong focus on character, romance with more at stake than "will they/won't they," and LGBTQ books across all genres).

REPRESENTS Novels. **Considers these nonfiction areas:** biography, business, film, history, humor, memoirs, military, popular culture, psychology, science, war. **Considers these fiction areas:** commercial, crime, historical, horror, literary, middle grade, mystery, suspense, thriller, westerns, women's, young adult.

HOW TO CONTACT Consult website for each agent's submission guidelines and e-mail addresses, as they differ. Accepts simultaneous submissions. Obtains most new clients through recommendations from others, conferences, submissions.

TERMS Agent receives 15% commission on domestic sales; 20% commission on foreign sales.

REGAL HOFFMANN & ASSOCIATES LLC

242 West 38th Street, Floor 2, New York NY 10018. (212)684-7900. **Fax:** (212)684-7906. **E-mail:** submissions@regal-literary.com. **Website:** www.regal-literary.com. London Office: 36 Gloucester Ave., Primrose Hill, London NW1 7BB, United Kingdom, uk@regal-literary.com Estab. 2002. Member of AAR. Represents 70 clients.

MEMBER AGENTS Claire Anderson-Wheeler (nonfiction: memoirs and biographies, narrative histories, popular science, popular psychology; adult fiction: primarily character-driven literary fiction, but open to genre fiction, high-concept fiction; all genres of young adult / middle grade fiction); Markus Hoffmann (international and literary fiction, crime, [pop] cultural studies, current affairs, economics, history, music, popular science, and travel literature); Joseph Regal (literary fiction, international thrillers, history, science, photography, music, culture, and whimsy).

REPRESENTS **Considers these nonfiction areas:** biography, creative nonfiction, current affairs, economics, history, memoirs, music, psychology, science, travel. **Considers these fiction areas:** literary, mainstream, middle grade, thriller, young adult.

HOW TO CONTACT Query with SASE or via e-mail to submissions@rhaliterary.com. No phone calls. Submissions should consist of a 1-page query letter detailing the book in question, as well as the qualifications of the author. For fiction, submissions may also include the first 10 pages of the novel or one short story from a collection. Responds if interested. Accepts simultaneous submissions. Responds in 4-8 weeks.

TERMS Agent receives 15% commission on domestic sales; 20% commission on foreign sales. "We charge no reading fees."

ANGELA RINALDI LITERARY AGENCY

P.O. Box 7875, Beverly Hills CA 90212-7875. (310)842-7665. **Fax:** (310)837-8143. **E-mail:** amr@rinaldiliterary.com. **Website:** www.rinaldiliterary.com. **Contact:** Angela Rinaldi. Member of AAR.

REPRESENTS Nonfiction, novels, TV and motion picture rights (for clients only). **Considers these nonfiction areas:** biography, business, cooking, current affairs, health, memoirs, parenting, psychology, self-help, women's issues, women's studies, narrative nonfiction, food narratives, wine, lifestyle, relationships, wellness, personal finance. **Considers these fiction areas:** commercial, historical, literary, mainstream, mystery, suspense, thriller, women's, contemporary, gothic, women's book club fiction.

HOW TO CONTACT E-queries only. E-mail submissions should be sent to info@RinaldiLiterary.com. Include the word "Query" in the subject line. For fiction, please send a brief synopsis and paste the first ten pages into an e-mail. Nonfiction queries should include a detailed cover letter, your credentials and platform information as well as any publishing history. Tell us if you have a completed proposal. Accepts simultaneous submissions. Responds in 2-4 weeks.

TERMS Agent receives 15% commission on domestic sales; 25% commission on foreign sales. Offers written contract.

ANN RITTENBERG LITERARY AGENCY, INC.

15 Maiden Lane, Suite 206, New York NY 10038. **E-mail:** info@rittlit.com. **Website:** www.rittlit.com. **Contact:** Ann Rittenberg, president. Member of AAR.

REPRESENTS Considers these nonfiction areas: creative nonfiction, women's issues.

HOW TO CONTACT Query via postal mail (with SASE) or via e-mail to info@rittlit.com. Submit 3 sample chapters (pasted in e-mail) with your query letter. "If you query by e-mail, we will only respond if interested." Accepts simultaneous submissions. Obtains most new clients through referrals from established writers and editors.

TERMS Agent receives 15% commission on domestic sales; 20% commission on foreign sales. Offers written contract. This agency charges clients for photocopying only.

RLR ASSOCIATES, LTD.

Literary Department, 7 W. 51st St., New York NY 10019. **E-mail:** sgould@rlrassociates.net. **Website:** www.rlrassociates.net. **Contact:** Scott Gould. Member of AAR. Represents 50 clients.

REPRESENTS Nonfiction, novels. **Considers these nonfiction areas:** biography, creative nonfiction, foods, history, humor, popular culture, sports. **Considers these fiction areas:** commercial, literary, mainstream, middle grade, picture books, romance, women's, young adult, genre.

HOW TO CONTACT Query by either e-mail or snail mail. For fiction, send a query and 1-3 chapters (pasted). For nonfiction, send query or proposal. Accepts simultaneous submissions. "If you do not hear from us within 3 months, please assume that your work is out of active consideration." Obtains most new clients through recommendations from others.

TERMS Agent receives 15% commission on domestic sales; 20% commission on foreign sales. Offers written contract.

B.J. ROBBINS LITERARY AGENCY

5130 Bellaire Ave., North Hollywood CA 91607-2908. **E-mail:** Robbinsliterary@gmail.com. **Website:** www.publishersmarketplace.com/members/bjrobbins. **Contact:** (Ms.) B.J. Robbins. Estab. 1992. Member of AAR.

REPRESENTS Nonfiction, fiction. **Considers these nonfiction areas:** autobiography, biography, cultural interests, current affairs, ethnic, film, health, history, investigative, medicine, memoirs, multicultural, music, popular culture, psychology, science, sociology, sports, theater, travel, true crime, women's issues, women's studies. **Considers these fiction areas:** contemporary issues, crime, detective, ethnic, historical, literary, mainstream, multicultural, mystery, sports, suspense, thriller, women's.

HOW TO CONTACT E-query with no attachments. For fiction, okay to include first 10 pages in body of e-mail. Accepts simultaneous submissions. Only responds to projects if interested. Obtains most new clients through conferences, referrals.

TERMS Agent receives 15% commission on domestic sales; 20% commission on foreign sales. Offers written contract; 3-month notice must be given to terminate contract.

RODEEN LITERARY MANAGEMENT

3501 N. Southport #497, Chicago IL 60657. **E-mail:** submissions@rodeenliterary.com. **Website:** www.rodeenliterary.com. **Contact:** Paul Rodeen. Estab. 2009. Member of AAR. Signatory of WGA.

REPRESENTS Nonfiction, novels, juvenile books, illustrations, graphic novels. **Considers these fiction areas:** juvenile, middle grade, picture books, young adult, graphic novels, comics.

HOW TO CONTACT Unsolicited submissions are accepted by e-mail only to submissions@rodeenliterary.com. Cover letters with synopsis and contact information should be included in the body of your e-mail. An initial submission of 50 pages from a novel or a longer work of nonfiction will suffice and should be pasted into the body of your e-mail. Electronic portfolios from illustrators are accepted but please keep the images at 72 dpi - a link to your website or blog is also helpful. Electronic picture book dummies and picture book texts are accepted. Graphic novels and comic books are accepted. Accepts simultaneous submissions. You will receive an auto-generated response to confirm your submission but please understand that further contact will be made only if we feel we can represent your work. Accepts simultaneous submissions.

LINDA ROGHAAR LITERARY AGENCY, LLC

133 High Point Dr., Amherst MA 01002. **E-mail:** linda@lindaroghaar.com. **E-mail:** contact@lindaroghaar.com. **Website:** www.lindaroghaar.com. **Contact:** Linda L. Roghaar. Member of AAR.

REPRESENTS Nonfiction.

HOW TO CONTACT "We prefer e-queries. Please mention 'query' in the subject line, and do not include attachments." For fiction, paste the first 5 pages of your ms below the query. For queries by mail, please include an SASE. Accepts simultaneous submissions. Responds within 12 weeks if interested.

TERMS Agent receives 15% commission on domestic sales; negotiable commission on foreign sales. Offers written contract.

THE ROSENBERG GROUP

23 Lincoln Ave., Marblehead MA 01945. (781)990-1341. **Fax:** (781)990-1344. **Website:** www.rosenberggroup.com. **Contact:** Barbara Collins Rosenberg. Estab. 1998. Member of AAR. Recognized agent of the RWA. Represents 25 clients.

REPRESENTS Nonfiction, novels, textbooks, college textbooks only. **Considers these nonfiction areas:** biography, current affairs, foods, music, popular culture, psychology, science, self-help, sports, women's issues, women's studies, women's health, wine/beverages. **Considers these fiction areas:** romance, women's, chick lit.

HOW TO CONTACT Query via snail mail. Your query letter should not exceed one page in length. It should include the title of your work, the genre and/or sub-genre; the manuscript's word count; and a brief description of the work. If you are writing category romance, please be certain to let her know the line for which your work is intended. Accepts simultaneous submissions. Obtains most new clients through recommendations from others, solicitations, conferences.

TERMS Agent receives 15% commission on domestic sales; 15% commission on foreign sales. Offers written contract; 1-month notice must be given to terminate contract. Charges maximum of $350/year for postage and photocopying.

RITA ROSENKRANZ LITERARY AGENCY

440 West End Ave., #15D, New York NY 10024. (212)873-6333. **Website:** www.ritarosenkranzliteraryagency.com. **Contact:** Rita Rosenkranz. Member of AAR. Represents 35 clients.

REPRESENTS Nonfiction. **Considers these nonfiction areas:** Americana, animals, anthropology, art, autobiography, biography, business, child guidance, computers, cooking, crafts, creative nonfiction, cultural interests, current affairs, dance, decorating, diet/nutrition, design, economics, education, ethnic, film, government, health, history, hobbies, how-to, humor, inspirational, interior design, language, law, literature, medicine, military, money, music, parenting, photography, popular culture, politics, psychology, religious, satire, science, self-help, sports, technology, theater, war, women's issues, women's studies.

HOW TO CONTACT Send query letter only (no proposal) via regular mail or e-mail. Submit proposal package with SASE only on request. No fax queries. Accepts simultaneous submissions. Responds in 2 weeks to queries. Obtains most new clients through directory listings, solicitations, conferences, word of mouth.

TERMS Agent receives 15% commission on domestic sales; 20% commission on foreign sales. Offers written contract, binding for 3 years; 3-month written notice must be given to terminate contract. Charges clients for photocopying. Makes referrals to editing services.

ANDY ROSS LITERARY AGENCY

767 Santa Ray Ave., Oakland CA 94610. (510)238-8965. **E-mail:** andyrossagency@hotmail.com. **Website:** www.andyrossagency.com. **Contact:** Andy Ross. Estab. 2008. Member of AAR. Represents see website for client list clients.

REPRESENTS Considers these nonfiction areas: anthropology, autobiography, biography, child guidance, creative nonfiction, cultural interests, current affairs, education, environment, ethnic, government, history, language, law, literature, military, parenting, popular culture, politics, psychology, science, sociology, technology, war. **Considers these fiction areas:** commercial, juvenile, literary, young adult.

HOW TO CONTACT Queries should be less than half page. Please put the word "query" in the title header of the e-mail. In the first sentence, state the category of the project. Give a short description of the book and your qualifications for writing. Accepts simultaneous submissions. Responds in 1 week to queries.

TERMS Agent receives 15% commission on domestic sales; 20% commission on foreign sales or other deals made through a sub-agent. Offers written contract.

ROSS YOON AGENCY

1666 Connecticut Ave. NW, Suite 500, Washington DC 20009. (202)328-3282. **E-mail:** submissions@rossyoon.com. **Website:** rossyoon.com. **Contact:** Jennifer Manguera. Member of AAR.

MEMBER AGENTS Gail Ross gail@rossyoon.com (represents important commercial nonfiction in a variety of areas; new projects must meet two criteria: it must make her daughters proud and offset their college educations); Howard Yoon, howard@rossyoon.com (specializes in narrative nonfiction, memoir, current events, history, science, cookbooks, and popular culture); Anna Sproul-Latimer, anna@rossyoon.com (nonfiction of all kinds, particularly working with clients who are driven by curiosity: exploring new worlds, uncovering hidden communities, and creating new connections with enthusiasm so infectious that national audiences have already begun to pay attention).

REPRESENTS Nonfiction.

HOW TO CONTACT E-query submissions@rossyoon.com with a query letter briefly explaining your idea, media platform, and qualifications for writing on this topic; or send a complete book proposal featuring an overview of your idea, author bio, media and marketing strategy, chapter outline, and 1-3 sample chapters. Please send these as attachments in .doc or .docx format. Accepts simultaneous submissions. Attempts to respond in 4-6 weeks to queries, but we cannot guarantee a reply. Obtains most new clients through referrals from current clients.

TERMS Agent receives 15% commission on domestic sales; 20% commission on foreign sales. Reserves the right to bill clients for office expenses.

JANE ROTROSEN AGENCY LLC

(212)593-4330. **Fax:** (212)935-6985. **Website:** www.janerotrosen.com. Estab. 1974. Member of AAR. Other memberships include Authors Guild. Represents more than 100 clients.

MEMBER AGENTS Jane Rotrosen Berkey (not taking on clients); Andrea Cirillo, acirillo@janerotrosen.com (general fiction, suspense, and women's fiction); Annelise Robey, arobey@janerotrosen.com (women's fiction, suspense, mystery, literary fiction, and select nonfiction); Meg Ruley, mruley@janerotrosen.com (commercial fiction, including suspense, mysteries, romance, and general fiction); Christina Hogrebe, chogrebe@janerotrosen.com (young adult, new adult, book club fiction, romantic comedies, mystery, and suspense); Amy Tannenbaum, atannenbaum@janerotrosen.com (contemporary romance, psychological suspense, thrillers, and new adult, as well as women's fiction that falls into that sweet spot between literary and commercial, memoir, narrative and prescriptive nonfiction in the areas of health, business, pop culture, humor, and popular psychology); Rebecca Scherer rscherer@janerotrosen.com (women's fiction, mystery, suspense, thriller, romance, upmarket/literary-leaning fiction); Jessica Errera (assistant to Christina and Rebecca).

REPRESENTS Nonfiction, novels. **Considers these nonfiction areas:** business, health, humor, memoirs, popular culture, psychology, narrative nonfiction.

Considers these fiction areas: commercial, literary, mainstream, mystery, new adult, romance, suspense, thriller, women's, young adult.

HOW TO CONTACT "Please e-mail the agent you think would best align with you and your work. Simultaneous e-mail submissions will not be considered. Send a query letter that includes a concise description of your work, relevant biographical information, and any relevant publishing history. Also include a brief synopsis and the first three chapters of your novel or proposal for nonfiction. Paste all text in the body of your e-mail. We will not open e-mail attachments." Accepts simultaneous submissions. Obtains most new clients through recommendations from others.

TERMS Agent receives 15% commission on domestic sales; 20% commission on foreign sales. Offers written contract, binding for 3 years; 2-month notice must be given to terminate contract. Charges clients for photocopying, express mail, overseas postage, book purchase.

SADLER CHILDREN'S LITERARY

(815)209-6252. **E-mail:** submissions.sadlerliterary@gmail.com. **Website:** www.sadlerchildrensliterary.com. **Contact:** Jodell Sadler. Member of AAR. Signatory of WGA.

REPRESENTS Nonfiction, fiction, novels, juvenile books. **Considers these nonfiction areas:** creative nonfiction, juvenile nonfiction, young adult. **Considers these fiction areas:** juvenile, middle grade, picture books, young adult.

HOW TO CONTACT "E-mail SUBMISSIONS ONLY from conferences and events, including participation in webinars and webinar series courses at KidLitCollege. Your subject line should read "CODE PROVIDED - (Genre) Title_by_Author" and specifically addressed to me. I prefer a short letter: Hook (why my agency), Pitch for you project, and Bio (brief background and other categories you work in). All submissions in body of the e-mail, no attachments. Query and complete picture book text; first 10 pages for longer genre category. If you are an illustrator or author-illustrator, I encourage you to contact me, and please send a link to your online portfolio." Accepts simultaneous submissions. "I only obtain clients through writing conferences and SCBWI, Writer's Digest, and KidLitCollege.com webinars and events."

THE SAGALYN AGENCY / ICM PARTNERS

Washington DC **E-mail:** info@sagalyn.com. **Website:** www.sagalyn.com. Estab. 1980. Member of AAR.

MEMBER AGENTS Raphael Sagalyn.

REPRESENTS Nonfiction. **Considers these nonfiction areas:** biography, business, creative nonfiction, economics, popular culture, science, technology.

HOW TO CONTACT Please send e-mail queries only. Accepts simultaneous submissions.

SALKIND LITERARY AGENCY

Part of Studio B, 62 Nassau Drive, Part of Studio B, Great Neck NY 11021. (516) 829-2102. **E-mail:** info@studiob.com. **Website:** www.salkindagency.com. **Contact:** Neil Salkind.

MEMBER AGENTS Neil Salkind, neil@studiob.com (general nonfiction and textbooks); Greg Aunapu, greg@studiob.com (nonfiction: biography, history, narrative, memoir, true-crime, adventure/true story, business/finance, current affairs, technology, pop culture, psychology, how-to, self-help, science, travel, pets/animals, relationships, parenting; fiction: commercial fiction, historical, thrillers/suspense, mystery, detective, adventure, humor, science-fiction / fantasy); Lynn Haller, lynn@studiob.com (technical, business, travel, self-help, health, photography, design, cooking, art, craft, politics, essays, culture, history, and textbooks).

REPRESENTS **Considers these nonfiction areas:** animals, art, biography, business, cooking, crafts, cultural interests, current affairs, design, health, history, how-to, memoirs, money, parenting, photography, popular culture, politics, psychology, science, self-help, technology, travel, true crime. **Considers these fiction areas:** adventure, commercial, detective, fantasy, historical, humor, mystery, science fiction, suspense, thriller.

HOW TO CONTACT Query electronically. Accepts simultaneous submissions. Obtains most new clients through recommendations from others.

TERMS Agent receives 15% commission on domestic sales; 15% commission on foreign sales.

VICTORIA SANDERS & ASSOCIATES

440 Buck Rd., Stone Ridge NY 12484. (212)633-8811. **Fax:** (212)633-0525. **E-mail:** queriesvsa@gmail.com. **Website:** www.victoriasanders.com. **Contact:** Victoria Sanders. Estab. 1992. Member of AAR. Signatory of WGA. Represents 135 clients.

MEMBER AGENTS Victoria Sanders, Chris Kepner, Bernadette Baker-Baughman.

REPRESENTS Nonfiction, fiction, novels, juvenile books. **Considers these nonfiction areas:** autobiography, biography, cultural interests, current affairs, ethnic, film, gay/lesbian, government, history, humor, law, literature, music, popular culture, politics, psychology, satire, theater, translation, women's issues, women's studies. **Considers these fiction areas:** action, adventure, comic books, contemporary issues, crime, detective, ethnic, family saga, feminist, lesbian, literary, mainstream, middle grade, mystery, new adult, picture books, thriller, young adult.

HOW TO CONTACT Query by e-mail only. "We will not respond to e-mails with attachments or attached files." Accepts simultaneous submissions.

TERMS Agent receives 15% commission on domestic sales; 20% commission on foreign/film sales. Offers written contract.

WENDY SCHMALZ AGENCY

402 Union St., #831, Hudson NY 12534. (518)672-7697. **E-mail:** wendy@schmalzagency.com. **Website:** www.schmalzagency.com. **Contact:** Wendy Schmalz. Estab. 2002. Member of AAR.

REPRESENTS Nonfiction, fiction, novels, juvenile books. **Considers these nonfiction areas:** biography, cultural interests, history, popular culture, young adult. Many nonfiction subjects are of interest to this agency. **Considers these fiction areas:** literary, mainstream, middle grade, young adult.

HOW TO CONTACT Accepts only e-mail queries. Paste synopsis into the e-mail. Do not attach the ms or sample chapters or synopsis. Replies to queries only if they want to read the ms. (2014: Not currently accepting submissions of genre fiction or children's picture books.) If you do not hear from this agency within 2 weeks, consider that a no. Accepts simultaneous submissions. Obtains clients through recommendations from others.

TERMS Agent receives 15% commission on domestic sales; 20% on foreign sales; 25% for Asian sales.

SUSAN SCHULMAN LITERARY AGENCY LLC

454 W. 44th St., New York NY 10036. (212)713-1633. **E-mail:** Susan@Schulmanagency.com. **Website:** www.publishersmarketplace.com/members/Schulman/. **Contact:** Susan Schulman. Estab. 1980. Member of AAR. Signatory of WGA. Other memberships include Dramatists Guild, Writers Guild of America, East, New York Women in Film, Women's Media Group, Agents' Roundtable, League of New York Theater Women

REPRESENTS Nonfiction, fiction, novels, juvenile books, feature film, TV scripts, theatrical stage play. **Considers these nonfiction areas:** anthropology, archeology, architecture, art, biography, business, child guidance, cooking, creative nonfiction, current affairs, economics, ethnic, government, health, history, juvenile nonfiction, law, money, popular culture, politics, psychology, religious, science, spirituality, women's issues, women's studies, young adult. **Considers these fiction areas:** commercial, contemporary issues, juvenile, literary, mainstream, new adult, religious, women's, young adult. **Considers these script areas:** theatrical stage play.

HOW TO CONTACT "For fiction: query letter with outline and three sample chapters, resume and SASE. For nonfiction: query letter with complete description of subject, at least one chapter, resume and SASE. Queries may be sent via regular mail or e-mail. Please do not submit queries via UPS or Federal Express. Please do not send attachments with e-mail queries Please incorporate the chapters into the body of the e-mail." Accepts simultaneous submissions. Responds in less than one week generally to a full query and six weeks to a full manuscript. Obtains most new clients through recommendations from others, solicitations, conferences.

TERMS Agent receives 15% commission on domestic sales; 20% commission on foreign sales. Offers written contract; 30-day notice must be given to terminate contract.

SCOVIL GALEN GHOSH LITERARY AGENCY, INC.

276 Fifth Ave., Suite 708, New York NY 10001. (212)679-8686. **Fax:** (212)679-6710. **Website:** www.sgglit.com. **Contact:** Russell Galen. Estab. 1992. Member of AAR. Represents 300 clients.

MEMBER AGENTS Russell Galen, russellgalen@sgglit.com (novels that stretch the bounds of reality; strong, serious nonfiction books on almost any subject that teach something new; no books that are merely entertaining, such as diet or pop psych books; serious interests include science, history, journalism, biography, business, memoir, nature, politics, sports, contemporary culture, literary nonfiction, etc.); Jack Scovil, jackscovil@sgglit.com; Anna Ghosh, annaghosh@sgglit.com (nonfiction proposals on all subjects, including literary nonfiction, history, science, social and cultural issues, memoir, food, art, adventure, and travel; adult commercial and literary fiction); Ann Behar, annbehar@sgglit.com (juvenile books for all ages).

HOW TO CONTACT E-mail queries only. Note how each agent at this agency has their own submission e-mail. Accepts simultaneous submissions.

THE SEYMOUR AGENCY

475 Miner St., Canton NY 13617. (315)386-1831. **E-mail:** marysue@twcny.rr.com; nicole@theseymouragency.com; julie@theseymouragency.com; lane@theseymouragency.com. **Website:** www.theseymouragency.com. Member of AAR. Signatory of WGA. Other memberships include RWA, Authors Guild, HWA.

MEMBER AGENTS Mary Sue Seymour (accepts queries in Christian, inspirational, romance, and nonfiction); Nicole Resciniti (accepts all genres of romance, young adult, middle grade, new adult, suspense, thriller, mystery, sci-fi, fantasy); Julie Gwinn (Christian and inspirational fiction and nonfiction, women's fiction [contemporary and historical], new adult, Southern fiction, literary fiction and young adult); Lane Heymont (science fiction, fantasy, romance, nonfiction).

REPRESENTS Novels. **Considers these nonfiction areas:** business, health, how-to, Christian books; cookbooks; any well-written nonfiction that includes a proposal in standard format and 1 sample chapter.. **Considers these fiction areas:** action, fantasy, inspirational, middle grade, mystery, new adult, religious, romance, science fiction, suspense, thriller, young adult.

HOW TO CONTACT For Mary Sue: E-query with synopsis, first 50 pages for romance. Accepts e-mail queries. For Nicole, Julie, and Lane: E-mail the query plus first 5 pages of the manuscript pasted into the e-mail. Accepts simultaneous submissions. Responds in 1 month to queries. Responds in 3 months to mss.

TERMS Agent receives 12-15% commission on domestic sales.

DENISE SHANNON LITERARY AGENCY, INC.

20 W. 22nd St., Suite 1603, New York NY 10010. **E-mail:** submissions@deniseshannonagency.com. **Website:** www.deniseshannonagency.com. **Contact:** Denise Shannon. Estab. 2002. Member of AAR.

REPRESENTS Nonfiction, novels. **Considers these nonfiction areas:** biography, business, health, narrative nonfiction, politics, journalism, social history. **Considers these fiction areas:** literary.

HOW TO CONTACT "Queries may be submitted by post, accompanied by a SASE, or by e-mail to submissions@deniseshannonagency.com. Please include a description of the available book project and a brief bio including details of any prior publications. We will reply and request more material if we are interested. We request that you inform us if you are submitting material simultaneously to other agencies." Accepts simultaneous submissions.

WENDY SHERMAN ASSOCIATES, INC.

27 W. 24th St., Suite 700B, New York NY 10010. (212)279-9027. **E-mail:** submissions@wsherman.com. **Website:** www.wsherman.com. **Contact:** Wendy Sherman. Member of AAR.

MEMBER AGENTS Wendy Sherman (women's fiction that hits that sweet spot between literary and mainstream, Southern voices, historical dramas, suspense with a well-developed protagonist, and writing that illuminates the multicultural experience, anything related to food, dogs, mothers and daughters).

REPRESENTS Nonfiction, fiction, novels. **Considers these nonfiction areas:** creative nonfiction, foods, humor, memoirs, parenting, popular culture, psychology, self-help, narrative nonfiction. **Considers these fiction areas:** mainstream, Mainstream fiction that hits the sweet spot between literary and commercial..

HOW TO CONTACT Query via e-mail only. "We ask that you include your last name, title, and the name of the agent you are submitting to in the subject line. For fiction, please include a query letter and your first 10 pages copied and pasted in the body of the e-mail. We will not open attachments unless they have been requested. For nonfiction, please include your query letter and author bio. Due to the large number of e-mail submissions that we receive, we can only reply to e-mail queries in the affirmative. We respectfully ask that you do not send queries to our individual e-mail addresses." Accepts simultaneous submissions. Obtains most new clients through recommendations from other writers.

TERMS Agent receives standard 15% commission. Offers written contract.

SPENCERHILL ASSOCIATES

8131 Lakewood Main St., Building M, Suite 205, Lakewood Ranch FL 34202. (941) 907-3700. **E-mail:** submission@spencerhillassociates.com. **Website:** www.spencerhillassociates.com. **Contact:** Karen Solem, Nalini Akolekar, Amanda Leuck or Sandy Harding. Member of AAR.

MEMBER AGENTS Karen Solem; Nalini Akolekar; Amanda Leuck; Sandy Harding.

REPRESENTS Novels. **Considers these fiction areas:** commercial, erotica, literary, mainstream, mystery, paranormal, romance, thriller.

HOW TO CONTACT "We accept electronic submissions and are no longer accepting paper queries. Please send us a query letter in the body of an e-mail, pitch us your project and tell us about yourself: Do you have prior publishing credits? Attach the first three chapters and synopsis preferably in .doc, rtf or txt format to your e-mail. Send all queries to submission@spencerhillassociates.com. We do not have a preference for exclusive submissions, but do appreciate knowing if the submission is simultaneous. We receive thousands of submissions a year and each query receives our attention. Unfortunately, we are unable to respond to each query individually. If we are interested in your work, we will contact you within 12 weeks." Accepts simultaneous submissions.

TERMS Agent receives 15% commission on domestic sales; 20% commission on foreign sales. Offers written contract; 3-month notice must be given to terminate contract.

PHILIP G. SPITZER LITERARY AGENCY, INC

50 Talmage Farm Lane, East Hampton NY 11937. (631)329-3650. **Fax:** (631)329-3651. **E-mail:** lukas.ortiz@spitzeragency.com; spitzer516@aol.com. **E-mail:** kim.lombardini@spitzeragency.com. **Website:** www.spitzeragency.com. **Contact:** Lukas Ortiz. Estab. 1969. Member of AAR.

MEMBER AGENTS Philip G. Spitzer; Lukas Ortiz.

REPRESENTS Novels. **Considers these nonfiction areas:** biography, current affairs, history, politics, sports, travel. **Considers these fiction areas:** juvenile, literary, mainstream, suspense, thriller.

HOW TO CONTACT E-mail query containing synopsis of work, brief biography, and two sample chapters (pasted into the e-mail). Be aware that this agency openly says their client list is quite full. Accepts simultaneous submissions. Obtains most new clients through recommendations from others.

TERMS Agent receives 15% commission on domestic sales; 20% commission on foreign sales. Charges clients for photocopying.

STIMOLA LITERARY STUDIO

308 Livingston Ct., Edgewater NJ 07020. **E-mail:** info@stimolaliterarystudio.com. **Website:** www.stimolaliterarystudio.com. **Contact:** Rosemary B. Stimola. Estab. 1997. Member of AAR. Represents 45 clients.

MEMBER AGENTS Rosemary B. Stimola.

REPRESENTS Juvenile books. **Considers these nonfiction areas:** cooking. **Considers these fiction areas:** young adult.

HOW TO CONTACT Query via e-mail. Author/illustrators of picture books may attach text and sample art. A PDF dummy is preferred. Accepts simultaneous submissions. Responds in 3 weeks to queries "we wish to pursue further." Responds in 2 months to requested mss. While unsolicited queries are welcome, most clients come through editor, agent, client referrals.

TERMS Agent receives 15% commission on domestic sales; 20% (if subagents are employed) commission on foreign sales. Offers written contract, binding for all children's projects. 60 days notice must be given to terminate contract.

STONESONG

270 W. 39th St. #201, New York NY 10018. (212)929-4600. **Fax:** (212)486-9123. **E-mail:** editors@stonesong.com. **E-mail:** submissions@stonesong.com. **Website:** stonesong.com. Member of AAR. Signatory of WGA.

MEMBER AGENTS Alison Fargis; Ellen Scordato; Judy Linden; Emmanuelle Morgen; Leila Campoli (business, science, technology, and self improvement); Maria Ribas (cookbooks, self-help, health, diet, home, parenting, and humor, all from authors with demonstrable platforms; she's also interested in narrative nonfiction and select memoir).

REPRESENTS Nonfiction, fiction, novels, juvenile books. **Considers these nonfiction areas:** architecture, art, biography, business, cooking, crafts, creative nonfiction, cultural interests, current affairs, dance, decorating, diet/nutrition, design, economics, foods, gay/lesbian, health, history, hobbies, how-to, humor, interior design, investigative, literature, memoirs, money, music, New Age, parenting, photography, popular culture, politics, psychology, science, self-help, sociology, spirituality, sports, technology, women's issues, young adult.

HOW TO CONTACT Accepts electronic queries for fiction and nonfiction. Submit query addressed to 1 agent. Include first chapter or first 10 pages of ms. Accepts simultaneous submissions.

ROBIN STRAUS AGENCY, INC.

229 E. 79th St., Suite 5A, New York NY 10075. (212)472-3282. **Fax:** (212)472-3833. **E-mail:** info@robinstrausagency.com. **Website:** www.robinstrausagency.com. **Contact:** Ms. Robin Straus. Estab. 1983. Member of AAR.

REPRESENTS Considers these nonfiction areas: biography, cooking, creative nonfiction, current affairs, history, memoirs, parenting, popular culture, psychology, mainstream science. **Considers these fiction areas:** commercial, literary, mainstream, women's.

HOW TO CONTACT E-query or query via snail mail with SASE. "Send us a query letter with contact information, an autobiographical summary, a brief synopsis or description of your book project, submission history, and information on competition. If you wish, you may also include the opening chapter of your manuscript (pasted). While we do our best to reply to all queries, you can assume that if you haven't heard from us after six weeks, we are not interested." Accepts simultaneous submissions.

TERMS Agent receives 15% commission on domestic sales; 20% commission on foreign sales. Offers written contract.

THE STRINGER LITERARY AGENCY LLC

PO Box 770365, Naples FL 34107. **E-mail:** mstringer@stringerlit.com. Use website form to submit. **Website:** www.stringerlit.com. **Contact:** Marlene Stringer. Estab. 2008; previously an agent with Barbara Bova Literary Agency. Member of AAR. Signatory of WGA. RWA, MWA, ITW, SBCWI Represents +/- 50 clients.

REPRESENTS Fiction, novels. **Considers these fiction areas:** commercial, crime, detective, fantasy, historical, mainstream, multicultural, mystery, new adult, paranormal, police, romance, science fiction, suspense, thriller, urban fantasy, women's, young adult.

HOW TO CONTACT Electronic submissions through website submission form only. Please make

sure your ms is as good as it can be before you submit. Agents are not first readers. For specific information on what we like to see in query letters, refer to the information at www.stringerlit.com under the heading "Learn." Accepts simultaneous submissions. "We strive to respond quickly, but current clients' work always comes first." Referrals, submissions, conferences.

TERMS Standard. We do not charge fees.

THE STROTHMAN AGENCY, LLC

63 East 9th St., 10X, New York NY 10003. **E-mail:** info@strothmanagency.com. **Website:** www.strothmanagency.com. **Contact:** Wendy Strothman, Lauren MacLeod. Member of AAR. Other memberships include Authors' Guild. Represents 50 clients.

MEMBER AGENTS Wendy Strothman (history, narrative nonfiction, narrative journalism, science and nature, and current affairs); Lauren MacLeod (young adult fiction and nonfiction, middle grade novels, as well as highly polished literary fiction and narrative nonfiction, particularly food writing, science, pop culture and history).

REPRESENTS Nonfiction, novels, juvenile books. **Considers these nonfiction areas:** business, current affairs, economics, environment, foods, history, language, popular culture, science. **Considers these fiction areas:** literary, middle grade, young adult.

HOW TO CONTACT Accepts queries only via e-mail at strothmanagency@gmail.com. See submission guidelines online. Accepts simultaneous submissions. "All e-mails received will be responded to with an auto-reply. If we have not replied to your query within six weeks, we do not feel that it is right for us." Accepts simultaneous submissions. Obtains most new clients through recommendations from others.

TERMS Agent receives 15% commission on domestic sales; 20% commission on foreign sales. Offers written contract; 30-day notice must be given to terminate contract.

EMMA SWEENEY AGENCY, LLC

245 E 80th St., Suite 7E, New York NY 10075. **E-mail:** queries@emmasweeneyagency.com. **Website:** www.emmasweeneyagency.com. Member of AAR. Other memberships include Women's Media Group. Represents 80 clients.

MEMBER AGENTS Emma Sweeney, president; Margaret Sutherland Brown (commercial and literary fiction, mysteries and thrillers, narrative nonfiction, lifestyle, and cookbook); Kasey Poserina (YA novels).

REPRESENTS Novels. **Considers these nonfiction areas:** cooking, history, memoirs, religious, science. **Considers these fiction areas:** commercial, historical, literary, mainstream, mystery, thriller, young adult.

HOW TO CONTACT "We accept only electronic queries, and ask that all queries be sent to queries@ emmasweeneyagency.com rather than to any agent directly. Please begin your query with a succinct (and hopefully catchy) description of your plot or proposal. Always include a brief cover letter telling us how you heard about ESA, your previous writing credits, and a few lines about yourself. We cannot open any attachments unless specifically requested, and ask that you paste the first 10 pages of your proposal or novel into the text of your e-mail." Accepts simultaneous submissions.

TERMS Agent receives 15% commission on domestic sales; 10% commission on foreign sales.

TESSLER LITERARY AGENCY, LLC

27 W. 20th St., Suite 1003, New York NY 10011. (212)242-0466. **Website:** www.tessleragency.com. **Contact:** Michelle Tessler. Estab. 2004. Member of AAR. Women's Media Group.

REPRESENTS Nonfiction, fiction. **Considers these nonfiction areas:** autobiography, biography, business, creative nonfiction, cultural interests, foods, health, history, investigative, memoirs, popular culture, psychology, science, self-help, travel, women's issues. **Considers these fiction areas:** commercial, literary, women's.

HOW TO CONTACT Submit query through online query form only. Accepts simultaneous submissions. New clients by queries/submissions through the website and recommendations from others.

TERMS Receives 15% commission on domestic sales; 20% on foreign sales. Offers written contract.

THOMPSON LITERARY AGENCY

115 West 29th Street, Third Floor, New York NY 10001. (347) 281-7685. **E-mail:** info@thompsonliterary.com; meg@thompsonliterary.com. **E-mail:** submissions@ thompsonliterary.com. **Website:** thompsonliterary. com. **Contact:** Meg Thompson. Estab. 2014. Member of AAR. Signatory of WGA.

MEMBER AGENTS Cindy Uh (Senior Agent), (picture book, middle grade and YA submissions,

including nonfiction queries. She loves compelling characters and distinct voices, and more diversity [of all types] is always welcome!); John Thorn (Affiliate Agent); Sandy Hodgman (Director of Foreign Rights).

REPRESENTS Nonfiction, fiction, novels, juvenile books. **Considers these nonfiction areas:** autobiography, biography, business, cooking, crafts, creative nonfiction, diet/nutrition, design, education, foods, health, history, how-to, humor, inspirational, interior design, juvenile nonfiction, memoirs, multicultural, popular culture, politics, science, self-help, sports, travel, women's issues, women's studies, young adult. **Considers these fiction areas:** commercial, historical, juvenile, literary, middle grade, picture books, women's, young adult.

HOW TO CONTACT "For fiction: Please send a query letter, including any salient biographical information or previous publications, and attach the first 25 pages of your manuscript. For nonfiction: Please send a query letter and a full proposal, including biographical information, previous publications, credentials that qualify you to write your book, marketing information, and sample material. You should address your query to whichever agent you think is best suited for your project." Accepts simultaneous submissions. Responds in 6 weeks if interested.

THREE SEAS LITERARY AGENCY

P.O. Box 8571, Madison WI 53708. (608)834-9317. **E-mail:** queries@threeseaslit.com. **Website:** three-seasagency.com. **Contact:** Michelle Grajkowski, Cori Deyoe. Estab. 2000. Member of AAR. Other memberships include RWA (Romance Writers of America), SCBWI Represents 55 clients.

MEMBER AGENTS Michelle Grajkowski (romance, women's fiction, young adult and middle grade fiction, select nonfiction projects); Cori Deyoe (all sub-genres of romance, women's fiction, young adult, middle grade, picture books, thrillers, mysteries and select nonfiction); Linda Scalissi (women's fiction, thrillers, young adult, mysteries and romance).

REPRESENTS Nonfiction, novels. **Considers these fiction areas:** middle grade, mystery, picture books, romance, thriller, women's, young adult.

HOW TO CONTACT E-mail queries only; no attachments, unless requested by agents. For fiction, please e-mail the first chapter and synopsis along with a cover letter. Also, be sure to include the genre and the number of words in your manuscript, as well as pertinent writing experience in your query letter. For nonfiction, e-mail a complete proposal, including a query letter and your first chapter. For picture books, query with complete text. Accepts simultaneous submissions. Obtains most new clients through recommendations from others, conferences.

TERMS Agent receives 15% commission on domestic sales; 20% commission on foreign sales. Offers written contract.

TRIADA U.S. LITERARY AGENCY, INC.

P.O. Box 561, Sewickley PA 15143. (412)401-3376. **E-mail:** uwe@triadaus.com; brent@triadaus.com; laura@triadaus.com; mallory@triadaus.com. **Website:** www.triadaus.com. **Contact:** Dr. Uwe Stender. Estab. 2004. Member of AAR.

MEMBER AGENTS Uwe Stender; Brent Taylor; Laura Crockett; Mallory Brown.

REPRESENTS Nonfiction, fiction, novels, juvenile books. **Considers these nonfiction areas:** biography, business, cooking, crafts, current affairs, diet/nutrition, economics, education, environment, foods, gardening, health, history, how-to, memoirs, music, parenting, popular culture, politics, science, self-help, sports, true crime, young adult. **Considers these fiction areas:** action, adventure, contemporary issues, crime, detective, ethnic, fantasy, gay, historical, horror, juvenile, literary, mainstream, middle grade, multicultural, mystery, new adult, occult, police, romance, suspense, thriller, urban fantasy, women's, young adult.

HOW TO CONTACT E-mail queries preferred. Accepts simultaneous submissions. Obtains most new clients through recommendations from others, conferences.

TERMS Agent receives 15% commission on domestic sales; 20% commission on foreign sales. Offers written contract; 30-day notice must be given to terminate contract.

TRIDENT MEDIA GROUP

41 Madison Ave., 36th Floor, New York NY 10010. (212)333-1511. **Website:** www.tridentmediagroup. com. **Contact:** Ellen Levine. Member of AAR.

MEMBER AGENTS Kimberly Whalen, ws.assistant@tridentmediagroup (commercial fiction and nonfiction, including women's fiction, romance, suspense, paranormal, and pop culture); Alyssa Eisner Henkin (picture books through young adult fic-

tion, including mysteries, period pieces, contemporary school-settings, issues of social justice, family sagas, eerie magical realism, and retellings of classics; children's/YA nonfiction: history, STEM/STEAM themes, memoir) Scott Miller, smiller@tridentmediagroup.com (commercial fiction, including thrillers, crime fiction, women's, book club fiction, middle grade, young adult; nonfiction, including military, celebrity and pop culture, narrative, sports, prescriptive, and current events); Melissa Flashman, mflashman@tridentmediagroup.com (nonfiction: pop culture, memoir, wellness, popular science, business and economics, technology; fiction: adult and YA, literary and commercial); Don Fehr, dfehr@tridentmediagroup.com (literary and commercial fiction, young adult fiction, narrative nonfiction, memoirs, travel, science, and health); John Silbersack, silbersack.assistant@tridentmediagroup.com (fiction: literary fiction, crime fiction, science fiction and fantasy, children's, thrillers/suspense; nonfiction: narrative nonfiction, science, history, biography, current events, memoirs, finance, pop culture); Erica Spellman-Silverman; Ellen Levine, levine.assistant@tridentmediagroup.com (popular commercial fiction and compelling nonfiction, including memoir, popular culture, narrative nonfiction, history, politics, biography, science, and the odd quirky book); Mark Gottlieb (fiction: science fiction, fantasy, young adult, graphic novels, historical, middle grade, mystery, romance, suspense, thrillers; nonfiction: business, finance, history, religious, health, cookbooks, sports, African-American, biography, memoir, travel, mind/body/spirit, narrative nonfiction, science, technology); Alexander Slater, aslater@tridentmdiagroup.com (children's, middle grade, and young adult fiction); Amanda O'Connor, aoconnor@tridentmediagroup.com; Tara Carberry, tcarberry@tridentmediagroup.com (women's commercial fiction, romance, new adult, young adult, and select nonfiction); Alexa Stark, astark@tridentmediagroup.com (literary fiction, upmarket commercial fiction, young adult, memoir, narrative nonfiction, popular science, cultural criticism and women's issues).

REPRESENTS Considers these nonfiction areas: biography, business, cooking, creative nonfiction, current affairs, economics, health, history, memoirs, military, popular culture, politics, religious, science, sports, technology, travel, women's issues, young adult, middle grade. **Considers these fiction areas:** commercial, crime, fantasy, historical, juvenile, literary, middle grade, mystery, new adult, paranormal, picture books, romance, science fiction, suspense, thriller, women's, young adult.

HOW TO CONTACT Submit through the agency's online submission form on the agency website. Query only one agent at a time. If you e-query, include no attachments. Accepts simultaneous submissions.

UNION LITERARY

30 Vandam St., Suite 5A, New York NY 10013. (212)255-2112. **E-mail:** info@unionliterary.com. **E-mail:** submissions@unionliterary.com. **Website:** unionliterary.com. Member of AAR. Signatory of WGA.

MEMBER AGENTS Trena Keating, tk@unionliterary.com (fiction and nonfiction, specifically a literary novel with an exotic setting, a YA/MG journey or transformation novel, a distinctly modern novel with a female protagonist, a creepy page-turner, a quest memoir that addresses larger issues, nonfiction based on primary research or a unique niche, a great essayist, and a voicy writer who is a great storyteller or makes her laugh); Sally Wofford-Girand, swg@unionliterary.com (history, memoir, women's issues, cultural studies, gripping literary fiction); Jenni Ferrari-Adler, jenni@unionliterary.com (fiction, cookbook/food, young adult and middle grade, narrative nonfiction); Christina Clifford, christina@unionliterary.com (literary fiction, international fiction, narrative nonfiction, specifically historical biography, memoir, business, and science); Shaun Dolan, sd@unionliterary.com (muscular and lyrical literary fiction, narrative nonfiction, memoir, pop culture, and sports narratives).

HOW TO CONTACT Nonfiction submissions: include a query letter, a proposal and a sample chapter. Fiction submissions: should include a query letter, synopsis, and either sample pages or full ms. "Due to the high volume of submissions we receive, we will only be in contact regarding projects that feel like a match for the respective agent." Accepts simultaneous submissions. Accepts simultaneous submissions. Responds in 1 month.

THE UNTER AGENCY

23 W. 73rd St., Suite 100, New York NY 10023. (212)401-4068. **E-mail:** Jennifer@theunteragency.com. **Website:** www.theunteragency.com. **Contact:** Jennifer Unter. Estab. 2008. Member of AAR. Signatory of WGA.

REPRESENTS Nonfiction, fiction, novels, short story collections, juvenile books. **Considers these nonfiction areas:** animals, art, autobiography, biography, cooking, creative nonfiction, current affairs, diet/nutrition, environment, foods, health, history, how-to, humor, juvenile nonfiction, law, memoirs, popular culture, politics, spirituality, sports, travel, true crime, women's issues, young adult, nature subjects. **Considers these fiction areas:** action, adventure, cartoon, commercial, family saga, inspirational, juvenile, mainstream, middle grade, mystery, paranormal, picture books, thriller, women's, young adult.

HOW TO CONTACT Send an e-query. There is also an online submission form. If you do not hear back from this agency within 3 months, consider that a no. Accepts simultaneous submissions. 3 months

UPSTART CROW LITERARY

244 Fifth Avenue, 11th Floor, New York NY 10001. **E-mail:** danielle.submission@gmail.com. **Website:** www.upstartcrowliterary.com. **Contact:** Danielle Chiotti, Alexandra Penfold. Estab. 2009. Member of AAR. Signatory of WGA.

MEMBER AGENTS Michael Stearns (not accepting submissions); Danielle Chiotti (all genres of young adult and middle grade fiction; adult upmarket commercial fiction [not considering romance, mystery/suspense/thriller, science fiction, horror, or erotica]; nonfiction in the areas of narrative/memoir, lifestyle, relationships, humor, current events, food, wine, and cooking); Ted Malawer (not accepting submissions); Alexandra Penfold (not accepting submissions).

REPRESENTS **Considers these nonfiction areas:** cooking, current affairs, foods, humor, memoirs. **Considers these fiction areas:** commercial, mainstream, middle grade, picture books, young adult.

HOW TO CONTACT Submit a query and 20 pages pasted into an e-mail. Accepts simultaneous submissions.

VERITAS LITERARY AGENCY

601 Van Ness Ave., Opera Plaza, Suite E, San Francisco CA 94102. (415)647-6964. **Fax:** (415)647-6965. **E-mail:** submissions@veritasliterary.com. **Website:** www.veritasliterary.com. **Contact:** Katherine Boyle. Member of AAR. Other memberships include Author's Guild and SCBWI.

MEMBER AGENTS Katherine Boyle, katherine@veritasliterary.com (literary fiction, middle grade, young adult, narrative nonfiction & memoir, historical fiction, crime & suspense, history, pop culture, popular science, business & career); Michael Carr, michael@veritasliterary.com (historical fiction, women's fiction, science fiction and fantasy, nonfiction), Chiara Rosati, chiara@veritasliterary.com (literary fiction, middle grade, young adult, new adult, women's studies, narrative nonfiction).

REPRESENTS Nonfiction, novels. **Considers these nonfiction areas:** business, history, memoirs, popular culture, women's issues. **Considers these fiction areas:** commercial, crime, fantasy, historical, literary, middle grade, new adult, science fiction, suspense, women's, young adult.

HOW TO CONTACT This agency accepts short queries or proposals via e-mail only. "Fiction: Please include a cover letter listing previously published work, a one-page summary and the first five pages in the body of the e-mail (not as an attachment). Nonfiction: If you are sending a proposal, please include an author biography, an overview, a chapter-by-chapter summary, and an analysis of competitive titles. We do our best to review all queries within 4-6 weeks; however, if you have not heard from us in 12 weeks, consider that a no." Accepts simultaneous submissions. If you have not heard from this agency in 12 weeks, consider that a no.

WALES LITERARY AGENCY, INC.

1508 10th Avenue East #401, Seattle WA 98102. (206)284-7114. **E-mail:** waleslit@waleslit.com. **Website:** www.waleslit.com. **Contact:** Elizabeth Wales; Neal Swain. Estab. 1990. Member of AAR. Other memberships include Authors Guild

MEMBER AGENTS Elizabeth Wales; Neal Swain.
REPRESENTS Nonfiction, fiction, novels.
HOW TO CONTACT E-query with no attachments. Accepts simultaneous submissions. Responds in 2 weeks to queries, 2 months to mss.
TERMS Agent receives 15% commission on domestic sales; 20% commission on foreign sales.

WATERSIDE PRODUCTIONS, INC.

2055 Oxford Ave., Cardiff CA 92007. (760)632-9190. **Fax:** (760)632-9295. **E-mail:** bgladstone@waterside.com. **E-mail:** admin@waterside.com. **Website:** www.waterside.com. Estab. 1982.
MEMBER AGENTS Bill Gladstone (big nonfiction books); Margot Maley Hutchinson (computer, health,

psychology, parenting, fitness, pop-culture, and business); Carole Jelen, carole@jelenpub.com (innovation and thought leaders especially in business, technology, lifestyle and self-help); David Nelson; Jill Kramer, WatersideAgentJK@aol.com (quality fiction with empowering themes for adults and YA (including crossovers); nonfiction, including mind-body-spirit, self-help, celebrity memoirs, relationships, sociology, finance, psychology, health and fitness, diet/nutrition, inspiration, business, family/parenting issues); Brad Schepp (e-commerce, social media and social commerce, careers, entrepreneurship, general business, health and fitness); Natasha Gladstone, (picture books, books with film tie-ins, books with established animated characters, and educational titles); Johanna Maaghul, johanna@waterside.com (nonfiction and select fiction).

REPRESENTS **Considers these nonfiction areas:** business, computers, diet/nutrition, health, inspirational, money, parenting, popular culture, psychology, self-help, sociology, technology, fitness. **Considers these fiction areas:** mainstream, picture books, young adult.

HOW TO CONTACT "Please read each agent bio [on the website] to determine who you think would best represent your genre of work. When you have chosen your agent, please write his or her name in the subject line of your e-mail and send it to admin@waterside.com with your query letter in the body of the e-mail, and your proposal or sample material as an attached word document." Nonfiction submission guidelines are available on the website. Accepts simultaneous submissions. Obtains most new clients through referrals from established client and publisher list.

WAXMAN LEAVELL LITERARY AGENCY, INC.

443 Park Ave. S, Suite 1004, New York NY 10016. (212)675-5556. **Fax:** (212)675-1381. **Website:** www.waxmanleavell.com.

MEMBER AGENTS Scott Waxman (nonfiction: history, biography, health and science, adventure, business, inspirational sports); Byrd Leavell (narrative nonfiction, sports, humor, and select commercial fiction); Holly Root (middle grade, young adult, women's fiction (commercial and upmarket), urban fantasy, romance, select nonfiction); Larry Kirschbaum (fiction and nonfiction; select self-published breakout books); Rachel Vogel (nonfiction: subject-driven narratives, memoirs and biography, journalism, popular culture and the occasional humor and gift book; selective fiction); Julie Stevenson (literary fiction, atmospheric thrillers, suspense-driven work); Taylor Haggerty (young adult, historical, contemporary and historical romance, middle grade, women's, new adult); Cassie Hanjian (new adult novels, plot-driven commercial and upmarket women's fiction, historical fiction, psychological suspense, cozy mysteries and contemporary romance; for nonfiction, mind/body/spirit, self-help, health and wellness, inspirational memoir, food/wine (narrative and prescriptive), and a limited number of accessible cookbooks); Fleetwood Robbins (fantasy and speculative fiction — all subgenres); Molly O'Neill (middle grade and YA fiction and picture book author/illustrators, and—more selectively—narrative nonfiction [including children's/YA/MG, pop science/pop culture, and lifestyle/food/travel/cookbook projects by authors with well-established platforms]).

REPRESENTS Nonfiction, novels. **Considers these nonfiction areas:** biography, business, foods, health, history, humor, inspirational, memoirs, popular culture, science, sports, adventure. **Considers these fiction areas:** fantasy, historical, literary, mainstream, middle grade, mystery, paranormal, romance, science fiction, suspense, thriller, urban fantasy, women's, young adult.

HOW TO CONTACT To submit a project, please send a query letter ONLY via e-mail to one of the addresses included on the website. Do not send attachments, though for fiction you may include 5-10 pages of your manuscript in the body of your e-mail. "Due to the high volume of submissions, agents will reach out to you directly if interested. The typical time range for consideration is 6-8 weeks." Accepts simultaneous submissions.

TERMS Agent receives 15% commission on domestic sales; 10% commission on foreign sales. Offers written contract; 2-month notice must be given to terminate contract.

CK WEBBER ASSOCIATES, LITERARY MANAGEMENT

E-mail: carlie@ckwebber.com. **Website:** ckwebber.com/. **Contact:** Carlie Webber. Member of AAR. Signatory of WGA.

REPRESENTS Nonfiction, novels. **Considers these nonfiction areas:** memoirs. **Considers these fiction areas:** fantasy, literary, mainstream, middle grade, mystery, new adult, romance, science fiction, suspense, thriller, women's, young adult.

HOW TO CONTACT To submit your work for consideration, please send a query letter, synopsis, and the first 30 pages or three chapters of your work, whichever is more, to carlie@ckwebber.com and put the word "query" in the subject line of your e-mail. You may include your materials either in the body of your e-mail or as a Word or PDF attachment. Blank e-mails that include an attachment will be deleted unread. We only accept queries via e-mail. Accepts simultaneous submissions.

WERNICK & PRATT AGENCY

E-mail: info@wernickpratt.com. **Website:** www.wernickpratt.com. **Contact:** Marcia Wernick; Linda Pratt; Emily Mitchell. Member of AAR. Signatory of WGA.

MEMBER AGENTS Marcia Wernick, Linda Pratt, Emily Mitchell.

HOW TO CONTACT Submit via e-mail only to submissions@wernickpratt.com. "Please indicate to which agent you are submitting." Detailed submission guidelines available on website. "Submissions will only be responded to further if we are interested in them. If you do not hear from us within six weeks of your submission, it should be considered declined." Accepts simultaneous submissions. Responds in 6 weeks.

⊘ WESTWOOD CREATIVE ARTISTS, LTD.

94 Harbord St., Toronto ON M5S 1G6 Canada. (416)964-3302. **E-mail:** wca_office@wcaltd.com. **Website:** www.wcaltd.com. Represents 350+ clients.

MEMBER AGENTS Jack Babad; Lix Culotti (foreign contracts and permissions); Carolyn Ford (literary fiction, commerical, women's/literary crossover, thrillers, serious narrative nonfiction, pop culture); Jackie Kaiser (president and CEO); Michael A. Levine; Linda McKnight; Hilary McMahon (fiction, nonfiction, children's); John Pearce (fiction and nonfiction); Meg Tobin-O'Drowsky; Bruce Westwood.

REPRESENTS Nonfiction, fiction, novels. **Considers these nonfiction areas:** biography, current affairs, history, parenting, science, journalism, practical nonfiction. **Considers these fiction areas:** commercial, juvenile, literary, thriller, women's, young adult.

HOW TO CONTACT E-query only. Include credentials, synopsis, and no more than 10 pages. No attachments. Accepts simultaneous submissions.

WOLF LITERARY SERVICES, LLC

Website: wolflit.com. Estab. 2008. Member of AAR. Signatory of WGA.

MEMBER AGENTS Kirsten Wolf (no queries); Kate Johnson (literary fiction, particularly character-driven stories, psychological investigations, modern-day fables, international tales, magical realism, and historical fiction; nonfiction: food, feminism, parenting, art, travel and the environment, and she loves working with journalists); Allison Devereux (literary and upmarket commercial fiction; nonfiction, including examinations of contemporary culture, pop science, and modern feminist perspectives; humor and blog-to-book; illustrated novels or memoir; and narrative nonfiction that uses a particular niche topic to explore larger truths about our culture).

REPRESENTS Considers these nonfiction areas: art, creative nonfiction, environment, foods, history, humor, memoirs, parenting, science, travel, women's issues. **Considers these fiction areas:** commercial, historical, literary, magical realism.

HOW TO CONTACT To submit a project, please send a query letter along with a 50-page writing sample (for fiction) or a detailed proposal (for nonfiction) to queries@wolflit.com. Samples may be submitted as an attachment or embedded in the body of the e-mail. Accepts simultaneous submissions.

WRITERS HOUSE

21 W. 26th St., New York NY 10010. (212)685-2400. **Fax:** (212)685-1781. **Website:** www.writershouse.com. Estab. 1973. Member of AAR.

MEMBER AGENTS Amy Berkower; Stephen Barr; Susan Cohen; Dan Conaway; Lisa DiMona; Susan Ginsburg; Susan Golomb; Merrilee Heifetz; Brianne Johnson; Daniel Lazar; Simon Lipskar; Steven Malk; Jodi Reamer, Esq.; Robin Rue; Rebecca Sherman; Geri Thoma; Albert Zuckerman; Alec Shane; Stacy Testa; Victoria Doherty-Munro; Beth Miller; Andrea Morrison; Soumeya Roberts.

REPRESENTS Nonfiction, novels. **Considers these nonfiction areas:** biography, business, cooking, economics, history, how-to, juvenile nonfiction, memoirs, parenting, psychology, science, self-help. **Considers these fiction areas:** commercial, fantasy, juvenile, literary, mainstream, middle grade, picture books, science fiction, women's, young adult.

HOW TO CONTACT Individual agent e-mail addresses are available on the website. "Please e-mail us a query letter, which includes your credentials, an explanation of what makes your book unique and special, and a synopsis. Some agents within our agency have different requirements. Please consult their individual Publisher's Marketplace (PM) profile for details. We respond to all queries, generally within six to eight weeks." If you prefer to submit my mail, address it to an individual agent, and please include a self-addressed-stamped-envelope for our reply. (If submitting to Steven Malk: Writers House, 7660 Fay Ave., #338H, La Jolla, CA 92037.) Accepts simultaneous submissions. "We respond to all queries, generally within six to eight weeks." Obtains most new clients through recommendations from authors and editors.

TERMS Agent receives 15% commission on domestic sales; 20% commission on foreign sales. Offers written contract, binding for 1 year. Agency charges fees for copying mss/proposals and overseas airmail of books.

TIPS "Do not send mss. Write a compelling letter. If you do, we'll ask to see your work. Follow submission guidelines and please do not simultaneously submit your work to more than one Writers House agent."

JASON YARN LITERARY AGENCY

3544 Broadway, No. 68, New York NY 10031. **E-mail:** jason@jasonyarnliteraryagency.com. **Website:** www.jasonyarnliteraryagency.com. Member of AAR. Signatory of WGA.

REPRESENTS Nonfiction, fiction. **Considers these nonfiction areas:** creative nonfiction, current affairs, foods, history, science. **Considers these fiction areas:** commercial, fantasy, literary, middle grade, science fiction, suspense, thriller, young adult, graphic novels, comics.

HOW TO CONTACT Please e-mail your query to jason@jasonyarnliteraryagency.com with the word "Query" in the subject line, and please paste the first 10 pages of your manuscript or proposal into the text of your e-mail, Do not send any attachments. "Visit the About page for information on what we are interested in, and please note that JYLA does not accept queries for film, TV, or stage scripts." Accepts simultaneous submissions.

RENÈE ZUCKERBROT LITERARY AGENCY

115 West 29th St., 3rd Floor, New York NY 10001. (212)967-0072. **Fax:** (212)967-0073. **E-mail:** renee@rzagency.com. **E-mail:** submissions@rzagency.com. **Website:** rzagency.com. **Contact:** Renèe Zuckerbrot.

Member of AAR. PEN and Authors Guild Represents 30 clients.

REPRESENTS Nonfiction, fiction, novels, short story collections. **Considers these nonfiction areas:** animals, biography, cultural interests, environment, hobbies, multicultural, politics, science, women's studies. **Considers these fiction areas:** commercial, ethnic, short story collections, women's.

HOW TO CONTACT Query by e-mail: submissions@rzagency.com. Include a synopsis, publication history and a brief personal bio. You may include up to the first 3 chapters. Accepts simultaneous submissions. Responds in approximately 4-6 weeks.

TERMS Agent receives 15% commission on domestic sales; 25% commission on foreign sales (10% to RZA; 15% to foreign rights co-agent).

BOOK PUBLISHERS

//

The markets in this year's Book Publishers section offer opportunities in nearly every area of publishing. Large, commercial houses are here as are their smaller counterparts.

The Book Publishers Subject Index is the best place to start your search. You'll find it in the back of the book, before the General Index. Subject areas for both fiction and non-fiction are broken out for all of the book publisher listings.

When you have compiled a list of publishers interested in books in your subject area, read the detailed listings. Pare down your list by cross-referencing two or three subject areas and eliminating the listings only marginally suited to your book. When you have a good list, send for those publishers' catalogs and manuscript guidelines, or check publishers' websites, which often contain catalog listings, manuscript preparation guidelines, current contact names, and other information helpful to prospective authors. You want to use this information to make sure your book idea is in line with a publisher's list but is not a duplicate of something already published.

You should also visit bookstores and libraries to see if the publisher's books are well represented. When you find a couple of books the house has published that are similar to yours, write or call the company to find out who edited those books. This extra bit of research could be the key to getting your proposal to precisely the right editor.

Publishers prefer different methods of submission on first contact. Most like to see a one-page query, especially for nonfiction. Others will accept a brief proposal package that might include an outline and/or a sample chapter. Some publishers will accept submissions from agents only. Each listing in the Book Publishers section includes specific submission methods, if provided by the publisher. Make sure you read each listing carefully to find out exactly what the publisher wants to receive.

When you write your one-page query, give an overview of your book, mention the intended audience, the competition for your book (check local bookstore shelves), and what sets your book apart from the competition. You should also include any previous publishing experience or special training relevant to the subject of your book. For more on queries, read "Query Letter Clinic."

Personalize your query by addressing the editor individually and mentioning what you know about the company from its catalog or books. Under the heading **Contact**, we list the names of editors who acquire new books for each company, along with the editors' specific areas of expertise. Try your best to send your query to the appropriate editor. Editors move around all the time, so it's in your best interest to look online or call the publishing house to make sure the editor you are addressing your query to is still employed by that publisher.

Author-subsidy publishers' not included

Writer's Market is a reference tool to help you sell your writing, and we encourage you to work with publishers that pay a royalty. Subsidy publishing involves paying money to a publishing house to publish a book. The source of the money could be a government, foundation or university grant, or it could be the author of the book. If one of the publishers listed in this book offers you an author-subsidy arrangement (sometimes called "co-operative publishing," "co-publishing," or "joint venture"); or asks you to pay for part or all of the cost of any aspect of publishing (editing services, manuscript critiques, printing, advertising, etc.); or asks you to guarantee the purchase of any number of the books yourself, we would like you to inform us of that company's practices immediately.

⊘ ABBEVILLE FAMILY

Abbeville Press, 116 W. 23rd St., New York NY 10011. (212)366-5585. **Fax:** (212)366-6966. **E-mail:** abbeville@abbeville.com. **Website:** www.abbeville.com. Estab. 1977. "Our list is full for the next several seasons." *Not accepting unsolicited book proposals at this time.* **Publishes 8 titles/year. 10% of books from first-time authors.** Accepts simultaneous submissions.

FICTION Picture books: animal, anthology, concept, contemporary, fantasy, folktales, health, hi-lo, history, humor, multicultural, nature/environment, poetry, science fiction, special needs, sports, suspense. Average word length 300-1,000 words. Please refer to website for submission policy.

⊘ ABBEVILLE PRESS

116 W. 23rd St., New York NY 10011. (646) 375-2136 or 1-800-ART-BOOK. **Fax:** (646)375-2359. **E-mail:** abbeville@abbeville.com. **Website:** www.abbeville.com. Estab. 1977. Mainstay in the art book publishing world. "Our list is full for the next several seasons." **10% of books from first-time authors.** Accepts simultaneous submissions.

NONFICTION Subjects include art. Not accepting unsolicited book proposals at this time.

FICTION Subjects include adventure. Picture books through imprint Abbeville Family. Not accepting unsolicited book proposals at this time.

⊘ ABC-CLIO/GREENWOOD

ABC-CLIO, P.O. Box 1911, Santa Barbara CA 93116. (805)968-1911. **E-mail:** acquisitions_inquiries@abc-clio.com. **Website:** www.abc-clio.com. **Contact:** Editorial Assistant. Publishes hardcover originals. ABC-CLIO/Greenwood publishes reference materials for high school, public and academic libraries in the humanities and the social and hard sciences. **Publishes 200 titles/year. 1,000 queries received/year. 25% of books from first-time authors. Pays variable royalty on net price. Pays rare advance.** Publishes book 1 year after acceptance. Accepts simultaneous submissions. Responds in 6 months to queries. Book catalog and ms guidelines online.

NONFICTION Subjects include humanities, literary criticism, social sciences, humanities and the social and hard sciences. Query with proposal package, including scope, organization, length of project, whether complete ms is available or when it will be, CV or resume and SASE. *No unsolicited mss.*

ABDO PUBLISHING CO.

8000 W. 78th St., Suite 310, Edina MN 55439. (800)800-1312. **Fax:** (952)831-1632. **E-mail:** nonfiction@abdopublishing.com. **E-mail:** fiction@abdopublishing.com; illustration@abdopublishing.com. **Website:** www.abdopublishing.com. **Contact:** Paul Abdo, editor-in-chief. Estab. 1985. Publishes hardcover originals. ABDO publishes nonfiction children's books (pre-kindergarten to 8th grade) for school and public libraries—mainly history, sports, biography, geography, science, and social studies. "Please specify each submission as either nonfiction, fiction, or illustration." **Publishes 300 titles/year.** Accepts simultaneous submissions. Guidelines online.

NONFICTION Subjects include animals, history, science, sports, geography, social studies.

ABINGDON PRESS

Imprint of The United Methodist Publishing House, 201 Eighth Ave. S., P.O. Box 801, Nashville TN 37202. (615)749-6000. **Fax:** (615)749-6512. **E-mail:** submissions@umpublishing.org. **Website:** www.abingdonpress.com. Estab. 1789. Publishes hardcover and paperback originals. "Abingdon Press, America's oldest theological publisher, provides an ecumenical publishing program dedicated to serving the Christian community—clergy, scholars, church leaders, musicians, and general readers—with quality resources in the areas of Bible study, the practice of ministry, theology, devotion, spirituality, inspiration, prayer, music and worship, reference, Christian education, and church supplies." **Publishes 120 titles/year. 3,000 queries received/year. 250 mss received/year. 85% from unagented writers. Pays 7½% royalty on retail price.** Publishes ms 2 years after acceptance. Responds in 2 months to queries. Book catalog available free. Guidelines online.

NONFICTION Subjects include education, religion, theology. Query with outline and samples only. The author should retain a copy of any unsolicited material submitted.

FICTION Publishes stories of faith, hope, and love that encourage readers to explore life. Agented submissions only for fiction.

⊘ HARRY N. ABRAMS, INC.

115 W. 18th St., 6th Floor, New York NY 10011. (212)206-7715. **Fax:** (212)519-1210. **E-mail:** abrams@abramsbooks.com. **Website:** www.abramsbooks.com. **Contact:** Managing Editor. Estab. 1951. Publishes

hardcover and a few paperback originals. **Publishes 250 titles/year.** Accepts simultaneous submissions.

IMPRINTS Stewart, Tabori & Chang; Abrams Appleseed; Abrams Books for Young Readers; Abrams Image; STC Craft; Amulet Books.

◖ Does not accept unsolicited materials.

NONFICTION Subjects include recreation.

FICTION Subjects include young adult. Publishes hardcover and "a few" paperback originals. Averages 150 total titles/year.

TIPS "We are one of the few publishers who publish almost exclusively illustrated books. We consider ourselves the leading publishers of art books and high-quality artwork in the U.S. Once the author has signed a contract to write a book for our firm the author must finish the manuscript to agreed-upon high standards within the schedule agreed upon in the contract."

⊘ ABRAMS BOOKS FOR YOUNG READERS

115 W. 18th St., New York NY 10011. **Website:** www. abramsyoungreaders.com. Accepts simultaneous submissions.

◖ Abrams no longer accepts unsolicted mss or queries.

ACADEMY CHICAGO PUBLISHERS

814 N. Franklin St., Chicago IL 60610. (312)337-0747. **Fax:** (312)337-5985. **Website:** www.academychicago. com. **Contact:** Yuval Taylor, senior editor. Estab. 1975. Publishes hardcover and some paperback originals and trade paperback reprints. "We publish quality fiction and nonfiction. Our audience is literate and discriminating. No novelized biography, history, or science fiction." No electronic submissions. **Publishes 10 titles/year. Pays 7-10% royalty on wholesale price.** Publishes ms 18 months after acceptance. Accepts simultaneous submissions. Responds in 3 months. Book catalog online. Guidelines online.

NONFICTION Subjects include history, travel. No religion, cookbooks, or self-help. Submit proposal package, outline, bio, 3 sample chapters.

FICTION Subjects include historical, mystery. "We look for quality work, but we do not publish experimental, avant garde, horror, science fiction, thrillers novels." Submit proposal package, synopsis, 3 sample chapters, and short bio.

TIPS "At the moment, we are looking for good non-fiction; we certainly want excellent original fiction,

but we are swamped. No fax queries, no disks. No electronic submissions. We are always interested in reprinting good out-of-print books."

ⒶⓄ ACE SCIENCE FICTION AND FANTASY

Imprint of the Berkley Publishing Group, Penguin Group (USA), Inc., 375 Hudson St., New York NY 10014. (212)366-2000. **Website:** www. us.penguingroup.com. Estab. 1953. Publishes hardcover, paperback, and trade paperback originals and reprints. Ace publishes science fiction and fantasy exclusively. **Publishes 75 titles/year. Pays royalty. Pays advance.**

◖ As imprint of Penguin, Ace is not open to unsolicited submissions.

FICTION Subjects include fantasy, science fiction. No other genre accepted. No short stories. Due to the high volume of manuscripts received, most Penguin Group (USA) Inc. imprints do not normally accept unsolicited mss.

ACTA PUBLICATIONS

4848 N. Clark St., Chicago IL 60640. **Website:** www. actapublications.com. **Contact:** Acquisitions Editor. Estab. 1958. Publishes trade paperback originals. "ACTA publishes nonacademic, practical books aimed at the mainline religious market." **Publishes 12 titles/year. 100 queries received/year. 25 mss received/year. 50% of books from first-time authors. 90% from unagented writers. Pays 10-12% royalty on wholesale price.** Publishes book 1 year after acceptance of ms. Responds in 2-3 months to proposals. Book catalog and guidelines online.

◖ "While some of ACTA's material is specifically Catholic in nature, most of the company's products are aimed at a broadly ecumenical audience."

NONFICTION Subjects include religion, spirituality. True Submit outline, 1 sample chapter. No e-mail submissions. Reviews artwork/photos. Send photocopies.

TIPS "Don't send a submission unless you have examined our catalog, website and several of our books."

ADAMS-BLAKE PUBLISHING

8041 Sierra St. #321, Fair Oaks CA 95628. (916)962-9296. **E-mail:** web@adams-blake.com. **Website:** www. adams-blake.com. **Contact:** Monica Blane, acquisitions editor. Estab. 1992. Publishes only e-books. "We are getting away from doing trade titles and are doing more short-run/high-priced specialized publications targeted to corporations, law, medicine, engineering, computers, etc." **Publishes 5 titles/year. 50 queries received/year. 15 mss received/year. 80% of books from first-time authors. 99% from unagented writers. Pays 15% royalty on wholesale price.** Publishes book 2 months after acceptance. Accepts simultaneous submissions. Responds in 2 months.

NONFICTION "We like titles in sales and marketing, but which are targeted to a specific industry. We don't look for retail trade titles but more to special markets where we sell 10,000 copies to a company to give to their employees." Query. Does not review artwork/photos.

TIPS "If you have a book that a large company might buy and give away at sales meetings, send us a query. We like books on sales, especially in specific industries—Like 'How to Sell Annuities' or 'How to Sell High-Tech.' We look for the title that a company will buy several thousand copies of at a time. We often 'personalize' for the company. We especially like short books, 50,000 words (more or less)."

ADAMS MEDIA

Division of F+W Media, Inc., 57 Littlefield St., Avon MA 02322. (508)427-7100. **Fax:** (800)872-5628. **E-mail:** adamsmediasubmissions@fwmedia.com. **Website:** www.adamsmedia.com. **Contact:** Acquisitions Editor. Estab. 1980. Publishes hardcover originals, trade paperback, e-book originals, and reprints. Adams Media publishes commercial nonfiction, including self-help, women's issues, pop psychology, relationships, business, careers, pets, parenting, New Age, gift books, cookbooks, how-to, reference, and humor. Does not return unsolicited materials. **Publishes more than 250 titles/year. 5,000 queries received/year. 1,500 mss received/year. 40% of books from first-time authors. Pays standard royalty or makes outright purchase. Pays variable advance.** Publishes book 12-18 months after acceptance. Accepts simultaneous submissions. Responds in 3 months to queries. Guidelines online.

ADDICUS BOOKS, INC.

P.O. Box 45327, Omaha NE 68145. (402)330-7493. **Fax:** (402)330-1707. **E-mail:** info@addicusbooks.com. **Website:** www.addicusbooks.com. **Contact:** Acquisitions Editor. Estab. 1994. Addicus Books, Inc. seeks mss with strong national or regional appeal. "We are dedicated to producing high-quality nonfiction books.

Our focus is on both consumer health titles and legal titles, but we will consider other topics. In addition to working with a master book distributor, IPG Books of Chicago, which delivers books to stores and libraries, we continually seek sales channels outside traditional bookstores. We need at least one solid sales channel outside the bookstore market. Due to the amount of queries we receive our editors are not available for phone inquiries. If we're interested in taking a closer look at your book, we'll contact you after we receive your e-mail inquiry." **Publishes 15 titles/year. 90% of books from first-time authors. 95% from unagented writers.** Publishes ms 9 months after acceptance. Accepts simultaneous submissions. Responds in 1 month to proposals. Catalog and guidelines online.

NONFICTION Subjects include business, economics, health, law, consumer health, consumer legal topics, economics, investment advice. "We are continuously expanding our line of consumer health and consumer legal titles." Query with a brief e-mail. "Tell us what your book is about, who the audience is, and how that audience would be reached. If we are interested, we may ask for a proposal, outlining the nature of your work. See proposal guidelines may be found on our website. Do not send entire ms unless requested. When querying electronically, send only a 1-page e-mail, giving an overview of your book and its market. Please do not mail queries or proposals by certified mail. Find additional submission guidelines online."

TIPS "We focus heavily on the quality of the editorial content of our books. We look for organization, clarity, and appropriate tone in a manuscript. Consumers are busy people. We serve them books that are compact, concise, and reader-friendly."

AHSAHTA PRESS

MFA Program in Creative Writing, Boise State University, 1910 University Dr., MS 1525, Boise ID 83725. (208)426-3414. **E-mail:** ahsahta@boisestate.edu. **Website:** ahsahtapress.org. **Contact:** Janet Holmes, director. Estab. 1974. Publishes trade paperback originals. **Publishes 7 titles/year. 1,000 mss received/year. 30% of books from first-time authors. 100% from unagented writers. Pays 8% royalty on retail price for first 1,000 sold; 10% thereafter.** Publishes ms 2 years after acceptance. Accepts simultaneous submissions. Responds in 3 months to mss. Book catalog online. Guidelines online; submit through submissions manager.

POETRY "We hold an open submissions period in May as well as the Sawtooth Poetry Prize competition, from which we publish 2-3 mss per year." Submit complete ms. The press publishes runners-up as well as winners of the Sawtooth Poetry Prize. Forthcoming, new, and backlist titles available on website. Most backlist titles: $9.95; most current titles: $18.

TIPS "Ahsahta's motto is that poetry is art, so our readers tend to come to us for the unexpected—poetry that makes them think, reflect, and even do something they haven't done before."

⊘ ALADDIN

Simon & Schuster, 1230 Avenue of the Americas, 4th Floor, New York NY 10020. (212)698-7000. **Website:** www.simonandschuster.com. **Contact:** Acquisitions Editor. Publishes hardcover/paperback originals and imprints of Simon & Schuster Children's Publishing Children's Division. Aladdin publishes picture books, beginning readers, chapter books, middle grade and tween fiction and nonfiction, and graphic novels and nonfiction in hardcover and paperback, with an emphasis on commercial, kid-friendly titles. Accepts simultaneous submissions.

FICTION Simon & Schuster does not review, retain or return unsolicited materials or artwork. "We suggest prospective authors and illustrators submit their mss through a professional literary agent."

⊘ ALGONQUIN BOOKS OF CHAPEL HILL

Workman Publishing, P.O. Box 2225, Chapel Hill NC 27515-2225. (919)967-0108. **Website:** www.algonquin. com. **Contact:** Editorial Department. Publishes hardcover originals. "Algonquin Books publishes quality literary fiction and literary nonfiction." **Publishes 24 titles/year.** Guidelines online.

IMPRINTS Algonquin Young Readers.

NONFICTION Does not accept unsolicited submissions at this time. "Visit our website for full submission policy to queries."

FICTION Subjects include literary. Does not accept unsolicited submissions at this time.

ALGONQUIN YOUNG READERS

P.O. Box 2225, Chapel Hill NC 27515. **Website:** algonquinyoungreaders.com. Algonquin Young Readers is a new imprint that features books for readers 7-17. "From short illustrated novels for the youngest independent readers to timely and topical crossover young adult fiction, what ties our books together are

unforgettable characters, absorbing stories, and superior writing." Accepts simultaneous submissions. Guidelines online.

FICTION Algonquin Young Readers publishes ficiton and a limited number of narrative nonfiction titles for middle grade and young adult readers. "We don't publish poetry, picture books, or genre fiction." Query with 15-20 sample pages and SASE.

ALGORA PUBLISHING

222 Riverside Dr., 16th Floor, New York NY 10025-6809. (212)678-0232. **Fax:** (212)666-3682. **Website:** www.algora.com. **Contact:** Martin DeMers, editor (sociology/philosophy/economics); Claudiu A. Secara, publisher (philosophy/international affairs). Estab. 1992. Publishes hardcover and trade paperback originals and reprints. Algora Publishing is an academic-type press, focusing on works by North and South American, European, Asian, and African authors for the educated general reader. **Publishes 25 titles/year. 1,500 queries received/year. 800 mss received/year. 20% of books from first-time authors. 85% from unagented writers. Pays $0-1,000 advance.** Publishes book 10-18 months after acceptance of ms. Accepts simultaneous submissions. Responds in 1 month to queries/proposals; 3 months to mss. Book catalog and guidelines online.

NONFICTION Subjects include anthropology, archeology, creative nonfiction, dance, education, environment, finance, government, history, language, literature, military, money, music, nature, philosophy, politics, psychology, religion, science, sociology, translation, war, womens issues, womens studies, economics. Algora Publishing welcomes proposals for original mss, but "we do not handle self-help, recovery, or children's books." Submit a query or ms by uploading file to our website.

TIPS "We welcome first-time writers; we help craft an author's raw manuscript into a literary work."

◐ IAN ALLAN PUBLISHING, LTD.

Terminal House, Shepperton TW17 8 AS, United Kingdom. (44)(193)283-4950. **E-mail:** info@ianallanpub.co.uk. **Website:** www.ianallanpublishing.com. **Contact:** Peter Waller, publishing manager. Publishes hardcover, trade paperback and mass market paperback originals and reprints. **Publishes 120 titles/year. 300 queries received/year. 50 mss received/year. 5% of books from first-time authors. 95% from unagented writers. Payment is subject to contract and**

type of publication. Publishes book 6 months after acceptance of ms. Accepts simultaneous submissions. Book catalog available free.

NONFICTION Subjects include history, hobbies, sports, travel. Query with SASE. Reviews artwork/photos.

TIPS "Audience is enthusiasts and historians. We don't publish books with a strong autobiographical bias—e.g., military reminiscences—and no fiction/children's/poetry."

ALLEN & UNWIN

406 Albert St., East Melbourne VIC 3002, Australia. (61)(3)9665-5000. **E-mail:** fridaypitch@allenandunwin.com. **Website:** www.allenandunwin.com. Allen & Unwin publish over 80 new books for children and young adults each year, many of these from established authors and illustrators. "However, we know how difficult it can be for new writers to get their work in front of publishers, which is why we've decided to extend our innovative and pioneering Friday Pitch service to emerging writers for children and young adults." Accepts simultaneous submissions. Guidelines online.

ALLWORTH PRESS

An imprint of Skyhorse Publishing, 307 West 36th St., 11th Floor, New York NY 10018. (212)643-6816. **Fax:** (212)643-6819. **E-mail:** allworthsubmissions@skyhorsepublishing.com. **Website:** www.allworth.com. Estab. 1989. Publishes hardcover and trade paperback originals. "Allworth Press publishes business and self-help information for artists, designers, photographers, authors and film and performing artists, as well as books about business, money and the law for the general public. The press also publishes the best of classic and contemporary writing in art and graphic design. Currently emphasizing photography, graphic and industrial design, performing arts, fine arts and crafts, et al." **Publishes 12-18 titles/year. Pays advance.** Responds in 4-6 weeks. Book catalog and ms guidelines free.

NONFICTION Subjects include photography, film, television, graphic design, performing arts, as well as business and legal guides for the public. "We are currently accepting query letters for practical, legal, and technique books targeted to professionals in the arts, including designers, graphic and fine artists, craftspeople, photographers, and those involved in film and the performing arts." Query with 1-2 page synopsis, chapter outline, market analysis, sample chapter, bio, SASE.

TIPS "We are helping creative people in the arts by giving them practical advice about business and success."

ALPINE PUBLICATIONS

38262 Linman Rd., Crawford CO 81415. (970)921-5005. **Fax:** (970)921-5081. **E-mail:** editorialdept@alpinepub.com. **Website:** alpinepub.com. Estab. 1975. Publishes hardcover and trade paperback originals and reprints. **Publishes 6-10 titles/year. 40% of books from first-time authors. 95% from unagented writers. Pays 8-15% royalty on wholesale price. Pays advance.** Publishes ms 18 months after acceptance. Accepts simultaneous submissions. Responds in 1 month. Book catalog available free. Guidelines online.

NONFICTION Subjects include animals. Alpine specializes in books that promote the enjoyment of and responsibility for companion animals with emphasis on dogs and horses. No biographies. Query with a brief synopsis, chapter outline, bio, 1-3 sample chapters, and market analysis.

TIPS "Our audience is pet owners, breeders, exhibitors, veterinarians, animal trainers, animal care specialists, and judges. Our books are in-depth and most are heavily illustrated. Look up some of our titles before you submit. See what is unique about our books. Write your proposal to suit our guidelines."

AMACOM BOOKS

American Management Association, 1601 Broadway, New York NY 10019. (212)586-8100. **Fax:** (212)903-8083. **E-mail:** ekadin@amanet.org; spower@amanet.org; astuart@amanet.org. **Website:** www.amacombooks.org. **Contact:** Ellen Kadin, executive editor (marketing, career, personal development); Stephen Power, senior editor (leadership, management, human resources, training); Airié Stuart, senior editor (sales, customer service, project management, finance); all editors (parenting, popular psychology, health & fitness). Book proposals on general business, education, science & technology, popular psychology, parenting, or health & fitness topics may be submitted to any editor.. Estab. 1923. Publishes trade hardcover and paperback originals and e-books. AMACOM Books—the publishing arm of the American Management Association (AMA)—is a nonfiction publisher devoted to helping readers lead more satisfying lives by publishing works that enhance their personal and professional growth and success. "Our authors—practitioners, journalists, and world-class educators—are noted experts and leaders in their fields. At AMACOM we can give authors the individual attention of a small publisher as well as the advantage of distributing and selling their books in both print and digital form through multiple channels around the world. Our high standards for both editing and packaging mean authors will have book of which they can be proud. We partner with our authors on creating the most effective marketing copy for their books. AMACOM's publicity department generates thousands of reviews, articles, excerpts, and other media placements for our books each year—in addition to promoting our books through our blog, e-newsletter, and social media outreach. Of course our books are showcased at international book fairs. Through such meetings millions of copies of our authors' books have been translated into 40 languages. We make our authors' books available through myriad electronic databases and partnerships with aggregators of content sold throughout the world. And our authors of business and personal development books have the unique opportunity to have their books selected for promotion directly to AMA's audiences—through AMA's website, podcasts, webcasts, blog, social media, e-newsletters, conferences, seminar catalogs and offerings, in AMA's own bookstores, and other means. At AMACOM we believe in what we publish—especially because we work toward publishing books that can make a positive difference in people's lives. (And unlike some publishers, we do not require that authors purchase copies of their books in bulk as a condition of publishing.) AMACOMers enjoy working with each other, and with our authors. Our authors feel the personal attention and camaraderie that publishing with AMACOM affords. This, and all the reasons above, may be why so many of our authors have chosen to publish with us multiple times." **Publishes 40-50 titles/year. Between 500 and 1000 Pays advance.** Depends on the circumstances. Usually 7 months to bound books. Accepts simultaneous submissions. Guidelines online.

NONFICTION Subjects include business, career guidance, child guidance, communications, economics, education, finance, government, nutrition, science, personal development; career. Publishes nonfiction books for consumer and professional markets, including all business topics, parenting, health & fitness, and popular psychology. Submit proposals including brief book description and rationale, TOC, author bio and platform, intended audience, competing books and sample chapters. Proposals returned with SASE only.

TIPS "Platform reflects author activities that demonstrate author's visibility, authority, and audience reach."

AMBERJACK PUBLISHING

P.O. Box 4668 #89611, New York NY 10163. (888)959-3352. **Website:** www.amberjackpublishing.com. Amberjack Publishing offers authors the freedom to write without burdening them with having to promote the work themselves. They retain all rights. "You will have no rights left to exploit, so you cannot resell, republish or use your story again." Accepts simultaneous submissions.

FICTION Amberjack Publishing is always on the lookout for the next great story. "We are interested in fiction, children's books, graphic novels, science fiction, fantasy, humor, and everything in between." Submit via online query form with book proposal and first 10 pages of ms.

AMERICAN CATHOLIC PRESS

16565 S. State St., South Holland IL 60473. (312)331-5845. **Fax:** (708)331-5484. **E-mail:** acp@acpress.org. **Website:** www.acpress.org. **Contact:** Rev. Michael Gilligan, PhD, editorial director. Estab. 1967. Publishes hardcover originals and hardcover and paperback reprints. **Publishes 4 titles/year. Makes outright purchase of $25-100.** Guidelines online.

NONFICTION Subjects include education, religion, spirituality. "We publish books on the Roman Catholic liturgy—for the most part, books on religious music and educational books and pamphlets. We also publish religious songs for church use, including Psalms, as well as choral and instrumental arrangements. We are interested in new music, meant for use in church services. Books, or even pamphlets, on the Roman Catholic Mass are especially welcome. We have no interest in secular topics and are not interested in religious poetry of any kind."

TIPS "Most of our sales are by direct mail, although we do work through retail outlets."

AMERICAN CHEMICAL SOCIETY

Publications/Books Division, 1155 16th St. NW, Washington DC 20036. (202)452-2120. **Fax:** (202)513-8819. **E-mail:** b_hauserman@acs.org. **Website:** pubs.

acs.org/books/. **Contact:** Bob Hauserman, senior acquisitions editor. Estab. 1876. Publishes hardcover originals. American Chemical Society publishes symposium-based books for chemistry. **Publishes 35 titles/year. Pays royalty.** Accepts simultaneous submissions. Responds in 2 months to proposals. Book catalog available free. Guidelines online.

NONFICTION Subjects include science. Emphasis is on meeting-based books. Log in to submission site online.

AMERICAN CORRECTIONAL ASSOCIATION

206 N. Washington St., Suite 200, Alexandria VA 22314. (703)224-0194. **Fax:** (703)224-0172. **E-mail:** kellim@aca.org. **Website:** www.aca.org. **Contact:** Kelli McAfee. Estab. 1870. Publishes trade paperback originals. "American Correctional Association provides practical information on jails, prisons, boot camps, probation, parole, community corrections, juvenile facilities and rehabilitation programs, substance abuse programs, and other areas of corrections." **Publishes 18 titles/year. 90% of books from first-time authors. 100% from unagented writers.** Publishes ms 1 year after acceptance. Accepts simultaneous submissions. Responds in 4 months to queries. Book catalog available free. Guidelines online.

NONFICTION "We are looking for practical, how-to texts or training materials written for the corrections profession. We are especially interested in books on management, development of first-line supervisors, and security-threat group/management in prisons." No autobiographies or true-life accounts by current or former inmates or correctional officers, theses, or dissertations. No fiction or poetry. Query with SASE. Reviews artwork/photos.

TIPS "Authors are professionals in the field of corrections. Our audience is made up of corrections professionals and criminal justice students. No books by inmates or former inmates. This publisher advises out-of-town freelance editors, indexers, and proofreaders to refrain from requesting work from them."

AMERICAN COUNSELING ASSOCIATION

6101 Stevenson Ave., Suite 600, Alexandria VA 22304. (703)823-9800, x356. **Fax:** (703)823-4786. **E-mail:** cbaker@counseling.org. **Website:** www.counseling.org. **Contact:** Carolyn C. Baker, associate publisher. Estab. 1952. Publishes paperback originals. "The American Counseling Association is dedicated to promoting public confidence and trust in the counseling profession. We publish scholarly texts for graduate level students and mental health professionals. We do not publish books for the general public." **Publishes 8-10 titles/year. 1% of books from first-time authors. 90% from unagented writers.** Accepts simultaneous submissions. Responds in 1 month to queries. Guidelines available free.

NONFICTION Subjects include career guidance, education, gay, lesbian, multicultural, psychology, religion, social sciences, spirituality, womens issues, womens studies, LGBTQ mental health, school counseling, marriage, family, couples counseling. ACA does not publish self-help books or autobiographies. Query with SASE. Submit proposal package, outline, 2 sample chapters, vitae.

TIPS "Target your market. Your books will not be appropriate for everyone across all disciplines."

AMERICAN FEDERATION OF ASTROLOGERS

6535 S. Rural Rd., Tempe AZ 85283. (480)838-1751. **Fax:** (480)838-8293. **E-mail:** info@astrologers.com. **Website:** www.astrologers.com. Estab. 1938. Publishes trade paperback originals and reprints. American Federation of Astrologers publishes astrology books, calendars, charts, and related aids. **Publishes 10-15 titles/year. 10 queries received/year. 20 mss received/year. 50% of books from first-time authors. 100% from unagented writers. Pays 10% royalty.** Publishes book 10 months after acceptance of ms. Accepts simultaneous submissions. Responds in 6 months to mss. Book catalog available free. Guidelines online.

NONFICTION "Our market for beginner books, Sun-sign guides, and similar material is limited and we thus publish very few of these. The ideal word count for a book-length manuscript published by AFA is about 40,000 words, although we will consider manuscripts from 20,000 to 60,000 words." Submit complete ms.

TIPS "AFA welcomes articles for *Today's Astrologer*, our monthly journal for members, on any astrological subject. Most articles are 1,500-3,000 words, but we do accept shorter and longer articles. Follow the guidelines online for book manuscripts. You also can e-mail your article to info@astrologers.com, but any charts or illustrations must be submitted as attachments and not embedded in the body of the e-mail or in an attached document."

AMERICAN QUILTER'S SOCIETY

5801 Kentucky Dam Rd., Paducah KY 42003. (270)898-7903. **Fax:** (270)898-1173. **E-mail:** editor@ aqsquilt.com. **Website:** www.americanquilter.com. **Contact:** Elaine Brelsford, executive book editor (primarily how-to and patterns, but other quilting books sometimes published, including quilt-related fiction). Estab. 1984. Publishes trade paperbacks. "American Quilter's Society publishes how-to and pattern books for quilters (beginners through intermediate skill level). We are not the publisher for non-quilters writing about quilts. We now publish quilt-related craft cozy romance and mystery titles, series only. Humor is good. Graphic depictions and curse words are bad." **Publishes 20-24 titles/year. 100 queries received/ year. 60% of books from first-time authors. Pays 5% royalty on retail price for both nonfiction and fiction.** Publishes nonfiction ms 9-18 months after acceptance. Fiction published on a different schedule TBD. Responds in 2 months to proposals. Guidelines online.

○ Accepts simultaneous nonfiction submissions. Does not accept simultaneous fiction submissions.

NONFICTION No queries; proposals only. Note: 1 or 2 completed quilt projects must accompany proposal.

FICTION Submit a synopsis and 2 sample chapters, plus an outline of the next 2 books in the series.

AMERICAN WATER WORKS ASSOCIATION

6666 W. Quincy Ave., Denver CO 80235. (303)347-6260. **Fax:** (303)794-7310. **E-mail:** submissions@ awwa.org. **Website:** www.awwa.org. **Contact:** David Plank, manager, business and product development. Estab. 1881. Publishes hardcover and trade paperback originals. "AWWA strives to advance and promote the safety and knowledge of drinking water and related issues to all audiences—from kindergarten through post-doctorate." **Publishes 25 titles/year.** Responds in 4 months to queries. Book catalog and ms guidelines free.

NONFICTION Subjects include science, software, drinking water- and wastewater-related topics, operations, treatment, sustainability. Query with SASE. Submit outline, bio, 3 sample chapters. Reviews artwork/photos. Send photocopies.

TIPS "See website to download submission instructions."

AMG PUBLISHERS

AMG International, Inc., 6815 Shallowford Rd., Chattanooga TN 37421-1755. (423)894-6060. **Fax:** (423)894-9511. **E-mail:** ricks@amgpublishers.com. **Website:** www.amgpublishers.com. **Contact:** Rick Steele, Product Development/Acquisitions. Estab. 1985. Publishes hardcover and trade paperback originals, electronic originals, and audio Bible and book originals. Publishing division of AMG International began in 1985 with release of the *Hebrew-Greek Key Word Study Bible* in the King James Version. This groundbreaking study Bible is now published in four other Bible translations. In-depth study and examination of original biblical languages provide some of our core Bible study and reference tools. In 1998, AMG launched the successful Following God Bible study series (primarily for women) that examine key characters of the Bible along with life application principles. AMG has also been publishing young adult inspirational fantasy fiction since 2005 but is not currently accepting fiction mss. "Profits from sales of our books and Bibles are funneled back into world missions and childcare efforts of parent organization, AMG Publishers." **Publishes 15-20 titles/year. 2,500 queries; 500 mss received/year. 25% of books from first-time authors. 35% from unagented writers. Pays 10-16% royalty on net sales. Advance negotiable.** Publishes book 12-18 months after acceptance of ms. Accepts simultaneous submissions. Responds in 1 month to queries, 4 months to proposals/mss. Book catalog and guidelines online.

IMPRINTS Living Ink Books; God and Country Press; AMG Bible Studies.

NONFICTION Subjects include Americana, education, history, military, parenting, religion, spirituality, war, womens issues, young adult. Bibles, trade nonfiction books, and workbook Bible studies Does not want self-help, memoir, autobiography, biography, New Age, prosperity gospel. Query with letter first, e-mail preferred.

FICTION Subjects include fantasy, young adult. "We are not presently acquiring fiction of any genre, though we continue to publish a number of titles in the young adult inspirational fantasy category."

TIPS "AMG is open to well-written, niche Bible study, reference, and devotional books that meet immediate needs."

AMHERST MEDIA, INC.

175 Rano St., Suite 200, Buffalo NY 14207. (716)874-4450. **Fax:** (716)874-4508. **E-mail:** submissions@amherstmedia.com. **Website:** www.amherstmedia.com. **Contact:** Craig Alesse, publisher. Estab. 1974. Publishes trade paperback originals and reprints. Amherst Media publishes how-to photography books. **Publishes 30 titles/year. 60% of books from first-time authors. 90% from unagented writers. Pays 8-12% royalty. Pays advance.** Publishes book 1 year after acceptance. Accepts simultaneous submissions. Responds in 2 months to queries. Book catalog online. Guidelines online.

NONFICTION Subjects include photography. Looking for well-written and illustrated photo books. 100 high quality photographs around a theme Reviews artwork/photos.

TIPS "Our audience is made up of beginning to advanced photographers. If I were a writer trying to market a book today, I would fill the need of a specific audience and self-edit in a tight manner."

AMULET BOOKS

Imprint of Abrams, 115 W. 18th St., 6th Floor, New York NY 10001. **Website:** www.amuletbooks.com. Estab. 2004. **10% of books from first-time authors.** Accepts simultaneous submissions.

 Does not accept unsolicited mss or queries.

FICTION Middle readers: adventure, contemporary, fantasy, history, science fiction, sports. Young adults/teens: adventure, contemporary, fantasy, history, science fiction, sports, suspense.

ANDERSEN PRESS

20 Vauxhall Bridge Rd., London SW1V 2SA, United Kingdom. **E-mail:** anderseneditorial@randomhouse.co.uk. **Website:** www.andersenpress.co.uk. Andersen Press is a specialist children's publisher. "We publish picture books, for which the required text would be approximately 500 words (maximum 1,000), juvenile fiction for which the text would be approximately 3,000-5,000 words and older fiction up to 75,000 words. We do not publish adult fiction, nonfiction, poetry, or short story anthologies." Accepts simultaneous submissions. Guidelines online.

FICTION Send all submissions by post: Query and full ms for picture books; synopsis and 3 chapters for longer fiction.

ANDREWS MCMEEL UNIVERSAL

1130 Walnut St., Kansas City MO 64106. (816)581-7500. **Website:** www.andrewsmcmeel.com. **Contact:** Christine Schillig, vice president/editorial director. Estab. 1973. Publishes hardcover and paperback originals. Andrews McMeel publishes general trade books, humor books, miniature gift books, calendars, and stationery products. **Publishes 300 titles/year. Pays royalty on retail price or net receipts. Pays advance.** Accepts simultaneous submissions. Guidelines online.

NONFICTION Subjects include cooking, games, comics, puzzles. Submit proposal.

ANHINGA PRESS

P.O. Box 3665, Tallahassee FL 32315. Phone/**Fax:** (850)577-0745. **E-mail:** info@anhinga.org. **Website:** www.anhinga.org. **Contact:** Kristine Snodgrass, co-director. Publishes hardcover and trade paperback originals. Publishes only full-length collections of poetry (60-80 pages). No individual poems or chapbooks. **Publishes 5 titles/year. Pays 10% royalty on retail price.** Accepts simultaneous submissions. Responds in 3 months. Guidelines online.

POETRY Not accepting any unsolicited submissions at this time. Enter Robert Dana-Anhinga Prize for Poetry.

ANKERWYCKE

American Bar Association, 321 N. Clark St., Chicago IL 60654. **Website:** www.ababooks.org. **Contact:** Tim Brandhorst, director of new product development. Estab. 1878. Publishes hardcover and trade paperback originals. "In 1215, the Magna Carta was signed underneath the ancient Ankerwycke Yew tree, starting the process which led to rule by constitutional law—in effect, giving rights and the law to the people. And today, the ABA's Ankerwycke line of books continues to bring the law to the people. With legal fiction, true crime books, popular legal histories, public policy handbooks, and prescriptive guides to current legal and business issues, Ankerwycke is a contemporary and innovative line of books for everyone from a trusted and vested authority." **Publishes 30-40 titles/year. 1,000's of queries received/year. 25% of books from first-time authors. 50% from unagented writers.** Publishes ms 12-18 months after acceptance. Accepts simultaneous submissions. Responds in 1 month to queries and proposals; 3 months to mss. Book catalog and ms guidelines online.

NONFICTION Subjects include business, consumer legal. "Extremely high quality nonfiction with a legal aspect; business books specifically for service professionals; consumer legal on a wide range of topics—we're actively acquiring in all these areas." Query with cover letter; outline or TOC; and CV/bio including other credits. Include e-mail address for response.

FICTION "We're actively acquiring legal fiction with extreme verisimilitude." Query with cover letter; outline or TOC; and CV/bio including other credits. Include e-mail address for response.

✪⊘ ANNICK PRESS, LTD.

15 Patricia Ave., Toronto ON M2M 1H9, Canada. (416)221-4802. **Fax:** (416)221-8400. **Website:** www. annickpress.com. **Contact:** The Editors. Publishes picture books, juvenile and YA fiction and nonfiction; specializes in trade books. "Annick Press maintains a commitment to high quality books that entertain and challenge. Our publications share fantasy and stimulate imagination, while encouraging children to trust their judgment and abilities." *Does not accept unsolicited mss.* **Publishes 25 titles/year. 5,000 queries received/year. 3,000 mss received/year. 20% of books from first-time authors. 80-85% from unagented writers. Pays authors royalty of 5-12% based on retail price. Offers advances (average amount: $3,000). Pays illustrators royalty of 5% minimum.** Publishes a book 2 years after acceptance. Accepts simultaneous submissions. Book catalog and guidelines online.

NONFICTION Works with 20 illustrators/year. Illustrations only: Query with samples.

FICTION Publisher of children's books. Not accepting picture books at this time.

✪ ANVIL PRESS

P.O. Box 3008 MPO, Vancouver BC V6B 3X5, Canada. (604)876-8710. **Fax:** (604)879-2667. **E-mail:** info@ anvilpress.com. **Website:** www.anvilpress.com. Estab. 1988. Publishes trade paperback originals. "Anvil Press publishes contemporary adult fiction, poetry, and drama, giving voice to up-and-coming Canadian writers, exploring all literary genres, discovering, nurturing, and promoting new Canadian literary talent. Currently emphasizing urban/suburban themed fiction and poetry; de-emphasizing historical novels." Canadian authors only. No e-mail submissions. **Publishes 8-10 titles/year. 300 queries received/year. 80% of books from first-time authors. 70% from un-**agented writers. Pays advance. Average advance is $500-2,000, depending on the genre.** Publishes book 8 months after acceptance of ms. Accepts simultaneous submissions. Responds in 2 months to queries; 6 months to mss. Book catalog for 9×12 SAE with 2 first-class stamps. Guidelines online.

NONFICTION Query with 20-30 pages and SASE.

FICTION Subjects include experimental, literary, short story collections. Contemporary, modern literature; no formulaic or genre. Query with 20-30 pages and SASE.

POETRY "Get our catalog, look at our poetry. We do very little poetry-maybe 1-2 titles per year." Query with 8-12 poems and SASE.

TIPS "Audience is informed, educated, aware, with an opinion, culturally active (films, books, the performing arts). No U.S. authors. Research the appropriate publisher for your work."

APA BOOKS

American Psychological Association, 750 First St., NE, Washington DC 20002. (202)336- 5792. **Website:** www.apa.org/pubs/books/index.aspx. Publishes hardcover and trade paperback originals. Accepts simultaneous submissions. Book catalog online. Guidelines online.

IMPRINTS Magination Press (children's books).

NONFICTION Subjects include education, multicultural, psychology, science, social sciences, sociology. Submit cv and prospectus with TOC, intended audience, selling points, and outside competition.

TIPS "Our press features scholarly books on empirically supported topics for professionals and students in all areas of psychology."

APPALACHIAN MOUNTAIN CLUB BOOKS

5 Joy St., Boston MA 02108. (617)523-0636. **Fax:** (617)523-0722. **E-mail:** amcbooks@outdoors.org. **E-mail:** amcbooks@outdoors.org. **Website:** www.outdoors.org. Estab. 1876. Publishes hardcover, trade paperback, and digital originals. AMC Books are written and published by the experts in the Northeast outdoors. "Our mission is to publish authoritative, accurate, and easy-to-use books and maps based on AMC's expertise in outdoor recreation, education, and conservation. We are committed to producing books and maps that appeal to novices and day visitors as well as outdoor enthusiasts in our core activity areas of hiking and paddling. By advancing the

interest of the public in outdoor recreation and helping our readers to access back country trails and waterways, and by using our books to educate the public about safety, conservation, and stewardship, we support AMC's mission of promoting the protection, enjoyment, and wise use of the Northeast outdoors. We work with the best professional writers possible and draw upon the experience of our programs staff and chapter leaders from Maine to Washington, DC." **Publishes 8-12 titles/year. 1% of books from first-time authors. 98% from unagented writers. Pays advance.** Publishes ms 1-2 years after acceptance. Responds in 4 weeks. Catalog online. Guidelines online.

NONFICTION Subjects include creative nonfiction, environment, nature, recreation, regional, Maps that are based on our direct work with land managers and our on-the-ground collection of data on trails, natural features, and points of interest.. Appalachian Mountain Club publishes hiking, paddling, nature, conservation, and mountain-subject guides for America's Northeast. "We also publish narrative titles related to outdoor recreation, mountaineering, and adventure, often with a historical perspective, and always with a deep connection to our region (from Maine to Washington, D.C.). We connect recreation to conservation and education." Please no Appalachian Trail memoirs. Send a query letter and the first three chapters of your ms to the publications department via e-mail. Your query letter should explain the subject of your book and why it would be appropriate for AMC Books to publish. Include information about word count (our guidebooks are typically between 80,000 and 100,000 words) and any special art or graphic treatment that you envision. Tell us how the book would be distinctive by comparing it to similar titles that are already on the market. Also explain the intended audience for your book and why you think your book would generate interest. Present some ideas of how you would help us market the book and reach readers. Conclude with a summary of your relevant experience and credentials, including previously published writing on related topics. Allow us four weeks to respond to your query.

TIPS "Our audience is outdoor recreationists, conservation-minded hikers and canoeists, family outdoor lovers, armchair enthusiasts. Visit our website for proposal submission guidelines and more information. Please no fiction, children's books, or poetry."

ARBORDALE PUBLISHING

612 Johnnie Dodds, Suite A2, Mt. Pleasant SC 29464. (843)971-6722. **Fax:** (843)216-3804. **E-mail:** katie@arbordalepublishing.com. **E-mail:** katie@arbordalepublishing.com. **Website:** www.arbordalepublishing.com. **Contact:** Katie Hall. Estab. 2004. Publishes hardcover, trade paperback, and electronic originals. "The picture books we publish are usually, but not always, fictional stories with nonfiction woven into the story that relate to science or math. All books should subtly convey an educational theme through a warm story that is fun to read and that will grab a child's attention. Each book has a 4-page *'For Creative Minds'* section to reinforce the educational component. This section will have a craft and/or game as well as 'fun facts' to be shared by the parent, teacher, or other adult. Authors do not need to supply this information with their submission, but if their ms is accepted, they may be asked to provide additional information for this section. Mss should be less than 1,000 words and meet all of the following 4 criteria: Fun to read—mostly fiction with nonfiction facts woven into the story; National or regional in scope; Must tie into early elementary school curriculum; must be marketable through a niche market such as a zoo, aquarium, or museum gift shop." **Publishes 14 titles/year. 1,000 mss received/year. 50% of books from first-time authors. 100% from unagented writers. Pays 6-8% royalty on wholesale price. Pays small advance.** Publishes book 18 months after acceptance. May hold onto mss of interest for 1 year until acceptance. Accepts simultaneous submissions. Accepts electronic submissions only. Snail mail submissions are discarded without being opened.

Acknowledges receipt of ms submission within 1 month. Book catalog and guidelines online. "All manuscripts should be submitted via e-mail to Katie Hall. Manuscripts should be less than 1,000 words.".

NONFICTION Reviews artwork/photos. Send 1-2 JPEGS.

FICTION Subjects include picture books. Picture books: animal, folktales, nature/environment, math-related. Word length—picture books: no more than 1,500.

POETRY "We do not accept books of poetry." Will consider mss written in rhyming verse, but prefer prose.

TIPS "Please make sure that you have looked at our website to read our complete submission guidelines and to see if we are looking for a particular subject. Manuscripts must meet all four of our stated criteria. We look for fairly realistic, bright and colorful art-no cartoons. We want the children excited about the books. We envision the books being used at home and in the classroom."

ARCADE PUBLISHING

Skyhorse Publishing, 307 W. 36th St., 11th Floor, New York NY 10018. (212)643-6816. **Fax:** (212)643-6819. **E-mail:** arcadesubmissions@skyhorsepublishing.com. **Website:** www.arcadepub.com. **Contact:** Acquisitions Editor. Estab. 1988. Publishes hardcover originals, trade paperback reprints. "Arcade prides itself on publishing top-notch literary nonfiction and fiction, with a significant proportion of foreign writers." **Publishes 35 titles/year. 5% of books from first-time authors. Pays royalty on retail price and 10 author's copies. Pays advance.** Publishes book 18 months after acceptance. Accepts simultaneous submissions. Responds in 2 months if interested. Book catalog and ms guidelines for #10 SASE.

NONFICTION Subjects include history, memoirs, travel, popular science, current events. Submit proposal with brief query, 1-2 page synopsis, chapter outline, market analysis, sample chapter, bio.

FICTION Subjects include literary, short story collections, translation. No romance, historical, science fiction. Submit proposal with brief query, 1-2 page synopsis, chapter outline, market analysis, sample chapter, bio.

ARCADIA PUBLISHING

420 Wando Park Blvd., Mt. Pleasant SC 29464. (843)853-2070. **Fax:** (843)853-0044. **Website:** www.arcadiapublishing.com. Estab. 1993. Publishes trade paperback originals. "Arcadia publishes photographic vintage regional histories. We have more than 3,000 Images of America series in print. We have expanded our California program." **Publishes 600 titles/year. Pays 8% royalty on retail price.** Publishes book 9 months after acceptance. Accepts simultaneous submissions. Book catalog online. Guidelines available free.

NONFICTION Subjects include history. "Arcadia accepts submissions year-round. Our editors seek proposals on local history topics and are able to provide authors with detailed information about our publishing program as well as book proposal submission guidelines. Due to the great demand for titles on local and regional history, we are currently searching for authors to work with us on new photographic history projects. Please contact one of our regional publishing teams if you are interested in submitting a proposal." Specific proposal form to be completed.

TIPS "Writers should know that we only publish history titles. The majority of our books are on a city or region, and contain vintage images with limited text."

ARCHAIA

Imprint of Boom! Studios, 5670 Wilshire Blvd., Suite 450, Los Angeles CA 90036. **Website:** www.archaia.com. **Contact:** Mark Smylie, chief creative officer. Use online submission form. Accepts simultaneous submissions.

FICTION Subjects include adventure, fantasy, horror, mystery, science fiction. Looking for graphic novel submissions that include finished art. "Archaia is a multi-award-winning graphic novel publisher with more than 75 renowned publishing brands, including such domestic and international hits as *Artesia, Mouse Guard*, and a line of Jim Henson graphic novels including *Fraggle Rock* and *The Dark Crystal*. Publishes creator-shared comic books and graphic novels in the adventure, fantasy, horror, pulp noir, and science fiction genres that contain idiosyncratic and atypical writing and art. *Archaia does not generally hire freelancers or arrange for freelance work, so submissions should only be for completed book and series proposals.*"

ARCH STREET PRESS

1122 County Line Rd., Bryn Mawr PA 19010. (877)732-ARCH. **E-mail:** contact@archstreetpress.org. **Website:** www.archstreetpress.org. **Contact:** Robert Rimm, managing editor. Estab. 2010. Publishes hardcover, trade paperback, mass market paperback, and electronic originals. Arch Street Press is an independent nonprofit publisher dedicated to the collaborative work of creative visionaries, social entrepreneurs and leading scholars worldwide. Arch Street Press is part of the Institute for Leadership Education, Advancement and Development, a Pennsylvania-based 501(c)(3) nonprofit with offices in Philadelphia and Bryn Mawr. It has served as a key force for community leadership development since 1995, fostering a degreed citizenry to tangibly improve and sustain the economic, civic and social well-being of communities throughout the United States. Please visit our website, www.archstreetpress.org, for further information, including our Innovate podcast series with international CEOs and leaders, current and upcoming books, wide-ranging blog et al. **Publishes 4 titles/ year. 100 queries; 5 mss received/year. 30% of books from first-time authors. 50% from unagented writers. Pays 6-20% royalty on retail price.** Publishes ms 1 year after acceptance. Accepts simultaneous submissions. Responds in 1-2 months. Book catalog and guidelines online.

NONFICTION Subjects include art, business, communications, community, contemporary culture, creative nonfiction, economics, education, environment, finance, government, health, history, humanities, labor, language, law, literary criticism, literature, memoirs, multicultural, music, nature, philosophy, social sciences, sociology, spirituality, translation, womens studies, world affairs, leadership. Query with SASE. Submit proposal package including outline and 3 sample chapters. Review artwork. Writers should send photocopies.

FICTION Subjects include literary. Query with SASE. Submit proposal package, including outline and 3 sample chapters.

ARC PUBLICATIONS

Nanholme Mill, Shaw Wood Rd., Todmorden, Lancashire OL14 6DA, United Kingdom. **E-mail:** info@ arcpublications.co.uk. **E-mail:** international-editor@ arcpublications.co.uk. **Website:** www.arcpublications. co.uk. **Contact:** John W. Clarke, domestic editor; James Byrne, international editor (outside Ireland/ England). Estab. 1969. Accepts simultaneous submissions. Responds in 6 weeks.

POETRY Publishes "contemporary poetry from new and established writers from the UK and abroad, specializing in the work of world poets writing in English, and the work of overseas poets in translation." Send 16-24 pages of poetry and short cover letter.

A-R EDITIONS, INC.

1600 Aspen Commons, Suite 100, Middleton WI 53562. (608)836-9000. **E-mail:** info@areditions. com. **Website:** www.areditions.com. Estab. 1962. "A-R Editions publishes modern critical editions of music based on current musicological research. Each edition is devoted to works by a single composer or to a single genre of composition. The contents are chosen for their potential interest to scholars and performers, then prepared for publication according

to the standards that govern the making of all reliable, historical editions." **Publishes 30 titles/year. 40 queries; 30 mss received/year. 75% of books from first-time authors. 100% from unagented writers. Pays royalty or honoraria.** Book catalog online. Guidelines online.

NONFICTION Subjects include historical music editions; computer music and digital audio topics. Computer Music and Digital Audio Series titles deal with issues tied to digital and electronic media, and include both textbooks and handbooks in this area.

ARROW PUBLICATIONS, LLC

20411 Sawgrass Dr., Montgomery Village MD 20886. (301)299-9422. **Fax:** (240)632-8477. **E-mail:** arrow_ info@arrowpub.com. **Website:** www.arrowpub. com. **Contact:** Tom King, managing editor; Maryan Gibson, acquisition editor. Estab. 1987. **Publishes 50 e-book titles. Paperback version launched in 2009 with 12 English and 12 Spanish titles/year. 150 queries received/year. 100 mss received/year. 80% of books from first-time authors. 100% from unagented writers. Makes outright purchase of accepted completed scripts.** Publishes book 4-6 months after acceptance of ms. Responds in 2 month to queries; 1 month to mss sent upon request. Guidelines online.

No graphic novels until further notice.

FICTION "We are looking for outlines of stories heavy on romance with elements of adventure/intrigue/mystery. We will consider other romance genres such as fantasy, western, inspirational, and historical as long as the romance element is strong." Query with outline first with SASE. Consult submission guidelines online before submitting.

TIPS "Our audience is primarily women 18 and older. Send query with outline only."

ARSENAL PULP PRESS

#202-211 East Georgia St., Vancouver BC V6A 1Z6, Canada. (604)687-4233. **Fax:** (604)687-4283. **E-mail:** info@arsenalpulp.com. **Website:** www.arsenalpulp. com. **Contact:** Editorial Board. Estab. 1980. Publishes trade paperback originals, and trade paperback reprints. "We are interested in literature that traverses uncharted territories, publishing books that challenge and stimulate and ask probing questions about the world around us." **Publishes 14-20 titles/year. 500 queries received/year. 300 mss received/year. 30% of books from first-time authors. 100% from**

unagented writers. Publishes ms 1 year after acceptance. Accepts simultaneous submissions. Responds in 2-4 months. Book catalog for 9×12 SAE with IRCs or online. Guidelines online.

NONFICTION Subjects include creative nonfiction, ethnic, history, multicultural, sex, sociology, travel, film, visual art. Rarely publishes non-Canadian authors. No poetry at this time. "We do not publish children's books." Each submission must include: "a synopsis of the work, a chapter by chapter outline for nonfiction, writing credentials, a 50-page excerpt from the ms (*do not send more, it will be a waste of postage; if we like what we see, we'll ask for the rest of the manuscript*), and a marketing analysis. If our editorial board is interested, you will be asked to send the entire ms. We do not accept discs or submissions by fax or e-mail, and we do not discuss concepts over the phone." Reviews artwork/photos.

FICTION Subjects include ethnic, feminist, literary, multicultural, short story collections. No children's books or genre fiction, i.e., westerns, romance, horror, mystery, etc. Submit proposal package, outline, clips, 2-3 sample chapters.

ARTE PUBLICO PRESS

University of Houston, 4902 Gulf Fwy, Bldg 19, Rm 100, Houston TX 77204-2004. **Fax:** (713)743-2847. **E-mail:** submapp@uh.edu. **Website:** artepublicopress. com. **Contact:** Nicolas Kanellos, editor. Estab. 1979. Publishes hardcover originals, trade paperback originals and reprints. Arte Publico Press is the oldest and largest publisher of Hispanic literature for children and adults in the United States. "We are a showcase for Hispanic literary creativity, arts and culture. Our endeavor is to provide a national forum for U.S.-Hispanic literature." **Publishes 25-30 titles/year. 1,000 queries received/year. 2,000 mss received/year. 50% of books from first-time authors. 80% from unagented writers. Pays 10% royalty on wholesale price. Provides 20 author's copies; 40% discount on subsequent copies. Pays $1,000-3,000 advance.** Publishes book 2 years after acceptance of ms. Accepts simultaneous submissions. Responds in 1 month to queries and proposals; 4 months to mss. Book catalog available free. Guidelines online.

NONFICTION Subjects include ethnic, regional, translation. Hispanic civil rights issues for new series: The Hispanic Civil Rights Series. Submissions made through online submission form.

FICTION Subjects include contemporary, ethnic, literary, mainstream. "Written by U.S.-Hispanics." Submissions made through online submission form.

POETRY Submissions made through online submission form.

TIPS "Include cover letter in which you 'sell' your book—why should we publish the book, who will want to read it, why does it matter, etc. Use our ms submission online form. Format files accepted are: Word, plain/text, rich/text files. Other formats will not be accepted. Manuscript files cannot be larger than 5MB. Once editors review your ms, you will receive an e-mail with the decision. Revision process could take up to 4 months."

ASA, AVIATION SUPPLIES & ACADEMICS

7005 132 Place SE, Newcastle WA 98059. (425)235-1500. **E-mail:** feedback@asa2fly.com. **Website:** www. asa2fly.com. "ASA is an industry leader in the development and sales of aviation supplies, publications, and software for pilots, flight instructors, flight engineers and aviation technicians. All ASA products are developed by a team of researchers, authors and editors." Book catalog available free.

NONFICTION Subjects include education. "We are primarily an aviation publisher. Educational books in this area are our specialty; other aviation books will be considered." All subjects must be related to aviation education and training. Query with outline. Send photocopies or MS Word files.

TIPS "Two of our specialty series include ASA's *Focus Series*, and ASA *Aviator's Library*. Books in our *Focus Series* concentrate on single-subject areas of aviation knowledge, curriculum and practice. The *Aviator's Library* is comprised of titles of known and/or classic aviation authors or established instructor/authors in the industry, and other aviation specialty titles."

ASCE PRESS

American Society of Civil Engineers, 1801 Alexander Bell Dr., Reston VA 20191. (703)295-6275. **E-mail:** ascepress@asce.org. **Website:** www.asce.org/bookstore. Estab. 1989. "ASCE Press publishes technical volumes that are useful to practicing civil engineers and civil engineering students, as well as allied professionals. We publish books by individual authors and editors to advance the civil engineering profession. Currently emphasizing geotechnical, structural engineering, sustainable engineering and engineering history. De-emphasizing highly specialized areas with narrow scope." **Publishes 10-15 titles/year. 20% of books from first-time authors. 100% from unagented writers.** Guidelines online.

NONFICTION Subjects include civil engineering. "We are looking for topics that are useful and instructive to the engineering practitioner." Query with proposal, sample chapters, CV, TOC, and target audience.

TIPS "As a traditional publisher of scientific and technical materials, ASCE Press applies rigorous standards to the expertise, scholarship, readability and attractiveness of its books."

ASHLAND POETRY PRESS

401 College Ave., Ashland OH 44805. (419)289-5098. **E-mail:** app@ashland.edu. **Website:** www.ashlandpoetrypress.com. **Contact:** Cassandra Brown, managing editor. Estab. 1969. Publishes trade paperback originals. **Publishes 2-3 titles/year. 400 mss received/ year in Snyder Prize. 50% of books from first-time authors. 100% from unagented writers. Makes outright purchase of $500-1,000.** Publishes book 10 months after acceptance. Accepts simultaneous submissions. Responds in 1 month to queries; 6 months to mss. Book catalog online. Guidelines online.

POETRY "We accept unsolicited manuscripts through the Snyder Prize competition each spring-the deadline is April 1. Judges are mindful of dedication to craftsmanship and thematic integrity."

TIPS "We rarely publish a title submitted off the transom outside of our Snyder Prize competition."

ASM PRESS

Book division for the American Society for Microbiology, 1752 N St., NW, Washington DC 20036. (202)737-3600. **Fax:** (202)942-9342. **E-mail:** books@ asmusa.org. **Website:** www.asmscience.org. **Contact:** Lindsay Williams, editorial and rights coordinator. Estab. 1899. Publishes hardcover, trade paperback and electronic originals. **Publishes 30 titles/year. 40% of books from first-time authors. 95% from unagented writers. Pays 5-15% royalty on wholesale price. Pays $1,000-10,000 advance.** Publishes book 6-9 months after acceptance. Accepts simultaneous submissions. Responds in 2 months. Book catalog online. Guidelines online.

NONFICTION Subjects include agriculture, animals, education, history, horticulture, science, microbiology and related sciences. "Must have bona fide

academic credentials in which they are writing." Query with SASE or by e-mail. Submit proposal package, outline, prospectus. Reviews artwork/photos. Send photocopies.

TIPS "Credentials are most important."

ASSOCIATION FOR SUPERVISION AND CURRICULUM DEVELOPMENT

1703 N. Beauregard St., Alexandria VA 22311-1714. (703)578-9600. **Fax:** (703)575-5400. **E-mail:** acquisitions@ascd.org. **Website:** www.ascd.org. **Contact:** Genny Ostertag, acquisitions editor; Allison Scott, acquisitions editor. Estab. 1943. Publishes trade paperback originals. ASCD publishes high-quality professional books for educators. **Publishes 24-30 titles/ year. 100 queries received/year. 100 mss received/ year. 50% of books from first-time authors. 95% from unagented writers. Pays negotiable royalty on actual monies received.** Publishes ms 1 year after acceptance. Accepts simultaneous submissions. Responds in 2-3 months to proposals. Book catalog and ms guidelines online.

NONFICTION Subjects include education. Submit full proposal, 2 sample chapters. Reviews artwork/ photos. Send photocopies.

ASTRAGAL PRESS

Finney Company, 5995 149th St. W., Suite 105, Apple Valley MN 55124. (866)543-3045. **E-mail:** info@finneyco.com. **Website:** www.astragalpress.com. Estab. 1983. Publishes trade paperback originals and reprints. "Our primary audience includes those interested in antique tool collecting, metalworking, carriage building, early sciences and early trades, and railroading." Accepts simultaneous submissions. Responds in 3 months. Book catalog and ms guidelines free.

NONFICTION Wants books on early tools, trades and technology, and railroads. Query with sample chapters, TOC, book overview, illustration descriptions.

TIPS "We sell to niche markets. We are happy to work with knowledgeable amateur authors in developing titles."

🅐∅ ATHENEUM BOOKS FOR YOUNG READERS

Simon & Schuster, 1230 Avenue of the Americas, New York NY 10020. **Website:** kids.simonandschuster.com. Estab. 1961. Publishes hardcover originals. Accepts simultaneous submissions. Guidelines for #10 SASE.

NONFICTION Subjects include Americana, animals, history, photography, psychology, recreation, religion, science, sociology, sports, travel. Publishes hardcover originals, picture books for young kids, nonfiction for ages 8-12 and novels for middle-grade and young adults. 100% require freelance illustration. Agented submissions only.

FICTION Subjects include adventure, ethnic, experimental, fantasy, gothic, historical, horror, humor, mystery, science fiction, sports, suspense, western, Animal. All in juvenile versions. "We have few specific needs except for books that are fresh, interesting and well written. Fad topics are dangerous, as are works you haven't polished to the best of your ability. We also don't need safety pamphlets, ABC books, coloring books and board books. In writing picture book texts, avoid the coy and 'cutesy,' such as stories about characters with alliterative names." Agented submissions only. No paperback romance-type fiction.

TIPS "Study our titles."

A.T. PUBLISHING

23 Lily Lake Rd., Highland NY 12528. (845)691-2021. **E-mail:** tjp2@optonline.net. **Contact:** Anthony Prizzia, publisher (education). Estab. 2001. Publishes trade paperback originals. **Publishes 1-3 titles/year. 5-10 queries received/year. 100% of books from first-time authors. 100% from unagented writers. Pays 15-25% royalty on retail price. Makes outright purchase of $500-2,500. Pays $500-1,000 advance.** Accepts simultaneous submissions. Responds in 1 month to queries; 2 months to proposals; 4 months to mss.

NONFICTION Subjects include education, recreation, science, sports. Query with SASE. Submit complete ms. Reviews artwork/photos. Send photocopies.

TIPS "Audience is people interested in a variety of topics, general. Submit typed manuscript for consideration, including a SASE for return of ms."

AUTUMN HOUSE PRESS

87½ Westwood St., Pittsburgh PA 15211. (412)381-4261. **E-mail:** info@autumnhouse.org. **Website:** www.autumnhouse.org. **Contact:** Christine Stroud, Senior Editor. Alison Taverna, Managing Editor Estab. 1998. Publishes hardcover, trade paperback, and electronic originals. Format: acid-free paper; offset printing; perfect and casebound (cloth) bound; sometimes contains illustrations. Average print order: 1,000. Debut novel print order: 1,000. "We are a non-profit literary press specializing in high-quality poetry, fiction, and nonfiction. Our editions are beautifully designed and printed, and they are distributed nationally. Approximately one-third of our sales are to college literature and creative writing classes." Member CLMP and Academy of American Poets. "We distribute our own titles. We do extensive national promotion through ads, web-marketing, reading tours, book fairs and conferences. We are open to all genres. The quality of writing concerns us, not the genre." You can also learn about our annual Fiction Prize, Poetry Prize, Nonfiction Prize, and Chapbook Award competitions, as well as our online journal, *Coal Hill Review.* (Please note that Autumn House accepts unsolicited mss *only* through these competitions.) **Publishes 8 titles/year. Receives 1,000 mss/year. 10% of books from first-time authors. 100% from unagented writers. Pays 7% royalty on wholesale price. Pays $0-2,500 advance.** Publishes 9 months after acceptance. Accepts simultaneous submissions. Responds in 1-3 days on queries and proposals; 3 months on mss. Catalog online. Guidelines online.

NONFICTION Subjects include memoirs. Enter the nonfiction contest.

FICTION Subjects include literary. Holds competition/award for short stories, novels, story collections, memoirs, nonfiction. *We ask that all submissions from authors new to Autumn House come through one of our annual contests.* See website for official guidelines. Responds to queries in 2 days. Accepts mss only through contest. Never critiques/comments on rejected mss. "Submit only through our annual contest. The competition is tough, so submit only your best work!"

POETRY *"We ask that all submissions from authors new to Autumn House come through one of our annual contests."* All finalists will be considered for publication. Submit only through our annual contest. See guidelines online.

TIPS "The competition to publish with Autumn House is very tough. Submit only your best work."

AVALON TRAVEL PUBLISHING

Avalon Publishing Group, 1700 4th St., Berkeley CA 94710. (510)595-3664. **Fax:** (510)595-4228. **E-mail:** avalon.acquisitions@perseusbooks.com. **Website:** www.avalontravelbooks.com. Estab. 1973. Publishes trade paperback originals. "Avalon travel guides feature practicality and spirit, offering a traveler-to-traveler perspective perfect for planning an afternoon

hike, around-the-world journey, or anything in between. ATP publishes 7 major series. Each one has a different emphasis and a different geographic coverage. We have expanded our coverage, with a focus on European and Asian destinations. Our main areas of interest are North America, Central America, South America, the Caribbean, and the Pacific. We are seeking only a few titles in each of our major series. Check online guidelines for our current needs. Follow guidelines closely." **Publishes 100 titles/year. 5,000 queries received/year. 25% of books from first-time authors. 95% from unagented writers. Pays up to $17,000 advance.** Publishes ms an average of 9 months after acceptance. Accepts simultaneous submissions. Responds in 4 months. Guidelines online.

NONFICTION Subjects include regional, travel. "We are not interested in fiction, children's books, and travelogues/travel diaries." Submit cover letter, resume, and up to 5 relevant clips.

AVON ROMANCE

Harper Collins Publishers, 10 E. 53 St., New York NY 10022. **E-mail:** info@avonromance.com. **Website:** www.avonromance.com. Estab. 1941. Publishes paperback and digital originals and reprints. "Avon has been publishing award-winning books since 1941. It is recognized for having pioneered the historical romance category and continues to bring the best of commercial literature to the broadest possible audience." **Publishes 400 titles/year.** Accepts simultaneous submissions.

FICTION Subjects include historical, literary, mystery, romance, science fiction, young adult. Submit a query and ms via the online submission form at www.avonromance.com/impulse.

BACKCOUNTRY GUIDES

Imprint of The Countryman Press, P. O. Box 748, Woodstock VT 05091. (802)457-4826. **Fax:** (802)457-1678. **E-mail:** countrymanpress@wwnorton.com. **Website:** www.countrymanpress.com. **Contact:** Submissions. Estab. 1973. Publishes trade paperback originals. "We publish books of the highest quality that take the reader where they want to go. Our books are promoted and sold to bookstores and to specialty markets throughout the United States, Canada, and other parts of the world." **Publishes 70 titles/year.** Accepts simultaneous submissions. Responds in 3 months to proposals. Book catalog available free. Guidelines online.

NONFICTION Subjects include recreation, sports, travel, food, gardening, country living, New England history. Query with SASE. Submit proposal package, outline, 2-3 sample chapters, market analysis. Reviews artwork/photos. Send transparencies.

TIPS "Look at our existing series of guidebooks to see how your proposal fits in."

THE BACKWATERS PRESS

1124 PACIFIC ST, #8392, Omaha NE 68108. **E-mail:** thebackwaterspress@gmail.com. **Website:** www.the-backwaterspress.org. **Contact:** James Cihlar, editor. Greg Kosmicki, Editor Emeritus Estab. 1998. Poetry in English. **Publishes 2-5 titles/year. 300-400 50% of books from first-time authors. 100% from unagented writers. Pays in copies, publication. Contest winner receives $1,000 and copies. Does not pay advance.** Publishes ms 6-12 months after acceptance. Accepts simultaneous submissions. Contest: 2-3 months. All others, up to 6 months. Catalog online. Guidelines online.

NONFICTION Subjects include literature.

POETRY Only considers submissions to Backwaters Prize. More details on website. Open to all styles and forms.

TIPS "Send your best work."

BAEN BOOKS

P.O. Box 1188, Wake Forest NC 27588. (919)570-1640. **E-mail:** info@baen.com. **Website:** www.baen.com. Estab. 1983. "We publish only science fiction and fantasy. Writers familiar with what we have published in the past will know what sort of material we are most likely to publish in the future: powerful plots with solid scientific and philosophical underpinnings are the sine qua non for consideration for science fiction submissions. As for fantasy, any magical system must be both rigorously coherent and integral to the plot, and overall the work must at least strive for originality." Accepts simultaneous submissions. Responds to mss within 12-18 months.

FICTION "Style: Simple is generally better; in our opinion good style, like good breeding, never calls attention to itself. Length: 100,000-130,000 words Generally we are uncomfortable with manuscripts under 100,000 words, but if your novel is really wonderful send it along regardless of length." "Query letters are not necessary. We prefer to see complete manuscripts accompanied by a synopsis. We prefer not to see si-

multaneous submissions. Electronic submissions are strongly preferred. *We no longer accept submissions by e-mail.* Send ms by using the submission form at: http://ftp.baen.com/Slush/submit.aspx. No disks unless requested. Attach ms as a Rich Text Format (.rtf) file. Any other format will not be considered."

BAILIWICK PRESS

309 East Mulberry St., Fort Collins CO 80524. (970)672-4878. **Fax:** (970)672-4731. **E-mail:** info@bailiwickpress.com. **E-mail:** aldozelnick@gmail.com. **Website:** www.bailiwickpress.com. "We're a micro-press that produces books and other products that inspire and tell great stories. Our motto is 'books with something to say.' We are now considering submissions, agented and unagented, for children's and young adult fiction. We're looking for smart, funny, and layered writing that kids will clamor for. Authors who already have a following have a leg up. We are only looking for humorous children's fiction. Please do not submit work for adults. Illustrated fiction is desired but not required. (Illustrators are also invited to send samples.) Make us laugh out loud, ooh and aah, and cry, 'Eureka!'" Accepts simultaneous submissions. Responds in 6 months.

FICTION "Please read the Aldo Zelnick series to determine if we might be on the same page, then fill out our submission form. Please do not send submissions via snail mail or phone calls. You must complete the online submission form to be considered. If, after completing and submitting the form, you also need to send us an e-mail attachment (such as sample illustrations or excerpts of graphics), you may e-mail them to aldozelnick@gmail.com."

Ⓐ⊘ BAKER ACADEMIC

Division of Baker Publishing Group, 6030 E. Fulton Rd., Ada MI 49301. (616)676-9185. **E-mail:** submissions@bakeracademic.com. **Website:** bakerpublishinggroup.com/bakeracademic. Estab. 1939. Publishes hardcover and trade paperback originals. "Baker Academic publishes religious academic and professional books for students and church leaders. Does not accept unsolicited queries. We will consider unsolicited work only through one of the following avenues. Materials sent to our editorial staff through a professional literary agent will be considered. In addition, our staff attends various writers' conferences at which prospective authors can develop relationships with those in the publishing industry." **Publishes 50**

titles/year. 10% of books from first-time authors. 85% from unagented writers. Pays advance.** Publishes book 1 year after acceptance. Accepts simultaneous submissions.

NONFICTION Subjects include education, psychology, religion, Biblical studies, Christian doctrine, books for pastors and church leaders, contemporary issues. Agented submissions only.

Ⓐ⊘ BAKER BOOKS

Division of Baker Publishing Group, 6030 East Fulton Rd., Ada MI 49301. (616)676-9185. **Website:** bakerpublishinggroup.com/bakerbooks. Estab. 1939. Publishes in hardcover and trade paperback originals, and trade paperback reprints. "We will consider unsolicited work only through one of the following avenues. Materials sent through a literary agent will be considered. In addition, our staff attends various writers' conferences at which prospective authors can develop relationships with those in the publishing industry." Accepts simultaneous submissions. Book catalog for 9½×12½ envelope and 3 first-class stamps. Guidelines online.

"Baker Books publishes popular religious nonfiction reference books and professional books for church leaders. Most of our authors and readers are evangelical Christians, and our books are purchased from Christian bookstores, mail-order retailers, and school bookstores. Does not accept unsolicited queries."

NONFICTION Subjects include Christian doctrines.

TIPS "We are not interested in historical fiction, romances, science fiction, biblical narratives or spiritual warfare novels. Do not call to 'pass by' your idea."

⊘ BAKER PUBLISHING GROUP

6030 E. Fulton Rd., Ada MI 49301. (616)676-9185. **Fax:** (616)676-2315. **Website:** www.bakerpublishinggroup.com. Accepts simultaneous submissions.

IMPRINTS Baker Academic; Baker Books; Bethany House; Brazos Press; Chosen; Fleming H. Revell.

Does not accept unsolicited queries.

Ⓐ BALLANTINE BANTAM DELL

Imprint of Penguin Random House, Inc., 1745 Broadway, 18th Floor, New York NY 10019. (212)782-9000. **Website:** www.penguinrandomhouse.com. Estab. 1952. Publishes hardcover, trade paperback, mass market paperback originals. Ballantine Bantam Dell publishes a wide variety of nonfiction and fiction. Accepts simultaneous submissions. Guidelines online.

NONFICTION Subjects include animals, child guidance, community, creative nonfiction, education, history, memoirs, recreation, religion, sex, spirituality, travel, true crime. Agented submissions only. Reviews artwork/photos. Send photocopies.

FICTION Subjects include confession, ethnic, fantasy, feminist, historical, humor, literary, multicultural, mystery, romance, short story collections, spiritual, suspense, translation, general fiction. Agented submissions only.

JONATHAN BALL PUBLISHERS

P.O. Box 6836, Roggebaai 8012, South Africa. (27)(11)622-2900. **Fax:** (27)(11)601-8183. **E-mail:** tercia.wyngaard@jonathanball.co.za. **Website:** www.jonathanball.co.za. **Contact:** Tercia Wyngaard. Publishes books about South Africa which enlighten and entertain. Accepts simultaneous submissions. Guidelines online.

NONFICTION Subjects include history, sports, travel, politics.

BALL PUBLISHING

P.O. Box 1660, West Chicago IL 60186. (630)231-3675. **Fax:** (630)231-5254. **E-mail:** cbeytes@ballpublishing.com. **Website:** www.ballpublishing.com. **Contact:** Chris Beytes, editor. Publishes hardcover and trade paperback originals. "We publish for the book trade and the horticulture trade. Books on both home gardening/landscaping and commercial production are considered." **Publishes 4-6 titles/year.** Accepts simultaneous submissions. Book catalog for 8 ½×11 envelope and 3 first-class stamps.

NONFICTION Subjects include agriculture, gardening, floriculture. Query with SASE. Submit proposal package, outline, 2 sample chapters. Reviews artwork/photos. Send photocopies.

TIPS "We are expanding our book line to home gardeners, while still publishing for green industry professionals. Gardening books should be well thought out and unique in the market. Actively looking for photo books on specific genera and families of flowers and trees."

BALZER & BRAY

HarperCollins Children's Books, 10 E. 53rd St., New York NY 10022. **Website:** www.harpercollinschildrens.com. Estab. 2008. "We publish bold, creative, groundbreaking picture books and novels that appeal directly to kids in a fresh way." **Publishes 10 titles/year. Offers advances. Pays illustrators by the project.** Publishes book 18 months after acceptance. Accepts simultaneous submissions.

NONFICTION Subjects include animals, cooking, dance, environment, history, multicultural, music, nature, science, social sciences, sports. "We will publish very few nonfiction titles, maybe 1-2 per year." Agented submissions only.

FICTION Picture Books, Young Readers: adventure, animal, anthology, concept, contemporary, fantasy, history, humor, multicultural, nature/environment, poetry, science fiction, special needs, sports, suspense. Middle readers, young adults/teens: adventure, animal, anthology, contemporary, fantasy, history, humor, multicultural, nature/environment, poetry, science fiction, special needs, sports, suspense. Agented submissions only.

BANCROFT PRESS

P.O. Box 65360, Baltimore MD 21209-9945. (410)358-0658. **Fax:** (410)764-1967. **E-mail:** bruceb@bancroftpress.com. **Website:** www.bancroftpress.com. **Contact:** Bruce Bortz, editor/publisher (health, investments, politics, history, humor, literary novels, mystery/thrillers, chick lit, young adult). Publishes hardcover and trade paperback originals. "Bancroft Press is a general trade publisher. We publish young adult fiction and adult fiction, as well as occasional nonfiction. Our only mandate is 'books that enlighten.'" **Publishes 4-6 titles/year. Pays 6-8% royalty. Pays various royalties on retail price. Pays $750 advance.** Publishes book up to 3 years after acceptance of ms. Accepts simultaneous submissions. Responds in 6-12 months. Guidelines online.

NONFICTION Subjects include regional, sports, popular culture. "We advise writers to visit the website." All quality books on any subject of interest to the publisher. Submit proposal package, outline, 5 sample chapters, competition/market survey.

FICTION Subjects include ethnic, feminist, historical, humor, literary, mystery, regional, science fiction, translation, young adult, thrillers. "Our current focuses are young adult fiction, women's fiction, and literary fiction." Submit complete ms.

TIPS "We advise writers to visit our website and to be familiar with our previous work. Patience is the number one attribute contributors must have. It takes us a very long time to get through submitted material, because we are such a small company. Also, we only publish 4-6 books per year, so it may take a long time for your optioned book to be published. We like to be able to market our books to be used in schools and in libraries. We prefer fiction that bucks trends and moves in a new direction. We are especially interested in mysteries and humor (especially humorous mysteries)."

Ⓐ⊘ BANTAM BOOKS

Imprint of Penguin Random House, Inc., 1745 Broadway, New York NY 10019. (212)782-9000. **Website:** www.randomhousebooks.com. *Not seeking mss at this time.* Accepts simultaneous submissions.

⊘ BARBOUR PUBLISHING, INC.

P.O. Box 719, Urichsville OH 44683. **E-mail:** submissions@barbourbooks.com. **Website:** www.barbourbooks.com. Estab. 1981. "Barbour Books publishes inspirational/devotional material that is nondenominational and evangelical in nature. We're a Christian evangelical publisher." Specializes in short, easy-to-read Christian bargain books. "Faithfulness to the Bible and Jesus Christ are the bedrock values behind every book Barbour's staff produces."

○ "We no longer accept unsolicited submissions unless they are submitted through professional literary agencies. For more information, we encourage new fiction authors to join a professional writers organization like American Christian Fiction Writers."

⊘ BAREFOOT BOOKS

2067 Massachusettes Ave., 5th Floor, Cambridge MA 02140. (617)576-0660. **Fax:** (617)576-0049. **E-mail:** help@barefootbooks.com. **Website:** www.barefootbooks.com. Publishes hardcover and trade paperback originals. "We are a small, independent publishing company that publishes high-quality picture books for children of all ages and specializes in the work of artists and writers from many cultures. We focus on themes that support independence of spirit, encourage openness to others, and foster a life-long love of learning. Prefers full manuscript." **Publishes 30 titles/year. 2,000 queries received/year. 3,000 mss received/year. 35% of books from first-time authors. 60% from unagented writers. Pays advance.** Accepts simultaneous submissions. Book catalog for 9x12 SAE stamped with $1.80 postage.

FICTION Subjects include juvenile. "Barefoot Books only publishes children's picture books and anthologies of folktales. We do not publish novels." Barefoot Books is not currently accepting ms queries or submissions.

BARRICADE BOOKS, INC.

2037 Lemoine Ave., Fort Lee NJ 07024. (201)944-7600. **Fax:** (201)917-4951. **Website:** www.barricadebooks.com. **Contact:** Carole Stuart, publisher. Estab. 1991. Publishes hardcover and trade paperback originals, trade paperback reprints. "Barricade Books publishes nonfiction, mostly of the controversial type, and books we can promote with authors who can talk about their topics on radio and television and to the press." **Publishes 12 titles/year. 200 queries received/year. 100 mss received/year. 80% of books from first-time authors. 50% from unagented writers. Pays 10-12% royalty on retail price for hardcover. Pays advance.** Publishes book 18 months after acceptance. Accepts simultaneous submissions. Responds in 1 month to queries.

NONFICTION Subjects include ethnic, history, psychology, sociology, true crime. "We look for quality nonfiction mss—preferably with a controversial lean." Query with SASE. Submit outline, 1-2 sample chapters. Material will not be returned or responded to without SASE. "We do not accept proposals on disk or via e-mail." Reviews artwork/photos. Send photocopies.

TIPS "Do your homework. Visit bookshops to find publishers who are doing the kinds of books you want to write. Always submit to a person—not just 'Editor.'"

Ⓐ⊘ BASIC BOOKS

Perseus Books, 250 W. 57th St., Suite 1500, New York NY 10107. **E-mail:** basic.books@perseusbooks.com. **Website:** www.basicbooks.com. **Contact:** Editor. Estab. 1952. Publishes hardcover and trade paperback originals and reprints. Accepts simultaneous submissions. Responds in at least 3 months to queries. Book catalog available free. Guidelines online.

NONFICTION Subjects include history, psychology, sociology, politics, current affairs.

BAYLOR UNIVERSITY PRESS

One Bear Place 97363, Waco TX 76798. (254)710-3164. **Fax:** (254)710-3440. **E-mail:** carey_newman@baylor.edu. **Website:** www.baylorpress.com. **Contact:** Dr. Carey C. Newman, director. Estab. 1897. Publishes hardcover and trade paperback originals. "We publish contemporary and historical scholarly works about culture, religion, politics, science, and the arts." **Publishes 30 titles/year. Pays 10% royalty on wholesale price.** Publishes ms 1 year after acceptance. Accepts simultaneous submissions. Responds in 2 months to proposals. Guidelines online.

NONFICTION Submit outline, 1-3 sample chapters via e-mail.

BAYWOOD PUBLISHING CO., INC.

26 Austin Ave., P.O. Box 337, Amityville NY 11701. (631)691-1270. **Fax:** (631)691-1770. **Website:** www.baywood.com. **Contact:** Stuart Cohen, managing editor. Estab. 1964. "Baywood Publishing publishes original and innovative books in the humanities and social sciences, including areas such as health sciences, gerontology, death and bereavement, psychology, technical communications, and archaeology." **Pays 7-15% royalty on retail price.** Publishes book within 1 year of acceptance. Book catalog and guidelines online.

NONFICTION Subjects include education, psychology, sociology, gerontology, technical writing, death and bereavement, environmental issues, recreational mathematics, health policy, labor relations, workplace rights.. Submit proposal package.

BEACON HILL PRESS OF KANSAS CITY

Nazarene Publishing House, P.O. Box 419527, Kansas City MO 64141. (816)931-1900. **Fax:** (816)753-4071. **E-mail:** crm@nph.com. **Website:** beaconhillbooks.com. Publishes hardcover and paperback originals. "Beacon Hill Press is a Christ-centered publisher that provides authentically Christian resources faithful to God's word and relevant to life." **Publishes 30 titles/year. Pays royalty.** Publishes ms 2 years after acceptance. Accepts simultaneous submissions. Responds in 3 months to queries.

NONFICTION "Accent on holy living; encouragement in daily Christian life." No fiction, autobiography, poetry, short stories, or children's picture books. Query or submit proposal electronically.

BEACON PRESS

24 Farnsworth St., Boston MA 02210. **E-mail:** editorial@beacon.org. **Website:** www.beacon.org. **Contact:** Melissa Nasson, acquisitions editor. Estab. 1854. Publishes hardcover originals and paperback reprints. Beacon Press publishes general interest books that promote the following values: the inherent worth and dignity of every person; justice, equity, and compassion in human relations; acceptance of one another; a free and responsible search for truth and meaning; the goal of world community with peace, liberty, and justice for all; respect for the interdependent web of all existence. Currently emphasizing innovative nonfiction writing by people of all colors. De-emphasizing poetry, children's stories, art books, self-help. **Publishes 60 titles/year. 10% of books from first-time authors. Pays royalty. Pays advance.** Accepts simultaneous submissions. Responds in 3 months to queries.

NONFICTION Subjects include child guidance, education, ethnic, philosophy, religion, world affairs. *Strongly prefers agented submissions.* Query by e-mail only. *Strongly prefers referred submissions, on exclusive.*

TIPS "We probably accept only 1 or 2 manuscripts from an unpublished pool of 4,000 submissions/year. No fiction, children's books, or poetry submissions invited. An academic affiliation is helpful."

BEARMANOR MEDIA

P.O. Box 71426, Albany GA 31708. **E-mail:** books@benohmart.com. **Website:** www.bearmanormedia.com. **Contact:** Ben Ohmart, publisher. Estab. 2000. Publishes trade paperback originals and reprints. **Publishes 70 titles/year. 90% of books from first-time authors. 90% from unagented writers. Negotiable per project. Pays upon acceptance.** Accepts simultaneous submissions. Responds only if interested. Book catalog available online, or free with a 9 x 12 SASE submission.

NONFICTION Subjects include cinema, dance, entertainment, memoirs, stage. Query with SASE. E-mail queries preferred. Submit proposal package, outline, list of credits on the subject.

TIPS "My readers love the past. Radio, old movies, old television. My own tastes include voice actors and scripts, especially of radio and television no longer available. I prefer books on subjects that haven't previously been covered as full books. It doesn't matter to me if you're a first-time author or have a track record. Just know your subject and know how to write a sentence!"

BEAR STAR PRESS

185 Hollow Oak Dr., Cohasset CA 95973. (530)891-0360. **Website:** www.bearstarpress.com. **Contact:** Beth Spencer, publisher/editor. Estab. 1996. Publishes trade paperback originals. "Bear Star is committed to publishing the best poetry it can attract. Each year it sponsors the Dorothy Brunsman contest, open to poets from Western and Pacific states. From time to time

we add to our list other poets from our target area whose work we admire." **Publishes 1-3 titles/year. Pays $1,000, and 25 copies to winner of annual Dorothy Brunsman contest.** Publishes book 9 months after acceptance. Accepts simultaneous submissions. Responds in 2 weeks to queries. Guidelines online.

POETRY Wants well-crafted poems. No restrictions as to form, subject matter, style, or purpose. "Poets should enter our annual book competition. Other books are occasionally solicited by publisher, sometimes from among contestants who didn't win." Online submissions strongly preferred.

TIPS "Send your best work, consider its arrangement. A 'wow' poem early keeps me reading."

BEHRMAN HOUSE INC.

11 Edison Place, Springfield NJ 07081. (973)379-7200. **Fax:** (973)379-7280. **E-mail:** customersupport@behrmanhouse.com. **Website:** www.behrmanhouse.com. Estab. 1921. Publishes books on all aspects of Judaism: history, cultural, textbooks, holidays. "Behrman House publishes quality books of Jewish content—history, Bible, philosophy, holidays, ethics—for children and adults." **12% of books from first-time authors. Pays authors royalty of 3-10% based on retail price or buys ms outright for $1,000-5,000. Offers advance. Pays illustrators by the project (range: $500-5,000).** Publishes book 18 months after acceptance. Accepts simultaneous submissions. Responds in 1 month to queries; 2 months to mss. Book catalog free on request. Guidelines online.

NONFICTION All levels: Judaism, Jewish educational textbooks. Average word length: young reader—1,200; middle reader—2,000; young adult—4,000. Submit outline/synopsis and sample chapters.

FREDERIC C. BEIL, PUBLISHER, INC.

609 Whitaker St., Savannah GA 31401. (912)233-2446. **E-mail:** fcb@beil.com. **Website:** www.beil.com. **Contact:** Frederic Beil. Estab. 1982. Publishes original titles in hardcover, softcover, and e-book. Frederic C. Beil publishes books in the subject areas of history, literature, and biography. **Publishes 8 titles/year. 950 queries; 8 mss received/year. 60% of books from first-time authors. 100% from unagented writers. Pays 7.5% royalty on retail price.** Publishes ms 12-15 months after acceptance. Accepts simultaneous submissions. Responds in 1 week to queries. Catalog online.

IMPRINTS The Sandstone Press.

NONFICTION Subjects include history, humanities, literature, memoirs. Query with SASE.

FICTION Subjects include historical, literary. Query with SASE.

TIPS "Our objectives are to offer to the reading public carefully selected texts, to adhere to high standards in the choice of materials and in bookmaking craftsmanship; to produce books that exemplify good taste in format and design; and to maintain the lowest cost consistent with quality."

BELLEBOOKS

P.O. Box 300921, Memphis TN 38130. (901)344-9024. **E-mail:** bellebooks@bellebooks.com. **Website:** www.bellebooks.com. Estab. 1999. BelleBooks began by publishing Southern fiction. It has become a "second home" for many established authors, who also continue to publish with major publishing houses. **Publishes 30-40 titles/year.** Accepts simultaneous submissions. Guidelines online.

FICTION Subjects include juvenile, young adult. "Yes, we'd love to find the next Harry Potter, but our primary focus for the moment is publishing for the teen market." Query e-mail with brief synopsis and credentials/credits with full ms attached (RTF format preferred).

TIPS "Our list aims for the teen reader and the crossover market. If you're a 'Southern Louise Rennison,' that would catch our attention. Humor is always a plus. We'd love to see books featuring teen boys as protagonists. We're happy to see dark edgy books on serious subjects."

BELLEVUE LITERARY PRESS

New York University School of Medicine, Dept. of Medicine, NYU School of Medicine, 550 First Avenue, OBV 612, New York NY 10016. (212)263-7802. **E-mail:** blpsubmissions@gmail.com. **Website:** blpress.org. **Contact:** Erika Goldman, publisher/editorial director. Estab. 2005. "Publishes literary and authoritative fiction and nonfiction at the nexus of the arts and the sciences, with a special focus on medicine. As our authors explore cultural and historical representations of the human body, illness, and health, they address the impact of scientific and medical practice on the individual and society." Accepts simultaneous submissions.

NONFICTION "If you have a completed ms, a sample of a ms or a proposal that fits our mission as a press feel free to submit it to us by e-mail."

FICTION Subjects include literary. Submit complete ms.

TIPS "We are a project of New York University's School of Medicine and while our standards reflect NYU's excellence in scholarship, humanistic medicine, and science, our authors need not be affiliated with NYU. We are not a university press and do not receive any funding from NYU. Our publishing operations are financed exclusively by foundation grants, private donors, and book sales revenue."

BENBELLA BOOKS

10300 N. Central Expressway, Suite 530, Dallas TX 75231. (214)750-3600. **E-mail:** glenn@benbellabooks. com. **Website:** www.benbellabooks.com. **Contact:** Glenn Yeffeth, publisher. Estab. 2001. Publishes hardcover and trade paperback originals. **Publishes 30-40 titles/year. Pays 6-15% royalty on retail price.** Publishes ms 10 months after acceptance. Accepts simultaneous submissions. Guidelines online.

NONFICTION Subjects include literary criticism, science. Submit proposal package, including: outline, 2 sample chapters (via e-mail).

BENTLEY PUBLISHERS

1734 Massachusetts Ave., Cambridge MA 02138. (617)547-4170. **Fax:** (617)876-9235. **Website:** www. bentleypublishers.com. **Contact:** Michael Bentley, president. Estab. 1950. Publishes hardcover and trade paperback originals and reprints. "Bentley Publishers publishes books for automotive enthusiasts. We are interested in books that showcase good research, strong illustrations, and valuable technical information." Automotive subjects only. Query with SASE. Submit sample chapters, bio, synopsis, target market. Reviews artwork/photos. Book catalog and ms guidelines online.

NONFICTION Query with SASE. Submit sample chapters, bio, synopsis, target market. Rreviews artwork/photos.

TIPS "Our audience is composed of serious, intelligent automobile, sports car, and racing enthusiasts, automotive technicians and high-performance tuners."

● BERGLI BOOKS

Schwabe Publishing, Steinentorstrasse II, Basel CH-4010, Switzerland. **E-mail:** info@bergli.ch. **Website:** www.bergli.ch. **Contact:** Richard Harvell, executive editor. Estab. 1991. Bergli Books publishes books in Switzerland that bridge intercultural gaps. "It's mostly English list has included many Swiss-interest bestsellers of the past two decades, including the *Ticking Along* Series, Margaret Oertig's *Beyond Chocolate*, and Sergio Lievano and Nicole Egger's *Hoi* books—the bestselling Swiss German guides of all time. An imprint of Schwabe since 2013, Bergli is unique in Switzerland—connecting English readers to Swiss culture and tradition." **Publishes 3-4 titles/year. Receives 50 queries/year. 50% of books from first-time authors. Pays 7-12% royalties on retail price. Pays $1,000-5,000 advance.** Publishes ms 12 months after acceptance. Accepts simultaneous submissions. Responds in 1 month to queries, proposals, and mss. Catalog available online. Guidelines available for SASE.

NONFICTION Subjects include travel, Swiss culture, Switzerland for expats. "Our chief market is among English speakers in Switzerland." Submit proposal package, outline, and 1 sample chapter. Reviews artwork, submit photocopies.

TIPS "We like illustrated books, show us something that has been done elsewhere but not in Switzerland."

ⒶⓄ BERKLEY/NAL

Penguin Group (USA) Inc., 375 Hudson St., New York NY 10014. **Website:** penguin.com. **Contact:** Leslie Gelbman, president and publisher. Estab. 1955. Publishes paperback and mass market originals and reprints. The Berkley Publishing Group publishes a variety of general nonfiction and fiction including the traditional categories of romance, mystery and science fiction. **Publishes 700 titles/year.**

IMPRINTS Ace; Jove; Heat; Sensation; Berkley Prime Crime; Berkley Caliber.

○ "Due to the high volume of manuscripts received, most Penguin Group (USA) Inc. imprints do not normally accept unsolicited mss. The preferred and standard method for having mss considered for publication by a major publisher is to submit them through an established literary agent."

NONFICTION Subjects include child guidance, creative nonfiction, history, New Age, psychology, true crime, job-seeking communication. No memoirs or personal stories. Prefers agented submissions.

FICTION Subjects include adventure, historical, literary, mystery, romance, spiritual, suspense, western, young adult. No occult fiction. Prefers agented submissions.

BERRETT-KOEHLER PUBLISHERS, INC.

1333 Broadway, Suite #1000, Oakland CA 94612. **E-mail:** bkpub@bkpub.com. **E-mail:** submissions@bk-pub.com. **Website:** www.bkconnection.com. **Contact:** Anna Leinberger, associate editor. Publishes hardcover and trade paperback originals, mass market paperback originals, hardcover and trade paperback reprints. "Berrett-Koehler Publishers' mission is to publish books that support the movement toward a world that works for all. Our titles promote positive change at personal, organizational and societal levels." Please see proposal guidelines online. **Publishes 40 titles/year. 1,300 queries received/year. 800 mss received/year. 20-30% of books from first-time authors. 70% from unagented writers. Pays 10-20% royalty.** Publishes book 10 months after acceptance. Accepts simultaneous submissions. Responds in 1 month. Book catalog online.

NONFICTION Subjects include community, New Age, spirituality. Submit proposal package, outline, bio, 1-2 sample chapters. Hard-copy proposals only. Do not e-mail, fax, or phone please. Reviews artwork/photos. Send photocopies or originals with SASE.

TIPS "Our audience is business leaders. Use common sense, do your research."

⊘ BETHANY HOUSE PUBLISHERS

Division of Baker Publishing Group, 6030 E. Fulton Rd., Ada MI 49301. (616)676-9185. **Fax:** (616)676-9573. **Website:** bakerpublishinggroup.com/bethanyhouse. Estab. 1956. Publishes hardcover and trade paperback originals, mass market paperback reprints. Bethany House Publishers specializes in books that communicate Biblical truth and assist people in both spiritual and practical areas of life. Considers unsolicited work only through a professional literary agent or through manuscript submission services, Authonomy or Christian Manuscript Submissions. Guidelines online. *All unsolicited mss returned unopened.* **Publishes 90-100 titles/year. 2% of books from first-time authors. 50% from unagented writers. Pays royalty on net price. Pays advance.** Publishes a book 1 year after acceptance. Accepts simultaneous submissions. Responds in 3 months to queries. Book catalog for 9 x 12 envelope and 5 first-class stamps.

NONFICTION Subjects include child guidance, Biblical disciplines, personal and corporate renewal, emerging generations, devotional, marriage and family, applied theology, inspirational.

FICTION Subjects include historical, young adult, contemporary.

TIPS "Bethany House Publishers' publishing program relates Biblical truth to all areas of life—whether in the framework of a well-told story, of a challenging book for spiritual growth, or of a Bible reference work. We are seeking high-quality fiction and nonfiction that will inspire and challenge our audience."

↻ BETWEEN THE LINES

401 Richmond St. W., Suite 277, Toronto ON M5V 3A8, Canada. (416)535-9914. **Fax:** (416)535-1484. **E-mail:** submissions@btlbooks.com. **Website:** www.btlbooks.com. **Contact:** Amanda Crocker, managing editor. Publishes trade paperback originals. "Between the Lines publishes nonfiction books in the following subject areas: politics and public policy issues, social issues, development studies, history, education, the environment, health, gender and sexuality, labour, technology, media, and culture. Please note that we do not publish fiction or poetry. We prefer to receive proposals rather than entire manuscripts for consideration." **Publishes 8 titles/year. 350 queries received/year. 50 mss received/year. 80% of books from first-time authors. 95% from unagented writers. Pays 8% royalty.** Publishes ms 1 year after acceptance. Accepts simultaneous submissions. Responds in 2-4 months. Book catalog online. Guidelines online.

NONFICTION Subjects include education, history, social sciences, sociology, development studies, labor, technology, media, culture. Submit proposal as a PDF by e-mail.

ⒶⓄ BEYOND WORDS PUBLISHING, INC.

20827 NW Cornell Rd., Suite 500, Hillsboro OR 97124. (503)531-8700. **Fax:** (503)531-8773. **E-mail:** info@beyondword.com. **Website:** www.beyondword.com. **Contact:** Submissions Department (for agents only). Estab. 1984. Publishes hardcover and trade paperback originals and paperback reprints. "At this time, we are not accepting any unsolicited queries or proposals, and recommend that all authors work with a literary agent in submitting their work." **Publishes 10-15 titles/year.** Accepts simultaneous submissions.

BIRCH BOOK PRESS

Birch Brook Impressions, P.O. Box 81, Delhi NY 13753. **Fax:** (607)746-7453. **E-mail:** birchbrook@copper.net. **Website:** www.birchbrookpress.info. **Contact:** Tom Tolnay, editor/publisher; Leigh Eckmair, art & research editor; Joyce Tolnay, account services. Estab. 1982. Occasionally publishes trade paperback originals. Birch Brook Press "is a book printer/typesetter/designer that uses monies from these activities to publish several titles of its own each year with cultural and literary interest." Specializes in literary work, flyfishing, baseball, outdoors, themed short fiction anthologies, and books about books. **Publishes 2 titles/year. 200+ queries received/year; 200+ mss received/year. 95% from unagented writers. Pays modest royalty on acceptance.** Publishes ms 10-18 months after acceptance. Accepts simultaneous submissions. Responds in 3 to 6 months. Book catalog online.

FICTION "Mostly we do anthologies around a particular theme generated inhouse. We make specific calls for fiction when we are doing an anthology." Query with SASE and submit sample chapter(s), synopsis.

POETRY Query first with a few sample poems or chapters, or send entire ms. No e-mail submissions; submissions by postal mail only. Must include SASE with submissions. Occasionally comments on rejected poems. Royalty on co-op contracts.

TIPS "Write well on subjects of interest to BBP, such as outdoors, flyfishing, baseball, music, literary stories, fine poetry, books about books."

BKMK PRESS

University of Missouri - Kansas City, 5101 Rockhill Rd., Kansas City MO 64110-2499. (816)235-2558. **Fax:** (816)235-2611. **E-mail:** bkmk@umkc.edu. **Website:** newletters.org. Estab. 1971. Publishes trade paperback originals. "BkMk Press publishes fine literature. Reading period February-June." **Publishes 4 titles/year.** Accepts simultaneous submissions. Responds in 4-6 months to queries. Guidelines online.

NONFICTION Creative nonfiction essays. Submit 25-50 sample pages and SASE.

FICTION Subjects include literary, short story collections. Query with SASE.

POETRY Submit 10 sample poems and SASE.

TIPS "We skew toward readers of literature, particularly contemporary writing. Because of our limited number of titles published per year, we discourage apprentice writers or 'scattershot' submissions."

BLACK DOME PRESS CORP.

649 Delaware Ave., Delmar NY 12054. (518)439-6512. **Fax:** (518)439-1309. **Website:** www.blackdomepress. com. Estab. 1990. Publishes cloth and trade paperback originals and reprints. Do not send the entire work. Mail a cover letter, TOC, introduction, sample chapter (or 2), and your CV or brief biography to the Editor. Please do not send computer disks or submit your proposal via e-mail. If your book will include illustrations, please send us copies of sample illustrations. Do not send originals. Accepts simultaneous submissions. Book catalog and guidelines online.

NONFICTION Subjects include history, photography, regional, Native Americans, grand hotels, genealogy, colonial life, French & Indian War (NYS), American Revolution (NYS), quilting, architecture, railroads, hiking and kayaking guidebooks. New York state regional material only. Submit proposal package, outline, bio.

TIPS "Our audience is comprised of New York state residents, tourists, and visitors."

BLACK HERON PRESS

P.O. Box 13396, Mill Creek WA 98082. **Website:** www. blackheronpress.com. Estab. 1984. Publishes hardcover and trade paperback originals, trade paperback reprints. "Black Heron Press publishes primarily literary fiction." **Publishes 4 titles/year. 1,500 queries received/year. 50% of books from first-time authors. 90% from unagented writers. Pays 8% royalty on retail price.** Publishes ms 2 years after acceptance. Accepts simultaneous submissions. Responds in 6 months. Catalog available online.

NONFICTION Submit proposal package, include cover letter and first 30-50 pages of your completed novel. "We do not review artwork."

FICTION Subjects include confession, erotica, Some science fiction—not fantasy, not Dungeons & Dragons—that makes or implies a social statement.. "All of our fiction is character driven. We don't want to see fiction written for the mass market. If it sells to the mass market, fine, but we don't see ourselves as a commercial press." Submit proposal package, including cover letter and first 40-50 pages pages of your completed novel.

TIPS "Our Readers love good fiction—they are scattered among all social classes, ethnic groups, and zip code areas. If you can't read our books, at least check out our titles on our website."

BLACK LAWRENCE PRESS

326 Bigham St., Pittsburgh PA 15211. **E-mail:** editors@blacklawrencepress.com. **Website:** www.blacklawrencepress.com. **Contact:** Diane Goettel, execu-

tive editor. Estab. 2003. Black Lawrence press seeks to publish intriguing books of literature—novels, short story collections, poetry collections, chapbooks, anthologies, and creative nonfiction. Will also publish the occasional translation from German. Publishes 15-20 books/year, mostly poetry and fiction. Mss are selected through open submission and competition. Books are 20-400 pages, offset-printed or high-quality POD, perfect-bound, with 4-color cover. **Accepts submissions during the months of June and November. Pays royalties.** Accepts simultaneous submissions. Responds in 6 months to mss.

FICTION Subjects include literary, short story collections, translation. Submit complete ms.

POETRY Submit complete ms.

BLACK LYON PUBLISHING, LLC

P.O. Box 567, Baker City OR 97814. **E-mail:** info@blacklyonpublishing.com. **E-mail:** queries@blacklyonpublishing.com. **Website:** www.blacklyonpublishing.com. **Contact:** The Editors. Estab. 2007. Publishes paperback and e-book originals. "Black Lyon Publishing is a small, independent publisher. We are very focused on giving new novelists a launching pad into the industry." **Publishes 15-20 titles/year.** Accepts simultaneous submissions. Responds in 2-3 months to queries. Guidelines online.

FICTION Subjects include gothic, historical, romance. Prefers e-mail queries.

TIPS "Write a good, solid romance with a setting, premise, character or voice just a little 'different' than what you might usually find on the market. We like unique books—but they still need to be romances."

BLACK OCEAN

P.O. Box 52030, Boston MA 02205. **Fax:** (617)849-5678. **E-mail:** carrie@blackocean.org. **Website:** www.blackocean.org. **Contact:** Carrie Olivia Adams, poetry editor. Estab. 2006. **Publishes 6 titles/year.** Accepts simultaneous submissions. Responds in 6 months to mss.

POETRY Wants poetry that is well-considered, risks itself, and by its beauty and/or bravery disturbs a tiny corner of the universe. Mss are selected through open submission. Books are 60+ pages. Book/chapbook mss may include previously published poems. "We have an open submission period in June of each year; specific guidelines are updated and posted on our website in the months preceding."

BLACK VELVET SEDUCTIONS PUBLISHING

E-mail: ric@blackvelvetseductions.com. **Website:** www.blackvelvetseductions.com. **Contact:** Richard Savage, acquisitions editor. Estab. 2005. Publishes trade paperback and electronic originals and reprints. "We publish two types of material: 1) romance novels and short stories and 2) romantic stories involving spanking between consenting adults. We look for well-crafted stories with a high degree of emotional impact. No first person point of view. All material must be in third person point of view." Publishes trade paperback and electronic originals. "We have a high interest in republishing backlist titles in electronic and trade paperback formats once rights have reverted to the author." Accepts only complete mss. Query with SASE. Submit complete ms. **Publishes about 20 titles/year. 500 queries; 1,000 mss received/year. 90% of books from first-time authors. 100% from unagented writers. Pays 10% royalty for paperbacks; 50% royalty for electronic books.** Publishes ms 6-12 months after acceptance. Accepts simultaneous submissions. Responds in 6 months to queries; 8 months to proposals; 8-12 months to mss. Catalog free or online. Guidelines online.

FICTION Subjects include romance, erotic romance, historical romance, multicultural romance, romance, short story collections romantic stories, romantic suspense, western romance. All stories must have a strong romance element. "There are very few sexual taboos in our erotic line. We tend to give our authors the widest latitude. If it is safe, sane, and consensual we will allow our authors latitude to show us the eroticism. However, we will not consider manuscripts with any of the following: bestiality (sex with animals), necrophilia (sex with dead people), pedophillia (sex with children)." Only accepts electronic submissions.

TIPS "We publish romance and erotic romance. We look for books written in very deep point of view. Shallow point of view remains the number one reason we reject manuscripts in which the storyline generally works."

JOHN F. BLAIR, PUBLISHER

1406 Plaza Dr., Winston-Salem NC 27103. (336)768-1374. **Fax:** (336)768-9194. **E-mail:** editorial@blairpub.com. **Website:** www.blairpub.com. **Contact:** Carolyn Sakowski, president. Estab. 1954. No poetry, young-adult, children's, science fiction. Fiction must be set in southern U.S. or author must have strong Southern connection. **Publishes 10-15 titles/year. 1,000 proposals received/year. Pays royalties. Pays negotiable advance.** Publishes ms 18 months after acceptance. Accepts simultaneous submissions. Responds in 3-6 months. Catalog online. Guidelines online.

NONFICTION Subjects include cooking, creative nonfiction, history, literature, memoirs, regional, travel. Does not want self-help or business.

FICTION "We specialize in regional books, with an emphasis on nonfiction categories such as history, travel, folklore, and biography. We publish only one or two works of fiction each year. Fiction submitted to us should have some connection with the Southeast. We do not publish children's books, poetry, or category fiction such as romances, science fiction, or spy thrillers. We do not publish collections of short stories, essays, or newspaper columns." Does not want fiction set outside southern U.S. Accepts unsolicited mss. Any fiction submitted should have some connection with the Southeast, either through setting or author's background. Send a cover letter, giving a synopsis of the book. Include the first 2 chapters (at least 50 pages) of the ms. "You may send the entire ms if you wish. If you choose to send only samples, please include the projected word length of your book and estimated completion date in your cover letter. Send a biography of the author, including publishing credits and credentials."

TIPS "We are primarily interested in nonfiction titles. Most of our titles have a tie-in with North Carolina or the southeastern United States, we do not accept short-story collections. Please enclose a cover letter and outline with the ms. We prefer to review queries before we are sent complete mss. Queries should include an approximate word count."

BLAZEVOX [BOOKS]

131 Euclid Ave., Kenmore NY 14217. **E-mail:** editor@blazevox.org. **Website:** www.blazevox.org. **Contact:** Geoffrey Gatza, editor/publisher. Estab. 2005. "We are a major publishing presence specializing in innovative fictions and wide-ranging fields of innovative forms of poetry and prose. Our goal is to publish works that are challenging, creative, attractive, and yet affordable to individual readers. Articles of submission depend on many criteria, but overall items submitted must conform to one ethereal trait, your work must not suck. This put plainly, bad art should be punished; we will not promote it. However, all sub-

missions will be reviewed and the author will receive feedback. We are human too." **65% of books from first-time authors. 100% from unagented writers. Pays 10% royalties on fiction and poetry books, based on net receipts. This amount may be split across multiple contributors. "We do not pay advances."** Accepts simultaneous submissions. Guidelines online.

FICTION Subjects include experimental, short story collections. Submit complete ms via e-mail.

POETRY Submit complete ms via e-mail.

TIPS "We actively contract and support authors who tour, read and perform their work, play an active part of the contemporary literary scene, and seek a readership."

BLOOMBERG PRESS

Imprint of John Wiley & Sons, Professional Development, 111 River St., Hoboken NJ 07030. **E-mail:** info@wiley.com. **Website:** www.wiley.com. Estab. 1995. Publishes hardcover and trade paperback originals. Bloomberg Press publishes professional books for practitioners in the financial markets. "We publish commercially successful, very high-quality books that stand out clearly from the competition by their brevity, ease of use, sophistication, and abundance of practical tips and strategies; books readers need, will use, and appreciate." **Publishes 18-22 titles/year. 200 queries; 20 mss received/year. 45% from unagented writers. Pays negotiable, competitive royalty. Pays negotiable advance for trade books.** Publishes book 9 months after acceptance. Accepts simultaneous submissions. Responds in 1 month to queries.

NONFICTION Subjects include professional books on finance, investment and financial services, and books for financial advisors.. "We are looking for authorities and for experienced service journalists. Do not send us unfocused books containing general information already covered by books in the marketplace. We do not publish business, management, leadership, or career books." Submit outline, sample chapters, SAE with sufficient postage. Submit complete ms.

⊘⊘ BLOOMSBURY CHILDREN'S BOOKS

Imprint of Bloomsbury USA, 1385 Broadway, 5th Floor, New York NY 10008. **Website:** www.bloomsbury.com/us/childrens. No phone calls or e-mails. *Agented submissions only.* **Publishes 60 titles/year. 25% of books from first-time authors. Pays royalty.**

Pays advance. Accepts simultaneous submissions. Responds in 6 months. Book catalog online. Guidelines online.

FICTION Subjects include adventure, fantasy, historical, humor, juvenile, multicultural, mystery, picture books, poetry, science fiction, sports, suspense, young adult, animal, anthology, concept, contemporary, folktales, problem novels. *Agented submissions only.*

⚫⚪ BLOOMSBURY CONTINUUM

Imprint of Bloomsbury Group, 1385 Broadway, 5th Floor, New York NY 10018. (212)419-5300. **Website:** http://www.bloomsbury.com/us/bloomsbury/bloomsbury-continuum/. Continuum publishes textbooks, monographs, and reference works in religious studies, the humanities, arts, and social sciences for students, teachers, and professionals worldwide. *Does not accept unsolicited submissions.* Book catalog online.

NONFICTION Subjects include education, history, philosophy, religion, sociology, linguistics.

BLUEBRIDGE

Imprint of United Tribes Media, Inc., (914)301-5901. **E-mail:** janguerth@bluebridgebooks.com. **Website:** www.bluebridgebooks.com. **Contact:** Jan-Erik Guerth, publisher (general nonfiction). Estab. 2004. Publishes hardcover and trade paperbacks. Blue-Bridge is an independent publisher of international nonfiction based near New York City. BlueBridge book subjects include Culture, History, Biography; Nature and Science; Inspiration and Self-Help. Blue-Bridge is an imprint of United Tribes Media Inc. **Publishes 4-6 titles/year. Pays variable advance.** Accepts simultaneous submissions.

NONFICTION Subjects include alternative lifestyles, Americana, animals, anthropology, archeology, architecture, art, community, contemporary culture, creative nonfiction, economics, environment, ethnic, gardening, history, humanities, literary criticism, multicultural, nature, philosophy, politics, psychology, public affairs, religion, science, social sciences, sociology, spirituality, travel, womens issues, womens studies, world affairs. BlueBridge only accepts submission queries per e-mail, without any attachments to the e-mail, and only for nonfiction.

TIPS "We target a broad general nonfiction audience."

BLUE LIGHT PRESS

1563 45th Ave., San Francisco CA 94122. **E-mail:** bluelightpress@aol.com. **Website:** www.bluelight-press.com. **Contact:** Diane Frank, chief editor. Estab. 1988. "We like poems that are imagistic, emotionally honest, and push the edge—where the writer pushes through the imagery to a deeper level of insight and understanding. No rhymed poetry." Has published poetry by Stephen Dunn, Kim Addonizio, Jane Hirshfield, Rustin Larson, Mary Kay Rummel, Daniel J. Langton, and K.B. Ballentine. "Books are elegantly designed and artistic. Our books are professionally printed, with original cover art, and we publish full-length books of poetry and chapbooks." Accepts simultaneous submissions. Catalog online.

NONFICTION Subjects include literature.

FICTION Subjects include poetry, poetry in translation, short story collections, flash fiction, micro fiction.

POETRY "We have an online poetry workshop with a wonderful group of American and international poets—open to new members 3 times/year. Send an e-mail for info." No rhymed poetry. Does not accept e-mail submissions. Deadlines: January 30 full-sized ms. and June 15 for chapbooks. "Read our guidelines before sending your ms."

BLUE MOUNTAIN PRESS

Blue Mountain Arts, Inc., P.O. Box 4219, Boulder CO 80306. (800)525-0642. **E-mail:** bmpbooks@sps.com. **Website:** www.sps.com. **Contact:** Patti Wayant, Director. Estab. 1971. Publishes hardcover originals, trade paperback originals, electronic originals. *"Please note: We are not accepting works of fiction, rhyming poetry, children's books, chapbooks, or memoirs."* **Pays royalty on wholesale price.** Publishes ms 12-16 months after acceptance. Accepts simultaneous submissions. Responds in 2-4 months. Guidelines by e-mail.

NONFICTION Subjects include personal growth, teens/tweens, family, relationships, motivational, and inspirational but not religious. Query with SASE. Submit proposal package including outline and 3-5 sample chapters.

POETRY "We publish poetry appropriate for gift books, self-help books, and personal growth books. We do not publish chapbooks or literary poetry." Query. Submit 10+ sample poems.

BLUE RIVER PRESS

Cardinal Publishers Group, 2402 N. Shadeland Ave., Suite A, Indianapolis IN 46219. (317)352-8200.

Fax: (317)352-8202. **E-mail:** msears@cardinalpub.com; tdoherty@cardinalpub.com. **Website:** www.brpressbooks.com; www.cardinalpub.com. **Contact:** Morgan Sears, editor; Tom Doherty, president (adult nonfiction). Estab. 2000. Publishes hardcover, trade paperback and electronic originals and reprints. Blue River Press released its first book in the spring of 2004. "Today we have more than 50 books and e-books in print on the subjects of sports, health, fitness, games, popular culture, and travel. Our books have been recognized with awards and national and regional review attention. We have had many titles reach Nielsen BookScan category top 50 status in retail sales; illustrating that readers have responded by purchasing Blue River Press titles. Our distributor, Cardinal Publishers Group, has placed our books in chain and independent book retailers, libraries of all sorts, mass-merchant retailers, gift shops, and many specialty retail and wholesale channels. Our authors, editors and designers always keep the reader in mind when creating and developing the content and designing attractive books that are competitively priced. At Blue River Press our mission is to produce, distribute and market books that present the reader with good educational and entertaining information at a value." **Publishes 8-12 titles/year. 200 queries received/year. 25% of books from first-time authors. 80% from unagented writers. Pays 10-15% on wholesale price. Outright purchase of $500-5,000. Offers advance up to $5,000.** Publishes ms 6-12 months after acceptance. Accepts simultaneous submissions. Responds to queries in 2 months. Book catalog for #10 SASE or online. Guidelines available by e-mail.

NONFICTION "Most non-religious adult nonfiction subjects are of interest. We like concepts that can develop into series products. Most of our books are paperback or hardcover in the categories of sport, business, health, fitness, lifestyle, yoga, and educational books for teachers and students."

BNA BOOKS

P.O. Box 7814, Edison NJ 08818. (800)960-1220. **Fax:** (723)346-1624. **Website:** www.bnabooks.com. Estab. 1929. Publishes hardcover and softcover originals. BNA Books publishes professional reference books written by lawyers, for lawyers. Accepts simultaneous submissions. Book catalog online. Guidelines online.

NONFICTION No fiction, biographies, bibliographies, cookbooks, religion books, humor, or trade books. Submit detailed TOC or outline, CV, intended market, estimated word length.

TIPS "Our audience is made up of practicing lawyers and law librarians. We look for authoritative and comprehensive treatises that can be supplemented or revised every year or 2 on legal subjects of interest to those audiences."

BOA EDITIONS, LTD.

P.O. Box 30971, Rochester NY 14603. (585)546-3410. **Fax:** (585)546-3913. **E-mail:** contact@boaeditions.org. **Website:** www.boaeditions.org. **Contact:** Jenna Fisher, Director of Marketing and Production; Peter Conners, Publisher. Melissa Hall, Director of Development and Operations Estab. 1976. Publishes hardcover, trade paperback, and digital e-book originals. BOA Editions, Ltd., a not-for-profit publisher of poetry, short fiction, and poetry-in-translation, fosters readership and appreciation of contemporary literature. By identifying, cultivating, and publishing both new and established poets and selecting authors of unique literary talent, BOA brings high quality literature to the public. **Publishes 10-12 titles/year. 1,000-2,000 queries and mss received/year. 15% of books from first-time authors. 90% from unagented writers. Negotiates royalties. Pays variable advance.** Publishes ms 18 months after acceptance. Accepts simultaneous submissions. Responds in 1 week to queries; 5 months to mss. Book catalog online. Guidelines online.

FICTION Subjects include literary, poetry, poetry in translation, short story collections. BOA publishes literary fiction through its American Reader Series. While aesthetic quality is subjective, our fiction will be by authors more concerned with the artfulness of their writing than the twists and turns of plot. "Our strongest current interest is in short story collections (and short-short story collections). We strongly advise you to read our published fiction collections." *Temporarily closed to novel/collection submissions.*

POETRY Readers who, like Whitman, expect the poet to 'indicate more than the beauty and dignity which always attach to dumb real objects . . They expect him to indicate the path between reality and their souls,' are the audience of BOA's books. BOA Editions, a Pulitzer Prize and National Book Award-winning not-for-profit publishing house, acclaimed for its work, reads poetry mss for the American Poets Continuum Series (new poetry by distinguished poets in mid-to-late career), the Lannan Translations Selection Series (publication of 2 new collections of contemporary international poetry annually, supported by the Lannan Foundation of Santa Fe, NM), the New Poets of America Series (publication of a poet's first book, selected through the A. Poulin, Jr. Poetry Prize), and the America Reader Series (short fiction and prose on poetics). Check BOA's website for reading periods for the American Poets Continuum Series and the Lannan Translation Selection Series. Please adhere to the general submission guidelines for each series. Guidelines online.

BOLD STROKES BOOKS, INC.

P.O. Box 249, Valley Falls NY 12185. (518)677-5127. **Fax:** (518)677-5291. **E-mail:** sandy.boldstrokes@gmail.com. **E-mail:** bsbsubmissions@gmail.com. **Website:** www.boldstrokesbooks.com. **Contact:** Sandy Lowe, senior editor. Publishes trade paperback originals and reprints; electronic originals and reprints. **Publishes 85+ titles/year. 300 queries/year; 300 mss/year. 10-20% of books from first-time authors. Sliding scale based on sales volume and format.** Publishes ms 6-16 months after acceptance. Responds in 1 month to queries; 2 months to proposals; 4 months to mss. Guidelines online.

IMPRINTS BSB Fiction; Victory Editions Lesbian Fiction; Liberty Editions Gay Fiction; Soliloquy Young Adult; Heat Stroke Erotica.

NONFICTION Subjects include gay, lesbian, memoirs, young adult. Submit completed ms with bio, cover letter, and synopsis electronically only. Does not review artwork.

FICTION Subjects include adventure, erotica, fantasy, gay, gothic, historical, horror, lesbian, literary, mainstream, mystery, romance, science fiction, suspense, western, young adult. "Submissions should have a gay, lesbian, transgendered, or bisexual focus and should be positive and life-affirming." Submit completed ms with bio, cover letter, and synopsis—electronically only.

TIPS "We are particularly interested in authors who are interested in craft enhancement, technical development, and exploring and expanding traditional genre definitions and boundaries and are looking for a long-term publishing relationship."

BOOKFISH BOOKS

E-mail: bookfishbooks@gmail.com. **Website:** bookfishbooks.com. **Contact:** Tammy Mckee, acquisitions editor. BookFish Books is looking for novel lengthed young adult, new adult, and middle grade works in all subgenres. Both published and unpublished, agented or unagented authors are welcome to submit. "Sorry, but we do not publish novellas, picture books, early reader/chapter books or adult novels." Responds to every query. Accepts simultaneous submissions. Guidelines online.

FICTION Query via e-mail with a brief synopsis and first 3 chapters of ms.

TIPS "We only accept complete manuscripts. Please do not query us with partial manuscripts or proposals."

BOOKOUTURE

StoryFire Ltd., 23 Sussex Rd., Ickenham UB10 8P, United Kingdom. **E-mail:** questions@bookouture.com. **E-mail:** pitch@bookouture.com. **Website:** www.bookouture.com. **Contact:** Oliver Rhodes, founder and publisher. Estab. 2012. Publishes mass market paperback and electronic originals and reprints. **Publishes 40 titles/year. Receives 200 queries/year; 300 mss/year. Pays 45% royalty on wholesale price.** Publishes ms 4 months after acceptance. Accepts simultaneous submissions. Responds in 1 month. Book catalog online.

IMPRINTS Imprint of StoryFire Ltd.

FICTION Subjects include contemporary, erotica, ethnic, fantasy, gay, historical, lesbian, mainstream, mystery, romance, science fiction, suspense, western, crime, thriller, new adult. "We are looking for entertaining fiction targeted at modern women. That can be anything from Steampunk to Erotica, Historicals to thrillers. A distinctive author voice is more important than a particular genre or ms length." Submit complete ms.

TIPS "The most important question that we ask of submissions is why would a reader buy the next book? What's distinctive or different about your storytelling that will mean readers will want to come back for more. We look to acquire global English language rights for e-book and Print on Demand."

BOREALIS PRESS, LTD.

8 Mohawk Crescent, Napean ON K2H 7G6, Canada. (613)829-0150. **Fax:** (613)829-7783. **E-mail:** drt@borealispress.com. **Website:** www.borealispress.com. Estab. 1972. Publishes hardcover and paperback originals and reprints. "Our mission is to publish work that will be of lasting interest in the Canadian book market." Currently emphasizing Canadian fiction, nonfic-

tion, drama, poetry. De-emphasizing children's books. **Publishes 20 titles/year. 80% of books from first-time authors. 95% from unagented writers. Pays 10% royalty on net receipts; plus 3 free author's copies.** Publishes book 18 months after acceptance. Responds in 2 months to queries; 4 months to mss. Book catalog online. Guidelines online.

IMPRINTS Tecumseh Press.

NONFICTION Subjects include history, regional. Only material Canadian in content. Looks for style in tone and language, reader interest, and maturity of outlook. Query with SASE. Submit outline, 2 sample chapters. *No unsolicited mss.* Reviews artwork/photos.

FICTION Subjects include adventure, ethnic, historical, juvenile, literary, romance, short story collections, young adult. Only material Canadian in content and dealing with significant aspects of the human situation. Query with SASE. Submit clips, 1-2 sample chapters. *No unsolicited mss.*

BOTTOM DOG PRESS, INC.

P.O. Box 425, Huron OH 44839. (419)433-3573. **E-mail:** lsmithdog@smithdocs.net. **Website:** smithdocs.net. **Contact:** Larry Smith, director; Susanna Sharp-Schwacke, associate editor. Bottom Dog Press, Inc., "is a nonprofit literary and educational organization dedicated to publishing the best writing and art from the Midwest and Appalachia." **4% of books from first-time authors. 8% from unagented writers. Pays 10 copies and 15% royalty. Does not pay advance.** Publishes ms 4 months after acceptance. Accepts simultaneous submissions.

○ "Query via e-mail first."

NONFICTION Subjects include alternative lifestyles, contemporary culture, humanities, memoirs, social sciences, spirituality, womens issues, sense of place.

FICTION Subjects include contemporary, ethnic, gay, historical, literary, short story collections, Appalachian, working-class.

BOYDS MILLS PRESS

Highlights for Children, Inc., 815 Church St., Honesdale PA 18431. (570)253-1164. **Website:** www.boydsmillspress.com. Estab. 1990. Boyds Mills Press publishes picture books, nonfiction, activity books, and paperback reprints. Their titles have been named notable books by the International Reading Association, the American Library Association, and the National Council of Teachers of English. They've earned numerous awards, including the National Jewish Book Award, the Christopher Medal, the NCTE Orbis Pictus Honor, and the Golden Kite Honor. Boyds Mills Press welcomes unsolicited submissions from published and unpublished writers and artists. Submit a ms with a cover letter of relevant information, including experience with writing and publishing. Label the package "Manuscript Submission" and include an SASE. For art samples, label the package "Art Sample Submission." All submissions will be evaluated for all imprints. Responds to mss within 3 months. Catalog online. Guidelines online.

POETRY Send a book-length collection of poems. Do not send an initial query. Keep in mind that the strongest collections demonstrate a facility with multiple poetic forms.

NICHOLAS BREALEY PUBLISHING

53 State St., 9th Floor, Boston MA 02109. (617)523-3801. **Fax:** (617)523-3708. **Website:** www.nicholasbrealey.com. **Contact:** Aquisitions Editor. Estab. 1992. "Nicholas Brealey Publishing has a reputation for publishing high-quality and thought-provoking business books with international appeal. Over time our list has grown to focus also on careers, professional and personal development, travel narratives and crossing cultures. We welcome fresh ideas and new insights in all of these subject areas." Submit via e-mail and follow the guidelines on the website. Accepts simultaneous submissions.

BREWERS PUBLICATIONS

Imprint of Brewers Association, 551 Westbury Ln., Georgetown TX 78633. **E-mail:** kristi@brewersassociation.org. **Website:** www.brewerspublications.com. **Contact:** Kristi Switzer, publisher. Estab. 1986. Publishes trade paperback originals. "BP is the largest publisher of contemporary and relevant brewing literature for today's craft brewers and homebrewers." **Publishes 2 titles/year. 50% of books from first-time authors. 100% from unagented writers. Pays advance.** Publishes book 9 months after acceptance. Accepts simultaneous submissions. Responds in 3 months to relevant queries. "Only those submissions relevant to our needs will receive a response to queries." Guidelines online.

NONFICTION Subjects include professional brewing, homebrewing, technical brewing. "We seek to do this in a positive atmosphere, create lasting relationships and shared pride in our contributions to the brewing and beer community. The books we select to carry out this mission include titles relevant to homebrewing, professional brewing, starting a brewery, books on particular styles of beer, industry trends, ingredients, processes and the occasional broader interest title on cooking or the history/impact of beer in our society." Query first with proposal and sample chapter.

BRICK BOOKS

Box 20081, 431 Boler Rd., London ON N6K 4G6, Canada. (519)657-8579. **E-mail:** brick.books@sympatico. ca. **Website:** www.brickbooks.ca. **Contact:** Kitty Lewis, General Manager. Estab. 1975. Publishes trade paperback originals. Brick Books has a reading period of January 1-April 30. Mss received outside that period will be returned. No multiple submissions. Pays 10% royalty in book copies only. **Publishes 7 titles/year. 100 mss received/year. 30% of books from first-time authors. 100% from unagented writers.** Publishes ms 2 years after acceptance. Responds in 3-4 months to queries. Book catalog free or online. Guidelines online.

"We publish only poetry."

POETRY Submit only poetry.

TIPS "Writers without previous publications in literary journals or magazines are rarely considered by Brick Books for publication."

BRICK ROAD POETRY PRESS, INC.

513 Broadway, Columbus GA 31901. (706)649-3080. **Fax:** (706)649-3094. **E-mail:** kbadowski@brickroadpoetrypress.com. **Website:** www.brickroadpoetrypress.com. **Contact:** Ron Self and Keith Badowski, co-editors/founders. Estab. 2009. Publishes poetry only: books (single author collections). The mission of Brick Road Poetry Press is to publish and promote poetry that entertains, amuses, edifies, and surprises a wide audience of appreciative readers. "We are not qualified to judge who deserves to be published, so we concentrate on publishing what we enjoy. Our preference is for poetry geared toward dramatizing the human experience in language rich with sensory image and metaphor, recognizing that poetry can be, at one and the same time, both familiar as the perspiration of daily labor and as outrageous as a carnival sideshow. We prefer poetry that offers a coherent human voice, a sense of humor, attentiveness to words and language, narratives with surprise twists, persona poems, and/or philosophical or spiritual themes explored through the concrete scenes and images." Does not want overemphasis on rhyme, intentional obscurity or riddling, highfalutin vocabulary, greeting card verse, overt religious statements of faith and/or praise, and/or abstractions. **Publishes 3-6 titles/year. 200 Pays royalties and 15 author copies. Initial print run of 150, print-on-demand thereafter.** Publishes ms 1 year after acceptance. Accepts simultaneous submissions. Responds in 3 months. "We accept .doc, .rtf, or .pdf file formats. We prefer electronic submissions but will reluctantly consider hard copy submissions by mail if USPS Flat Rate Mailing Envelope is used and with the stipulation that, should the author's work be chosen for publication, an electronic version (.doc or .rtf) must be prepared in a timely manner and at the poet's expense." Please include cover letter with poetry publication/recognition highlights and something intriguing about your life story or ongoing pursuits. "We would like to develop a connection with the poet as well as the poetry." Please include the collection title in the cover letter.

POETRY Publishes poetry only: books (single author collections) "We prefer poetry that offers a coherent human voice, a sense of humor, attentiveness to words and language, narratives with surprise twists, persona poems, and/or philosophical or spiritual themes explored through the concrete scenes and images." Publishes 3-6 poetry books/year Mss accepted through open submission December-January and competition August-November. "We accept .doc, .rtf, or .pdf file formats. We prefer electronic submissions but will reluctantly consider hard copy submissions by mail if USPS Flat Rate Mailing Envelope is used and with the stipulation that, should the author's work be chosen for publication, an electronic version (.doc or .rtf) must be prepared in a timely manner and at the poet's expense." Please include cover letter with poetry publication/recognition highlights and something intriguing about your life story or ongoing pursuits. "We would like to develop a connection with the poet as well as the poetry." Please include the collection title in the cover letter. "We want to publish poets who are engaged in the literary community, including regular submission of work to various publications and participation in poetry readings, workshops, and writers' groups. That said, we would never rule out an emerging poet who demonstrates ability and motivation to move in that direction." Does not want overemphasis on rhyme, intentional obscurity or riddling, highfalutin vocabulary, greeting card verse, overt religious statements of faith and/or praise, and/or abstractions. Publishes poetry only: books (single author collections) "We accept .doc, .rtf, or .pdf file formats. We prefer electronic submissions but will reluctantly consider hard copy submissions by mail if USPS Flat Rate Mailing Envelope is used and with the stipulation that, should the author's work be chosen for publication, an electronic version (.doc or .rtf) must be prepared in a timely manner and at the poet's expense." Please include cover letter with poetry publication/recognition highlights and something intriguing about your life story or ongoing pursuits. "We would like to develop a connection with the poet as well as the poetry." Please include the collection title in the cover letter. "We want to publish poets who are engaged in the literary community, including regular submission of work to various publications and participation in poetry readings, workshops, and writers' groups. That said, we would never rule out an emerging poet who demonstrates ability and motivation to move in that direction."

TIPS "The best way to discover all that poetry can be and to expand the limits of your own poetry is to read expansively. We recommend the following poets: Kim Addonizio, Ken Babstock, Coleman Barks, Billy Collins, Morri Creech, Cynthia Cruz, Alice Friman, John Glenday, Beth A. Gylys, Jane Hirshfield, Jane Kenyon, Ted Kooser, Stanley Kunitz, Thomas Lux, Barry Marks, Michael Meyerhofer, Linda Pastan, Mark Strand, and Natasha D. Trethewey."

BROADVIEW PRESS, INC.

P.O. Box 1243, Peterborough ON K9J 7H5, Canada. (705)743-8990. **Fax:** (705)743-8353. **E-mail:** customerservice@broadviewpress.com. **Website:** www.broadviewpress.com. Estab. 1985. "We publish in a broad variety of subject areas in the arts and social sciences. We are open to a broad range of political and philosophical viewpoints, from liberal and conservative to libertarian and Marxist, and including a wide range of feminist viewpoints." **Publishes over 40 titles/year. 500 queries received/year. 200 mss received/year. 10% of books from first-time authors. 99% from unagented writers. Pays royalty.** Publishes ms 12 months after acceptance. Accepts simultaneous submissions. Responds in 1 month to queries; 2 months to proposals; 4 months to mss. Book catalog available free. Guidelines online.

NONFICTION Subjects include philosophy, religion, politics. "Our focus is very much on English studies and Philosophy, but within those two core subject areas we are open to a broad range of academic approaches and political viewpoints. We welcome feminist perspectives, and we have a particular interest in addressing environmental issues. Our publishing program is internationally-oriented, and we publish for a broad range of geographical markets-but as a canadian company we also publish a broad range of titles with a canadian emphasis." Query with SASE. Submit proposal package. Reviews artwork/photos. Send photocopies.

TIPS "Our titles often appeal to a broad readership; we have many books that are as much of interest to the general reader as they are to academics and students."

BROADWAY BOOKS

Penguin Random House, 1745 Broadway, New York NY 10019. (212)782-9000. **Fax:** (212)782-9411. **Website:** crownpublishing.com/imprint/broadway-books. Estab. 1995. Publishes hardcover and trade paperback books. "Broadway publishes high quality general interest nonfiction and fiction for adults." **Receives thousands of mss/year. Pays royalty on retail price. Pays advance.** Accepts simultaneous submissions.

IMPRINTS Broadway Books; Broadway Business; Doubleday; Doubleday Image; Doubleday Religious Publishing; Main Street Books; Nan A. Talese.

NONFICTION Subjects include child guidance, contemporary culture, history, memoirs, multicultural, New Age, psychology, sex, spirituality, sports, travel, current affairs, motivational/inspirational, popular culture, consumer reference. *Agented submissions only.*

FICTION *Agented submissions only.*

BRONZE MAN BOOKS

Millikin University, 1184 W. Main, Decatur IL 62522. (217)424-6264. **E-mail:** rbrooks@millikin.edu. **Website:** www.bronzemanbooks.com. **Contact:** Dr. Randy Brooks, editorial board; Edwin Walker, editorial board. Estab. 2006. Publishes hardcover, trade paperback, literary chapbooks and mass market paperback originals. A student-owned and operated press located on Millikin University's campus in Decatur, Ill., Bronze Man Books is dedicated to integrating quality design and meaningful content. The company exposes undergraduate students to the process of publishing by combining the theory of writing, publishing, editing and designing with the practice of running a book publishing company. This emphasis on performance learning is a hallmark of Millikin's brand of education. **Publishes 3-4 titles/year. 80% of books from first-time authors. 100% from unagented writers. Outright purchase based on wholesale value of 10% of a press run.** Publishes book 6-12 months after acceptance. Accepts simultaneous submissions. Responds in 1-3 months.

NONFICTION Subjects include architecture, art, literature, parenting. Query with SASE. E-mail inquiries are welcome.

FICTION Subjects include picture books, poetry. Subjects include art, graphic design, exhibits, general. Submit completed ms.

POETRY Submit completed ms.

TIPS "The art books are intended for serious collectors and scholars of contemporary art, especially of artists from the Midwestern US. These books are published in conjunction with art exhibitions at Millikin University or the Decatur Area Arts Council. The children's books have our broadest audience, and the literary chapbooks are intended for readers of contemporary fiction, drama, and poetry."

☺ THE BRUCEDALE PRESS

P.O. Box 2259, Port Elgin ON N0H 2C0, Canada. (519)832-6025. **E-mail:** info@brucedalepress.ca. **Website:** brucedalepress.ca. Publishes hardcover and trade paperback originals. The Brucedale Press publishes books and other materials of regional interest and merit, as well as literary, historical, and/or pictorial works. **Publishes 3 titles/year. 50 queries received/year. 30 mss received/year. 75% of books from first-time authors. 100% from unagented writers. Pays royalty.** Publishes book 1 year after acceptance. Accepts simultaneous submissions. Book catalog online. "Unless responding to an invitation to submit, query first by Canada Post with outline and sample chapter to book-length manuscripts. Send full manuscripts for work intended for children." Guidelines online.

 ◒ *Accepts works by Canadian authors only. Book submissions reviewed November to January. Submissions to* The Leaf Journal *accepted in September and March only. Manuscripts must be in English and thoroughly proofread before being sent. Use Canadian spellings and style.*

NONFICTION Subjects include history, memoirs, photography. Reviews artwork/photos.

FICTION Subjects include fantasy, feminist, historical, humor, juvenile, literary, mystery, plays, poetry, romance, short story collections, young adult.

TIPS "Our focus is very regional. In reading submissions, I look for quality writing with a strong connection to the Queen's Bush area of Ontario. All authors should visit our website, get a catalog, and read our books before submitting."

BUCKNELL UNIVERSITY PRESS

Bucknell University, 1 Dent Dr., Lewisburg PA 17837. (570)577-3674. **E-mail:** universitypress@bucknell.edu. **Website:** www.bucknell.edu/universitypress. **Contact:** Greg Clingham, director. Estab. 1968. Publishes hardcover, paperback, and e-books on various platforms. "In all fields, our criteria are scholarly excellence, critical originality, and interdisciplinary and theoretical expertise and sensitivity." **Publishes 35-40 titles/year.** Book catalog available free. Guidelines online.

NONFICTION Subjects include environment, ethnic, history, law, literary criticism, multicultural, philosophy, psychology, sociology, Luso-Hispanic studies, Latin American studies, 18-century studies, ecocriticism, African studies, Irish literature, cultural studies, historiography, legal theory. Series: Transits: Literature, Thought & Culture 1650-1850; Bucknell Series in Latin American Literature and Theory; Eighteenth-Century Scotland; New Studies in the Age of Goethe; Contemporary Irish Writers; Griot Project Book Series; Apercus: Histories Texts Cultures. Submit full proposal and CV by Word attachment.

BULLITT PUBLISHING

P.O. Box, Austin TX 78729. **E-mail:** bullittpublishing@yahoo.com. **E-mail:** submissions@bullittpublishing.com. **Website:** bullittpublishing.com. **Contact:** Pat Williams, editor. Estab. 2012. Publishes trade paperback and electronic originals. "Bullitt Publishing is a royalty-offering publishing house specializing in smart, contemporary romance. We are proud to provide print on demand distribution through the world's most comprehensive distribution channel including Amazon.com and BarnesandNoble.com. Digital distribution is available through the world's largest distibutor of e-books and can be downloaded to reading devices such as the iPhone, Ipod Touch, Amazon Kindle, Sony Reader or Barnes & Noble nook. E-books are distributed to the Apple iBookstore, Barnes & Noble, Sony, Kobo and the Diesel eBook

Store. Whether this is your first novel or your 101st novel, Bullitt Publishing will treat you with the same amount of professionalism and respect. While we expect well-written entertaining manuscripts from all of our authors, we promise to provide high quality, professional product in return." **Publishes 12 titles/year.** Accepts simultaneous submissions.

IMPRINTS Includes imprint Tempo Romance.

FICTION Subjects include romance.

BULL PUBLISHING CO.

P.O. Box 1377, Boulder CO 80306. (800)676-2855. **Fax:** (303)545-6354. **Website:** www.bullpub.com. **Contact:** James Bull, publisher. Estab. 1974. Publishes hardcover and trade paperback originals. "Bull Publishing publishes health and nutrition books for the public with an emphasis on self-care, nutrition, women's health, weight control and psychology." **Publishes 6-8 titles/year. Pays 10-16% royalty on wholesale price (net to publisher).** Publishes ms 6 months after acceptance. Accepts simultaneous submissions. Book catalog available free.

NONFICTION Subjects include education. Subjects include self-care, nutrition, fitness, child health and nutrition, health education, mental health. "We look for books that fit our area of strength: responsible books on health that fill a substantial public need, and that we can market primarily through professionals." Submit outline, sample chapters. Reviews artwork/photos.

BURFORD BOOKS

101 E. State St., #301, Ithaca NY 14850. (607)319-4373. **E-mail:** info@burfordbooks.com. **Website:** www.burfordbooks.com. **Contact:** Burford Books Editorial Department. Estab. 1997. Publishes hardcover originals, trade paperback originals and reprints. Burford Books publishes books on all aspects of the outdoors, from backpacking to sports, practical and literary, as well as books on food & wine, military history, and the Finger Lakes region of New York State. **Publishes 12 titles/year. 300 queries; 200 mss received/year. 30% of books from first-time authors. 60% from unagented writers. Pays royalty on wholesale price.** Publishes book 18 months after acceptance. Accepts simultaneous submissions. Responds in 1 week to queries; 1 month to proposals; 2 months to mss. Book catalog and ms guidelines online.

NONFICTION Subjects include Americana, animals, cooking, foods, history, hobbies, military, recre-

ation, sports, travel, fitness. "Burford Books welcomes proposals on new projects, especially in the subject areas in which we specialize: sports, the outdoors, golf, nature, gardening, food and wine, travel, and military history. We are not currently considering fiction or children's books. In general it's sufficient to send a brief proposal letter that outlines your idea, which should be e-mailed to info@burfordbooks.com with the word 'query' in the subject line." Reviews artwork/photos. Send digital images.

BUSTER BOOKS

16 Lion Yard, Tremadoc Rd., London WA SW4 7NQ, United Kingdom. (020)7720-8643. **Fax:** (022)7720-8953. **E-mail:** enquiries@mombooks.com. **Website:** www.busterbooks.co.uk. "We are dedicated to providing irresistible and fun books for children of all ages. We typically publish black & white nonfiction for children aged 8-12 novelty titles-including doodle books." Accepts simultaneous submissions.

NONFICTION Prefers synopsis and sample text over complete ms.

TIPS "We do not accept picturebook or poetry submissions. Please do not send original artwork as we cannot guarantee its safety." Visit website before submitting.

BUTTE PUBLICATIONS, INC.

P.O. Box 1328, Hillsboro OR 97123-1328. (503)648-9791. **E-mail:** service@buttepublications.com. **Website:** www.buttepublications.com. Estab. 1992. Butte Publications, Inc., publishes classroom books related to deafness and language. **Publishes several titles/year.** Accepts simultaneous submissions. Responds in 6 months to mss. Book catalog and ms guidelines for #10 SASE or online.

NONFICTION Subjects include education. Not seeking autobiographies or novels. Submit proposal package, including author bio, synopsis, market survey, 2-3 sample chapters, SASE and ms (if completed). Reviews artwork/photos. Send photocopies.

TIPS "Audience is students, teachers, parents, and professionals in the arena dealing with deafness and hearing loss."

BY LIGHT UNSEEN MEDIA

20 Heald St, Pepperell MA 01463. (978)433-8866. **Fax:** (978)433-8866. **E-mail:** vyrdolak@bylightunseenmedia.com. **Website:** bylightunseenmedia.com. **Contact:** Inanna Arthen, owner/editor-in-chief. Estab.

2006. Publishes hardcover, paperback and electronic originals. The only small press owned and operated by a recognized expert in vampire folklore, media and culture, By Light Unseen Media was founded in 2006. "Our mission is to explore and celebrate the variety, imagination and ambiguities of the vampire theme in fiction, history and the human psyche." **Publishes 5 titles/year. 5 mss; 50 queries received/year. 80% of books from first-time authors. 100% from unagented writers. Pays royalty of 50-70% on net as explicitly defined in contract. Payment quarterly. No advance.** Publishes book 4 months after acceptance. Accepts simultaneous submissions. Responds in 3 months. Catalog online. Ms guidelines online.

NONFICTION Subjects include creative nonfiction, vampire-related. "We are a niche small press that will *only* consider nonfiction on the theme of vampires (vampire folklore, movies, television, literature, vampires in culture, etc.). We're especially interested in academic or other well-researched material, but will consider self-help/New Age types of books (e.g. the kind of material published by Llewellyn). We use digital printing so all interiors would need to be black and white, including illustrations." Does not want anything that does not focus on vampires! Submit proposal package including outline, 3 sample chapters, brief author bio. *No unsolicited mss will be considered.* Reviews artwork. Send photocopies/scanned PDF/jpeg.

FICTION Subjects include contemporary, fantasy, feminist, gay, gothic, horror, lesbian, mystery, occult, science fiction, suspense, western, young adult, magical realism, thriller. "We are a niche small press that *only* publishes fiction relating in some way to vampires. Within that guideline, we're interested in almost any genre that includes a vampire trope, the more creative and innovative, the better. Restrictions are noted in the submission guidelines (no derivative fiction based on other works, such as Dracula, no gore-for-gore's-sake 'splatter' horror, etc.) We do not publish anthologies." Does not want anything that does not focus on vampires as the major theme. Submit proposal package including synopsis, 3 sample chapters, brief author bio. "We encourage electronic submissions." *Unsolicited mss will not be considered.*

TIPS "We strongly urge authors to familiarize themselves with the vampire genre and not imagine that they're doing something new and amazingly different just because they're not imitating the current fad."

C&T PUBLISHING

1651 Challenge Dr., Concord CA 94520-5206. (925)677-0377. **Fax:** (925)677-0373. **E-mail:** support@ctpub.com. **Website:** www.ctpub.com. Estab. 1983. Publishes hardcover and trade paperback originals. "C&T publishes well-written, beautifully designed books on quilting and fiber crafts, embroidery, dollmaking, knitting and paper crafts." **Publishes 70 titles/year.** Accepts simultaneous submissions. Responds in 3 months to queries. Book catalog free; guidelines online.

IMPRINTS Stash Books.

NONFICTION Subjects include hobbies, quilting books, occasional quilt picture books, quilt-related crafts, wearable art, needlework, fiber and surface embellishments, other books relating to fabric crafting and paper crafting.. Extensive proposal guidelines are available on the company's website.

TIPS "In our industry, we find that how-to books have the longest selling life. Quiltmakers, sewing enthusiasts, needle artists, fiber artists and paper crafters are our audience. We like to see new concepts or techniques. Include some great samples, and you'll get our attention quickly. Dynamic design is hard to resist, and if that's your forte, show us what you've done."

⊘ CALAMARI PRESS

Via Titta Scarpetta #28, Rome 00153, Italy. **E-mail:** derek@calamaripress.net. **Website:** www.calamaripress.com. Publishes paperback originals. Calamari Press publishes books of literary text and art. Mss are selected by invitation. Occasionally has open submission period—check website. Helps to be published in *SleepingFish* first. **Publishes 1-2 titles/year. Pays in author's copies.** Ms published 2-6 months after acceptance. Accepts simultaneous submissions. Responds to mss in 2 weeks. Guidelines online.

FICTION Query with outline/synopsis and 3 sample chapters. Accepts queries by e-mail only. Include brief bio. Send SASE or IRC for return of ms.

CALKINS CREEK

Boyds Mills Press, 815 Church St., Honesdale PA 18431. **Website:** www.calkinscreekbooks.com. Estab. 2004. "We aim to publish books that are a well-written blend of creative writing and extensive research, which emphasize important events, people, and places in U.S. history." **Pays authors royalty or work purchased outright.** Accepts simultaneous submissions. Guidelines online.

NONFICTION Subjects include history. Submit outline/synopsis and 3 sample chapters.

FICTION Subjects include historical. Submit outline/synopsis and 3 sample chapters.

TIPS "Read through our recently published titles and review our catalog. When selecting titles to publish, our emphasis will be on important events, people, and places in U.S. history. Writers are encouraged to submit a detailed bibliography, including secondary and primary sources, and expert reviews with their submissions."

⚊⊘ CANDLEWICK PRESS

99 Dover St., Somerville MA 02144. (617)661-3330. **Fax:** (617)661-0565. **E-mail:** bigbear@candlewick.com. **Website:** www.candlewick.com. Estab. 1991. Publishes hardcover and trade paperback originals, and reprints. "Candlewick Press publishes high-quality, illustrated children's books for ages infant through young adult. We are a truly child-centered publisher." **Publishes 200 titles/year. 5% of books from first-time authors. Pays authors royalty of 2½-10% based on retail price. Offers advance.** Accepts simultaneous submissions.

🖲 *Candlewick Press is not accepting queries or unsolicited mss at this time.*

NONFICTION Picture books: concept, biography, geography, nature/environment. Young readers: biography, geography, nature/environment.

FICTION Subjects include juvenile, picture books, young adult. Picture books: animal, concept, contemporary, fantasy, history, humor, multicultural, nature/environment, poetry. Middle readers, young adults: contemporary, fantasy, history, humor, multicultural, poetry, science fiction, sports, suspense/mystery. "We currently do not accept unsolicited editorial queries or submissions. If you are an author or illustrator and would like us to consider your work, please read our submissions policy (online) to learn more."

TIPS *"We no longer accept unsolicited mss.* See our website for further information about us."

CANTERBURY HOUSE PUBLISHING, LTD.

4535 Ottawa Trail, Sarasota FL 34233. (941)312-6912. **Website:** www.canterburyhousepublishing.com. **Contact:** Sandra Horton, editor. Estab. 2009. Publishes hardcover, trade paperback, and electronic originals. "Our audience is made up of readers looking for wholesome fiction with good southern stories, with elements of mystery, romance, and inspiration

and/or are looking for true stories of achievement and triumph over challenging circumstances. We are very strict on our submission guidelines due to our small staff, and our target market of Southern regional settings." **Publishes 3-6 titles/year. 35% of books from first-time authors. 100% from unagented writers. Pays 10-15% royalty on wholesale price.** Publishes ms 9-12 months after acceptance. Accepts simultaneous submissions. Responds in 1 month to queries; 3 months to mss. Book catalog online. Guidelines online.

NONFICTION Subjects include memoirs, regional. Query with SASE and through website e-mail upon request. Reviews artwork. Send photocopies.

FICTION Subjects include contemporary, historical, literary, mainstream, mystery, regional, romance, suspense. Query with SASE and through website.

TIPS "Because of our limited staff, we prefer authors who have good writing credentials and submit edited manuscripts. We also look at authors who are business and marketing savvy and willing to help promote their books."

⚫ CAPALL BANN PUBLISHING

Auton Farm, Milverton, Somerset TA4 1NE, United Kingdom. (44)(182)340-1528. **E-mail:** enquiries@capallbann.co.uk. **Website:** www.capallbann.co.uk. **Contact:** Julia Day (MBS, healing, animals and religion). Publishes trade and mass market paperback originals and trade paperback and mass market paperback reprints. "Our mission is to publish books of real value to enhance and improve readers' lives." **Publishes 46 titles/year. 800 queries; 450 mss received/year. 50% of books from first-time authors. 100% from unagented writers. Pays 10% royalty on net sales.** Publishes ms 4-8 months after acceptance. Accepts simultaneous submissions. Responds in 2-6 weeks to queries; 2 months to proposals and mss. Book catalog free. Guidelines online.

NONFICTION Subjects include animals, astrology, crafts, creative nonfiction, gardening, New Age, philosophy, psychic, religion, spirituality, witchcraft, paganism, druidry, ritual magic. Submit outline. Reviews artwork/photos. Send photocopies.

CAPSTONE PRESS

Capstone Young Readers, 1710 Roe Crest Dr., North Mankato MN 56003. **E-mail:** nf.il.sub@capstonepub.com; author.sub@capstonepub.com; il.sub@capstonepub.com. **Website:** www.capstonepub.com. Estab. 1991. The Capstone Press imprint publishes nonfiction with accessible text on topics kids love to capture interest and build confidence and skill in beginning, struggling, and reluctant readers, grades pre-K-9. Responds only if submissions fit needs. Mss and writing samples will not be returned. "If you receive no reply within 6 months, you should assume the editors are not interested." Catalog available upon request. Guidelines online.

CAPSTONE PROFESSIONAL

Maupin House, Capstone, 1710 Roe Crest Dr., North Mankato MN 56003. (312) 324-5200. **Fax:** (312) 324-5201. **E-mail:** info@maupinhouse.com. **Website:** www.capstonepd.com. **Contact:** Karen Soll, Managing Editor, acquisitions. Marketing Director: David Willette. Marketing Specialist: Mary McCarthy. Associate Marketing Manager: Patty Corcoran. Estab. 2013. Capstone Professional publishes professional learning resources for K-12 educators under the imprint of Maupin House. **Publishes 6-8 titles/year. Receives 25 submissions/year. 60% of books from first-time authors. 100% from unagented writers. Pays royalty. Not usually.** Publishes 6 months after acceptance. Accepts simultaneous submissions. Responds in less than 1 month. Catalog and guidelines online.
IMPRINTS Maupin House.
NONFICTION Subjects include education. Professional development offerings by Capstone Professional range from webinars and workshops to conference speakers and author visits. Submissions for products that speak to the needs of educators today are always accepted. "We continue to look for professional development resources that support grades K–8 classroom teachers in areas, such as these: Literacy, Language Arts, Content-Area Literacy, Research-Based Practices, Assessment, Inquiry, Technology, Differentiation, Standards-Based Instruction, School Safety, Classroom Management, and School Community." Reviews artwork/photos as part of the ms package. Writers should send photocopies, digital.

CARCANET PRESS

Alliance House, 4th Floor, 30 Cross St., Manchester England M2 7AQ, United Kingdom. 44(0)161 834 8730. **Fax:** 44(0)161 832 0084. **E-mail:** info@carcanet.co.uk. **Website:** www.carcanet.co.uk. **Contact:** Michael Schmidt, editorial and managing director. Estab. 1969. Publishes hardcover and trade paperback originals. "Carcanet Press is one of Britain's leading poetry publishers. It provides a comprehensive and diverse list of modern and classic poetry in English and in translation. It now incorpprates Anvil Press Poetry and represents Northern House."
IMPRINTS Fyfield Books, Lives & Letters.
NONFICTION Subjects include literature.
FICTION Subjects include poetry.
POETRY Familiarize yourself with our books, and then submit between 6 and 10 pages or work (poetry or translations) and SASE. Replies are usually sent within 6 weeks. Writers wishing to propose other projects should send a full synopsis and cover letter, with sample pages, having first ascertained that the kind of book proposed is suitable for our programme. Do not call in person.

THE CAREER PRESS, INC.

12 Parish Dr., Wayne NJ 07470. **E-mail:** aschwartz@careerpress.com. **Website:** www.careerpress.com. **Contact:** Michael Pye, senior acquisitions editor; Adam Schwartz, acquisitions editor.. Estab. 1985. Publishes hardcover and paperback originals. Career Press publishes books for adult readers seeking practical information to improve themselves in careers, business, HR, sales, entrepreneurship, and other related topics, as well as titles on supervision, management and CEOs. New Page Books publishes in the areas of New Age, new science, paranormal, the unexplained, alternative history, spirituality. Accepts simultaneous submissions. Guidelines online.
NONFICTION Subjects include recreation, nutrition. Look through our catalog; become familiar with our publications. "We like to select authors who are specialists on their topic." Submit outline, bio, TOC, 2-3 sample chapters, marketing plan, SASE. Or, send complete ms (preferred).

CARNEGIE MELLON UNIVERSITY PRESS

5032 Forbes Ave., Pittsburgh PA 15289-1021. (412)268-2861. **Fax:** (412)268-8706. **E-mail:** carnegiemellonuniversitypress@gmail.com. **Website:** www.cmu.edu/universitypress/. Estab. 1972. Publishes hardcover and trade paperback originals. **Publishes 6 titles/year.** Accepts simultaneous submissions. Book catalog and guidelines online.
NONFICTION Subjects include education, history, literary criticism, memoirs, science, sociology, translation. Query with SASE.

FICTION Subjects include literary, poetry, poetry in translation, short story collections, drama, epistolary novel.

POETRY Holds annual reading period. "This reading period is only for poets who have not previously been published by CMP." Submit complete ms. **Requires reading fee of $15**.

CAROLINA WREN PRESS

120 Morris St., Durham NC 27701. (919)560-2738. **E-mail:** carolinawrenpress@earthlink.net. **Website:** www.carolinawrenpress.org. **Contact:** Andrea Selch, president. Estab. 1976. "We publish poetry, fiction, and memoirs by, and/or about people of color, women, gay/lesbian issues, and work by writers from, living in, or writing about the U.S. South." Publishes ms 2 year after acceptance. Accepts simultaneous submissions. Responds in 3 months to queries; 6 months to mss. Guidelines online.

◯   Accepts simultaneous submissions, but "let us know if work has been accepted elsewhere."

NONFICTION Subjects include ethnic, gay, lesbian, literature, multicultural, womens issues.

FICTION Subjects include ethnic, experimental, feminist, literary, poetry, short story collections. "We are no longer publishing children's literature of any topic." Books: 6×9 paper; typeset; various bindings; illustrations. Distributes titles through Amazon.com, Barnes & Noble, Baker & Taylor, and on their website. "We very rarely accept any unsolicited manuscripts, but we accept submissions for the Doris Bakwin Award for Writing by a Woman in Jan-March of even-numbered years." Query by mail. "We will accept e-mailed queries—a letter in the body of the e-mail describing your project—but please do not send large attachments."

POETRY Publishes 2 poetry books/year, "usually through the Carolina Wren Press Poetry Series Contest. Otherwise we primarily publish women, minorities, and authors from, living in, or writing about the U.S. South." Not accepting unsolicited submissions except through Poetry Series Contest. Accepts e-mail queries, but send only letter and description of work, no large files. Carolina Wren Press Poetry Contest for a First or Second Book takes submissions, electronically, from January to March of odd-numbered years.

TIPS "Best way to get read is to submit to a contest."

⊘ CAROLRHODA BOOKS, INC.

1251 Washington Ave. N., Minneapolis MN 55401. **E-mail:** info@lernerbooks.com. **Website:** www.lernerbooks.com. Estab. 1959. "We will continue to seek targeted solicitations at specific reading levels and in specific subject areas. The company will list these targeted solicitations on our website and in national newsletters, such as the SCBWI Bulletin." Interested in "boundary-pushing" teen fiction. *Lerner Publishing Group no longer accepts submissions to any of their imprints except for Kar-Ben Publishing.* Accepts simultaneous submissions.

CARSON-DELLOSA PUBLISHING CO., INC.

P.O. Box 35665, Greensboro NC 27425-5665. (336)632-0084. **E-mail:** freelancesamples@carsondellosa.com. **Website:** www.carsondellosa.com. **Publishes 80-90 titles/year. 15-20% of books from first-time authors. 95% from unagented writers. Makes outright purchase.** Accepts simultaneous submissions. Responds in 3 months to proposals. Book catalog online. Guidelines available free.

NONFICTION Subjects include education. "We publish supplementary educational materials, such as teacher resource books, workbooks, and activity books." No textbooks or trade children's books, please. Submit proposal package, sample chapters or pages, SASE. Reviews artwork/photos. Send photocopies.

🅐⊘ CARTWHEEL BOOKS

Imprint of Scholastic Trade Division, 557 Broadway, New York NY 10012. (212)343-6100. **Website:** www.scholastic.com. Estab. 1991. Publishes novelty books, easy readers, board books, hardcover and trade paperback originals. Cartwheel Books publishes innovative books for children, up to age 8. "We are looking for 'novelties' that are books first, play objects second. Even without its gimmick, a Cartwheel Book should stand alone as a valid piece of children's literature." Accepts simultaneous submissions. Guidelines available free.

NONFICTION Subjects include animals, history, recreation, science, sports. Cartwheel Books publishes for the very young, therefore nonfiction should be written in a manner that is accessible to preschoolers through 2nd grade. Often writers choose topics that are too narrow or "special" and do not appeal to the mass market. Also, the text and vocabulary are frequently too difficult for our young audience. *Accepts mss from agents only.* Reviews artwork/photos. Send Please do not send original artwork.

FICTION Subjects include humor, juvenile, mystery, picture books. Again, the subject should have mass market appeal for very young children. Humor can be helpful, but not necessary. Mistakes writers make are a reading level that is too difficult, a topic of no interest or too narrow, or mss that are too long. *Accepts mss from agents only.*

CATHOLIC UNIVERSITY OF AMERICA PRESS

620 Michigan Ave. NE, 240 Leahy Hall, Washington DC 20064. (202)319-5052. **Fax:** (202)319-4985. **E-mail:** cua-press@cua.edu. **Website:** cuapress.cua.edu. **Contact:** Trevor Lipscombe, director. Estab. 1939. The Catholic University of America Press publishes in the fields of history (ecclesiastical and secular), literature and languages, philosophy, political theory, social studies, and theology. "We have interdisciplinary emphasis on patristics, and medieval studies. We publish works of original scholarship intended for academic libraries, scholars and other professionals and works that offer a synthesis of knowledge of the subject of interest to a general audience or suitable for use in college and university classrooms." **Publishes 30-35 titles/year. 50% of books from first-time authors. 100% from unagented writers. Pays variable royalty on net receipts.** Publishes book 18 months after acceptance. Accepts simultaneous submissions. Responds in 5 days to queries. Book catalog on request. Guidelines online.

NONFICTION Subjects include history, philosophy, religion, Church-state relations. No unrevised doctoral dissertations. Length: 40,000-120,000 words. Query with outline, sample chapter, CV, and list of previous publications.

TIPS "Scholarly monographs and works suitable for adoption as supplementary reading material in courses have the best chance."

CATO INSTITUTE

1000 Massachusetts Ave. NW, Washington DC 20001. (202)842-0200. **Website:** www.cato.org. **Contact:** Submissions Editor. Estab. 1977. Publishes hardcover originals, trade paperback originals and reprints. Cato Institute publishes books on public policy issues from a free-market or libertarian perspective. **Publishes 12 titles/year. 25% of books from first-time authors. 90% from unagented writers. Makes outright purchase of $1,000-10,000. Pays advance.** Publishes ms 9 months after acceptance. Accepts simultaneous submissions. Responds in 3 months to queries. Book catalog online.

NONFICTION Subjects include education, sociology, public policy. Query with SASE.

CAVE BOOKS

Cave Research Foundation, Hamilton Valley Rd., Cave City KY 42127. (609)530-9743. **E-mail:** editor@cavebooks.com. **Website:** www.cavebooks.com. **Contact:** Elizabeth Winkler, managing editor. Estab. 1980. Publishes hardcover and trade paperback originals and reprints. Cave Books publishes books only on caves, karst, and speleology. **Publishes 2 titles/year. 20 queries received/year. 10 mss received/year. 75% of books from first-time authors. 100% from unagented writers. Pays 10% royalty on retail price.** Publishes ms 18 months after acceptance. Responds in 2 weeks to queries; 3 months to mss.

NONFICTION Subjects include science, studies of caves, karst and animals found in karst areas, history of caves and cave exploration. Submit complete ms. Reviews artwork/photos. Send photocopies.

FICTION Subjects include adventure, historical, literary, caves, karst, speleology only. Must be realistic and centrally concerned with cave exploration. The cave and action in the cave must be central, authentic, and realistic. No gothic, no science fiction, no fantasy, no romance, no mystery, or no poetry. No novels that are not entirely about caves. We will not respond to manuscripts that do not fit this very limited category. Query with SASE. Submit complete ms.

TIPS "Our readers are interested only in caves, karst, and speleology. Please do not send manuscripts on other subjects."

CAVE HOLLOW PRESS

P.O. Drawer J, Warrensburg MO 64093. **E-mail:** gbcrump@cavehollowpress.com. **Website:** www.cavehollowpress.com. **Contact:** G.B. Crump, editor. Estab. 2001. Publishes trade paperback originals. **Publishes 1 titles/year. 85 queries received/year. 6 mss received/year. 80% of books from first-time authors. 100% from unagented writers. Pays 7-12% royalty on wholesale price. Pays negotiable amount in advance.** Publishes ms 1 year after acceptance. Accepts simultaneous submissions. Responds in 1-2 months to queries and proposals; 3-6 months to mss. Available online. Guidelines available free.

FICTION Subjects include contemporary, literary, mainstream, mystery. "We publish fiction by Midwestern authors and/or with Midwestern themes and/

or settings. Our website is updated frequently to reflect the current type of fiction Cave Hollow Press is seeking." Query with SASE.

TIPS "Our audience varies based on the type of book we are publishing. We specialize in Missouri and Midwest regional fiction. We are interested in talented writers from Missouri and the surrounding Midwest. Check our submission guidelines on the website for what type of fiction we are interested in currently."

CEDAR FORT, INC.

2373 W. 700 S, Springville UT 84663. (801)489-4084. **Fax:** (801)489-1097. **Website:** www.cedarfort.com. Estab. 1986. Publishes hardcover, trade paperback originals and reprints, mass market paperback and electronic reprints. "Each year we publish well over 100 books, and many of those are by first-time authors. At the same time, we love to see books from established authors. As one of the largest book publishers in Utah, we have the capability and enthusiasm to make your book a success, whether you are a new author or a returning one. We want to publish uplifting and edifying books that help people think about what is important in life, books people enjoy reading to relax and feel better about themselves, and books to help improve lives. Although we do put out several children's books each year, we are extremely selective. Our children's books must have strong religious or moral values, and must contain outstanding writing and an excellent storyline." **Publishes 150 titles/year. Receives 200 queries/year; 600 mss/year. 60% of books from first-time authors. 95% from unagented writers. Pays 10-12% royalty on wholesale price. Pays $2,000-50,000 advance.** Publishes book 10-14 months after acceptance. Accepts simultaneous submissions. Responds in 1 month on queries; 2 months on proposals; 4 months on mss. Catalog and guidelines online.

IMPRINTS Council Press, Sweetwater Books, Bonneville Books, Front Table Books, Hobble Creek Press, CFI, Plain Sight Publishing, Horizon Publishers, Pioneer Plus.

NONFICTION Subjects include agriculture, Americana, animals, anthropology, archeology, business, child guidance, communications, cooking, crafts, creative nonfiction, economics, education, foods, gardening, health, history, hobbies, horticulture, house and home, military, nature, recreation, regional, religion, social sciences, spirituality, war, womens is-

sues, young adult. Query with SASE; submit proposal package, including outline, 2 sample chapters; or submit completed ms. Reviews artwork as part of the ms package. Send photocopies.

FICTION Subjects include adventure, contemporary, fantasy, historical, humor, juvenile, literary, mainstream, military, multicultural, mystery, regional, religious, romance, science fiction, spiritual, sports, suspense, war, western, young adult. Submit completed ms.

TIPS "Our audience is rural, conservative, mainstream. The first page of your ms is very important because we start reading every submission, but good writing and plot keep us reading."

CENTERSTREAM PUBLISHING

P.O. Box 17878, Anaheim Hills CA 92817. (714)779-9390. **Fax:** (714)779-9390. **E-mail:** centerstrm@aol. com. **Website:** www.centerstream-usa.com. Estab. 1980. Publishes music hardcover and mass market paperback originals, trade paperback and mass market paperback reprints. Centerstream publishes music history and instructional books, all instruments plus DVDs. **Publishes 12 titles/year. 15 queries; 15 mss received/year. 80% of books from first-time authors. 100% from unagented writers. Pays 10-15% royalty on wholesale price. Pays $300-3,000 advance.** Publishes ms 8 months after acceptance. Accepts simultaneous submissions. Responds in 3 months to queries. Book catalog and ms guidelines for #10 SASE.

NONFICTION Query with SASE.

CHALICE PRESS

483 E. Lockwood Ave., Suite 100, St. Louis MO 63119. (314)231-8500. **Fax:** (314)231-8524. **E-mail:** submissions@chalicepress.com. **Website:** www.chalicepress. com. **Contact:** Bradley Lyons, president and publisher. Estab. 1911. Publishes hardcover and trade paperback originals. The mission of CBP/Chalice Press is to publish resources inviting all people into deeper relationship with God, equipping them as disciples of Jesus Christ, and sending them into ministries as the Holy Spirit calls them. CBP is a 501(c)3 not-for-profit organization. **Publishes 20 titles/year. 300 queries received/year. 50 mss received/year. 10% of books from first-time authors. 95% from unagented writers.** Publishes ms 1 year after acceptance. Accepts simultaneous submissions. Responds in 2 months to queries; 3 months to proposals and mss. Book catalog online. Guidelines online.

IMPRINTS Chalice Press, TCP Books, CBP, Inside-Out Church Camp Curriculum

NONFICTION Subjects include religion, Christian spirituality, Social justice. Submit query as directed on www.chalicepress.com.

TIPS "We publish for lay Christian readers, church ministers, and educators."

⬤ S. CHAND & COMPANY LTD.

7361 Ram Nagar, Qutab Rd., New Delhi 110055, India. (91)(11)2367-2080. **Fax:** (91)(11)2367-7446. **E-mail:** info@schandpublishing.com. **Website:** www.schandpublishing.com. Accepts simultaneous submissions. Guidelines online.

NONFICTION Subjects include history, botany, chemistry, engineering, technical, English, mathematics, physics, political science, zoology. Query through website.

CHANGELING PRESS LLC

315 N. Centre St., Martinsburg WV 25404. **E-mail:** submissions@changelingpress.com. **Website:** www.changelingpress.com. **Contact:** Margaret Riley, publisher. Estab. 2004. Publishes e-books. Erotic romance, novellas only (8,000-25,000 words). "We're currently looking for contemporary and futuristic short fiction, single title, series, and serials in the following genres and themes: sci-fi/futuristic, dark and urban fantasy, paranormal, BDSM, action adventure, guilty pleasures (adult contemporary kink), new adult, menage, bisexual and more, gay, interracial, BBW, cougar (M/F), silver fox (M/M), men and women in uniform, vampires, werewolves, elves, dragons and magical creatures, other shape shifters, magic, dark desires (demons and horror), and hentai (tentacle monsters)." **Publishes 114 titles/year. 240 5% of books from first-time authors. 100% from unagented writers. Pays 35% gross royalties on site, 50% gross off site monthly. Does not pay advance.** Publishes ms 60-90 days after acceptance. Responds in 1 week to queries. Catalog online. Guidelines available.

IMPRINTS Razor's Edge Press.

FICTION Subjects include erotica, ethnic, fantasy, gay, historical, horror, juvenile, literary, military, multicultural, mystery, romance, science fiction, spiritual, suspense, war, western, young adult. Accepts unsolicited submissions. No lesbian fiction submissions without prior approval, please. Absolutely no lesbian fiction written by men. E-mail submissions only.

CHARLESBRIDGE PUBLISHING

85 Main St., Watertown MA 02472. (617)926-0329. **Fax:** (617)926-5720. **E-mail:** tradeeditorial@charlesbridge.com. **E-mail:** yasubs@charlesbridge.com. **Website:** www.charlesbridge.com. Estab. 1980. Publishes hardcover and trade paperback nonfiction and fiction, children's books for the trade and library markets. "Charlesbridge publishes high-quality books for children, with a goal of creating lifelong readers and lifelong learners. Our books encourage reading and discovery in the classroom, library, and home. We believe that books for children should offer accurate information, promote a positive worldview, and embrace a child's innate sense of wonder and fun. To this end, we continually strive to seek new voices, new visions, and new directions in children's literature. As of September 2015, we are now accepting young adult novels for consideration." **Publishes 30 titles/year. 10-20% of books from first-time authors. 80% from unagented writers. Pays royalty. Pays advance.** Publishes ms 2-4 years after acceptance. Accepts simultaneous submissions. Responds in 3 months. Guidelines online.

NONFICTION Subjects include animals, creative nonfiction, history, multicultural, science, social science. Strong interest in nature, environment, social studies, and other topics for trade and library markets. Please submit only 1 or 2 chapters at a time. For nonfiction books longer than 30 ms pages, send a detailed proposal, a chapter outline, and 1-3 chapters of text.

FICTION Subjects include young adult. Strong stories with enduring themes. Charlesbridge publishes both picture books and transitional bridge books⊠ (books ranging from early readers to middle-grade chapter books). Our fiction titles include lively, plot-driven stories with strong, engaging characters. No alphabet books, board books, coloring books, activity books, or books with audiotapes or CD-ROMs. Please submit only 1 ms at a time. For picture books and shorter bridge books, please send a complete ms. For fiction books longer than 30 ms pages, please send a detailed plot synopsis, a chapter outline, and 3 chapters of text. If sending a young adult novel, mark the front of the envelope w/ YA NOVEL ENCLOSED. Please note, for YA, e-mail submissions are preferred to the following address; YAsubs@charlesbridge.com. Only responds if interested. Full guidelines on site.

TIPS "To become acquainted with our publishing program, we encourage you to review our books and visit our website where you will find our catalog."

CHELSEA GREEN PUBLISHING CO.

85 N. Main St., Suite 120, White River Junction VT 05001. (802)295-6300. **Fax:** (802)295-6444. **E-mail:** editorial@chelseagreen.com. **E-mail:** submissions@chelseagreen.com. **Website:** www.chelseagreen.com. Estab. 1984. Publishes hardcover and trade paperback originals and reprints. "Since 1984, Chelsea Green has been the publishing leader for books on the politics and practice of sustainable living." **Publishes 18-25 titles/year. 600-800 queries received/year. 200-300 mss received/year. 30% of books from first-time authors. 80% from unagented writers. Pays royalty on publisher's net. Pays $2,500-10,000 advance.** Publishes book 18 months after acceptance. Accepts simultaneous submissions. Responds in 2 weeks to queries; 1 month to proposals/mss. Book catalog online. Guidelines online.

NONFICTION Subjects include agriculture, alternative lifestyles, business, community, cooking, economics, environment, foods, gardening, government, health, medicine, politics, science, simple living, renewable energy, and other sustainability topics. Autobiography, memoir, and self-help. Prefers electronic queries and proposals via e-mail (as a single attachment). If sending via snail mail, submissions will only be returned with SASE. Please review our guidelines carefully before submitting. Reviews artwork/photos.

TIPS "Our readers and our authors are passionate about finding sustainable and viable solutions to contemporary challenges in the fields of energy, food production, economics, and building. It would be helpful for prospective authors to have a look at several of our current books, as well as our website."

CHEMICAL PUBLISHING CO., INC.

1309 Zuni Ln., Topanga CA 90290. (888)439-3976. **Fax:** (888)439-3976. **E-mail:** info@chemical-publishing.com. **Website:** www.chemical-publishing.com. **Contact:** B. Carr, publisher. Estab. 1934. Publishes hardcover originals. Chemical Publishing Co., Inc., publishes professional chemistry-technical titles aimed at people employed in the chemical industry, libraries and graduate courses. "We invite the submission of manuscripts whether they are technical, scientific or serious popular expositions. All submitted manuscripts and planned works will receive prompt attention. The staff will consider finished and proposed manuscripts by authors whose works have not been previously published as sym-

pathetically as those by experienced authors. Please do not hesitate to consult us about such manuscripts or about your ideas for writing them." **Publishes 10-15 titles/year. 20 queries received/year. 50% of books from first-time authors. 100% from unagented writers. Pays 10% royalty on retail price or makes negotiable outright purchase. Pays negotiable advance.** Publishes ms 8 months after acceptance. Responds in 3 weeks to queries; 5 weeks to proposals; 1 months to mss. Book catalog available free. Guidelines online.

NONFICTION Subjects include science, analytical methods, chemical technology, cosmetics, dictionaries, engineering, environmental science, food technology, formularies, industrial technology, medical, metallurgy, textiles. Submit outline, a few pages of 3 sample chapters, SASE. Download CPC submission form online and include with submission. Reviews, artwork and photos should also be part of the ms package.

TIPS "Audience is professionals in various fields of chemistry, corporate and public libraries, college libraries. We request a fax letter with an introduction of the author and the kind of book written. Afterwards, we will reply. If the title is of interest, then we will request samples of the manuscript."

CHICAGO REVIEW PRESS

814 N. Franklin St., Chicago IL 60610. (312)337-0747. **Fax:** (312)337-5110. **E-mail:** frontdesk@chicagoreviewpress.com. **Website:** www.chicagoreviewpress.com. **Contact:** Cynthia Sherry, publisher; Yuval Taylor, senior editor; Jerome Pohlen, senior editor; Lisa Reardon, senior editor. Estab. 1973. "Chicago Review Press publishes high-quality, nonfiction, educational activity books that extend the learning process through hands-on projects and accurate and interesting text. We look for activity books that are as much fun as they are constructive and informative." **Pays authors royalty of 7.5-12.5% based on retail price. Offers advances of $3,000-6,000. Pays illustrators and photographers by the project (range varies considerably).** Publishes a book 1-2 years after acceptance. Accepts simultaneous submissions. Responds in 2 months. Book catalog available for $3. Ms guidelines available for $3.

IMPRINTS Academy Chicago; Ball Publishing; Chicago Review Press; Lawrence Hill Books; Zephyr Press.

NONFICTION Young readers, middle readers and young adults: activity books, arts/crafts, multicultural, history, nature/environment, science. "We're interested in hands-on, educational books; anything else probably will be rejected." Average length: young readers and young adults—144-160 pages. Enclose cover letter and a brief synopsis of book in 1-2 paragraphs, table of contents and first 3 sample chapters; prefers not to receive e-mail queries. For children's activity books include a few sample activities with a list of the others. Full guidelines available on site.

FICTION Guidelines now available on website.

TIPS "We're looking for original activity books for small children and the adults caring for them—new themes and enticing projects to occupy kids' imaginations and promote their sense of personal creativity. We like activity books that are as much fun as they are constructive. Please write for guidelines so you'll know what we're looking for."

⊘ CHILDREN'S BRAINS ARE YUMMY (CBAY) BOOKS

P.O. Box 670296, Dallas TX 75367. **E-mail:** submissions@cbaybooks.com. **Website:** www.cbaybooks.com. **Contact:** Madeline Smoot, publisher. Estab. 2008. "CBAY Books currently focuses on quality fantasy and science fiction books for the middle grade and teen markets. We are not currently accepting unsolicited submissions." **Publishes 3-6 titles/year. 30% of books from first-time authors. 80% from unagented writers. Pays authors royalty 10%-15% based on wholesale price. Offers advances against royalties. Average amount $500. Pays advance.** Publishes ms 24 months after acceptance. Accepts simultaneous submissions. Responds in 2 months. "We are distributed by IPG. Our books can be found in their catalog at www.ipgbooks.com.". Brochure and guidelines online.

FICTION Subjects include adventure, fantasy, juvenile, mystery, science fiction, short story collections, suspense, young adult, folktales.

◕⊘ CHILD'S PLAY (INTERNATIONAL) LTD.

Child's Play, Ashworth Rd. Bridgemead, Swindon, Wiltshire SN5 7YD, United Kingdom. **E-mail:** neil@childs-play.com; office@childs-play.com. **Website:** www.childs-play.com. **Contact:** Sue Baker, Neil Burden, manuscript acquisitions. Art Director: Annie Kubler. Estab. 1972. Specializes in nonfiction, fiction, educational material, multicultural material. Produces 30 picture books/year; 10 young readers/year. "A child's early years are more important than any other. This is when children learn most about the world around them and the language they need to survive and grow. Child's Play aims to create exactly the right material for this all-important time." **Publishes 40 titles/year.** Publishes book 2 years after acceptance. Accepts simultaneous submissions.

○ "Due to a backlog of submissions, Child's Play is currently no longer able to accept anymore manuscripts."

NONFICTION Picture books: activity books, animal, concept, multicultural, music/dance, nature/environment, science. Young readers: activity books, animal, concept, multicultural, music/dance, nature/environment, science. Average word length: picture books—2,000; young readers—3,000.

FICTION Picture books: adventure, animal, concept, contemporary, folktales, multicultural, nature/environment. Young readers: adventure, animal, anthology, concept, contemporary, folktales, humor, multicultural, nature/environment, poetry. Average word length: picture books—1,500; young readers—2,000.

TIPS "Look at our website to see the kind of work we do before sending. Do not send cartoons. We do not publish novels. We do publish lots of books with pictures of babies/toddlers."

CHOSEN BOOKS

a division of Baker Publishing Group, 3985 Bradwater St., Fairfax VA 22031. (703)764-8250. **E-mail:** jcampbell@chosenbooks.com. **Website:** www.chosenbooks.com. **Contact:** Jane Campbell, editorial director. Estab. 1971. Publishes hardcover and trade paperback originals. "We publish well-crafted books that recognize the gifts and ministry of the Holy Spirit, and help the reader live a more empowered and effective life for Jesus Christ." **Publishes 24 titles/year. 15% of books from first-time authors. 85% from unagented writers. Pays modest advance.** Publishes book 18–24 months after acceptance. Accepts simultaneous submissions. Responds in 2-3 months to queries. Guidelines online.

NONFICTION "We publish books reflecting the current acts of the Holy Spirit in the world, books with a charismatic Christian orientation, or a very few thematic first-person narratives. (No autobiographies, please.) Query briefly by e-mail first." No New Age, poetry, fiction, autobiographies, biographies, compilations, Bible studies, booklets, academic, or children's books.

TIPS "We look for solid, practical advice for the mature Christian. Platform essential. No chronicling of life events, please. State the topic or theme of your book clearly in your query."

CHRISTIAN FOCUS PUBLICATIONS

Geanies House, Fearn, Tain Ross-shire Scotland IV20 1TW, United Kingdom. (44)1862-871-011. **Fax:** (44)1862-871-699. **E-mail:** submissions@christian-focus.com. **Website:** www.christianfocus.com. **Contact:** Director of Publishing. Estab. 1975. Specializes in Christian material, nonfiction, fiction, educational material. **Publishes 22-32 titles/year. 2% of books from first-time authors.** Publishes book 1 year after acceptance. Accepts simultaneous submissions. Responds to queries in 2 weeks; mss in 3 to 6 months.

NONFICTION All levels: activity books, biography, history, religion, science. Average word length: picture books—5,000; young readers—5,000; middle readers—5,000-10,000; young adult/teens—10,000-20,000. Query or submit outline/synopsis and 3 sample chapters. Include Author Information Form from site with submission. Will consider electronic submissions and previously published work.

FICTION Picture books, young readers, adventure, history, religion. Middle readers: adventure, problem novels, religion. Young adult/teens: adventure, history, problem novels, religion. Average word length: young readers—5,000; middle readers—max 10,000; young adult/teen—max 20,000.

TIPS "Be aware of the international market as regards writing style/topics as well as illustration styles. Our company sells rights to European as well as Asian countries. Fiction sales are not as good as they were. Christian fiction for youngsters is not a product that is performing well in comparison to nonfiction such as Christian biography/Bible stories/church history, etc."

CHRONICLE BOOKS

680 Second St., San Francisco CA 94107. **E-mail:** submissions@chroniclebooks.com. **Website:** www.chroniclebooks.com. "We publish an exciting range of books, stationery, kits, calendars, and novelty formats. Our list includes children's books and interactive formats; young adult books; cookbooks; fine art, design, and photography; pop culture; craft, fashion,

beauty, and home decor; relationships, mind-body-spirit; innovative formats such as interactive journals, kits, decks, and stationery; and much, much more." **Publishes 90 titles/year. Generally pays authors in royalties based on retail price, "though we do occasionally work on a flat fee basis." Advance varies. Illustrators paid royalty based on retail price or flat fee.** Publishes a book 1-3 years after acceptance. Accepts simultaneous submissions. Responds to queries in 1 month. Book catalog for 9x12 SAE and 8 first-class stamps. Ms guidelines for #10 SASE.

NONFICTION Subjects include art, beauty, cooking, crafts, house and home, New Age, pop culture. "We're always looking for the new and unusual. We do accept unsolicited manuscripts and we review all proposals. However, given the volume of proposals we receive, we are not able to personally respond to unsolicited proposals unless we are interested in pursuing the project." Submit via mail or e-mail (prefers e-mail for adult submissions; only by mail for children's submissions). Submit proposal (guidelines online) and allow 3 months for editors to review and for children's submissions, allow 6 months. If submitting by mail, do not include SASE since our staff will not return materials.

FICTION Only interested in fiction for children and young adults. No adult fiction. Submit complete ms (picture books); submit outline/synopsis and 3 sample chapters (for older readers). Will not respond to submissions unless interested. Will not consider submissions by fax, e-mail or disk. Do not include SASE; do not send original materials. No submissions will be returned.

CHRONICLE BOOKS FOR CHILDREN

680 Second St., San Francisco CA 94107. (415)537-4200. **Fax:** (415)537-4460. **E-mail:** submissions@chroniclebooks.com. **Website:** www.chroniclekids.com. Publishes hardcover and trade paperback originals. "Chronicle Books for Children publishes an eclectic mixture of traditional and innovative children's books. Our aim is to publish books that inspire young readers to learn and grow creatively while helping them discover the joy of reading. We're looking for quirky, bold artwork and subject matter." **Publishes 100-110 titles/year. 30,000 queries received/year. 6% of books from first-time authors. 25% from unagented writers. Pays variable advance.** Publishes a book 18-24 months after acceptance. Accepts simulta-

neous submissions. Responds in 2-4 weeks to queries; 6 months to mss. Book catalog for 9x12 envelope and 3 first-class stamps. Guidelines online.

NONFICTION Subjects include animals, multicultural, science. Query with synopsis. Reviews artwork/photos.

FICTION Subjects include multicultural, young adult, picture books. Does not accept proposals by fax, via e-mail, or on disk. When submitting artwork, either as a part of a project or as samples for review, do not send original art.

TIPS "We are interested in projects that have a unique bent to them—be it in subject matter, writing style, or illustrative technique. As a small list, we are looking for books that will lend our list a distinctive flavor. Primarily we are interested in fiction and nonfiction picture books for children ages up to 8 years, and nonfiction books for children ages up to 12 years. We publish board, pop-up, and other novelty formats as well as picture books. We are also interested in early chapter books, middle grade fiction, and young adult projects."

CHURCH PUBLISHING INC.

19 E. 34th St., New York NY 10016. (800)223-6602. **Fax:** (212)779-3392. **E-mail:** nabryan@cpg.org. **Website:** www.churchpublishing.org. **Contact:** Nancy Bryan, editorial director. Estab. 1884. "With a religious publishing heritage dating back to 1918 and headquartered today in New York City, CPI is an official publisher of worship materials and resources for The Episcopal Church, plus a multi-faceted publisher and supplier to the broader ecumenical marketplace. In the nearly 100 years since its first publication, Church Publishing has emerged as a principal provider of liturgical and musical resources for The Episcopal Church, along with works on church leadership, pastoral care and Christian formation. With its growing portfolio of professional books and resources, Church Publishing was recognized in 1997 as the official publisher for the General Convention of the Episcopal Church in the United States. Simultaneously through the years, Church Publishing has consciously broadened its program, reach, and service to the church by publishing books for and about the worldwide Anglican Communion." Accepts simultaneous submissions.

IMPRINTS Church Publishing, Morehouse Publishing, Seabury Books.

TIPS "Prefer using freelancers who are located in central Pennsylvania and are available for meetings when necessary."

CINCO PUNTOS PRESS

701 Texas Ave., El Paso TX 79901. (915)838-1625. **Fax:** (915)838-1635. **E-mail:** info@cincopuntos.com. **Website:** www.cincopuntos.com. **Contact:** Lee Byrd, acquisitions editor. "We don't always know what we're looking for until we actually see it, but the one thing that matters to us is that the writing is good, that it is work that comes from the heart and soul of the author and that it fits well with the concerns of our press." Call first for submission details.

FICTION "We do not look at unsolicited mss or at work that comes via e-mail."

CLARION BOOKS

Houghton Mifflin Co., 215 Park Ave. S., New York NY 10003. **Website:** www.hmhco.com. Estab. 1965. Publishes hardcover originals for children. "Clarion Books publishes picture books, nonfiction, and fiction for infants through grade 12. Avoid telling your stories in verse unless you are a professional poet. *We are no longer responding to your unsolicited submission unless we are interested in publishing it. Please do not include a SASE. Submissions will be recycled, and you will not hear from us regarding the status of your submission unless we are interested. We regret that we cannot respond personally to each submission, but we do consider each and every submission we receive.*" **Publishes 50 titles/year. Pays 5-10% royalty on retail price. Pays minimum of $4,000 advance.** Publishes a book 2 years after acceptance. Accepts simultaneous submissions. Responds in 2 months to queries. Guidelines online.

NONFICTION Subjects include Americana, history, photography, holiday. No unsolicited mss. Query with SASE. Submit proposal package, sample chapters, SASE. Reviews artwork/photos. Send photocopies.

FICTION Subjects include adventure, historical, humor, mystery, suspense, strong character studies, contemporary. "Clarion is highly selective in the areas of historical fiction, fantasy, and science fiction. A novel must be superlatively written in order to find a place on the list. Mss that arrive without an SASE of adequate size will *not* be responded to or returned. Accepts fiction translations." Submit complete ms. No queries, please. Send to only *one* Clarion editor.

TIPS "Looks for freshness, enthusiasm—in short, life."

CLARITY PRESS, INC.

2625 Piedmont Rd. NE, Suite 56, Atlanta GA 30324. (404)647-6501. **Fax:** (877)613-7868. **E-mail:** claritypress@usa.net. **Website:** www.claritypress.com. **Contact:** Diana G. Collier, editorial director (contemporary social justice issues). Estab. 1984. Publishes hardcover and trade paperback originals and e-books. **Publishes 8 titles/year. 20% of books from first-time authors. 100% from unagented writers.** Accepts simultaneous submissions. Responds to queries only if interested. Guidelines available.

IMPRINTS Clear Day Books.

NONFICTION Subjects include contemporary culture, economics, environment, ethnic, government, history, labor, law, military, multicultural, politics, world affairs, human rights/socioeconomic and minority issues, globalization, social justice. Publishes books on contemporary global issues in U.S., Middle East and Africa, on US public and foreign policy. No fiction. Query by e-mail only with synopsis, TOC, résumé, publishing history.

FICTION quality fiction which addresses social/political context and issues

TIPS "Check our titles on the website."

Ⓐ CLARKSON POTTER

Penguin Random House, 1745 Broadway, New York NY 10019. (212)782-9000. **Website:** www.clarksonpotter.com. Estab. 1959. Publishes hardcover and trade paperback originals. Accepts agented submissions only. Clarkson Potter specializes in publishing cooking books, decorating and other around-the-house how-to subjects.

NONFICTION Subjects include child guidance, memoirs, photography, psychology, translation. Agented submissions only.

CLEIS PRESS

Cleis Press & Viva Editions, 101 Hudson St., 37th Floor, Suite 3705, Jersey City NJ 07302. **Fax:** (510)845-8001. **E-mail:** kthomas@cleispress.com. **Website:** www.cleispress.com. **Contact:** KAren Thomas, publisher. Estab. 1980. Publishes books that inform, enlighten, and entertain. Areas of interest include gift, inspiration, health, family and childcare, self-help, women's issues, reference, cooking. "We do our best to bring readers quality books that celebrate life, inspire the mind, revive the spirit, and enhance lives all around. Our authors are practical visionaries; people who offer deep wisdom in a hopeful and helpful manner.". Cleis Press publishes provocative, intelligent books in the areas of sexuality, gay and lesbian studies, erotica, fiction, gender studies, and human rights. **Publishes 45 titles/year. 10% of books from first-time authors. 40% from unagented writers.** Publishes ms 2 years after acceptance. Accepts simultaneous submissions. Responds in 2 month to queries.

NONFICTION Subjects include sexual politics. "Cleis Press is interested in books on topics of sexuality, human rights and women's and gay and lesbian literature. Please consult our website first to be certain that your book fits our list." Query or submit outline and sample chapters.

FICTION Subjects include feminist, literary. "We are looking for high quality fiction and nonfiction." Submit complete ms. Include brief bio, list of publishing credits. Send SASE for return of ms or send a disposable ms and SASE for reply only.

TIPS "Be familiar with publishers' catalogs; be absolutely aware of your audience; research potential markets; present fresh new ways of looking at your topic; avoid 'PR' language and include publishing history in query letter."

CLEVELAND STATE UNIVERSITY POETRY CENTER

2121 Euclid Ave., RT 1841, Cleveland OH 44115. (216)687-3986. **Fax:** (216)687-6943. **E-mail:** poetrycenter@csuohio.edu. **Website:** www.csupoetrycenter.com. **Contact:** Amber Allen, managing editor. Estab. 1962. The Cleveland State University Poetry Center was established in 1962 at the former Fenn College of Engineering to promote poetry through readings and community outreach. In 1971, it expanded its mission to become a national non-profit independent press under the auspices of the Cleveland State University Department of English, and has since published nearly 200 rangy, joyful, profound, astonishing, complicated, surprising, and aesthetically diverse collections of contemporary poetry and prose by established and emerging authors. The Cleveland State University Poetry Center publishes between three and five collections of contemporary poetry and prose a year, with a national distribution and reach. The Poetry Center currently acquires manuscripts through three annual contests (one dedicated to publishing and promoting first books of poetry, one to supporting an established poet's career, and one to publishing collections of literary essays). **Publishes 3-5 titles/year. 500-1,200 submissions received/year. 50% of books from first-time authors. 100% from unagented writers. Pays $1,000 for competition winners.** Publishes ms 1-2 years after acceptance. Accepts simultaneous submissions. Responds in less than a year. Catalog online. Guidelines online.

POETRY Most mss are accepted through the competitions. All mss sent for competitions are considered for publication. Outside of competitions, mss are accepted by solicitation only.

COACHES CHOICE

P.O. Box 1828, Monterey CA 93942. (888)229-5745. **E-mail:** info@coacheschoice.com. **Website:** www. coacheschoice.com. Publishes trade paperback originals and reprints. "We publish books for anyone who coaches a sport or has an interest in coaching a sport— all levels of competition." Detailed descriptions, step-by-step instructions, and easy-to-follow diagrams set our books apart. Accepts simultaneous submissions. Book catalog available free.

NONFICTION Subjects include sports, sports specific training. Submit proposal package, outline, resume, 2 sample chapters. Reviews artwork/photos. Send photocopies and diagrams.

◎ COACH HOUSE BOOKS

80 bpNichol Ln., Toronto ON M5S 3J4, Canada. (416)979-2217. **Fax:** (416)977-1158. **E-mail:** editor@ chbooks.com. **Website:** www.chbooks.com. **Contact:** Alana Wilcox, editorial director. Publishes trade paperback originals by Canadian authors. **Publishes 18 titles/year. 80% of books from first-time authors. Pays 10% royalty on retail price.** Publishes ms 1 year after acceptance. Responds in 6-8 months to queries. Guidelines online.

NONFICTION Query.

FICTION Subjects include experimental, literary, poetry. "Electronic submissions are welcome. Please send your complete ms, along with an introductory letter that describes your work and compares it to at least 2 current Coach House titles, explaining how your book would fit our list, and a literary CV listing your previous publications and relevant experience. If you would like your ms back, please enclose a large enough self-addressed envelope with adequate postage. If you don't want your ms back,

a small stamped envelope or e-mail address is fine. We prefer electronic submissions. Please e-mail PDF files to editor@chbooks.com and include the cover letter and CV as a part of the ms. Please send your manuscript only once. Revised and updated versions will not be read, so make sure you're happy with your text before sending. You can also mail your ms. Please do not send it by ExpressPost or Canada Post courier—regular Canada Post mail is much more likely to arrive here. Be patient. We try to respond promptly, but we do receive hundreds of submissions, so it may take us several months to get back to you. Please do not call or e-mail to check on the status of your submission. We will answer you as promptly as possible."

TIPS "We are not a general publisher, and publish only Canadian poetry, fiction, select nonfiction and drama. We are interested primarily in innovative or experimental writing."

COFFEE HOUSE PRESS

79 13th NE, Suite 110, Minneapolis MN 55413. (612)338-0125. **Fax:** (612)338-4004. **E-mail:** info@ coffeehousepress.org. **Website:** www.coffeehouse-press.org. **Contact:** Molly Fuller, production editor. Estab. 1984. Publishes hardcover and trade paperback originals. This successful nonprofit small press has received numerous grants from various organizations including the NEA, the McKnight Foundation and Target. Books published by Coffee House Press have won numerous honors and awards. Example: *The Book of Medicines*, by Linda Hogan won the Colorado Book Award for Poetry and the Lannan Foundation Literary Fellowship. **Publishes 16-18 titles/year.** Accepts simultaneous submissions. Responds in 4-6 weeks to queries; up to 6 months to mss. Book catalog and ms guidelines online.

NONFICTION Subjects include creative nonfiction, memoirs, book-length essays, collections of essays. Query with outline and sample pages during annual reading periods (March 1-31 and September 1-30).

FICTION Seeks literary novels, short story collections and poetry. Query first with outline and samples (20-30 pages) during annual reading periods (March 1-31 and September 1-30).

POETRY Coffee House Press will not accept unsolicited poetry submissions. Please check our web page periodically for future updates to this policy.

TIPS "Look for our books at stores and libraries to get a feel for what we like to publish. No phone calls, e-mails, or faxes."

THE COLLEGE BOARD

College Entrance Examination Board, 250 Vesey St., New York NY 10281. (212)713-8000. **Website:** www.collegeboard.com. Publishes trade paperback originals. The College Board publishes guidance information for college-bound students. **Publishes 2 titles/year. 25% of books from first-time authors. 50% from unagented writers. Pays royalty on retail price. Pays advance.** Publishes ms 9 months after acceptance. Accepts simultaneous submissions. Responds in 2 months to queries. Book catalog available free.

NONFICTION Subjects include education, college guidance. "We want books to help students make a successful transition from high school to college." Query with SASE. Submit outline, sample chapters, SASE.

COLLEGE PRESS PUBLISHING CO.

P.O. Box 1132, 2111 N. Main St., Suite C, Joplin MO 64801. (800)289-3300. **Fax:** (417)623-1929. **E-mail:** collpressbooks@gmail.com. **Website:** www.collegepress.com. **Contact:** Acquisitions Editor. Estab. 1959. Publishes hardcover and trade paperback originals and reprints. College Press is a traditional Christian publishing house. Seeks proposals for Bible studies, topical studies (biblically based), apologetic studies, historical biographies of Christians, Sunday/Bible School curriculum (adult electives). Accepts simultaneous submissions. Responds in 3 months to proposals; 2 months to mss. Book catalog for 9x12 envelope and 5 first-class stamps. Guidelines online.

NONFICTION Seeks Bible studies, topical studies, apologetic studies, historical biographies of Christians, and Sunday/Bible school curriculum. No poetry, games/puzzles, books on prophecy from a premillennial or dispensational viewpoint, or any book without a Christian message. Query with SASE.

TIPS "Our core market is Christian Churches/Churches of Christ and conservative evangelical Christians. Have your material critically reviewed prior to sending it. Make sure that it is non-Calvinistic and that it leans more amillennial (if it is apocalyptic writing)."

◉ COLOURPOINT BOOKS

Jubilee Business Park, 21 Jubilee Rd., Newtownards, Northern Ireland BT23 4YH, United Kingdom. (44)(289)182-0505. **Fax:** (44)(289)182-1900. **E-mail:** info@colourpoint.co.uk. **Website:** www.colourpoint.co.uk. Estab. 1993. **Publishes 25 titles/year. Pays royalty.** Accepts simultaneous submissions. Responds in 2-3 months. Guidelines online.

NONFICTION Subjects include education. "Our specialisms are educational textbooks and transport subjects—mainly trains and buses. When e-mailing queries, please put 'submission query' in the subject line." Does not want fiction, poetry or plays. Query with SASE. Submit outline, outline/proposal, resume, publishing history, bio, 2 sample pages, SASE.

TIPS "Before approaching any publisher with a proposal, be sure that you are sending it to the right company. Publishing houses have their own personalities and specialisms and much time can be saved—including yours—by not submitting to a totally unsuitable publisher."

CONARI PRESS

Red Wheel/Weiser, LLC., 665 Third St., Suite 400, San Francisco CA 94107. **E-mail:** info@rwwbooks.com. **E-mail:** submissions@rwwbooks.com. **Website:** www.redwheelweiser.com. Estab. 1987. "Conari Press, an imprint of Red Wheel/Weiser, publishes books on topics ranging from spirituality, personal growth, and relationships to women's issues, parenting, and social issues. Our mission is to publish quality books that will make a difference in people's lives—how we feel about ourselves and how we relate to one another. We value integrity, compassion, and receptivity, both in the books we publish and in the way we do business." Accepts simultaneous submissions.

NONFICTION Subjects include foods, health, parenting, spirituality, womens issues, womens studies. "Inspire, literally to breathe life into. That's what Conari Press books aim to do—inspire all walks of life, mind, body, and spirit; inspire creativity, laughter, gratitude, good food, good health, and all good things in life." Submit proposal, including: an overview of the book; a complete TOC; a market/audience analysis, including similar titles; an up-to-date listing of your own marketing and publicity experience and/or plans; your vita and/or qualifications to write the book; and 2-3 sample chapters. Send cover letter including author information and brief description of proposed work.

TIPS "Review our website to make sure your work is appropriate."

CONCORDIA PUBLISHING HOUSE

3558 S. Jefferson Ave., St. Louis MO 63118. (314)268-1187. **Fax:** (314)268-1329. **E-mail:** publicity@cph.org. **Website:** www.cph.org. Estab. 1869. Publishes hardcover and trade paperback originals. Concordia Publishing House is the publishing arm of The Lutheran Church—Missouri Synod. "We develop, produce, and distribute (1) resources that support pastoral and congregational ministry, and (2) scholary and professional books in exegetical, historical, dogmatic, and practical theology." Accepts simultaneous submissions.

ⒶⓈⓄ CONSTABLE & ROBINSON, LTD.

50 Victoria Embankment, London EC4Y 0DZ, United Kingdom. **E-mail:** info@littlebrown.co.uk. **Website:** https://www.littlebrown.co.uk/ConstableRobinson/about-constable-publisher.page. Publishes hardcover and trade paperback originals. **Publishes 60 titles/year. 3,000 queries/year; 1,000 mss/year. Pays royalty. Pays advance.** Publishes book 1 year after acceptance. Accepts simultaneous submissions. Responds in 1-3 months. Book catalog available free.

NONFICTION Subjects include health, history, medicine, military, photography, politics, psychology, science, travel, war. Query with SASE. Submit synopsis. Reviews artwork/photos. Send photocopies.

FICTION Subjects include historical, mystery. Publishes "crime fiction (mysteries) and historical crime fiction." Length 80,000 words minimum; 130,000 words maximum. *Agented submissions only.*

CORNELL UNIVERSITY PRESS

Sage House, 512 E. State St., Ithaca NY 14850. (607)277-2338. **Fax:** (607)277-2374. **Website:** www.cornellpress.cornell.edu. **Contact:** Emily Powers and Bethany R. Wasik, acquisitions assistants. Estab. 1869. Publishes hardcover and paperback originals. "Cornell Press is an academic publisher of nonfiction with particular strengths in anthropology, Asian studies, biological sciences, classics, history, labor and business, literary criticism, politics and international relations, women's studies, Slavic studies, philosophy, urban studies, health care work, regional titles, and security studies. Currently emphasizing sound scholarship that appeals beyond the academic community." **Publishes 150 titles/year. Pays royalty. Pays $0-5,000 advance.** Publishes ms 1 year after acceptance. Accepts simultaneous submissions. Book catalog and guidelines online.

NONFICTION Subjects include agriculture, ethnic, history, philosophy, regional, sociology, translation, classics, life sciences. Submit résumé, cover letter, and prospectus.

CORWIN PRESS, INC.

2455 Teller Rd., Thousand Oaks CA 91320. (800)818-7243. **Fax:** (805)499-2692. **E-mail:** lisa.shaw@corwin.com. **Website:** www.corwinpress.com. **Contact:** Lisa Shaw, vice president (publishing and professional group); Jessica Allan, senior acquisitions editor (science, special education, gifted education, early childhood education, and counseling); Dan Alpert, program director (equity/diversity, professional learning); Arnis Burvikos, executive editor (educational leadership, technology); Lisa Luedeke, publisher (Corwin Literacy); Erin Null, acquisitions editor (math, science, STEM, general methods); Ariel Bartlett, acquisitions editor (educational technology and general methods). Estab. 1990. Publishes paperback originals. **Publishes 150 titles/year.** Publishes ms 7 months after acceptance. Accepts simultaneous submissions. Responds in 1-2 months to queries. Guidelines online.

○ "Corwin Press, Inc., publishes leading-edge, user-friendly publications for education professionals."

NONFICTION Subjects include education. Seeking fresh insights, conclusions, and recommendations for action. Prefers theory or research-based books that provide real-world examples and practical, hands-on strategies to help busy educators be successful. Professional-level publications for administrators, teachers, school specialists, policymakers, researchers and others involved with Pre K-12 education. No textbooks that simply summarize existing knowledge or mass-market books. Query with SASE.

○ COTEAU BOOKS

Thunder Creek Publishing Co-operative Ltd., 2517 Victoria Ave., Regina SK S4P 0T2, Canada. (306)777-0170. **Fax:** (306)522-5152. **E-mail:** coteau@coteaubooks.com. **Website:** www.coteaubooks.com. **Contact:** Geoffrey Ursell, publisher. Estab. 1975. Publishes trade paperback originals and reprints. "Our mission is to publish the finest in Canadian fiction, nonfiction, poetry, drama, and children's literature, with an emphasis on Saskatchewan and prairie writers. De-emphasizing science fiction, picture books." Publishes chapter books for young readers aged 9-12 and novels for older kids ages 13-15 and for ages 15 and up. **Publishes 12 titles/year. 200 queries received/year. 40 mss received/year. 25% of books from first-time authors. 90% from unagented writers. Pays 10% royalty on retail price.** Publishes book 1 year after acceptance. Responds in 3 months. Book catalog available free. Guidelines online.

NONFICTION Subjects include creative nonfiction, ethnic, history, memoirs, regional, sports, travel. *Canadian authors only.* Submit hard copy query, bio, 3-4 sample chapters, SASE.

FICTION Subjects include ethnic, fantasy, feminist, historical, humor, juvenile, literary, multicultural, multimedia, mystery, plays, poetry, regional, short story collections, spiritual, sports, novels/short fiction, adult/middle years. No science fiction. No children's picture books. Query.

POETRY Submit 20-25 sample poems.

TIPS "Look at past publications to get an idea of our editorial program. We do not publish romance, horror, or picture books but are interested in juvenile and teen fiction from Canadian authors. Submissions, even queries, must be made in hard copy only. We do not accept simultaneous/multiple submissions. Check our website for new submission timing guidelines."

COUNCIL ON SOCIAL WORK EDUCATION

1701 Duke St., Suite 200, Alexandria VA 22314. (703)683-8080. **Fax:** (703)683-8099. **E-mail:** info@cswe.org. **Website:** www.cswe.org. **Contact:** Elizabeth Simon, publications manager. Estab. 1952. Publishes trade paperback originals. "Council on Social Work Education produces books and resources for social work educators, students and practitioners." **Publishes 4 titles/year. 12 queries; 8 mss received/year. 25% of books from first-time authors. 100% from unagented writers. Pays sliding royalty scale, starting at 12%.** Publishes ms 1 year after acceptance. Responds in 2-3 months. Book catalog and guidelines online.

NONFICTION Subjects include counseling, education, social work. Books for social work and other educators. Does not want how-to, self-help, or personal memoir. Query via e-mail only with proposal package, including CV, outline, expected audience, and 2 sample chapters.

FICTION Subjects include contemporary, Social work, social workers. Short stories/novels illustrative of specific themes for use in social work classes. Query

via e-mail only with proposal package, including CV, synopsis, expected audience, and brief excerpt.

TIPS "Audience is social work educators and students and others in the helping professions. Check areas of publication interest on website."

COVENANT COMMUNICATIONS, INC.

920 E. State Rd., Suite F, P.O. Box 416, American Fork UT 84003. (801)756-1041. **Fax:** (801)756-1049. **E-mail:** submissionsdesk@covenant-lds.com. **Website:** www.covenant-lds.com. **Contact:** Kathryn Gordon, managing editor. Estab. 1958. "Currently emphasizing inspirational, doctrinal, historical, biography, and fiction." **Publishes 80-100 titles/year. Receives 1,200 mss/year. 30% of books from first-time authors. 99% from unagented writers. Pays 6-15% royalty on retail price.** Publishes book 6-12 months after acceptance. Responds in 1 month on queries; 4-6 months on mss. Guidelines online.

NONFICTION Subjects include history, religion, spirituality. "We target an audience of members of The Church of Jesus Christ of Latter-day Saints, LDS, or Mormon. All mss must be acceptable to that audience." Submit complete ms. Reviews artwork. Send photocopies.

FICTION Subjects include adventure, historical, mystery, regional, religious, romance, spiritual, suspense. "Manuscripts do not necessarily have to include LDS/Mormon characters or themes, but cannot contain profanity, sexual content, gratuitous violence, witchcraft, vampires, and other such material." Submit complete ms.

TIPS "We are actively looking for new, fresh regency romance authors."

CQ PRESS

2455 Teller Rd., Thousand Oaks CA 91320. (805)410-7582. **Website:** www.cqpress.com. **Contact:** Jim Brace-Thompson, senior acquisitions editor. Estab. 1945. Publishes hardcover and online paperback titles. CQ Press seeks to educate the public by publishing authoritative works on American and international politics, policy, and people. Accepts simultaneous submissions. Book catalog available free.

NONFICTION Subjects include history. "We are interested in American government, public administration, comparative government, and international relations." Submit proposal package, including prospectus, TOC, 1-2 sample chapters.

TIPS "Our books present important information on American government and politics, and related issues, with careful attention to accuracy, thoroughness, and readability."

⊘ CRABTREE PUBLISHING COMPANY

PMB 59051, 350 Fifth Ave., 59th Floor, New York NY 10118. (212)496-5040; (800)387-7650. **Fax:** (800)355-7166. **Website:** www.crabtreebooks.com. Estab. 1978. Crabtree Publishing Company is dedicated to producing high-quality books and educational products for K-8+. Each resource blends accuracy, immediacy, and eye-catching illustration with the goal of inspiring nothing less than a life-long interest in reading and learning in children. The company began building its reputation in 1978 as a quality children's nonfiction book publisher with acclaimed author Bobbie Kalman's first series about the early pioneers. The Early Settler Life Series became a mainstay in schools as well as historic sites and museums across North America. Accepts simultaneous submissions.

○ "Crabtree does not accept unsolicited manuscripts. Crabtree Publishing has an editorial team in-house that creates curriculum-specific book series."

TIPS "Since our books are for younger readers, lively photos of children and animals are always excellent." Portfolio should be diverse and encompass several subjects rather than just 1 or 2; depth of coverage of subject should be intense so that any publishing company could, conceivably, use all or many of a photographer's photos in a book on a particular subject."

CRAFTSMAN BOOK CO.

6058 Corte Del Cedro, Carlsbad CA 92011. (760)438-7828 or (800)829-8123. **Fax:** (760)438-0398. **E-mail:** jacobs@costbook.com. **Website:** www.craftsman-book.com. **Contact:** Laurence D. Jacobs, editorial manager. Estab. 1957. Publishes paperback originals. Publishes how-to manuals for professional builders. Currently emphasizing construction software for cost estimating, contract writing and construction forms. **Publishes 12 titles/year. 85% of books from first-time authors. 98% from unagented writers. Pays 7-12% royalty on wholesale price and 12-1/2% on retail price.** Publishes ms 2 years after acceptance. Accepts simultaneous submissions. Responds in 2 months to queries. Book catalog and ms guidelines free.

NONFICTION Subjects include business, software. All titles are related to construction for professional builders. Reviews artwork/photos.

TIPS "The book submission should be loaded with step-by-step instructions, illustrations, charts, reference data, forms, samples, cost estimates, rules of thumb, and examples that solve actual problems in the builder's office and in the field. It must cover the subject completely, become the owner's primary reference on the subject, have a high utility-to-cost ratio, and help the owner make a better living in his chosen field."

CRAIGMORE CREATIONS

PMB 114, 4110 SE Hawthorne Blvd., Portland OR 97124. (503)477-9562. **E-mail:** info@craigmorecreations.com. **Website:** www.craigmorecreations.com. Estab. 2009. Accepts simultaneous submissions.

NONFICTION Subjects include animals, anthropology, archeology, creative nonfiction, environment, multicultural, nature, regional, science, young adult, Earth sciences, natural history. "We publish books that make time travel seem possible: nonfiction that explores pre-history and Earth sciences for children." Submit proposal package. See website for detailed submission guidelines. Send photocopies.

FICTION Subjects include juvenile, picture books, young adult. Submit proposal package. See website for detailed submission guidelines.

CREATIVE COMPANY

P.O. Box 227, Mankato MN 56002. **E-mail:** info@thecreativecompany.us. **Website:** www.thecreative-company.us. **Contact:** Kate Riggs, Managing Editor. Estab. 1932. "We are currently not accepting fiction submissions." **Publishes 140 titles/year.** Publishes a book 2 years after acceptance. Accepts simultaneous submissions. Responds in 3-6 months. Guidelines available for SAE.

IMPRINTS Creative Editions (picture books); Creative Education (nonfiction).

NONFICTION Picture books, young readers, young adults: animal, arts/crafts, biography, careers, geography, health, history, hobbies, multicultural, music/dance, nature/environment, religion, science, social issues, special needs, sports. Average word length: young readers—500; young adults—6,000. Submit outline/synopsis and 2 sample chapters, along with division of titles within the series.

TIPS "We are accepting nonfiction, series submissions only. Fiction submissions will not be reviewed or returned. Nonfiction submissions should be presented in series (4, 6, or 8) rather than single."

CRESCENT MOON PUBLISHING

P.O. Box 1312, Maidstone Kent ME14 5XU, United Kingdom. (44)(162)272-9593. **E-mail:** cresmopub@yahoo.co.uk. **Website:** www.crmoon.com. **Contact:** Jeremy Robinson, director (arts, media, cinema, literature); Cassidy Hughes (visual arts). Estab. 1988. Publishes hardcover and trade paperback originals. "Our mission is to publish the best in contemporary work, in poetry, fiction, and critical studies, and selections from the great writers. Currently emphasizing nonfiction (media, film, music, painting). De-emphasizing children's books." **Publishes 25 titles/year. 300 queries; 400 mss received/year. 1% of books from first-time authors. 1% from unagented writers. Pays royalty. Pays negotiable advance.** Publishes ms 18 months after acceptance. Accepts simultaneous submissions. Responds in 2 months to queries; 4 months to proposals and mss. Book catalog and ms guidelines free.

IMPRINTS Joe's Press; Pagan America Magazine; Passion Magazine.

NONFICTION Subjects include Americana, gardening, philosophy, religion, travel, cinema, the media, cultural studies. Query with SASE. Submit outline, 2 sample chapters, bio. Reviews artwork/photos. Send photocopies.

FICTION Subjects include erotica, experimental, feminist, literary, short story collections, translation. "We do not publish much fiction at present but will consider high quality new work." Query with SASE. Submit outline, clips, 2 sample chapters, bio.

POETRY "We prefer a small selection of the poet's very best work at first. We prefer free verse or non-rhyming poetry. Do not send too much material." Query and submit 6 sample poems.

TIPS "Our audience is interested in new contemporary writing."

CRESTON BOOKS

P.O. Box 9369, Berkeley CA 94709. **E-mail:** submissions@crestonbooks.co. **Website:** crestonbooks.co. Creston Books is author-illustrator driven, with talented, award-winning creators given more editorial freedom and control than in a typical New York house.

50% of books from first-time authors. 50% from unagented writers. **Pays advance.** Accepts simultaneous submissions. Catalog online. Guidelines available.

FICTION Subjects include juvenile, multicultural, picture books, young adult. Please paste text of picture books or first chapters of novels in the body of e-mail. Words of Advice for submitting authors listed on the site.

CRIMSON ROMANCE

Adams Media, a division of F+W Media, Inc., 57 Littlefield St., Avon MA 02322. (508)427-7100. **E-mail:** editorcrimson@gmail.com. **Website:** crimsonromance.com. **Contact:** Tara Gelsomino, Executive Editor. Publishes electronic originals. "Direct to e-book romance imprint of Adams Media." Accepts simultaneous submissions.

FICTION Subjects include romance. "We're open to romance submissions in 5 popular subgenres: romantic suspense, contemporary, paranormal, historical, and erotic romance. Within those subgenres, we are flexible about what happens. It's romance, so there must be a happily-ever-after, but we're open to how your characters get there. You won't come up against preconceived ideas about what can or can't happen in romance or what kind of characters you can or can't have. Our only rule is everyone has to be a consenting adult. Other than that, we're looking for smart, savvy heroines, fresh voices, and new takes on old favorite themes." Length: 55,000-90,000 words. Please see current submission guidelines online.

CROSS-CULTURAL COMMUNICATIONS

Cross-Cultural Literary Editions, CROSS-CULTURAL COMMUNICATIONS, 239 Wynsum Ave., Merrick NY 11566-4725. (516)869-5635. **Fax:** (516)379-1901. **E-mail:** info@cross-culturalcommunications.com; cccpoetry@aol.com. **Website:** www.cross-culturalcommunications.com. **Contact:** Stanley H. Barkan; Bebe Barkan. Estab. 1971. Publishes hardcover and trade paperback originals. **Publishes 10 titles/year. 200 queries; 50 mss received/year. 10-25% of books from first-time authors. 100% from unagented writers.** Publishes book 1 year after acceptance. Responds in 1 month to proposals; 2 months to mss. Book catalog (sample flyers) for #10 SASE.

NONFICTION Subjects include memoirs, multicultural. "Query first; we basically do not want the focus on nonfiction." Query with SASE. Reviews artwork/photos. Send photocopies.

FICTION Subjects include historical, multicultural, poetry, poetry in translation, translation, bilingual poetry. Query with SASE.

POETRY For bilingual poetry submit 3-6 short poems in original language with English translation, a brief (3-5 lines) bio of the author and translator(s).

TIPS "Best chance: poetry from a translation."

THE CROSSROAD PUBLISHING COMPANY

83 Chestnut Ridge Rd., Chestnut Ridge NY 10977. **Fax:** (845)517-0181. **E-mail:** submissions@crossroadpublishing.com. **Website:** www.crossroadpublishing.com. Estab. 1980. Publishes hardcover and trade paperback originals and reprints. **Publishes 45 titles/year. 1,000 queries received/year. 200 mss received/year. 10% of books from first-time authors. 75% from unagented writers. Pays 6-14% royalty on wholesale price.** Publishes ms 14 months after acceptance. Accepts simultaneous submissions. Responds in 6 weeks to queries and proposals; 12 weeks to mss. Book catalog available free. Guidelines online.

IMPRINTS Crossroad (trade); Herder (classroom/academic).

NONFICTION Subjects include creative nonfiction, ethnic, religion, spirituality, leadership, Catholicism. "We want hopeful, well-written books on religion and spirituality." Query with SASE.

TIPS "Refer to our website and catalog for a sense of the range and kinds of books we offer. Follow our application guidelines as posted on our website."

CROSSWAY

A publishing ministry of Good News Publishing, 1300 Crescent St., Wheaton IL 60174. (630)682-4300. **Fax:** (630)682-4785. **E-mail:** info@crossway.org. **E-mail:** submissions@crossway.org. **Website:** www.crossway.org. **Contact:** Jill Carter, editorial administrator. Estab. 1938. "'Making a difference in people's lives for Christ' as its maxim, Crossway Books lists titles written from an evangelical Christian perspective." Member ECPA. Distributes titles through Christian bookstores and catalogs. Promotes titles through magazine ads, catalogs. **Publishes 85 titles/year. Pays negotiable royalty.** Publishes ms 18 months after acceptance. Accepts simultaneous submissions.

○ *Does not accept unsolicited mss.*

NONFICTION "Send us an e-mail query and, if your idea fits within our acquisitions guidelines, we'll invite a proposal."

Ⓐ CROWN BUSINESS

Penguin Random House, 1745 Broadway, New York NY 10019. (212)572-2275. **Fax:** (212)572-6192. **E-mail:** crownosm@randomhouse.com. **Website:** crownpublishing.com. Estab. 1995. Publishes hardcover and trade paperback originals. *Agented submissions only.* Accepts simultaneous submissions. Book catalog online.

Ⓐ⊘ CROWN PUBLISHING GROUP

Penguin Random House, 1745 Broadway, New York NY 10019. (212)782-9000. **E-mail:** crownosm@randomhouse.com. **Website:** crownpublishing.com. Estab. 1933. Publishes popular fiction and nonfiction hardcover originals. Accepts simultaneous submissions. *Agented submissions only.* See website for more details.

IMPRINTS Amphoto Books; Back Stage Books; Billboard Books; Broadway Books; Clarkson Potter; Crown; Crown Archetype; Crown Business; Crown Forum; Harmony Books; Image Books; Potter Craft; Potter Style; Ten Speed Press; Three Rivers Press; Waterbrook Multnomah; Watson-Guptill.

CRYSTAL SPIRIT PUBLISHING, INC.

P.O. Box 12506, Durham NC 27709. **E-mail:** crystalspiritinc@gmail.com. **E-mail:** submissions@crystalspiritinc.com. **Website:** www.crystalspiritinc.com. **Contact:** Vanessa S. O'Neal, Senior Managing Editor. Estab. 2004. Publishes hardcover, trade paperback, mass market paperback, and electronic originals. "Our readers are lovers of high-quality books that are sold as direct sales, in bookstores, gift shops and placed in libraries and schools. They support independent authors and they expect works that will provide them with entertainment, inspiration, romance, and education. Our audience loves to read and will embrace niche authors that love to write." **Publishes 3-5 titles/year. Receives 80 mss/year. 80% of books from first-time authors. 100% from unagented writers. Pays 20-45% royalty on retail price.** Publishes ms 3-6 months after acceptance. Accepts simultaneous submissions. Responds in 1-3 months to mss. Book catalog and ms guidelines online. Guidelines for submissions are stated on the website.

NONFICTION Subjects include alternative lifestyles, business, creative nonfiction, economics, ethnic, memoirs, multicultural, religion, sex, spirituality, womens issues, womens studies, young adult, inspirational, Christian romance. Submit cover letter, synopsis, and 30 pages by USPS mail, e-mail or website submission.

FICTION Subjects include confession, contemporary, erotica, ethnic, feminist, gay, humor, juvenile, literary, mainstream, multicultural, religious, romance, short story collections, spiritual, young adult, inspirational, Christian romance. Submit cover letter, synopsis, and 30 pages by USPS mail, e-mail or website submission.

TIPS "Submissions are accepted for publication throughout the year. Works should be positive and non-threatening. Typed pages only. Non-typed entries will not be reviewed or returned. Ensure that all contact information is correct, abide by the submission guidelines and do not send follow-up e-mails or calls."

CSLI PUBLICATIONS

Condura Hall, Stanford University, 210 Panama St., Stanford CA 94305. (650)723-1839. **Fax:** (650)725-2166. **E-mail:** pubs@csli.stanford.edu. **Website:** csli-publications.stanford.edu. Publishes hardcover and scholarly paperback originals. CSLI Publications, part of the Center for the Study of Language and Information, specializes in books in the study of language, information, logic, and computation. Book catalog available free. Guidelines online.

NONFICTION Subjects include science, logic, cognitive science. "We do not accept unsolicited mss."

CURIOSITY QUILLS

Whampa, LLC, P.O. Box 2160, Reston VA 20195. (800)998-2509. **Fax:** (800)998-2509. **E-mail:** editor@curiosityquills.com. **Website:** curiosityquills.com. **Contact:** Alisa Gus. Eugene Teplitsky, Nikki Tetreault Estab. 2011. Firm publishes sci-fi, speculative fiction, steampunk, paranormal and urban fantasy, and corresponding romance titles under its new Rebel Romance imprint. Curiosity Quills is a publisher of hard-hitting dark sci-fi, speculative fiction, and paranormal works aimed at adults, young adults, and new adults. **Publishes 75 titles/year. 1,000 submissions/year. 60% of books from first-time authors. 65% from unagented writers. Pays variable royalty. Does not pay advance.** Publishes ms 9 months after acceptance. Accepts simultaneous submissions. Responds in 1-6 weeks. Catalog available. Guidelines online.

IMPRINTS Curiosity Quills Press, Rebel Romance.

NONFICTION Writer's guides, on a strictly limited basis.

FICTION Subjects include adventure, contemporary, erotica, fantasy, gay, gothic, hi-lo, historical, horror, humor, juvenile, lesbian, literary, mainstream, multicultural, multimedia, mystery, romance, science fiction, suspense, young adult, steampunk, dieselpunk, space opera. Looking for "thought-provoking, mind-twisting rollercoasters—challenge our mind, turn our world upside down, and make us question. Those are the makings of a true literary marauder." Submit ms using online submission form or e-mail to acquisitions@curiosityquills.com.

CURIOUS FOX

Brunel Rd., Houndmills, Basingstoke Hants RG21 6XS, United Kingdom. **E-mail:** submissions@curious-fox.com. **Website:** www.curious-fox.com. "Do you love telling good stories? If so, we'd like to hear from you. Curious Fox is on the lookout for UK-based authors, whether new talent or established authors with exciting ideas. We take submissions for books aimed at ages 3-young adult. If you have story ideas that are bold, fun, and imaginative, then please do get in touch!" Accepts simultaneous submissions. Guidelines online.

FICTION "Send your submission via e-mail to submissions@curious-fox.com. Include the following in the body of the e-mail, not as attachments: Sample chapters, Résumé, List of previous publishing credits, if applicable. We will respond only if your writing samples fit our needs."

CYCLE PUBLICATIONS, INC.

Van der Plas Publications, 1282 Seventh Ave., San Francisco CA 94112. (415)665-8214. **Fax:** (415)753-8572. **Website:** www.cyclepublishing.com. Estab. 1985. "Van der Plas Publications/Cycle Publishing was started in 1997 with 4 books. Since then, we have introduced about 4 new books each year, and in addition to our 'mainstay' of cycling books, we now also have books on manufactured housing, golf, baseball, and strength training. Our offices are located in San Francisco, where we do editorial work, as well as administration, publicity, and design. Our books are warehoused in Kimball, Michigan, which is close to the companies that print most of our books and is conveniently located to supply our book trade distributors and the major book wholesalers." Accepts simultaneous submissions.

CYCLOTOUR GUIDE BOOKS

160 Harvard St., Rochester NY 14607. **E-mail:** cyclotour@cyclotour.com. **Website:** www.cyclotour.com. Estab. 1994. Publishes trade paperback originals. **Publishes 2 titles/year. Receives 25 queries/year and 2 mss/year. 25% of books from first-time authors. 100% from unagented writers.** Publishes ms 2 years after acceptance. Accepts simultaneous submissions. Responds in 1 month. Book catalog and ms guidelines online.

NONFICTION Subjects include travel. Query with SASE. Reviews artwork/photos as part of ms package. Send photocopies.

TIPS Bicyclists. Folks with a dream of bicycle touring. "Check your grammar and spelling. Write logically."

🅐🅞 DA CAPO PRESS

Perseus Books Group, 44 Farnsworth St., 3rd Floor, Boston MA 02210. (617)252-5200. **Website:** www.dacapopress.com. Estab. 1975. Publishes hardcover originals and trade paperback originals and reprints. **Publishes 115 titles/year. 500 queries received/year. 300 mss received/year. 25% of books from first-time authors. 1% from unagented writers. Pays 7-15% royalty. Pays $1,000-225,000 advance.** Publishes book 1 year after acceptance. Accepts simultaneous submissions. Book catalog and guidelines online.

NONFICTION Subjects include contemporary culture, creative nonfiction, history, memoirs, social sciences, sports, translation, travel, world affairs. No unsolicited mss or proposals. Agented submissions only.

🅢 DARTON, LONGMAN & TODD

1 Spencer Ct., 140-142 Wandsworth High St., London SW18 4JJ, United Kingdom. (44)(208)875-0155. **Fax:** (44)(208)875-0133. **E-mail:** editorial@darton-longman-todd.co.uk. **Website:** www.dltbooks.com. **Contact:** Editorial Department. Estab. 1959. Darton, Longman and Todd is an internationally-respected publisher of brave, ground-breaking, independent books and e-books on matters of heart, mind, and soul that meet the needs and interests of ordinary people. **Publishes 50 titles/year. Pays royalty.** Accepts simultaneous submissions. Guidelines online.

NONFICTION Subjects include religion, spirituality. Simultaenous submissions accepted, but inform publisher if submitting elsewhere. Does not want poetry, scholarly monographs or children's books. Query by e-mail only.

TIPS "Our books are read by people inside and outside the Christian churches, by believers, seekers and sceptics, and by thoughtful non-specialists as well as students and academics. The books are widely sold throughout the religious and the general trade."

🅞 JONATHAN DAVID PUBLISHERS, INC.

68-22 Eliot Ave., Middle Village NY 11379. (718)456-8611. **Fax:** (718)894-2818. **Website:** www.jdbooks.com. **Contact:** David Kolatch, editorial director. Estab. 1948. Publishes hardcover and trade paperback originals and reprints. Jonathan David publishes popular Judaica. **Publishes 20-25 titles/year. 50% of books from first-time authors. 90% from unagented writers. Pays royalty, or makes outright purchase.** Publishes ms 18 months after acceptance. Accepts simultaneous submissions. Responds in 1-2 months. Book catalog and guidelines online.

NONFICTION Subjects include creative nonfiction, ethnic, multicultural, religion, sports. Unsolicited mss are not being accepted at this time.

DAW BOOKS, INC.

Penguin Random House, 375 Hudson St., New York NY 10014-3658. (212)366-2096. **Fax:** (212)366-2090. **E-mail:** daw@us.penguingroup.com. **Website:** www.dawbooks.com. **Contact:** Peter Stampfel, submissions editor. Estab. 1971. Publishes hardcover and paperback originals and reprints. DAW Books publishes science fiction and fantasy. **Publishes 50-60 titles/year. Pays in royalties with an advance negotiable on a book-by-book basis.** Responds in 3 months. Guidelines online.

FICTION Subjects include fantasy, science fiction. "Currently seeking modern urban fantasy and paranormals. We like character-driven books with appealing protagonists, engaging plots, and well-constructed worlds. We accept both agented and unagented manuscripts." Submit entire ms, cover letter, SASE. "Do not submit your only copy of anything. The average length of the novels we publish varies but is almost never less than 80,000 words."

DAWN PUBLICATIONS

12402 Bitney Springs Rd., Nevada City CA 95959. (530)274-7775. **Fax:** (530)274-7778. **Website:** www.dawnpub.com. **Contact:** Glenn Hovemann, editor. Estab. 1979. Publishes hardcover and trade paperback originals. "Dawn Publications is dedicated to inspiring in children a sense of appreciation for all life on earth. Dawn looks for nature awareness and appreciation titles that promote a relationship with the natural world and specific habitats, usually through inspiring treatment and nonfiction." **Publishes 6 titles/year. 2,500 queries or mss received/year. 15% of books from first-time authors. 90% from unagented writers. Pays advance.** Publishes book 1-2 years after acceptance. Accepts simultaneous submissions. Responds in 2 months to queries. Book catalog and guidelines online.

○ Dawn accepts mss submissions by e-mail; follow instructions posted on website. Submissions by mail still OK.

NONFICTION Subjects include animals.

TIPS "Publishes mostly creative nonfiction with lightness and inspiration." Looking for "picture books expressing nature awareness with inspirational quality leading to enhanced self-awareness." Does not publish anthropomorphic works; no animal dialogue.

KATHY DAWSON BOOKS

Penguin Random House, 375 Hudson St., New York NY 10014. (212)366-2000. **Website:** kathydawsonbooks.tumblr.com. **Contact:** Kathy Dawson, vicepresident and publisher. Estab. 2014. Mission statement: Publish stellar novels with unforgettable characters for children and teens that expand their vision of the world, sneakily explore the meaning of life, celebrate the written word, and last for generations. The imprint strives to publish tomorrow's award contenders: quality books with strong hooks in a variety of genres with universal themes and compelling voices—books that break the modl and the heart. Responds only if interested. Guidelines online.

FICTION Accepts fiction queries via snail mail only. Include cover sheet with one-sentence elevator pitch, main themes, author version of catalog copy for book, first 10 pages of ms (double-spaced, Times Roman, 12 point type), and publishing history. No SASE needed. Responds only if interested.

Ⓐ⊘ DELACORTE PRESS

an imprint of Random House Children's Books, a division of Penguin Random House LLC, New York, 1745 Broadway, New York NY 10019. (212)782-9000. **Website:** randomhousekids.com; randomhouseteens.com. Publishes middle grade and young adult fiction in hard cover, trade paperback, mass market and digest formats. Accepts simultaneous submissions.

○ All query letters and manuscript submissions must be submitted through an agent or at the request of an editor.

Ⓐ⊘ DEL REY BOOKS

Penguin Random House, 1745 Broadway, 18th Floor, New York NY 10019. (212)782-9000. **Website:** www.penguinrandomhouse.com. Estab. 1977. Publishes hardcover, trade paperback, and mass market originals and mass market paperback reprints. Del Rey publishes top level fantasy, alternate history, and science fiction. **Pays royalty on retail price. Pays competitive advance.**

IMPRINTS Del Rey/Manga, Del Rey/Lucas Books.

FICTION Subjects include fantasy, science fiction, alternate history. *Agented submissions only.*

TIPS "Del Rey is a reader's house. Pay particular attention to plotting, strong characters, and dramatic, satisfactory conclusions. It must be/feel believable. That's what the readers like. In terms of mass market, we basically created the field of fantasy bestsellers. Not that it didn't exist before, but we put the mass into mass market."

DIAL BOOKS FOR YOUNG READERS

Imprint of Penguin Group (USA), 345 Hudson St., New York NY 10014. (212)366-2000. **Website:** www.penguin.com/children. Estab. 1961. Publishes hardcover originals. "Dial Books for Young Readers publishes quality picture books for ages 18 months-6 years; lively, believable novels for middle readers and young adults; and occasional nonfiction for middle readers and young adults." **Publishes 50 titles/year. 5,000 queries received/year. 20% of books from first-time authors. Pays royalty. Pays varies advance.** Responds in 4-6 months to queries. Book catalog and guidelines online.

NONFICTION Only responds if interested. "We accept entire picture book manuscripts and a maximum of 10 pages for longer works (novels, easy-to-reads). When submitting a portion of a longer work, please provide an accompanying cover letter that briefly describes your manuscript's plot, genre (i.e. easy-to-read, middle grade or YA novel), the intended age group, and your publishing credits, if any."

FICTION Subjects include adventure, fantasy, juvenile, picture books, young adult. Especially looking for lively and well-written novels for middle grade and young adult children involving a convincing plot and believable characters. The subject matter or theme should not already be overworked in previously published books. The approach must not be demeaning to any minority group, nor should the roles of female characters (or others) be stereotyped, though we don't think books should be didactic, or in any way message-y. No topics inappropriate for the juvenile, young adult, and middle grade audiences. No plays. Accepts unsolicited queries and up to 10 pages for longer works and unsolicited mss for picture books. Will only respond if interested.

TIPS "Our readers are anywhere from preschool age to teenage. Picture books must have strong plots, lots of action, unusual premises, or universal themes treated with freshness and originality. Humor works well in these books. A very well-thought-out and intelligently presented book has the best chance of being taken on. Genre isn't as much of a factor as presentation."

DIVERTIR

P.O. Box 232, North Salem NH 03073. **E-mail:** info@divertirpublishing.com. **E-mail:** query@divertirpublishing.com. **Website:** www.divertirpublishing.com. **Contact:** Kenneth Tupper, publisher. Estab. 2009. Publishes trade paperback and electronic originals. Divertir Publishing is an independent publisher located in Salem, NH. "Our goal is to provide interesting and entertaining books to our readers, as well as to offer new and exciting voices in the writing community the opportunity to publish their work. We seek to combine an understanding of traditional publishing with a unique understanding of the modern market to best serve both our authors and readers." **Publishes 6-12 titles/year. 1,000 submissions received/year. 70% of books from first-time authors. 100% from unagented writers. Pays 10-15% royalty on wholesale price (for novels and nonfiction). Does not pay advance.** Publishes ms 9-12 months after acceptance. Accepts simultaneous submissions. Responds in 1-3 months on queries; 3-4 months on proposals and mss. Catalog online. Guidelines online.

NONFICTION Subjects include contemporary culture, crafts, government, history, hobbies, politics, public affairs, world affairs. "We are particularly interested in the following: political/social commentary, current events, history, humor and satire, and crafts and hobbies." Reviews artwork/photos as part of the ms package. Submit electronically.

FICTION Subjects include adventure, contemporary, fantasy, gothic, historical, horror, humor, mainstream, mystery, occult, romance, science fiction, suspense, young adult. "We are particularly interested in the following: science fiction, fantasy, historical, alternate history, contemporary mythology, mystery and suspense, paranormal, and urban fantasy." Does not consider erotica or mss with excessive violence. Electronically submit proposal package, including synopsis and query letter with author's bio.

TIPS "Please see our Author Info page (online) for more information."

Ⓐ🖐⊘ DK PUBLISHING

Penguin Random House, 80 Strand, London WC2R 0RL, United Kingdom. **Website:** www.dk.com. "DK publishes photographically illustrated nonfiction for children of all ages." *DK Publishing does not accept unagented mss or proposals.* Accepts simultaneous submissions.

DOVER PUBLICATIONS, INC.

31 E. Second St., Mineola NY 11501. (516)294-7000. **Fax:** (516)873-1401. **Website:** www.doverpublications.com. Estab. 1941. Publishes trade paperback originals and reprints. **Publishes 660 titles/year. Makes outright purchase.** Accepts simultaneous submissions. Book catalog online.

NONFICTION Subjects include agriculture, Americana, animals, history, hobbies, philosophy, photography, religion, science, sports, translation, travel. Publishes mostly reprints. Accepts original paper doll collections, game books, coloring books (juvenile). Query with SASE. Reviews artwork/photos.

DOWN THE SHORE PUBLISHING

P.O. Box 100, West Creek NJ 08092. **Fax:** (609)597-0422. **E-mail:** info@down-the-shore.com. **Website:** www.down-the-shore.com. **Contact:** Acquisitions Editor. Publishes hardcover and trade paperback originals and reprints. "Bear in mind that our market is regional-New Jersey, the Jersey Shore, the mid-Atlantic, and seashore and coastal subjects." **Publishes 4-10 titles/year. Pays royalty on wholesale or retail price, or makes outright purchase.** Accepts simultaneous submissions. Responds in 3 months to queries. Book catalog online. Guidelines online.

NONFICTION Subjects include Americana, history, regional. Query with SASE. Submit proposal package,

1-2 sample chapters, synopsis. Reviews artwork/photos. Send photocopies.

FICTION Subjects include regional. Query with SASE. Submit proposal package, clips, 1-2 sample chapters.

POETRY "We do not publish poetry, unless it is to be included as part of an anthology."

TIPS "Carefully consider whether your proposal is a good fit for our established market."

DREAM OF THINGS

P.O. Box 872, Downers Grove IL 60515. **Website:** dreamofthings.com. Estab. 2009. Publishes trade paperback originals and reprints, electronic originals and reprints. Publishes memoirs, essay collections, and creative nonfiction. **Publishes 3-4 titles/ year. 90% of books from first-time authors. 90% from unagented writers. Pays 10% royalties on retail price. No advance.** Accept to publish time is 6 months. Accepts simultaneous submissions. Catalog online. Guidelines online.

NONFICTION Subjects include creative nonfiction, memoirs, essay collections. Submit via online form. For memoirs, submit 1 sample chapter. For essay collections, submit 2-3 essays. Does not review artwork.

DUFOUR EDITIONS

P.O. Box 7, 124 Byers Rd., Chester Springs PA 19425. (610)458-5005. **Fax:** (610)458-7103. **Website:** www.dufoureditions.com. Estab. 1948. Publishes hardcover originals, trade paperback originals and reprints. "We publish literary fiction by good writers which is well received and achieves modest sales. De-emphsazing poetry and nonfiction." **Publishes 3-4 titles/year. 200 queries; 15 mss received/year. 20-30% of books from first-time authors. 80% from unagented writers. Pays $100-500 advance.** Publishes ms 18 months after acceptance. Accepts simultaneous submissions. Responds in 3-6 months. Book catalog available free.

NONFICTION Subjects include history, translation. Query with SASE. Reviews artwork/photos. Send photocopies.

FICTION Subjects include literary, short story collections, translation. "We like books that are slightly offbeat, different and well-written." Query with SASE.

POETRY Query.

DUNDURN PRESS, LTD.

3 Church St., Suite 500, Toronto ON M5E 1M2, Canada. (416)214-5544. **Fax:** (416)214-5556. **E-mail:** info@ dundurn.com. **E-mail:** submissions@dundurn.com. **Website:** www.dundurn.com. **Contact:** Acquisitions Editor. Estab. 1972. Publishes hardcover, trade paperback, and e-book originals and reprints. Dundurn publishes books by Canadian authors. **600 queries received/year. 25% of books from first-time authors. 50% from unagented writers.** Publishes ms 1-2 year after acceptance. Accepts simultaneous submissions. Responds in 3 months to queries. Guidelines online.

NONFICTION Subjects include history, regional, art history, theater, serious and popular nonfiction. Submit cover letter, synopsis, CV, TOC, writing sample, e-mail contact. Accepts submissions via postal mail only. Do not submit original materials. Submissions will not be returned.

FICTION Subjects include literary, mystery, young adult. No romance, science fiction, or experimental. "Important note: Dundurn is not currently accepting fiction submissions, including mysteries or YA, nor is it accepting children's nonfiction submissions."

DUNEDIN ACADEMIC PRESS LTD

Hudson House, 8 Albany St., Edinburgh EH1 3QB, United Kingdom. (44)(131)473-2397. **E-mail:** mail@ dunedinacademicpress.co.uk. **Website:** www.dunedinacademicpress.co.uk. **Contact:** Anthony Kinahan, director. Estab. 2001. Dunedin Academic Press Ltd is a lively small independent academic publishing house. **Publishes 15-20 titles/year. 10% of books from first-time authors. 100% from unagented writers. Pays royalty.** Book catalog and proposal guidelines online.

"Read and respond to the proposal guidelines on our website before submitting. Do not send mss unless requested to do so. Do not send hard copy proposals. Approach first by e-mail, outlining proposal and identifying the market."

NONFICTION Subjects include earth science, health and social care, child protection. Reviews artwork/photos.

TIPS "Dunedin's list contains authors and subjects from across the international the academic world. DAP's horizons are far broader than our immediate Scottish environment. One of the strengths of Dunedin is that we are able to offer our authors that individual support that comes from dealing with a small independent publisher committed to growth through careful treatment of its authors."

ⓐ⊘ THOMAS DUNNE BOOKS

Imprint of St. Martin's Press, 175 Fifth Ave., New York NY 10010. (212)674-5151. **E-mail:** thomasdunnebooks@stmartins.com. **Website:** www.thomasdunnebooks.com. Estab. 1986. Publishes hardcover and trade paperback originals, and reprints. "Thomas Dunne Books publishes popular trade fiction and nonfiction. With an output of approximately 175 titles each year, his group covers a range of genres including commercial and literary fiction, thrillers, biography, politics, sports, popular science, and more. The list is intentionally eclectic and includes a wide range of fiction and nonfiction, from first books to international bestsellers." Accepts simultaneous submissions. Book catalog and ms guidelines free.

NONFICTION Subjects include history, sports, political commentary. *Accepts agented submissions only.*

FICTION Subjects include mystery, suspense, thrillers, women's. *Accepts agented submissions only.*

DUQUESNE UNIVERSITY PRESS

600 Forbes Ave., Pittsburgh PA 15282. (412)396-6610. **Fax:** (412)396-5984. **E-mail:** dupress@duq.edu. **Website:** www.dupress.duq.edu. **Contact:** Susan Wadsworth-Booth, director. Estab. 1927. Publishes hardcover and trade paperback originals. "Duquesne publishes scholarly monographs in the fields of literary studies (medieval and Renaissance), continental philosophy, ethics, religious studies, philosophy of communication, and humanistic psychology. Interdisciplinary works are also of interest. Duquesne University Press does not publish fiction, poetry, children's books, technical or 'hard' science works, or unrevised theses or dissertations." **Publishes 8-12 titles/year. 400 queries; 65 mss received/year. 30% of books from first-time authors. 95% from unagented writers. Pays royalty on net price. Pays (some) advance.** Publishes ms 1 year after acceptance. Accepts simultaneous submissions. Responds in 1-3 months. Book catalog available. Guidelines online.

NONFICTION Subjects include communications, humanities, literary criticism, philosophy, psychology, religion, social sciences. "We look for quality of scholarship." For scholarly books, query or submit outline, 1 sample chapter, and SASE.

ⓐ⊘ DUTTON ADULT TRADE

Penguin Random House, 375 Hudson St., New York NY 10014. (212)366-2000. **Website:** penguin.com. Estab. 1852. Publishes hardcover originals. "Dutton currently publishes 45 hardcovers a year, roughly half fiction and half nonfiction." **Pays royalty. Pays negotiable advance.** Book catalog online.

NONFICTION Agented submissions only. *No unsolicited mss.*

FICTION Subjects include adventure, historical, literary, mystery, short story collections, suspense. Agented submissions only. *No unsolicited mss.*

TIPS "Write the complete ms and submit it to an agent or agents. They will know exactly which editor will be interested in a project."

DUTTON CHILDREN'S BOOKS

Penguin Random House, 375 Hudson St., New York NY 10014. **Website:** www.penguin.com. **Contact:** Julie Strauss-Gabel, vice president and publisher. Estab. 1852. Publishes hardcover originals as well as novelty formats. Dutton Children's Books publishes high-quality fiction and nonfiction for readers ranging from preschoolers to young adults on a variety of subjects. Currently emphasizing middle grade and young adult novels that offer a fresh perspective. De-emphasizing photographic nonfiction and picture books that teach a lesson. **Publishes 100 titles/year. 15% of books from first-time authors. Pays royalty on retail price. Pays advance.** Accepts simultaneous submissions.

"Cultivating the creative talents of authors and illustrators and publishing books with purpose and heart continue to be the mission and joy at Dutton."

NONFICTION Subjects include animals, history, science. Query. Only responds if interested.

FICTION Subjects include juvenile, young adult. Dutton Children's Books has a diverse, general interest list that includes picture books; easy-to-read books; and fiction for all ages, from first chapter books to young adult readers. Query. Responds only if interested.

EAGLE'S VIEW PUBLISHING

6756 N. Fork Rd., Liberty UT 84310. (801)393-4555. **Website:** www.eaglesviewpub.com. Estab. 1982. Publishes trade paperback originals. "Eagle's View primarily publishes how-to craft books with a subject related to historical or contemporary Native American/Mountain Man/frontier crafts/bead crafts. Currently emphasizing bead-related craft books. De-emphasizing history except for historical Indian crafts." **Publishes 2-4 titles/year. 40 queries received/year. 20 mss received/year. 90% of books from first-time authors. 100% from unagented writers. Pays 8-10% royalty on net selling price.** Publishes ms 1 year after acceptance. Accepts simultaneous submissions. Responds in 1 year to proposals.

NONFICTION Subjects include ethnic, history, hobbies. Submit outline, 1-2 sample chapters. Reviews artwork/photos. Send photocopies and sample illustrations.

EASTLAND PRESS

P.O. Box 99749, Seattle WA 98139. (206)217-0204. **Fax:** (206)217-0205. **E-mail:** info@eastlandpress.com. **Website:** www.eastlandpress.com. **Contact:** John O'Connor, Managing Editor. Estab. 1981. Publishes hardcover and trade paperback originals. "Eastland Press is interested in textbooks for practitioners of alternative medical therapies, primarily Chinese and physical therapies, and related bodywork." **Publishes 3-4 titles/year. 25 queries received/year. 30% of books from first-time authors. 90% from unagented writers. Pays 12-15% royalty on receipts.** Publishes ms 1-2 years after acceptance. Accepts simultaneous submissions. Responds in 1 month to queries. Catalog online.

NONFICTION Subjects include medicine. "We prefer that a ms be completed or close to completion before we will consider publication. Proposals are rarely considered, unless submitted by a published author or teaching institution." Submit TOC and 2-3 sample chapters. Reviews artwork/photos

ⒶⓍ THE ECCO PRESS

195 Broadway, New York NY 10007. (212)207-7000. **Fax:** (212)702-2460. **Website:** www.harpercollins.com. Estab. 1970. Publishes hardcover and trade paperback originals and reprints. **Publishes 60 titles/year. Pays royalty. Pays negotiable advance.** Publishes ms 1 year after acceptance. Accepts simultaneous submissions.

FICTION Literary, short story collections. "We can publish possibly 1 or 2 original novels a year." *Does not accept unsolicited mss.*

TIPS "We are always interested in first novels and feel it's important that they be brought to the attention of the reading public."

◔ EDGE SCIENCE FICTION AND FANTASY PUBLISHING

Hades Publications, Box 1714, Calgary AB T2P 2L7, Canada. (403)254-0160. **Website:** www.edgewebsite. com. **Contact:** Editorial Manager. Estab. 1996. Publishes hardcover, trade paperback and e-book originals. EDGE publishes thought-provoking full length novels and anthologies of Science Fiction, Fantasy and Horror. Featuring works by established authors and emerging new voices, EDGE is pleased to provide quality literary entertainment in both print and pixels. **Publishes 20+ titles/year. 300-400 20% of books from first-time authors. 90% from unagented writers. Pays 10% royalty on net price. Negotiable advance.** Publishes ms 18-20 months after acceptance. Responds in 4-5 months to mss. Catalog online. Guidelines online.

IMPRINTS EDGE, EDGE-Lite, Absolute XPress.

FICTION Subjects include fantasy, horror, science fiction, young adult. "We are looking for all types of fantasy, science fiction, and horror - except juvenile, erotica, and religious fiction. Short stories and poetry are only required for announced anthologies." Length: 75,000-100,000/words. Does not want juvenile, erotica, and religious fiction. Submit first 3 chapters and synopsis. Check website for guidelines. Include estimated word count.

◕ ÉDITIONS DU NOROÎT

4609 D'Iberville, Bureau 202, Montreal QC H2H 2L9, Canada. (514)727-0005. **Fax:** (514)723-6660. **E-mail:** lenoroit@lenoroit.com. **Website:** www.lenoroit.com. **Contact:** Paul Belanger, director. Publishes trade paperback originals and reprints. "Editions du Noiroît publishes poetry and essays on poetry." **Publishes 20 titles/year. 500 queries; 500 mss received/year. Pays 10% royalty on retail price.** Publishes ms 1 year after acceptance. Accepts simultaneous submissions. Responds in 4 months to mss.

POETRY Submit 40 sample poems.

EDUPRESS, INC.

P.O. Box 8610, Madison WI 53708. (608)242-1201. **E-mail:** edupress@highsmith.com. **E-mail:** lbowie@highsmith.com. **Website:** www.edupress.com. **Contact:** Liz Bowie. Estab. 1979. Edupress, Inc., publishes supplemental curriculum resources for PK-6th grade. Currently emphasizing Common Core reading and math games and materials. **Work purchased outright from authors.** Publishes ms 1-2 years after acceptance. Accepts simultaneous submissions. Responds in 2-4 months. Catalog online.

◔ "Our mission is to create products that make kids want to go to school."

NONFICTION Submit complete ms via mail or e-mail with "Manuscript Submission" as the subject line.

TIPS "We are looking for unique, research-based, quality supplemental materials for Pre-K through 6th grade. We publish mainly reading and math materials in many different formats, including games. Our materials are intended for classroom and home schooling use. We do not publish picture books."

WILLIAM B. EERDMANS PUBLISHING CO.

2140 Oak Industrial Dr. NE, Grand Rapids MI 49505. (616)459-4591. **Fax:** (616)459-6540. **E-mail:** info@eerdmans.com. **E-mail:** submissions@eerdmans.com. **Website:** www.eerdmans.com. Estab. 1911. Publishes hardcover and paperback originals and reprints. "The majority of our adult publications are religious and most of these are academic or semi-academic in character (as opposed to inspirational or celebrity books), though we also publish general trade books on the Christian life. Our nonreligious titles, most of them in regional history or on social issues, aim, similarly, at an educated audience." Accepts simultaneous submissions. Responds in 4 weeks. Book catalog and ms guidelines free.

NONFICTION Subjects include history, philosophy, psychology, regional, religion, sociology, translation, Biblical studies. "We prefer that writers take the time to notice if we have published anything at all in the same category as their manuscript before sending it to us." Query with TOC, 2-3 sample chapters, and SASE for return of ms. Reviews artwork/photos.

FICTION Subjects include religious. Query with SASE.

EDWARD ELGAR PUBLISHING, INC.

The William Pratt House, 9 Dewey Ct., Northampton MA 01060. (413)584-5551. **Fax:** (413)584-9933. **E-mail:** elgarinfo@e-elgar.com. **Website:** www.e-elgar.com. Estab. 1986. "Specializing in research monographs, reference books and upper-level textbooks in highly focused areas, we are able to offer a unique service in terms of editorial, production and worldwide marketing. We have three offices, Cheltenham and Camberley in the UK and Northampton, MA, US. We are actively commissioning new titles and are happy to consider and advise on ideas for monograph books, textbooks, professional law books and academic journals at any stage. Please complete a proposal form in as much detail as possible. We review all prososals

with our academic advisors." Accepts simultaneous submissions.

ELLORA'S CAVE PUBLISHING, INC.

1056 Home Ave., Akron OH 44310. **E-mail:** submissions@ellorascave.com. **Website:** www.ellorascave.com. Estab. 2000. Publishes electronic originals and reprints; print books. **Pays 45% royalty on amount received.** Accepts simultaneous submissions. Responds in 2-4 months to mss. No queries. Guidelines online. "Read and follow detailed submission instructions."

FICTION Erotic romance and erotica fiction of every subgenre, including gay/lesbian, menage and more, and BDSM. All must have abundant, explicit, and graphic erotic content. Submit electronically only; cover e-mail as defined in our submission guidelines plus 1 attached .docx file containing full synopsis, first 3 chapters, and last chapter.

TIPS "Our audience is romance readers who want explicit sexual detail. They come to us because we offer sex with romance, plot, emotion. In addition to erotic romance with happy-ever-after endings, we also publish pure erotica, detailing sexual adventure, and experimentation."

ELM BOOKS

1175 Hwy. 130, Laramie WY 82070. (610)529-0460. **E-mail:** leila.elmbooks@gmail.com. **Website:** www.elm-books.com. **Contact:** Leila Monaghan, publisher. "We are eager to publish stories by new writers that have real stories to tell. We are looking for short stories (5,000-10,000 words) with real characters and true-to-life stories. Whether your story is fictionalized autobiography, or other stories of real-life mayhem and debauchery, we are interested in reading them!" **Pays royalties.** Accepts simultaneous submissions.

FICTION "We are looking for short stories (1,000-5,000 words) about kids of color that will grab readers' attentions—mysteries, adventures, humor, suspense, set in the present, near past or near future that reflect the realities and hopes of life in diverse communities." Also looking for middle grade novels (20,000-50,000 words). Send complete ms for short stories; synopsis and 3 sample chapters for novels.

EMIS, INC.

P.O. Box 270666, Fort Collins CO 80527. (800)225-0694. **Fax:** (970)672-8606. **Website:** www.emispub.

com. Publishes trade paperback originals. "Medical text designed for physicians; fit in the lab coat pocket as a quick reference. Currently emphasizing women's health." **Publishes 2 titles/year. Pays 12% royalty on retail price.** Accepts simultaneous submissions. Responds in 3 months to queries. Book catalog available free. Guidelines available free.

NONFICTION Subjects include psychology, women's health/medicine. Submit 3 sample chapters with SASE.

ENCANTE PRESS, LLC

1572 Blue Lupine Ln., Victor MT 59875. (406)642-3333. **Fax:** (406)642-6373. **E-mail:** books@encantepress.com. **Website:** www.encantepress.com. **Contact:** Marty Essen, president. Estab. 2007. Nonfiction publisher interested in nature, wildlife, animals, environment, travel, sciences, and politics. **Publishes 3-6 titles/year. 75% of books from first-time authors. 75% from unagented writers. Pays 10-20% royalty on net. "We offer a small advance, depending on the author and the book."** Publishes book 1 year after acceptance. Accepts simultaneous submissions. Responds in 1 month to queries/proposals; 2 months to mss. Guidelines via e-mail.

NONFICTION Subjects include animals, environment, government, nature, politics, science, travel, wildlife. Query via e-mail with proposal package, including 2 sample chapters. Reviews artwork as part of package (PDF or Word files only).

TIPS "We are only interested in books that fit the nonfiction categories we have listed. As an eco-friendly publishing company, we only accept queries and sample chapters via e-mail (in a PDF file attachment). Make sure whatever you send us is free of spelling and punctuation errors. Poorly proofed correspondence and/or manuscripts will be quickly rejected. Although queries are accepted, authors are welcome to skip that step and just send 2 sample chapters. Your cover letter must include the elevator pitch for your book, a brief description of your book's potential market, and what you will do to help promote your book."

⚠️⊘ ENCOUNTER BOOKS

900 Broadway, Suite 601, New York NY 10003. (212)871-6310. **Fax:** (212)871-6311. **Website:** www.encounterbooks.com. **Contact:** Acquisitions. Publisher/President: Roger Kimball. Publishes hardcover, trade paperback, and e-book originals and trade paperback reprints. Encounter Books publishes serious nonfic-

tion—books that can alter our society, challenge our morality, stimulate our imaginations—in the areas of history, politics, religion, biography, education, public policy, current affairs, and social sciences. Encounter Books is an activity of Encounter for Culture and Education, a tax-exempt, non profit corporation dedicated to strengthening the marketplace of ideas and engaging in educational activities to help preserve democratic culture. Accepts simultaneous submissions. Book catalog online. Guidelines online.

NONFICTION Subjects include child guidance, education, ethnic, history, memoirs, multicultural, philosophy, psychology, religion, science, sociology, gender studies. Only considers agented submissions.

ENETE ENTERPRISES

1321 Upland Dr. #6536, Houston TX 77043. **E-mail:** eneteenterprises@gmail.com. **E-mail:** eneteenterprises@gmail.com. **Website:** www.eneteenterprises.com. **Contact:** Shannon Enete, editor. Estab. 2011. Publishes trade paperback originals, mass market paperback originals, electronic originals. **Publishes 6 titles/year. 290 queries received/year. 95% of books from first-time authors. 100% from unagented writers. Pays royalties of 10-20%.** Publishes book 3-6 months after acceptance. Accepts simultaneous submissions. Responds to queries/proposals in 1 month; mss in 1-3 months. Guidelines online.

NONFICTION Subjects include education, health, memoirs, travel, travel guides, travel memoirs, life abroad, retired living abroad. Submit query, proposal, or ms with marketing plan by e-mail.

TIPS "Send me your best work. Do not rush a draft."

ENSLOW PUBLISHERS, INC.

101 W. 23rd St., Suite 240, New York NY 10011. (973)771-9400. **E-mail:** customerservice@enslow.com. **Website:** www.enslow.com. Estab. 1977. Publishes hardcover originals. 10% require freelance illustration. Enslow publishes nonfiction and fiction series books for young adults and school-age children. **Publishes 250 titles/year. Pays royalty on net price with advance or flat fee. Pays advance.** Publishes ms 1 year after acceptance. Accepts simultaneous submissions. Responds in 1 month to queries. Guidelines via e-mail.

NONFICTION Subjects include history, recreation, science, sociology, sports. "Interested in new ideas for series of books for young people." No fiction, fictionalized history, or dialogue.

TIPS "We love to receive resumes from experienced writers with good research skills who can think like young people."

ENTANGLED TEEN

Website: www.entangledteen.com. "Entangled Teen and Entangled digiTeen, our young adult imprints publish the swoonworthy young adult romances readers crave. Whether they're dark and angsty or fun and sassy, contemporary, fantastical, or futuristic. We are seeking fresh voices with interesting twists on popular genres." **Pays royalty.** Accepts simultaneous submissions.

IMPRINTS Teen Crush; Teen Crave.

FICTION "We are seeking novels in the subgenres of romantic fiction for contemporary, upper young adult with crossover appeal." E-mail using site. "All submissions must have strong romantic elements. YA novels should be 50K to 100K in length. Revised backlist titles will be considered on a case by case basis." Agented and unagented considered.

ENTREPRENEUR PRESS

Entrepreneur Media Inc., 18061 Fitch, Irvine CA 92614. (949)261-2325. **Fax:** (949)622-7106. **E-mail:** press@entrepreneur.com. **Website:** www.entrepreneurbookstore.com. **Contact:** Vanessa Campos, marketing manager. Acquisitions Director: Jen Dorsey. "We specialize in quality paperbacks and e-books that focus on the entrepreneur in us all. Addressing the diverse challenges at all stages of business, each Entrepreneur Press book aims to provide actionable solutions to help entrepreneurs excel in all ventures they take on." **Publishes 20+ titles/year. Pays competitive net royalty.** Accepts simultaneous submissions. Catalog online. Guidelines online.

NONFICTION Subjects include business, career guidance, business start-up, small business management, business planning, marketing, finance, careers, personal finance, accounting, motivation, leadership, legal advise, management. When submitting work to us, please send as much of the proposed book as possible. Proposal should include: cover letter, preface, marketing plan, analysis of competition and comparative titles, author bio, TOC, 2 sample chapters. Go to website for more details. Reviews artwork/photos. Send transparencies and all other applicable information.

TIPS "We are currently seeking proposals covering sales, small business, startup, online businesses, marketing, etc."

EPICENTER PRESS, INC.

6524 NE 181st St. #2, Kenmore WA 98028. **Fax:** (425)481-8253. **E-mail:** lael@epicenterpress.com. **Website:** www.epicenterpress.com. **Contact:** Lael Morgan, acquisitions editor. Estab. 1987. Publishes hardcover and trade paperback originals. "We are a regional press founded in Alaska whose interests include but are not limited to the arts, history, environment, and diverse cultures and lifestyles of the North Pacific and high latitudes." **Publishes 4-8 titles/ year. 200 queries received/year. 100 mss received/ year. 75% of books from first-time authors. 90% from unagented writers.** Publishes book 1-2 years after acceptance. Accepts simultaneous submissions. Responds in 3 months to queries. Book catalog and guidelines online.

◗ "Our affiliated company, Aftershocks Media, provides a range of services to self-publisher industry distributors."

NONFICTION Subjects include animals, ethnic, history, recreation, regional. "Our focus is Alaska and the Pacific Northwest. We do not encourage nonfiction titles from outside this region." Submit outline and 3 sample chapters. Reviews artwork/photos. Send photocopies.

F+W, A CONTENT + ECOMMERCE COMPANY (BOOK DIVISION)

10151 Carver Rd., Suite 200, Blue Ash OH 45242. (513)531-2690. **Website:** www.fwcommunity.com. President: Sara Domville. Estab. 1913. Publishes trade paperback originals and reprints. F+W connects passionate, like-minded groups of people to share an ongoing exchange of information, ideas, and inspiration. "We are committed to providing the very best experience for our consumers across our niche categories–craft, art, writing, design, outdoors, and lifestyle. We offer exclusive programs and products, best-in-industry customer service, curated kit flash sales, rewards and VIP programs, personalized 1-to-1 marketing, and more." **Publishes 400+ titles/year.** Accepts simultaneous submissions. Guidelines online.

IMPRINTS Adams Media (general interest series); HOW Books (graphic design, illustrated, humor, pop culture); IMPACT Books (fantasy art, manga, creative comics and popular culture); Interweave (knitting, beading, crochet, jewelry, sewing); Krause Books (antiques and collectibles, automotive, coins and paper money, comics, crafts, games, firearms, militaria, outdoors and hunting, records and CDs, sports, toys); North Light Books (crafts, decorative painting, fine art); Popular Woodworking Books (shop skills, woodworking); Tyrus Books (mystery and literary fiction); Warman's (antiques and collectibles, field guides); Writer's Digest Books (writing and reference).

Please see individual listings for specific submission information about the company's imprints.

FACTS ON FILE, INC.

Infobase Learning, 132 W. 31st St., 17th Floor, New York NY 10001. (800)322-8755. **Fax:** (800)678-3633. **E-mail:** llikoff@factsonfile.com; custserv@factsonfile.com. **Website:** www.factsonfile.com. Estab. 1941. Publishes hardcover originals and reprints and e-books as well as reference databases. Facts On File produces high-quality reference materials in print and digital format on a broad range of subjects for the school and public library market and the general nonfiction trade. **Publishes 150-200 titles/year. 10% of books from first-time authors. 25% from unagented writers. Pays 10% royalty on retail price. Pays $5,000 advance.** Accepts simultaneous submissions. Responds in 2 months to queries. Book catalog available free. Guidelines online.

NONFICTION Subjects include career guidance, contemporary culture, education, history, literary criticism, multicultural, nutrition, politics, religion, sports, womens studies, young adult, careers, entertainment, natural history, popular culture. "We publish serious, informational books and e-books for a targeted audience. All our books must have strong library interest, but we also distribute books effectively to the trade. Our library books fit the junior and senior high school curriculum." No computer books, technical books, cookbooks, biographies (except YA), pop psychology, humor, fiction or poetry. Query or submit outline and sample chapter with SASE. No submissions returned without SASE.

TIPS "Our audience is school and public libraries for our more reference-oriented books and libraries, schools and bookstores for our less reference-oriented informational titles."

FAIRLEIGH DICKINSON UNIVERSITY PRESS

285 Madison Ave., M-GH2-01, Madison NJ 07940. (973)443-8564. **Fax:** (973)443-8364. **E-mail:** fdupress@fdu.edu. **Website:** www.fdupress.org. **Contact:** Harry Keyishian, Director. Estab. 1967. Publishes in hardcover originals and all electronic formats. Publishes a selection of volumes in paperback. Fairleigh Dickinson publishes scholarly books for the academic market, in the humanities and social sciences through a co-publishing partnership with Rowman & Littlefield, Lanham, MD. **Publishes 35-45 titles/year. 33% of books from first-time authors. 95% from unagented writers.** Publishes ms 6-7 months after acceptance. Responds in 2 weeks to queries.

"Contracts are arranged through The Rowman & Littlefield Publishing Group, which also handles editing and production. Publication decisions are made by our Editorial and Advisory Board. FDU Press is open to quality scholarly submissions in all humanities/social science field. We also have developed several book series: American History and Culture; Communication Studies; Italian Studies; Law, Culture and the Humanities; Mormon Studies; Shakespeare and the Stage; Studies in Willa Cather."

NONFICTION Subjects include architecture, art, cinema, communications, contemporary culture, dance, economics, ethnic, film, gay, government, history, law, lesbian, literary criticism, multicultural, music, philosophy, psychology, regional, religion, sociology, womens issues, womens studies, world affairs, local, world literature, Italian Studies (series), Communication Studies (series), Willa Cather (series), American history and culture, Civil War, Jewish studies. "The Press discourages submissions of unrevised dissertations. We will consider scholarly editions of literary works in all fields, in English, or translation. We welcome inquiries about essay collections if the the material is previously unpublished, he essays have a unifying and consistent theme, and the editors provide a substantial scholarly introduction." No nonscholarly books. "We do not publish textbooks, or original fiction, poetry or plays." Query with outline, detailed abstract, and sample chapters (if possible), and CV. Does not review artwork.

FAMILIUS

1254 Commerce Way, Sanger CA 93657. (559)876-2170. **Fax:** (559)876-2180. **E-mail:** bookideas@familius.com. **Website:** familius.com. **Contact:** Michele Robbins, acquisitions editor. David Miles: Design & Digital, Brooke Jorden: Managing Editor, Erika Riggs: Marketing & Publicity Estab. 2011. Publishes hardcover, trade paperback, and electronic originals and reprints. Familius is all about strengthening families. Collective, the authors and staff have experienced a wide slice of the family-life spectrum. Some come from broken homes. Some are married and in the throes of managing a bursting household. Some are preparing to start families of their own. Together, they publish books and articles that help families be happy. **Publishes 40 titles/year. 200 queries; 100 mss received/year. 30% of books from first-time authors. 70% from unagented writers. Authors are paid 10-30% royalty on wholesale price.** Publishes book 12 months after acceptance. Accepts simultaneous submissions. Responds in 1 month to queries and proposals; 2 months to mss. Catalog online. Guidelines online.

NONFICTION Subjects include Americana, beauty, child guidance, cooking, counseling, finance, foods, health, hobbies, medicine, memoirs, nutrition, parenting, young adult. All mss must align with Familius mission statement to help families succeed. Submit a proposal package, including an outline, one sample chapter, competition evaluation, and your author platform. Reviews JPEGS if sent as part of the submission package.

FICTION Subjects include juvenile, picture books, young adult. All fiction must align with Familius values statement listed on the website footer. Submit a proposal package, including a synopsis, 3 sample chapters, and your author platform.

FAMILYLIFE PUBLISHING

FamilyLife, a division of Campus Crusade for Christ, P.O. Box 7111, Little Rock AR 72223. (800)358-6329. **Website:** www.familylife.com. Publishes hardcover and trade paperback originals. FamilyLife is dedicated to effectively developing godly families. We publish connecting resources—books, videos, audio resources, and interactive multi-piece packs—that help husbands and wives communicate better, and parents and children build stronger relationships. **Publishes 3-12 titles/year. 250 queries received/year. 50 mss received/year. 1% of books from first-time authors. 90% from unagented writers. Pays 2-18% royalty on wholesale price. Makes outright purchase of 250.** Publishes ms 2 years after acceptance. Accepts simultaneous submissions. Responds in 3 months to queries; 6 months to proposals and mss. Book catalog online.

NONFICTION Subjects include child guidance, education, religion, sex, spirituality. FamilyLife Publish-

ing exists to create resources to connect your family. "We publish very few books. Become familiar with what we offer. Our resources are unique in the marketplace. Discover what makes us unique, match your work to our style, and then submit." Query with SASE. Submit proposal package, outline, 2 sample chapters. Reviews artwork/photos.

FANTAGRAPHICS BOOKS, INC.

7563 Lake City Way NE, Seattle WA 98115. (206)524-1967. **Fax:** (206)524-2104. **Website:** www.fantagraphics.com. **Contact:** Submissions Editor. Estab. 1976. Publishes original trade paperbacks. Publishes comics for thinking readers. Does not want mainstream genres of superhero, vigilante, horror, fantasy, or science fiction. Accepts simultaneous submissions. Responds in 2-3 months to queries. Book catalog online. Guidelines online.

FICTION Subjects include comic books. "Fantagraphics is an independent company with a modus operandi different from larger, factory-like corporate comics publishers. If your talents are limited to a specific area of expertise (i.e. inking, writing, etc.), then you will need to develop your own team before submitting a project to us. We want to see an idea that is fully fleshed-out in your mind, at least, if not on paper. Submit a minimum of 5 fully-inked pages of art, a synopsis, SASE, and a brief note stating approximately how many issues you have in mind."

TIPS "Take note of the originality and diversity of the themes and approaches to drawing in such Fantagraphics titles as *Love & Rockets* (stories of life in Latin America and Chicano L.A.), *Palestine* (journalistic autobiography in the Middle East), *Eightball* (surrealism mixed with kitsch culture in stories alternately humorous and painfully personal), and *Naughty Bits* (feminist humor and short stories which both attack and commiserate). Try to develop your own, equally individual voice; originality, aesthetic maturity, and graphic storytelling skill are the signs by which Fantagraphics judges whether or not your submission is ripe for publication."

FARCOUNTRY PRESS

P.O. Box 5630, Helena MT 59604. (800)821-3874. **Fax:** (406)443-5480. **E-mail:** will@farcountrypress.com. **Website:** www.farcountrypress.com. **Contact:** Will Harmon. Award-winning publisher Farcountry Press specializes in softcover and hardcover color photography books showcasing the nation's cities, states, national parks, and wildlife. Farcountry also publishes several children's series, as well as guidebooks, cookbooks, and regional history titles nationwide. **Publishes The staff produces about 30 books annually; the backlist has grown to more than 300 titles titles/year.** Accepts simultaneous submissions. Guidelines online.

FARRAR, STRAUS & GIROUX

18 W. 18th St., New York NY 10011. (646)307-5151. **Website:** us.macmillan.com/fsg. **Contact:** Editorial Department. Estab. 1946. Publishes hardcover originals and trade paperback reprints. "We publish original and well-written material for all ages." **Publishes 75 titles/year. 6,000 queries and mss received/year. 5% of books from first-time authors. 50% from unagented writers. Pays 2-6% royalty on retail price for paperbacks, 3-10% for hardcovers. Pays $3,000-25,000 advance.** Publishes ms 18 months after acceptance. Accepts simultaneous submissions. Responds in 2-3 months. Catalog available by request. Guidelines online.

NONFICTION All levels. Send cover letter describing submission with first 50 pages.

FICTION Subjects include juvenile, picture books, young adult. Do not query picture books; just send ms. Do not fax or e-mail queries or mss. Send cover letter describing submission with first 50 pages.

POETRY Send cover letter describing submission with 3-4 poems. By mail only.

FARRAR, STRAUS & GIROUX FOR YOUNG READERS

Macmillan Children's Publishing Group, 175 Fifth Ave., New York NY 10010. (212)741-6900. **Fax:** (212)633-2427. **E-mail:** childrens.editorial@fsgbooks.com. **Website:** www.fsgkidsbooks.com. Estab. 1946. Accepts simultaneous submissions. Book catalog available by request. Ms guidelines online.

NONFICTION All levels: all categories. "We publish only literary nonfiction." Submit cover letter, first 50 pages by mail only.

FICTION All levels: all categories. "Original and well-written material for all ages." Submit cover letter, first 50 pages by mail only.

POETRY Submit cover letter, 3-4 poems by mail only.

TIPS "Study our catalog before submitting. We will see illustrators' portfolios by appointment. Don't ask for criticism and/or advice—due to the volume of submissions we receive, it's just not possible. Never send originals. Always enclose SASE."

FAT FOX BOOKS

The Den, P.O. Box 579, Tonbridge TN9 9NG, United Kingdom. (44)(0)1580-857249. **E-mail:** hello@fatfoxbooks.com. **Website:** fatfoxbooks.com. "Can you write engaging, funny, original and brilliant stories? We are looking for fresh new talent as well as exciting new ideas from established writers and illustrators. We publish books for children from 3-14, and if we think the story is brilliant and fits our list, then as one of the few publishers who accepts unsolicited material, we will take it seriously. We will consider books of all genres." Accepts simultaneous submissions. Guidelines online. Currently closed to submissions.

FICTION For picture books, send complete ms; for longer works, send first 3 chapters and estimate of final word count.

FATHER'S PRESS

590 N.W. 1921 St. Rd., Kingsville MO 64063. (816)566-0654. **E-mail:** mike@fatherspress.com. **Website:** www.fatherspress.com. **Contact:** Mike Smitley, owner (fiction, nonfiction). Estab. 2006. Publishes hardcover, trade paperback, and mass market paperback originals and reprints. **Publishes 6-10 titles/year. Pays 10-15% royalty on wholesale price.** Publishes ms 6 months after acceptance. Responds in 1-3 months. Guidelines online.

NONFICTION Subjects include animals, creative nonfiction, history, religion. Query with SASE. Unsolicited mss returned unopened. Call or e-mail first. Reviews artwork/photos. Send photocopies.

FICTION Subjects include adventure, historical, juvenile, literary, mystery, regional, religious, suspense, western, young adult. Query with SASE. Unsolicited mss returned unopened. Call or e-mail first.

FAWCETT

The Ballantine Publishing Group, A Division of Penguin Random House, 1745 Broadway, New York NY 10019. **Website:** www.penguinrandomhouse.com. Estab. 1955. Publishes paperback originals and reprints. Major publisher of mystery mass market and trade paperbacks. Accepts simultaneous submissions.

FICTION Subjects include mystery. Agented submissions only. *All unsolicited mss returned.*

FEIWEL AND FRIENDS

Macmillan Children's Publishing Group, 175 Fifth Ave., New York NY 10010. (646)307-5151. **Website:** us.macmillan.com. Feiwel and Friends is a publisher of innovative children's fiction and nonfiction literature, including hardcover, paperback series, and individual titles. The list is eclectic and combines quality and commercial appeal for readers ages 0-16. The imprint is dedicated to "book by book" publishing, bringing the work of distinctive and oustanding authors, illustrators, and ideas to the marketplace. This market does not accept unsolicited mss due to the volume of submissions; they also do not accept unsolicited queries for interior art. The best way to submit a ms is through an agent. Catalog online.

FENCE BOOKS

Science Library 320, Univ. of Albany, 1400 Washington Ave., Albany NY 12222. (518)591-8162. **E-mail:** fencesubmissions@gmail.com. **Website:** www.fence-portal.org. **Contact:** Submissions Manager. Publishes hardcover originals. "Fence Books publishes poetry, fiction, and critical texts and anthologies, and prioritizes sustained support for its authors, many of whom come to us through our book contests and then go on to publish second, third, fourth books." Accepts simultaneous submissions. Guidelines online.

FICTION Subjects include literary, poetry. Submit via contests and occasional open reading periods.

POETRY Submit via contests and occasional open reading periods.

FERGUSON PUBLISHING CO.

Infobase Publishing, 132 W. 31st St., 17th Floor, New York NY 10001. (800)322-8755. **E-mail:** editorial@factsonfile.com. **Website:** www.infobasepublishing.com. Estab. 1940. Publishes hardcover and trade paperback originals. "We are primarily a career education publisher that publishes for schools and libraries. We need writers who have expertise in a particular career or career field (for possible full-length books on a specific career or field)." **Publishes 50 titles/year. Pays by project.** Accepts simultaneous submissions. Responds in 6 months to queries. Guidelines online.

NONFICTION "We publish work specifically for the elementary/junior high/high school/college library reference market. Works are generally encyclopedic in nature. Our current focus is career encyclopedias and young adult career sets and series. We consider manuscripts that cross over into the trade market." No mass market, poetry, scholarly, or juvenile books, please. Query or submit an outline and 1 sample chapter.

TIPS "We like writers who know the market—former or current librarians or teachers or guidance counselors."

☺ FERNWOOD PUBLISHING, LTD.

32 Ocenavista Ln., Black Point NS B0J 1B0, Canada. (902)857-1388. **Fax:** (902) 857-1328. **E-mail:** info@fernpub.ca. **E-mail:** editorial@fernpub.ca. **Website:** www.fernwoodpublishing.ca. **Contact:** Errol Sharpe, publisher. Estab. 1993. Publishes trade paperback originals. "Fernwood's objective is to publish critical works which challenge existing scholarship. We are a political and academic publisher. We publish critical books in the social sciences and humanities and for the trade market." **Publishes 35-40 titles/year. 120 queries received/year. 50 mss received/year. 40% of books from first-time authors. 100% from unagented writers. Pays 7-10% royalty on wholesale price. Pays advance.** Publishes ms 12-18 months after acceptance. Accepts simultaneous submissions. Responds in 6 weeks to proposals. Guidelines online.

IMPRINTS Roseway Publishing.

NONFICTION Subjects include agriculture, anthropology, communications, community, contemporary culture, creative nonfiction, economics, education, environment, ethnic, gay, government, health, history, humanities, labor, law, lesbian, multicultural, philosophy, politics, regional, sex, social sciences, sociology, translation, womens issues, womens studies, world affairs, young adult, contemporary culture, world affairs. "Our main focus is in the social sciences and humanities, emphasizing Indigenous resistance and resurgence, politics, capitalism, political economy, women, gender, sexuality, crime and law, international development and social work-for use in college and university courses." Submit proposal package, outline, sample chapters. Reviews artwork/photos. Send photocopies.

FICTION Subjects include ethnic, feminist, gay, historical, lesbian, literary, multicultural, regional, young adult, environment. Roseway Publishing is our social justice literary imprint. Roseway publishes fiction, young adult fiction, children's fiction and autobiography that deals with social justice issues. Guidelines online.

☺ DAVID FICKLING BOOKS

31 Beamont St., Oxford OX1 2NP, United Kingdom. (018)65-339000. **Fax:** (018)65-339009. **Website:** www.

davidficklingbooks.co.uk. **Contact:** Simon Mason, managing editor. David Fickling Books is a story house."For nearly twelve years DFB has been run as an imprint—first as part of Scholastic, then of Random House. Now we've set up as an independent business." **Publishes 12-20 titles/year.** Accepts simultaneous submissions. Responds to mss in 3 months, if interested. Guidelines online. Closed to submissions. Check website for when they open to submissions and for details on the Inkpot competition.

FICTION Considers all categories. Submit cover letter and 3 sample chapters as PDF attachment saved in format "Author Name_Full Title."

TIPS "We adore stories for all ages, in both text and pictures. Quality is our watch word."

FILBERT PUBLISHING

140 3rd St. N., Kandiyohi MN 56251-0326. (320)444-5080. **E-mail:** filbertpublishing@filbertpublishing.com. **Website:** filbertpublishing.com. **Contact:** Maurice Erickson, acquisitions. Estab. 2001. Publishes trade paperback and electronic originals and reprints. "We really like to publish books that creative people can use to help them make a living following their dream. This includes books on marketing, books that encourage living a full life, freelancing, we'll consider a fairly wide range of subjects under this umbrella. The people who purchase our books (and visit our website) tend to be in their fifties, female, well-educated; many are freelancers who want to make a living writing. Any well-written title that would appeal to that audience is nearly a slam dunk to get added to our catalog." **Publishes 6-12 titles/year. 85% of books from first-time authors. 99% from unagented writers. Authors receive 10% royalty on retail price. E-books receive 50% net.** Publishes book 2-3 months after acceptance. Accepts simultaneous submissions. Responds in 1 month. Catalog online. Guidelines online.

NONFICTION Subjects include communications, creative nonfiction, spirituality, reference books for freelancers and creative people with an emphasis on marketing. "Our projects tend to be evergreen. If you've got a great project that's as relevant today as it will be 10 years from now, something that you're passionate about, query." Submit a query via SASE with a proposal package, including an outline and 2 sample chapters. Will review artwork. Writers should send photocopies or query about sending electronically.

FICTION Subjects include contemporary, mainstream, mystery, romance, suspense. "We're slow to accept new fiction, however, we are thrilled when we find a story that sweeps us off our feet. Fiction queries have been very sparse the last couple of years, and we're keen on expanding that line in the coming months." Query via SASE with a proposal package, including a synopsis, 5 sample chapters, information regarding your web platform, and a brief mention of your current marketing plan.

RECENT TITLE(S) *A Writer's Vehicle: Henry Ford's Way*, by Billie Williams; *365 Tips for Writer's*, by Dawn Colclasure; and *Some of the Best Destinations in Life Begin With a Detour*, by Lois Silverman.

TIPS "Get to know us. Subscribe to Writing Etc. to capture our preferred tone. Dig through our website, you'll get many ideas of what we're looking for. We love nurturing new writing careers and most of our authors have stuck with us since our humble beginning. We love words. We really love the publishing business. If you share those passions, feel free to query."

FILTER PRESS, LLC

P.O. Box 95, Palmer Lake CO 80133. (888)570-2663. **Fax:** (719)481-2420. **E-mail:** info@filterpressbooks.com. **Website:** www.filterpressbooks.com. **Contact:** Doris Baker, president. Estab. 1957. Publishes trade paperback originals and reprints. "Filter Press specializes in nonfiction of the West." **Publishes 4-6 titles/year. Pays 10-12% royalty on wholesale price.** Publishes ms 18 months after acceptance. Accepts simultaneous submissions.

NONFICTION Subjects include Americana, ethnic, history, regional, crafts and crafts people of the Southwest. Query with outline and SASE. Reviews artwork/photos.

⬤ FINDHORN PRESS

Delft Cottage, Dyke, Forres Scotland IV36 2TF, United Kingdom. (44)(1309)690-582. **Fax:** (44)(131)777-2711. **E-mail:** submissions@findhornpress.com. **Website:** www.findhornpress.com. **Contact:** Thierry Bogliolo, publisher. Estab. 1971. Publishes trade paperback originals and e-books. **Publishes 20 titles/year. 1,000 queries received/year. 50% of books from first-time authors. 80% from unagented writers. Pays 10-15% royalty on wholesale price.** Publishes ms 12-18 months after acceptance. Accepts simultaneous submissions. Responds in 3-4 months to proposals. Book catalog and ms guidelines online.

IMPRINTS Earthdancer, Camino Guides.

NONFICTION Subjects include alternative lifestyles, animals, community, health, nature, New Age, psychology, spirituality, alternative health. No autobiographies.

FINNEY COMPANY, INC.

5995 149th St. W., Suite 105, Apple Valley MN 55124. **E-mail:** info@finneyco.com. **Website:** www.finneyco.com. **Contact:** Acquisitions. Publishes trade paperback originals. **Publishes 2 titles/year. Pays 10% royalty on wholesale price. Pays advance.** Publishes ms 1 year after acceptance. Accepts simultaneous submissions. Responds in 2-3 months to queries.

NONFICTION Subjects include education, career exploration/development. Finney publishes career development educational materials. Query with SASE. Reviews artwork/photos.

🅐🚫 FIRST SECOND

Macmillan Children's Publishing Group, 175 5th Ave., New York NY 10010. **E-mail:** mail@firstsecondbooks.com. **Website:** www.firstsecondbooks.com. First Second is a publisher of graphic novels and an imprint of Macmillan Children's Publishing Group. First Second does not accept unsolicited submissions. Responds in about 6 weeks. Catalog online.

☯ FITZHENRY & WHITESIDE LTD.

195 Allstate Pkwy., Markham ON L3R 4T8, Canada. (905)477-9700, Toll Free 1-800-387-9776. **Fax:** (905)477-9179, 1-800-260-9777. **E-mail:** fitzkids@fitzhenry.ca; godwit@fitzhenry.ca. **Website:** www.fitzhenry.ca/. **Contact:** Sharon Fitzhenry (adult books); Cheryl Chen (children's books). Emphasis on Canadian authors and illustrators, subject or perspective. **Publishes 15 titles/year. 10% of books from first-time authors. Pays authors 8-10% royalty with escalations. Offers "respectable" advances for picture books, split 50/50 between author and illustrator. Pays illustrators by project and royalty. Pays photographers per photo.** Publishes book 1-2 years after acceptance. Accepts simultaneous submissions.

NONFICTION For works of nonfiction, please include a proposal with two or three sample chapters.

FICTION For picture book submissions, please include the entire text. For novels, please submit a proposal/ synopsis and the first three chapters only. Full guidelines on site.

TIPS "We respond to quality."

FLASHLIGHT PRESS

527 Empire Blvd., Brooklyn NY 11225. (718)288-8300. **Fax:** (718)972-6307. **E-mail:** submissions@flashlightpress.com. **Website:** www.flashlightpress.com. **Contact:** Shari Dash Greenspan, editor. Estab. 2004. Publishes hardcover and trade paperback original children's picture books for 4-8 year olds. **Publishes 2-3 titles/year. 2000 queries received/year 50% of books from first-time authors. 50% from unagented writers. Pays 8-10% royalty on wholesale price. Pays advance.** Publishes ms up to 3 years after acceptance. Accepts simultaneous submissions. "Only accepts e-mail queries according to submission guidelines." Responds in 3 months to requested mss. Book catalog available online. Guidelines online.

NONFICTION See art submission guidelines online.

FICTION Subjects include picture books. Average word length: 1,000 words. Picture books: contemporary, humor, multicultural. "Query by e-mail only, after carefully reading our submission guidelines online. No e-mail attachments. Do not send anything by snail mail."

FLOATING BRIDGE PRESS

909 NE 43rd St., #205, Seattle WA 98105. **E-mail:** floatingbridgepress@yahoo.com. **Website:** www.floatingbridgepress.org. Estab. 1994. Accepts simultaneous submissions.

💬 Floating Bridge Press publishes the work of poets residing in Washington State.

POETRY Floating Bridge Press publishes chapbooks and anthologies by Washington State poets, selected through an annual competition.

🅐🚫 FLUX

Llewellyn Worldwide, Ltd., Llewellyn Worldwide, Ltd., 2143 Wooddale Dr., Woodbury MN 55125. (651)312-8613. **Fax:** (651)291-1908. **Website:** https://www.fluxnow.com. Estab. 2005. "Flux seeks to publish authors who see YA as a point of view, not a reading level. We look for books that try to capture a slice of teenage experience, whether in real or imagined worlds." **Publishes 21 titles/year. 50% of books from first-time authors. Pays royalties of 10-15% based on wholesale price.** Accepts simultaneous submissions. Book catalog and guidelines online.

FICTION Young Adults: adventure, contemporary, fantasy, history, humor, problem novels, religion, science fiction, sports, suspense. Average word length: 50,000. *Accepts agented submissions only.*

TIPS "Read contemporary teen books. Be aware of what else is out there. If you don't read teen books, you probably shouldn't write them. Know your audience. Write incredibly well. Do not condescend."

FLYING EYE BOOKS

62 Great Eastern St., London EC2A 3QR, United Kingdom. (44)(0)207-033-4430. **E-mail:** picturbksubs@nobrow.net. **Website:** www.flyingeyebooks.com. Estab. 2013. Flying Eye Books is the children's imprint of award-winning visual publishing house Nobrow. FEB seeks to retain the same attention to detail and excellence in illustrated content as its parent publisher, but with a focus on the craft of children's storytelling and nonfiction. Accepts simultaneous submissions. Guidelines online.

FLYLEAF PRESS

Ancestor Network Ltd, 4 Spencer Villas, Glenageary, County Dublin , Ireland. (353)(1)285-4658. **E-mail:** books@flyleaf.ie. **Website:** www.flyleaf.ie. **Contact:** James Ryan, managing editor (family history). Sales: Brian Smith. Estab. 1987. Publishes Irish-interest family history and genealogy titles. Flyleaf Press is the publishing arm of Ancestor Network Ltd. (http://ancestornetwork.ie) which provides research services to personal and professional clients. Flyleaf Press was founded in 1987 and is Ireland's major specialist publisher of family history and genealogy titles. Flyleaf specialize in high-quality 'how-to' guides for research in various counties of Ireland. To date guides for 12 counties have been published. They also publish reference works on Church Records, Census records and wills. **Publishes 3 titles/year. 15 queries; 10 mss received/year. 60% of books from first-time authors. 100% from unagented writers. Pays 7-10% royalty on wholesale price. Does not pay advance.** Publishes book 6 months after acceptance. Responds in 1 month to mss. Book catalog online.

NONFICTION Subjects include history, hobbies, family history. Submit proposal package, outline, 1 sample chapter.

TIPS "Audience is family history hobbyists, history students, local historians."

FOCAL PRESS

Imprint of Elsevier (USA), Inc., 711 3rd Ave., 8th Floor, New York NY 10017. **Website:** routledge.com/focal-press. Estab. US, 1981; UK, 1938. Publishes hardcover and paperback originals and reprints. "Focal Press provides excellent books for students, advanced amateurs, and working professionals involved in all areas of media technology. Topics of interest include photography (digital and traditional techniques), film/video, audio, broadcasting, and cinematography, through to journalism, radio, television, video, and writing. Currently emphasizing graphics, gaming, animation, and multimedia." **Publishes 80-120 UK-US titles/year; entire firm publishes over 1,000 titles/year. 25% of books from first-time authors. 90% from unagented writers.** Publishes ms 6 months after acceptance. Accepts simultaneous submissions. Responds in 2 months to queries. Guidelines online.

NONFICTION Subjects include photography, film, cinematography, broadcasting, theater and performing arts, audio, sound and media technology. Does not publish collections of photographs or books composed primarily of photographs. To submit a proposal for consideration by Elsevier, complete the proposal form online. "Once we have had a chance to review your proposal in line with our publishing plan and budget, we will contact you to discuss the next steps." Reviews artwork/photos.

FODOR'S TRAVEL PUBLICATIONS, INC.

Imprint of Random House, Inc., 1745 Broadway, 15th Floor, New York NY 10019. **E-mail:** editors@fodors.com. **Website:** www.fodors.com. Estab. 1936. Publishes trade paperback originals. Fodor's publishes travel books on many regions and countries. "Remember that most Fodor's writers live in the areas they cover. Note that we do not accept unsolicited mss." **Most titles are collective works, with contributions as works for hire. Most contributions are updates of previously published volumes.** Accepts simultaneous submissions. Responds in 2 months to queries. Book catalog available free.

NONFICTION Subjects include travel. "We are interested in unique approaches to favorite destinations. Writers seldom review our catalog or our list and often query about books on topics that we're already covering. Beyond that, it's important to review competition and to say what the proposed book will add. Do not send originals without first querying as to our interest in the project. We're not interested in travel literature or in proposals for general travel guidebooks." Submit writing clips and résumé via mail or e-mail. In cover letter, explain qualifications and areas of expertise.

TIPS "In preparing your query or proposal, remember that it's the only argument Fodor's will hear about why your book will be a good one, and why you think it will sell; and it's also best evidence of your ability to create the book you propose. Craft your proposal well and carefully so that it puts your best foot forward."

FOLDED WORD

79 Tracy Way, Meredith NH 03253. **Website:** www. foldedword.com. **Contact:** Barbara Flaherty, Submissions Editor. Editor-in-Chief: J.S. Graustein. Poetry Editor: Rose Auslander. Fiction Editor: Casey Tingle. Estab. 2008. Folded Word is a literary micro-press that explores the world, one voice at a time. "Our list includes globally-distributed work by authors from four continents. We give individualized attention to the editing and design of each title." **Publishes 12 titles/year. 30% of books from first-time authors. 99% from unagented writers. Pays royalty. Advance only in rare cases with solicited books.** Publishes ms 2 years after acceptance. Accepts simultaneous submissions. Responds in 60 days for queries. If a full ms is requested, it may take 6 months for a final decision. Catalog online. Guidelines online.

NONFICTION Subjects include creative nonfiction, literature, nature, travel. "We are seeking creative nonfiction that is well-researched, concise, and poetic. We are looking for a respite from the predictable and formulaic. We are also looking for manuscripts that are ecologically and culturally aware. We enjoy humor, word-play, and strong images. Please, surprise us." We are especially seeking 5000 word travel and literary essays that can be published as stand-alone chapbooks.

FICTION Subjects include contemporary, historical, humor, literary, poetry, poetry in translation, regional, short story collections. "We are seeking non-formulaic narratives that have a strong sense of place and/or time, especially the exploration of unfamiliar place/time. We are looking for manuscripts that are an escape from the everyday, be it a cleansing laugh, a cathartic cry, a virtual holiday, or even a respite from predictable plots. We are also looking for manuscripts that are ecologically aware. We enjoy quirky characters, voices that take a chance, humor, and word-play. Please, surprise us." "We are especially seeking 5,000-word short stories that can be published as stand-alone chapbooks and chapbook-length collections of flash fiction."

POETRY "We enjoy narrative poetry that has a strong sense of place and/or time, especially the exploration of unfamiliar place/time. We enjoy mind-bending images and creative spacing on the page. We are also looking for poetry that is ecologically and culturally aware. We enjoy humor, word-play, and voices that take a chance. Please, surprise us." "We are especially seeking regional poetry (any region), haiku (and other Japanese-form poetry), and bilingual chapbooks of poetry in translation."

TIPS "Please be sure you have read some of our titles prior to submitting; our ebooks are reasonably priced to make exploring our list easier."

FORDHAM UNIVERSITY PRESS

2546 Belmont Ave., University Box L, Bronx NY 10458. (718)817-4795. **Fax:** (718)817-4785. **Website:** www.fordhampress.com. **Contact:** Tom Lay, acquisitions editor. Editorial Director: Richard W. Morrison. Publishes hardcover and trade paperback originals and reprints. "We are a publisher in humanities, accepting scholarly monographs, collections, occasional reprints and general interest titles for consideration. No fiction." Accepts simultaneous submissions. Book catalog and ms guidelines free.

NONFICTION Subjects include education, history, philosophy, regional, religion, science, sociology, translation, business, Jewish studies, media, music. Submit query letter, CV, SASE.

TIPS "We have an academic and general audience."

FOREIGN POLICY ASSOCIATION

470 Park Ave. S., New York NY 10016. (212)481-8100. **Fax:** (212)481-9275. **E-mail:** krohan@fpa.org. **Website:** www.fpa.org. **Contact:** Karen Rohan, editorial department. Publishes 2 periodicals, an annual eight episode PBS Television series with DVD and an occasional hardcover and trade paperback original. The Foreign Policy Association, a nonpartisan, not-for-profit educational organization founded in 1918, is a catalyst for developing awareness, understanding of and informed opinion on US foreign policy and global issues. Through its balanced, nonpartisan publications, FPA seeks to encourage individuals in schools, communities and the workplace to participate in the foreign policy process. Accepts simultaneous submissions. Book catalog available free.

IMPRINTS Headline Series (quarterly); Great Decisions (annual).

NONFICTION Subjects include history, foreign policy.

TIPS "Audience is students and people with an interest, but not necessarily any expertise, in foreign policy and international relations."

FORMAC PUBLISHING CO. LTD.

5502 Atlantic St., Halifax NS B3H 1G4, Canada. (902)421-7022. **Fax:** (902)425-0166. **Website:** www.formac.ca. **Contact:** Acquisitions Editor. Estab. 1977. Publishes hardcover and trade paperback originals. **Publishes 15-20 titles/year. 200 queries received/year. 150 mss received/year. 20% of books from first-time authors. 75% from unagented writers. Pays 5-10% royalty on wholesale price.** Publishes book 1 year after acceptance of ms. Accepts simultaneous submissions. Responds in 2 months to queries and to proposals; 4 months to mss. Book catalog available free. Guidelines online.

NONFICTION Subjects include animals, creative nonfiction, history, multicultural, regional, travel, marine subjects, transportation. Submit proposal package, outline, 2 sample chapters, CV or résumé of author(s).

TIPS "For our illustrated books, our audience includes adults interestsed in regional topics. For our travel titles, the audience is Canadians and visitors looking for cultural and outdoor experiences. Check out our website to see if you think your books fits anywhere in our list before submitting it. We are primarily interested in the work of Canadian authors."

FORTRESS PRESS

P.O. Box 1209, Minneapolis MN 55440. (612)330-3300. **Website:** www.fortresspress.com. Publishes hardcover and trade paperback originals. "Fortress Press publishes academic books in Biblical studies, theology, Christian ethics, church history, and professional books in pastoral care and counseling." **Pays royalty on retail price.** Accepts simultaneous submissions. Book catalog free. Guidelines online.

NONFICTION Subjects include religion, church history, African-American studies. Use online form. Please study guidelines before submitting.

FORWARD MOVEMENT

412 Sycamore St., Cincinnati OH 45202. (513)721-6659; (800)543-1813. **Fax:** (513)721-0729. **E-mail:** editorial@forwardmovement.org. **Website:** www.forwardmovement.org. **Contact:** Richelle Thompson, managing editor. Estab. 1934. "Forward Movement was established to help reinvigorate the life of the church. Many titles focus on the life of prayer, where our relationship with God is centered, death, marriage, baptism, recovery, joy, the Episcopal Church and more. Currently emphasizing prayer/spirituality." **Publishes 30 titles/year.** Accepts simultaneous submissions. Responds in 1 month. Book catalog free. Guidelines online.

NONFICTION Subjects include religion. "We are an agency of the Episcopal Church. There is a special need for tracts of under 8 pages. (A page usually runs about 200 words.) On rare occasions, we publish a full-length book." Query with SASE or by e-mail with complete ms attached.

FICTION Subjects include juvenile.

TIPS "Audience is primarily Episcopalians and other Christians."

WALTER FOSTER PUBLISHING, INC.

3 Wrigley, Suite A, Irvine CA 92618. (800)426-0099. **Fax:** (949)380-7575. **E-mail:** walterfoster@quartous.com. **Website:** www.walterfoster.com. **Contact:** Submissions. Estab. 1922. Publishes trade paperback originals. "Walter Foster publishes instructional how-to/craft instruction as well as licensed products." Accepts simultaneous submissions. Guidelines online.

NONFICTION Art, craft, activity books. Submit proposal package.

FOUR WAY BOOKS

Box 535, Village Station, New York NY 10014. **E-mail:** editors@fourwaybooks.com. **Website:** www.fourwaybooks.com. **Contact:** Martha Rhodes, director. Estab. 1993. "Four Way Books is a not-for-profit literary press dedicated to publishing poetry and short fiction by emerging and established writers. Each year, Four Way Books publishes the winners of its national poetry competitions, as well as collections accepted through general submission, panel selection, and solicitation by the editors." Accepts simultaneous submissions.

FICTION Open reading period: June 1-30. Book-length story collections and novellas. Submission guidelines will be posted online at end of May. Does not want novels or translations.

POETRY Four Way Books publishes poetry and short fiction. Considers full-length poetry mss only.

Books are about 70 pages, offset-printed digitally, perfect-bound, with paperback binding, art/graphics on covers. Does not want individual poems or poetry intended for children/young readers. See website for complete submission guidelines and open reading period in June. Book mss may include previously published poems. Responds to submissions in 4 months. Payment varies. Order sample books from Four Way Books online or through bookstores.

FOX CHAPEL PUBLISHING

1970 Broad St., East Petersburg PA 17520. (800)457-9112. **Fax:** (717)560-4702. **E-mail:** acquisitions@foxchapelpublishing.com. **Website:** www.foxchapelpublishing.com. Publishes hardcover and trade paperback originals and trade paperback reprints. Fox Chapel publishes craft, lifestyle, and woodworking titles for professionals and hobbyists. **Publishes 90-150 titles/year. 30% of books from first-time authors. 100% from unagented writers. Pays royalty or makes outright purchase. Pays variable advance.** Accepts simultaneous submissions. Submission guidelines online.

NONFICTION Subjects include cooking, crafts, creative nonfiction.

TIPS "We're looking for knowledgeable artists, craftspeople and woodworkers, all experts in their fields, to write books of lasting value."

⬤ FRANCES LINCOLN BOOKS

74-77 White Lion St., Islington, London N1 9PF, United Kingdom. (44)(20)7284-4009. **Website:** www.franceslincoln.com. Estab. 1977. **Publishes 100 titles/year. 6% of books from first-time authors.** Publishes book 18 months after acceptance. Accepts simultaneous submissions. Responds in 6 weeks to mss.

NONFICTION Subjects include animals, career guidance, cooking, environment, history, multicultural, nature, religion, social issues, special needs. Query by e-mail.

⬤ FRANCES LINCOLN CHILDREN'S BOOKS

Frances Lincoln, 74-77 White Lion St., Islington, London N1 9PF, United Kingdom. (44)(20)7284-4009. **Website:** www.franceslincoln.com. Estab. 1977. "Our company was founded by Frances Lincoln in 1977. We published our first books two years later, and we have been creating illustrated books of the highest quality ever since, with special emphasis on gardening, walking and the outdoors, art, architecture, design and landscape. In 1983, we started to publish illustrated books for children. Since then we have won many awards and prizes with both fiction and nonfiction children's books." **Publishes 100 titles/year. 6% of books from first-time authors.** Publishes book 18 months after acceptance. Accepts simultaneous submissions. Responds in 6 weeks to mss.

NONFICTION Subjects include animals, career guidance, cooking, environment, history, multicultural, nature, religion, young adult, social issues, special needs. Average word length: picture books—1,000; middle readers—29,768. Query by e-mail.

FICTION Subjects include adventure, fantasy, historical, humor, juvenile, multicultural, picture books, sports, young adult, anthololgy, folktales, nature. Average word length: picture books—1,000; young readers— 9,788; middle readers— 20,653; young adults— 35,407. Query by e-mail.

FRANCISCAN MEDIA PRESS

28 W. Liberty St., Cincinnati OH 45202-6498. (513)241-5615. **Fax:** (513)241-0399. **E-mail:** mlombard@franciscanmedia.org. **Website:** www.americancatholic.org. **Contact:** Mark Lombard, book publishing division and foreign rights. Estab. 1970. Publishes trade paperback originals. "St. Anthony Messenger Press/Franciscan Communications seeks to communicate the word that is Jesus Christ in the styles of Saints Francis and Anthony. Through print and electronic media marketed in North America and worldwide, we endeavor to evangelize, inspire, and inform those who search for God and seek a richer Catholic, Christian, human life. Our efforts help support the life, ministry, and charities of the Franciscan Friars of St. John the Baptist Province, who sponsor our work. Currently emphasizing prayer/spirituality." **Publishes 20-25 titles/year. 300 queries received/year. 50 mss received/year. 5% of books from first-time authors. 99% from unagented writers. Pays $1,000 average advance.** Publishes ms 18 months after acceptance. Accepts simultaneous submissions. Responds in 2 months. Guidelines online.

IMPRINTS Servant Books.

NONFICTION Query with SASE. Submit outline. Reviews artwork/photos.

ⒶⓈ⊘ FRANKLIN WATTS

Hachette Children's Books, Carmelite House, 50 Victoria Embankment, London EC4Y 0DZ, United

Kingdom. (44)(20)7873-6000. **Fax:** (44)(20)7873-6024. **E-mail:** ad@hachettechildrens.co.uk. **Website:** www. franklinwatts.co.uk. Estab. 1942. Franklin Watts is well known for its high quality and attractive information books, which support the National Curriculum and stimulate children's enquiring minds. *Generally does not accept unsolicited mss.* Accepts simultaneous submissions.

FREE SPIRIT PUBLISHING, INC.

6325 Sandburg Rd., Suite 100, Golden Valley MN 55427-3674. (612)338-2068. **Fax:** (612)337-5050. **E-mail:** acquisitions@freespirit.com. **Website:** www. freespirit.com. Estab. 1983. Publishes trade paperback originals and reprints. "We believe passionately in empowering kids to learn to think for themselves and make their own good choices." Free Spirit does not accept general fiction, poetry or storybook submissions. **Publishes 25-30 titles/year. Pays advance.** Accepts simultaneous submissions. Responds to proposals in 2-6 months. Book catalog and ms guidelines online.

NONFICTION Subjects include child guidance, counseling, education, educator resources; early childhood education. "Many of our authors are educators, mental health professionals, and youth workers involved in helping kids and teens." No general fiction or picture storybooks, poetry, single biographies or autobiographies, books with mythical or animal characters, or books with religious or New Age content. We are not looking for academic or religious materials, or books that analyze problems with the nation's school systems. Query with cover letter stating qualifications, intent, and intended audience and market analysis (comprehensive list of similar titles and detailed explanation of how your book stands out from the field), along with your promotional plan, outline, 2 sample chapters (note: for early childhood submissions, the entire text is required for evaluation), resume, SASE. Do not send original copies of work.

FICTION "Please review catalog and author guidelines (both available online) for details before submitting proposal. If you'd like material returned, enclose a SASE with sufficient postage." Accepts queries only—not submissions—by e-mail.

TIPS "Our books are issue-oriented, jargon-free, and solution-focused. Our audience is children, teens, teachers, parents and youth counselors. We are especially concerned with kids' social and emotional well-being and look for books with ready-to-use strategies for coping with today's issues at home or in school—written in everyday language. We are not looking for academic or religious materials, or books that analyze problems with the nation's school systems. Instead, we want books that offer practical, positive advice so kids can help themselves, and parents and teachers can help kids succeed."

FULCRUM PUBLISHING

4690 Table Mountain Dr., Suite 100, Golden CO 80403. **E-mail:** acquisitions@fulcrumbooks.com. **Website:** www.fulcrum-books.com. **Contact:** T. Baker, acquisitions editor. Estab. 1984. **Pays authors royalty based on wholesale price. Offers advances.** Accepts simultaneous submissions. Catalog for SASE. Guidelines online.

NONFICTION Looking for nonfiction-based graphic novels and comics, U.S. history and culture, Native American history or culture studies, conservation-oriented materials. "We do not accept memoir or fiction manuscripts." "Your submission must include: a proposal of your work, including a brief synopsis, 2-3 sample chapters, brief biography of yourself, description of your audience, your assessment of the market for the book, list of competing titles, and what you can do to help market your book. We are a green company and therefore only accept e-mailed submissions. Paper queries submitted via US Mail or any other means (including fax, FedEx/UPS, and even door-to-door delivery) will not be reviewed or returned. Please help us support the preservation of the environment by e-mailing your query to acquisitions@fulcrumbooks. com."

TIPS "Research our line first. We look for books that appeal to the school market and trade. "

FUTURECYCLE PRESS

Website: www.futurecycle.org. **Contact:** Diane Kistner, director/editor-in-chief. Estab. 2007. Publishes English-language poetry books, chapbooks, and anthologies in print-on-demand and digital editions. Awards the FutureCycle Poetry Book Prize and honorarium for the best full-length book the press publishes each year. **Pays in deeply discounted author copies (no purchase required).** Accepts simultaneous submissions. Responds in 3 months. Guidelines, sample contract, and detailed *Guide for Authors* online.

POETRY Wants "poetry from imaginative, highly skilled poets, whether well known or emerging. We abhor the myopic, self-absorbed, and sloppy, but otherwise are eclectic in our tastes." Does not want concrete or visual poetry. Publishes 15+ poetry books/year and 5+ chapbooks/year. Ms. selected through open submission. Books average 62-110 pages; chapbooks 30-42 pages; anthologies 100+ pages. Submit complete ms. No need to query.

FUTURE HORIZONS

721 W. Abram St., Arlington TX 76013. (817)277-0727. **Fax:** (817)277-2270. **Website:** www.fhautism.com. **Contact:** Jennifer Gilpin-Yacio, editorial director. Publishes hardcover originals, trade paperback originals and reprints. **Publishes 10 titles/year. 250 queries received/year. 125 mss received/year. 75% of books from first-time authors. 95% from unagented writers. Pays 10% royalty. Makes outright purchase.** Publishes book 2 months after acceptance of ms. Accepts simultaneous submissions. Responds in 1 month to queries; 2 months to proposals. Book catalog available free. Guidelines online.

NONFICTION Subjects include education, autism. Submit proposal package, outline by mail (no e-mail). Reviews artwork/photos. Send photocopies.

TIPS "Audience is parents, teachers."

GENEALOGICAL PUBLISHING CO., IND

Genealogical.com, 3600 Clipper Mill Rd., Suite 260, Baltimore MD 21211. (410)837-8271. **Fax:** (410)752-8492. **E-mail:** info@genealogical.com. **E-mail:** jgaronzi@genealogical.com. **Website:** www.genealogical.com. **Contact:** Joe Garonzik, marketing director. Eileen Perkins, Production Manager Estab. 1959. Publishes hardcover and trade paperback originals and reprints. **Publishes 50 titles/year. Receives 100 queries/year; 20 mss/year. 10% of books from first-time authors. 99% from unagented writers. Pays 10-15% royalty on selling price. Does not pay advance.** Publishes book 6 months after acceptance. Accepts simultaneous submissions. Responds in 1 month. Catalog free on request.

IMPRINTS Clearfield Company.

NONFICTION Subjects include Americana, ethnic, history, hobbies. Submit outline, 1 sample chapter. Reviews artwork/photos as part of the mss package.

TIPS "Our audience is genealogy hobbyists."

GERTRUDE PRESS

P.O. Box 28281, Portland OR 97228. (503)515-8252. **E-mail:** editor@gertrudepress.org. **Website:** www.gertrudepress.org. Estab. 2005. "Gertrude Press is a nonprofit organization developing and showcasing the creative talents of lesbian, gay, bisexual, trans, queer-identified and allied individuals. We publish limited-edition fiction and poetry chapbooks plus the biannual literary journal, *Gertrude*." Reads chapbook mss only through contests. Accepts simultaneous submissions.

FICTION Subjects include ethnic, experimental, feminist, gay, humor, lesbian, literary, mainstream, multicultural, short story collections.

TIPS Sponsors poetry and fiction chapbook contest. Prize is $175 and 50 contributor's copies. Submission guidelines and fee information on website. "Read the journal and sample published work. We are not impressed by pages of publications; your work should speak for itself."

GIANT SQUID BOOKS

E-mail: editors@giantsquidbooks.com. **Website:** giantsquidbooks.com. Editors: Rachel Miller and Anna McCormally. "Our mission is to publish, support, and promote debut authors—and help them navigate the world of online publishing." Accepts simultaneous submissions. Guidelines online.

FICTION Giant Squid Books is currently closed to submissions. "See website or follow us on Twitter @ giantsquidbooks to be notified when we reopen submissions." Accepts young adult novels in any genre. Query with the first 3 chapters or 50 pages of book.

TIPS "We read every submission and try to respond within two weeks but due to a high volume of submissions sometimes get behind! If it's been more than 2 weeks since you queried us, please feel free to send a follow-up e-mail."

GIBBS SMITH

P.O. Box 667, Layton UT 84041. (801)544-9800. **Fax:** (801)544-8853. **E-mail:** debbie.uribe@gibbs-smith.com. **Website:** www.gibbs-smith.com. Estab. 1969. **Publishes 3 titles/year. 50% of books from first-time authors. 50% from unagented writers. Pays authors royalty of 2% based on retail price or work purchased outright ($500 minimum). Offers advances (average amount: $2,000).** Publishes ms 1-2 years after acceptance. Accepts simultaneous submissions. Responds in 2 months. Book catalog available for 9×12 SAE and $2.30 postage. Ms guidelines available by e-mail.

NONFICTION Middle readers: activity, arts/crafts, cooking, how-to, nature/environment, science. Average word length: picture books—under 1,000 words; activity books—under 15,000 words. Submit an outline and writing samples for activity books; query for other types of books.

TIPS "We target ages 5-11. We do not publish young adult novels or chapter books."

⊘ GIFTED EDUCATION PRESS

10201 Yuma Ct., Manassas VA 20109. (703)369-5017. **E-mail:** mfisher345@comcast.net. **Website:** www.giftedstemeducation.com. **Contact:** Maurice Fisher, publisher. Estab. 1981. Publishes trade paperback originals. "Searching for rigorous texts on teaching science, math and humanities to gifted students." **Publishes 5 titles/year. 20 queries; 10 mss received/ year. 90% of books from first-time authors. 100% from unagented writers. Pays 10% royalty on retail price.** Publishes ms 4 months after acceptance. Accepts simultaneous submissions. Responds in 1 month. Book catalog online. Guidelines online.

NONFICTION Subjects include child guidance, education, history, humanities, philosophy. Query with SASE. *All unsolicited mss returned unopened.* Reviews artwork/photos.

TIPS "Audience includes teachers, parents, gifted program supervisors, professors. Be knowledgeable about your subject. Write clearly and don't use educational jargon."

GIVAL PRESS

Gival Press, LLC, P.O. Box 3812, Arlington VA 22203. (703)351-0079. **E-mail:** givalpress@yahoo.com. **Website:** www.givalpress.com. **Contact:** Robert L. Giron, editor-in-chief (area of interest: literary). Estab. 1998. Publishes trade paperback, electronic originals, and reprints. "We publish literary works: fiction, nonfiction (essays, academic), and poetry in English, Spanish, and French." **Publishes 4-5 titles/year. 200 queries; 60 mss received/year. 50% of books from first-time authors. 70% from unagented writers. Pays royalty.** Publishes ms 12 months after acceptance. Accepts simultaneous submissions. Responds in 3-5 months. Book catalog online. Guidelines online.

NONFICTION Subjects include creative nonfiction, education, gay, lesbian, literature, memoirs, multicultural, translation, womens issues, womens studies, scholarly. Submit between May 15-August 15. Always query first via e-mail; provide plan/ms content,

bio, and supportive material. Best to submit via our portal at: www.givalpress.submittable.com. Reviews artwork/photos; query first.

FICTION Subjects include contemporary, feminist, gay, historical, lesbian, literary, multicultural, poetry, poetry in translation, translation. Always query first via e-mail; provide description, author's bio, and supportive material.

POETRY Query via e-mail; provide description, bio, etc.; submit 5-6 sample poems via e-mail.

TIPS "Our audience is those who read literary works with depth to the work. Visit our website—there is much to be read/learned from the numerous pages."

GLENBRIDGE PUBLISHING, LTD.

19923 E. Long Ave., Centennial CO 80016. (800)986-4135. **Fax:** (720)230-1209. **E-mail:** glenbridge10@gmail.com. **Website:** www.glenbridgepublishing.com. Estab. 1986. Publishes hardcover originals and reprints, trade paperback originals. "Glenbridge has an eclectic approach to publishing. We look for titles that have long-term capabilities." **Publishes 6-8 titles/year. Pays 10% royalty.** Publishes ms 1 year after acceptance. Accepts simultaneous submissions. Responds in 2 months to queries. Book catalog online. Guidelines for #10 SASE.

NONFICTION Subjects include Americana, history, philosophy, sociology. Send e-mail on website. Query with outline/synopsis, sample chapters.

THE GLENCANNON PRESS

P.O. Box 1428, El Cerrito CA 94530. (510)528-4216. **E-mail:** merships@yahoo.com. **Website:** www.glencannon.com. **Contact:** Bill Harris (maritime, maritime children's). Estab. 1993. Publishes hardcover and paperback originals and hardcover reprints. "We publish quality books about ships and the sea." Average print order: 1,000. Member PMA, BAIPA. Distributes titles through Baker & Taylor. Promotes titles through direct mail, magazine advertising and word of mouth. Accepts unsolicited mss. Often comments on rejected mss. **Publishes 4-5 titles/year. 25% of books from first-time authors. 100% from unagented writers. Pays 10-20% royalty.** Publishes ms 6-24 months after acceptance. Accepts simultaneous submissions. Responds in 1 month to queries; 2 months to mss.

IMPRINTS Smyth: perfect binding; illustrations.

NONFICTION Subjects include history, marine subjects, transportation, travel, war.

FICTION Subjects include adventure, historical, mainstream, military, multicultural, mystery, war, western, young adult. Submit complete ms. Include brief bio, list of publishing credits. Send SASE for return of ms or send a disposable ms and SASE for reply only.

TIPS "Write a good story in a compelling style."

✪✪⊘ DAVID R. GODINE, PUBLISHER

15 Court Square, Suite 320, Boston MA 02108. (617)451-9600. **Fax:** (617)350-0250. **E-mail:** info@godine.com. **Website:** www.godine.com. Estab. 1970. "We publish books that matter for people who care." This publisher is no longer considering unsolicited mss of any type. Only interested in agented material. Accepts simultaneous submissions.

IMPRINTS Black Sparrow Books, Verba Mundi, Nonpareil.

NONFICTION Subjects include Americana, art, creative nonfiction, gardening, history, language, law, literary criticism, literature, photography, young adult, typography.

FICTION Subjects include literary, multicultural, poetry, poetry in translation, translation, young adult.

✪✪⊘ GOLDEN BOOKS FOR YOUNG READERS GROUP

1745 Broadway, New York NY 10019. **Website:** www.penguinrandomhouse.com. Estab. 1935. "Random House Books aims to create books that nurture the hearts and minds of children, providing and promoting quality books and a rich variety of media that entertain and educate readers from 6 months to 12 years." *Random House-Golden Books does not accept unsolicited mss, only agented material.* They reserve the right not to return unsolicited material. **2% of books from first-time authors. Pays authors in royalties; sometimes buys mss outright.** Accepts simultaneous submissions. Book catalog free on request.

GOLDEN WEST BOOKS

P.O. Box 80250, San Marino CA 91118. (626)458-8148. **Fax:** (626)458-8148. **Website:** www.goldenwestbooks.com. Publishes hardcover originals. "Golden West Books specializes in railroad history. We are always interested in new material. Please use the form online to contact us; we will follow up with you as soon as possible." **Publishes 3-4 titles/year. 8-10 queries; 5 mss received/year. 75% of books from first-time authors. 100% from unagented writers. Pays 8-10%**

royalty on wholesale price. Publishes ms 3 months after acceptance. Responds in 3 months to queries. Book catalog and ms guidelines free.

NONFICTION Subjects include Americana, history. Use online form. Reviews artwork/photos.

GOOSEBOTTOM BOOKS

543 Trinidad Ln., Foster City CA 94404. **Fax:** (888)407-5286. **E-mail:** submissions@goosebottombooks.com. **Website:** goosebottombooks.com. **Contact:** Shirin Bridges. Estab. 2010. **1,000 submissions received/year. 50% of books from first-time authors. 100% from unagented writers. Goosebottom Books: Pays advance plus royalties; Gosling Press: Pays royalties only.** Publishes ms 18 months after acceptance. Responds in 1 month. Catalog online. Guidelines available.

IMPRINTS Goosebottom Books, Gosling Press.

NONFICTION Subjects include creative nonfiction, history, multicultural, social sciences, womens studies, young adult.

FICTION Subjects include adventure, ethnic, fantasy, feminist, gay, historical, horror, humor, juvenile, literary, mainstream, multicultural, mystery, picture books, science fiction, suspense, young adult. Gosling Press is a new partnership publishing imprint for children's, middle grade and young adult fiction. Please query with first ten pages. Any fiction for adults. Gosling Press focuses on picture book to YA. Query with first 10 pages.

☯ GOOSE LANE EDITIONS

500 Beaverbrook Ct., Suite 330, Fredericton NB E3B 5X4, Canada. (506)450-4251. **Fax:** (506)459-4991. **E-mail:** submissions@gooselane.com. **Website:** www.gooselane.com. **Contact:** Angela Williams, publishing assistant. Estab. 1954. Publishes hardcover and paperback originals and occasional reprints. "Goose Lane publishes literary fiction and nonfiction from well-read and highly skilled Canadian authors." **Publishes 16-20 titles/year. 20% of books from first-time authors. 60% from unagented writers. Pays 8-10% royalty on retail price. Pays $500-3,000, negotiable advance.** Responds in 6 months to queries.

NONFICTION Subjects include history, regional. Query with SASE.

FICTION Subjects include literary, short story collections, contemporary. Our needs in fiction never change: Substantial, character-centered literary fiction. No children's, YA, mainstream, mass market, genre, mystery, thriller, confessional or science fiction. Query with SAE with Canadian stamps or IRCs. No U.S. stamps.

POETRY Considers mss by Canadian poets only. Submit cover letter, list of publications, synopsis, entire ms, SASE.

TIPS "Writers should send us outlines and samples of books that show a very well-read author with highly developed literary skills. Our books are almost all by Canadians living in Canada; we seldom consider submissions from outside Canada. We consider submissions from outside Canada only when the author is Canadian and the book is of extraordinary interest to Canadian readers. We do not publish books for children or for the young adult market."

GRANITE PUBLISHING, LLC

P.O. Box 1429, Columbus NC 28722. (828)894-8444. **Fax:** (828)894-8454. **E-mail:** info@granitepublishing. us. **Website:** www.granite-planet.net. Publishes trade paperback originals and reprints. "Granite Publishing strives to preserve the Earth by publishing books that develop new wisdom about our emerging planetary citizenship, bringing information from the outerworlds to our world. Currently emphasizing indigenous ideas, planetary healing. Granite Publishing accepts only a few very fine mss in our niches each year, and those that are accepted must follow our rigid guidelines online. Our Little Granite Books imprint publishes only our own writings for children." **Publishes 4 titles/year. 50 queries; 150 mss received/year. 70% of books from first-time authors. 90% from unagented writers. Pays 7-10% royalty.** Publishes ms 16 months after acceptance. Accepts simultaneous submissions. Responds in 6 months to mss.

NONFICTION Subjects include New Age, planetary paradigm shift. Submit proposal. Reviews artwork/photos. Send photocopies.

⚠⊘ GRAYWOLF PRESS

250 Third Ave. N.,, Suite 600, Minneapolis MN 55401. (651)641-0077. **Fax:** (651)641-0036. **Website:** www. graywolfpress.org. Estab. 1974. Publishes trade cloth and paperback originals. "Graywolf Press is an independent, nonprofit publisher dedicated to the creation and promotion of thoughtful and imaginative contemporary literature essential to a vital and diverse culture." **Publishes 30 titles/year. Pays royalty on retail price. Pays $1,000-25,000 advance.** Publishes

18 months after acceptance. Accepts simultaneous submissions. Responds in 3 months to queries. Book catalog free. Guidelines online.

NONFICTION Subjects include contemporary culture, culture. Agented submissions only.

FICTION Subjects include short story collections, literary novels. "Familiarize yourself with our list first." No genre books (romance, western, science fiction, suspense) Agented submissions only.

POETRY "We are interested in linguistically challenging work." Agented submissions only.

GREAT POTENTIAL PRESS

1650 N. Kolb Rd., #200, Tucson AZ 85715. (520)777-6161. **Fax:** (520)777-6217. **Website:** www.greatpotentialpress.com. President: James T. Webb, Ph.D. Estab. 1986. Publishes trade paperback originals. Specializes in nonfiction books that address academic, social and emotional issues of gifted and talented children and adults. **Publishes 6-10 titles/year. 75 queries; 20-30 mss received/year. 50% of books from first-time authors. 100% from unagented writers. Pays 10% royalty on retail price.** Publishes book 1 year after acceptance. Accepts simultaneous submissions. Responds in 2 months to queries; 3 months to proposals; 4 months to mss. Book catalog free or on website. Guidelines online.

NONFICTION Subjects include child guidance, education, multicultural, psychology, translation, travel, gifted/talented children and adults, misdiagnosis of gifted, parenting gifted, teaching gifted, meeting the social and emotional needs of gifted and talented, and strategies for working with gifted children and adults. Use online submission form.

TIPS "Mss should be clear, cogent, and well-written and should pertain to gifted, talented, and creative persons and/or issues."

GREENHAVEN PRESS

27500 Drake Rd., Farmington Hills MI 48331. (800)877-4523. **Website:** www.gale.com/greenhaven. Estab. 1970. Publishes 220 young adult academic reference titles/year. 50% of books by first-time authors. Greenhaven continues to print quality nonfiction anthologies for libraries and classrooms. "Our well-known Opposing Viewpoints series is highly respected by students and librarians in need of material on controversial social issues." Greenhaven accepts no unsolicited mss. Send query, resume, and list of published works by e-mail. Work purchased outright from authors; write-for-hire, flat fee. Accepts simultaneous submissions.

NONFICTION Young adults (high school): controversial issues, social issues, history, literature, science, environment, health.

Ⓐ⊘ GREENWILLOW BOOKS

HarperCollins Publishers, 10 E. 53rd St., New York NY 10022. (212)207-7000. **Website:** www.greenwillowblog.com. Estab. 1974. Publishes hardcover originals, paperbacks, e-books, and reprints. *Does not accept unsolicited mss.* "Unsolicited mail will not be opened and will not be returned." **Publishes 40-50 titles/year. Pays 10% royalty on wholesale price for first-time authors. Offers variable advance.** Publishes ms 2 years after acceptance. Accepts simultaneous submissions.

FICTION Subjects include fantasy, humor, literary, mystery, picture books. *Agented submissions only.*

GREY GECKO PRESS

565 S. Mason Rd., Suite 154, Katy TX 77450. Phone/Fax: (866)535-6078. **E-mail:** info@greygeckopress.com. **E-mail:** submissions@greygeckopress.com. **Website:** www.greygeckopress.com. **Contact:** Submissions Coordinator. Estab. 2011. Publishes hardcover, trade paperback, audiobook, and electronic originals. Grey Gecko focuses on new and emerging authors and great books that might not otherwise get a chance to see the light of day. "We publish all our titles in hardcover, trade paperback, and e-book formats (both Kindle and ePub), as well as audiobook and foreign-language editions. Our books are available worldwide, for readers of all types, kinds, and interests." **Publishes 5-15 titles/year. 200+ queries received/year; 30-40 mss received/year. 55% of books from first-time authors. 100% from unagented writers. Pays 50-75% royalties on net revenue. Does not pay advance.** Publishes ms 12-18 months after acceptance. Accepts simultaneous submissions. Responds in 6-12 months. Catalog online. Guidelines online.

NONFICTION Subjects include architecture, art, contemporary culture, cooking, creative nonfiction, environment, foods, history, marine subjects, military, nature, photography, travel, war. All nonfiction submissions are evaluated on a case-by-case basis. "We focus mainly on fiction, but we'll take a look at nonfiction works." Use online submission page. Re-

views artwork. Send photocopies or link to photo website.

FICTION Subjects include adventure, contemporary, ethnic, fantasy, feminist, gay, historical, horror, humor, juvenile, lesbian, literary, mainstream, military, multicultural, mystery, occult, regional, romance, science fiction, short story collections, sports, suspense, war, western, young adult. "We do not publish extreme horror, erotica, or religious fiction. New and interesting stories by unpublished authors will always get our attention. Innovation is a core value of our company." Extreme horror (e.g. *Saw* or *Hostel*), religious, or erotica. Use online submission page.

TIPS "Be willing to be a part of the Grey Gecko family. Publishing with us is a partnership, not indentured servitude. Authors are expected and encouraged to be proactive and contribute to their book's success."

Ⓐ⊘ GROSSET & DUNLAP PUBLISHERS

Penguin Random House, 345 Hudson St., New York NY 10014. **Website:** www.penguin.com. **Contact:** Francesco Sedita, president/publisher. Estab. 1898. Publishes hardcover (few) and mass market paperback originals. Grosset & Dunlap publishes children's books that show children that reading is fun, with books that speak to their interests, and that are affordable so that children can build a home library of their own. Focus on licensed properties, series and readers. "Grosset & Dunlap publishes high-interest, affordable books for children ages 0-10 years. We focus on original series, licensed properties, readers and novelty books." **Publishes 140 titles/year. Pays royalty. Pays advance.**

NONFICTION Subjects include science. *Agented submissions only.*

FICTION Subjects include juvenile. *Agented submissions only.*

◔ GROUNDWOOD BOOKS

128 Sterling Road, Lower Level, Attention: Submissions, Toronto Ontario M6R 2B7, Canada. (416)363-4343. **Fax:** (416)363-1017. **E-mail:** submissions@groundwoodbooks.com. **Website:** groundwoodbooks.com. "We are always looking for new authors of novel-length fiction for children of all ages. Our mandate is to publish high-quality, character-driven literary fiction. We do not generally publish stories with an obvious moral or message, or genre fiction such as thrillers or fantasy." Publishes 19 picture books/

year; 2 young readers/year; 3 middle readers/year; 3 young adult titles/year, approximately 2 nonfiction titles/year. **Offers advances.** Accepts simultaneous submissions. Responds to mss in 6-8 months. Visit website for guidelines: www.houseofanansi.com/ Groundwoodsubmissions.aspx.

NONFICTION Recently published: *The Amazing Travels of IBN Batutta*, by Fatima Sharafeddine, Illustrated by Intelaq Mohammed Ali. Picture books recently published: *Mr. Frank*, by Irene Luxbacher; *The Tweedles Go Electric*, by Monica Kulling, illustrated by Marie LaFrance; *Morris Micklewhite and the Tangerine Dress*, by Christine Baldacchino, illustrated by Isabelle Malenfant; *Why Are You Doing That?*, by Elisa Amado, illustrated by Manuel Monroy; *Don't*, by Litsa Trochatos, illustrated by Virginia Johnson.

FICTION Recently published: *Lost Girl Found*, by Leah Bassoff and Laura Deluca; *A Simple Case of Angels*, by Carolnie Adderson; *This One Summer*, by Mariko Tamaki and Jillian Tamaki. Submit a cover letter, synopsis and sample chapters via e-mail. "Due to the large number of submissions we receive, Groundwood regrets that we cannot accept unsolicited manuscripts for picture books."

GROUP PUBLISHING, INC.

1515 Cascade Ave., Loveland CO 80539. **E-mail:** info@group.com. **Website:** www.group.com. Estab. 1974. Publishes trade paperback originals. "Our mission is to equip churches to help children, youth, and adults grow in their relationship with Jesus." **Publishes 65 titles/year. 500 queries; 500 mss received/year. 40% of books from first-time authors. 95% from unagented writers. Pays up to 10% royalty on wholesale price or makes outright purchase or work for hire. Pays up to $1,000 advance.** Publishes ms 18 months after acceptance. Accepts simultaneous submissions. Responds in 1 month to queries; 6 months to proposals and mss. Book catalog for 9x12 envelope and 2 first-class stamps.

NONFICTION Subjects include education, religion. "We're an interdenominational publisher of resource materials for people who work with adults, youth or children in a Christian church setting. We also publish materials for use directly by youth or children (such as devotional books, workbooks or Bibles stories). Everything we do is based on concepts of active and interactive learning as described in *Why Nobody Learns Much of Anything at Church: And How to Fix*

It, by Thom and Joani Schultz. We need new, practical, hands-on, innovative, out-of-the-box ideas—things that no one's doing.. yet." Query with SASE. Submit proposal package, outline, 3 sample chapters, cover letter, introduction to book, and sample activities if appropriate.

TIPS "Our audience consists of pastors, Christian education directors, youth leaders, and Sunday school teachers."

ⒶⒸ GROVE/ATLANTIC, INC.

154 W. 14th St., 12th Floor, New York NY 10011. **E-mail:** info@groveatlantic.com. **Website:** www.grove-atlantic.com. Estab. 1917. Publishes hardcover and trade paperback originals, and reprints. "Due to limited resources of time and staffing, Grove/Atlantic cannot accept manuscripts that do not come through a literary agent. In today's publishing world, agents are more important than ever, helping writers shape their work and navigate the main publishing houses to find the most appropriate outlet for a project." **Publishes 100 titles/year. 1,000+ queries; 1,000+ mss received/year. 10% of books from first-time authors. Pays 7 ½-12 ½% royalty. Makes outright purchase of $5-500,000.** Book published 9 months after acceptance of ms. Accepts simultaneous submissions. Responds in 1 month to queries; 2 months to proposals; 4 months to mss. Book catalog available online.

IMPRINTS Black Cat, Atlantic Monthly Press, Grove Press.

NONFICTION Subjects include creative nonfiction, education, memoirs, philosophy, psychology, science, social sciences, sports, translation. Agented submissions only.

FICTION Subjects include erotica, horror, literary, science fiction, short story collections, suspense, western. Agented submissions only.

POETRY Agented submissions only.

GRYPHON HOUSE, INC.

P.O. Box 10, 6848 Leon's Way, Lewisville NC 27023. (800)638-0928. **E-mail:** info@ghbooks.com. **Website:** www.gryphonhouse.com. Estab. 1981. Publishes trade paperback originals. "At Gryphon House, our goal is to publish books that help teachers and parents enrich the lives of children from birth through age 8. We strive to make our books useful for teachers at all levels of experience, as well as for parents, caregivers, and anyone interested in working with children." Query. Submit outline/synopsis and 2 sample chapters. Responds to queries/mss in 6 months. Publishes a book 18 months after acceptance. Will consider simultaneous submissions, e-mail submissions. Book catalog and ms guidelines available via website or with SASE. **Publishes 12-15 titles/year. Pays royalty on wholesale price.** Responds in 3-6 months to queries. Guidelines available online.

NONFICTION Subjects include child guidance, education. Currently emphasizing social-emotional intelligence and classroom management; de-emphasizing literacy after-school activities. "We prefer to receive a letter of inquiry and/or a proposal, rather than the entire manuscript. Please include: the proposed title, the purpose of the book, table of contents, introductory material, 20-40 sample pages of the actual book. In addition, please describe the book, including the intended audience, why teachers will want to buy it, how it is different from other similar books already published, and what qualifications you possess that make you the appropriate person to write the book. If you have a writing sample that demonstrates that you write clear, compelling prose, please include it with your letter."

TIPS "We are looking for books of creative, participatory learning experiences that have a common conceptual theme to tie them together. The books should be on subjects that parents or teachers want to do on a daily basis."

♻⊘ GUERNICA EDITIONS

1569 Heritage Way, Oakville Ontario L6M 2Z7, Canada. (905)599-5304. **Fax:** (416)981-7606. **E-mail:** michaelmirolla@guernicaeditions.com. **Website:** www.guernicaeditions.com. **Contact:** Michael Mirolla, editor/publisher (poetry, nonfiction, short stories, novels). Estab. 1978. Publishes trade paperback originals and reprints. Guernica Editions is a literary press that produces works of poetry, fiction and nonfiction often by writers who are ignored by the mainstream. **Publishes 25-30 titles/year. Several hundred mss received/year. 20% of books from first-time authors. 99% from unagented writers. Pays 8-10% royalty on retail price, or makes outright purchase of $200-5,000. Pays $450-750 advance.** Publishes 24-36 months after acceptance. Responds in 1 month to queries. Responds in 6 months to proposals. Responds in 1 year to manuscripts. Book catalog available online. Queries and submissions accepted via e-mail.

IMPRINTS MiroLand

NONFICTION Subjects include creative nonfiction, ethnic, history, literary criticism, literature, memoirs, multicultural, philosophy, politics, pop culture, psychology, regional, social sciences, translation. Query by e-mail only. Reviews artwork/photos. Send photocopies.

FICTION Subjects include comic books, contemporary, ethnic, experimental, feminist, gay, lesbian, literary, multicultural, plays, poetry, poetry in translation, short story collections, translation. "We wish to open up into the fiction world and focus less on poetry. We specialize in European, especially Italian, translations." E-mail queries only.

POETRY Feminist, gay/lesbian, literary, multicultural, poetry in translation. We wish to have writers in translation. Any writer who has translated Italian poetry is welcomed. Full books only. No single poems by different authors, unless modern, and used as an anthology. Query.

GULF PUBLISHING COMPANY

P.O. Box 2608, Houston TX 77252. (713)529-4301. **Fax:** (713)520-4433. **Website:** www.gulfpub.com. Estab. 1916. Publishes hardcover originals and reprints; electronic originals and reprints. "Gulf Publishing Company is the leading publisher to the oil and gas industry. Our specialized publications reach over 100,000 people involved in energy industries worldwide. Our magazines and catalogs help readers keep current with information important to their field and allow advertisers to reach their customers in all segments of petroleum operations. More than half our editorial staff have engineering degrees. The others are thoroughly trained and experienced business journalists and editors." **Publishes 12-15 titles/year. 3-5 queries and mss received in a year. 30% of books from first-time authors. 80% from unagented writers. Royalties on retail price. Pays $1,000-$1,500 advance.** Publishes ms 8-9 months after acceptance. Accepts simultaneous submissions. Responds in 2 months to queries; 1 month to proposals and mss. Catalog free on request. Guidelines available by e-mail.

NONFICTION Subjects include Engineering. "We don't publish a lot in the year, therefore we are able to focus more on marketing and sales—we are hoping to grow in the future." Submit outline, 1-2 sample chapters, completed ms. Reviews artwork. Send high res file formats with high dpi in b&w.

TIPS "Our audience would be engineers, engineering students, academia, professors, well managers, construction engineers. We recommend getting contributors to help with the writing process—this provides a more comprehensive overview for technical and scientific books. Work harder on artwork. It's expensive and time-consuming for a publisher to redraw a lot of the figures."

HACHAI PUBLISHING

527 Empire Blvd., Brooklyn NY 11225. (718)633-0100. **Fax:** (718)633-0103. **Website:** www.hachai.com. **Contact:** Devorah Leah Rosenfeld, editor. Estab. 1988. Publishes hardcover originals. Hachai is dedicated to producing high quality Jewish children's literature, ages 2-10. Story should promote universal values such as sharing, kindness, etc. **Publishes 5 titles/year. 75% of books from first-time authors. Work purchased outright from authors for $800-1,000.** Accepts simultaneous submissions. Responds in 2 months to mss. Guidelines online.

○ "All books have spiritual/religious themes, specifically traditional Jewish content. We're seeking books about morals and values; the Jewish experience in current and Biblical times; and Jewish observance, Sabbath and holidays."

NONFICTION Subjects include ethnic, religion. Submit complete ms. Reviews artwork/photos. Send photocopies.

FICTION Subjects include juvenile. Picture books and young readers: contemporary, historical fiction, religion. Middle readers: adventure, contemporary, problem novels, religion. Does not want to see fantasy, animal stories, romance, problem novels depicting drug use or violence. Submit complete ms.

TIPS "We are looking for books that convey the traditional Jewish experience in modern times or long ago; traditional Jewish observance such as Sabbath and holidays and mitzvos such as mezuzah, blessings etc.; positive character traits (middos) such as honesty, charity, respect, sharing, etc. We are also interested in historical fiction for young readers (7-10) written with a traditional Jewish perspective and highlighting the relevance of Torah in making important choices. Please, no animal stories, romance, violence, preachy sermonizing. Write a story that incorporates a moral, not a preachy morality tale. Originality is the key. We feel Hachai publications will appeal to a wider readership as parents become more interested in positive values for their children."

HADLEY RILLE BOOKS

P.O. Box 25466, Overland Park KS 66225. **E-mail:** contact@hadleyrillebooks.com. **E-mail:** subs@hadleyrillebooks.com. **Website:** https://hadleyrillebks.wordpress.com. **Contact:** Eric T. Reynolds, editor/publisher. Estab. 2005. Currently closed to submissions. Check website for future reading periods. Accepts simultaneous submissions.

FICTION Subjects include fantasy, science fiction, short story collections.

TIPS "We aim to produce books that are aligned with current interest in the genres. Anthology markets are somewhat rare in SF these days, we feel there aren't enough good anthologies being published each year and part of our goal is to present the best that we can. We like stories that fit well within the guidelines of the particular anthology for which we are soliciting manuscripts. Aside from that, we want stories with strong characters (not necessarily characters with strong personalities, flawed characters are welcome). We want a sense of wonder and awe. We want to feel the world around the character and so scene description is important (however, this doesn't always require a lot of text, just set the scene well so we don't wonder where the character is). We strongly recommend workshopping the story or having it critiqued in some way by readers familiar with the genre. We prefer clichés be kept to a bare minimum in the prose and avoid re-working old story lines."

HAMPTON ROADS PUBLISHING CO., INC.

665 Third St., Suite 400, San Francisco CA 94107. **E-mail:** submissions@rwwbooks.com. **Website:** www.redwheelweiser.com. Estab. 1989. Publishes and distributes hardcover and trade paperback originals on subjects including metaphysics, health, complementary medicine, visionary fiction, and other related topics. "Our reason for being is to impact, uplift, and contribute to positive change in the world. We publish books that will enrich and empower the evolving consciousness of mankind. Though we are not necessarily limited in scope, we are most interested in manuscripts on the following subjects: Body/Mind/Spirit, Health and Healing, Self-Help. Please be advised that at the moment we are not accepting: Fiction or Novelized material that does not pertain to body/mind/spirit, Channeled writing." " **Publishes 35-40 titles/year. 1,000 queries; 1,500 mss received/year. 50% of books from first-time authors. 70% from unagented writers. Pays royalty. Pays $1,000-50,000 advance.**

Publishes ms 1 year after acceptance. Accepts simultaneous submissions. Responds in 2-4 months to queries; 1 month to proposals; 6-12 months to mss. Guidelines online.

○ "Please know that we only publish a handful of books every year, and that we pass on many well written, important works, simply because we cannot publish them all. We review each and every proposal very carefully. However, due to the volume of inquiries, we cannot respond to them all individually. Please give us 30 days to review your proposal. If you do not hear back from us within that time, this means we have decided to pursue other book ideas that we feel fit better within our plan."

NONFICTION Subjects include New Age, spirituality. Query with SASE. Submit synopsis, SASE. No longer accepting electronic submissions. Reviews artwork/photos. Send photocopies.

FICTION Subjects include literary, spiritual, visionary fiction, past-life fiction based on actual memories. Fiction should have 1 or more of the following themes: spiritual, inspirational, metaphysical, i.e., past-life recall, out-of-body experiences, near-death experience, paranormal. Query with SASE. Submit outline, 2 sample chapters, clips. Submit complete ms.

HANCOCK HOUSE PUBLISHERS

1431 Harrison Ave., Blaine WA 98230. (604)538-1114. **Fax:** (604)538-2262. **E-mail:** submissions@hancockhouse.com. **Website:** www.hancockhouse.com. Estab. 1971. Publishes hardcover, trade paperback, and e-book originals and reprints. "Hancock House Publishers is the largest North American publisher of wildlife and Native Indian titles. We also cover Pacific Northwest, fishing, history, Canadiana, biographies. We are seeking agriculture, natural history, and popular science titles with a regional (Pacific Northwest), national, or international focus. Currently emphasizing nonfiction wildlife, cryptozoology, guide books, native history, biography, fishing." **Publishes 12-20 titles/year. 50% of books from first-time authors. 90% from unagented writers. Pays 10% royalty.** Publishes book 1 year after acceptance. Accepts simultaneous submissions. Responds to proposals in 3-6 months. Book catalog available free. Guidelines online.

NONFICTION Subjects include agriculture, animals, ethnic, history, horticulture, regional. Centered around Pacific Northwest, local history, nature guide books, international ornithology, and Native Americans. Query via e-mail, including outline with word count, a short author bio, table of contents, 3 sample chapters. Accepts double-spaced word .docs or PDFs. Reviews artwork/photos. Send photocopies.

HANSER PUBLICATIONS

6915 Valley Ave., Cincinnati OH 45244. (800)950-8977. **Fax:** (513)527-8801. **E-mail:** info@hanserpublications.com. **Website:** www.hanserpublications.com. **Contact:** Development Editor. Estab. 1993. Publishes hardcover and paperback originals, and digital educational and training programs. "Hanser Publications publishes books and electronic media for the manufacturing (both metalworking and plastics) industries. Publications range from basic training materials to advanced reference books." **Publishes 10-15 titles/year. 100 queries received/year. 10-20 mss received/year. 50% of books from first-time authors. 100% from unagented writers.** Publishes ms 10 months after acceptance. Accepts simultaneous submissions. Responds in 2 weeks to queries; 1 month to proposals/mss. Book catalog available free. Guidelines available online.

○ "Hanser Publications is currently seeking technical experts with strong writing skills to author training and reference books and related products focused on various aspects of the manufacturing industry. Our goal is to provide manufacturing professionals with insightful, easy-to-reference information, and to educate and prepare students for technical careers through accessible, concise training manuals. Do your publishing ideas match this goal? If so, we'd like to hear from you. Submit your detailed product proposals, resume of credentials, and a brief writing sample to: Development Editor, Prospective Authors."

NONFICTION "We publish how-to texts, references, technical books, and computer-based learning materials for the manufacturing industries. Titles include award-winning management books, encyclopedic references, and leading references." Submit outline, sample chapters, resume, preface, and comparison to competing or similar titles.

TIPS "E-mail submissions speed up response time."

⊘⊘ HARCOURT, INC., TRADE DIVISION

Imprint of Houghton Mifflin Harcourt Book Group, 215 Park Ave. S., New York NY 10003. **Website:** www.

harcourtbooks.com. Publishes hardcover and trade paperback originals and trade paperback reprints. **Publishes 120 titles/year. 5% of books from first-time authors. 5% from unagented writers. Pays 6-15% royalty on retail price. Pays $2,000 minimum advance.** Accepts simultaneous submissions. Book catalog for 9×12 envelope and first-class stamps. Guidelines available online.

NONFICTION *No unsolicited mss.* Agented submissions only.

FICTION Agented submissions only.

HARKEN MEDIA

4308 201st Ave. NE, Sammamish WA 98074-6120. **E-mail:** info@harkenmedia.com. **E-mail:** hmeditors@gmail.com. **Website:** www.harkenmedia.com. **Contact:** Robert Sappington, editor-in-chief; Sheila Sappington, editor. Publishes hardcover originals, trade paperback originals, and electronic originals. Harken Media publishes original, unpublished novels possessing unique insights on compelling themes for young adult, new adult, or adult audiences. Compelling themes explore our humanity and in the process expand awareness and understand. **Publishes 1-5 titles/year. Receives 1,000 queries and 50 mss from writers/year. 100% of books from first-time authors. 100% from unagented writers. Authors are paid 15-50% royalty on net wholesale price. Does not pay advance.** Publishes in 6-12 months after acceptance. Accepts simultaneous submissions. Responds in 1 month to queries and proposals, 1-3 months to mss. Catalog online. Guidelines online.

FICTION Subjects include adventure, contemporary, fantasy, gothic, historical, humor, literary, mainstream, multicultural, multimedia, mystery, science fiction, suspense, young adult. "Our notion of entertainment encompasses a broad range of emotional responses from readers. We're as likely to publish a story that makes us cry as laugh. Manipulate our emotions; we like that. A novel's emotional impact is as important as its message. Thus, a successful story for Harken Media both entertains and enlightens." Submit a proposal package following the guidelines on our submissions page, including a synopsis and a detailed description of theme(s) and unique insight(s). "We will not consider physical submissions."

HARLEQUIN AMERICAN ROMANCE

225 Duncan Mill Rd., Don Mills ON M3B 3K9, Canada. **E-mail:** submisssions@harlequin.com. **Website:** www.harlequin.com. **Contact:** Kathleen Scheibling, senior editor. "Upbeat and lively, fast paced and well plotted, American Romance celebrates the pursuit of love in the backyards, big cities and wide-open spaces of America." Publishes paperback originals and reprints. Books: newspaper print paper; web printing; perfect bound. Length: 55,000 words. "American Romance features heartwarming romances with strong family elements. These are stories about the pursuit of love, marriage and family in America today." **Pays royalty. Offers advance.** Accepts simultaneous submissions. Guidelines online.

FICTION Subjects include romance. Needs "all-American stories with a range of emotional and sensual content that are supported by a sense of community within the plot's framework. In the confident and caring heroine, the tough but tender hero, and their dynamic relationship that is at the center of this series, real-life love is showcased as the best fantasy of all!" Submit online.

HARLEQUIN BLAZE

225 Duncan Mill Rd., Don Mills ON M3B 3K9, Canada. (416)445-5860. **Website:** www.harlequin.com. **Contact:** Kathleen Scheibling, senior editor. Publishes paperback originals. "Harlequin Blaze is a red-hot series. It is a vehicle to build and promote new authors who have a strong sexual edge to their stories. It is also the place to be for seasoned authors who want to create a sexy, sizzling, longer contemporary story." Accepts simultaneous submissions. Guidelines online.

FICTION Subjects include romance. "Sensuous, highly romantic, innovative plots that are sexy in premise and execution. The tone of the books can run from fun and flirtatious to dark and sensual. Submissions should have a very contemporary feel—what it's like to be young and single today. We are looking for heroes and heroines in their early 20s and up. There should be a a strong emphasis on the physical relationship between the couples. Fully described love scenes along with a high level of fantasy and playfulness." Length: 55,000-60,000 words.

TIPS "Are you a *Cosmo* girl at heart? A fan of *Sex and the City*? Or maybe you have a sexually adventurous spirit. If so, then Blaze is the series for you!"

HARLEQUIN DESIRE

233 Broadway, Suite 1001, New York NY 10279. (212)553-4200. **Website:** www.harlequin.com. **Contact:** Stacy Boyd, senior editor. Publishes paperback

originals and reprints. Always powerful, passionate, and provocative. "Desire novels are sensual reads and a love scene or scenes are still needed. But there is no set number of pages that needs to be fulfilled. Rather, the level of sensuality must be appropriate to the storyline. Above all, every Silhouette Desire novel must fulfill the promise of a powerful, passionate and provocative read." **Pays royalty. Offers advance.** Accepts simultaneous submissions. Guidelines online.

FICTION Subjects include romance. Looking for novels in which "the conflict is an emotional one, springing naturally from the unique characters you've chosen. The focus is on the developing relationship, set in a believable plot. Sensuality is key, but lovemaking is never taken lightly. Secondary characters and subplots need to blend with the core story. Innovative new directions in storytelling and fresh approaches to classic romantic plots are welcome." Manuscripts must be 50,000-55,000 words.

⬙ HARLEQUIN HQN

Imprint of Harlequin, 225 Duncan Mill Rd., Don Mills ON M3B 3K9, Canada. **Website:** harlequin. com. **Contact:** Margo Lipschultz, senior editor. Publishes hardcover, trade paperback, and mass market paperback originals. "HQN publishes romance in all subgenres—historical, contemporary, romantic suspense, paranormal—as long as the story's central focus is romance. Prospective authors can familiarize themselves with the wide range of books we publish by reading work by some of our current authors. The imprint is looking for a wide range of authors from known romance stars to first-time authors. At the moment, we are accepting only agented submissions—unagented authors may send a query letter to determine if their project suits our needs. Please send your projects to our New York Editorial Office." **Pays royalty. Pays advance.** Accepts simultaneous submissions.

FICTION Subjects include romance. Accepts unagented material. Length: 90,000 words.

⬙ HARLEQUIN INTRIGUE

225 Duncan Mill Rd., Don Mills ON M3B 3K9, Canada. **Website:** www.harlequin.com. **Contact:** Denise Zaza, senior editor. Wants crime stories tailored to the series romance market packed with a variety of thrilling suspense and whodunit mystery. Word count: 55,000-60,000. Accepts simultaneous submissions. Guidelines online.

FICTION Subjects include mystery, romance, suspense. Submit online.

⬙ HARLEQUIN SUPERROMANCE

225 Duncan Mill Rd., Don Mills ON M3B 3K9, Canada. **Website:** www.harlequin.com. **Contact:** Victoria Curran, senior editor. Publishes paperback originals. "The Harlequin Superromance line focuses on believable characters triumphing over true-to-life drama and conflict. At the heart of these contemporary stories should be a compelling romance that brings the reader along with the hero and heroine on their journey of overcoming the obstacles in their way and falling in love. Because of the longer length relevant subplots and secondary characters are welcome but not required. This series publishes a variety of story types—family sagas, romantic suspense, Westerns, to name a few—and tones from light to dramatic, emotional to suspenseful. Settings also vary from vibrant urban neighborhoods to charming small towns. The unifying element of Harlequin Superromance stories is the realistic treatment of character and plot. The characters should seem familiar to readers—similar to people they know in their own lives—and the circumstances within the realm of possibility. The stories should be layered and complex in that the conflicts should not be easily resolved. The best way to get an idea of we're looking for is to read what we're currently publishing. The aim of Superromance novels is to produce a contemporary, involving read with a mainstream tone in its situations and characters, using romance as the major theme. To achieve this, emphasis should be placed on individual writing styles and unique and topical ideas." **Pays royalties. Pays advance.** Accepts simultaneous submissions. Guidelines online.

FICTION Subjects include romance. "The criteria for Superromance books are flexible. Aside from length (80,000 words), the determining factor for publication will always be quality. Authors should strive to break free of stereotypes, clichés and worn-out plot devices to create strong, believable stories with depth and emotional intensity. Superromance novels are intended to appeal to a wide range of romance readers." Submit online.

TIPS "A general familiarity with current Superromance books is advisable to keep abreast of ever-changing trends and overall scope, but we don't want imitations. We look for sincere, heartfelt writing based on true-to-life experiences the reader can identify with. We are interested in innovation."

Ⓐ⊘ HARLEQUIN TEEN

Harlequin, 195 Broadway, 24th Floor, New York NY 10007. **Website:** www.harlequin.com. **Contact:** Natashya Wilson, executive editor. Harlequin Teen is a single-title program dedicated to building authors and publishing unique, memorable young-adult fiction. Accepts simultaneous submissions.

FICTION Harlequin Teen looks for fresh, authentic fiction featuring extraordinary characters and extraordinary stories set in contemporary, paranormal, fantasy, science-fiction, and historical worlds. Wants commercial, high-concept stories that capture the teen experience and will speak to readers with power and authenticity. All subgenres are welcome, so long as the book delivers a relevant reading experience that will resonate long after the book's covers are closed. Expects that most stories will include a compelling romantic element. *Agented submissions only.*

HARMONY INK PRESS

5032 Capital Circle SW, Suite 2 PMB 279, Tallahassee FL 32305. (850)632-4648. **Fax:** (888)308-3739. **E-mail:** submissions@harmonyinkpress.com. **Website:** harmonyinkpress.com. Harmony Ink is accepting mss for teen and new adult fiction featuring at least 1 strong LGBTQ+ main character who shows significant personal growth through the course of the story. **Pays royalty. Pays $500-1,000 advance.** Accepts simultaneous submissions.

FICTION "We are looking for stories in all subgenres, featuring primary characters across the whole LGBTQ+ spectrum between the ages of 14 and 21 that explore all the facets of young adult, teen, and new adult life. Sexual content should be appropriate for the characters and the story." Submit complete ms.

Ⓐ⊘ HARPERBUSINESS

Imprint of HarperCollins General Books Group, 195 Broadway, New York NY 10007. (212)207-7000. **Website:** www.harpercollins.com. Estab. 1991. Publishes hardcover, trade paperback originals and reprints. HarperBusiness publishes the inside story on ideas that will shape business practices with cutting-edge information and visionary concepts. **Pays royalty on retail price. Pays advance.** Accepts simultaneous submissions.

○ "The gold standard of business book publishing for 50 years, Harper Business brings you innovative, authoritative, and creative works from world-class thinkers. Building upon this rich legacy of paradigm-shifting books, Harper Business authors continue to help readers see the future and to lead and live successfully."

NONFICTION Subjects include marketing subjects. "We don't publish how-to, textbooks or things for academic market; no reference (tax or mortgage guides), our reference department does that. Proposals need to be top notch. We tend not to publish people who have no business standing. Must have business credentials." Agented submissions only.

Ⓐ⊘ HARPERCOLLINS

195 Broadway, New York NY 10007. (212)207-7000. **Website:** www.harpercollins.com. Publishes hardcover and paperback originals and paperback reprints. HarperCollins, one of the largest English language publishers in the world, is a broad-based publisher with strengths in academic, business and professional, children's, educational, general interest, and religious and spiritual books, as well as multimedia titles. **Pays royalty. Pays negotiable advance.** Accepts simultaneous submissions.

NONFICTION Agented submissions only. Unsolicited mss returned unopened.

FICTION Subjects include adventure, fantasy, gothic, historical, literary, mystery, science fiction, suspense, western. "We look for a strong story line and exceptional literary talent." Agented submissions only. *All unsolicited mss returned.*

TIPS "We do not accept any unsolicited material."

○⊘ HARPERCOLLINS CANADA, LTD.

2 Bloor St. E., 20th Floor, Toronto ON M4W 1A8, Canada. (416)975-9334. **Fax:** (416)975-5223. **Website:** www.harpercollins.ca. Estab. 1989. *HarperCollins Canada is not accepting unsolicited material at this time.* Accepts simultaneous submissions.

Ⓐ HARPERCOLLINS CHILDREN'S BOOKS/ HARPERCOLLINS PUBLISHERS

195 Broadway, New York NY 10007. (212)207-7000. **Website:** www.harpercollins.com. Publishes hardcover and paperback originals and paperback reprints. HarperCollins, one of the largest English language publishers in the world, is a broad-based publisher with strengths in academic, business and professional, children's, educational, general interest, and religious and spiritual books, as well as multimedia

titles. **Publishes 500 titles/year. Negotiates payment upon acceptance.** Accepts simultaneous submissions. Responds in 1 month, will contact only if interested. Does not accept any unsolicited texts. Catalog online.

IMPRINTS HarperCollins Australia/New Zealand: Angus & Robertson, Fourth Estate, HarperBusiness, HarperCollins, HarperPerenniel, HarperReligious, HarperSports, Voyager; **HarperCollins Canada:** HarperFlamingoCanada, PerennialCanada; **HarperCollins Children's Books Group:** Amistad, Julie Andrews Collection, Avon, Joanna Cotler Books, Eos, Laura Geringer Books, Greenwillow Books, HarperAudio, HarperCollins Children's Books, HarperFestival, HarperTempest, HarperTrophy, Rayo, Katherine Tegen Books; **HarperCollins General Books Group:** Access, Amistad, Avon, Caedmon, Ecco, Eos, Fourth Estate, HarperAudio, HarperBusiness, HarperCollins, HarperEntertainment, HarperLargePrint, HarperResource, HarperSanFrancisco, HarperTorch, Harper Design International, Perennial, PerfectBound, Quill, Rayo, ReganBooks, William Morrow, William Morrow Cookbooks; **HarperCollins UK:** Collins Bartholomew, Collins, HarperCollins Crime & Thrillers, Collins Freedom to Teach, HarperCollins Children's Books, Thorsons/Element, Voyager Books; **Zondervan:** Inspirio, Vida, Zonderkidz, Zondervan.

NONFICTION *No unsolicited mss or queries.* Agented submissions only. Unsolicited mss returned unopened.

FICTION Subjects include picture books, young adult, chapter books, middle grade, early readers. "We look for a strong story line and exceptional literary talent." Agented submissions only. *All unsolicited mss returned.*

TIPS "We do not accept any unsolicited material."

Ⓐ HARPERTEEN

195 Broadway, New York NY 10007. (212)207-7000. **Website:** www.harpercollins.com. HarperTeen is a teen imprint that publishes hardcovers, paperback reprints and paperback originals. **Publishes 100 titles/year.** Accepts simultaneous submissions.

◯ *HarperCollins Children's Books is not accepting unsolicited and/or unagented mss or queries.* Unfortunately the volume of these submissions is so large that they cannot receive the attention they deserve. Such submissions will not be reviewed or returned.

Ⓐ⊘ HARPER VOYAGER

Imprint of HarperCollins General Books Group, 195 Broadway, New York NY 10007. (212)207-7000. **Website:** www.harpercollins.com. Estab. 1998. Publishes hardcover originals, trade and mass market paperback originals, and reprints. Eos publishes quality science fiction/fantasy with broad appeal. **Pays royalty on retail price. Pays variable advance.** Accepts simultaneous submissions. Guidelines online.

FICTION Subjects include fantasy, science fiction. No horror or juvenile. Agented submissions only. *All unsolicited mss returned.*

HARTMAN PUBLISHING, INC.

1313 Iron Ave. SW, Albuquerque NM 87102. **E-mail:** info@hartmanonline.com. **Website:** www.hartmanonline.com. **Contact:** Managing Editor. Publishes trade paperback originals. "We publish educational books for employees of nursing homes, home health agencies, hospitals, and providers of eldercare." **Publishes 5-10 titles/year. 50 queries received/year. 25 mss received/year. 50% of books from first-time authors. 100% from unagented writers. Pays 6-12% royalty on wholesale or retail price, or makes outright purchase of $200-600.** Publishes book 4-12 months after acceptance of ms. Accepts simultaneous submissions. Responds in 2 months to proposals; 3 months to mss. Book catalog available free. Guidelines online.

IMPRINTS Care Spring.

NONFICTION "Writers should request our books-wanted list, as well as view samples of our published material." Submit via online form.

THE HARVARD COMMON PRESS

535 Albany St., 5th Floor, Boston MA 02118. (617)423-5803. **Fax:** (617)695-9794. **E-mail:** info@harvardcommonpress.com. **E-mail:** editorial@harvardcommonpress.com. **Website:** www.harvardcommonpress.com. **Contact:** Submissions. Estab. 1976. Publishes hardcover and trade paperback originals and reprints. "We want strong, practical books that help people gain control over a particular area of their lives. Currently emphasizing cooking, child care/parenting, health. De-emphasizing general instructional books, travel." **Publishes 16 titles/year. 20% of books from first-time authors. 40% from unagented writers. Pays royalty. Pays average $2,500-10,000 advance.** Publishes ms 1 year after acceptance. Accepts simultane-

ous submissions. Responds in 2 months to queries. Guidelines online.

NONFICTION Subjects include child guidance. "A large percentage of our list is made up of books about cooking, child care, and parenting; in these areas we are looking for authors who are knowledgeable, if not experts, and who can offer a different approach to the subject. We are open to good nonfiction proposals that show evidence of strong organization and writing, and clearly demonstrate a need in the marketplace. First-time authors are welcome." Submit outline. Potential authors may also submit a query letter or e-mail of no more than 300 words, rather than a full proposal; if interested, will ask to see a proposal. Queries and questions may be sent via e-mail. "We will not consider e-mail attachments containing proposals. No phone calls, please."

TIPS "We are demanding about the quality of proposals; in addition to strong writing skills and thorough knowledge of the subject matter, we require a detailed analysis of the competition."

Ⓐ⊘ HARVEST HOUSE PUBLISHERS

990 Owen Loop N., Eugene OR 97402. (541)343-0123. **Fax:** (541)302-0731. **Website:** www.harvesthousepublishers.com. Estab. 1974. Publishes hardcover, trade paperback, and mass market paperback originals and reprints. **Publishes 160 titles/year. 1,500 queries received/year. 1,000 mss received/year. 1% of books from first-time authors. Pays royalty.** Accepts simultaneous submissions.

NONFICTION Subjects include child guidance, religion, Bible studies. *No unsolicited mss.*

FICTION *No unsolicited mss, proposals, or artwork.* Agented submissions only.

TIPS "For first time/nonpublished authors we suggest building their literary résumé by submitting to magazines, or perhaps accruing book contributions."

Ⓐ HAY HOUSE, INC.

P.O. Box 5100, Carlsbad CA 92018. (760)431-7695. **Fax:** (760)431-6948. **E-mail:** editorial@hayhouse.com. **Website:** www.hayhouse.com. Estab. 1985. Publishes hardcover, trade paperback and e-book/POD originals. "We publish books, audios, and videos that help heal the planet." **Publishes 50 titles/year. Pays standard royalty.** Accepts simultaneous submissions. Guidelines online.

IMPRINTS Hay House Lifestyles; Hay House Insights; Hay House Visions; SmileyBooks.

NONFICTION Subjects include alternative lifestyles, astrology, cooking, education, foods, health, New Age, nutrition, philosophy, psychic, psychology, sociology, spirituality, womens issues, mind/body/spirit. "Hay House is interested in a variety of subjects as long as they have a positive self-help slant to them. No poetry, children's books, or negative concepts that are not conducive to helping/healing ourselves or our planet." Accepts e-mail submissions from agents.

TIPS "Our audience is concerned with our planet, the healing properties of love, and general self-help principles. If I were a writer trying to market a book today, I would research the market thoroughly to make sure there weren't already too many books on the subject I was interested in writing about. Then I would make sure I had a unique slant on my idea. Simultaneous submissions from agents must include SASE's."

HEALTH COMMUNICATIONS, INC.

3201 SW 15th St., Deerfield Beach FL 33442. (954)360-0909, ext. 232. **Fax:** (954)360-0034. **E-mail:** editorial@hcibooks.com. **Website:** www.hcibooks.com. **Contact:** Editorial Committee. Estab. 1976. Publishes hardcover and trade paperback nonfiction only. "While HCI is a best known for recovery publishing, today recovery is only one part of a publishing program that includes titles in self-help and psychology, health and wellness, spirituality, inspiration, women's and men's issues, relationships, family, teens and children, memoirs, mind/body/spirit integration, and gift books." **Publishes 60 titles/year.** Accepts simultaneous submissions. Responds in 3-6 months. Guidelines online.

NONFICTION Subjects include child guidance, health, parenting, psychology, young adult, self-help.

TIPS "Due to the volume of submissions, Health Communications cannot guarantee response times or personalize responses to individual proposals. Under no circumstances do we accept phone calls or e-mails pitching submissions."

HEALTH PROFESSIONS PRESS

P.O. Box 10624, Baltimore MD 21285-0624. (410)337-9585. **Fax:** (410)337-8539. **E-mail:** mmagnus@healthpropress.com. **Website:** www.healthpropress.com. **Contact:** Acquisitions Department. Publishes hardcover and trade paperback originals. "We are a specialty publisher. Our primary audiences are professionals, students, and educated consumers interested in topics related to aging, eldercare, and healthcare management." **Publishes 6-8 titles/year. 70 queries received/year. 12 mss received/year. 50% of books from first-time authors. 100% from unagented writers. Pays 8-15% royalty on wholesale price.** Publishes ms 8-10 months after acceptance. Accepts simultaneous submissions. Responds in 1 month to queries; 3 months to proposals; 4 months to mss. Book catalog free or online. Guidelines online.

NONFICTION Subjects include health, psychology. Query with SASE. Submit proposal package, outline, resume, 1-2 sample chapters, cover letter.

WILLIAM S. HEIN & CO., INC.

2350 N. Forest Rd., Getzville NY 14068. (716)882-2600. **Fax:** (716)883-8100. **E-mail:** mail@wshein.com. **Website:** www.wshein.com. **Contact:** Sheila Jarrett, senior editor. Estab. 1961. "William S. Hein & Co. publishes reference books for law librarians, legal researchers, and those interested in legal writing. Currently emphasizing legal research, legal writing, and legal education." **Publishes 18 titles/year. 30 queries received/year. 15 mss received/year. 30% of books from first-time authors. 99% from unagented writers. Pays 10-20% royalty on net price for print; higher royalties if published as an e-book.** Publishes book 9 months after acceptance. Accepts simultaneous submissions. Responds in 6 weeks to queries. Book catalog online. Guidelines by e-mail.

NONFICTION Subjects include education, law, world affairs, legislative histories.

● HEINEMANN EDUCATIONAL PUBLISHERS

P.O. Box 781940, Sandton 2146, South Africa. **E-mail:** customerliaison@heinemann.co.za. **Website:** www.heinemann.co.za. Interested in textbooks for primary schools, literature and textbooks for secondary schools, and technical publishing for colleges/universities. Accepts simultaneous submissions.

NONFICTION Subjects include animals, education, ethnic, history, humanities, psychology, regional, religion, science, social sciences, sports, math, engineering, management, nursing, marketing.

HELLGATE PRESS

P.O. Box 3531, Ashland OR 97520. (541)973-5154. **E-mail:** sales@hellgatepress.com. **Website:** www.hellgatepress.com. **Contact:** Harley B. Patrick. Estab. 1996. "Hellgate Press specializes in military history, veteran memoirs, other military topics, travel adventure, and historical/adventure fiction." **Publishes 15-**

20 **titles/year. 85% of books from first-time authors. 95% from unagented writers. Pays royalty.** Publishes ms 6-9 months after acceptance. Accepts simultaneous submissions. Responds in 2 months to queries.

NONFICTION Subjects include history, memoirs, military, war, womens issues, world affairs, travel adventure. Query/proposal by e-mail only. *Do not send mss.*

HENDRICK-LONG PUBLISHING CO., INC.

10635 Tower Oaks, Suite D, Houston TX 77070. (832)912-READ. **Fax:** (832)912-7353. **E-mail:** hendrick-long@worldnet.att.net. **Website:** hendricklongpublishing.com. **Contact:** Vilma Long. Estab. 1969. Publishes hardcover and trade paperback originals and hardcover reprints. "Hendrick-Long publishes historical fiction and nonfiction about Texas and the Southwest for children and young adults." **Publishes 4 titles/year. 90% from unagented writers. Pays royalty on selling price. Pays advance.** Publishes ms 18 months after acceptance. Responds in 3 months to queries. Book catalog available. Guidelines online.

NONFICTION Subjects include history, regional. Subject must be Texas related; other subjects cannot be considered. "We are particularly interested in material from educators that can be used in the classroom as workbooks, math, science, history with a Texas theme or twist." Query, or submit outline and 2 sample chapters. Reviews artwork/photos. Send photocopies.

FICTION Subjects include juvenile, young adult. Query with SASE. Submit outline, clips, 2 sample chapters.

⊘ HENDRICKSON PUBLISHERS, INC.

P.O. Box 3473, Peabody MA 01961. **Fax:** (978)573-8276. **E-mail:** editorial@hendrickson.com. **Website:** www.hendrickson.com. Estab. 1981. Publishes trade reprints, bibles, and scholarly material in the areas of New Testament; Hebrew Bible; religion and culture; patristics; Judaism; and practical, historical, and Biblical theology. "Hendrickson is an academic publisher of Biblical scholarship and trade books that encourage spiritual growth. Currently emphasizing Biblical language and reference, pastoral resources, and Biblical studies." **Publishes 35 titles/year. 800 queries received/year. 10% of books from first-time authors. 90% from unagented writers.** Publishes ms 1 year after acceptance. Guidelines online.

NONFICTION Subjects include contemporary culture, creative nonfiction, education, entertainment, film, history, humanities, language, literature, religion, social sciences, spirituality. "We cannot accept unsolicited mss or book proposals except through one of the 2 following avenues: Materials sent to our editorial staff through a professional literary agent will be considered; Our staff would be happy to discuss book ideas at the various conferences we attend throughout the year (most notably the AAR/SBL annual meeting)."

HERITAGE BOOKS, INC.

5810 Ruatan St., Berwyn Heights MD 20740. (800)876-6103. **E-mail:** info@heritagebooks.com. **E-mail:** submissions@heritagebooks.com. **Website:** www.heritagebooks.com. Estab. 1978. Publishes hardcover and paperback originals and reprints. "Our goal is to celebrate life by exploring all aspects of American life: settlement, development, wars, and other significant events, including family histories, memoirs, etc. Currently emphasizing early American life, early wars and conflicts, ethnic studies." **Publishes 200 titles/year. 25% of books from first-time authors. 100% from unagented writers. Pays 10% royalty on list price.** Accepts simultaneous submissions. Responds in 3 months to queries. Book catalog and ms guidelines free.

NONFICTION Subjects include Americana, ethnic, history, memoirs, military, regional. Military memoirs. Query with SASE. Submit outline via e-mail. Reviews artwork/photos.

TIPS "The quality of the book is of prime importance; next is its relevance to our fields of interest."

♻ HERITAGE HOUSE PUBLISHING CO., LTD.

103-1075 Pendergast St., Victoria BC V8V 0A1, Canada. (250)360-0829. **E-mail:** heritage@heritagehouse.ca. **Website:** www.heritagehouse.ca. **Contact:** Lara Kordic, senior editor. Publishes mostly trade paperback and some hardcovers. "Heritage House publishes books that celebrate the historical and cultural heritage of Canada, particularly Western Canada and the Pacific Northwest. We also publish some children's titles, titles of national interest and a series of books aimed at young and casual readers, called *Amazing Stories*. We accept simultaneous submissions, but indicate on your query that it is a simultaneous submission." **Publishes 25-30 titles/year. 200 queries;**

100 mss received/year. **50% of books from first-time authors. 90% from unagented writers. Pays 12-15% royalty on net proceeds. Advances are rarely paid.** Publishes book within 1-2 years of acceptance. Accepts simultaneous submissions. Responds in 6 months to queries. Catalog and guidelines online.

NONFICTION Subjects include animals, anthropology, art, business, community, contemporary culture, creative nonfiction, environment, ethnic, history, humanities, marine subjects, multicultural, politics, pop culture, public affairs, regional, war, womens issues, adventure, contemporary Canadian culture. Query by e-mail. Include synopsis, outline, 2-3 sample chapters with indication of illustrative material available, and marketing strategy.

TIPS "Our books appeal to residents of and visitors to the northwest quadrant of the continent. We're looking for good stories and good storytellers. We focus on work by Canadian authors."

HEYDAY BOOKS

c/o Acquisitions Editor, Box 9145, Berkeley CA 94709. **Fax:** (510)549-1889. **E-mail:** heyday@heydaybooks. com. **Website:** www.heydaybooks.com. **Contact:** Gayle Wattawa, acquisitions and editorial director. Estab. 1974. Publishes hardcover originals, trade paperback originals and reprints. "Heyday Books publishes nonfiction books and literary anthologies with a strong California focus. We publish books about Native Americans, natural history, history, literature, and recreation, with a strong California focus." **Publishes 12-15 titles/year. 50% of books from first-time authors. 90% from unagented writers. Pays 8% royalty on net price.** Publishes book 18 months after acceptance. Responds in 3 months. Book catalog online. Guidelines online.

NONFICTION Subjects include Americana, ethnic, history, recreation, regional, travel. Books about California only. Query with outline and synopsis. "Query or proposal by traditional post. Include a cover letter introducing yourself and your qualifications, a brief description of your project, a table of contents and list of illustrations, notes on the market you are trying to reach and why your book will appeal to them, a sample chapter, and a SASE if you would like us to return these materials to you." Reviews artwork/photos.

FICTION Publishes picture books, beginning readers, and young adult literature. Submit complete ms for picture books; proposal with sample chapters for longer works. include a chapter by chapter summary. Mark attention: Children's Submission. Reviews manuscript/illustration packages; but may consider art and text separately. Tries to respond to query within 12 weeks.

HIGHLAND PRESS PUBLISHING

P.O. Box 2292, High Springs FL 32655. **E-mail:** the.highland.press@gmail.com; submissions.hp@gmail.com. **Website:** www.highlandpress.org. **Contact:** Leanne Burroughs, CEO (fiction); she will forward all mss to appropriate editor. Estab. 2005. Publishes paperback originals, both historical and contemporary. Also publishes some nonfiction books. "With our focus on historical romances, Highland Press Publishing is known as your 'Passport to Romance.' We focus on historical romances and our award-winning anthologies. Our short stories/novellas are heart warming. As for our historicals, we publish historical novels like many of us grew up with and loved. History is a big part of the story and is tactfully woven throughout the romance. We have opened our submissions up to all genres, with the exception of erotica. Our newest lines are inspirational, regency, and young adult." **Publishes 30 titles/year. 25% of books from first-time authors. 90% from unagented writers. Pays royalties.** Publishes ms within 18 months of acceptance. Accepts simultaneous submissions. Responds in 3 months to queries; 3-12 months to mss. Catalog and guidelines online.

FICTION Subjects include contemporary, historical, military, mystery, religious, romance, short story collections, suspense, western, young adult. Query with proposal and sample chapters. Accepts queries by snail mail, e-mail. Include estimated word count, target market, promotional strategy.

TIPS "I don't publish based on industry trends. We buy what we like and what we believe readers are looking for. However, often this proves to be the genres and time-periods larger publishers are not currently interested in. Be professional at all times. Present your manuscript in the best possible light. Be sure you have run spell check and that the manuscript has been vetted by at least one critique partner, preferably more. Many times we receive manuscripts that have wonderful stories involved, but would take far too much time to edit to make it marketable."

HIGH PLAINS PRESS

P.O. Box 123, 403 Cassa Rd., Glendo WY 82213. (307)735-4370. **Fax:** (307)735-4590. **E-mail:** editor@highplainspress.com. **Website:** www.highplainspress.com. **Contact:** Nancy Curtis, publisher. Estab. 1984. Publishes hardcover and trade paperback originals. High Plains Press is a regional book publishing company specializing in books about the American West, with special interest in things relating to Wyoming. **Publishes 4 titles/year. 50 queries; 75 mss received/year. 75% of books from first-time authors. 100% from unagented writers. Pays 10% royalty on wholesale price. Pays $200-2000 advance.** Publishes book 2 years after acceptance of ms. Accepts simultaneous submissions. Responds in 1 month to queries and proposals; 6 months on mss. Book catalog and guidelines online.

NONFICTION Subjects include agriculture, Americana, environment, history, horticulture, memoirs, nature, regional. "We consider only books with strong connection to the West." Query with SASE. Reviews artwork/photos. Send photocopies.

POETRY "We publish 1 poetry volume a year. Sometimes we skip a year. Require connection to West. Consider poetry in August." Submit 5 sample poems.

TIPS "Our audience comprises general readers interested in history and culture of the Rockies."

Ⓐ Ⓞ HILL AND WANG

Farrar Straus & Giroux, Inc., 18 W. 18th St., New York NY 10011. (212)741-6900. **Fax:** (212)633-9385. **Website:** www.fsgbooks.com. Estab. 1956. Publishes hardcover and trade paperbacks. "Hill and Wang publishes serious nonfiction books, primarily in history, science, mathematics and the social sciences. We are not considering new fiction, drama, or poetry." **Publishes 12 titles/year. 1,500 queries received/year. 50% of books from first-time authors. 50% from unagented writers.** Publishes ms 1 year after acceptance. Accepts simultaneous submissions. Book catalog available free.

NONFICTION Subjects include history. *Agented submissions only.*

LAWRENCE HILL BOOKS

Chicago Review Press, 814 N. Franklin St., 2nd Floor, Chicago IL 60610. (312)337-0747. **Fax:** (312)337-5110. **Website:** www.chicagoreviewpress.com. **Contact:** Yuval Taylor, senior editor. Publishes hardcover originals and trade paperback originals and reprints. **Publishes 3-10 titles/year. 20 queries; 10 mss received/year. 40% of books from first-time authors. 50%**

from unagented writers. **Pays 7-12% royalty on re-tail price. Pays $3,000-10,000 advance.** Publishes ms 1 year after acceptance. Accepts simultaneous submissions. Responds in 1 month to queries; 2 months to proposals and mss. Book catalog available free.

NONFICTION Subjects include ethnic, history, multicultural. Submit proposal package, outline, 2 sample chapters.

HIPPOCRENE BOOKS, INC.

171 Madison Ave., Suite 1605, New York NY 10016, USA. 212-685-4371. **E-mail:** info@hippocrenebooks. com. **Website:** www.hippocrenebooks.com. Estab. 1971. *Mastering Arabic 1 and 2, Beginner's Russian with Interactive Online Workbook, Farsi Concise Dictionary, Tagalog Standard Dictionary, The Ghana Cookbook, Muy Bueno, Latin Twist, Healthy South Indian Cooking.* "Over the last forty years, Hippocrene Books has become one of America's foremost publishers of foreign language reference books and ethnic cookbooks. As a small publishing house in a marketplace dominated by conglomerates, Hippocrene has succeeded by continually reinventing its list while maintaining a strong international and ethnic orientation." Accepts simultaneous submissions. Please include summary, author background/resume including ability to promote book, sample chapter, table of contents, and audience. Do not send entire manuscript (hard copy or document file).

⬤   Hippocrene Books offers guides to over 120 languages and cookbooks in 80 inernational cuisines. We're seeking new languages not a part of our catalog, or additional titles in top-selling languages. Our cookbooks highlight a specific region or country, and stay clear of trends or fads.

FICTION No fiction is accepted.

POETRY Not seeking new poetry submissions.

⬤ HIPPOPOTAMUS PRESS

22 Whitewell Rd., Frome Somerset BA11 4EL, United Kingdom. (44)(173)466-6653. **E-mail:** rjhippopress@ aol.com. **Contact:** R. John, editor; M. Pargitter (poetry); Anna Martin (translation). Estab. 1974. Publishes hardcover and trade paperback originals. "Hippopotamus Press publishes first, full collections of verse by those well represented in the mainstream poetry magazines of the English-speaking world." **Publishes 6-12 titles/year. 90% of books from first-time authors. 90% from unagented writers. Pays 7½-10%**

royalty on retail price. Pays advance.** Publishes book 10 months after acceptance. Accepts simultaneous submissions. Responds in 1 month to queries. Book catalog available free.

NONFICTION Subjects include translation. Query with SASE. Submit complete ms.

POETRY "Read one of our authors—poets often make the mistake of submitting poetry without knowing the type of verse we publish." Query and submit complete ms.

TIPS "We publish books for a literate audience. We have a strong link to the Modernist tradition. Read what we publish."

HIPSO MEDIA

8151 E. 29th Ave., Denver CO 80238. **Website:** www. hipsomedia.com. Estab. 2012. Publishes trade and mass market paperback and electronic originals. **Publishes 6 titles/year. 10% of books from first-time authors. 100% from unagented writers. Authors receive between 15-30% on royalty.** Averages 6 months between acceptance of a book-length ms and publication. Accepts simultaneous submissions. Responds in 1 month. Catalog online. Guidelines online.

NONFICTION Subjects include alternative lifestyles, contemporary culture, cooking, foods, health, medicine, nutrition, travel. Looking for books that can be enhanced with media, video, audio, animation, and interactivity. Query via online form. Reviews artwork as part of the ms package. Artwork or photos must be in JPG form.

FICTION Subjects include erotica, experimental, humor, multicultural, multimedia, mystery, short story collections, young adult. Query via online form.

TIPS Describes ideal audience as "hip readers of e-books. We are going digital first, so tell us why someone would want to read your book."

HISTORY PUBLISHING COMPANY, LLC

P.O. Box 700, Palisades NY 10964. (845)398-8161. **Fax:** (845)231-6167. **E-mail:** djb@historypublishingco.com. **Website:** www.historypublishingco.com. **Contact:** Don Bracken, editorial director. Estab. 2001. Publishes hardcover and trade paperback originals and electronic books. "History Publishing is looking for interesting stories that make up history. If you have a story about an aspect of history that would have an appeal to a large niche or broad readership, History Publishing is interested." **Publishes 20 titles/ year. Receives 45 submissions/year. 50% of books** from first-time authors. **50% from unagented writers. Pays 7-10% royalty on wholesale list price. Does not pay advances to unpublished authors.** Publishes ms 1 year after acceptance. Responds in 4 months to full mss. Guidelines online.

IMPRINTS Chronology Books; Today's Books.

NONFICTION Subjects include Americana, business, contemporary culture, creative nonfiction, economics, government, history, military, politics, social sciences, sociology, war, world affairs. Query with SASE. Submit proposal package, outline, 3 sample chapters or submit complete ms. Reviews artwork/photos. Send photocopies.

TIPS "We focus on an audience interested in the events that shaped the world we live in and the events of today that continue to shape that world. Focus on interesting and serious events that will appeal to the contemporary reader who likes easy-to-read history that flows from one page to the next."

HOBAR PUBLICATIONS

A division of Finney Co., 5995 149th St. W., Suite 105, Apple Valley MN 55124. (952)469-6699. **Fax:** (952)469-1968. **E-mail:** feedback@finney-hobar.com; info@finneyco.com. **Website:** www.finney-hobar.com. **Contact:** Alan E. Krysan, president. Publishes trade paperback originals. "Hobar publishes career and technical educational materials." **Publishes 4-6 titles/year. 30 queries received/year. 10 mss received/year. 35% of books from first-time authors. 100% from unagented writers. Pays 10% royalty on wholesale price. Pays advance.** Publishes ms 1 year after acceptance. Accepts simultaneous submissions. Responds in 10-12 weeks to queries.

NONFICTION Subjects include agriculture, animals, education, gardening, science, building trades. Query with SASE. Reviews artwork/photos.

HOHM PRESS

P.O. Box 4410, Chino Valley AZ 86323. (800)381-2700. **Fax:** (928)717-1779. **Website:** www.hohmpress.com. **Contact:** Acquisitions Editor. Estab. 1975. Publishes hardcover and trade paperback originals. "*Hohm Press* publishes a range of titles in the areas of transpersonal psychology and spirituality, herbistry, alternative health methods, and nutrition. Not interested in personal health survival stories." **Publishes 6-8 titles/year. 50% of books from first-time authors. Pays 10% royalty on net sales.** Publishes

ms 18 months after acceptance. Accepts simultaneous submissions. Responds in 3 months to queries.

NONFICTION Subjects include philosophy, religion, yoga. "We look for writers who have an established record in their field of expertise. The best buy of recent years came from 2 women who fully substantiated how they could market their book. We believed they could do it. We were right." No children's books please. Query with SASE. No e-mail inquiries, please.

POETRY "We are not accepting poetry at this time except for translations of recognized religious/spiritual classics."

HOLIDAY HOUSE, INC.

425 Madison Ave., New York NY 10017. (212)688-0085. **Fax:** (212)421-6134. **E-mail:** info@holidayhouse.com. **Website:** holidayhouse.com. Estab. 1935. Publishes hardcover originals and paperback reprints. "Holiday House publishes children's and young adult books for the school and library markets. We have a commitment to publishing first-time authors and illustrators. We specialize in quality hardcovers from picture books to young adult, both fiction and nonfiction, primarily for the school and library market." **Publishes 50 titles/year. 5% of books from first-time authors. 50% from unagented writers. Pays royalty on list price, range varies.** Publishes 1-2 years after acceptance. Responds in 4 months. Guidelines for #10 SASE.

NONFICTION Subjects include Americana, history, science, Judaica. Please send the entire ms, whether submitting a picture book or novel. "All submissions should be directed to the Editorial Department, Holiday House. We do not accept certified or registered mail. There is no need to include a SASE. We do not consider submissions by e-mail or fax. Please note that you do not have to supply illustrations. However, if you have illustrations you would like to include with your submission, you may send detailed sketches or photocopies of the original art. Do not send original art." Reviews artwork/photos. Send photocopies-no originals.

FICTION Subjects include adventure, historical, humor, literary, Judaica and holiday, animal stories for young readers.. Children's books only. Query with SASE. No phone calls, please.

TIPS "We need manuscripts with strong stories and writing."

Ⓐ Ⓞ HENRY HOLT

175 Fifth Ave., New York NY 10011. (646)307-5095. **Fax:** (212)633-0748. **Website:** www.henryholt.com.

Agented submissions only. Accepts simultaneous submissions.

HOLY CROSS ORTHODOX PRESS

Hellenic College, 50 Goddard Ave., Brookline MA 02445. (617)850-1321. **Fax:** (617)850-1457. **E-mail:** press@hchc.edu. **Website:** www.hchc.edu/community/administrative_offices/holy.cross.orthodox.press/. **Contact:** Dr. Anton C. Vrame. Estab. 1974. Publishes trade paperback originals. "Holy Cross publishes titles that are rooted in the tradition of the Eastern Orthodox Church." **Publishes 8 titles/year. 10-15 queries; 10-15 mss received/year. 85% of books from first-time authors. 100% from unagented writers. Pays 10% royalty on net revenue from retail sales.** Publishes ms 2 years after acceptance. Accepts simultaneous submissions. Responds in 6 months to mss. Book catalog available online through Holy Cross Bookstore.

NONFICTION Subjects include ethnic, religion. Holy Cross Orthodox Press publishes scholarly and popular literature in the areas of Orthodox Christian theology and Greek letters. Submissions are often far too technical usually with very limited audiences. Submit outline. Submit complete ms. Reviews artwork/photos. Send photocopies.

Ⓐ HOPEWELL PUBLICATIONS

P.O. Box 11, Titusville NJ 08560. **Website:** www.hopepubs.com. **Contact:** E. Martin, publisher. Estab. 2002. Format publishes in hardcover, trade paperback, and electronic originals; trade paperback and electronic reprints. "Hopewell Publications specializes in classic reprints—books with proven sales records that have gone out of print—and the occasional new title of interest. Our catalog spans from one to sixty years of publication history. We print fiction and nonfiction, and we accept agented and unagented materials. Submissions are accepted online only." **Publishes 20-30 titles/year. Receives 2,000 queries/year; 500 mss/year. 25% of books from first-time authors. 75% from unagented writers. Pays royalty on retail price.** Publishes ms 6-12 months after acceptance. Accepts simultaneous submissions. Responds in 3 months to queries; 6 months to proposals; 9 months to mss. Catalog online. Guidelines online.

IMPRINTS Egress Books, Legacy Classics.

NONFICTION Subjects include All nonfiction subjects acceptable. Query online using online guidelines.

FICTION Subjects include adventure, contemporary, experimental, fantasy, gay, historical, humor, juvenile, literary, mainstream, mystery, plays, short story collections, spiritual, suspense, young adult, All fiction subjects acceptable. Query online using our online guidelines.

HOUGHTON MIFFLIN HARCOURT BOOKS FOR CHILDREN

Imprint of Houghton Mifflin Trade & Reference Division, 222 Berkeley St., Boston MA 02116. (617)351-5000. **Fax:** (617)351-1111. **Website:** www.houghtonmifflinbooks.com. Publishes hardcover originals and trade paperback originals and reprints. Houghton Mifflin Harcourt gives shape to ideas that educate, inform, and above all, delight. *Does not respond to or return mss unless interested.* **Publishes 100 titles/year. 5,000 queries received/year. 14,000 mss received/year. 10% of books from first-time authors. 60% from unagented writers. Pays 5-10% royalty on retail price. Pays variable advance.** Publishes ms 2 years after acceptance. Accepts simultaneous submissions. Responds in 4-6 months to queries. Guidelines online.

NONFICTION Subjects include animals, ethnic, history, science, sports. Interested in innovative books and subjects about which the author is passionate. Query with SASE. Submit sample chapters, synopsis. Reviews artwork/photos. Send photocopies.

FICTION Subjects include adventure, ethnic, historical, humor, juvenile, literary, mystery, picture books, suspense, young adult, board books. Submit complete ms.

Ⓐⓞ HOUGHTON MIFFLIN HARCOURT CO.

222 Berkeley St., Boston MA 02116. (617)351-5000. **Website:** www.hmhco.com. Estab. 1832. Publishes hardcover originals and trade paperback originals and reprints. "Houghton Mifflin Harcourt gives shape to ideas that educate, inform and delight. In a new era of publishing, our legacy of quality thrives as we combine imagination with technology, bringing you new ways to know." Accepts simultaneous submissions.

NONFICTION "We are not a mass market publisher. Our main focus is serious nonfiction. We do practical self-help but not pop psychology self-help." *Agented submissions only. Unsolicited mss returned unopened.*

✪⊘ HOUSE OF ANANSI PRESS

128 Sterling Rd., Lower Level, Toronto ON M6R 2B7, Canada. (416)363-4343. **Fax:** (416)363-1017. **Website:** www.anansi.ca. Estab. 1967. House of Anansi publishes literary fiction and poetry by Canadian and international writers. **Pays 8-10% royalties. Pays $750 advance and 10 author's copies.** Responds to queries within 1 year; to mss (if invited) within 4 months. Accepts simultaneous submissions.

NONFICTION Avoids dry, jargon-filled academic prose and has a literary twist that will interest general readers and experts alike. Query with SASE.

FICTION Publishes literary fiction that has a unique flair, memorable characters, and a strong narrative voice. Query with SASE.

POETRY "We seek to balance the list between well-known and emerging writers, with an interest in writing by Canadians of all backgrounds. We publish Canadian poetry only, and poets must have a substantial publication record—if not in books, then definitely in journals and magazines of repute." Does not want "children's poetry or poetry by previously unpublished poets." Canadian poets should query first with 10 sample poems (typed double-spaced) and a cover letter with brief bio and publication credits. Considers simultaneous submissions. Poems are circulated to an editorial board. Often comments on rejected poems.

HOW BOOKS

F+W, a Content + eCommerce Company, 10151 Carver Rd., Suite 200, Blue Ash OH 45242. (513)531-2690. **Website:** www.howdesign.com. **Contact:** Brendan O'Neill, editorial director. Estab. 1985. Publishes hardcover and trade paperback originals. **Publishes 15 titles/year. 50 queries; 5 mss received/year. 50% of books from first-time authors. 50% from unagented writers. Pays 10% royalty on wholesale price. Pays $2,000-6,000 advance.** Publishes ms 18-24 months after acceptance. Accepts simultaneous submissions. Responds in 1 month to queries and proposals; 3 months to mss. Book catalog available online. Guidelines available online.

NONFICTION Subjects include graphic design, web design, creativity, pop culture. "We look for material that reflects the cutting edge of trends, graphic design, and culture. Nearly all HOW Books are intensely visual, and authors must be able to create or supply art/illustration for their books." Query via e-mail. Submit proposal package, outline, 1 sample chapter, sample art or sample design. Reviews artwork/photos. Send as PDF's.

TIPS "Audience comprised of graphic designers. Your art, design, or concept."

HUMAN KINETICS PUBLISHERS, INC.

P.O. Box 5076, Champaign IL 61825-5076. (800)747-4457. **Fax:** (217)351-1549. **E-mail:** acquisitions@hkusa.com. **Website:** www.humankinetics.com. Estab. 1974. Publishes hardcover, ebooks, and paperback text and reference books, trade paperback originals, course software and audiovisual. "*Human Kinetics* publishes books which provide expert knowledge in sport and fitness training and techniques, physical education, sports sciences and sports medicine for coaches, athletes and fitness enthusiasts and professionals in the physical action field." **Publishes 160 titles/year. Pays 10-15% royalty on net income.** Publishes ms up to 18 months after acceptance. Accepts simultaneous submissions. Responds in 2 months to queries. Book catalog available free. Guidelines online.

NONFICTION Subjects include education, psychology, recreation, sports. "Here is a current listing of our divisions: Amer. Sport Education; Aquatics Edu.; Professional Edu.; HPERD Div., Journal Div.; STM Div., Trade Div." Submit outline, sample chapters. Reviews artwork/photos.

IBEX PUBLISHERS

P.O. Box 30087, Bethesda MD 20824. (301)718-8188. **Fax:** (301)907-8707. **E-mail:** info@ibexpub.com. **Website:** www.ibexpublishers.com. Estab. 1979. Publishes hardcover and trade paperback originals and reprints. "IBEX publishes books about Iran and the Middle East and about Persian culture and literature." **Publishes 10-12 titles/year. Payment varies.** Accepts simultaneous submissions. Book catalog available free.

IMPRINTS Iranbooks Press.

NONFICTION Subjects include history, humanities, language, literature, spirituality, translation. Query with SASE, or submit proposal package, including outline and 2 sample chapters.

POETRY "Translations of Persian poets will be considered."

ICONOGRAFIX/ENTHUSIAST BOOKS

2017 O'Neil Rd., Hudson WI 54016. (715)381-9755. **E-mail:** info@enthusiastbooks.com. **Website:** www.enthusiastbooks.com. Estab. 1992. Publishes trade paperback originals. "Iconografix publishes special, historical-interest photographic books for transportation equipment enthusiasts. Currently emphasizing emergency vehicles, buses, trucks, railroads, automobiles, auto racing, construction equipment, snowmobiles." **Publishes 6-10 titles/year. 50 queries received/year. 20 mss received/year. 50% of books from first-time authors. 100% from unagented writers. Pays 8-12% royalty on wholesale price. Pays $1,000-3,000 advance.** Publishes book 1 year after acceptance. Accepts simultaneous submissions. Responds in 1 month to queries; 3 months to proposals and mss. Book catalog and ms guidelines free.

NONFICTION Subjects include Americana, history, hobbies, transportation (older photos of specific vehicles). Interested in photo archives. Query with SASE, or submit proposal package, including outline. Reviews artwork/photos. Send photocopies.

ICS PUBLICATIONS

Institute of Carmelite Studies, 2131 Lincoln Rd. NE, Washington DC 20002. (202)832-8489. **Fax:** (202)832-8967. **E-mail:** editor@icspublications.org. **Website:** www.icspublications.org. **Contact:** Patricia Morrison, editorial director. Publishes hardcover and trade paperback originals and reprints. "Our audience consists of those interested in the Carmelite tradition and in developing their life of prayer and spirituality." **Publishes 3 titles/year. 10-20 queries received/year. 10 mss received/year. 10% of books from first-time authors. 90-100% from unagented writers. Pays 2-6% royalty on retail price or makes outright purchase. Pays $500 advance.** Publishes ms 3 years after acceptance. Accepts simultaneous submissions. Responds in 6 months to proposals.

NONFICTION "Too often we receive proposals for works that merely repeat what has already been done, are too technical for a general audience, or have little to do with the Carmelite tradition and spirit. We are looking for significant works on Carmelite history, spirituality, and main figures (Saints Teresa, John of the Cross, Therese of Lisieux, etc.)."

IDW PUBLISHING

2765 Truxtun Rd., San Diego CA 92106. **E-mail:** letters@idwpublishing.com. **Website:** www.idwpublishing.com. Estab. 1999. Publishes hardcover, mass market and trade paperback originals. IDW Publishing currently publishes a wide range of comic books and graphic novels including titles based on GI Joe, Star Trek, Terminator: Salvation, and Transformers. Creator-driven titles include Fallen Angel by Peter David and JK Woodward, Locke & Key by Joe Hill and Gabriel Rodriguez, and a variety of titles by writer Steve Niles including Wake the Dead, Epilogue, and Dead, She Said. Accepts simultaneous submissions.

IDYLL ARBOR, INC.

39129 264th Ave. SE, Enumclaw WA 98022. (360)825-7797. **Fax:** (360)825-5670. **E-mail:** editors@idyllarbor.com. **Website:** www.idyllarbor.com. **Contact:** Tom Blaschko. Estab. 1984. Publishes hardcover and trade paperback originals, and trade paperback reprints. "Idyll Arbor publishes practical information on the current state and art of healthcare practice. Currently emphasizing therapies (recreational, horticultural), and activity directors in long-term care facilities. Issues Press looks at problems in society from video games to returning veterans and their problems reintegrating into the civilian world. Pine Winds Press publishes books about strange phenomena such as Bigfoot and the life force." **Publishes 6 titles/year. 50% of books from first-time authors. 100% from unagented writers. Pays 8-15% royalty on wholesale price or retail price.** Publishes book 1 year after acceptance. Accepts simultaneous submissions. Responds in 1 month; 2 months to proposals; 6 months to mss. Book catalog and ms guidelines free.

IMPRINTS Issues Press; Pine Winds Press.

NONFICTION Subjects include health, medicine, New Age, psychic, psychology, recreation, science, spirituality, horticulture (used in long-term care activities or health care therapy). "Idyll Arbor is currently developing a line of books under the imprint Issues Press, which treats emotional issues in a clear-headed manner. We look for mss from authors with recent clinical experience. Good grounding in theory is required, but practical experience is more important." Query preferred with outline and 1 sample chapter. Reviews artwork/photos. Send photocopies.

TIPS "The books must be useful for the health practitioner who meets face to face with patients or the books must be useful for teaching undergraduate and graduate level classes. Pine Winds Press books should be compatible with the model of the soul found on calculatingsoulconnections.com."

ILIUM PRESS

2407 S. Sonora Dr., Spokane WA 99037. (509)701-8866. **E-mail:** iliumpress@outlook.com. **E-mail:** iliumpress@outlook.com. **Contact:** John Lemon, owner/

editor. Estab. 2010. Publishes trade paperback originals and reprints, electronic originals and reprints. "Ilium is a small, 1-man press that I run in my spare time that was created to cultivate and promote the relevance of epic poetry in today's world. I am very selective about my projects, but I provide extensive editorial care to those I take on." **Publishes 1-3 titles/year. Pays 20-50% royalties on receipts. Does not pay advance.** Publishes ms up to 1 year after acceptance. Accepts simultaneous submissions. Responds in 6 months.

POETRY Ilium Press specializes in original, book-length narrative epic poems written in blank or sprung (non-rhyming) metered verse in contemporary language. "I'm looking for original work that shows how epic poetry is still relevant in today's world. Please query via e-mail if you have questions." Submit via e-mail (preferred) or via mail with first 20 pages.

ILLUSIO & BAQER

1827 W. Shannon Ave., Spokane WA **E-mail:** submissions@zharmae.com. **Website:** illusiobaqer.com. Illusio & Baqer publishes high quality middle grade, young adult, and new adult fiction of all genres. "We are a young adult, new adult, and middle grade imprint of The Zharmae Publishing Press." Accepts simultaneous submissions.

FICTION Query with synopsis and 3-5 sample chapters.

ILR PRESS

Cornell University Press, Sage House, 512 E. State St., Ithaca NY 14850. (607)277-2338. **Fax:** (607)277-2374. **E-mail:** fgb2@cornell.edu. **Website:** www.ilr.cornell.edu/ilrpress. **Contact:** Frances Benson, editorial director. Estab. 1945. Publishes hardcover and trade paperback originals and reprints. "We are interested in manuscripts with innovative perspectives on current workplace issues that concern both academics and the general public." **Publishes 10-15 titles/year. Pays royalty.** Responds in 2 months to queries. Book catalog available free.

NONFICTION Subjects include history, sociology. All titles relate to labor relations and/or workplace issues including relevant work in the fields of history, sociology, political science, economics, human resources, and organizational behavior. Special series: culture and politics of health care work. Query with SASE. Submit outline, sample chapters, CV.

TIPS "Manuscripts must be well documented to pass our editorial evaluation, which includes review by academics in related fields."

IMAGE COMICS

2001 Center St., 6th Floor, Berkeley CA 94704. **E-mail:** submissions@imagecomics.com. **Website:** www.imagecomics.com. **Contact:** Eric Stephenson, publisher. Estab. 1992. Publishes creator-owned comic books, graphic novels. See this company's website for detailed guidelines. Does not accept writing samples without art. Accepts simultaneous submissions.

FICTION Query with 1-page synopsis and 5 pages or more of samples. "We do not accept writing (that is plots, scripts, whatever) samples! If you're an established pro, we might be able to find somebody willing to work with you but it would be nearly impossible for us to read through every script that might find its way our direction. Do not send your script or your plot unaccompanied by art—it will be discarded, unread."

TIPS "We are not looking for any specific genre or type of comic book. We are looking for comics that are well written and well drawn, by people who are dedicated and can meet deadlines."

IMMEDIUM

P.O. Box 31846, San Francisco CA 94131. (415)452-8546. **Fax:** (360)937-6272. **Website:** www.immedium.com. Estab. 2005. Publishes hardcover and trade paperback originals. "Immedium focuses on publishing eye-catching children's picture books, Asian American topics, and contemporary arts, popular culture, and multicultural issues." **Publishes 4 titles/year. 50 queries received/year. 25 mss received/year. 50% of books from first-time authors. 90% from unagented writers. Pays 5% royalty on wholesale price. Pays on publication.** Publishes book 2 years after acceptance. Accepts simultaneous submissions. Responds in 1-3 months. Catalog online. Guidelines online.

NONFICTION Subjects include multicultural. Submit complete ms. Reviews artwork/photos. Send photocopies.

FICTION Subjects include comic books, picture books. Submit complete ms.

TIPS "Our audience is children and parents. Please visit our site."

IMMORTAL INK PUBLISHING

E-mail: immortalinkpublishing@gmail.com. **Website:** www.immortalinkpublishing.com. Immortal

Ink Publishing is open to most genres, but specifically wants literary fiction, women's fiction, crime/mystery/thriller, young adult, and dark and paranormal fiction that is original, character-based, and literary in flavor. Immortal Ink Publishing is currently closed to submissions. Accepts simultaneous submissions.

FICTION Submit query with first 10 pages via e-mail.

TIPS "Due to time constraints, we will not be giving reasons for our rejections (as you really shouldn't be making changes just because of something we personally didn't like anyway), but we will get back to you with either a 'no thanks' or a request for your full manuscript."

IMPACT BOOKS

F+W Media, Inc., 10151 Carver Rd., Suite 200, Blue Ash OH 45242. **Fax:** (513)531-2686. **E-mail:** mona.clough@fwcommunity.com. **Website:** www.northlightshop.com; www.impact-books.com. **Contact:** Mona Clough, content director (art instruction for fantasy, comics, manga, anime, popular culture, science fiction, cartooning and body art). Estab. 2004. Publishes trade paperback originals. **Publishes 9 titles/year. 50 queries received/year. 10-12 mss received/year. 70% of books from first-time authors. 80% from unagented writers.** 11 months Accepts simultaneous submissions. Responds in 4 months to queries. Responds in 4 months to proposals. Responds in 4 months to manuscripts. Visit website for booklist. Guidelines available at www.artistsnetwork.com/contactus.

IMPACT Books publishes titles that emphasize illustrated how-to-draw-manga, science-fiction, fantasy and comics art instruction. Currently emphasizing manga and anime art, science fiction, traditional American comics styles, including humor, and pop art. Looking for good science fiction art instruction. This market is for experienced artists who are willing to work with an IMPACT editor to produce a step-by-step how-to book about how to create the art and the artist's creative process. See also separate listing for F+W Media in this section.

NONFICTION Subjects include art, contemporary culture, creative nonfiction, hobbies. Via e-mail only. Submit proposal package, outline, 1 sample chapter, at least 20 examples of sample art. Reviews artwork/photos. Send digital art.

TIPS "Audience comprised primarily of 12- to 18-year-old beginners along the lines of comic buyers, in general—mostly teenagers—but also appealing to a broader audience of young adults 19-30 who need basic techniques. Art must appeal to teenagers and be submitted in a form that will reproduce well. Authors need to know how to teach beginners step-by-step. A sample step-by-step demonstration is important."

IMPACT PUBLISHERS, INC.

5674 Shattuck Ave., Oakland CA 94609. **E-mail:** proposals@newharbinger.com. **Website:** www.newharbinger.com/imprint/impact-publishers. Estab. 1970. "Our purpose is to make the best human services expertise available to the widest possible audience. We publish only popular psychology and self-help materials written in everyday language by professionals with advanced degrees and significant experience in the human services." **Publishes 3-5 titles/year. 20% of books from first-time authors. Pays authors royalty of 10-12%. Offers advances.** Accepts simultaneous submissions. Responds in 3 months. Book catalog for #10 SASE with 2 first-class stamps. Guidelines for SASE.

IMPRINTS Little Imp Books, Rebuilding Books, The Practical Therapist Series.

NONFICTION Young readers, middle readers, young adults: self-help. Query or submit complete ms, cover letter, résumé.

TIPS "Please do not submit fiction, poetry or narratives."

INCENTIVE PUBLICATIONS, INC.

233 N. Michigan Ave., Suite 2000, Chicago IL 60601. **E-mail:** incentive@worldbook.com. **Website:** www.incentivepublications.com. **Contact:** Paul Kobasa, editor-in-chief. Estab. 1970. Publishes paperback originals. "Incentive publishes developmentally appropriate teacher/school administrator/parent resource materials and supplementary instructional materials for children in grades K-12. Actively seeking proposals for student workbooks, all grades/all subjects, and professional development resources for pre K-12 classroom teachers and school administrators." **Publishes 10-15 titles/year. 25% of books from first-time authors. 100, but agent proposals welcome% from unagented writers. Pays royalty, or makes outright purchase.** an average of 1 year Accepts simultaneous submissions. Responds in 1 month to queries.

NONFICTION Subjects include education. Instructional, teacher/administrator professional development books in pre-K through 12th grade. Query with synopsis and detailed outline.

INDIANA HISTORICAL SOCIETY PRESS

450 W. Ohio St., Indianapolis IN 46202-3269. (317)233 6073. **Fax:** (317)233-0857. **E-mail:** ihspress@indianahistory.org. **Website:** www.indianahistory.org. **Contact:** Submissions Editor. Estab. 1830. Publishes hardcover and paperback originals. **Publishes 10 titles/year.** Accepts simultaneous submissions. Responds in 1 month to queries.

NONFICTION Subjects include agriculture, ethnic, history, sports, family history, children's books. All topics must relate to Indiana. "We seek book-length manuscripts that are solidly researched and engagingly written on topics related to Indiana: biography, history, literature, music, politics, transportation, sports, agriculture, architecture, and children's books." Query with SASE.

INFORMATION TODAY, INC.

143 Old Marlton Pike, Medford NJ 08055. (609)654-6266. **Fax:** (609)654-4309. **E-mail:** rcolding@infotoday.com. **Website:** www.infotoday.com. **Contact:** Rob Colding, Book Marketing Manager. Publishes hardcover and trade paperback originals. "We look for highly-focused coverage of cutting-edge technology topics. Written by established experts and targeted to a tech-savvy readership. Virtually all our titles focus on how information is accessed, used, shared, and transformed into knowledge that can benefit people, business, and society. Currently emphasizing Internet/online technologies, including their social significance: biography, how-to, technical, reference, scholarly. De-emphasizing fiction." **Publishes 15-20 titles/year. 200 queries received/year. 30 mss received/year. 30% of books from first-time authors. 90% from unagented writers. Pays 10-15% royalty on wholesale price. Pays $500-2,500 advance.** Publishes book 9 months after acceptance. Accepts simultaneous submissions. Responds in 1 month to queries; 2 months to proposals; 3 months to mss. Book catalog free or on website. Proposal guidelines free or via e-mail as attachment.

IMPRINTS ITI (academic, scholarly, library science); CyberAge Books (high-end consumer and business technology books-emphasis on Internet/WWW topics including online research).

NONFICTION Subjects include business, education, science, Internet and cyberculture. Query with SASE. Reviews artwork/photos. Send photocopies.

TIPS "Our readers include scholars, academics, educators, indexers, librarians, information professionals (ITI imprint), as well as high-end consumer and business users of Internet/WWW/online technologies, and people interested in the marriage of technology with issues of social significance (i.e., cyberculture)."

⊙ INSOMNIAC PRESS

520 Princess Ave., London ON N6B 2B8, Canada. (416)504-6270. **E-mail:** mike@insomniacpress.com. **Website:** www.insomniacpress.com. **Contact:** Mike O'Connor, publisher. Estab. 1992. Publishes trade paperback originals and reprints, mass market paperback originals, and electronic originals and reprints. **Publishes 20 titles/year. 250 queries received/year. 1,000 mss received/year. 50% of books from first-time authors. 80% from unagented writers. Pays 10-15% royalty on retail price. Pays $500-1,000 advance.** Publishes ms 6 months after acceptance. Accepts simultaneous submissions. Guidelines online.

NONFICTION Subjects include multicultural, religion, true crime. Very interested in areas such as true crime and well-written and well-researched nonfiction on topics of wide interest. Query via e-mail, submit proposal package including outline, 2 sample chapters, or submit complete ms. Reviews artwork/photos. Send photocopies.

FICTION Subjects include comic books, ethnic, experimental, humor, literary, mystery, poetry, suspense. "We publish a mix of commercial (mysteries) and literary fiction." Query via e-mail, submit proposal.

POETRY "Our poetry publishing is limited to 2-4 books per year and we are often booked up a year or two in advance." Submit complete ms.

TIPS "We envision a mixed readership that appreciates up-and-coming literary fiction and poetry as well as solidly researched and provocative nonfiction. Peruse our website and familiarize yourself with what we've published in the past."

INTERLINK PUBLISHING GROUP, INC.

46 Crosby St., Northampton MA 01060. (413)582-7054. **Fax:** (413)582-7057. **E-mail:** info@interlinkbooks.com. **Website:** www.interlinkbooks.com. Estab. 1987. Publishes hardcover and trade paperback originals. Interlink is an independent publisher of general

trade adult fiction and nonfiction with an emphasis on books that have a wide appeal while also meeting high intellectual and literary standards. **Publishes 90 titles/year. 30% of books from first-time authors. 50% from unagented writers. Pays 6-8% royalty on retail price. Pays small advance.** Publishes ms 18 months after acceptance. Accepts simultaneous submissions. Responds in 3-6 months to queries. Book catalog and guidelines online.

NONFICTION Submit outline and sample chapters.

FICTION Subjects include ethnic, international. "We are looking for translated works relating to the Middle East, Africa or Latin America." No science fiction, romance, plays, erotica, fantasy, horror. Query with SASE. Submit outline, sample chapters.

TIPS "Any submissions that fit well in our publishing program will receive careful attention. A visit to our website, your local bookstore, or library to look at some of our books before you send in your submission is recommended."

INTERNATIONAL FOUNDATION OF EMPLOYEE BENEFIT PLANS

18700 W. Bluemound Rd., Brookfield WI 53045. (262)786-6700. **Fax:** (262)786-8780. **Website:** www.if-ebp.org. Estab. 1954. Publishes trade paperback originals. IFEBP publishes general and technical monographs on all aspects of employee benefits—pension plans, health insurance, etc. **Publishes 6 titles/year. 15% of books from first-time authors. 80% from unagented writers. Pays 5-15% royalty on wholesale and retail price.** Publishes ms 1 year after acceptance. Accepts simultaneous submissions. Responds in 3 months to queries. Book catalog online. Guidelines online.

NONFICTION Subjects limited to health care, pensions, retirement planning and employee benefits and compensation. Query with outline.

TIPS "Be aware of interests of employers and the marketplace in benefits topics, for example, pension plan changes, healthcare cost containment."

INTERNATIONAL MARINE

The McGraw-Hill Companies, 90 Mechanic St., Camden ME 04843. (207)236-4838. **Fax:** (207)236-6314. **Website:** www.internationalmarine.com. **Contact:** Acquisitions Editor. Estab. 1969. Publishes hardcover and paperback originals. International Marine publishes the best books about boats. **Publishes 50 titles/year. 500-700 mss received/year. 30% of books from**

first-time authors. 60% from unagented writers. Pays standard royalties based on net price. Pays advance.** Publishes ms 1 year after acceptance. Accepts simultaneous submissions. Responds in 2 months to queries. Guidelines online.

IMPRINTS Ragged Mountain Press (sports and outdoor books that take you off the beaten path).

NONFICTION All books are illustrated. Material in all stages welcome. Publishes a wide range of subjects include: sea stories, seamanship, boat maintenance, etc. Query first with outline and 2-3 sample chapters. Reviews artwork/photos.

TIPS "Writers should be aware of the need for clarity, accuracy and interest. Many progress too far in the actual writing."

INTERNATIONAL PRESS

P.O. Box 502, Somerville MA 02143. (617)623-3855. **Fax:** (617)623-3101. **E-mail:** ipb-mgmt@intlpress.com. **Website:** www.intlpress.com. **Contact:** Brian Bianchini. Estab. 1992. Publishes hardcover originals and reprints. International Press of Boston, Inc. is an academic publishing company that welcomes book publication inquiries from prospective authors on all topics in Mathematics and Physics. International Press also publishes high-level mathematics and mathematical physics book titles and textbooks. **Publishes 12 titles/year. 200 queries received/year. 500 mss received/year. 10% of books from first-time authors. 100% from unagented writers. Pays 3-10% royalty.** Publishes ms 6 months after acceptance. Responds in 5 months to queries and proposals; 1 year to mss. Book catalog available free. Guidelines online.

NONFICTION Subjects include science. All our books will be in research mathematics. Authors need to provide ready to print latex files. Submit complete ms. Reviews artwork/photos. Send EPS files.

TIPS "Audience is PhD mathematicians, researchers and students."

INTERNATIONAL SOCIETY FOR TECHNOLOGY IN EDUCATION (ISTE)

180 W. 8th St., Suite 300, Eugene OR 97401. (541)434-8928. **E-mail:** iste@iste.org. **Website:** www.iste.org. Publishes trade paperback originals. "Currently emphasizing books on educational technology standards, curriculum integration, professional development, and assessment. De-emphasizing software how-to books." **Publishes 10 titles/year. 100 queries received/year. 40 mss received/year. 75% of books**

from first-time authors. **95% from unagented writers. Pays 10% royalty on retail price.** Publishes ms 6-9 months after acceptance. Accepts simultaneous submissions. Responds in 2 weeks to queries; 1 month to proposals and mss. Book catalog and guidelines online.

NONFICTION Submit proposal package, outline, sample chapters, TOC, vita. Reviews artwork/photos. Send photocopies.

TIPS "Our audience is K-12 teachers, teacher educators, technology coordinators, and school and district administrators."

INTERNATIONAL WEALTH SUCCESS

IWS, Inc., P.O. Box 186, Merrick NY 11570. (516)766-5850. **Fax:** (516)766-5919. **E-mail:** admin@iwsmoney. com. **Website:** www.iwsmoney.com. **Contact:** Tyler G. Hicks, President. Estab. 1966. International Wealth Success Inc. (IWS) is a full-service newsletter, book and self-study course publisher of print and digital media on small business and income real estate. The company's mission is to help beginning and experienced business people choose, start, finance, and succeed in their own small businesses. Topics include real estate investment, import-export, mail order, home-based business, marketing, fundraising, and financing. **Publishes 10 titles/year. Pays 10% royalty on wholesale or retail price.** Publishes ms 4 months after acceptance. Accepts simultaneous submissions. Responds within 1 month to queries.

NONFICTION Subjects include business, finance, real estate, private money, financial institutions, homebased business, marketing, export-import, grants and fundraising. Techniques, methods, sources for building wealth. Personal, how-to-do-it with case histories and examples. Publications are aimed at aspiring wealth builders and are sympathetic to their problems and challenges. Publications present a wide range of business opportunities while providing practical, hands-on, step-by-step instructions aimed at helping readers achieve their personal goals in as short a time as possible while adhering to ethical and professional business standards. Length: 60,000-70,000 words. Query. Reviews artwork/photos.

INTERVARSITY PRESS

P.O. Box 1400, Downers Grove IL 60515. **E-mail:** e-mail@ivpress.com. **Website:** www.ivpress.com/submissions. Estab. 1947. Publishes hardcover originals, trade paperback and mass market paperback originals. "InterVarsity Press publishes a full line of books from an evangelical Christian perspective targeted to an open-minded audience. We serve those in the university, the church, and the world, by publishing books from an evangelical Christian perspective." **Publishes 115 titles/year. 1,000 queries; 900 mss received/year. 13% of books from first-time authors. 80% from unagented writers. Pays 14-16% royalty on retail price. Outright purchase is $75-1,500. Pays negotiable advance.** Publishes book 18 months after acceptance. Accepts simultaneous submissions. "We are unable to provide updates on the review process or personalized responses to unsolicited proposals. We regret that submissions will not be returned.". Book catalog online. Guidelines online.

IMPRINTS IVP Academic; IVP Connect; IVP Books.

NONFICTION Subjects include business, child guidance, contemporary culture, economics, ethnic, history, multicultural, philosophy, psychology, religion, science, social sciences, sociology, spirituality. "InterVarsity Press publishes a full line of books from an evangelical Christian perspective targeted to an open-minded audience. We serve those in the university, the church, and the world, by publishing books from an evangelical Christian perspective." "We review The Writer's Edge at writersedgeservice.com." Does not review artwork.

TIPS "The best way to submit to us is to go to a conference where one of our editors is attending. Networking is key. We are seeking writers who have good ideas and a presence/platform where they have been testing out their ideas (a church, university, on a prominent blog). We need authors who will bring resources to the table for helping to publicize and sell their books (speaking at seminars and conferences, writing for national magazines or newspapers, etc.)."

INTERWEAVE PRESS

201 E. Fourth St., Loveland CO 80537. (970)669-7672. **Fax:** (970)667-8317. **E-mail:** Kerry.bogert@fwcommunity.com. **Website:** www.interweave.com. **Contact:** Kerry Bogert, Editorial Director. Estab. 1975. Publishes hardcover and trade paperback originals. Interweave Press publishes instructive titles relating to the fiber arts and beadwork topics. **Publishes 40-45 titles/year. 60% of books from first-time authors. 90% from unagented writers.** Publishes ms 6-18 months after acceptance. Accepts simultaneous

submissions. Responds in 2 months to queries. Book catalog and guidelines online.

NONFICTION Subjects include crafts, hobbies. Subjects limited to fiber arts (spinning, knitting, dyeing, weaving, sewing/stiching, art quilting, mixed media/collage) and jewelry making (beadwork, stringing, wireworking, metalsmithing). Submit outline, sample chapters. Accepts simultaneous submissions if informed of non-exclusivity. Reviews artwork/photos.

TIPS "We are looking for very clear, informally written, technically correct manuscripts, generally of a how-to nature, in our specific fiber and beadwork fields only. Our audience includes a variety of creative self-starters who appreciate inspiration and clear instruction. They are often well educated and skillful in many areas."

INVERTED-A

P.O. Box 267, Licking MO 65542. **E-mail:** amnfn@well.com. **Contact:** Aya Katz, chief editor (poetry, novels, political); Nets Katz, science editor (scientific, academic). Estab. 1985. Publishes paperback originals. Books: POD. Distributes through Amazon, Bowker, Barnes Noble. **Pays 10 author's copies.** Publishes ms 1 year after acceptance. Accepts simultaneous submissions. Responds in 1 month to queries; 3 months to mss. Guidelines for SASE.

NONFICTION Subjects include Americana, politics, stage, translation.

FICTION Subjects include historical, picture books, translation, war, young adult, Utopian, political. Does not accept unsolicited mss. Query with SASE. Reading period open from January 2 to March 15. Accepts queries by e-mail. Include estimated word count.

TIPS "Read our books. Read the *Inverted-A Horn*. We are different. We do not follow industry trends."

♥ IRISH ACADEMIC PRESS

8 Chapel Ln., Sallins Co. Kildare , Ireland. (353) (45)895562. **E-mail:** info@iap.ie. **E-mail:** conor.graham@iap.ie. **Website:** www.iap.ie. **Contact:** Conor Graham. Estab. 1974. Publishes nonfiction. **Publishes 10 titles/year. Pays royalty.** Accepts simultaneous submissions. Guidelines online.

IMPRINTS Merrion Press.

NONFICTION Subjects include history, literary criticism, genealogy, Irish history. Does not want fiction or poetry.

IRON GATE PUBLISHING

P.O. Box 999, Niwot CO 80544. (303)530-2551. **Fax:** (303)530-5273. **E-mail:** editor@irongate.com. **Website:** www.irongate.com. **Contact:** Dina C. Carson, publisher (how-to, genealogy, local history). Publishes hardcover and trade paperback originals. "Our readers are people who are looking for solid, how-to advice on self-publishing a family or local history, or who are conducting genealogical or local history research in Colorado." **Publishes 20-30 titles/year. 100 queries; 20 mss received/year. 30% of books from first-time authors. 10% from unagented writers. Pays royalty on a case-by-case basis.** Publishes book 6 months after acceptance. Accepts simultaneous submissions. Responds in 2 months to proposals. Book catalog and writer's guidelines free or online.

NONFICTION Subjects include history, genealogy, local history. Query with SASE, or submit proposal package, including outline, 2 sample chapters, and marketing summary. Reviews artwork/photos. Send photocopies.

TIPS "Please look at the other books we publish and tell us in your query letter why your book would fit into our line of books."

ITALICA PRESS

595 Main St., Suite 605, New York NY 10044-0047. (917)371-0563. **E-mail:** inquiries@italicapress.com. **Website:** www.italicapress.com. **Contact:** Ronald G. Musto and Eileen Gardiner, publishers. Estab. 1985. Publishes hardcover and trade paperback originals. "Italica Press publishes English translations of modern Italian fiction and medieval and Renaissance nonfiction." **Publishes 6 titles/year. 600 queries; 60 mss received/year. 5% of books from first-time authors. 100% from unagented writers. Pays 7-15% royalty on wholesale price; author's copies.** Publishes ms 1 year after acceptance. Accepts simultaneous submissions. Responds in 1 month to queries; 4 months to mss. Book catalog and guidelines online.

NONFICTION Subjects include translation. "We publish English translations of medieval and Renaissance source materials and English translations of modern Italian fiction." Query via e-mail. Reviews artwork/photos.

FICTION "First-time translators published. We would like to see translations of Italian writers who are well-known in Italy who are not yet translated for an American audience." Query via e-mail.

POETRY Poetry titles are always translations and generally dual language. Query with 10 sample translations of medieval and Renaissance Italian poets. Include cover letter, bio, and list of publications.

TIPS "We are interested in considering a wide variety of medieval and Renaissance topics (not historical fiction), and for modern works we are only interested in translations from Italian fiction by well-known Italian authors. *Only* fiction that has been previously published in Italian. A *brief* e-mail saves a lot of time. 90% of proposals we receive are completely off base—but we are very interested in things that are right on target."

JAIN PUBLISHING CO.

P.O. Box 3523, Fremont CA 94539. (510)659-8272. **Fax:** (510)659-0501. **E-mail:** mail@jainpub.com. **Website:** www.jainpub.com. **Contact:** Mukesh Jain, editor-in-chief. Estab. 1989. Publishes hardcover and paperback originals and reprints. Jain Publishing Co. is a humanities and social sciences publisher that publishes academic and scholarly references, as well as books for the general reader in both print and electronic formats. A substantial part of its publishing program pertains to books dealing with Asia, commonly categorized as "Asian Studies." **Publishes 6-8 titles/year. 300 queries received/year. 100% from unagented writers. Pays 5-10% royalty on net sales.** Publishes ms 1-2 years after acceptance. Accepts simultaneous submissions. Responds in 3 months to mss. Book catalog and ms guidelines online.

NONFICTION Subjects include cinema, environment, film, humanities, multicultural, philosophy, psychology, religion, social sciences, spirituality, Asian studies. Submit proposal package, publishing history. Reviews artwork/photos. Send photocopies.

ALICE JAMES BOOKS

114 Prescott St., Farmington ME 04938. (207)778-7071. **Fax:** (207)778-7766. **E-mail:** info@alicejamesbooks.org. **Website:** www.alicejamesbooks.org. **Contact:** Carey Salerno, executive director. Estab. 1973. Publishes trade paperback originals. "Alice James Books is a nonprofit cooperative poetry press. The founders' objectives were to give women access to publishing and to involve authors in the publishing process. The cooperative selects mss for publication through both regional and national competitions." **Publishes 6 titles/year. Approximately 1,000 mss received/year. 50% of books from first-time au-** thors. **100% from unagented writers. Pays through competition awards.** Publishes ms 1 year after acceptance. Accepts simultaneous submissions. Responds promptly to queries; 4 months to mss. Book catalog online. Guidelines online.

POETRY "Alice James Books is a nonprofit cooperative poetry press. The founders' objectives were to give women access to publishing and to involve authors in the publishing process. The cooperative selects mss for publication through both regional and national competitions." Does not want children's poetry or light verse.

TIPS "Send SASE for contest guidelines or check website. Do not send work without consulting current guidelines."

JEWISH LIGHTS PUBLISHING

LongHill Partners, Inc., Sunset Farm Offices, Rt. 4, P.O. Box 237, Woodstock VT 05091. (802)457-4000. **Fax:** (802)457-4004. **E-mail:** editorial@jewishlights.com; sales@jewishlights.com. **Website:** www.jewishlights.com. **Contact:** Acquisitions Editor. Estab. 1990. Publishes hardcover and trade paperback originals, trade paperback reprints. "Jewish Lights publishes books for people of all faiths and all backgrounds who yearn for books that attract, engage, educate and spiritually inspire. Our authors are at the forefront of spiritual thought and deal with the quest for the self and for meaning in life by drawing on the Jewish wisdom tradition. Our books cover topics including history, spirituality, life cycle, children, self-help, recovery, theology and philosophy. We do not publish autobiography, biography, fiction, haggadot, poetry or cookbooks. At this point we plan to do only two books for children annually, and one will be for younger children (ages 4-10)." **Publishes 30 titles/year. 50% of books from first-time authors. 75% from unagented writers. Pays authors royalty of 10% of revenue received; 15% royalty for subsequent printings.** Publishes ms 1 year after acceptance. Accepts simultaneous submissions. Responds in 6 months to queries. Book catalog and guidelines online.

NONFICTION Subjects include history, philosophy, religion, spirituality. Picture book, young readers, middle readers: activity books, spirituality. "We do *not* publish haggadot, biography, poetry, memoirs, or cookbooks." Query. Reviews artwork/photos. Send photocopies.

FICTION Picture books, young readers, middle readers: spirituality. "We are not interested in anything other than spirituality." Query with outline/synopsis and 2 sample chapters; submit complete ms for picture books.

TIPS "We publish books for all faiths and backgrounds that also reflect the Jewish wisdom tradition. Explain in your cover letter why you're submitting your project to us in particular. Make sure you know what we publish."

JIST PUBLISHING

875 Montreal Way, St. Paul MN 55102. **E-mail:** educate@emcp.com. **Website:** www.jist.emcp.com. Estab. 1981. Publishes hardcover and trade paperback originals. "Our purpose is to provide quality job search, career development, occupational, and life skills information, products, and services that help people manage and improve their lives and careers-and the lives of others. Publishes practical, self-directed tools and training materials that are used in employment and training, education, and business settings. Whether reference books, trade books, assessment tools, workbooks, or videos, JIST products foster self-directed job-search attitudes and behaviors." **Publishes 60 titles/year. Receives 40 submissions/year. 25% of books from first-time authors. 75% from unagented writers. Pays 8-10% royalty on net receipts.** Accepts simultaneous submissions. Responds in 6 months. Book catalog and guidelines online.

NONFICTION Subjects include business, economics, education. "We want text/workbook formats that would be useful in a school or other institutional setting. We also publish trade titles for all reading levels. Will consider books for professional staff and educators, appropriate software and videos." Submit proposal package, including outline, 1 sample chapter, and author resume, competitive analysis, marketing ideas. Does not review artwork/photos.

TIPS "Our audiences are students, job seekers, and career changers of all ages and occupations who want to find good jobs quickly and improve their futures. We sell materials through the trade as well as to institutional markets like schools, colleges, and one-stop career centers."

THE JOHNS HOPKINS UNIVERSITY PRESS

2715 N. Charles St., Baltimore MD 21218. (410)516-6900. **Fax:** (410)516-6968. **Website:** www.press.jhu.edu. **Contact:** Jacqueline C. Wehmueller, executive editor (consumer health, psychology and psychiatry, and history of medicine; jcw@press.jhu.edu); Matthew McAdam, editor (mxm@jhu.press.edu); Robert J. Brugger, senior acquisitions editor (American history; rjb@press.jhu.edu); Vincent J. Burke, exec. editor (biology; vjb@press.jhu.edu). Estab. 1878. Publishes hardcover originals and reprints, and trade paperback reprints. **Publishes 140 titles/year. Pays royalty.** Publishes ms 1 year after acceptance. Accepts simultaneous submissions.

NONFICTION Subjects include history, humanities, literary criticism, regional, religion, science. Submit proposal package, outline, 1 sample chapter, CV. Reviews artwork/photos. Send photocopies.

POETRY "One of the largest American university presses, Johns Hopkins publishes primarily scholarly books and journals. We do, however, publish short fiction and poetry in the series Johns Hopkins: Poetry and Fiction, edited by John Irwin."

JOHNSON BOOKS

Imprint of Big Earth Publishing, 3005 Center Green Dr., Suite 225, Boulder CO 80301. (303)443-9766. **Fax:** (303)443-9687. **E-mail:** books@bigearthpublishing.com. **Website:** bigearthpublishing.com/johnson-books. Estab. 1979. Publishes hardcover and paperback originals and reprints. Johnson Books specializes in books on the American West, primarily outdoor, useful titles that will have strong national appeal. **Publishes 20-25 titles/year. 30% of books from first-time authors. 90% from unagented writers. Royalties vary.** Publishes ms 1 year after acceptance. Accepts simultaneous submissions. Responds in 4 months to queries. Book catalog for 9 x 12 SAE with 5 first-class stamps. Guidelines available.

NONFICTION Subjects include history, recreation, regional, science, travel, general nonfiction. "We are primarily interested in books for the informed popular market, though we will consider vividly written scholarly works. Looks for good writing, thorough research, professional presentation, and appropriate style. Marketing suggestions from writers are helpful." Submit outline/synopsis, 3 sample chapters and a author bio.

JOLLY FISH PRESS

P.O. Box 1773, Provo UT 84603. **E-mail:** submit@jollyfishpress.com. **Website:** jollyfishpress.com. **Publishes 17 titles/year. 600 70% of books from first-time authors. 70% from unagented writers. Does** not pay advance. Publishes ms 2 years after acceptance. Accepts simultaneous submissions. Guidelines online.

NONFICTION Nonfiction mss do not have to be completed, but the status of the ms should be noted. Submit query and proposal.

FICTION "We accept literary fiction, fantasy, sci-fi, mystery, suspense, horror, thriller, children's literature, young adult, trade." Submit query with synopsis and first 3 chapters.

JOSSEY-BASS

John Wiley & Sons, Inc., One Montgomery St., Suite 1200, San Francisco CA 94104. **Website:** www.wiley.com. Jossey-Bass is an imprint of Wiley, specializing in books and periodicals for thoughtful professionals and researchers in the areas of business and management, leadership, human resource development, education, health, psychology, religion, and the public and nonprofit sectors. **Publishes 250 titles/year. Pays variable royalties. Pays occasional advance.** Publishes ms 1 year after acceptance. Accepts simultaneous submissions. Responds in 2-3 months to queries. Guidelines online.

NONFICTION Subjects include education, psychology, religion. Jossey-Bass publishes first-time and unagented authors. Publishes books on topics of interest to a wide range of readers: business and management, conflict resolution, mediation and negotiation, K-12 education, higher and adult education, healthcare management, psychology/behavioral healthcare, nonprofit and public management, religion, human resources and training. Also publishes 25 periodicals. See guidelines online.

JOURNEYFORTH

Imprint of BJU Press, 1700 Wade Hampton Blvd., Greenville SC 29614. (864)770-1317
800-845-5731. **Fax:** (864)271-8151
800-525-8398. **E-mail:** journeyforth@bjupress.com. **Website:** www.journeyforth.com. Estab. 1974. Publishes paperback originals. "Small independent publisher of trustworthy novels and biographies for readers in primary school through high school from a conservative Christian perspective as well as Christian living books and Bible studies for teens and adults." **Publishes 12 titles/year. 400+ 4% of books from first-time authors. 4% from unagented writers. Pays royalty.** Publishes book 12-18 months after acceptance. Accepts simultaneous submissions. Re-

sponds in 1 month to queries; 3 months to mss. Book catalog available free or online. Guidelines online.

NONFICTION Subjects include animals, contemporary culture, creative nonfiction, environment, history, music, nature, religion, spirituality, sports, young adult. Christian living, Bible studies, church and ministry, church history. "We produce books for the adult Christian market that are from a conservative Christian worldview."

FICTION Subjects include adventure, hi-lo, historical, juvenile, mystery, sports, western, young adult. "Our fiction is all based on a Christian worldview." Does not want short stories. Submit 5 sample chapters, synopsis, market analysis of competing works.

TIPS "Study the publisher's guidelines. No picture books. Fiction for the youth market only."

JUDAICA PRESS

123 Ditmas Ave., Brooklyn NY 11218. (718)972-6200. **Fax:** (718)972-6204. **E-mail:** submissions@judaicapress.com. **Website:** www.judaicapress.com. Estab. 1963. Publishes hardcover and trade paperback originals and reprints. "We cater to the Orthodox Jewish market." **Publishes 12 titles/year.** Accepts simultaneous submissions. Responds in 3 months to queries. Book catalog in print and online.

NONFICTION Subjects include religion, prayer, holidays, life cycle. Looking for Orthodox Judaica in all genres. Submit ms with SASE.

JUDSON PRESS

P.O. Box 851, Valley Forge PA 19482. (610)768-2127. **Fax:** (610)768-2441. **E-mail:** acquisitions@judsonpress.com. **Website:** www.judsonpress.com. Estab. 1824. Publishes hardcover and paperback originals. "Our audience is comprised primarily of pastors, leaders, and Christians who seek a more fulfilling personal spiritual life and want to serve God in their churches, communities, and relationships. We have a large African American and multicultural readership. Currently emphasizing Baptist identity and small group resources. Not accepting biography, memoir, children's books, poetry." **Publishes 10-12 titles/year. 500 queries received/year. 50% of books from first-time authors. 85% from unagented writers. Pays royalty or makes outright purchase.** Publishes ms 12-18 months after acceptance. Accepts simultaneous submissions. Responds in 3-6 months to queries. Catalog online. Guidelines online.

NONFICTION Subjects include community, multicultural, parenting, religion, spirituality, womens issues. Adult religious nonfiction of 30,000-80,000 words. Does not want biography, autobiography, memoir. Query by e-mail or mail. Submit annotated outline, sample chapters, CV, competing titles, marketing plan.

TIPS "Writers have the best chance selling us practical books assisting clergy or laypersons in their ministry and personal lives. Our audience consists of Protestant church leaders and members. Be informed about the market's needs and related titles. Be clear about your audience, and be practical in your focus. Books on multicultural issues are very welcome. Also seeking books that respond to real (felt) needs of pastors and churches."

⊘ JUPITER GARDENS PRESS

Jupiter Gardens, LLC, P.O. Box 191, Grimes IA 50111. **Website:** www.jupitergardens.com. **Contact:** Mary Wilson, publisher. Estab. 2007. Format publishes in trade paperback originals and reprints; electronic originals and reprints. **Publishes 30+ titles/year. Pays 40% royalty on retail price.** Publishes ms 4 months after acceptance. Accepts simultaneous submissions. Responds in 1 month on proposals; 2 months on mss. Catalog online. Guidelines online.

NONFICTION Subjects include alternative lifestyles, animals, astrology, environment, gay, health, lesbian, medicine, nature, psychic, religion, sex, spirituality, womens issues, world affairs, young adult, romance, science fiction, fantasy, and metaphysical fiction & nonfiction. "We only publish metaphysical/New Age nonfiction, or nonfiction related to science fiction and fantasy." Use online form. Currently closed to submissions.

FICTION Subjects include fantasy, gay, lesbian, occult, religious, romance, science fiction, spiritual. "We only publish romance (all sub-genres), science fiction & fantasy & metaphysical fiction. Our science fiction and fantasy covers a wide variety of topics, such as feminist fantasy, or more hard science fiction and fantasy which looks at the human condition. Our young adult imprint, Jupiter Storm, with thought provoking reads that explore the full range of speculative fiction, includes science fiction or fantasy and metaphysical fiction. These readers would enjoy edgy contemporary works. Our romance readers love seeing a couple, no matter the gender, overcome obstacles and grow in order to find true love. Like our readers, we believe that love can come in many forms." Use online submission form. Currently closed to submissions.

TIPS "No matter which line you're submitting to, know your genre and your readership. We publish a diverse catalog, and we're passionate about our main focus. We want romance that takes your breath away and leaves you with that warm feeling that love does conquer all. Our science fiction takes place in wild and alien worlds, and our fantasy transports readers to mythical realms and finds strange worlds within our own. And our metaphysical nonfiction will help readers gain new skills and awareness for the coming age. We want authors who engage with their readers and who aren't afraid to use social media to connect. Read and follow our submission guidelines."

JUST US BOOKS, INC.

P.O. Box 5306, East Orange NJ 07019. (973)672-7701. **Fax:** (973)677-7570. **Website:** justusbooks.com. Estab. 1988. "Just Us Books is the nation's premier independent publisher of Black-interest books for young people. Our books focus primarily on the culture, history, and contemporary experiences of African Americans." Accepts simultaneous submissions. Guidelines online.

IMPRINTS Marimba Books.

NONFICTION Query with synopsis and 3-5 sample pages.

FICTION Subjects include juvenile. Just Us Books is currently accepting queries for chapter books and middle reader titles only. "We are not considering any other works at this time."

TIPS "We are looking for realistic, contemporary characters; stories and interesting plots that introduce both conflict and resolution. We will consider various themes and story-lines, but before an author submits a query we urge them to become familiar with our books."

KAEDEN BOOKS

P.O. Box 16190, Rocky River OH 44116. **Website:** www.kaeden.com. Estab. 1986. Publishes paperback originals. "Children's book publisher for education K-3 market: reading stories, fiction/nonfiction, chapter books, science, and social studies materials." **Publishes 12-20 titles/year. 1,000 mss received/year. 30% of books from first-time authors. 95% from unagented writers. Work purchased outright from au-**

thors. **Pays royalties to previous authors.** Publishes ms 6-9 months after acceptance. Accepts simultaneous submissions. Responds only if interested. Book catalog and guidelines online.

NONFICTION Subjects include animals, creative nonfiction, science, social sciences. Mss should have interesting topics and information presented in language comprehensible to young students. Content should be supported with details and accurate facts. Submit complete ms. "Can be as minimal as 25 words for the earliest reader or as much as 2,000 words for the fluent reader. Beginning chapter books are welcome. Our readers are in kindergarten to third grade, so vocabulary and sentence structure must be appropriate for young readers. Make sure that all language used in the story is of an appropriate level for the students to read independently. Sentences should be complete and grammatically correct." Reviews artwork/photos. Send photocopies.

FICTION Subjects include adventure, fantasy, historical, humor, mystery, short story collections, sports, suspense. "We are looking for stories with humor, surprise endings, and interesting characters that will appeal to children in kindergarten through third grade." No sentence fragments. Please do not submit: queries, ms summaries, or résumés, mss that stereotype or demean individuals or groups, mss that present violence as acceptable behavior. Submit complete ms. "Can be as minimal as 25 words for the earliest reader or as much as 2,000 words for the fluent reader. Beginning chapter books are welcome. Our readers are in kindergarten to third grade, so vocabulary and sentence structure must be appropriate for young readers. Make sure that all language used in the story is of an appropriate level for the students to read independently. Sentences should be complete and grammatically correct."

TIPS "Our audience ranges from kindergarten-third grade school children. We are an educational publisher. We are particularly interested in humorous stories with surprise endings and beginning chapter books."

KALMBACH PUBLISHING CO.

21027 Crossroads Circle, P.O. Box 1612, Waukesha WI 53186. (262)796-8776. **Fax:** (262)798-6468. **Website:** www.kalmbach.com. Estab. 1934. Publishes paperback originals and reprints. **Publishes 40-50 titles/ year. 50% of books from first-time authors. 99% from unagented writers. Pays 7% royalty on net re-** ceipts. **Pays $1,500 advance.** Publishes ms 18 months after acceptance. Accepts simultaneous submissions. Responds in 2 months to queries.

NONFICTION "Focus on beading, wirework, and one-of-a-kind artisan creations for jewelry-making and crafts and in the railfan, model railroading, plastic modeling and toy train collecting/operating hobbies. Kalmbach publishes reference materials and how-to publications for hobbyists, jewelry-makers, and crafters." Query with 2-3 page detailed outline, sample chapter with photos, drawings, and how-to text. Reviews artwork/photos.

TIPS "Our how-to books are highly visual in their presentation. Any author who wants to publish with us must be able to furnish good photographs and rough drawings before we'll consider his or her book."

◑ KANE/MILLER BOOK PUBLISHERS

4901 Morena Blvd., Suite 213, San Diego CA 92117. (858)456-0540. **Fax:** (858)456-9641. **E-mail:** submissions@kanemiller.com. **Website:** www.kanemiller.com. **Contact:** Editorial Department. Estab. 1985. "Kane/Miller Book Publishers is a division of EDC Publishing, specializing in award-winning children's books from around the world. Our books bring the children of the world closer to each other, sharing stories and ideas, while exploring cultural differences and similarities. Although we continue to look for books from other countries, we are now actively seeking works that convey cultures and communities within the US. We are committed to expanding our picture book list and are interested in great stories with engaging characters, especially those with particularly American subjects. When writing about the experiences of a particular community, we will express a preference for stories written from a firsthand experience." Submission guidelines on site. Accepts simultaneous submissions. If interested, responds in 90 days to queries.

NONFICTION Subjects include Americana, history, sports, young adult.

FICTION Subjects include adventure, fantasy, historical, juvenile, multicultural, mystery, picture books. Picture Books: concept, contemporary, health, humor, multicultural. Young Readers: contemporary, multicultural, suspense. Middle Readers: contemporary, humor, multicultural, suspense. "At this time, we are not considering holiday stories (in any age range) or self-published works."

TIPS "We like to think that a child reading a Kane/Miller book will see parallels between his own life and what might be the unfamiliar setting and characters of the story. And that by seeing how a character who is somehow or in some way dissimilar—an outsider—finds a way to fit comfortably into a culture or community or situation while maintaining a healthy sense of self and self-dignity, she might be empowered to do the same."

KAR-BEN PUBLISHING

Lerner Publishing Group, 241 First Ave. N, Minneapolis MN 55401. (612)215-6229. **E-mail:** editorial@karben.com. **Website:** www.karben.com. Estab. 1974. Publishes hardcover, trade paperback and electronic originals. Kar-Ben publishes exclusively children's books on Jewish themes. **Publishes 20 titles/year. 800 mss received/year. 20% of books from first-time authors. 70% from unagented writers. Pays 5% royalty on NET sale. Pays $500-2,500 advance.** Most mss published within 2 years. Accepts simultaneous submissions. Responds in 6 weeks. Book catalog online; free upon request. Guidelines online.

NONFICTION Subjects include religion. "In addition to traditional Jewish-themed stories about Jewish holidays, history, folktales and other subjects, we especially seek stories that reflect the rich diversity of the contemporary Jewish community." Picture books, young readers: activity books, arts/crafts, biography, careers, concept, cooking, history, how-to, multicultural, religion, social issues, special needs; must be of Jewish interest. No textbooks, games, or educational materials. Submit completed ms. Reviews artwork separately. Works with 10-12 illustrators/year. Prefers four-color art in any medium that is scannable. Reviews illustration packages from artists. Submit sample of art or online portfolio (no originals).

FICTION "We seek picture book mss 800-1,000 words on Jewish-themed topics for children." Picture books: Adventure, concept, folktales, history, humor, multicultural, religion, special needs; must be on a Jewish theme. Average word length: picture books–1,000. Recently published titles: *The Count's Hanukkah Countdown*, *Sammy Spider's First Book of Jewish Holidays*, *The Cats of Ben Yehuda Street*. Submit full ms. Picture books only.

TIPS "Authors: Do a literature search to make sure similar title doesn't already exist. Illustrators: Look at our online catalog for a sense of what we like—bright colors and lively composition."

🅰 ⊘ KATHERINE TEGEN BOOKS

HarperCollins, 10 E. 53rd St., New York NY 10022. **Website:** www.harpercollins.com. **Contact:** Katherine Tegen, vice-president and publisher. Estab. 2003. Katherine Tegen Books publishes high-quality, commercial literature for children of all ages, including teens. Talented authors and illustrators who offer powerful narratives that are thought-provoking, well-written, and entertaining are the core of the Katherine Tegen Books imprint. *Katherine Tegen Books accepts agented work only.*

KAYA PRESS

c/o USC ASE, 3620 S. Vermont Ave. KAP 462, Los Angeles CA 90089. (213) 740-2285. **E-mail:** info@kaya.com. **Website:** www.kaya.com. **Contact:** Sunyoung Lee, editor. Estab. 1994. Publishes hardcover originals and trade paperback originals and reprints. Kaya is an independent literary press dedicated to the publication of innovative literature from the Asian Pacific diaspora. Accepts simultaneous submissions. Responds in 6 months to mss. Book catalog available free. Guidelines online.

NONFICTION Subjects include multicultural. Submit proposal package, outline, sample chapters, previous publications, SASE. Reviews artwork/photos. Send photocopies.

FICTION Submit 2-4 sample chapters, clips, SASE.

POETRY Submit complete ms.

TIPS "Audience is people interested in a high standard of literature and who are interested in breaking down easy approaches to multicultural literature."

KELSEY STREET PRESS

Poetry by Women, 2824 Kelsey St., Berkeley CA 94705. **E-mail:** info@kelseyst.com. **Website:** www.kelseyst.com. Estab. 1974. Hardcover and trade paperback originals and electronic originals. "A Berkeley, California press publishing collaborations between women poets and artists. Many of the press's collaborations focus on a central theme or conceit, like the sprawl and spectacle of New York in *Arcade* by Erica Hunt and Alison Saar." Accepts simultaneous submissions.

FICTION Subjects include experimental, horror, multicultural, mystery, poetry, prose, women of color.

POETRY Query.

KENSINGTON PUBLISHING CORP.

119 W. 40th St., New York NY 10018. (212)407-1500. **Fax:** (212)935-0699. **E-mail:** jscognamiglio@kensingtonbooks.com. **Website:** www.kensingtonbooks.com. **Contact:** John Scognamiglio, editorial director, fiction (historical romance, Regency romance, women's contemporary fiction, gay and lesbian fiction and nonfiction, mysteries, suspense, mainstream fiction); Michaela Hamilton, editor-in-chief, Citadel Press (thrillers, mysteries, mainstream fiction, true crime, current events); Selena James, executive editor, Dafina Books (African American fiction and nonfiction, inspirational, young adult, romance); Peter Senftleben, assistant editor (mainstream fiction, women's contemporary fiction, gay and lesbian fiction, mysteries, suspense, thrillers, romantic suspense, paranormal romance). Estab. 1975. Publishes hardcover and trade paperback originals, mass market paperback originals and reprints. "Kensington focuses on profitable niches and uses aggressive marketing techniques to support its books." **Publishes over 500 titles/year. 5,000 queries received/year. 2,000 mss received/year. 10% of books from first-time authors. Pays 6-15% royalty on retail price. Makes outright purchase. Pays $2,000 and up advance.** Publishes ms 9-12 months after acceptance. Accepts simultaneous submissions. Responds in 1 month to queries and proposals; 4 months to mss. Book catalog and guidelines online.

NONFICTION Subjects include Americana, animals, child guidance, contemporary culture, history, hobbies, memoirs, multicultural, philosophy, psychology, recreation, regional, sex, sports, travel, true crime, pop culture. Query.

FICTION Subjects include ethnic, historical, horror, mainstream, multicultural, mystery, occult, romance, suspense, western, thrillers, women's. No science fiction/fantasy, experimental fiction, business texts or children's titles. Query.

TIPS "Agented submissions only, except for submissions to romance lines. For those lines, query with SASE or submit proposal package including 3 sample chapters, synopsis."

KENT STATE UNIVERSITY PRESS

P.O. Box 5190, 1118 University Library, Kent OH 44242. **Fax:** (330)672-3104. **E-mail:** ksupress@kent.edu. **Website:** www.kentstateuniversitypress.com. **Contact:** Joyce Harrison, acquiring editor. Estab. 1965. Publishes hardcover and paperback originals and some reprints. "Kent State publishes primarily scholarly works and titles of regional interest. Currently emphasizing US history, US literary criticism." **Publishes 30-35 titles/year. Non-author subsidy publishes 20% of books. Standard minimum book contract on net sales.** Accepts simultaneous submissions. Responds in 4 months to queries. Book catalog available free.

NONFICTION Subjects include history, literary criticism, regional, true crime, literary criticism, material culture, textile/fashion studies, US foreign relations.. "Especially interested in scholarly works in history (US and world) and US literary studies of high quality, any titles of regional interest for Ohio, scholarly biographies and general nonfiction. Send a letter of inquiry before submitting mss. Decisions based on in-house readings and 2 by outside scholars in the field of study." Please, no faxes, phone calls, or e-mail submissions.

KIDS CAN PRESS

25 Dockside Dr., Toronto ON M5A 0B5, Canada. (416)479-7000. **Fax:** (416)960-5437. **Website:** www.kidscanpress.com. **Contact:** Corus Quay, acquisitions. Estab. 1973. Publishes book 18-24 months after acceptance. Accepts simultaneous submissions. Responds in 6 months only if interested.

Kids Can Press is currently accepting unsolicited mss from Canadian adult authors only.

NONFICTION Picture books: activity books, animal, arts/crafts, biography, careers, concept, health, history, hobbies, how-to, multicultural, nature/environment, science, social issues, special needs, sports. Young readers: activity books, animal, arts/crafts, biography, careers, concept, history, hobbies, how-to, multicultural. Middle readers: cooking, music/dance. Average word length: picture books 500-1,250; young readers 750-2,000; middle readers 5,000-15,000.

FICTION Picture books, young readers: concepts. "We do not accept young adult fiction or fantasy novels for any age." Adventure, animal, contemporary, folktales, history, humor, multicultural, nature/environment, special needs, sports, suspense/mystery. Average word length: picture books 1,000-2,000; young readers 750-1,500; middle readers 10,000-15,000; young adults over 15,000. Submit outline/synopsis and 2-3 sample chapters. For picture books submit complete ms.

KIRKBRIDE BIBLE CO., INC.

1102 Deloss St., Indianapolis IN 46203. (800)428-4385. **Fax:** (317)633-1444. **E-mail:** info@kirkbride.com. **Website:** www.kirkbride.com. Estab. 1915. Publishes Thompson Chain-Reference Bible hardcover originals and quality leather bindings styles and translations of the Bible. Types of books include reference and religious. Specializes in reference and study material. Accepts simultaneous submissions.

DENIS KITCHEN PUBLISHING CO., LLC

P.O. Box 2250, Amherst MA 01004. (413)259-1627. **Fax:** (413)259-1812. **E-mail:** help@deniskitchen. com. **Website:** www.deniskitchen.com. **Contact:** Denis Kitchen, publisher. Publishes hardcover and trade paperback originals and reprints. **Publishes 4 titles/year. 15% of books from first-time authors. 50% from unagented writers. Pays 6-10% royalty on retail price. Occasionally makes deals based on percentage of wholesale if idea and/or bulk of work is done in-house. Pays $1-5,000 advance.** Publishes ms 9-12 months after acceptance. Responds in 4-6 weeks.

◯ This publisher strongly discourages e-mail submissions.

NONFICTION Query with SASE. Submit proposal package, outline, illustrative matter. Submit complete ms. Reviews artwork/photos. Send photocopies and transparencies.

FICTION Subjects include adventure, erotica, historical, horror, humor, literary, mystery, occult, science fiction. "We do not want pure fiction. We seek cartoonists or writer/illustrator teams who can tell compelling stories with a combination of words and pictures." No pure fiction (meaning text only). Query with SASE. Submit sample illustrations/comic pages. Submit complete ms.

TIPS "Our audience is readers who embrace the graphic novel revolution, who appreciate historical comic strips and books, and those who follow popular and alternative culture. We like to discover new talent. The artist who has a day job but a great idea is encouraged to contact us. The pop culture historian who has a new take on an important figure is likewise encouraged. We have few preconceived notions about manuscripts or ideas, though we are decidedly selective. Historically, we have published many first-time authors and artists, some of whom developed into award-winning creators with substantial followings. Artists or illustrators who do

not have confidence in their writing should send us self-promotional postcards (our favorite way of spotting new talent)."

KNOPF

Imprint of Random House, 1745 Broadway, New York NY 10019. **Fax:** (212)940-7390. **Website:** knopfdoubleday.com/imprint/knopf. Estab. 1915. Publishes hardcover and paperback originals. **Publishes 200 titles/year. Royalties vary. Offers advance.** Publishes ms 1 year after acceptance. Accepts simultaneous submissions. Responds in 2-6 months to queries.

NONFICTION Usually only accepts mss submitted by agents. However, writers may submit sample 25-50 pages with SASE.

FICTION Publishes book-length fiction of literary merit by known or unknown writers. Length: 40,000-150,000 words. Usually only accepts mss submitted by agents. However, writers may submit sample 25-50 pages with SASE.

KNOX ROBINSON PUBLISHING

Knox Robinson Holdings, LLC, 3104 Briarcliff RD NE #98414, Atlanta GA 30345. (404)478-8696. **E-mail:** info@knoxrobinsonpublishing.com. **E-mail:** subs@knoxrobinsonpublishing.com. **Website:** www. knoxrobinsonpublishing.com. **Contact:** Dr. Dana Celeste Robinson, Publisher. Estab. 2010. Publishes fiction and nonfiction. Knox Robinson Publishing began as an international, independent, specialist publisher of historical fiction, historical romance and fantasy. Now open to well-written literature in all genres. **Publishes 20 titles/year. Pays royalty.** Accepts simultaneous submissions. Responds within 6 months to submissions of first 3 chapters. "We do not accept proposals.". Catalog available. Guidelines online.

IMPRINTS Under The Maple Tree Books (Children's Literature), Mithras Books (Young Adult Literature).

NONFICTION Subjects include history, humanities, religion, general nonfiction. "Our goal is to publish history books, monographs and historical fiction that satisfies history buffs and encourages general readers to learn more." Submit first 3 chapters and author questionnaire found on website. Reviews artwork/photos. Send photocopies. Does not accept printed submissions; electronic only.

FICTION Subjects include adventure, contemporary, fantasy, historical, horror, literary, mainstream, romance, science fiction. "We are seeking historical fiction featuring obscure historical figures." Submit first 3 chapters and author questionnaire found on website.

KRAUSE PUBLICATIONS

A Division of F+W Media, Inc., 700 E. State St., Iola WI 54990. (715)445-2214. **Fax:** (715)445-4087. **E-mail:** paul.kennedy@fwcommunity.com. **Website:** www.krausebooks.com. **Contact:** Paul Kennedy (antiques and collectibles, rocks, gems and minerals, music, sports, militaria, numismatics); Corrina Peterson (firearms); Chris Berens (outdoors); Brian Earnest (automotive). Publishes hardcover and trade paperback originals. "We are the world's largest hobby and collectibles publisher." **Publishes 60 titles/year. 200 queries received/year. 150 mss received/year. 50% of books from first-time authors. 95% from unagented writers. Pays advance. Photo budget.** Publishes ms 18 months after acceptance. Responds in 1month to proposals; 1 month to mss. Guidelines available free upon request.

NONFICTION Submit proposal package, including outline, TOC, a sample chapter, and letter explaining your project's unique contributions. Reviews artwork/photos. Accepts only digital photography. Send sample photos.

TIPS Audience consists of serious hobbyists. "Your work should provide a unique contribution to the special interest."

⊘ KREGEL PUBLICATIONS

2450 Oak Industrial Dr. NE, Grand Rapids MI 49505. (616)451-4775. **Fax:** (616)451-9330. **E-mail:** kregelbooks@kregel.com. **Website:** www.kregelpublications.com. **Contact:** Dennis R. Hillman, publisher. Estab. 1949. Publishes hardcover and trade paperback originals and reprints. "Our mission as an evangelical Christian publisher is to provide—with integrity and excellence—trusted, Biblically based resources that challenge and encourage individuals in their Christian lives. Works in theology and Biblical studies should reflect the historic, orthodox Protestant tradition." **Publishes 90 titles/year. 20% of books from first-time authors. 10% from unagented writers. Pays royalty on wholesale price. Pays negotiable advance.** Publishes ms 12-16 months after acceptance. Accepts simultaneous submissions. Responds in 2-3 months. Guidelines online.

IMPRINTS Kregel Publications, Kregel Academic, Kregel Childrens, Kregel Classics.

NONFICTION Subjects include history, religion. "We serve evangelical Christian readers and those in career Christian service." Finds works through The Writer's Edge and Christian Manuscript Submissions ms screening services.

FICTION Subjects include religious, young adult. Fiction should be geared toward the evangelical Christian market. Wants books with fast-paced, contemporary storylines presenting a strong Christian message in an engaging, entertaining style. Finds works through The Writer's Edge and Christian Manuscript Submissions ms screening services.

TIPS "Our audience consists of conservative, evangelical Christians, including pastors and ministry students."

KRIEGER PUBLISHING CO.

1725 Krieger Ln., Malabar FL 32950. (321)724-9542. **Fax:** (321)951-3671. **E-mail:** info@krieger-publishing. com. **Website:** www.krieger-publishing.com. **Contact:** Sharan B. Merriam and Ronald M. Cervero, series editor (adult education); David E. Kyvig, series director (local history); James B. Gardner, series editor (public history). Also publishes in the fields of natural sciences, history and space sciences.. Estab. 1969. Publishes hardcover and paperback originals and reprints. "We are a short-run niche publisher providing accurate and well-documented scientific and technical titles for text and reference use, college level and higher." **Publishes 30 titles/year. 30% of books from first-time authors. 100% from unagented writers. Pays royalty on net price.** Publishes ms 9-18 months after acceptance. Accepts simultaneous submissions. Responds in 3 months to queries. Book catalog online.

IMPRINTS Anvil Series; Orbit Series; Public History; Professional Practices in Adult Education and Lifelong Learning Series.

NONFICTION Subjects include agriculture, animals, education, history, science, herpetology. Query with SASE. Reviews artwork/photos.

◐ KWELA BOOKS

Imprint of NB Publishers, P.O. Box 6525, Roggebaai 8012, South Africa. (27)(21)406-3605. **Fax:** (27) (21)406-3712. **E-mail:** kwela@kwela.com. **Website:** www.kwela.com. Estab. 1994. Accepts simultaneous submissions.

NONFICTION Subjects include contemporary culture, ethnic, history, memoirs, social sciences.

FICTION Subjects include literary.

LAKE CLAREMONT PRESS

Everything Goes Media, LLC, P.O. Box 1524, Chicago IL 60690. (312)226-8400. **Fax:** (312)226-8420. **E-mail:** sharon@lakeclaremont.com. **Website:** www.lakeclaremont.com. **Contact:** Sharon Woodhouse, publisher. Estab. 1994. Publishes trade paperback originals. "We specialize in nonfiction books on the Chicago area and its history, particularly by authors with a passion or organizations with a mission." **Publishes 2-3 titles/year. 250 queries; 100 mss received/year. 50% of books from first-time authors. 100% from unagented writers. Pays 10-15% royalty on net sales. Pays $500-1,000 advance.** Publishes ms 12-18 months after acceptance. Accepts simultaneous submissions. Responds in 1 month to queries; 2 months to proposals; 2-6 months to mss. Book catalog online.

NONFICTION Subjects include Americana, ethnic, history, regional, travel, film/cinema/stage (regional)—as long as it is primarily a Chicago book. Query with SASE, or submit proposal package, including outline and 2 sample chapters, or submit complete ms (e-mail queries and proposals preferred).

TIPS "Please include a market analysis in proposals (who would buy this book and where) and an analysis of similar books available for different regions. Please know what else is out there."

LANGMARC PUBLISHING

P.O. Box 90488, Austin TX 78709-0488. (512)394-0989. **Fax:** (512)394-0829. **E-mail:** langmarc@booksails.com. **Website:** www.langmarc.com. **Contact:** Lois Qualben, president (inspirational). Publishes trade paperback originals. **Publishes 3 titles/year. 150 queries; 80 mss received/year. 60% of books from first-time authors. 80% from unagented writers. Pays 14% royalty on sales price.** Publishes ms 8-14 months after acceptance. Accepts simultaneous submissions. Responds in 3 months to queries. Book catalog online. Guidelines online.

NONFICTION Subjects include creative nonfiction. Query with SASE.

LANTANA PUBLISHING

London , United Kingdom. **E-mail:** info@lantanapublishing.com. **E-mail:** submissions@lantanapublishing.com. **Website:** www.lantanapublishing.com. Estab. 2014. "Lantana Publishing is an independent publishing company committed to addressing the widespread lack of cultural diversity in children's publishing in the UK. As a publishing house with a strong social mission to increase the availability and visibility of diverse children's writing, we provide opportunities for authors and illustrators of minority backgrounds to create children's books that are resonant of their own experiences, places and cultures." **Pays royalty. Pays advance.** Accepts simultaneous submissions. Responds in 6 weeks. Guidelines online.

○ "We are currently focusing on picture books for 4 to 8 year olds."

FICTION Subjects include adventure, ethnic, experimental, fantasy, multicultural, picture books. "We love writing that is new, unusual or quirky, and that interweaves mythic, historical or spiritual elements into fun, contemporary stories full of colour and excitement. We particularly like stories with modern-day settings and strong role models, positive relationships between communities and their environment, and evocative storylines that can provide a glimpse into the belief systems, traditions or world views of other cultures." No nonfiction. "If you are a picture book author, please send us the complete text of your ms. Illustrations are not necessary. If we like your story, we will commission an illustrator to work with you. A picture book ms should not normally exceed 1,000 words. If your story does exceed this word limit please include a justification for its length in your covering letter."

LAPWING PUBLICATIONS

1 Ballysillan Dr., Belfast BT14 8HQ, Northern Ireland. (44)2890-500-796. **Fax:** (44)2890-295-800. **E-mail:** lapwing.poetry@ntlworld.com. **Website:** www.lapwingpoetry.com. **Contact:** Dennis Greig, editor. Estab. 1989. **Pays 20 author's copies, no royalties.** Accepts simultaneous submissions. Responds to queries in 1 month; mss in 2 months.

○ Lapwing will produce work only if and when resources to do so are available.

POETRY Lapwing publishes "emerging Irish poets and poets domiciled in Ireland, plus the new work of a suitable size by established Irish writers. Non-Irish poets are also published. Poets based in continental Europe have become a major feature. Emphasis on first collections preferrably not larger than 80 pages. "Submit 6 poems in the first instance; depending on these, an invitation to submit more may follow." Considers simultaneous submissions. Accepts e-mail submissions in body of message or in DOC format. Cover letter is required. "All submissions receive a first reading. If these poems have minor errors or faults, the writer is advised. Those which appeal at first reading are retained, and a conditional offer is sent." Often comments on rejected poems. "After initial publication, irrespective of the quantity, the work will be permanently available using 'print-on-demand' production; such publications may not always be printed exactly as the original, although the content will remain the same."

TIPS "We are unable to accept new work from beyond mainland Europe and the British Isles due to delivery costs."

LEAPFROG PRESS

Box 505, Fredonia NY 14063. (508)274-2710. **E-mail:** leapfrog@leapfrogpress.com. **E-mail:** acquisitions@ leapfrogpress.com. **Website:** www.leapfrogpress.com. **Contact:** Rebecca Schwab, acquisitions editor; Layla Al-Bedawi, publicity. Estab. 1996. **Publishes 4-6 titles/year. 2,000-3,000 submissions received/year. 50% of books from first-time authors. 50% from unagented writers. Pays 10% royalty on net receipts. Average advance: negotiable.** Publishes ms approximately 1 year after acceptance. Accepts simultaneous submissions. Response time varies. Guidelines online.

FICTION Subjects include adventure, ethnic, experimental, feminist, gay, historical, juvenile, lesbian, literary, mainstream, multicultural, poetry, science fiction, short story collections, young adult. "We search for beautifully written literary titles and market them aggressively to national trade and library accounts. We also sell film, translation, foreign, and book club rights." Publishes paperback originals. Books: acid-free paper; sewn binding. Average print order: 3,000. First novel print order: 2,000 (average). Member, Publishers Marketing Association, PEN. Distributes titles through Consortium Book Sales and Distribution, St. Paul, MN. Promotes titles through all national review media, bookstore readings, author tours, website, radio shows, chain store promotions, advertisements, book fairs. "Genres often blur; look for good writing. We are most interested in works that are quirky, that fall outside of any known genre, and of course well written and finely crafted. We are most interested in literary fiction." Query by e-mail only. Send letter and first 5 to 10 ms pages within e-mail message. No attachments. Responds in 2-3 weeks to queries by e-

mail; 6 months to mss. May consider simultaneous submissions.

TIPS "We like anything that is superbly written and genuinely original. We like the idiosyncratic and the peculiar. We rarely publish nonfiction. Send only your best work, and send only completed work that is ready. That means the completed ms has already been through extensive editing and is ready to be judged. We consider submissions from both previously published and unpublished writers. We are uninterested in an impressive author bio if the work is poor; if the work is excellent, the author bio is equally unimportant."

LEE & LOW BOOKS

95 Madison Ave., #1205, New York NY 10016. (212)779-4400. **E-mail:** general@leeandlow.com. **Website:** www.leeandlow.com. Estab. 1991. Publishes hardcover originals and trade paperback reprints. "Our goals are to meet a growing need for books that address children of color, and to present literature that all children can identify with. We only consider multicultural children's books. Sponsors a yearly New Voices Award for first-time picture book authors of color. Contest rules online at website or for SASE." **Publishes 12-14 titles/year. Receives 100 queries/year; 1,200 mss/year. 20% of books from first-time authors. 50% from unagented writers. Pays net royalty. Pays authors advances against royalty. Pays illustrators advance against royalty. Photographers paid advance against royalty.** Publishes book 2 years after acceptance. Responds in 6 months to mss if interested. Book catalog available online. Guidelines available online or by written request with SASE.

NONFICTION Picture books: concept. Picture books, middle readers: biography, history, multicultural, science and sports. Average word length: picture books-1,500-3,000. Submit complete ms. Reviews artwork/photos only if writer is also a professional illustrator or photographer. Send photocopies and nonreturnable art samples only.

FICTION Picture books, young readers: anthology, contemporary, history, multicultural, poetry. Picture book, middle reader: contemporary, history, multicultural, nature/environment, poetry, sports. Average word length: picture books—1,000-1,500 words. "We do not publish folklore or animal stories." Submit complete ms.

POETRY Submit complete ms.

TIPS "Check our website to see the kinds of books we publish. Do not send mss that don't fit our mission."

LEGACY PRESS

17909 Adria Maru, Carson CA 90746. (800)532-4278. **E-mail:** info@rainbowpublishers.com. **Website:** www.rainbowpublishers.com. Estab. 1979. "Our mission is to publish Bible-based, teacher resource materials that contribute to and inspire spiritual growth and development in kids ages 2-12." **Publishes 4 young readers/year; 4 middle readers/year; 4 young adult titles/year. 50% of books from first-time authors. For authors work purchased outright (range: $500 and up). Pays illustrators by the project (range: $300 and up). Sends galleys to authors.** Accepts simultaneous submissions. Responds to queries in 6 weeks, mss in 3 months.

NONFICTION Young readers, middle readers, young adult/teens: activity books, arts/crafts, how-to, reference, religion. Works with 10 illustrators/year. Reviews ms/illustration packages from artists. Submit ms with 2-5 pieces of final art. Illustrations only: Query with samples. Responds in 6 weeks. Samples returned with SASE; samples filed.

TIPS "Our Rainbow imprint publishes reproducible books for teachers of children in Christian ministries, including crafts, activities, games and puzzles. Our Legacy imprint publishes titles for children such as devotionals, fiction and Christian living. Please see website and study the market before submitting material."

LEHIGH UNIVERSITY PRESS

B040 Christmas-Saucon Hall, 14 E. Packer Ave., Bethlehem PA 18015. (610)758-3933. **Fax:** (610)758-6331. **E-mail:** inlup@lehigh.edu. **Website:** https://lupress.cas2.lehigh.edu. **Contact:** Kate Crassons. Estab. 1985. Publishes nonfiction hardcover originals. Currently emphasizing works on 18th-century studies, history of technology, literary criticism, and topics involving Asian Studies. **Publishes 10 titles/year. 90-100 queries; 50-60 mss received/year. 70% of books from first-time authors. 100% from unagented writers. Pays royalty.** Publishes ms 18 months after acceptance. Responds in 3 months to queries. Book catalog available free. Guidelines online.

NONFICTION Subjects include Americana, history, science. Lehigh University Press is a conduit for nonfiction works of scholarly interest to the academic community. Submit proposal package with cover letter, several sample chapters, current CV and SASE.

◐ LES ÉDITIONS DU VERMILLON

305 Saint Patrick St., Ottawa ON K1N 5K4, Canada. (613)241-4032. **Fax:** (613)241-3109. **E-mail:** leseditionsduvermillon@rogers.com. **Website:** www.leseditionsduvermillon.ca. Publishes trade paperback originals. **Publishes 15-20 titles/year. Pays 10% royalty.** Publishes ms 18 months after acceptance. Accepts simultaneous submissions. Responds in 6 months to mss. Book catalog available free.

FICTION Subjects include juvenile, literary, religious, short story collections, young adult.

LES FIGUES PRESS

P.O. Box 7736, Los Angeles CA 90007. **E-mail:** info@lesfigues.com. **Website:** www.lesfigues.com. **Contact:** Teresa Carmody, director. Les Figues Press is an independent, nonprofit publisher of poetry, prose, visual art, conceptual writing, and translation. With a mission is to create aesthetic conversations between readers, writers, and artists, Les Figues Press favors projects which push the boundaries of genre, form, and general acceptability. Submissions are only reviewed through its annual NOS Book Contest. Accepts simultaneous submissions.

LETHE PRESS

118 Heritage Ave., Maple Shade NJ 08052. (609)410-7391. **E-mail:** lethepress@aol.com. **Website:** www.lethepressbooks.com. Estab. 2001. "Welcomes submissions from authors of any sexual or gender identity." Accepts simultaneous submissions. Guidelines online.

NONFICTION Query via e-mail.

FICTION Subjects include gay, lesbian, occult, science fiction. "Named after the Greek river of memory and forgetfulness (and pronounced Lee-Thee), Lethe Press is a small press devoted to ideas that are often neglected or forgotten by mainstream, profit-oriented publishers." Distributes/promotes titles. Lethe Books are distributed by Ingram Publications and Bookazine, and are available at all major bookstores, as well as the major online retailers. Query via e-mail.

POETRY "Lethe Press is a small press seeking gay and lesbian themed poetry collections." Lethe Books are distributed by Ingram Publications and Bookazine, and are available at all major bookstores, as well as the major online retailers. Query with 7-10 poems, list of publications.

ARTHUR A. LEVINE BOOKS

Scholastic, Inc., 557 Broadway, New York NY 10012. (212)343-4436. **Fax:** (212)343-6143. **Website:** www.arthuralevinebooks.com. Estab. 1996. Publishes hardcover, paperback, and e-book editions. Publishes a book 18 months after acceptance. Accepts simultaneous submissions. Responds in 1 month to queries; 5 months to mss. Picture Books: Query letter and full text of pb. Novels: Send Query letter, first 2 chapters and synopsis. Other: Query letter, 10-page sample and synopsis/proposal.

NONFICTION Please follow submission guidelines. Works with 8 illustrators/year. Will review ms/illustration packages from artists. Query first. Illustrations only: Send postcard sample with tearsheets. Samples not returned.

FICTION Subjects include juvenile, picture books, young adult. "Arthur A. Levine is looking for distinctive literature, for children and young adults, for whatever's extraordinary." Averages 18-20 total titles/year. Query.

☯ LEXISNEXIS CANADA, INC.

111 Gordon Baker Rd., Suite 900, Toronto ON M2H 3R1, Canada. (905)479-2665. **Fax:** (905)479-2826. **Website:** www.lexisnexis.ca. **Contact:** Product Development Director. LexisNexis Canada, Inc., publishes professional reference material for the legal, business, and accounting markets under the Butterworths imprint and operates the Quicklaw and LexisNexis online services. **Publishes 100 titles/year. 50% of books from first-time authors. 100% from unagented writers. Pays 5-15% royalty on wholesale price.** Publishes ms 4 months after acceptance. Accepts simultaneous submissions. Responds in 1 month to queries. Book catalog available free. Guidelines online.

TIPS "Audience is legal community, business, medical, accounting professions."

LIFE CYCLE BOOKS

20 - 1085 Bellamy Rd N, Toronto ON M1H 3C7, Canada. **Website:** www.lifecyclebooks.com. **Contact:** Paul Broughton, general manager. Estab. 1973. Publishes trade paperback originals and reprints, and mass market reprints. **Publishes 6 titles/year. 50+ queries received/year. 50% of books from first-time authors. 100% from unagented writers. Pays 8-10% royalty on wholesale price. Pays $250+ advance.** Publishes book 1 year after acceptance. Responds within 1-2 months. Catalog online.

NONFICTION Subjects include pro-life issues. "We specialize in pro-life issues. Please look at our website before submitting your manuscript." Query with SASE. Submit complete ms.

LIGUORI PUBLICATIONS

One Liguori Dr., Liguori MO 63057. (636)464-2500. **Fax:** (636)464-8449. **E-mail:** manuscript_submission@liguori.org. **Website:** www.liguori.org. **Contact:** Acquisitions Editor. Estab. 1947. Publishes paperback originals and reprints under the Ligouri and Libros Ligouri imprints. Liguori Publications, faithful to the charism of St. Alphonsus, is an apostolate within the mission of the Denver Province. Its mission, a collaborative effort of Redemptorists and laity, is to spread the gospel of Jesus Christ primarily through the print and electronic media. It shares in the Redemptorist priority of giving special attention to the poor and the most abandoned. Currently emphasizing practical spirituality, prayers and devotions, how-to spirituality. **Publishes 20-25 titles/year. Pays royalty. Makes outright purchase. Pays varied advance.** Publishes ms 2 years after acceptance. Responds in 2-3 months. Guidelines online.

NONFICTION Subjects include religion, spirituality. Mostly adult audience; limited children/juvenile. Mss with Catholic sensibility. Query with SASE. Submit outline, 1 sample chapter.

TIPS "As a rule, Liguori Publications does not accept unsolicited fiction, poetry, art books, biography, autobiography, private revelations."

LILLENAS PUBLISHING CO.

Imprint of Lillenas Drama Resources, P.O. Box 419527, Kansas City MO 64141. (800)877-0700. **Fax:** (816)412-8390. **E-mail:** drama@lillenas.com. **Website:** www.lillenasdrama.com. Publishes mass market paperback and electronic originals. "We purchase only original, previously unpublished materials. Also, we require that all scripts be performed at least once before it is submitted for consideration. We do not accept scripts that are sent via fax or e-mail. Direct all manuscripts to the Drama Resources Editor." **Publishes 50+ titles/year. Pays royalty on net price. Makes outright purchase.** Responds in 4-6 months to material. Guidelines online.

NONFICTION No musicals. Query with SASE. Submit complete ms.

FICTION "Looking for sketch and monologue collections for all ages – adults, children and youth. For these collections, we request 12 - 15 scripts to be submitted at one time. Unique treatments of spiritual themes, relevant issues and biblical messages are of interest. Contemporary full-length and one-act plays that have conflict, characterization, and a spiritual context that is neither a sermon nor an apologetic for youth and adults. We also need wholesome so-called secular full-length scripts for dinner theatres and schools." No musicals.

TIPS "We never receive too many manuscripts."

LINDEN PUBLISHING, INC.

2006 S. Mary, Fresno CA 93721. (559)233-6633. **Fax:** (559)233-6933. **E-mail:** richard@lindenpub.com. **Website:** www.lindenpub.com and www.quilldriverbooks.com. **Contact:** Richard Sorsky, president; Kent Sorsky, vice president. Estab. 1976. Publishes hardcover and trade paperback originals; hardcover and trade paperback reprints. **Publishes 10-12 titles/year. 30+ queries; 5-15 mss received/year. 40% of books from first-time authors. 50% from unagented writers. Pays 7½ -12% royalty on wholesale price. Pays $500-6,000 advance.** Publishes ms 18 months after acceptance. Responds in 1 month. Book catalog online. Guidelines available via e-mail.

IMPRINTS Quill Driver Books, Craven Street Books.

NONFICTION Subjects include crafts, history, hobbies, regional, true crime, Regional California history. Submit proposal package, outline, 3 sample chapters, bio. Reviews artwork/photos. Send electronic files, if available.

R.C. LINNELL PUBLISHING

2100 Tyler Ln., Louisville KY 40205. **E-mail:** info@linnellpublishing.com. **Website:** www.linnellpublishing.com. **Contact:** Cheri Powell, owner. Estab. 2010. Publishes print on demand paperbacks. "We are currently very small and have published a limited number of books. We would review books on other subjects on a case-by-case basis. If a book is well-written and has an audience we would consider it. We offer publishing services. Please review our web page to understand our business model and what we can do for you." **Publishes 3 titles/year. 100 queries/ mss received/ year. 83% of books from first-time authors. 100% from unagented writers. Pays 10-40% royalty on retail price.** Publishes ms 3 months after acceptance.

Accepts simultaneous submissions. Responds in 1 month to mss. Book catalog and guidelines online.

NONFICTION Subjects include alternative lifestyles, Americana, astrology, career guidance, contemporary culture, cooking, counseling, creative nonfiction, ethnic, foods, language, literature, memoirs, multicultural, New Age, philosophy, psychic, psychology, regional, religion, sociology, spirituality, translation, travel, womens issues, womens studies, young adult. Submit complete ms.

FICTION Subjects include adventure, confession, contemporary, experimental, fantasy, feminist, gay, gothic, hi-lo, historical, humor, lesbian, literary, mainstream, multicultural, mystery, occult, regional, religious, romance, science fiction, short story collections, spiritual, suspense, translation, western, young adult. Submit complete ms.

TIPS "Visit our website to understand the business model and the relationship with authors. All sales are through the internet. Author should have a marketing plan in mind. We can help expand the plan but we do not market books. Author should be comfortable with using the internet and should know their intended readers. We are especially interested in books that inspire, motivate, amuse and challenge readers."

LIQUID SILVER BOOKS

10509 Sedgegrass Dr., Indianapolis IN 46235. **E-mail:** submissions@liquidsilverbooks.com. **Website:** www.lsbooks.com. **Contact:** Chrissie Henderson, editorial director. Estab. 1999. Liquid Silver Books is an imprint of Atlantic Bridge Publishing, a royalty paying, full-service ePublisher. Atlantic Bridge has been in business since June 1999. Liquid Silver Books is dedicated to bringing high quality erotic romance to our readers. Liquid Silver Books, Romance's Silver Lining. Publishes ms 105 days after contract. Accepts simultaneous submissions. Responds to mss in 10-15 days.

○ "We are foremost an e-publisher. We believe the market will continue to grow for e-books. It is our prime focus. At this time our print publishing is on hiatus. We will update the submission guidelines if we reinstate this aspect of our publishing."

FICTION Subjects include romance. Needs contemporary, gay and lesbian, paranormal, supernatural, sci-fi, fantasy, historical, suspense, and western romances. "We do not accept literary erotica submissions." E-mail entire ms as an attachment in .RTF format in Arial 12 pt. "Include in the body of the e-mail: author bio, your thoughts on ePublishing, a blurb of your book, including title and series title if applicable. Ms must include Pen name, real name, snail mail and e-mail contact information on the first page, top left corner."

LISTEN & LIVE AUDIO

1700 Manhattan Ave., Union City NJ 07087. (201)558-9000. **Website:** www.listenandlive.com. **Contact:** Alfred C. Martino, president. Independent audiobook publisher. "We also license audiobooks for the download market. We specialize in the following genres: fiction, mystery, nonfiction, self-help, business, children's, and teen." **Publishes 10+ titles/year.** Accepts simultaneous submissions. Catalog online.

Ⓐ⊘ LITTLE, BROWN AND CO. ADULT TRADE BOOKS

1290 Avenue of the Americas, New York NY 10104. **Website:** www.littlebrown.com. Estab. 1837. Publishes hardcover originals and paperback originals and reprints. "The general editorial philosophy for all divisions continues to be broad and flexible, with high quality and the promise of commercial success as always the first considerations." **Publishes 100 titles/year. Pays royalty. Offer advance.** Accepts simultaneous submissions. Guidelines online.

NONFICTION *Agented submissions only.*

FICTION Subjects include contemporary, literary, mainstream. *Agented submissions only.*

Ⓐ⊘ LITTLE, BROWN BOOKS FOR YOUNG READERS

Hachette Book Group USA, 1290 Avenue of the Americas, New York NY 10104. (212)364-1100. **Fax:** (212)364-0925. **Website:** littlebrown.com. Estab. 1837. "Little, Brown and Co. Children's Publishing publishes all formats including board books, picture books, middle grade fiction, and nonfiction YA titles. We are looking for strong writing and presentation, but no predetermined topics." *Only interested in solicited agented material.* **Publishes 100-150 titles/year. Pays authors royalties based on retail price. Pays illustrators and photographers by the project or royalty based on retail price. Sends galleys to authors; dummies to illustrators. Pays negotiable advance.** Publishes ms 2 years after acceptance. Accepts simultaneous submissions. Responds in 1-2 months.

NONFICTION Subjects include animals, ethnic, history, hobbies, recreation, science, sports. "Writers should avoid looking for the 'issue' they think publishers want to see, choosing instead topics they know best and are most enthusiastic about/inspired by." *Agented submissions only.*

FICTION Subjects include adventure, fantasy, feminist, historical, humor, mystery, science fiction, suspense, chick lit, multicultural. Average word length: picture books—1,000; young readers—6,000; middle readers—15,000- 50,000; young adults—50,000 and up. *Agented submissions only.*

TIPS "In order to break into the field, authors and illustrators should research their competition and try to come up with something outstandingly different."

LITTLE PICKLE PRESS

3701 Sacramento St., #494, San Francisco CA 94118. (415)340-3344. **Fax:** (415)366-1520. **E-mail:** info@littlepicklepress.com. **Website:** www.littlepicklepress.com. Little Pickle Press is a 21st Century publisher dedicated to helping parents and educators cultivate conscious, responsible little people by stimulating explorations of the meaningful topics of their generation through a variety of media, technologies, and techniques. Submit through submission link on site. Includes YA imprint Relish Media Accepts simultaneous submissions. Uses Author.me for submissions for Little Pickle and YA imprint Relish Media. Guidelines available on site.

TIPS "We have lots of manuscripts to consider, so it will take up to 8 weeks before we get back to you."

Ⓐ⊘ LITTLE SIMON

Imprint of Simon & Schuster, 1230 Avenue of the Americas, New York NY 10020. (212)698-1295. **Fax:** (212)698-2794. **Website:** www.simonandschuster.com/kids. Publishes novelty and branded books only. "Our goal is to provide fresh material in an innovative format for preschool to age 8. Our books are often, if not exclusively, format driven." **Offers advance and royalties.** Accepts simultaneous submissions.

NONFICTION "We publish very few nonfiction titles." No picture books. *Currently not accepting unsolicited mss.*

FICTION Novelty books include many things that do not fit in the traditional hardcover or paperback format, such as pop-up, board book, scratch and sniff, glow in the dark, lift the flap, etc. Children's/juvenile. No picture books. Large part of the list is holiday-themed. *Currently not accepting unsolicited mss.*

⊜⊘ LITTLE TIGER PRESS

1 The Coda Centre, 189 Munster Rd., London SW6 6AW, United Kingdom. (44)(20)7385-6333. **Website:** www.littletigerpress.com. Little Tiger Press is a dynamic and busy independent publisher. Also includes imprints: Caterpillar Books and Stripes Publishing.

FICTION Picture books: animal, concept, contemporary, humor. Average word length: picture books—750 words or less. "We are no longer accepting unsolicited manuscripts. We will however, continue to accept illustration submissions and samples."

⊘ LIVINGSTON PRESS

University of West Alabama, 100 N. Washington St., Station 22, University of West Alabama, Livingston AL 35470. **Fax:** (205)653-3717. **E-mail:** jwt@uwa.edu. **Website:** www.livingstonpress.uwa.edu. **Contact:** Joe Taylor, director. Estab. 1974. Publishes hardcover and trade paperback originals, plus Kindle. "Livingston Press, as do all literary presses, looks for authorial excellence in style. Currently emphasizing novels." Reading in June only. Check back for details. **Publishes 7-10 titles/year. 50% of books from first-time authors. 100% from unagented writers. Pays 100 contributor's copies, after sales of 1,500, standard royalty.** Publishes ms 18 months after acceptance. Accepts simultaneous submissions. Responds in 4 months to queries; 6-12 months to mss. Book catalog online. Guidelines online.

IMPRINTS Swallow's Tale Press.

FICTION Subjects include experimental, literary, offbeat or Southern. "We are interested in form and, of course, style." No genre fiction, please.

TIPS "Our readers are interested in literature, often quirky literature that emphasizes form and style. Please visit our website for current needs."

⊛⊘ LIZZIE SKURNICK BOOKS

Ig Publishing, (718)797-0676. **Website:** lizzieskurnickbooks.com. Estab. 2013. Lizzie Skurnick Books, an imprint of Ig Publishing, is devoted to reissuing the very best in young adult literature, from the classics of the 1930s and 1940s to the social novels of the 1970s and 1980s. Ig does not accept unsolicited mss, either by e-mail or regular mail. If you have a ms that you would like Ig to take a look at, send a query through online contact form. If interested, they will contact. All unsolicited mss will be discarded. Accepts simultaneous submissions.

LLEWELLYN PUBLICATIONS

Imprint of Llewellyn Worldwide, Ltd., 2143 Wooddale Dr., Woodbury MN 55125. (651)291-1970. **Fax:** (651)291-1908. **E-mail:** customerservice@llewellyn.com. **E-mail:** submissions@llewellyn.com. **Website:** www.llewellyn.com. Estab. 1901. Publishes trade and mass market paperback originals. "Llewellyn publishes New Age fiction and nonfiction exploring new worlds of mind and spirit. Currently emphasizing astrology, alternative health and healing, tarot. De-emphasizing fiction, channeling." **Publishes 100+ titles/year. 30% of books from first-time authors. 50% from unagented writers. Pays 10% royalty on wholesale or retail price.** Accepts simultaneous submissions. Responds in 3 months to queries. Book catalog online.

NONFICTION Subjects include New Age, psychology. Submit outline, sample chapters. Reviews artwork/photos.

LONELY PLANET PUBLICATIONS

150 Linden St., Oakland CA 94607-2538. (510)893-8555. **Fax:** (510)893-8563. **Website:** www.lonelyplanet.com. Estab. 1973. Publishes trade paperback originals. "Lonely Planet publishes travel guides, atlases, travel literature, phrasebooks, condensed pocket guides, diving and snorkeling guides." **Work-for-hire: on contract, 1/3 on submission, 1/3 on approval. Pays advance.** Accepts simultaneous submissions. Responds in 3 months to queries. Book catalog online. Guidelines online.

NONFICTION Subjects include travel. "We only work with contract writers on book ideas that we originate. We do not accept original proposals. Request our writer's guidelines. Send resume and clips of travel writing." Query with SASE.

LOOSE ID

P.O. Box 806, San Francisco CA 94104. **E-mail:** submissions@loose-id.com. **Website:** www.loose-id.com. **Contact:** Treva Harte, editor-in-chief. Estab. 2004. "*Loose Id* is love unleashed. We're taking romance to the edge." Publishes e-books and some print books. Distributes/promotes titles. "The company promotes itself through web and print advertising wherever readers of erotic romance may be found, creating a recognizable brand identity as the place to let your id run free and the people who unleash your fantasies. It is currently pursuing licensing agreements for foreign translations, and has a print program of 2 to 5 titles per month." **Pays e-book royalties of 40%.** Publishes ms within 1 year after acceptance. Accepts simultaneous submissions. Responds to queries in 1 month. Guidelines online.

◐ "Loose Id is actively acquiring stories from both aspiring and established authors."

FICTION Subjects include erotica, romance. Wants nontraditional erotic romance stories, including gay, lesbian, heroes and heroines, multi-culturalism, cross-genre, fantasy, and science fiction, straight contemporary or historical romances. Query with outline/synopsis and 3 sample chapters. Accepts queries by e-mail. Include estimated word count, list of publishing credits, and why your submission is love unleashed. "Before submitting a query or proposal, please read the guidelines on our website. Please don't hesitate to contact us by e-mail for any information you don't see there."

LOST HORSE PRESS

105 Lost Horse Ln., Sandpoint ID 83864. (208)255-4410. E-mail: losthorsepress@mindspring.com. **Website:** www.losthorsepress.org. **Contact:** Christine Holbert, publisher. Estab. 1998. Publishes hardcover and paperback originals. Distributed by University of Washington Press. **Publishes 8-10 titles/year.** Publishes ms 3-9 months after acceptance. Accepts simultaneous submissions.

◐ "*Does not accept unsolicited mss.* However, we welcome submissions for the Idaho Prize for Poetry, a national competition offering $1,000 prize money plus publication for a book-length ms. Please check the submission guidelines for the Idaho Prize for Poetry online."

Ⓞ LOVING HEALING PRESS INC.

5145 Pontiac Trail, Ann Arbor MI 48105. (888)761-6268. **Fax:** (734)663-6861. **E-mail:** info@lovinghealing.com. **Website:** www.lovinghealing.com. **Contact:** Victor R. Volkman, senior editor (psychology, self-help, personal growth, trauma recovery). Estab. 2003. Publishes hardcover and trade paperback originals and reprints. *Currently not accepting mss.* **Publishes 20 titles/year. Receives 200 queries/year; 100 mss/year. 50% of books from first-time authors. 80% from unagented writers. Pays 6-12% royalty on retail price.** Publishes book 10 months after acceptance. Accepts simultaneous submissions. Responds in 1 month. Catalog and guidelines online.

IMPRINTS Modern History Press, Marvelous Spirit Press.

NONFICTION Subjects include child guidance, health, memoirs, psychology, social work. "We are primarily interested in self-help books which are person-centered and non-judgmental." Submit proposal package, including outline, 3 sample chapters. Reviews artwork/photos as part of the ms package; send JPEG files.

LOYOLA PRESS

3441 N. Ashland Ave., Chicago IL 60657. (773)281-1818. **Fax:** (773)281-0152. **E-mail:** durepos@loyolapress.com. **Website:** www.loyolapress.org. **Contact:** Joseph Durepos, acquisitions editor.. Estab. 1912. Publishes hardcover and trade paperback. **Publishes 20-30 titles/year. 500 queries received/year. Pays standard royalties. Offers reasonable advance.** Accepts simultaneous submissions. Book catalog online. Guidelines online.

NONFICTION Subjects include memoirs, religion, spirituality, inspirational, prayer, Catholic life, parish and adult faith formation resources with a special focus on Ignatian spirituality and Jesuit history. E-mail query, or snail mail query with SASE.

TIPS "Check our submission guidelines."

LRP PUBLICATIONS, INC.

360 Hiatt Dr., Palm Beach Gardens FL 33418. **Website:** www.lrp.com. Estab. 1977. Publishes hardcover and trade paperback originals. "LRP publishes two industry-leading magazines, *Human Resource Executive®* and *Risk & Insurance®*, as well as hundreds of newsletters, books, videos and case reporters in the fields of: human resources, federal employment, workers' compensation, public employment law, disability, bankruptcy, education administration and law." **Pays royalty.** Book catalog free. Guidelines free.

NONFICTION Subjects include education. Submit proposal package, outline.

Ⓞ LUNA BISONTE PRODS

137 Leland Ave., Columbus OH 43214-7505. **E-mail:** bennettjohnm@gmail.com. **Website:** www.johnmbennett.net. **Contact:** John M. Bennett, editor/publisher. Estab. 1967. **Publishes 5 titles/year. Pays copy or copies of book; further copies at cost. Does not pay advance.**

NONFICTION Subjects include language, literature, poetry, visual poetry.

POETRY "Interested in avant-garde and highly experimental work only." Has published poetry by Jim Leftwich, Sheila E. Murphy, Al Ackerman, Richard Kostelanetz, Carla Bertola, Olchar Lindsann, and many others. Query first, with a few sample poems and cover letter with brief bio and publication credits. "Keep it brief. Chapbook publishing usually depends on grants or other subsidies, and is usually by solicitation. **Will also consider subsidy arrangements on negotiable terms.**" A sampling of various Luna Bisonte Prods products is available for $20.

⊘ THE LYONS PRESS

The Globe Pequot Press, Inc., Box 480, 246 Goose Ln., Guilford CT 06437. (203)458-4500. **Fax:** (203)458-4668. **E-mail:** editorial@lyonspress.com. **Website:** www.lyonspress.com. Estab. 1984 (Lyons & Burford), 1997 (The Lyons Press). Publishes hardcover and trade paperback originals and reprints. The Lyons Press publishes practical and literary books, chiefly centered on outdoor subjects—natural history, all sports, gardening, horses, fishing, hunting, survival, self-reliant living, plus cooking, memoir, bio, nonfiction. "At this time, we are not accepting unsolicited mss or proposals." Check back for updates. **Pays $3,000-25,000 advance.** Book catalog online. Guidelines online.

NONFICTION Subjects include agriculture, Americana, animals, history, recreation, sports, adventure, fitness, the sea, woodworking.

☯ MAGENTA FOUNDATION

151 Winchester St., Toronto ON M4X 1B5, Canada. **E-mail:** info@magentafoundation.org. **Website:** www.magentafoundation.org. **Contact:** Submissions. Estab. 2004. "Established in 2004, The Magenta Foundation is Canada's pioneering non-profit, charitable arts publishing house. Magenta was created to organize promotional opportunities for artists, in an international context, through circulated exhibitions and publications. Projects mounted by Magenta are supported by credible international media coverage and critical reviews in all mainstream-media formats (radio, television and print). Magenta works with respected individuals and international organizations to help increase recognition for artists while uniting the global photography community." Accepts simultaneous submissions.

MAGE PUBLISHERS, INC.

1780 Crossroads Dr., Odenton MD 21113. (202)342-1642. **Fax:** (202)342-9269. **E-mail:** as@mage.com. **Website:** www.mage.com. Estab. 1985. Publishes hardcover originals and reprints, trade paperback originals. Mage publishes books relating to Persian/Iranian culture. **Pays royalty.** Accepts simultaneous submissions. Responds in 1 month to queries. Book catalog available free. Guidelines online.

NONFICTION Subjects include ethnic, history, sociology, translation. Submit outline, bio, SASE. Query via mail or e-mail. Reviews artwork/photos. Send photocopies.

FICTION Subjects include ethnic, feminist, historical, literary, short story collections. Must relate to Persian/Iranian culture. Submit outline, SASE. Query via mail or e-mail.

POETRY Must relate to Persian/Iranian culture. Query.

TIPS "Audience is the Iranian-American community in America and Americans interested in Persian culture."

MAGINATION PRESS

750 First St. NE, Washington DC 20002. (202)336-5618. **Fax:** (202)336-5624. **E-mail:** magination@apa.org. **Website:** www.apa.org. Estab. 1988. Magination Press is an imprint of the American Psychological Association. "We publish books dealing with the psycho/therapeutic resolution of children's problems and psychological issues with a strong self-help component." Submit complete ms. Full guidelines available on site. Materials returned only with SASE. **Publishes 12 titles/year. 75% of books from first-time authors.** Publishes a book 18-24 months after acceptance. Accepts simultaneous submissions. Responds to queries in 1-2 months; mss in 2-6 months.

NONFICTION All levels: psychological and social issues, self-help, health, multicultural, special needs.

FICTION All levels: psychological and social issues, self-help, health, parenting concerns and, special needs. Picture books, middle school readers.

MANDALA PUBLISHING

Mandala Publishing and Earth Aware Editions, 800 A St., San Rafael CA 94901. **E-mail:** info@mandalapublishing.com. **Website:** www.mandalaeartheditions.com. Estab. 1989. Publishes hardcover, trade paperback, and electronic originals. "In the traditions of the East, wisdom, truth, and beauty go hand in-hand. This is reflected in the great arts, music, yoga, and philosophy of India. Mandala Publishing strives to bring to its readers authentic and accessible renderings of thousands of years of wisdom and philosophy from this unique culture-timeless treasures that are our inspirations and guides. At Mandala, we believe that the arts, health, ecology, and spirituality of the great Vedic traditions are as relevant today as they were in sacred India thousands of years ago. As a distinguished publisher in the world of Vedic literature, lifestyle, and interests today, Mandala strives to provide accessible and meaningful works for the modern reader." **Publishes 12 titles/year. 200 queries received/year. 100 mss received/year. 40% of books from first-time authors. 100% from unagented writers. Pays 3-15% royalty on retail price.** Publishes ms 8 months after acceptance. Accepts simultaneous submissions. Responds in 6 months. Book catalog online.

NONFICTION Subjects include education, philosophy, photography, religion, spirituality. Query with SASE. Reviews artwork/photos. Send photocopies and thumbnails.

FICTION Subjects include juvenile, religious, spiritual. Query with SASE.

✪ MANOR HOUSE PUBLISHING, INC.

452 Cottingham Crescent, Ancaster ON L9G 3V6, Canada. **E-mail:** mbdavie@manor-house.biz. **E-mail:** mbdavie@manor-house.biz. **Website:** www.manor-house.biz. **Contact:** Mike Davie, president (novels and nonfiction). Estab. 1998. Publishes hardcover, trade paperback, and mass market paperback originals reprints. **Publishes 5-6 titles/year. 30 queries; 20 mss received/year. 90% of books from first-time authors. 90% from unagented writers. Pays 10% royalty on retail price.** Publishes book 1 year after acceptance. Accepts simultaneous submissions. Queries and mss to be sent by e-mail only. "We will respond in 30 days if interested-if not, there is no response. Do not follow up unless asked to do so.". Book catalog online. Guidelines available via e-mail.

NONFICTION Subjects include history, sex, social sciences, sociology, spirituality. "We are a Canadian publisher, so mss should be Canadian in content and aimed as much as possible at a wide, general audience. At this point in time, we are only publishing books by Canadian citizens residing in Canada." Query via e-mail. Submit proposal package, outline, bio, 3 sample chapters. Submit complete ms. Reviews artwork/photos. Send photocopies.

FICTION Subjects include adventure, experimental, gothic, historical, horror, humor, juvenile, literary, mystery, occult, poetry, regional, romance, short story collections, young adult. Stories should have Canadian settings and characters should be Canadian, but content should have universal appeal to wide audience. Query via e-mail. Submit proposal package, clips, bio, 3 sample chapters. Submit complete ms.

POETRY Poetry should engage, provoke, involve the reader.

TIPS "Our audience includes everyone-the general public/mass audience. Self-edit your work first, make sure it is well written with strong Canadian content."

MARINE TECHNIQUES PUBLISHING

126 Western Ave., Suite 266, Augusta ME 04330. (207)622-7984. **E-mail:** info@marinetechpublishing.com. **Website:** www.marinetechpublishing.com. **Contact:** James L. Pelletier, president/owner(commercial maritime); Maritime Associates Globally (commercial maritime). Estab. 1983. Trade paperback originals and reprints. "Publishes only books related to the commercial marine/maritime industry." **Publishes 2-5 titles/year. 20+ queries received/year. 40+ mss received/year. 50% of books from first-time authors. 75% from unagented writers. Pays 25-55% royalty on wholesale or retail price. Makes outright purchase.** Publishes ms 1 year after acceptance. Accepts simultaneous submissions. Responds in 2 months. Book catalog online. Guidelines available by e-mail.

💬 This publishing business is now for sale.

NONFICTION "We are concerned with 'maritime related works' and not recreational boating, but rather commercial maritime industries, such as deep-sea water transportation, offshore oil & gas, inland towing, coastal tug boat, 'water transportation industries.'" Submit proposal package, including all sample chapters; submit completed ms. Reviews artwork/photos as part of the ms package; send photocopies.

FICTION Subjects include adventure, military, war, maritime. Must be commercial maritime/marine related. Submit proposal package, including all sample chapters. Submit complete ms.

TIPS "Audience consists of commercial marine/maritime firms, persons employed in all aspects of the marine/maritime commercial water-transportation-related industries and recreational fresh and salt water fields, persons interested in seeking employment in the commercial marine industry; firms seeking to sell their products and services to vessel owners, operators, and managers; shipyards, vessel repair yards, recreational and yacht boat building and national and international ports and terminals involved with the commercial marine industry globally worldwide, etc."

MARTIN SISTERS PUBLISHING COMPANY, INC

P.O. Box 1154, Barbourville KY 40906-1499. **E-mail:** submissions@martinsisterspublishing.com. **Website:** www.martinsisterspublishing.com. **Contact:** Publisher/Editor (fiction/nonfiction). Estab. 2011. Firm/imprint publishes trade and mass market paperback originals; electronic originals. **Publishes 12 titles/year. 75% of books from first-time authors. 100% from unagented writers. Pays 7.5% royalty/max on print net. Pays 35% royalty/max on eBook net. No advance offered.** Publishes ms 9 months after acceptance. Accepts simultaneous submissions. Responds in 1 month on queries, 2 months on proposals, 3-6 months on mss. Catalog and guidelines online.

NONFICTION Subjects include Americana, child guidance, contemporary culture, cooking, creative nonfiction, education, gardening, history, house and home, humanities, labor, language, law, literature, memoirs, money, nutrition, parenting, psychology, regional, sociology, spirituality, womens issues, womens studies, western. Does not review artwork.

FICTION Subjects include adventure, confession, fantasy, historical, humor, juvenile, literary, mainstream, military, mystery, poetry in translation, regional, religious, romance, science fiction, short story collections, spiritual, sports, suspense, war, western, young adult. "Please place query letter, marketing plan and the first 5-10 pages of your manuscript (if you are submitting fiction) directly into your e-mail." Guidelines available on site.

MARVEL COMICS

135 W. 50th St., 7th Floor, New York NY 10020. **Website:** www.marvel.com. Publishes hardcover originals and reprints, trade paperback reprints, mass market comic book originals, electronic reprints. **Pays on a per page work for hire basis or creator-owned which is then contracted. Pays negotiable advance.** Responds in 3-5 weeks to queries. Guidelines online.

FICTION Subjects include adventure, comic books, fantasy, horror, humor, science fiction, young adult. Our shared universe needs new heroes and villains; books for younger readers and teens needed. Submit inquiry letter, idea submission form (download from website), SASE.

MASTER BOOKS

P.O. Box 726, Green Forest AR 72638. (870)438-5288. **Fax:** (870)438-5120. **E-mail:** submissions@newleafpress.net. **Website:** www.masterbooks.com. **Contact:** Craig Froman, acquisitions editor. Estab. 1975. Publishes 3 middle readers/year; 2 young adult nonfiction titles/year; 10 homeschool curriculum titles; 20 adult trade books/year. **10% of books from first-time authors. Pays authors royalty of 3-15% based on wholesale price.** Publishes book 1 year after acceptance. Accepts simultaneous submissions. Responds in 90 days. Book catalog available upon request. Guidelines online.

NONFICTION Picture books: activity books, animal, nature/environment, creation. Young readers, middle readers, young adults: activity books, animal, biography Christian, nature/environment, science, creation. Submission guidelines on website.

TIPS "All of our children's books are creation-based, including topics from the Book of Genesis. We look also for home school educational material that would be supplementary to a home school curriculum, especially elementary material."

MAVEN HOUSE PRESS

4 Snead Ct., Palmyra VA 22963. (610)883-7988. **Fax:** (888)894-3403. **E-mail:** jim@mavenhousepress.com. **Website:** www.mavenhousepress.com. **Contact:** Jim Pennypacker, publisher. Estab. 2012. Publishes hardcover, trade paperback, and electronic originals. Maven House Press publishes business books for executives and managers to help them lead their organizations to greatness. **Publishes 6 titles/year. Pays 10-50% royalty based on wholesale price. Does not pay advance.** Publishes ms 12 months after acceptance. Accepts simultaneous submissions. Responds in 1 month.

NONFICTION Subjects include business, economics, business/management. Submit proposal package including: outline, 1-2 sample chapters. See submission form online.

⊘ MAVERICK DUCK PRESS

E-mail: maverickduckpress@yahoo.com. **Website:** www.maverickduckpress.com. **Contact:** Kendall A. Bell, editor. Assistant Editors: Kayla Marie Middlebrook and Brielle Kelton. Estab. 2005. Maverick Duck

Press is a "publisher of chapbooks from undiscovered talent. We are looking for fresh and powerful work that shows a sense of innovation or a new take on passion or emotion. Previous publication in print or online journals could increase your chances of us accepting your manuscript." Does not want "unedited work." **Pays 20 author's copies.**

POETRY Send ms in Microsoft Word format with a cover letter with brief bio and publication credits. Chapbook mss may include previously published poems. "Previous publication is always a plus, as we may be more familiar with your work. Chapbook mss should have 16-24 poems, but no more than 24 poems."

MAVERICK MUSICALS AND PLAYS

89 Bergann Rd., Maleny QLD 4552, Australia. Phone/Fax: (61)(7)5494-4007. **E-mail:** gail@maverickmusicals.com. **Website:** www.maverickmusicals.com. **Contact:** Gail Denver, editor. Estab. 1978. Accepts simultaneous submissions. Guidelines online.

FICTION "Looking for two-act musicals and one- and two-act plays. See website for more details."

MCBOOKS PRESS

ID Booth Building, 520 N. Meadow St., Ithaca NY 14850. (607)272-2114. **E-mail:** mcbooks@mcbooks.com. **Website:** www.mcbooks.com. **Contact:** Alexander G. Skutt, publisher. Estab. 1979. Publishes trade paperback and hardcover originals and reprints. **Publishes 5 titles/year.** Accepts simultaneous submissions. Guidelines online.

"Currently not accepting submissions or queries for fiction or nonfiction." The only exception that we would look at is excellent nautical historical fiction that could be expanded into a series.

NONFICTION Subjects include history, marine subjects.

FICTION Subjects include adventure, military, war. Publishes Julian Stockwin, John Biggins, Colin Sargent, and Douglas W. Jacobson. Distributes titles through Independent Publishers Group.

TIPS "We are currently only publishing authors with whom we have a pre-existing relationship. If this policy changes, we will announce the change on our website."

MCCLELLAND & STEWART, LTD.

The Canadian Publishers, 320 Front St. W., Suite 1400, Toronto ON M5V 3B6, Canada. (416)364-4449. **Fax:** (416)598-7764. **Website:** www.mcclelland.com. Publishes hardcover, trade paperback, and mass market paperback originals and reprints. **Publishes 80 titles/year. 1,500 queries received/year. 10% of books from first-time authors. 30% from unagented writers. Pays 10-15% royalty on retail price (hardcover rates). Pays advance.** Publishes ms 1 year after acceptance. Accepts simultaneous submissions. Responds in 3 months to proposals.

NONFICTION Subjects include history, philosophy, photography, psychology, recreation, religion, science, sociology, sports, translation, travel, Canadiana. "We publish books primarily by Canadian authors." Submit outline. *All unsolicited mss returned unopened.*

FICTION "We publish work by established authors, as well as the work of new and developing authors." Query. *All unsolicited mss returned unopened.*

POETRY Only Canadian poets should apply. We publish only 4 titles each year. Query. *No unsolicted mss.*

THE MCDONALD & WOODWARD PUBLISHING CO.

695 Tall Oaks Dr., Newark OH 43055. (740)641-2691. **Fax:** (740)641-2692. **E-mail:** mwpubco@mwpubco.com. **Website:** www.mwpubco.com. **Contact:** Jerry N. McDonald, publisher. Estab. 1986. Publishes hardcover and trade paperback originals. McDonald & Woodward publishes books in natural history, cultural history, and natural resources. Currently emphasizing travel, natural and cultural history, and natural resource conservation. **Publishes 5 titles/year. 25 queries received/year. 20 mss received/year. Pays 10% royalty.** Accepts simultaneous submissions. Responds in less than 1 month. Book catalog online. Guidelines free on request; by e-mail.

NONFICTION Subjects include animals, architecture, environment, history, nature, science, travel, natural history. Query with SASE. Reviews artwork/photos. Photos are not required.

FICTION Subjects include historical. Query with SASE.

TIPS "Our books are meant for the curious and educated elements of the general population."

MARGARET K. MCELDERRY BOOKS

Imprint of Simon & Schuster Children's Publishing Division, 1230 Sixth Ave., New York NY 10020. (212)698-7200. **Website:** imprints.simonandschuster.

biz/margaret-k-mcelderry-books. Estab. 1971. "Margaret K. McElderry Books publishes hardcover and paperback trade books for children from pre-school age through young adult. This list includes picture books, middle grade and teen fiction, poetry, and fantasy. The style and subject matter of the books we publish is almost unlimited. We do not publish textbooks, coloring and activity books, greeting cards, magazines, pamphlets, or religious publications." **Publishes 30 titles/year. 15% of books from first-time authors. 50% from unagented writers. Pays authors royalty based on retail price. Pays illustrator royalty of by the project. Pays photographers by the project. Original artwork returned at job's completion. Offers $5,000-8,000 advance for new authors.** Accepts simultaneous submissions. Guidelines for #10 SASE.

NONFICTION Subjects include history, adventure. *No unsolicited mss. Agented submissions only.*

FICTION Subjects include adventure, fantasy, historical, mystery, picture books, young adult. *No unsolicited mss. Agented submissions only.*

TIPS "Read! The children's book field is competitive. See what's been done and what's out there before submitting. We look for high quality: an originality of ideas, clarity and felicity of expression, a well organized plot, and strong character-driven stories. We're looking for strong, original fiction, especially mysteries and middle grade humor. We are always interested in picture books for the youngest age reader. Study our titles."

MCFARLAND & CO., INC., PUBLISHERS

Box 611, Jefferson NC 28640. (336)246-4460. **Fax:** (336)246-5018. **E-mail:** info@mcfarlandpub.com. **Website:** www.mcfarlandpub.com. **Contact:** Editorial Department. Estab. 1979. Publishes hardcover and quality paperback originals. "McFarland publishes serious nonfiction in a variety of fields, including general reference, performing arts, popular culture, sports (particularly baseball); women's studies, librarianship, literature, Civil War, history and international studies. Currently emphasizing medieval history, automotive history. De-emphasizing memoirs." **Publishes 350 titles/year. 50% of books from first-time authors. 95% from unagented writers.** Publishes book 10 months after acceptance. Accepts simultaneous submissions. Responds in 1 month to queries. Guidelines online.

NONFICTION Subjects include history, recreation, sociology, African-American studies (very strong).

Reference books are particularly wanted—fresh material (i.e., not in head-to-head competition with an established title). "We prefer manuscripts of 250 or more double-spaced pages or at least 75,000 words." No fiction, New Age, exposes, poetry, children's books, devotional/inspirational works, Bible studies, or personal essays. Query with SASE. Submit outline, sample chapters. Reviews artwork/photos.

TIPS "We want well-organized knowledge of an area in which there is not information coverage at present, plus reliability so we don't feel we have to check absolutely everything. Our market is worldwide and libraries are an important part."

MCGRAW-HILL PROFESSIONAL BUSINESS

Imprint of The McGraw-Hill Companies, 2 Penn Plaza, New York NY 10121. (212)438-1000. **Website:** www.mcgraw-hill.com. McGraw Hill Professional is a publishing leader in business/investing, management, careers, self-help, consumer health, language reference, test preparation, sports/recreation, and general interest titles. Publisher not responsible for returning mss or proposals. Accepts simultaneous submissions. Guidelines online.

NONFICTION Subjects include child guidance, education, sports, management, consumer reference, English and foreign language reference. Current, up-to-date, original ideas are needed. Good self-promotion is key. Submit proposal package, outline, concept of book, competition and market info, CV.

MC PRESS

3695 W. Quail Heights Ct., Boise ID 83703. (208)629-7275. **Fax:** (208)639-1231. **E-mail:** duptmor@mcpressonline.com. **Website:** www.mc-store.com. **Contact:** David Uptmor, publisher. Editor: Anne Grubb. Estab. 2001. Publishes trade paperback originals. **Publishes 12 titles/year. 50 queries received/year. 15 mss received/year. 50% of books from first-time authors. 100% from unagented writers. Pays 10-16% royalty on wholesale price.** Publishes book 5 months after acceptance. Accepts simultaneous submissions. Responds in 1 month. Book catalog and ms guidelines free.

IMPRINTS MC Press, IBM Press.

NONFICTION "We specialize in computer titles targeted at IBM technologies." Submit proposal package, outline, 2 sample chapters, abstract. Reviews artwork/photos. Send photocopies.

MEDALLION PRESS

4222 Meridian Pkwy., Aurora IL 60504. (630)513-8316. **E-mail:** emily@medallionpress.com. **Website:** medallionpress.com. **Contact:** Emily Steele, editorial director. Estab. 2003. Publishes trade paperback, hardcover, e-book originals, book apps, and TREE-book. "We are an independent, innovative publisher looking for compelling, memorable stories told in distinctive voices." **Offers advance.** Publishes ms 1-2 years after acceptance. Accepts simultaneous submissions. Responds in 2-3 months to mss. Guidelines online. Currently closed to submissions.

NONFICTION Subjects include art, health, celebrity, design, fitness. *Agented only.* Please query.

FICTION Subjects include fantasy, historical, horror, literary, mainstream, mystery, romance, science fiction, suspense, young adult, thriller, YA-YA (YA written by young adults). Word count: 40,000-90,000 for YA; 60,000-120,000 for all others. No short stories, anthologies, erotica. Submit first 3 consecutive chapters and a synopsis through our online submission form. Please check if submissions are currently open before submitting.

TIPS "We are not affected by trends. We are simply looking for well-crafted, original, compelling works of fiction and nonfiction. Please visit our website for the most current guidelines prior to submitting anything to us. Please check if submissions are currently open before submitting."

MEDICAL GROUP MANAGEMENT ASSOCIATION

104 Inverness Terrace E., Englewood CO 80112. (303)799-1111. **E-mail:** support@mgma.com. **Website:** www.mgma.org. Estab. 1926. Publishes professional and scholarly hardcover, paperback, and electronic originals, and trade paperback reprints. **Publishes 6 titles/year. 18 queries received/year. 6 mss received/year. 30% of books from first-time authors. 100% from unagented writers. Pays 8-17% royalty on net sales (twice a year). Pays $2,000-5,000 advance.** Publishes ms 6 months after acceptance. Accepts simultaneous submissions. Responds in less than 3 weeks to queries. Book catalog online. Guidelines online.

NONFICTION Subjects include education, health. Submit proposal package, outline, 3 sample chapters. Submit complete ms. Reviews artwork/photos. Send photocopies.

TIPS "Audience includes medical practice managers and executives. Our books are geared at the business side of medicine."

MEDICAL PHYSICS PUBLISHING

4555 Helgesen Dr., Madison WI 53718. (608)224-4508. **Fax:** (608)224-5016. **E-mail:** todd@medicalphysics.org. **Website:** www.medicalphysics.org. **Contact:** Todd Hanson, editor. Estab. 1985. Publishes hardcover and paperback originals and reprints. "We are a nonprofit, membership organization publishing affordable books in medical physics and related fields. Currently emphasizing biomedical engineering. De-emphasizing books for the general public." **Publishes 5-6 titles/year. 10-20 queries received/year. 100% from unagented writers. Pays 10% royalty on wholesale price.** Publsihes ms 1 year after acceptance. Accepts simultaneous submissions. Responds in 6 months to mss. Book catalog available via website or upon request.

NONFICTION Subjects include symposium proceedings in the fields of medical physics and radiology.. Submit complete ms. Reviews artwork/photos. Send disposable copies.

MELANGE BOOKS, LLC

White Bear Lake MN 55110-5538. **E-mail:** melange-books@melange-books.com. **E-mail:** submissions@melange-books.com. **Website:** www.melange-books.com. **Contact:** Nancy Schumacher, publisher and acquiring editor for Melange and Satin Romance; Caroline Andrus, acquiring editor for Fire and Ice for Young Adult. Estab. 2011. Publishes trade paperback originals and electronic originals. Melange is a royalty-paying company publishing e-books and print books. **Publishes 75 titles/year. Receives 1,000 queries/year; 700 mss/year. 65% of books from first-time authors. 75% from unagented writers. Authors receive a minimum of 20% royalty on print sales, 40% on electronic book sales. Does not offer an advance.** Publishes book 12-15 months after acceptance. Accepts simultaneous submissions. Responds in 1 month on queries; 2 months on proposals; 4-6 months on mss. Send SASE for book catalog. Guidelines online.

IMPRINTS Fire and Ice (young and new adult); Satin Romance.

FICTION Subjects include adventure, contemporary, erotica, fantasy, gay, gothic, historical, lesbian, mainstream, multicultural, mystery, romance, science fiction, suspense, western, young adult. Submit a clean mss by following guidelines on website. Query electronically by clicking on "submissions" on website. Include a synopsis and 4 chapters.

⚫ MELBOURNE UNIVERSITY PUBLISHING, LTD.

Subsidiary of University of Melbourne, Level 1, 11-15 Argyle Pl. S., Carlton VIC 3053, Australia. (61)(3)934-20300. **Fax:** (61)(3)9342-0399. **E-mail:** mup-contact@unimelb.edu.au. **E-mail:** mup-submissions@unimelb.edu.au. **Website:** www.mup.com.au. **Contact:** The Executive Assistant. Estab. 1922. **Publishes 80 titles/year.** Accepts simultaneous submissions. Responds to queries in 4 months if interested. Guidelines online.

IMPRINTS Melbourne University Press; The Miegunyah Press (strong Australian content); Victory Books.

NONFICTION Subjects include philosophy, science, social sciences, Aboriginal studies, cultural studies, gender studies, natural history. Submit using MUP Book Proposal Form available online.

MENASHA RIDGE PRESS

2204 First Ave. S., Suite 102, Birmingham AL 35233. (205)322-0439. **E-mail:** tim@keencommunication.com. **Website:** www.menasharidge.com. **Contact:** Tim Jackson, acquisitions editor. Publishes hardcover and trade paperback originals. Menasha Ridge Press publishes distinctive books in the areas of outdoor sports, travel, and diving. "Our authors are among the best in their fields." **Publishes 20 titles/year. 30% of books from first-time authors. 85% from unagented writers. Pays varying royalty. Pays varying advance.** Publishes ms 1 year after acceptance. Accepts simultaneous submissions. Responds in 2 months to queries.

NONFICTION Subjects include nature, recreation, sports, travel, outdoors. Most concepts are generated in-house, but a few come from outside submissions. Submit proposal package, resume, clips. Reviews artwork/photos.

MERRIAM PRESS

133 Elm St., Suite 3R, Bennington VT 05201. (802)447-0313. **E-mail:** ray@merriam-press.com. **Website:** www.merriam-press.com. Estab. 1988. Publishes hardcover and softcover trade paperback originals and reprints. Many titles are also made available in PDF and eBook editions. "Merriam Press specializes in military history, particularly World War II history. We are also branching out into other genres, including fiction, historical fiction, poetry, children." **Publishes 50+ titles/year. 70-90% of books from first-time authors. 100% from unagented writers. Pays 10% royalty on actual selling price. Does not pay advance.** Publishes ms 6 months or less after acceptance. Responds quickly (e-mail preferred) to queries. Book catalog and guidelines online.

NONFICTION Subjects include Americana, history, memoirs, military, war. Especially but not limited to military history. Query with SASE or by e-mail first. Send copies of sample chapters or entire ms by mail or on disk/flash drive or as an e-mail attachment (preferred in Word .doc/.docx file format). Reviews artwork/photos.

FICTION Subjects include historical, military, poetry, war. Especially but not limited to military history. Query with SASE or by e-mail first.

POETRY Especially but not limited to military topics. Query with SASE or by e-mail first.

TIPS "Our military history books are geared for military historians, collectors, model kit builders, wargamers, veterans, general enthusiasts. We now publish some historical fiction and poetry and will consider well-written books on a variety of non-military topics."

MESSIANIC JEWISH PUBLISHERS

6120 Day Long Ln., Clarksville MD 21029. (410)531-6644. **E-mail:** editor@messianicjewish.net. **Website:** www.messianicjewish.net. Publishes hardcover and trade paperback originals and reprints. **Publishes 6-12 titles/year. Pays 7-15% royalty on wholesale price.** Accepts simultaneous submissions. Guidelines via e-mail.

NONFICTION Subjects include religion. Text must demonstrate keen awareness of Jewish culture and thought, and Biblical literacy. Jewish themes only. Query with SASE. Unsolicited mss are not returned.

FICTION Subjects include religious. "We publish very little fiction. Jewish or Biblical themes are a must. Text must demonstrate keen awareness of Jewish culture and thought." Query with SASE. Unsolicited mss are not return.

METAL POWDER INDUSTRIES FEDERATION

105 College Rd. E., Princeton NJ 08540. (609)452-7700. **Fax:** (609)987-8523. **Website:** www.mpif.org. Estab. 1946. Publishes hardcover originals. "Metal

Powder Industries publishes monographs, textbooks, handbooks, design guides, conference proceedings, standards, and general titles in the field of powder metallurgy or particulate materials." **Publishes 10 titles/year. Pays 3-12% royalty on wholesale or retail price. Pays $3,000-5,000 advance.** Accepts simultaneous submissions. Responds in 1 month to queries.

NONFICTION Work must relate to powder metallurgy or particulate materials.

◐ METHUEN PUBLISHING LTD

Editorial Department, 35 Hospital Fields Rd., York YO10 4DZ, United Kingdom. **E-mail:** editorial@ metheun.co.uk. **Website:** www.methuen.co.uk. Estab. 1889. **Pays royalty.** Accepts simultaneous submissions. Guidelines online.

◐ No unsolicited mss; synopses and ideas welcome. Prefers to be approached via agents or a letter of inquiry. No first novels, cookery books or personal memoirs.

NONFICTION Subjects include contemporary culture, history, psychology, sports. No cookbooks or memoirs. Query with SASE. Submit outline, resume, publishing history, clips, bio, SASE.

FICTION No first novels. Query with SASE. Submit proposal package, outline, outline/proposal, resume, publishing history, clips, bio, SASE.

TIPS "We recommend that all prospective authors attempt to find an agent before submitting to publishers and we do not encourage unagented submissions."

⊘ MIAMI UNIVERSITY PRESS

356 Bachelor Hall, Miami University, Oxford OH 45056. **E-mail:** mupress@miamioh.edu. **Website:** www.miamioh.edu/mupress. **Contact:** Keith Tuma, editor; Amy Toland, managing editor. Estab. 1992. Publishes 1-2 books of poetry/year and 1 novella, in paperback editions. Accepts simultaneous submissions.

POETRY Miami University Press is unable to respond to unsolicited mss and queries.

MICHIGAN STATE UNIVERSITY PRESS

1405 S. Harrison Rd., Suite 25, East Lansing MI 48823. (517)355-9543. **Fax:** (517)432-2611. **E-mail:** msupress@msu.edu. **Website:** msupress.org. **Contact:** Alex Schwartz and Julie Loehr, acquisitions. Estab. 1947. Publishes hardcover and softcover originals. Michigan State University Press has notably represented both scholarly publishing and the mission of Michigan State University with the publication of numerous award-winning books and scholarly journals. In addition, they publish nonfiction that addresses, in a more contemporary way, social concerns, such as diversity and civil rights. They also publish literary fiction and poetry. **Pays variable royalty.** Book catalog and ms guidelines online.

NONFICTION Distributes books for: University of Calgary Press, University of Alberta Press, and University of Manitoba Press. Submit proposal/outline and sample chapter. Hard copy is preferred but e-mail proposals are also accepted. Initial submissions to MSU Press should be in the form of a short letter of inquiry and a sample chapter(s), as well as our preliminary Marketing Questionnaire, which can be downloaded from their website. We do not accept: Festschrifts, conference papers, or unrevised dissertations. Reviews artwork/photos.

FICTION Subjects include literary. Publishes literary fiction. Submit proposal.

POETRY Publishes poetry collections. Submit proposal with sample poems.

MICROSOFT PRESS

E-mail: 4bkideas@microsoft.com. **Website:** www.microsoft.com/learning/en/us/microsoft-press-books.aspx. **Publishes 80 titles/year. 25% of books from first-time authors. 90% from unagented writers.** Accepts simultaneous submissions. Book proposal guidelines online.

NONFICTION Subjects include software. A book proposal should consist of the following information: TOC, a resume with author biography, a writing sample, and a questionnaire. "We place a great deal of emphasis on your proposal. A proposal provides us with a basis for evaluating the idea of the book and how fully your book fulfills its purpose."

MILKWEED EDITIONS

1011 Washington Ave. S., Suite 300, Minneapolis MN 55415. (612)332-3192. **Fax:** (612)215-2550. **Website:** www.milkweed.org. **Contact:** Patrick Thomas, managing editor. Estab. 1979. Publishes hardcover, trade paperback, and electronic originals; trade paperback and electronic reprints. "Milkweed Editions publishes with the intention of making a humane impact on society, in the belief that literature is a transformative art uniquely able to convey the essential experiences of the human heart and spirit. To that end, Milkweed Editions publishes distinctive voices of literary merit in handsomely designed, visually dynamic books, exploring the ethical, cultural, and esthetic issues that free societies need continually to address." **Publishes 15-20 titles/year. 25% of books from first-time authors. 75% from unagented writers. Pays authors variable royalty based on retail price. Offers advance against royalties. Pays varied advance from $500-10,000.** Publishes book in 18 months. Accepts simultaneous submissions. Responds in 6 months. Book catalog online. Only accepts submissions during open submission periods. See website for guidelines.

NONFICTION Subjects include agriculture, animals, art, contemporary culture, creative nonfiction, environment, gardening, gay, government, history, humanities, language, literature, multicultural, nature, politics, translation, world affairs. Does not review artwork.

FICTION Subjects include experimental, short story collections, translation, young adult. Novels for adults and for readers 8-13. High literary quality. For adult readers: literary fiction, nonfiction, poetry, essays. Middle readers: adventure, contemporary, fantasy, multicultural, nature/environment, suspense/mystery. Average length: middle readers—90-200 pages. No romance, mysteries, science fiction. "Please submit a query letter with three opening chapters (of a novel) or three representative stories (of a collection). Publishes YR."

POETRY Milkweed Editions is "looking for poetry manuscripts of high quality that embody humane values and contribute to cultural understanding." Not limited in subject matter. Open to writers with previously published books of poetry or a minimum of 6 poems published in nationally distributed commercial or literary journals. Considers translations and bilingual mss. Query with SASE; submit completed ms.

TIPS "We are looking for excellent writing with the intent of making a humane impact on society. Please read submission guidelines before submitting and acquaint yourself with our books in terms of style and quality before submitting. Many factors influence our selection process, so don't get discouraged. Nonfiction is focused on literary writing about the natural world, including living well in urban environments."

MILKWEED FOR YOUNG READERS

Milkweed Editions, Open Book Building, 1011 Washington Ave. S., Suite 300, Minneapolis MN 55415.

(612)332-3192. **Fax:** (612)215-2550. **Website:** www.milkweed.org. **Contact:** Patrick Thomas, managing editor. Estab. 1984. Publishes hardcover and trade paperback originals. "We are looking first of all for high quality literary writing. We publish books with the intention of making a humane impact on society." **Publishes 3-4 titles/year. 25% of books from first-time authors. 50% from unagented writers. Pays 7% royalty on retail price. Pays variable advance.** Publishes ms 1 year after acceptance. Accepts simultaneous submissions. Responds in 6 months to queries. Book catalog for $1.50. Guidelines online.

FICTION Subjects include adventure, fantasy, historical, humor, animal, environmental. "Milkweed Editions now accepts manuscripts online through our Submission Manager. If you're a first-time submitter, you'll need to fill in a simple form and then follow the instructions for selecting and uploading your manuscript. Please make sure that your manuscript follows the submission guidelines."

⊘ THE MILLBROOK PRESS

Lerner Publishing Group, 1251 Washington Ave N, Minneapolis MN 55401. **E-mail:** info@lernerbooks.com. **Website:** www.lernerbooks.com. **Contact:** Carol Hinz, editorial director. "Millbrook Press publishes informative picture books, illustrated nonfiction titles, and inspiring photo-driven titles for grades K–5. Our authors approach curricular topics with a fresh point of view. Our fact-filled books engage readers with fun yet accessible writing, high-quality photographs, and a wide variety of illustration styles. We cover subjects ranging from the parts of speech and other language arts skills; to history, science, and math; to art, sports, crafts, and other interests. Millbrook Press is the home of the best-selling Words Are CATegorical® series and Bob Raczka's Art Adventures. We do not accept unsolicited manuscripts from authors. Occasionally, we may put out a call for submissions, which will be announced on our website." Accepts simultaneous submissions.

MINNESOTA HISTORICAL SOCIETY PRESS

Minnesota Historical Society, 345 Kellogg Blvd. W., St. Paul MN 55102. (651)259-3200. **Fax:** (651)297-1345. **E-mail:** ann.regan@mnhs.org. **Website:** www.mnhs.org/mnhspress. **Contact:** Ann Regan, editor-in-chief. Estab. 1852. Publishes hardcover, trade paperback and electronic originals; trade paperback and electronic reprints. The Minnesota Historical Society Press is a leading publisher of the history and culture of Minnesota and the Upper Midwest. The Minnesota Historical Society Press seeks proposals for book manuscripts relating to the history and culture of Minnesota and the Upper Midwest. We are especially interested in excellent works of history and in well-researched and well-written manuscripts that use the best tools of narrative journalism to tell history for general audiences. Successful manuscripts will address themes or issues that are important to understanding life in this region and will reveal a strong sense of place. Preferred topics include Native American studies, Scandinavian studies, nature and environment, women's history, popular culture, food, adventure and travel, true crime, war and conflict, and the histories of Minnesota's diverse peoples. **Publishes 20 titles/year. 300 queries; 150 mss received/year. 60% of books from first-time authors. 95% from unagented writers. Royalties are negotiated; 5-10% on wholesale price. Pays $1,000 and up.** Publishes ms 16 months after acceptance. Accepts simultaneous submissions. Responds in 1-4 months. Book catalog online. Guidelines online.

NONFICTION Subjects include Americana, community, contemporary culture, cooking, creative nonfiction, ethnic, history, memoirs, multicultural, music, photography, politics, pop culture, regional, Native American studies. Books must have a connection to the Midwest. Regional works only. Submit proposal package, outline, 1 sample chapter and other materials listed in our online website in author guidelines: CV, brief description, intended audience, readership, length of ms, schedule. Reviews artwork/photos. Send photocopies.

MISSOURI HISTORICAL SOCIETY PRESS

The Missouri Historical Society, P.O. Box 11940, St. Louis MO 63112. (314)746-4558 or (314)746-4556. **Fax:** (314)746-4548. **E-mail:** lmitchell@mohistory.org. **Website:** www.mohistory.org. **Contact:** Lauren Mitchell, director of publications. Publishes hardcover and trade paperback originals and reprints. **Publishes 2-4 titles/year. 30 queries; 20 mss received/year. 10% of books from first-time authors. 80% from unagented writers. Pays 5-10% royalty.** Accepts simultaneous submissions. Responds in 1-2 months.

NONFICTION Subjects include history, multicultural, regional, sports, popular culture, photography,

children's nonfiction. Query with SASE and request author-proposal form.

TIPS "We're looking for new perspectives, even if the topics are familiar. You'll get our attention with non-traditional voices and views."

MITCHELL LANE PUBLISHERS, INC.

P.O. Box 196, Hockessin DE 19707. (302)234-9426. **Fax:** (866)834-4164. **E-mail:** barbaramitchell@mitchelllane.com; customerservice@mitchelllane.com. **Website:** www.mitchelllane.com. **Contact:** Barbara Mitchell, publisher. Estab. 1993. Publishes hardcover and library bound originals. **Publishes 80 titles/year. 100 queries received/year. 5 mss received/year. 0% of books from first-time authors. 90% from unagented writers. Work purchased outright from authors (range: $350-2,000). Pays illustrators by the project (range: $40-400).** Publishes ms 1 year after acceptance. Responds only if interested to queries. Book catalog available free.

NONFICTION Subjects include ethnic, multicultural. Young readers, middle readers, young adults: biography, nonfiction, and curriculum-related subjects. Average word length: 4,000-50,000 words. Recently published: *My Guide to US Citizenship*, *Rivers of the World* and *Vote America*. Query with SASE. *All unsolicited mss discarded.*

TIPS "We hire writers on a 'work-for-hire' basis to complete book projects we assign. Send résumé and writing samples that do not need to be returned."

MONDIAL

203 W. 107th St., Suite 6C, New York NY 10025. 212-864-7095. **Fax:** (208)361-2863. **E-mail:** contact@mondialbooks.com. **Website:** www.mondialbooks.com; www.librejo.com. **Contact:** Andrew Moore, editor. Estab. 1996. Publishes hard cover, trade paperback originals and reprints. **Publishes 20 titles/year. 2,000 queries received/year. 500 mss received/year. 20% of books from first-time authors. Pays 10% royalty on wholesale price.** Publishes ms 4 months after acceptance. Accepts simultaneous submissions. Responds to queries in 3 months. Responds only if interested. Guidelines available online.

NONFICTION Subjects include ethnic, history, literary criticism, memoirs, multicultural, philosophy, psychology, sex, sociology, translation. Submit proposal package, outline, 1 sample chapters. Send only electronically by e-mail.

FICTION Subjects include adventure, erotica, ethnic, historical, literary, multicultural, mystery, poetry, romance, short story collections, translation. Query through online submission form.

MONTANA HISTORICAL SOCIETY PRESS

225 N. Roberts St., Helene MT 59620-1201. (406)444-4741. **E-mail:** mholz@mt.gov. **Website:** https://mhs.mt.gov/pubs/press. **Contact:** Molly Holz, editor. Estab. 1956. Publishes hardcover originalsand trade paperback originals and reprints. **Publishes 4 titles/year. 24 queries received/year. 16 mss received/year. 50% of books from first-time authors. 100% from unagented writers. Pays 5-10% royalty on wholesale price.** Publishes ms 1 year after acceptance. Responds in 1 month to queries; 2 months to proposals; 4 months to mss. Book catalog online. Guidelines online.

NONFICTION Subjects include history, regional, travel. "We publish history and environmental studies books focusing on the northern plains and Rocky Mountains." Query with SASE.

TIPS "Audience includes history buffs; people with an interest in Yellowstone National Park."

🅐⊘ MOODY PUBLISHERS

Moody Bible Institute, 820 N. LaSalle Blvd., Chicago IL 60610. (800)678-8812. **Fax:** (312)329-4157. **E-mail:** authors@moody.edu. **Website:** www.moodypublishers.org. **Contact:** Acquisitions Coordinator. Estab. 1894. Publishes hardcover, trade, and mass market paperback originals. "The mission of Moody Publishers is to educate and edify the Christian and to evangelize the non-Christian by ethically publishing conservative, evangelical Christian literature and other media for all ages around the world, and to help provide resources for Moody Bible Institute in its training of future Christian leaders." **Publishes 60 titles/year. 1,500 queries received/year. 2,000 mss received/year. 1% of books from first-time authors. 80% from unagented writers. Royalty varies.** Publishes book 1 year after acceptance. Responds in 2-3 months to queries. Book catalog for 9×12 envelope and 4 first-class stamps. Guidelines online.

NONFICTION Subjects include child guidance, religion, spirituality. "We are no longer reviewing queries or unsolicited manuscripts unless they come to us through an agent,are from an author who has published with us, an associate from a Moody Bible Institute ministry or a personal contact at a writer's conference. Unsolicited proposals will be returned only if proper postage is included. We are not able to acknowledge the receipt of your unsolicited proposal." Does not accept unsolicited nonfiction submissions.

FICTION Subjects include fantasy, historical, mystery, religious, science fiction, young adult. *Agented submissions only.*

TIPS "In our fiction list, we're looking for Christian storytellers rather than teachers trying to present a message. Your motivation should be to delight the reader. Using your skills to create beautiful works is glorifying to God."

MOREHOUSE PUBLISHING CO.

Church Publishing Incorporated, 19 E. 34th St., New York NY 10016. **Fax:** (717)541-8136. **E-mail:** dperkins@cpg.org. **Website:** www.christianpublishing.org. **Contact:** Davis Perkins. Estab. 1884. Publishes hardcover and paperback originals. Morehouse Publishing publishes mainline Christian books, primarily Episcopal/Anglican works. Currently emphasizing Christian spiritual direction. **Publishes 35 titles/year. 50% of books from first-time authors. Pays small advance.** Publishes book 18 months after acceptance. Accepts simultaneous submissions. Responds in 2-3 months to queries. Guidelines online.

NONFICTION Subjects include religion, Christian spirituality, liturgies, congregational resources, issues around Christian life. Submit outline, résumé, 1-2 sample chapters, market analysis.

MOTORBOOKS

Quayside Publishing Group, 400 First Ave. N., Suite 400, Minneapolis MN 55401. (612)344-8100. **Fax:** (612)344-8691. **E-mail:** zack.miller@quartous.com. **Website:** www.motorbooks.com. **Contact:** Zack Miller. Estab. 1973. Publishes hardcover and paperback originals. "Motorbooks is one of the world's leading transportation publishers, covering subjects from classic motorcycles to heavy equipment to today's latest automotive technology. We satisfy our customers' high expectations by hiring top writers and photographers and presenting their work in handsomely designed books that work hard in the shop and look good on the coffee table." **Publishes 200 titles/year. 300 queries; 50 mss received/year. 95% from unagented writers. Pays $5,000 average advance.** Publishes ms 1 year after acceptance. Accepts simultaneous submissions. Responds in 6-8 months to proposals. Book catalog available free. Guidelines online.

NONFICTION Subjects include Americana, history, hobbies, photography, translation. State qualifications for doing book. Transportation-related subjects. Query with SASE. Reviews artwork/photos. Send photocopies.

MOUNTAINEERS BOOKS

1001 SW Klickitat Way, Suite 201, Seattle WA 98134-1162. (206)223-6303. **Fax:** (206)223-6306. **E-mail:** submissions@mountaineersbooks.org. **Website:** www.mountaineersbooks.org. **Contact:** Kate Rogers, editor in chief. Estab. 1961. Publishes hardcover and trade paperback originals and reprints. "Mountaineers Books specializes in expert, authoritative books dealing with mountaineering, hiking, backpacking, skiing, snowshoeing, etc. These can be either how-to-do-it or where-to-do-it (guidebooks). Currently emphasizing regional conservation and natural history." **Publishes 40 titles/year. 25% of books from first-time authors. 98% from unagented writers. Pays advance.** Publishes ms 1 year after acceptance. Responds in 3 months to queries. Guidelines online.

NONFICTION Subjects include recreation, regional, sports, translation, travel, natural history, conservation. Accepts nonfiction translations. Looks for expert knowledge, good organization. Also interested in nonfiction adventure narratives. Does not want to see anything dealing with hunting, fishing, or motorized travel. Submit outline, 2 sample chapters, bio.

TIPS "The type of book the writer has the best chance of selling to our firm is an authoritative guidebook (*in our field*) to a specific area not otherwise covered; or a how-to that is better than existing competition (again, *in our field*)."

MOUNTAIN PRESS PUBLISHING CO.

P.O. Box 2399, Missoula MT 59806. (406)728-1900 or (800)234-5308. **Fax:** (406)728-1635. **E-mail:** info@mtnpress.com. **Website:** www.mountain-press.com. **Contact:** Jennifer Carey, editor. Estab. 1948. Publishes hardcover and trade paperback originals. "We are expanding our Roadside Geology, Geology Underfoot, and Roadside History series (done on a state-by-state basis). We are interested in well-written regional field guides—plants and flowers—and readable history and natural history." **Publishes 15 titles/year. 50% of books from first-time authors. 90% from unagented writers. Pays 7-12% royalty on wholesale price.** Publishes ms 2 years after acceptance. Accepts simultaneous submissions. Responds in 3 months to queries. Book catalog online.

⬤ Expanding children's/juvenile nonfiction titles.

NONFICTION Subjects include animals, history, regional, science. No personal histories or journals, poetry or fiction. Query with SASE. Submit outline, sample chapters. Reviews artwork/photos.

TIPS "Find out what kind of books a publisher is interested in and tailor your writing to them; research markets and target your audience. Research other books on the same subjects. Make yours different. Don't present your manuscript to a publisher—sell it. Give the information needed to make a decision on a title. Please learn what we publish before sending your proposal. We are a 'niche' publisher."

⊘ MOVING PARTS PRESS

10699 Empire Grade, Santa Cruz CA 95060. (831)427-2271. **E-mail:** frice@movingpartspress.com. **Website:** www.movingpartspress.com. **Contact:** Felicia Rice, poetry editor. Estab. 1977. Moving Part Press publishes handsome, innovative books, broadsides, and prints that "explore the relationship of word and image, typography and the visual arts, the fine arts and popular culture." Accepts simultaneous submissions.

POETRY *Does not accept unsolicited mss.*

MSI PRESS

1760-F Airline Hwy, #203, Hollister CA 95023. **Fax:** (831)886-2486. **E-mail:** editor@msipress.com. **Website:** www.msipress.com. **Contact:** Betty Leaver, managing editor (self-help, spirituality, religion, memoir, mind/body/spirit, some humor, popular psychology, foreign tales, parenting). Estab. 2003. Publishes trade paperback originals and corresponding e-books. "We are a small, 'boutique' press that specializes in award-winning quality publications, refined through strong personal interactions and productive working relationships between our editors and our authors. A small advance may be offered to previously published authors with a strong book and strong platform. We will accept first-time authors with credibility in their fields and a strong platform, but we do not offer advances to first-time authors. We may refer authors with a good book but little credibility or lacking a strong platform to San Juan Books, our co-publishing venture." **Publishes 20-25 titles/year. 100-200 10% of books from first-time authors. 100% from unagented writers. Pays 10% royalty on retail price.**

Pays small advance to previously published authors with good sales history. Does not pay advance to first-time authors or to authors whose previously published books do not have a good track record. Publishes ms 8-12 months after acceptance. Responds in 2 weeks to queries sent by e-mail and to proposals submitted via the template on our website. Catalog online. Guidelines online.

IMPRINTS MSI Press, LLC; San Juan Books.

NONFICTION Subjects include creative nonfiction, education, health, humanities, memoirs, parenting, philosophy, psychology, religion, spirituality, travel, womens issues, Ask; we are open to new ideas.. "We continue to expand our spirituality, psychology, and self-help lines and are interested in adding to our collection of books in Spanish. We do not do or publish translations." Does not want erotica. Submit proposal package, including: outline, 1 sample chapter, professional resume, platform. Prefers electronic submissions. Note that we are open to foreign writers (non-native speakers of English), but please have an English editor proofread the submission prior to sending. Reviews artwork/photos; send computer disk, or, preferably, e-file.

TIPS "Learn the mechanics of writing. Too many submissions are full of grammar and punctuation errors and poorly worded and trite expressions. Read to write; observe and analyze how the great authors of all time use language to good avail. Capture our attention with active verbs, not bland description. Before writing your book, determine its audience, write to that audience, and go about developing your credibility with that audience—and then tell us what you have done and are doing in your proposal."

☹ MUSSIO VENTURES PUBLISHING LTD.

106 - 1500 Hartley Ave., Coquitlam BC V3K 7A1, Canada. **E-mail:** info@backroadmapbooks.com. **Website:** www.backroadmapbooks.com. Estab. 1993. "We are in the business of producing, publishing, distributing and marketing Outdoor Recreation guidebooks and maps. We are also actively looking to advance our digital side of the business including making our products Google Earth, cell phone or iPhone and GPS compatible." **Publishes 5 titles/year. 5 queries received/year. 2 mss received/year. 25% of books from first-time authors. Makes outright purchase of $2,000-4,800. Pays $1,000 advance.** Publishes ms 12 months after acceptance. Accepts simultaneous submissions. Responds in 1 month. Book catalog available free.

NONFICTION Subjects include maps and guides. Submit proposal package, outline/proposal, 1 sample chapter. Reviews artwork/photos. Send photocopies and digital files.

TIPS "Audience includes outdoor recreation enthusiasts and travellers. Provide a proposal including an outline and samples."

NATIONAL ASSOCIATION FOR MUSIC EDUCATION

1806 Robert Fulton Dr., Reston VA 20191-4348. **Fax:** (703)860-1531. **E-mail:** carolinea@nafme.org. **Website:** www.nafme.org. **Contact:** Caroline Arlington. Estab. 1907. Publishes hardcover and trade paperback originals. "Our mission is to advance music education by encouraging the study and making of music by all." **Publishes 5 titles/year. 75 queries received/year. 50 mss received/year. 40% of books from first-time authors. 100% from unagented writers. Pays royalty on retail price. Does not pay advance.** Publishes ms 1-2 years after acceptance. Responds in 2 months to queries; 4 months to proposals. Catalog and guidelines online.

◯   All our books are currently published in partnership with Rowman & Littlefield.

NONFICTION Subjects include education, multicultural, music, music education. Mss evaluated by professional music educators. "We don't publish books that are effectively ads for a program or product." Submit proposal package, outline, 1-3 sample chapters, bio, CV, marketing strategy. For journal articles, submit electronically to http://mc.manuscriptcentral.com/mej. Authors will be required to set up an online account on the SAGET-RACK system powered by ScholarOne (this can take about 30 minutes). From their account, a new submission can be initiated.

TIPS "Look online at nafme.org for book proposal guidelines. No telephone calls. We are committed to music education books that will serve as the very best resources for music educators, students and their parents."

Ⓐ⊘ NATIONAL GEOGRAPHIC CHILDREN'S BOOKS

1145 17th St. NW, Washington DC 20090-8199. (800)647-5463. **Website:** www.ngchildrensbooks.org. National Geographic CHildren's Books provides quality nonfiction for children and young adults by award-winning authors. *This market does not currently accept unsolicited mss.*

NATUREGRAPH PUBLISHERS, INC.

P.O. Box 1047, 3543 Indian Creek Rd., Happy Camp CA 96039. (530)493-5353. **Fax:** (530)493-5240. **E-mail:** nature@sisqtel.net. **Website:** www.naturegraph.com. **Contact:** Barbara Brown, owner. Estab. 1946. Publishes trade paperback originals. **Publishes 2 titles/year. 300 queries; 12 mss received/year. 80% of books from first-time authors. Pays royalties. Does not pay advance.** Publishes ms 2 years after acceptance. Accepts simultaneous submissions. Responds in 1 month to queries; 2 months to mss. Book catalog for #10 SASE.

NONFICTION Subjects include ethnic, multicultural, New Age, science, crafts.

TIPS "Please-always send a stamped reply envelope. Publishers get hundreds of manuscripts yearly."

THE NAUTICAL & AVIATION PUBLISHING CO. OF AMERICA

845 A Lowcountry Blvd., Mt. Pleasant SC 29464. (843)856-0561. **Fax:** (843)856-3164. **E-mail:** nauticalaviationpublishing@comcast.net. **Website:** www.nauticandaviation.com. Estab. 1979. Publishes hardcover and trade paperback originals and reprints. **Publishes 6 titles/year. 200 queries received/year. Pays royalty.** Accepts simultaneous submissions. Book catalog and guidelines available free.

NONFICTION Subjects include military history, fiction and reference. Query with SASE. Submit 3 sample chapters, synopsis.

FICTION Subjects include adventure, historical, military, war. Submit complete ms with cover letter and brief synopsis.

TIPS "We are primarily a nonfiction publisher, but we will review historical fiction of military interest with strong literary merit."

NAVAL INSTITUTE PRESS

US Naval Institute, 291 Wood Rd., Annapolis MD 21402. (410)268-6110. **Fax:** (410)295-1084. **Website:** www.usni.org. Estab. 1873. "The Naval Institute Press publishes trade and scholarly nonfiction. We are interested in national and international security, naval, military, military jointness, intelligence, and special warfare, both current and historical." **Publishes 80-90 titles/year. 50% of books from first-time authors. 90% from unagented writers.** Accepts simultaneous submissions. Guidelines online.

NONFICTION Submit proposal package with outline, author bio, TOC, description/synopsis, sample chapter(s), page/word count, number of illustrations, ms completion date, intended market; or submit complete ms. Send SASE with sufficient postage for return of ms. Send by postal mail only. No e-mail submissions, please.

⊘ NAVPRESS

3820 N. 30th St., Colorado Springs CO 80904. **Website:** www.navpress.com. Estab. 1975. Publishes hardcover, trade paperback, direct and mass market paperback originals and reprints; electronic books and Bible studies. **Pays royalty. Pays low or no advances.** Accepts simultaneous submissions. Book catalog available free.

NONFICTION Subjects include child guidance.

NBM PUBLISHING

160 Broadway, Suite 700, East Bldg., New York NY 10038. **E-mail:** nbmgn@nbmpub.com. **Website:** nbmpub.com. **Contact:** Terry Nantier, editor/art director. Estab. 1976. Publishes graphic novels for an audience of YA/adults. Types of books include fiction, mystery and social parodies. **Publishes 16 titles/year. 5% of books from first-time authors. 90% from unagented writers. Advance negotiable.** Publishes ms 1 year after acceptance. Accepts simultaneous submissions. Responds to e-mail 1-2 days; mail 1 week. Catalog online.

FICTION Subjects include comic books, contemporary, erotica, humor, literary, translation, young adult.

❶⊘ THOMAS NELSON, INC.

HarperCollins Christian Publishing, Box 141000, Nashville TN 37214. (615)889-9000. **Website:** www.thomasnelson.com. Publishes hardcover and paperback orginals. Thomas Nelson publishes Christian lifestyle nonfiction and fiction, and general nonfiction. **Publishes 100-150 titles/year. Rates negotiated for each project. Pays advance.** Publishes ms 1-2 years after acceptance. Accepts simultaneous submissions.

NONFICTION Subjects include gardening, religion, spirituality, adult inspirational, motivational, devotional, Christian living, prayer and evangelism, Bible study, personal development, political, biography/autobiography. *Does not accept unsolicited mss.* No phone queries.

FICTION Publishes authors of commercial fiction who write for adults from a Christian perspective. *Does not accept unsolicited mss.* No phone queries.

⊘ TOMMY NELSON

Imprint of Thomas Nelson, Inc., P.O. Box 141000, Nashville TN 37214-1000. (615)889-9000. **Fax:** (615)902-2219. **Website:** www.tommynelson.com. Publishes hardcover and trade paperback originals. "Tommy Nelson publishes children's Christian nonfiction and fiction for boys and girls up to age 14. We honor God and serve people through books, videos, software and Bibles for children that improve the lives of our customers." **Publishes 50-75 titles/year.** Guidelines online.

NONFICTION Subjects include religion. *Does not accept unsolicited mss.*

FICTION Subjects include adventure, juvenile, mystery, picture books, religious. No stereotypical characters. *Does not accept unsolicited mss.*

TIPS "Know the Christian Booksellers Association market. Check out the Christian bookstores to see what sells and what is needed."

NEW DIRECTIONS

80 Eighth Ave., New York NY 10011. **Fax:** (212)255-0231. **E-mail:** editorial@ndbooks.com. **Website:** www.ndbooks.com. **Contact:** Editorial Assistant. Estab. 1936. Hardcover and trade paperback originals. "Currently, New Directions focuses primarily on fiction in translation, avant garde American fiction, and experimental poetry by American and foreign authors. If your work does not fall into one of those categories, you would probably do best to submit your work elsewhere." **Publishes 30 titles/year.** Responds in 3-4 months to queries. Book catalog and guidelines online.

FICTION Subjects include ethnic, experimental, historical, humor, literary, poetry, poetry in translation, regional, short story collections, suspense, translation. No juvenile or young adult, occult or paranormal, genre fiction (formula romances, sci-fi or westerns), arts & crafts, and inspirational poetry. Brief query only.

POETRY Query.

TIPS "Our books serve the academic community."

◯ NEWEST PUBLISHERS LTD.

201, 8540-109 St., Edmonton AB T6G 1E6, Canada. (780)432-9427. **Fax:** (780)433-3179. **E-mail:** info@newestpress.com. **E-mail:** submissions@newestpress.com. **Website:** www.newestpress.com. Estab. 1977. Publishes trade paperback originals. NeWest publishes Western Canadian fiction, nonfiction, poetry, and drama. **Publishes 13-16 titles/year. 40% of books from first-time authors. 85% from unagented writers. Pays 10% royalty.** Publishes ms 2-3 years after acceptance. Accepts simultaneous submissions. Responds in 6-8 months to queries. Book catalog for 9×12 SASE. Guidelines online.

NONFICTION Subjects include ethnic, history, Canadian. Query.

FICTION Subjects include literary. Submit complete ms.

NEW FORUMS PRESS

New Forums, 1018 S. Lewis St., Stillwater OK 74074. (405)372-6158. **Fax:** (405)377-2237. **E-mail:** contact@newforums.com. **E-mail:** submissions@newforums.com. **Website:** www.newforums.com. **Contact:** Doug Dollar, president (interests: higher education, Oklahoma-Regional, US military). Estab. 1981. Hardcover and trade paperback originals. "New Forums Press is an independent publisher offering works devoted to various aspects of professional development in higher education, home and office aides, US military, and various titles of a regional interest. We welcome suggestions for thematic series of books and thematic issues of our academic journals—addressing a single issue, problem, or theory." **60% of books from first-time authors. 100% from unagented writers.** Accepts simultaneous submissions. Guidelines online.

NONFICTION Subjects include business, education, history, literature, military, regional, sociology, war. "We are actively seeking new authors—send for review copies and author guidelines, and visit our website." Mss should be submitted as a Microsoft Word document, or a similar standard word processor document (saved in RTF rich text), as an attachment to an e-mail sent to submissions@newforums.com. Otherwise, submit your ms on 8 ½ x 11 inch white bond paper (one original). The name and complete address, telephone, fax number, and e-mail address of each author should appear on a separate cover page, so it can be removed for the blind review process.

NEW HARBINGER PUBLICATIONS

5674 Shattuck Ave., Oakland CA 94609. (510)652-0215. **Fax:** (510)652-5472. **E-mail:** proposals@newharbinger.com. **Website:** www.newharbinger.com. Estab. 1973. "We look for psychology and health self-help books that teach readers how to master essential life skills. Mental health professionals who want simple, clear explanations or important psychological techniques and health issues also read our books. Thus, our books must be simple ane easy to understand but also complete and authoritative. Most of our authors are therapists or other helping professionals." **Publishes 55 titles/year. 1,000 queries received/year. 300 mss received/year. 60% of books from first-time authors. 75% from unagented writers.** Publishes ms 1 year after acceptance. Accepts simultaneous submissions. Responds in 2 weeks to queries; 1 month to proposals; 2 months to mss. Book catalog free. Guidelines online.

NONFICTION Subjects include psychology, psycho spirituality, anger management, anxiety, coping, mindfulness skills. Authors need to be qualified psychotherapists or health practitioners to publish with us. Submit proposal package, outline, 2 sample chapters, TOC, competing titles, and a compelling, supported reason why the book is unique.

TIPS "Audience includes psychotherapists and lay readers wanting step-by-step strategies to solve specific problems. Our definition of a self-help psychology or health book is one that teaches essential life skills. The primary goal is to train the reader so that, after reading the book, he or she can deal more effectively with health and/or psychological challenges."

⊘ NEW HOPE PUBLISHERS

Woman's Missionary Union, P.O. Box 12065, Birmingham AL 35202-2065. (205)991-4950. **Fax:** (205)991-4015. **E-mail:** newhopereader@wmu.org. **Website:** www.newhopepublishers.com. **Contact:** Acquisitions Editor. "Our vision is to challenge believers to understand and be radically involved in the missions of God. This market does not accept unsolicited mss. We encourage you to post your proposal at ChristianManuscriptSubmissions.com." **Publishes 20-28 titles/year. 25% of books from first-time authors.** Publishes ms 2 years after acceptance. Accepts simultaneous submissions.

NONFICTION Subjects include child guidance, education, multicultural, religion, church leadership. "We publish books dealing with all facets of Christian life for women and families, including health, discipleship, missions, ministry, Bible studies, spiritual development, parenting, and marriage. We currently do not accept adult fiction or children's picture books. We are particularly interested in niche categories and books on lifestyle development and change." "We do not accept or review any unsolicited queries, proposals, or manuscripts."

NEW HORIZON PRESS

P.O. Box 669, Far Hills NJ 07931. (908)604-6311. **Fax:** (908)604-6330. **E-mail:** nhp@newhorizonpressbooks.com. **Website:** www.newhorizonpressbooks.com. **Contact:** Acquisitions Editor. Estab. 1983. Publishes hardcover and trade paperback originals. "New Horizon publishes adult nonfiction featuring true stories of uncommon heroes, true crime, social issues, and self help." **Publishes 12 titles/year. 90% of books from first-time authors. 50% from unagented writers. Pays standard royalty on net receipts. Pays advance.** Publishes book within 2 years of acceptance. Accepts simultaneous submissions. Book catalog available free. Guidelines online.

IMPRINTS Small Horizons.

NONFICTION Subjects include child guidance, creative nonfiction, psychology, true crime. Submit proposal package, outline, résumé, bio, 3 sample chapters, photo, marketing information.

TIPS "We are a small publisher, thus it is important that the author/publisher have a good working relationship. The author must be willing to promote his book."

NEW ISSUES POETRY & PROSE

Western Michigan University, 1903 W. Michigan Ave., Kalamazoo MI 49008-5463. (269)387-8185. **Fax:** (269)387-2562. **E-mail:** new-issues@wmich.edu. **Website:** wmich.edu/newissues. **Contact:** Managing Editor. Estab. 1996. **50% of books from first-time authors. 95% from unagented writers.** Publishes 18 months after acceptance. Accepts simultaneous submissions. Guidelines online.

FICTION Subjects include literary, poetry. Only considers submissions to book contests.

POETRY New Issues Poetry & Prose offers two contests annually. The Green Rose Prize is awarded to an author who has previously published at least one full-length book of poems. The New Issues Poetry Prize, an award for a first book of poems, is chosen by a guest judge. Past judges have included Philip Levine, C.K. Williams, C.D. Wright, and Campbell McGrath. New Issues does not read mss outside our contests. Graduate students in the Ph.D. and M.F.A. programs of Western Michigan Univ. often volunteer their time reading mss. Finalists are chosen by the editors. New

Issues often publishes up to 2 additional mss selected from the finalists.

NEW LIBRI PRESS

4907 Meridian Ave. N., Seattle WA 98103. **E-mail:** query@newlibri.com. **Website:** www.newlibri.com. **Contact:** Michael Muller, editor; Stanislav Fritz, editor. Estab. 2011. Publishes trade paperback, electronic original, electronic reprints. "We only accept e-mail submissions, not USPS." **Publishes 5 titles/year. Receives over 100 submissions/year. 90% of books from first-time authors. 100% from unagented writers. Pays 20-35% royalty on wholesale price. No advance.** Publishes ms 9-12 months after acceptance. Accepts simultaneous submissions. Responds in 3 months to mss. Catalog online. Guidelines online. Electronic submissions only.

NONFICTION Subjects include agriculture, automotive, business, child guidance, computers, cooking, creative nonfiction, economics, electronics, environment, gardening, hobbies, house and home, nature, parenting, recreation, science, sex, software, translation, travel. "Writers should know we embrace e-books. This means that some formats and types of books work well and others don't." Religious. Prefers e-mail. Submit proposal package, including outline, 2 sample chapters, and summary of market from author's perspective. Prefers complete ms.

FICTION Subjects include adventure, experimental, fantasy, historical, horror, literary, mainstream, military, mystery, science fiction, translation, war, western, young adult. "Open to most ideas right now; this will change as we mature as a press. As a new press, we are more open than most and time will probably shape the direction. That said, trite as it is, we want good writing that is fun to read. While we currently are not looking for some sub-genres, if it is well written and a bit off the beaten path, submit to us. We are e-book focused. **We may not create a paper version if the e-book does not sell**, which means some fiction may be less likely to currently sell (e.g. picture books are problematic). Submit query, synopsis, and full manuscript (so we don't have to ask for it later if we like it. We will read about 50 pages to start).

TIPS "Our audience is someone who is comfortable reading an e-book, or someone who is tired of the recycled authors of mainstream publishing, but still wants a good, relatively fast, reading experience. The industry is changing, while we accept for the traditional model, we are searching for writers who are interested in sharing the risk and controlling their own destiny. We embrace writers with no agent."

NEW RIVERS PRESS

1104 Seventh Ave. S., Moorhead MN 56563. **Website:** www.newriverspress.com. **Contact:** Nayt Rundquist, managing editor. Estab. 1968. New Rivers Press publishes collections of poetry, novels, nonfiction, translations of contemporary literature, and collections of short fiction and nonfiction. "We continue to publish books regularly by new and emerging writers, but we also welcome the opportunity to read work of every character and to publish the best literature available nationwide. Each fall through the Many Voices Project competition, we choose 2 books: 1 poetry and 1 prose." Accepts simultaneous submissions.

FICTION Sponsors American Fiction Prize to find best unpublished short stories by American writers.

POETRY The Many Voices Project awards $1,000, a standard book contract, publication of a book-length ms by New Rivers Press, and national distribution. All previously published poems must be acknowledged. "We will consider simultaneous submissions if noted as such. If your manuscript is accepted elsewhere during the judging, you must notify New Rivers Press immediately. If you do not give such notification and your manuscript is selected, your entry gives New Rivers Press permission to go ahead with publication." Guidelines online.

NEWSAGE PRESS

P.O. Box 607, Troutdale OR 97060-0607. (503)695-2211. **E-mail:** info@newsagepress.com. **Website:** www.newsagepress.com. Estab. 1985. Publishes trade paperback originals. "We focus on nonfiction books. No 'how-to' books or cynical, despairing books. Photo-essay books in large format are no longer published by Newsage Press. No novels or other forms of fiction." Accepts simultaneous submissions. Guidelines online.

NONFICTION Subjects include animals, multicultural, death/dying. Submit 2 sample chapters, proposal (no more than 1 page), SASE.

NEW SOCIETY PUBLISHERS

P.O. Box 189, Gabriola Island BC V0R 1X0, Canada. (250)247-9737. **Fax:** (250)247-7471. **E-mail:** editor@newsociety.com. **Website:** www.newsociety.com. Publishes trade paperback originals and reprints and electronic originals. **Publishes 25 titles/year.**

400 queries; 300 mss received/year. 50% of books from first-time authors. 80% from unagented writers. Pays 10-12% royalty on wholesale price. Pays $0-5,000 advance. Publishes ms about 9 months after acceptance. Accepts simultaneous submissions. Responds in 1-2 months. Book catalog and guidelines online.

NONFICTION Subjects include agriculture, alternative lifestyles, animals, beauty, business, child guidance, communications, community, contemporary culture, cooking, economics, education, environment, fashion, finance, foods, gardening, health, horticulture, house and home, humanities, labor, money, nature, nutrition, parenting, philosophy, politics, regional, science, social sciences, spirituality, sustainability, open building, peak oil, renewable energy, post carbon prep, sustainable living, gardening & cooking, green building, natural building, ecological design & planning, environment & economy. Query with SASE. Submit proposal package, outline, 2 sample chapters. Reviews artwork/photos. Send photocopies.

TIPS "Audience is activists, academics. Don't get an agent!"

NEW WORLD LIBRARY

14 Pamaron Way, Novato CA 94949. (415)884-2100. **Fax:** (415)884-2199. **E-mail:** submit@newworldlibrary.com. **Website:** www.newworldlibrary.com. **Contact:** Joel Prins, submissions editor. Estab. 1979. Publishes hardcover and trade paperback originals and reprints. "NWL is dedicated to publishing books that inspire and challenge us to improve the quality of our lives and our world." Prefers e-mail submissions. No longer accepting children's mss. **Publishes 35-40 titles/year. 10% of books from first-time authors. 25% from unagented writers. Pays advance.** Publishes ms 12 months after acceptance. Accepts simultaneous submissions. Responds in 3 months to queries if interested. Reviews all queries. Book catalog free. Guidelines online.

NONFICTION Subjects include alternative lifestyles, animals, business, career guidance, child guidance, contemporary culture, counseling, environment, nature, New Age, parenting, religion, spirituality, womens issues. Submit outline, overview, bio, 2-3 sample chapters, SASE. Does not review artwork.

NEW YORK UNIVERSITY PRESS

838 Broadway, 3rd Floor, New York NY 10003. (212)998-2575. **Fax:** (212)995-3833. **E-mail:** information@nyupress.org. **Website:** www.nyupress.org. **Contact:** Ellen Chodosh, director. Estab. 1916. Hardcover and trade paperback originals. "New York University Press embraces ideological diversity. We often publish books on the same issue from different poles to generate dialogue, engender and resist pat categorizations." **Publishes 100 titles/year. 800-1,000 queries received/year. 30% of books from first-time authors. 90% from unagented writers.** Publishes ms 9-11 months after acceptance. Accepts simultaneous submissions. Responds in 1-4 months (peer reviewed) to proposals. Guidelines online.

NONFICTION Subjects include ethnic, psychology, regional, religion, sociology, American history, anthropology. New York University Press is a publisher primarily of academic books and is a department of the New York University Division of Libraries. NYU Press publishes in the humanities and social sciences, with emphasis on sociology, law, cultural and American studies, religion, American history, anthropology, politics, criminology, media and film, and psychology. The Press also publishes books on New York regional history, politics, and culture. Query with SASE. Submit proposal package, outline, 1 sample chapter. Reviews artwork/photos. Send photocopies.

NIGHTSCAPE PRESS

P.O. Box 1948, Smyrna TN 37167. **E-mail:** info@nightscapepress.com. **E-mail:** submissions@nightscapepress.com. **Website:** www.nightscapepress.com. Estab. 2012. Nightscape Press is seeking quality book-length words of at least 50,000 words (40,000 for young adult). **Pays monthly royalties. Offers advance.** Accepts simultaneous submissions. Guidelines online. Currently closed to submissions. Will announce on site when they re-open to submissions.

FICTION Subjects include experimental, fantasy, horror, science fiction, short story collections, suspense, young adult. "We are not interested in erotica or graphic novels." Query.

⊘ NINETY-SIX PRESS

Special Collections, James B. Duke Library, 3300 Poinsett Hwy., Greenville SC 29613. (864)294-2194. **E-mail:** specialcollections@furman.edu. **Website:** library.furman.edu/specialcollections/96Press/index.htm. **Contact:** Jeffrey Makala, Special Collections Librarian and University Archivist. Estab. 1991. For a sample, send $10.

TIPS "Between 1991 and 2015, the Ninety-Six Press published only poetry by South Carolina authors. The Press is not considering new publishing projects at this time. Check our website for up-to-date information."

NOLO

950 Parker St., Berkeley CA 94710. (510)549-1976. **Fax:** (510)859-0025. **Website:** www.nolo.com. **Contact:** Editorial Department. Estab. 1971. Publishes trade paperback originals. "We publish practical, do-it-yourself books, software and various electronic products on financial and legal issues that affect individuals, small business, and nonprofit organizations. We specialize in helping people handle their own legal tasks; i.e., write a will, file a small claims lawsuit, start a small business or nonprofit, or apply for a patent." **Publishes 75 new editions and 15 new titles/year. 20% of books from first-time authors. Pays advance.** Accepts simultaneous submissions. Responds in 3 weeks to queries. Responds in 5 weeks to proposals. Guidelines online.

NONFICTION Subjects include legal guides in various topics including employment, small business, intellectual property, parenting and education, finance and investment, landlord/tenant, real estate, and estate planning. Query with SASE. Submit outline, 1 sample chapter.

NOMAD PRESS

2456 Christain St., White River Junction VT 05001. (802)649-1995. **E-mail:** rachel@nomadpress.net; info@nomadpress.net. **Website:** www.nomadpress.net. **Contact:** Alex Kahan, publisher. Estab. 2001. "We produce nonfiction children's activity books that bring a particular science or cultural topic into sharp focus. Nomad Press does not accept unsolicited manuscripts. If authors are interested in contributing to our children's series, please send a writing resume that includes relevant experience/expertise and publishing credits." **Pays authors royalty based on retail price or work purchased outright. Offers advance against royalties.** Publishes book 1 year after acceptance. Accepts simultaneous submissions. Responds to queries in 3-4 weeks. Catalog online.

◯ Nomad Press does not accept picture books, fiction, or cookbooks.

NONFICTION Middle readers: activity books, history, science. Average word length: middle readers—30,000.

TIPS "We publish a very specific kind of nonfiction children's activity book. Please keep this in mind when querying or submitting."

NORTH ATLANTIC BOOKS

2526 Martin Luther King Jr. Way, Berkeley CA 94704. **Website:** www.northatlanticbooks.com. **Contact:** Acquisitions Board. Estab. 1974. Publishes hardcover, trade paperback, and electronic originals; trade paperback and electronic reprints. **Publishes 60 titles/year. Receives 200 mss/year. 50% of books from first-time authors. 75% from unagented writers. Pays royalty percentage on wholesale price.** Publishes ms 14 months after acceptance. Accepts simultaneous submissions. Responds in 3-6 months. Book catalog free on request (if available). Guidelines online.

IMPRINTS Evolver Editions, Blue Snake Books.

NONFICTION Subjects include agriculture, anthropology, archeology, architecture, art, astrology, business, child guidance, community, contemporary culture, cooking, economics, electronics, environment, finance, foods, gardening, gay, health, horticulture, lesbian, medicine, memoirs, money, multicultural, nature, New Age, nutrition, philosophy, politics, psychic, psychology, public affairs, religion, science, social sciences, sociology, spirituality, sports, travel, womens issues, womens studies, world affairs. Submit proposal package including an outline, 3-4 sample chapters, and "a 75-word statement about the book, your qualifications as an author, marketing plan/audience, for the book, and comparable titles." Reviews artwork with ms package.

FICTION Subjects include adventure, literary, multicultural, mystery, regional, science fiction, spiritual. "We only publish fiction on rare occasions." Submit proposal package including an outline, 3-4 sample chapters, and "a 75-word statement about the book, your qualifications as an author, marketing plan/audience, for the book, and comparable titles."

POETRY Submit 15-20 sample poems.

NORTH CAROLINA OFFICE OF ARCHIVES AND HISTORY

Historical Publications Section, 4622 Mail Service Center, Raleigh NC 27699. (919)733-7442. **Fax:** (919)733-1439. **E-mail:** historical.publications@ncdcr.gov. **Website:** www.ncdcr.gov/about/history/historical-publications. **Contact:** Michael Hill, supervisor (michael.hill@ncdcr.gov). Publishes hardcover and trade paperback originals. "We publish *only* titles that

relate to North Carolina. The North Carolina Office of Archives and History also publishes the *North Carolina Historical Review*, a quarterly scholarly journal of history." **Publishes 1 titles/year. 10 queries received/year. 5 mss received/year. 5% of books from first-time authors. 100% from unagented writers. Makes one-time payment upon delivery of completed ms.** Publishes ms 2 years after acceptance. Accepts simultaneous submissions. Responds in 1 week to queries and to proposals; 2 months to mss. Guidelines for $3.
NONFICTION Subjects include history, regional. Query with SASE. Reviews artwork/photos. Send photocopies.

NORTHERN ILLINOIS UNIVERSITY PRESS

2280 Bethany Rd., DeKalb IL 60115-2854. (815)753-1075. **Fax:** (815)753-1845. **E-mail:** afarranto@niu.edu. **E-mail:** lmanning2@niu.edu. **Website:** www.niupress.niu.edu. **Contact:** Amy Farranto, editor; Linda Manning, director. Estab. 1965. The NIU Press publishes nonfiction on a variety of topics in the humanities, arts, and social sciences. With more than 500 books in print, each year it publishes 20-25 new books on aspects of history, politics, religion, regional studies, and literature. In fulfilling its broadly educational mission, the Press publishes books for inquiring general readers as well as for specialists. **Publishes 20-25 titles/year. 50% of books from first-time authors. 100% from unagented writers. Pays royalties on net sales price** Book catalog available free.
IMPRINTS Switchgrass Books.
NONFICTION Subjects include history, humanities, literature, memoirs, philosophy, politics, regional, religion, translation. No collections of previously published essays or unsolicited poetry. Submit (preferably via e-mail) a brief prospectus, consisting of a TOC, an introduction, a sample chapter, and vita to the appropriate editor.

Ⓐ NORTHFIELD PUBLISHING

Imprint of Moody Publishers, 820 N. La Salle Blvd., Chicago IL 60610. (800)678-8001. **Fax:** (312)329-2019. **Website:** www.moodypublishers.org. **Contact:** Acquisitions Coordinator. Northfield publishes a line of books for non-Christians or those exploring the Christian faith. "While staying true to Biblical principles, we eliminate some of the Christian wording and scriptural references to avoid confusion." **Publishes 5-10 titles/year. Pays $500-50,000 advance.**

Publishes ms 1 year after acceptance. Accepts simultaneous submissions.
NONFICTION Subjects include child guidance, religion. Agented submissions only.

NORTH LIGHT BOOKS

F+W, a Content + eCommerce Company, 10151 Carver Rd., Suite 200, Blue Ash OH 45242. **Fax:** (513)891-7153. **E-mail:** mona.clough@fwcommunity.com. **Website:** www.fwcommunity.com; www.artistsnetwork.com; www.createmixedmedia.com. **Contact:** Mona Clough, content director art and mixed media. Publishes hardcover and trade paperback how-to books. "North Light Books publishes art books, including watercolor, drawing, mixed media, acrylic that emphasize illustrated how-to art instruction. Currently emphasizing drawing including traditional, zen, doodle, and creativity and inspiration." **Publishes 50 titles/year. Pays 8% royalty on net receipts and $3,000 advance. Yes.** Accepts simultaneous submissions. Responds in approx. 3 months to queries. Visit www.northlightshop.com. Does not return submissions.

Ⓞ This market is for experienced fine artists and workshop instructors who are willing to work with an North Light editor to produce a step-by-step how-to book that teaches readers how to accomplish art techniques. See also separate listing for F+W Media, Inc., in this section.

NONFICTION Subjects include art, watercolor, realistic drawing, creativity, decorative painting, paper arts, collage and other craft instruction books.. Interested in books on acrylic painting, basic drawing and sketching, journaling, pen and ink, colored pencil, decorative painting, art and how-to. Do not submit coffee table art books without how-to art instruction. Query via e-mail only. Submit outline with JPEG low-resolution images. Submissions via snail mail will not be returned.

Ⓐ Ⓞ NORTH POINT PRESS

Imprint of Farrar Straus & Giroux, Inc., 175 Fifth Ave., New York NY 10010. **Website:** www.fsgbooks.com. Estab. 1980. Publishes hardcover and paperback originals. "We are a broad-based literary trade publisher-high quality writing only." **Pays standard royalty. Pays varied advance.** Accepts simultaneous submissions.
NONFICTION Subjects include history, travel, cultural criticism, music, cooking/food. Be familiar with our list. No genres. *Agented submissions only.*

NORTHSOUTH BOOKS

600 Third Ave., 2nd Floor, New York NY 10016. (917)210-5868. **E-mail:** hlennon@northsouth.com. **E-mail:** submissionsnsb@gmail.com. **Website:** www.northsouth.com. Accepts simultaneous submissions. Guidelines online.

FICTION Looking for fresh, original fiction with universal themes that could appeal to children ages 3-8. "We typically do not acquire rhyming texts, since our books must also be translated into German." Submit picture book mss (1,000 words or less) via e-mail.

NORTIA PRESS

Santa Ana CA **E-mail:** acquisitions@nortiapress.com. **Website:** www.nortiapress.com. Estab. 2009. Publishes trade paperback and electronic originals. **Publishes 6 titles/year. 0% of books from first-time authors. 80% from unagented writers. Pays negotiable royalties on wholesale price.** Publishes ms 7 months after acceptance. Accepts simultaneous submissions. Responds in 1 month.

NONFICTION Subjects include ethnic, government, humanities, military, public affairs, religion, social sciences, sociology, war, womens issues.

FICTION Subjects include ethnic, historical, literary, military, war. "We focus mainly on nonfiction as well as literary and historical fiction, but are open to other genres. No vampire stories, science fiction, or erotica, please." Submit a brief e-mail query. Please include a short bio, approximate word count of book, and expected date of completion (fiction titles should be completed before sending a query, and should contain a sample chapter in the body of the e-mail). All unsolicited snail mail or attachments will be discarded without review.

TIPS "We specialize in working with experienced authors who seek a more collaborative and fulfilling relationship with their publisher. As such, we are less likely to accept pitches form first-time authors, no matter how good the idea. As with any pitch, please make your e-mail very brief and to the point, so the reader is not forced to skim it. Always include some biographic information. Your life is interesting."

W.W. NORTON & COMPANY, INC.

500 Fifth Ave., New York NY 10110. (212)354-5500. **Fax:** (212)869-0856. **Website:** www.wwnorton.com. Estab. 1923. "W. W. Norton & Company, the oldest and largest publishing house owned wholly by its employees, strives to carry out the imperative of its founder to 'publish books not for a single season, but for the years' in fiction, nonfiction, poetry, college textbooks, cookbooks, art books and professional books. Due to the workload of our editorial staff and the large volume of materials we receive, *Norton is no longer able to accept unsolicited submissions*. If you are seeking publication, we suggest working with a literary agent who will represent you to the house." Accepts simultaneous submissions.

NO STARCH PRESS, INC.

245 8th St., San Francisco CA 94103. (415)863-9900. **Fax:** (415)863-9950. **E-mail:** editors@nostarch.com. **Website:** www.nostarch.com. **Contact:** William Pollock, publisher. Estab. 1994. Publishes trade paperback originals. "No Starch Press publishes the finest in geek entertainment—unique books on technology, with a focus on open source, security, hacking, programming, alternative operating systems, LEGO, science, and math. Our titles have personality, our authors are passionate, and our books tackle topics that people care about." **Publishes 20-25 titles/year. 100 queries; 5 mss received/year. 80% of books from first-time authors. 90% from unagented writers. Pays 10-15% royalty on wholesale price. Pays advance.** Publishes ms 4 months after acceptance. Accepts simultaneous submissions. Book catalog online.

NONFICTION Subjects include science, technology, computing, lego. Submit outline, bio, 1 sample chapter, market rationale. Reviews artwork/photos. Send photocopies.

TIPS "Books must be relevant to tech-savvy, geeky readers."

NOSY CROW PUBLISHING

The Crow's Nest, 10a Lant St., London SE1 1QR, United Kingdom. (44)(0)207-089-7575. **Fax:** (44)(0)207-089-7576. **E-mail:** hello@nosycrow.com. **E-mail:** submissions@nosycrow.com. **Website:** nosycrow.com. "We publish books for children 0-14. We're looking for 'parent-friendly' books, and we don't publish books with explicit sex, drug use or serious violence, so no edgy YA or edgy cross-over. And whatever New Adult is, we don't do it. We also publish apps for children from 2-7, and may publish apps for older children if the idea feels right." Accepts simultaneous submissions. Guidelines online.

NONFICTION Prefers submissions by e-mail, but post works if absolutely necessary.

FICTION "As a rule, we don't like books with 'issues' that are in any way overly didactic." Prefers submissions by e-mail, but post works if absolutely necessary.

TIPS "Please don't be too disappointed if we reject your work! We're a small company and can only publish a few new books and apps each year, so do try other publishers and agents: publishing is necessarily a hugely subjective business. We wish you luck!"

NOVA PRESS

9058 Lloyd Place, West Hollywood CA 90069. (310)275-3513. **Fax:** (310)281-5629. **E-mail:** novapress@aol.com. **Website:** www.novapress.net. **Contact:** Jeff Kolby, president. Estab. 1993. Publishes trade paperback originals. "Nova Press publishes only test prep books for college entrance exams (SAT, GRE, GMAT, LSAT, etc.), and closely related reference books, such as college guides and vocabulary books." **Publishes 6 titles/year.** Publishes book 6 months after acceptance. Accepts simultaneous submissions. Book catalog available free.

NONFICTION Subjects include education, software.

NURSESBOOKS.ORG

American Nurses Association, 8515 Georgia Ave., Suite 400, Silver Spring MD 20901. (800)274-4ANA. **Fax:** (301)628-5003. **E-mail:** anp@ana.org. **E-mail:** joseph.vanilla@ana.org. **Website:** www.nursesbooks.org. **Contact:** Joseph Vanilla, publisher. Publishes professional paperback originals and reprints. "Nursebooks. org publishes books designed to help professional nurses in their work and careers. Through the publishing program, Nursebooks.org provides nurses in all practice settings with publications that address cutting edge issues and form a basis for debate and exploration of this century's most critical health care trends." **Publishes 10 titles/year. 50 queries received/year. 8-10 mss received/year. 75% of books from first-time authors. 100% from unagented writers.** Publishes ms 4 months after acceptance. Responds in 3 months. Book catalog online. Guidelines available free.

NONFICTION Subjects include advanced practice, computers, continuing education, ethics, health care policy, nursing administration, psychiatric and mental health, quality, nursing history, workplace issues, key clinical topics, such as geriatrics, pain management, public health, spirituality and home health. Submit outline, 1 sample chapter, CV, list of 3 reviewers and paragraph on audience and how to reach them. Reviews artwork/photos. Send photocopies.

OAK KNOLL PRESS

310 Delaware St., New Castle DE 19720. (302)328-7232. **Fax:** (302)328-7274. **E-mail:** publishing@oak-knoll.com. **Website:** www.oakknoll.com. **Contact:** Robert D. Fleck, president. Estab. 1976. Publishes hardcover and trade paperback originals and reprints. "Oak Knoll specializes in books about books and manuals on the book arts: preserving the art and lore of the printed word." **Publishes 40 titles/year. 250 queries; 100 mss received/year. 50% of books from first-time authors. 100% from unagented writers.** Publishes ms 1 year after acceptance. Accepts simultaneous submissions. Guidelines online.

NONFICTION Reviews artwork/photos. Send photocopies.

OAK TREE PRESS

1700 Dairy Ave., #49, Corcoran CA 93212. **E-mail:** query@oaktreebooks.com. **Website:** www.oaktreebooks.com. **Contact:** Billie Johnson, publisher. Estab. 1998. Publishes trade paperback and hardcover books. Oak Tree Press is an independent publisher that is looking for mainstream, genre fiction especially mysteries, narrative nonfiction, how-to. Sponsors 3 contests annually: Dark Oak Mystery, Timeless Love Romance and CopTales for true crime and other stories of law enforcement professionals." **Publishes 40-60 titles/year. 2,000+ submissions received/year. 30% of books from first-time authors. 90% from unagented writers. Royalties based on sales. Does not pay advance.** Publishes ms 9-18 months after acceptance. Accepts simultaneous submissions. Responds in 4-6 weeks. Catalog and guidelines online. "We require a marketing plan, and author participation in the book promotion process.".

IMPRINTS Dark Oak Mysteries, Timeless Love, Wild Oaks (stories of the old West).

FICTION Subjects include adventure, confession, contemporary, ethnic, fantasy, feminist, humor, mainstream, mystery, picture books, suspense, young adult. Emphasis on mystery and romance novels. "No science fiction or fantasy novels, or stories set far into the future. Next, novels substantially longer than our stated word count are not considered, regardless of genre. We look for manuscripts of 70-90,000 words. If the story really charms us, we will bend some on either end of the range. No right-wing political or racist agenda, gratuitous sex or violence, especially against women, or depict harm of animals." Does not accept or return unsolicited mss. Query with SASE. Accepts queries by e-mail. Include estimated word count, brief bio, list of publishing credits, brief description of ms.

TIPS "Perhaps my most extreme pet peeve is receiving queries on projects which we've clearly advertised we don't want: science fiction, fantasy, epic tomes, bigoted diatribes and so on. Second to that is a practice I call 'over-taping,' or the use of yards and yards of tape, or worse yet, the filament tape so that it takes forever to open the package. Finding story pitches on my voice mail is also annoying."

OBERLIN COLLEGE PRESS

50 N. Professor St., Oberlin OH 44074. (440)775-8408. **Fax:** (440)775-8124. **E-mail:** oc.press@oberlin.edu. **Website:** www.oberlin.edu/ocpress. **Contact:** Marco Wilkinson, managing editor. Estab. 1969. Publishes hardcover and trade paperback originals. **Publishes 2-3 titles/year. Pays 7½-10% royalty.** Accepts simultaneous submissions. Responds promptly to queries; 2 months to mss.

POETRY *FIELD Magazine*—submit 2-6 poems through website "submissions" tab; FIELD Translation Series—query with SASE and sample poems; FIELD Poetry Series—*no unsolicited mss.* Enter mss in FIELD Poetry Prize ($1,000 and a standard royalty contract) held annually in May. Submit complete ms.

TIPS "Queries for the FIELD Translation Series: send sample poems and letter describing project. Winner of the annual FIELD poetry prize determines publication. Do not send unsolicited manuscripts."

OCEANVIEW PUBLISHING

595 Bay Isles Rd., Suite 120-G, Longboat Key FL 34228. **E-mail:** mail@oceanviewpub.com. **E-mail:** submissions@oceanviewpub.com. **Website:** www.oceanviewpub.com. **Contact:** Robert Gussin, CEO. Estab. 2006. Publishes hardcover and electronic originals. "Independent publisher of nonfiction and fiction, with primary interest in original mystery, thriller and suspense titles. Accepts new and established writers." Accepts simultaneous submissions. Responds in 3 months on mss. Catalog and guidelines online.

FICTION Subjects include mystery, suspense, thriller. Accepting adult mss with a primary interest in the mystery, thriller and suspense genres—from new and established writers. No children's or YA literature, poetry, cookbooks, technical manuals or short stories. Within body of e-mail only, include author's name and brief bio (Indicate if this is an agent sub-mission), ms title and word count, author's mailing address, phone number and e-mail address. Attached to the e-mail should be the following: A synopsis of 750 words or fewer. The first 30 pages of the ms. Please note that we accept only Word documents as attachments to the submission e-mail. Do not send query letters or proposals.

OHIO STATE UNIVERSITY PRESS

1070 Carmack Rd., 180 Pressey Hall, Columbus OH 43210-1002. (614)292-6930. **Fax:** (614)292-2065. **E-mail:** eugene@osupress.org. **E-mail:** lindsay@osupress.org. **Website:** www.ohiostatepress.org. **Contact:** Eugene O'Connor, acquisitions editor (medieval studies and classics); Lindsay Martin, acquisitions editor (literary studies). Estab. 1957. The Ohio State University Press publishes scholarly nonfiction, and offers short fiction and short poetry prizes. Currently emphasizing history, literary studies, political science, women's health, classics, Victoria studies. **Publishes 30 titles/year. Pays royalty. Pays advance.** Accepts simultaneous submissions. Responds in 3 months to queries. Guidelines online.

NONFICTION Subjects include education, history, literary criticism, multicultural, regional, sociology, criminology, literary criticism, women's health. Query.

POETRY Offers poetry competition through *The Journal*.

OHIO UNIVERSITY PRESS

31 S. Court St., Suite 143, Athens OH 45701. (740)593-1154. **Fax:** (740)593-4536. **Website:** www.ohioswallow.com. **Contact:** Gillian Berchowitz, director. Estab. 1964. Publishes hardcover and trade paperback originals and reprints. "Ohio University Press publishes and disseminates the fruits of research and creative endeavor, specifically in the areas of literary studies, regional works, philosophy, contemporary history, and African studies. Its charge to produce books of value in service to the academic community and for the enrichment of the broader culture is in keeping with the university's mission of teaching, research and service to its constituents." **Publishes 45-50 titles/year. 500 queries received/year. 50 mss received/year. 20% of books from first-time authors. 95% from unagented writers.** Publishes ms 1 year after acceptance. Accepts simultaneous submissions. Responds in 1-3 months. Book catalog available free. Guidelines online.

NONFICTION Subjects include Americana, anthropology, government, history, language, literature, military, nature, politics, regional, sociology, African studies. "We prefer queries or detailed proposals, rather than manuscripts, pertaining to scholarly projects that might have a general interest." Proposals should explain the thesis and details of the subject matter, not just sell a title. Query with SASE. Reviews artwork/photos. Send photocopies.

TIPS "Rather than trying to hook the editor on your work, let the material be compelling enough and well-presented enough to do it for you."

ONEWORLD PUBLICATIONS

10 Bloomsbury St., London WC1B 3SR, United Kingdom. **E-mail:** submissions@oneworld-publications. com. **Website:** www.oneworld-publications.com. Estab. 1986. Publishes hardcover and trade paperback originals and mass market paperback reprints. "We publish general trade nonfiction, which must be accessible but authoritative, mainly by academics or experts for a general readership and where appropriate a cross-over student market. Currently emphasizing current affairs, popular science, history, psychology, politics and business; de-emphasizing self-help. We also publish literary fiction by international authors, both debut and established, throughout the English language world as well as selling translation rights. Our focus is on well-written literary and high-end commercial fiction from a variety of cultures and periods, many exploring interesting themes and issues. In addition we publish fiction in translation and YA fiction." **Publishes 80 titles/year. 300 queries; 200 mss received/year. 20% of books from first-time authors. 20% from unagented writers. Payment varies. Pays advance.** Publishes ms 12-15 months after acceptance. Book catalog online. Guidelines online.

NONFICTION Subjects include business, economics. Submit through online proposal form.

FICTION Subjects include multicultural. Submit through online proposal forms.

TIPS "We don't require agents—just good proposals with enough hard information."

ONSTAGE PUBLISHING

190 Lime Quarry Rd., Suite 106-J, Madison AL 35758-8962. (256)461-0661. **E-mail:** onstage123@knology. net. **Website:** www.onstagepublishing.com. **Contact:** Dianne Hamilton, senior editor. Estab. 1999. "At this time, we only produce fiction books for ages 8-18. We have added an eBook only side of the house for mysteries for grades 6-12. See our website for more information. We will not do anthologies of any kind. Query first for nonfiction projects as nonfiction projects must spark our interest. Now accepting e-mail queries and submissions. For submissions: Put the first 3 chapters in the body of the e-mail. Do not use attachments! We will no longer return any mss. Only an SASE envelope is needed. Send complete ms if under 20,000 words, otherwise send synopsis and first 3 chapters." **80% of books from first-time authors. Pays authors/illustrators/photographers advance plus royalties.** Accepts simultaneous submissions.

Suggested manuscript lengths: Chapter books: 3,000 to 9,000 words, Middle Grade novels: 10,000 to 40,000 words, Young adult novels: 40,000 to 60,000 words.

FICTION Middle readers: adventure, contemporary, fantasy, history, nature/environment, science fiction, suspense/mystery. Young adults: adventure, contemporary, fantasy, history, humor, science fiction, suspense/mystery. Average word length: chapter books—4,000-6,000 words; middle readers—5,000 words and up; young adults—25,000 and up. Recently published *Mission: Shanghai* by Jamie Dodson (an adventure for boys ages 12+); *Birmingham, 1933: Alice* (a chapter book for grades 3-5). "We do not produce picture books."

TIPS "Study our titles and get a sense of the kind of books we publish, so that you know whether your project is likely to be right for us."

ON THE MARK PRESS

15 Dairy Ave., Napanee ON K7R 1M4, Canada. (800)463-6367. **Fax:** (800)290-3631. **E-mail:** lisa@onthemarkpress.com. **Website:** www.onthemarkpress. com. Estab. 1986. Publishes books for the Canadian curriculum. **15% of books from first-time authors.** Accepts simultaneous submissions.

OOLICHAN BOOKS

P.O. Box 2278, Lantzville BC V0R 1M0, Canada. (250)390-4839. **Fax:** (866)299-0026. **E-mail:** info@ oolichan.com. **Website:** www.oolichan.com. Publisher: Randal Macnair. Estab. 1974. Publishes hardcover and trade paperback originals and reprints. **Publishes 8 titles/year. 2,000 mss received/year. 30% of books from first-time authors. Pays royalty on retail price.** Publishes ms 6-12 months after acceptance.

Accepts simultaneous submissions. Responds in 1-3 months. Book catalog online. Guidelines online.

🖙 Only publishes Canadian authors.

NONFICTION Subjects include history. "We try to publish creative nonfiction titles each year which are of regional, national, and international interest." Submit proposal package, publishing history, bio, cover letter, 3 sample chapters, SASE.

FICTION Subjects include literary. "We try to publish at least 2 literary fiction titles each year. We receive many more deserving submissions than we are able to publish, so we publish only outstanding work. We try to balance our list between emerging and established writers, and have published many first-time writers who have gone on to win or be shortlisted for major literary awards, both nationally and internationally." Submit proposal package, publishing history, clips, bio, cover letter, 3 sample chapters, SASE.

POETRY "We are one of the few small literary presses in Canada that still publishes poetry. We try to include 2-3 poetry titles each year. We attempt to balance our list between emerging and established poets. Our poetry titles have won or been shortlisted for major national awards, including the Governor General's Award, the BC Book Prizes, and the Alberta Awards." Submit 10 sample poems.

TIPS "Our audience is adult readers who love good books and good literature. Our audience is regional and national, as well as international. Follow our submission guidelines. Check out some of our titles at your local library or bookstore to get an idea of what we publish. Don't send us the only copy of your manuscript. Let us know if your submission is simultaneous, and inform us if it is accepted elsewhere. Above all, keep writing!"

OOLIGAN PRESS

369 Neuberger Hall, 724 SW Harrison St., Portland OR 97201. (503)725-9410. **E-mail:** acquisitions@ooliganpress.pdx.edu. **Website:** ooligan.pdx.edu. **Contact:** Acquisitions Co-Managers. Estab. 2001. Publishes trade paperbacks, electronic originals, and reprints. "We seek to publish regionally significant works of literary, historical, and social value. We define the Pacific Northwest as Northern California, Oregon, Idaho, Washington, British Columbia, and Alaska. We recognize the importance of diversity, particularly within the publishing industry, and are committed to building a literary community that includes traditionally underrepresented voices; therefore, we are interested in works originating from, or focusing on, marginalized communities of the Pacific Northwest." **Publishes 3-4 titles/year. 250-500 queries; 50-75 mss received/year. 90% of books from first-time authors. 90% from unagented writers. Pays negotiable royalty on retail price.** Publishes ms 12-18 months after acceptance. Accepts simultaneous submissions. Responds in 2 weeks for queries; 3 months for proposals. Catalog online. Guidelines online.

NONFICTION Subjects include alternative lifestyles, Americana, community, contemporary culture, creative nonfiction, education, environment, ethnic, gay, history, humanities, lesbian, literary criticism, literature, memoirs, multicultural, philosophy, regional, social sciences, sociology, spirituality, translation, travel, womens issues, womens studies, young adult. Cookbooks, self-help books, how-to manuals. Submit a query through Submittable. If accepted, then submit proposal package, outline, 4 sample chapters, projected page count, audience, marketing ideas, and a list of similar titles.

FICTION Subjects include adventure, contemporary, ethnic, experimental, fantasy, feminist, gay, historical, humor, lesbian, literary, mainstream, multicultural, mystery, plays, poetry, poetry in translation, regional, science fiction, short story collections, spiritual, suspense, young adult, Middle grade.. "We seek to publish regionally significant works of literary, historical, and social value. We define the Pacific Northwest as Northern California, Oregon, Idaho, Washington, British Columbia, and Alaska."

POETRY Ooligan is a not-for-profit general trade press that publishes books honoring the cultural and natural diversity of the Pacific Northwest. "We are limited in the number of poetry titles that we publish as poetry represents only a small percentage of our overall acquisitions. We are open to all forms of style and verse; however, we give special preference to prose poetry and traditional verse. Although spoken word, slam, and rap poetry are of interest to the press, we will consider such work if it does not translate well to the written page. Ooligan does not publish chapbooks." Query first through e-mail or Submittable.

TIPS "Search the blog for tips."

OPEN COURT PUBLISHING CO.

70 E. Lake St., Suite 800, Chicago IL 60601. **E-mail:** opencourt@cricketmedia.com. **Website:** www.open-

courtbooks.com. **Contact:** Acquisitions Editor. Estab. 1887. Publishes hardcover and trade paperback originals. "Regrettably, now, and for the forseeable future, Open Court can consider no new unsolicited manuscripts for publication, with the exception of works suitable for our Popular Culture and Philosophy series." **Publishes 20 titles/year. Pays 5-15% royalty on wholesale price.** Publishes ms 2 years after acceptance. Book catalog online. Guidelines online.

NONFICTION Subjects include philosophy, Asian thought, religious studies and popular culture. Query with SASE. Submit proposal package, outline, 1 sample chapter, TOC, author's cover letter, intended audience.

TIPS "Audience consists of philosophers and intelligent general readers. Only accepting submissions to Popular Culture and Philosophy series."

OPEN ROAD TRAVEL GUIDES

P.O. Box 284, Cold Spring Harbor NY 11724. (631)692-7172. **E-mail:** jonathan@openroadguides.com. **Website:** www.openroadguides.com. **Contact:** Jonathan Stein, publisher. Estab. 1993. Publishes trade paperback originals. "Open Road publishes travel guides and, in its Cold Spring Press imprint, now publishes genealogy books (8 in print to date) and welcomes submissions in this area." **Publishes 20-22 titles/year. 200 queries received/year. 75 mss received/year. 30% of books from first-time authors. 98% from unagented writers. Pays 5-6% royalty on retail price. Pays $1,000-3,500 advance.** Publishes ms 3 months after acceptance. Accepts simultaneous submissions. Responds in 1 month to queries; 2 months to proposals. Book catalog online.

NONFICTION Query.

◐ ORCA BOOK PUBLISHERS

P.O. Box 5626, Stn. B, Victoria BC V8R 6S4, Canada. (250)380-1229. **Fax:** (877)408-1551. **E-mail:** orca@orcabook.com. **Website:** www.orcabook.com. **Contact:** Amy Collins, editor (picture books); Sarah Harvey, editor (young readers); Andrew Wooldridge, editor (juvenile and teen fiction); Bob Tyrrell, publisher (YA, teen); Ruth Linka, associate editor (rapid reads).. Estab. 1984. Publishes hardcover and trade paperback originals, and mass market paperback originals and reprints. Only publishes Canadian authors. **Publishes 30-50 titles/year. 2,500 queries; 1,000 mss received/year. 20% of books from first-time authors. 75% from unagented writers. Pays 10% royalty.** Pub-

lishes book 12-18 months after acceptance. Responds in 1 month to queries; 2 months to proposals and mss. Book catalog for 8½x11 SASE. Guidelines online.

NONFICTION Subjects include gay, lesbian, marine subjects, multicultural, sports, young adult, picture books. Only publishes Canadian authors. Query with a SASE.

FICTION Subjects include adventure, gay, hi-lo, juvenile, lesbian, literary, multicultural, mystery, picture books, sports, young adult. Picture books: animals, contemporary, history, nature/environment. Middle readers: contemporary, history, fantasy, nature/environment, problem novels, graphic novels. Young adults: adventure, contemporary, hi-lo (Orca Soundings), history, multicultural, nature/environment, problem novels, suspense/mystery, graphic novels. Average word length: picture books—500-1,500; middle readers—20,000-35,000; young adult—25,000-45,000; Orca Soundings—13,000-15,000; Orca Currents—13,000-15,000. No romance, science fiction. Query with SASE. Submit proposal package, outline, clips, 2-5 sample chapters, SASE.

TIPS "Our audience is students in grades K-12. Know our books, and know the market."

⚫⊘ ORCHARD BOOKS (US)

557 Broadway, New York NY 10012. **Website:** www.scholastic.com. *Orchard is not accepting unsolicited mss.* **Publishes 20 titles/year. 10% of books from first-time authors. Most commonly offers an advance against list royalties.** Accepts simultaneous submissions.

FICTION Picture books, early readers, and novelty: animal, contemporary, history, humor, multicultural, poetry.

⊘ ORCHISES PRESS

P.O. Box 320533, Alexandria VA 22320. (703)683-1243. **E-mail:** lathbury@gmu.edu. **Website:** mason.gmu.edu/~lathbury. **Contact:** Roger Lathbury, editor-in-chief. Estab. 1983. Publishes hardcover and trade paperback originals and reprints. Orchises Press is a general literary publisher specializing in poetry with selected reprints and textbooks. No new fiction or children's books. **Publishes 2-3 titles/year. 1% of books from first-time authors. 95% from unagented writers. Pays 36% of receipts after Orchises has recouped its costs.** Publishes book 1 year after acceptance. Accepts simultaneous submissions. Responds in 3 months to queries. Guidelines online.

NONFICTION No real restrictions on subject matter. Query with SASE. Reviews artwork/photos. Send photocopies.

POETRY Poetry must have been published in respected literary journals. *Orchises Press no longer reads unsolicited mss.* Publishes free verse, but has strong formalist preferences. Query and submit 5 sample poems.

OREGON STATE UNIVERSITY PRESS

121 The Valley Library, Corvallis OR 97331. (541)737-3873. **Fax:** (541)737-3170. **E-mail:** mary.braun@oregonstate.edu. **Website:** osupress.oregonstate.edu. **Contact:** Mary Elizabeth Braun, acquisitions editor. Estab. 1962. Publishes hardcover, paperback, and e-book originals. **Publishes 20-25 titles/year. 40% of books from first-time authors.** Publishes book 1 year after acceptance. Responds in 3 months to queries. Book catalog for 6x9 SAE with 2 first-class stamps. Guidelines online.

NONFICTION Subjects include regional, science. Publishes scholarly books in history, biography, geography, literature, natural resource management, with strong emphasis on Pacific or Northwestern topics and Native American and indigenous studies. Submit outline, sample chapters.

O'REILLY MEDIA

1005 Gravenstein Highway N., Sebastopol CA 95472. (707)827-7000. **Fax:** (707)829-0104. **E-mail:** workwithus@oreilly.com. **Website:** www.oreilly.com. **Contact:** Acquisitions Editor. "We're always looking for new authors and new book ideas. Our ideal author has real technical competence and a passion for explaining things clearly." Accepts simultaneous submissions. Guidelines online.

NONFICTION "At the same time as you might say that our books are written 'by and for smart people,' they also have a down to earth quality. We like straight talk that goes right to the heart of what people need to know." Submit proposal package, outline, publishing history, bio.

TIPS "It helps if you know that we tend to publish 'high end' books rather than books for dummies, and generally don't want yet another book on a topic that's already well covered."

OUR SUNDAY VISITOR, INC.

200 Noll Plaza, Huntington IN 46750. **E-mail:** jlindsey@osv.com. **Website:** www.osv.com. Publishes paperback and hardbound originals. "We are a Catholic publishing company seeking to educate and deepen our readers in their faith. Currently emphasizing devotional, inspirational, Catholic identity, apologetics, and catechetics." **Publishes 40-50 titles/year. Pays authors royalty of 10-12% net. Pays illustrators by the project (range: $25-1,500).** Publishes ms 1-2 years after acceptance. Accepts simultaneous submissions. Responds in 2 months. Book catalog for 9×12 envelope and first-class stamps; ms guidelines available online.

Our Sunday Visitor, Inc. is publishing only those children's books that are specifically Catholic. See website for submission guidelines.

NONFICTION Prefers to see well-developed proposals as first submission with annotated outline and definition of intended market; Catholic viewpoints on family, prayer, and devotional books, and Catholic heritage books. Picture books, middle readers, young readers, young adults. Query, submit complete ms, or submit outline/synopsis and 2-3 sample chapters. Reviews artwork/photos.

TIPS "Stay in accordance with our guidelines."

RICHARD C. OWEN PUBLISHERS, INC.

P.O. Box 585, Katonah NY 10536. (914)232-3903; (800)262-0787. **E-mail:** richardowen@rcowen.com. **Website:** www.rcowen.com. **Contact:** Richard Owen, publisher. Estab. 1982. "We publish child-focused books, with inherent instructional value, about characters and situations with which 5, 6, and 7-year-old children can identify—books that can be read for meaning, entertainment, enjoyment and information. We include multicultural stories that present minorities in a positive and natural way. Our stories show the diversity in America." Not interested in lesson plans, or books of activities for literature studies or other content areas. Submit complete ms and cover letter. **Pays authors royalty of 5% based on net price or outright purchase (range: $25-500). Offers no advances. Pays illustrators by the project (range: $100-2,000) or per photo (range: $50-150).** Publishes book 2-3 years after acceptance. Accepts simultaneous submissions. Responds to mss in 1 year. Book catalog available with SASE. Ms guidelines with SASE or online.

"Due to high volume and long production time, we are currently limiting to nonfiction submissions only."

NONFICTION Subjects include history, recreation, science, sports, music, diverse culture, nature. "Our books are for kindergarten, first- and second-grade children to read on their own. The stories are very brief—up to 2,000 words—yet well structured and crafted with memorable characters, language, and plots. Picture books, young readers: animals, careers, history, how-to, music/dance, geography, multicultural, nature/environment, science, sports. Multicultural needs include: Good stories respectful of all heritages, races, cultural—African-American, Hispanic, American Indian, Asian, European, Middle Eastern." Wants lively stories. No "encyclopedic" type of information stories. Average word length: under 500 words.

☙ PETER OWEN PUBLISHERS

81 Bridge Rd., London N8 9NP, United Kingdom. (44)(208)350-1775. **Fax:** (44)(208)340-9488. **E-mail:** info@peterowen.com. **Website:** www.peterowen.com. Publishes hardcover originals and trade paperback originals and reprints. "We are far more interested in proposals for nonfiction than fiction at the moment. No poetry or short stories." **Publishes 20-30 titles/year. 3,000 queries received/year. 800 mss received/year. 70% from unagented writers. Pays 7½-10% royalty. Pays negotiable advance.** Publishes ms 1 year after acceptance. Responds in 2 months to queries; 3 months to proposals and mss. Book catalog for SASE, SAE with IRC or on website.

NONFICTION Subjects include history, literature, memoirs, translation, travel, art, drama, literary, biography. Query with synopsis, sample chapters.

FICTION "No first novels. Authors should be aware that we publish very little new fiction these days." Query with synopsis, sample chapters.

OXFORD UNIVERSITY PRESS

198 Madison Ave., New York NY 10016. (212)726-6000. **E-mail:** custserv.us@oup.com. **Website:** www. oup.com/us. World's largest university press with the widest global audience. Accepts simultaneous submissions. Guidelines online.

NONFICTION Query with outline, proposal, sample chapters.

☙ OXFORD UNIVERSITY PRESS: SOUTHERN AFRICA

P.O. Box 12119, NI City Cape Town 7463, South Africa. (27)(21)596-2300. **Fax:** (27)(21)596-1234. **E-mail:** oxford.za@oup.com. **Website:** www.oxford.co.za. Academic publisher known for its educational books for southern African schools. Also publishes general and reference titles. **Publishes 150 titles/year.** Accepts simultaneous submissions. Book catalog online. Guidelines online.

NONFICTION Submit cover letter, synopsis, first few chapters, and submission form (available online) via mail.

FICTION Submit cover letter, synopsis.

OZARK MOUNTAIN PUBLISHING, INC.

Cannon Holdings, LLC, P.O. Box 754, Huntsville AR 72740. (479)738-2348. **Fax:** (479)738-2448. **E-mail:** brandy@ozarkmt.com. **Website:** www.ozarkmt. com. **Contact:** Nancy Vernon, general manager. Estab. 1992. Publishes trade paperback originals. "We publish New Age/metaphysical, spiritual nonfiction books." **Publishes 8-10 titles/year. 50-75 queries; 150-200 mss received/year. 50% of books from first-time authors. 95% from unagented writers. Pays 10-15% royalty on retail or wholesale price. Pays $250-500 advance.** Publishes ms within 18 months after acceptance. Accepts simultaneous submissions. Responds in 6 months to queries; 7 months to mss. Book catalog online. Guidelines online. Postcard included for notification of receipt. No phone call please.

NONFICTION Subjects include New Age, philosophy, spirituality, metaphysical. No phone calls please. Query with SASE. Submit TOC and 4-5 sample chapters.

Guidelines online.

TIPS "We envision our audience to be open minded, spiritually expanding. Please do not call to check on submissions. Do not submit electronically. Send hard copy only."

P & R PUBLISHING CO.

P.O. Box 817, Phillipsburg NJ 08865. **Fax:** (908)859-2390. **E-mail:** editorial@prpbooks.com. **Website:** www.prpbooks.com. Estab. 1930. Publishes hardcover originals and trade paperback originals and reprints. **Publishes 40 titles/year. Up to 300 queries received/year. 100 mss received/year. 5% of books from first-time authors. 95% from unagented writers. Pays 10-16% royalty on wholesale price.** Accepts simultaneous submissions. Responds in 3 months to proposals. Guidelines online.

NONFICTION Subjects include history, religion, spirituality, translation. Only accepts electronic submission with completion of online Author Guidelines. Hard copy mss will not be returned.

TIPS "Our audience is evangelical Christians and seekers. All of our publications are consistent with Biblical teaching, as summarized in the Westminster Standards."

PACIFIC PRESS PUBLISHING ASSOCIATION

Trade Book Division, 1350 N. Kings Rd., Nampa ID 83687. (208)465-2500. **Fax:** (208)465-2531. **Website:** www.pacificpress.com. Estab. 1874. Publishes hardcover and trade paperback originals and reprints. "We publish books that fit Seventh-day Adventist beliefs only. All titles are Christian and religious. For guidance, see www.adventist.org/beliefs/index.html. Our books fit into the categories of this retail site: www.adventistbookcenter.com." **Publishes 35 titles/year. 35% of books from first-time authors. 100% from unagented writers. Pays 8-16% royalty on wholesale price.** Publishes book 2 years after acceptance. Responds in 3 months to queries. Guidelines online.

NONFICTION Subjects include child guidance, philosophy, religion, spirituality, family living, Christian lifestyle, Bible study, Christian doctrine, prophecy. Query with SASE or e-mail, or submit 3 sample chapters, cover letter with overview of book. Electronic submissions accepted. Reviews artwork/photos.

FICTION Subjects include religious. "Pacific Press rarely publishes fiction, but we're interested in developing a line of Seventh-day Adventist fiction in the future. Only proposals accepted; no full manuscripts."

TIPS "Our primary audience is members of the Seventh-day Adventist denomination. Almost all are written by Seventh-day Adventists. Books that do well for us relate the Biblical message to practical human concerns and focus more on the experiential rather than theoretical aspects of Christianity. We are assigning more titles, using less unsolicited material—although we still publish manuscripts from freelance submissions and proposals."

PAGESPRING PUBLISHING

P.O. Box 2113, Columbus OH 43221. **E-mail:** sales@pagespringpublishing.com. **E-mail:** submissions@pagespringpublishing.com. **Website:** www.pagespringpublishing.com. **Contact:** Lucky Marble Books Editor or Cup of Tea Books Editor. Estab. 2012. Publishes trade paperback and electronic originals. "PageSpring Publishing publishes young adult and middle grade titles under the Lucky Marble Books imprint and women's fiction under the Cup of Tea imprint. See PageSpring website for submission de-tails." **Publishes 7-10 titles/year. 75% of books from first-time authors. 100% from unagented writers. Pays royalty on wholesale price.** Publishes ms 9-12 months after acceptance. Accepts simultaneous submissions. "We endeavor to respond to all queries within six weeks.". Catalog online. Guidelines online.

IMPRINTS Lucky Marble Books, Cup of Tea Books.

FICTION Subjects include adventure, contemporary, historical, humor, juvenile, mainstream, mystery, regional, romance, science fiction, young adult. Cup of Tea Books publishes women's fiction. Lucky Marble books specializes in middle grade and young adult fiction. Looking for YA submissions."Our favorite genres include historical fiction, fantasy, science fiction, mystery, supernatural fiction, romantic comedy, and humor. Send submissions to submissions@pagespringpublishing.com."Please send a query, synopsis, and the first 30 pages of your manuscript in the body of the e-mail. No attachments, please. In the subject line, please write Young Adult Submission."

TIPS "Cup of Tea Books would love to see more cozy mysteries and humor. Lucky Marble Books is looking for humor and engaging contemporary stories for middle grade and young adult readers."

PAGESPRING PUBLISHING

PageSpring Publishing, P.O. Box 21133, Columbus OH 43221. **E-mail:** submissions@pagespringpublishing.com. **Website:** www.pagespringpublishing.com. Estab. 2012. Publishes trade paperback and electronic originals. PageSpring Publishing is a small independent publisher with two imprints: Cup of Tea Books and Lucky Marble Books. Cup of Tea Books publishes women's fiction, with particular emphasis on mystery and humor. Lucky Marble Books publishes young adult and middle grade fiction. **Publishes 6-10 titles/year. 75% of books from first-time authors. 100% from unagented writers. Pays royalty.** Publishes ms 12 months after acceptance. Accepts simultaneous submissions. Responds in 3 months. Guidelines online.

IMPRINTS Cup of Tea Books and Lucky Marble Books.

○ "We are looking for engaging characters and well-crafted plots that keep our readers turning the page. We accept e-mail queries only; see our website for details."

FICTION Subjects include adventure, contemporary, fantasy, feminist, hi-lo, historical, humor, juvenile, literary, mainstream, multicultural, mystery, regional, romance, science fiction, sports, suspense, young adult. Cup of Tea Books publishes women's fiction. Lucky Marble Books publishes middle grade and young adult novels. No children's picture books. Submit proposal package via e-mail only. Include synopsis and 30 sample pages.

TIPS "Cup of Tea Books is particularly interested in cozy mystery novels. Lucky Marble Books is looking for funny, age-appropriate tales for middle grade and young adult readers."

⊘ PAJAMA PRESS

181 Carlaw Ave., Suite 207, Toronto ON M4M 2S1, Canada. **E-mail:** info@pajamapress.ca. **E-mail:** annfeatherstone@pajamapress.ca. **Website:** pajamapress.ca. "We publish picture books—both for the very young and for school-aged readers—as well as novels for middle grade readers and for young adults aged 12+. Our nonfiction titles typically contain a strong narrative element." Accepts simultaneous submissions.

FICTION Query with an excerpt. Guidelines on site.

PALADIN PRESS

5540 Central Ave., Suite 200, Boulder CO 80301. (303)443-7250. **Fax:** (303)442-8741. **E-mail:** editorial@paladin-press.com. **Website:** www.paladin-press.com. Estab. 1970. Publishes hardcover originals and paperback originals and reprints, videos. "Paladin Press publishes the action library of nonfiction in military science, police science, weapons, combat, personal freedom, self-defense, survival." **Publishes 50 titles/year. 50% of books from first-time authors. 95% from unagented writers. "We pay royalties in full and on time." Pays advance.** Publishes ms 1 year after acceptance. Accepts simultaneous submissions. Responds in 2 months to proposals. Book catalog available free.

IMPRINTS Sycamore Island Books; Flying Machines Press; Outer Limits Press; Romance Book Classics.

NONFICTION If applicable, send sample photographs and line drawings with complete outline and sample chapters. Paladin Press primarily publishes original manuscripts on military science, weaponry, self-defense, personal privacy, financial freedom, espionage, police science, action careers, guerrilla warfare, and fieldcraft. To submit a book proposal to Paladin Press, send an outline or chapter description along with 1-2 sample chapters (or the entire ms) to the address below. If applicable, samples of illustrations or photographs are also useful. Do not send a computer disk at this point, and be sure keep a copy of everything you send us. We are not accepting mss as electronic submissions at this time. Please allow 2-6 weeks for a reply. If you would like your sample material returned, a SASE with proper postage is required. Editorial Department, Paladin Press Gunbarrel Tech Center, 5540 Central Ave., Boulder, CO 80301, or e-mail us at: editorial@paladin-press.com. Query with SASE. Submitting a proposal for a video project is not much different than a book proposal. See guidelines online and send to: All materials related to video proposals should be addressed directly to: David Dubrow, Video Production Manager.

TIPS "We need lucid, instructive material aimed at our market and accompanied by sharp, relevant illustrations and photos. As we are primarily a publisher of 'how-to' books, a manuscript that has step-by-step instructions, written in a clear and concise manner (but not strictly outline form) is desirable. No fiction, first-person accounts, children's, religious, or joke books. We are also interested in serious, professional videos and video ideas (contact Michael Rigg)."

PALETTES & QUILLS

1935 Penfield Rd., Penfield NY 14526. (585)383-0812. **E-mail:** palettesnquills@gmail.com. **Website:** www.palettesnquills.com. **Contact:** Donna M. Marbach, publisher/owner. Estab. 2002. Publishes chapbooks, broadsides, e-newsletter. Palettes & Quills is devoted to the celebration and expansion of the literary and visual arts, offering both commissioned and consulting services. It works to support beginning and emerging writers and artists to expand their knowledge, improve their skills, and connect to other resources in the community. Further, Palettes & Quills seeks to increase the public's awareness and appreciation of these arts through education, advocacy, hands-on program assistance, and functioning as a small literary press. "We publish a chapbook every other year in a contest judged by a well-known poet. We also publish a monthly e-newsletter, and chapbooks/anthologies/ and broadsides on an irregular schedule. Reprints accepted only for our e-newsletter." **Contest winner gets $200 and 50 books. Others are paid copies.** Accepts simultaneous submissions. Response time varies. "We try to respond as quick as we can.". Guidelines online.

NONFICTION Subjects include art, crafts, creative nonfiction, entertainment, literary criticism, literature, music, photography. Does not want political and religious diatribes. Our preference is for book reviews, how to for literature and the arts, interviews with artists/authors/essay of interest for writing style or art and literature interest. Artwork can be photos, copies of paintings, collages , photos of scuptures, Photos can be on any subject but should be of interest to literary and visual artists. Reviews art work and photos for covers.

FICTION "We prefer short-shorts and stories. We might consider a novella, but we are too small for long epic novels. Encourage short essays, short stories, reviews for our monthy newsletter."

POETRY Palettes & Quills "is at this point is only considering chapbooks that are poetry, creative nonfiction, or fiction, a poetry press only, and produces only a handful of publications each year, specializing in anthologies, individual chapbooks, and broadsides." Wants "work that should appeal to a wide audience." Does not want "poems that are sold blocks of text, long-lined and without stanza breaks. Wildly elaborate free-verse would be difficult and in all likelihood fight with art background, amateurish rhyming poem, overly sentimental poems, poems that use excessive profanity, or which denigrate other people, or political and religious diatribes." Query first with 3-5 poems and a cover letter with brief bio and publication credits for individual unsolicited chapbooks. May include previously published poems. Chapbook poets would get 20 copies of a run; broadside poets and artists get 5-10 copies and occasionally paid $10 for reproduction rights. Anthology poets get 1 copy of the anthology. All poets and artists get a discount on purchases that include their work.

TIPS "We are very small and the best bet with us with our monthly e-newsletter Pencil Marks."

PALGRAVE MACMILLAN

St. Martin's Press, 175 Fifth Ave., New York NY 10010. (212)982-3900. **Fax:** (212)777-6359. **E-mail:** proposals@palgrave.com. **Website:** www.palgrave.com. Publishes hardcover and trade paperback originals. "Palgrave wishes to expand on our already successful academic, trade, and reference programs so that we will remain at the forefront of publishing in the global information economy of the 21st century. We publish high-quality academic works and a distin-

guished range of reference titles, and we expect to see many of our works available in electronic form. We do not accept fiction or poetry." Accepts simultaneous submissions. Book catalog and ms guidelines online.

○ Palgrave Macmillan is a cross-market publisher specializing in cutting edge academic and trade nonfiction titles. Our list consists of top authors ranging from academics making original contributions in their disciplines to trade authors, including journalists and experts, writing news-making books for a broad, educated readership.

NONFICTION Subjects include creative nonfiction, education, ethnic, history, multicultural, philosophy, regional, religion, sociology, spirituality, translation, humanities. We are looking for good solid scholarship. Query with proposal package including outline, 3-4 sample chapters, prospectus, cv and SASE. Reviews artwork/photos.

PANKHEARST

Website: pankhearst.wordpress.com. Estab. 2012. Pankhearst is a collective of independent writers. "We exist to develop and promote new writers, and to learn while doing. We have published 4 spiffing full-length collections of fiction, 2 novels, and more than a dozen Kindle 'singles' to date. We've also published 2 collections of poetry and flash fiction." Accepts simultaneous submissions. Guidelines online.

TIPS "Pankhearst welcomes everybody, regardless of age, color, disability, familial or parental status, gender identity, marital status, national origin, race, religion, sex, sexual orientation, and anything else you or we can think of."

Ⓐⵁ PANTHEON BOOKS

Penguin Random House, 1745 Broadway, New York NY 10019. **Website:** www.pantheonbooks.com. Estab. 1942. Publishes hardcover and trade paperback originals and trade paperback reprints. Accepts simultaneous submissions.

○ Pantheon Books publishes both Western and non-Western authors of literary fiction and important nonfiction. "We only accept mss submitted by an agent."

NONFICTION *Does not accept unsolicited mss.* Agented submissions only.

FICTION *Does not accept unsolicited mss.* Agented submissions only.

PANTS ON FIRE PRESS

2062 Harbor Cove Way, Winter Garden FL 34787. (863)546-0760. **E-mail:** submission@pantsonfirepress.com. **Website:** www.pantsonfirepress.com. **Contact:** Becca Goldman, senior editor; Emily Gerety, editor. Estab. 2012. Publishes hardcover originals and reprints, trade paperback originals and reprints, and electronic originals and reprints. Pants On Fire Press is an award-winning book publisher of picture, middle-grade, young adult, and adult books. They are a digital-first book publisher, striving to follow a high degree of excellence while maintaining quality standards. **Publishes 10-15 titles/year. Receives 2,500 queries and mss per year. 60% of books from first-time authors. 80% from unagented writers. Pays 10-50% royalties on wholesale price.** Publishes ms approximately 7 months after acceptance. Accepts simultaneous submissions. Responds in 3 months. Catalog online. Guidelines online.

FICTION Subjects include adventure, fantasy, historical, humor, juvenile, romance, science fiction, suspense, young adult. Publishes big story ideas with high concepts, new worlds, and meaty characters for children, teens, and discerning adults. Always on the lookout for action, adventure, animals, comedic, dramatic, dystopian, fantasy, historical, paranormal, romance, sci-fi, supernatural, and suspense stories. Submit a proposal package including a synopsis, 3 sample chapters, and a query letter via e-mail.

PAPERCUTZ

160 Broadway, Suite 700E, New York NY 10038. (646)559-4681. **Fax:** (212)643-1545. **Website:** www.papercutz.com. Estab. 2004. Publisher of graphic novels. **Publishes 10 titles/year.** Accepts simultaneous submissions.

FICTION Subjects include comic books, fantasy, humor, juvenile, translation, young adult. "Independent publisher of graphic novels based on popular existing properties aimed at the teen and tween market."

TIPS "Be familiar with our titles—that's the best way to know what we're interested in publishing. If you are somehow attached to a successful tween or teen property and would like to adapt it into a graphic novel, we may be interested."

PARACLETE PRESS

P.O. Box 1568, Orleans MA 02653. (508)255-4685. **Fax:** (508)255-5705. **E-mail:** phil@paracletepress.

com. **Website:** www.paracletepress.com. **Contact:** Editorial Review Committee. Estab. 1981. Publishes hardcover and trade paperback originals. Publisher of devotionals, new editions of classics, books on prayer, Christian living, spirituality, fiction, compact discs, and videos. **Publishes 40 titles/year. 250 mss received/year.** Publishes ms up to 2 years after acceptance. Responds in 2 months.

○ "Does not publish poetry, memoirs, or children's books. "

NONFICTION Subjects include art, religion. Query with SASE. Submit 2-3 sample chapters, TOC, chapter summaries.

PARADISE CAY PUBLICATIONS

P.O. Box 29, Arcata CA 95518-0029. (800)736-4509. **Fax:** (707)822-9163. **E-mail:** info@paracay.com. **Website:** www.paracay.com. Publishes hardcover and trade paperback originals and reprints. "Paradise Cay Publications, Inc. is a small independent publisher specializing in nautical books, videos, and art prints. Our primary interest is in manuscripts that deal with the instructional and technical aspects of ocean sailing. We also publish and will consider fiction if it has a strong nautical theme." **Publishes 5 titles/year. 360-480 queries received/year. 240-360 mss received/year. 10% of books from first-time authors. 100% from unagented writers. Pays 10-15% royalty on wholesale price. Makes outright purchase of $1,000-10,000. Does not normally pay advances to first-time or little-known authors.** Publishes book 4 months after acceptance. Accepts simultaneous submissions. Responds in 1 month to queries/proposals; 2 months to mss. Book catalog and ms guidelines free on request or online.

IMPRINTS Pardey Books.

NONFICTION Subjects include recreation, sports, travel. Must have strong nautical theme. Include a cover letter containing a story synopsis and a short bio, including any plans to promote their work. The cover letter should describe the book's subject matter, approach, distinguishing characteristics, intended audience, author's qualifications, and why the author thinks this book is appropriate for Paradise Cay. Call first. Reviews artwork/photos. Send photocopies.

FICTION Subjects include adventure. All fiction must have a nautical theme. Query with SASE. Submit proposal package, clips, 2-3 sample chapters.

TIPS "Audience is recreational sailors. Call Matt Morehouse (publisher)."

PARADISE RESEARCH PUBLICATIONS, INC.

P.O. Box 837, Kihei HI 96753. (808)874-4876. **Fax:** (808)874-4876. **E-mail:** dickb@dickb.com. **Website:** www.dickb.com/index.shtml. Publishes trade paperback originals. Paradise Research Publications wants only books on Alcoholics Anonymous and its spiritual roots. **Publishes 3 titles/year. 5 queries received/year. 1 mss received/year. 20% of books from first-time authors. 100% from unagented writers. Pays 10% royalty.** Publishes ms 3 months after acceptance. Accepts simultaneous submissions. Responds in 1 month to queries. Book catalog available online.

NONFICTION Subjects include psychology, religion, spirituality, recovery, alcoholism, addictions, Christian recovery, history of Alcoholics Annonymous. Query with SASE.

PARAGON HOUSE PUBLISHERS

3600 Labore Rd., Suite 1, St. Paul MN 55110. (651)644-3087. **Fax:** (651)644-0997. **E-mail:** paragon@paragonhouse.com. **Website:** www.paragonhouse.com. **Contact:** Gordon Anderson, acquisitions editor. Estab. 1962. Publishes hardcover and trade paperback originals and trade paperback reprints and e-books. "We publish general-interest titles and textbooks that provide the readers greater understanding of society and the world. Currently emphasizing religion, philosophy, economics, and society." **Publishes 5-10 titles/year. 1,500 queries received/year. 150 mss received/year. 7% of books from first-time authors. 90% from unagented writers. Not generally. Royalties paid as earned.** Publishes ms 1 year after acceptance. Accepts simultaneous submissions. Guidelines online.

IMPRINTS Omega Books.

NONFICTION Subjects include anthropology, economics, government, history, military, New Age, parenting, philosophy, politics, psychology, religion, social sciences, spirituality, world affairs, integral studies. Submit proposal package, outline, 2 sample chapters, market breakdown, SASE.

PARALLAX PRESS

P.O. Box 7355, Berkeley CA 94707. (510)525-0101, ext. 113. **Fax:** (510)525-7129. **E-mail:** rachel.neumann@parallax.org. **Website:** www.parallax.org. **Contact:** Rachel Neumann, publisher. Estab. 1985. Publishes hardcover and trade paperback originals. "We focus primarily on engaged Buddhism." **Publishes 5-8 titles/year.** Responds in 6-8 weeks to queries. Guidelines online.

NONFICTION Subjects include multicultural, religion, spirituality. Query with SASE. Submit 1 sample chapter, 1-page proposal. Reviews artwork/photos. Send photocopies.

PASSKEY PUBLICATIONS

P.O. Box 580465, Elk Grove CA 95758. (916)917-5376. **Fax:** (916)427-5765. **E-mail:** frontdesk@passkeypublications.com. **Website:** www.passkeypublications.com. Estab. 2007. Publishes trade paperback originals. **Publishes 15 titles/year. Receives 375 queries/year; 120 mss/year. 15% of books from first-time authors. 90% from unagented writers. Pay varies on retail price.** Publishes ms 1 year after acceptance. Accepts simultaneous submissions. Responds in 1 month. Catalog and guidelines online.

IMPRINTS Passkey Publications, PassKey EA Review.

NONFICTION Subjects include business, economics, finance, money, real estate, accounting, taxation, study guides for professional examinations. "Books on taxation and accounting are generally updated every year to reflect tax law changes, and the turnaround on a ms must be less than 3 months for accounting and tax subject matter. Books generally remain in publication only 11 months and are generally published every year for updates." Submit complete ms. Nonfiction mss only. Reviews artwork/photos as part of ms package. Send electronic files on disk, via e-mail, or jump drive.

TIPS "Accepting business, accounting, tax, finance and other related subjects only."

PAUL DRY BOOKS

1700 Sansom St., Suite 700, Philadelphia PA 19103. (215)231-9939. **Fax:** (215)231-9942. **E-mail:** editor@pauldrybooks.com. **E-mail:** pdry@pauldrybooks.com. **Website:** pauldrybooks.com. Hardcover and trade paperback originals, trade paperback reprints. "We publish fiction, both novels and short stories, and nonfiction, biography, memoirs, history, and essays, covering subjects from Homer to Chekhov, bird watching to jazz music, New York City to shogunate Japan." Accepts simultaneous submissions. Book catalog available online. Guidelines available online.

○ "Take a few minutes to familiarize yourself with the books we publish. Then if you think your book would be a good fit in our line, we invite you to submit the following: A one- or two-page summary of the work. Be sure to tell us how many pages or words the full book will be; a sample of 20-30 pages; your bio. A brief description of how you think the book (and you, the author) could be marketed."

NONFICTION Subjects include agriculture, contemporary culture, history, literary criticism, memoirs, multicultural, philosophy, religion, translation, popular mathematics. Submit proposal package.

FICTION Subjects include literary, short story collections, translation, young adult, novels. Submit sample chapters, clips, bio.

TIPS "Our aim is to publish lively books 'to awaken, delight, and educate'—to spark conversation. We publish fiction and nonfiction, and essays covering subjects from Homer to Chekhov, bird watching to jazz music, New York City to shogunate Japan."

PAULINE BOOKS & MEDIA

50 St. Paul's Ave., Boston MA 02130. (617)522-8911. **Fax:** (617)541-9805. **E-mail:** design@paulinemedia. com; editorial@paulinemedia.com. **Website:** www. pauline.org. Estab. 1932. Publishes trade paperback originals and reprints. "Submissions are evaluated on adherence to Gospel values, harmony with the Catholic faith tradition, relevance of topic, and quality of writing." For board books and picture books, the entire manuscript should be submitted. For easy-to-read, young readers, and middle reader books and teen books, please send a cover letter accompanied by a synopsis and two sample chapters. "Electronic submissions are encouraged. We make every effort to respond to unsolicited submissions within 2 months." **Publishes 40 titles/year. 15- for adult books; about 40% for children's books% of books from first-time authors. 5% from unagented writers. Varies by project, but generally are royalties with advance. Flat fees sometimes considered for smaller works.** Publishes a book approximately 11-18 months after acceptance. Responds in 2 months to queries, proposals, & mss. Book catalog available online. Guidelines available online & by e-mail.

NONFICTION Subjects include child guidance, religion, spirituality, young adult. Picture books, young readers, middle readers, teen: religion and fiction. Average word length: picture books—500-1,000; young readers—8,000-10,000; middle read-

ers—15,000-25,000; teen—30,000-50,000. Recently published children's titles: *Bible Stores for Little Ones* by Genny Monchapm; *I Forgive You: Love We Can Hear, Ask For and Give* by Nicole Lataif; *Shepherds To the Rescue* (first place Catholic Book Award Winner) by Maria Grace Dateno; *FSP*; *Jorge from Argentina*; *Prayers for Young Catholics.* Teen Titles: *Teens Share the Mission* by Teens; *Martyred: The Story of Saint Lorenzo Ruiz*; *Ten Commandmenst for Kissing Gloria Jean* by Britt Leigh; *A.K.A. Genius* (2nd Place Catholic Book Award Winner) by Marilee Haynes; *Tackling Tough Topics* with Faith and Fiction by Diana Jenkins. No memoir/autobiography, poetry, or strictly nonreligious works currently considered. Submit proposal package, including outline, 1- 2 sample chapters, cover letter, synopsis, intended audience and proposed length.

FICTION Subjects include adventure, contemporary, juvenile, picture books, religious, romance, spiritual, young adult. Children's and teen fiction only. We are now accepting submissions for easy-to-read and middle reader chapter, and teen well documented historical fiction. We would also consider well-written fantasy, fairy tales, myths, science fiction, mysteries, or romance if approached from a Catholic perspective and consistent with church teaching. Please see our Writer's Guidelines. "Submit proposal package, including synopsis, 2 sample chapters, and cover letter; complete ms."

TIPS "Manuscripts may or may not be explicitly catechetical, but we seek those that reflect a positive worldview, good moral values, awareness and appreciation of diversity, and respect for all people. All material must be relevant to the lives of readers and must conform to Catholic teaching and practice."

PAULIST PRESS

997 Macarthur Blvd., Mahwah NJ 07430. (201)825-7300. **Fax:** (201)825-8345. **E-mail:** submissions@ paulistpress.com. **Website:** www.paulistpress.com. **Contact:** Trace Murphy, editorial director. Estab. 1865. Paulist Press publishes ecumenical theology, Roman Catholic studies, and books on scripture, liturgy, spirituality, church history, and philosophy, as well as works on faith and culture. "Our publishing is oriented toward adult-level nonfiction. We do not publish memoirs, poetry, or works of fiction, and we have scaled back on children's books. Offer of a subsidy is no guarantee of acceptance—we are not a vanity

press." **Receives 250 submissions/year. 10% of books from first-time authors. 95% from unagented writers. Royalties and advances are negotiable. Pays negotiable advance.** Publishes a book 12-18 months after receipt of final, edited ms. Responds in 3 months to queries and proposals; 3-4 months on mss. Book catalog available online. Guidelines available on website and by e-mail.

NONFICTION Subjects include religion. Accepts submissions via e-mail. Hard copy submissions returned only if accompanied by self-addressed envelope with adequate postage.

PAYCOCK PRESS

3819 N. 13th St., Arlington VA 22201. (703)525-9296. **E-mail:** rchrdpeabody9@gmail.com. **Website:** www.gargoylemagazine.com. **Contact:** Richard Peabody. Estab. 1976. "Too academic for the underground, too outlaw for the academic world. We tend to be edgy and look for ultra-literary work." Publishes paperback originals. Books: POD printing. Average print order: 500. Averages 1 total title/year. Member CLMP. Distributes through Amazon and website. Publishes ms 1 year after acceptance. Accepts simultaneous submissions. Responds to queries in 1 month; mss in 4 months.

FICTION Subjects include experimental, literary, poetry, short story collections. Accepts unsolicited mss. Accepts queries by e-mail. Include brief bio. Send SASE for return of ms or send a disposable ms and SASE for reply only.

POETRY Considers experimental, edgy poetry collections. Accepts unsolicited mss. Accepts queries by e-mail. Include brief bio. Send SASE for return of ms or send a disposable ms and SASE for reply only.

TIPS "Check out our website. Two of our favorite writers are Paul Bowles and Jeanette Winterson."

ⓐ⊘ PEACE HILL PRESS

Affiliate of W.W. Norton, 18021 The Glebe Ln., Charles City VA 23030. (804)829-5043. **Fax:** (804)829-5704. **Website:** www.peacehillpress.com. Estab. 2001. Publishes hardcover and trade paperback originals. **Publishes 4-8 titles/year. Pays 6-10% royalty on retail price. Pays $500-1,000 advance.** Publishes a book 18 months after acceptance.

NONFICTION Subjects include education, history. Does not take submissions. Reviews artwork/photos. Send photocopies.

FICTION Subjects include historical, juvenile, picture books, young adult. Does not take submissions.

PEACHTREE CHILDREN'S BOOKS

Peachtree Publishers, Ltd., 1700 Chattahoochee Ave., Atlanta GA 30318-2112. (404)876-8761. **Fax:** (404)875-2578. **E-mail:** hello@peachtree-online.com. **Website:** www.peachtree-online.com. **Contact:** Helen Harriss, submissions editor. Publishes hardcover and trade paperback originals. "We publish a broad range of subjects and perspectives, with emphasis on innovative plots and strong writing." **Publishes 30 titles/year. 25% of books from first-time authors. 25% from unagented writers. Pays royalty on retail price.** Publishes ms 1 year after acceptance. Accepts simultaneous submissions. Responds in 6 months and mss. Book catalog for 6 first-class stamps. Guidelines online.

NONFICTION Subjects include animals, child guidance, creative nonfiction, education, ethnic, gardening, history, literary criticism, multicultural, recreation, regional, science, social sciences, sports, travel. No e-mail or fax queries of mss. Submit complete ms with SASE, or summary and 3 sample chapters with SASE.

FICTION Subjects include juvenile, picture books, young adult. Looking for very well-written middle grade and young adult novels. No adult fiction. No collections of poetry or short stories; no romance or science fiction. Submit complete ms with SASE.

PEACHTREE PUBLISHERS, LTD.

1700 Chattahoochee Ave., Atlanta GA 30318. (404)876-8761. **Fax:** (404)875-2578. **E-mail:** hello@peachtree-online.com. **Website:** www.peachtree-online.com. Estab. 1977. **Publishes 30-35 titles/year.** Publishes book 1-2 years after acceptance. Accepts simultaneous submissions. Responds in 6-7 months.

NONFICTION Picture books: animal, history, nature/environment. Young readers, middle readers, young adults: animal, biography, nature/environment. Does not want to see religion. Submit complete ms or 3 sample chapters by postal mail only.

FICTION Picture books, young readers: adventure, animal, concept, history, nature/environment. Middle readers: adventure, animal, history, nature/environment, sports. Young adults: fiction, mystery, adventure. Does not want to see science fiction, romance. Submit complete ms or 3 sample chapters by postal mail only.

☘⊘ PEDLAR PRESS

113 Bond St., St. John's NL A16 1T6, Canada. (709)738-6702. **E-mail:** feralgrl@interlog.com. **Website:** www.pedlarpress.com. **Contact:** Beth Follett, owner/editor. **Publishes 7 titles/year. Pays 10% royalty on retail price. Average advance: $200-400.** Publishes ms 18 months after acceptance. Accepts simultaneous submissions.

NONFICTION Subjects include creative nonfiction, gay, literary criticism, literature.

FICTION Subjects include experimental, feminist, gay, lesbian, literary, poetry, short story collections. Experimental, feminist, gay/lesbian, literary, short story collections. Canadian writers only. Query with SASE, sample chapter(s), synopsis.

TIPS "I select manuscripts according to my taste, which fluctuates. Be familiar with some if not most of Pedlar's recent titles."

PELICAN PUBLISHING COMPANY

1000 Burmaster St., Gretna LA 70053. (504)368-1175. **Fax:** (504)368-1195. **E-mail:** editorial@pelicanpub.com. **Website:** www.pelicanpub.com. Estab. 1926. Publishes hardcover, trade paperback and mass market paperback originals and reprints. "We believe ideas have consequences. One of the consequences is that they lead to a best-selling book. We publish books to improve and uplift the reader. Currently emphasizing business and history titles." Publishes 20 young readers/year; 1 middle reader/year. "Our children's books (illustrated and otherwise) include history, biography, holiday, and regional. Pelican's mission is to publish books of quality and permanence that enrich the lives of those who read them." **Pays authors in royalties; buys ms outright "rarely." Illustrators paid by "various arrangements." Advance considered.** Publishes a book 9-18 months after acceptance. Responds in 1 month to queries; 3 months to mss. Requires exclusive submission. Book catalog and ms guidelines online.

NONFICTION Subjects include Americana, ethnic, history, multicultural, regional, religion, sports, motivational (with business slant). "We look for authors who can promote successfully. We require that a query be made first. This greatly expedites the review process and can save the writer additional postage expenses." Young readers: biography, history, holiday, multicultural. Middle readers: Louisiana history, holiday, regional. No multiple queries or submissions. Reviews artwork/photos.

FICTION Subjects include historical, juvenile. We publish no adult fiction. Young readers: history, holiday, science, multicultural and regional. Middle readers: Louisiana History. Multicultural needs include stories about African-Americans, Irish-Americans, Jews, Asian-Americans, and Hispanics. Does not want animal stories, general Christmas stories, "day at school" or "accept yourself" stories. Maximum word length: young readers—1,100; middle readers—40,000. No young adult, romance, science fiction, fantasy, gothic, mystery, erotica, confession, horror, sex, or violence. Also no psychological novels. Submit outline, clips, 2 sample chapters, SASE. Full guidelines on website.

POETRY Considers poetry for "hardcover children's books only (1,100 words maximum), preferably with a regional focus. However, our needs for this are very limited; we publish 20 juvenile titles per year, and most of these are prose, not poetry." Books are 32 pages, magazine-sized, include illustrations.

TIPS "We do extremely well with cookbooks, popular histories, and business. We will continue to build in these areas. The writer must have a clear sense of the market and knowledge of the competition. A query letter should describe the project briefly, give the author's writing and professional credentials, and promotional ideas."

Ⓐ☘ PENGUIN CANADA, LTD.

The Penguin Group, 320 Front St. W., Suite 1400, Toronto ON M5V 3B6, Canada. (416)364-4449. **Fax:** (416)598-7764. **Website:** www.penguinrandomhouse.ca. Estab. 1974. **Pays advance.**

NONFICTION Canadian subject by any Canadian authors. Agented submissions only.

Ⓐ⊘ PENGUIN GROUP USA

375 Hudson St., New York NY 10014. (212)366-2000. **Website:** www.penguin.com. General interest publisher of both fiction and nonfiction. *No unsolicited mss.* Submit work through a literary agent. DAW Books is the lone exception. Guidelines online.

Ⓐ⊘ PENGUIN RANDOM HOUSE, LLC

Division of Bertelsmann Book Group, 1745 Broadway, New York NY 10019. (212)782-9000. **Website:** www.penguinrandomhouse.com. Estab. 1925. Penguin Random House LLC is the world's largest English-language general trade book publisher. *Agented submissions only. No unsolicited mss.* Accepts simultaneous submissions.

IMPRINTS Crown Publishing Group; Knopf Doubleday Publishing Group; Random House Publishing Group; Random House Children's Books; RH Digital Publishing Group; RH International.

THE PERMANENT PRESS

Attn: Judith Shepard, 4170 Noyac Rd., Sag Harbor NY 11963. (631)725-1101. **Fax:** (631)725-8215. **E-mail:** judith@thepermanentpress.com; shepard@thepermanentpress.com. **Website:** www.thepermanentpress.com. **Contact:** Judith and Martin Shepard, acquisitions/co-publishers. Estab. 1978. Publishes hardcover originals. Mid-size, independent publisher of literary fiction. "We keep titles in print and are active in selling subsidiary rights." Average print order: 1,000-2,500. Averages 16 total titles. Accepts unsolicited mss. Pays 10-15% royalty on wholesale price. Offers $1,000 advance. *Will not accept simultaneous submissions.* **Pays 10-15% royalty on wholesale price. Offers $1,000 advance.** Publishes ms within 18 months after acceptance. Responds in weeks or months.

FICTION Promotes titles through reviews. Literary, mainstream/contemporary, mystery. Especially looking for high-line literary fiction, "artful, original and arresting." Accepts any fiction category as long as it is a "well-written, original full-length novel."

TIPS "We are looking for good books—be they 10th novels or first ones, it makes little difference. The fiction is more important than the track record. Send us the first 25 pages; it's impossible to judge something that begins on page 302. Also, no outlines—let the writing present itself."

PERSEA BOOKS

277 Broadway, Suite 708, New York NY 10007. (212)260-9256. **Fax:** (212)267-3165. **E-mail:** info@perseabooks.com. **Website:** www.perseabooks.com. Estab. 1975. The aim of Persea is to publish works that endure by meeting high standards of literary merit and relevance. "We have often taken on important books other publishers have overlooked, or have made significant discoveries and rediscoveries, whether of a single work or writer's entire oeuvre. Our books cover a wide range of themes, styles, and genres. We have published poetry, fiction, essays, memoir, biography, titles of Jewish and Middle Eastern interest, women's studies, American Indian folklore, and revived classics, as well as a notable selection of works in translation." Accepts simultaneous submissions. Responds in 8 weeks to proposals; 10 weeks to mss. Guidelines online.

NONFICTION Subjects include contemporary culture, literary criticism, literature, memoirs, translation, travel, young adult.

FICTION Subjects include contemporary, literary, short story collections, translation, young adult. Queries should include a cover letter, author background and publication history, a detailed synopsis of the proposed work, and a sample chapter. Please indicate if the work is simultaneously submitted.

POETRY "We have a longstanding commitment to publishing extraordinary contemporary poetry and maintain an active poetry program. At this time, due to our commitment to the poets we already publish, we are limited in our ability to add new collections." Send an e-mail to poetry@perseabooks.com describing current project and publication history, attaching a pdf or Word document with up to 12 sample pages of poetry. "If the timing is right and we are interested in seeing more work, we will contact you."

⊘ PERUGIA PRESS

P.O. Box 60364, Florence MA 01062. **Website:** www.perugiapress.com. **Contact:** Susan Kan, director. Estab. 1997. The best new women poets, for 20 years. "Contact us through our website." Accepts simultaneous submissions.

PETER PAUPER PRESS, INC.

202 Mamaroneck Ave., 4th Floor, White Plains NY 10601. **Website:** www.peterpauper.com. Estab. 1928. Publishes hardcover originals. "PPP publishes small and medium format, illustrated gift books for occasions and in celebration of specific relationships such as mom, sister, friend, teacher, grandmother, granddaughter. PPP has expanded into the following areas: books for teens and tweens, activity books for children, organizers, books on popular topics of nonfiction for adults and licensed books by best-selling authors." **Publishes 40-50 titles/year. 100 queries received/year. 150 mss received/year. 5% from unagented writers. Makes outright purchase only. Pays advance.** Publishes ms 1 year after acceptance. Responds in 2 months to queries.

NONFICTION "We do not publish fiction or poetry. We publish brief, original quotes, aphorisms, and wise sayings. Please do not send us other people's quotes." Submit cover letter and hard copy ms.

TIPS "Our readers are primarily female, age 10 and over, who are likely to buy a 'gift' book or gift book set in a stationery, gift, book, or boutique store or national book chain. Writers should become familiar with our previously published work. We publish only small- and medium-format, illustrated, hardcover gift books and sets of between 1,000-4,000 words. We have much less interest in work aimed at men."

PETERSON'S

115 W. Century Rd., Paramus NJ 07652. **E-mail:** support@petersons.com. **Website:** www.petersons.com. Estab. 1966. Publishes trade and reference books. Peterson's publishes guides to graduate and professional programs, colleges and universities, financial aid, distance learning, private schools, summer programs, international study, executive education, job hunting and career opportunities, educational and career test prep, as well as online products and services offering educational and career guidance and information for adult learners and workplace solutions for education professionals. **Pays royalty. Pays advance.** Book catalog available free.

NONFICTION Subjects include education, careers. Looks for appropriateness of contents to our markets, author's credentials, and writing style suitable for audience.

PFEIFFER

John Wiley & Sons, Inc., 989 Market St., San Francisco CA 94103. **Website:** www.wiley.com. Pfeiffer is an imprint of Wiley. **Publishes 250 titles/year. Pays variable royalties. Pays occasional advance.** Publishes ms 1 year after acceptance. Accepts simultaneous submissions. Responds in 2-3 months to queries. Guidelines online.

NONFICTION Subjects include education, psychology, religion. See proposal guidelines online.

PFLAUM PUBLISHING GROUP

2621 Dryden Rd., Dayton OH 45439. (800)543-4383. **Website:** www.pflaum.com. "Pflaum Publishing Group, a division of Peter Li, Inc., serves the specialized market of religious education, primarily Roman Catholic. We provide high quality, theologically sound, practical, and affordable resources that assist religious educators of and ministers to children from preschool through senior high school." **Pub-**lishes 20 titles/year. Payment by outright purchase. Accepts simultaneous submissions. Book catalog and ms guidelines free.

NONFICTION Query with SASE.

PHAIDON PRESS

65 Bleecker St., 8th Floor, New York NY 10012. (212)652-5400. **Fax:** (212)652-5410. **E-mail:** submissions@phaidon.com. **Website:** www.phaidon.com. Estab. 1923. Publishes hardcover and trade paperback originals and reprints. Phaidon Press is the world's leading publisher of books on the visual arts, with offices in London, Paris, Berlin, Barcelona, Milan, New York and Tokyo. Their books are recognized worldwide for the highest quality of content, design, and production. They cover everything from art, architecture, photography, design, performing arts, decorative arts, contemporary culture, fashion, film, travel, cookery and children's books. **Publishes 100 titles/year. 500 mss received/year. 40% of books from first-time authors. 90% from unagented writers. Pays royalty on wholesale price, if appropriate. Offers advance, if appropriate.** Publishes ms 1 year after acceptance. Accepts simultaneous submissions. Responds in 3 months to proposals. Book catalog available free. Guidelines online.

NONFICTION Subjects include photography, design. Submit proposal package and outline, or submit complete ms. Submissions by e-mail or fax will not be accepted. Reviews artwork/photos. Send photocopies.

TIPS "Please do not contact us to obtain an update on the status of your submission until we have had your submission for at least three months, as we will not provide updates before this period of time has elapsed. Phaidon does not assume any responsibility for any unsolicited submissions, or any materials included with a submission."

❶❷ PHILOMEL BOOKS

Imprint of Penguin Group (USA), Inc., 375 Hudson St., New York NY 10014. (212)414-3610. **Website:** www.penguin.com. **Contact:** Michael Green, president/publisher. Estab. 1980. Publishes hardcover originals. "We look for beautifully written, engaging manuscripts for children and young adults." **Publishes 8-10 titles/year. 5% of books from first-time authors. 20% from unagented writers. Pays authors in royalties. Average advance payment "varies." Illustrators paid by advance and in royalties. Pays negotiable advance.** Accepts simultaneous submissions.

NONFICTION Picture books. *Agented submissions only.*

FICTION Subjects include adventure, ethnic, fantasy, historical, juvenile, literary, picture books, regional, short story collections, translation, western, young adult. *No unsolicited mss.*

PHILOSOPHY DOCUMENTATION CENTER

P.O. Box 7147, Charlottesville VA 22906-7147. (434)220-3300. **Fax:** (434)220-3301. **E-mail:** leaman@pdcnet.org. **Website:** www.pdcnet.org. **Contact:** Dr. George Leaman, director. Estab. 1966. The Philosophy Documentation Center specializes in the publication of reference materials, scholarly journals, book series, and conference proceedings. It has a unique commitment to support teaching, research, and professional activities in philosophy and related fields. **Publishes 10 titles/year. 20 queries; 4-6 mss received/year. 20% of books from first-time authors. Pays 2-10% royalty. Pays advance (special cases only).** Publishes ms 1 year after acceptance. Responds in 1 week to queries.

NONFICTION Subjects include philosophy, software. "We want to increase the range of philosophical titles that are available online, and we support online publication of philosophical work in multiple languages." Query with SASE. Submit outline.

PIANO PRESS

P.O. Box 85, Del Mar CA 92014. (619)884-1401. **Fax:** (858)755-1104. **E-mail:** pianopress@pianopress.com. **Website:** www.pianopress.com. **Contact:** Elizabeth C. Axford, editor. Estab. 1984. "We publish music-related books, either fiction or nonfiction, music-related coloring books, songbooks, sheet music, CDs, and music-related poetry." **Pays authors, illustrators, and photographers royalties based on the retail price.** Publishes book 1 year after acceptance. Accepts simultaneous submissions. Electronic queries ONLY may be sent to: pianopress@pianopress.com. Please include a brief bio and/or web link(s) with your inquiry. Please DO NOT send MP3s, manuscript .docs, or picture .jpgs unless requested to do so by the acquisitions editor. Responds if interested. Book catalog available online.

NONFICTION Subjects include music. Picture books, young readers, middle readers, young adults: multicultural, music/dance. Average word length: picture books—1,500-2,000.

FICTION Subjects include multicultural, multimedia, picture books. Picture books, young readers, middle readers, young adults: folktales, multicultural, poetry, music. Average word length: picture books—1,500-2,000.

TIPS "We are looking for music-related material only for the juvenile market. Please do not send non-music-related materials. Query by e-mail first before submitting anything."

PIÑATA BOOKS

Imprint of Arte Publico Press, University of Houston, 4902 Gulf Fwy., Bldg. 19, Room 100, Houston TX 77204-2004. (713)743-2845. **Fax:** (713)743-3080. **E-mail:** submapp@uh.edu. **Website:** www.artepublicopress.com. Estab. 1994. Publishes hardcover and trade paperback originals. "Piñata Books is dedicated to the publication of children's and young adult literature focusing on U.S. Hispanic culture by U.S. Hispanic authors. Arte Publico's mission is the publication, promotion and dissemination of Latino literature for a variety of national and regional audiences, from early childhood to adult, through the complete gamut of delivery systems, including personal performance as well as print and electronic media." **Publishes 10-15 titles/year. 80% of books from first-time authors. Pays 10% royalty on wholesale price. Pays $1,000-3,000 advance.** Publishes book 2 years after acceptance. Accepts simultaneous submissions. Responds in 2-3 months to queries; 4-6 months to mss. Book catalog and guidelines online.

NONFICTION Subjects include ethnic. Piñata Books specializes in publication of children's and young adult literature that authentically portrays themes, characters and customs unique to U.S. Hispanic culture. Submissions made through online submission form.

FICTION Subjects include adventure, juvenile, picture books, young adult. Submissions made through online submission form.

POETRY Appropriate to Hispanic theme. Submissions made through online submission form.

TIPS "Include cover letter with submission explaining why your manuscript is unique and important, why we should publish it, who will buy it, etc."

ⒶⒺ⊘ PIATKUS BOOKS

Little, Brown Book Group, Carmelite House, 50 Victoria Embankment, London EC4Y 0DZ, United Kingdom. (020)3122-7000. **Fax:** (020)3122-7000. **E-mail:** info@littlebrown.co.uk. **Website:** piatkus.co.uk. Estab. 1979. Publishes hardcover originals, paperback originals, and paperback reprints. **10% from un-agented writers.** Publishes ms 1 year after acceptance. Accepts simultaneous submissions. Guidelines online.

NONFICTION *Agented submissions only.*

FICTION Romance fiction, women's fiction, book-club fiction. *Agented submissions only.*

Ⓐ⊘ PICADOR USA

MacMillan, 175 Fifth Ave., New York NY 10010. (212)674-5151. **Website:** us.macmillan.com/picador. Estab. 1994. Picador publishes high-quality liter-ary fiction and nonfiction. "We are open to a broad range of subjects, well written by authoritative au-thors." Publishes hardcover and trade paperback originals and reprints. Does not accept unsolicited mss. *Agented submissions only.* **Publishes 70-80 titles/year. Pays 7-15% on royalty. Advance varies.** Publishes ms 18 months after acceptance. Accepts si-multaneous submissions.

PICCADILLY BOOKS, LTD.

P.O. Box 25203, Colorado Springs CO 80936. (719)550-9887. **Fax:** (719)550-8810. **E-mail:** info@ piccadillybooks.com. **Website:** www.piccadillybooks. com. Estab. 1985. Publishes hardcover originals and trade paperback originals and reprints. "Picadilly publishes nonfiction, diet, nutrition, and health-re-lated books with a focus on alternative and natural medicine." **Publishes 5-8 titles/year. 70% of books from first-time authors. 95% from unagented writ-ers. Pays 6-10% royalty on retail price.** Publishes ms 1 year after acceptance. Accepts simultaneous sub-missions. Responds only if interested, unless accom-panied by a SASE to queries. Responds to all e-mail queries.

NONFICTION Subjects include health, medicine, nutrition, Health, nutrition, diet, and physical fit-ness. "Do your research. Let us know why there is a need for your book, how it differs from other books on the market, and how you will promote the book. No phone calls. We prefer to see the entire ms, but will accept a minimum of 3 sample chapters on your first inquiry. A cover letter is also required; please provide a brief overview of the book, information about simi-lar books already in print and explain why yours is different or better. Tell us the prime market for your book and what you can do to help market it. Also, pro-vide us with background information on yourself and explain what qualifies you to write this book."

TIPS "We publish nonfiction, general interest, self-help books currently emphasizing alternative health."

⊘ THE PILGRIM PRESS

700 Prospect Ave. E., Cleveland OH 44115-1100. (216)736-3755. **Fax:** (216)736-2207. **Website:** www. thepilgrimpress.com. Publishes hardcover and trade paperback originals. No longer accepting unsolicited ms proposals. **Publishes 25 titles/year. 60% of books from first-time authors. 80% from unagented writ-ers. Pays standard royalties. Pays advance.** Publish-es ms an average of 18 months after acceptance. Re-sponds in 3 months to queries. Book catalog and ms guidelines online.

NONFICTION Subjects include religion, ethics, so-cial issues with a strong commitment to justice—ad-dressing such topics as public policy, sexuality and gender, human rights and minority liberation—pri-marily in a Christian context, but not exclusively.

PINEAPPLE PRESS, INC.

P.O. Box 3889, Sarasota FL 34230. (941)706-2507. **Fax:** (800)746-3275. **E-mail:** info@pineapplepress. com. **Website:** www.pineapplepress.com. **Contact:** June Cussen, executive editor. Estab. 1982. Publish-es hardcover and trade paperback originals. "We are seeking quality nonfiction on diverse topics for the li-brary and book trade markets. Our mission is to pub-lish good books about Florida." **Publishes 21 titles/ year. 1,000 queries; 500 mss received/year. 50% of books from first-time authors. 95% from unagented writers. Pays authors royalty of 10-15%.** Publishes a book 1 year after acceptance. Accepts simultaneous submissions. Responds in 2 months. Book catalog for 9×12 SAE with $1.32 postage. Guidelines online.

NONFICTION Subjects include regional, Florida. Picture books: animal, history, nature/environmental, science. Young readers, middle readers, young adults: animal, biography, geography, history, nature/envi-ronment, science. Query or submit outline/synopsis and intro and 3 sample chapters. Reviews artwork/ photos. Send photocopies.

FICTION Subjects include regional. Picture books, young readers, middle readers, young adults: animal, folktales, history, nature/environment. Query or sub-mit outline/synopsis and 3 sample chapters.

TIPS "Quality first novels will be published, though we usually only do one or two novels per year and they must be set in Florida. We regard the author/editor relationship as a trusting relationship with communication open both ways. Learn all you can about the publishing process and about how to promote your book once it is published. A query on a novel without a brief sample seems useless."

⊘ PLAN B PRESS

2714 Jefferson Dr., Alexandria VA 22303. (215)732-2663. **E-mail:** planbpress@gmail.com. **Website:** www.planbpress.com. **Contact:** Steven Allen May, president. Estab. 1999. Plan B Press is a "small publishing company with an international feel. Our intention is to have Plan B Press be part of the conversation about the direction and depth of literary movements and genres. Plan B Press's new direction is to seek out authors rarely-to-never published, sharing new voices that might not otherwise be heard. Plan B Press is determined to merge text with image, writing with art." Publishes poetry and short fiction. Wants "experimental poetry, concrete/visual work." **Pays author's copies.** Accepts simultaneous submissions. Responds to queries in 1 month; mss in 3 months.

NONFICTION Subjects include literature.

POETRY Wants to see: experimental, concrete, visual poetry. Does not want "sonnets, political or religious poems, work in the style of Ogden Nash."

PLANNERS PRESS

Imprint of the American Planning Association, 205 N. Michigan Ave., Suite 1200, Chicago IL 60601. (312)431-9100. **Fax:** (312)786-6700. **E-mail:** plannerspress@planning.org. **Website:** www.planning.org/plannerspress. **Contact:** Camille Fink (planning practice, urban issues, land use, transportation). Estab. 1970. Publishes hardcover, electronic, and trade paperback originals; and trade paperback and electronic reprints. "We publish titles of interest to planning practitioners, researchers, and the general public, with the aim of stimulating readers, creating an engaged citizenry, and influencing policy development—all by telling the many stories of planning. Our books often have a narrow audience of city planners and frequently focus on the tools of city planning." **Publishes 10 titles/year. 50 queries; 35 mss received/year. 25% of books from first-time authors. 100% from unagented writers. Pays 10-15% royalty on net receipts. Pays advance against royalties.** Publishes ms 15 months after acceptance. Accepts simultaneous submissions. Responds in 1 month to queries; 2 months to proposals and mss. Book catalog online. Guidelines online.

NONFICTION Subjects include agriculture, architecture, community, contemporary culture, economics, environment, finance, government, history, horticulture, law, politics, real estate, science, transportation, world affairs. Submit proposal package, including: outline, 1 sample chapter and CV. Submit completed ms. Reviews artwork/photos. Send photocopies.

TIPS "Our audience is professional planners but also anyone interested in community development, urban affairs, sustainability, and related fields."

⊜ PLAYLAB PRESS

P.O. Box 3701, South Brisbane BC 4101, Australia. **E-mail:** info@playlab.org.au. **Website:** www.playlab.org.au. Estab. 1978. **Publishes 1 titles/year.** Accepts simultaneous submissions. Responds in 3 months to mss. Guidelines online.

NONFICTION Subjects include literary criticism.

FICTION Subjects include plays. Submit 2 copies of ms, cover letter.

TIPS "Playlab Press is committed to the publication of quality writing for and about theatre and performance, which is of significance to Australia's cultural life. It values socially just and diverse publication outcomes and aims to promote these outcomes in local, national, and international contexts."

PLEXUS PUBLISHING, INC.

143 Old Marlton Pike, Medford NJ 08055. (609)654-6500. **Fax:** (609)654-4309. **E-mail:** rcolding@plexuspublishing.com. **Website:** www.plexuspublishing.com. **Contact:** Rob Colding, Book Marketing Manager. Estab. 1977. Publishes hardcover and paperback originals. Plexus publishes regional-interest (southern New Jersey and the greater Philadelphia area) fiction and nonfiction including mysteries, field guides, nature, travel and history. **Pays $500-1,000 advance.** Accepts simultaneous submissions. Responds in 3 months to proposals. Book catalog and book proposal guidelines for 10x13 SASE.

NONFICTION Query with SASE.

FICTION Subjects include adventure, mystery. Mysteries and literary novels with a strong regional (southern New Jersey) angle. Query with SASE.

⊕⊘ POCKET BOOKS

Simon & Schuster, 1230 Avenue of the Americas, New York NY 10020. (212)698-7000. **Website:** www.simonandschuster.com. Estab. 1939. Publishes paperback originals and reprints, mass market and trade paperbacks. Pocket Books publishes commercial fiction and genre fiction (WWE, Downtown Press, Star Trek). Book catalog available free. Guidelines online.

NONFICTION *Agented submissions only.*

FICTION Subjects include mystery, romance, suspense, western. *Agented submissions only.*

POCOL PRESS

Box 411, Clifton VA 20124. (703)830-5862. **Website:** www.pocolpress.com. **Contact:** J. Thomas Hetrick, editor. Estab. 1999. Publishes trade paperback originals. "Pocol Press is dedicated to producing high-quality print books and e-books from first-time, non-agented authors. However, all submissions are welcome. We're dedicated to good storytellers and to the written word, specializing in short fiction and baseball. Several of our books have been used as literary texts at universities and in book group discussions around the nation. Pocol Press does not publish children's books, romance novels, or graphic novels. Our authors are comprised of veteran writers and emerging talents." **Publishes 6 titles/year. 90 queries received/year. 20 mss received/year. 90% of books from first-time authors. 100% from unagented writers. Pays 10-12% royalty on wholesale price.** Publishes book less than 1 year after acceptance. Responds in 1 month to queries; 2 months to mss. Book catalog and guidelines online.

FICTION Subjects include historical, horror, literary, mystery, short story collections, spiritual, sports, western, baseball fiction. "We specialize in thematic short fiction collections by a single author, westerns, war stories, and baseball fiction. Expert storytellers welcome." Does not accept or return unsolicited mss. Query with SASE or submit 1 sample chapter.

TIPS "Our audience is aged 18 and over. Pocol Press is unique; we publish good writing and great storytelling. Write the best stories you can. Read them to you friends/peers. Note their reaction. Publishes some of the finest fiction by a small press."

THE POISONED PENCIL

Poisoned Pen Press, 6962 E. 1st Ave., Suite 103, Scottsdale AZ 85251. (480)945-3375. **Fax:** (480)949-1707. **E-mail:** info@thepoisonedpencil.com. **E-mail:** ellen@thepoisonedpencil.com. **Website:** www.thepoisonedpencil.com. **Contact:** Ellen Larson, editor. Robert Rosenwald, publisher Estab. 2012. Publishes trade paperback and electronic originals. **Publishes 4-6 titles/year. 150 submissions received/year. Pays 9-15%**

for trade paperback; **25-35% for e-books. Pays advance of $1,000.** Publishes ms 15 months after acceptance. Responds in 6 weeks to mss. Guidelines online.

◐ *Accepts young adult mysteries only.*

FICTION Subjects include mystery, young adult. "We publish only young adult mystery novels, 45,000 to 90,000 words in length. For our purposes, a young adult book is a book with a protagonist between the ages of 13 and 18. We are looking for both traditional and cross-genre young adult mysteries. We encourage off-beat approaches and narrative choices that reflect the complexity and ambiguity of today's world. Submissions from teens are very welcome. Avoid serial killers, excessive gore, and vampires (and other heavy supernatural themes). We only consider authors who live in the US or Canada, due to practicalities of marketing promotion. Avoid coincidence in plotting. Avoid having your sleuth leap to conclusions rather than discover and deduce. Pay attention to the resonance between character and plot; between plot and theme; between theme and character. We are looking for clean style, fluid storytelling, and solid structure. Unrealistic dialogue is a real turn-off." Submit proposal package including synopsis, complete ms, and cover letter.

TIPS "Our audience is made up of young adults and adults who love YA mysteries."

POISONED PEN PRESS

6962 E. 1st Ave., Suite 103, Scottsdale AZ 85251. (480)945-3375. **Fax:** (480)949-1707. **E-mail:** submissions@poisonedpenpress.com. **Website:** www.poisonedpenpress.com. **Contact:** Robert Rosenwald, publisher; Barbara Peters, editor-in-chief. Estab. 1996. Publishes hardcover originals, and hardcover and trade paperback reprints. "Our publishing goal is to offer well-written mystery novels of crime and/or detection where the puzzle and its resolution are the main forces that move the story forward." **Publishes 36 titles/year. 1,000 queries received/year. 300 mss received/year. 35% of books from first-time authors. 65% from unagented writers. Pays 9-15% royalty on retail price.** Publishes book 10-12 months after acceptance. Responds in 2-3 months to queries and proposals; 6 months to mss. Book catalog and guidelines online.

IMPRINTS The Poisoned Pencil (Young adult titles. Contact: Ellen Larson).

◐ *Not currently accepting submissions. Check website.*

FICTION Subjects include mystery. Mss should generally be longer than 65,000 words and shorter than 100,000 words. Member Publishers Marketing Associations, Arizona Book Publishers Associations, Publishers Association of West. Distributes through Ingram, Baker & Taylor, Brodart. Does not want novels centered on serial killers, spousal or child abuse, drugs, or extremist groups, although we do not entirely rule such works out. Accepts unsolicited mss. Electronic queries only. "Query with SASE. Submit clips, first 3 pages. We must receive both the synopsis and ms pages electronically as separate attachments to an e-mail message or as a disk or CD which we will not return."

TIPS "Audience is adult readers of mystery fiction and young adult readers."

POLIS BOOKS

E-mail: info@polisbooks.com. **E-mail:** submissions@polisbooks.com. **Website:** www.polisbooks.com. Estab. 2013. "Polis Books is an independent publishing company actively seeking new and established authors for our growing list. We are actively acquiring titles in mystery, thriller, suspense, procedural, traditional crime, science fiction, fantasy, horror, supernatural, urban fantasy, romance, erotica, commercial women's fiction, commercial literary fiction, young adult and middle grade books." **Publishes 40 titles/year. 500+ 33% of books from first-time authors. 10% from unagented writers. Offers advance against royalties.** For e-book originals, ms published 6-9 months after acceptance. For front list print titles, 9-15 months. Accepts simultaneous submissions. Only responds to submissions if interested. Guidelines online.

FICTION Query with 3 sample chapters and bio via e-mail.

POPULAR WOODWORKING BOOKS

Imprint of F+W Media, Inc., 10151 Carver Rd., Suite 200, Blue Ash OH 45242. (513)531-2690. **Website:** www.popularwoodworking.com. **Contact:** Scott Francis, content editor. Publishes trade paperback and hardcover originals and reprints. "Popular Woodworking Books is one of the largest publishers of woodworking books in the world. From perfecting a furniture design to putting on the final coat of finish, our books provide step-by-step instructions and trusted advice from the pros that make them valuable tools for both beginning and advanced woodworkers. Currently emphasizing woodworking jigs and fixtures, woodworking techniques, furniture and cabinet projects, smaller finely crafted boxes, all styles of furniture." **Publishes 8-10 titles/year. 20 queries; 10 mss received/year. 20% of books from first-time authors. 95% from unagented writers.** Accepts simultaneous submissions. Responds in 1 month to queries.

NONFICTION "We publish heavily illustrated how-to woodworking books that show, rather than tell, our readers how to accomplish their woodworking goals." Query with SASE, or electronic query. Proposal package should include an outline and digital photos.

TIPS "Our books are for beginning to advanced woodworking enthusiasts."

PPI (PROFESSIONAL PUBLICATIONS, INC.)

1250 Fifth Ave., Belmont CA 94002. (650)593-9119. **Fax:** (650)592-4519. **E-mail:** info@ppi2pass.com. **E-mail:** acquisitions@ppi2pass.com. **Website:** www.ppi2pass.com. Estab. 1975. Publishes hardcover, paperback, and electronic products, CD-ROMs and DVDs. "PPI publishes professional, reference, and licensing preparation materials. PPI wants submissions from both professionals practicing in the field and from experienced instructors. Currently emphasizing engineering, interior design, architecture, landscape architecture and LEED exam review." **Publishes 10 titles/year. 5% of books from first-time authors. 100% from unagented writers.** Publishes ms 4-18 months after acceptance. Accepts simultaneous submissions. Responds in 1 month to queries. Book catalog and ms guidelines free.

NONFICTION Subjects include architecture, science, landscape architecture, engineering mathematics, engineering, surveying, interior design, greenbuilding, sustainable development, and other professional licensure subjects.. Especially needs review and reference books for all professional licensing examinations. Please submit ms and proposal outlining market potential, etc. Proposal template available upon request. Reviews artwork/photos.

TIPS "We specialize in books for those people who want to become licensed and/or accredited professionals: engineers, architects, surveyors, interior designers, LEED APs, etc. Demonstrating your understanding of the market, competition, appropriate delivery methods, and marketing ideas will help sell us on your proposal."

PRAKKEN PUBLICATIONS, INC.

P.O. Box 8623, Ann Arbor MI 48107. (734)975-2800. **Fax:** (734)975-2787. **E-mail:** pam@eddigest.com. **E-**

mail: susanne@eddigest.com. **Contact:** Susanne Peckham, book editor; Sharon K. Miller, art/design/production manager. Estab. 1934. Publishes educational hardcover and paperback originals, as well as educational magazines. "We publish books for educators in career/vocational and technology education, as well as books for the machine trades and machinists' education. Currently emphasizing machine trades." **Publishes 3 titles/year.** Accepts simultaneous submissions. Responds in 2 months to queries. Book catalog for #10 SASE.

NONFICTION Subjects include education. "We are currently interested in manuscripts with broad appeal in any of the specific subject areas of machine trades, technology education, career-technical education, and reference for the general education field." Submit outline, sample chapters.

TIPS "We have a continuing interest in magazine and book manuscripts which reflect emerging issues and trends in education, especially career-technical, industrial, and technology education."

PRESA PRESS

P.O. Box 792, 8590 Belding Rd. NE, Rockford MI 49341. **E-mail:** presapress@aol.com. **Website:** www.presapress.com. **Contact:** Roseanne Ritzema, editor. Estab. 2003. Presa Press publishes perfect-bound paperbacks of poetry. Wants "imagistic poetry where form is an extension of content, surreal, experimental, and personal poetry." Does not want "overtly political or didactic material." **Pays 10-25 author/quotes copies.** Time between acceptance and publication is 8-12 weeks. Accepts simultaneous submissions. Responds to queries in 2-4 weeks; to mss in 8-12 weeks.

POETRY Acquires first North American serial rights and the right to reprint in anthologies. Rights include e-book publishing rights. Rights revert to poets upon publication. Accepts postal submissions only. Cover letter is preferred. Reads submissions year round. Poems are circulated to an editorial board. Send materials for review consideration to Roseanne Ritzema. Query first, with a few sample poems and a cover letter with brief bio and publication credits. Book/chapbook mss may include previously published poems.

PRESS 53

560 N. Trade St., Suite 103, Winston-Salem NC 27101. (336)770-5353. **E-mail:** kevin@press53.com. **Website:** www.press53.com. **Contact:** Kevin Morgan Watson, publisher.. Estab. 2005. Poetry and short fiction collections only. "Press 53 was founded in October 2005 and quickly began earning a reputation as a quality publishing house of short fiction and poetry collections." **Publishes 14-15 titles/year. Finds mss through contest and referrals. 60% of books from first-time authors. 90% from unagented writers.** Catalog online. Guidelines online.

FICTION Subjects include literary, short story collections. "We publish roughly 4-6 short fiction collections each year by writers who are active and earning recognition through publication and awards, plus the winner of our Press 53 Award for Short Fiction." Collections should be between 100 and 250 pages (give or take) with 70% or more of those stories previously published. Does not want novels. Finds mss through contest and referrals.

POETRY "We love working with poets who have been widely published and are active in the poetry community. We publish roughly 6-8 full-length poetry collections of around 70 pages or more each year, plus the winner of our Press 53 Award for Poetry." Prefers that at least 30-40% of the poems in the collection be previously published. Experimental. Overtly political or religious. Finds mss through contest and referrals.

TIPS "We are looking for writers who are actively involved in the writing community, writers who are submitting their work to journals, magazines and contests, and who are getting published, building readership, and earning a reputation for their work."

⚙ PRESSES DE L'UNIVERSITÉ DE MONTREAL

C.P. 6128, succ. Centre-ville, Montreal QC H3C 3J7, Canada. (514)343-6933. **Fax:** (514)343-2232. **E-mail:** sb@editionspum.ca. **Website:** www.pum.umontreal.ca. **Contact:** Sylvie Brousseau, rights and sales. Publishes hardcover and trade paperback originals. **Publishes 40 titles/year.** Publishes ms 6 months after acceptance. Accepts simultaneous submissions. Responds in 1 month. Book catalog and ms guidelines free.

NONFICTION Subjects include education, history, philosophy, psychology, sociology, translation. Submit outline, 2 sample chapters.

PRESS HERE

22230 NE 28th Place, Sammamish WA 98074-6408. **Website:** www.gracecuts.com/press-here. Estab. 1989. Press Here publishes award-winning books of haiku, tanka, and related poetry by the leading poets of these genres, as well as essays, criticism, and interviews about these genres. "We publish work only by those poets who are already frequently published in the leading haiku and tanka journals." Publishes 1-2 poetry books/year, plus occasional books of essays or interviews. Mss are selected through open submission. **Pays a negotiated percentage of author's copies (out of a press run of 200-1,000).** Accepts simultaneous submissions. Responds to queries in up to 1 month; to mss in up to 2 months. Catalog available for #10 SASE.

○ Press Here publications have won the 1st-place Merit Book Award and other awards from the Haiku Society of America.

POETRY Does not want any poetry other than haiku, tanka, and related genres. Has published poetry by Lee Gurga, paul m., Paul O. Williams, Adele Kenny, Pat Shelley, Cor van den Heuvel, and William J. Higginson. Query first, with a few sample poems and a cover letter with brief bio and publication credits. Book mss may include previously published poems ("previous publication strongly preferred"). "All proposals must be by well-established haiku or tanka poets, and must be for haiku or tanka poetry, or criticism/discussion of these genres. If the editor does not already know your work well from leading haiku and tanka publications, then he is not likely to be interested in your manuscript."

PRESTWICK HOUSE, INC.

P.O. Box 658, Clayton DE 19938. **E-mail:** info@prestwickhouse.com. **Website:** www.prestwickhouse.com. Estab. 1980. Accepts simultaneous submissions.

NONFICTION Submit proposal package, outline, resume, 1 sample chapter, TOC.

TIPS "We market our books primarily for middle and high school English teachers. Submissions should address a direct need of grades 7-12 language arts teachers. Current and former English teachers are encouraged to submit materials developed and used by them successfully in the classroom."

○○ PRICE STERN SLOAN, INC.

Penguin Group, 375 Hudson St., New York NY 10014. (212)366-2000. **Website:** www.penguin.com. **Contact:** Francesco Sedita, president/publisher. Estab. 1963. "Price Stern Sloan publishes quirky mass market novelty series for childrens as well as licensed movie tie-in books." Price Stern Sloan only responds to submissions it's interested in publishing. Accepts simultaneous submissions. Book catalog online.

FICTION Publishes picture books and novelty/board books. *Agented submissions only.*

TIPS "Price Stern Sloan publishes unique, fun titles."

PRINCETON ARCHITECTURAL PRESS

37 E. 7th St., New York NY 10003. (212)995-9620. **Fax:** (212)995-9454. **E-mail:** submissions@papress.com. **Website:** www.papress.com. Publishes hardcover and trade paperback originals. **Publishes 50 titles/year. 300 queries; 150 mss received/year. 65% of books from first-time authors. 95% from unagented writers. Pays royalty on wholesale price.** Publishes ms 1 year after acceptance. Accepts simultaneous submissions. Responds in 2 months. Book catalog online. Guidelines online.

NONFICTION Submit proposal package, outline, 1 sample chapter, TOC, sample of art, and survey of competitive titles. Reviews artwork/photos. Do not send originals.

TIPS "Princeton Architecture Press publishes fine books on architecture, design, photography, landscape, and visual culture. Our books are acclaimed for their strong and unique editorial vision, unrivaled design sensibility, and high production values at affordable prices."

PRINCETON BOOK CO.

614 Route 130, Hightstown NJ 08520. (609)426-0602. **Fax:** (609)426-1344. **E-mail:** pbc@dancehorizons.com. **Website:** www.dancehorizons.com. **Contact:** Charles Woodford, president. Publishes hardcover and trade paperback originals and reprints. **Publishes 5-6 titles/year. 50 queries received/year. 100 mss received/year. 80% of books from first-time authors. 100% from unagented writers. Pays negotiable royalty on net receipts.** Publishes ms 9-12 months after acceptance. Accepts simultaneous submissions. Responds in 1 week. Book catalog and guidelines online.

IMPRINTS Dance Horizons, Elysian Editions.

NONFICTION "We publish all sorts of dance-related books including those on fitness and health." Does not accept memoir. Submit proposal package, outline, 3 sample chapters. Reviews artwork/photos. Send photocopies.

PRINCETON UNIVERSITY PRESS

41 William St., Princeton NJ 08540. (609)258-4900. **Fax:** (609)258-6305. **Website:** press.princeton.edu.

"The Lockert Library of Poetry in Translation embraces a wide geographic and temporal range, from Scandinavia to Latin America to the subcontinent of India, from the Tang Dynasty to Europe of the modern day. It especially emphasizes poets who are established in their native lands and who are being introduced to an English-speaking audience. Manuscripts are judged with several criteria in mind: the ability of the translation to stand on its own as poetry in English; fidelity to the tone and spirit of the original, rather than literal accuracy; and the importance of the translated poet to the literature of his or her time and country." Accepts simultaneous submissions. Responds in 3-4 months. Guidelines online.

NONFICTION Query with SASE.

POETRY Submit hard copy of proposal with sample poems or full ms. Cover letter is required. Reads submissions year round. Mss will not be returned. Comments on finalists only.

PRINTING INDUSTRIES OF AMERICA

301 Brush Creek Rd., Warrendale PA 15086. (412)741-6860. **Fax:** (412)741-2311. **E-mail:** sshea@printing.org. **Website:** www.printing.org. **Contact:** Sam Shea, manager. Estab. 1921. Publishes trade paperback originals and reference texts. "Printing Industries of America, along with its affiliates, delivers products and services that enhance the growth and profitability of its members and the industry through advocacy, education, research, and technical information." Printing Industries of America's mission is to serve the graphic communications community as the major resource for technical information and services through research and education. **Publishes 8-10 titles/year. 20 mss; 30 queries received/year. 50% of books from first-time authors. 100% from unagented writers. Pays 15% royalty on wholesale price.** Publishes ms 18 months after acceptance. Accepts simultaneous submissions. Responds in 1 month to queries.

NONFICTION Subjects include business, communications, economics, education, printing and graphic arts reference, technical, textbook. Currently emphasizing technical textbooks as well as career guides for graphic communications and turnkey training curricula. Query with SASE, or submit outline, sample chapters, and SASE. Reviews artwork. Send photocopies.

PROMETHEUS BOOKS

59 John Glenn Dr., Amherst NY 14228-2119. (800)421-0351. **Fax:** (716)564-2711. **E-mail:** editorial@prometheusbooks.com. **Website:** www.prometheusbooks.com. **Contact:** Steven L. Mitchell, editor-in-chief. Estab. 1969. Publishes hardcover originals, trade paperback originals and reprints. "Prometheus Books is a leading independent publisher in philosophy, social science, popular science, and critical thinking. We publish authoritative and thoughtful books by distinguished authors in many categories. Currently emphasizing popular science, health, psychology, social science, current events, business and economics, atheism and critiques of religion." **Publishes 90-100 titles/year. 30% of books from first-time authors. 40% from unagented writers.** Accepts simultaneous submissions. Responds in 2 months to queries; 3 months to proposals; 4 months to mss. Book catalog and guidelines online.

NONFICTION Subjects include education, history, New Age, philosophy, psychology, religion, contemporary issues. Ask for a catalog, go to the library or our website, look at our books and others like them to get an idea of what our focus is. Submit proposal package including outline, synopsis, potential market, tentative ms length, résumé, and a well-developed query letter with SASE, two or three of author's best chapters. Reviews artwork/photos. Send photocopies.

TIPS "Audience is highly literate with multiple degrees; an audience that is intellectually mature and knows what it wants. They are aware, and we try to provide them with new information on topics of interest to them in mainstream and related areas."

PRUFROCK PRESS, INC.

P.O. Box 8813, Waco TX 76714. (800)988-2208. **Fax:** (800)240-0333. **E-mail:** info@prufrock.com. **Website:** www.prufrock.com. **Contact:** Joel McIntosh, publisher and marketing director. "Prufrock Press offers award-winning products focused on gifted education, gifted children, advanced learning, and special needs learners, including trade nonfiction (not narrative nonfiction, however) for adults and children/teens. For more than 20 years, Prufrock has supported gifted children and their education and development. The company publishes more than 300 products that enhance the lives of gifted children and the teachers and parents who support them." Accepts simultaneous submissions, but must be notified about it. **50 queries; 40 mss received/year. 20% of books from first-time authors. 100% from unagented writers.** Publishes ms 1-2 year after acceptance. Accepts simultaneous submissions. Book catalog available. Guidelines online.

NONFICTION Subjects include education. "We are always looking for truly original, creative materials for teachers." Query with SASE. Submit outline, 1-3 sample chapters.

FICTION Prufrock Press "offers award-winning products focused on gifted education, gifted children, advanced learning, and special needs learners. For more than 20 years, Prufrock has supported gifted children and their education and development. The company publishes more than 300 products that enhance the lives of gifted children and the teachers and parents who support them." No picture books. "Prufrock Press does not consider unsolicited manuscripts."

Ⓐ⊘ PUFFIN BOOKS

Imprint of Penguin Group (USA), Inc., 375 Hudson St., New York NY 10014. (212)366-2000. **Website:** www.penguin.com. **Contact:** Eileen Bishop Kreit, publisher. Publishes trade paperback originals and reprints. "Puffin Books publishes high-end trade paperbacks and paperback reprints for preschool children, beginning and middle readers, and young adults." **Publishes 175-200 titles/year.** Publishes book 1 year after acceptance.

NONFICTION Subjects include education, history, womens issues, womens studies. "Women in history books interest us." *No unsolicited mss. Agented submissions only.*

FICTION Subjects include fantasy, picture books, science fiction, young adult, middle grade, easy-to-read grades 1-3, graphic novels, classics. *No unsolicited mss. Agented submissions only.*

TIPS "Our audience ranges from little children 'first books' to young adult (ages 14-16). An original idea has the best luck."

PURDUE UNIVERSITY PRESS

504 West State St., West Lafayette IN 47907-2058. (765)494-2038. **E-mail:** pupress@purdue.edu. **Website:** www.thepress.purdue.edu. **Contact:** Rebecca Corbin, administrative assistant. Estab. 1960. Purdue University Press is administratively a unit of Purdue University Libraries and its Director reports to the Dean of Libraries. There are 3 full-time staff and 2 part-time staff, as well as student assistants. Dedicated to the dissemination of scholarly and professional information, the Press provides quality resources in several key subject areas including business, technology, health, veterinary sciences, and other selected disciplines in the humanities and sciences. As well as publishing 30 books a year, and 5 subscription-based journals, the Press is committed to broadening access to scholarly information using digital technology. As part of this initiative, the Press distributes a number of Open Access electronic-only journals. An editorial board of 9 Purdue faculty members is responsible for the imprint of the Press and meets twice a semester to consider mss and proposals, and guide the editorial program. A management advisory board advises the Director on strategy, and meets twice a year. Purdue University Press is a member of the Association of American University Presses.

G.P. PUTNAM'S SONS, PENGUIN YOUNG READERS GROUP

345 Hudson St., 14th Floor, New York NY 10014. (212)366-2000. **Website:** http://www.penguin.com. **Contact:** Dave Kopka, Art Assistant. Accepts simultaneous submissions.

Ⓐ⊘ G.P. PUTNAM'S SONS HARDCOVER

Imprint of Penguin Group (USA), Inc., 375 Hudson, New York NY 10014. (212)366-2000. **Fax:** (212)366-2664. **Website:** www.penguin.com. **Contact:** Christine Ball, vice president/deputy publisher; Mark Tavani, vice president/executive editor. Publishes hardcover originals. **Pays variable royalties on retail price. Pays varies advance.** Accepts simultaneous submissions. Request book catalog through mail order department.

NONFICTION Subjects include animals, child guidance, contemporary culture, religion, science, sports, travel, celebrity-related topics. *Agented submissions only. No unsolicited mss.*

FICTION Subjects include adventure, literary, suspense, women's. *Agented submissions only.*

QUE

Pearson Education, 800 E. 96th St., Indianapolis IN 46240. (317)581-3500. **E-mail:** greg.wiegand@pearson.com. **Website:** www.quepublishing.com. **Contact:** Greg Wiegand, associate publisher. Estab. 1981. Publishes hardcover, trade paperback and mass market paperback originals and reprints. **Publishes 100 titles/year. 80% from unagented writers. Pays variable royalty on wholesale price or makes work-for-hire arrangements. Pays varying advance.** Accepts simultaneous submissions. Book catalog and guidelines online.

NONFICTION Subjects include technology, certification. Submit proposal package, resume, TOC, writing sample, competing titles.

QUILL DRIVER BOOKS

2006 S. Mary St., Fresno CA 93721. (559)233-6633. **E-mail:** kent@lindenpub.com. **Website:** www.quilldriverbooks.com. **Contact:** Kent Sorsky. Publishes hardcover and trade paperback originals and reprints. Quill Driver Books publishes a mix of nonfiction titles, with an emphasis on how-to books. "Our books, we hope, make a worthwhile contribution to the human community, and we have a little fun along the way." **Publishes 10-12 titles/year. 50% of books from first-time authors. 75% from unagented writers. Pays 4-10% royalty on retail price. Pays $500-5,000 advance.** Publishes ms 12 months after acceptance. Accepts simultaneous submissions. Responds in 1 month to queries and proposals; 3 months to mss. Book catalog and ms guidelines for #10 SASE.

NONFICTION Subjects include regional, writing, aging. Query with SASE. Submit proposal package. Reviews artwork/photos. Send photocopies.

⊘ QUITE SPECIFIC MEDIA GROUP, LTD.

7373 Pyramid Place, Hollywood CA 90046. (323-646-9934. **E-mail:** info@quitespecificmedia.com. **Website:** www.quitespecificmedia.com. Estab. 1967. Publishes hardcover originals, trade paperback originals and reprints. "Quite Specific Media Group is an umbrella company of 5 imprints specializing in costume and fashion, theater and design." **Publishes 12 titles/year. 75 queries received/year. 30 mss received/year. 75% of books from first-time authors. 85% from unagented writers. Pays royalty on wholesale price. Pays varies advance.** Publishes ms 18 months after acceptance. Accepts simultaneous submissions. Responds to queries. Book catalog online.

NONFICTION Subjects include fashion, history, literary criticism, translation. Query by e-mail please. Reviews artwork/photos.

RAGGED SKY PRESS

P.O. Box 312, Annandale NJ 08801. **E-mail:** raggedskyanthology@gmail.com. **Website:** www.raggedsky.com. **Contact:** Ellen Foos, publisher; Vasiliki Katsarou, managing editor; Arlene Weiner, editor. Produces poetry anthologies and single-author poetry collec-

tions along with occasional inspired prose. Ragged Sky is a small, highly selective cooperative press. "We work with our authors closely." Individual poetry collections currently by invitation only. Learn more online. Accepts simultaneous submissions.

Ⓐ⊘ RANDOM HOUSE CHILDREN'S BOOKS

1745 Broadway, New York NY 10019. (212)782-9000. **Website:** www.randomhouse.com. Estab. 1925. "Producing books for preschool children through young adult readers, in all formats from board to activity books to picture books and novels, Random House Children's Books brings together world-famous franchise characters, multimillion-copy series and top-flight, award-winning authors, and illustrators." Submit mss through a literary agent. Accepts simultaneous submissions.

IMPRINTS Kids@Random; Golden Books; Princeton Review; Sylvan Learning.

FICTION "Random House publishes a select list of first chapter books and novels, with an emphasis on fantasy and historical fiction." Chapter books, middle-grade readers, young adult. *Does not accept unsolicited mss.*

TIPS "We look for original, unique stories. Do something that hasn't been done before."

Ⓐ🌑⊘ RANDOM HOUSE CHILDREN'S PUBLISHERS UK

20 Vauxhall Bridge Rd., London SW1V 2SA, United Kingdom. **Website:** www.randomhousechildrens.co.uk. *Only interested in agented material.* **Publishes 250 titles/year. Pays authors royalty. Offers advances.** Accepts simultaneous submissions.

IMPRINTS Bantam, Doubleday, Corgi, Johnathan Cape, Hutchinson, Bodley Head, Red Fox, Tamarind Books.

FICTION Picture books: adventure, animal, anthology, contemporary, fantasy, folktales, humor, multicultural, nature/environment, poetry, suspense/mystery. Young readers: adventure, animal, anthology, contemporary, fantasy, folktales, humor, multicultural, nature/environment, poetry, sports, suspense/mystery. Middle readers: adventure, animal, anthology, contemporary, fantasy, folktales, humor, multicultural, nature/environment, problem novels, romance, sports, suspense/mystery. Young adults: adventure, contemporary, fantasy, humor, multicultural, nature/environment, problem novels, romance, science fiction, suspense/mystery. Average word length: picture books—800; young readers—1,500-6,000; middle readers—10,000-15,000; young adults—20,000-45,000.

TIPS "Although Random House is a big publisher, each imprint only publishes a small number of books each year. Our lists for the next few years are already full. Any book we take on from a previously unpublished author has to be truly exceptional. Manuscripts should be sent to us via literary agents."

⊘⊘ RANDOM HOUSE PUBLISHING GROUP

Division of Random House, Inc., 1745 Broadway, New York NY 10019. (212)782-9000. **Website:** www.penguinrandomhouse.com. Estab. 1925. Publishes hardcover and paperback trade books. Random House is the world's largest English-language general trade book publisher. It includes an array of prestigious imprints that publish some of the foremost writers of our time. **Publishes 120 titles/year.** Accepts simultaneous submissions.

IMPRINTS Ballantine Books; Bantam; Delacorte; Dell; Del Rey; Modern Library; One World; Presidio Press; Random House Trade Group; Random House Trade Paperbacks; Spectra; Spiegel & Grau; Triumph Books; Villard.

NONFICTION *Agented submissions only.*

FICTION *Agented submissions only.*

RAZORBILL

Penguin Young Readers Group, 345 Hudson St., New York NY 10014. (212)414-3720. **E-mail:** jharriton@penguinrandomhouse.com; bschrank@penguinrandomhouse.com. **Website:** www.razorbillbooks.com. **Contact:** Jessica Almon, senior editor; Elizabeth Tingue, editor; Casey McIntyre, associate publisher; Deborah Kaplan, vice president and executive art director, Marissa Grossman; assistant editor, Tiffany Liao; associate editor. Estab. 2003. "This division of Penguin Young Readers is looking for the best and the most original of commercial contemporary fiction titles for middle grade and YA readers. A select quantity of nonfiction titles will also be considered." **Publishes 30 titles/year. Offers advance against royalties.** Publishes book 1-2 after acceptance. Accepts simultaneous submissions. Responds in 1-3 months.

NONFICTION Middle readers and young adults/teens: concept. Submit cover letter with up to 30 sample pages.

FICTION Middle Readers: adventure, contemporary, graphic novels, fantasy, humor, problem novels. Young adults/teens: adventure, contemporary, fantasy, graphic novels, humor, multicultural, suspense, paranormal, science fiction, dystopian, literary, romance. Average word length: middle readers—40,000; young adult—60,000. Submit cover letter with up to 30 sample pages.

TIPS "New writers will have the best chance of acceptance and publication with original, contemporary material that boasts a distinctive voice and well-articulated world. Check out website to get a better idea of what we're looking for."

◑ REBELIGHT PUBLISHING, INC.

23-845 Dakota St., Suite 314, Winnipeg Manitoba R2M 5M3, Canada. **E-mail:** submit@rebelight.com. **Website:** www.rebelight.com. **Contact:** Editor. Estab. 2014. Publishes paperback and electronic originals. Rebelight Publishing is interested in "crack the spine, blow your mind" manuscripts for middle grade, young adult and new adult novels. *Only considers submissions from Canadian writers.* **Publishes 6-10 titles/year. Receive about 500 submissions/year. 25-50% of books from first-time authors. 100% from unagented writers. Pays 12-22% royalties on retail price. Does not offer an advance.** Publishes ms 12-18 months after acceptance. Accepts simultaneous submissions. Responds in 3 months to queries and mss. Submissions accepted via e-mail only. Catalog online or PDF available via e-mail request. Guidelines online.

FICTION Subjects include adventure, contemporary, fantasy, historical, horror, humor, juvenile, mainstream, multicultural, mystery, romance, science fiction, sports, suspense, young adult. All genres are considered, provided they are for a middle grade, young adult, or new adult audience. "Become familiar with our books. Study our website. Stick within the guidelines. Our tag line is 'crack the spine, blow your mind'—we are looking for well-written, powerful, fresh, fast-paced fiction. Keep us turning the pages. Give us something we just have to spread the word about." Submit proposal package, including a synopsis and 3 sample chapters. Read guidelines carefully.

TIPS "Review your manuscript for passive voice prior to submitting! (And that means get rid of it.)"

RED DEER PRESS

195 Allstate Pkwy., Markham ON L3R 4TB, Canada. (905)477-9700. **Fax:** (905)477-9179. **E-mail:** rdp@reddeerpress.com. **Website:** www.reddeerpress.com. **Contact:** Richard Dionne, publisher. Estab. 1975. Red Deer Press publishes upscale children's picture books, including illustrated children's Aboriginal titles, contemporary juvenile and young-adult fiction, adult fiction and nonfiction. "We produce creative and contemporary books by enlisting a balance of established and emerging authors and illustrators guided by a production team of expert editors, designers and production personnel. We enlist publishing talent from across Canada, publish to the national and international markets, and continually strive to creatively promote and market our books." **Pays 8-10% royalty.** Publishes ms 18 months after acceptance. Accepts simultaneous submissions. Responds to queries in 6 months. Book catalog for 9 x 12 SASE.
Red Deer Press is an award-winning publisher of children's and young adult literary titles.

NONFICTION Submit query with outline and sample chapter.

FICTION Publishes young adult, adult science fiction, fantasy, and paperback originals "focusing on books by, about, or of interest to Canadians." Books: offset paper; offset printing; hardcover/perfect-bound. Average print order: 5,000. First novel print order: 2,500. Distributes titles in Canada and the US, the UK, Australia and New Zealand. Young adult (juvenile and early reader), contemporary. No romance or horror. Accepts unsolicited mss. Query with SASE. No submissions on disk.

TIPS "We're very interested in young adult and children's fiction from Canadian writers with a proven track record (either published books or widely published in established magazines or journals) and for manuscripts with regional themes and/or a distinctive voice. We publish Canadian authors exclusively."

RED HEN PRESS

P.O. Box 40820, Pasadena CA 91114. (626)356-4760. **Fax:** (626)356-9974. **Website:** www.redhen.org. **Contact:** Mark E. Cull, publisher/executive director. Managing Editor: Kate Gale. Estab. 1993. Publishes trade paperback originals. "At this time, the best opportunity to be published by Red Hen is by entering one of our contests. Please find more information in our award submission guidelines." **Publishes 22 titles/**year. 2,000 queries; 500 mss received/year. 10% of books from first-time authors. 90% from unagented writers. Publishes ms 1 year after acceptance. Accepts simultaneous submissions. Responds in 1-2 months. Book catalog available free. Guidelines online.

NONFICTION Subjects include ethnic, memoirs, political/social interest. Query with synopsis and either 20-30 sample pages or complete ms using online submission manager.

FICTION Subjects include ethnic, experimental, feminist, historical, literary, poetry, poetry in translation, short story collections. Query with synopsis and either 20-30 sample pages or complete ms using online submission manager.

POETRY Submit to Benjamin Saltman Poetry Award.

TIPS "Audience reads poetry, literary fiction, intelligent nonfiction. If you have an agent, we may be too small since we don't pay advances. Write well. Send queries first. Be willing to help promote your own book."

REDLEAF LANE

10 Yorkton Ct., St. Paul MN 55117. (800)423-8309. **E-mail:** info@redleafpress.org. **E-mail:** acquisitions@redleafpress.org. **Website:** www.redleafpress.org. **Contact:** David Heath, director. Redleaf Lane publishes engaging, high-quality picture books for children. "Our books are unique because they take place in group-care settings and reflect developmentally appropriate practices and research-based standards." Accepts simultaneous submissions. Guidelines online.

RED MOON PRESS

P.O. Box 2461, Winchester VA 22604. (540)722-2156. **E-mail:** jim.kacian@redmoonpress.com. **Website:** www.redmoonpress.com. **Contact:** Jim Kacian, editor/publisher. Estab. 1993. English-language haiku, contemporary haiku in other languages in English translation, haiku anthologies, books of haiku theory and criticism, books on related genres (tanka, haibun, haiga, renga, renku, etc.). Red Moon Press "is the largest and most prestigious publisher of English-language haiku and related work in the world." Publishes 8-10 volumes/year, usually 2-3 anthologies, 4-5 individual collections of English-language haiku, and 1-3 books of essays, translations, or criticism of haiku. Under other imprints, the press also publishes chapbooks of various sizes and formats. **Publishes 8-10 titles/year. 100+ 75% of books from first-time** authors. **100% from unagented writers. Every book is a separate consideration.** Publishes ms 1 month after acceptance. Accepts simultaneous submissions. Catalog online. Guidelines available.

NONFICTION Subjects include alternative lifestyles, art, contemporary culture, education, environment, ethnic, history, hobbies, humanities, language, literary criticism, literature, memoirs, multicultural, music, nature, New Age, philosophy, photography, pop culture, psychology, recreation, spirituality, translation, travel.

POETRY Query first with book concept (not just "I've written a few haiku . ."); if interested we'll ask for samples. "Each contract separately negotiated."

RED ROCK PRESS

205 W. 57th St., Suite 8B, New York NY 10024. **Fax:** (212)362-6216. **Website:** www.redrockpress.com. **Contact:** Ilene Barth. Estab. 1998. Publishes hardcover and trade paperback originals. **Publishes 6-8 titles/year. Pays royalty on wholesale price. The amount of the advance offered depends on the project.** Responds in 3-4 months to queries.

NONFICTION Subjects include creative nonfiction. All of our books are pegged to gift-giving holidays.

RED SAGE PUBLISHING, INC.

P.O. Box 4844, Seminole FL 33775. (727)391-3847. **E-mail:** submissions@eredsage.com. **Website:** www. eredsage.com. Estab. 1995. Publishes books of romance fiction, written for the adventurous woman. **Publishes 4 titles/year. 50% of books from first-time authors. Pays advance.** Guidelines online.

FICTION Read guidelines.

✪ RED TUQUE BOOKS, INC.

477 Martin St., Unit #6, Penticton BC V2A 5L2, Canada. (778)476-5750. **Fax:** (778)476-5651. **E-mail:** dave@redtuquebooks.ca. **Website:** www.redtuquebooks.ca. **Contact:** David Korinetz, executive editor. Publishes Canadian authors only, other than in the Annual Canadian Tales Anthology, which will accept stories written about Canada or Canadians by non-Canadians. Publication in the anthology is only through submissions to the Canadian Tales writing contest. See website for details. **Pays 5-7% royalties on net sales. Pays $250 advance.** Publishes ms 1-2 years after acceptance. Accepts simultaneous submissions. Responds in 3-6 weeks.

FICTION Subjects include short story collections. Submit a query letter, 1-page synopsis, and first 5 pages only. Include total word count. Accepts ms only by mail. SASE or e-mail address for reply.

TIPS "Well-plotted, character-driven stories, preferably with happy endings, will have the best chance of being accepted. Keep in mind that authors who like to begin sentences with 'and, or, and but' are less likely to be considered. Don't send anything gruesome or overly explicit; tell us a good story, but think PG."

RED WHEEL/WEISER

65 Parker Street, Suite 7, Newburyport MA 01950. 978-465-0504. **Fax:** 978-465-0504. **E-mail:** submissions@rwwbooks.com; info@rwwbooks.com;. **Website:** www.redwheelweiser.com. **Contact:** Pat Bryce, acquisitions editor; Jim Warner, creative director. Estab. 1956. Publishes hardcover and trade paperback originals and reprints. **Publishes 60-75 titles/year. 2,000 queries received/year; 2,000 mss received/year. 20% of books from first-time authors. 50% from unagented writers. Pays royalty.** Publishes ms 1 year after accceptance. Accepts simultaneous submissions. Responds in 3-6 months. Book catalog available free. Guidelines online.

NONFICTION Subjects include New Age, spirituality, parenting. Query with SASE. Submit proposal package, outline, 2 sample chapters, TOC. Reviews artwork/photos. Send photocopies.

ROBERT D. REED PUBLISHERS

P.O. Box 1992, Bandon OR 97411. (541)347-9882. **Fax:** (541)347-9883. **E-mail:** cleone@rdrpublishers.com; bob@rdrpublishers.com. **Website:** www.rdrpublishers.com. **Contact:** Cleone L. Reed. Estab. 1991. Publishes hardcover and trade paperback originals and e-books. **Publishes 5-10 titles/year. 75% of books from first-time authors. 90% from unagented writers. Pays 12-17% royalty on wholesale price.** Publishes ms 5 months after acceptance. Accepts simultaneous submissions. Responds in 1 month. Catalog and guidelines online.

NONFICTION Subjects include alternative lifestyles, business, career guidance, child guidance, communications, community, contemporary culture, counseling, education, entertainment, environment, ethnic, gay, health, history, humanities, language, lesbian, literature, memoirs, military, money, multicultural, nature, New Age, nutrition, parenting, philosophy, psychology, social sciences, sociology, spirituality, travel, true crime, womens issues, womens studies, world affairs. "We want titles that have a large audience with at least 10-year sales potential, and author's workshop, speaking and seminar participation. We like titles that are part of author's career." Submit proposal package with outline. Reviews artwork.

TIPS "We publish books to make this a better world. Nonfiction only."

REFERENCE SERVICE PRESS

1945 Golden Way, Mountain View CA 94040. (650)861 3170. **Fax:** (650)861 3171. **E-mail:** info@rsp funding.com. **Website:** www.rspfunding.com. Estab. 1977. Publishes hardcover originals. "Reference Service Press focuses on the development and publication of financial aid resources in any format (print, electronic, e-book, etc.). We are interested in financial aid publications aimed at specific groups (e.g., minorities, women, veterans, the disabled, undergraduates majoring in specific subject areas, specific types of financial aid, etc.)." **Publishes 10-20 titles/year. 100% from unagented writers. Pays 10% royalty. Pays advance.** Publishes book 6 months after acceptance. Accepts simultaneous submissions. Responds in 2 months to queries. Book catalog for #10 SASE.

NONFICTION Subjects include agriculture, education, ethnic, history, religion, science, sociology, disabled. Submit outline, sample chapters.

TIPS "Our audience consists of librarians, counselors, researchers, students, re-entry women, scholars, and other fundseekers."

ⒶⓄ REVELL

Division of Baker Publishing Group, 6030 E. Fulton Rd., Ada MI 49301. (616)676-9185. **Fax:** (616)676-9573. **Website:** www.bakerbooks.com. Estab. 1870. Publishes hardcover, trade paperback and mass market paperback originals. "Revell publishes to the heart (rather than to the head). For 125 years, Revell has been publishing evangelical books for the personal enrichment and spiritual growth of general Christian readers." Accepts simultaneous submissions. Book catalog and ms guidelines online.

Ⓠ *No longer accepts unsolicited mss.*

NONFICTION Subjects include child guidance, religion, Christian living, marriage.

FICTION Subjects include historical, religious, suspense, contemporary.

Ⓞ RING OF FIRE PUBLISHING LLC

6523 California Ave. SW #409, Seattle WA 98136. **E-mail:** contact@ringoffirebooks.com. **Website:** www.

ringoffirebooks.com. Estab. 2011. Publishes trade paperback and electronic originals. "We are currently closed to submissions." Check website for updates. **Publishes 6-12 titles/year. 75% of books from first-time authors. 100% from unagented writers. Pays royalties.** Publishes ms 6 months after acceptance. Accepts simultaneous submissions. Book catalog and ms guidelines online.

FICTION Subjects include adventure, contemporary, experimental, fantasy, gothic, horror, juvenile, literary, mainstream, mystery, occult, romance, science fiction, short story collections, suspense, western, young adult.

RIO NUEVO PUBLISHERS

Imprint of Treasure Chest Books, P.O. Box 5250, Tucson AZ 85703. **Fax:** (520)624-5888. **E-mail:** info@rionuevo.com. **Website:** www.rionuevo.com. Estab. 1975. Publishes hardcover and trade paperback originals and reprints. **Publishes 12-20 titles/year. 30 queries received/year. 10 mss received/year. 30% of books from first-time authors. 100% from unagented writers. Pays $1,000-4,000 advance.** Publishes book 1 year after acceptance. Accepts simultaneous submissions. Responds in 6 months. Book catalog online. Guidelines online.

NONFICTION Subjects include animals, gardening, history, regional, religion, spirituality, travel. "We cover the Southwest but prefer titles that are not too narrow in their focus. We want our books to be of broad enough interest that people from other places will also want to read them." Query with SASE or via e-mail. Submit proposal package, outline, 2 sample chapters. Reviews artwork/photos. Send photocopies.

TIPS "We have a general audience of intelligent people interested in the Southwest-nature, history, culture. Many of our books are sold in gift shops throughout the region. Look at our books and website for inspiration and to see what we do."

RIPPLE GROVE PRESS

P.O. Box 86740, Portland OR 97286. **E-mail:** submit@ripplegrovepress.com. **Website:** www.ripplegrovepress.com. Estab. 2013. Publishes hardcover originals. "We started Ripple Grove Press because we have a passion for well-written and beautifully illustrated children's picture books. Each story selected has been read dozens of times, then slept on, then walked away from, then talked about again and again. If the story has the same intrigue and the same interest that it had when we first read it, we move forward." **Publishes 3-6 titles/year. Authors receive between 10-12% royalty on net receipts.** Average length of time between acceptance of a book-length ms and publication is 12-18 months. Accepts simultaneous submissions. "Given the volume of submissions we receive we are no longer able to individually respond to each. Please allow 5 months for us to review your submission. If we are interested in your story, you can expect to hear from us within that time. If you do not hear from us after that time, we are not interested in publishing your story. It's not you, it's us! We receive thousands of submissions and only publish a few books each year. Don't give up!". Catalog online. Guidelines online.

NONFICTION We do review artwork. Writers should send photo copies or links to their website and online portfolio.

FICTION Subjects include contemporary, humor, juvenile, literary, mainstream, multicultural, picture books. We are looking for something unique, that hasn't been done before; an interesting story that captures a moment with a timeless feel. We are looking for picture driven stories for children ages 2-6. Please do not send early readers, middle grade, or YA mss. No religious or holiday themed stories. Please do not submit your story with page breaks or illustration notes. Do not submit a story with doodles or personal photographs. Do not send your "idea" for a story, send your story in manuscript form. Submit completed mss. Accepts submissions by mail and e-mail. Please submit a cover letter including a summary of your story, the age range of the story, a brief biography of yourself, and contact information.

TIPS "Please read children's picture books. We create books that children and adults want to read over and over again. Our books showcase art as well as stories and tie them together to create a unique and creative product."

RIVER CITY PUBLISHING

1719 Mulberry St., Montgomery AL 36106. **E-mail:** fnorris@rivercitypublishing.com. **Website:** www.rivercitypublishing.com. **Contact:** Fran Norris, editor. Estab. 1989. Publishes hardcover and trade paperback originals. Midsize independent publisher. River City publishes literary fiction, regional, short story collections. No poetry, memoir, or children's books. We also consider narrative histories, sociological accounts, and travel; however, only biographies and memoirs

from noted persons will be considered. **Publishes 6 titles/year.** Accepts simultaneous submissions. Responds within 9 months.

NONFICTION "We do not publish self-help, how-to, business, medicine, religion, education, or psychology." Accepts unsolicited submissions and submissions from unagented authors, as well as those from established and agented writers. Submit 5 consecutive sample chapters or entire ms for review. "Please include a short biography that highlights any previous writing and publishing experience, sales opportunities the author could provide, ideas for marketing the book, and why you think the work would be appropriate for River City." Send appropriate-sized SASE or IRC, "otherwise, the material will be recycled." Also accepts queries by e-mail.

FICTION Subjects include literary, regional, short story collections. No poetry, memoir, or children's books. Send appropriate-sized SASE or IRC, "otherwise, the material will be recycled." Also accepts queries by e-mail. "Please include your electronic query letter as inline text and not an as attachment; we do not open unsolicited attachments of any kind." No multiple submissions. Rarely comments on rejected mss.

TIPS "Only send your best work after you have received outside opinions. From approximately 1,000 submissions each year, we publish no more than 8 books and few of those come from unsolicited material. Competition is fierce, so follow the guidelines exactly. First-time novelists are also encouraged to send work."

Ⓐ⊘ RIVERHEAD BOOKS

Penguin Putnam, 375 Hudson St., New York NY 10014. **Website:** www.penguin.com. **Contact:** Rebecca Saletan, vice president/editorial director. Accepts simultaneous submissions.

FICTION Subjects include contemporary, literary, mainstream. *Submit through agent only. No unsolicited mss.*

Ⓐ⊘ ROARING BROOK PRESS

Macmillan Children's Publishing Group, 175 Fifth Ave., New York NY 10010. (646)307-5151. **Website:** us.macmillan.com. Estab. 2000. Roaring Brook Press is an imprint of MacMillan, a group of companies that includes Henry Holt and Farrar, Straus & Giroux. *Roaring Brook is not accepting unsolicited mss.*

Pays authors royalty based on retail price. Accepts simultaneous submissions.

NONFICTION Picture books, young readers, middle readers, young adults: adventure, animal, contemporary, fantasy, history, humor, multicultural, nature/environment, poetry, religion, science fiction, sports, suspense/mystery. *Not accepting unsolicited mss or queries.*

FICTION Picture books, young readers, middle readers, young adults: adventure, animal, contemporary, fantasy, history, humor, multicultural, nature/environment, poetry, religion, science fiction, sports, suspense/mystery. *Not accepting unsolicited mss or queries.*

TIPS "You should find a reputable agent and have him/her submit your work."

○ ROCKY MOUNTAIN BOOKS

103 - 1075 Pendergast St., Victoria BC V8V 0A1, Canada. (250)360-0829. **E-mail:** don@rmbooks.com. **Website:** www.rmbooks.com. **Contact:** Don Gorman, publisher. Publishes trade paperback and hardcover books. "RMB is a dynamic book publisher located in western Canada. We specialize in quality nonfiction on the outdoors, travel, environment, social and cultural issues." **Rarely offers advance.** Accepts simultaneous submissions. Responds in 2-6 months to queries. Book catalog and ms guidelines online.

NONFICTION "Our main area of publishing is outdoor recreation guides to Western and Northern Canada."

⊙⊘ RODALE BOOKS

400 S. Tenth St., Emmaus PA 18098. (610)967-5171. **Fax:** (610)967-8961. **Website:** www.rodaleinc.com. Estab. 1932. "Rodale Books publishes adult trade titles in categories such health & fitness, cooking, spirituality, and pet care." Accepts simultaneous submissions.

○ RONSDALE PRESS

3350 W. 21st Ave., Vancouver BC V6S 1G7, Canada. (604)738-4688. **Fax:** (604)731-4548. **E-mail:** ronsdale@shaw.ca. **Website:** ronsdalepress.com. **Contact:** Ronald B. Hatch (fiction, poetry, nonfiction, social commentary); Veronica Hatch (YA novels and short stories). Estab. 1988. Publishes trade paperback originals. "Ronsdale Press is a Canadian literary publishing house that publishes 12 books each year, four of which are young adult titles. Of particular interest are books involving children exploring and discovering new aspects of Ca-

nadian history." **Publishes 12 titles/year. 40 queries; 800 mss received/year. 40% of books from first-time authors. 95% from unagented writers. Pays 10% royalty on retail price.** Publishes book 1 year after acceptance. Accepts simultaneous submissions. Responds to queries in 2 weeks; mss in 2 months. Book catalog for #10 SASE. Guidelines online.

NONFICTION Subjects include history, literary criticism, literature, regional. Middle readers, young adults: animal, biography, history, multicultural, social issues. Average word length: young readers—90; middle readers—90. "We publish a number of books for children and young adults in the age 10 to 15 range. We are especially interested in YA historical novels. We regret that we can no longer publish picture books." Submit complete ms.

FICTION Subjects include literary, short story collections, novels. Young adults: Canadian novels. Average word length: middle readers and young adults—50,000. Submit complete ms.

POETRY Poets should have published some poems in magazines/journals and should be well-read in contemporary masters. Submit complete ms.

TIPS "Ronsdale Press is a literary publishing house, based in Vancouver, and dedicated to publishing books from across Canada, books that give Canadians new insights into themselves and their country. We aim to publish the best Canadian writers."

ROSE ALLEY PRESS

4203 Brooklyn Ave. NE, #103A, Seattle WA 98105-5911, USA. (206)633-2725. **E-mail:** rosealleypress@juno.com. **Website:** www.rosealleypress.com. **Contact:** David D. Horowitz. Estab. 1995. "Rose Alley Press primarily publishes books featuring rhymed metrical poetry and an annually updated booklet about writing and publication. We do not read or consider unsolicited manuscripts." Accepts simultaneous submissions.

NONFICTION Subjects include literature, philosophy.

ROSEN PUBLISHING

29 E. 21st St., New York NY 10010. (800)237-9932. **Fax:** (888)436-4643. **Website:** www.rosenpublishing. com. Estab. 1950. Rosen Publishing is an independent educational publishing house, established to serve the needs of students in grades Pre-K-12 with high interest, curriculum-correlated materials. Rosen publishes

more than 700 new books each year and has a backlist of more than 7,000.

ROTOVISION

Sheridan House, 114 Western Rd., Hove East Sussex BN3 IDD, England. (44)(127)371-6010. **Fax:** (44)(127)372-7269. **E-mail:** isheetam@rotovision.com. **Website:** www.rotovision.com. **Contact:** Isheeta Mustafi. Publishes hardcover and trade paperback originals, and trade paperback reprints. Accepts simultaneous submissions. Book catalog available free. Guidelines available free.

"RotoVision books showcase the works of top writers and designers reflecting excellence and innovation in the visual arts. If you wish to submit a book proposal, in the first instance please familiarise yourself with our publishing portfolio to ensure your proposal fits into our focus area."

NONFICTION Subjects include art, creative nonfiction. "Our books are aimed at keen amateurs and professionals who want to improve their skills." Submit an e-mail with "Book Proposal" in the subject line. Reviews artwork/photos. Send transparencies and PDFs.

TIPS "Our audience includes professionals, keen amateurs, and students of visual arts including graphic design, general design, advertising, and photography. Make your approach international in scope. Content not to be less than 35% US."

ROWMAN & LITTLEFIELD PUBLISHING GROUP

4501 Forbes Blvd., Suite 200, Lanham MD 20706. (301)459-3366. **Fax:** (301)429-5748. **Website:** www.rowmanlittlefield.com. Estab. 1949. Publishes hardcover and trade paperback originals and reprints. "We are an independent press devoted to publishing scholarly books in the best tradition of university presses; innovative, thought-provoking texts for college courses; and crossover trade books intended to convey scholarly trends to an educated readership. Our approach emphasizes substance and quality of thought over ephemeral trends. We offer a forum for responsible voices representing the diversity of opinion on college campuses, and take special pride in several series designed to provide students with the pros and cons of hotly contested issues." **Pays advance.** Book catalog online. Guidelines online.

NONFICTION "Rowman & Littlefield is seeking proposals in the serious nonfiction areas of history, politics, current events, religion, sociology, philosophy, communication and education. All proposal inquiries can be e-mailed or mailed to the respective acquisitions editor listed on the contacts page on our website."

RUKA PRESS

P.O. Box 1409, Washington DC 20013. **E-mail:** contact@rukapress.com. **E-mail:** submissions@rukapress.com. **Website:** www.rukapress.com. **Contact:** Daniel Kohan, owner. Estab. 2010. Publishes in trade paperback originals, electronic. "We publish nonfiction books with a strong environmental component for a general audience. We are looking for books that explain things, that make an argument, that demystify. We are interested in economics, science, nature, climate change, and sustainability. We like building charts and graphs, tables and timelines. Our politics are progressive, but our books need not be political." **Publishes 2-4 titles/year. 40% of books from first-time authors. 80% from unagented writers. Pays advance. Royalties are 10-25% on wholesale price.** Publishes book an average of 9-12 months after acceptance of ms. Accepts simultaneous submissions. Responds in 1 month. Book catalog online. Guidelines online.

NONFICTION Subjects include environment, nature, science. Submit proposal package, including outline, resume, bio, or CV, and 1 sample chapter.

TIPS "We appeal to an audience of intelligent, educated readers with broad interests. Be sure to tell us why your proposal is unique, and why you are especially qualified to write this book. We are looking for originality and expertise."

RUTGERS UNIVERSITY PRESS

106 Somerset St., 3rd Floor, New Brunswick NJ 08901. (732)445-7762. **Fax:** (732)445-7039. **E-mail:** lmitch@rutgers.edu. **Website:** rutgerspress.rutgers.edu. **Contact:** Leslie Mitchner, editor-in-chief/associate director (humanities); Peter Micklaus, editor (social sciences); Dana Dreibelbis, editor (science, health and medicine); Marlie Wasserman, associate editor (Jewish studies), Kimberly Guinta, editor (women's studies). Estab. 1936. Publishes hardcover and trade paperback originals and reprints. "Our press aims to reach audiences beyond the academic community with accessible scholarly and regional books." **Publishes 100 titles/year. 1,500 queries; 300 mss received/year. 30% of books from first-time authors.**

70% from unagented writers. **Pays 7 1/2-15% royalty. Pays $1,000-10,000 advance.** Publishes ms 1 year after acceptance. Accepts simultaneous submissions. Responds in 1 month to proposals. Book catalog online. Guidelines online.

NONFICTION Subjects include ethnic, history, multicultural, regional, religion, sociology, African-American studies. Books for use in undergraduate courses. Submit outline, 2-3 sample chapters. Reviews artwork/photos. Send photocopies.

TIPS "Both academic and general audiences. Many of our books have potential for undergraduate course use. We are more trade-oriented than most university presses. We are looking for intelligent, well-written, and accessible books. Avoid overly narrow topics."

SADDLEBACK EDUCATIONAL PUBLISHING

3120-A Pullman St., Costa Mesa CA 92626. (888)735-2225. **E-mail:** contact@sdlback.com. **Website:** www.sdlback.com. Saddleback is always looking for fresh, new talent. "Please note that we primarily publish books for kids ages 12-18." Accepts simultaneous submissions.

FICTION "We look for diversity for our characters and content." Mail typed submission along with a query letter describing the work simply and where it fits in with other titles.

SAE INTERNATIONAL

400 Commonwealth Dr., Warrendale PA 15096-0001. (724)776-4841. **E-mail:** writeabook@sae.org; mailtowriteabook@sae.org. **Website:** www.sae.org/writeabook. Estab. 1905. Publishes hardcover and trade paperback originals, e-books. Automotive means anything self-propelled. "We are a professional society serving engineers, scientists, and researchers in the automobile, aerospace, and off-highway industries." **Publishes approximately 10 titles/year. 50 queries received/year. 20 mss received/year. 70% of books from first-time authors. 100% from unagented writers. Pays royalty. Pays possible advance.** Publishes ms 9-10 months after acceptance. Accepts simultaneous submissions. Responds in 4 months to queries. Book catalog free. Guidelines online.

NONFICTION Query with proposal.

TIPS "Audience is automotive and aerospace engineers and managers, automotive safety and biomechanics professionals, students, educators, enthusiasts, and historians."

SAFER SOCIETY PRESS

P.O. Box 340, Brandon VT 05733. (802)247-3132. **Fax:** (802)247-4233. **Website:** www.safersociety.org. **Contact:** Mary Falcon, editorial director. Estab. 1985. Publishes trade paperback originals. "Our mission is the prevention and treatment of sexual abuse." **Publishes 3-4 titles/year. 15-20 queries received/year. 15-20 mss received/year. 90% of books from first-time authors. 100% from unagented writers. Pays 10% royalty on retail price.** Publishes ms 1 year after acceptance. Accepts simultaneous submissions. Book catalog available free. Guidelines online.

NONFICTION Subjects include psychology. "We are a small, nonprofit, niche press. We want well-researched books dealing with any aspect of sexual abuse: treatment, prevention, understanding; works on subject in Spanish." Memoirs generally not accepted. Query with SASE, submit proposal package, or complete ms Reviews artwork/photos. Send photocopies.

TIPS "Audience is persons working in mental health/persons needing self-help books. Pays small fees or low royalties."

SAGUARO BOOKS, LLC

16201 E. Keymar Dr., Fountain Hills AZ 85268. **Fax:** (480)284-4855. **E-mail:** mjnickum@saguarobooks.com. **Website:** www.saguarobooks.com. **Contact:** Mary Nickum, CEO. Estab. 2012. Publishes trade paperback and electronic originals. Saguaro Books, LLC is a publishing company specializing in middle grade and young adult ficiton by first-time authors. **Publishes 4-6 titles/year. Receives 60-80 queries/year, 8-10 mss/year. 100% of books from first-time authors. 100% from unagented writers. Pays 20% royalties after taxes and publication costs. Does not offer advance.** Publishes ms 18-24 months after acceptance. Responds within 3 months only if we're interested. Catalog available online. Guidelines available by e-mail.

FICTION Subjects include adventure, fantasy, historical, juvenile, military, multicultural, mystery, occult, science fiction, sports, suspense, war, western, young adult. Ms should be well-written; signed letter by a professional editor is required. Does not want agented work. Query via e-mail before submitting work. Any material sent before requested will be ignored.

TIPS "Visit our website before sending us a query. Pay special attention to the For Authors Only page."

ST. AUGUSTINE'S PRESS

P.O. Box 2285, South Bend IN 46680. (574)-291-3500. **Fax:** (574)291-3700. **E-mail:** bruce@staugustine.net. **Website:** www.staugustine.net. **Contact:** Bruce Fingerhut, president (philosophy). Publishes hardcover originals and trade paperback originals and reprints. "Our market is scholarly in the humanities. We publish in philosophy, religion, cultural history, and history of ideas only." **Publishes 30+ titles/year. 350 queries; 300 mss received/year. 2% of books from first-time authors. 95% from unagented writers. Pays 6-15% royalty. Pays $500-5,000 advance.** Publishes book 8-18 months after acceptance. Accepts simultaneous submissions. Responds in 2-6 months to queries; 3-8 months to proposals; 4-8 months to mss. Book catalog available free.

IMPRINTS Carthage Reprints.

NONFICTION Subjects include philosophy, religion. Query with SASE. Reviews artwork/photos. Send photocopies.

TIPS "Scholarly and college student audience."

ST. JOHANN PRESS

P.O. Box 241, Haworth NJ 07641. (201)387-1529. **E-mail:** d.biesel@verizon.net. **Website:** www.stjohannpress.com. Estab. 1991. Publishes hardcover originals, trade paperback originals and reprints. **Publishes 6-8 titles/year. Receives 30-50 submissions/year. 50% of books from first-time authors. 95% from unagented writers. Pays 10-15% royalty on wholesale price.** Publishes book 15 months after acceptance. Accepts simultaneous submissions. Responds in 1 month on queries. Catalog online. Guidelines free on request.

NONFICTION Subjects include cooking, crafts, foods, history, hobbies, military, nutrition, religion, spirituality, sports, Black history in sports.. "We are a niche publisher with interests in titles that will sell over a long period of time. For example, the World Football League Encyclopedia, Chicago Showcase of Basketball, will not need to be redone. We do baseball but prefer soccer, hockey, etc." Query with SASE. Reviews artwork/photos as part of the ms package. Send photocopies.

TIPS "Our readership is libraries, individuals with special interests, (e.g. sports historians); we also do specialized reference."

⚠️⊘ ST. MARTIN'S PRESS, LLC

Holtzbrinck Publishers, 175 Fifth Ave., New York NY 10010. (212)674-5151. **Fax:** (212)420-9314. **Website:** www.stmartins.com. Estab. 1952. Publishes hardcover, trade paperback and mass market originals. General interest publisher of both fiction and nonfiction. **Publishes 1,500 titles/year. Pays royalty. Pays advance.** Accepts simultaneous submissions.

NONFICTION Subjects include sports, general nonfiction. *Agented submissions only. No unsolicited mss.*

FICTION Subjects include contemporary, fantasy, historical, horror, literary, mystery, science fiction, suspense, western, general fiction. *Agented submissions only. No unsolicited mss.*

SAINT MARY'S PRESS

702 Terrace Heights, Winona MN 55987. (800)533-8095. **Fax:** (800)344-9225. **E-mail:** submissions@smp.org. **Website:** www.smp.org. Accepts simultaneous submissions. Ms guidelines online or by e-mail.

NONFICTION Subjects include religion. Titles for Catholic youth and their parents, teachers, and youth ministers. High school Catholic religious education textbooks and primary source readings. Query with SASE. Submit proposal package, outline, 1 sample chapter, SASE. Brief author biography.

TIPS "Request product catalog and/or do research online of Saint Mary Press book lists before submitting proposal."

ST PAULS

Society of St. Paul, 2187 Victory Blvd., Staten Island NY 10314. (718)761-0047. **Fax:** (718)761-0057. **E-mail:** edmund_lane@juno.com. **Website:** www.stpauls.us. **Contact:** Edmund C. Lane, SSP, acquisitions editor. Estab. 1957. Publishes trade paperback and mass market paperback originals and reprints. **Publishes 22 titles/year. 250 queries; 150 mss received/year. 10% of books from first-time authors. 100% from unagented writers. Pays 5-10% royalty.** Publishes ms 10 months after acceptance. Responds in 1 month to queries and proposals; 2 months to mss. Book catalog and ms guidelines free.

NONFICTION Subjects include philosophy, religion, spirituality. Alba House is the North American publishing division of the Society of St. Paul, an International Roman Catholic Missionary Religious Congregation dedicated to spreading the Gospel message via the media of communications. Does not want fiction, children's books, poetry, personal testimonies, or autobiographies. Submit complete ms. Reviews artwork/photos. Send photocopies.

TIPS "Our audience is educated Roman Catholic readers interested in matters related to the Church, spirituality, Biblical and theological topics, moral concerns, lives of the saints, etc."

SAKURA PUBLISHING & TECHNOLOGIES

805 Lindaraxa Park North, Alhambra CA 91801. (330)360-5131. **E-mail:** skpublishing124@gmail.com. **Website:** www.sakura-publishing.com. **Contact:** Derek Vasconi, submissions coordinator. Estab. 2007. Publishes hardcover, trade paperback, mass market paperback and electronic originals and reprints. Currently accepts only the following genres: Asian fiction, Japanese fiction (in English), Nonfiction, and horror. Please do not send queries for any other genres. Mss that don't follow guidelines will not be considered. Sakura Publishing is a traditional, independent book publishing company that focuses on fiction, Asian culture-related books, nonfiction, and horror books. **Publishes 1-3 titles/year. 90% of books from first-time authors. 80% from unagented writers. Royalty payments on paperback, e-book, wholesale, and merchandise Does not pay advance.** Publishes ms 6 months after acceptance. Accepts simultaneous submissions. Responds in 1 week. Book catalog available for #10 SASE. Guidelines online.

NONFICTION Subjects include contemporary culture, creative nonfiction, entertainment, ethnic, film, games, history, hobbies, humanities, literature, memoirs, military, music, philosophy, pop culture, psychology, regional, religion, sex, travel, true crime, world affairs. Looking for memoirs by Asians, nonfiction dealing with American Wars, anything to do with terrorism, anything to do with sex, or any type of edgy nonfiction No memoirs other than what we have listed above, cookbooks, humor, textbooks, technical, and definitely no books about suffering from diseases and overcoming them. Follow guidelines online.

FICTION Subjects include contemporary, ethnic, horror, multicultural, occult, Asian, horror, occult. Looking mostly for horror and anything relating to Asians, and Asian Americans, with top preference given to Japanese writers and books based in or around Japan. Follow guidelines online.

POETRY Follow guidelines online.

TIPS "Please make sure you visit our submissions page at our website and follow all instructions exactly as written. Also, Sakura Publishing has a preference for fiction/nonfiction books specializing in Asian culture."

SALEM PRESS, INC.

P.O. Box 56, Amenia NY 12501. **E-mail:** lmars@greyhouse.com. **Website:** www.salempress.com. **Contact:** Laura Mars, editorial director. **Publishes 20-22 titles/year. 15 queries received/year. Work-for-hire pays 5-15¢/word.** Accepts simultaneous submissions. Responds in 3 months to queries; 1 month to proposals. Book catalog online.

NONFICTION Subjects include ethnic, history, philosophy, psychology, science, sociology. "We accept vitas for writers interested in supplying articles/entries for encyclopedia-type entries in library reference books. Will also accept multi-volume book ideas from people interested in being a general editor." Query with SASE.

SALINA BOOKSHELF

1120 W. University Ave., Suite 102, Flagstaff AZ 86001. (877)527-0070. **Fax:** (928)526-0386. **Website:** www.salinabookshelf.com. Publishes trade paperback originals and reprints. **Publishes 4-5 titles/year. 50% of books from first-time authors. 100% from unagented writers. Pays varying royalty. Pays advance.** Publishes ms 1 year after acceptance. Accepts simultaneous submissions. Responds in 3 months to queries.

NONFICTION Subjects include education, ethnic, science. "We publish children's bilingual readers." Nonfiction should be appropriate to science and social studies curriculum grades 3-8. Query with SASE.

FICTION Subjects include juvenile. Submissions should be in English or Navajo. "All our books relate to the Navajo language and culture." Query with SASE.

POETRY "We accept poetry in English/Southwest language for children." Submit 3 sample poems.

🐟 SALMON POETRY

Knockeven, Cliffs of Moher, County Clare , Ireland. 353(0)852318909. **E-mail:** info@salmonpoetry.com. **E-mail:** jessie@salmonpoetry.com. **Website:** www.salmonpoetry.com. **Contact:** Jessie Lendennie, editor. Estab. 1981. Publishes contemporary poetry and literary nonfiction. **Publishes 30 titles/year. 300+ 5% of books from first-time authors. 100% from unagented writers. Pays advance.** Publishes ms 2 years after acceptance. Responds in 3 months. Guidelines available.

NONFICTION Subjects include literature, marine subjects.

POETRY "Salmon Press is one of the most important publishers in the Irish literary world; specializing in the promotion of new poets, particularly women. Established in 1981 as an alternative voice in Irish literature, Salmon is known for its international list and over the years has developed a cross-cultural literary dialog, broadening Irish Literature and urging new perspectives on established traditions." E-mail query with short biographical note and 5-10 sample poems.

TIPS "Read as much poetry as you can, and always research the publisher before submitting!"

SALVO PRESS

An imprint of Start Publishing, 101 Hudson St., 37th Floor, Suite 3705, Jersey City NJ 07302. **E-mail:** info@salvopress.com. **E-mail:** submissions@start-media.com. **Website:** www.salvopress.com. Estab. 1998. Salvo Press proudly publishes mysteries, thrillers, and literary books in e-book and audiobook formats. **Publishes 6-12 titles/year. 75% from unagented writers. Pays 10% royalty.** Publishes ms 9-12 months after acceptance. Responds in 5 minutes to 1 month to queries; 2 months to mss. Book catalog and ms guidelines online.

FICTION Subjects include adventure, literary, mystery, science fiction, suspense, thriller/espionage. "We are a small press specializing in mystery, suspense, espionage and thriller fiction. Our press publishes in trade paperback and most e-book formats." Query by e-mail.

SANTA MONICA PRESS

P.O. Box 850, Solana Beach CA 92075. (858)793-1890; (800)784-9553. **E-mail:** books@santamonicapress.com. **E-mail:** acquisitions@santamonicapress.com. **Website:** www.santamonicapress.com. Estab. 1994. Publishes hardcover and trade paperback originals. Santa Monica Press has been publishing an eclectic line of books since 1994. "Our critically acclaimed titles are sold in chain, independent, online, and university bookstores around the world, as well as in some of the most popular retail outlets in North America. Our authors are recognized experts who are sought after by the media and receive newspaper, magazine, radio, and television coverage both nationally and internationally. At Santa Monica Press, we're not afraid to cast a wide editorial net. Our list of lively and modern nonfiction titles includes books in such categories as popular culture, film history, photography, humor, biography, travel, and reference." **Publishes 12 titles/year. 25% of books from first-time authors. 75% from unagented writers. Pays 6-10% royalty on net price. Pays $500-10,000+ advance.** Publishes book 1 year after acceptance. Accepts simultaneous submissions. Responds in 1-2 months to proposals. Guidelines available.

NONFICTION Subjects include Americana, art, cinema, contemporary culture, creative nonfiction, education, entertainment, film, history, humanities, language, literature, memoirs, music, parenting, photography, pop culture, regional, social sciences, sports, stage, travel. Submit proposal package, including outline, 2-3 sample chapters, biography, marketing and publicity plans, analysis of competitive titles, SASE with appropriate postage. Reviews artwork/photos. Send photocopies.

TIPS "Visit our website before submitting to view our author guidelines and to get a clear idea of the types of books we publish. Carefully analyze your book's competition and tell us what makes your book different—and what makes it better. Also let us know what promotional and marketing opportunities you, as the author, bring to the project."

SARABANDE BOOKS, INC.

2234 Dundee Rd., Suite 200, Louisville KY 40205. (502)458-4028. **Fax:** (502)458-4065. **E-mail:** info@sarabandebooks.org. **Website:** www.sarabandebooks.org. **Contact:** Sarah Gorham, Editor-in-Chief. Estab. 1994. Publishes trade paperback originals. "Sarabande Books was founded to publish poetry, short fiction, and creative nonfiction. We look for works of lasting literary value. Please see our titles to get an idea of our taste. Accepts submissions through contests and open submissions." **Publishes 10 titles/year. 1,500 queries received/year. 3,000 mss received/year. 35% of books from first-time authors. 75% from unagented writers. Pays royalty. 10% on actual income received. Also pays in author's copies. Pays $500-1,000 advance.** Publishes ms 18 months after acceptance. Accepts simultaneous submissions. Book catalog available free. Contest guidelines for #10 SASE or on website.

○ Charges $15 handling fee with alternative option of purchase of book from website (e-mail confirmation of sale must be included with submission).

FICTION Subjects include literary, short story collections, novellas, short novels (300 pages maximum, 150 pages minimum). "We consider novels and nonfiction in a wide variety of genres. We do not consider genre fiction such as science fiction, fantasy, or horror. Our target length is 70,000-90,000 words." Queries can be sent via e-mail, fax, or regular post.

POETRY Poetry of superior artistic quality; otherwise no restraints or specifications. Sarabande Books publishes books of poetry of 48 pages minimum. Wants "poetry that offers originality of voice and subject matter, uniqueness of vision, and a language that startles because of the careful attention paid to it—language that goes beyond the merely competent or functional." Mss selected through literary contests, invitation, and recommendation by a well-established writer.

TIPS "Sarabande publishes for a general literary audience. Know your market. Read-and buy-books of literature. Sponsors contests for poetry and fiction. Make sure you're not writing in a vacuum, that you've read and are conscious of contemporary literature. Have someone read your manuscript, checking it for ordering, coherence. Better a lean, consistently strong manuscript than one that is long and uneven. We like a story to have good narrative, and we like to be engaged by language."

SAS PUBLISHING

100 SAS Campus Dr., Cary NC 27513-2414. (919)531-0585. **Fax:** (919)677-4444. **E-mail:** saspress@sas.com. **Website:** support.sas.com/saspress. Estab. 1976. Publishes hardcover and trade paperback originals. "SAS publishes books for SAS and JMP software users, both new and experienced." **Publishes 40 titles/year. 50% of books from first-time authors. 100% from unagented writers. Payment negotiable. Pays negotiable advance.** Responds in 2 weeks to queries. Book catalog and ms guidelines online.

NONFICTION Subjects include software, statistics. SAS Publishing jointly Wiley and SAS Business Series titles. "Through SAS, we also publish books by SAS users on a variety of topics relating to SAS software. SAS titles enhance users' abilities to use SAS effectively. We're interested in publishing manuscripts that describe or illustrate using any of SAS products, including JMP software. Books must be aimed at SAS or JMP users, either new or experienced." Mss must reflect current or upcoming software releases, and the author's writing should indicate an understanding of SAS and the technical aspects covered in the ms. Query with SASE. Submit outline, sample chapters. Reviews artwork/photos.

SASQUATCH BOOKS

1904 Third Ave., Suite 710, Seattle WA 98101. (206)467-4300. **Fax:** (206)467-4301. **E-mail:** cust serv@sasquatchbooks.com. **Website:** www.sasquatchbooks.com. Estab. 1986. Publishes regional hardcover and trade paperback originals. "Sasquatch Books publishes books for and from the Pacific Northwest, Alaska, and California is the nation's premier regional press. Sasquatch Books' publishing program is a veritable celebration of regionally written words. Undeterred by political or geographical borders, Sasquatch defines its region as the magnificent area that stretches from the Brooks Range to the Gulf of California and from the Rocky Mountains to the Pacific Ocean. Our top-selling Best Places® travel guides serve the most popular destinations and locations of the West. We also publish widely in the areas of food and wine, gardening, nature, photography, children's books, and regional history, all facets of the literature of place. With more than 200 books brimming with insider information on the West, we offer an energetic eye on the lifestyle, landscape, and worldview of our region. Considers queries and proposals from authors and agents for new projects that fit into our West Coast regional publishing program. We can evaluate query letters, proposals, and complete mss." **Publishes 30 titles/year. 20% of books from first-time authors. 75% from unagented writers. Pays royalty on cover price. Pays wide range advance.** Publishes book 6-9 months after acceptance. Accepts simultaneous submissions. Responds to queries in 3 months. Guidelines online.

NONFICTION Subjects include animals, gardening, history, recreation, regional, sports, travel, outdoors. "We are seeking quality nonfiction works about the Pacific Northwest and West Coast regions (including Alaska to California). The literature of place includes how-to and where-to as well as history and narrative nonfiction." Picture books: activity books, animal, concept, nature/environment. "We publish a variety of nonfiction books, as well as children's books under our Little Bigfoot imprint." Query first, then submit outline and sample chapters with SASE. Send submissions to The Editors. E-mailed submissions and queries are not recommended. Please include return postage if you want your materials back.

FICTION Young readers: adventure, animal, concept, contemporary, humor, nature/environment.

TIPS "We sell books through a range of channels in addition to the book trade. Our primary audience consists of active, literate residents of the West Coast."

SATURNALIA BOOKS

105 Woodside Rd., Ardmore PA 19003. (267)278-9541. **E-mail:** info@saturnaliabooks.com. **Website:** www.saturnaliabooks.org. **Contact:** Henry Israeli, publisher. Estab. 2002. Publishes trade paperback originals and digital versions for e-readers. "We do not accept unsolicited submissions. We hold a contest, the Saturnalia Books Poetry Prize, annually in which 1 anonymously submitted title is chosen by a poet with a national reputation for publication. Submissions are accepted during the month of March. The submission fee is $30, and the prize is $2,000 and 20 copies of the book. See website for details." **Publishes 5 titles/year. Receives 600 mss/year. 33% of books from first-time authors. 100% from unagented writers. Pays authors 4-6% royalty on retail price. Pays $400-2,000 advance.** Accepts simultaneous submissions. Responds in 4 months on mss. Catalog online. No unsolicited submissions. Contest guidelines online.

POETRY "Saturnalia Books has no bias against any school of poetry, but we do tend to publish writers who take chances and push against convention in some way, whether it's in form, language, content, or musicality." Submit complete ms to contest only.

TIPS "Our audience tend to be young avid readers of contemporary poetry. Read a few sample books first."

SCARECROW PRESS, INC.

Imprint of Rowman & Littlefield Publishing Group, 4501 Forbes Blvd., Suite 200, Lanham MD 20706. (301)459-3366. **Fax:** (301)429-5748. **Website:** www.scarecrowpress.com. Estab. 1955. Publishes hardcover originals. Scarecrow Press publishes several series: Historical Dictionaries (includes countries, religions, international organizations, and area studies); Studies and Documentaries on the History of Popular Entertainment (forthcoming); Society, Culture and Libraries. Emphasis is on any title likely to appeal to libraries. Currently emphasizing jazz, Africana, and educational issues of contemporary interest. **Publishes 165 titles/year. 70% of books from first-time authors. 99% from unagented writers. Pays 8% royalty on net of**

first 1,000 copies; 10% of net price thereafter. Publishes ms 18 months after acceptance. Responds in 2 months to queries. Catalog and ms guidelines online.

NONFICTION Subjects include religion, sports, annotated bibliographies, handbooks and biographical dictionaries in the areas of women's studies and ethnic studies, parapsychology, fine arts and handicrafts, genealogy, sports history, music, movies, stage, library and information science.. Query with SASE.

SCHIFFER PUBLISHING, LTD.

4880 Lower Valley Rd., Atglen PA 19310. (610)593-1777. **Fax:** (610)593-2002. **E-mail:** info@schifferbooks.com. **Website:** www.schifferbooks.com. Estab. 1975. **Publishes 10-20 titles/year. Pays royalty on wholesale price.** Accepts simultaneous submissions. Responds in 2 weeks to queries. Book catalog available free. Guidelines online.

NONFICTION Art-quality illustrated regional histories. Looking for informed, entertaining writing and lots of subject areas to provide points of entry into the text for non-history buffs who buy a beautiful book because they are from, or love, an area. Full color possible in the case of historic postcards. Fax or e-mail outline, photos, and book proposal.

TIPS "We want to publish books for towns or cities with relevant population or active tourism to support book sales. A list of potential town vendors is a helpful start toward selling us on your book idea."

ⒶⓍ SCHOCKEN BOOKS

Imprint of Knopf Publishing Group, Division of Random House, Inc., 1745 Broadway, New York NY 10019. (212)572-9000. **Fax:** (212)572-6030. **Website:** www.schocken.com. Estab. 1945. Publishes hardcover and trade paperback originals and reprints. "Schocken publishes quality Judaica in all areas-fiction, history, biography, current affairs, spirituality and religious practices, popular culture, and cultural studies." *Does not accept unsolicited mss. Agented submissions only.* **Publishes 9-12 titles/year. Pays varied advance.** Accepts simultaneous submissions.

SCHOLASTIC, INC.

557 Broadway, New York NY 10012. (212)343-6100. **Website:** www.scholastic.com. Accepts simultaneous submissions.

IMPRINTS Arthur A. Levine Books, Cartwheel Books®, Chicken House®, David Fickling Books, Graphix™, Little Shepherd™, Orchard Books®, Point™,

PUSH, Scholastic en Español, Scholastic Licensed Publishing, Scholastic Nonfiction, Scholastic Paperbacks, Scholastic Press, Scholastic Reference™, and The Blue Sky Press® are imprints of the Scholastic Trade Books Division. In addition, Scholastic Trade Books included Klutz®, a highly innovative publisher and creator of "books plus" for children.

- Scholastic Trade Books is an award-winning publisher of original children's books. Scholastic publishes approximately 600 new hardcover, paperback and novelty books each year. The list includes the phenomenally successful publishing properties Harry Potter®, Goosebumps®, The 39 Clues™, I Spy™, and *The Hunger Games*; best-selling and award-winning authors and illustrators, including Blue Balliett, Jim Benton, Suzanne Collins, Christopher Paul Curtis, Ann M. Martin, Dav Pilkey, J.K. Rowling, Pam Muñoz Ryan, Brian Selznick, David Shannon, Mark Teague, and Walter Wick, among others; as well as licensed properties such as Star Wars® and Rainbow Magic®.

SCHOLASTIC CHILDREN'S BOOKS UK

Euston House, 24 Eversholt St., London VI NW1 1DB, United Kingdom. **E-mail:** contactus@scholastic.co.uk. **Website:** www.scholastic.co.uk. Accepts simultaneous submissions.

- Scholastic UK does not accept unsolicited submissions. Unsolicited illustrations are accepted, but please do not send any original artwork as it will not be returned.

TIPS "Getting work published can be a frustrating process, and it's often best to be prepared for disappointment, but don't give up."

SCHOLASTIC LIBRARY PUBLISHING

90 Old Sherman Turnpike, Danbury CT 06816. (203)797-3500. **Fax:** (203)797-3197. **E-mail:** slpservice@scholastic.com. **Website:** www.scholastic.com/librarypublishing. **Contact:** Phil Friedman, vice president/publisher; Kate Nunn, editor-in-chief; Marie O'Neil, art director. Estab. 1895. Publishes hardcover and trade paperback originals. "Scholastic Library is a leading publisher of reference, educational, and children's books. We provide parents, teachers, and librarians with the tools they need to enlighten children to the pleasure of learning and prepare them for the road ahead. Publishes informational (nonfiction) for K-12;

picture books for young readers, grades 1-3." **Pays authors royalty based on net or work purchased outright. Pays illustrators at competitive rates.**

IMPRINTS Grolier; Children's Press; Franklin Watts; Grolier Online.

- *Accepts agented submissions only.*

NONFICTION Photo-illustrated books for all levels: animal, arts/crafts, biography, careers, concept, geography, health, history, hobbies, how-to, multicultural, nature/environment, science, social issues, special needs, sports. Average word length: young readers—2,000; middle readers—8,000; young adult—15,000. Query; submit outline/synopsis, resume, and/or list of publications, and writing sample. SASE required for response.

FICTION Publishes 1 picture book series, Rookie Readers, for grades 1-2. Does not accept unsolicited mss. *Does not accept fiction proposals.*

SCHOLASTIC PRESS

Imprint of Scholastic, Inc., 557 Broadway, New York NY 10012. (212)343-6100. **Fax:** (212)343-4713. **Website:** www.scholastic.com. Publishes hardcover originals. Scholastic Press publishes fresh, literary picture book fiction and nonfiction; fresh, literary nonseries or nongenre-oriented middle grade and young adult fiction. Currently emphasizing subtly handled treatments of key relationships in children's lives; unusual approaches to commonly dry subjects, such as biography, math, history, or science. De-emphasizing fairy tales (or retellings), board books, genre, or series fiction (mystery, fantasy, etc.). **Publishes 60 titles/year. 2,500 queries received/year. 1% of books from first-time authors. Pays royalty on retail price. Pays variable advance.** Publishes book 2 years after acceptance. Responds in 3 months to queries; 6-8 months to mss.

NONFICTION Agented submissions and previously published authors only.

FICTION Subjects include juvenile, picture books, novels. Looking for strong picture books, young chapter books, appealing middle grade novels (ages 8-11) and interesting and well-written young adult novels. Wants fresh, exciting picture books and novels—inspiring, new talent. *Agented submissions only.*

TIPS "Read *currently* published children's books. Revise, rewrite, rework and find your own voice, style and subject. We are looking for authors with a strong and unique voice who can tell a great story and have the ability to evoke genuine emotion. Children's publishers are becoming more selective, looking for irresistible talent and fairly broad appeal, yet still very willing to take risks, just to keep the game interesting."

SCRIBE PUBLICATIONS

18-20 Edward St., Brunswick VIC 3056, Australia. (61)(3)9388-8780. **E-mail:** info@scribepub.com.au. **Website:** www.scribepublications.com.au. **Contact:** Anna Thwaites. Estab. 1976. Scribe has been operating as a wholly independent trade-publishing house for almost 40 years. What started off in 1976 as a desire on publisher Henry Rosenbloom's part to publish 'serious nonfiction' as a one-man band has turned into a multi-award-winning company with 20 staff members in two locations — Melbourne, Australia and London, England — and a scout in New York. Scribe publishes over 65 nonfiction and fiction titles annually in Australia and about 40 in the United Kingdom. "We currently have acquiring editors working in both our Melbourne and London offices. We spend each day sifting through submissions and manuscripts from around the world, and commissioning and editing local titles, in an uncompromising pursuit of the best books we can find, help create, and deliver to readers. We love what we do, and we hope you will, too." **Publishes 70 titles/year. 10-20% from unagented writers.** Guidelines online.

IMPRINTS Scribble.

NONFICTION Subjects include environment, history, memoirs, psychology, current affairs, social history. "Please refer first to our website before contacting us or submitting anything, because we explain there who we will accept proposals from."

FICTION Subjects include contemporary, historical, humor, literary, military, mystery, picture books, poetry, short story collections, suspense, translation, war, young adult. Submit synopsis, sample chapters, CV.

TIPS "We are only able to consider unsolicited submissions if you have a demonstrated background of writing and publishing for general readers."

SCRIBNER

Imprint of Simon & Schuster Adult Publishing Group, 1230 Avenue of the Americas, 12th Floor, New York NY 10020. (212)698-7000. **E-mail:** info@simonsays.com. **Website:** www.simonsays.com. Publishes hardcover originals. **Publishes 70-75 titles/year. Thousands queries received/year. 20% of books from** first-time authors. **Pays 7-15% royalty. Pays variable advance.** Publishes ms 9 months after acceptance. Accepts simultaneous submissions. Responds in 3 months to queries.

NONFICTION Subjects include education, ethnic, history, philosophy, psychology, religion, science, criticism. *Agented submissions only.*

FICTION Subjects include literary, mystery, suspense. *Agented submissions only.*

SEAL PRESS

Perseus Books Group, 1700 4th St., Berkeley CA 94710. (510)595-3664. **E-mail:** seal.press@perseusbooks.com. **E-mail:** emma.rose@perseusbooks.com. **Website:** www.sealpress.com. Estab. 1976. Publishes hardcover and trade paperback originals. "Seal Press is an imprint of the Perseus Book Group, a feminist book publisher interested in original, lively, radical, empowering and culturally diverse nonfiction by women addressing contemporary issues with the goal of informing women's lives. Currently emphasizing women outdoor adventurists, young feminists, political issues, health and fitness, parenting, personal finance, sex and relationships, and LGBT and gender topics. *Not accepting fiction at this time.*" **Publishes 30 titles/year. 1,000 queries received/year. 750 mss received/year. 25% of books from first-time authors. 50% from unagented writers. Pays 7-10% royalty on retail price. Pays variable royalty on retail price. Pays wide ranging advance.** Publishes ms 1 year after acceptance. Accepts simultaneous submissions. Responds in 2 months to queries. Book catalog and ms guidelines for SASE or online.

NONFICTION Subjects include alternative lifestyles, Americana, child guidance, contemporary culture, creative nonfiction, ethnic, gay, health, lesbian, memoirs, multicultural, parenting, politics, pop culture, sex, travel, womens issues, womens studies, popular culture, politics, domestic violence, sexual abuse. Query with SASE. Reviews artwork/photos. Send photocopies. No original art or photos accepted.

TIPS "Seeking empowering and progressive nonfiction that can impact a woman's life across categories."

SEARCH INSTITUTE PRESS

Search Institute, 615 First Ave. NE, Suite 125, Minneapolis MN 55413. (612)376-8955. **Fax:** (612)692-5553. **E-mail:** si@search-institute.org. **Website:** www.search-institute.org. Estab. 1958. Publishes trade paperback originals. **Publishes 12-15 titles/year. Pays**

royalty. Publishes book 1 year after acceptance. Accepts simultaneous submissions. Responds in 6 months. Catalog and guidelines online.

NONFICTION Subjects include career guidance, child guidance, community, counseling, education, entertainment, games, parenting, public affairs, social sciences, youth leadership, prevention, activities. Does not want children's picture books, poetry, New Age and religious-themes, memoirs, biographies, and autobiographies. Query with SASE. Does not review artwork/photos.

TIPS "Our audience is educators, youth program leaders, mentors, parents."

SEAWORTHY PUBLICATIONS, INC.

2023 N. Atlantic Ave., #226, Cocoa Beach FL 32931. (321)610-3634. **E-mail:** queries@seaworthy.com. **Website:** www.seaworthy.com. **Contact:** Joseph F. Janson, publisher. Publishes trade paperback originals, hardcover originals, and reprints. "Seaworthy Publications is a nautical book publisher that primarily publishes books of interest to recreational boaters and bluewater cruisers, including cruising guides, how-to books about boating. Currently emphasizing cruising guides." **Publishes 8 titles/year. 50 queries; 10 mss received/year. 60% of books from first-time authors. 100% from unagented writers. Pays 10% starting royalty based on wholesale price with increases up to 15% based on sales. Pays $1,000 advance.** Publishes ms 6 months after acceptance. Responds in 1 month to queries. Book catalog and guidelines online.

NONFICTION Subjects include environment, marine subjects, regional, sports, travel, sailing, boating, regional, boating guide books, boating how-to, Bahamas, Caribbean, travel. Regional guide books, first-person adventure, reference, how-to, technical—all dealing with boating. Query with SASE. Submit 3 sample chapters, TOC. Prefers electronic query via e-mail. Reviews artwork/photos. Send photocopies, color prints, or jpeg files.

TIPS "Our audience consists of sailors, boaters, and those interested in the sea, sailing, or long-distance cruising."

☉ SECOND STORY PRESS

20 Maud St., Suite 401, Toronto ON M5V 2M5, Canada. (416)537-7850. **Fax:** (416)537-0588. **E-mail:** info@secondstorypress.ca. **Website:** www.second-storypress.ca. "Please keep in mind that as a feminist press, we are looking for non-sexist, non-racist and non-violent stories, as well as historical fiction, chapter books, novels and biography." Accepts simultaneous submissions.

NONFICTION Subjects include community, contemporary culture, creative nonfiction, environment, gay, health, history, labor, lesbian, literature, memoirs, multicultural, politics, sociology, womens issues, womens studies, young adult. Picture books: biography. Accepts appropriate material from residents of Canada only. "Send a synopsis and up to 3 sample chapters. If you are submitting a picture book you can send the entire manuscript.

Illustrations are not necessary." No electronic submissions or queries. Guidelines on site.

FICTION Considers non-sexist, non-racist, and non-violent stories, as well as historical fiction, chapter books, picture books.

SEEDLING CONTINENTAL PRESS

520 E. Bainbridge St., Elizabethtown PA 17022. (800)233-0759; **Fax:** 888-834-1303. **Website:** www.continentalpress.com. "Continental publishes educational materials for grades K-12, specializing in reading, mathematics, and test preparation materials. We are not currently accepting submissions for Seedling leveled readers or instructional materials." **Work purchased outright from authors.** Publishes book 1-2 years after acceptance. Accepts simultaneous submissions. Responds to mss in 6 months.

NONFICTION Young readers: animal, arts/crafts, biography, careers, concept, multicultural, nature/environment, science. Does not accept texts longer than 12 pages or over 300 words. Average word length: young readers—100.

FICTION Young readers: adventure, animal, folktales, humor, multicultural, nature/environment. Does not accept texts longer than 12 pages or over 300 words. Average word length: young readers—100. Submit complete ms.

TIPS "See our website. Follow writers' guidelines carefully and test your story with children and educators."

☉ SELF-COUNSEL PRESS

1481 Charlotte Rd., North Vancouver BC V7J 1H1, Canada. (360)676-4530. **E-mail:** editor@self-counsel.com. **Website:** www.self-counsel.com. Estab. 1971.

Publishes trade paperback originals. Self-Counsel Press publishes a range of quality self-help books written in practical, nontechnical style by recognized experts in the fields of business, financial, or legal guidance for people who want to help themselves. **Publishes 30 titles/year. 1,500 queries received/year. 30% of books from first-time authors. 90% from unagented writers. Pays rare advance.** Publishes ms 8 months after acceptance. Accepts simultaneous submissions. Responds in 2 months to queries. Book catalog online. Guidelines online.

NONFICTION Subjects include legal issues for lay people. Submit proposal package, outline, resume, 2 sample chapters.

⊘ SENTIENT PUBLICATIONS

P.O. Box 7204, Boulder CO 80306. **Website:** www.sentientpublications.com. **Contact:** Connie Shaw, acquisitions editor. Estab. 2001. Publishes hardcover and trade paperback originals; trade paperback reprints. "We are not currently accepting submissions." **Publishes 4 titles/year. 200 queries; 100 mss received/year. 70% of books from first-time authors. 50% from unagented writers. Pays royalty on wholesale price. Sometimes pays advance.** Publishes ms 10 months after acceptance. Responds in 1 month to queries; 2 months to proposals and mss. Book catalog online.

NONFICTION Subjects include child guidance, contemporary culture, creative nonfiction, education, environment, gardening, history, philosophy, photography, psychology, science, social sciences, sociology, spirituality, travel. Does not review artwork/photos.

SERIOUSLY GOOD BOOKS

999 Vanderbilt Beach Rd., Naples FL 34108. **E-mail:** seriouslygoodbks@aol.com. **Website:** www.seriouslygoodbks.net. Estab. 2010. Publishes trade paperback and electronic originals. Publishes historical fiction only. **Publishes 2-5 titles/year. Pays 15% minimum royalties (print); more on digital.** Accepts simultaneous submissions. Responds in 1 month to queries. Book catalog and guidelines online.

FICTION Subjects include historical. Query letter by e-mail. See Submissions tab on website.

TIPS "Looking for historial fiction with substance. We seek well-researched historical fiction in the vein of Rutherfurd, Mary Renault, Maggie Anton, Robert Harris, etc. Please don't query with historical fiction mixed with other genres (romance, time travel, vampires, etc.)."

SEVEN STORIES PRESS

140 Watts St., New York NY 10013. (212)226-8760. **Fax:** (212)226-1411. **E-mail:** info@sevenstories.com. **Website:** www.sevenstories.com. **Contact:** Acquisitions. Estab. 1995. Publishes hardcover and trade paperback originals. Founded in 1995 in New York City, and named for the seven authors who committed to a home with a fiercely independent spirit, Seven Stories Press publishes works of the imagination and political titles by voices of conscience. While most widely known for its books on politics, human rights, and social and economic justice, Seven Stories continues to champion literature, with a list encompassing both innovative debut novels and National Book Award–winning poetry collections, as well as prose and poetry translations from the French, Spanish, German, Swedish, Italian, Greek, Polish, Korean, Vietnamese, Russian, and Arabic. **Publishes 40-50 titles/year. 15% of books from first-time authors. 50% from unagented writers. Pays 7-15% royalty on retail price. Pays advance.** Publishes ms 1-3 years after acceptance. Accepts simultaneous submissions. Responds in 1 month. Book catalog and ms guidelines free.

NONFICTION Responds only if interested. Submit cover letter with 2 sample chapters.

FICTION Subjects include literary. Submit cover letter with 2 sample chapters.

🅐🅢⊘ SEVERN HOUSE PUBLISHERS

Salatin House, 19 Cedar Rd., Sutton, Surrey SM2 5DA, United Kingdom. (44)(208)770-3930. **Fax:** (44)(208)770-3850. **Website:** www.severnhouse.com. Publishes hardcover and trade paperback originals and reprints. Severn House is currently emphasizing suspense, romance, mystery. Large print imprint from existing authors. **Publishes 150 titles/year. 400-500 queries received/year. 50 mss received/year. Pays 7-15% royalty on retail price. Pays $750-5,000 advance.** Accepts simultaneous submissions. Responds in 3 months to proposals. Book catalog available free.

FICTION Subjects include adventure, fantasy, historical, horror, mystery, romance, short story collections, suspense. *Agented submissions only.*

SHAMBHALA PUBLICATIONS, INC.

4720 Walnut St., Boulder CO 80304. **E-mail:** editors@shambhala.com. **Website:** www.shambhala.com. Estab. 1969. Publishes hardcover and trade paperback originals and reprints. **Publishes 90-100 titles/year. 500 queries; 1,200 mss/proposals received/year. 30% of books from first-time authors. 70% from unagented writers. Pays 8% royalty on retail price.** Publishes ms 1 year after acceptance. Accepts simultaneous submissions. Responds in 4 months. Book catalog free. Guidelines online.

IMPRINTS Roost Books; Snow Lion.

NONFICTION Subjects include cooking, crafts, parenting, Buddhism, martial arts, yoga, natural health, Eastern philosophy, creativity, green living, nature writing. To send a book proposal, include a synopsis of the book, see the submissions guidelines online. "We strongly prefer electronic submissions and do not take phone calls regarding book ideas or proposals."

⬤ SHEARSMAN BOOKS, LTD

50 Westons Hills Dr., Emersons Green Bristol BS16 7DF, United Kingdom. **E-mail:** editor@shearsman. com. **Website:** www.shearsman.com. **Contact:** Tony Frazer, editor. Estab. 1981. Publishes trade paperback originals. **Publishes 45-60 titles/year. Receives 2,000 submissions/year. 10% of books from first-time authors. 95% from unagented writers. Pays 10% royalty on retail price after 150 copies have sold; authors also receive 10 free copies of their books. Does not pay advance.** Publishes ms 9-12 months after acceptance. Accepts simultaneous submissions. Responds in 3 months to mss. Book catalog online. Guidelines online.

NONFICTION Subjects include literature, memoirs, translation, essays. All nonfiction has to do with poetry in some way. "We don't publish nonfiction unless it's related to poetry."

POETRY "Shearsman only publishes poetry, poetry collections, and poetry in translation (from any language but with an emphasis on work in Spanish & in German). Some critical work on poetry and also memoirs and essays by poets. Mainly poetry by British, Irish, North American, and Australian poets." No children's books. No devotional or religious verse.

TIPS "Book ms submission: most of the ms must have already appeared in the UK or USA magazines of some repute, and it has to fill 70-72 pages of half letter or A5 pages. You must have sufficient return postage. Submissions can also be made by e-mail. It is unlikely that a poet with no track record will be accepted for publication as there is no obvious audience for the work. Try to develop some exposure to UK and US magazines and try to assemble a MS only later."

SHIPWRECKT BOOKS PUBLISHING COMPANY LLC

309 W. Stevens Ave., Rushford MN 55971. (507)458-8190. **E-mail:** editor@shipwrecktbooks.com. **E-mail:** contact@shipwrecktbooks.com. **Website:** www.shipwrecktbooks.com. **Contact:** Tom Driscoll, managing editor. Publishes trade paperback originals, mass market paperback originals, and electronic originals. **Publishes 6 titles/year. Receives 1,000 submissions/ year. 50% of books from first-time authors. 100% from unagented writers. Authors receive a maximum of 35% royalties.** Average length of time between acceptance of a book-length ms and publication is 6 months. Accepts simultaneous submissions. Responds to queries within 6 months. Catalog and guidelines online.

IMPRINTS Rocket Science Press (literary); Up On Big Rock Poetry Series; Lost Lake Folk Art (memoir, biography, essays, and nonfiction).

NONFICTION Subjects include agriculture, alternative lifestyles, Americana, animals, creative nonfiction, environment, ethnic, foods, gardening, gay, government, health, history, hobbies, horticulture, house and home, lesbian, medicine, memoirs, military, multicultural, nature, nutrition, politics, recreation, regional, spirituality, sports, war, womens issues, world affairs, young adult. E-mail query first. All unsolicited mss returned unopened. Does not review artwork.

FICTION Subjects include adventure, comic books, ethnic, experimental, fantasy, historical, humor, literary, multicultural, mystery, poetry, regional, science fiction, suspense, young adult. E-mail query first. All unsolicited mss returned unopened.

POETRY Submit 3 sample poems by e-mail.

TIPS "Quality writing. Query first. Development and full editorial services available."

SILMAN-JAMES PRESS

3624 Shannon Rd., Los Angeles CA 90027. (323)661-9922. **Fax:** (323)661-9933. **Website:** www.silman-jamespress.com. Publishes trade paperback originals and reprints. **Pays variable royalty on retail price.** Accepts simultaneous submissions. Book catalog available free.

NONFICTION Pertaining to film, theatre, music, performing arts. Submit proposal package, outline, 1+

sample chapters. Will accept phone queries. Reviews artwork/photos. Send photocopies.

TIPS "Our audience ranges from people with a general interest in film (fans, etc.) to students of film and performing arts to industry professionals. We will accept 'query' phone calls."

SILVER DOLPHIN BOOKS

(858)457-2500. **E-mail:** infosilverdolphin@readerlink.com. **Website:** www.silverdolphinbooks.com. Silver Dolphin Books publishes activity, novelty, and educational nonfiction books for preschoolers to 12-year-olds. Highly interactive formats such as the Field Guides and Uncover series both educate and entertain older children. "We will consider submissions only from authors with previously published works." Accepts simultaneous submissions.

FICTION Submit cover letter with full proposal and SASE.

SILVERFISH REVIEW PRESS

P.O. Box 3541, Eugene OR 97403. (541)344-5060. **E-mail:** sfrpress@earthlink.net. **Website:** www.silverfishreviewpress.com. Estab. 1978. Publishes trade paperback originals. "Sponsors the Gerald Cable Book Award. This prize is awarded annually to a book length manuscript of original poetry by an author who has not yet published a full-length collection. There are no restrictions on the kind of poetry or subject matter; translations are not acceptable. Winners will receive $1,000, publication, and 25 copies of the book. Entries must be postmarked by October 15. Entries may be submitted by e-mail. See website for instructions." **Publishes 2-3 titles/year. 50% of books from first-time authors. 100% from unagented writers.** Accepts simultaneous submissions. Guidelines online.

TIPS "Read recent Silverfish titles."

SILVER LAKE PUBLISHING

P.O. Box 173, Aberdeen WA 98520. (360)532-5758. **Fax:** (360)532-5728. **E-mail:** publisher@silverlakepub.com. **Website:** www.silverlakepub.com. Estab. 1998. Publishes hardcover and trade paperback originals and reprints. **Pays royalty.** Accepts simultaneous submissions. Responds in 6-8 weeks to proposals. Book catalog available free. Guidelines available free.

NONFICTION No fiction or poetry. Submit outline, resume, 2 sample chapters, cover letter, synopsis. Submit via mail only.

SIMON & SCHUSTER

1230 Avenue of the Americas, New York NY 10020. (212)698-7000. **Website:** www.simonandschuster.com. *Accepts agented submissions only.* Accepts simultaneous submissions.

IMPRINTS Aladdin; Atheneum Books for Young Readers; Atria; Beach Lane Books; Folger Shakespeare Library; Free Press; Gallery Books; Howard Books; Little Simon; Margaret K. McElderry Books; Pocket; Scribner; Simon & Schuster; Simon & Schuster Books for Young Readers; Simon Pulse; Simon Spotlight; Threshold; Touchstone; Paula Wiseman Books.

SIMON & SCHUSTER BOOKS FOR YOUNG READERS

Imprint of Simon & Schuster Children's Publishing, 1230 Avenue of the Americas, New York NY 10020. (212)698-7000. **Fax:** (212)698-2796. **Website:** www.simonsayskids.com. Publishes hardcover originals. "Simon and Schuster Books For Young Readers is the Flagship imprint of the S&S Children's Division. We are committed to publishing a wide range of contemporary, commercial, award-winning fiction and nonfiction that spans every age of children's publishing. BFYR is constantly looking to the future, supporting our foundation authors and franchises, but always with an eye for breaking new ground with every publication. We publish high-quality fiction and nonfiction for a variety of age groups and a variety of markets. Above all, we strive to publish books that we are passionate about." *No unsolicited mss.* All unsolicited mss returned unopened. **Publishes 75 titles/year. Pays variable royalty on retail price.** Publishes ms 2-4 years after acceptance. Accepts simultaneous submissions. Guidelines online.

NONFICTION Subjects include history, biography. Picture books: concept. All levels: narrative, current events, biography, history. "We're looking for picture books or middle grade nonfiction that have a retail potential. No photo essays." *Agented submissions only.*

FICTION Subjects include fantasy, historical, humor, juvenile, mystery, picture books, science fiction, young adult. *Agented submissions only.*

TIPS "We're looking for picture books centered on a strong, fully-developed protagonist who grows or changes during the course of the story; YA novels that are challenging and psychologically complex; also imaginative and humorous middle-grade fiction. And we want nonfiction that is as engaging as fiction.

Our imprint's slogan is 'Reading You'll Remember.' We aim to publish books that are fresh, accessible and family-oriented; we want them to have an impact on the reader."

SIMPLY READ BOOKS

501-5525 W. Blvd., Vancouver BC V6M 3W6, Canada. E-mail: go@simplyreadbooks.com. Website: www.simplyreadbooks.com. Simply Read Books is current seeking mss in picture books, early readers, early chapter books, middle grade fiction, and graphic novels. Accepts simultaneous submissions.

FICTION Query or submit complete ms.

SKINNER HOUSE BOOKS

The Unitarian Universalist Association, 24 Farnsworth St., Boston MA 02210. (617)742-2100, ext. 603. **Fax:** (617)948-6466. **E-mail:** bookproposals@uua.org. **Website:** www.uua.org/publications/skinnerhouse. **Contact:** Betsy Martin. Estab. 1975. Publishes trade paperback originals and reprints. "We publish titles in Unitarian Universalist faith, liberal religion, history, biography, worship, and issues of social justice. Most of our children's titles are intended for religious education or worship use. They reflect Unitarian Universalist values. We also publish inspirational titles of poetic prose and meditations. Writers should know that Unitarian Universalism is a liberal religious denomination committed to progressive ideals. Currently emphasizing social justice concerns." **Publishes 10-20 titles/year. 30% of books from first-time authors. 100% from unagented writers.** Publishes book 1 year after acceptance. Accepts simultaneous submissions. Responds to queries in 1 month. Book catalog for 6×9 SAE with 3 first-class stamps. Guidelines online.

NONFICTION Subjects include religion, inspirational, church leadership. All levels: activity books, multicultural, music/dance, nature/environment, religion. Query or submit proposal with cover letter, TOC, 2 sample chapters. Reviews artwork/photos. Send photocopies.

FICTION Only publishes fiction for children's titles for religious instruction. Query.

TIPS "From outside our denomination, we are interested in manuscripts that will be of help or interest to liberal churches, Sunday School classes, parents, ministers, and volunteers. Inspirational/spiritual and children's titles must reflect liberal Unitarian Universalist values."

SKY PONY PRESS

307 W. 36th St., 11th Floor, New York NY 10018. (212)643-6816. **Fax:** (212)643-6819. **Website:** skyponypress.com. Estab. 2011. Sky Pony Press is the children's book imprint of Skyhorse Publishing. "Following in the footsteps of our parent company, our goal is to provide books for readers with a wide variety of interests." Accepts simultaneous submissions. Guidelines online.

NONFICTION "Our parent company publishes many excellent books in the fields of ecology, independent living, farm living, wilderness living, recycling, and other green topics, and this will be a theme in our children's books. We are also searching for books that have strong educational themes and that help inform children of the world in which they live." Submit proposal via e-mail.

FICTION "We will consider picture books, early readers, midgrade novels, novelties, and informational books for all ages." Submit ms or proposal.

SLEEPING BEAR PRESS

2395 South Huron Parkway #200, Ann Arbor MI 48104. (800)487-2323. **Fax:** (734)794-0004. **E-mail:** submissions@sleepingbearpress.com. **Website:** www.sleepingbearpress.com. **Contact:** Manuscript Submissions. Estab. 1998. Accepts simultaneous submissions. Book catalog available via e-mail.

FICTION Picture books: adventure, animal, concept, folktales, history, multicultural, nature/environment, religion, sports. Young readers: adventure, animal, concept, folktales, history, humor, multicultural, nature/environment, religion, sports. Average word length: picture books—1,800. Accepts unsolicited queries three times per year. See website for details. Query with sample of work (up to 15 pages) and SASE. Please address packages to Manuscript Submissions.

SMALL BEER PRESS

150 Pleasant St., #306, Easthampton MA 01027. (413)203-1636. **Fax:** (413)203-1636. **E-mail:** info@smallbeerpress.com. **Website:** www.smallbeerpress.com. Estab. 2000. Small Beer Press also publishes the zine *Lady Churchill's Rosebud Wristlet.* "SBP's books have recently received the Tiptree and Crawford Awards." **Publishes 6-10 titles/year.** Accepts simultaneous submissions.

FICTION Subjects include experimental, literary, short story collections, speculative. Does not accept unsolicited novel or short story collection mss. Send queries with first 10-20 pages and SASE.

TIPS "Please be familiar with our books first to avoid wasting your time and ours, thank you. E-mail queries will be deleted. Really."

SMITH AND KRAUS PUBLISHERS, INC.

177 Lyme Rd., Hanover NH 03755. (603)643-6431. **E-mail:** editor@smithandkraus.com. **Website:** smithandkraus.com. Estab. 1990. Publishes hardcover and trade paperback originals. **Publishes 35-40 titles/year. 10% of books from first-time authors. 10-20% from unagented writers. Pays 7% royalty on retail price. Pays $500-2,000 advance.** Publishes ms 1 year after acceptance. Responds in 1 month to queries; 2 months to proposals; 4 months to mss. Book catalog available free.

NONFICTION Subjects include drama. Does not return submissions. Query with SASE.

FICTION Does not return submissions. Query with SASE.

GIBBS SMITH, PUBLISHER

P.O. Box 667, Layton UT 84041. (801)544-9800. **Fax:** (801)546-8853. **E-mail:** debbie.uribe@gibbs-smith. com. **Website:** www.gibbs-smith.com. Estab. 1969. Publishes hardcover and trade paperback originals. "We publish books that enrich and inspire humankind. Currently emphasizing interior decorating and design, home reference. De-emphasizing novels and short stories." **Publishes 80 titles/year. 3,000-4,000 queries received/year. 50% of books from first-time authors. 75% from unagented writers. Pays 8-14% royalty on gross receipts. Offers advance based on first year saleability projections.** Publishes ms 1-2 years after acceptance. Accepts simultaneous submissions. Responds in 1 month to queries; 10 weeks to proposals and mss. Guidelines online.

NONFICTION Subjects include regional, interior design, cooking, business, western, outdoor/sports/recreation. Query by e-mail only.

SOFT SKULL PRESS INC.

Counterpoint, 2650 Ninth St., Suite 318, Berkeley CA 94710. (510)704-0230. **Fax:** (510)704-0268. **E-mail:** info@counterpointpress.com. **Website:** www.softskull.com. Publishes hardcover and trade paperback originals. "Here at Soft Skull we love books that are new, fun, smart, revelatory, quirky, groundbreaking, cage-rattling and/or/otherwise unusual." **Publishes**

40 titles/year. Pays 7-10% royalty. Average advance: $100-15,000. Publishes ms 6 months after acceptance. Accepts simultaneous submissions. Responds in 2 months to proposals; 3 months to mss. Book catalog and guidelines online.

NONFICTION Subjects include contemporary culture, creative nonfiction, entertainment, literature, pop culture. Send a cover letter describing your project and a full proposal along with 2 sample chapters.

FICTION Subjects include comic books, confession, contemporary, erotica, experimental, gay, lesbian, literary, mainstream, multicultural, short story collections. Does not consider poetry. Soft Skull Press no longer accepts digital submissions. Send a cover letter describing your project in detail and a completed ms. For graphic novels, send a minimum of five fully inked pages of art, along with a synopsis of your storyline. "Please do not send original material, as it will not be returned."

TIPS "See our website for updated submission guidelines."

SOHO PRESS, INC.

853 Broadway, New York NY 10003. (212)260-1900. **E-mail:** soho@sohopress.com. **Website:** www.sohopress. com. **Contact:** Bronwen Hruska, publisher; Mark Doten, senior editor. Estab. 1986. Publishes hardcover and trade paperback originals; trade paperback reprints. Soho Press publishes primarily fiction, as well as some narrative literary nonfiction and mysteries set abroad. No electronic submissions, only queries by e-mail. **Publishes 60-70 titles/year. 15-25% of books from first-time authors. 10% from unagented writers. Pays 10-15% royalty on retail price (varies under certain circumstances).** Publishes ms 18 months after acceptance. Accepts simultaneous submissions. Responds in 3 months. Guidelines online.

NONFICTION Subjects include creative nonfiction, ethnic, memoirs. "Independent publisher known for sophisticated fiction, mysteries set abroad, women's interest (no genre) novels and multicultural novels." Publishes hardcover and trade paperback originals and reprint editions. Books: perfect binding; halftone illustrations. First novel print order varies. We do not buy books on proposal. We always need to see a complete ms before we buy a book, though we prefer an initial submission of 3 sample chapters. We do not publish books with color art or photographs or a lot of graphical material." No self-help, how-to, or cookbooks. Submit 3 sample chapters and a cover letter with a synopsis and author bio; SASE. Send photocopies.

FICTION Subjects include ethnic, historical, humor, literary, mystery, In mysteries, we only publish series with foreign or exotic settings, usually procedurals.. Adventure, ethnic, feminist, historical, literary, mainstream/contemporary, mystery (police procedural), suspense, multicultural. Submit 3 sample chapters and cover letter with synopsis, author bio, SASE. *No e-mailed submissions.*

TIPS "Soho Press publishes discerning authors for discriminating readers, finding the strongest possible writers and publishing them. Before submitting, look at our website for an idea of the types of books we publish, and read our submission guidelines."

SOURCEBOOKS, INC.

1935 Brookdale Rd., Suite 139, Naperville IL 60563. (630)961-3900. **Fax:** (630)961-2168. **E-mail:** editorialsubmissions@sourcebooks.com. **Website:** www.sourcebooks.com. Estab. 1987. Publishes hardcover and trade paperback originals. "Sourcebooks publishes many forms of fiction and nonfiction titles, including books on parenting, self-help/psychology, business, and health. Focus is on practical, useful information and skills. It also continues to publish in the reference, New Age, history, current affairs, and humor categories. Currently emphasizing gift, women's interest, history, reference, historical fiction, romance genre, and children's." **Publishes 300 titles/year. 30% of books from first-time authors. 25% from unagented writers. Pays royalty on wholesale or list price. Pays advance.** Publishes ms 1 year after acceptance. Accepts simultaneous submissions. Responds in 3 months to queries. Book catalog online. Guidelines online.

NONFICTION Subjects include child guidance, history, psychology, science, sports, contemporary culture. Books for small business owners, entrepreneurs, and students. A key to submitting books to us is to explain how your book helps the reader, why it is different from the books already out there (please do your homework), and the author's credentials for writing this book. Books likely to succeed with us are self-help, parenting and childcare, psychology, women's issues, how-to, history, reference, biography, humor, gift books, or books with strong artwork. "We seek unique books on traditional subjects and authors who are smart and aggressive." Query with SASE, 2-3 sample chapters (not the first). *No complete mss.* Reviews artwork/photos.

TIPS "Our market is a decidedly trade-oriented bookstore audience. We also have very strong penetration into the gift-store market. Books which cross over between these 2 very different markets do extremely well with us. Our list is a solid mix of unique and general audience titles and series-oriented projects. We are looking for products that break new ground either in their own areas or within the framework of our series of imprints."

SOURCEBOOKS CASABLANCA

Sourcebooks, Inc., 232 Madison Ave., Suite 1100, New York NY 10016. **E-mail:** romance@sourcebooks.com. **Website:** www.sourcebooks.com. **Contact:** Deb Werksman (deb.werksman@sourcebooks.com). "Our romance imprint, Sourcebooks Casablanca, publishes single title romance in all subgenres." Accepts simultaneous submissions. Responds in 2-3 months. Guidelines online.

FICTION "Our editorial criteria call for: a heroine the reader can relate to, a hero she can fall in love with, a world gets created that the reader can escape into, there's a hook that we can sell within 2-3 sentences, and the author is out to build a career with us."

TIPS "We are actively acquiring single-title and single-title series romance fiction (90,000-100,000 words) for our Casablanca imprint. We are looking for strong writers who are excited about marketing their books and building their community of readers, and whose books have something fresh to offer in the genre of romance."

SOURCEBOOKS FIRE

1935 Brookdale Rd., Suite 139, Naperville IL 60563. (630)961-3900. **Fax:** (630)961-2168. **E-mail:** submissions@sourcebooks.com. **Website:** www.sourcebooks.com. "We're actively acquiring knockout books for our YA imprint. We are particularly looking for strong writers who are excited about promoting and building their community of readers, and whose books have something fresh to offer the ever-growing young adult audience. We are not accepting any unsolicited or unagented manuscripts at this time. Unfortunately, our staff can no longer handle the large volume of manuscripts that we receive on a daily basis. We will continue to consider agented manuscripts."

See website for details. Accepts simultaneous submissions.

FICTION Query with the full ms attached in Word doc.

SOURCEBOOKS LANDMARK

Sourcebooks, Inc., 232 Madison Ave., Suite 1100, New York NY 10016. **E-mail:** editorialsubmissions@sourcebooks.com. **Website:** www.sourcebooks.com. "Our fiction imprint, Sourcebooks Landmark, publishes a variety of commercial fiction, including specialties in historical fiction and Austenalia. We are interested first and foremost in books that have a story to tell." Accepts simultaneous submissions. Responds in 2-3 months.

FICTION "We are actively acquiring contemporary, book club, and historical fiction for our Landmark imprint. We are looking for strong writers who are excited about marketing their books and building their community of readers." Submit synopsis and full ms preferred. Receipt of e-mail submissions acknowledged within 3 weeks of e-mail.

SOUTHERN ILLINOIS UNIVERSITY PRESS

1915 University Press Dr., SIUC Mail Code 6806, Carbondale IL 62901. (618)453-6613. **Fax:** (618)453-1221. **E-mail:** kageff@siu.edu. **Website:** www.siupress.com. **Contact:** Karl Kageff, editor-in-chief. Estab. 1956. Publishes hardcover and trade paperback originals and reprints. Scholarly press specializes in theater studies, rhetoric and composition studies, American history, Civil War, regional and nonfiction trade, poetry. No fiction. Currently emphasizing theater and American history, especially Civil War. **Publishes 36-40 titles/year. 300 queries; 80 mss received/year. 40% of books from first-time authors. 99% from unagented writers. Pays 5-10% royalty on wholesale price. Rarely offers advance.** Publishes ms 1 year after acceptance. Responds in 2 months to queries. Book catalog and ms guidelines free.

NONFICTION Subjects include archeology, history, language, military, regional, stage, war, womens studies.

POETRY Crab Orchard Series in Poetry. Guidelines online.

SPENCER HILL PRESS

P.O. Box 243, Marlborough CT 06447. (860)207-2206. **E-mail:** submissions@spencerhillpress.com. **Website:** www.spencerhillpress.com. **Contact:** Jennifer Carson. Spencer Hill Press is an independent publishing house specializing in sci-fi, urban fantasy, and paranormal romance for young adult readers. "Our books have that 'I couldn't put it down!' quality." Accepts simultaneous submissions. Guidelines online.

FICTION "We are interested in young adult, new adult, and middle grade sci-fi, psych-fi, paranormal, or urban fantasy, particularly those with a strong and interesting voice." Check website for open submission periods.

SPINNER BOOKS

University Games, 2030 Harrison St., San Francisco CA 94110. (415)503-1600. **Fax:** (415)503-0085. **E-mail:** info@ugames.com. **Website:** www.ugames.com. Estab. 1985. "Spinners Books publishes books of puzzles, games and trivia." Publishes book 6 months after acceptance. Accepts simultaneous submissions. Responds to queries in 3 months; mss in 2 months only if interested.

NONFICTION Picture books: games and puzzles. Query.

SPLASHING COW BOOKS

P.O. Box 867, Manchester VT 05254. **Website:** www.splashingcowbooks.com. **Contact:** Gordon McClellan, publisher. Estab. 2014. Publishes mass market paperback and electronic originals. Splashing Cow Books publishes books under three imprints: Splashing Cow (children), Blue Boot (women) and Yellow Dot (any other topic that interests us!). Four Splashing Cow authors in the last year (our first year) won national awards for their work. Splashing Cow also recently launched DartFrog, which selects self-published books of distinction for distribution. **Publishes 10 titles/year. 100% of books from first-time authors. 100% from unagented writers. Pays royalties on retail price. Does not offer an advance.** Accepts simultaneous submissions. We try to respond in 1 week to all inquiries, but it can take longer. Catalog available online. Guidelines available online.

IMPRINTS Blue Boot Books imprint publishes books for women. Yellow Dot publishes general interest topics.

NONFICTION Open to any topic that would be of interest to children, women or general interest.

FICTION Subjects include adventure, comic books, contemporary, ethnic, fantasy, historical, humor, juvenile, literary, mainstream, multicultural, mystery, picture books, science fiction, short story collections, spiritual, sports, suspense, western. Interested in a wide range of subject matter for children and women. Please check our website for submission guidelines.

SQUARE ONE PUBLISHERS, INC.

115 Herricks Rd., Garden City Park NY 11040. (516)535-2010. **Fax:** (516)535-2014. **E-mail:** sq1publish@aol.com. **Website:** www.squareonepublishers.com. **Contact:** Acquisitions Editor. Publishes trade paperback originals. **Publishes 20 titles/year. 500 queries; 100 mss received/year. 95% of books from first-time authors. 95% from unagented writers. Pays 10-15% royalty on wholesale price. Pays variable advance.** Publishes ms 10 months after acceptance. Accepts simultaneous submissions. Responds in 1 month. Book catalog and ms guidelines online.

NONFICTION Subjects include child guidance, cooking, health, hobbies, nutrition, psychology, religion, spirituality, sports, travel, writers' guides, cooking/foods, gaming/gambling. Query with SASE. Submit proposal package, outline, bio, introduction, synopsis, SASE. Reviews artwork/photos. Send photocopies.

TIPS "We focus on making our books accessible, accurate, and interesting. They are written for people who are looking for the best place to start, and who don't appreciate the terms 'dummy,' 'idiot,' or 'fool,' on the cover of their books. We look for smartly written, informative books that have a strong point of view, and that are authored by people who know their subjects well."

STANDARD PUBLISHING

Standex International Corp., 4050 Lee Vance View, Colorado Springs CO 80918. (800)323-7543. **Fax:** (800)323-0726. **Website:** www.standardpub.com. Estab. 1866. Publishes resources that meet church and family needs in the area of children's ministry. Guidelines online.

STANFORD UNIVERSITY PRESS

425 Broadway St., Redwood City CA 94063. (650)723-9434. **Fax:** (650)725-3457. **E-mail:** kwahl@stanford.edu. **Website:** www.sup.org. **Contact:** Kate Wahl, publishing director, editor-in-chief. Estab. 1925. "Stanford University Press publishes scholarly books in the humanities and social sciences, along with professional books in business, economics and management science; also high-level textbooks and some

books for a more general audience." *Submit to specific editor*. **Pays variable royalty (sometimes none). Pays occasional advance.** Guidelines online.

NONFICTION Subjects include ethnic, history, humanities, literary criticism, philosophy, psychology, religion, science, social sciences, sociology, political science, law, education, history and culture of China, Japan and Latin America, European history, linguistics, geology, medieval and classical studies. Query with prospectus and an outline. Reviews artwork/photos.

TIPS "The writer's best chance is a work of original scholarship with an argument of some importance."

STAR BRIGHT BOOKS

13 Landsdowne St., Cambridge MA 02139. (617)354-1300. **Fax:** (617)354-1399. **E-mail:** info@starbrightbooks.com. **Website:** www.starbrightbooks.com. Star Bright Books does accept unsolicited mss and art submissions. "We welcome submissions for picture books and longer works, both fiction and nonfiction." Also beginner readers and chapter books. Query first. **Publishes 18 titles/year. 75% of books from first-time authors. 99% from unagented writers. Pays advance.** Publishes ms 1-2 years after acceptance. Accepts simultaneous submissions. Responds in several months. Catalog available.

NONFICTION Almost anything of interest to children. Very keen on Biographies and any thing of interest to children.

STC CRAFT

Imprint of Abrams, 115 W. 18th St., New York NY 10011. **E-mail:** stccraft@abramsbooks.com; abrams@abramsbooks.com. **Website:** www.abramsbooks.com. **Contact:** STC craft editorial. Publishes a vibrant collection of exciting and visually stunning craft books specializing in knitting, sewing, quilting, felting, and other popular craft genres. Accepts simultaneous submissions. Guidelines online.

NONFICTION Subjects include crafts. Please submit via e-mail.

STEEL TOE BOOKS

Department of English, Western Kentucky University, 1906 College Heights Blvd. #11086, Bowling Green KY 42101. (270)745-5769. **E-mail:** tom.hunley@wku.edu. **Website:** www.steeltoebooks.com. **Contact:** Dr. Tom C. Hunley, director. Estab. 2003. Steel Toe Books publishes "full-length, single-author poetry collections. Our books are professionally designed and printed. We look for workmanship (economical use of language, high-energy verbs, precise literal descriptions, original figurative language, poems carefully arranged as a book); a unique style and/or a distinctive voice; clarity; emotional impact; humor (word plays, hyperbole, comic timing); performability (a Steel Toe poet is at home on the stage as well as on the page)." Does not want "dry verse, purposely obscure language, poetry by people who are so wary of being called 'sentimental' they steer away from any recognizable human emotions, poetry that takes itself so seriously that it's unintentionally funny." Has published poetry by Allison Joseph, Susan Browne, James Doyle, Martha Silano, Mary Biddinger, John Guzlowski, Jeannine Hall Gailey, and others. Publishes 1-3 poetry books/year. Mss are normally selected through open submission. Accepts simultaneous submissions.

POETRY "Check the website for news about our next open reading period." Book mss may include previously published poems. Responds to mss in 3 months. Pays $500 advance on 10% royalties and 10 author's copies. Order sample books by sending $12 to Steel Toe Books. *Must purchase a ms in order to submit.* See website for submission guidelines.

STENHOUSE PUBLISHERS

480 Congress St., Floor 2, Portland ME 04101. **E-mail:** editors@stenhouse.com. **Website:** www.stenhouse.com. **Contact:** Philippa Stratton, editorial director. Estab. 1993. Publishes paperback originals. Stenhouse publishes exclusively professional books for teachers, K-12. **Publishes 15 titles/year. 300 queries received/year. 30% of books from first-time authors. 99% from unagented writers. Pays royalty on wholesale price.** Accepts simultaneous submissions. Responds in 2 weeks to queries; 1 month to mss. Book catalog free or online. Guidelines online.

NONFICTION Subjects include education, specializing in literary with offerings in elementary and middle level math and science. All of our books are a combination of theory and practice. No children's books or student texts. Query by e-mail (preferred) or SASE. Reviews artwork/photos. Send photocopies.

STERLING PUBLISHING CO., INC.

1166 Avenue of the Americas, 17th Floor, New York NY 10036. (212)532-7160. **Fax:** (212)981-0508. **Website:** www.sterlingpublishing.com. Publishes hard-cover and paperback originals and reprints. "Sterling publishes highly illustrated, accessible, hands-on, practical books for adults and children. Our mission is to publish high-quality books that educate, entertain, and enrich the lives of our readers." **15% of books from first-time authors. Pays royalty or work purchased outright. Offers advances (average amount: $2,000).** Accepts simultaneous submissions. Catalog online. Guidelines online.

NONFICTION Subjects include animals, ethnic, gardening, hobbies, New Age, recreation, science, sports, fiber arts, games and puzzles, children's humor, children's science, nature and activities, pets, wine, home decorating, dolls and puppets, ghosts, UFOs, woodworking, crafts, medieval, Celtic subjects, alternative health and healing, new consciousness. Proposals on subjects such as crafting, decorating, outdoor living, and photography should be sent directly to Lark Books at their Asheville, North Carolina offices. Complete guidelines can be found on the Lark site: www.larkbooks.com/submissions. Publishes nonfiction only. Submit outline, publishing history, 1 sample chapter (typed and double-spaced), SASE. "Explain your idea. Send sample illustrations where applicable. For children's books, please submit full mss. We do not accept electronic (e-mail) submissions. Be sure to include information about yourself with particular regard to your skills and qualifications in the subject area of your submission. It is helpful for us to know your publishing history—whether or not you've written other books and, if so, the name of the publisher and whether those books are currently in print." Reviews artwork/photocopies.

FICTION Publishes fiction for children. Submit to attention of "Children's Book Editor."

TIPS "We are primarily a nonfiction activities-based publisher. We have a picture book list, but we do not publish chapter books or novels. Our list is not trend-driven. We focus on titles that will backlist well. "

STIPES PUBLISHING LLC

P.O. Box 526, Champaign IL 61824. (217)356-8391. **Fax:** (217)356-5753. **E-mail:** stipes01@sbcglobal.net. **Website:** www.stipes.com. Estab. 1925. Publishes hardcover and paperback originals. "Stipes Publishing is oriented towards the education market and educational books with some emphasis in the trade market." **Publishes 15-30 titles/year. 50% of books from first-time authors. 95% from unagented writ-**

ers. **Pays 15% maximum royalty on retail price.** Publishes ms 4 months after acceptance. Responds in 2 months to queries. Guidelines online.

NONFICTION Subjects include agriculture, recreation, science. "All of our books in the trade area are books that also have a college text market. No books unrelated to educational fields taught at the college level." Submit outline, 1 sample chapter.

STONE ARCH BOOKS

1710 Roe Crest Rd., North Mankato MN 56003. **E-mail:** author.sub@capstonepub.com. **Website:** www.stonearchbooks.com. **Work purchased outright from authors.** Accepts simultaneous submissions. Catalog online.

FICTION Imprint of Capstone Publishers. Young readers, middle readers, young adults: adventure, contemporary, fantasy, humor, light humor, mystery, science fiction, sports, suspense. Average word length: young readers—1,000-3,000; middle readers and early young adults—5,000-10,000. Submit outline/synopsis and 3 sample chapters. Electronic submissions preferred. Full guidelines available on website.

TIPS "A high-interest topic or activity is one that a young person would spend their free time on without adult direction or suggestion."

STONE BRIDGE PRESS

P.O. Box 8208, Berkeley CA 94707. **E-mail:** sbp@stonebridge.com. **Website:** www.stonebridge.com. **Contact:** Peter Goodman, publisher. Estab. 1989. "Independent press focusing on books about Japan and Asia in English (business, language, culture, literature, animation)." Publishes hardcover and trade paperback originals. Books: 60-70 lb. offset paper; web and sheet paper; perfect bound; some illustrations. Distributes titles through Consortium. Promotes titles through Internet announcements, special-interest magazines and niche tie-ins to associations. **Publishes 12 titles/year. 75% from unagented writers. Pays royalty on wholesale price.** Publishes ms 2 years after acceptance. Accepts simultaneous submissions. Responds to queries in 4 months; mss in 8 months. Available for download from company website. Ms guidelines online.

NONFICTION Subjects include business, cinema, crafts, creative nonfiction, film, house and home, language, literature, memoirs, nature, philosophy, pop culture, sex, spirituality, travel, womens issues.

FICTION Subjects include comic books, contemporary, erotica, literary, translation. Experimental, gay/lesbian, literary, Asia-themed. "Primarily looking at material relating to Asia, especially Japan and China. " Does not accept unsolicited mss. Accepts queries by e-mail.

POETRY No poetry.

TIPS "Fiction translations only for the time being. No poetry. Looking also for graphic novels, not manga or serializations."

STONESLIDE BOOKS

Stoneslide Media LLC, P.O. Box 8331, New Haven CT 06530. **E-mail:** editors@stoneslidecorrective.com. **E-mail:** submissions@stoneslidecorrective.com. **Website:** www.stoneslidecorrective.com. **Contact:** Jonathan Weisberg, editor; Christopher Wachlin, editor. Estab. 2012. Publishes trade paperback and electronic originals. "We like novels with strong character development and narrative thrust, brought out with writing that's clear and expressive." **Publishes 3-5 titles/year. Receives 300 queries/year; 150 mss/year. 100% of books from first-time authors. 100% from unagented writers. Pays 20-80% royalty.** Publishes book 8 months after acceptance. Responds in 1-2 months. Book catalog and guidelines online.

FICTION Subjects include adventure, contemporary, experimental, fantasy, gothic, historical, humor, literary, mainstream, mystery, science fiction, short story collections, suspense. "We will look at any genre. The important factor for us is that the story use plot, characters, emotions, and other elements of storytelling to think and move the mind forward." Submit proposal package via online submission form including: synopsis and 3 sample chapters.

TIPS "Read the Stoneslide Corrective to see if your work fits with our approach."

STOREY PUBLISHING

210 MASS MoCA Way, North Adams MA 01247. (800)793-9396. **Fax:** (413)346-2196. **E-mail:** feedback@storey.com. **Website:** www.storey.com. Estab. 1983. Publishes hardcover and trade paperback originals and reprints. "The mission of Storey Publishing is to serve our customers by publishing practical information that encourages personal independence in harmony with the environment. We seek to do this in a positive atmosphere that promotes editorial quality, team spirit, and profitability. The books we select

to carry out this mission include titles on gardening, small-scale farming, building, cooking, home brewing, crafts, part-time business, home improvement, woodworking, animals, nature, natural living, personal care, and country living. We are always pleased to review new proposals, which we try to process expeditiously. We offer both work-for-hire and standard royalty contracts." **Publishes 40 titles/year. 600 queries received/year. 150 mss received/year. 25% of books from first-time authors. 60% from unagented writers. We offer both work-for-hire and standard royalty contracts. Pays advance.** Publishes book 2 years after acceptance. Accepts simultaneous submissions. Responds in 1-3 months. Book catalog available free. Guidelines online.

NONFICTION Subjects include animals, gardening, home, mind/body/spirit, birds, beer and wine, crafts, building, cooking. Submit a proposal. Reviews artwork/photos.

STRATEGIC MEDIA BOOKS

782 Wofford St., Rock Hill SC 29730. (803)366-5440. **E-mail:** contact@strategicmediabooks.com. **Website:** strategicmediabooks.com. Estab. 2010. Publishes hardcover, trade paperback, and electronic originals. "Strategic Media Books, LLC is an independent U.S. publisher that aims to bring extraordinary true-life stories to the widest possible audience. Founded in 2010, Strategic Media Books intends to be one of the most energetic and hard-hitting nonfiction publishers in the business. While we currently specialize in true crime, we plan to expand and publish great books in any nonfiction genre." **Publishes 16-20 titles/year. 100 queries received/year. 30-35 mss received/year. 20% of books from first-time authors. 85% from unagented writers. Authors receive 15-20% royalty on retail price.** Publishes book 9 months after acceptance. Accepts simultaneous submissions. Responds in 1-2 months. Catalog online. Guidelines via e-mail.

NONFICTION Subjects include Americana, contemporary culture, environment, ethnic, government, history, memoirs, military, multicultural, nature, politics, regional, war, world affairs, true crime. Planning to increase the number of books for the 2014 and 2015 seasons. Query with SASE. Will review artwork. Writers should send photocopies.

FICTION Subjects include mystery, suspense. "We are very selective in our publication of fiction. If writers want to submit, make sure mss fits the mystery or suspense genres." Query with SASE.

STRAWBERRIES PRESS

750 Pinehurst Dr., Rio Vista CA 94571. (707)398-6430. **E-mail:** books@strawberriespress.com. **Website:** www.strawberriespress.com. **Contact:** Susan Zhang, Executive Editor. Estab. 2015. Publishes interactive flipbooks on CDs. Strawberries Press publishes full-color, interactive and digitally enhanced, children's picture flipbooks on CDs that are designed to be viewed and read on computer screens and that explore exciting subjects that stimulate young minds. **Publishes 6 titles/year. Receives 12-20 queries/year; 12 mss/year. 50% of books from first-time authors. 100% from unagented writers. Pays for outright purchase between $250-500.** Publishes mss in 3-4 months upon acceptance. Responds in 1 month. Catalog available online. Guidelines available by e-mail.

NONFICTION Subjects include anthropology, archeology, architecture, art, creative nonfiction, education, environment, ethnic, hobbies, marine subjects, nature, photography, science, sports, transportation, young adult. Interested in topics that explore exciting subjects that stimulate young minds in both the fiction and nonfiction genres. For examples of subject matter and format requirements, see online catalog of flipbook titles. "We only publish wholesome learning resources and educationally constructive subject matter that retains, promotes, and enhances the innocence of children. Political, immoral, antisocial, propagandist, and other age-inappropriate themes are strictly prohibited at Strawberries Press. We do not use our publications as social engineering and brainwashing tools." Submit completed ms. Writers should sent artwork/photographs with manuscript, if available. All art/photo submissions are provided as unsolicited; Strawberries Press is not responsible for the loss or damage of art/photos; therefore, do not send irreplaceable original work. Send copies only.

TIPS "Although there are no restrictions on the number of sentences on a single page, all flipbooks are limited to 40 pages. For text, illustrating, and formatting examples, view our sample online flipbook."

STYLUS PUBLISHING, LLC

22883 Quicksilver Dr., Sterling VA 20166. **E-mail:** sylusinfo@styluspub.com. **Website:** styluspub.com. Estab. 1996. Publishes hardcover and trade paperback originals. "We publish in higher education (diversity, professional development, distance education, teaching, administration)." **Publishes 10-15 titles/year. 50 queries received/year. 6 mss received/year. 50% of books from first-time authors. 100% from unagented writers. Pays 5-10% royalty on wholesale price. Pays advance.** Publishes ms 6 months after acceptance. Responds in 1 month to queries. Book catalog available free. Guidelines online.

NONFICTION Query or submit outline, 1 sample chapter with SASE. Reviews artwork/photos. Send photocopies.

SUBITO PRESS

University of Colorado at Boulder, Dept. of English, 226 UCB, Boulder CO 80309-0226. **E-mail:** subitopressucb@gmail.com. **Website:** www.subitopress.org. Publishes trade paperback originals. Subito Press is a non-profit publisher of literary works. Each year Subito publishes one work of fiction and one work of poetry through its contest. Accepts simultaneous submissions. Guidelines online.

FICTION Subjects include experimental, literary, translation. Submit complete ms to contest.

POETRY Submit complete ms to contest.

TIPS "We publish 2 books of innovative writing a year through our poetry and fiction contests. All entries are also considered for publication with the press."

SUN BOOKS / SUN PUBLISHING

P.O. Box 5588, Santa Fe NM 87502. (505)471-5177. **E-mail:** info@sunbooks.com. **Website:** www.sunbooks.com; www.abooksource.com. **Contact:** Skip Whitson, director. Estab. 1973. Publishes trade paperback originals and reprints. Not accepting new mss at this time. **Publishes 10-15 titles/year. 5% of books from first-time authors. 90% from unagented writers. Pays 5% royalty on retail price. Occasionally makes outright purchase.** Publishes ms 16-18 months after acceptance. Accepts simultaneous submissions. "Will respond within 2 months, via e-mail, to queries if interested.". Book catalog online. Queries via e-mail only, please.

NONFICTION Subjects include agriculture, alternative lifestyles, Americana, astrology, career guidance, environment, history, New Age, regional, self-help, leadership, motivational, recovery, inspirational.

SUNBURY PRESS, INC.

105 S Market St., Mechanicsburg PA 17055. **E-mail:** info@sunburypress.com. **E-mail:** proposals@sunburypress.com. **Website:** www.sunburypress.com. Estab. 2004. Publishes trade paperback and hardcover originals and reprints; electronic originals and reprints. Sunbury Press, Inc., headquartered in Mechanicsburg, PA is a publisher of trade paperback, hard cover and digital books featuring established and emerging authors in many fiction and nonfiction categories. Sunbury's books are printed in the USA and sold through leading booksellers worldwide. "Please use our online submission form." **Publishes 60 titles/year. Receives 1,000 queries/year; 500 mss/year. 40% of books from first-time authors. 90% from unagented writers. Pays 10% royalty on wholesale price.** Publishes ms 6 months after acceptance. Accepts simultaneous submissions. Responds in 3 months. Catalog and guidelines online.

NONFICTION Subjects include agriculture, Americana, animals, anthropology, archeology, architecture, art, astrology, business, career guidance, child guidance, communications, computers, contemporary culture, counseling, crafts, creative nonfiction, economics, education, electronics, entertainment, ethnic, government, health, history, hobbies, house and home, humanities, language, literature, memoirs, military, money, music, nature, New Age, psychic, public affairs, regional, religion, science, sex, spirituality, sports, transportation, travel, war, world affairs, young adult. "We are currently seeking war memoirs of all kinds and local / regional histories and biographies." Reviews artwork.

FICTION Subjects include adventure, confession, contemporary, ethnic, experimental, fantasy, gothic, historical, horror, humor, juvenile, mainstream, military, multicultural, mystery, occult, regional, religious, romance, science fiction, short story collections, spiritual, sports, suspense, western, young adult. "We are especially seeking climate change / dystopian fiction and books of regional interest."

POETRY Submit complete ms.

TIPS "Our books appeal to very diverse audiences. We are building our list in many categories, focusing on many demographics. We are not like traditional publishers—we are digitally adept and very creative. Don't be surprised if we move quicker than you are accustomed to!"

SUNRISE RIVER PRESS

838 Lake St. S., Forest Lake MN 55025. (800)895-4585. **Fax:** (651)277-1203. **E-mail:** info@sunriserpress.

com. **Website:** www.sunriseriverpress.com. Estab. 1992. "E-mail is preferred method of contact." **Publishes 30 titles/year. Pays advance.** Accepts simultaneous submissions. Guidelines online.

○ Sunrise River Press is part of a 3-company publishing house that also includes CarTech Books and Specialty Press. "Sunrise River Press is currently seeking book proposals from health/medical writers or experts who are interested in authoring consumer-geared trade paperbacks on healthcare, fitness, and nutrition topics."

NONFICTION Subjects include genetics, immune system maintenance, fitness; also some professional healthcare titles. Check website for submission guidelines. No phone calls, please; no originals.

SUNSTONE PRESS

Box 2321, Santa Fe NM 87504. (800)243-5644. **Website:** www.sunstonepress.com. **Contact:** Submissions Editor. Sunstone's original focus was on nonfiction subjects that preserved and highlighted the richness of the American Southwest but it has expanded its view over the years to include mainstream themes and categories—both nonfiction and fiction—that have a more general appeal. Accepts simultaneous submissions. Guidelines online.

NONFICTION Query with 1 sample chapter.

FICTION Query with 1 sample chapter.

SUPERCOLLEGE

3286 Oak Ct., Belmont CA 94002. (650)618-2221. **Website:** www.supercollege.com. Estab. 1998. Publishes trade paperback originals. "We only publish books on admission, financial aid, scholarships, test preparation, student life, and career preparation for college and graduate students." **Publishes 8-10 titles/year. 50% of books from first-time authors. 70% from unagented writers. Pays royalty on wholesale price or makes outright purchase.** Publishes ms 7-9 months after acceptance. Accepts simultaneous submissions. Book catalog and writers guidelines online.

NONFICTION Subjects include education. Submit complete ms. Reviews artwork/photos. Send photocopies.

TIPS "We want titles that are student and parent friendly, and that are different from other titles in this category. We also seek authors who want to work with a small but dynamic and ambitious publishing company."

SWAN ISLE PRESS

P.O. Box 408790, Chicago IL 60640. (773)728-3780. **E-mail:** info@swanislepress.com. **Website:** www.swanislepress.com. Estab. 1999. Publishes hardcover and trade paperback originals. *"We do not accept unsolicited mss."* **Publishes 3 titles/year. 1,500 queries received/year. Pays 7-10% royalty on wholesale price.** Publishes book 18 months after acceptance. Accepts simultaneous submissions. Responds in 6-12 months. Book catalog online. Guidelines online.

NONFICTION Subjects include creative nonfiction, ethnic, history, humanities, literary criticism, memoirs, multicultural, translation. Query with SASE.

FICTION Subjects include ethnic, historical, literary, multicultural, poetry, poetry in translation, short story collections, translation. Query with SASE.

POETRY Query with SASE.

SWAN SCYTHE PRESS

1468 Mallard Way, Sunnyvale CA 94087. **E-mail:** robert.pesich@gmail.com. **Website:** www.swanscythe.com. **Contact:** Robert Pesich, editor. Estab. 1999. Accepts simultaneous submissions.

POETRY "After publishing 25 chapbooks, a few full-sized poetry collections, and 1 anthology, then taking a short break from publishing, Swan Scythe Press is now re-launching its efforts with some new books, under a new editorship. We have also begun a new series of books, called Poetas/Puentes, from emerging poets writing in Spanish, translated into English. We will also consider mss in indigenous languages from North, Central and South America, translated into English." Query first before submitting a ms via e-mail or through website.

SWEDENBORG FOUNDATION

320 N. Church St., West Chester PA 19380. (610)430-3222. **Fax:** (610)430-7982. **E-mail:** editor@swedenborg.com. **Website:** www.swedenborg.com. **Contact:** John Connolly, editor. Estab. 1849. Publishes trade paperback originals and reprints. The Swedenborg Foundation publishes books by and about Emanuel Swedenborg (1688-1772), his ideas, how his ideas have influenced others, and related topics. Appropriate topics include Swedenborgian concepts, such as: near-death experience, angels, Biblical interpretation, mysteries of good and evil, etc. A work must actively engage the thought of Emanuel Swedenborg and show an understanding of his philosophy in order to

be accepted for publication. **Publishes 5 titles/year.** Responds in 1 month to queries; 3 months to proposals and mss. Book catalog available free. Guidelines online.

NONFICTION Subjects include philosophy, religion, spirituality. Submit proposal package, outline, sample chapters, synopsis via e-mail. Reviews artwork/photos. Send photocopies.

SWEET CHERRY PUBLISHING

Unit E, Vulcan Business Complex, Vulcan Rd., Leicester Leicestershire LE5 3EB, United Kingdom. **E-mail:** info@sweetcherrypublishing.com. **E-mail:** submissions@sweetcherrypublishing.com. **Website:** www.sweetcherrypublishing.com. Estab. 2011. Sweet Cherry Publishing publishes fiction for children between the ages of 0 and 16. "We specialize in sets and series: our aim is to give our readers the opportunity to revisit their favorite characters again and again, and to create stories that will stand the test of time. If you have written an original series with strong themes and characters, we would like to hear from you." **Offers a one-time fee for work that is accepted.** Accepts simultaneous submissions. Guidelines online.

NONFICTION Freelance illustrators are welcome to submit via our website.

FICTION Subjects include adventure, comic books, contemporary, fantasy, gothic, horror, humor, juvenile, mainstream, picture books, science fiction, young adult. No erotica. Submit a cover letter and a synopsis with 3 sample chapters via post or e-mail. "Please note that we strongly prefer e-mail submissions."

TIPS "We strongly prefer e-mail submissions over postal submissions. If your work is accepted, Sweet Cherry may consider commissioning you for future series."

TAFELBERG PUBLISHERS

Imprint of NB Publishers, P.O. Box 879, Cape Town 8000, South Africa. (27)(21)406-3033. **Fax:** (27)(21)406-3812. **E-mail:** kristin@nb.co.za. **Website:** www.tafelberg.com. **Contact:** Kristin Paremoer. General publisher best known for Afrikaans fiction, authoritative political works, children's/youth literature, and a variety of illustrated and nonillustrated nonfiction. **Publishes 10 titles/year. Pays authors royalty of 15-18% based on wholesale price.** Publishes book 1 year after acceptance. Accepts simultaneous submissions. Responds to queries in 2 weeks; mss in 6 months.

NONFICTION Subjects include memoirs, politics. Submit outline, information on intended market, bio, and 1-2 sample chapters.

FICTION Subjects include juvenile, romance. Picture books, young readers: animal, anthology, contemporary, fantasy, folktales, hi-lo, humor, multicultural, nature/environment, scient fiction, special needs. Middle readers, young adults: animal (middle reader only), contemporary, fantasy, hi-lo, humor, multicultural, nature/environment, problem novels, science fiction, special needs, sports, suspense/mystery. Average word length: picture books—1,500-7,500; young readers—25,000; middle readers—15,000; young adults—40,000. Submit complete ms.

TIPS "Writers: Story needs to have a South African or African style. Illustrators: I'd like to look, but the chances of getting commissioned are slim. The market is small and difficult. Do not expect huge advances. Editorial staff attended or plans to attend the following conferences: IBBY, Frankfurt, SCBWI Bologna."

NAN A. TALESE

Imprint of Doubleday, Random House, 1745 Broadway, New York NY 10019. (212)782-8918. **Fax:** (212)782-8448. **Website:** www.nanatalese.com. Publishes hardcover originals. Nan A. Talese publishes nonfiction with a powerful guiding narrative and relevance to larger cultural interests, and literary fiction of the highest quality. **Publishes 15 titles/year. 400 queries received/year. 400 mss received/year. Pays variable royalty on retail price. Pays varying advance.** Accepts simultaneous submissions.

NONFICTION Subjects include contemporary culture, history, philosophy, sociology. *Agented submissions only.*

FICTION Subjects include literary. Well-written narratives with a compelling story line, good characterization and use of language. We like stories with an edge. *Agented submissions only.*

TIPS "Audience is highly literate people interested in story, information and insight. We want well-written material submitted by agents only. See our website."

TANTOR MEDIA

6 Business Park Rd., Old Saybrook CT 06475. (860)395-1155. **Fax:** (860)395-1154. **E-mail:** rightsemail@tantor.com. **Website:** www.tantor.com. **Contact:** Ron Formica, director of acquisitions. Estab. 2001. Publishes audiobooks. Tantor Media, a division

of Recorded Books, is a leading audiobook publisher, producing more than 100 new titles every month. **Publishes 1,000 titles/year. Pays 5-15% royalty on wholesale price.** Publishes book 3 months after acceptance. Accepts simultaneous submissions. Responds in 2 months. Catalog online.

NONFICTION Subjects include agriculture, alternative lifestyles, Americana, animals, anthropology, astrology, business, child guidance, communications, contemporary culture, cooking, creative nonfiction, economics, education, entertainment, foods, games, gay, government, health, history, horticulture, law, lesbian, literary criticism, marine subjects, memoirs, military, money, multicultural, music, New Age, philosophy, psychology, religion, science, sex, social sciences, sociology, spirituality, sports, womens issues, womens studies, world affairs, young adult. Not accepted print submissions.

FICTION Subjects include adventure, contemporary, erotica, experimental, fantasy, feminist, gay, gothic, historical, horror, humor, juvenile, lesbian, literary, mainstream, military, multicultural, multimedia, mystery, occult, religious, romance, science fiction, short story collections, spiritual, sports, suspense, western, young adult. Query with SASE, or submit proposal package including synopsis and 3 sample chapters.

TARPAULIN SKY PRESS

P.O. Box 189, Grafton VT 05146. **Website:** www.tarpaulinsky.com. **Contact:** Resh Daily, managing editor. Estab. 2006. Tarpaulin Sky Press publishes cross- and trans-genre works as well as innovative poetry and prose. Produces full-length books and chapbooks, hand-bound books and trade paperbacks, and offers both hand-bound and perfect-bound paperback editions of full-length books. "We're a small, author-centered press endeavoring to create books that, as objects, please our authors as much their texts please us." Accepts simultaneous submissions.

POETRY Writers whose work has appeared in or been accepted for publication in *Tarpaulin Sky* may submit chapbook or full-length mss at any time, with no reading fee. Tarpaulin Sky Press also considers chapbook and full-length mss from writers whose work has not appeared in the journal, but **asks for a $20 reading fee.** Make checks/money orders to Tarpaulin Sky Press. Cover letter is preferred. Reading periods may be found on the website.

TEACHERS COLLEGE PRESS

1234 Amsterdam Ave., New York NY 10027. (212)678-3929. **Fax:** (212)678-4149. **E-mail:** tcpress@tc.columbia.edu. **Website:** www.teacherscollegepress.com. Estab. 1904. Publishes hardcover and paperback originals and reprints. "Teachers College Press publishes a wide range of educational titles for all levels of students: early childhood to higher education. Publishing books that respond to, examine, and confront issues pertaining to education, teacher training, and school reform." **Publishes 60 titles/year. Pays industry standard royalty. Pays advance.** Publishes ms 1 year after acceptance. Responds in 2 months to queries. Book catalog available free. Guidelines online.

NONFICTION Subjects include education, history, philosophy, sociology. This university press concentrates on books in the field of education in the broadest sense, from early childhood to higher education: good classroom practices, teacher training, special education, innovative trends and issues, administration and supervision, film, continuing and adult education, all areas of the curriculum, computers, guidance and counseling, and the politics, economics, philosophy, sociology, and history of education. We have recently added women's studies to our list. The Press also issues classroom materials for students at all levels, with a strong emphasis on reading and writing and social studies. Submit outline, sample chapters.

TEBOT BACH

P.O. Box 7887, Huntington Beach CA 92615. (714)968-0905. **Fax:** 714-968-0905. **E-mail:** info@tebotbach.org. **Website:** www.tebotbach.org. **Contact:** Mifanwy Kaiser, editor/publisher. Publishes mss 6 months-1 years after acceptance. Accepts simultaneous submissions. Responds in 3 months.

POETRY Offers 2 contests per year. The Patricia Bibby First Book Contest and The Clockwise Chapbook contest. Go online for more information. Query first via e-mail, with a few sample poems and cover letter with brief bio.

TEMPLE UNIVERSITY PRESS

1852 N. 10th St., Philadelphia PA 19122. (215)926-2140. **Fax:** (215)926-2141. **E-mail:** sara.cohen@temple.edu. **Website:** www.temple.edu/tempress/. **Contact:** Sara Cohen, editor. Estab. 1969. "Temple University Press has been publishing path-breaking books on Asian-Americans, law, gender issues, film, women's studies and other interesting areas for nearly 40 years."

Publishes 60 titles/year. **Pays advance.** Publishes ms 10 months after acceptance. Responds in 2 months to queries. Book catalog available free. Guidelines online.

NONFICTION Subjects include ethnic, history, photography, regional, sociology, labor studies, urban studies, Latin American/Latino, Asian American, African American studies, public policy, women's studies. No memoirs, fiction or poetry. Query with SASE. Reviews artwork/photos.

Ⓐ⊘ TEN SPEED PRESS

Penguin Random House, The Crown Publishing Group, Attn: Acquisitions, 2625 Alcatraz Ave. #505, Berkeley CA 94705. (510)559-1600. **Fax:** (510)524-1052. **E-mail:** crownbiz@randomhouse.com. **Website:** crownpublishing.com/imprint/ten-speed-press. Estab. 1971. Publishes trade paperback originals and reprints. "Ten Speed Press publishes authoritative books for an audience interested in innovative ideas. Currently emphasizing cookbooks, career, business, alternative education, and offbeat general nonfiction gift books." **Publishes 120 titles/year. 40% of books from first-time authors. 40% from unagented writers. Pays $2,500 average advance.** Publishes ms 1 year after acceptance. Accepts simultaneous submissions. Responds in 3 months to queries; 6-8 weeks to proposals. Book catalog for 9×12 envelope and 6 first-class stamps. Guidelines online.

NONFICTION Subjects include business, career guidance, cooking, crafts, relationships, how-to, humor, and pop culture. *Agented submissions only.*

TIPS "We like books from people who really know their subject, rather than people who think they've spotted a trend to capitalize on. We like books that will sell for a long time, rather than 9-day wonders. Our audience consists of a well-educated, slightly weird group of people who like food, the outdoors, and take a light, but serious, approach to business and careers. Study the backlist of each publisher you're submitting to and tailor your proposal to what you perceive as their needs. Nothing gets a publisher's attention like someone who knows what he or she is talking about, and nothing falls flat like someone who obviously has no idea who he or she is submitting to."

TEXAS TECH UNIVERSITY PRESS

1120 Main St., Second Floor, Box 41037, Lubbock TX 79415. (806)742-2982. **Fax:** (806)742-2979. **E-mail:** ttup@ttu.edu. **Website:** www.ttupress.org. Estab.

1971. Texas Tech University Press, the book publishing office of the university since 1971 and an AAUP member since 1986, publishes nonfiction titles in the areas of natural history and the natural sciences; 18th century and Joseph Conrad studies; studies of modern Southeast Asia, particularly the Vietnam War; costume and textile history; Latin American literature and culture; and all aspects of the Great Plains and the American West, especially history, biography, memoir, sports history, and travel. In addition, the Press publishes several scholarly journals, acclaimed series for young readers, an annual invited poetry collection, and literary fiction of Texas and the West. Accepts simultaneous submissions. Guidelines online.

NONFICTION Subjects include environment, ethnic, history, law, literary criticism, literature, regional, sports. Submit proposal that includes introduction, 2 sample chapters, cover letter, working title, anticipated ms length, description of audience, comparison of book to others published on the subject, brief bio or CV.

FICTION Subjects include ethnic, multicultural, religious, western. Fiction rooted in the American West and Southwest, Jewish literature, Latin American and Latino fiction (in translation or English).

POETRY "TTUP publishes an annual invited first-book poetry manuscript (please note that we cannot entertain unsolicited poetry submissions)."

⊘ TEXAS WESTERN PRESS

The University of Texas at El Paso, 500 W. University Ave., El Paso TX 79968. (915)747-5688. **Fax:** (915)747-5345. **E-mail:** ctavarez@utep.edu. **Website:** twp.utep.edu. **Contact:** Carmen P. Tavarez. Estab. 1952. Publishes hardcover and paperback originals. "Texas Western Press publishes books on the history and cultures of the American Southwest, particularly historical and biographical works about West Texas, New Mexico, northern Mexico, and the U.S. borderlands." **Publishes 1 titles/year. Pays standard 10% royalty. Pays advance.** Responds in 2 months to queries. Book catalog available free. Guidelines online.

IMPRINTS Southwestern Studies.

NONFICTION Subjects include education, history, regional, science, social sciences. "Historic and cultural accounts of the Southwest (West Texas, New Mexico, northern Mexico). Also art, photographic books, Native American and limited regional fiction reprints." *Not currently seeking mss.*

TIPS "We try to treat our authors professionally, produce handsome, long-lived books and aim for quality, rather than quantity of titles carrying our imprint."

THISTLEDOWN PRESS LTD.

410 2nd Ave., Saskatoon SK S7K 2C3, Canada. (306)244-1722. **Fax:** (306)244-1762. **E-mail:** editorial@thistledownpress.com. **Website:** www.thistledownpress.com. **Contact:** Allan Forrie, publisher. "Thistledown originates books by Canadian authors only, although we have co-published titles by authors outside Canada. We do not publish children's picture books." **Pays authors royalty of 10-12% based on net dollar sales. Pays illustrators and photographers by the project (range: $250-750).** Publishes book 1 year after acceptance. Responds to queries in 6 months. Book catalog on website.

NONFICTION Subjects include literature, young adult.

FICTION Subjects include literary, short story collections. Young adults: adventure, anthology, contemporary, fantasy, humor, poetry, romance, science fiction, suspense/mystery, short stories. Average word length: young adults—40,000. Submit outline/synopsis and sample chapters. *Does not accept mss.* Do not query by e-mail. "Please note: we are not accepting middle years (ages 8-12) nor children's manuscripts at this time." See Submission Guidelines on Website.

POETRY "We do not publish cowboy poetry, inspirational poetry, or poetry for children."

TIPS "Send cover letter including publishing history and SASE."

THOMSON CARSWELL

One Corporate Plaza, 2075 Kennedy Rd., Toronto ON M1T 3V4, Canada. (416)298-5024. **Fax:** (416)298-5094. **Website:** www.carswell.com. Publishes hardcover originals. "Thomson Carswell is Canada's national resource of information and legal interpretations for law, accounting, tax and business professionals." **Publishes 150-200 titles/year. 30-50% of books from first-time authors. Pays 5-15% royalty on wholesale price.** Publishes ms 6 months after acceptance. Accepts simultaneous submissions. Responds in 3 months to queries. Book catalog and ms guidelines free.

NONFICTION Canadian information of a regulatory nature is our mandate. Submit proposal package, outline, resume.

TIPS "Audience is Canada and persons interested in Canadian information; professionals in law, tax, accounting fields; business people interested in regulatory material."

THUNDERSTONE BOOKS

6575 Horse Dr., Las Vegas NV 89131. **E-mail:** info@thunderstonebooks.com. **Website:** www.thunderstonebooks.com. **Contact:** Rachel Noorda, editorial director. Estab. 2014. Publishes hardcover, trade paperback, mass market paperback, and electronic originals. "At ThunderStone Books, we aim to publish children's books that have an educational aspect. We are not looking for curriculum for learning certain subjects, but rather stories that encourage learning for children, whether that be learning about a new language/culture or learning more about science and math in a fun, fictional format. We want to help children to gain a love for other languages and subjects so that they are curious about the world around them. We are currently accepting fiction and nonfiction submissions. Picture books without accompanying illustration will not be accepted." **Publishes 2-5 titles/year. Receives 30 queries and mss/year. 100% of books from first-time authors. 100% from unagented writers. Pays 5-15% royalties on retail price. Pays $300-1,000 advance.** Publishes ms 6 months after acceptance. Accepts simultaneous submissions. Responds in 3 months. Catalog available for SASE. Guidelines available.

NONFICTION Subjects include creative nonfiction, education, language, literature, multicultural, regional, science, translation. Looking for engaging educational materials, not a set curriculum, but books that teach as well as have some fun. Open to a variety of educational subjects, but specialty and main interest lies in language exposure/learning, science, math, and history. Reviews photocopies of artwork.

FICTION Subjects include multicultural, picture books, regional. Interested in multicultural stories with an emphasis on authentic culture and language (these may include mythology). "If you think your book is right for us, send a query letter with a word attachment of the first 50 pages to info@thunderstonebooks.com. If it is a picture book or chapter book for young readers that is shorter than 50 pages send the entire manuscript."

TIA CHUCHA PRESS

13197 Gladstone Ave., Unit A, Sylmar CA 91342. (818)939-3433. **Fax:** (818)367-5600. **E-mail:** info@tiachucha.com. **Website:** www.tiachucha.com. **Contact:** Luis Rodriguez, director. Estab. 1989. Publishes hardcover and trade paperback originals. Tia Chucha's Centro Cultural is a nonprofit learning and cultural arts center. "We support and promote the continued growth, development and holistic learning of our community through the many powerful means of the arts. Tia Centra provides a positive space for people to activate what we all share as humans: the capacity to create, to imagine and to express ourselves in an effort to improve the quality of life for our community." **Publishes 2-4 titles/year. 25-30 queries received/year. 150 mss received/year. Pays 10% royalty on wholesale price.** Publishes ms 1 year after acceptance. Responds in 9 months to mss. Guidelines online.

POETRY No restrictions as to style or content. "We only publish poetry at this time. We do cross-cultural and performance-oriented poetry. It has to work on the page, however." Query and submit complete ms.

TIPS "We will cultivate the practice. Audience is those interested."

♻⊘ TIGHTROPE BOOKS

#207-2 College St., Toronto ON M5G 1K3, Canada. (416)928-6666. **E-mail:** tightropeasst@gmail.com. **Website:** www.tightropebooks.com. **Contact:** Jim Nason, publisher. Estab. 2005. Publishes trade paperback originals. **Publishes 12 titles/year. 60% of books from first-time authors. 90% from unagented writers. Pays 5-15% royalty on retail price. Pays advance of $200-300.** Publishes book 1-2 years after acceptance. Accepts simultaneous submissions. Responds if interested. Catalog and guidelines online.

○ Accepting submissions for literary fiction, nonfiction and poetry from Canadian citizens and permanent Canadian residents only.

NONFICTION Subjects include alternative lifestyles, art, contemporary culture, creative nonfiction, ethnic, gay, language, lesbian, literary criticism, literature, memoirs, multicultural, womens issues, womens studies. No genres

FICTION Subjects include contemporary, ethnic, experimental, feminist, gay, lesbian, literary, multicultural, poetry, poetry in translation, short story collections, young adult.

TIPS "Audience is urban, literary, educated, unconventional."

TILBURY HOUSE PUBLISHERS

WordSplice Studio, Inc., 12 Starr St., Thomaston ME 04861. (800)582-1899. **Fax:** (207)582-8772. **E-mail:**

tilbury@tilburyhouse.com. **Website:** www.tilburyhouse.com. **Contact:** Audrey Maynard, children's book editor; Jonathan Eaton, publisher. Estab. 1990. **Publishes 10 titles/year. Pays royalty based on wholesale price.** Publishes ms 1 year after acceptance. Accepts simultaneous submissions. Responds to mss in 3 months. Guidelines and catalog online.

NONFICTION Regional adult biography/history/maritime/nature, and children's picture books that deal with issues, such as bullying, multiculturalism, etc., science/nature. Submit complete ms for picture books or outline/synopsis for longer works. Now uses online submission form. Reviews artwork/photos. Send photocopies.

FICTION Picture books: multicultural, nature/environment. Special needs include books that teach children about tolerance and honoring diversity. Send art/photography samples and/or complete ms to Audrey Maynard, children's book editor.

TIPS "We are always interested in stories that will encourage children to understand the natural world and the environment, as well as stories with social justice themes. We really like stories that engage children to become problem solvers as well as those that promote respect, tolerance and compassion." We do not publish books with personified animal characters; historical fiction; YA or middle grade fiction or chapter books; fantasy."

⊘ TIN HOUSE BOOKS

2617 NW Thurman St., Portland OR 97210. (503)473-8663. **Fax:** (503)473-8957. **E-mail:** meg@tinhouse.com. **Website:** www.tinhouse.com. **Contact:** Meg Storey, editor; Tony Perez, editor; Masie Cochran, editor. Publishes hardcover originals, paperback originals, paperback reprints. "We are a small independent publisher dedicated to nurturing new, promising talent as well as showcasing the work of established writers." Distributes/promotes titles through W. W. Norton. **Publishes 10-12 titles/year.** Publishes ms 1 year after acceptance. Accepts simultaneous submissions. Responds to queries in 2-3 weeks; mss in 2-3 months. Guidelines online.

NONFICTION *Agented mss only.* "We no longer read unsolicited submissions by authors with no representation. We will continue to accept submissions from agents."

FICTION *Agented mss only.* "We no longer read unsolicited submissions by authors with no representation. We will continue to accept submissions from agents."

TITAN PRESS

PMB 17897, Encino CA 91416. **E-mail:** titan91416@ yahoo.com. **Website:** https://www.facebook.com/ RVClef. **Contact:** Romana V. Clef, editor. Estab. 1981. Publishes hardcover and paperback originals. Little literary publisher. **Publishes 12 titles/year. 50% from unagented writers. Pays 20-40% royalty.** Publishes ms 1 year after acceptance. Accepts simultaneous submissions. Responds to queries in 3 months.

NONFICTION Subjects include creative nonfiction, entertainment, literary criticism.

FICTION Subjects include contemporary, literary, mainstream, short story collections. Does not accept unsolicited mss. Query with SASE. Include brief bio, list of publishing credits.

POETRY Literary, not MFA banality.

TIPS "Look, act, sound, and *be* professional."

⊘ TOP COW PRODUCTIONS, INC.

3812 Dunn Dr., Culver City CA 90232. **E-mail:** fanmail@topcow.com. **Website:** www.topcow.com. Accepts simultaneous submissions. Guidelines online.

FICTION *No unsolicited submissions.* Prefers submissions from artists. See website for details and advice on how to break into the market.

TOR BOOKS

Tom Doherty Associates, 175 Fifth Ave., New York NY 10010. **Website:** www.tor-forge.com. Tor Books is the "world's largest publisher of science fiction and fantasy, with strong category publishing in historical fiction, mystery, western/Americana, thriller, YA." **Publishes 10-20 titles/year. Pays author royalty. Pays illustrators by the project.** Accepts simultaneous submissions. Book catalog available. Guidelines online.

FICTION Subjects include adventure, fantasy, historical, humor, mystery, picture books, science fiction, suspense, young adult. Submit first 3 chapters, 3-10 page synopsis, dated cover letter, SASE.

TORQUERE PRESS LLC

P.O. Box 37, Waldo AR 71770. **E-mail:** editor@torquerepress.com. **E-mail:** submissions@torquerepress.com. **Website:** www.torquerepress.com. **Contact:** Kristi Boulware, submissions editor (homoerotica, suspense, gay/lesbian). Estab. 2015. Publishes trade paperback originals and electronic originals and reprints. "We are a gay and lesbian press focusing on romance and genres of romance. We particularly like paranormal and western romance." **Publishes 140 titles/year. 500 queries; 200 mss received/year. 25% of books from first-time authors. 100% from unagented writers. Pays 8-40% royalty. Pays $35-75 for anthology stories. Does not pay advance.** Publishes ms 6 months after acceptance. Responds in 1 month to queries and proposals; 2-4 months to mss. Book catalog online. Guidelines online.

FICTION Subjects include adventure, erotica, historical, horror, multicultural, mystery, occult, romance, science fiction, short story collections, suspense, western. All categories gay and lesbian themed. Submit proposal package, 3 sample chapters, clips.

TIPS "Our audience is primarily people looking for a familiar romance setting featuring gay or lesbian protagonists. Please read guidelines carefully and familiarize yourself with our lines."

TORREY HOUSE PRESS, LLC

2806 Melony Dr., Salt Lake City UT 84124. **E-mail:** anne@torreyhouse.com. **Website:** torreyhouse.com. **Contact:** Anne Terashima. Estab. 2010. Publishes hardcover, trade paperback, and electronic originals. Torrey House Press is an independent nonprofit publisher promoting environmental conservation through literature. **Publishes 6 titles/year. Receives 500 queries/year; 200 mss/year. 50% of books from first-time authors. 80% from unagented writers. Pays 5-15% royalty on retail price.** Publishes ms 12-18 months after acceptance. Accepts simultaneous submissions. Responds in 3 months. Catalog online. Guidelines online.

NONFICTION Subjects include creative nonfiction, environment, nature. Query; submit proposal package, including: outline, ms, bio. Does not review artwork.

FICTION Subjects include historical, literary. "Torrey House Press publishes literary fiction and creative nonfiction about the world environment and the American West." Submit proposal package including: synopsis, complete ms, bio.

POETRY Query; submit complete ms.

TIPS "Include writing experience (none okay)."

◎ TOUCHWOOD EDITIONS

The Heritage Group, 103-1075 Pendergast St., Victoria BC V8V 0A1, Canada. (250)360-0829. **Fax:** (250)386-

0829. **E-mail:** edit@touchwoodeditions.com. **Website:** www.touchwoodeditions.com. **Contact:** Renée Layberry, Editor. Publishes trade paperback, originals and reprints. **Publishes 20-25 titles/year. 40% of books from first-time authors. 70% from unagented writers. Pays 15% royalty on net price.** Publishes ms 12-24 months after acceptance. Accepts simultaneous submissions. Responds in 6 months to queries. Book catalog and guidelines online.

NONFICTION Subjects include cooking, creative nonfiction, history, memoirs, recreation, regional, regional travel or guidebooks with a focus on food, wine, art or similar topics, regional history or biography, biography (well-known and western Canadian figures only), cultural studies, aboriginal history and writing, for adult and young readers, historical fiction, relating to western Canada. Submit TOC, outline, word count, 2-3 sample chapters, synopsis. Reviews artwork/photos. Send photocopies.

FICTION Subjects include historical, mainstream, mystery, regional. Submit bio/CV, marketing plan, TOC, outline, word count.

TIPS "Our area of interest is western Canada. We would like more creative nonfiction and fiction from First Nations authors, and welcome authors who write about notable individuals in Canada's history. Please note we do not publish poetry."

TOWER PUBLISHING

588 Saco Rd., Standish ME 04084. (207)642-5400. **Fax:** (207)642-5463. **E-mail:** info@towerpub.com. **E-mail:** michaell@towerpub.com. **Website:** www.towerpub.com. **Contact:** Michael Lyons, president. Estab. 1772. Publishes hardcover originals and reprints, trade paperback originals. Tower Publishing specializes in business and professional directories and legal books. **Publishes 22 titles/year. 60 queries; 30 mss received/year. 10% of books from first-time authors. 90% from unagented writers.** Publishes ms 6 months after acceptance. Accepts simultaneous submissions. Responds in 1 month to queries; 2 months to proposals and mss. Book catalog and ms guidelines online.

NONFICTION Looking for legal books of a national stature. Query with SASE. Submit outline.

✪ TRADEWIND BOOKS

202-1807 Maritime Mews, Granville Island, Vancouver BC V6H 3W7, Canada. (604)662-4405. **Website:** www.tradewindbooks.com. Publishes hardcover and trade paperback originals. "Tradewind Books publishes juvenile picture books and young adult novels. Requires that submissions include evidence that author has read at least 3 titles published by Tradewind Books." **Publishes 5 titles/year. 15% of books from first-time authors. 50% from unagented writers. Pays 7% royalty on retail price. Pays variable advance.** Publishes book 3 years after acceptance. Accepts simultaneous submissions. Responds to mss in 2 months. Book catalog and ms guidelines online.

FICTION Subjects include juvenile, multicultural, picture books. Average word length: 900 words. Send complete ms for picture books. *YA novels by Canadian authors only. Chapter books by US authors considered.* For chapter books/Middle Grade Fiction, submit the first three chapters, a chapter outline and plot summary.

POETRY Please send a book-length collection only.

TRAFALGAR SQUARE BOOKS

388 Howe Hill Rd., P.O. Box 257, North Pomfret VT 05053. (802)457-1911. **E-mail:** submissions@trafalgarbooks.com. **Website:** www.horseandriderbooks.com. Estab. 1985. Publishes hardcover and trade paperback originals. "We publish high-quality instructional books for horsemen and horsewomen, always with the horse's welfare in mind." **Publishes 12 titles/year. 50% of books from first-time authors. 80% from unagented writers. Pays royalty. Pays advance.** Publishes ms 18 months after acceptance. Responds in 1 month to queries; 2 months to proposals; 2-3 months to mss. Catalog free on request and by e-mail.

NONFICTION Subjects include animals. "We rarely consider books for complete novices." Query with SASE. Submit proposal package including outline, 1-3 sample chapters, letter of introduction including qualifications for writing on the subject and why the proposed book is an essential addition to existing publications. Reviews artwork/photos as part of the ms package. We prefer color laser thumbnail sheets or duplicate prints (do not send original photos or art!).

TIPS "Our audience is comprised of horse lovers and riders interested in pursuing their passion and/or sport while doing what is best for horses."

TRAVELERS' TALES

Solas House, Inc., 2320 Bowdoin St., Palo Alto CA 94306. (650)462-2110. **Fax:** (650)462-6305. **E-mail:** submit@travelerstales.com. **Website:** www.travelerstales.com. **Contact:** James O'Reilly, Larry Habegger,

Sean O'Reilly, series editors. Estab. 1993. Publishes inspirational travel books, mostly anthologies and travel advice books. "Due to the volume of submissions, we do not respond unless the material submitted meets our immediate editorial needs. All stories are read and filed for future use contingent upon meeting editorial guidelines." **Publishes 4-6 titles/year. Receives hundreds of submissions/year. 30% of books from first-time authors. 80% from unagented writers. Pays $100 honorarium for anthology pieces. Does not pay advance.** Accepts simultaneous submissions. "We contact you if we'd like to publish your work." Guidelines online.

NONFICTION Subjects include creative nonfiction, literature, memoirs, spirituality, travel, womens issues, world affairs. Subjects include all aspects of travel.

TIPS "We publish personal nonfiction stories and anecdotes—funny, illuminating, adventurous, frightening, or grim. Stories should reflect that unique alchemy that occurs when you enter unfamiliar territory and begin to see the world differently as a result. Stories that have already been published, including book excerpts, are welcome as long as the authors retain the copyright or can obtain permission from the copyright holder to reprint the material."

TRIANGLE SQUARE

Seven Stories Press, 140 Watts St., New York NY 10013. (212)226-8760. **Fax:** (212)226-1411. **E-mail:** info@sevenstories.com. **Website:** www.sevenstories.com/trianglesquare/. Triangle Square is a children's and young adult imprint of Seven Story Press. Accepts simultaneous submissions.

FICTION Send a cover letter with 2 sample chapters and SASE. Send c/o Acquisitions.

THE TRINITY FOUNDATION

P.O. Box 68, Unicoi TN 37692. (423)743-0199. **Fax:** (423)743-2005. **E-mail:** tjtrinityfound@aol.com. **Website:** www.trinityfoundation.org. **Contact:** Thomas W. Juodaitis, editor. Publishes hardcover and paperback originals and reprints. **Publishes 2-3 titles/year.** Publishes ms 9 months after acceptance. Accepts simultaneous submissions. Responds in 1 month to queries and proposals; 3 months to mss. Book catalog online.

NONFICTION Only books that conform to the philosophy and theology of the Westminster Confession of Faith. Textbooks subjects include business/economics, education, government/politics, history, philosophy, religion, science. Query with SASE.

TRISTAN PUBLISHING

2355 Louisiana Ave. N, Golden Valley MN 55427. (763)545-1383. **Fax:** (763)545-1387. **E-mail:** info@tristanpublishing.com; manuscripts@tristanpublishing.com. **Website:** www.tristanpublishing.com. **Contact:** Brett Waldman, publisher. Estab. 2002. Publishes hardcover originals. **Publishes 6-10 titles/year. 1,000 queries and mss/year. 15% of books from first-time authors. 100% from unagented writers. Pays royalty on wholesale or retail price; outright purchase.** Publishes book 2 years after acceptance. Accepts simultaneous submissions. Responds in 3 months. Catalog and guidelines online.

NONFICTION Subjects include inspirational. "Our mission is to create books with a message that inspire and uplift in typically 1,000 words or less." Query with SASE; submit completed mss. Reviews artwork/photos; send photocopies.

FICTION Subjects include inspirational, gift books. Query with SASE; submit completed mss.

TIPS "Our audience is adults and children."

TRIUMPH BOOKS

814 N. Franklin St., Chicago IL 60610. (312)337-0747. **Fax:** (312)280-5470. **Website:** www.triumphbooks.com. Estab. 1990. Publishes hardcover originals and trade paperback originals and reprints. Accepts simultaneous submissions. Book catalog available free.

NONFICTION Subjects include recreation, sports, health, sports business/motivation. Query with SASE. Reviews artwork/photos. Send photocopies.

TRUMAN STATE UNIVERSITY PRESS

100 E. Normal Ave., Kirksville MO 63501. (660)785-7336. **Fax:** (660)785-4480. **E-mail:** tsup@truman.edu. **E-mail:** bsm@truman.edu. **Website:** tsup.truman.edu. **Contact:** Barbara Smith-Mandell, editor-in-chief. Estab. 1986. Truman State University Press (TSUP) publishes peer-reviewed research in the humanities for the scholarly community and the broader public, and publishes creative literary works. Accepts simultaneous submissions. Guidelines online.

NONFICTION Subjects include contemporary nonfiction, early modern, American studies, poetry. Submit book ms proposals in American Midwest/American history to Barbara Smith-Mandell at bsm@truman.edu; nonfiction to Monica Barron at tsupnonfiction@truman.edu; early modern studies to Michael. Wolfe@qc.cuny.edu.

POETRY Not accepting unsolicited mss. Submit to annual T.S. Eliot Prize for Poetry.

TU BOOKS

Lee & Low Books, 95 Madison Ave., Suite #1205, New York NY 10016. **Website:** www.leeandlow.com/imprints/3. **Contact:** Stacy Whitman, Publisher. Estab. 2010. The Tu imprint spans many genres: science fiction, fantasy, mystery, contemporary, and more. "We don't believe in labels or limits, just great stories. Join us at the crossroads where fantasy and real life collide. You'll be glad you did." **25% of books from first-time authors. Pays advance.** Accepts simultaneous submissions. Responds only if interested. Guidelines online. Electronic submissions can be submitted here (only): https://tubooks.submittable.com/submit.

NONFICTION Subjects include young adult.

FICTION Subjects include young adult. "At Tu Books, an imprint of Lee & Low Books, our focus is on well-told, exciting, adventurous fantasy, science fiction, and mystery novels starring people of color. We also selectively publish realism that explores the contemporary and historical experiences of people of color. We look for fantasy set in worlds inspired by non-Western folklore or culture, contemporary mysteries and fantasy set all over the world starring people of color, and science fiction that centers the possibilities for people of color in the future. We welcome intersectional narratives that feature LGBTQIA and disabled POC as heroes in their own stories. We are looking specifically for stories for both middle grade (ages 8-12) and young adult (ages 12-18) readers. Occasionally a manuscript might fall between those two categories; if your manuscript does, let us know. We are not looking for picture books, chapter books, or short stories at this time. Please do not send submissions in these categories. (See the Lee & Low Books guidelines for books for younger young readers.)" Only submissions sent through Submittable or regular post will be considered. "We cannot accept submissions through e-mail or fax. Mss should be accompanied by a cover letter that includes a brief biography of the author, including publishing history. The letter should also state if the ms is a simultaneous or an exclusive submission. Include a synopsis and the first 3 chapters of the novel. Include full contact information on the cover letter and the first page of the ms."

TUMBLEHOME LEARNING

P.O. Box 71386, Boston MA 02117. **E-mail:** info@tumblehomelearning.com. **E-mail:** submissions@tumblehomelearning.com. **Website:** www.tumblehomelearning.com. **Contact:** Pendred Noyce, editor. Estab. 2011. Publishes hardcover, trade paperback, and electronic originals. Tumblehome Learning helps kids imagine themselves as young scientists or engineers and encourages them to experience science through adventure and discovery. "We do this with exciting mystery and adventure tales as well as experiments carefully designed to engage students from ages 8 and up." **Publishes 8-10 titles/year. Receives 20 queries and 20 mss/year. 50% of books from first-time authors. 100% from unagented writers. Pays authors 8-12% royalties on retail price. Pays $500 advance.** Publishes ms 8 months after acceptance. Accepts simultaneous submissions. Responds in 1 month to queries and proposals, and 2 months to mss. Catalog available online. Guidelines available on request for SASE.

NONFICTION Subjects include science. Rarely publishes nonfiction. Book would need to be sold to trade, not just the school market.

FICTION Subjects include adventure, juvenile. "All our fiction has science at its heart. This can include using science to solve a mystery (see *The Walking Fish* by Rachelle Burk or *Something Stinks!* by Gail Hedrick), realistic science fiction, books in our Galactic Academy of Science series, science-based adventure tales, and the occasional picture book with a science theme, such as appreciation of the stars and constellations in *Elizabeth's Constellation Quilt* by Olivia Fu. A graphic novel about science would also be welcome." Submit completed ms electronically.

TIPS "Please don't submit to us if your book is not about science. We don't accept generic books about animals or books with glaring scientific errors in the first chapter. That said, the book should be fun to read and the science content can be subtle. We work closely with authors, including first-time authors, to edit and improve their books. As a small publisher, the greatest benefit we can offer is this friendly and respectful partnership with authors."

TUPELO PRESS

P.O. Box 1767, North Adams MA 01247. (413)664-9611. **E-mail:** publisher@tupelopress.org. **Website:** www.tupelopress.org. **Contact:** Jeffrey Levine, publish/editor-in-chief; Jim Schley, managing editor. Estab. 2001. "We're an independent nonprofit literary press. We accept book-length poetry, poetry collections (48+ pages), short story collections, novellas, literary nonfiction/memoirs and up to 80 pages of a novel." Accepts simultaneous submissions. Guidelines online.

NONFICTION Subjects include memoirs. No cookbooks, children's books, inspirational books, graphic novels, or religious books. **Charges $45 reading fee.**

FICTION Subjects include poetry, short story collections, novels. "For Novels—submit no more than 100 pages along with a summary of the entire book. If we're interested we'll ask you to send the rest. We accept very few works of prose (1 or 2 per year)." Submit complete ms. **Charges a $45 reading fee.**

POETRY "Our mission is to publish thrilling, visually and emotionally and intellectually stimulating books of the highest quality, inside and out. We want contemporary poetry, etc. by the most diverse list of emerging and established writers in the U.S." Submit complete ms. **Charges $28 reading fee.**

TURNING POINT

WordTech Communications LLC, P.O. Box 541106, Cincinnati OH 45254. **E-mail:** connect@wordtech-communications.com. **Website:** www.turningpoint-books.com. **Pays in royalties.** Accepts simultaneous submissions. Catalog and guidelines online.

POETRY "Dedicated to the art of story in poetry. We seek to publish collections of narrative poetry that tell the essential human stories of our times." No e-mail submissions. No calls for book-length poetry right now.

✪ TURNSTONE PRESS

Artspace Building, 206-100 Arthur St., Winnipeg MB R3B 1H3, Canada. (204)947-1555. **Fax:** (204)942-1555. **Website:** www.turnstonepress.com. **Contact:** Submissions Assistant. Estab. 1976. "Turnstone Press is a literary publisher, not a general publisher, and therefore we are only interested in literary fiction, literary nonfiction—including literary criticism—and poetry. We do publish literary mysteries, thrillers, and noir under our Ravenstone imprint. We publish only Canadian authors or landed immigrants, we strive to publish a significant number of new writers, to publish in a variety of genres, and to have 50% of each year's list be Manitoba writers and/or books with

Manitoba content." Publishes ms 2 years after acceptance. Accepts simultaneous submissions. Responds in 4-7 months. Guidelines online.

NONFICTION "Samples must be 40 to 60 pages, typed/printed in a minimum 12 point serif typeface such as Times, Book Antiqua, or Garamond."

FICTION "Samples must be 40 to 60 pages, typed/printed in a minimum 12 point serif typeface such as Times, Book Antiqua, or Garamond."

POETRY Poetry mss should be a minimum 70 pages. Submit complete ms. Include cover letter.

TIPS "As a Canadian literary press, we have a mandate to publish Canadian writers only. Do some homework before submitting works to make sure your subject matter/genre/writing style falls within the publishers area of interest."

TUTTLE PUBLISHING

364 Innovation Dr., North Clarendon VT 05759. (802)773-8930. **Fax:** (802)773-6993. **E-mail:** submissions@tuttlepublishing.com. **Website:** www.tuttle-publishing.com. Estab. 1832. Publishes hardcover and trade paperback originals and reprints. Tuttle is America's leading publisher of books on Japan and Asia. "Familiarize yourself with our catalog and/or similar books we publish. Send complete book proposal with cover letter, table of contents, 1-2 sample chapters, target audience description, SASE. No e-mail submissions." **Publishes 125 titles/year. 1,000 queries received/year. 20% of books from first-time authors. 40% from unagented writers. Pays 5-10% royalty on net or retail price, depending on format and kind of book. Pays advance.** Publishes book 18 months after acceptance. Accepts simultaneous submissions. Responds in 2-3 months to proposals. Tuttle accepts submissions by mail or e-mail. In the interest of environmental responsibility, we prefer digital submissions. (See below for more detail on where to send).

NONFICTION Publishes Asian cultures, language, martial arts, textbooks, art and design, craft books and kits, cookbooks, religion, philosophy, and more. Query with SASE.

TWILIGHT TIMES BOOKS

P.O. Box 3340, Kingsport TN 37664. **E-mail:** publisher@twilighttimesbooks.com. **Website:** www.twilighttimesbooks.com. **Contact:** Andy M. Scott, managing editor. Estab. 1999. "We publish compelling literary fiction by authors with a distinctive voice."

Published 5 debut authors within the last year. Averages 120 total titles; 15 fiction titles/year. Member: AAP, PAS, SPAN, SLF. **90% from unagented writers. Pays 8-15% royalty.** Accepts simultaneous submissions. Responds in 4 weeks to queries; 2 months to mss. Guidelines online.

NONFICTION Subjects include creative nonfiction, literary criticism, memoirs, military, nature, New Age, womens studies, young adult.

FICTION Subjects include fantasy, historical, humor, juvenile, literary, mainstream, military, mystery, regional, science fiction, suspense, war, young adult. Accepts unsolicited mss. Do not send complete mss. Queries via e-mail only. Include estimated word count, brief bio, list of publishing credits, marketing plan.

TIPS "The only requirement for consideration at Twilight Times Books is that your novel must be entertaining and professionally written."

TWO DOLLAR RADIO

Website: www.twodollarradio.com. **Contact:** Eric Obenauf, editorial director. Estab. 2005. Two Dollar Radio is a boutique family-run press, publishing bold works of literary merit, each book, individually and collectively, providing a sonic progression that "we believe to be too loud to ignore." Targets readers who admire ambition and creativity. Range of print runs: 2,000-7,500 copies. **Publishes 5-6 (plus a biannual journal of nonfiction essays, *Frequencies*) titles/year. Advance: $500-$1,000.**

FICTION Submit entire, completed ms with a brief cover letter, via Submittable. No previously published work. No proposals. No excerpts. There is a $2 reading fee per submission. Accepts submissions every other month (January, March, May, July, September, November).

TIPS "We want writers who show an authority over language and the world that is being created, from the very first sentence on."

Ⓐ⦸ TYNDALE HOUSE PUBLISHERS, INC.

351 Executive Dr., Carol Stream IL 60188. (800)323-9400. **Fax:** (800)684-0247. **Website:** www.tyndale.com. Estab. 1962. Publishes hardcover and trade paperback originals and mass paperback reprints. "Tyndale House publishes practical, user-friendly Christian books for the home and family." **Publishes 15 titles/year. Pays negotiable royalty. Pays negotiable**

advance. Accepts simultaneous submissions. Guidelines online.

NONFICTION Subjects include child guidance, religion, devotional/inspirational. *Agented submissions only. No unsolicited mss.*

FICTION Subjects include juvenile, romance, Christian (children's, general, inspirational, mystery/suspense, thriller, romance). "Christian truths must be woven into the story organically. No short story collections. Youth books: character building stories with Christian perspective. Especially interested in ages 10-14. We primarily publish Christian historical romances, with occasional contemporary, suspense, or standalones." *Agented submissions only. No unsolicited mss.*

TIPS "All accepted manuscripts will appeal to Evangelical Christian children and parents."

⦸ TYRUS BOOKS

F+W Media, 1213 N. Sherman Ave., #306, Madison WI 53704. (508)427-7100. **Fax:** (508)427-6790. **Website:** tyrusbooks.com. "We publish crime and literary fiction. We believe in the life changing power of the written word." Accepts simultaneous submissions.

FICTION Subjects include literary, mystery. Submissions currently closed; check website for updates.

UMI (URBAN MINISTRIES, INC.)

P.O. Box 436987, Chicago IL 60643. **Website:** www.urbanministries.com. Estab. 1970. Publishes trade paperback originals and reprints. **Publishes 2-3 titles/year.**

NONFICTION Subjects include education, religion, spirituality, Christian living, Christian doctrine, theology. "The books we publish are generally those we have a specific need for (i.e., Vacation Bible School curriculum topics); to complement an existing resource or product line; or those with a potential to develop into a curriculum." Query with SASE. Submit proposal package, outline, 2-3 sample chapters, letter why UMI should publish the book and why the book will sell.

UNBRIDLED BOOKS

8201 E. Highway WW, Columbia MO 65201. **E-mail:** michalsong@unbridledbooks.com. **Website:** unbridledbooks.com. **Contact:** Greg Michalson. Estab. 2004. "Unbridled Books is a premier publisher of works of rich literary quality that appeal to a broad audience." Accepts simultaneous submissions.

FICTION Please query first by e-mail. "Due to the heavy volume of submissions, we regret that at this time we are not able to consider uninvited mss."

TIPS "We try to read each ms that arrives, so please be patient."

⊘ UNITY HOUSE

1901 N.W. Blue Pkwy., Unity Village MO 64065-0001. (816)524-3550. **Fax:** (816)347-5518. **E-mail:** unity@ unityonline.org. **Website:** www.unityonline.org. Estab. 1889. Publishes hardcover, trade paperback, and electronic originals. Unity House publishes metaphysical Christian books based on Unity principles, as well as inspirational books on metaphysics and practical spirituality. All manuscripts must reflect a spiritual foundation and express the Unity philosophy, practical Christianity, universal principles, and/ or metaphysics. **Publishes 5-7 titles/year. 50 queries received/year. 5% of books from first-time authors. 95% from unagented writers. Pays 10-15% royalty on retail price. Pays advance.** Publishes ms 13 months after acceptance. Responds in 6-8 months. Catalog and guidelines online.

NONFICTION Subjects include religion. "Writers should be familiar with principles of metaphysical Christianity but not feel bound by them. We are interested in works in the related fields of holistic health, spiritual psychology, and the philosophy of other world religions." *Not accepting mss for new books at this time.* Reviews artwork/photos. Writers should send photocopies.

FICTION Subjects include spiritual, inspirational, metaphysical, visionary fiction. "We are a bridge between traditional Christianity and New Age spirituality. Unity is based on metaphysical Christian principles, spiritual values and the healing power of prayer as a resource for daily living." *Not accepting mss for new books at this time.*

TIPS "We target an audience of spiritual seekers."

THE UNIVERSITY OF AKRON PRESS

120 E. Mill St., Suite 415, Akron OH 44325. **E-mail:** uapress@uakron.edu. **Website:** www.uakron.edu/uapress. **Contact:** Jon Miller, transitional director and acquisitions. Estab. 1988. Publishes hardcover and paperback originals and reissues. "The University of Akron Press is the publishing arm of The University of Akron and is dedicated to the dissemination of scholarly, professional, and regional books and other content." **Publishes 10-12 titles/year. 100 queries received/year. 50-75 mss received/year. 40% of books from first-time authors. 80% from unagented writers. Pays 7-15% royalty.** Publishes book 9-12 months after acceptance. Accepts simultaneous submissions. Responds in 2 weeks to queries/ proposals; 3-4 months to solicited mss. Query prior to submitting. Guidelines online.

IMPRINTS Ringtaw Books, Buchtel Books.

NONFICTION Subjects include Americana, anthropology, archeology, creative nonfiction, environment, history, humanities, labor, law, literary criticism, multicultural, politics, psychology, regional. Query by email. Mss cannot be returned unless SASE is included.

POETRY Follow the guidelines and submit mss only for the contest: www.uakron.edu/uapress/poetry. html. "We publish two books of poetry annually, one of which is the winner of The Akron Poetry prize. We also are interested in literary collections based around one theme, especially collections of translated works." If you are interested in publishing with The University of Akron Press, please fill out form online.

THE UNIVERSITY OF ALABAMA PRESS

200 Hackberry Lane, 2nd Floor, Tuscaloosa AL 35487. (205)348-5180 or (205)348-1571. **Fax:** (205)348-9201. **E-mail:** waterman@uapress.ua.edu. **Website:** www. uapress.ua.edu. **Contact:** Daniel Waterman, editor-in-chief. Publishes nonfiction hardcover and paperbound originals. **Publishes 70-75 titles/year. 70% of books from first-time authors. 95% from unagented writers. Pays advance in very limited number of circumstances.** Accepts simultaneous submissions. Responds in 2-3 weeks to queries. Book catalog available free.

NONFICTION Subjects include history, literary criticism, politics, religion. Considers upon merit almost any subject of scholarly interest, but specializes in communications, military history, public administration, literary criticism and biography, history, Judaic studies, and American archaeology. Accepts nonfiction translations. Query with SASE.

TIPS "Please direct inquiry to appropriate acquisitions editor. University of Alabama Press responds to an author within 2-3 weeks upon receiving the ms or proposal. If they think it is unsuitable for Alabama's program, they tell the author as soon as possible. If the ms warrants it, they begin the peer-review process, which may take 2-4 months to complete. During that process, they keep the author fully informed."

UNIVERSITY OF ALASKA PRESS

P.O. Box 756240, Fairbanks AK 99775-6240. (907)474-5831 or (888)252-6657. **Fax:** (907)474-5502. **E-mail:** amy.simpson@alaska.edu. **Website:** www.uaf.edu/uapress. **Contact:** Acquisitions Editor. Estab. 1967. Publishes hardcover originals, trade paperback originals and reprints. "The mission of the University of Alaska Press is to encourage, publish, and disseminate works of scholarship that will enhance the store of knowledge about Alaska and the North Pacific Rim, with a special emphasis on the circumpolar regions." **Publishes 10 titles/year.** Publishes ms within 2 years of acceptance. Accepts simultaneous submissions. Responds in 2 months to queries. Book catalog available free. Guidelines online.

NONFICTION Subjects include Americana, animals, education, ethnic, history, regional, science, translation. Northern or circumpolar only. Query with SASE and proposal. Reviews artwork/photos.

FICTION Subjects include literary. Alaska literary series with Peggy Shumaker as series editor. Publishes 1-3 works of fiction/year. Submit proposal.

TIPS "Writers have the best chance with scholarly nonfiction relating to Alaska, the circumpolar regions and North Pacific Rim. Our audience is made up of scholars, historians, students, libraries, universities, individuals, and the general Alaskan public."

◑⊘ THE UNIVERSITY OF ALBERTA PRESS

Ring House 2, Edmonton AB T6G 2E1, Canada. (780)492-3662. **Fax:** (780)492-0719. **E-mail:** pmidgley@ualberta.ca. **Website:** www.uap.ualberta.ca. **Contact:** Peter Midgley. Estab. 1969. Publishes originals and reprints. "We do not accept unsolicited novels, short story collections, or poetry. Please see our website for details." **Publishes 18-25 titles/year. Royalties are negotiated.** Publishes ms within 2 years after acceptance. Responds in 3 months to queries. Guidelines online.

NONFICTION Subjects include history, regional, natural history, social policy. Submit cover letter, word count, CV, 1 sample chapter, TOC.

UNIVERSITY OF ARIZONA PRESS

Main Library Building, 5th Floor, 1510 E. University Blvd., Tucson AZ 85721. (520)621-1441. **Fax:** (520)621-8899. **E-mail:** kbuckles@uapress.arizona.edu. **Website:** www.uapress.arizona.edu. **Contact:** Kristen Buckles, acquiring editor. Estab. 1959. Publishes hardcover and paperback originals and reprints. "University of Arizona is a publisher of scholarly books and books of the Southwest." **Royalty terms vary; usual starting point for scholarly monography is after sale of first 1,000 copies. Pays advance.** Responds in 3 months to queries. Book catalog online. Guidelines online.

NONFICTION Subjects include Americana, ethnic, regional, environmental studies, western, and environmental history. Scholarly books about anthropology, Arizona, American West, archeology, Native American studies, Latino studies, environmental science, global change, Latin America, Native Americans, natural history, space sciences, and women's studies. Submit sample chapters, resume, TOC, ms length, audience, comparable books. Reviews artwork/photos.

TIPS "Perhaps the most common mistake a writer might make is to offer a book manuscript or proposal to a house whose list he or she has not studied carefully. Editors rejoice in receiving material that is clearly targeted to the house's list ('I have approached your firm because my books complement your past publications in') and presented in a straightforward, businesslike manner."

THE UNIVERSITY OF ARKANSAS PRESS

McIlroy House, 105 N. McIlroy Ave., Fayetteville AR 72701. (479)575-3246. **Fax:** (479)575-6044. **E-mail:** mbieker@uark.edu. **Website:** uapress.com. **Contact:** Mike Bieker, director. Estab. 1980. Publishes hardcover and trade paperback originals and reprints. "The University of Arkansas Press publishes series on Ozark studies, the Civil War in the West, poetry and poetics, food studies, and sport and society." **Publishes 22 titles/year. 30% of books from first-time authors. 95% from unagented writers.** Publishes book 1 year after acceptance. Accepts simultaneous submissions. Responds in 3 months to proposals. Book catalog and ms guidelines online.

NONFICTION Subjects include architecture, foods, history, humanities, literary criticism, regional, Arkansas. Accepted mss must be submitted electronically. Query with SASE. Submit outline, sample chapters, resume.

FICTION Subjects include historical, regional.

POETRY University of Arkansas Press publishes 4 poetry books per year through the Miller Williams Poetry Prize.

☾ UNIVERSITY OF CALGARY PRESS

2500 University Dr. NW, Calgary AB T2N 1N4, Canada. (403)220-7578. **Fax:** (403)282-0085. **E-mail:** ucpress@ucalgary.ca. **Website:** www.uofcpress.com. **Contact:** Brian Scrivener, Director. Estab. 1984. Publishes scholarly and trade paperback originals and reprints. **Publishes 10 titles/year. 40% of books from first-time authors. 90% from unagented writers.** Publishes ms 20 months after acceptance. Book catalog available for free. Guidelines online.

NONFICTION Subjects include architecture, art, cinema, communications, environment, film, history, humanities, literary criticism, literature, memoirs, military, politics, public affairs, regional, social sciences, womens studies, Canadian studies, postmodern studies, native studies, history, international relations, arctic studies, Africa, Latin American and Caribbean studies, and heritage of the Canadian and American heartland.

UNIVERSITY OF CALIFORNIA PRESS

155 Grand Ave., Suite 400, Oakland CA 94612. **Website:** www.ucpress.edu. **Contact:** Kate Marshall, acquisitions editor. Estab. 1893. Publishes hardcover and paperback originals and reprints. "University of California Press publishes mostly nonfiction written by scholars." **Pays advance.** Accepts simultaneous submissions. Response time varies, depending on the subject. Enclose return postage to queries. Guidelines online.

NONFICTION Subjects include history, translation, art, literature, natural sciences, some high-level popularizations. No length preference. Submit proposal package.

FICTION Publishes fiction only in translation.

⊘ THE UNIVERSITY OF CHICAGO PRESS

1427 East 60th St., Chicago IL 60637. (773)702-7700. **Fax:** (773)702-9756. **Website:** www.press.uchicago. edu. **Contact:** Randolph Petilos, Poetry and Medieval Studies Editor. Estab. 1891. "The University of Chicago Press has been publishing scholarly books and journals since 1891. Annually, we publish an average of 4 books in our Phoenix Poets series and 2 books of poetry in translation. Occasionally, we may publish a book of poetry outside Phoenix Poets, or as a paperback reprint from another publisher." Has recently published work by Peter Balakian, Charles Bernstein, Maggie Dietz, Reginald Gibbons, Nate Klug, Gail Ma-

zur, Robert Pack, Vanesha Pravin, Alan Shapiro, and Connie Voisine. Accepts simultaneous submissions.

UNIVERSITY OF GEORGIA PRESS

Main Library, Third Floor, 320 S. Jackson St., Athens GA 30602. (706)369-6130. **Fax:** (706)369-6131. **Website:** www.ugapress.org. **Contact:** Mick Gusinde-Duffy, assistant director for acquisitions and editor-in-chief; Walter Biggins, senior acquisitions editor; Pat Allen, acquisitions editor; Beth Snead, assistant acquisitions editor. Estab. 1938. Publishes hardcover originals, trade paperback originals, and reprints. University of Georgia Press is a midsized press that publishes fiction only through the Flannery O'Connor Award for Short Fiction competition. **Publishes 85 titles/year. Pays 7-10% royalty on net receipts. Pays rare, varying advance.** Publishes book 1 year after acceptance. Responds in 2 months to queries. Book catalog and guidelines online.

NONFICTION Subjects include history, regional, environmental studies, literary nonfiction.. Query with SASE. Submit bio, 1 sample chapter. Reviews artwork/photos. Send if essential to book.

FICTION Short story collections published in Flannery O'Connor Award Competition.

TIPS "Please visit our website to view our book catalogs and for all manuscript submission guidelines."

UNIVERSITY OF ILLINOIS PRESS

1325 S. Oak St., Champaign IL 61820-6903. (217)333-0950. **Fax:** (217)244-8082. **E-mail:** uipress@uillinois. edu. **Website:** www.press.uillinois.edu. **Contact:** Laurie Matheson, director; Daniel Nasset, acquisitions editor; Dawn Durante, acquisitions editor; James Engelhardt, acquisitions editor. Estab. 1918. Publishes hardcover and trade paperback originals and reprints. University of Illinois Press publishes scholarly books and serious nonfiction with a wide range of study interests. Currently emphasizing American history, especially immigration, labor, African-American, and military; American religion, music, women's studies, and film. **Publishes 150 titles/year. 35% of books from first-time authors. 95% from unagented writers. Pays $1,000-1,500 (rarely) advance.** Publishes ms 1 year after acceptance. Accepts simultaneous submissions. Responds in 1 month to queries. Guidelines online.

NONFICTION Subjects include Americana, animals, history, philosophy, regional, sociology, sports, translation, film/cinema/stage. "Always looking for solid, scholarly books in American history, especially social history; books on American popular music, and books in the broad area of American studies." Query with SASE. Submit outline.

TIPS "As a university press, we are required to submit all mss to rigorous scholarly review. Mss need to be clearly original, well written, and based on solid and thorough research. We cannot encourage memoirs or autobiographies."

UNIVERSITY OF IOWA PRESS

100 Kuhl House, 119 W. Park Rd., Iowa City IA 52242. (319)335-2000. **Fax:** (319)335-2055. **E-mail:** james-mccoy@uiowa.edu; elisabeth-chretien@uiowa.edu; cathcampbell@uiowa.edu. **Website:** www.uiowapress.org. **Contact:** James McCoy, director (short fiction, poetry, general trade); Elisabeth Chretien, acquisitions editor (literary criticism, literary and general nonfiction, military and veterans' studies); Catherine Cocks, acquisitions editor (book arts, fan studies, food studies, Midwestern history and culture, theater history and culture). Estab. 1969. Publishes hardcover and paperback originals. The University of Iowa Press publishes both trade and academic work in a variety of fields. **Publishes 35 titles/year. 30% of books from first-time authors. 95% from unagented writers.** Accepts simultaneous submissions. Book catalog available free. Guidelines online.

NONFICTION Subjects include agriculture, contemporary culture, creative nonfiction, environment, history, humanities, literary criticism, multicultural, nature, pop culture, regional, travel, true crime, womens studies. "Looks for evidence of original research, reliable sources, clarity of organization, complete development of theme with documentation, supportive footnotes and/or bibliography, and a substantive contribution to knowledge in the field treated. Use *Chicago Manual of Style*." Query with SASE. Submit outline. Reviews artwork/photos.

FICTION Currently publishes the Iowa Short Fiction Award selections. "We do not accept any fiction submissions outside of the Iowa Short Fiction Award. See www.uiowapress.org for contest details."

POETRY Currently publishes winners of the Iowa Poetry Prize Competition and Kuhl House Poets (by invitation only). Competition guidelines available on website.

UNIVERSITY OF MAINE PRESS

5729 Fogler Library, Orono ME 04469. (207)581-1652. **Fax:** (207)581-1653. **E-mail:** michael.alpert@umit.

maine.edu. **Website:** www.umaine.edu/umpress. **Contact:** Michael Alpert, editorial director. Publishes hardcover and trade paperback originals and reprints. **Publishes 4 titles/year. 50 queries received/year. 25 mss received/year. 50% of books from first-time authors. 90% from unagented writers.** Publishes ms 1 year after acceptance. Accepts simultaneous submissions.

NONFICTION Subjects include history, regional, science. "We are an academic book publisher, interested in scholarly works on regional history, regional life sciences, Franco-American studies. Authors should be able to articulate their ideas on the potential market for their work." Query with SASE.

UNIVERSITY OF MICHIGAN PRESS

839 Greene St., Ann Arbor MI 48106. (734)764-4388. **Fax:** (734)615-1540. **Website:** www.press.umich. edu.. **Contact:** Mary Francis, editorial director. "In partnership with our authors and series editors, we publish in a wide range of humanities and social sciences disciplines." Accepts simultaneous submissions. Guidelines online.

NONFICTION Submit proposal.

FICTION Subjects include literary, regional. In addition to the annual Michigan Literary Fiction Awards, this publishes literary fiction linked to the Great Lakes region. Submit cover letter and first 30 pages.

UNIVERSITY OF NEVADA PRESS

Morrill Hall, Mail Stop 0166, Reno NV 89557. (775)784-6573. **Fax:** (775)784-6200. **Website:** www.unpress.nevada.edu. **Contact:** Justin Race, director. Estab. 1961. Publishes hardcover and paperback originals and reprints. "Small university press. Publishes fiction that primarily focuses on the American West." Member: AAUP **Publishes 25 titles/year.** Publishes ms 18 months after acceptance. Responds in 2 months. Guidelines online.

NONFICTION Subjects include ethnic, history, regional, western literature, current affairs, gambling and gaming, Basque studies. No juvenile books. Submit proposal. No online submissions. Reviews artwork/photos. Send photocopies.

FICTION "We publish in Basque Studies, Gambling Studies, Western literature, Western history, Natural science, Environmental Studies, Travel and Outdoor books, Archeology, Anthropology, and Political Studies, all focusing on the West". The Press also publishes creative nonfiction and books on regional topics for a general audience. *Does not publish unsolicited fiction.*

UNIVERSITY OF NEW MEXICO PRESS

1717 Roma Ave. NE, Albuquerque NM 87106. (505)277-3495 or (800)249-7737. **Fax:** (505)277-3343. **Website:** www.unmpress.com. **Contact:** John W. Byram, Director. Estab. 1929. Publishes hardcover originals and trade paperback originals and reprints. "The Press is well known as a publisher in the fields of anthropology, archeology, Latin American studies, art and photography, architecture and the history and culture of the American West, fiction, some poetry, Chicano/a studies and works by and about American Indians. We focus on American West, Southwest and Latin American regions." **Publishes 75 titles/ year. 1,500 submissions received/year. 20% of books from first-time authors. 80% from unagented writers. Pays variable royalty. Pays advance.** Publishes ms 10 months after acceptance. Responds in 6 weeks. Book catalog available free. Guidelines online.

NONFICTION Subjects include Americana, anthropology, archeology, architecture, art, ethnic, gardening, history, humanities, literary criticism, literature, memoirs, multicultural, nature, photography, pop culture, regional, religion, science, social sciences, translation, travel, true crime, womens issues, womens studies, contemporary culture, cinema/stage, true crime, general nonfiction. No how-to, humor, juvenile, self-help, software, technical or textbooks. Query with SASE. Reviews artwork/photos. Send photocopies.

FICTION Subjects include ethnic, literary, multicultural, regional, translation.

THE UNIVERSITY OF NORTH CAROLINA PRESS

116 S. Boundary St., Chapel Hill NC 27514. (919)966-3561. **Fax:** (919)966-3829. **E-mail:** uncpress@unc.edu. **Website:** www.uncpress.unc.edu. **Contact:** Mark Simpson-Vos, editorial director. Publishes hardcover originals, trade paperback originals and reprints. "UNC Press publishes nonfiction books for academic and general audiences. We have a special interest in trade and scholarly titles about our region. We do not, however, publish original fiction, drama, or poetry, memoirs of living persons, or festshriften." **Publishes 90 titles/year. 500 queries received/year. 200 mss received/year. 50% of books from first-time authors. 90% from unagented writers. Pays variable royalty**

on wholesale price. Offers variable advance. Publishes ms 1 year after acceptance. Accepts simultaneous submissions. Responds in 3-4 weeks. Book catalog and guidelines online.

NONFICTION Subjects include Americana, gardening, history, multicultural, philosophy, photography, regional, religion, translation, African-American studies, American studies, cultural studies, Latin-American studies, American-Indian studies, media studies, gender studies, social medicine, Appalachian studies. Submit proposal package, outline, CV, cover letter, abstract, and TOC. Reviews artwork/photos. Send photocopies.

UNIVERSITY OF NORTH TEXAS PRESS

1155 Union Circle, #311336, Denton TX 76203. (940)565-2142. **Fax:** (940)565-4590. **E-mail:** bonnie.stufflebeam@unt.edu. **Website:** untpress.unt.edu. **Contact:** Ronald Chrisman, director; Karen De Vinney, assistant director; Amy Pierce, administrative assistant; Bonnie Stufflebeam, Marketing Manager. Estab. 1987. Publishes hardcover and trade paperback originals and reprints. "We are dedicated to producing the highest quality scholarly, academic, and general interest books. We are committed to serving all peoples by publishing stories of their cultures and experiences that have been overlooked. Currently emphasizing military history, Texas history, music, Mexican-American studies." **Publishes 14-16 titles/ year. 500 queries received/year. 50% of books from first-time authors. 95% from unagented writers.** Publishes ms 1-2 years after acceptance. Responds in 1 month to queries. Book catalog for 8 ½×11 SASE. Guidelines online.

NONFICTION Subjects include Americana, art, cooking, creative nonfiction, ethnic, government, history, humanities, military, multicultural, music, nature, photography, politics, regional, social sciences, war, womens issues, womens studies. Query by e-mail. Reviews artwork/photos. Send photocopies.

FICTION Subjects include short story collections. "The only fiction we publish is the winner of the Katherine Anne Porter Prize in Short Fiction, an annual, national competition with a $1,000 prize, and publication of the winning ms each Fall."

POETRY "The only poetry we publish is the winner of the Vassar Miller Prize in Poetry, an annual, national competition with a $1,000 prize and publication of the winning ms each Spring." Query.

TIPS "We publish series called War and the Southwest; Texas Folklore Society Publications; the Western Life Series; Practical Guide Series; Al-Filo: Mexican-American studies; North Texas Crime and Criminal Justice; Katherine Anne Porter Prize in Short Fiction; and the North Texas Lives of Musicians Series."

UNIVERSITY OF OKLAHOMA PRESS

2800 Venture Dr., Norman OK 73069. (405)325-5609. E mail: ccrankin@ou.edu. **Website:** www.oupress. com. **Contact:** Charles E. Rankin, editor-in-chief. Estab. 1928. Publishes hardcover and paperback originals and reprints. University of Oklahoma Press publishes books for both scholarly and nonspecialist readers. **Publishes 90 titles/year. Pays standard royalty.** Responds promptly to queries. Book catalog for 9×12 SAE with 6 first-class stamps.

IMPRINTS Plains Reprints.

NONFICTION Subjects include political science (Congressional, area and security studies), history (regional, military, natural), language/literature (American Indian, US West), American Indian studies, classical studies. Query with SASE or by e-mail. Submit outline, resume, 1-2 sample chapters. Use *Chicago Manual of Style* for ms guidelines. Reviews artwork/photos.

☺ UNIVERSITY OF OTTAWA PRESS

542 King Edward Ave., Ottawa ON K1N 6N5, Canada. (613)562-5246. **Fax:** (613)562-5247. **E-mail:** puo-uop@ uottawa.ca. **Website:** www.press.uottawa.ca. **Contact:** Lara Mainville, director; Dominike Thomas, acquisitions editor. Estab. 1936. "UOP publishes books and journals, in French and English, and in any and all editions and formats, that touch upon the human condition: anthropology, sociology, political science, psychology, criminology, media studies, economics, education, language and culture, law, history, literature, translation studies, philosophy, public administration, health sciences, and religious studies." Accepts simultaneous submissions. Book catalog and ms guidelines online.

NONFICTION Submit outline, proposal form (please see website), CV, 1-2 sample chapters (for monographs only), ms (for collected works only), TOC, 2-5 page proposal/summary, contributor names, short bios, and citizenships (for collected works only).

TIPS "Please note that the University of Ottawa Press does not accept: bilingual works (texts must be either entirely in English or entirely in French), undergraduate or masters theses, or doctoral theses that have not been substantially revised."

UNIVERSITY OF PENNSYLVANIA PRESS

3905 Spruce St., Philadelphia PA 19104. (215)898-6261. **Fax:** (215)898-0404. **E-mail:** agree@upenn.edu. **Website:** www.pennpress.org. **Contact:** Peter Agree, editor-in-chief. Estab. 1890. Publishes hardcover and paperback originals, and reprints. "Manuscript submissions are welcome in fields appropriate for Penn Press's editorial program. The Press's acquiring editors, and their fields of responsibility, are listed in the Contact Us section of our Web site. Although we have no formal policies regarding manuscript proposals and submissions, what we need minimally, in order to gauge our degree of interest, is a brief statement describing the manuscript, a copy of the contents page, and a reasonably current vita. Initial inquiries are best sent by letter, in paper form, to the appropriate acquiring editor." **Publishes 100+ titles/year. 20-30% of books from first-time authors. 95% from unagented writers. Royalty determined on book-by-book basis. Pays advance.** Publishes ms 10 months after acceptance. Responds in 3 months to queries. Book catalog online. Guidelines online.

NONFICTION Subjects include Americana, history, literary criticism, sociology, anthropology, literary criticism, cultural studies, ancient studies, medieval studies, urban studies, human rights. Follow the *Chicago Manual of Style*. "Serious books that serve the scholar and the professional, student and general reader." Query with SASE. Submit outline, resume.

UNIVERSITY OF SOUTH CAROLINA PRESS

1600 Hampton St., 5th Floor, Columbia SC 29208. (803)777-5243. **Fax:** (803)777-0160. **Website:** www. sc.edu/uscpress. **Contact:** Jonathan Haupt, director. Estab. 1944. Publishes hardcover originals, trade paperback originals and reprints. "We focus on scholarly monographs and regional trade books of lasting merit." **Publishes 50 titles/year. 500 queries received/ year. 150 mss received/year. 30% of books from first-time authors. 95% from unagented writers.** Publishes ms 1 year after acceptance. Accepts simultaneous submissions. Responds in 3 months to mss. Book catalog available free. Guidelines online.

NONFICTION Subjects include history, regional, religion, rhetoric, communication. Query with SASE, or submit proposal package and outline, and 1 sample chapter and resume with SASE Reviews artwork/photos. Send photocopies.

POETRY Palmetto Poetry Series, a South Carolina-based original poetry series edited by Nikky Finney. Director: Jonathan Haupt, director (jhaupt@mailbox. sc.edu).

UNIVERSITY OF TAMPA PRESS

University of Tampa, 401 W. Kennedy Blvd., Tampa FL 33606. (813)253-6266. **Fax:** (813)258-7593. **E-mail:** utpress@ut.edu. **Website:** www.ut.edu/tampapress. **Contact:** Richard Mathews, editor. Estab. 1952. Publishes hardcover originals and reprints; trade paperback originals and reprints. "We are a small university press publishing a limited number of titles each year, primarily in the areas of local and regional history and printing history." **Publishes 4-6 titles/year. Does not pay advance.** Publishes ms 6 months-2 years after acceptance. Responds in 3-4 months to queries. Book catalog online. "We do not accept unsolicited book manuscripts except for poetry manuscripts submitted through the annual Tampa Review Prize for Poetry.".

NONFICTION Subjects include Florida history. "We do not consider unsolicited nonfiction manuscripts. We do not consider e-mail submissions." Reviews artwork/photos.

FICTION Subjects include literary, poetry.

POETRY "We consider original poetry collections through the annual Tampa Review Prize for Poetry competition, with a deadline of December 31 each year." Submit to the Tampa Review Prize for Poetry.

THE UNIVERSITY OF TENNESSEE PRESS

The University of Tennessee, 110 Conference Center, 600 Henley St., Knoxville TN 37996-4108. (865)974-3321. **Fax:** (865)974-3724. **E-mail:** twells@utk.edu. **Website:** www.utpress.org. **Contact:** Thomas Wells, acquisitions editor. Estab. 1940. "Our mission is to stimulate scientific and scholarly research in all fields; to channel such studies, either in scholarly or popular form, to a larger number of people; and to extend the regional leadership of the University of Tennessee by stimulating research projects within the South and by nonuniversity authors." **Publishes 35 titles/year. 35% of books from first-time authors. 99% from unagented writers. Pays negotiable royalty on net receipts. Rarely offers advance.** Publishes ms 18 months after acceptance. Accepts simultaneous submissions. Guidelines online.

NONFICTION Subjects include Americana, archeology, architecture, history, literary criticism, military, music, regional, religion, war, African-American studies, Appalachian studies, folklore/folklife, material culture. Prefers scholarly treatment and a readable style. Authors usually have advanced degrees. Submissions in other fields, fiction or poetry, textbooks, and plays and translations are not invited Submit cover letter, outline, bio or CV, and sample chapters. Reviews artwork/photos.

FICTION The press no longer publishes works of fiction.

UNIVERSITY OF TEXAS PRESS

P.O. Box 7819, Austin TX 78713-7819. **Fax:** (512)232-7178. **E-mail:** rdevens@utpress.utexas.edu. **Website:** www.utexaspress.com. **Contact:** Robert Devens, editor-in-chief. Estab. 1952. "In addition to publishing the results of advanced research for scholars worldwide, UT Press has a special obligation to the people of its state to publish authoritative books on Texas. We do not publish fiction or poetry, except as invited by a series editor, and some Latin American and Middle Eastern literature in translation." **Publishes 90 titles/year. 50% of books from first-time authors. 99% from unagented writers. Pays occasional advance.** Publishes ms 18-24 months after acceptance. Responds in 3 months to queries. Guidelines online.

NONFICTION Subjects include ethnic, history, literary criticism, regional, science, translation, natural history, American, Latin American, Native American, Latino, and Middle Eastern studies; classics and the ancient world, film, contemporary regional architecture, geography, ornithology, biology. Also uses specialty titles related to Texas and the Southwest, national trade titles and regional trade titles. Submit cover letter, TOC, CV, sample chapter.

UNIVERSITY OF WASHINGTON PRESS

P.O. Box 359570, Seattle WA 98195. (206)543-4050. **Fax:** (206)543-3932. **E-mail:** uwapress@uw.edu. **E-mail:** lmclaugh@uw.edu. **Website:** www.washington. edu/uwpress/. **Contact:** Laurin McLaughlin, editor-in-chief. Publishes in hardcover originals. **Publishes 70 titles/year.** Accepts simultaneous submissions. Book catalog guidelines online.

NONFICTION Subjects include ethnic, history, multicultural, photography, regional, social sciences. Go to our Book Search page for complete subject listing. We publish academic and general books, especially in anthropology, Asian studies, art, environmental studies, Middle Eastern Studies & regional interests. International Studies with focus on Asia; Jewish Studies; Art & Culture of the Northwest coast; Indians & Alaskan Eskimos; The Asian-American Experience; Southeast Asian Studies; Korean and Slavic Studies; Studies in Modernity & National Identity; Scandinavian Studies. Query with SASE. Submit proposal package, outline, sample chapters.

UNIVERSITY OF WISCONSIN PRESS

1930 Monroe St., 3rd Floor, Madison WI 53711. (608)263-1110. **Fax:** (608)263-1132. **E-mail:** gcwalker@wisc.edu. **E-mail:** kadushin@wisc.edu. **Website:** uwpress.wisc.edu. **Contact:** Raphael Kadushin, senior acquisitions editor; Gwen Walker, acquisitions editor. Estab. 1937. Publishes hardcover originals, paperback originals, and paperback reprints. **Publishes 98 titles/year. Pays royalty.** Publishes ms 9-18 months after acceptance. Accepts simultaneous submissions. Responds in 2 weeks to queries; 8 weeks to mss. Rarely comments on rejected mss. Guidelines online.

NONFICTION Subjects include anthropology, dance, environment, film, foods, gay, history, lesbian, memoirs, travel, African Studies, classical studies, human rights, Irish studies, Jewish studies, Latin American studies, Latino/a memoirs, modern Western European history, performance studies, Slavic studies, Southeast Asian studies.. Does not accept unsolicited mss. Query with SASE or submit outline, 1-2 sample chapter(s), synopsis.

FICTION Subjects include gay, hi-lo, lesbian, mystery, regional, short story collections. Query with SASE or submit outline, 1-2 sample chapter(s), synopsis.

POETRY The University of Wisconsin Press Awards the Brittingham Prize in Poetry and Felix Pollack Prize in Poetry. More details online.

TIPS "Make sure the query letter and sample text are well-written, and read guidelines carefully to make sure we accept the genre you are submitting."

UNIVERSITY PRESS OF KANSAS

2502 Westbrooke Circle, Lawrence KS 66045. (785)864-4154. **Fax:** (785)864-4586. **E-mail:** upress@ku.edu. **Website:** www.kansaspress.ku.edu; www.facebook.com/kansaspress. **Contact:** Charles T. Myers, director; Michael J. Briggs, editor-in-chief; Kim Hogeland, acquisitions editor. Estab. 1946. Publishes hardcover originals, trade paperback originals and reprints. "The University Press of Kansas publishes scholarly books that advance knowledge and regional books that contribute to the understanding of Kansas, the Great Plains, and the Midwest." **Publishes 55 titles/year. 600 queries received/year. 20% of books from first-time authors. 98% from unagented writers. Pays selective advance.** Publishes book 10 months after acceptance. Responds in 1 month to proposals. Book catalog and ms guidelines free.

NONFICTION Subjects include Americana, archeology, environment, government, military, nature, politics, regional, war, American History, Native Studies, American Cultural Studies. "We are looking for books on topics of wide interest based on solid scholarship and written for both specialists and informed general readers. Do not send unsolicited, complete manuscripts." Submit outline, sample chapters, cover letter, CV, prospectus. Reviews artwork/photos. Send photocopies.

UNIVERSITY PRESS OF KENTUCKY

663 S. Limestone St., Lexington KY 40508. (859)257-8434. **Fax:** (859)323-1873. **E-mail:** adwatk0@e-mail.uky.edu. **Website:** www.kentuckypress.com. **Contact:** Anne Dean Dotson, senior acquisitions editor. Estab. 1943. Publishes hardcover and paperback originals and reprints. "We are a scholarly publisher, publishing chiefly for an academic and professional audience, as well as books about Kentucky, the upper South, Appalachia, and the Ohio Valley." **Publishes 60 titles/year. Royalty varies.** Publishes ms 1 year after acceptance. Accepts simultaneous submissions. Responds in 2 months to queries. Book catalog available free. Guidelines online.

NONFICTION Subjects include history, regional, political science. No textbooks, genealogical material, lightweight popular treatments, how-to books, or books unrelated to our major areas of interest. The Press does not consider original works of fiction or poetry. Query with SASE.

UNIVERSITY PRESS OF MISSISSIPPI

3825 Ridgewood Rd., Jackson MS 39211. (601)432-6205. **Fax:** (601)432-6217. **E-mail:** press@mississippi.edu. **Website:** www.upress.state.ms.us. **Contact:** Craig Gill, editor-in-chief (regional studies, history, folklore, music). Estab. 1970. Publishes hardcover and paperback originals and reprints and e-books. "University Press of Mississippi publishes scholarly and trade titles, as well as special series, including: American Made Music; Conversations with Comic

Artists; Conversations with Filmmakers; Faulkner and Yoknapatawpha; Literary Conversations; Hollywood Legends; Caribbean Studies." **Publishes 70 titles/year. 80% of books from first-time authors. 90% from unagented writers. Pays competitive royalties and terms. Pays advance.** Publishes ms 1 year after acceptance. Responds in 3 months to queries.

NONFICTION Subjects include Americana, ethnic, literary criticism, regional, folklife, literary criticism, popular culture with scholarly emphasis, literary studies. "We prefer a proposal that describes the significance of the work and a chapter outline." Submit outline, sample chapters, CV.

Ⓐ🌑⊘ USBORNE PUBLISHING

83-85 Saffron Hill, London En EC1N 8RT, United Kingdom. (44)207430-2800. **Fax:** (44)207430-1562. **E-mail:** mail@usborne.co.uk. **Website:** www.usborne.com. "Usborne Publishing is a multiple-award-winning, worldwide children's publishing company publishing almost every type of children's book for every age from baby to young adult." **Pays authors royalty.** Accepts simultaneous submissions.

FICTION Young readers, middle readers: adventure, contemporary, fantasy, history, humor, multicultural, nature/environment, science fiction, suspense/mystery, strong concept-based or character-led series. Average word length: young readers—5,000-10,000; middle readers—25,000-50,000; young adult—50,000-100,000. *Agented submissions only.*

TIPS "Do not send any original work and, sorry, but we cannot guarantee a reply."

UTAH STATE UNIVERSITY PRESS

3078 Old Main Hill, Logan UT 84322. **Website:** www.usu.edu/usupress. **Contact:** Darrin Pratt, director. Estab. 1972. Publishes hardcover and trade paperback originals and reprints. Utah State University Press publishes scholarly works in the academic areas noted below. Currently interested in book-length scholarly mss dealing with folklore studies, composition studies, Native American studies, and history. **Publishes 18 titles/year. 8% of books from first-time authors.** Publishes ms 18 months after acceptance. Responds in 1 month to queries. Book catalog available free. Guidelines online.

NONFICTION Subjects include history, regional, folklore, the West, Native-American studies, studies

in composition and rhetoric. Query via online submission form. Reviews artwork/photos. Send photocopies.

TIPS "Utah State University Press also sponsors the annual May Swenson Poetry Award."

VANDERBILT UNIVERSITY PRESS

PMB 351813, 2301 Vanderbilt Place, Nashville TN 37235. (615)322-3585. **Fax:** (615)343-8823. **E-mail:** vupress@vanderbilt.edu. **Website:** www.vanderbiltuniversitypress.com. **Contact:** Michael Ames, director. Publishes hardcover originals and trade paperback originals and reprints. "Vanderbilt University Press publishes books on healthcare, social sciences, education, and regional studies, for both academic and general audiences that are intellectually significant, socially relevant, and of practical importance." **Publishes 20-25 titles/year. 500 queries received/year. 25% of books from first-time authors. 90% from unagented writers. Pays rare advance.** Publishes ms 10 months after acceptance. Accepts simultaneous submissions. Responds in 2 weeks to proposals. Book catalog online. Guidelines online.

NONFICTION Subjects include Americana, education, ethnic, history, multicultural, philosophy. Submit cover letter, TOC, CV, 1-2 sample chapters.

TIPS "Our audience consists of scholars and educated, general readers."

🌑 VAN SCHAIK PUBLISHERS

1059 Francis Baard St., Hatfield 0083, South Africa. **E-mail:** vanschaik@vanschaiknet.com. **Website:** www.vanschaiknet.com. **Contact:** Julia Read. Accepts simultaneous submissions. Guidelines online.

NONFICTION Subjects include education, social sciences, nursing/medicine, language, accounting, public administration. Submit proposal package, outline, sample text.

⟳ VÉHICULE PRESS

P.O.B. 42094 BP Roy, Montreal QC H2W 2T3, Canada. (514)844-6073. **Fax:** (514)844-7543. **E-mail:** sd@vehiculepress.com. **E-mail:** admin@vehiculepress.com. **Website:** www.vehiculepress.com. **Contact:** Simon Dardick, nonfiction; Carmine Starnino, poetry; Dimitri Nasrallah, fiction. Estab. 1973. Publishes trade paperback originals by Canadian authors mostly. "Montreal's Véhicule Press has published the best of Canadian and Quebec literature-fiction, poetry, essays, translations, and social history." **Publishes**

15 titles/year. 20% of books from first-time authors. 95% from unagented writers. Pays 10-15% royalty on retail price. Pays $200-500 advance. Publishes ms 1 year after acceptance. Accepts simultaneous submissions. Responds in 4 months to queries. Book catalog for 9 x 12 SAE with IRCs.

IMPRINTS Signal Editions (poetry); Esplanade Editions (fiction).

NONFICTION Subjects include history, memoirs, regional, sociology. Especially looking for Canadian social history. Query with SASE. Reviews artwork/photos.

FICTION Subjects include feminist, literary, regional, translation, literary novels. No romance or formula writing. Query with SASE.

POETRY Vehicle Press is a "literary press with a poetry series, Signal Editions, publishing the work of Canadian poets only." Publishes flat-spined paperbacks. Publishes Canadian poetry that is "first-rate, original, content-conscious."

TIPS "Quality in almost any style is acceptable. We believe in the editing process."

VELÁZQUEZ PRESS

Division of Academic Learning Press, 9682 Telstar Ave., Suite 110, El Monte CA 91731. (626)448-3448. **Website:** www.velazquezpress.com. Publishes hardcover and trade paperback originals and reprints. **Publishes 5-10 titles/year. Pays 10% royalty on retail price.** Publishes ms 6 months after acceptance. Accepts simultaneous submissions. Responds in 2 months. Book catalog and guidelines via e-mail.

IMPRINTS WBusiness Books; ZHealth.

NONFICTION Subjects include education. "We are interested in publishing bilingual educational materials." Submit proposal package, outline, 2 sample chapters, cover letter. Submit complete ms. Reviews artwork/photos. Send photocopies.

VENTURE PUBLISHING, INC.

1999 Cato Ave., State College PA 16801. (814)234-4561. **Fax:** (814)234-1651. **Website:** www.venture-publish.com. Estab. 1978. Publishes hardcover and paperback originals and reprints. "Venture Publishing produces quality educational publications, also workbooks for professionals, educators, and students in the fields of recreation, parks, leisure studies, therapeutic recreation and long term care." **Pays royalty on wholesale price. Pays advance.** Book catalog and ms guidelines online.

NONFICTION Subjects include recreation, sociology, long-term care nursing homes, therapeutic recreation. Textbooks and books for recreation activity leaders high priority. Submit 1 sample chapter, book proposal, competing titles.

VERSO

20 Jay St., 10th Floor, Brooklyn NY 11201. (718)246-8160. **Fax:** (718)246-8165. **E-mail:** verso@versobooks.com. **Website:** www.versobooks.com. **Contact:** Editorial Department. Estab. 1970. Publishes hardcover and trade paperback originals. "Our books cover economics, politics, cinema studies, and history (among other topics), but all come from a critical, Leftist viewpoint, on the border between trade and academic." **Publishes 100 titles/year. Pays royalty. Pays advance.** Accepts simultaneous submissions. Book catalog available free. Guidelines online.

NONFICTION Subjects include history, philosophy, sociology. Submit proposal package.

✪ VERTIGO

DC Universe, Vertigo-DC Comics, 1700 Broadway, New York NY 10019. **Website:** www.vertigocomics.com. At this time, DC Entertainment does not accept unsolicited artwork or writing submissions. Accepts simultaneous submissions.

✪✪ VIKING

Imprint of Penguin Group (USA), Inc., 375 Hudson St., New York NY 10014. (212)366-2000. **Website:** www.penguin.com. Estab. 1925. Publishes hardcover and originals. Viking publishes a mix of academic and popular fiction and nonfiction. **Publishes 100 titles/year. Pays 10-15% royalty on retail price.** Publishes ms 18 months after acceptance. Accepts simultaneous submissions.

NONFICTION Subjects include child guidance, history, philosophy. *Agented submissions only.*

FICTION Subjects include literary, mystery, suspense. *Agented submissions only.*

✪✪ VIKING CHILDREN'S BOOKS

375 Hudson St., New York NY 10014. **Website:** www.penguin.com. Publishes hardcover originals. "Viking Children's Books is known for humorous, quirky picture books, in addition to more traditional fiction. We publish the highest quality fiction, nonfiction, and picture books for pre-schoolers through young adults." *Does not accept unsolicited submissions.* **Pub-**

lishes 70 titles/year. **Pays 2-10% royalty on retail price or flat fee. Pays negotiable advance.** Publishes book 1-2 years after acceptance. Accepts simultaneous submissions. Responds in 6 months.

NONFICTION All levels: biography, concept, history, multicultural, music/dance, nature/environment, science, and sports. *Agented submissions only.*

FICTION All levels: adventure, animal, contemporary, fantasy, history, humor, multicultural, nature/environment, poetry, problem novels, romance, science fiction, sports, suspense/mystery. *Accepts agented mss only.*

TIPS "No 'cartoony' or mass-market submissions for picture books."

Ⓐ Ⓞ VILLARD BOOKS

Penguin Random House, 1745 Broadway, New York NY 10019. (212)572-2600. **Website:** www.penguinrandomhouse.com. Estab. 1983. "Villard Books is the publisher of savvy and sometimes quirky, best-selling hardcovers and trade paperbacks." **Pays negotiable royalty. Pays negotiable advance.**

NONFICTION *Agented submissions only.*

FICTION Commercial fiction. *Agented submissions only.*

Ⓐ Ⓞ VINTAGE ANCHOR PUBLISHING

Penguin Random House, 1745 Broadway, New York NY 10019. **Website:** www.penguinrandomhouse.com. **Pays 4-8% royalty on retail price. Average advance: $2,500 and up.** Publishes ms 1 year after acceptance. Accepts simultaneous submissions.

FICTION Subjects include contemporary, literary, mainstream, short story collections. *Agented submissions only.*

VIVISPHERE PUBLISHING

675 Dutchess Turnpike, Poughkeepsie NY 12603. (845)463-1100, ext. 314. **Fax:** (845)463-0018. **E-mail:** cs@vivisphere.com. **Website:** www.vivisphere.com. **Contact:** Submissions. Estab. 1995. Publishes trade paperback originals and reprints and e-books. Vivisphere Publishing is now considering new submissions from any genre as follows: game of bridge (cards), nonfiction, history, military, new age, fiction, feminist/gay/lesbian, horror, contemporary, self-help, science fiction and cookbooks. **Pays royalty.** Publishes ms 6 months-2 years after acceptance. Accepts simultaneous submissions. Responds in 6-24 months. Book catalog and ms guidelines online.

"Cookbooks should have a particular slant or appeal to a certain niche. Also publish out-of-print books."

NONFICTION Subjects include contemporary culture, game of bridge. Query with SASE. Please submit a proposal package (printed paper copy) including: outline and 1st chapter along with your contact information. If submitting, please use above guidelines and e-mail cs@vivisphere.com.

FICTION Query with SASE.

Ⓞ VIZ MEDIA LLC

P.O. Box 77010, San Francisco CA 94107. (415)546-7073. **Website:** www.viz.com. "VIZ Media, LLC is one of the most comprehensive and innovative companies in the field of manga (graphic novel) publishing, animation and entertainment licensing of Japanese content. Owned by three of Japan's largest creators and licensors of manga and animation, Shueisha Inc., Shogakukan Inc., and Shogakukan-Shueisha Productions, Co., Ltd., VIZ Media is a leader in the publishing and distribution of Japanese manga for English speaking audiences in North America, the United Kingdom, Ireland, and South Africa and is a global ex-Asia licensor of Japanese manga and animation. The company offers an integrated product line including magazines such as *Shonen Jump* and *Shojo Beat*, graphic novels, and DVDs, and develops, markets, licenses, and distributes animated entertainment for audiences and consumers of all ages." Accepts simultaneous submissions.

FICTION "At the present, all of the manga that appears in our magazines come directly from manga that has been serialized and published in Japan."

VOLCANO PRESS, INC.

P.O. Box 270, Volcano CA 95689-0270. (209)296-7989. **Fax:** (209)296-4995. **Website:** www.volcanopress. com. Estab. 1969. Publishes trade paperback originals. **Publishes 4-6 titles/year. Pays $500-1,000 advance.** Responds in 1 month to queries. Book catalog available free.

NONFICTION Subjects include multicultural. "We publish women's health and social issues, particularly in the field of domestic violence." Query with SASE. No e-mail or fax submissions

TIPS "Look at our titles on the Web or in our catalog, and submit materials consistent with what we already publish."

VOYAGEUR PRESS

Quayside Publishing Group, 400 First Ave. N., Suite 400, Minneapolis MN 55401. (800)458-0454. **Fax:** (612)344-8691. **Website:** voyageurpress.com. Estab. 1972. Publishes hardcover and trade paperback originals. "Voyageur Press (and its sports imprint MVP Books) is internationally known as a leading publisher of quality music, sports, country living, crafts, natural history, and regional books. No children's or poetry books." **Publishes 80 titles/year. 1,200 queries received/year. 500 mss received/year. 10% of books from first-time authors. 90% from unagented writers. Pays royalty. Pays advance.** Publishes ms 1 year after acceptance. Accepts simultaneous submissions. Responds in 3 months to queries.

NONFICTION Subjects include Americana, cooking, environment, history, hobbies, music, nature, regional, sports, collectibles, country living, knitting and quilting, outdoor recreation. Query with SASE. Submit outline. Send sample digital images or transparencies (duplicates and tearsheets only).

TIPS "We publish books for an audience interested in regional, natural, and cultural history on a wide variety of subjects. We seek authors strongly committed to helping us promote and sell their books. Please present as focused an idea as possible in a brief submission (1-page cover letter; 2-page outline or proposal). Note your credentials for writing the book. Tell all you know about the market niche and marketing possibilities for proposed book. We use more book designers than artists or illustrators, since most of our books are illustrated with photographs."

⊘ WAKE FOREST UNIVERSITY PRESS

P.O. Box 7333, Winston-Salem NC 27109. (336)758-5448. **Fax:** (336)758-5636. **E-mail:** wfupress@wfu.edu. **Website:** wfupress.wfu.edu. **Contact:** Jefferson Holdridge, director/poetry editor; Dillon Johnston, advisory editor. Estab. 1976. "We publish only poetry from Ireland. I am able to consider only poetry written by native Irish poets. I must return, unread, poetry from American poets." Query with 4-5 samples and cover letter. Sometimes sends prepublication galleys. Buys North American or U.S. rights. **Publishes 4-6 titles/year. Pays on 8% list royalty contract, plus 6-8 author's copies. Negotiable advance.** Responds to queries in 1-2 weeks; to submissions (*if invited*) in 2-3 months.

WALCH PUBLISHING

40 Walch Dr., Portland ME 04103. (207)772-3105. **Fax:** (207)774-7167. **Website:** www.walch.com. Estab. 1927. "We focus on English/language arts, math, social studies and science teaching resources for middle school through adult assessment titles." **Publishes 100 titles/year. 10% of books from first-time authors. 95% from unagented writers. Pays 5-8% royalty on flat rate.** Publishes ms 6 months after acceptance. Accepts simultaneous submissions. Responds in 2 months to queries.

NONFICTION Subjects include education, history, science, technology. "Most titles are assigned by us, though we occasionally accept an author's unsolicited submission. We have a great need for author/artist teams and for authors who can write at third- to seventh-grade levels." Looks for sense of organization, writing ability, knowledge of subject, skill of communicating with intended audience. Formats include teacher resources, reproducibles. "We do *not* want textbooks or anthologies. All authors should have educational writing experience." Query first.

WASHINGTON STATE UNIVERSITY PRESS

P.O. Box 645910, Pullman WA 99164-5910. (800)354-7360. **Fax:** (509)335-8568. **E-mail:** wsupress@wsu.edu. **E-mail:** robert.clark@wsu.edu. **Website:** wsupress.wsu.edu. **Contact:** Robert A. Clark, acquisitions editor. Estab. 1928. Publishes hardcover originals, trade paperback originals, and reprints. WSU Press publishes scholarly nonfiction books on the history, prehistory, culture, and politics of the West, particularly the Pacific Northwest. **Publishes 8-10 titles/year. 40% of books from first-time authors. 95% from unagented writers. Pays 5% royalty graduated according to sales.** Publishes ms 18 months after acceptance. Accepts simultaneous submissions. Responds in 2 months to queries. Guidelines online.

NONFICTION Subjects include essays. "We welcome engaging and thought-provoking mss that focus on the greater Pacific Northwest (primarily Washington, Oregon, Idaho, British Columbia, western Montana, and southeastern Alaska). Currently we are not accepting how-to books, literary criticism, memoirs, novels, or poetry." Submit outline, sample chapters. Reviews artwork/photos.

TIPS "We have developed our marketing in the direction of regional and local history, and use this as the base upon which to expand our publishing program.

For history, the secret is to write strong narratives on significant topics or events. Stories should be told in imaginative, clever ways and be substantiated factually. Have visuals (photos, maps, etc.) available to help the reader envision what has happened. Explain stories in ways that tie them to wider-ranging regional, national—or even international—events. Weave them into the large pattern of history."

WASHINGTON WRITERS' PUBLISHING HOUSE

P.O. Box 15271, Washington DC 20003. **E-mail:** wwphpress@gmail.com. **Website:** www.washingtonwriters.org. Estab. 1975. **Offers $1,000 and 50 copies of published book plus additional copies for publicity use.** Accepts simultaneous submissions. Guidelines online.

FICTION Washington Writers' Publishing House considers book-length mss for publication by fiction writers living within 75 driving miles of the U.S. Capitol, Baltimore area included, through competition only. Mss may include previously published stories and excerpts. "Author should indicate where they heard about WWPH." Submit an electronic copy by e-mail (use PDF, .doc, or rich text format) or 2 hard copies by snail mail of a short story collection or novel (no more than 350 pages, double or 1-1/2 spaced; author's name should not appear on any ms pages). Include separate page of publication acknowledgments plus 2 cover sheets: one with ms title, poet's name, address, telephone number, and e-mail address, the other with ms title only. Include SASE for results only; mss will not be returned (will be recycled).

POETRY Washington Writers' Publishing House considers book-length mss for publication by poets living within 75 driving miles of the U.S. Capitol (Baltimore area included) through competition only. Publishes 1-2 poetry books/year. "No specific criteria, except literary excellence."

⊘⊘ WATERBROOK MULTNOMAH PUBLISHING GROUP

Penguin Random House, 12265 Oracle Blvd., Suite 200, Colorado Springs CO 80921. (719)590-4999. **Fax:** (719)590-8977. **E-mail:** info@waterbrookmultnomah.com. **Website:** www.waterbrookmultnomah.com. Estab. 1996. Publishes hardcover and trade paperback originals. **Publishes 70 titles/year. 2,000 queries received/year. 15% of books from first-time authors. Pays royalty.** Publishes book 1 year after acceptance.

Accepts simultaneous submissions. Responds in 2-3 months. Book catalog online.

NONFICTION Subjects include child guidance, religion, spirituality, marriage, Christian living. "We publish books on unique topics with a Christian perspective." *Agented submissions only.*

FICTION Subjects include adventure, historical, literary, mystery, religious, romance, science fiction, spiritual, suspense. *Agented submissions only.*

WAVE BOOKS

1938 Fairview Ave. E., Suite 201, Seattle WA 98102. (206)676-5337. **E-mail:** info@wavepoetry.com. **Website:** www.wavepoetry.com. Estab. 2005. Publishes hardcover and trade paperback originals. "Wave Books is an independent poetry press based in Seattle, Washington, dedicated to publishing the best in contemporary American poetry, poetry in translation, and writing by poets. The Press was founded in 2005, merging with established publisher Verse Press. By publishing strong innovative work in finely crafted trade editions and handmade ephemera, we hope to continue to challenge the values and practices of readers and add to the collective sense of what's possible in contemporary poetry." Accepts simultaneous submissions. Catalog online.

POETRY "Please no unsolicited mss or queries. We will post calls for submissions on our website."

WAVELAND PRESS, INC.

4180 Illinois Rt. 83, Suite 101, Long Grove IL 60047. (847)634-0081. **Fax:** (847)634-9501. **E-mail:** info@waveland.com. **Website:** www.waveland.com. Estab. 1975. Waveland Press, Inc. is a publisher of college textbooks and supplements. "We are committed to providing reasonably priced teaching materials for the classroom and actively seek to add new titles to our growing lists in a variety of academic disciplines. If you are currently working on a project you feel serves a need and would have promise as an adopted text in the college market, we would like to hear from you." Accepts simultaneous submissions.

WESLEYAN PUBLISHING HOUSE

P.O. Box 50434, Indianapolis IN 46250. (800)493-7539. **E-mail:** submissions@wesleyan.org. **Website:** www.wesleyan.org/wg. **Contact:** Katie Long, Communications Coordinator. Estab. 1843. Publishes hardcover and trade paperback originals. **100 submissions received/year. Pays royalty on wholesale** price. **Pays advance occasionally.** Publishes book 11 months after acceptance. Accepts simultaneous submissions. Responds within 2 months to proposals. Catalog online. Guidelines online.

NONFICTION Subjects include religion, Christianity. Does not want biographies, memoirs, children's products, plays, poems, art work. No hard-copy submissions. Submit proposal package, including outline, 5 sample chapters, bio. See writer's guidelines. Does not review artwork.

TIPS "Our books help evangelical Christians learn about the faith or grow in their relationship with God."

⊘ WESLEYAN UNIVERSITY PRESS

215 Long Ln., Middletown CT 06459. (860)685-7711. **Fax:** (860)685-7712. **E-mail:** stamminen@wesleyan. edu. **Website:** www.wesleyan.edu/wespress. **Contact:** Suzanna Tamminen, director and editor-in-chief. Estab. 1959. Publishes hardcover originals and paperbacks. "Wesleyan University Press is a scholarly press with a focus on poetry, music, dance and cultural studies." Wesleyan University Press is one of the major publishers of poetry in the nation. Poetry publications from Wesleyan tend to get widely (and respectfully) reviewed. **"We are accepting manuscripts by invitation only until further notice." Pays royalties, plus 10 author's copies.** Accepts simultaneous submissions. Responds to queries in 2 months; to mss in 4 months. Book catalog available free. Guidelines online.

NONFICTION Subjects include film/TV & media studies, science fiction studies, dance and poetry. *Does not accept unsolicited mss.*

POETRY *Does not accept unsolicited mss.*

WESTERN PSYCHOLOGICAL SERVICES

625 Alaska Ave., Torrance CA 90503. (424)201-8800 or (800)648-8857. **Fax:** (424)201-6950. **Website:** www. wpspublish.com. Estab. 1948. Publishes psychological and educational assessments and some trade paperback originals. "Western Psychological Services publishes psychological and educational assessments that practitioners trust. Our products allow helping professionals to accurately screen, diagnose, and treat people in need. WPS publishes practical books and games used by therapists, counselors, social workers, and others in the helping professions who work with children and adults." **Publishes 2 titles/year. 60 queries received/year. 30 mss received/year. 90% of** books from first-time authors. 95% from unagented writers. Pays 5-10% royalty on wholesale price. Publishes ms 1 year after acceptance. Accepts simultaneous submissions. Responds in 2 months to queries. Book catalog available free. Guidelines online.

NONFICTION Subjects include child guidance. "We publish children's books dealing with feelings, anger, social skills, autism, family problems." Submit complete ms. Reviews artwork/photos. Send photocopies.

WESTMINSTER JOHN KNOX PRESS

Division of Presbyterian Publishing Corp., 100 Witherspoon St., Louisville KY 40202. **Fax:** (502)569-5113. **E-mail:** jkelley@wjkbooks.com. **Website:** www.wjkbooks.com. **Contact:** Jessica Miller Kelley, acquisitions editor. Publishes hardcover and paperback originals and reprints. "All WJK books have a religious/spiritual angle, but are written for various markets—scholarly, professional, and the general reader. Westminster John Knox is affiliated with the Presbyterian Church USA. No phone queries. We do not publish fiction, poetry, memoir, children's books, or dissertations. We will not return or respond to submissions without an accompanying SASE with sufficient postage." **Publishes 70 titles/year. 2,500 queries received/year. 750 mss received/year. 10% of books from first-time authors. Pays royalty on net price.** Responds in 3 months. Proposal guidelines online.

NONFICTION Subjects include religion, spirituality. Submit proposal package according to the WJK book proposal guidelines found online.

WHITAKER HOUSE

1030 Hunt Valley Circle, New Kensington PA 15068. **E-mail:** publisher@whitakerhouse.com. **Website:** www.whitakerhouse.com. **Contact:** Editorial Department. Estab. 1970. Publishes hardcover, trade paperback, and mass market originals. **Publishes 70 titles/year. 600 queries; 200 mss received/year. 15% of books from first-time authors. 60% from unagented writers. Pays 5-15% royalty on wholesale price.** Publishes ms 9 months after acceptance. Accepts simultaneous submissions. Responds in 3 months. Book catalog online. Guidelines online.

NONFICTION Subjects include religion. Accepts submissions on topics with a Christian perspective. Query with SASE. Does not review artwork/photos.

FICTION Subjects include religious. All fiction must have a Christian perspective. Query with SASE.

TIPS "Audience includes those seeking uplifting and inspirational fiction and nonfiction."

WHITECAP BOOKS, LTD.

210 - 314 W. Cordova St., Vancouver BC V6B 1 E8, Canada. (604)681-6181. **Fax:** (905)477-9179. **E-mail:** steph@whitecap.ca. **Website:** www.whitecap.ca. Publishes hardcover and trade paperback originals. "Whitecap Books is a general trade publisher with a focus on food and wine titles. Although we are interested in reviewing unsolicited ms submissions, please note that we only accept submissions that meet the needs of our current publishing program. Please see some of most recent releases to get an idea of the kinds of titles we are interested in." **Publishes 30 titles/year. 500 queries received/year; 1,000 mss received/year. 20% of books from first-time authors. 90% from unagented writers. Pays royalty. Pays negotiated advance.** Publishes book 1 year after acceptance. Accepts simultaneous submissions. Responds in 2-3 months to proposals. Catalog and guidelines online.

NONFICTION Subjects include animals, gardening, history, recreation, regional, travel. Young children's and middle reader's nonfiction focusing mainly on nature, wildlife and animals. "Writers should take the time to research our list and read the submission guidelines on our website. This is especially important for children's writers and cookbook authors. We will only consider submissions that fall into these categories: cookbooks, wine and spirits, regional travel, home and garden, Canadian history, North American natural history, juvenile series-based fiction. At this time, we are not accepting the following categories: self-help or inspirational books, political, social commentary, or issue books, general how-to books, biographies or memoirs, business and finance, art and architecture, religion and spirituality." Submit cover letter, synopsis, SASE via ground mail. See guidelines online. Reviews artwork/photos. Send photocopies.

FICTION No children's picture books or adult fiction. See guidelines.

TIPS "We want well-written, well-researched material that presents a fresh approach to a particular topic."

WHITE MANE KIDS

73 W. Burd St., P.O. Box 708, Shippensburg PA 17257. (717)532-2237. **Fax:** (717)532-6110. **E-mail:** marketing@whitemane.com. **Website:** www.whitemane.com. **Contact:** Harold Collier, acquisitions editor. Estab.

1987. **Pays authors royalty of 7-10%. Pays illustrators and photographers by the project.** Publishes book 18 months after acceptance. Accepts simultaneous submissions. Responds to queries in 1 month, mss in 6-9 months. Book catalog and writer's guidelines available for SASE.

IMPRINTS White Mane Books, Burd Street Press, White Mane Kids, Ragged Edge Press.

NONFICTION Middle readers, young adults: history. Average word length: middle readers—30,000. Does not publish picture books. Submit outline/synopsis and 2-3 sample chapters. Book proposal form on website.

FICTION Middle readers, young adults: history (primarily American Civil War). Average word length: middle readers—30,000. Does not publish picture books. Query.

TIPS "Make your work historically accurate. We are interested in historically accurate fiction for middle and young adult readers. We do *not* publish picture books. Our primary focus is the American Civil War and some America Revolution topics."

WHITE PINE PRESS

P.O. Box 236, Buffalo NY 14201. (716)627-4665. **Fax:** (716)627-4665. **E-mail:** wpine@whitepine.org. **Website:** www.whitepine.org. **Contact:** Dennis Maloney, editor. Estab. 1973. Publishes trade paperback originals. **Publishes 8-10 titles/year. Receives 500 queries/year. 1% of books from first-time authors. 100% from unagented writers. Pays contributor's copies.** Publishes ms 18 months after acceptance. Accepts simultaneous submissions. Responds in 1 month to queries and proposals; 4 months to mss. Catalog online. Guidelines online.

NONFICTION Subjects include language, literature, multicultural, translation, poetry. *"We are currently not considering nonfiction mss."*

POETRY "Only considering submissions for our annual poetry contest."

ALBERT WHITMAN & COMPANY

250 S. Northwest Hwy., Suite 320, Park Ridge IL 60068. (800)255-7675. **Fax:** (847)581-0039. **E-mail:** submissions@albertwhitman.com. **Website:** www.albertwhitman.com. Estab. 1919. Publishes in original hardcover, paperback, boardbooks. Albert Whitman & Company publishes books for the trade, library, and school library market. Interested in re-

viewing the following types of projects: Picture book manuscripts for ages 2-8; novels and chapter books for ages 8-12; young adult novels; nonfiction for ages 3-12 and YA; art samples showing pictures of children. Best known for the classic series The Boxcar Children® Mysteries. "We are no longer reading unsolicited queries and manuscripts sent through the US mail. We now require these submissions to be sent by e-mail. You must visit our website for our guidelines, which include instructions for formatting your e-mail. E-mails that do not follow this format may not be read. We read every submission within 4 months of receipt, but we can no longer respond to every one. If you do not receive a response from us after four months, we have declined to publish your submission." **Publishes 60 titles/year. 10% of books from first-time authors. 50% from unagented writers.** Accepts simultaneous submissions. Guidelines online.

NONFICTION Picture books up to 1,000 words. Submit cover letter, brief description.

FICTION Picture books (up to 1,000 words); middle grade (up to 35,000 words); young adult (up to 70,000 words). For picture books, submit cover letter and brief description. For middle grade and young adult, send query, synopsis, and first 3 chapters.

WILD CHILD PUBLISHING

P.O. Box 4897, Culver City CA 90231. (310) 721-4461. **E-mail:** admin@wildchildpublishing.com. **Website:** www.wildchildpublishing.com. Estab. 1999. "We are known for working with newer/unpublished authors and editing to the standards of NYC publishers." **Publishes 12 titles/year. Pays royalties 10-40%.** Publishes ms 2-4 months after acceptance. Accepts simultaneous submissions. Responds in 1 month to queries and mss. Book catalogs on website.

FICTION Subjects include adventure, erotica, ethnic, experimental, fantasy, feminist, gay, historical, horror, humor, juvenile, lesbian, literary, mainstream, military, mystery, romance, science fiction, short story collections, suspense, western, young adult. Multiple anthologies planned. Query with outline/synopsis and 1 sample chapter. Accepts queries by e-mail only. Include estimated word count, brief bio. Often critiques/comments on rejected mss.

TIPS "Read our submission guidelines thoroughly. Send in entertaining, well-written stories. Be easy to work with and upbeat."

WILDERNESS PRESS

2204 First Ave. S., Suite 102, Birmingham AL 35233. (800)443-7227. **Fax:** (205)326-1012. **E-mail:** tim@keencommunications.com. **Website:** www.wildernesspress.com. **Contact:** Tim Jackson, acquisitions editor. Estab. 1967. Publishes paperback originals. "Wilderness Press has a long tradition of publishing the highest quality, most accurate hiking and other outdoor activity guidebooks." **Publishes 12 titles/year.** Publishes ms 8-12 months after acceptance. Accepts simultaneous submissions. Responds in 2 months to queries. Book catalog and ms guidelines online.

NONFICTION Subjects include recreation, trail guides for hikers and backpackers. "We publish books about the outdoors and some general travel guides. Many are trail guides for hikers and backpackers, but we also publish climbing, kayaking, and other outdoor activity guides, how-to books about the outdoors and urban walking books. The manuscript must be accurate. The author must research an area in person. If writing a trail guide, you must walk all the trails in the area your book is about. Outlook must be strongly conservationist. Style must be appropriate for a highly literate audience." Download proposal guidelines from website.

JOHN WILEY & SONS, INC.

111 River St., Hoboken NJ 07030. (201)748-6000. **Fax:** (201)748-6088. **Website:** www.wiley.com. Estab. 1807. Publishes hardcover originals, trade paperback originals and reprints. **Pays competitive rates.** Accepts simultaneous submissions. Book catalog online. Guidelines online.

NONFICTION Subjects include business, communications, computers, economics, education, finance, health, psychology, science. Wiley is a global publisher of print and electronic products—including scientific, scholarly, professional, consumer, and educational content. "Please visit our website to review our submissions guidelines for Books and Journals authors."

⊘⊘ WILLIAM MORROW

HarperCollins, 195 Broadway, New York NY 10007. (212)207-7000. **Fax:** (212)207-7145. **Website:** www.harpercollins.com. Estab. 1926. "William Morrow publishes a wide range of titles that receive much recognition and prestige—a most selective house." **Pays standard royalty on retail price. Pays varying**

advance. Accepts simultaneous submissions. Book catalog available free.

NONFICTION Subjects include history. Length 50,000-100,000 words. *No unsolicited mss or proposals. Agented submissions only.*

FICTION Publishes adult fiction. Morrow accepts only the highest quality submissions in adult fiction. *No unsolicited mss or proposals. Agented submissions only.*

WILLIAMSON BOOKS

6100 Tower Circle, Suite 210, Franklin TN 37067. **Website:** www.idealsbooks.com. Estab. 1983. Publishes "very successful nonfiction series (Kids Can! Series) on subjects such as history, science, arts/crafts, geography, diversity, multiculturalism. Little Hands series for ages 2-6, Kaleidoscope Kids series (age 7 and up) and Quick Starts for Kids! series (ages 8 and up). Our goal is to help every child fulfill his/her potential and experience personal growth." **Pays authors advance against future royalties based on wholesale price or purchases outright. Pays illustrators by the project. Pays photographers per photo.** Publishes book 1 year after acceptance. Accepts simultaneous submissions. Responds in 4 months. Guidelines online.

NONFICTION Hands-on active learning books, animals, African-American, arts/crafts, Asian, biography, diversity, careers, geography, health, history, hobbies, how-to, math, multicultural, music/dance, nature/environment, Native American, science, writing and journaling. Does not want to see textbooks, picture books, fiction. "Looking for all things African American, Asian American, Hispanic, Latino, and Native American including crafts and traditions, as well as their history, biographies, and personal retrospectives of growing up in U.S. for grades pre K-8th. We are looking for books in which learning and doing are inseparable." Query with annotated TOC/synopsis and 1 sample chapter.

WILLOW CREEK PRESS

P.O. Box 147, Minocqua WI 54548. (715)358-7010. **Fax:** (715)358-2807. **Website:** www.willowcreekpress. com. **Contact:** Sarah Olson, Designer. Estab. 1986. Publishes hardcover and trade paperback originals and reprints. "We specialize in nature, outdoor, and sporting topics, including gardening, wildlife, and animal books. Pets, cookbooks, and a few humor books and essays round out our titles. Currently emphasizing pets (mainly dogs and cats), wildlife, out-door sports (hunting, fishing). De-emphasizing essays, fiction." **Publishes 25 titles/year. 400 queries received/year. 150 mss received/year. 15% of books from first-time authors. 50% from unagented writers. Pays 6-15% royalty on wholesale price. Pays $2,000-5,000 advance.** Publishes ms 18 months after acceptance. Accepts simultaneous submissions. Responds in 2 months to queries. Guidelines online.

NONFICTION Subjects include animals, gardening, recreation, sports, travel, wildlife, pets. Submit cover letter, chapter outline, 1-2 sample chapters, brief bio, SASE. Reviews artwork/photos.

WINDWARD PUBLISHING

Finney Company, 5995 149th St. W., Suite 105, Apple Valley MN 55124. **E-mail:** info@finneyco.com. **Website:** www.finneyco.com. **Contact:** Alan E. Krysan, president. Estab. 1973. Publishes trade paperback originals. Windward publishes illustrated natural history, recreation books, and children's books. "Covers topics of natural history and science, outdoor recreation, and children's literature. Its principal markets are book, retail, and specialty stores. While primarily a nonfiction publisher, we will occasionally accept fiction books with educational value." **Publishes 6-10 titles/year. 120 queries received/year. 50 mss received/year. 50% of books from first-time authors. 100% from unagented writers. Pays 10% royalty on wholesale price. Pays advance.** Publishes book 1 year after acceptance. Accepts simultaneous submissions. Responds in 8-10 weeks to queries.

NONFICTION Subjects include agriculture, animals, gardening, recreation, science, sports, natural history. Young readers, middle readers, young adults: activity books, animal, careers, nature/environment, science. Young adults: textbooks. Query with SASE. Does not accept e-mail or fax submissions. Reviews artwork/photos.

WISCONSIN HISTORICAL SOCIETY PRESS

816 State St., Madison WI 53706. (608)264-6465. **Fax:** (608)264-6486. **E-mail:** whspress@wisconsinhistory. org. **Website:** www.wisconsinhistory.org/whspress/. **Contact:** Kate Thompson, editor. Estab. 1855. Publishes hardcover and trade paperback originals; trade paperback reprints. **Publishes 12-14 titles/year. 60-75 queries received/year. 20% of books from first-time authors. 90% from unagented writers. Pays royalty on wholesale price.** Publishes ms 2 years after

acceptance. Accepts simultaneous submissions. Book catalog available free. Guidelines online.

NONFICTION Subjects include history. Submit book proposal, form from website. Reviews artwork/photos. Send photocopies.

TIPS "Our audience reads about Wisconsin. Carefully review the book."

WISDOM PUBLICATIONS

199 Elm St., Somerville MA 02144. (617)776-7416, ext. 28. **Fax:** (617)776-7841. **E-mail:** editors@wisdompubs.org. **Website:** www.wisdompubs.org. **Contact:** David Kittelstrom, senior editor. Estab. 1976. Publishes hardcover originals and trade paperback originals and reprints. "Wisdom Publications is dedicated to making available authentic Buddhist works for the benefit of all. We publish translations, commentaries, and teachings of past and contemporary Buddhist masters and original works by leading Buddhist scholars. Currently emphasizing popular applied Buddhism, scholarly titles." **Publishes 20-25 titles/year. 300 queries received/year. 50% of books from first-time authors. 95% from unagented writers. Pays 4-8% royalty on wholesale price. Pays advance.** Publishes ms within 2 years of acceptance. Book catalog and ms guidelines online.

NONFICTION Subjects include philosophy, psychology, religion, spirituality, Buddhism, Tibet. Submissions should be made electronically.

TIPS "Wisdom Publications is the leading publisher of contemporary and classic Buddhist books and practical works on mindfulness. Please see our catalog or our website before you send anything to us to get a sense of what we publish."

Ⓐ⊘ PAULA WISEMAN BOOKS

1230 Sixth Ave., New York NY 10020. (212)698-7000. **Fax:** (212)698-2796. **E-mail:** paula.wiseman@simonandschuster.com; sylvie.frank@simonandschuster.com; sarahjane.abbott@simonandschuster.com. **Website:** kids.simonandschuster.com. Estab. 2003. Paula Wiseman Books is an imprint of Simon & Schuster Children's Publishing that launched in 2003. It has since gone on to publish over 70 award-winning and bestselling books, including picture books, novelty books, and novels. The imprint focuses on stories and art that are childlike, timeless, innovative, and centered in emotion. "We strive to publish books that entertain while expanding the experience of the children who read them, as well as stories that will endure, including those based in other cultures. We are committed to publishing new talent in both picture books and novels. We are actively seeking submissions from new and published authors and artists through agents and from SCBWI conferences." **Publishes 30 titles/year. 15% of books from first-time authors.** Accepts simultaneous submissions.

NONFICTION Picture books: animal, biography, concept, history, nature/environment. Young readers: animal, biography, history, multicultural, nature/environment, sports. Average word length: picture books—500; others standard length. Does not accept unsolicited or unagented mss. By mail preferably.

FICTION Considers all categories. Average word length: picture books—500; others standard length.

WOODBINE HOUSE

6510 Bells Mill Rd., Bethesda MD 20817. (301)897-3570. **Fax:** (301)897-5838. **E-mail:** info@woodbinehouse.com. **Website:** www.woodbinehouse.com. **Contact:** Acquisitions Editor. Estab. 1985. Publishes trade paperback originals. Woodbine House publishes books for or about individuals with disabilities to help those individuals and their families live fulfilling and satisfying lives in their homes, schools, and communities. **Publishes 10 titles/year. 15% of books from first-time authors. 90% from unagented writers. Pays 10-12% royalty.** Publishes ms 18 months after acceptance. Accepts simultaneous submissions. Responds in 3 months to queries. Guidelines online.

NONFICTION Publishes books for and about children with disabilities. No personal accounts or general parenting guides. Submit outline, and at least 3 sample chapters. Reviews artwork/photos.

FICTION Subjects include picture books. Receptive to stories re: developmental and intellectual disabilities, e.g., autism and cerebral palsy. Submit complete ms with SASE.

TIPS "Do not send us a proposal on the basis of this description. Examine our catalog or website and a couple of our books to make sure you are on the right track. Put some thought into how your book could be marketed (aside from in bookstores). Keep cover letters concise and to the point; if it's a subject that interests us, we'll ask to see more."

Ⓐ WORDSONG

815 Church St., Honesdale PA 18431. **Fax:** (570)253-0179. **Website:** www.wordsongpoetry.com. Estab.

1990. "We publish fresh voices in contemporary poetry." **Pays authors royalty or work purchased outright.** Accepts simultaneous submissions. Responds to mss in 3 months.

POETRY *Agented submissions only.*

TIPS "Collections of original poetry, not anthologies, are our biggest need at this time. Keep in mind that the strongest collections demonstrate a facility with multiple poetic forms and offer fresh images and insights. Check to see what's already on the market and on our website before submitting."

WORKMAN PUBLISHING CO.

225 Varick St., New York NY 10014. **E-mail:** submissions@workman.com. **Website:** www.workman.com. Estab. 1967. Publishes hardcover and trade paperback originals, as well as calendars. "We are a trade paperback house specializing in a wide range of popular nonfiction. We publish no adult fiction and very little children's fiction. We also publish a full range of full-color wall and Page-A-Day calendars." **Publishes 40 titles/year. thousands of queries received/year. Open to first-time authors. Pays variable royalty on retail price. Pays variable advance.** Publishes ms approximately 1 year after acceptance. Accepts simultaneous submissions. Responds in 5 months to queries. Guidelines online.

NONFICTION Subjects include child guidance, gardening, sports, travel. Query.

TIPS "We prefer electronic submissions."

WORLD BOOK, INC.

180 N. LaSalle St., Suite 900, Chicago IL 60601. (312)729-5800. **Fax:** (312)729-5600. **E-mail:** service@worldbook.com. **Website:** www.worldbook.com. World Book, Inc. (publisher of The World Book Encyclopedia), publishes reference sources and nonfiction series for children and young adults in the areas of science, mathematics, English-language skills, basic academic and social skills, social studies, history, and health and fitness. "We publish print and non-print material appropriate for children ages 3-14. WB does not publish fiction, poetry, or wordless picture books." **Payment negotiated on project-by-project basis.** Publishes book 18 months after acceptance. Accepts simultaneous submissions. Responds to queries in 2 months.

NONFICTION Young readers: animal, arts/crafts, careers, concept, geography, health, reference. Middle readers: animal, arts/crafts, careers, geography, health, history, hobbies, how-to, nature/environment, reference, science. Young adult: arts/crafts, careers, geography, health, history, hobbies, how-to, nature/environment, reference, science. Query.

WORLD WEAVER PRESS

Alpena Michigan 49707. **E-mail:** submissions@worldweaverpress.com. **Website:** www.worldweaverpress.com. **Contact:** WWP Editors. Estab. 2012. World Weaver Press publishes digital and print editions of speculative fiction at various lengths for adult, young adult, and new adult audiences. We believe in great storytelling. **Publishes 10-12 titles/year. 85% from unagented writers. Average royalty rate of 39% net on all editions. No advance.** Publishes ms 6-24 months after acceptance. Accepts simultaneous submissions. Responds to query letters within 3 weeks. Responses to mss requests take longer. Catalog online. Guidelines online.

IMPRINTS Red Moon Romance, publishing sweet to erotic romances. Hot romance, it's what we do. Information at redmoonromance.com.

NONFICTION Subjects include cinema, pop culture, folk lore and fairy tale studies. We're interested in nonfiction that relates to pop culture and genre studies (i.e. essays on genre fiction/TV/film), folklore and fairy tale explorations, and books on writing and/or for genre writers. Unless you walked the Hobbit path to Mordor, we don't want your travelogue or memoir.

FICTION Subjects include erotica, fantasy, romance, science fiction. "We believe that publishing speculative fiction isn't just printing words on the page — it's the act of weaving brand new worlds. Seeking speculative fiction in many varieties: protagonists who have strength, not fainting spells; intriguing worlds with well-developed settings; characters that are to die for (we'd rather find ourselves in love than just in lust)." Full list of interests on website. Does not want giant bugs, ghosts, post-apocalyptic and/or dystopia, angels, zombies, magical realism, surrealism, middle grade (MG) or younger. Query letter with first 5,000 words in body of e-mail. Queries accepted only during February and September annually, unless agented.

TIPS "Use your letter to pitch us the story, not talk about its themes or inception."

WORTHY KIDS/IDEALS BOOKS

6100 Tower Circle, Suite 210, Franklin TN 37067. **Website:** www.idealsbooks.com. **Contact:** Submissions. Estab. 1944. Accepts simultaneous submissions.

NONFICTION Worthy Kids/Ideals publishes for ages birth to 8, no longer than 800 words. Submit complete ms.

FICTION Subjects include juvenile. Picture books: animal, concept, history, religion. Board books: animal, history, nature/environment, religion. Worthy Kids/Ideals publishes for ages birth to 8, no longer than 800 words. Submit complete ms.

WRITER'S DIGEST BOOKS

Imprint of F+W, a Content + eCommerce Company, 10151 Carver Rd., Suite #200, Cincinnati OH 45242. **E-mail:** writersdigest@fwcommunity.com. **Website:** www.writersdigest.com. **Contact:** Rachel Randall. Estab. 1920. Publishes hardcover originals and trade paperbacks. "Writer's Digest Books is the premiere source for instructional books on writing and publishing for an audience of aspirational writers. Typical mss are 80,000 words. E-mail queries strongly preferred; no phone calls please." **Publishes 18-20 titles/year. 300 queries; 50 mss received/year. 30% from unagented writers. Pays average $3,000 advance.** Publishes book 1 year after acceptance. Accepts simultaneous submissions. Responds in 3 months to queries. "Our catalog of titles is available to view online at www.WritersDigestShop.com.".

○ Writer's Digest Books accepts query letters and complete proposals via e-mail at writersdigest@fwcommunity.com.

NONFICTION "Our instruction books stress results and how to achieve them. Should be well-researched, yet lively and readable. We do not want to see books telling readers how to crack specific nonfiction markets: *Writing for the Computer Market* or *Writing for Trade Publications*, for instance. We are most in need of fiction-technique books written by published authors. Be prepared to explain how the proposed book differs from existing books on the subject." No fiction or poetry. Query with SASE. Submit outline, sample chapters, SASE.

TIPS "Most queries we receive are either too broad (how to write fiction) or too niche (how to write erotic horror), and don't reflect a knowledge of our large backlist of 150 titles. We rarely publish new books on journalism, freelancing, magazine article writing or marketing/promotion. We are actively seeking fiction and nonfiction writing technique books with fresh perspectives, interactive and visual writing instruction books, similar to *The Pocket Muse* by Monica

Wood, and general reference works that appeal to an audience beyond writers."

YALE UNIVERSITY PRESS

P.O. Box 209040, New Haven CT 06520. (203)432-0960. **Fax:** (203)432-0948. **E-mail:** chris.rogers@yale.edu. **Website:** yalebooks.com. **Contact:** Christopher Rogers, executive editor for history and current events. Estab. 1908. Publishes hardcover and trade paperback originals. "Yale University Press publishes scholarly and general interest books." Accepts simultaneous submissions. Catalog and guidelines online.

NONFICTION Subjects include Americana, education, history, philosophy, psychology, religion, science, sociology. "Our nonfiction has to be at a very high level. Most of our books are written by professors or journalists, with a high level of expertise. *Submit proposals only.* We'll ask if we want to see more. *No unsolicited mss.* We won't return them." Submit sample chapters, cover letter, prospectus, CV, TOC, SASE. Reviews artwork/photos. Send photocopies.

POETRY Submit to Yale Series of Younger Poets Competition. Guidelines online.

TIPS "Audience is scholars, students and general readers."

YELLOW SHOE FICTION SERIES

P.O. Box 25053, Baton Rouge LA 70894. **Website:** www.lsu.edu/lsupress. **Contact:** Michael Griffith, editor. Estab. 2004. **Publishes 2 titles/year. Pays royalty. Offers advance.** Accepts simultaneous submissions.

○ "Looking first and foremost for literary excellence, especially good manuscripts that have fallen through the cracks at the big commercial presses. I'll cast a wide net."

FICTION Does not accept unsolicited mss. Accepts queries by mail, Attn: James W. Long.

YMAA PUBLICATION CENTER

P.O. Box 480, Wolfeboro NH 03894. (603)569-7988. **Fax:** (603)569-1889. **Website:** ymaa.com. **Contact:** David Ripianzi, director. Estab. 1982. Publishes trade paperback originals and reprints. Publishes 6-8 DVD titles/year. YMAA publishes books on Chinese Chi Kung (Qigong), Taijiquan, (Tai Chi) and Asian martial arts. We are expanding our focus to include books on healing, wellness, meditation and subjects related to Asian culture and Asian medicine. **Publishes 6-8 titles/year. 50 queries received/year. 20 mss received/year. 25% of books from first-time**

authors. 100% from unagented writers. Publishes ms 18 months after acceptance. Accepts simultaneous submissions. Responds in 3 months to proposals. Book catalog online. Guidelines available free.

NONFICTION Subjects include ethnic, history, philosophy, spirituality, sports, Asian martial arts, Chinese Qigong. "We no longer publish or solicit books for children. We also produce instructional DVDs and videos to accompany our books on traditional Chinese martial arts, meditation, massage, and Chi Kung. We are most interested in Asian martial arts, Chinese medicine, and Chinese Qigong. We publish Eastern thought, health, meditation, massage, and East/West synthesis." Submit proposal package, outline, bio, 1 sample chapter, SASE. Reviews artwork/photos. Send Send photocopies and 1-2 originals to determine quality of photo/line art.

FICTION "We are seeking mss that bring the venerated tradition of true Asian martial arts to readers. Your novel length ms should be a thrilling story that conveys insights into true martial techniques and philosophies."

TIPS "If you are submitting health-related material, please refer to an Asian tradition. Learn about author publicity options as your participation is mandatory."

● YOGI IMPRESSIONS BOOKS PVT. LTD.

1711, Centre 1, World Trade Centre, Cuffe Parade Mumbai 400 005, India. **E-mail:** yogi@yogiimpressions.com. **Website:** www.yogiimpressions.com. Estab. 2000. "Yogi Impressions are Self-help, Personal Growth and Spiritual book publishers based in Mumbai, India. Established at the turn of the millennium, at Mumbai, Yogi Impressions publishes books which seek to revive interest in spirituality, enhance the quality of life and, thereby, create the legacy of a better world for future generations." Accepts simultaneous submissions. Guidelines online.

NONFICTION Subjects include child guidance, multicultural, religion, spirituality, alternative health, enlightened business, self-improvement/personal growth. Submit outline/proposal, bio, 2-3 sample chapters, market assessment, SASE.

ZEBRA BOOKS

Kensington, 119 W. 40th St., New York NY 10018. (212)407-1500. **E-mail:** esogah@kensingtonbooks.com. **Website:** www.kensingtonbooks.com. **Contact:** Esi Sogah, senior editor. Publishes hardcover

originals, trade paperback and mass market paperback originals and reprints. Zebra Books is dedicated to women's fiction, which includes, but is not limited to romance. Publishes ms 12-18 months after acceptance. Accepts simultaneous submissions. Book catalog online.

FICTION Query.

ZENITH PRESS

Quayside Publishing Group, 400 First Ave. N., Suite 300, Minneapolis MN 55401. (612)344-8100; (800)328-0590. **Fax:** (612)344-8691. **E-mail:** erik.gilg@quartous.com. **Website:** zenithpress.com. **Contact:** Erik Gilg, editorial director. Senior Acquisitions Editor: Dennis Pernu. Estab. 2004. Publishes hardcover and trade paperback originals, electronic originals and reprints, hardcover and trade paperback reprints. "Zenith Press publishes an eclectic collection of historical nonfiction and current affairs in both narrative and illustrated formats. Building on a core of military history, particularly from World War II forward, Zenith reaches out to other historical, aviation, and science topics with compelling narrative hooks or eye-catching photography. From a history of WWII aviation wrecks to an illustrated celebration of the space shuttle program, Zenith books are engaging true stories with historical, military, or science foundations—sometimes all 3 at once." **Publishes 210 titles/year. Receives 250 queries/year; 100 mss/year. 25% of books from first-time authors. 50% from unagented writers. Pays authors 8-15% royalty on wholesale price.** Publishes ms 1 year after acceptance. Accepts simultaneous submissions. Responds in 1 month. Catalog and guidelines online.

NONFICTION Subjects include history, military, politics, science, world affairs, aviation. Submit proposal package, including outline, 1-3 sample chapters, and author biography. Reviews artwork. Send digital files.

ZEST BOOKS

2443 Fillmore St., Suite 340, San Francisco CA 94115. (415)777-8654. **Fax:** (415)777-8653. **E-mail:** info@zestbooks.net. **Website:** zestbooks.net. **Contact:** Dan Harmon, publishing director. Zest Books is a leader in young adult nonfiction, publishing books on entertainment, history, science, health, fashion, and lifestyle advice since 2006. Zest Books is distributed by Houghton Mifflin Harcourt. Accepts simultaneous submissions. Guidelines online.

NONFICTION Submit proposal.

TIPS "If you're interested in becoming a member of our author pool, send a cover letter stating why you are interested in young adult nonfiction, plus your specific areas of interest and specialties, your resume, 3-5 writing samples."

ZUMAYA PUBLICATIONS, LLC

3209 S. Interstate 35, Austin TX 78741. (512)537-3145. **Fax:** (512)276-6745. **E-mail:** business@zumayapublishing.com. **E-mail:** acquisitions@zumayapublications.com. **Website:** www.zumayapublications.com. **Contact:** Rie Sheridan Rose, acquisitions editor. Estab. 1999. Publishes trade paperback and electronic originals and reprints. Zumaya Publications is a digitally-based micro-press publishing mainly in on-demand trade paperback and e-book formats. "We currently offer approximately 190 fiction titles in the mystery, SF/F, historical, romance, LGBTQ, horror, and occult genres in adult, young adult, and middle reader categories. In 2016, we plan to officially launch our graphic and illustrated novel imprint, Zumaya Fabled Ink. We publish approximately 10-15 new titles annually, at least five of which are from new authors. We do not publish erotica or graphic erotic romance at this time. We accept only electronic queries; all others will be discarded unread. A working knowledge of computers and relevant software is a necessity, as our production process is completely digital." **Publishes 10-15 titles/year. 1,000 queries received/year. 50 mss requested/year. 5% of books from first-time authors. 98% from unagented writers. Pay 20% of net on paperbacks, net defined as cover price less printing and other associated costs; 50% of net on all e-books. Does not pay advance.** Publishes book 2 years after acceptance. Responds in 3 months to queries and proposals; 6 months to mss. Guidelines online.

IMPRINTS Zumaya Arcane (New Age, inspirational fiction & nonfiction), Zumaya Boundless (GLBTQ); Zumaya Embraces (romance/women's fiction); Zumaya Enigma (mystery/suspense/thriller); Zumaya Thresholds (YA/middle grade); Zumaya Otherworlds (SF/F/H), Zumaya Yesterdays (memoirs, historical fiction, fiction, western fiction); Zumaya Fabled Ink (graphic and illustrated novels).

NONFICTION Subjects include creative nonfiction, memoirs, New Age, spirituality, true ghost stories. "The easiest way to figure out what we're looking for is to look at what we've already done. Our main nonfiction interests are in collections of true ghost stories, ones that have been investigated or thoroughly documented, memoirs that address specific regions and eras from a 'normal person' viewpoint and books on the craft of writing. That doesn't mean we won't consider something else." Electronic query only. Reviews artwork/photos. Send digital format.

FICTION Subjects include adventure, contemporary, ethnic, fantasy, feminist, gay, gothic, historical, horror, humor, juvenile, lesbian, literary, military, multicultural, mystery, occult, romance, science fiction, short story collections, spiritual, suspense, war, western, young adult. "We are open to all genres, particularly GLBT and YA/middle grade, historical and western, New Age/inspirational (no overtly Christian materials, please), non-category romance, thrillers. We encourage people to review what we've already published so as to avoid sending us more of the same, at least, insofar as the plot is concerned. While we're always looking for good mysteries, especially cozies, mysteries with historical settings, and police procedurals, we want original concepts rather than slightly altered versions of what we've already published. We do not publish erotica or graphically erotic romance at this time." Does not want erotica, graphically erotic romance, experimental, literary (unless it fits into one of our established imprints). A copy of our rules of submission is posted on our website and can be downloaded. They are rules rather than guidelines and should be read carefully before submitting. It will save everyone time and frustration.

TIPS "We're catering to readers who may have loved last year's best seller but not enough to want to read 10 more just like it. Have something different. If it does not fit standard pigeonholes, that's a plus. On the other hand, it has to have an audience. And if you're not prepared to work with us on promotion and marketing, particularly via social media, it would be better to look elsewhere."

CONSUMER MAGAZINES

//

Selling your writing to consumer magazines is as much an exercise of your marketing skills as it is of your writing abilities. Editors of consumer magazines are looking for good writing which communicates pertinent information to their readers.

Marketing skills will help you successfully discern a magazine's editorial slant, and write queries and articles that prove your knowledge of the magazine's readership. You can gather clues about a magazine's readership—and establish your credibility with the editor—in a number of ways: Read the listing in *Writer's Market*; study a magazine's writer's guidelines; check a magazine's website; and read current issues of the magazine.

Writers who can correctly and consistently discern a publication's audience and deliver stories that speak to that target readership will win out every time over writers who submit haphazardly.

In nonfiction, editors continue to look for short feature articles covering specialized topics. Editors want crisp writing and expertise. If you are not an expert in the area about which you are writing, make yourself one through research. Always query before sending your manuscript.

Fiction editors prefer to receive complete manuscripts. Writers must keep in mind that fiction is competitive, and editors receive far more material than they can publish. For this reason, they often do not respond to submissions unless they are interested in using the story.

Most magazines listed here have indicated pay rates; some give very specific payment-per-word rates, while others state a range. Any agreement you come to with a magazine, whether verbal or written, should specify the payment you are to receive and when you are to receive it.

ANIMAL

💲💲 APPALOOSA JOURNAL

2720 West Pullman Rd., Moscow ID 83843. (208)882-5578. **Fax:** (208)882-8150. **E-mail:** editor@appaloosajournal.com; designer2@appaloosajournal.com. **Website.** www.appaloosajournal.com. **Contact:** Dana Russell, editor; John Langston, art director. **40% freelance written.** Monthly magazine covering Appaloosa horses. "*Appaloosa Journal* is the authoritative, association-based source for information about the Appaloosa Horse Club, the Appaloosa breed and the Appaloosa industry. Our mission is to cultivate a broader membership base and instill enthusiasm for the breed by recognizing the needs and achievements of the Appaloosa, ApHC members, enthusiasts and our readers. The Appaloosa Horse Club is a not-for-profit organization. Serious inquiries within specified budget only." Estab. 1946. Circ. 25,000. Byline given. Pays on publication. Publishes ms an average of 3 months after acceptance. Accepts simultaneous submissions. Responds in 1 month to queries. Responds in 2 months to mss. Sample copy free. Guidelines online.

NONFICTION Needs historical, interview. **Buys 15-20 mss/year.** Send complete ms. *Appaloosa Journal* is not responsible for unsolicited materials. All freelance correspondence should be directed to editor Dana Russell via e-mail, with the subject line "'Freelance.' Article-length reports of timely and newsworthy events, such as shows, races, and overseas competition, are welcome but must be pre-approved by the editor. Mss exceeding the preferred word length will be evaluated according to relevance and content matter. Lengthy stories, opinion pieces, or poorly written pieces will be rejected. Mss may be sent on a CD or via e-mail in Microsoft Word or text-only format. If sent via CD, an accompanying hard copy should be printed, double spaced, following the guidelines." Length: 1,500-1,800 words (features); 600-800 words (article-length). **Pays $200-400.**

💲💲 THE CHRONICLE OF THE HORSE

P.O. Box 46, Middleburg VA 20118. (540)687-6341. **Fax:** (540)687-3937. **E-mail:** slieser@chronofhorse.com. **E-mail:** bethr@chronofhorse.com (feature stories); results@chronofhorse.com (news stories). **Website:** www.chronofhorse.com. **Contact:** Sara Lieser, managing editor; Beth Rasin, executive editor. **50%**

freelance written. Weekly magazine covering horse sport. "We cover English riding sports, including horse showing, grand prix jumping competitions, steeplechase racing, foxhunting, dressage, endurance riding, handicapped riding, and combined training. We are the official publication for the national governing bodies of many of the above sports. We feature news, how-to articles on equitation and horse care and interviews with leaders in the various fields." Estab. 1937. Byline given. Pays for features, news and other items on publication. Publishes an average of 4 months after acceptance. Submit seasonal material 3 months in advance. Accepts queries by mail, e-mail. Accepts simultaneous submissions. Responds in 5-6 weeks to queries. Guidelines online.

NONFICTION Needs general interest, historical, how-to, humor, interview, technical. Special issues: Steeplechase Racing (January); American Horse in Sport and Grand Prix Jumping (February); Horse Show (March); Intercollegiate (April); Kentucky 4-Star Preview (April); Junior and Pony (April); Dressage (June); Horse Care (July); Combined Training (August); Hunt Roster (September); Amateur (November); Stallion (December). No poetry, Q&A interviews, clinic reports, Western riding articles, personal experience or wild horses. **Buys 300 mss/year.** Send complete ms. Length: 1,500-2,500 words. **Pays $150-400.**

COLUMNS Dressage, Combined Training, Horse Show, Horse Care, Racing over Fences, Young Entry (about young riders, geared for youth), Horses and Humanities, Hunting, Vaulting, Handicapped Riding, Trail Riding, 1,000-1,225 words; News of major competitions (clear assignment with us first), 1,500 words. Query with or without published clips or send complete ms. **Pays $25-200.**

💲 EQUINE JOURNAL

83 Leicester St., North Oxford MA 01537. (508)987-5886. **Fax:** (508)987-5887. **E-mail:** editorial@morris.com. **Website:** www.equinejournal.com. **Contact:** Kelly Ballou, editor. **90% freelance written.** Monthly tabloid covering horses—all breeds, all disciplines. *Equine Journal* is a monthly, all-breed/discipline regional publication for horse enthusiasts. "The purpose of our editorial is to educate, entertain, and enable amateurs and professionals alike to stay on top of new developments in the field. Every month, the *Equine Journal* presents feature articles and columns span-

ning the length and breadth of horse-related activities and interests from all corners of the country." Estab. 1988. Circ. 26,000. Byline given. Pays on publication. Editorial lead time 4 months. Accepts queries by e-mail. Accepts simultaneous submissions. Responds in 2 months to queries. Guidelines online.

NONFICTION Needs general interest, how-to, interview. Does not accept poetry, fiction, or stories told from a first-person perspective. **Buys 100 mss/year.** Query with published clips, or send complete ms. Length: 1,200-1,800 words for features; 300-500 words for event write-ups.

COLUMNS Horse Health (health-related topics), 1,200-1,500 words. **Buys 12 mss/year.** Query.

$ THE GREYHOUND REVIEW

P.O. Box 543, Abilene KS 67410. (785)263-4660. **E-mail:** nga@ngagreyhounds.com. **Website:** www.ngagreyhounds.com. **20% freelance written.** Monthly magazine covering greyhound breeding, training, and racing. Estab. 1911. Circ. 3,500. Byline given. Pays on acceptance. No kill fee. Submit seasonal material 2 months in advance. Accepts simultaneous submissions. Responds in 2 weeks to queries. Responds in 1 month to mss. Sample copy for $3. Guidelines free.

NONFICTION Needs how-to, interview, personal experience. Do not submit gambling systems. **Buys 24 mss/year.** Query. Length: 1,000-10,000 words. **Pays $85-150.**

🍁 HORSE CANADA

Horse Publications Group, Box 670, Aurora ON L4G 4J9 Canada. (905)727-0107. **Fax:** (905)841-1530. **E-mail:** hceditor@horse-canada.com. **Website:** www.horse-canada.com. **Contact:** Amy Harris, managing editor. **80% freelance written.** National magazine for horse lovers of all ages. Readers are committed horse owners with many different breeds involved in a variety of disciplines—from beginner riders to industry professionals. Circ. 20,000. No kill fee. Editorial lead time 2 months. Accepts queries by e-mail. Accepts simultaneous submissions. Guidelines online.

NONFICTION Query. Length: 750-1,500 words. **Payment varies.**

COLUMNS Tail End (humor). **Payment varies.**

$$ HORSE ILLUSTRATED

I-5 Publishing, P.O. Box 12106, Lexington KY 40580. (800)546-7730. **E-mail:** horseillustrated@i5publishing.com. **Website:** www.horseillustrated.com. **Contact:** Elizabeth Moyer, editor. **90% freelance written. Prefers to work with published/established writers, but will work with new/unpublished writers.** Monthly magazine covering all aspects of horse ownership. "Our readers are adults, mostly women, between the ages of 18 and 40; stories should be geared to that age group and reflect responsible horse care." Estab. 1976. Circ. 160,660. Byline given. Pays on publication. Publishes ms an average of 8 months after acceptance. Submit seasonal material 6 months in advance. Accepts queries by mail. Accepts simultaneous submissions. Responds in 3 months to queries. Guidelines available at www.horsechannel.com/horse-magazines/horse-illustrated/submission-guidelines.aspx.

NONFICTION Needs general interest, how-to, inspirational, photo feature. "No little girl horse stories, cowboy and Indian stories, or anything not *directly* relating to horses." **Buys 20 mss/year.** Query or send complete ms. Length: 1,000-2,000 words. **Pays $200-475.**

$$ JUST LABS

Willow Creek Press, 2779 Aero Park Dr., Traverse City MI 49686. (231)946-3712; (800)447-7367. **E-mail:** jake@villagepress.com; jillias@villagepress.com. **Website:** www.justlabsmagazine.com. **Contact:** Jason Smith, editor; Jill LaCross, managing and Web editor. **50% freelance written.** Bimonthly magazine covering all aspects of the Labrador Retriever. "*Just Labs* is targeted toward the family Labrador Retriever, and all of our articles help people learn about, live with, train, take care of, and enjoy their dogs. We do not look for articles that pull at the heart strings (those are usually staff-written), but rather we look for articles that teach, inform, and entertain." Estab. 2001. Circ. 15,000. Byline given. Pays on publication. Offers 40% kill fee. Publishes ms an average of 6 months after acceptance. Editorial lead time 6 months. Submit seasonal material 6-8 months in advance. Accepts queries by mail, e-mail. Accepts simultaneous submissions. Responds in 4-6 weeks to queries; in 2 months to mss. Guidelines by e-mail.

NONFICTION Needs essays, how-to, humor, inspirational, interview, photo feature, technical, travel. "We don't want tributes to dogs that have passed on. This is a privilege we reserve for our subscribers." **Buys 30 mss/year.** Query. Length: 1,000-1,800 words. **Pays $250-400.**

$ MINIATURE DONKEY TALK

Miniature Donkey Talk, Inc., P.O. Box 982, Cripple Creek CO 80813. (719)689-2904. **E-mail:** mike@

donkeytalk.info. **Website:** www.web-donkeys.com. **Contact:** Mike Gross. **65% freelance written.** Quarterly magazine covering donkeys, with articles on healthcare, promotion, and management of donkeys for owners, breeders, and donkey lovers. Estab. 1987. Circ. 4,925. Byline given. Pays on acceptance. Publishes ms an average of 4 months after acceptance. Editorial lead time 2 months. Submit seasonal material 3 months in advance. Accepts queries by mail, e-mail. Accepts simultaneous submissions. Responds in 2 weeks to queries. Responds in 1 month to mss. Sample copy for $5. Guidelines free.

NONFICTION Needs book excerpts, humor, interview, personal experience. **Buys 6 mss/year.** Query with published clips. Length: 700-5,000 words. **Pays $25-150.**

COLUMNS Columns: Humor: 2,000 words; Healthcare: 2,000-5,000 words; Management: 2,000 words. **Buys 50 mss/year.** Query. **Pays $25-100.**

💲💲 PAINT HORSE JOURNAL

American Paint Horse Association, P.O. Box 961023, Ft. Worth TX 76161-0023. (817)834-2742. **Fax:** (817)834-3152. **E-mail:** jhein@apha.com. **Website:** apha.com/phj/welcome. **Contact:** Jessica Hein, editor. **10% freelance written. Works with a small number of new/unpublished writers each year.** Monthly magazine for people who raise, breed, and show Paint Horses. Estab. 1966. Circ. 12,000. Byline given. Pays on acceptance. Offers negotiable kill fee. Submit seasonal material 3 months in advance. Accepts queries by mail, e-mail, fax. Accepts simultaneous submissions. Sample copy for $7 (includes shipping). Guidelines online.

NONFICTION Needs general interest, historical, how-to. **Buys 4-5 mss/year.** Query. Length: 1,000-2,000 words. **Pays $100-500.**

💲💲 REPTILES

i-5 Publishing, 3 Burroughs, Irvine CA 92618. (949)855-8822. **E-mail:** reptiles@i5publishing.com. **Website:** www.reptilesmagazine.com. **20% freelance written.** Monthly magazine covering reptiles and amphibians. *Reptiles* covers "a wide range of topics relating to reptiles and amphibians, including breeding, captive care, field herping, etc." Estab. 1992. Byline given. Pays on publication. Offers 20% kill fee. Publishes ms an average of 6-8 months after acceptance. Accepts queries by mail, e-mail. Accepts simultane-

ous submissions. Responds in 1 month to queries. Responds in 1-2 months to mss. Sample copy online. Guidelines online.

NONFICTION Needs general interest, historical, how-to, interview, personal experience, photo feature, travel. **Buys 10 mss/year.** Query. Length: 1,000-2,000 words. **Pays $350-500.**

💲💲 TROPICAL FISH HOBBYIST MAGAZINE

TFH Publications, Inc., One TFH Plaza, Neptune City NJ 07753. **E-mail:** associateeditor@tfh.com. **Website:** www.tfhmagazine.com. **90% freelance written.** Monthly magazine covering tropical fish. Estab. 1952. Circ. 35,000. Byline given. Pays on acceptance. No kill fee. Editorial lead time 3 months. Submit seasonal material 6 months in advance. Accepts queries by e-mail. Responds immediately on electronic queries. Guidelines online.

NONFICTION **Buys 100-150 mss/year.** "Manuscripts should be submitted as e-mail attachments. Please break up the text using subheads to categorize topics. We prefer articles that are submitted with photos. Do not insert photos into the text. Photos must be submitted separately." Length: 10,000-20,000 characters with spaces. **Pays $100-250.**

💲💲 USDF CONNECTION

United States Dressage Federation, 4051 Iron Works Pkwy., Lexington KY 40511. **E-mail:** connection@usdf.org. **E-mail:** editorial@usdf.org. **Website:** www.usdf.org. **Contact:** Jennifer Bryant. **40% freelance written.** Magazine published 10 times/year covering dressage (an equestrian sport). All material must relate to the sport of dressage in the U.S. Estab. 2000. Circ. 35,000. Byline given. Pays on acceptance. Offers 50% kill fee. Publishes ms an average of 6 months after acceptance. Editorial lead time 3 months. Submit seasonal material 6 months in advance. Accepts queries by mail, e-mail. Responds in 1 month to queries; in 1-2 months to mss. Sample copy: $5. Guidelines online.

NONFICTION Needs book excerpts, essays, how-to, interview, opinion, personal experience. Does not want general-interest equine material or stories that lack a U.S. dressage angle. **Buys 20 mss/year.** Query. Length: 500-2,000 words. **Pays $100-400 for assigned articles. Pays $100-300 for unsolicited articles. Byline only for "The Tail End," a one-page**

personal or op/ed column pertaining to USDF members' dressage experiences.

COLUMNS Amateur Hour (profiles of and service pieces of interest to USDF's adult amateur members), 1,200-1,500 words; Under 21 (profiles of and service pieces of interest to USDF's young members), 1,200-1,500 words; Horse-Health Connection (dressage-related horse health), 1,200-1,800 words. **Buys 12 mss/year.** Query with published clips. **Pays $150-300.**

ART & ARCHITECTURE

⊕⊕ THE ARTIST'S MAGAZINE

F+W, a Content + eCommerce Company, 10151 Carver Rd., Blue Ash OH 45242. (513)531-2690, ext. 11731. **Fax:** (513)891-7153. **Website:** www.artistsmagazine. com. **Contact:** Maureen Bloomfield, editor-in-chief; Brian Roeth, senior art director. **80% freelance written.** Magazine published 10 times/year covering primarily two-dimensional art for working artists. Maureen Bloomfield says, "Ours is a highly visual approach to teaching serious amateur and professional artists techniques that will help them improve their skills and market their work. The style should be crisp and immediately engaging, written in a voice that speaks directly to artists. We do not accept unsolicited manuscripts. Artists should send digital images of their work; writers should send clips of previously published work, along with a query letter." Circ. 100,000. Bionote given for feature material. Pays on publication. Offers 8% kill fee. Publishes ms an average of 6 months-1 year after acceptance. Accepts simultaneous submissions. Responds in 6 months to queries. Sample copy for $5.99. Guidelines online.

NONFICTION No unillustrated articles. **Buys 60 mss/year.** Length: 500-1,200 words. **Pays $300-500 and up.**

⊕⊕⊕ ARTLINK

Artlink Australia, P.O. Box 182, Fullarton SA 5063 Australia. (61)(8)8271-6228. **E-mail:** info@artlink. com.au. **Website:** www.artlink.com.au. **Contact:** Eve Sullivan, executive editor. Quarterly magazine covering contemporary art in Australia. Estab. 1981. Accepts simultaneous submissions. Guidelines online.

NONFICTION Needs general interest. Special issues: "*Artlink* welcomes proposals for writing and information on associated projects and exhibition programs that relate to forthcoming themed issues."

See website for upcoming themes. Write or e-mail the editor with your CV and 2-3 examples of previously published writing. **Pays $300/1,000 words.**

⊕⊕⊕⊕⊕ AZURE (ARCHITECTURE, DESIGN, INTERIORS, CURIOSITY)

460 Richmond St W, Suite 601, Toronto ON M5V 1Y1 Canada. 416-203-9674. **E-mail:** editorial@azureonline.com; azure@azureonline.com. **Website:** www.azuremagazine.com. **Contact:** David Dick-Agnew, senior editor. **75% freelance written.** Magazine covering design and architecture. "*AZURE* is an award-winning magazine with a focus on contemporary architecture and design. In 8 visually stunning issues per year, *AZURE* explores inventive projects, emerging trends, and design issues that relate to our changing society. In recent years, *AZURE* has evolved into a media brand offering digital editions, weekly e-newsletters featuring the latest design news, an interactive website updated daily, and an international awards program celebrating excellence in design." Estab. 1985. Byline given. Pays on publication. Offers variable kill fee. Publishes ms an average of 1 month after acceptance. Editorial lead time up to 45 days. Accepts queries by e-mail. Accepts simultaneous submissions. Responds in 6 weeks to queries.

NONFICTION Needs new product, profile, technical, travel. Special issues: January/February: Houses; March/April: Iconic Buildings; June: Office Spaces; July/August: AZ Awards Annual; October: Trends; December: Interiors and Higher Ed. Does not want "anything other than architecture, design, urbanism and landscape, and tangentially related topics." **Buys 25-30 mss/year.** Length: 300-1,500 words. **Pays $1/word (Canadian).**

COLUMNS Groundbreaker (profiles of new, large architectural projects) 350 words; book and documentary reviews, 300 words; Field Trip (profiles of hospitality/travel spaces with design angle), 800 words; Trailer (idiosyncratic design stories) 300 words. **Buys 30 mss/year.** Query. **Pays $1/word (Canadian).**

⊕⊕⊕ C MAGAZINE

C The Visual Arts Foundation, P.O. Box 5, Station B, Toronto ON M5T 2T2 Canada. (416)539-9495. **Fax:** (416)539-9903. **E-mail:** info@cmagazine.com. **E-mail:** amishmorrell@cmagazine.com. **Website:** www. cmagazine.com. **Contact:** Amish Morrell, editor. **80% freelance written.** Quarterly magazine covering international contemporary art. "*C Magazine* is a Toronto-based contemporary art and criticism periodical devoted to providing a forum for significant ideas in visual art and culture. Each quarterly issue explores a new theme through original art writing, criticism, and artists' projects." Estab. 1983. Circ. 7,000. Byline given. Pays on publication. Offers kill fee. Publishes ms an average of 4 months after acceptance. Editorial lead time 3 months. Accepts queries by e-mail. Accepts simultaneous submissions. Responds in 6 weeks to queries; in 4 months to mss. Sample copy: $10 (US). Guidelines online.

NONFICTION Needs essays, general interest, opinion, personal experience. "*C Magazine* welcomes writing on contemporary art and culture that is lively and rigorously engaged with current ideas and debates. *C* is interested in writing that addresses emergent practices and places them in critical context." **Buys 50 mss/year.** Query with published clips and brief bio by e-mail: amishmorrell@cmagazine.com. Length: 800-1,000 words for book reviews; 2,500-4,000 words for features, cultural analysis, artist profiles, and interviews. **Pays $150-500 (Canadian), $105-350 (US).**

⊙🌑💲 ESPACE

Le Centre de Diffusion 3D, 423-5445 Avenue De Gaspé, Montreal QC H2J 3B2 Canada. (514)907-6147. **E-mail:** info@espaceartactuel.com. **Website:** www.espaceartactuel.com. **Contact:** Serge Fisette, editor. **95% freelance written.** Quarterly magazine covering sculpture events. Estab. 1987. Circ. 1,400. Byline given. Pays on publication. No kill fee. Publishes ms an average of 3 months after acceptance. Editorial lead time 5 months. Submit seasonal material 3 months in advance. Accepts queries by e-mail. Accepts simultaneous submissions. Sample copy free. Guidelines online.

NONFICTION Needs interview, reviews, sculpture events. **Buys 60 mss/year.** Send complete ms. Length: up to 1,000 words for reviews; 1,500-2,000 words for interviews, events. **Pays $65/page.**

💲💲 THE MAGAZINE ANTIQUES

Brant Publications, 110 Greene St., New York NY 10012. (212)941-2800. **Fax:** (212)941-2819. **E-mail:** tmaedit@artnews.com (JavaScript required to view). **Website:** www.themagazineantiques.com. **75% freelance written.** Bimonthly. "Articles should present new information in a scholarly format (with footnotes) on the fine and decorative arts, architecture, historic preservation, and landscape architecture." Estab. 1922. Circ. 40,000. Byline given. Pays on publication. No kill fee. Publishes ms an average of 6 months after acceptance. Editorial lead time 6 months. Submit seasonal material 6 months in advance. Accepts simultaneous submissions. Responds in 3 weeks to queries. Responds in 6 months to mss. Sample copy $12 plus shipping costs. Contact tmacustserv@cdsfulfillment.com.

NONFICTION Buys 50 mss/year. "For submission guidelines and questions about our articles, please contact the editorial department at tmaedit@artnews.com; you need JavaScript enabled to view it." Length: 2,850-3,500 words. **Pays $250-500.**

💲💲💲💲 METROPOLIS

Bellerophon Publications, 205 Lexington Ave., 17th Floor, New York NY 10016. (212)627-9977. **Fax:** (212)627-9988. **E-mail:** edit@metropolismag.com. **Website:** www.metropolismag.com. **Contact:** Claire Barliant, managing editor. **80% freelance written.** Monthly magazine (combined issue July/August) for consumers interested in architecture and design. "*Metropolis* examines contemporary life through design—architecture, interior design, product design, graphic design, crafts, planning, and preservation. Subjects range from the sprawling urban environment to intimate living spaces to small objects of everyday use. In looking for why design happens in a certain way, *Metropolis* explores the economic, environmental, social, cultural, political, and technological context. With its innovative graphic presentation and its provocative voice, *Metropolis* shows how richly designed our world can be." Estab. 1981. Circ. 45,000. Byline given. Pays 60-90 days after acceptance. No kill fee. Publishes ms an average of 3 months after acceptance. Submit seasonal material 3 months in advance. Accepts queries by e-mail. Accepts simultaneous submissions. Responds in 8 months to queries. Sample copy: $7. Guidelines online.

NONFICTION Needs essays, interview. No profiles on individual architectural practices, information from public relations firms, or fine arts. **Buys 30 mss/year.** Send query via e-mail; no mss. "Describe your idea and why it would be good for our magazine. Be concise, specific, and clear. Also, please include clips or links to a few of your recent stories. The ideal *Metropolis* story is based on strong reporting and includes an examination of current critical issues. A design firm's newest work isn't a story, but the issues that its work brings to light might be." Length: 1,500-4,000 words. **Pays $1,500-4,000.**

COLUMNS The Metropolis Observed (architecture, design, and city planning news features), 100-1,200 words, pays $100-1,200; Perspective (opinion or personal observation of architecture and design), 1,200 words, pays $1,200; Enterprise (the business/development of architecture and design), 1,500 words, pays $1,500; In Review (architecture and book review essays), 1,500 words, pays $1,500. **Buys 40 mss/year.** Query with published clips.

SOUTHWEST ART

10901 W. 120th Ave., Suite 340, Broomfield CO 80021. (303)442-0427. **Fax:** (303)449-0279. **E-mail:** southwestart@fwmedia.com. **Website:** www.southwestart.com. **Contact:** Kristin Hoerth, editor in chief. **60% freelance written.** Monthly magazine directed to art collectors interested in artists, market trends, and art history of the American West. Estab. 1971. Circ. 60,000. Byline given. Pays on acceptance. Publishes ms an average of 1 year after acceptance. Submit seasonal material 8 months in advance. Accepts queries by mail, fax. Accepts simultaneous submissions. Responds in 6 months to mss.

NONFICTION Needs book excerpts, interview. No fiction or poetry. **Buys 70 mss/year.** Query with published clips. Length: 1,400-1,600 words.

ASSOCIATIONS

BUGLE

Rocky Mountain Elk Foundation, 5705 Grant Creek, Missoula MT 59808. (406)523-4500. **Fax:** (800)225-5355. **E-mail:** bugle@rmef.org. **E-mail:** conservationeditor@rmef.org; huntingeditor@rmef.org; assistanteditor@rmef.org; photos@rmef.org. **Website:** www.rmef.org. *Bugle* is the membership publication of the Rocky Mountain Elk Foundation, a nonprofit wildlife conservation group. "Our readers are predominantly hunters, many of them conservationists who care deeply about protecting wildlife habitat." Bimonthly. Estab. 1984. Circ. 185,000. Pays on acceptance. Accepts simultaneous submissions. Responds in 1 month to queries; 3 months to mss. Sample copy for $5. Writer's guidelines online.

NONFICTION Needs essays, personal experience, conservation, natural history, wildlife management, hunting and human interest, essays on women in the outdoors. Query or submit complete ms to appropriate e-mail address; see website for guidelines. Length:

750-4,500 words, depending on type of piece. **Pays 20¢/word and 3 contributor's copies.**

FICTION "We accept fiction and nonfiction stories pertaining in some way to elk, other wildlife, hunting, habitat conservation, and related issues. We would like to see more humor." Needs adventure, historical, humorous, novel excerpts, slice-of-life vignettes, western, children's/juvenile, satire, human interest, natural history, conservation—as long as they related to elk. Query or submit complete ms to appropriate e-mail address; see website for guidelines. Length: 1,500-4,500 words; average length: 2,500 words. **Pays 20¢/word and 3 contributor's copies.**

DATA CENTER MANAGEMENT

AFCOM, 742 E. Chapman Ave., Orange CA 92866. **Fax:** (714)997-9743. **E-mail:** afcom@afcom.com; jmoore@afcom.com. **Website:** www.afcom.com. **Contact:** Karen Riccio, managing editor. **50% freelance written.** Bimonthly magazine covering data center management. *Data Center Management* is the slick, 4-color, bimonthly publication for members of AFCOM, the leading association for data center management. Estab. 1988. Circ. 4,000 worldwide. Byline given. Pays on acceptance for assigned articles and on publication for unsolicited articles. Offers up to 10% kill fee. Publishes ms an average of 3 months after acceptance. Editorial lead time 6-12 months. Submit seasonal material 6 months in advance. Accepts queries by e-mail. Accepts simultaneous submissions. Responds in 1-3 weeks to queries; in 1-3 months to mss. Guidelines online.

NONFICTION Needs how-to. Special issues: The January/February issue is the annual 'Emerging Technologies' issue. Articles for this issue are visionary and product neutral. No product reviews or general tech articles. **Buys 15+ mss/year.** Query with published clips. Length: up to 2,000 word. **Pays 50¢/word minimum, based on writer's expertise.**

THE ELKS MAGAZINE

425 W. Diversey Pkwy., Chicago IL 60614. (773)755-4900. **E-mail:** magnews@elks.org. **Website:** www.elks.org/elksmag. **Contact:** John P. Sheridan, Managing Editor. **25% freelance written.** Magazine covers nonfiction only; published 10 times/year with basic mission of being the voice of the elks. All fraternal is written in-house. Estab. 1922. Circ. 800,000. Pays on acceptance. No kill fee. Accepts queries by mail, e-mail.

Responds in 1 month with a yes/no on ms purchase. Guidelines online.

NONFICTION Needs general interest, historical, travel. No fiction, religion, controversial issues, first-person, fillers, or verse. **Buys 20-30 mss/year.** Send complete ms. Length: 1,500-2,000 words. **Pays 25¢/word.**

COLUMNS "The invited columnists are already selected."

💲💲 FCA MAGAZINE

Fellowship of Christian Athletes, 8701 Leeds Rd., Kansas City MO 64129. (816)921-0909; (800)289-0909. **Fax:** (816)921-8755. **E-mail:** mag@fca.org. **Website:** www.fca.org/mag. **Contact:** Clay Meyer, editor; Matheau Casner, creative director. **50% freelance written. Prefers to work with published/established writers, but works with a growing number of new/unpublished writers each year.** Published 6 times/year. *FCA Magazine*'s mission is to serve as a ministry tool of the Fellowship of Christian Athletes by informing, inspiring and involving coaches, athletes and all whom they influence, that they may make an impact for Jesus Christ. Estab. 1959. Circ. 75,000. Byline given. Pays on publication. No kill fee. Publishes ms an average of 4 months after acceptance. Submit seasonal material 6 months in advance. Accepts simultaneous submissions. Responds to queries/mss in 3 months. Sample copy for $2 and 9x12 SASE with 3 first-class stamps. Guidelines available at www.fca.org/mag/media-kit.

NONFICTION Needs inspirational, personal experience, photo feature. **Buys 5-20 mss/year.** Articles should be accompanied by at least 3 quality photos. Query and submit via e-mail. Length: 1,000-2,000 words. **Pays $150-400 for assigned and unsolicited articles.**

💲💲 LION

Lions Clubs International, 300 W. 22nd St., Oak Brook IL 60523-8842. (630)468-6909. **Fax:** (630)571-1685. **E-mail:** magazine@lionsclubs.org. **Website:** www.lionsclubs.org. **Contact:** Jay Copp, senior editor. **35% freelance written. Works with a small number of new/unpublished writers each year.** Monthly magazine covering service club organization for Lions Club members and their families. Estab. 1918. Circ. 490,000. Byline given. Pays on acceptance. No kill fee. Publishes ms an average of 5 months after acceptance.

Accepts queries by mail, e-mail, fax, phone. Accepts simultaneous submissions. Responds in 1 month to queries. Sample copy and writer's guidelines free.

NONFICTION Needs photo feature. No travel, biography, or personal experiences. **Buys 40 mss/year.** "Article length should not exceed 2,000 words, and is subject to editing. No gags, fillers, quizzes or poems are accepted. Photos must be color prints or sent digitally. *LION* magazine pays upon acceptance of material. Advance queries save your time and ours. Address all submissions to Jay Copp, senior editor, by mail or e-mail text and .tif or .jpg (300 dpi) photos." Length: 500-2,000 words. **Pays $100-750.**

💲💲💲⊘ NATIONAL PARKS MAGAZINE

National Parks Conservation Association, 777 Sixth St. NW, Suite 700, Washington DC 20001. (202)223-6722; (800)628-7275. **Fax:** (202)454-3333. **E-mail:** npmag@npca.org. **Website:** www.npca.org/magazine/. **Contact:** Scott Kirkwood, editor-in-chief. **60% freelance written. Prefers to work with published/established writers.** Quarterly magazine for a largely unscientific but highly educated audience interested in preservation of National Park System units, natural areas, and protection of wildlife habitat. "*National Parks* magazine publishes articles about areas in the National Park System, proposed new areas, threats to parks or park wildlife, scientific discoveries, legislative issues, and endangered species of plants or animals relevant to national parks. We do not publish articles on general environmental topics, nor do we print articles about land managed by the Fish and Wildlife Service, Bureau of Land Management, or other federal agencies." Estab. 1919. Circ. 340,000. Pays on acceptance. Offers 33% kill fee. Publishes ms an average of 2 months after acceptance. Accepts simultaneous submissions. Responds in 3-4 months to queries. Sample copy for $3 and 9x12 SASE or online. Guidelines online.

NONFICTION Needs expose, descriptive articles about new or proposed national parks and wilderness parks. No poetry, philosophical essays, or first-person narratives. No unsolicited mss. Length: 1,500 words. **Pays $1,300 for 1,500-word features and travel articles.**

💲💲 NEW MOBILITY

United Spinal Association, 120-34 Queens Blvd., #320, Kew Gardens NY 11415. (718)803-3782. **E-mail:** tgilmer@unitedspinal.org; jbyzek@unitedspinal.org.

Website: www.spinalcord.org/. **Contact:** Tim Gilmer, editor; Josie Byzek, managing editor. **50% freelance written.** Bimonthly magazine covering living with spinal cord injury/disorder (SCI/D). The bimonthly membership magazine for the National Spinal Cord Injury Association, a program of United Spinal Association. Members include people with spinal cord injury or disorder, as well as caregivers, parents, and some spinal cord injury/disorder professionals. All articles should reflect this common interest of the audience. Assume that your audience is better educated in the subject of spinal cord injury than average, but be careful not to be too technical. Each issue has a theme (available from editor) that unites features in addition to a series of departments focused on building community and providing solutions for the SCI/D community. Articles that feature members, chapters or the organization are preferred, but any article that deals with issue pertinent to SCI/D community will be considered. Estab. 2011. Circ. 35,000. Byline given. Pays on publication. No kill fee. Publishes ms an average of 1-2 months after acceptance. Accepts queries by e-mail. Accepts simultaneous submissions. Sample copy and guidelines available on website.

NONFICTION Needs essays, general interest, how-to, humor, interview, new product, personal experience, photo feature, travel, medical research. Does not want "articles that treat disabilities as an affliction or cause for pity, or that show the writer does not get that people with disabilities are people like anyone else. We aren't interested in 'courageous' or 'inspiring' tales of 'overcoming disability.'" **Buys 36 mss/year.** Query. Length: 800-1,600 words. **Pays 15¢/word for new writers.**

COLUMNS Travel (report on access of a single travel destination based on conversations with disabled travelers), Access (hands-on look at how to improve access for a specific type of area), Ask Anything (tap members and experts to answer community question relating to life w/SCI/D), Advocacy (investigation of ongoing advocacy issue related to SCI/D). **Buys 40 mss/year.** Length: 800 words. Query with published clips. **Pays 15¢/word for new writers.**

PENN LINES

Pennsylvania Rural Electric Association, P.O. Box 1266, Harrisburg PA 17108. **E-mail:** editor@prea.com. **Website:** www.prea.com/content/pennlines.asp. Monthly magazine covering rural life in Pennsylvania. News magazine of Pennsylvania electric cooperatives. Features should be balanced, and they should have a rural focus. Electric cooperative sources (such as consumers) should be used. Estab. 1966. Circ. 165,000. Byline given. Pays on publication. No kill fee. Publishes ms an average of 3 months after acceptance. Editorial lead time 4 months. Submit seasonal material 4 months in advance. Accepts queries by mail, e-mail. Accepts simultaneous submissions. Sample copy online.

NONFICTION Needs general interest, historical, how-to, interview. Query or send complete ms. Length: 500-2,000 words. **Negotiates payment individually.**

THE ROTARIAN

Rotary International, One Rotary Center, 1560 Sherman Ave., Evanston IL 60201. (847)866-3000. **Fax:** (847)328-8554. **E-mail:** rotarian@rotary.org. **Website:** www.rotary.org. **40% freelance written.** Monthly magazine for Rotarian business and professional men and women and their families, schools, libraries, hospitals, etc. "Articles should appeal to an international audience and in some way help Rotarians help other people. The organization's rationale is one of hope, encouragement, and belief in the power of individuals talking and working together." Estab. 1911. Circ. 510,000. Byline sometimes given. Pays on acceptance. Offers kill fee. Kill fee negotiable. Editorial lead time 4-8 months. Accepts queries by mail, e-mail. Accepts simultaneous submissions. Sample copy for $1 (edbrookc@rotaryintl.org). Guidelines online.

NONFICTION Needs general interest, humor, inspirational, photo feature, technical, travel, sports, business/finance, environmental, health/medicine, social issues. No fiction, religious, or political articles. Query with published clips. Length: 1,500-2,500 words. **Pays negotiable rate.**

COLUMNS Health; Management; Finance; Travel, all 550-900 words. Query.

SCOUTING

Boy Scouts of America, 1325 W. Walnut Hill Lane, P.O. Box 152079, Irving TX 75015-2079. **Website:** www.scoutingmagazine.org. **80% freelance written.** Magazine published 6 times/year covering Scouting activities for adult leaders of the Boy Scouts, Cub Scouts, and Venturing. Estab. 1913. Circ. 1 million. Byline given. Pays on acceptance for major features and some shorter features. Publishes ms an average of

18 months after acceptance. Editorial lead time 1 year. Submit seasonal material 1 year in advance. Accepts queries by mail. Accepts simultaneous submissions. Responds in 3 weeks to queries; in 2 months to mss. Sample copy: $2.50 and 9x12 SAE with 4 first-class stamps, or online.

NONFICTION Needs inspirational, interview. **Buys 20-30 mss/year.** Query with SASE. Length: short features, 500-700 words; some longer features, up to 1,200 words, usually the result of a definite assignment to a professional writer. **Pays $650-800 for major articles, $300-500 for shorter features. Rates depend on professional quality of article.**

COLUMNS Way It Was (Scouting history), 600-750 words; Family Talk (family, raising kids, etc.), 600-750 words. **Buys 8-12 mss/year.** Query. **Pays $300-500.**

FILLERS Limited to personal accounts of humorous or inspirational Scouting experiences. Needs anecdotes, short humor. **Buys 15-25 mss/year.** Length: 50-150 words. **Pays $25 on publication.**

TOASTMASTER MAGAZINE

Toastmasters International, P.O. Box 9052, Mission Viejo CA 92690. 949-858-8255. **E-mail:** submissions@toastmasters.org. **Website:** www.toastmasters.org. **Contact:** submissions@toastmasters.org. **50% freelance written.** Monthly magazine covers public speaking, leadership, communication and club-related topics. The monthly Toastmaster magazine is distributed to members of Toastmasters International, a nonprofit organization and world leader in communication and leadership development. The publications team prizes article originality, depth of research, timeliness and excellence of expression. Unsolicited article queries and photos are accepted via e-mail. All accepted articles are subject to editing for length and/or clarity. Articles and photos may be published in print and digital versions. Estab. Toastmasters International: Established in 1924. Read more at www.toastmasters.org/About/History. Circ. To 332,000 members in more than 15,400 clubs in 135 countries. Byline given. Pays upon acceptance. No kill fee. Submit seasonal material 3-4 months in advance. Accepts queries by e-mail, online submission form. Accepts simultaneous submissions. Guidelines available at www.toastmasters.org/Submissions. Please refer to the submissions guidelines on the Toastmasters website first, and then submit your query via e-mail to submissions@toastmasters.org. Tip: We highly recommend that you review several issues of the Toastmaster magazine before submitting a query.

NONFICTION Needs how-to, humor, interview, profile, communications, leadership, language use. Articles with political or religious slants or sexist or nationalist language will not be accepted. **Buys 50 mss/year.** Need: Leadership and communication "How To ..." articles, expert advice and tips for public speakers, impromptu speaking, humorous speeches, persuasive speeches, storytelling and cross-cultural communication. Profiles of prominent international speakers and leaders relative to an international audience. Length: 650-1,800 words. **Compensation for accepted articles (word count: 650–1,800) is $200–$650, and is based on readability, thoroughness of the research performed, compliance with submissions guidelines, and the article's value to the publications team and to members of Toastmasters.**

TRAIL & TIMBERLINE

The Colorado Mountain Club, 710 Tenth St., Suite 200, Golden CO 80401. (303)279-3080. **E-mail:** editor@cmc.org. **Website:** www.cmc.org/about/newsroom/trailandtimberline.aspx. **Contact:** Editor. **80% freelance written.** Official quarterly publication for the Colorado Mountain Club. "Articles in *Trail & Timberline* conform to the mission statement of the Colorado Mountain Club to unite the energy, interest, and knowledge of lovers of the Colorado mountains, to collect and disseminate information 'regarding the Colorado mountains in the areas of art, science, literature, and recreation,' to stimulate public interest, and to encourage preservation of the mountains of Colorado and the Rocky Mountain region." Estab. 1918. Circ. 10,500. Byline given. Pays on acceptance. No kill fee. Publishes ms an average of 2 months after acceptance. Editorial lead time 6 months. Submit seasonal material 6 months in advance. Accepts queries by mail, e-mail. Accepts simultaneous submissions. Responds in 1 week to queries.; in 1 month to mss. Sample copy: online, or $3 plus catalog-sized SASE. Make checks payable to CMC. Guidelines online.

NONFICTION Needs essays, humor, opinion, personal experience, photo feature, travel. **Buys 10-15 mss/year.** Send complete ms. Length: 500-2,000 words. **Pays $50.**

VFW MAGAZINE

Veterans of Foreign Wars of the United States, 406 W. 34th St., Kansas City MO 64111. (816)756-3390. **Fax:**

(816)968-1169. **E-mail:** kgibson@vfw.org; magazine@vfw.org. **Website:** www.vfwmagazine.org. **Contact:** Kelly Gibson, senior writer. **40% freelance written.** Monthly magazine on veterans' affairs, military history, patriotism, defense, and current events. *VFW Magazine* goes to its members worldwide, all having served honorably in the armed forces overseas from World War II through the Iraq and Afghanistan Wars. Estab. 1904. Circ. 1.5 million. Byline given. Pays on acceptance. Offers 50% kill fee. Publishes ms 3-6 months after acceptance. Editorial lead time is 6 months. Submit seasonal material 6 months in advance. Accepts queries by mail, e-mail, fax. Accepts simultaneous submissions. Responds in 2 months to queries. Sample copy for 9x12 SAE with 5 first-class stamps. Guidelines online.

NONFICTION Needs general interest, historical, inspirational. **Buys 25-30 mss/year.** Query with 1-page outline, résumé, and published clips. Do not send unsolicited mss. Length: 1,000 words. **Pays up to $500-1,000 maximum for assigned articles; $500-750 maximum for unsolicited articles.**

VINTAGE SNOWMOBILE MAGAZINE

Meagher, Inc., P.O. Box 130, Grey Eagle MN 56336. (320)285-7066. **E-mail:** vsca@vsca.com. **Website:** www.vsca.com. **Contact:** Mike Meagher. **75% freelance written.** Quarterly magazine covering vintage snowmobiles and collectors. *Vintage Snowmobile Magazine* is sent to members of the Vintage Snowmobile Club of America. "It is published quarterly in March, June, September and December and features restoration articles, stories about vintage snowmobile events and features articles about the great people in the early days of the sport." Estab. 1987. Circ. 2,400. Byline sometimes given. Pays on acceptance. No kill fee. Publishes ms an average of 3 months after acceptance. Editorial lead time 2 months. Submit seasonal material 3 months in advance. Accepts queries by mail, e-mail, fax, phone. Accepts simultaneous submissions.

NONFICTION Needs general interest, historical, humor, photo feature, coverage of shows. Query with published clips. Length: 200-2,000 words.

COLUMNS Featured Sleds Stories, 500 words. Query with published clips.

🢒 WALK MAGAZINE

The Ramblers' Association, 2nd Floor, Camelford House, 87-90 Albert Embankment, London England SE1 7TW United Kingdom. +44 020 7339 8500. **Fax:** +44 020 7339 8501. **E-mail:** ramblers@ramblers.org.uk. **Website:** www.ramblers.org.uk. "Quarterly magazine that encourages people to participate in walking, educates people about the countryside, and promotes wider access to—and protection of—the countryside. The magazine is distributed to Ramblers' Association members, organizations, and individuals who want to stay informed on the group's policies." Circ. 140,000. Pays on publication. No kill fee. Editorial lead time 6 weeks. Accepts queries by mail. Accepts simultaneous submissions. Sample copy online or for a SASE (A4 and 73 pence). Guidelines available by e-mail.

NONFICTION Query with synopsis/outline, published clips, SASE. Length: 500-800 words. **Payment is negotiable.**

ASTROLOGY, METAPHYSICAL & NEW AGE

💲 🢒 FATE MAGAZINE

Fate Magazine, Inc., P.O. Box 460, Lakeville MN 55044. (952)431-2050. **Fax:** (952)891-6091. **E-mail:** fate@fatemag.com. **Website:** www.fatemag.com. **Contact:** Phyllis Galde, editor in chief. **75% freelance written.** Covers the paranormal, ghosts, UFOs, strange science. "Reports a wide variety of strange and unknown phenomena. We are open to receiving any well-written, well-documented article. Our readers especially like reports of current investigations, experiments, theories, and experiences." Estab. 1948. Circ. 15,000. Byline given. Pays after publication. Publishes ms 3-6 months after acceptance. Editorial lead time 3-6 months. Accepts queries by mail, e-mail. Accepts simultaneous submissions. Responds in 1-3 months to queries. Sample copy available for free online, by e-mail. Guidelines online.

NONFICTION Needs general interest, historical, how-to, personal experience, photo feature, technical. "We do not publish poetry, fiction, editorial/opinion pieces, or book-length mss." **Buys 100 mss/year.** Submit complete ms by e-mail or on CD accompanied by hard copy. Length: 1,500-3,000 words. **Pays $50.** Pays with merchandise or ad space if requested.

COLUMNS True Mystic Experiences (short reader-submitted stories of strange experiences); My Proof of Survival (short reader-submitted stories of proof of life after death), up to 500 words. Submit complete ms by e-mail or on CD accompanied by hard copy. **Pays $25.**

FILLERS Fillers are especially welcomed and must be fully authenticated. Needs anecdotes and facts. Length: 150-500 words. **Pays $10.**

$ WHOLE LIFE TIMES

Whole Life Media, LLC, 23705 Vanowen St., #306, West Hills CA 91307. (877)807-2599. **Fax:** (310)933-1693. **E-mail:** editor@wholelifemagazine.com. **Website:** www.wholelifemagazine.com. Bimonthly regional glossy on holistic living. *Whole Life Times* relies almost entirely on freelance material. Open to stories on natural health, alternative healing, green living, sustainable and local food, social responsibility, conscious business, the environment, spirituality and personal growth—anything relevant to a progressive, healthy lifestyle. Estab. 1978. Circ. 40,000 (print); 5,000 (digital). Byline given. Pays within 30-45 days of publication. 50% kill fee on assigned stories. No kill fee to first-time *WLT* writers or for unsolicited submissions. Publishes ms 2-4 months after acceptance. Accepts simultaneous submissions. Sample copy and writer's Guidelines online.

NONFICTION Special issues: Special issues include: Healing Arts, Food and Nutrition, Spirituality, New Beginnings, Relationships, Longevity, Arts/Cultures Travel, Vitamins and Supplements, Women's Issues, Sexuality, Science and Metaphysics, Eco Lifestyle. **Buys 60 mss/year.** Send complete ms. Submissions are accepted via e-mail. Artwork should also be sent via e-mail as hard copies will not be returned. "Queries should be professionally written and show an awareness of our style and current topics of interest in our subject area. We welcome investigative reporting and are happy to see queries that address topics in a political context. We are especially looking for articles on health and nutrition. No regular columns sought. Submissions should be double-spaced in AP style as an attached unformatted MS Word file (.docx). If you do not have Microsoft Word and must e-mail in another program, please also copy and paste your story in the message section of your e-mail." **Payment varies. "*WLT* accepts up to 3 longer stories (800-1,100 words) per issue, and pay ranges from $100-175 depending on topic, research required, and writer experience. In addition, we have a number of regular departments that pay $35-150 depending on topic, length, research required, and writer experience. We pay by invoice, so please be sure to submit one and to name the file with your name."**

COLUMNS Local News, Taste of Health (food), Yoga & Spirit, Whole Living, Success Track, Art & Soul (media reviews). Length: 600-750 words. Send complete ms or well-developed query and links to previously published work. Submissions are accepted via e-mail. Artwork should also be sent via e-mail as hard copies will not be returned. **"City of Angels is our FOB section featuring short, newsy blurbs on our coverage topics, generally in the context of Los Angeles. These are generally 350-450 words and pay $25-35 depending on length and topic. This is a great section for writers who are new to us. BackWords is a 650-word personal essay that often highlights a seminal moment or event in the life of the writer and pays $100. We pay by invoice, so please be sure to submit one, and name the file with your name."**

AUTOMOTIVE & MOTORCYCLE

$ AMERICAN MOTORCYCLIST

American Motorcyclist Association, 13515 Yarmouth Dr., Pickerington OH 43147. (614)856-1900. **E-mail:** submissions@ama-cycle.org. **Website:** www.americanmotorcyclist.com. **Contact:** Grant Parsons, director of communications; James Holter, managing editor. **25% freelance written.** Monthly magazine for enthusiastic motorcyclists investing considerable time and money in the sport, emphasizing the motorcyclist, not the vehicle. Monthly magazine of the American Motorcyclist Association. Emphasizes people involved in, and events dealing with, all aspects of motorcycling. Readers are "enthusiastic motorcyclists, investing considerable time in road riding or all aspects of the sport." Estab. 1947. Circ. 200,000. Byline given. Pays on publication. No kill fee. Editorial lead time 3 months. Submit seasonal material 4 months in advance. Accepts queries by mail, e-mail. Accepts simultaneous submissions. Responds in 5 weeks to queries. Responds in 6 weeks to mss. Sample copy for $1.50. Guidelines free.

NONFICTION Needs interview, personal experience, travel. **Buys 8 mss/year.** Send complete ms. Length: 1,000-2,500 words. **Pays minimum $8/published column inch.**

✪❸❸❸ CANADIAN BIKER MAGAZINE

108-2220 Sooke Rd., Victoria BC V9B 0G9 Canada. (250)384-0333. **E-mail:** edit@canadianbiker.com. **Website:** www.canadianbiker.com. **Contact:** John Campbell, editor. **65% freelance written.** Magazine covering motorcycling. Estab. 1980. Circ. 20,000. Byline given. Publishes ms an average of 1 year after acceptance. Editorial lead time 3 months. Accepts queries by mail, e-mail. Accepts simultaneous submissions. Responds in 6 weeks to queries; in 6 months to mss. Sample copy: $5 or online.

NONFICTION Needs general interest, historical, how-to, interview, new product, technical, travel. **Buys 12 mss/year.** Query. Length: 500-1,500 words. **Pays $100-200 for assigned articles. Pays $80-150 for unsolicited articles.**

❸❸❸❸⊘ CAR AND DRIVER

Hearst Communications, Inc., 1585 Eisenhower Place, Ann Arbor MI 48108. **E-mail:** editors@caranddriver.com. **Website:** www.caranddriver.com. **Contact:** Eddie Alterman, editor in chief; Mike Fazioli, managing editor. Monthly magazine for auto enthusiasts; readers are college-educated, professional, median 24-35 years of age. Estab. 1956. Circ. 1,212,555. Byline given. Pays on acceptance. Offers 25% kill fee. Accepts queries by mail, e-mail. Accepts simultaneous submissions. Responds in 2 months to queries.

NONFICTION Query with published clips before submitting.

MOTOR TREND

TEN: The Enthusiast Network, 831 S. Douglas St., El Segundo CA 90245. **Website:** www.motortrend.com. **5-10% freelance written. Only works with published/established writers.** Monthly magazine for automotive enthusiasts and general interest consumers. Estab. 1949. Circ. 1,250,000. No kill fee. Publishes ms an average of 3 months after acceptance. Accepts queries by mail. Accepts simultaneous submissions. Responds in 1 month to queries.

NONFICTION Query before submitting.

⊘ SUPER CHEVY

Source Interlink Media, Inc., 1733 Alton Parkway, Suite 100, Irvine CA 92606. **Website:** www.superchevy-web.com. "Monthly magazine covering various forms of motorsports where Cheverolet cars and engines are in competition." Circ. 198,995. No kill fee. Accepts simultaneous submissions.

TRUCK TREND

Primedia, 831 S. Douglas Street, El Segundo CA 90245. **Website:** www.trucktrend.com. **60% freelance written.** Bimonthly magazine covering light trucks, SUVs, minivans, vans, and travel. *Truck Trend* readers want to know about what's new in the world of sport-utilities, pickups, and vans. What to buy, how to fix up, and where to go. Estab. 1998. Circ. 125,000. Byline given. Pays on publication. No kill fee. Publishes ms an average of 3 months after acceptance. Editorial lead time 5 months. Submit seasonal material 6 months in advance. Accepts queries by mail. Accepts simultaneous submissions. Sample copy for #10 sase. Guidelines online.

NONFICTION Needs how-to, travel. **Buys 12 mss/year.** "Contributions are welcomed but editors recommend that contributors query first. Contributions must be accompanied by return postage, and we assume no responsibility for loss or damage thereto. Manuscripts must be typewritten on white paper."

⬛ WHEELS

ACP Magazines, Ltd., Locked Bag 12, 73 Atherton Rd., Oakleigh VIC 3166 Australia. **E-mail:** wheels@bauertrader.com.au. **Website:** http://wheelsmag.com.au. **Contact:** Glenn Butler, editor. Monthly magazine covering all aspects of motoring. Estab. 1953. Circ. 63,200. Accepts simultaneous submissions.

NONFICTION Needs general interest, new product, technical. Query.

AVIATION

⬛ AFRICAN PILOT

Wavelengths 10 (Pty) Ltd., 6 Barbeque Heights, 9 Dytchley Rd., Barbeque Downs, Midrand 1684 South Africa. +27 (0)11 466 8524/6. **Fax:** +27 (0)86 767 4333. **E-mail:** editor@africanpilot.co.za. **Website:** www.africanpilot.co.za. **Contact:** Athol Franz, editor. **50% freelance written.** "*African Pilot* is southern Africa's premier monthly aviation magazine. It publishes a high-quality magazine that is well known and respected within the aviation community of southern Africa. The magazine offers a number of benefits to readers and advertisers, including a weekly e-mail, Aviation News, annual service guide, aviation training supplement, executive wall calendar, and an extensive website. The monthly aviation magazine is also available online as an exact replica of the paper edition but where all major advertising pages are hyperlinked to the advertisers' websites. The magazine offers clean layouts with outstanding photography and reflects editorial professionalism as well as a responsible approach to journalism. The magazine offers a complete and tailored promotional solution for all aviation businesses operating in the African region." Estab. 2001. Circ. 7,000+ online; 6,600+ print. Byline given. No kill fee. Editorial lead time 2-3 months. Accepts queries by e-mail. Accepts simultaneous submissions. Responds only if interested; send nonreturnable samples. Sample copies available upon request. Writer's guidelines online or via e-mail.

NONFICTION Needs general interest, historical, interview, new product, personal experience, photo feature, technical. No articles on aircraft accidents. **Buys up to 60 mss/year.** Send complete ms. Length: 1,200-2,800 words.

AIR & SPACE

Smithsonian Institution, P.O. Box 37012, MRC 513, Washington DC 20013. (202)633-6070. **Fax:** (202)633-6085. **E-mail:** editors@si.edu. **Website:** www.air-spacemag.com. **80% freelance written.** Bimonthly magazine covering aviation and aerospace for a nontechnical audience. "*Air & Space* is a general interest magazine about flight. Its goal is to show readers, both the knowledgeable and the novice, facets of the enterprise of flight that they are unlikely to encounter elsewhere. The emphasis is on the human rather than the technological, on the ideas behind events, rather than a simple recounting of details." Estab. 1985. Circ. 225,000. Byline given. Pays on acceptance. Offers kill fee. Accepts queries by mail, e-mail, online submission form. Accepts simultaneous submissions. Responds in 3 months to queries. Sample copy: $7. Guidelines online.

NONFICTION Needs book excerpts, essays, general interest, historical, humor, photo feature, technical. **Buys 50 mss/year.** Query with published clips. Length: 1,500-3,000 words. **Pay varies.**

COLUMNS Above & Beyond (first-person narrative of an adventure in air or space), 1,500 words; Flights & Fancy (whimsical, brief reflection), 800-1,000 words; Soundings (short, current news items reporting oddball or amusing events, efforts, or situations), 300-1,000 words; Reviews & Previews (a description and critique of a recent or soon-to-be-released book, video, movie, aerospace-related recreational product, or software), 200-450 words. **Buys 25 mss/year.** Query with published clips. **Pay varies.**

AUSTRALIAN FLYING

Yaffa Publishing, 17-21 Bellevue St., Surry Hills NSW 2010 Australia. (61)(2)9281-2333. **Fax:** (61)(2)9281-2750. **E-mail:** stevehitchen@yaffa.com.au. **Website:** www.australianflying.com.au. **Contact:** Steve Hitchen, editor. Bimonthly magazine offering hands-on tips to better flying as well as the latest technologies, accessories, and techniques, and all the relevant news that affects the day-to-day operation of the industry. Accepts simultaneous submissions.

NONFICTION Needs general interest, how-to, interview, new product, technical. Query.

AVIATION HISTORY

HistoryNet, LLC, 1600 Tysons Blvd., Ste. 1140, Tysons VA 22102. **E-mail:** aviationhistory@historynet.com. **Website:** www.historynet.com/aviation-history. **Contact:** Carl Von Wodtke, editor. **95% freelance written.** Bimonthly magazine covering military and civilian aviation from first flight to the space age. "*Aviation History* aims to make aeronautical history not only factually accurate and complete but also enjoyable to a varied subscriber and newsstand audience." Estab. 1990. Circ. 40,000. Byline given. Pays on publication. No kill fee. Publishes ms an average of 2 years after acceptance. Editorial lead time 6 months. Submit seasonal material 1 year in advance. Accepts queries by mail, e-mail. Accepts simultaneous submissions. Responds in 2 months to queries; in 3 months to mss. Sample copy: $6. Guidelines with #10 SASE or online.

NONFICTION Needs historical, interview, personal experience. **Buys 24 mss/year.** Query. Length: up to 3,000 words, with a 500-word sidebar where appropriate, author bio, and book suggestions for further reading. **Pays minimum of $300.**

COLUMNS Aviators; Restored; Extremes, all up to 1,500 words. **Pays minimum of $150. Book reviews, 250-500 words, pays minimum $50.**

FLYING ADVENTURES

Aviation Publishing Corporation, El Monte Airport (EMT), P.O. Box 93613, Pasadena CA 91109-3613. (626)618-4000. **E-mail:** editor@flyingadventures.com; info@flyingadventures.com. **Website:** www.flyingadventures.com. **Contact:** Lyn Freeman, editor in chief. **20% freelance written.** Bimonthly magazine covering lifestyle travel for owners and passengers of private aircraft. Articles cover upscale travelers. Estab. 1994. Circ. 135,000. Byline given for features. Pays on acceptance. No kill fee. Editorial lead time 2-8 weeks. Accepts queries by e-mail. Accepts simultaneous submissions. Responds immediately. Sample copy and guidelines free.

NONFICTION "Nothing nonrelevant or not our style. See magazine." Query with published clips. Length: 500-1,500 words. **Pays $150-300 for assigned and unsolicited articles.**

COLUMNS Publication has numerous departments; see magazine. **Buys 100+ mss/year.** Query with published clips. **Pays up to $150.**

💲💲 PILOT GETAWAYS MAGAZINE

Airventure Publishing LLC, P.O. Box 550, Glendale CA 91209. (818)241-1890; (877)745-6849. **Fax:** (818)241-1895. **E-mail:** info@pilotgetaways.com; editor@pilotgetaways.com. **Website:** www.pilotgetaways.com. **Contact:** George A. Kounis, editor/publisher. **90% freelance written.** Bimonthly magazine covering aviation travel for private pilots. *Pilot Getaways* is a travel magazine for private pilots. Our articles cover destinations that are easily accessible by private aircraft, including details such as airport transportation, convenient hotels, and attractions. Other regular features include fly-in dining, flying tips, and bush flying. Estab. 1999. Circ. 10,000. Byline given. Pays on publication. No kill fee. Editorial lead time 4 months. Submit seasonal material 9 months in advance. Accepts queries by mail, e-mail, phone. Accepts simultaneous submissions. Responds in 2 weeks to queries; 2 months to mss. Sample copy and writer's guidelines free.

NONFICTION Needs travel. "We rarely publish articles about events that have already occurred, such as travel logs about trips the authors have taken or air show reports." **Buys 24 mss/year.** Query. Length: 1,000-3,500 words. **Pays $100-500.**

COLUMNS Weekend Getaways (short fly-in getaways), 2,000 words; Fly-in Dining (reviews of airport restaurants), 1,200 words; Flying Tips (tips and pointers on flying technique), 1,000 words; Bush Flying (getaways to unpaved destinations), 1,500 words. **Buys 20 mss/year.** Query. **Pays $100-500.**

BUSINESS & FINANCE

💲💲 ALASKA BUSINESS MONTHLY

Alaska Business Publishing, 501 W. Northern Lights Blvd., Suite 100, Anchorage AK 99503-2577. (907)276-4373; (800)770-4373. **Fax:** (907)279-2900. **E-mail:** editor@akbizmag.com. **Website:** www.akbizmag.com. **Contact:** Susan Harrington, Managing Editor; David Geiger, Art Director. **75% freelance written.** "Our audience is Alaska businessmen and businesswomen who rely on us for timely features and up-to-date information about doing business in Alaska." Estab. 1985. Circ. 12,000-15,000. Byline given. Pays month of publication. Offers $50 kill fee. Publishes ms an average of 2 months after acceptance. Assignments are due 2 months before date published. Editorial lead time 3-6 months. Submit seasonal material 6 months in advance. Accepts queries by e-mail, online submission form. Responds in 1 month to queries. Order sample copy through website store or download off website under "archives." Guidelines online.

NONFICTION Special issues: "A different industry is featured each month in a special section. Read our magazine and editorial calendar for an idea of the material we assign." No fiction, poetry, or anything not pertinent to Alaska business. Rarely uses any unsolicited or unassigned articles. **Buys approximately 200 mss/year.** Send query and half a dozen clips of previously published articles. Do not send complete mss. Does not republish blog posts. Length: 500-1,800 words. **Pays $100-350 for assigned articles.**

💲💲 BUSINESS NH MAGAZINE

Millyard Communications, 55 S. Commercial St., Manchester NH 03101. (603)626-6354. **Fax:** (603)626-6359. **E-mail:** edit@BusinessNHmagazine.com. **E-mail:** edit@businessnhmagazine.com. **Website:** www.millyardcommunications.com. **Contact:** Erika Cohen, associate editor. **25% freelance written.** Monthly magazine covering business, politics, and people of New Hampshire. "Our audience consists of the owners and top managers of New Hampshire businesses." Estab. 1983. Circ. 15,000. Byline given. Pays on publication. Publishes ms an average of 2 months after acceptance. three months Accepts queries by e-mail.

NONFICTION Needs how-to, interview. No unsolicited mss; interested in New Hampshire writers only. **Buys 24 mss/year.** Query with published clips and résumé. Length: 750-2,500 words. **Payment varies.**

💲💲 DOLLARS & SENSE: THE MAGAZINE OF ECONOMIC JUSTICE

Economic Affairs Bureau, Inc., 95 Berkeley St., Suite 305, Boston MA 02116. (617)447-2177. **Fax:** (617)477-2179. **E-mail:** dollars@dollarsandsense.org. **Website:**

www.dollarsandsense.org. **Contact:** Alejandro Reuss and Chris Sturr, co-editors. **10% freelance written.** Bimonthly magazine covering economic, environmental, and social justice. "*Dollars & Sense* publishes economic news and analysis, reports on economic justice activism, primers on economic topics, and critiques of the mainstream media's coverage of the economy. Our readers include professors, students, and activists who value our smart and accessible economic coverage. We explain the workings of the U.S. and international economics and provide left perspectives on current economic affairs." Estab. 1974. Circ. 8,000. Byline given. Pays on publication. No kill fee. Publishes ms an average of 4 months after acceptance. Editorial lead time 3 months. Submit seasonal material 2 months in advance. Accepts queries by mail, e-mail. Accepts simultaneous submissions. Sample copy: $5 or on website. Guidelines online.

NONFICTION Special issues: Wants in-depth articles on a broad range of topics. **Buys 6 mss/year.** Query with published clips. Length: 1,500-3,000 words. **Pays up to $200.**

COLUMNS Active Culture (briefs on activism), 250-400 words; Reviews (coverage of recent books, movies, and other media), 700 words. Query with published clips.

THE ECONOMIST

The Economist Group, 1730 Rhode Island Ave. NW, Suite 1210, Washington DC 20036. (202)429-0890. **Fax:** (202)429-0899. **Website:** www.economist.com. Weekly newspaper that is not just a chronicle of economics. Takes "part in a severe contest between intelligence, which presses forward, and an unworthy, timid ignorance obstructing our progress." Targets highly educated readers. Offers authoritative insight and opinion on international news, politics, business, finance, science, and technology. Estab. 1843. Accepts simultaneous submissions.

💲💲 ENTREPRENEUR MAGAZINE

Entrepreneur Media Inc., 18061 Fitch, Irvine CA 92614. **E-mail:** entmag@entrepreneur.com. **Website:** www.entrepreneur.com. **Contact:** Amy Cosper, editor in chief. **60% freelance written.** "*Entrepreneur* readers already run their own businesses. They have been in business for several years and are seeking innovative methods and strategies to improve their business operations. They are also interested in new business ideas and opportunities, as well as current issues that

affect their companies." Circ. 600,000. Byline given. Pays on acceptance. No kill fee. Publishes ms an average of 5 months after acceptance. Submit seasonal material 6 months in advance. Accepts queries by e-mail. Accepts simultaneous submissions. Responds in 3 months to queries. Sample copy: $7.20.

NONFICTION Needs how-to. **Buys 10-20 mss/year.** Query with published clips. Length: 1,800 words. **Payment varies.**

COLUMNS Snapshots (profiles of interesting entrepreneurs who exemplify innovation in their marketing/sales technique, financing method or management style, or who have developed an innovative product/service or technology); Money Smarts (financial management); Marketing Smarts; Web Smarts (Internet news); Tech Smarts; Management Smarts; Viewpoint (first-person essay on entrepreneurship), all 300 words. **Pays $1/word.**

FAST COMPANY

7 World Trade Center, New York NY 10007-2195. (212) 389-5300. **Fax:** (212) 389-5496. **E-mail:** pr@fastcompany.com. **Website:** www.fastcompany.com. **Contact:** Lori Hoffman, managing editor. Magazine published 10 times/year that inspires readers and users to think beyond traditional boundaries, lead conversations, and create the future of business. *Fast Company* is the world's leading progressive business media brand, with a unique editorial focus on innovation in technology, ethonomics (ethical economics), leadership, and design. Estab. 1996. Circ. 750,000. Accepts queries by e-mail. Accepts simultaneous submissions. No formal guidelines. Familiarize yourself with the magazine.

NONFICTION Rarely accepts unsolicited freelancer contributions. If you have a person, company, product, or any other story idea you'd like to see in *Fast Company*, query with a pitch. If interested, *Fast Company* will contact you.

FORTUNE

Time, Inc., 1271 Avenue of the Americas, New York NY 10020. (212)522-1212. **Fax:** (212)522-0810. **E-mail:** letters@fortune.com. **Website:** www.fortune.com. **Contact:** Eric Danetz, publisher; Michael Schneider, associate publisher. Biweekly magazine covering business and finance. Edited primarily for high-demographic business people. Specializes in big stories about companies, business personalities, technology, managing, Wall Street, media, marketing, personal finance, politics, and policy. Circ. 1,066,000. No kill fee. Editorial lead time 6 weeks. Accepts simultaneous submissions.

⊛⊛ INGRAM'S

Show-Me Publishing, Inc., 2049 Wyandotte, Kansas City MO 64108. (816)268-6402. **E-mail:** editorial@ingramsonline.com. **Website:** www.ingramsonline.com. **Contact:** Dennis Boone, managing editor. **10% freelance written.** Monthly magazine covering Kansas City business and economic development. "*Ingram's* readers are top-level corporate executives and community leaders, officials, and decision makers. Our editorial content must provide such readers with timely, relevant information and insights." Estab. 1975. Circ. 105,000. Byline given. Pays on publication. No kill fee. Publishes ms an average of 1 month after acceptance. Editorial lead time 1 month. Submit seasonal material 5 months in advance. Accepts queries by e-mail. Accepts simultaneous submissions. Sample copy free.

NONFICTION Needs interview, technical. Does not want humor, inspirational, or anything not related to Kansas City business. **Buys 4-6 mss/year.** Query. Length: 500-1,500 words. **Pays $75-200 depending on research/feature length.**

COLUMNS Say So (opinion), 1,500 words. **Buys 12 mss/year. Pays $75-100 maximum.**

⊛⊛ THE LANE REPORT

Lane Communications Group, 210 E. Main St., 14th Floor, Lexington KY 40507. (859)244-3500. **E-mail:** markgreen@lanereport.com. **Website:** www.lanereport.com. **Contact:** Mark Green, managing editor. **60% freelance written.** Monthly magazine covering statewide business. *The Lane Report* is an intelligent, enterprising magazine that informs readers and drives a statewide dialogue by highlighting important business stories in Kentucky. Estab. 1985. Circ. 15,000. Byline given. Pays on publication. No kill fee. Editorial lead time 6 weeks. Submit seasonal material 3 months in advance. Accepts queries by mail, e-mail. Accepts simultaneous submissions. Responds in 1 month to queries. Sample copy and writer's guidelines free.

NONFICTION Needs essays, interview, new product, photo feature. **Buys 30-40 mss/year.** Query with published clips. Do not send unsolicited mss. Looking for major trends shaping the state, noteworthy business and practices, and stories with sweeping implications across industry sectors and state regions. Length: 750-3,000 words. **Pays $150-375.**

COLUMNS Fast Lane Briefs (recent news and trends and how they might shape the future), 100-400 words; Opinion (opinion on a business or economic issue about which you, the writer, feel passionate and qualified to write), 750 words; Entrepreneurs (profile of a particularly interesting or quirky member of the business community), 750-1,400 words. Query.

MONEY

Time, Inc., 1271 Avenue of the Americas, 17th Floor, New York NY 10020. (212)522-1212. **E-mail:** editor@money.timeinc.com. **Website:** time.com/money. Monthly magazine covering finance. *Money* magazine offers sophisticated coverage in all aspects of personal finance for individuals, business executives, and personal investors. Estab. 1972. Circ. 1,967,420. No kill fee. Accepts simultaneous submissions.

⊛⊛⊛⊛ NATIONAL BLACK MBA MAGAZINE

1 E. Wacker, Suite 3500, Chicago IL 60601. (312)236-2622. **Fax:** (312)236-0390. **E-mail:** elaine@naylor.com. **Website:** www.nbmbaa.org. **80% freelance written.** Online magazine covering business career strategy, economic development, and financial management. Estab. 1997. Circ. 45,000. Byline given. Pays after publication. Offers 10-20% or $500 kill fee. Publishes ms an average of 1 month after acceptance. Editorial lead time 2-3 months. Submit seasonal material 3-4 months in advance. Accepts queries by mail, e-mail, fax.

COLUMNS Management Strategies (leadership development), 1,200-1,700 words; Features (business management, entreprenuerial finance); Finance; Technology. Send complete ms. **Pays $500-1,000.**

⊛⊛ THE NETWORK JOURNAL

The Network Journal Communication, 39 Broadway, Suite 2430, New York NY 10006. (212)962-3791. **Fax:** (212)962-3537. **E-mail:** tnjeditors@tnj.com. **Website:** www.tnj.com. **25% freelance written.** Monthly magazine covering business and career articles. *The Network Journal* caters to black professionals and small-business owners, providing quality coverage on business, financial, technology, and career news germane to the black community. Estab. 1993. Circ. 25,000. Byline given. Pays on publication. Editorial lead time 2 months. Submit seasonal material 3 months in advance. Accepts queries by mail, e-mail, fax, phone. Accepts simultaneous submissions. Sample copy for $1 or online. Writer's guidelines for SASE.

NONFICTION Needs how-to, interview. Send complete ms. Length: 1,200-1,500 words. **Pays $150-200.**

COLUMNS Book reviews, 700-800 words; career management and small business development, 800 words. **Pays $100.**

$$ PACIFIC COAST BUSINESS TIMES

14 E. Carrillo St., Suite A, Santa Barbara CA 93101. (805)560-6950. **E-mail:** hdubroff@pacbiztimes.com. **Website:** www.pacbiztimes.com. **Contact:** Henry Dubroff, founder and editor. **10% freelance written.** Weekly tabloid covering financial news specific to Santa Barbara, Ventura, San Luis Obispo counties in California. Estab. 2000. Circ. 5,000. Byline given. No kill fee. Editorial lead time 1 month. Accepts queries by e-mail, phone. Accepts simultaneous submissions. Sample copy free. Guidelines free.

NONFICTION Needs interview, opinion, personal finance. Does not want first person, promo or fluff pieces. **Buys 20 mss/year.** Query. Length: 500-800 words. **Pays $75-175.**

$$ SMARTCEO MEDIA

SmartCEO, 2700 Lighthouse Point E., Suite 220A, Baltimore MD 21224. (410)342-9510. **Fax:** (410)675-5280. **E-mail:** editorial@smartceo.com. **Website:** www.smartceo.com. **25% freelance written.** Publishes four bi-monthly print magazines covering regional business in the Baltimore, MD, Philadelphia, PA, New York, NY, and Washington, DC areas. Nearly 50,000 offensive-minded, growth-oriented CEOs turn to *SmartCEO* magazine to find ideas and inspiration to help them grow their businesses. Each issue includes behind-the-scenes looks at local success stories, columns written by key opinion leaders and other resources to help the region's middle-market CEOs conquer the daily challenges of running a business. *SmartCEO* magazine is published on a bi-monthly basis with editions in four major markets: *Baltimore SmartCEO, New York SmartCEO, Philadelphia SmartCEO* and *Washington SmartCEO.* Estab. 2001. Circ. 45,000. Byline given. Pays on publication. No kill fee. Publishes ms an average of 2 months after acceptance. Editorial lead time 5 months. Submit seasonal material 5 months in advance. Accepts queries by e-mail, phone. Accepts simultaneous submissions. Responds in 4 weeks to queries. Responds in 2 months to mss. Sample copy online. Guidelines by e-mail.

NONFICTION Needs interview, Business features or tips. "We do not want pitches on CEOs or companies outside the Baltimore, MD, Philadelphia, PA, New York, NY or Washington, DC areas; no product reviews, lifestyle content or book reviews, please." **Buys 20 mss/year. mss/year.** Query. Length: varies. **Pay varies.**

COLUMNS Project to Watch (overview of a local development project in progress and why it is of interest to the business community), 600 words; Q&A and tip-focused coverage of business issues and challenges (each article includes the opinions of 10-20 CEOs), 500-1,000 words. **Buys 0-5 mss/year mss/year.** Query.

$$ TECHNICAL ANALYSIS OF STOCKS & COMMODITIES

4757 California Ave. SW, Seattle WA 98116. (206)938-0570. **E-mail:** editor@traders.com. **Website:** www.traders.com. **90% freelance written.** "Magazine covers methods of investing and trading stocks, bonds and commodities (futures), options, mutual funds, and precious metals using technical analysis." Estab. 1982. Circ. 60,000. Byline given. Pays on publication. No kill fee. Publishes ms an average of 4 months after acceptance. Accepts simultaneous submissions. Responds in 2 months to queries. Sample copy: $5. Guidelines online.

NONFICTION Needs how-to. No newsletter-type, buy-sell recommendations. The article subject must relate to technical analysis, charting, or a numerical technique used to trade securities or futures. Almost universally requires graphics with every article. **Buys 150 mss/year.** Send complete ms. Length: 1,000-4,000 words. **Pays $3/column inch (two-column format) or $2/column inch (three-column format); $50 minimum.**

FILLERS "Must relate to trading stocks, bonds, options, mutual funds, commodities, or precious metals." **Buys 20 mss/year.** Length: 500 words. **Pays $20-50.**

$$ VERMONT BUSINESS MAGAZINE

365 Dorset St., South Burlington VT 05403. (802)863-8038. **Fax:** (802)863-8069. **Website:** www.vermontbiz.com. **Contact:** Tim McQuiston, editor. **80% freelance written.** Monthly tabloid covering business in Ver-

mont. Circ. 8,000. Byline given. Pays on publication. No kill fee. Publishes ms an average of 1 month after acceptance. Accepts simultaneous submissions. Responds in 2 months to queries. Sample copy for SAE with 11x14 envelope and 7 first-class stamps.

NONFICTION **Buys 200 mss/year.** Query with published clips. Length: 800-1,800 words. **Pays $100-200.**

CAREER, COLLEGE & ALUMNI

💲💲 AFRICAN-AMERICAN CAREER WORLD

Equal Opportunity Publications, Inc., 445 Broad Hollow Rd., Suite 425, Melville NY 11747. (631)421-9421. **E-mail:** info@eop.com. **Website:** www.eop.com. **Contact:** Joann Whitcher, editorial director. **60% freelance written.** Semiannual magazine focused on African-American students and professionals in all disciplines. Estab. 1969. Byline given. Pays on publication. No kill fee. Publishes ms an average of 3 months after acceptance. Editorial lead time 3 months. Accepts queries by mail, e-mail. Accepts simultaneous submissions. Sample copy free. Guidelines free.

NONFICTION Needs how-to, interview, personal experience. "We do not want articles that are too general." Query. Length: 1,500-2,500 words. **Pays $350 for assigned articles.**

💲💲 EQUAL OPPORTUNITY

Equal Opportunity Publications, Inc., 445 Broad Hollow Rd., Suite 425, Melville NY 11747. (631)421-9421. **Fax:** (631)421-0359. **E-mail:** jwhitcher@eop.com. **Website:** www.eop.com. **Contact:** Joann Whitcher, director, editorial and production. **70% freelance written. Prefers to work with published/established writers.** Triannual magazine dedicated to advancing the professional interests of African Americans, Hispanics, Asian Americans, and Native Americans. Audience is 90% college juniors and seniors; 10% working graduates. An understanding of educational and career problems of minorities is essential. Estab. 1967. Circ. 11,000. Byline given. Pays on publication. Publishes ms an average of 6 months after acceptance. Editorial lead time 6 months. Submit seasonal material 6 months in advance. Accepts queries by mail, e-mail, fax, phone. Accepts simultaneous submissions. Responds in 2 weeks to queries; in 1 month to mss. Sample copy and writer's guidelines for 9x12 SAE with 5 first-class stamps.

NONFICTION Needs general interest, how-to, interview, opinion, personal experience, technical, coverage of minority interests. **Buys 10 mss/year.** Send complete ms. Length: 1,000-2,000 words. **Pays 10¢/word.**

💲💲💲💲 HARVARD MAGAZINE

7 Ware St., Cambridge MA 02138. (617)495-5746. **Fax:** (617)495-0324. **E-mail:** john_rosenberg@harvard. edu. **Website:** www.harvardmagazine.com. **Contact:** John S. Rosenberg, editor. **35-50% freelance written.** Bimonthly magazine for Harvard University faculty, alumni, and students. Estab. 1898. Circ. 245,000. Byline given. Pays on publication. No kill fee. Publishes ms an average of 4 months after acceptance. Editorial lead time 1 year. Accepts queries by mail, e-mail. Accepts simultaneous submissions. Responds in 1 month to queries and mss. Sample copy online.

NONFICTION Needs book excerpts, essays, interview, journalism on Harvard-related intellectual subjects. **Buys 20-30 mss/year.** Query with published clips. Length: 800-10,000 words. **Pays $400-3,000.**

💲💲💲💲 NOTRE DAME MAGAZINE

University of Notre Dame, 500 Grace Hall, Notre Dame IN 46556-5612. (574)631-5335. **Fax:** (574)631-6767. **E-mail:** ndmag@nd.edu. **Website:** magazine. nd.edu. **Contact:** Kerry Temple, editor; Kerry Prugh, art director. **50% freelance written.** "We are a university magazine with a scope as broad as that found at a university, but we place our discussion in a moral, ethical, and spiritual context reflecting our Catholic heritage." Estab. 1972. Circ. 150,000. Byline given. Pays on acceptance. No kill fee. Publishes ms an average of 1 year after acceptance. Accepts queries by mail, e-mail. Accepts simultaneous submissions. Responds in 2 months to queries. Sample copy available online and by request. Guidelines online.

NONFICTION Needs essays, general interest, opinion, personal experience. **Buys 35 mss/year.** Query with published clips. Length: 600-3,000 words. **Pays $250-3,000.**

COLUMNS CrossCurrents (essays, deal with a wide array of issues—some topical, some personal, some serious, some light). Query with or without published clips or send complete ms.

THE PENN STATER

Penn State Alumni Association, 218 Hintz Family Alumni Center, University Park PA 16802

USA. (814)865-2709. **Fax:** (814)863-5690. **E-mail:** pennstater@psu.edu. **E-mail:** pennstater@psu.edu. **Website:** www.pennstatermag.com. **Contact:** Tina Hay, editor. **60% freelance written.** Bimonthly magazine covering Penn State and Penn Staters. Estab. 1910. Circ. 135,000. Byline given. Pays on acceptance. Offers 50% kill fee. Publishes ms an average of 4 months after acceptance. Editorial lead time 3 months. Submit seasonal material 8 months in advance. Accepts queries by mail, e-mail, fax. Responds in 3 months to queries. Sample copy and writer's guidelines free.

NONFICTION Needs book excerpts, general interest, historical, interview, photo feature, profile, book reviews, science/research. No unsolicited mss. **Buys 20 mss/year.** Query with published clips. Length: 200-3,000 words. **Pays competitive rates.**

💲💲💲 UAB MAGAZINE

UAB Office of Public Relations and Marketing (University of Alabama at Birmingham), AB 340, 1720 2nd Ave. S., Birmingham AL 35294-0103. (205)975-6577. **E-mail:** charlesb@uab.edu; uabmagazine@uab.edu. **Website:** www.uab.edu/uabmagazine. **Contact:** Charles Buchanan, editor. **70% freelance written.** University magazine published 2 times/year covering University of Alabama at Birmingham. *UAB Magazine* informs readers about the innovation and creative energy that drives UAB's renowned research, educational, and health care programs. The magazine reaches active alumni, faculty, friends and donors, patients, corporate and community leaders, media, and the public. Estab. 1980. Circ. 33,000. Byline given. Pays on acceptance. Offers 50% kill fee. Publishes ms an average of 3-4 months after acceptance. Editorial lead time 3 months. Accepts queries by mail, e-mail. Accepts simultaneous submissions. Sample copy online.

NONFICTION general interest/interview, science/research. **Buys 40-50 mss/year.** Query with published clips. Length: 500-5,000 words. **Pays $100-1,200.**

💲💲 WORKFORCE DIVERSITY FOR ENGINEERING & IT PROFESSIONALS

Equal Opportunity Publications, Inc., 445 Broad Hollow Rd., Suite 425, Melville NY 11747. (631)421-9421. **Fax:** (631)421-1352. **E-mail:** info@eop.com; jwhitcher@eop.com. **Website:** www.eop.com. **Contact:** Joann Whitcher, director, editorial and production. **60% freelance written.** Quarterly magazine addressing workplace issues affecting technical professional

women, members of minority groups, and people with disabilities. Estab. 1969. Byline given. Pays on publication. No kill fee. Publishes ms an average of 3 months after acceptance. Editorial lead time 3 months. Accepts queries by mail, e-mail, fax, phone. Accepts simultaneous submissions. Responds in 2 weeks to queries. Responds in 2 months to mss. Sample copy free. Guidelines free.

NONFICTION Needs how-to, interview, personal experience. We do not want articles that are too general. Query. Length: 1,500-2,500 words. **Pays $350 for assigned articles.**

CHILD CARE & PARENTAL GUIDANCE

💲 ATLANTA PARENT

2346 Perimeter Park Dr., Atlanta GA 30341. (770)454-7599. **E-mail:** editor@atlantaparent.com; atlantaparent@atlantaparent.com. **Website:** www.atlantaparent.com. **Contact:** Editor. **50% freelance written.** Monthly magazine for parents in the Atlanta metro area with children from birth to 18 years old. "*Atlanta Parent* magazine has been a valuable resource for Atlanta families since 1983. It is the only magazine in the Atlanta area providing pertinent, local, and award-winning family-oriented articles and information. Atlanta parents rely on us for features that are timely, informative, and reader-friendly on important issues such as childcare, family life, education, adolescence, motherhood, health, and teens. Fun, easy, and inexpensive family activities and crafts as well as the humorous side of parenting are also important to our readers." Estab. 1983. Byline given. Pays on publication. Publishes ms an average of 3 months after acceptance. Submit seasonal material 6 months in advance. Accepts queries by mail, e-mail. Accepts simultaneous submissions. Responds in 4 months to queries. Sample copy: $3.

NONFICTION Needs general interest, how-to, humor, interview, travel. No religious or philosophical discussions. **Buys 60 mss/year.** Send complete ms by mail or e-mail. Length: 800-1,200 words. **Pays $5-50.**

💲💲 BIRMINGHAM PARENT

Evans Publishing LLC, 3590-B Hwy 31S. #289, Pelham AL 35124. (205)987-7700. **Fax:** (205)987-7600. **E-mail:** carol@biringhamparent.com. **Website:** www.

birminghamparent.com. **Contact:** Carol Evans, publisher/editor. **75% freelance written.** Monthly magazine covering family issues, parenting, education, babies to teens, health care, anything involving parents raising children. "We are a free, local parenting publication in central Alabama. All of our stories carry some type of local slant. Parenting magazines abound: we are the source for the local market." Estab. 2004. Circ. 30,000. Byline given. Pays within 30 days of publication. Offers 20% kill fee. Publishes ms an average of 3-4 months after acceptance. Editorial lead time 3-4 months. Submit seasonal material 4 months in advance. Accepts queries by e-mail. Accepts simultaneous submissions. Responds in 2-3 weeks to queries. Responds in 2-3 months to mss. Sample copy for $3. Guidelines online.

NONFICTION Needs book excerpts, general interest, how-to, interview, parenting. Does not want first person pieces. "Our pieces educate and inform; we don't take stories without sources." **Buys 24 mss/year.** Send complete ms. Length: 350-2,500 words. **Pays $50-350 for assigned articles. Pays $35-200 for unsolicited articles.**

COLUMNS Parenting Solo (single parenting), 650 words; Baby & Me (dealing with newborns or pregnancy), 650 words; Teens (raising teenagers), 650-1,500 words. **Buys 36 mss/year.** Query with published clips or send complete ms. **Pays $35-200.**

BRAIN, CHILD

Erielle Media, LLC, 341 Newtown Turnpike, Wilton CT 06897. **E-mail:** editorial@brainchildmag.com. **Website:** www.brainchildmag.com. **Contact:** Marcelle Soviero, editor in chief. **75% freelance written.** Quarterly magazine covering the experience of motherhood. "*Brain, Child: The Magazine for Thinking Mothers*, reflects modern motherhood—the way it really is. It is the largest print literary magazine devoted to motherhood. *Brain, Child* is a community for and by mothers who like to think about what raising kids does for (and to) the mind and soul. *Brain, Child* isn't your typical parenting magazine. We couldn't cupcake-decorate our way out of a paper bag. We are more 'literary' than 'how-to,' more *New Yorker* than *Parents*. We shy away from expert advice on childrearing in favor of first-hand reflections by great writers (Jane Smiley, Barbara Ehrenreich, Anne Tyler) on life as a mother. Each quarterly issue is full of essays, features, humor, reviews, fiction, art, cartoons, and our readers' own stories. Our philosophy is pretty simple: Motherhood is worthy of literature. And there are a lot of ways to mother, all of them interesting. We're proud to be publishing articles and essays that are smart, down to earth, sometimes funny, and sometimes poignant." Estab. 2000. Circ. 36,000. Byline given. Pays on publication. 20% kill fee. Publishes ms an average of 3-4 months after acceptance. Editorial lead time 3 months. Submit seasonal material 6 months in advance. Accepts queries by mail, e-mail, online submission form. Accepts simultaneous submissions. Responds in 1 month to queries; in 2-3 months to mss. Sample copy online. Guidelines online.

NONFICTION Needs essays, humor, opinion, reviews. No how-to articles, advice, or tips. **Buys 240 mss/year.** Submit complete ms. Length: 800-4,000 words. **Pays competitive rate.**

FICTION "We publish fiction that has a strong motherhood theme." Needs mainstream, literary. No genre fiction. **Buys 4 mss/year.** Send complete ms. Length: 800-4,000 words. **Payment varies.**

⊗⊗ CHICAGO PARENT

141 S. Oak Park Ave., Oak Park IL 60302. (708)386-5555. **E-mail:** tamara@chicagoparent.com; chiparent@chicagoparent.com. **Website:** www.chicagoparent.com. **Contact:** Tamara O'Shaughnessy, editor. **80% freelance written.** Monthly parenting magazine covering the six-county Chicago metropolitan area. *Chicago Parent* has a distinctly local approach. Offers information, inspiration, perspective, and empathy to Chicago-area parents. Lively editorial mix has a "we're all in this together" spirit, and articles are thoroughly researched and well written. Estab. 1988. Circ. 100,000. Byline given. Pays on publication. Offers 10-50% kill fee. Publishes ms an average of 2 months after acceptance. Editorial lead time 4 months. Submit seasonal material 4 months in advance. Accepts queries by e-mail. Responds in 6 weeks to queries. Sample copy for $4.95 and 11×17 SAE with $1.65 postage direct to circulation. Guidelines available on website.

NONFICTION Needs essays, expose, general interest, how-to, humor, interview, personal experience, profile, travel. No pot-boiler parenting pieces or nonlocal writers (from outside the six-county Chicago metropolitan area). **Buys 40-50 mss/year.** Query with links to published clips. Length: 200-2,500 words. **Pays $25-450 for assigned articles.**

⊗ GRAND RAPIDS FAMILY MAGAZINE

Gemini Publications, 549 Ottawa Ave. NW, Suite 201, Grand Rapids MI 49503-1444. (616)459-4545.

Fax: (616)459-4800. **E-mail:** cvalade@geminipub.com. **Website:** www.grfamilymag.com. **Contact:** Carole Valade, editor. Monthly magazine covering local parenting issues. *Grand Rapids Family* seeks to inform, instruct, amuse, and entertain its readers and their families. Circ. 30,000. Byline given. Pays on publication. Offers $25 kill fee. Editorial lead time 3 months. Submit seasonal material 4 months in advance. Accepts simultaneous submissions. Responds in 2 months to queries. Responds in 6 months to mss. Guidelines with #10 SASE.

NONFICTION Query. **Pays $25-50.**

COLUMNS All local: law, finance, humor, opinion, mental health. **Pays $25.**

$ HUDSON VALLEY PARENT

The Professional Image, 174 South St., Newburgh NY 12550. (845)562-3606. **E-mail:** editor@excitingread.com. **Website:** www.hvparent.com. **Contact:** Felicia Hodges. **95% freelance written.** Monthly magazine covering local parents and families. Estab. 1994. Circ. 80,000. Byline given. Pays on publication. No kill fee. Publishes ms an average of 3 months after acceptance. Editorial lead time 4 months. Submit seasonal material 4 months in advance. Accepts queries by e-mail. Accepts simultaneous submissions. Responds in 2-4 weeks to mss. Sample copy free. Guidelines online.

NONFICTION Needs expose, general interest, humor, interview, personal experience. **Buys 20 mss/year.** Query. Length: 700-1,200 words. **Pays $80-120 for assigned articles. Pays $25-35 for unsolicited articles.**

$$ INDY'S CHILD MAGAZINE

Midwest Parenting Publications, 6340 Westfield Blvd., Suite 200, Indianapolis IN 46220. (317)722-8500. **E-mail:** indyschild@indyschild.com. **E-mail:** susan@indyschild.com. **Website:** www.indyschild.com. **Contact:** Susan Bryant, editor. **100% freelance written.** *Indy's Child* Parenting Magazine is a local and nationally award-winning parenting magazine. As an independent publication, we strive to make sure we give our readers exactly what they are looking for. We are a valuable guide for parents, educators, and child care providers, and we are 1 of the only publications to be distributed to a majority of schools, libraries, child care agencies, and other family-oriented facilities." Estab. 1985. Byline given. Pays on publication. No kill fee. Publishes ms an average of 6 months after acceptance. Editorial lead time 3 months. Submit seasonal material 6 months in advance. Accepts queries by e-mail. Accepts simultaneous submissions. Guidelines online.

NONFICTION Needs expose, general interest, historical, how-to, humor, inspirational, interview, opinion, photo feature, travel. **Buys 50 mss/year.** Query by e-mail. See editorial calendar for upcoming topics. **Pay based on assigned word count.**

COLUMNS Query by e-mail. **Pay based on assigned word count.**

[C] $ ISLAND PARENT MAGAZINE

Island Parent Group, 830-A Pembroke St., Victoria BC V8T 1H9 Canada. (250)388-6905. **E-mail:** editor@islandparent.ca. **Website:** www.islandparent.ca. **Contact:** Sue Fast, editor. **98% freelance written.** Monthly magazine covering parenting. Estab. 1988. Circ. 20,000. Byline given. No kill fee. Publishes ms an average of 3 months after acceptance. Editorial lead time 3 months. Submit seasonal material 3 months in advance. Accepts queries by e-mail. Accepts simultaneous submissions. Responds in 6 weeks to queries. Sample copy and guidelines online.

NONFICTION Needs book excerpts, essays, general interest, how-to, humor, inspirational, interview, opinion, personal experience, travel. **Buys 80 mss/year.** Query. Length: 1,000 words average. **Pays $35.**

FILLERS Needs anecdotes, facts, gags, newsbreaks, short humor. **Buys 10 mss/year.** Length: 400-650 words. **Pays $35.**

$ MEDIA FOR LIVING, VALLEY LIVING MAGAZINE

Shalom Foundation, 1251 Virginia Ave., Harrisonburg VA 22802. (540)433-5351. **E-mail:** info@valleyliving.org. **E-mail:** melodie@valleyliving.org. **Website:** www.valleyliving.org. Lindsey Shantz. **90% freelance written.** Quarterly tabloid covering family living. Articles focus on giving general encouragement for families of all ages and stages. Estab. 1990. Circ. 11,000. Byline given. Pays on publication. No kill fee. Publishes ms an average of 6-12 months after acceptance. Editorial lead time 4-6 months. Submit seasonal material 6 months in advance. Accepts queries by mail, e-mail, online submission form. Accepts simultaneous submissions. Responds in 2 months to queries; in 2-4 months to mss. Sample copy for SAE with 9x12 envelope and 4 first-class stamps.

NONFICTION Needs general interest, how-to, humor, inspirational, personal experience. "We do not use devotional materials intended for Christian audiences. We seldom use pet stories and receive way too many grief/death/dealing-with-serious-illness stories to use. We publish in March, June, September, and December, so holidays that occur in other months are not usually the subject of articles." **Buys 48-52 mss/year.** Query. Length: 500-1,200 words. **Pays $35-60.**

🟢 METROFAMILY MAGAZINE

Inprint Publishing, 318 NW 13th St., Suite 101, Oklahoma City OK 73103. (405)818-5025. **E-mail:** editor@metrofamilymagazine.com. **Website:** www.metrofamilymagazine.com. **Contact:** Hannah Schmitt, editor. **20% freelance written.** Monthly tabloid covering parenting. Circ. 35,000. Byline given. Pays on publication. No kill fee. Requests ms an average of 2-3 months after acceptance. Editorial lead time 3-6 months. Accepts queries by e-mail. Accepts simultaneous submissions. Responds in 3 weeks to queries (only if interested). Responds in 1 month to mss. Sample copy for SAE with 10x13 envelope and 3 first-class stamps. Guidelines online.

NONFICTION Family or mom-specific articles; see website for themes. No poetry, fiction (except for humor column), or anything that doesn't support good, solid family values. Submit via e-mail only. "We are interested in well-written, thought-provoking feature stories (800-1,500 words), short features (400-750 words) or shorts (up to 400 words) that focus on timely issues and highlight local experts or conditions." **Pays $40-60, plus 1 contributor's copy.**

COLUMNS "Our columns are all written by our regular, staff writers and freelance submissions will not be considered for columns."

🟢 METROKIDS

Kidstuff Publications, Inc., 1412-1414 Pine St., Philadelphia PA 19102. (215)291-5560, ext. 102. **Fax:** (215)291-5565. **E-mail:** editor@metrokids.com. **Website:** www.metrokids.com. **Contact:** Sara Murphy, managing editor. **25% freelance written.** Monthly magazine providing information for parents and kids in Philadelphia and surrounding counties, South Jersey, and Delaware. "*MetroKids*, a free monthly magazine, is a resource for parents living in the greater Delaware Valley. The Pennsylvania, South Jersey, and Delaware editions of *MetroKids* are available in supermarkets, libraries, daycares, and hundreds of other locations. The magazine and website feature the area's most extensive calendar of day-by-day family events;

child-focused camp, day care, and party directories; local family fun suggestions; and articles that offer parenting advice and insights. Other *MetroKids* publications include *The Ultimate Family Guide*, a guide to area attractions, service providers and community resources; SpecialKids, a resource guide for families of children with special needs; and Educator's Edition, a directory of field trips, assemblies, and school enrichment programs." Estab. 1990. Circ. 115,000. Byline given. Pays on publication. Submit seasonal material 4 months in advance. Accepts queries by e-mail. Accepts simultaneous submissions. Guidelines available by e-mail.

NONFICTION Needs general interest, how-to, new product. Special issues: See editorial calendar online for current needs. **Buys 40 mss/year.** Query with published clips. Length: 575-1,500 words. **Pays $50.**

COLUMNS Tech Talk, Mom Matters, Health, Money, Your Home, Parenting, Toddlers, Tweens/Teens, Education, Food & Nutrition, Play, Toddlers, Camp, Classes, Features, all 650-850 words. **Buys 25 mss/year.** Query. **Pays $25-50.**

🟢🟢 METRO PARENT MAGAZINE

Metro Parent Publishing Group, 22041 Woodward Ave., Ferndale MI 48220. (248)398-3400. **Fax:** (248)339-4215. **E-mail:** editor@metroparent.com; jelliott@metroparent.com. **Website:** www.metroparent.com. **Contact:** Julia Elliott, editor. **75% freelance written.** Monthly magazine covering parenting, women's health, education. "MetroParent.com is an online parenting community offering expert advice, stories on parenting trends and issues, and numerous ways for parents to enrich their experience raising the next generation. It is part of Metro Parent Publishing Group, which began in suburban Detroit in 1986. Publications include Metro Parent magazine, Metro Baby, Going Places, Special Edition, Party Book and Big Book of Schools. Metro Parent Publishing Group also brings family-friendly events to southeast Michigan as part of its events department." Circ. 60,000. Byline given. Pays on publication. Publishes ms an average of 3 months after acceptance. Editorial lead time 3 months. Submit seasonal material 3 months in advance. Accepts queries by mail, e-mail. Accepts simultaneous submissions. Responds in 2 weeks to queries. Responds in 3 months to mss. Sample copy for $2.50. Guidelines online.

NONFICTION Needs essays, humor, inspirational, personal experience. **Buys 100 mss/year.** Send complete ms. Length: 1,500-2,500 words for features, 500-700 words for Getaway pieces, 100-600 words for Parent Pipeline pieces. **Pays $150-300 for feature articles, $35-50 for Parent Pipeline pieces.**

COLUMNS Women's Health (latest issues of 20-40 year olds), 750-900 words; Solo Parenting (advice for single parents); Family Finance (making sense of money and legal issues); Tweens 'N Teens (handling teen issues), 750-800 words. **Buys 50 mss/year.** Send complete ms. **Pays $50-75.**

PARENTGUIDE

PG Media, 101 E. Park Ave., #358, Long Beach NY 11561. (212)213-8840. **Fax:** (646)224-9682. **E-mail:** samantha@parentguidenews.com. **Website:** www. parentguidenews.com. **80% freelance written.** Monthly magazine covering parenting and family issues. "We are a tabloid-sized publication catering to the needs and interests of parents who have children under the age of 12. Our print publication is distributed in New York City, New Jersey, Long Island, Westchester County, Rockland County, and Queens. Our website (one of the most popular online parenting sites) is read by parents, psychologists, teachers, caretakers, and others concerned about family matters worldwide. Our columns and feature articles cover health, education, child-rearing, current events, parenting issues, recreational activities and social events. We also run a complete calendar of local events. We welcome articles from professional authors as well as never-before-published writers." Estab. 1982. Circ. 285,000. Byline given. Does not offer financial compensation. No kill fee. Publishes ms an average of 5 months after acceptance. Editorial lead time 3 months. Submit seasonal material 6 months in advance. Accepts queries by e-mail. Accepts simultaneous submissions. Sample copy online. Guidelines online.

NONFICTION Needs how-to, inspirational, interview, personal experience, travel, education, health, fitness, special needs, parenting. Length: 750 words max. Include a 3-sentence bio.

FICTION Needs humorous, slice-of-life vignettes. Query. Length: 700-1,000 words.

PARENTS

Meredith Corp., 805 Third Ave., New York NY 10022. (212)499-2000. **Website:** www.parents.com. **Contact:** See masthead for specific department editors. Monthly magazine that focuses on the daily needs and concerns of mothers with young children. Provides high-quality content that informs, entertains, and joins parents in celebrating the joys of parenthood. Features information about child health, safety, behavior, discipline, and education. There are also stories on women's health, nutrition, pregnancy, marriage, and beauty. Estab. 1926. Circ. 2,215,645. Pays on acceptance. Offers 25% kill fee. Submit seasonal material 6-8 months in advance. Accepts queries by mail, e-mail. Accepts simultaneous submissions. Responds in 4-6 weeks to queries.

NONFICTION Query before submitting. "Include one-page letter detailing the topic you'd like to address as well as your strategy for writing the story. Demonstrate that you are adept at doing research by mentioning the kinds of sources you intend to use. Keep in mind that all of our articles include expert advice and real-parent examples as well as study data." Include SASE.

$ PEDIATRICS FOR PARENTS

Pediatrics for Parents, Inc., P.O. Box 219, Gloucester MA 01931. (215)253-4543. **Fax:** (973)302-4543. **E-mail:** editor@pedsforparents.com. **E-mail:** submissions@pedsforparents.com. **Website:** www.pedsforparents.com. **Contact:** Richard J. Sagall, M.D., editor. **50% freelance written.** Monthly newsletter covering children's health. "*Pediatrics For Parents* emphasizes an informed, common sense approach to childhood health care. We stress preventative action, accident prevention, when to call the doctor, and when and how to handle a situation at home. We are also looking for articles that describe general, medical, and pediatric problems, advances, new treatments, etc. All articles must be medically accurate and useful to parents with children—prenatal to adolescence." Estab. 1981. Circ. 120,000. Byline given. Pays on publication. Publishes ms an average of 4 months after acceptance. Accepts queries by mail, e-mail, fax. Accepts simultaneous submissions. Responds in 1 month to queries. Sample copy online. Guidelines online.

NONFICTION No first person or experience. **Buys 25 mss/year.** Send complete ms with cover letter containing contact info. Prefers electronic submissions: Send to submissions@pedsforparents.com. Length: 1,000-1,500 words. **Pays $25 and either a 1-year subscription of print issue or a lifetime subscription to PDF version of the newsletter.**

$ SACRAMENTO PARENT

Family Publishing Inc., 457 Grass Valley Hwy., Suite 5, Auburn CA 95603. (530)888-0573. **Fax:** (530)888-1536. **E-mail:** shelly@sacramentoparent.com. **E-mail:** shannon@sacramentoparent.com. **Website:** www.sacramentoparent.com. **Contact:** Shelly Bokman, editor in chief; Shannon Smith, editor. **50% freelance written.** Monthly magazine covering parenting in the Sacramento region. "We look for articles that promote a developmentally appropriate, healthy, and peaceful environment for children." Estab. 1992. Circ. 50,000. Byline given. Pays on publication. Offers 10% kill fee. Publishes ms an average of 2 months after acceptance. Editorial lead time 3 months. Submit seasonal material 4 months in advance. Accepts queries by e-mail. Accepts simultaneous submissions. Sample copy free. Guidelines online.

NONFICTION Needs book excerpts, general interest, how-to, humor, interview, opinion, personal experience. **Buys 36 mss/year.** Query. Length: 300-1,000 words. **Pays $50-200 for original articles.**

COLUMNS Let's Go! (Sacramento regional family-friendly day trips/excursions/activities), 600 words. **Pays $25-45.**

$ SAN DIEGO FAMILY MAGAZINE

1475 6th Ave., 5th Floor, San Diego CA 92101-3200. (619)685-6970. **Fax:** (619)685-6978. **E-mail:** family@sandiegofamily.com. **E-mail:** editor@sandiegofamily.com. **Website:** www.sandiegofamily.com. **100% freelance written.** "*SDFM* is a regional family monthly publication. We focus on providing current, informative and interesting editorial about parenting and family life that educates and entertains." Estab. 1982. Circ. 100,000. Byline given. Pays on publication. No kill fee. Publishes ms an average of 1-6 months after acceptance. Editorial lead time 4 months. Submit seasonal material 6 months in advance. Accepts queries by mail, e-mail. Accepts simultaneous submissions. Responds in 1 month to queries. Responds in 2 months to mss. Sample copy for $4.50 to P.O. Box 23960, San Diego CA 92193. Guidelines online.

NONFICTION Needs essays, general interest, how-to, interview, technical, travel, informational articles. Does not want humorous personal essays, opinion pieces, religious or spiritual. **Buys 350-500 mss/year.** Query. Length: 600-1,250 words. **Pays $22-90.**

FILLERS **Buys 0-12 mss/year.** Send complete ms. Length: 200-600 words.

$$ SOUTH FLORIDA PARENTING

6501 Nob Hill Rd., Tamarac FL 33321. (954)698-6397. **Fax:** (954)421-9002. **E-mail:** editor@sfparenting.com. **Website:** www.sfparenting.com. **Contact:** Jennifer Jhon, editor. **90% freelance written.** Monthly magazine covering parenting, family. "*South Florida Parenting* provides news, information, and a calendar of events for readers in Southeast Florida (Palm Beach, Broward and Miami-Dade counties). The focus is on parenting issues, things to do, information about raising children in South Florida." Estab. 1990. Circ. 110,000. Byline given. Pays on publication. No kill fee. Editorial lead time 4 months. Submit seasonal material 4 months in advance. Accepts queries by e-mail, fax. Accepts simultaneous submissions. Responds in 3 months to queries.

NONFICTION family, parenting and children's issues. Special issues: family fitness, education, spring party guide, fall party guide, kids and the environment, toddler/preschool, preteen. **Pays $25-115.**

COLUMNS Dad's Perspective, Family Deals, Products for Families, Health/Safety, Nutrition, Baby Basics, Travel, Toddler/Preschool, Preteen, South Florida News.

$$ TWINS™ MAGAZINE

30799 Pinetree Road, #256, Cleveland OH 44124. (855)758-9567. **Fax:** (855)758-9567. **E-mail:** twinseditor@twinsmagazine.com. **Website:** www.twinsmagazine.com. **Contact:** Christa Reed, editor. **50% freelance written.** "We now publish 8 issues/year—4 print/4 digital covering all aspects of parenting twins/multiples. *Twins* is a national/international publication that provides informational and educational articles regarding the parenting of twins, triplets, and more. All articles must be multiple specific and have an upbeat, hopeful, and/or positive ending." Estab. 1984. Circ. 35,000. Byline given. Pays on publication. Editorial lead time 4 months. Submit seasonal material 6 months in advance. Response time varies. Sample copy for $5 or on website. Guidelines online.

NONFICTION Needs personal experience, professional experience as it relates to multiples. Nothing on cloning, pregnancy reduction, or fertility issues. **Buys 12 mss/year.** Send complete ms. Length: 650-1,100 words. **Pays $25-250 for assigned articles. Pays $25-125 for unsolicited articles.**

COLUMNS A Word From Dad; Double Takes; Mom-2-Mom; LOL: Laugh Out Loud; Family Health; Resource Round Up; Tales From Twins; Twins in the News; Twin Start Spotlight; & Research. Pays $25-75. **Buys 8-10 mss/year.** Query with or without published clips or send complete ms. **Pays $40-75.**

CONSUMER SERVICE & BUSINESS OPPORTUNITY

💲💲 HOME BUSINESS MAGAZINE

20711 Holt Ave., #807, Lakeville MN 55044. **E-mail:** editor@homebusinessmag.com. **Website:** www.homebusinessmag.com. **75% freelance written.** Covers every angle of the home-based business market including: cutting edge editorial by well-known authorities on sales and marketing, business operations, the home office, franchising, business opportunities, network marketing, mail order, and other subjects to help readers choose, manage, and prosper in a home-based business; display advertising, classified ads and a directory of home-based businesses; technology, the Internet, computers, and the future of home-based business; home-office editorial including management advice, office set-up, and product descriptions; business opportunities, franchising and work-from-home success stories. Estab. 1993. Circ. 105,000. No kill fee. Publishes ms an average of 6 months after acceptance. Editorial lead time 6 months. Submit seasonal material 6 months in advance. Accepts queries by e-mail. Accepts simultaneous submissions. Sample copy for sae with 9x12 envelope and 8 first-class stamps. Guidelines for #10 SASE.

NONFICTION Needs book excerpts, general interest, how-to, inspirational, interview, new product, personal experience, photo feature. No non-home business related topics. **Buys 40 mss/year.** Send complete ms. "Send complete information by e-mail. We encourage writers to submit feature articles (2-3 pages) and departmental articles (1 page). Please submit polished, well-written, organized material. It helps to provide subheadings within the article. Boxes, lists, and bullets are encouraged because they make your article easier to read, use, and reference by the reader. A primary problem in the past is that articles do not stick to the subject of the title. Please pay attention to the focus of your article and to your title. Please don't call to get the status of your submission. We will call if we're interested in publishing the submission."

Length: 200-1,000 words. **Pays 20¢/published word for work-for-hire assignments; 50-word byline for unsolicited articles.**

COLUMNS Marketing & Sales; Money Corner; Home Office; Management; Technology; Working Smarter; Franchising; Network Marketing, all 650 words. Send complete ms.

KIPLINGER'S PERSONAL FINANCE

1100 13th St. NW, Washington DC 20005. (202)887-6400; (646) 695-7046. **E-mail:** jbodnar@kiplinger.com; alex@rosengrouppr.com. **Website:** www.kiplinger.com. **Contact:** Janet Bodnar, editor; Stacie Harrison, art director; Alex Kutler, account executive. **10% freelance written. Prefers to work with published/established writers.** Monthly magazine for general, adult audience interested in personal finance and consumer information. "*Kiplinger's* is a highly trustworthy source of information on saving and investing, taxes, credit, home ownership, paying for college, retirement planning, automobile buying, and many other personal finance topics." Estab. 1947. Circ. 800,000. Pays on acceptance. No kill fee. Publishes ms an average of 2 months after acceptance. Accepts simultaneous submissions. Responds in 1 month to queries.

NONFICTION Query with published clips.

CONTEMPORARY CULTURE

💲💲 A&U

Art & Understanding, Inc., 25 Monroe St., Suite 205, Albany NY 12210-2729. (518)426-9010. **Fax:** (518)436-5354. **E-mail:** aumaglit@gmail.com; chaelneedle@mac.com. **Website:** www.aumag.org. Brent Calderwood, literary editor. **Contact:** Chael Needle, managing editor. **50% freelance written.** Monthly national nonprofit print magazine covering cultural, political, and medical responses to HIV/AIDS. Estab. 1991. Circ. 180,000. Byline given. Pays 1-3 months after publication. Publishes ms an average of 1-3 months after acceptance. Editorial lead time 6 months. Accepts queries by mail, e-mail. Accepts simultaneous submissions. Responds in 1 month to queries; in 2 months to mss. Sample copy: $5. Guidelines online.

NONFICTION Needs book excerpts, essays, general interest, how-to, humor, interview, opinion, personal experience, photo feature, reviews (film, theater, art exhibits, video, music, other media), medical news, artist profiles. **Buys 6 mss/year.** Query with published clips. Length: 800-1,200 words. **Pays $150-300 for assigned articles.**

COLUMNS The Culture of AIDS (reviews of books, music, film), 300 words; Viewpoint (personal opinion), 750 words. **Buys 8 mss/year.** Send complete ms. **Pays $50-150.**

FICTION Literary electronic submissions, as Word attachments, may be mailed to Brent Calderwood, literary editor, at aumaglit@gmail.com. Pay rate schedule available upon request. Send complete ms. Length: up to 1,500 words. **Pays $50.**

POETRY Accepts any length/style (shorter works preferred). **Pays $25.**

🍁 $ $ $ ADBUSTERS

Adbusters Media Foundation, 1243 W. Seventh Ave., Vancouver BC V6H 1B7 Canada. (604)736-9401. **E-mail:** editor@adbusters.org. **Website:** www.adbusters.org. **50% freelance written.** Bimonthly magazine on consumerism. "Based in Vancouver, British Columbia, Canada, *Adbusters* is a not-for-profit, reader-supported magazine concerned with the erosion of our physical and cultural environments by commercial forces. Since 1989, the magazine has been featured in hundreds of alternative and mainstream newspapers, magazines, television, and radio shows. Known worldwide for sparking Occupy Wall Street, *Adbusters* is also responsible for social media campaigns such as Buy Nothing Day and Digital Detox Week. Included in the magazine are incisive philosophical articles and activist commentary, coupled with impact design that seeks to unbound the traditional magazine format. Issues relevant to our contemporary moment, such as media concentration, climate change, and genetically modified foods, are regularly featured. We seek out a world where economy and ecology exist in harmony. By challenging people to become participants as opposed to spectators, *Adbusters* takes aim at corporate disinformation, global injustice, and the industries and governments who actively pollute and destroy our physical and mental commons." Estab. 1989. Circ. 90,000. Byline given. Pays 1 month after publication. Accepts queries by mail, e-mail, fax. Accepts simultaneous submissions. Guidelines online.

NONFICTION Needs essays, expose, interview, opinion. **Buys variable mss/year.** Query. Length: 250-3,000 words. **Pays $100/page for unsolicited articles; 50¢/word for solicited articles.**

FICTION Inquire about themes.

POETRY Inquire about themes.

$ $ ALBEMARLE

Carden Jennings Publishing, 375 Greenbrier Dr., Suite 100, Charlottesville VA 22901. (434)817-2010. **Fax:** (434)817-2020. **E-mail:** info@albemarlemagazine.com. **E-mail:** editorial@albemarlemagazine.com. **Website:** www.albemarlemagazine.com. **80% freelance written.** Bimonthly magazine covering lifestyle for central Virginia. "*albemarle* is a lifestyle magazine originating from the birthplace of Thomas Jefferson. We are committed to Jeffersonian ideals: intellectual depth, love for the land, historic and cultural significance, humor, and celebration of life. Much of the content is regional and seeks to enlighten, educate, and entertain readers who are longtime residents, newcomers, and visitors to Charlottesville and Albemarle County." Estab. 1987. Circ. 10,000. Byline given. Pays on publication. Offers 30% kill fee. Publishes ms an average of 4 months after acceptance. Editorial lead time 6-8 months. Submit seasonal material 6 months in advance. Accepts queries by e-mail. Accepts simultaneous submissions. Responds in 1 month to queries; in 2 months to mss. Sample copy for $6; e-mail eden@cjp.com. Guidelines online.

NONFICTION Needs essays, historical, interview, photo feature, travel. No fiction, poetry, or anything without a direct tie to central Virginia. **Buys 30-35 mss/year.** Query with published clips. Length: 900-3,500 words. **Payment varies based on type of article.**

COLUMNS Etcetera (personal essay), 900-1,200 words; Leisure (travel, sports), 3,000 words. **Buys 20 mss/year.** Query with published clips. **Pays $75-150.**

🍁 $ $ BROKEN PENCIL

P.O. Box 203, Station P, Toronto ON M5S 2S7 Canada. **E-mail:** editor@brokenpencil.com. **Website:** www.brokenpencil.com. Hal Niedzviecki, publisher. **Contact:** Alison Lang, editor. **80% freelance written.** Quarterly magazine covering arts and culture. "*Broken Pencil* is one of the few magazines in the world devoted exclusively to underground culture and the independent arts. We are a great resource and a lively read! *Broken Pencil* reviews the best zines, books, websites, videos, and artworks from the underground and reprints the best articles from the alternative press.

From the hilarious to the perverse, *Broken Pencil* challenges conformity and demands attention." Estab. 1995. Circ. 5,000. Byline given. Pays on publication. Publishes ms an average of 2-3 months after acceptance. Accepts queries by mail, e-mail. Accepts simultaneous submissions. Guidelines online.

NONFICTION Needs essays, general interest, historical, humor, interview, opinion, personal experience, photo feature, reviews, travel. Special issues: Canzine Issue (Fall); Deathmatch Issue (Spring). Does not want anything about mainstream art and culture. **Buys 8 mss/year.** Query with published clips. Length: 400-2,500 words. **Pays $30-300.**

COLUMNS Books (book reviews and feature articles); Music (music reviews and feature articles); Film (film reviews and feature articles), all 200-300 words for reviews, and up to 1,000 words for features. **Buys 8 mss/year.** Query with published clips. **Pays $30-300.**

FICTION "We're particularly interested in work from emerging writers." Reads fiction submissions February 1-September 15. Needs adventure, erotica, ethnic, experimental, fantasy, historical, horror, humorous, mystery, romance, science fiction, short stories. Submit via online submissions manager. Length: 50-3,000 words. **Pays $30-300.**

♻️💲 BUST MAGAZINE

Bust, Inc., 253 36th St., Suite C307, Brooklyn NY 11232. **E-mail:** debbie@bust.com. **E-mail:** submissions@bust.com. **Website:** www.bust.com. **Contact:** Debbie Stoller, editor in chief/publisher. **60% freelance written.** Bimonthly magazine covering pop culture for young women. "*Bust* is the groundbreaking, original women's lifestyle magazine and website that is unique in its ability to connect with bright, cutting-edge, influential young women." Estab. 1993. Circ. 100,000. Byline given. Pays on publication. No kill fee. Publishes ms an average of 4 months after acceptance. Editorial lead time 3-4 months. Submit seasonal material 6 months in advance. Accepts queries by mail, e-mail. Accepts simultaneous submissions. Response time varies. Guidelines online at www.bust.com/info/submit.html.

NONFICTION Needs book excerpts, general interest, historical, how-to, humor, inspirational, interview, new product, personal experience, photo feature, travel. Special issues: "No dates are currently set, but we usually have a fashion issue, a music issue and a *Men We Love* issue periodically." We do not want po-

etry; no stories not relating to women. **Buys 60+ mss/year.** Query with published clips. Length: 350-3,000 words. **Pays up to $250.**

COLUMNS Contact: Emily Rems, managing editor. Books (reviews of books by women); Music (reviews of music by/about women); Movies (reviews of movies by/about women), all 300 words; One-Handed-Read (Erotic Fiction for Women), 1,200 words. **Buys 6 mss/year.** Query with published clips. **Pays up to $100.**

FICTION Contact: Jenni Miller, Sex Files editor. Needs erotica. "We only publish erotic fiction. All other content is nonfiction." **Buys 6 mss/year.** Query with published clips. Length: 1,000-1,500 words. **Pays up to $50.**

♻️💲 CANADIAN DIMENSION

2E-91 Albert St., Winnipeg MB R3B 1G5 Canada. (204)957-1519. **E-mail:** editor@canadiandimension.com. **Website:** www.canadiandimension.com. **Contact:** Cy Gonick, publisher and coordinating editor. **80% freelance written.** Bimonthly magazine covering politics and world issues from a socialist perspective. "We bring a socialist perspective to bear on events across Canada and around the world. Our contributors provide in-depth coverage on popular movements, peace, labour, women, aboriginal justice, environment, third world, and eastern Europe." Estab. 1963. Circ. 3,000. Pays on publication. Publishes ms an average of 6 months after acceptance. Submit seasonal materials 2-3 months in advance. Accepts queries by e-mail. Accepts simultaneous submissions. Responds in 6 weeks to queries. Sample copy: $2. Guidelines online.

NONFICTION Needs interview, opinion, reviews. Special issues: See website for list of upcoming themes. **Buys 8 mss/year.** Query. Length: 500-2,000 words. **Pays $25-100.**

♻️💲💲 COMMON GROUND

Common Ground Publishing, 3152 W 8th Ave., Vancouver BC V6K 2C3 Canada. (604)733-2215. **Fax:** (604)733-4415. **E-mail:** editor@commonground.ca. **Website:** www.commonground.ca. **90% freelance written.** Monthly tabloid covering health, environment, spirit, creativity, and wellness. "We serve the cultural creative community." Estab. 1982. Circ. 70,000. Byline given. Pays on publication. No kill fee. Publishes ms an average of 1 month after acceptance. Editorial lead time 2 months. Submit seasonal material 3 months in advance. Accepts queries by e-mail. Accepts simultaneous submissions. Responds in 6 weeks to queries. Responds in 3 months to mss. Sample copy for $5. Guidelines online.

NONFICTION Needs book excerpts, how-to, inspirational, interview, opinion, personal experience, travel, call to action. Send complete ms. Length: 500-2,500 words. **Pays 10¢/word (Canadian).**

❸❸❸❸ MOTHER JONES

Foundation for National Progress, 222 Sutter St., Suite 600, San Francisco CA 94108. (415)321-1700. **E-mail:** query@motherjones.com. **Website:** www.motherjones.com. **Contact:** Mark Murrmann, photo editor; Ivylise Simones, creative director; Monika Bauerlein and Clara Jeffery, editors. **80% freelance written.** Bimonthly magazine covering politics, investigative reporting, social issues, and pop culture. *"Mother Jones* is a 'progressive' magazine—but the core of its editorial well is reporting (i.e., fact-based). No slant required. Estab. 1976. Circ. 240,000. Byline given. Pays on publication. Offers 33% kill fee. Publishes ms an average of 4 months after acceptance. Editorial lead time 4 months. Submit seasonal material 6 months in advance. Accepts simultaneous submissions. Responds in 2 months to queries. Sample copy for $6 and 9x12 SASE. Guidelines online.

NONFICTION Needs interview, photo feature, current issues, policy, investigative reporting. **Buys 70-100 mss/year.** Query with published clips. "Please also include your résumè and two or three of your most relevant clips. If the clips are online, please provide the complete URLs. Web pieces are generally less than 1,500 words. Because we have staff reporters it is extremely rare that we will pay for a piece whose timeliness or other qualities work for the Web only. Magazine pieces can range up to 5,000 words. There is at least a two-month lead time. No phone calls please." Length: 2,000-5,000 words. **Pays $1/word.**

COLUMNS Outfront (short, newsy and/or outrageous and/or humorous items), 200-800 words; Profiles of Hellraisers, 500 words. **Pays $1/word.**

❷ THE OLDIE MAGAZINE

Oldie Publications Ltd, 65 Newman St., London England W1T 3EG United Kingdom. (44)(207)436-8801. **Fax:** (44)(207)436-8804. **E-mail:** jeremylewis@theoldie.co.uk. **Website:** www.theoldie.co.uk. **Contact:** Jeremy Lewis, features editor. No kill fee. Accepts queries by mail. Accepts simultaneous submissions. Responds in 1 month to mss. Sample copy by e-mail. Guidelines online.

NONFICTION Send complete ms. Length: 600-1,300 words.

COLUMNS Modern Life (puzzling aspects of today's world); Anorak (owning up to an obsession); The Old Un's Diary (oldun@theoldie.co.uk).

PEOPLE STYLEWATCH

Time Inc., 1271 Avenue of the Americas, 27th Floor, New York NY 10020. (212)522-1388. **Fax:** (212)467-3127. **E-mail:** editors@people.com. **Website:** www.peoplestylewatch.com. **Contact:** Susan Kaufman, editor. Monthly magazine focusing on celebrity style, fashion, and beauty. *People StyleWatch* is an extension of *People Magazine's* StyleWatch column. Estab. 2002. Accepts simultaneous submissions.

❸❸❸ THE SUN

107 N. Roberson St., Chapel Hill NC 27516. (919)942-5282. **Fax:** (919)932-3101. **Website:** www.thesunmagazine.org. **Contact:** Sy Safransky, editor. **90% freelance written.** *The Sun* publishes essays, interviews, fiction, and poetry. "We are open to all kinds of writing, though we favor work of a personal nature." Estab. 1974. Circ. 72,000. Byline given. Pays on publication. Publishes ms an average of 6-12 months after acceptance. Accepts queries by mail. Responds in 3-6 months to queries and mss. Sample copy online. Guidelines online.

NONFICTION Needs essays, interview, memoir, personal experience, Also needs spiritual fields; in-depth philosophical; thoughtful essays on political, cultural, and philosophical themes. **Buys 50 mss/year.** Send complete ms. No fax or e-mail submissions. Length: up to 7,000 words. **Pays $300-2,000 and 1-year subscription.**

FICTION Open to all fiction. Receives 800 unsolicited mss/month. Accepts 20 short stories/year. Recently published work by Sigrid Nunez, Susan Straight, Lydia Peelle, Stephen Elliott, David James Duncan, Linda McCullough Moore, and Brenda Miller. No science fiction, horror, fantasy, or other genre fiction. "Read an issue before submitting." **Buys 20 mss/year.** Send complete ms. Accepts reprint submissions. Length: up to 7,000 words. **Pays $300-1,500 and 1-year subscription.**

POETRY Needs free verse. Submit up to 6 poems at a time. Considers previously published poems but strongly prefers unpublished work. "Poems should be typed and accompanied by a cover letter and SASE." Recently published poems by Tony Hoagland, Ellen Bass, Steve Kowit, Brian Doyle, and Alison Luterman. Rarely publishes poems that rhyme. **Pays $100-200 and 1-year subscription.**

⊘ VANITY FAIR

Conde Nast Publications, Inc., 1472 Broadway, New York NY 10036. **E-mail:** letters@vf.com. **Website:** www.vanityfair.com. Monthly magazine. *Vanity Fair* is edited for readers with an interest in contemporary society. No kill fee. Accepts simultaneous submissions.

DISABILITIES

⊛$$ ABILITIES

Canadian Abilities Foundation, 340 College St., Suite 270, Toronto ON M5T 3A9 Canada. (416)421-7944. **Fax:** (416)923-9829. **E-mail:** jennifer@abilities.ca. **Website:** www.abilities.ca. **Contact:** Jennifer Rivkin, managing editor. **50% freelance written.** Quarterly magazine covering disability issues. "*Abilities* is Canada's foremost cross-disability lifestyle magazine. The mission of the magazine is to provide **information** about lifestyle topics, including travel, health, careers, education, relationships, parenting, new products, social policy and much more; **inspiration** to participate in organizations, events, and activities and pursue opportunities in sports, education, careers, and more; and **opportunity** to learn about a wealth of Canadian resources that facilitate self empowerment of people with disabilities." Estab. 1987. Circ. 20,000. Byline given. Pays on publication. Offers 50% kill fee. Publishes ms an average of 3 months after acceptance. Editorial lead time 3 months. Submit seasonal material 4 months in advance. Accepts queries by mail, e-mail. Responds in 3 months to queries. Sample copy free. Writer's guidelines for #10 SASE, online, or by e-mail.

NONFICTION Needs general interest, how-to, humor, inspirational, interview, new product, personal experience, photo feature, travel. Does not want articles that 'preach to the converted'—this means info that people with disabilities likely already know, such as what it's like to have a disability. **Buys 30-40 mss/year.** Query or send complete ms. Length: 500-2,000 words. **Pays $50-325 (Canadian) for assigned articles.**

COLUMNS The Lighter Side (humor), 700 words; Profile, 1,200 words.

$$$$ ARTHRITIS TODAY

Arthritis Foundation, 1330 W. Peachtree St., Suite 100, Atlanta GA 30309. **Website:** www.arthritistoday.org. **50% freelance written.** Bimonthly magazine covering living with arthritis and the latest in research/treatment. *Arthritis Today* is a consumer health magazine and is written for the more than 70 million Americans who have arthritis and for the millions of others whose lives are touched by an arthritis-related disease. The editorial content is designed to help the person with arthritis live a more productive, independent, and pain-free life. The articles are upbeat and provide practical advice, information, and inspiration. Estab. 1987. Circ. 650,000. Byline given. Pays on acceptance. Offers kill fee. Offers kill fee. Editorial lead time 6 months. Submit seasonal material 6 months in advance. Accepts queries by mail, online submission form. Accepts simultaneous submissions. Responds in 2 months to queries. Sample copy for 9x11 SAE with 4 first-class stamps.

NONFICTION Needs general interest, how-to, inspirational, new product, opinion, personal experience, photo feature, technical, travel. **Buys 12 unsolicited mss/year.** Query with published clips. Length: 150-2,500 words. **Pays $100-2,500.**

COLUMNS Nutrition, 100-600 words; Fitness, 100-600 words; Balance (emotional coping), 100-600 words; MedWatch, 100-800 words; Solutions, 100-600 words; Life Makeover, 400-600 words.

FILLERS Needs facts, gags, short humor. **Buys 2 mss/year.** Length: 40-100 words. **Pays $80-150.**

$$ CAREERS & THE DISABLED

Equal Opportunity Publications, 445 Broad Hollow Rd., Suite 425, Melville NY 11747. (631)421-9421, ext. 12. **E-mail:** jwhitcher@eop.com. **Website:** www.eop.com. **Contact:** Joann Whitcher, editorial and production director. **60% freelance written.** Magazine published 6 times/year, with Fall, Winter, Spring, Summer, and Expo editions, offering role-model profiles and career guidance articles geared toward disabled college students and professionals, and promoting personal and professional growth. Estab. 1967. Circ. 10,000. Byline given. Pays on publication. Publishes ms an average of 6 months after acceptance. Editorial lead time 6 months. Submit seasonal material 6 months in advance. Accepts queries by mail, e-mail, phone. Accepts simultaneous submissions. Responds in 3 weeks to queries. Sample copy for 9x12 SAE with 5 first-class stamps. Guidelines free.

NONFICTION Needs essays, general interest, how-to, interview, new product, opinion, personal experience. **Buys 30 mss/year.** Query. Length: 1,000-2,500 words. **Pays 10¢/word.**

$$ DIABETES HEALTH

P.O. Box 1199, Woodacre CA 94973. **E-mail:** editor@diabeteshealth.com. **Website:** www.diabeteshealth.com. **Contact:** Nadia Al-Samarrie, editor in chief. **40% freelance written.** Monthly tabloid covering diabetes care. "*Diabetes Health* covers the latest in diabetes care, medications, and patient advocacy. Personal accounts are welcome as well as medical-oriented articles by MDs, RNs, and CDEs (certified diabetes educators)." Estab. 1991. Circ. 40,000. Byline given. Pays on publication. No kill fee. Publishes ms an average of 2 months after acceptance. Editorial lead time 2 months. Submit seasonal material 2 months in advance. Accepts queries by e-mail. Accepts simultaneous submissions. Sample copy online. Guidelines free.

NONFICTION Needs essays, how-to, humor, inspirational, interview, new product, opinion, personal experience. *Diabetes Health* does not accept mss that promote a product, philosophy, or personal view. **Buys 25 mss/year.** Send complete ms. Length: 500-1,500 words. **Pays about 20¢/word. "Payment varies with experience and is based on the final length as it appears in the magazine."**

$$ DIABETES SELF-MANAGEMENT

Madavor Media, LLC, 150 W. 22nd St., Suite 800, New York NY 10011. **E-mail:** dsmwebeditor@madavor.com. **Website:** www.diabetesselfmanagement.com. **20% freelance written.** Bimonthly magazine. "We publish how-to health care articles for motivated, intelligent readers who have diabetes and who are actively involved in their own health care management. All articles must have immediate application to their daily living." Estab. 1983. Circ. 410,000. Byline given. Pays on publication. Offers 20% kill fee. Submit seasonal material 6 months in advance. Accepts queries by e-mail. Accepts simultaneous submissions. Responds in 6 weeks to queries. Guidelines online.

NONFICTION Needs how-to, technical, travel. No personal experiences, personality profiles, exposés, or research breakthroughs. **Buys 10-12 mss/year.** Query with published clips. Length: 2,000-3,000 words. **Pay varies.**

$ DIALOGUE

Blindskills, Inc., P.O. Box 5181, Salem OR 97304. **E-mail:** magazine@blindskills.com. **Website:** www.blindskills.com. **60% freelance written.** Quarterly journal covering visually impaired people. Estab. 1962. Circ. 1,100. Byline given. Pays on publication. Publishes ms an average of 6 months after acceptance. Editorial lead time 3 months. Accepts queries by e-mail. Accepts simultaneous submissions. Sample copy: 1 free copy on request. Available in large print, Braille, digital audio cassette, and e-mail. Guidelines online.

NONFICTION Needs essays, general interest, historical, how-to, humor, interview, personal experience, sports, recreation, hobbies. No controversial, explicit sex, religious, or political topics. **Buys 50-60 mss/year.** Send complete ms. Length: 200-1,200 words. **Pays $15-35 for assigned articles. Pays $15-25 for unsolicited articles.**

COLUMNS All material should be relative to blind and visually impaired readers. Living with Low Vision, 1,000 words; Hear's How (dealing with sight loss), 1,000 words; Technology Answer Book, 1,000 words. **Buys 80 mss/year.** Send complete ms. **Pays $10-25.**

$ KALEIDOSCOPE

701 S. Main St., Akron OH 44311-1019. (330)762-9755. **Fax:** (330)762-0912. **E-mail:** kaleidoscope@udsakron.org. **Website:** www.kaleidoscopeonline.org. **Contact:** Gail Willmott, editor in chief. **75% freelance written. Eager to work with new/unpublished writers.** Semiannual free online magazine. "*Kaleidoscope* magazine creatively focuses on the experiences of disability through literature and the fine arts. Unique to the field of disability studies, this award-winning publication expresses the diversity of the disability experience from a variety of perspectives including: individuals, families, friends, caregivers, educators, and healthcare professionals, among others." Estab. 1979. Byline given. Pays on publication. No kill fee. Accepts simultaneous submissions. Responds in 6-9 months. Guidelines online. Submissions and queries electronically via website and e-mail.

NONFICTION Needs essays, interview, personal experience, reviews, articles relating to both literary and visual arts. For book reviews: "Reviews that are substantive, timely, powerful works about publications in the field of disability and/or the arts. The writer's opinion of the work being reviewed should be clear. The review should be a literary work in its own right." **Buys 40-50 mss/year.** Submit complete ms by website or e-mail. Include cover letter. Length: up to 5,000 words. **Pays $10-100.**

FICTION Wants short stories with a well-crafted plot and engaging characters. Needs short stories. No fiction that is stereotypical, patronizing, sentimental, erotic, or maudlin. No romance, religious or dogmatic fiction; no children's literature. Submit complete ms by website or e-mail. Include cover letter. Length: up to 5,000 words. **Pays $10-100.**

POETRY Wants poems that have strong imagery, evocative language. Submit up to 5 poems by website or e-mail. Include cover letter. "Do not get caught up in rhyme scheme. We want high quality with strong imagery and evocative language." Reviews any style.

$$$$ POZ

CDM Publishing, LLC, 462 Seventh Ave., 19th Floor, New York NY 10018. (212)242-2163. **Fax:** (212)675-8505. **E-mail:** website@poz.com; editor-in-chief@poz.com. **Website:** www.poz.com. **Contact:** Doriot Kim, art director. **25% freelance written.** Monthly national magazine for people impacted by HIV and AIDS. "*POZ* is a trusted source of conventional and alternative treatment information, investigative features, survivor profiles, essays and cutting-edge news for people living with AIDS and their caregivers. *POZ* is a lifestyle magazine with both health and cultural content." Estab. 1994. Circ. 125,000. Byline given. Pays 30 days after publication. Offers 25% kill fee. Publishes ms an average of 3 months after acceptance. Editorial lead time 4 months. Submit seasonal material 4 months in advance. Accepts simultaneous submissions. Sample copy and writer's guidelines free.

NONFICTION Needs book excerpts, essays, historical, how-to, humor, inspirational, interview, opinion, personal experience, photo feature. Query with published clips. "We take unsolicited mss on speculation only." Length: 200-3,000 words. **Pays $1/word.**

ENTERTAINMENT

$ CINEASTE

Cineaste, Inc., 708 Third Ave., 5th Floor, New York NY 10017-4201. (212)209-3856. **E-mail:** cineaste@cineaste.com. **Website:** www.cineaste.com. **30% freelance written.** Quarterly magazine covering motion pictures with an emphasis on social and political perspective on cinema. Estab. 1967. Circ. 11,000. Byline given. Pays on publication. Offers 50% kill fee. Publishes ms an average of 4 months after acceptance. Editorial lead time 3 months. Submit seasonal material 4 months in advance. Accepts queries by mail, e-mail, fax. Accepts simultaneous submissions. Responds in 1 month to queries. Sample copy: $8. Writer's guidelines on website.

NONFICTION Needs book excerpts, essays, expose, historical, humor, interview, opinion. **Buys 20-30 mss/year.** Query with published clips. Length: 2,000-5,000 words. **Pays $30-100.**

COLUMNS Homevideo (topics of general interest or a related group of films); A Second Look (new interpretation of a film classic or a reevaluation of an unjustly neglected release of more recent vintage); Lost and Found (film that may or may not be released or otherwise seen in the U.S. but which is important enough to be brought to the attention of our readers); all 1,000-1,500 words. Query with published clips. **Pays $50 minimum.**

$$ DANCE INTERNATIONAL

Scotiabank Dance Centre, Level 6 - 677 Davie St., Vancouver BC V6B 2G6 Canada. (604)681-1525. **Fax:** (604)681-7732. **E-mail:** editor@danceinternational.org; info@danceinternational.org. **Website:** www.danceinternational.org. **100% freelance written.** Quarterly magazine covering dance arts. Articles and reviews on current activities in world dance, with occasional historical features, reviews, and reports from the world of dance. Estab. 1977. Circ. 3,000. Byline given. Pays on publication. Offers 50% kill fee. Publishes ms an average of 3 months after acceptance. Editorial lead time 3 months. Long lead times necessary for quarterly publication. Accepts queries by mail, e-mail. Responds promptly to queries. Sample copy: $7.50 plus p&p, or on Kobo.

NONFICTION Needs book excerpts, essays, historical, interview, memoir, personal experience, profile, reviews, technical. **Buys 100 mss/year.** Query with a brief proposal and short bio. Length: 1,200-2,200 words.

COLUMNS Mediawatch (recent books, DVDs, media reviewed), 700-800 words; Regional Reports (events in each region), 800 words. **Buys 100 mss/year.** Query. **Pays $80.**

⚙ EAST END LIGHTS

11-4040 Creditview Rd., P.O. Box 188, Mississauga ON L5C 3Y8 Canada. (416)763-8500. **Fax:** (905)566-7369. **E-mail:** eastendlights0@gmail.com. **Website:** www.eastendlightsmagazine.com. **90% freelance written.** Quarterly magazine covering Elton John. Estab. 1990. Circ. 1,700. Byline given. Pays 3 weeks after publication. Publishes ms an average of 3 months after acceptance. Submit seasonal material 6 months in advance. Accepts queries by mail, e-mail, fax. Accepts simultaneous submissions. Responds in 2 months to queries. Sample copy: $5.

NONFICTION Needs book excerpts, essays, expose, general interest, historical, humor, interview. **Buys 20 mss/year.** Send complete ms. Length: 400-1,000 words.

COLUMNS Clippings (nonwire references to Elton John in other publications), 200 words. **Buys 12 mss/year.** Send complete ms.

ENTERTAINMENT WEEKLY

Time, Inc., 1675 Broadway, 30th Floor, New York NY 10019. (212)522-5600. **Fax:** (212)522-0074. **Website:** www.ew.com. **Contact:** Matt Bean, editor. Weekly magazine. *Entertainment Weekly* is an all-access pass to Hollywood's most creative minds and fascinating stars. Written for readers who want the latest reviews, previews, and updates of the entertainment world. Circ. 1,600,000. No kill fee. Editorial lead time 4 weeks. Accepts simultaneous submissions.

⚙ IN TOUCH WEEKLY

270 Sylvan Ave., Englewood Cliffs NJ 07632. (201)569-6699. **E-mail:** contactus@intouchweekly.com. **Website:** www.intouchweekly.com. **10% freelance written.** Weekly magazine covering celebrity news and entertainment. Estab. 2002. Circ. 1,300,000. No byline given. Pays on publication. Editorial lead time 1 week. Accepts queries by mail, e-mail. Accepts simultaneous submissions.

NONFICTION Needs interview, gossip. **Buys 1,300 mss/year.** Query. Send a tip about a celebrity by e-mail. Length: 100-1,000 words. **Pays $50.**

⚙ METRO MAGAZINE (AUSTRALIA)

Australian Teachers of Media (ATOM), P.O. Box 2040, St. Kilda West VIC 3182 Australia. (61)(3)9525-5302. **Fax:** (61)(3)9537-2325. **E-mail:** metro@atom.org.au. **Website:** www.metromagazine.com.au. **Contact:** Adolfo Aranjuez. Quarterly magazine specializing in longform articles, analytical reviews, and critical essays on film, TV, and media from Australia, New Zealand, and the Asia-Pacific region. Estab. 1968. Accepts simultaneous submissions. Guidelines online.

NONFICTION Needs essays, general interest, interview, reviews. Send complete ms via e-mail. Length: 1,000-3,000 words.

⚙⚙ MOVIEMAKER MAGAZINE

MovieMaker Media LLC, 2525 Michigan Ave., Building I, Santa Monica CA 90404. (310)828-8388. **E-mail:** tim@moviemaker.com. **Website:** www.moviemaker. com. **Contact:** Timothy Rhys, editor in chief. **75% freelance written.** Bimonthly magazine covering film, independent cinema, and Hollywood. "*MovieMaker's* editorial is a progressive mix of in-depth interviews and criticism, combined with practical techniques and advice on financing, distribution, and production strategies. Behind-the-scenes discussions with Hollywood's top moviemakers, as well as independents from around the globe, are routinely found in *MovieMaker's* pages. E-mail is the preferred submission method, but we will accept queries via mail as well. Please, no telephone pitches. We want to read the idea with clips." Estab. 1993. Circ. 55,000. Byline given. Pays 30 days after newsstand publication. Offers variable kill fee. Publishes ms an average of 2 months after acceptance. Editorial lead time 3 months. Submit seasonal material 4 months in advance. Accepts queries by mail, e-mail. Accepts simultaneous submissions. Responds in 2-4 weeks to queries; in 4-6 weeks to mss. Sample copy online. Guidelines by e-mail.

NONFICTION Needs expose, general interest, historical, how-to, interview, new product, technical. **Buys 20 mss/year.** Query with published clips. Length: 800-3,000 words. **Pays $75-500 for assigned articles.**

COLUMNS Documentary; Home Cinema (home video/DVD reviews); How They Did It (first-person filmmaking experiences); Festival Beat (film festival reviews); World Cinema (current state of cinema from a particular country). Query with published clips **Pays $75-300.**

TV GUIDE

11 W. 42nd St., 16th Floor, New York NY 10036. (212)852-7500. **Fax:** (212)852-7470. **Website:** www. tvguide.com. **Contact:** Mickey O'Connor, editor in chief. Weekly magazine. Focuses on all aspects of network, cable, and pay television programming and how

it affects and reflects audiences. Estab. 1953. Circ. 9 million. No kill fee. Accepts simultaneous submissions.

ETHNIC & MINORITY

💲💲 AMBASSADOR MAGAZINE

National Italian American Foundation, 1860 19th St. NW, Washington DC 20009. (202)939 3108. **Fax:** (202)387-0800. **E-mail:** don@niaf.org. **Website:** www. niaf.org. **Contact:** Don Oldenburg, editor and director of publications. **50% freelance written.** "We publish original nonfiction articles on the Italian American experience, culture, and traditions. We also publish profiles of Italian Americans (famous and not famous but doing something exceptional) and travels features, especially in Italy, but also relevant U.S. travel pieces." Estab. 1989. Circ. 28,000. Byline given. Pays on publication. $50 kill fee for assigned stories. Time between acceptance and publication varies. Editorial lead time 4 months. Accepts queries by e-mail. Responds within 2 months to e-mailed queries. Sample copy free. Writer's guidelines available by e-mail.

NONFICTION Needs general interest, interview, personal experience, photo feature, profile, reviews, travel. Query via e-mail before submitting ms. When submitting ms, send as a Word e-mail attachment. Phone and mailed queries and mss are discouraged. Length: 800-1,500 words. **Pays $300 for full feature or profile; $350 for full feature or profile with photo taken by writer.**

☮💲 CELTIC LIFE INTERNATIONAL

Clansman Publishing, Ltd., P.O. Box 8805, Station A, Halifax NS B3K 5M4 Canada. (902)835-2358. **Fax:** (902)835-0080. **E-mail:** editor@celticlife.ca. **Website:** www.celticlifeintl.com. **Contact:** Patrick Smart, editor. **50% freelance written.** Quarterly magazine covering culture of those with an interest in Celtic culture around the world. *Celtic Life International* is a global community for a living, breathing Celtic culture. Home to an extensive collection of feature stories, interviews, history, heritage, news, views, reviews, recipes, events, trivia, humor, and tidbits from across all Seven Celtic Nations and beyond. The flagship publication, *Celtic Life International Magazine*, is published 4 times/year in both print and digital formats, and is distributed around the world. The online home, CelticLife.ca, is an informative and interactive

community that engages Celts from all walks of life. Estab. 1987. Circ. 201,340. Byline given. Pays after publication. No kill fee. Editorial lead time 2 months. Submit seasonal material 3 months in advance. Responds in 1 week to queries; in 1 month to mss.

NONFICTION Needs essays, general interest, historical, interview, opinion, personal experience, profile, travel, Gaelic language, Celtic music reviews, profiles of Celtic musicians, Celtic history, traditions, and folklore. Also buys short fiction. No fiction, poetry, historical stories already well publicized. **Buys 100 mss/year.** Query or send complete ms. Length: 700-2,500 words. **All writers receive a complimentary subscription.**

COLUMNS Query.

💲💲 GERMAN LIFE

Zeitgeist Publishing, Inc., 1068 National Hwy., La-Vale MD 21502. **E-mail:** mslider@germanlife.com. **Website:** www.germanlife.com. **Contact:** Mark Slider. **80% freelance written.** Bimonthly magazine covering German-speaking Europe (Germany, Austria, Switzerland). *"German Life* is for all interested in the diversity of German-speaking culture—past and present—and in the various ways that the US (and North America in general) has been shaped by its German immigrants. The magazine is dedicated to solid reporting on travel, cultural, historical, social, genealogical, culinary and political topics." Estab. 1994. Circ. 40,000. Byline given. Pays on publication. Editorial lead time 4 months. Submit seasonal material 6-12 months in advance. Accepts queries by mail, e-mail. Responds in 2 months to queries; in 3 months to mss. Sample copy for $4.95 and SASE with 4 first-class stamps. Guidelines available online at www.germanlife.com.

NONFICTION Needs general interest, historical, interview, photo feature, reviews, travel. Special issues: February/March: Food, wine, beer; April/May: travel in Germany and other parts of German-speaking Europe; June/July: German-American travel destinations; August/September: Education; October/November: Oktoberfest;. December/January:Holiday Issue. **Buys 50 mss/year.** Query with published clips. Length: up to 1,200 words. **Pays $100-500.**

COLUMNS German-Americana (regards specific German-American communities, organizations, and/or events past or present), 1,200 words; Profile (portrays prominent Germans, Americans, or German-Americans), 1,000 words; At Home (cuisine, etc. relating to German-speaking Europe), 800 words; Library (reviews of books, videos, CDs, etc.), 300 words. **Buys 30 mss/year.** Query with published clips. **Pays $100-130.**

FILLERS Needs facts, newsbreaks. Length: 100-300 words. **Pays $80.**

HADASSAH MAGAZINE

40 Wall St., 8th Floor, New York NY 10005. **Fax:** (212)451-6257. **E-mail:** magazine@hadassah.org. **Website:** www.hadassahmagazine.org. **Contact:** Elizabeth Barnea. **90% freelance written.** Monthly magazine. Circ. 255,000. Pays on acceptance. Accepts simultaneous submissions. Responds in 4 months to mss. Sample copy and writer's guidelines with 9x12 SASE.

NONFICTION Buys 10 unsolicited mss/year. Query. Length: 1,500-2,000 words.

COLUMNS "We have a family column and a travel column, but a query for topic or destination should be submitted first to make sure the area is of interest and the story follows our format."

FICTION Contact: Zelda Shluker, managing editor. Short stories with strong plots and positive Jewish values. Needs ethnic. Length: 1,500-2,000 words. **Pays $500 minimum.**

INTERNATIONAL EXAMINER

409 Maynard Ave. S., #203, Seattle WA 98104. (206)624-3925. **Fax:** (206)624-3046. **E-mail:** editor@iexaminer.org. **Website:** www.iexaminer.org. **Contact:** Travis Quezon, editor in chief. **75% freelance written.** Biweekly journal of Asian American news, politics, and arts. "*International Examiner* is about Asian American issues and things of interest to Asian Americans. We do not want stuff about Asian things (stories on your trip to China, Japanese Tea Ceremony, etc. will be rejected). Yes, we are in English." Estab. 1974. Circ. 12,000. Pays on publication. No kill fee. Publishes ms an average of 1 month after acceptance. Editorial lead time 1 month. Submit seasonal material 2 months in advance. Accepts queries by mail, e-mail, fax. Accepts simultaneous submissions. Guidelines for #10 SASE.

NONFICTION Needs essays, general interest, historical, humor, interview, opinion, personal experience, photo feature. **Buys 100 mss/year.** Query with published clips. Length: 750-5,000 words, depending on subject. **Pays $25-100.**

FICTION Asian American authored fiction by or about Asian Americans only. **Buys 1-2 mss/year.** Query.

ITALIAN AMERICA

219 E St. NE, Washington DC 20002. (202)547-2900. **Fax:** (202)546-8168. **E-mail:** ddesanctis@osia.org. **Website:** www.osia.org. **Contact:** Dona De Sanctis, editor. **20% freelance written.** Quarterly magazine. *Italian America* provides timely information about OSIA, while reporting on individuals, institutions, issues, and events of current or historical significance in the Italian-American community. Estab. 1996. Circ. 65,000. Byline given. Pays on publication. Offers 50% kill fee. Publishes ms an average of 3 months after acceptance. Editorial lead time 3 months. Accepts queries by mail, e-mail, fax. Accepts simultaneous submissions. Sample copy free. Guidelines online.

NONFICTION Needs historical, interview, opinion, current events. **Buys 8 mss/year.** Query with published clips. Length: 750-1,000 words. **Pays $50-250.**

KHABAR

3635 Savannah Place Dr., Suite 400, Duluth GA 30096. (770)451-3067, ext. 4. **E-mail:** editor@khabar.com. **Website:** www.khabar.com. **50% freelance written.** "*Khabar* is a monthly magazine for the Indian community, free in Georgia, Alabama, Tennessee, and South Carolina. Besides Indian-Americans, *Khabar* also reaches other South Asian immigrants in Georgia—those from countries such as Pakistan, Bangladesh, Nepal, and Sri Lanka who share common needs for good and services. 'Khabar' means 'news' or 'to know' in many Indian languages, but we are a features magazine rather than a news publication." Estab. 1992. Circ. 27,000. Pays on publication. Offers 25% kill fee. Publishes ms an average of 2 months after acceptance. Editorial lead time 2 months. Submit seasonal material 2 months in advance. Accepts queries by e-mail. Accepts simultaneous submissions. Sample copy free. Guidelines by e-mail.

NONFICTION Needs essays, interview, opinion, personal experience, travel. **Buys 5 mss/year.** Send complete ms. Length: 750-4,000 words. **Pays $100-300 for assigned articles. Pays $75 for unsolicited articles.**

COLUMNS Book Review, 1,200 words; Music Review, 800 words; Spotlight (profiles), 1,200-3,000 words. **Buys 5 mss/year.** Query with or without published clips or send complete ms. **Pays $75 minimum.**

FICTION Needs ethnic. **Buys 5 mss/year.** Query or send complete ms. **Pays $50-100.**

ⓢⓢⓢ MOMENT

4115 Wisconsin Ave. NW, Suite LL10, Washington DC 20016. (202)363-6422. **Fax:** (202)362-2514. **E-mail:** editor@momentmag.com. **Website:** www.momentmag.com. **90% freelance written.** Bimonthly magazine on Judaism. *Moment* is committed to portraying intellectual, political, cultural, and religious debates within the community, and to educating readers about Judaism's rich history and contemporary movements, ranging from left to right, fundamentalist to secular. Estab. 1975. Circ. 65,000. Byline given. Pays on publication. Publishes ms an average of 6 months after acceptance. Editorial lead time 3 months. Submit seasonal material 6 months in advance. Accepts queries by mail, e-mail. Accepts simultaneous submissions. Responds in 1 month to queries; in 3 months to mss. Sample copy for $4.50 and SAE. Guidelines online.

NONFICTION **Buys 25-30 mss/year.** Query with published clips. Length: 2,500-7,000 words. **Pays $200-1,200.**

COLUMNS 5765 (snappy pieces about quirky events in Jewish communities, news and ideas to improve Jewish living), 250 words maximum; Olam (first-person pieces, humor, and colorful reportage), 600-1,500 words; book eviews (fiction and nonfiction) are accepted but generally assigned, 400-800 words. **Buys 30 mss/year.** Query with published clips. **Pays $50-250.**

ⓢⓢ NATIVE PEOPLES MAGAZINE

5333 N. Seventh St., Suite C-224, Phoenix AZ 85014. (602)265-4855. **Fax:** (602)265-3113. **E-mail:** editorial@nativepeoples.com; twalker@nativepeoples.com; kcoochwytewa@nativepeoples.com. **Website:** www.nativepeoples.com. **Contact:** Taté Walker, editor; Kevin Coochwytewa, creative director. Bimonthly magazine covering Native Americans. High-quality reproduction with full color throughout. The primary purpose of this magazine is to offer a sensitive portrayal of the arts and lifeways of native peoples of the Americas. Estab. 1987. Circ. 40,000. Byline given. Pays on publication. Accepts queries by mail, e-mail, fax. Accepts simultaneous submissions. Responds in 2 months to queries. Guidelines by request.

NONFICTION Needs personal experience. **Buys 35 mss/year.** Length: 1,000-2,500 words. **Pays 25¢/word.**

ⓢⓢ RUSSIAN LIFE

RIS Publications, P.O. Box 567, Montpelier VT 05601. **E-mail:** editors@russianlife.com. **Website:** russianlife.com. **Contact:** Paul Richardson. **75% freelance written.** Bimonthly magazine covering Russian culture, history, travel, and business. "Our readers are informed Russophiles with an avid interest in all things Russian. But we do not publish personal travel journals or the like." Estab. 1956. Circ. 15,000. Byline given. Pays on publication. No Publishes ms an average of 3-6 months after acceptance. Editorial lead time 2 months. Submit seasonal material 3 months in advance. Accepts queries by mail, e-mail. Responds in 1 month to queries. Sample copy with 9x12 SASE and 6 first-class stamps. Guidelines online.

NONFICTION Needs book excerpts, general interest, interview, photo feature, travel. No personal stories, i.e., How I came to love Russia. **Buys 15-20 mss/year.** Query. Length: 1,000-6,000 words. **Pays $100-300.**

ⓢⓢ WINDSPEAKER

Aboriginal Multi-Media Society, 13245-146 St., Edmonton AB T5L 4S8 Canada. (780)455-2700. **Fax:** (780)455-7639. **E-mail:** market@ammsa.com; dsteel@ammsa.com. **Website:** www.ammsa.com/publications/windspeakerwww.ammsa.com/windspeaker. **Contact:** Paul Macedo, director of publishing operations; Debora Steel, contributing news editor. **25% freelance written.** Monthly tabloid covering native issues. Focus on events and issues that affect and interest native peoples, national or local. Estab. 1983. Circ. 27,000. Byline given. Pays on publication. Offers kill fee. Publishes ms an average of 1 month after acceptance. Editorial lead time 1 month. Submit seasonal material 2 months in advance. Accepts queries by mail, e-mail, phone. Accepts simultaneous submissions. Sample copy free. Guidelines online.

NONFICTION Needs opinion, photo feature, travel, news interview/profile, reviews: books, music, movies. Special issues: Powwow (June); Travel supplement (May). **Buys 200 mss/year.** Query with published clips and SASE or by e-mail. Length: 500-800 words. **Pays $3-3.60/published inch for a single source story and $4.15/published inch for a multi-source story.**

FOOD & DRINK

CHEF

704 N. Wells St., 2nd Floor, Chicago IL 60654. (312)849-2220. **Fax:** (312)849-2174. **E-mail:** cjohnson@talcott.com; moneill@talcott.com. **Website:** www.chefmagazine.com. **Contact:** Claire Johnson, managing editor; Megan O'Neill, associate editor. **40% freelance written.** Monthly magazine covering chefs in all food-service segments. *Chef* is the one magazine that communicates food production to a commercial, professional audience in a meaningful way. Circ. 42,000. Byline given. No kill fee. Editorial lead time 2 months. Submit seasonal material 4 months in advance. Accepts queries by mail, e-mail, fax. Accepts simultaneous submissions. Guidelines free.

NONFICTION Needs book excerpts, essays, expose, general interest, historical, how-to, inspirational, interview, new product, opinion, personal experience, photo feature, technical. **Buys 30-50 mss/year.** Length: 750-1,500 words.

COLUMNS Flavor (traditional and innovative applications of a particular flavor) 1,000-1,200 words; Dish (professional chef profiles) 1,000-1,200 words; Savor (themed recipes) 1,000-1,500 words.

THE DAILY TEA

1000 Germantown Pike, Suite F2, Plymouth Meeting PA 19462. (484)688-0299. **E-mail:** alexis@thedailytea.com. **Website:** www.thedailytea.com. **75% freelance written.** Annual magazine covering anything tea related. "Around the office, we have a saying—'It's not just about dry brown leaves, or hot brown liquid.' For sure, *The Daily Tea* is for tea lovers of all levels, but we aim to be much more than a text book. It's the culture that surrounds tea that we find even more fascinating—the lives of the people who grow it, the rituals and traditions around tea, the peace we find in drinking it, and the fact that tea is a common denominator to so many around the world. This is what *The Daily Tea* is all about." Estab. 1994. Circ. 9,500. Byline given. Pays on publication. Publishes ms an average of 1 year after acceptance. Editorial lead time 9 months. Submit seasonal material 6 months in advance. Accepts queries by mail, e-mail. Accepts simultaneous submissions. Responds in 6 months to mss. Guidelines by e-mail.

NONFICTION Needs book excerpts, essays, general interest, historical, how-to, humor, interview, personal experience, photo feature, travel. Send complete ms or query with proprosal. **Pays negotiable amount.**

COLUMNS Readers' Stories (personal experience involving tea); Book Reviews (review on tea books). Send complete ms. **Pays negotiable amount.**

⑤⑤⑤ DRAFT

300 W. Clarendon Ave., Suite 155, Phoenix AZ 85013. **E-mail:** editorial@draftmag.com. **Website:** www.draftmag.com. **60% freelance written.** Bimonthly magazine covering beer and men's lifestyle (including food, travel, sports, and leisure). "*DRAFT* is a national men's magazine devoted to beer, breweries, and the lifestyle and culture that surrounds it. Read by nearly 300,000 men aged 21-45, *DRAFT* offers formal beer reviews, plus coverage of food, travel, sports, and leisure. Writers need not have formal beer knowledge (though that's a plus!), but they should be experienced journalists who can appreciate beer and beer culture." Estab. 2006. Circ. 275,000. Byline given. Pays on publication. Offers 20% kill fee. Publishes ms an average of 2 months after acceptance. Editorial lead time 4 months. Submit seasonal material 6 months in advance. Accepts queries by e-mail. Accepts simultaneous submissions. Responds in 1 month to queries. Sample copy: $3 (magazine can also be found on most newsstands for $4.99). Guidelines available at draftmag.com/submissions.

NONFICTION Do not want unsolicited mss, beer reviews, brewery profiles. **Buys 80 mss/year.** Query with published clips. Length: 250-2,500 words. **Pays 50-90¢ for assigned articles.** Expenses limit agreed upon in advance.

FOOD & WINE

American Express Publishing Corp., 1120 Avenue of the Americas, 9th Floor, New York NY 10036. (212)522-1387. **Fax:** (212)764-2177. **Website:** www.foodandwine.com. **Contact:** Morgan Goldberg. Monthly magazine for the reader who enjoys the finer things in life. Editorial focuses on upscale dining, covering resturants, entertaining at home, and travel destinations. Circ. 964,000. No kill fee. Editorial lead time 6 months. Accepts simultaneous submissions.

⑤ GOURMET TRAVELLER WINE

GT Wine Magazine Pty Limited, Level 7, 233 Castlereagh St., GPO Box 4088, Sydney NSW 2000 Australia. (61)(2)91990601. **E-mail:** jsarris@gourmettravellerwine.com. **Website:** www.gourmettravellerwine.com

com. James Kilmartin. **Contact:** Judy Sarris, editor. Bimonthly magazine for the world of wine, celebrating both local and overseas industries. "*Gourmet Traveller Wine* is for wine lovers: It's for those who love to travel, to eat out, and to entertain at home, and for those who want to know more about the wine in their glass." Estab. 1996. Circ. 22,088. Accepts queries by e-mail. Accepts simultaneous submissions.

NONFICTION Needs general interest, how-to, interview, new product, profile, reviews, travel. Query.

💲💲 KASHRUS MAGAZINE

The Kashrus Institute, P.O. Box 204, Brooklyn NY 11204. (718)336-8544. **Fax:** (718)336-8550. **E-mail:** editorial@kashrusmagazine.com. **Website:** www. kashrusmagazine.com. **Contact:** Rabbi Yosef Wikler, editor. *Kashrus Magazine* is the kosher consumer's most established, authoritative, and independent source of news about kosher foods. Estab. 1981. Circ. 10,000. Byline given. Pays on publication. Offers 50% kill fee. Publishes ms an average of 2 months after acceptance. Submit seasonal material 2 months in advance. Accepts queries by mail, phone. Accepts simultaneous submissions. Responds in 2 weeks. Sample copy by e-mail.

NONFICTION Needs personal experience, photo feature, religious, technical. Special issues: International Kosher Travel (October); Passover Shopping Guide (March); Domestic Kosher Travel Guide (June). **Buys 8-12 mss/year.** Query with published clips. Length: 1,000-1,500 words. **Pays $100-250 for assigned articles. Pays up to $100 for unsolicited articles.**

COLUMNS Health/Diet/Nutrition, 1,000-1,500 words; Book Review (cookbooks, food technology, kosher food), 250-500 words; People in the News (interviews with kosher personalities), 1,000-1,500 words; Regional Kosher Supervision (report on kosher supervision in a city or community), 1,000-1,500 words; Food Technology (new technology or current technology with accompanying pictures), 1,000-1,500 words; Kosher Travel (international, national—must include Kosher information and Jewish communities), 1,000-1,500 words; Regional Kosher Cooking, 1,000-1,500 words. **Buys 8-12 mss/year.** Query with published clips. **Pays $50-250.**

SAVEUR MAGAZINE

Bonnier Publications, 15 East 32nd St., 12th Floor, New York NY 10016. (212)219-7400. **Website:** www. saveur.com. **Contact:** Adam Sachs, editor in chief.

Magazine published 9 times/year. "Saveur seeks out stories from around the globe that weave together culture, tradition, and people through the language of food. On every page the magazine honors a fundamental truth: cooking is one of the most universal—and beautiful—means of human expression. It is written for sophisticated, upscale lovers of food, wine, travel, and adventure." Estab. 1994. Circ. 365,000. No kill fee. Accepts queries by mail, e-mail. Accepts simultaneous submissions. Sample copy for $5 at newsstands. Guidelines online.

NONFICTION Query with published clips.

COLUMNS Query with published clips.

TASTE OF HOME

Reader's Digest Association, Inc., 1610 N. 2nd St., Suite 102, Milwaukee WI 53207. (414)423-0100. **Fax:** (414)423-8463. **E-mail:** feedback@tasteofhome.com; editors@tasteofhome.com. **Website:** www.tasteofhome. com. Bimonthly magazine. *Taste of Home* is dedicated to home cooks, from beginners to the very experienced. Editorial includes recipes and serving suggestions, interviews and ideas from the publication's readers and field editors based around the country, and reviews of new cooking tools and gadgets. Circ. 3.5 million. No kill fee. Accepts simultaneous submissions.

VEGETARIAN JOURNAL

P.O. Box 1463, Baltimore MD 21203-1463. (410)366-8343. **E-mail:** vrg@vrg.org. **Website:** www.vrg.org. **Contact:** Debra Wasserman, editor. Quarterly non-profit vegetarian magazine that examines the health, ecological and ethical aspects of vegetarianism. "Highly-educated audience including health professionals." Estab. 1982. Circ. 20,000. Accepts simultaneous submissions. Sample copy: $4.

NONFICTION "The articles we publish are usually written by registered dietitians and individuals with a science background. We are open to non-paid articles by others, and possibly a paid feature for a super idea. If you have a great idea that you would like to be paid for, please send a query letter along with a résumé, and indicate that you would like to be paid." **Pays $100-200/article.**

POETRY "Please, no submissions of poetry from adults; 18 and under only."

💲💲💲💲 WINE ENTHUSIAST MAGAZINE

Wine Enthusiast Media, 333 North Bedford Rd., Mt. Kisco NY 10549. **E-mail:** editor@wineenthusiast.net.

E-mail: jczerwin@wineenthusiast.net; jfink@wineenthusiast.net. **Website:** www.winemag.com. **Contact:** Joe Czerwinski, managing editor; Jameson Fink, senior editor. **25% freelance written.** Monthly magazine covering the lifestyle of wine. Demystifying wine without dumbing it down, and tapping into current trends of spirits, travel, entertaining and art through a savvy wine lovers' lens, Wine Enthusiast is the modern tome of popular wine culture—a magazine that provokes and drives global dialogue in one of the world's most vibrant and fast-paced lifestyle categories, educating and entertaining legions of smart and sophisticated consumers. Estab. 1988. Circ. 180,000. Byline given. Pays on acceptance. Offers 25% kill fee. Editorial lead time 4 months. Submit seasonal material 5 months in advance. Accepts queries by e-mail. Responds in 2 weeks to queries. Responds in 2 months to mss.

NONFICTION Needs essays, humor, interview, new product, nostalgic, personal experience, travel. **Buys 5 mss/year.** Submit a proposal (1 or 2 paragraphs) with clips and a résumé. Submit short, front-of-book items to Jameson Fink; submit feature proposals to Joe Czerwinski. **$1/word**

🟢🟢 WINE PRESS NORTHWEST

333 W. Canal Dr., Kennewick WA 99336. (509)582-1564. **Fax:** (509)585-7221. **E-mail:** editor@winepressnw.com; info@winepressnw.com. **Website:** www.winepressnw.com. **50% freelance written.** Quarterly magazine covering Pacific Northwest wine (Washington, Oregon, British Columbia, Idaho). "Wine Press Northwest is a quarterly magazine for those with an interest in wine, from the novice to the veteran. We publish in March, June, September and December. We focus on Washington, Oregon, Idaho and British Columbia's talented winemakers and the wineries, vintners and restaurants that showcase Northwest wines. We are dedicated to all who savor the fruits of their labor." Estab. 1998. Circ. 12,000. Byline given. Pays on publication. Offers 20% kill fee. Publishes ms an average of 3 months after acceptance. Editorial lead time 3 months. Submit seasonal material 3 months in advance. Accepts queries by mail, e-mail, fax. Accepts simultaneous submissions. Responds in 1 month to queries. Sample copy free or online. Guidelines free.

NONFICTION Needs general interest, historical, interview, new product, photo feature, travel. No beer, spirits, non-NW (California wine, etc.). **Buys 30 mss/year.** Query with published clips. Length: 1,500-2,500 words. **Pays $300.**

GAMES & PUZZLES

🟢 THE BRIDGE BULLETIN

American Contract Bridge League, 6575 Windchase Dr., Horn Lake MS 38637-1523. (662)253-3156. **Fax:** (662)253-3187. **E-mail:** editor@acbl.org; brent.manley@acbl.org. **Website:** www.acbl.org. Paul Linxwiler, managing editor. **Contact:** Brent Manley, editor. **20% freelance written.** Monthly magazine covering duplicate (tournament) bridge. Estab. 1938. Circ. 155,000. Byline given. Pays on publication. Publishes ms an average of 3 months after acceptance. Editorial lead time 2 months. Accepts queries by mail, e-mail. Accepts simultaneous submissions.

NONFICTION Needs book excerpts, essays, how-to, humor, interview, new product, personal experience, photo feature, technical, travel. **Buys 6 mss/year.** Query. Length: 500-2,000 words. **Pays $100/page.**

🟢🟢 CHESS LIFE

P.O. Box 3967, Crossville TN 38557. (931)787-1234. **Fax:** (931)787-1200. **E-mail:** dlucas@uschess.org; fbutler@uschess.org. **Website:** www.uschess.org. **Contact:** Daniel Lucas, editor; Francesca "Frankie" Butler, art director. **15% freelance written. Works with a small number of new/unpublished writers/year.** Monthly magazine. "*Chess Life* is the official publication of the United States Chess Federation, covering news of most major chess events, both here and abroad, with special emphasis on the triumphs and exploits of American players." Estab. 1939. Circ. 85,000. Byline given. No kill fee. Publishes ms an average of 6 months after acceptance. Submit seasonal material 6 months in advance. Accepts simultaneous submissions. Responds in 3 months to mss. Sample copy via PDF is available.

NONFICTION Needs general interest, historical, humor, interview, photo feature, technical. No stories about personal experiences with chess. **Buys 30-40 mss/year.** Query with samples if new to publication. 3,000 words maximum. **Pays $100/page (800-1,000 words).**

FILLERS Submit with samples and clips. Buys first or negotiable rights to cartoons and puzzles. **Pays $25 upon acceptance.**

❷ GAME INFORMER

GameStop, 724 N. First St., 4th Floor, Minneapolis MN 55401. (612)486-6154. **Fax:** (612)486-6101. **Website:** www.gameinformer.com. **Contact:** Andy McNamara, editor in chief; Matt Bertz, managing editor. Monthly video game magazine featuring articles, news, strategy, and reviews of video games and associated consoles. Estab. 1991. Circ. 7.6 million. Accepts simultaneous submissions.

❸❸❸ GAMES WORLD OF PUZZLES

Kappa Publishing Group, Inc., 6198 Butler Pike, Suite 200, Blue Bell PA 19422. (215)643-6385. **Fax:** (215)628-3571. **E-mail:** games@kappapublishing.com. **Website:** www.gamesmagazine-online.com. **Contact:** Jennifer Orehowsky, senior editor. **50% freelance written.** *Games World of Puzzles*, published 10 times/year, features visual and verbal puzzles, quizzes, game reviews, contests, and feature articles. Estab. 1977. Circ. 75,000. Byline given. Pays on publication. Offers 25% kill fee. Publishes ms an average of 4 months after acceptance. Editorial lead time 3 months. Submit seasonal material 6 months in advance. Accepts queries by mail, e-mail. Accepts simultaneous submissions. Responds in 6-8 weeks to queries and mss. Sample copy: $5. Guidelines online.

NONFICTION Needs humor, photo feature, game- and puzzle-related events or people, wordplay. Query or submit complete ms by e-mail. Length: 2,000-2,500 words. **Pays $500-1,000.**

COLUMNS Puzzles, tests, quizzes. **Buys 50 mss/ year.** Query or send complete ms. **Payment varies.**

GAY & LESBIAN INTEREST

❸❸ THE ADVOCATE

Here Media, Inc., 10990 Wilshire Blvd., Penthouse, Los Angeles CA 90024. (310)806-4288. **Fax:** (310)806-4268. **E-mail:** newsroom@advocate.com. **Website:** www.advocate.com. **Contact:** Matthew Breen, editor in chief; Meg Thomann, managing editor. Biweekly magazine covering national news events with a gay and lesbian perspective on the issues. Estab. 1967. Circ. 120,000. Byline given. Pays on publication. Accepts simultaneous submissions. Responds in 1 month to queries. Sample copy: $3.95. Guidelines on website.

NONFICTION Needs expose. Query. Length: 800 words. **Pays $550.**

COLUMNS Arts & Media (news and profiles of well-known gay or lesbians in entertainment); 750 words. Query. **Pays $100-500.**

❸ ECHO MAGAZINE

ACE Publishing, Inc., P.O. Box 16630, Phoenix AZ 85011. (602)266-0550, ext. 110. **Fax:** (602)266-0773. **E-mail:** editor@echomag.com. **Website:** www.echo-mag.com. **Contact:** KJ Philp, managing editor. **30-40% freelance written.** Biweekly magazine covering gay and lesbian issues. *Echo Magazine* is a newsmagazine for gay, lesbian, bisexual, and transgendered persons in the Phoenix metro area and throughout the state of Arizona. Editorial content needs to be pro-gay, that is, supportive of LGBTQ equality in all areas of American life. Estab. 1989. Circ. 15,000-18,000. Byline given. Pays on publication. No kill fee. Publishes ms an average of less than 1 month after acceptance. Editorial lead time 1-2 months. Submit seasonal material 1-2 months in advance. Accepts queries by e-mail. Accepts simultaneous submissions. Responds in 2 weeks to queries; in 1 month to mss. Sample copy online. Guidelines by e-mail.

NONFICTION Needs book excerpts, essays, historical, humor, interview, opinion, personal experience, photo feature, travel. Special issues: Pride Festival (April); Arts issue (August); Holiday Gift/ Decor (December). No articles on topics unrelated to our LGBTQ readers, or anything that is not pro-gay. **Buys 10-20 mss/year.** Query. Length: 500-2,000 words. **Pays $30-40.**

COLUMNS Guest Commentary (opinion on GLBT issues), 500-1,000 words; Arts/Entertainment (profiles of GLBT or relevant celebrities, or arts issues), 800-1,500 words. **Buys 5-10 mss/year.** Query. **Pays $30-40.**

❸ THE GAY & LESBIAN REVIEW

Gay & Lesbian Review, Inc., P.O. Box 16477, Hollywood CA 91615. (844)752-7829. **E-mail:** richard. schneider@glreview.org. **Website:** www.glreview. org. **Contact:** Richard Schneider, Jr., editor. **100% freelance written.** "*The Gay & Lesbian Review* is a bimonthly magazine targeting an educated readership of gay, lesbian, bisexual, and transgendered (GLBT) men and women. Under the tagline 'a bimonthly journal of history, culture, and politics,' the

G&LR publishes essays in a wide range of disciplines as well as reviews of books, movies, and plays." Estab. 1994. Circ. 12,000. Byline given. Pays on publication. No kill fee. Editorial lead time 2 months. Accepts simultaneous submissions. Sample copy free. Guidelines online.

NONFICTION Needs essays, historical, humor, interview, opinion, book reviews. Does not want fiction, memoirs, personal reflections. Query or send complete ms by e-mail. Length: 2,000-4,000 words for features; 600-1,200 words for book reviews. **Pays $50-100.**

COLUMNS Guest Opinion (op-ed pieces by GLBT writers and activists), 500-1,000 words; Artist's Profile (focuses on the creative output of a visual artist, musician, or writer), 1,000-1,500 words; Art Memo (reflections on a work or artist of the past who made a difference for gay culture), 1,000-1,500 words; International Spectrum (the state of GLBT rights or culture in city or region outside the U.S.), 1,000-1,500 words. Query or submit complete ms by e-mail.

POETRY Needs avant-garde, free verse, traditional. Submit poems by postal mail (no e-mail submissions) with SASE for reply. Submit maximum 3 poems. Length: "While there is no hard-and-fast limit on length, poems of over 50 lines become hard to accommodate."

INSTINCT MAGAZINE

11856 Balboa Blvd., #312, Granada Hills CA 91344. (818)284-4525. **E-mail:** editor@instinctmag.com. **Website:** instinctmagazine.com. **Contact:** Mike Wood, editor-in-chief. **40% freelance written.** Gay men's monthly lifestyle and entertainment magazine. "*Instinct* is a blend of *Cosmo* and *Maxim* for gay men. We're smart, sexy, irreverent, and we always have a sense of humor—a unique style that has made us the #1 gay men's magazine in the US." Estab. 1997. Circ. 115,000. Byline given. Pays on publication. Offers 20% kill fee. Editorial lead time 2-3 months. Accepts queries by mail, e-mail. Accepts simultaneous submissions. Sample copy online. Guidelines online. Register online first.

NONFICTION Needs expose, general interest, humor, interview, travel, basically anything of interest to gay men will be considered. Does not want first-person accounts or articles. Send complete ms via online submissions manager. Length: 850-2,000 words. **Pays $50-300.**

COLUMNS Health (gay, off-kilter), 800 words; Fitness (irreverent), 500 words; Movies, Books (edgy, sardonic), 800 words; Music, Video Games (indie, underground), 800 words. **Pays $150-250.**

METROSOURCE MAGAZINE

137 W. 19th St., 2nd Floor, New York NY 10011. (212)691-5127. **E-mail:** letters@metrosource.com. **Website:** www.metrosource.com. **75% freelance written.** Magazine published 6 times/year. "*MetroSource* is an upscale, glossy, 4-color lifestyle magazine targeted to an urban, professional gay and lesbian readership." Estab. 1990. Circ. 145,000. Byline given. Pays on publication. Publishes ms an average of 2 months after acceptance. Editorial lead time 4 months. Submit seasonal material 4 months in advance. Accepts simultaneous submissions. Sample copy for $5.

NONFICTION **Buys 20 mss/year.** Query with published clips. Length: 1,000-1,800 words. **Pays $100-400.**

COLUMNS Book, film, television, and stage reviews; health columns; and personal diary and opinion pieces. Word lengths vary. Query with published clips. **Pays $200.**

RAINBOW RUMPUS

P.O. Box 6881, Minneapolis MN 55406. **Website:** www.rainbowrumpus.org. **Contact:** Liane Bonin Starr, editor in chief and fiction editor. "*Rainbow Rumpus* is the world's only online literary magazine for children and youth with lesbian, gay, bisexual, and transgender (LGBT) parents. We are creating a new genre of children's and young adult fiction. Please carefully read and observe the guidelines on our website." Estab. 2005. Circ. 300 visits/day. Byline given. Pays on publication. Accepts simultaneous submissions. Guidelines online.

FICTION "Stories should be written from the point of view of children or teens with lesbian, gay, bisexual, or transgender parents or other family members, or who are connected to the LGBT community. Stories featuring families of color, bisexual parents, transgender parents, family members with disabilities, and mixed-race families are particularly welcome." Query editor through website's Contact page. Be sure to select the Submissions category. Length: 800-2,500 words for stories for 4- to 12-year-olds; up to 5,000 words for stories for 13- to 18-year-olds. **Pays $300/ story.**

ST. SEBASTIAN REVIEW

1308 Sherman Ave., #2S, Evanston IL 60201. **E-mail:** editor@stsebastianreview.com. **Website:** www.stsebastianreview.com. **Contact:** Carolyn E.M. Gibney, editor. The *St. Sebastian Review* is a semiannual LGBTQ Christian literary magazine, founded to give voice to a community often disenfranchised and unheard. "We exist as a forum within and from which LGBTQ Christians of any denomination can engage both critically and compassionately the culture in which they find themselves. We are purveyors of fine poetry, fiction, nonfiction essays, and visual art from among the LGBTQ Christian community and its allies." Estab. 2011. Byline given. Does not offer payment. Publishes ms an average of 2-3 months after acceptance. Accepts queries by e-mail. Accepts simultaneous submissions. Responds in 2 weeks to queries and 3 months to mss. Sample copy online. Guidelines online.

NONFICTION Needs essays, personal experience. Writer should query before submitting. Length: 2,000 words maximum.

FICTION Length: 2,000 words maximum.

POETRY Needs avant-garde, free verse, light verse, traditional. Submit maximum 5 poems.

$ THE WASHINGTON BLADE

P.O. Box 53352, Washington DC 20009. (202)747-2077. **Fax:** (202)747-2070. **E-mail:** knaff@washblade.com. **Website:** www.washblade.com. **Contact:** Kevin Naff, editor. **20% freelance written.** Nation's oldest and largest weekly newspaper covering the lesbian, gay, bisexual and transgender issues. Articles (subjects) should be written from or directed to a gay perspective. Estab. 1969. Circ. 30,000. Byline given. No kill fee. Submit seasonal material 1 month in advance. Accepts queries by mail, e-mail, fax. Accepts simultaneous submissions. Responds in 1 month to queries.

COLUMNS Send feature submissions to Joey DiGuglielmo, arts editor (joeyd@washblade.com). Send opinion submissions to Kevin Naff, editor (knaff@washblade.com). Pay varies. No sexually explicit material.

GENERAL INTEREST

$ THE ALMANAC FOR FARMERS & CITY FOLK

Greentree Publishing, Inc., Box 319, 840 S. Rancho Dr., Suite 4, Las Vegas NV 89106. (702)387-6777. **Fax:** (702)385-1370. **Website:** www.thealmanac.com. **30-40% freelance written.** Annual almanac of "down-home, folksy material pertaining to farming, gardening, homemaking, animals, etc." Estab. 1983. Circ. 300,000. Byline given. Pays on publication. No kill fee. Publishes ms an average of 6 months after acceptance. Accepts queries by mail. Accepts simultaneous submissions. Sample copy: $4.99.

NONFICTION Needs essays, general interest, historical, how-to, humor. "No fiction or controversial topics. Please, no first-person pieces!" **Buys 30-40 mss/year.** No queries, please. Editorial decisions made from mss only. Send complete ms by mail. Length: 350-1,400 words. **Pays $45/page.**

FILLERS Needs anecdotes, facts, short humor, gardening hints. Length: up to 125 words. **Pays $15 for short fillers or page rate for longer fillers.**

$$ THE AMERICAN LEGION MAGAZINE

P.O. Box 1055, Indianapolis IN 46206-1055. (317)630-1253; (317) 630-1298. **Fax:** (317)630-1280. **E-mail:** magazine@legion.org; mgrills@legion.org; hsoria@legion.org. **Website:** www.legion.org. **Contact:** Matt Grills, cartoon editor; Holly Soria, art director. **70% freelance written. Prefers to work with published/established writers, but works with a small number of new/unpublished writers each year.** Monthly magazine. Working through 15,000 community-level posts, the honorably discharged wartime veterans of The American Legion dedicate themselves to God, country, and traditional American values. They believe in a strong defense; adequate and compassionate care for veterans and their families; community service; and the wholesome development of our nation's youth. Publishes articles that reflect these values. Informs readers and their families of significant trends and issues affecting the nation, the world and their way of life. Major features focus on the American flag, national security, foreign affairs, business trends, social issues, health, education, ethics, and the arts. Also publishes selected general feature articles, articles of special interest to veterans, and question-and-answer interviews with prominent national and world figures. Estab. 1919. Circ. 2,550,000. Byline given. Pays on acceptance. No kill fee. Publishes ms an average of 6 months after acceptance. Accepts queries by mail, e-mail, fax. Accepts simultaneous submissions. Responds in 2 months to queries. Sample copy for $3.50 and 9x12 SAE with 6 first-class stamps. Guidelines for #10 SASE.

NONFICTION Needs general interest, interview. No regional topics or promotion of partisan political agendas. No personal experiences or war stories. **Buys 50-60 mss/year.** Query with SASE should explain the subject or issue, article's angle and organization, writer's qualifications, and experts to be interviewed. Length: 300-2,000 words. **Pays 40¢/word and up.**

$ THE CHRISTIAN SCIENCE MONITOR

210 Massachussetts Ave., Boston MA 02115. **E-mail:** homeforum@csmonitor.com. **Website:** www.csmonitor.com. **Contact:** Editor, The Home Forum. **95% freelance written.** *The Christian Science Monitor*, a Web-first publication that also publishes a weekly print magazine, regularly features personal nonfiction essays and, occasionally, poetry in its Home Forum section. "We're looking for upbeat essays of 600-800 words and short (20 lines maximum) poems that explore and celebrate daily life." Estab. 1908. Pays on publication. Offers 50% kill fee. Publishes ms 1-8 months after acceptance. Editorial lead time 6-8 weeks. Accepts queries by e-mail, online submission form. Responds in 3 weeks to mss; only responds to accepted mss. Sample copy online. Guidelines available online or by e-mail.

NONFICTION Needs essays, humor, personal experience. **Buys 2,500+ mss/year.** 600-800 **Pays $75-150.**

POETRY Accepts submissions via online form. Does not want "work that presents people in helpless or hopeless states; poetry about death, aging, or illness; or dark, violent, sensual poems. No poems that are overtly religious or falsely sweet." Submit maximum 5 poems. Length: up to 20 lines/poem. **Pays $25/haiku; $50/poem.**

CONTINENTAL NEWSTIME

Continental Features/Continental News Service, 501 W. Broadway, Plaza A, PMB #265, San Diego CA 92101-3802. (858)492-8696. **E-mail:** continentalnewsservice@yahoo.com. **Website:** www.continentalnewsservice.com. **Contact:** Gary P. Salamone, editor-in-chief. See above. Twice-monthly general interest magazine of news and commentary on U.S. national and world news, with travel columns, science articles, entertainment features, analytical pieces, investigative journalism, humor pieces, comic strips, general humor panels, and editorial cartoons. "Writers who offer the kind and quality of writing we seek stand an equal chance regardless of experience. *CF/CNS* specializes in covering the unreported/under-reported news/information and requires 3 letters of recommendation, 1 of which must be from a current subscriber to our general-interest newsmagazine, *Continental Newstime*, to ensure consistency with this mission and with our quality and format standards." CF/CNS publishes special Washington D.C., Chicago, San Diego, Minneapolis, Boston, Atlanta, Houston, Anchorage, Honolulu, Miami, Rochester (NY), and Seattle News Editions of Continental Newstime general-interest newsmagazine in a monthly rotation. Estab. 1987. Varies Acceptance Usually one month Accepts queries by mail, e-mail. Accepts simultaneous submissions. Responds in 1 month. Sample copy available for $4.50 in US and $6.50 CAN/foreign. Guidelines for #10 SASE.

NONFICTION Contact: Same as above. **Buys Varies mss/year.** 300 to 700/800 words

DEPARTURES

Affluent Media Group, 1120 Avenue of the Americas, 9th Floor, New York NY 10036. (212)382-5600. **E-mail:** depeditors@timeinc.com. **Website:** www.departures.com. Bimonthly magazine. Contains feature articles on travel, art and culture, men's and women's style, and interior design with an eye on global adventures and purchases. Circ. 680,000. No kill fee. Editorial lead time 4 months. Accepts queries by e-mail. Accepts simultaneous submissions.

NONFICTION Needs general interest, travel. Query.

EBONY

Johnson Publishing Co., Inc., 820 S. Michigan Ave., Chicago IL 60605. **E-mail:** digitalpitches@ebony.com. **Website:** www.ebony.com. **Contact:** Najja Parker, editorial assistant. Monthly magazine covering topics ranging from education and history to entertainment, art, government, health, travel, sports, and social events. "*Ebony* is the top source for an authoritative perspective on the Black-American community. *Ebony* features the best thinkers, trendsetters, hottest celebrities, and next-generation leaders of Black America. It ignites conversation, promotes empowerment, and celebrates aspiration." Circ. 11,000,000. No kill fee. Editorial lead time 3 months. Accepts queries by e-mail. Accepts simultaneous submissions.

NONFICTION Needs interview, profile. Query.

$$$$ FAMILY CIRCLE

Meredith Corp., 805 Third Ave., 24th Floor, New York NY 10022. **Website:** www.familycircle.com. Lisa Kelsey, art director. **Contact:** Cassie Kreitner, editorial assistant; Lisa Kelsey, art director. **80% freelance written.** Magazine published every 3 weeks. A national women's service magazine which covers many stages of a woman's life, along with her everyday concerns about social, family, and health issues. Submissions should focus on families with children ages 8-16. Estab. 1932. Circ. 4.2 million. Byline given. Offers 20% kill fee. Editorial lead time 4 months. Submit seasonal material 4 months in advance. Accepts simultaneous submissions. Responds in 2 months to queries. Responds in 2 months to mss. For back issues, send $6.95 to P.O. Box 3156, Harlan IA 51537. Guidelines online.

NONFICTION Needs essays, opinion, personal experience, women's interest subjects such as family and personal relationships, children, physical and mental health, nutrition and self-improvement. No fiction or poetry. **Buys 200 mss/year.** Submit detailed outline, 2 clips, cover letter describing your publishing history, SASE or IRCs. Length: 1,000-2,500 words. **Pays $1/word.**

GRIT MAGAZINE

Ogden Publications, Inc., 1503 SW 42nd St., Topeka KS 66609-1265. (800)678-5779. **E-mail:** editor@grit.com; editor@cappersfarmer.com. **Website:** www.grit.com; www.cappersfarmer.com. **Contact:** Caleb Regan, managing editor. **80% freelance written.** "*GRIT* is a bimonthly rural lifestyle magazine that focuses on small-town life, country and rural lifestyles, and small-scale farms." Estab. 1879. Circ. 160,000. Byline given. Pays for articles on publication. Publishes manuscripts an average of 2-15 months after acceptance. Submit seasonal queries 6-8 months in advance. Responds to queries within a month's time. Sample copies and guidelines available online or by e-mailing ireid@grit.com.

NONFICTION Needs feature-length articles (1,000-1,750 words with photos) on topics of interest to those living in rural areas, on farms or ranches, or those simply interested in the rural lifestyle; department articles (500-1,500 words with photos) on nostalgia, farm equipment and animals, DIY projects, gardening and cooking. Send queries via e-mail (ktrimble@grit.com). Include complete contact information. Articles (except Heart of the Home) are assigned in most cases; no editorial calendar is published." Approximately 1500 words.

COLUMNS Departments include Gazette (news and quirky briefs of interest to lifestyle farmers); Heart of the Home (nostalgic remembrances on specific topics asked for in each issue); Country Tech (looking at equipment necessary for the farm life); Looking Back (nostalgic look at life on the farm); and In the Shop (how-to for those specialty farm items). Other departments are Comfort Foods, Recipe Box, In the Wild, and Sow Hoe (gardening topics). A query should be sent via e-mail to cregan@grit.com for all departments except Heart of the Home. Send complete article via e-mail to tsmith@cappers.com or mail them to GRIT/Capper's Farmer Editorial Department, 1503 SW 42nd St., Topeka, KS 66609. **Payment varies depending on experience and expertise. Payment will also include 2 contributor's copies. For Heart of the Home articles, we pay a standard $25 rate and a standard $5 payment for Heart of the Home articles that appear on our website but not in the magazines.**

HARPER'S MAGAZINE

666 Broadway, 11th Floor, New York NY 10012. (212)420-5720. **E-mail:** readings@harpers.org; scg@harpers.org. **Website:** www.harpers.org. **Contact:** Ellen Rosenbush, editor. **90% freelance written.** Monthly magazine for well-educated, socially concerned, widely read men and women who value ideas and good writing. *Harper's Magazine* encourages national discussion on current and significant issues in a format that offers arresting facts and intelligent opinions. By means of its several shorter journalistic forms—Harper's Index, Readings, Forum, and Annotation—as well as with its acclaimed essays, fiction, and reporting, *Harper's* continues the tradition begun with its first issue in 1850: to inform readers across the whole spectrum of political, literary, cultural, and scientific affairs. Estab. 1850. Circ. 230,000. Pays on acceptance. Offers negotiable kill fee. Publishes ms an average of 3 months after acceptance. Accepts queries by mail. Accepts simultaneous submissions. Responds in 6 weeks to queries. Guidelines online.

NONFICTION Needs humor. No interviews or profiles. **Buys 2 mss/year.** Query. Length: 4,000-6,000 words. **Generally pays 50¢-$1/word.**

FICTION Will consider unsolicited fiction. Has published work by Rebecca Curtis, George Saunders, Haruki Murakami, Margaret Atwood, Allan Gurganus, Evan Connell, and Dave Bezmosgis. Needs humorous. **Buys 12 mss/year.** Submit complete ms by postal mail. Length: 3,000-5,000 words. **Generally pays 50¢-$1/word.**

$ INSPIRED SENIOR LIVING

Stratis Publishing Ltd., 3, 3948 Quadra St., Victoria BC V8X 1J6 Canada. (250)479-4705. **Fax:** (250)479-4808. **E-mail:** editor@seniorlivingmag.com. **Website:** www.seniorlivingmag.com. **Contact:** Bobbie Jo Reid, managing editor. **100% freelance written.** Magazine published 12 times/year covering active 55+ living. Inspiration for people over 55. Monthly magazine distributed throughout British Columbia, extensive website, 2 annual 55+ Lifestyle Shows. Estab. 2004. Circ. 50,000. Byline given. Pays quarterly. No kill fee. Publishes an average of 2-3 months after acceptance. Editorial lead time 3 months. Submit seasonal material 6 months in advance. Accepts queries by e-mail. Accepts simultaneous submissions. Sample copy online. Guidelines available.

NONFICTION Needs historical, how-to, humor, inspirational, interview, personal experience, travel, profiles of inspiring people age 55+ who live in British Columbia. Special issues: Special issues: housing, travel, charitable giving, fashion. Does not want politics, religion, promotion of business, service or products, humor that demeans senior demographic or aging process. Query. Does not accept previously published material. Length: 500-1,200 words. **Pays $35-150 for assigned articles. Pays $35-150 for unsolicited articles.** Sometimes pays expenses (limit agreed upon in advance).

COLUMNS Buys 5-6 mss/year. Query with published clips. **Pays $25-50.**

$ JOURNAL PLUS

654 Osos St., San Luis Obispo CA 93401. (805)546-0609; (805)544-8711. **Fax:** (805)546-8827. **E-mail:** slojournal@fix.net. **Website:** slojournal.com. **Contact:** Steve Owens, publisher. **60% freelance written.** Monthly magazine that can be read online covering the 25-year old age group and up, but young-at-heart audience. "The *Journal Plus* is a combination of the *SLO County Journal* and *Plus Magazine*. It is the community magazine written for and by the local people of the Central Coast." Estab. 1981. Circ. 25,000. Byline given. Pays on publication. No kill fee. Publishes ms an average of 2 months after acceptance. Editorial lead time 2 months. Submit seasonal material 2 months in advance. Accepts queries by mail. Accepts simultaneous submissions. Responds in 2 weeks to queries; in 1 month to mss. Sample copy for 9x12 SAE with $2 postage. Guidelines online.

NONFICTION Needs historical, humor, interview, personal experience, travel, book reviews, entertainment, health. Special issues: Christmas (December); Travel (October, April). No finance, automotive, heavy humor, poetry, or fiction. **Buys 60-70 mss/year.** Send complete ms. Length: 600-1,400 words. **Pays $50-75.**

✪ $ $ MAISONNEUVE

Maisonneuve Magazine Association, 1051 Boulevard Decarie, P.O. Box 53527, St. Laurent QC H4L 5J9 Canada. **E-mail:** submissions@maisonneuve.org. **Website:** www.maisonneuve.org. **90% freelance written.** Quarterly magazine covering eclectic curiousity. *Maisonneuve* has been described as a new *New Yorker* for a younger generation, or as *Harper's* meets *Vice*, or as *Vanity Fair* without the vanity—but *Maisonneuve* is its own creature. *Maisonneuve*'s purpose is to keep its readers informed, alert, and entertained, and to dissolve artistic borders between regions, countries, languages, and genres. It does this by providing a diverse range of commentary across the arts, sciences, and daily and social life. The magazine has a balanced perspective and "brings the news" in a wide variety of ways. Estab. 2002. Circ. under 10,000. Byline given. Pays on publication. Offers 25% kill fee. Publishes ms an average of 4-6 months after acceptance. Editorial lead time 4 months. Submit seasonal material 8 months in advance. Accepts simultaneous submissions. Responds in 2 weeks to queries; in 3 months to mss. Sample copy online. Guidelines online.

NONFICTION Needs essays, general interest, historical, humor, interview, personal experience, photo feature. Submit ms via online submissions manager (maisonneuvemagazine.submittable.com) or by mail. Length: 50-5,000 words. **Pays 10¢/word.**

$ $ $ $ NATIONAL GEOGRAPHIC

P.O. Box 98199, Washington DC 20090-8199. (202)857-7000. **Fax:** (202)828-5460. **Website:** www.nationalgeographic.com. **Contact:** Susan Goldberg, editor in chief; David Brindley, managing editor. **60% freelance written. Prefers to work with published/established writers.** Monthly magazine for members of the National Geographic Society. Looking for timely articles written in a compelling, "eyewitness" style. Arresting photographs that speak to the beauty, mystery, and harsh realities of life on earth. Maps of unprecedented detail and accuracy. These are the hallmarks of *National Geographic* magazine. Estab.

1888. Circ. 6,800,000. Accepts queries by mail. Accepts simultaneous submissions. Guidelines online.

NONFICTION Query (500 words with clips of published articles). Do not send mss. Length: 2,000-8,000 words.

NATIONAL REVIEW

215 Lexington Ave., New York NY 10016. (212)679-7330. **E-mail:** submissions@nationalreview.com. **Website:** www.nationalreview.com. Accepts simultaneous submissions. Guidelines available on website.

NEWSWEEK

The Daily Beast, 251 W. 57th St., New York NY 10019. (212)445-4000. **Website:** www.newsweek.com. **Contact:** Kira Bindrim, managing editor. *Newsweek* is edited to report the week's developments on the newsfront of the world and the nation through news, commentary, and analysis. Estab. 1933. Circ. 3.2 million. No kill fee. Accepts simultaneous submissions.

COLUMNS Contact: myturn@newsweek.com. No longer accepting submissions for the print edition. To submit an essay to website, please e-mail. The My Turn essay should be: A) an original piece, B) 850-900 words, C) generally personal in tone, and D) about any topic, but not framed as a response to a Newsweek story or another My Turn essay. Submissions must not have been published elsewhere. Please include full name, phone number, and address with your entry. The competition is very stiff. Receives 600 entries per month and only prints 1 a week. **Pays $1,000 on publication.**

THE NEW YORKER

1 World Trade Center, New York NY 10007. **E-mail:** the-mail@newyorker.com. **Website:** www.newyorker.com. **Contact:** David Remnick, editor in chief. A quality weekly magazine of distinct news stories, articles, essays, and poems for a literate audience. Estab. 1925. Circ. 938,600. Pays on acceptance. No kill fee. Accepts queries by mail, e-mail. Responds in 3 months to mss. Subscription: $59.99/year (47 issues), $29.99 for 6 months (23 issues).

NONFICTION Submissions should be sent as PDF attachments. Do not paste them into the message field. Due to volume, cannot consider unsolicited "Talk of the Town" stories or other nonfiction.

FICTION Contact: fiction@newyorker.com. Publishes 1 ms/issue. Send complete ms by e-mail (as PDF attachment) or mail (address to Fiction Editor). **Payment varies.**

POETRY Contact: poetry@newyorker.com. Submit up to 6 poems at a time by e-mail (as PDF attachment) or mail (address to Poetry Department). **Pays top rates.**

THE NEW YORK TIMES MAGAZINE

620 Eighth Ave., New York NY 10018. (212)556-1234. **Fax:** (212)556-3830. **E-mail:** magazine@nytimes.com; nytnews@nytimes.com; executive-editor@nytimes.com. **Website:** www.nytimes.com/pages/magazine. **Contact:** Margaret Editor, public editor. *The New York Times Magazine* appears in the New York Times on Sunday. The 'Arts and Leisure' section appears during the week. The 'Op Ed' page appears daily. Circ. 1.8 million. No kill fee. Accepts simultaneous submissions.

THE OLD FARMER'S ALMANAC

Yankee Publishing, Inc., P.O. Box 520, Dublin NH 03444. (603)563-8111. **Website:** www.almanac.com. **Contact:** Janice Stillman, editor. **95% freelance written.** Annual magazine covering weather, gardening, history, oddities, and lore. *"The Old Farmer's Almanac* is the oldest continuously published periodical in North America. Since 1792, it has provided useful information for people in all walks of life: tide tables for those who live near the ocean; sunrise tables and planting charts for those who live on the farm or simply enjoy gardening; recipes for those who like to cook; and forecasts for those who don't like the question of weather left up in the air. The words of the *Almanac*'s founder, Robert B. Thomas, guide us still: 'Our main endeavor is to be useful, but with a pleasant degree of humour.'" Estab. 1792. Circ. 3,100,000. Byline given. Pays on acceptance. Offers 25% kill fee. Publishes ms an average of 9 months after acceptance. Editorial lead time 6 months. Submit seasonal material 1 year in advance. Accepts queries by mail. Accepts simultaneous submissions. Responds in 3 weeks to queries. Responds in 2 months to mss. Sample copy for $6 at bookstores or online. Guidelines online.

NONFICTION Needs general interest, historical, how-to. No personal recollections/accounts, personal/family histories. Query with published clips via mail or online contact form. Length: 800-2,500 words. **Pays 65¢/word.**

FILLERS Needs anecdotes, short humor. **Buys 1-2 mss/year.** Length: 100-200 words. **Pays $25.**

◎◎◎◎ PARADE

ParadeNet, Inc., 60 E. 42nd St., New York NY 10165-1910. (212)478-1910. **Website:** parade.com. **95% freelance written.** Weekly magazine for a general interest audience. *Parade* magazine is distributed by more than 600 Sunday newspapers, including the *Atlanta Journal & Constitution*, *The Baltimore Sun*, *Boston Globe*, *Chicago Tribune*, *Dallas Morning News*, *Houston Chronicle*, *The Los Angeles Times*, *The Miami Herald*, *The New York Post*, *The Philadelphia Inquirer*, *San Francisco Chronicle*, *Seattle Times & Post Intelligencer*, and *The Washington Post*. Estab. 1941. Circ. 22,000,000. Pays on acceptance. Offers kill fee. Kill fee varies in amount. Publishes ms an average of 5 months after acceptance. Editorial lead time 1 month. Accepts queries by mail, online submission form. Accepts simultaneous submissions. Sample copy and guidelines online.

NONFICTION Spot news events are not accepted, as *Parade* has a 2-month lead time. No fiction, fashion, travel, poetry, cartoons, nostalgia, regular columns, personal essays, quizzes, or fillers. Unsolicited queries concerning celebrities, politicians or sports figures are rarely assigned. **Buys 150 mss/year.** Query with published clips. Length: 1,200-1,500 words. **Pays very competitive amount.**

PEOPLE

Time, Inc., 1271 Avenue of the Americas, 28th Floor, New York NY 10020. (212)522-1212. **Fax:** (212)522-1359. **E-mail:** editor@people.com. **Website:** www.people.com. Weekly magazine. Designed as a forum for personality journalism through the use of short articles on contemporary news events and people. Circ. 3.7 million. No kill fee. Editorial lead time 3 months. Accepts simultaneous submissions.

◎◎ READER'S DIGEST

The Reader's Digest Association, Inc., Box 100, Pleasantville NY 10572. **E-mail:** letters@rd.com. **E-mail:** articleproposals@rd.com. **Website:** www.rd.com. *Reader's Digest* is an American general interest family magazine, published monthly. Estab. 1922. Circ. 4.6 million. Accepts queries by e-mail. Accepts simultaneous submissions. Guidelines online.

NONFICTION Accepts 1-page queries that clearly detail the article idea, with special emphasis on the arc of the story, interview access to the main characters, access to documents, etc. Looks for dramatic narratives, articles about everyday heroes, crime dramas, adventure stories. Include a separate page for writing credentials.

COLUMNS Life; @Work; Off Base, **pays $300.** Laugh; Quotes, **pays $100.** Address your submission to the appropriate humor category.

◎◎◎◎ READER'S DIGEST (CANADA)

1100 Rene Levesque Blvd. W, Montreal QC H3B 5H5 Canada. **E-mail:** editor@rd.com. **Website:** www.readersdigest.ca. **30-50% freelance written.** Monthly magazine of general interest articles and subjects. Estab. 1948. Circ. 1,000,000. Byline given. **Pays on acceptance for original works.** Pays on publication for pickups. Offers $500 (Canadian) kill fee. Submit seasonal material 5 months in advance. Accepts queries by mail, online submission form. Accepts simultaneous submissions. Guidelines online.

NONFICTION Needs general interest, how-to, humor, inspirational, personal experience, travel, crime, health. Query with published clips. Proposals can be mailed to the above address. We are looking for dramatic narratives, inspirational stories, articles about crime, adventure, travel and health issues. Download our writer's guidelines. If we are interested in pursuing your idea, an editor will contact you. Length: up to 2,500 words. **Pays $1/word (CDN) or more depending on story type.**

◎ REUNIONS MAGAZINE

P.O. Box 11727, Milwaukee WI 53211-0727. (414)263-4567. **Fax:** (414)263-6331. **E-mail:** editor@reunionsmag.com. **Website:** www.reunionsmag.com. **Contact:** Edith Wagner, editor. **85% freelance written.** Quarterly magazine covering reunions—all aspects and types. "*Reunions Magazine* is primarily for people actively planning family, class, military, and other reunions. We want easy, practical ideas about organizing, planning, researching/searching, attending, or promoting reunions." Estab. 1990. Circ. 20,000. Byline given. Pays on publication. Publishes ms an average of 1 year after acceptance. Editorial lead time 6 months. Submit seasonal material 1 year in advance. Accepts queries by mail, e-mail. Accepts simultaneous submissions. Responds in about 1 year. Sample copy and writer's guidelines for #10 SASE or online.

NONFICTION Needs how-to, humor, new product, personal experience, photo feature, travel, reunion recipes with reunion anecdote. **Buys 40 mss/year.** Query with published clips. Length: 500-2,500 (prefers work on the short side). **"Rarely able to pay anymore, but when we can pays $25-50."**

FILLERS Must be reunion-related. Needs anecdotes, facts, short humor. **Buys 20-40 fillers/year mss/year.** Length: 50-250 words. **Pays $5.**

$$$$ ROBB REPORT

CurtCo Robb Media, LLC, 29160 Heathercliff Rd., Suite #200, Malibu CA 90265. (310)589-7700. **Fax:** (310)589-7701. **E-mail:** editorial@robbreport.com. **Website:** www.robbreport.com. **60% freelance written.** Monthly lifestyle magazine geared toward active, affluent readers. Addresses upscale autos, luxury travel, boating, technology, lifestyles, watches, fashion, sports, investments, collectibles. "For over 30 years, *Robb Report* magazine has served as the definitive authority on connoisseurship for ultra-affluent consumers. *Robb Report* not only showcases the products and services available from the most prestigious luxury brands around the globe, but it also provides its sophisticated readership with detailed insight into a range of these subjects, which include sports and luxury automobiles, yachts, real estate, travel, private aircraft, fashion, fine jewelry and watches, art, wine, state-of-the-art home electronics, and much more. For connoisseurs seeking the very best that life has to offer, *Robb Report* remains the essential luxury resource." Estab. 1976. Circ. 104,000. Byline given. Pays on publication. Offers 25% kill fee. Submit seasonal material 5 months in advance. Accepts queries by mail, fax. Accepts simultaneous submissions. Responds in 2 months to queries; in 1 month to mss. Sample copy: $14, plus s&h.

NONFICTION Needs new product, travel. Special issues: Home (October); Recreation (March). **Buys 60 mss/year.** Query with published clips. Length: 500-2,000 words. **Pays $1/word.**

$$$$ SMITHSONIAN MAGAZINE

Capital Gallery, Suite 6001, MRC 513, P.O. Box 37012, Washington DC 20013. (202)275-2000. **E-mail:** smithsonianmagazine@si.edu. **Website:** www.smithsonianmag.com. **Contact:** Molly Roberts, photo editor; Jeff Campagna, art services coordinator. **90% freelance written.** Monthly magazine for associate members of the Smithsonian Institution; 85% with college education. *Smithsonian Magazine's* mission is to inspire fascination with all the world has to offer by featuring unexpected and entertaining editorial that explores different lifestyles, cultures and peoples, the arts, the wonders of nature and technology, and much more. The highly educated, innovative readers of *Smithsonian* share a unique desire to celebrate life, seeking out the timely as well as timeless, the artistic as well as the academic, and the thought-provoking as well as the humorous. Circ. 2.3 million. Pays on acceptance. Offers 33% kill fee. Publishes ms an average of 6 months after acceptance. Editorial lead time 2 months. Submit seasonal material 3 months in advance. Accepts simultaneous submissions. Sample copy for $5. Guidelines online.

NONFICTION Buys 120-130 feature (up to 5,000 words) and 12 short (500-650 words) mss/year. Use online submission form. *Smithsonian* magazine accepts unsolicited proposals from established freelance writers for features and some departments. Submit a proposal of 250 to 300 words as a preliminary query. Background information and writing credentials are helpful. The proposal text box on the Web submission form holds 10,000 characters (approximately 2,000 words), ample room for a cover letter and proposal. All unsolicited proposals are sent on speculation. Supporting material or clips of previously published work can be provided with links. Article length ranges from a 700-word humor column to a 4,000-word full-length feature. Considers focused subjects that fall within the general range of Smithsonian Institution interests, such as: cultural history, physical science, art and natural history. **Pays various rates per feature, $1,500 per short piece.**

COLUMNS Length: 1,000-2,000 words. Last Page humor, 550-700 words. **Buys 12-15 mss/year.** Use online submission form. **Pays $1,000-1,500.**

🌐⊘ TAKE 5

Bauer Media Group, 54-58 Park St., Sydney NSW 2000 Australia. (61)(2)9282-8089. **E-mail:** take5@bauer-media.com.au. **Website:** www.bauer-media.com.au/brands/take-5/. **Contact:** Paul Merrill, editor in chief. "*Take 5* is a weekly mix of exciting and emotional real-life stories, 40 puzzle prizes, and a good mix of traditional women's magazine fare. Each week, we tell stories of scandal, betrayal, love and loss, from quirky and fun tales to heartbreaking accounts of tragedy and crime. Written in their own voice, the magazine is a conduit for the readers to tell each other their stories, share their experiences and dream about winning a puzzle prize." Circ. 155,723. Accepts simultaneous submissions.

🌐$$ THAT'S LIFE!

H Bauer Publishing, Freepost LON12043, London England NW1 1YU United Kingdom. (44)(207)241-8000. **E-mail:** stories@thatslife.co.uk. **Website:** www.thatslife.co.uk. **Contact:** Sophie Hearsey, editor. "*that's life!* is packed with the most amazing true-life stories and fab puzzles offering big-money prizes including family sunshine holidays and even a car! We also have bright, up-to-date fashion, health, and beauty pages with top tips and readers' letters. And just to make sure we get you smiling too, there's our rib-tickling rude jokes and 'aren't men daft' tales." Estab. 1995. Circ. 550,000. No kill fee. Submit seasonal material 3 months in advance. Accepts queries by mail, online submission form. Responds in 6 weeks to mss. Guidelines by e-mail.

NONFICTION true-life stories, humor, health. Special issues: "Have you got a story to tell? It can be sexy, saucy, wicked or sad." Submit via online submissions form. **Pay varies.**

TIME

1271 Avenue of the Americas, New York NY 10020. **E-mail:** letters@time.com. **Website:** www.time.com. **Contact:** Nancy Gibbs, managing editor. Weekly magazine. *TIME* covers the full range of information that is important to people today—breaking news, national and world affairs, business news, societal and lifestyle issues, culture and entertainment news and reviews. Estab. 1923. Circ. 4 million. No kill fee. Accepts simultaneous submissions.

$$$ YES! MAGAZINE

284 Madrona Way NE, Suite 116, Bainbridge Island WA 98110. **E-mail:** editors@yesmagazine.org. **E-mail:** submissions@yesmagazine.org. **Website:** www.yesmagazine.org. **70% freelance written.** Quarterly magazine covering sustainability, social justice, grassroots activism, contemporary culture; nature, conservation, ecology, politics, and world affairs. "*YES! Magazine* documents how people are creating a more just, sustainable and compassionate world. Each issue includes articles focused on a theme—about solutions to a significant challenge facing our world—and a number of timely, non-theme articles. Our non-theme section provides ongoing coverage of issues like health, climate change, globalization, media reform, faith, democracy, economy and labor, social and racial justice and peace building. To inquire about upcoming themes, send an e-mail to submissions@yesmagazine.org; please be sure to type 'themes' as the subject line." Estab. 1997. Circ. 55,000. Byline given. Pays on publication. Rarely offers kill fee. Publishes ms an average of 1-6 months after acceptance. Editorial lead time 3-6 months. Submit seasonal material 2-6 months in advance. Accepts queries by e-mail. Accepts simultaneous submissions. Responds in 3 months. Sample copy and writer's guidelines online.

NONFICTION Needs book excerpts, opinion. "We don't want stories that are negative or too politically partisan." **Buys 30 mss/year mss/year.** Query with published clips. Length: 100-2,500 words. **Pays $50-1,250 for assigned articles. Pays $50-600 for unsolicited articles.**

COLUMNS Signs of Life (positive news briefs), 100-250 words; Commentary (opinion from thinkers and experts), 500 words; Book and film reviews, 500-800 words. **Pays $20-300.**

HEALTH & FITNESS

$$ AMERICAN FITNESS

15250 Ventura Blvd., Suite 200, Sherman Oaks CA 91403. (800)446-2322, ext. 200. **E-mail:** americanfitness@afaa.com. **Website:** www.afaa.com. **Contact:** Meg Jordan, editor. **75% freelance written.** Bimonthly magazine covering exercise and fitness, health, and nutrition. "We need timely, in-depth, informative articles on health, fitness, aerobic exercise, sports nutrition, age-specific fitness, and outdoor activity. Absolutely no first-person accounts. Need well-researched articles for professional readers." Estab. 1983. Circ. 42,900. Byline given. Pays 30 days after publication. No kill fee. Publishes ms an average of 6 months after acceptance. Submit seasonal material 4 months in advance. Accepts queries by mail, fax. Accepts simultaneous submissions. Responds in 2 months to queries. Sample copy for $4.50 and SASE with 6 first-class stamps.

NONFICTION Needs historical, inspirational, interview, new product, personal experience, photo feature, travel. No articles on unsound nutritional practices, popular trends, or unsafe exercise gimmicks. **Buys 18-25 mss/year.** Send complete ms. Length: 800-1,200 words. **Pays $200 for features, $80 for news.**

COLUMNS Research (latest exercise and fitness findings); Alternative paths (nonmainstream approaches to health, wellness, and fitness); Strength (latest breakthroughs in weight training); Clubscene (profiles and highlights of fitness club industry); Adventure (treks, trails, and global challenges); Food (low-fat/nonfat, high-flavor dishes); Homescene (home-workout alternatives); Clip 'n' Post (concise exercise research to post in health clubs, offices or on refrigerators). Length: 800-1,000 words. Query with published clips or send complete ms. **Pays $100-200.**

🌑🌑 HEALING LIFESTYLES & SPAS

P.O. Box 271207, Louisville CO 80027. (202)441-9558. **E-mail:** editorial@healinglifestyles.com. **Website:** www.healinglifestyles.com. **Contact:** Melissa Williams, editor in chief. **90% freelance written.** "*Healing Lifestyles & Spas* is a bimonthly magazine committed to healing, health, and living a well-rounded, more natural life. In each issue we cover retreats, spas, organic living, natural food, herbs, beauty, yoga, alternative medicine, bodywork, spirituality, and features on living a healthy lifestyle." Estab. 1996. Circ. 45,000. Pays on publication. No kill fee. Publishes ms an average of 2-10 months after acceptance. Editorial lead time 6 months. Submit seasonal material 6-9 months in advance. Accepts queries by mail, e-mail. Accepts simultaneous submissions. Responds in 6 weeks to queries.

NONFICTION Needs travel. No fiction or poetry. Query. Length: 1,000-2,000 words. **Pays $150-500, depending on length, research, experience, and availability and quality of images.**

COLUMNS All Things New & Natural (short pieces outlining new health trends, alternative medicine updates, and other interesting tidbits of information), 50-200 words; Urban Retreats (focuses on a single city and explores its spas and organic living features), 1,200-1,600 words; Health (features on relevant topics ranging from nutrition to health news and updates), 900-1,200 words; Food (nutrition or spa-focused food articles and recipes), 1,000-1,200 words; Ritual (highlights a specific at-home ritual), 500 words; Seasonal Spa (focuses on a seasonal ingredient on the spa menu), 500-700 words; Spa Origins (focuses on particular modalities and healing beliefs from around the world, 1,000-1,200 words; Yoga, 400-

800 words; Retreat (highlights a spa or yoga retreat), 500 words; Spa a la carte (explores a new treatment or modality on the spa menu), 600-1,000 words; Insight (focuses on profiles, theme-related articles, and new therapies, healing practices, and newsworthy items), 1,000-2,000 words. Query.

🌑🌑🌑🌑 HEALTH

Time, Inc., Southern Progress Corp., 1271 Avenue of Americas, New York NY 10020. **E-mail:** christine. mattheis@health.com; theresa_tamkins@health.com. **Website:** www.health.com. **Contact:** Christine Mattheis, senior editor; Theresa Tamkins, editor in chief. Magazine published 10 times/year covering health, fitness, and nutrition. Readers are predominantly college-educated women in their 30s, 40s, and 50s. Edited to focus not on illness but on wellness news, events, ideas, and people. Estab. 1987. Circ. 1,360,000. Byline given. Pays on acceptance. Offers 33% kill fee. Accepts queries by mail, e-mail. Accepts simultaneous submissions. Responds in 2 months to queries. Sample copy: $5. Guidelines for #10 SASE or via e-mail.

NONFICTION No unsolicited mss. **Buys 25 mss/year.** Query with published clips and SASE. Length: up to 1,200 words.

COLUMNS Body, Mind, Fitness, Beauty, Food.

HEALTH FREEDOM NEWS

National Health Federation, P.O. Box 688, Monrovia CA 91017. (626)357-2181. **Fax:** (626)303-0642. **E-mail:** contact-us@thenhf.com. **Website:** www.thenhf.com. **50-60% freelance written.** *Health Freedom News* is the quarterly magazine of the National Health Federation. It contains feature articles on the latest methods of alternative healing, threats to health, nutrition centers and makers of nutrition, health products, and more. Estab. 1982. Circ. 16,000. Byline given. Editorial lead time 2 months. Submit ms 2 months in advance. Accepts queries by mail, e-mail, fax. Accepts simultaneous submissions. Responds in 1-2 weeks on queries; in 1-2 months on mss. Sample copy: $5.

NONFICTION Needs essays, expose, general interest, humor, inspirational, interview. No product articles. Query. Length: 750-2,000 words.

COLUMNS Open to suggestions for new columns. Query.

🌑🌑🌑 IMPACT MAGAZINE

IMPACT Productions, 2007 Second St. SW, Calgary AB T2S 1S4 Canada. (403)228-0605. **E-mail:** editor@

impactmagazine.ca. **E-mail:** info@impactmagazine.ca. **Website:** www.impactmagazine.ca. **Contact:** Chris Welner, editor. **10% freelance written.** Bimonthly magazine covering fitness and sport performance. A leader in the industry, *IMPACT Magazine* is committed to publishing content provided by the best experts in their fields for those who aspire to higher levels of health, fitness, and sport performance. Estab. 1991. Circ. 90,000. Byline given. Pays 30 days after publication. Offers 25% kill fee. Publishes ms an average of 4-6 months after acceptance. Editorial lead time 6 months. Submit seasonal material 6 months in advance. Accepts queries by e-mail. Accepts simultaneous submissions. Responds in 4 weeks to queries. Sample copy and guidelines online.

NONFICTION Needs general interest, how-to, interview, new product, opinion, technical. **Buys 4 mss/year.** Query before submitting. Length: 600-1,800 words. **Pays 25¢/word maximum for assigned articles. Pays 25¢/word maximum for unsolicited articles.**

MEN'S HEALTH

Rodale, 33 E. Minor St., Emmaus PA 18098. (610)967-5171. **Fax:** (610)967-7725. **E-mail:** mhletters@rodale.com. **Website:** www.menshealth.com. **50% freelance written.** Magazine published 10 times/year covering men's health and fitness. *Men's Health* is a lifestyle magazine showing men the practical and positive actions that make their lives better, with articles covering fitness, nutrition, relationships, travel, careers, grooming, and health issues. Estab. 1986. Circ. 1,600,000. Pays on acceptance. Offers 25% kill fee. Accepts queries by mail, e-mail. Accepts simultaneous submissions. Responds in 3 weeks to queries. Guidelines for #10 SASE.

NONFICTION Buys 30 features/year; 360 short mss/year. Query with published clips. Length: 1,200-4,000 words for features; 100-300 words for short pieces. **Pays $1,000-5,000 for features; $100-500 for short pieces.**

COLUMNS Length: 750-1,500 words. **Buys 80 mss/year. Pays $750-2,000.**

NATURE & HEALTH

Yaffa Publishing, 17-21 Bellevue St., Surry Hills NSW 2010 Australia. (61)(2)9281-2333. **Fax:** (61)(2)9281-2750. **E-mail:** pamelaallardice@yaffa.com.au. **Website:** www.natureandhealth.com.au. **Contact:** Pamela Allardice, editor. Bimonthly magazine for people interested in maintaining a naturally healthy lifestyle. Circ. 30,000. Accepts simultaneous submissions.

NONFICTION Query.

OXYGEN

Robert Kennedy Publishing, 400 Matheson Blvd. W., Mississauga ON L5R 3M1 Canada. (905)507-3545; (888)254-0767. **Fax:** (905)507-2372. **Website:** www.oxygenmag.com. **70% freelance written.** Monthly magazine covering women's health and fitness. *Oxygen* encourages various exercise, good nutrition to shape, and condition the body. Estab. 1997. Circ. 340,000. Byline given. Pays on acceptance. Offers 25% kill fee. Publishes ms an average of 4 months after acceptance. Editorial lead time 3 months. Submit seasonal material 6 months in advance. Accepts queries by mail, fax. Accepts simultaneous submissions. Responds in 5 weeks to queries. Responds in 2 months to mss. Sample copy for $5.

NONFICTION Needs expose, how-to, humor, inspirational, interview, new product, personal experience, photo feature. No poorly researched articles that do not genuinely help the readers toward physical fitness, health, and physique. **Buys 100 mss/year.** Send complete ms with SASE and $5 for return postage. Length: 1,400-1,800 words. **Pays $250-1,000.**

COLUMNS Nutrition (low-fat recipes), 1,700 words; Weight Training (routines and techniques), 1,800 words; Aerobics (how-tos), 1,700 words. **Buys 50 mss/year.** Send complete ms. **Pays $150-500.**

REMEDYMD HEALTH GUIDES

Remedy Health Media, 750 Third Ave., 6th Floor, New York NY 10017. (212)695-2223. **Fax:** (212)695-2936. **Website:** www.remedyhealthmedia.com. Magazine published 8 times/year, dealing with specific and current health issues in each issue. See editorial calendar online for details. Accepts simultaneous submissions.

SPIRITUALITY & HEALTH MAGAZINE

Spirituality & Health Media, LLC, 444 Hana Hwy., Suite D, Kahului HI 96732. (231)933-5660. **E-mail:** editors@spiritualityhealth.com. **Website:** www.spiritualityhealth.com. **Contact:** Karen Bouris, editor in chief; Ilima Loomis, managing editor. Bimonthly magazine covering research-based spirituality and health. "We look for formally credentialed writers in their fields. We are nondenominational and non-proselytizing. We are not New Age. We appreciate well-written work that offers spiritual seekers from all different traditions help in their unique journeys." Estab. 1998. Circ. 95,000. Byline given. Pays on acceptance. Offers 25% kill fee. Editorial lead time 4 months. Submit seasonal material 6 months in advance. Accepts queries by e-mail. Accepts simultaneous submissions. Responds in 3-4 months to queries. Responds in 2-4 months to mss. Sample copy and writer's guidelines online.

NONFICTION Does not want proselytizing, New Age cures with no scientific basis, "how I recovered from a disease personal essays," psychics, advice columns, profiles of individual healers or practitioners, pieces promoting one way or guru, reviews, poetry or columns. Query.

💲 💲 ⊘   VIBRANT LIFE

Review and Herald Publishing Association, P.O. Box 5353, Nampa ID 83653-5353. (208)465-2579. **Fax:** (208)465-2531. **E-mail:** vibrantlife@pacificpress.com, hquintana@rhpa.org. **Website:** www.vibrantlife.com. **Contact:** Heather Quintana, editor. **80% freelance written. Enjoys working with published/established writers; works with a small number of new/unpublished writers each year.** Bimonthly magazine covering health articles (especially from a prevention angle and with a Christian slant). "Whether you are fit and vigorous or have just received a frightening diagnosis, *Vibrant Life* has health information that will help you move closer to the life you were designed to live. It is perfect for sharing with people who may have never heard of this Christian approach to whole-person health. It's a wonderful way to introduce people to God's plan for us to have harmony of mind, body, and spirit. You can give a subscription to neighbors, friends, or coworkers; order a stack to place in a local grocery store, business, or doctor's office; or use it as a part of local church health initiatives, such as blood drives or cooking classes." Estab. 1885. Circ. 30,000. Byline given. Pays on acceptance. Offers 50% kill fee. Submit seasonal material 9 months in advance. Accepts queries by mail, e-mail, fax. Accepts simultaneous submissions. Responds in 1 month to queries. Sample copy for $1. Guidelines online.

NONFICTION Needs interview. **Buys 50-60 feature articles/year and 6-12 short mss/year.** Send complete ms. Length: 500-1,500 words for features; 25-250 words for short pieces. **Pays $100-300 for articles.**

WEBMD THE MAGAZINE

WebMD, 111 8th Ave, 7th Floor, New York NY 10011. (212)624-3700. **Website:** www.webmd.com/magazine. **80% freelance written.** Bimonthly magazine covering health, lifestyle health, and well-being, some medical. Published by WebMD Health, *WebMD the Magazine* is the print sibling of the website WebMD.com. It aims to broaden the company-wide mandate: "Better information, better health." It is a health magazine, with a difference. It is specifically designed and written for people who are about to have what may be the most important conversation of the year with their physician or other medical professional. The magazine's content is therefore developed to be most useful at this critical point of care, to improve and enhance the dialogue between patient and doctor. Readers are adults (65% women, 35% men) in their 30s, 40s, and 50s (median age is 41) who care about their health, take an active role in their own and their family's wellness, and want the best information possible to make informed healthcare decisions. Estab. 2005. Circ. 1 million. Byline given. Pays on acceptance. Offers 30% kill fee. Publishes ms an average of 3 months after acceptance. Editorial lead time 3-4 months. Submit seasonal material 3-4 months in advance. Accepts queries by e-mail. Accepts simultaneous submissions. Sample copy online.

WEIGHT WATCHERS

14 W. 23rd St. #2, New York NY 10010. (212)929-7054. **Website:** www.weightwatchers.com/magazine. The official magazine of Weight Watchers International, an international company that offers various products and services to assist weight loss and service. Estab. 1963. Accepts simultaneous submissions.

WOMEN'S HEALTH

Rodale Inc., 400 South 10th St., Emmaus PA 18098. **E-mail:** womenshealth@rodale.com; whonline@womenshealthmag.com. **Website:** www.womenshealthmag.com. Magazine published 10 times/year for the woman who wants to reach a healthy, attractive weight. *Women's Health* reaches a new generation of women who don't like the way most women's magazines make them feel. Estab. 2005. Circ. 1.5 million. Accepts queries by e-mail. Accepts simultaneous submissions.

💲   WOMEN'S HEALTH & FITNESS

Blitz Publications, P.O. Box 4075, Mulgrave VIC 3170 Australia. (61)(3)9574-8999. **Fax:** (61)(3)9574-

8899. **E-mail:** rebecca@blitzmag.com.au. **Website:** www.womenshealthandfitness.com.au. **Contact:** Rebecca Long, editor. Monthly glossy magazine covering health, fitness, beauty, sex, and travel. *Women's Health & Fitness Magazine* is a holistic guide to a happier and healthier lifestyle, offering information on weight training, nutrition, mental well-being, health, beauty, fat loss, life coaching, home workouts, low-fat recipes, fitness fashion, fitness tips, diet, supplementation, natural remedies, pregnancy, and body shaping. Estab. 1994. Accepts simultaneous submissions.

NONFICTION Needs general interest, how-to, new product. Query.

❸❸❸❸ YOGA JOURNAL

Active Interest Media, Healthy Living Group, 475 Sansome St., Suite 850, San Francisco CA 94111. (415)591-0555. **Fax:** (415)591-0733. **E-mail:** queries@yjmag.com. **Website:** www.yogajournal.com. **Contact:** Kaitlin Quistgaard, editor in chief. **75% freelance written.** Magazine published 9 times a year covering the practice and philosophy of yoga. Estab. 1975. Circ. 300,000. Byline given. Pays within 90 days of acceptance. Offers kill fee. Offers kill fee on assigned articles. Publishes ms an average of 10 months after acceptance. Submit seasonal material 7 months in advance. Accepts queries by e-mail. Accepts simultaneous submissions. Responds in 6 weeks to queries if interested. Sample copy: $4.99. Guidelines on website.

NONFICTION Needs book excerpts, how-to, interview, opinion, photo feature, travel. Does not want unsolicited poetry or cartoons. "Please avoid New Age jargon and in-house buzz words as much as possible." **Buys 50-60 mss/year.** Query with SASE. Length: 3,000-5,000 words. **Pays $800-2,000.**

COLUMNS Om: Covers myriad aspects of the yoga lifestyle (150-400 words). This department includes Yoga Diary, a 250-word story about a pivotal moment in your yoga practice. Eating Wisely: A popular, 1,400-word department about relationship to food. Most stories focus on vegetarian and whole-foods cooking, nutritional healing, and contemplative pieces about the relationship between yoga and food. Yoga Scene: Featured on the back page of the magazine, this photo depicts some expression of your yoga practice. Please tell us where the photo is from, what was going on during the moment the photo was taken, and any other information that will help put the photo into context. E-mail a well-written query.

HISTORY

❸ THE ARTILLERYMAN

Jack W. Melton Jr. LLC, 96 Craig St., Suite 112-333, East Ellijay GA 30540. (706)940-2673. **E-mail:** mail@artillerymanmagazine.com. **Website:** www.artillerymanmagazine.com. **Contact:** Jack Melton, Publisher. **60% freelance written.** Quarterly magazine covering antique artillery, fortifications, and crew-served weapons 1750-1900 for competition shooters, collectors, and living history reenactors using artillery. Estab. 1979. Circ. 1,200. Byline given. Pays on publication. Publishes ms an average of 6 months after acceptance. Accepts queries by mail, e-mail, fax. Accepts simultaneous submissions. Responds in 3 weeks to queries. Sample copy online.

NONFICTION Needs historical, how-to, interview, photo feature, technical, travel. **Buys 12 mss/year.** Send complete ms. Length: 300 words minimum. **Pays $40-60.**

❸❸ GATEWAY

Missouri History Museum, P.O. Box 11940, St. Louis MO 63112. (314)746-4558. **Fax:** (314)746-4548. **E-mail:** kmcbride@mohistory.org. **Website:** www.mohistory.org. **Contact:** Keri McBride, managing editor. **75% freelance written.** Annual magazine covering Missouri history and culture. "*Gateway* is a popular cultural history magazine that is primarily a member benefit of the Missouri History Museum. Thus, we have a general audience with an interest in the history and culture of Missouri and St. Louis in particular." Estab. 1980. Circ. 9,000. Byline given. Publishes ms an average of 6 months-1 year after acceptance. Editorial lead time 6 months. Accepts queries by mail, e-mail. Accepts simultaneous submissions. Responds in 1 month to queries; in 2 months to mss. Sample copy: $10. Guidelines online.

NONFICTION Needs book excerpts, essays, historical, interview, photo feature, scholarly essays, Missouri biographies, viewpoints on events, first-hand historical accounts, regional architectural history, literary history. No genealogies. **Buys 4-6 mss/year.** Query with writing samples or complete ms. Length: 2,000-5,000 words.

❸ GOOD OLD DAYS

Annie's, 306 E. Parr Rd., Berne IN 46711. **Fax:** (260)589-8093. **E-mail:** editor@goodolddaysmagazine.

com. **Website:** www.goodolddaysmagazine.com. **Contact:** Mary Beth Weisenburger, editor. **75% freelance written.** Bimonthly magazine of first-person nostalgia, 1935-1960. "We look for strong narratives showing life as it was in the middle decades of the 20th century. Our readership is composed of nostalgia buffs, history enthusiasts, and the people who actually lived and grew up in this era." Byline given. Pays on contract. No kill fee. Publishes ms an average of 8 months after acceptance. Submit seasonal material 10 months in advance. Accepts queries by mail, e-mail, fax. Responds in 2 months to queries. Sample copy: $2. Guidelines online.

NONFICTION Needs historical, humor, personal experience, photo feature, favorite food/recipes, year-round seasonal material, biography, memorable events, fads, fashion, sports, music, literature, entertainment. No fiction accepted. **Buys 350 mss/year.** Query or send complete ms. Length: 500-1,500 words. **Pays $15-50, depending on quality and photos.**

HISTORY MAGAZINE

Moorshead Magazines, 82 Church St. S., Suite 101, Ajax ON L1S 6B3 Canada. **E-mail:** edward@moorshead.com. **E-mail:** edward@moorshead.com. **Website:** www.history-magazine.com. **Contact:** Edward Zapletal, publisher/editor. **99% freelance written.** Bimonthly magazine covering social history. A general interest history magazine, focusing on social history up to about 1960. Estab. 1999. Byline given. Pays on publication. Publishes ms an average of 6 months after acceptance. Editorial lead time 6 months. Submit seasonal material 6 months in advance. Accepts queries by mail, e-mail. Accepts simultaneous submissions. Responds in 1 month to queries. Sample PDF copy available on request. Guidelines online.

NONFICTION Needs book excerpts, historical. Does not want first-person narratives or revisionist history. **Buys 50 mss/year.** Query. Do not submit complete ms. "PLEASE NOTE: Submissions must be accompanied by the author's name, telephone number, postal address, and e-mail address. If not present in the ms, we will delay publication until we receive the necessary contact information." Length: 500-2,500 words. **Pays 8¢/word; $7/image submitted and used in the final layout.**

MHQ: THE QUARTERLY JOURNAL OF MILITARY HISTORY

World History Group, 19300 Promenade Dr., Leesburg VA 20176-6500. **E-mail:** mhq@historynet.com.

Website: www.historynet.com/magazines/mhq. **Contact:** Dr. Michael W. Robbins, editor. **100% freelance written.** Quarterly journal covering military history. "*MHQ* offers readers in-depth articles on the history of warfare from ancient times into the 21st century. Authoritative features and departments cover military strategies, philosophies, campaigns, battles, personalities, weaponry, espionage, and perspectives, all written in a lively and readable style. Articles are accompanied by classic works of art, photographs, and maps. Readers include serious students of military tactics, strategy, leaders, and campaigns, as well as general world history enthusiasts. Many readers are currently in the military or retired officers." Estab. 1988. Circ. 22,000. Byline given. Pays on publication. No kill fee. Editorial lead time 1 year. Submit seasonal material 1 year in advance. Accepts queries by mail, e-mail. Accepts simultaneous submissions. Sample copy: $6. Guidelines online.

NONFICTION Needs historical, personal experience, photo feature. No fiction or stories pertaining to collectibles or reenactments. **Buys 36 mss/year.** Query by mail or e-mail with published clips. Length: 1,500-6,000 words.

COLUMNS Artists on War (description of artwork of a military nature); Experience of War (first-person accounts of military incidents); Strategic View (discussion of military theory, strategy); Arms & Men (description of military hardware or unit), all up to 2,500 words. **Buys 16 mss/year.** Send complete ms.

MILITARY HISTORY

HistoryNet, 1600 Tysons Blvd., Suite 1140, Tysons VA 22102. (703)771-9400. **Fax:** (703)779-8345. **E-mail:** militaryhistory@historynet.com. **Website:** www.historynet.com/magazines/military_history. **Contact:** Stephen Harding, editor. **70% freelance written.** Magazine published 6 times/year covering world military history of all ages. "We strive to give the general reader accurate, highly readable, often narrative popular history, richly accompanied by period art." Byline given. Pays on publication. No kill fee. Submit seasonal material 1 year in advance. Accepts queries by mail, e-mail. Accepts simultaneous submissions. Sample: $6. Guidelines for #10 SASE or by e-mail.

NONFICTION Needs historical, interview. **Buys 20-30 mss/year.** Query by mail or e-mail with published clips. Length: 2,000-3,000 words with a 200- to 500-word sidebar.

COLUMNS Interview; What We Learned (lessons from history); Valor (those who have earned medals/awards); Hallowed Ground (battlegrounds of significance); and Reviews (books, video, games, all relating to military history). Length: 700-1,300 words.

💲💲 PERSIMMON HILL

1700 NE 63rd St., Oklahoma City OK 73111. (405)478-2250, ext. 213. **Fax:** (405)478-4714. **E-mail:** editor@nationalcowboymuseum.org. **Website:** www.nationalcowboymuseum.org. **Contact:** Judy Hilovsky. **70% freelance written. Prefers to work with published/established writers; works with a small number of new/unpublished writers each year.** Biannual magazine for an audience interested in Western art, Western history, ranching, and rodeo, including historians, artists, ranchers, art galleries, schools, and libraries. Publication of the National Cowboy and Western Heritage Museum. Estab. 1970. Circ. 7,500. Byline given. Pays on publication. No kill fee. Publishes ms an average of 18 months after acceptance. Accepts simultaneous submissions. Responds in 3 months to queries. Sample copy for $11. Writer's guidelines available on website.

NONFICTION Buys 50-75 mss/year. Query with clips. Length: 1,500 words. **Pays $150-300.**

💲 RENAISSANCE MAGAZINE

703 Post Rd., Fairfield CT 06824. (800)232-2224. **Fax:** (800)775-2729. **E-mail:** editortom@renaissancemagazine.com. **Website:** www.renaissancemagazine.com. **Contact:** Tom Hauck, editor. **90% freelance written.** Bimonthly magazine covering the history of the Middle Ages and the Renaissance. "Our readers include historians, reenactors, roleplayers, medievalists, and Renaissance Faire enthusiasts." Estab. 1996. Circ. 33,000. Byline given. Pays 3 weeks after publication. Publishes ms an average of 1 year after acceptance. Editorial lead time 6 months. Submit seasonal material 4 months in advance. Accepts queries by mail, e-mail, fax, phone. Accepts simultaneous submissions. Responds in 3 weeks to queries. Responds in 2 months to mss. Sample copy for $9. Guidelines online.

NONFICTION Needs essays, expose, historical, how-to, interview, new product, opinion, photo feature, religious, travel. **Buys 25 mss/year.** Query or send ms. Length: 2,000 words. **Pays 10¢/word and 1 contributor's copy.**

💲💲💲⊘ TRUE WEST

True West Publishing, Inc., 6702 E. Cave Creek Rd., Suite 5, P.O. Box 8008, Cave Creek AZ 85327.

(888)687-1881. **Fax:** (480)575-1903. **E-mail:** editor@twmag.com. **Website:** www.truewestmagazine.com. **Contact:** Meghan Saar, editor; Bob Boze Bell, executive editor. **45% freelance written. Works with a small number of new/unpublished writers each year.** Magazine published 10 times/year covering Western American history from prehistory 1800 to 1930. "We want reliable research on significant historical topics written in lively prose for an informed general audience. More recent topics may be used if they have a historical angle or retain the Old West flavor of trail dust and saddle leather. True West magazine's features and departments tie the history of the American West (between 1800-1930) to the modern western lifestyle through enticing narrative and intelligent analyses." Estab. 1953. Byline given. Pays on publication. Kill fee applicable only to material assigned by the editor, not for stories submitted on spec based on query written to the editor. 50% of original fee should the story have run in the publication. Editorial lead time 6 months. Accepts queries by mail, e-mail. Accepts simultaneous submissions. Sample copy for $3. Guidelines online.

NONFICTION No fiction, poetry, or unsupported, undocumented tales. **Buys 30 mss/year.** No unsolicited mss. *True West* seeks to establish long-term relationships with writers who conduct excellent research, provide a fresh look at an old subject, write well, hit deadlines and provide manuscripts at the assigned word length. Such writers tend to get repeat assignments. Send your query and accompanying MSS and photos to: **Meghan Saar**, editor-in-chief, via mail (SASE). Length: 1,500 words for features; 450 words for short features; 200 words for snapshot coverage. **Pays 25¢/word with a $20 payment for each photo the author provides that is published with the article and not already part of True West archives."**

FILLERS Needs anecdotes, facts, gags, newsbreaks, short humor. **Buys 30 mss/year.** Length: 50-300 words.

VIETNAM

World History Group, Vietnam Story Idea, 1600 Tysons Blvd., Suite 1140, Tysons VA 22102-4883. **E-mail:** vietnam@historynet.com. **Website:** www.historynet.com/vietnam. **Contact:** Chuck Springston, editor. **90% freelance written.** Bimonthly magazine providing in-depth and authoritative accounts of the many complexities that made the war in Vietnam unique, including the people, battles, strategies, perspectives, analysis, and weaponry. Estab. 1988. Circ. 46,000. Byline given. Pays on publication. No kill fee. Accepts queries by mail, e-mail. Accepts simultaneous submissions. Sample copy: $9.95. Guidelines for #10 SASE or by e-mail.

NONFICTION Needs historical, interview, personal experience. "Absolutely no fiction or poetry; we want straight history, as much personal narrative as possible, but not the gung-ho, shoot-'em-up variety, either." **Buys 24 mss/year.** Query by mail or e-mail with published clips. Length: up to 4,000 words with 500-word sidebar.

COLUMNS Arsenal (about weapons used, all sides); Personality (profiles of the players, all sides); Fighting Forces (various units or types of units: air, sea, rescue); Perspectives. Length: 2,000 words. Query.

💲💲 WILD WEST

World History Group, Wild West Story Idea, 1600 Tysons Blvd. Suite 1140, Tysons VA 22102-4883. **E-mail:** wildwest@historynet.com. **Website:** www.historynet.com. **Contact:** Gregory J. Lalire, editor. **95% freelance written.** Bimonthly magazine covering the history of the American frontier, from its eastern beginnings to its western terminus. "*Wild West* covers the popular (narrative) history of the American West—events, trends, personalities, anything of general interest." Estab. 1988. Circ. 83,500. Byline given. Pays on publication. No kill fee. Publishes ms an average of 2 years after acceptance. Editorial lead time 10 months. Submit seasonal material 1 year in advance. Accepts queries by mail, e-mail. Accepts simultaneous submissions. Responds in 3 months to queries; in 6 months to mss. Single issue: $9.95. Writer's guidelines for #10 SASE or online.

NONFICTION Needs historical. No excerpts, travel, etc. Articles can be adapted from book. No fiction or poetry. Nothing current. **Buys 36 mss/year.** Query. Length: 3,500 words with a 500-word sidebar. **Pays $300.**

COLUMNS Gunfighters & Lawmen, 2,000 words; Westerners, 2,000 words; Warriors & Chiefs, 2,000 words; Western Lore, 2,000 words; Guns of the West, 1,500 words; Artists West, 1,500 words; Books Reviews, 250 words. **Buys 36 mss/year.** Query. **Pays $150 for departments; book reviews paid by the word, minimum $40.**

🌑💲💲 WORLD WAR II

World History Group, World War II, 19300 Promenade Dr., Leesburg VA 20176. **E-mail:** worldwar2@ weiderhistorygroup.com; worldwar2@historynet.com. **Website:** www.historynet.com/magazines/world-war-ii-magazine. **Contact:** Karen Jensen, editor. **25% freelance written. "Most of our stories are assigned by our staff to professional writers. However, we do accept written proposals for features and for our Time Travel department."** Bimonthly magazine covering military operations in World War II—events, personalities, strategy, the home front, etc. Estab. 1986. Circ. 146,000. Byline given. Pays on acceptance. Offers kill fee. Accepts queries by mail, e-mail. Accepts simultaneous submissions. Writer's guidelines available on website or for SASE.

NONFICTION No fiction. **Buys 24 mss/year.** Query by mail or e-mail with published clips. "Your proposal should convince the editors to cover the subject, describe how you would treat the subject, and give the editors an opportunity to judge your writing ability. Please include your writing credentials and background with your proposal. A familiarity with recent issues of the magazine is the best guide to our editorial needs." Length: 2,500-4,000 words.

HOBBY & CRAFT

💲💲💲💲 AMERICAN CRAFT

American Craft Council, 1224 Marshall St. NE, Suite 200, Minneapolis MN 55413. (612)206-3115. **E-mail:** mmoses@craftcouncil.org. **E-mail:** query@craftcouncil.org. **Website:** www.americancraftmag.org. **Contact:** Monica Moses, editor in chief. **75% freelance written.** Bimonthly magazine covering art, craft, design. "American Craft Council is a national nonprofit aimed at supporting artists and craft enthusiasts. We want to inspire people to live a creative life. *American Craft* magazine celebrates the age-old human impulse to make things by hand." Estab. 1941. Circ. 40,000. Byline given. Pays on acceptance. Offers 25% kill fee. Publishes ms an average of 2 months after acceptance. Editorial lead time 4-6 months. Submit seasonal material 4-6 months in advance. Accepts queries by mail, e-mail. Accepts simultaneous submissions. Responds in 1 month to queries; in 2 months to mss. See writer's guidelines online.

NONFICTION Needs essays, interview, profile, travel, craft artist profiles, art travel pieces, interviews with creative luminaries, essays on creativity. Query with images. Include medium (glass, clay, fiber, metal, wood, paper, etc.) and department in subject line.

Length: 500-2,000 words. **Pays $1/word, according to assigned length.**

COLUMNS On Our Radar (profiles of emerging artists doing remarkable work); Product Placement (stylish, inventive, practical, and generally affordable goods in production and the people who design them); Shop Talk (Q&As with owners of galleries); Material Matters (an artist using unusual materials to make fine craft); Personal Paths (an artist doing very individual—even idiosyncratic—work from a personal motivation); Spirit of Craft (art forms that might not typically be considered fine craft but may entail the sort of devotion generally associated with craft); Craft in Action (artists or organizations using craft to make the world better); Crafted Lives (photo-driven Q&A with a person or people living in a particularly creative space); Ideas (Q&A with a thinker or practitioner whose views represent a challenge to the status quo); Wide World of Craft (foreign or U.S. travel destination for craft lovers). **Buys 10-12 mss/year.** Query with published clips.

⊜⊛ BEAD & BUTTON

Kalmbach Publishing, P.O. Box 1612, 21027 Crossroads Circle, Waukesha WI 53187-1612. **E-mail:** editor@beadandbutton.com. **Website:** www.beadandbutton.com. **Contact:** Julia Gerlach, editor. **50% freelance written.** "*Bead & Button* is a bimonthly magazine devoted to techniques, projects, designs, and materials relating to making beaded jewelry. Our readership includes both professional and amateur bead and button makers, hobbyists, and enthusiasts who find satisfaction in making beautiful things." Estab. 1994. Circ. 100,000. Byline given. Pays on acceptance. Offers $75 kill fee. Publishes ms an average of 4-12 months after acceptance. Editorial lead time 4-5 months. Accepts queries by e-mail. Accepts simultaneous submissions. Responds to queries in 4-6 weeks. Guidelines online.

NONFICTION Needs how-to, interview, profile. **Buys 20-25 mss/year.** Query. Length: 1,000-1,200 words. **Pays $75-400.**

⊜⊛ BLADE MAGAZINE

F+W, A Content and Ecommerce Company, 700 E. State St., Iola WI 54990-0001. (715)445-2214. **Fax:** (715)445-4087. **E-mail:** joe.kertzman@fwcommunity.com. **Website:** www.blademag.com. **Contact:** Joe Kertzman, managing editor. **5% freelance written.** Monthly magazine covering working and using collectible, popular knives. *Blade* prefers in-depth articles focusing on groups of knives, whether military, collectible, high-tech, pocket knives, or hunting knives, and how they perform. Estab. 1973. Circ. 39,000. Byline given. Pays on publication. No kill fee. Publishes ms an average of 9 months after acceptance. Editorial lead time 9 months. Submit seasonal material 9 months in advance. Accepts queries by mail, e-mail, fax. Accepts simultaneous submissions. Responds in 3 months to queries; in 6 months to mss. Sample copy: $4.99. Guidelines for SAE with 8x11 envelope and 3 first-class stamps.

NONFICTION Needs general interest, historical, how-to, interview, new product, photo feature, technical. "We assign profiles, show stories, hammer-in stories, etc. We don't need those. If you've seen the story on the Internet or in another knife or knife/gun magazine, we don't need it. We don't do stories on knives used for self-defense." Send complete ms. Length: 700-1,400 words. **Pays $150-300.**

FILLERS Needs anecdotes, facts, newsbreaks. **Buys 1-2 mss/year.** Length: 50-200 words. **Pays $25-50.**

⊙⊛⊜ CANADIAN WOODWORKING AND HOME IMPROVEMENT

Sawdust Media, Inc., 51 Maple Ave. N., RR #3, Burford ON N0E 1A0 Canada. (519)449-2444. **Fax:** (519)449-2445. **E-mail:** pfulcher@canadianwoodworking.com. **Website:** www.canadianwoodworking.com. **20% freelance written.** Bimonthly magazine covering woodworking; only accepts work from Canadian writers. Estab. 1999. Byline given. Pays on publication. Offers 50% kill fee. Accepts queries by e-mail. Accepts simultaneous submissions. Sample copy online. Guidelines available by e-mail.

NONFICTION Needs how-to, humor, inspirational, new product, personal experience, photo feature, technical. Does not want profile on a woodworker. Query. Length: 500-4,000 words. **Pays $100-600 for assigned articles. Pays $50-400 for unsolicited articles.**

⊜⊛ CLASSIC TOY TRAINS

Kalmbach Publishing Co., P.O. Box 1612, 21027 Crossroads Circle, Waukesha WI 53187. (262)796-8776, ext. 524. **Fax:** (262)796-1142. **E-mail:** manuscripts@classictoytrains.com. **Website:** www.classictoytrains.com. **Contact:** Carl Swanson, editor. **80% freelance written.** Magazine published 9 times/year covering collectible toy trains (O, S, Standard) like Lionel and

American Flyer, etc. "For the collector and operator of toy trains, *CTT* offers full-color photos of layouts and collections of toy trains, restoration tips, operating information, new product reviews and information, and insights into the history of toy trains." Estab. 1987. Circ. 40,000. Byline given. Pays on acceptance. Publishes ms an average of 1 year after acceptance. Editorial lead time 3 months. Submit seasonal material 6 months in advance. Accepts queries by mail, e-mail. Accepts simultaneous submissions. Responds in 3 weeks to queries; in 1 month to mss. Sample copy for $6.95, plus postage. Guidelines online.

NONFICTION Needs general interest, historical, how-to, interview, personal experience, photo feature, technical. **Buys 90 mss/year.** Query. Length: 500-3,000 words. **Pays $75-500.**

🟢🟢 DOLLHOUSE MINIATURES

68132 250th Ave., Kasson MN 55944. (507)634-3143. **E-mail:** traci@ashdown.co.uk. **Website:** www.dh-miniatures.com. **Contact:** Traci Nigon. **70% freelance written.** Monthly magazine covering dollhouse scale miniatures. *Dollhouse Miniatures* is America's best-selling miniatures magazine and the definitive resource for artisans, collectors, and hobbyists. It promotes and supports the large national and international community of miniaturists through club columns, short reports, and by featuring reader projects and ideas. Estab. 1971. Circ. 25,000. Byline given. Pays on acceptance. Editorial lead time 6 months. Submit seasonal material 6 months in advance. Accepts queries by mail, e-mail. Accepts simultaneous submissions. Responds in 1 month to queries; in 2 months to mss. Sample copy: $6.95, plus shipping. Guidelines available by e-mail.

NONFICTION Needs how-to, interview, photo feature. No essays or articles on miniature shops. **Buys 50-60 mss/year.** Send complete ms. Length: 500-1,500 words. **Pays $30-250 for assigned articles and up to $150 for unsolicited articles.**

🟢🟢 DOLLS

Jones Publishing, Inc., P.O. Box 5000, N7528 Aanstad Rd., Iola WI 54945. (715)445-5000. **Fax:** (715)445-4053. **E-mail:** joyceg@jonespublishing.com; jonespub@jonespublishing.com. **Website:** www.dollsmagazine.com. **Contact:** Joyce Greenholdt, editor. **75% freelance written.** Magazine published 10 times/year covering dolls, doll artists, and related topics of interest to doll collectors and enthusiasts. "*Dolls* enhances the joy of collecting by introducing readers to the best new dolls from around the world, along with the artists and designers who create them. It keeps readers up to date on shows, sales, and special events in the doll world. With beautiful color photography, *Dolls* offers an array of easy-to-read, informative articles that help our collectors select the best buys." Estab. 1982. Circ. 100,000. Byline given. Pays on publication. No kill fee. Accepts queries by mail, e-mail. Accepts simultaneous submissions. Responds in 1 month to queries.

NONFICTION Needs historical, how-to, interview, new product, photo feature. **Buys 55 mss/year.** Send complete ms. Length: 750-1,200 words. **Pays $75-300.**

F+W, A CONTENT + ECOMMERCE COMPANY (MAGAZINE DIVISION)

(formerly F+W Media, Inc.), 10151 Carver Rd., Suite 200, Cincinnati OH 45242. (513)531-2690. **E-mail:** dave.pulvermacher@fwcommunity.com. **Website:** www.fwcommunity.com. **Contact:** Dave Pulvermacher, Marketing Research. Each month, millions of enthusiasts turn to the magazines from F+W for inspiration, instruction, and encouragement. Readers are as varied as our categories, but all are assured of getting the best possible coverage of their favorite hobby. Publishes magazines in the following categories: antiques and collectibles (*Antique Trader*); astronomy (*Sky & Telescope*); automotive (*Military Vehicles, Old Cars Report Price Guide, Old Cars Weekly*); beading (*Beadwork*); coins and paper money (*Bank Note Reporter, Coins Magazine, Numismatic News, World Coin News*); construction (*Frame Building News, Metal Roofing Magazine, Rural Builder*); crocheting (*Interweave Crochet, Love of Crochet*); fine art (*Acrylic Artist, Collector's Guide, Drawing, Pastel Journal, Southwest Art, The Artist's Magazine, Watercolor Artist*); firearms and knives (*Blade, Gun Digest The Magazine*); genealogy (*Family Tree Magazine*); graphic design (*HOW Magazine, PRINT*); horticulture (*Horticulture*); jewelry (*Jewelry Stringing, Lapidary Journal Jewelry Artist, Step by Step Wire Jewelry*); knitting (*Interweave Knits, Knitscene, Love of Knitting*) militaria (*Military Trader*); mixed media (*Cloth Paper Scissors*); outdoors and hunting (*Deer & Deer Hunting, Trapper & Predator Caller*); quilting (*Fons & Porter's Easy Quilts, Fons & Porter's Love of Quilting, McCall's Quick Quilts, McCall's Quilting, Quilters Newsletter, Quilting Arts Magazine, Quiltmaker*); records and CDs (*Goldmine*); sewing (*Burda-*

style, Creative Machine Embroidery, Piecework, Sew News); spinning (*Spin-off*); sports (*Sports Collectors Digest*); woodworking (*Popular Woodworking Magazine*); weaving (*Handwoven*); writing (*Writer's Digest*). Accepts simultaneous submissions.

- Please see individual listings in the Consumer Magazines and Trade Journals sections for specific submission information about each magazine.

⊕⊕⊕ FAMILY TREE MAGAZINE

F+W, a Content and eCommerce Company, 10151 Carver Rd., Suite 200, Blue Ash OH 45242. (513)531-2690. **Fax:** (513)891-7153. **E-mail:** ftmedit@fwpubs.com. **Website:** www.familytreemagazine.com. **75% freelance written.** Magazine covering family history, heritage, and genealogy research. "*Family Tree Magazine* is a special-interest consumer magazine that helps readers discover, preserve, and celebrate their family's history. We cover genealogy, ethnic heritage, genealogy websites and software, photography and photo preservation, and other ways that families connect with their past." Estab. 1999. Circ. 75,000. Byline given. Pays on acceptance. Offers 25% kill fee. Publishes ms an average of 6 months after acceptance. Editorial lead time 8 months. Submit seasonal material 8 months in advance. Accepts queries by mail, e-mail. Responds in 6-8 weeks to queries. Sample copy: $8 from website. Guidelines online.

NONFICTION Needs book excerpts, historical, how-to, new product, technical. Does not publish personal experience stories (except brief stories in the Tree Talk column, which does not pay) or histories of specific families. Does not cover general family or parenting topics. **Buys 40 mss/year.** Query with a specific story idea and published clips. Length: 250-4,500 words. **Pays up to $800.**

⊕⊕ FIBRE FOCUS

The Ontario Handweavers & Spinners, 1188 Walker Lake Dr., RR4, Huntsville ON P1H 2J6 Canada. **E-mail:** ffeditor@ohs.on.ca. **Website:** www.ohs.on.ca. **Contact:** Dawna Beatty, editor. **75% freelance written.** Quarterly magazine covering handweaving, spinning, basketry, beading, and other fiber arts. "Our readers are weavers and spinners who also do dyeing, knitting, basketry, feltmaking, papermaking, sheep raising, and craft supply. All articles deal with some aspect of these crafts." Estab. 1957. Circ. 700. Byline given. Pays within 30 days after publication. Publishes

ms 2-5 months after acceptance. Editorial lead time 3 months. Submit seasonal material 6 months in advance. Accepts simultaneous submissions. Responds in 1 month to queries. Sample copy: $8 (Canadian). Guidelines online.

NONFICTION Needs historical, how-to, interview, new product, opinion, personal experience, photo feature, profile, reviews, technical, travel. **Buys 40-60 mss/year.** Contact the *Fibre Focus* editor before undertaking a project or an article. Mss may be submitted c/o Dawna Beatty by e-mail for anything you have to contribute for upcoming issues. Feature article deadlines: December 31, March 31, June 30, and September 15. Length: varies, but generally 600-1,800 words. **Pays $30 (Canadian)/published page.**

⊕ FINESCALE MODELER

Kalmbach Publishing Co., 21027 Crossroads Circle, P.O. Box 1612, Waukesha WI 53187-1612. (414)796-8776. **Website:** www.finescale.com. **80% freelance written. Eager to work with new/unpublished writers.** Magazine published 10 times/year devoted to how-to-do-it modeling information for scale model builders who build non-operating aircraft, tanks, boats, automobiles, figures, dioramas, and science fiction and fantasy models. Circ. 60,000. Byline given. Pays on acceptance. No kill fee. Publishes ms an average of 14 months after acceptance. Accepts simultaneous submissions. Responds in 6 weeks to queries. Responds in 3 months to mss. Sample copy with 9x12 SASE and 3 first-class stamps. Guidelines available on website.

NONFICTION Needs how-to, technical. Query or send complete ms via www.contribute.kalmbach.com. Length: 750-3,000 words. **Pays $60/published page minimum.**

COLUMNS *FSM* Showcase (photos plus description of model); *FSM* Tips and Techniques (model building hints and tips). **Buys 25-50 mss/year.** Send complete ms. **Pays $25-50.**

HANDWOVEN

F+W, a Content and eCommerce Company, 4868 Innovation Dr., Fort Collins CO 80525. **E-mail:** aosterhaug@interweave.com; cgarton@interweave.com. **Website:** www.weavingtoday.com. **Contact:** Anita Osterhaug, editor; Christina Garton, assistant editor. "The main goal of *Handwoven* articles is to inspire our readers to weave. Articles and projects should be accessible to weavers of all skill levels, even when the material is technical. The best way to prepare an article for *Handwoven* is to study the format and style of articles in recent issues." Pays on acceptance. Editorial lead time is 6-12 months. Accepts queries by mail, e-mail. Responds in 6 weeks to queries. Guidelines available on website.

NONFICTION Special issues: Query or submit full ms by e-mail or mail. Include written intro, relevant photos or other visuals (include photo credits), 25-word author bio, and photo.

COLUMNS Roving Reporters, What's Happening, Spotlight. Submit materials to Christina Garton, assistant editor.

INTERWEAVE CROCHET

F+W, a Content and eCommerce Company, 4868 Innovation Dr., Fort Collins CO 80525. **E-mail:** crochet@interweave.com. **Website:** www.crochetme.com. **Contact:** Dana Bincer. "*Interweave Crochet* is a quarterly publication for all those who love to crochet. In each issue we present beautifully finished projects, accompanied by clear step-by-step instructions, as well as stories and articles of interest to crocheters. The projects range from quick but intriguing projects that can be accomplished in a weekend to complex patterns that may take months to complete. Engaging and informative feature articles come from around the country and around the world. Fashion sensibility and striking examples of craft technique are important to us." Pays on publication. Accepts queries by mail. Guidelines available on website.

NONFICTION Special issues: "We are interested in articles on a broad range of topics, including technical pieces, profiles of inspiring crochet designers, and features about regions of the world where crochet has played or continues to play an important role." See website for current calls for submission. Query by mail. Include submission form (available online). "Please send a detailed proposal—complete outline, written description—to give us a clear idea of what to expect in the finished piece."

INTERWEAVE KNITS

Interweave Press, 201 E. Fourth St., Loveland CO 80537. **Website:** www.knittingdaily.com. *Interweave Knits* is a quarterly publication of Interweave Press for all those who love to knit. In each issue we present beautifully finished projects, accompanied by clear step-by-step instruction, and stories and articles of interest to knitters. The projects range from quick but intriguing items that can be accomplished in a weekend, to complex patterns that may take months to complete. Feature articles (personally arresting but information rich) come from around the country and around the world. Fashion sensibility and striking examples of craft technique are important to us. *Interweave Knits* is published quarterly. Pays on publication. Editorial lead time is 6-12 months. Responds in 6 weeks to queries. Guidelines available on website.

NONFICTION Special issues: "We are interested in articles of all lengths on a broad range of topics, including technical pieces; profiles of inspiring knitwear designers and others in textile industries; and features about regions of the world where knitting has played or continues to play an important role. We take knitting seriously and want articles that do the same. The best way to understand what we're looking for is to read a recent issue of the magazine carefully. For all article queries, send a detailed proposal: For shorter submissions, a brief description will do; for feature articles, send an outline and a sample paragraph or two. If the proposal is accepted, and once we've made any adjustments to the concept and agreed on the details, you will begin work on the article." Query by mail. Include submission form (available online). Do not address queries to Eunny Jang. "Beyond the Basics" (useful, accurate, high-quality technical information; 2,000-2,200 words); "Ravelings" (the personal side of knitting; 700-750 words, send whole articles)

COLUMNS "Knitted Artifact" (examines a knitted artifact, exploring the societal and cultural importance of the craft; 250-300 words); "Where it Comes From (educates readers about fiber and yarn; 250-300 words); "Yarn Review" (1,200-1,400 words); Profiles (showcasing a designer; 1,500-1,800 words).

🟡🟡 KITPLANES

P.O. Box 1295, Dayton NV 89403. **E-mail:** editorial@kitplanes.com. **Website:** www.kitplanes.com. **Contact:** Paul Dye, editor in chief; Mark Schrimmer, managing editor. **50% freelance written. Eager to work with new/unpublished writers.** Monthly magazine covering self-construction of private aircraft for pilots and builders. Estab. 1984. Circ. 72,000. Byline given. Pays on publication. Publishes ms an average of 3 months after acceptance. Submit seasonal material 6 months in advance. Accepts queries by mail, e-mail. Accepts simultaneous submissions. Responds in 1 month to queries; in 6 weeks to mss. Sample copy: $6. Guidelines online.

NONFICTION Needs general interest, how-to, interview, new product, personal experience, photo feature, technical. No general-interest aviation articles, or "My First Solo" type of articles. **Buys 80 mss/year.** Query. Interested in articles on all phases of aircraft construction, from basic design to flight trials to construction technique in wood, metal, and composite. Length: varies, but feature articles average about 2,000 words. **Pays $250-1,000, including story photos.**

🚫 LOST TREASURE, INC.

P.O. Box 451589, Grove OK 74345. (866)469-6224. **Fax:** (918)786-2192. **E-mail:** managingeditor@losttreasure.com. **Website:** www.losttreasure.com. **Contact:** Carla Nielsen, managing editor. **75% freelance written.** Monthly and annual magazines covering lost treasure. Estab. 1966. Circ. 55,000. Byline given. Pays on publication. Accepts queries by mail, e-mail, fax. Accepts simultaneous submissions. Responds in 1 month to queries; in 2 months to mss. Sample copy for #10 SASE. Submission guidelines can be requested by e-mailing managingeditor@losttreasure.com.

NONFICTION Buys 225 mss/year. Query on *Treasure Cache* only. "Will buy articles, photographs, and cartoons that meet our editorial approval." Enclose SASE with all editorial submissions. Length: 1,000-2,000 words. **Pays 4¢/word.**

MCCALL'S QUILTING

Primedia Enthusiast Group, 741 Corporate Circle, Suite A, Golden CO 80401. (303)278-1010. **Fax:** (303)277-0370. **Website:** www.mccallsquilting.com. Bimonthly magazine covering quiltmaking. Attracts quilters of all skill levels with a variety of complete, how-to quilting projects, including bed size quilts, wall hangings, wearables, and small projects. Estab. 1993. Circ. 162,000. No kill fee. Editorial lead time 6-9 months. Submit seasonal material 6-9 months in advance. Accepts queries by mail. Accepts simultaneous submissions. Sample copy for $5.95. Guidelines by e-mail.

🚫🚫 MILITARY VEHICLES

F+W Media, Inc., 700 E. State St., Iola WI 54990-0001. (715)445-4612. **Fax:** (715)445-4087. **E-mail:** john.adams-graf@fwmedia.com. **Website:** www.militarytrader.com. **Contact:** John Adams-Graf, editor. **50% freelance written.** Bimonthly magazine covering historic military vehicles. Dedicated to serving people who collect, restore, and drive historic military vehicles. Estab. 1987. Circ. 18,500. Byline given. Pays on publication. No kill fee. Publishes ms an average of 1 month after acceptance. Accepts queries by mail, e-mail. Accepts simultaneous submissions. Responds in 1 week to queries. Responds in 1 month to mss. Sample copy for $5.

NONFICTION Needs historical, how-to, technical. **Buys 20 mss/year.** Send complete ms. Length: 1,300-2,600 words. **Pays $0-200.**

COLUMNS Pays $0-75.

🚫 MODEL CARS MAGAZINE

Golden Bell Press, 2403 Champa St., Denver CO 80205. (808)754-1378. **E-mail:** gregg@modelcarsmag.com. **Website:** www.modelcarsmag.com. **25% freelance written.** Magazine published 9 times/year covering model cars, trucks, and other automotive models. *Model Cars Magazine* is the how-to authority for the automotive modeling hobbiest. This magazine is on the forefront of the hobby, the editorial staff are model car builders, and every single one of the writers has a passion for the hobby that is evident in the articles and stories that we publish. This is the model car magazine written by and for model car builders. Estab. 1999. Circ. 7,000. Byline given. Pays on publication. Publishes ms an average of 2-3 months after acceptance. Editorial lead time 2-3 months. Accepts queries by mail, e-mail. Accepts simultaneous submissions. Sample copy online. Guidelines online.

NONFICTION Needs how-to. Send ms or queries via e-mail or to *Model Cars Magazine*, P.O. Box 89530, Honolulu, HI 96830. Length: 600-3,000 words. **Pays $50/page. Pays $25/page for unsolicited articles.**

🚫 NATIONAL COMMUNICATIONS MAGAZINE

SCAN Services Co., P.O. Box 1, Aledo IL 61231-0001. (309)228-8000. **Fax:** (888)287-SCAN. **E-mail:** editor@NatComMag.com. **E-mail:** editor@NatComMag.com. **Website:** www.NatComMag.com. **Contact:** Chuck Gysi, editor and publisher. **50% freelance written.** We cover scanner radios and listening (VHF/UHF), citizens band (CB) radio and other hobby two-way radio services such as GMRS, FRS and MURS. National Communications Magazine was created for the hobby radio user. Estab. 1988. Circ. 5,000. Byline given. Pays immediately on publication. No kill fee. Publishes ms an average of 2 months after acceptance. 3 months.

Submit seasonal material 3 months in advance. Accepts queries by e-mail. One day to one week. Current issue sample copy: $6. Free recent PDF sample download at www.nat-com.org/sample.pdf. Inquire before writing with an outline of your proposed article. We're also interested in working with new authors, but we like to work with them in shaping articles before they are started. Photos and graphics are needed for all articles.

NONFICTION Contact: Chuck Gysi. Needs how-to, interview, new product, personal experience, photo feature, technical. Does not want articles off topic of the publication's audience (radio hobbyists). If you aren't writing about police scanners, CB radios, or two-way radios and don't know our audience, we're not interested in your article. It's essential to know your subject matter well. **Buys 18 mss/year.** Query by e-mail only. Length: 2,500 to 3,000 words. **Pays $75 or more.** No expenses paid.

$$ PAPER CRAFTS MAGAZINE

Primedia Magazines, 14512 S. Center Point Way, Suite 600, Bluffdale UT 84065. (801)816-8300. **Fax:** (801)816-8302. **E-mail:** editor@papercraftsmag.com. **Website:** www.papercraftsmag.com. **Contact:** Jennifer Schaerer, editor-in-chief; Kerri Miller, managing editor. Magazine published 10 times/year designed to help readers make creative and rewarding handmade crafts. The main focus is fresh, craft-related projects our reader can make and display in her home or give as gifts. Estab. 1978. Circ. 300,000. Byline given. Pays on acceptance. Editorial lead time 6 months. Accepts queries by mail, e-mail. Accepts simultaneous submissions. Responds in 1 month to queries. Guidelines for #10 SASE and available online.

NONFICTION Needs how-to. **Buys 300 mss/year.** Query with photo or sketch of how-to project. Do not send the actual project until request. **Pays $100-500.**

$$ POPULAR WOODWORKING MAGAZINE

F+W, A Content + Ecommerce Company, 8469 Blue Ash Rd., Suite 100, Cincinnati OH 45236. (513)531-2690, ext. 11348. **E-mail:** megan.fitzpatrick@fwcommunity.com. **Website:** www.popularwoodworking.com. **Contact:** Megan Fitzpatrick. **75% freelance written.** Magazine published 7 times/year. "*Popular Woodworking Magazine* invites woodworkers of all skill levels into a community of professionals who share their hard-won shop experience through in-depth projects and technique articles, which help readers hone their existing skills and develop new ones for both hand and power tools. Related stories increase the readers' understanding and enjoyment of their craft. Any project submitted must be aesthetically pleasing, of sound construction, and offer a challenge to readers. On the average, we use 5 freelance features per issue. Our primary needs are 'how-to' articles on woodworking. Our secondary need is for articles that will inspire discussion concerning woodworking. Tone of articles should be conversational and informal but knowledgeable, as if the writer is speaking directly to the reader. Our readers are the woodworking hobbyist and small woodshop owner. Writers should have an extensive knowledge of woodworking and excellent woodworking techniques and skills." Estab. 1981. Circ. 150,000. Byline given. Pays on acceptance. No kill fee. Publishes ms an average of 10 months after acceptance. Submit seasonal material 6 months in advance. Accepts queries by mail, e-mail. Responds in 2 months to queries. Sample copy: $6.99 plus 9x12 SAE with 6 first-class stamps, or online. Guidelines online.

NONFICTION Needs how-to, profile, technical. No tool reviews. **Buys 35 mss/year.** Query first; see guidelines and sample query on website. Length: 1,200-2,500 words. **Pay starts at $275/published page.**

COLUMNS Tricks of the Trade (helpful techniques) 250 words; End Grain (thoughts on woodworking as a profession or hobby, can be humorous or serious) 500-550 words. **Buys 20 mss/year.** Query. **Pays $350 for End Grain and $50-100 for Tricks of the Trade.**

$ QST

American Radio Relay League, 225 Main St., Newington CT 06111. (860)594-0200. **Fax:** (860)594-0259. **E-mail:** qst@arrl.org. **Website:** www.arrl.org. **Contact:** Steve Ford, editor. **90% freelance written.** Monthly magazine covering amateur radio. "*QST* is the monthly membership journal of ARRL, the national association for amateur radio, covering subjects of interest to amateur ('ham') radio operators." Estab. 1915. Circ. 150,000. Byline given. Pays on publication. No kill fee. Publishes ms an average of 6 months after acceptance. Editorial lead time 6 months. Submit seasonal material 6 months in advance. Accepts queries by mail, e-mail, fax, phone. Accepts simultaneous submissions. Responds in 1 week to queries; in 1 month to mss. Guidelines available online at: www.arrl.org/qst-author-guide.

NONFICTION Needs general interest, how-to, technical. Send complete ms by mail or e-mail. Length: 900-3,000 words. **Pays $65/published page.**

💲 SCALE AUTO

Kalmbach Publishing Co., 21027 Crossroads Circle, P.O. Box 1612, Waukesha WI 53187-1612. (262)796-8776. **Fax:** (262)796-1383. **E-mail:** jhaught@kalmbach.com. **Website:** www.scaleautomag.com. **70% freelance written.** Bimonthly magazine covering model car building. We are looking for model builders, collectors, and enthusiasts who feel their models and/or modeling techniques and experiences would be of interest and benefit to our readership. Estab. 1979. Circ. 35,000. Byline given. Pays on publication. Publishes ms an average of 1 year after acceptance. Editorial lead time 4 months. Submit seasonal material 4 months in advance. Accepts queries by mail, e-mail, fax, phone. Accepts simultaneous submissions. Responds in 3 months to queries. Responds in 3 months to mss. Sample copy online. Guidelines online.

NONFICTION Needs book excerpts, historical, how-to, interview, personal experience, photo feature, technical. Query or send complete ms Length: 750-3,000 words.

COLUMNS **Buys 50 mss/year.** Query.

SPIN-OFF

Interweave Press, 201 E. 4th St., Loveland CO 80537-5655. **E-mail:** spinoff@interweave.com. **Website:** www.spinningdaily.com. "*Spin-Off* is a quarterly magazine devoted to the interests of handspinners at all skill levels. Informative articles in each issue aim to encourage the novice, challenge the expert, and increase every spinner's working knowledge of this ancient and complex craft." Pays on publication. Editorial lead time is 6-12 months. Responds in 6 months to ms. Guidelines available on website.

NONFICTION Special issues: Wants articles on the following subjects: spinning tips (400 words or less); spinning basics (1,200 words); back page essay (650 words); methods for dyeing with natural and chemical dyes; tools for spinning and preparing fibers; fiber basics (2,000 words); ideas for using handspun yarn in a variety of techniques; profiles of people who spin; a gallery of your work; tips on blending fibers; the history and/or cultural role of spinning. Query or submit

full ms by e-mail or mail. Length: 200-2,700 words. **Pays $50/published page.**

💲💲 TEDDY BEAR & FRIENDS

P.O. Box 5000, Iola WI 54945-5000. (800)331-0038, ext. 150. **Fax:** (715)445-4053. **E-mail:** joyceg@jonespublishing.com. **Website:** www.teddybearandfriends.com. **Contact:** Joyce Greenholdt, editor. **65% freelance written. Works with a small number of new/unpublished writers each year.** Bimonthly magazine on teddy bears for collectors, enthusiasts, and bearmakers. Estab. 1985. Byline given. Payment upon publication on the last day of the month the issue is mailed. Submit seasonal material 6 months in advance. Accepts simultaneous submissions. Sample copy and writer's guidelines for $2 and 9x12 SAE.

NONFICTION Needs historical, how-to, interview. No articles from the bear's point of view. **Buys 30-40 mss/year.** Query with published clips. Length: 900-1,500 words. **Pays $100-350.**

💲💲 THREADS

Taunton Press, 63 S. Main St., P.O. Box 5506, Newtown CT 06470. (203)426-8171. **Fax:** (203)426-3434. **E-mail:** th@taunton.com. **Website:** www.threadsmagazine.com. Bimonthly magazine covering garment sewing, garment design, and embellishments (including quilting and embroidery). Written by sewing experts; magazine is geared primarily to intermediate/advanced sewers. "We're seeking proposals from hands-on authors who first and foremost have a skill. Being an experienced writer is of secondary consideration." Estab. 1985. Circ. 129,000. Byline given. Offers $150 kill fee. Editorial lead time minimum 4 months. Accepts simultaneous submissions. Responds in 1-2 months to queries. Guidelines online.

NONFICTION Send proposal that includes: "a brief 1- or 2-paragraph summary; an outline of the ideas and points you'll cover; sample photographs of work illustrating the topic (quick snapshots are fine) or supporting fabric swatches if you have them. **Payment varies.**

COLUMNS Product reviews; book reviews; Tips; Closures (stories of a humorous nature). Query. **Closures pays $150/page. Each sewing tip printed pays $25.**

⊘ VOGUE KNITTING

Soho Publishing Co., Inc., 161 Avenue of the Americas, Suite 1301, New York NY 10013. (212)937-2555.

Fax: (646)336-3960. **E-mail:** editors@vogueknitting.com. **Website:** www.vogueknitting.com. Bimonthly magazine created for participants in and enthusiasts of high-fashion knitting. Circ. 175,000. No kill fee. Accepts simultaneous submissions.

$ WESTERN & EASTERN TREASURES

People's Publishing Co., Inc., P.O. Box 647, Pacific Grove CA 93950-0647. **E-mail:** editor@wetreasures.com. **Website:** www.wetreasures.com. **100% freelance written.** Monthly magazine covering hobby/sport of metal detecting/treasure hunting. "*Western & Eastern Treasures* provides concise yet comprehensive coverage of every aspect of the sport/hobby of metal detecting and treasure hunting with a strong emphasis on current, accurate information; innovative, field-proven advice and instruction; and entertaining, effective presentation." Estab. 1966. Circ. 50,000. Byline given. Pays on publication. No kill fee. Publishes ms an average of 4+ months after acceptance. Editorial lead time 4 months. Submit seasonal material 3-4 months in advance. Responds in 2 months to mss. Sample copy for SAE with 9x12 envelope and 5 first-class stamps. Guidelines for #10 SASE or online.

NONFICTION Needs how-to, personal experience. Special issues: *Silver & Gold Annual* (editorial deadline February each year)—looking for articles 1,500+ words, plus photos on the subject of locating silver and/or gold using a metal detector. No fiction, poetry, or puzzles. **Buys 150+ mss/year.** Send complete ms by e-mail or mail (include SASE). Length: 1,000-2,000 words. **Pays 5¢/word.**

$$ WOOD MAGAZINE

Meredith Corporation, 1716 Locust St., LS221, Des Moines IA 50309. **E-mail:** woodmail@woodmagazine.com. **Website:** www.woodmagazine.com. **3% freelance written.** Magazine published 7 times/year covering woodworking. *Wood* manuscripts are friendly, informative, authoritative in the subject of woodworking, and full of helpful service-related content. Estab. 1984. Circ. 550,000. Byline given. Pays on publication. Editorial lead time 2 months. Submit seasonal material 1 year in advance. Accepts queries by e-mail. Accepts simultaneous submissions. Responds in 3 weeks to queries. Responds in 3 weeks to mss.

NONFICTION Does not want nonwoodworking. **Buys 3-4 mss/year.** Query. Length: 500-2,000 words. **Pays $300/page.**

HOME & GARDEN

$$ THE AMERICAN GARDENER

American Horticultural Society, 7931 E. Boulevard Dr., Alexandria VA 22308-1300. (703)768-5700. **E-mail:** editor@ahs.org;. **E-mail:** editor@ahs.org. **Website:** www.ahs.org. **Contact:** David Ellis, Editor. **60% freelance written.** Bimonthly, 64-page, four-color magazine covering gardening and horticulture. "This is the official publication of the American Horticultural Society (AHS), a national, nonprofit, membership organization for gardeners, founded in 1922. The AHS mission is 'to open the eyes of all Americans to the vital connection between people and plants, and to inspire all Americans to become responsible caretakers of the earth, to celebrate America's diversity through the art and science of horticulture, and to lead this effort by sharing the society's unique national resources with all Americans.' All articles are also published on members-only website." Estab. 1922. Circ. 20,000. Byline given. Pays on publication. Offers 25% kill fee. Publishes ms an average of 6 months after acceptance. Editorial lead time 6 months. Submit seasonal material at least 1 year in advance. Accepts queries by mail, e-mail. Responds in 3 months to queries. Sample copy: $8. Writer's guidelines by e-mail and online.

NONFICTION **Buys 20 mss/year.** Query with published clips. No fax, phone, or e-mail submissions. Length: 1,500-2,500 words. **Pays $300-500, depending on complexity and author's experience.**

COLUMNS Natural Connections (explains a natural phenomenon—plant and pollinator relationships, plant and fungus relationships, parasites—that may be observed in nature or in the garden), 750-1,200 words; Homegrown Harvest (articles on edible plants delivered in a personal, reassuring voice. Each issue focuses on a single crop, such as carrots, blueberries, or parsley), 800-900 words; Plant in the Spotlight (profiles of a single plant species or cultivar, including a personal perspective on why it's a favored plant), 600 words. **Buys 5 mss/year.** Query with published clips. **Pays $100-250.**

$$ ATLANTA HOMES AND LIFESTYLES

Network Communications, Inc., 1117 Perimeter Center West, Suite N118, Atlanta GA 30338. (404)252-6670. **E-mail:** editor@atlantahomesmag.com. **Web-**

site: www.atlantahomesmag.com. **Contact:** Elizabeth Ralls, editor-in-chief; Elizabeth Anderson, art director. **65% freelance written.** Magazine published 12 times/year. *Atlanta Homes and Lifestyles* is designed for the action-oriented, well-educated reader who enjoys his/her shelter, its design and construction, its environment, and living and entertaining in it. Estab. 1983. Circ. 30,000. Byline given. Pays on publication. Publishes ms an average of 6 months after acceptance. Accepts queries by mail, fax. Accepts simultaneous submissions. Responds in 3 months to queries. Sample copy online.

NONFICTION Needs interview, new product. "We do not want articles outside the respective market area, not written for magazine format, or that are excessively controversial, investigative, or that cannot be appropriately illustrated with attractive photography." **Buys 35 mss/year.** Query with published clips. Length: 500-1,200 words. **Pays $100-500.** Sometimes pays expenses of writer on assignment.

COLUMNS Pays $50-200.

CALIFORNIA HOMES

McFadden-Bray Publishing Corp., 567 San Nicolas Dr., Suite 130, Newport Beach CA 92660. (949)640-1484. **E-mail:** susan@calhomesmagazine.com; mike@calhomesmagazine.com. **Website:** www.calhomesmagazine.com. **Contact:** Susan McFadden, editor in chief; Michael McFadden, senior editor. **80% freelance written.** Bimonthly magazine covering California interiors, architecture, some food, travel, history, and current events in the field. Estab. 1997. Circ. 80,000. Byline given. Pays on publication. Offers 50% kill fee. Publishes ms an average of 3 months after acceptance. Editorial lead time 3 months. Submit seasonal material 6 months in advance. Accepts queries by mail, e-mail. Accepts simultaneous submissions. Responds in 1 month to queries; in 2 months to mss. Sample copy: $7.50. Guidelines for #10 SASE.

NONFICTION Query. Length: 500-1,000 words. **Pays $250-750.**

CANADIAN GARDENING

Transcontinental Media G.P., TVA Publications, 1010 Sérigny Street, Longueuil QC J4k 5G7 Canada. (416)733-7600; (514) 848-7000. **E-mail:** online form. **Website:** www.canadiangardening.com. **Mostly freelance written by assignment.** Magazine published 8 times/year covering Canadian gardening. *Canadian*

Gardening is a national magazine aimed at the avid home gardener. Our readers are city gardeners with tiny lots, country gardeners with rolling acreage, indoor gardeners, rooftop gardeners, and enthusiastic beginners and experienced veterans. Estab. 1990. Circ. 152,000. Byline given. Pays on acceptance. Offers 25-50% kill fee. Editorial lead time 4 months. Accepts queries by mail, fax. Accepts simultaneous submissions. Responds in 4 months to queries. Guidelines online.

NONFICTION Needs how-to, humor, personal experience, technical, plant and garden profiles, practical advice. **Buys 100 mss/year.** Query. Length: 200-1,500 words. **Pays variable amount.**

CANADIAN HOMES & COTTAGES

The In-Home Show, Ltd., 2650 Meadowvale Blvd., Unit 4, Mississauga ON L5N 6M5 Canada. (905)567-1440. **Fax:** (905)567-1442. **E-mail:** jnaisby@homesandcottages.com; editorial@homesandcottages.com. **Website:** www.homesandcottages.com. **Contact:** Janice E. Naisby, editor-in-chief. **75% freelance written.** Magazine published 6 times/year covering home building and renovating in Canada. "*Homes & Cottages* is Canada's largest home improvement magazine. Publishes articles that have a technical slant, as well as those with a more general lifestyle feel." Estab. 1987. Circ. 92,340. Byline given. Pays on acceptance. Offers 10% kill fee. Publishes ms an average of 6 months after acceptance. Editorial lead time 3 months. Submit seasonal material 6 months in advance. Accepts queries by mail. Accepts simultaneous submissions. Sample copy for SAE. Guidelines for #10 SASE.

NONFICTION Needs humor, new product, technical. **Buys 32 mss/year.** Query. Length: 800-1,500 words. **Pays $3500-650.**

CHARLESTON STYLE & DESIGN

P.O. Box 20098, Charleston SC 29413. **E-mail:** editor@charlestonstyleanddesign.com. **Website:** www.charlestonstyleanddesign.com. **Contact:** Mary K. Love, editor. **85% freelance written.** Quarterly magazine covering design (architecture and interior design) and lifestyle (wines, restaurants, fashion, local retailers, and travel). "*Charleston Style & Design* is a full-color magazine for discriminating readers eager to discover new horizons in Charleston and the world beyond. We offer vivid, well-researched articles on trends in home design, fashion, food and wine, health/fitness, antiques/collectibles, the arts, travel, and more. We also profile celebrities and opinion leaders who have a link with Charleston or the area." Need personal essays and local writers for assignments. Estab. 2008. Circ. 45,000. Byline given. Pays on publication. Pays 50% kill fee. Publishes ms 4 months after acceptance. Editorial lead time 3-6 months. Submit seasonal material 3 months in advance. Accepts queries by e-mail. Accepts simultaneous submissions. Responds in 2 weeks to queries; in 2 months to mss. Sample copy online. Guidelines via e-mail.

NONFICTION Needs essays, general interest. Query with published clips. Length: 300-1,200 words. **Pays $120-500.** Sometimes

COLUMNS Reflections (personal essays), 600 words. "Your essay should present an idea, concept, or experience that you think would be of interest to our readers. We believe that the best personal essays have all the characteristics of a good story, offering compelling descriptions, a narrative line, and, of course, a personal point of view. Beyond that, we look for essays that give readers a 'takeaway,' a thought or insight to which they can relate." Submit personal essay and short two-sentence bio via e-mail with the words "personal essay" in the subject line. **Pays $180.**

💲💲 EARLY AMERICAN LIFE

Firelands Media Group LLC, P.O. Box 221228, Shaker Heights OH 44122. **E-mail:** queries@firelandsmedia.com. **Website:** www.ealonline.com. **Contact:** Jeanmarie Andrews, executive editor. **60% freelance written.** Bimonthly magazine for people who are interested in capturing the warmth and beauty of the 1600-1840 period and using it in their homes and lives today. Readers are interested in antiques, traditional crafts, architecture, restoration, and collecting. Estab. 1970. Circ. 90,000. Byline given. Pays on acceptance. 25% kill fee. Publishes ms an average of 1 year after acceptance. Accepts queries by mail, e-mail. Accepts simultaneous submissions. Responds in 3 months to queries. Sample copy for 9x12 SAE with $2.50 postage. Guidelines available online at: www.ealonline.com/editorial/guidelines.php.

NONFICTION Needs historical, travel, architecture and decorating, antiques, studio crafts. **Buys 40 mss/year.** Query. Length: 750-2,500 words. **Pays $250-700; additional payment for photos.**

💲💲💲💲 GOOD HOUSEKEEPING

Hearst Corp., 300 W. 57th St., 28th Floor, New York NY 10019. **Website:** www.goodhousekeeping.com. Monthly magazine covering women's interests. *Good Housekeeping* is edited for the new traditionalist. Articles which focus on food, fitness, beauty, and childcare draw upon the resources of the Good Housekeeping Institute. Editorial includes human interest stories, articles that focus on social issues, money management, health news, and travel. Circ. 4,000,000. Byline given. Pays on acceptance. Offers 25% kill fee. Submit seasonal material 6 months in advance. Accepts queries by mail. Accepts simultaneous submissions. Responds in 2-3 months to queries and mss. Call for a sample copy. Guidelines online.

NONFICTION Needs personal experience, travel. **Buys 4-6 mss/year.** Query by mail with published clips. Include SASE. Length: 500 words.

COLUMNS Blessings (about a person or event that proved to be a blessing), 500 words. Query by mail with published clips. Include SASE. **Pays $1/word.**

💲 GREENPRINTS

P.O. Box 1355, Fairview NC 28730. (828)628-1902. **E-mail:** pat@greenprints.com. **Website:** www.greenprints.com. **Contact:** Pat Stone, managing editor. **90% freelance written.** "*GreenPrints* is the 'Weeder's Digest.' We share the human—*not* how-to—side of gardening. We publish true personal gardening stories and essays: humorous, heartfelt, insightful, inspiring." Estab. 1990. Circ. 11,000. Byline given. No editorial lead time. Accepts queries by mail, e-mail. Accepts simultaneous submissions. Responds in 3 months to mss. Sample: $5. Guidelines online.

NONFICTION Needs essays, general interest, historical, humor, inspirational, nostalgic, personal experience. Does not want how-to. **Buys 60 mss/year.** Submit complete ms. Length: 250-2,500 words. **Pays $50-200 for unsolicited articles.**

COLUMNS Broken Trowel (the story of your funniest garden mistake), 300 words. **Buys 12 mss/year.** Submit complete ms. **Pays $50-75.**

FICTION "We run very little fiction." **Buys 2 mss/year.** Submit complete ms. **Pays $75-200.**

POETRY Needs free verse, light verse, traditional. "If it's not hands-on and gardening based, please don't send it." Buys 4 poems/year. Submit maximum 3 poems. **Pays $25.**

FILLERS Wants anecdotes, short humor. Length: 100-300 words. **Pays $50-75.**

HGTV MAGAZINE

Hearst Corporation, 320 W. 57th St., 5th Floor, New York NY 10019. **E-mail:** hgtvmagazine@hearst.com.

Website: hgtvmagonline.com. *HGTV Magazine* is a fresh home lifestyle magazine that gives readers inspiring, real-life solutions for all the things that homeowners deal with every day in an upbeat and engaging way. The magazine offers value of insider advice from trusted experts, as well as the enjoyment of taking a look inside real people's homes. Accepts queries by mail, e-mail. Accepts simultaneous submissions.

NONFICTION Query.

🌕🌕🌕🌕 HORTICULTURE

F+W, a Content + eCommerce Company, 10151 Carver Rd., Suite #200, Blue Ash OH 45242. (513)531-2690. **Fax:** (513)891-7153. **E-mail:** edit@hortmag.com. **Website:** www.hortmag.com. Bimonthly magazine. *Horticulture*, the country's oldest gardening magazine, is designed for active home gardeners. Our goal is to offer a blend of text, photographs and illustrations that will both instruct and inspire readers. Circ. 160,000. Byline given. Offers kill fee. Submit seasonal material 10 months in advance. Accepts queries by mail, e-mail, fax. Accepts simultaneous submissions. Responds in 3 months to queries. Guidelines for SASE or by e-mail.

NONFICTION Buys 70 mss/year. Query with published clips, subject background material and SASE. Length: 800-1,000 words. **Pays $500.**

COLUMNS Length: 200-600 words. Query with published clips, subject background material and SASE. Include disk where possible. **Pays $250.**

LOG HOME LIVING

Home Buyer Publications, Inc., 4125 Lafayette Center Dr., Suite 100, Chantilly VA 20151. (703)222-9411; (800)826-3893. **Fax:** (703)222-3209. **E-mail:** editor@timberhomeliving.com. **Website:** www.loghome.com. **90% freelance written.** Monthly magazine for enthusiasts who are dreaming of, planning for, or actively building a log home. Estab. 1989. Circ. 132,000. Byline given. Pays on acceptance. Offers $100 kill fee. Publishes ms an average of 6 months after acceptance. Editorial lead time 6 months. Submit seasonal material 6 months in advance. Accepts queries by mail, e-mail. Accepts simultaneous submissions. Responds in 6 weeks to queries. Sample copy for $4. Guidelines online.

NONFICTION Needs personal experience, technical, travel. **Buys 60 mss/year.** Query with SASE. Length: 1,000-2,000 words. **Payment depends on length, nature of the work, and writer's expertise.**

MIDWEST HOME

Greenspring Media, 706 S. Second Ave. S., Suite 1000, Minneapolis MN 55402. (612)371-5800. **Fax:** (612)371-5801. **E-mail:** clee@greenspring.com. **Website:** midwesthomemag.com. **Contact:** Chris Lee, editor. **50% freelance written.** "*Midwest Home* is an upscale shelter magazine showcasing innovative architecture, interesting interior design, and beautiful gardens of Minnesota. Estab. 1997. Circ. 50,000. Byline given. Pays on acceptance. Offers 20% kill fee. Accepts queries by e-mail. Accepts simultaneous submissions. Guidelines online.

NONFICTION Needs book excerpts, how-to, interview, new product, photo feature, profile. Query with résumé and published clips. Length: 300-1,000 words. **Payment negotiable.**

🌕🌕 MOUNTAIN LIVING

Wiesner Media Network Communications, Inc., 1780 S. Bellaire St., Suite 505, Denver CO 80222. (303)248-2060. **Fax:** (303)248-2066. **E-mail:** greatideas@mountainliving.com; hscott@mountainliving.com; cdeorio@mountainliving.com. **Website:** www.mountainliving.com. **Contact:** Holly Scott, publisher; Christine DeOrio, editor-in-chief. **50% freelance written.** Magazine published 7 times/year covering architecture, interior design, and lifestyle issues for people who live in, visit, or hope to live in the mountains. Estab. 1994. Circ. 40,000. Byline given. Pays on acceptance. Offers 15% kill fee. Publishes ms an average of 4 months after acceptance. Editorial lead time 6 months. Submit seasonal material 8-12 months in advance. Responds in 6-8 weeks to queries. Responds in 2 months to mss. Sample copy for $7. Guidelines by e-mail.

NONFICTION Needs photo feature, travel, home features. **Buys 30 mss/year.** Query with published clips. Length: 200-600 words. **Pays $250-600.**

COLUMNS ML Recommends; Short Travel Tips; New Product Information; Art; Insider's Guide; Entertaining. Length: 150-400 words.

🌕🌕 ROMANTIC HOMES

Y-Visionary Publishing, 22840 Savi Ranch Pkwy., Suite 200, Yorba Linda CA 92887. **E-mail:** jdemontravel@beckett.com. **Website:** www.romantichomes.com. **Contact:** Jacqueline DeMontravel, editor. **70% freelance written.** Monthly magazine covering home decor. *Romantic Homes* is the magazine for women who want to create a warm, intimate, and casually elegant home—a haven that is both a gathering place for family and friends and a private refuge from the pressures of the outside world. The *Romantic Homes* reader is personally involved in the decor of her home. Features offer unique ideas and how-to advice on decorating, home furnishings, and gardening. Departments focus on floor and wall coverings, paint, textiles, refinishing, architectural elements, artwork, travel, and entertaining. Every article responds to the reader's need to create a beautiful, attainable environment, providing her with the style ideas and resources to achieve her own romantic home. Estab. 1994. Circ. 200,000. Byline given. Pays 30-60 days upon receipt of invoice. No kill fee. Publishes ms an average of 4 months after acceptance. Editorial lead time 5 months. Submit seasonal material 6 months in advance. Accepts queries by mail, fax. Accepts simultaneous submissions. Responds in 2 weeks to queries. Responds in 2 months to mss. Guidelines for #10 SASE.

NONFICTION Needs essays, how-to, new product, personal experience, travel. **Buys 150 mss/year.** Query with published clips. Length: 1,000-1,200 words. **Pays $500.**

COLUMNS Departments cover antiques, collectibles, artwork, shopping, travel, refinishing, architectural elements, flower arranging, entertaining, and decorating. Length: 400-600 words. **Pays $250.**

$$ **SAN DIEGO HOME/GARDEN LIFESTYLES**

McKinnon Enterprises, 4577 Viewridge Avenue, San Diego CA 92123. (858)571-1818. **Fax:** (858)571-1889. **E-mail:** ditler@sdhg.net; nboynton@sdhg.net. **Website:** www.sdhg.net. **Contact:** Eva Ditler, managing editor; Nicole Boynton, associate editor. **30% freelance written.** Monthly magazine covering homes, gardens, food, intriguing people, real estate, art and culture for residents of San Diego city and county. Estab. 1979. Circ. 50,000. Byline given. Pays on publication. No kill fee. Publishes ms an average of 3 months after acceptance. Submit seasonal material 3 months in advance. Accepts queries by mail. Accepts simultaneous submissions. Responds in 3 months to queries. Sample copy: $5.

NONFICTION Query with published clips. Length: 500-1,000 words. **Pays $50-375.**

MARTHA STEWART LIVING

Omnimedia, 601 W. 26th St., New York NY 10001. (212)827-8000. **Fax:** (212)827-8204. **Website:** http://livingblog.marthastewart.com; www.marthastewart.com. Monthly magazine for gardening, entertaining, renovating, cooking, collecting, and creating. Magazine, featuring Martha Stewart, that focuses on the domestic arts. Estab. 1990. Circ. 2,000,000. Accepts simultaneous submissions.

$$ **TEXAS GARDENER**

Suntex Communications, Inc., P.O. Box 9005, 10566 N. River Crossing, Waco TX 76714. (254)848-9393. **Fax:** (254)848-9779. **E-mail:** info@texasgardener.com. **Website:** www.texasgardener.com. **80% freelance written. Works with a small number of new/unpublished writers each year.** Bimonthly magazine covering vegetable and fruit production, ornamentals, and home landscape information for home gardeners in Texas. Estab. 1981. Circ. 20,000. Byline given. Pays on publication. No kill fee. Publisher pays at time of publication. Submit seasonal material 6 months in advance. Accepts queries by mail, e-mail, fax. Accepts simultaneous submissions. Responds in 2 months to queries. Sample copy for $4.95 and SAE with postage attached (five first class stamps). Writers' guidelines available online at website.

NONFICTION Needs how-to, humor, interview, photo feature. **Buys 50-60 mss/year.** Query with published clips. Length: 800-2,400 words. **Pays $50-200.**

COLUMNS Between Neighbors. See sample issue for style and content. **Buys 6 mss/year. Pays $50.**

$$$$ **THIS OLD HOUSE**

Time Inc., 135 W. 50th St., 10th Floor, New York NY 10020. (212)522-9465. **Fax:** (212)522-9435. **E-mail:** toh_letters@thisoldhouse.com; scott@thisoldhouse.com. **Website:** www.thisoldhouse.com. **Contact:** Scott Omelianuk, editor. **40% freelance written.** Magazine published 10 times/year covering home design, renovation, and maintenance. "*This Old House* is the ultimate resource for readers whose homes are their passions. The magazine's mission is threefold: to inform with lively service journalism and reporting on innovative new products and materials, to inspire with beautiful examples of fine craftsmanship and elegant architectural design, and to instruct with clear step-by-step projects that will enhance a home or help a homeowner maintain one. The voice of the magazine is not that of a rarefied design maven or a linear Mr. Fix It but rather that of an eyes-wide-open, in-the-trenches homeowner who's eager for advice, tools, and techniques that'll help him realize his dream of a home." Estab. 1995. Circ.

960,000. Byline given. Pays on acceptance. Publishes ms an average of 3-6 months after acceptance. Editorial lead time 3-12 months. Submit seasonal material 1 year in advance. Accepts queries by mail, e-mail. Accepts simultaneous submissions.

NONFICTION Needs essays, how-to, new product. **Buys 70 mss/year.** Query with published clips. Length: 250-2,500 words. **Pays $1/word.**

COLUMNS Around the House (news, new products), 250 words. **Pays $1/word.**

$ $ UNIQUE HOMES

Network Communications, Inc., 327 Wall St., Princeton NJ 08540. (609)688-1110. **Fax:** (609)688-0201. **Website:** www.uniquehomes.com. **30% freelance written.** Bimonthly magazine covering luxury real estate for consumers and the high-end real estate industry. Our focus is the luxury real estate market, i.e., the business of buying and selling luxury homes, as well as regional real estate market trends. Byline given. Pays on publication. No kill fee. Publishes ms an average of 3 months after acceptance. Editorial lead time 4 months. Submit seasonal material 4 months in advance. Accepts queries by mail, e-mail, fax. Accepts simultaneous submissions. Responds in 1 month to queries. Responds in 4 months to mss. Sample copy online.

NONFICTION Special issues: Golf Course Living; Resort Living; Ski Real Estate; Farms, Ranches and Country Estates; Waterfront Homes; International Homes. **Buys 36 mss/year.** Query with published clips and résumé. Length: 500-1,500 words. **Pays $150-500.**

$ $ $ VAIL VALLEY HOME

Vail Board of Realtors, 0275 Main St., Suites 003 and 004, Edwards CO 81632. (970)766-1028. **E-mail:** pconnolly@vaildaily.com. **Website:** www.vvhmag.com. **Contact:** Wren Bova, editor. **80% freelance written.** Quarterly magazine covering building, remodeling Colorado homes. "We cater to an affluent population of homeowners (including primary, second and third homeowners) who are planning to build or remodel their Colorado home in the mountains or on the western slope. While we feature luxury homes, we also have a slant toward green building." Estab. 2005. Circ. 35,000. Byline given. Pays on publication. No kill fee. Publishes ms an average of 2-3 months after acceptance. Editorial lead time 1 year. Submit seasonal material 6 months in advance. Accepts queries by e-mail. Accepts simultaneous submissions.

Responds in 2-4 weeks to queries; in 1 month to mss. Sample copy online.

NONFICTION Needs interview, new product, profiles of Colorado homes and features related to them. "We do not want do-it-yourself projects." Query with published clips. **Pays $200-650 for assigned articles.** "We do not buy articles; we only assign articles."

COLUMNS Your Green Home (tips for environmentally-conscious building, remodeling and living), 300 words. **Buys 4 mss/year.** Query.

⊘ VERANDA

The Hearst Corp., Veranda, Attn: Carolyn Englefield, 300 W. 57th St., New York NY 10019. **Website:** www.veranda.com. Bimonthly magazine. "Written as an interior design magazine featuring creative design across the country and around the world." Circ. 380,890. No kill fee. Editorial lead time 5 months. Accepts queries by mail. Accepts simultaneous submissions. Guidelines on website. Hard-copy submissions only.

$ $ VICTORIAN HOMES

Beckett Media, 22840 Savi Ranch Pkwy., Suite 200, Yorba Linda CA 92887. (714)939-9991. **Fax:** (714)939-9909. **E-mail:** ephillips@beckett.com. **Website:** www.victorianhomesmag.com. **Contact:** Elaine K. Phillips, editor; Jacqueline deMontravel, editorial director. **90% freelance written.** Quarterly magazine covering Victorian home restoration and decoration. *Victorian Homes* is read by Victorian home owners, restorers, house museum management, and others interested in the Victorian revival. Feature articles cover home architecture, interior design, furnishings, and the home's history. Photography is very important to the feature. Estab. 1981. Circ. 100,000. Byline given. Pays on acceptance. Offers $50 kill fee. Publishes ms an average of 1 year after acceptance. Editorial lead time 4 months. Submit seasonal material 1 year in advance. Accepts simultaneous submissions. Responds in 6 weeks to queries; in 2 months to mss. Sample copy and writer's guidelines for SAE.

NONFICTION **Buys 30-35 mss/year.** Query. Length: 500-1,200 words. **Pays $50-150.**

HUMOR

$ $ MAD MAGAZINE

DC Entertainment, 1700 Broadway, New York NY 10019. (212)506-4850. **E-mail:** submissions@mad-magazine.com. **Website:** www.madmag.com. **100% freelance written.** Monthly magazine always on the lookout for new ways to spoof and to poke fun at hot trends. Estab. 1952. Byline given. Pays on acceptance. Publishes ms an average of 6 months after acceptance. Submit seasonal material 6 months in advance. Accepts simultaneous submissions. Responds in 10 weeks to queries. Sample copy online. Guidelines online.

NONFICTION "We're not interested in formats we're already doing or have done to death like 'what they say and what they really mean.' Don't send previously published submissions, riddles, advice columns, TV or movie satires, book manuscripts, top 10 lists, articles about Alfred E. Neuman, poetry, essays, short stories or other text pieces." **Buys 400 mss/year. Pays minimum of $500/page.**

INFLIGHT

😊 💲 HORIZON EDITION MAGAZINE

Paradigm Communications Group, 2701 First Ave., Suite 250, Seattle WA 98121. (206)441-5871. **Fax:** (206)448-6939. **Website:** www.alaskaairlinesmagazine.com/horizonedition. **Contact:** Michele Andrus Dill, editor. **90% freelance written.** Monthly inflight magazine covering travel, business, and leisure in the Pacific Northwest. "*Horizon Edition Magazine* is the monthly in-flight magazine for Horizon Air, reaching more than 574,000 travelers in Washington, Oregon, Idaho, Montana, California, Nevada, Western Canada and Baja, Mexico, each month." Estab. 1990. Byline given. Pays on publication. Offers 33% kill fee. Publishes ms an average of 1 year after acceptance. Editorial lead time 6 months. Submit seasonal material 6 months in advance. Accepts queries by mail, fax. Accepts simultaneous submissions. Sample copy for 9x12 SASE. Guidelines online.

NONFICTION Needs essays, general interest, historical, how-to, humor, interview, personal experience, photo feature, travel, business. Special issues: Meeting planners' guide, golf, gift guide. No material unrelated to the Pacific Northwest. **Buys approximately 36 mss/year.** Query with published clips. Length: 2,000-2,500 words. **Pays $250 minimum.**

COLUMNS Region (Northwest news/profiles), 200-500 words. **Buys 15 mss/year.** Query with published clips. **Pays $100 minimum.**

JUVENILE

ASK

Cricket Media.Inc., **E-mail:** ask@askmagkids.com. **Website:** www.cricketmag.com. "*Ask* is a magazine of arts and sciences for curious kids ages 7-10 who like to find out how the world works." Estab. 2002. Byline given. Accepts queries by e-mail, online submission form. Accepts simultaneous submissions. Guidelines online.

NONFICTION Needs humor, photo feature, profile. "*ASK* commissions most articles but welcomes queries from authors on all nonfiction subjects. Particularly looking for odd, unusual, and interesting stories likely to interest science-oriented kids. Writers interested in working for *ASK* should send a résumé and writing sample (including at least 1 page unedited) for consideration." Length: 200-1,600.

💲 BABYBUG

Cricket Media, Inc., 13625A Dulles Technology Dr., Herndon VA 20171. (703)885-3400. **Website:** www.cricketmedia.com. **50% freelance written.** "*Babybug*, a look-and-listen magazine, presents simple poems, stories, nonfiction, and activities that reflect the natural playfulness and curiosity of babies and toddlers." Estab. 1994. Circ. 45,000. Byline given. Pays on publication. Accepts simultaneous submissions. Responds in 3-6 months to mss. Guidelines available online: www.cricketmedia.com/babybug-submission-guidelines.

NONFICTION "First Concepts," a playful take on a simple idea, expressed through very short nonfiction. See recent issues for examples. **Buys 10-20 mss/year.** Submit through online submissions manager: cricketmag.submittable.com/submit. Length: up to 6 sentences. **Pays up to 25¢/word.**

FICTION Wants very short, clear fiction. , rhythmic, rhyming. **Buys 10-20 mss/year.** Submit complete ms via online submissions manager. Length: up to 6 sentences. **Pays up to 25¢/word.**

POETRY "We are especially interested in rhythmic and rhyming poetry. Poems may explore a baby's day, or they may be more whimsical." Submit via online submissions manager. **Pays up to $3/line; $25 minimum.**

😊😊😊💲 BOYS' LIFE

Boy Scouts of America, P.O. Box 152079, 1325 W. Walnut Hill Ln., Irving TX 75015. **Website:** www.

boyslife.org. **Contact:** Paula Murphey, senior editor; Clay Swartz, associate editor. **75% freelance written. Prefers to work with published/established writers; works with small number of new/unpublished writers each year.** *Boys' Life* is a monthly 4-color general interest magazine for boys 7-18, most of whom are Cub Scouts, Boy Scouts, or Venturers. Estab. 1911. Circ. 1.1 million. Byline given. Pays on acceptance. Publishes ms approximately 1 year after acceptance. Accepts queries by mail. Accepts simultaneous submissions. Responds to queries/mss in 2 months. Sample copy: $3.95 plus 9x12 SASE. Guidelines online.

NONFICTION scouting activities and general interests. **Buys 60 mss/year.** Query senior editor with SASE. No phone or e-mail queries. Length: 500-1,500 words. **Pay ranges from $400-1,500.**

COLUMNS Science; Nature; Earth; Health; Sports; Space and Aviation; Cars; Computers; Entertainment; Pets; History; Music, all 600 words. Query associate editor. **Pays $100-400.**

BREAD FOR GOD'S CHILDREN

P.O. Box 1017, Arcadia FL 34265. (863)494-6214. **E-mail:** bread@breadministries.org. **Website:** www.breadministries.org. **Contact:** Judith M. Gibbs, editor. **10% freelance written.** An interdenominational Christian teaching publication published 4-6 times/year written to aid children and youth in leading a Christian life. Estab. 1972. Circ. 10,000 (U.S. and Canada). Byline given. No kill fee. Publishes ms an average of 6 months after acceptance. Accepts queries by mail. Accepts simultaneous submissions. Responds in 6 months to mss. Sample copy for 9x12 SAE and 5 first-class stamps. Guidelines for #10 SASE.

NONFICTION All levels: how-to. "We do not want anything detrimental to solid family values. Most topics will fit if they are slanted to our basic needs." **Buys 3-4 mss/year.** Send complete ms. Length: 500-800 words.

COLUMNS Freelance columns: Let's Chat (children's Christian values), 500-700 words; Teen Page (youth Christian values), 600-800 words; Idea Page (games, crafts, Bible drills). **Buys 5-8 mss/year.** Send complete ms. **Pays $30.**

FICTION "We are looking for writers who have a solid knowledge of Biblical principles and are concerned for the youth of today living by those principles. Stories must be well written, with the story itself getting the message across—no preaching, moralizing, or tag endings." , Young readers, middle readers, young adult/teen: adventure, religious, problem-solving, sports. Looks for "teaching stories that portray Christian lifestyles without preaching." **Buys 10-15 mss/year.** Send complete ms. Length: 600-800 words for young children; 900-1,500 words for older children. **Pays $40-50.**

TIPS "We want stories or articles that illustrate overcoming obstacles by faith and living solid, Christian lives. Know our publication and what we have used in the past. Know the readership and publisher's guidelines. Stories should teach the value of morality and honesty without preaching. Edit carefully for content and grammar."

$ CADET QUEST MAGAZINE

1333 Alger St. SE, Grand Rapids MI 49507. (616)241-5616. **Fax:** (616)241-5558. **E-mail:** submissions@calvinistcadets.org. **Website:** www.calvinistcadets.org. **Contact:** Steve Bootsma, editor. Magazine published 7 times/year. *Cadet Quest Magazine* shows boys 9-14 how God is at work in their lives and in the world around them. Estab. 1958. Circ. 6,000. Byline given. Pays on acceptance. No kill fee. Publishes ms 4-11 months after acceptance. Accepts simultaneous submissions. Responds in 2 months to mss. Sample copy for 9x12 SASE and $1.45 postage. Guidelines online.

NONFICTION Needs how-to, humor, inspirational, interview, personal experience, informational. Special issues: New themes list available online in January or for SASE. "Articles about Christian athletes, coaching tips, and developing Christian character through sports are appreciated. Photos of these sports or athletes are also welcomed. Be original in presenting these topics to boys. Articles about camping, nature, and survival should be practical—the 'how-to' approach is best. 'God in nature' articles, if done without being preachy, are appreciated." Send complete ms via postal mail or e-mail (in body of e-mail; no attachments). Length: up to 1,500 words. **Pays 5¢/word and 1 contributor's copy.**

COLUMNS Project/Hobby articles (simple projects boys 9-14 can do on their own, made with easily accessible materials; must provide clear, accurate instructions); Cartoons and Puzzles (wholesome and boy-oriented logic puzzles, crosswords, and hidden pictures).

FICTION "Fast-moving, entertaining stories that appeal to a boy's sense of adventure or to his sense of humor are welcomed. Stories must present Christian life realistically and help boys relate Christian values to their own lives. Stories must have action without long dialogues. Favorite topics for boys include sports and athletes, humor, adventure, mystery, friends, etc. They must also fit the theme of that issue of *Cadet Quest*. Stories with preachiness and/or clichés are not of interest to us.", middle readers, boys/early teens: adventure, arts/craft, games/puzzles, hobbies, humorous, multicultural, religious, science, sports. No fantasy, science fiction, fashion, horror, or erotica. Send complete ms by postal mail or e-mail (in body of e-mail; no attachments). Length: 1,000-1,300 words. **Pays 5¢/word and 1 contributor's copy.**

CLICK

Cricket Media, Inc., **E-mail:** click@cricketmedia.com. **Website:** www.cricketmag.com. Magazine covering areas of interest for children ages 3-7. "*Click* is a science and exploration magazine for children ages 3-7. Designed and written with the idea that it's never too early to encourage a child's natural curiosity about the world, *Click*'s 40 full-color pages are filled with amazing photographs, beautiful illustrations, and stories and articles that are both entertaining and thought-provoking." Accepts queries by e-mail. Accepts simultaneous submissions. Sample copy online. Guidelines online.

NONFICTION Query by e-mail with résumé and published clips. Length: 200-500 words.

$$ COBBLESTONE

Cricket Media, Inc., **E-mail:** cobblestone@cricketmedia.com. **Website:** www.cricketmedia.com. **50% freelance written.** "*Cobblestone* is interested in articles of historical accuracy and lively, original approaches to the subject at hand." American history magazine for ages 8-14. Circ. 15,000. Byline given. Pays on publication. Offers 50% kill fee. Accepts queries by e-mail. Accepts simultaneous submissions. Sample copy online. Guidelines online.

NONFICTION Needs historical, humor, interview, personal experience, photo feature. No material that editorializes rather than reports. **Buys 45-50 mss/year.** Query by e-mail with published clips. Length: 700-800 words for feature articles; 300-600 words for supplemental nonfiction. **Pays 20-25¢/word.**

FICTION Needs adventure. **Buys 5 mss/year.** Query by e-mail with published clips. Length: up to 800 words. **Pays 20-25¢/word.**

POETRY Needs free verse, light verse, traditional. Serious and light verse considered. Must have clear, objective imagery. Buys 3 poems/year. Length: up to 100 lines/poem. **Pays on an individual basis.**

FILLERS Crossword and other word puzzles (no word finds), mazes, and picture puzzles that use the vocabulary of the issue's theme or otherwise relate to the theme. Query by e-mail with published clips. **Pays on an individual basis.**

$$ CRICKET

Cricket Media, Inc., **Website:** www.cricketmag.com. *Cricket* is a monthly literary magazine for ages 9-14. Publishes 9 issues/year. Estab. 1973. Circ. 73,000. Byline given. Pays on publication. Accepts queries by online submission form. Accepts simultaneous submissions. Responds in 3-6 months to mss. Sample copy online. Guidelines online.

NONFICTION *Cricket* publishes thought-provoking nonfiction articles on a wide range of subjects: history, biography, true adventure, science and technology, sports, inventors and explorers, architecture and engineering, archaeology, dance, music, theater, and art. Articles should be carefully researched and include a solid bibliography that shows that research has gone beyond reviewing websites. Submit via online submissions manager (cricketmag.submittable.com). Length: 1,200-1,800 words. **Pays up to 25¢/word.**

FICTION Needs realistic, contemporary, historic, humor, mysteries, fantasy, science fiction, folk/fairy tales, legend, myth. No didactic, sex, religious, or horror stories. **Buys 75-100 mss/year.** Submit via online submissions manager (cricketmag.submittable.com). Length: 1,200-1,800 words. **Pays up to 25¢/word.**

POETRY *Cricket* publishes both serious and humorous poetry. Poems should be well-crafted, with precise and vivid language and images. Poems can explore a variety of themes, from nature, to family and friendships, to whatever you can imagine that will delight our readers and invite their wonder and emotional response. Buys 20-30 poems/year. Submit maximum 6 poems. Length: up to 35 lines/poem. Most poems run 8-15 lines. **Pays up to $3/line.**

FILLERS Crossword puzzles, logic puzzles, math puzzles, crafts, recipes, science experiments, games and activities from other countries, plays, music, art. **Pays $75.**

DEVOZINE

1908 Grand Ave., P.O. Box 340004, Nashville TN 37203-0004. **E-mail:** devozine@upperroom.org. **Website:** www.devozine.org. **Contact:** Sandy Miller, editor. *devozine,* published bimonthly, is a 64-page devotional magazine for youth (ages 14-19) and adults who care about youth. Offers meditations, scripture, prayers, poems, stories, songs, and feature articles to "aid youth in their prayer life, introduce them to spiritual disciplines, help them shape their concept of God, and encourage them in the life of discipleship." Accepts queries by mail, e-mail, online submission form. Accepts simultaneous submissions.

NONFICTION Special issues: Submit by postal mail with SASE, or by e-mail. Include name, age/birth date (if younger than 25), mailing address, e-mail address, phone number, and fax number (if available). Always publishes theme issues (available for SASE or online). Indicate theme you are writing for. Submit devotionals by mail or e-mail listed above. Submit feature article **queries** by e-mail to smiller@upperroom. org. Length: 150-250 words for devotionals; 500-600 words for feature articles. **Pays $25-100.**

POETRY Needs religious. Considers poetry by teens. Submit by postal mail with SASE, or by e-mail. Include name, age/birth date (if younger than 25), mailing address, e-mail address, phone number, and fax number (if available). Always publishes theme issues (available for SASE or online). Indicate theme you are writing for. Length: 10-20 lines/poem. **Pays $25.**

💲💲 FACES

Cricket Media, Inc., **E-mail:** faces@cricketmedia.com. **Website:** www.cricketmedia.com. **90-100% freelance written.** "Published 9 times/year, *Faces* covers world culture for ages 9-14. It stands apart from other children's magazines by offering a solid look at 1 subject and stressing strong editorial content, color photographs throughout, and original illustrations. *Faces* offers an equal balance of feature articles and activities, as well as folktales and legends." Estab. 1984. Circ. 15,000. Byline given. Pays on publication. Offers 50% kill fee. Accepts simultaneous submissions. Sample copy online. Guidelines online.

NONFICTION Needs historical, interview, personal experience, photo feature, feature articles (in-depth nonfiction highlighting an aspect of the featured culture, interviews, and personal accounts), 700-800 words; supplemental nonfiction (subjects directly and indirectly related to the theme), 300-600 words. Special issues: See website for upcoming themes. **Buys 45-50 mss/year.** Query by e-mail with cover letter, one-page outline, bibliography. **Pays 20-25¢/word.**

FICTION Fiction accepted: retold legends, folktales, stories, and original plays from around the world, etc., relating to the theme. Needs ethnic. Query with cover letter, one-page outline, bibliography. **Pays 20-25¢/word.**

FILLERS Needs Puzzles and Games (word puzzles using the vocabulary of the edition's theme, mazes and picture puzzles that relate to the theme); Activities (crafts, games, recipes, projects, etc., which children can do either alone or with adult supervision; should be accompanied by sketches and description of how activity relates to theme), up to 700 words. No crossword puzzles. **Pays on an individual basis.**

💲💲 GIRLS' LIFE

3 S. Frederick St., Suite 806, Baltimore MD 21202. (410)426-9600. **Fax:** (866)793-1531. **E-mail:** writeforgl@girlslife.com. **Website:** www.girlslife.com. **Contact:** Karen Bokram, founding editor and publisher; Kelsey Haywood, senior editor; Chun Kim, art director. Bimonthly magazine covering girls ages 9-15. Estab. 1994. Circ. 2.16 million. Byline given. Pays on publication. Publishes an average of 3 months after acceptance. Editorial lead time 4 months. Submit seasonal material 5 months in advance. Accepts queries by mail, e-mail. Accepts simultaneous submissions. Responds in 1 month to queries. Sample copy for $5 or online. Guidelines online.

NONFICTION Needs book excerpts, essays, general interest, how-to, humor, inspirational, interview, new product, travel. Special issues: Special issues: Back to School (August/September); Fall, Halloween (October/November); Holidays, Winter (December/January); Valentine's Day, Crushes (February/March); Spring, Mother's Day (April/May); and Summer, Father's Day (June/July). **Buys 40 mss/year.** Query by mail with published clips. Submit complete ms on spec only. "Features and articles should speak to young women ages 10-15 looking for new ideas about relationships, family, friends, school, etc. with fresh, savvy advice. Front-of-the-book columns and quizzes are a good place to start." Length: 700-2,000 words. **Pays $350/regular column; $500/feature.**

COLUMNS Buys 20 mss/year. Query with published clips. **Pays $150-450.**

FICTION "We accept short fiction. They should be stand-alone stories and are generally 2,500-3,500 words." Needs short stories.

💲 HIGHLIGHTS FOR CHILDREN

803 Church St., Honesdale PA 18431. (570)253-1080. **Fax:** (570)251-7847. **E-mail:** customerservice@highlights.com. **Website:** www.highlights.com. **Contact:** Christine French Cully, editor-in-chief. **80% freelance written.** Monthly magazine for children up to ages 6-12. "This book of wholesome fun is dedicated to helping children grow in basic skills and knowledge, in creativeness, in ability to think and reason, in sensitivity to others, in high ideals, and worthy ways of living—for children are the world's most important people. We publish stories for beginning and advanced readers. Up to 500 words for beginning readers, up to 800 words for advanced readers." Estab. 1946. Circ. approximately 1.5 million. Pays on acceptance. Accepts queries by mail. Accepts simultaneous submissions. Responds in 2 months to queries. Sample copy free. Guidelines on website in "Company" area.

NONFICTION "Generally we prefer to see a manuscript rather than a query. However, we will review queries regarding nonfiction." Length: 800 words maximum. **Pays $25 for craft ideas and puzzles; $25 for fingerplays; $150 and up for articles.**

FICTION Meaningful stories appealing to both girls and boys, up to age 12. Vivid, full of action. Engaging plot, strong characterization, lively language. Prefers stories in which a child protagonist solves a dilemma through his or her own resources. Seeks stories that the child ages 8-12 will eagerly read, and the younger child will like to hear when read aloud (500-800 words). Stories require interesting plots and a number of illustration possiblities. Also need rebuses (picture stories 100 words), stories with urban settings, stories for beginning readers (100-500 words), sports and humorous stories, adventures, holiday stories, and mysteries. We also would like to see more material of 1-page length (300 words), both fiction and factual. Needs adventure, fantasy, historical, humorous, animal, contemporary, folktales, multi-cultural, problem-solving, sports. No stories glorifying war, crime or violence. Send complete ms. **Pays $150 minimum plus 2 contributor's copies.**

POETRY Lines/poem: 16 maximum ("most poems are shorter"). Considers simultaneous submissions ("please indicate"); no previously published poetry. No e-mail submissions. "Submit typed manuscript with very brief cover letter." Occasionally comments on submissions "if manuscript has merit or author seems to have potential for our market." Guidelines available for SASE. Responds "generally within 2 months." Always sends prepublication galleys. Pays 2 contributor's copies; "money varies." Acquires all rights.

💲💲 JACK AND JILL

U.S. Kids, P.O. Box 567, Indianapolis IN 46206. (317)634-1100. **E-mail:** jackandjill@saturdayeveningpost.org. **Website:** www.uskidsmags.com. **50% freelance written.** Bimonthly magazine published for children ages 8-12. "*Jack and Jill* is an award-winning magazine for children ages 6-12. It promotes the healthy educational and creative growth of children through interactive activities and articles. The pages are designed to spark a child's curiosity in a wide range of topics through articles, games, and activities. Inside you will find: current real-world topics in articles in stories; challenging puzzles and games; and interactive entertainment through experimental crafts and recipes." Estab. 1938. Circ. 200,000. Byline given. Pays on publication. Publishes ms an average of 8 months after acceptance. Submit seasonal material 8 months in advance. Accepts queries by mail. Accepts simultaneous submissions. Responds to mss in 3 months. Guidelines online.

NONFICTION Buys 8-10 mss/year. Submit complete ms via postal mail; no e-mail submissions. Queries not accepted. "We are especially interested in features or Q&As with regular kids (or groups of kids) in the *Jack and Jill* age group who are engaged in unusual, challenging, or interesting activities. No celebrity pieces, please." Length: up to 700 words. **Pays 25$ minimum.**

FICTION Submit complete ms via postal mail; no e-mail submissions. "The tone of the stories should be fun and engaging. Stories should hook readers right from the get-go and pull them through the story. Humor is very important! Dialogue should be witty instead of just furthering the plot. The story should convey some kind of positive message. Possible themes could include self-reliance, being kind to others, appreciating other cultures, and so on. There are a million positive messages, so get creative! Kids can see preachy coming from a mile away, though, so please focus on telling a good story over teaching a lesson. The message—if there is one—should come organically from the story and not feel tacked on." **Buys 30-35 mss/year.** Length: 600-800 words. **Pays $25 minimum.**

POETRY Submit via postal mail; no e-mail submissions. Wants light-hearted poetry appropriate for the age group. Mss must be typewritten with poet's contact information in upper-right corner of each poem's page. SASE required. Length: up to 30 lines/poem. **Pays $25-50.**

FILLERS Needs puzzles, activities, games. "In general, we prefer to use in-house generated material for this category but on occasion we do receive unique and fun puzzles, games, or activities through submissions. Please make sure you are submitting a truly unique activity for our consideration." **Pays $25-40.**

KEYS FOR KIDS DEVOTIONAL

Box 1001, Grand Rapids MI 49501-1001. **E-mail:** editorial@keysforkids.org. **Website:** www.keysforkids. org. **Contact:** Courtney Lasater. **90%.** "*Keys for Kids Devotional*, published by Keys for Kids Ministries, features stories and Key Verses of the day for children ages 6-12. Our devotions teach kids about God's love." Estab. 1982. Circ. 60,000 print (not including digital circulation). Byline given. Pays on acceptance. Publishes ms 6-9 months after acceptance. Editorial lead time 6-8 months. Accepts queries by e-mail. Responds in 2-4 months. Sample copy online. Guidelines online.

FICTION "Propose a title and suggest an appropriate Scripture passage, generally 3-10 verses, to reinforce the theme of your story. Tell a contemporary story (not a Bible story) with a spiritual application. Avoid fairy-tale endings. Include some action and message illustration—not conversation only. Some humor is good." Needs religious. Submit complete ms. Length: up to 350 words. **Pays $25.**

🌐🌐 LADYBUG

Cricket Media, Inc., **Website:** www.cricketmag.com. *Ladybug* magazine is an imaginative magazine with art and literature for young children ages 3-6. Publishes 9 issues/year. Estab. 1990. Circ. 125,000. Byline given. Pays on publication. Accepts queries by online submission form. Accepts simultaneous submissions. Responds in 6 months to mss. Guidelines online.

NONFICTION Seeks "simple explorations of interesting places in a young child's world (such as the li-brary and the post office), different cultures, nature, and science. These articles can be straight nonfiction, or they may include story elements, such as a fictional child narrator." **Buys 35 mss/year.** Submit via online submissions manager: cricketmag.submittable.com. Length: up to 400 words. **Pays up to 25¢/word.**

FICTION imaginative contemporary stories, original retellings of fairy and folk tales, multicultural stories. **Buys 30 mss/year.** Submit via online submissions manager: cricket.submittable.com. Length: up to 800 words. **Pays up to 25¢/word.**

POETRY Needs light verse, traditional. Wants poetry that is "rhythmic, rhyming; serious, humorous." Submit via online submissions manager: cricket.submittable.com. Length: up to 20 lines/poem. **Pays up to $3/line ($25 minimum).**

FILLERS Learning activities, games, crafts, songs, finger games. See back issues for types, formats, and length.

🌐🌐🌐🚫 MUSE

Cricket Media, Inc., **E-mail:** muse@cricketmedia. com. **Website:** www.cricketmag.com. "The goal of *Muse* is to give as many children as possible access to the most important ideas and concepts underlying the principal areas of human knowledge. Articles should meet the highest possible standards of clarity and transparency, aided, wherever possible, by a tone of skepticism, humor, and irreverence." Estab. 1996. Circ. 40,000. Accepts queries by e-mail. Accepts simultaneous submissions.

NONFICTION Needs interview, photo feature, profile, entertaining stories from the fields of science, technology, engineering, art, and math. Query by e-mail with published clips. Length: 1,200-1,800 words for features; 500-800 words for profiles and interviews; 100-300 words for photo essays.

FICTION Needs science fiction. Query with published clips. Length: 1,000-1,600 words

🌐🌐🌐🌐 NATIONAL GEOGRAPHIC KIDS

National Geographic Society, 1145 17th St. NW, Washington DC 20036. **E-mail:** ashaw@ngs.org. **E-mail:** chughes@ngs.org; asilen@ngs.org; kboatner@ ngs.org. **Website:** www.kids.nationalgeographic.com. **Contact:** Catherine Hughes, science editor; Andrea Silen, associate editor; Kay Boatner, associate editor; Jay Sumner, photo director. **70% freelance written.** Magazine published 10 times/year. "It's our mission to find fresh ways to entertain children while educating and exciting them about their world." Estab. 1975. Circ. 1.3 million. Byline given. Pays on acceptance. Offers 10% kill fee. Publishes ms an average of 6 months after acceptance. Editorial lead time 6+ months. Submit seasonal material 6+ months in advance. Accepts queries by mail. Accepts simultaneous submissions. Sample copy for #10 SASE. Guidelines online.

NONFICTION Needs general interest, humor, interview, technical. Query with published clips and résumé. Length: 100-1,000 words. **Pays $1/word for assigned articles.**

COLUMNS Freelance columns: Amazing Animals (animal heroes, stories about animal rescues, interesting/funny animal tales), 100 words; Inside Scoop (fun, kid-friendly news items), 50-70 words. Query with published clips. **Pays $1/word.**

🄢 NATURE FRIEND MAGAZINE

4253 Woodcock Lane, Dayton VA 22821. (540)867-0764. **E-mail:** info@naturefriendmagazine.com; editor@naturefriendmagazine.com; photos@naturefriendmagazine.com. **Website:** www.naturefriendmagazine.com. **Contact:** Kevin Shank, editor. **80% freelance written.** Monthly children's magazine covering creation-based nature. "*Nature Friend* includes stories, puzzles, science experiments, nature experiments—all submissions need to honor God as creator." Estab. 1982. Circ. 13,000. Byline given. Pays on publication. No kill fee. Editorial lead time 4 months. Submit seasonal material 6 months in advance. Accepts simultaneous submissions. Responds in 6 months to mss. Sample copy: $5, postage paid. Guidelines available on website.

NONFICTION Needs how-to. No poetry, evolution, animals depicted in captivity, talking animal stories, or evolutionary material. **Buys 50 mss/year.** Send complete ms. Length: 250-900 words. **Pays 5¢/word.**

COLUMNS Learning By Doing, 500-900 words. **Buys 12 mss/year.** Send complete ms.

FILLERS Needs facts, puzzles, short essays on something current in nature. **Buys 35 mss/year.** Length: 150-250 words. **5¢/word.**

🄢🄢 NEW MOON GIRLS

New Moon Girl Media, P.O. Box 161287, Duluth MN 55816. (218)728-5507. **Fax:** (218)728-0314. **Website:** www.newmoon.com. **25% freelance written.** Bi-monthly magazine covering girls ages 8-14, edited by girls ages 8-14. "*New Moon Girls* is for every girl who wants her voice heard and her dreams taken seriously. *New Moon* celebrates girls, explores the passage from girl to woman, and builds healthy resistance to gender inequities. The *New Moon* girl is true to herself, and *New Moon Girls* helps her as she pursues her unique path in life, moving confidently into the world." Estab. 1992. Circ. 30,000. Byline given. Pays on publication. Publishes ms an average of 6 months after acceptance. Editorial lead time 6 months. Submit seasonal material 8 months in advance. Accepts queries by mail, e-mail, fax. Accepts simultaneous submissions. Responds in 2 months to mss. Sample copy: $7.50 or online. Guidelines available at website.

NONFICTION Needs essays, general interest, humor, inspirational, interview, opinion, personal experience, photo feature, religious. No fashion, beauty, or dating. **Buys 20 mss/year.** Send complete ms by e-mail. Publishes nonfiction by adults in Herstory and Women's Work departments only. Length: 600 words. **Pays 6-12¢/word.**

COLUMNS Women's Work (profile of a woman and her job relating the the theme), 600 words; Herstory (historical woman relating to theme), 600 words. **Buys 10 mss/year.** Query. **Pays 6-12¢/word.**

FICTION Prefers girl-written material. All girl-centered. Needs adventure, fantasy, historical, humorous, slice-of-life vignettes. **Buys 6 mss/year.** Send complete ms by e-mail. Length: 900-1,600 words. **Pays 6-12¢/word.**

ON COURSE

The General Council of the Assemblies of God, 1445 Boonville Ave., Springfield MO 65802-1894. (417)862-2781. **Fax:** (417)862-1693. **E-mail:** oncourse@ag.org. **Website:** www.oncourse.ag.org. **Contact:** Amber Weigand-Buckley, editor; Josh Carter, art director. *ONCOURSE* is a magazine to empower students to grow in a real-life relationship with Christ. Estab. 1991. Byline given. Pays on acceptance. Accepts simultaneous submissions. Sample copy free for 9x11 SASE. Guidelines on website.

NONFICTION "Submit an audition manuscript of less than 1,200 words. *ONCOURSE* evaluates manuscripts to determine if you, as a writer, fit our magazine. We will not print them—we do not purchase unsolicited articles. Article assignments go to writers listed in our Writer's File and focus on scheduled topics. If we approve you for our Writers File, we will also issue you a password for Writers Only, where we post these themes." **Pays $40 for columns, $80 for two-page features, $15 for sidebars/reviews, and $30 for Web-only features.**

FICTION Length: 800 words.

$$ POCKETS

The Upper Room, P.O. Box 340004, Nashville TN 37203. (615)340-7333. **E-mail:** pockets@upperroom.org. **Website:** pockets.upperroom.org. **Contact:** Lynn W. Gilliam, editor. **60% freelance written.** Magazine published 11 times/year. "*Pockets* is a Christian devotional magazine for children ages 6-12. All submissions should address the broad theme of the magazine. Each issue is built around a theme with material which can be used by children in a variety of ways. Scripture stories, fiction, poetry, prayers, art, graphics, puzzles and activities are included. Submissions do not need to be overtly religious. They should help children experience a Christian lifestyle that is not always a neatly wrapped moral package but is open to the continuing revelation of God's will. Seasonal material, both secular and liturgical, is desired." Estab. 1981. Byline given. Pays on acceptance. No kill fee. Publishes ms an average of 1 year after acceptance. Submit seasonal material 1 year in advance. Accepts simultaneous submissions. Responds in 8 weeks to mss. Each issue reflects a specific theme. Guidelines online.

NONFICTION Picture-oriented, young readers, middle readers: cooking, games/puzzles. Special issues: "*Pockets* seeks biographical sketches of persons, famous or unknown, whose lives reflect their Christian commitment, written in a way that appeals to children." Does not accept how-to articles. "Nonfiction should read like a story." Multicultural needs include stories that feature children of various racial/ethnic groups and do so in a way that is true to those depicted. **Buys 10 mss/year.** Submit complete ms by mail. No e-mail submissions. Length: 400-1,000 words. **Pays 14¢/word.**

COLUMNS Family Time, 200-300 words; Peacemakers at Work (profiles of children working for peace, justice, and ecological concerns), 400-600 words. **Pays 14¢/word.** Activities/Games (related to themes). **Pays $25 and up.** Kids Cook (simple recipes children can make alone or with minimal help from an adult). **Pays $25.**

FICTION "Stories should contain lots of action, use believable dialogue, be simply written, and be rele-

vant to the problems faced by this age group in everyday life." Submit complete ms by mail. No e-mail submissions. Length: 600-1,000 words.

POETRY Both seasonal and theme poems needed. Considers poetry by children. Buys 14 poems/year. Length: up to 20 lines. **Pays $25 minimum.**

$ SHINE BRIGHTLY

GEMS Girls' Clubs, 1333 Alger St., SE, Grand Rapids MI 49507. (616)241-5616. Fax: (616)241-5558. **E-mail:** shinebrightly@gemsgc.org. **Website:** www.gemsgc.org. **Contact:** Kelli Gilmore, managing editor. **60% freelance written. Works with new and published/established writers.** Monthly magazine (with combined May/June/July/August summer issue). "Our purpose is to lead girls into a living relationship with Jesus Christ and to help them see how God is at work in their lives and the world around them. Puzzles, crafts, stories, and articles for girls ages 9-14." Estab. 1970. Circ. 14,000. Byline given. Pays on publication. No kill fee. Publishes ms an average of 4 months after acceptance. Submit seasonal material 1 year in advance. Accepts simultaneous submissions. Responds in 2 months to mss. Sample copy with 9x12 SASE with 3 first class stamps and $1. Guidelines online.

NONFICTION Needs humor, inspirational, interview, personal experience, photo feature, religious, travel, adventure, mystery. Avoid the testimony approach. **Buys 15 unsolicited mss/year.** Submit complete ms in body of e-mail. No attachments. Length: 100-800 words. **Pays up to $35, plus 2 copies.**

COLUMNS How-to (crafts); puzzles and jokes; quizzes. Length: 200-400 words. Send complete ms. **Pay varies.**

FICTION Does not want "unrealistic stories and those with trite, easy endings. We are interested in manuscripts that show how real girls can change the world." Needs ethnic, historical, humorous, mystery, religious, slice-of-life vignettes. Believable only. Nothing too preachy. **Buys 30 mss/year.** Submit complete ms in body of e-mail. No attachments. Length: 700-900 words. **Pays up to $35, plus 2 copies.**

POETRY Needs free verse, haiku, light verse, traditional. **Limited need for poetry. Pays $5-15.**

$ SPARKLE

GEMS Girls' Clubs, 1333 Alger St. SE, Grand Rapids MI 49507. (616)241-5616. Fax: (616)241-5558. **E-mail:** kelli@gemsgc.org. **Website:** www.gemsgc.org. **Contact:** Kelli Gilmore, managing editor; Lisa Hunter, art director/photo editor. **40% freelance written.** Monthly magazine for girls ages 6-9 from October to March. Mission is to prepare young girls to live out their faith and become world-changers. Strives to help girls make a difference in the world. Looks at the application of scripture to everyday life. Also strives to delight the reader and cause the reader to evalute her own life in light of the truth presented. Finally, attempts to teach practical life skills. Estab. 2002. Circ. 9,000. Byline given. Pays on publication. Editorial lead time 3 months. Submit seasonal material 1 year in advance. Accepts queries by e-mail. Accepts simultaneous submissions. Responds 3 months to mss. Sample copy for 9x13 SAE, 3 first-class stamps, and $1 for coverage/publication cost. Guidelines available for #10 SASE or online.

NONFICTION Contact: Kelli Gilmore. , Young readers: animal, arts/crafts, biography, careers, cooking, concept, games/puzzles, geography, health, history, hobbies, how-to, humor, inspirational, interview/profile, math, multicultural, music/drama/art, nature/environment, personal experience, photo feature, problem-solving, quizzes, recipes, religious, science, social issues, sports, travel. Looking for inspirational biographies, stories from Zambia, and ideas on how to live a green lifestyle. Constant mention of God is not necessary if the moral tone of the story is positive. **Buys 10 mss/year.** Send complete ms. Length: 100-400 words. **Pays $35 maximum.**

COLUMNS Crafts; puzzles and jokes; quizzes, all 200-400 words. Send complete ms. **Payment varies.**

FICTION Young readers: adventure, animal, contemporary, ethnic/multicultural, fantasy, folktale, health, history, humorous, music and musicians, mystery, nature/environment, problem-solving, religious, recipes, service projects, slice-of-life, sports, suspense/mystery, vignettes, interacting with family and friends. **Buys 10 mss/year.** Send complete ms. Length: 100-400 words. **Pays $35 maximum.**

POETRY Prefers rhyming. "We do not wish to see anything that is too difficult for a first grader to read. We wish it to remain light. The style can be fun but should also teach a truth." No violence or secular material. Buys 4 poems/year. Submit maximum 4 poems.

FILLERS Needs facts, short humor. **Buys 6 mss/year.** Length: 50-150 words. **Pays $10-15.**

⑨⑨ SPIDER

Cricket Media, Inc., **Website:** www.cricketmag.com. **85% freelance written.** Monthly reading and activity magazine for children ages 6-9. "*Spider* introduces children to the highest-quality stories, poems, illustrations, articles, and activities. It was created to foster in beginning readers a love of reading and discovery that will last a lifetime. We're looking for writers who respect children's intelligence." Estab. 1994. Circ. 70,000. Byline given. Pays on publication. Accepts queries by online submission form. Accepts simultaneous submissions. Responds in 6 months to mss. Sample copy online. Guidelines online.

NONFICTION Special issues: Wants "well-researched articles about animals, kids their own age doing amazing things, and cool science discoveries (such as wetsuits for penguins and real-life invisibility cloaks). Nonfiction articles should rise above a simple list of facts; we look for kid-friendly nonfiction shaped into an engaging narrative." Submit complete ms via online submissions manager (cricketmag.submittable.com). Length: 300-800 words. **Pays up to 25¢/word.**

FICTION Wants "complex and believable" stories. Needs fantasy, humorous. No romance, horror, religious. Submit complete ms via online submissions manager (cricketmag.submittable.com). Length: 300-1,000 words. **Pays up to 25¢/word.**

POETRY Needs free verse, traditional. Submit up to 5 poems via online submissions manager (cricketmag.submittable.com). "Poems should be succinct, imaginative, and accessible; we tend to avoid long narrative poems." Length: up to 20 lines/poem. **Pays up to $3/line.**

FILLERS Needs recipes, crafts, puzzles, games, brainteasers, math and word activities. Submit via online submissions manager (cricketmag.submittable.com). Length: 1-4 pages. **Pays $75.**

⑨ STONE SOUP

Children's Art Foundation, P.O. Box 83, Santa Cruz CA 95063-0083. (831)426-5557. **E-mail:** editor@stonesoup.com. **Website:** http://stonesoup.com. **Contact:** Ms. Gerry Mandel, editor. **100% freelance written.** Bimonthly magazine of writing and art by children age 13 under, including fiction, poetry, book reviews, and art. *Stone Soup* is 48 pages, 7×10, professionally printed in color on heavy stock, saddle-stapled, with coated cover with full-color illustration. Receives 5,000 poetry submissions/year, accepts about 12. Press run is 15,000. Subscription: $37/year (U.S.). "We have a preference for writing and art based on real-life experiences; no formula stories or poems. We only publish writing by children ages 8 to 13. We do not publish writing by adults." Estab. 1973. Pays on publication. Publishes ms an average of 4 months after acceptance. Submit seasonal material 6 months in advance. View a PDF sample copy at www.stonesoup.com.

NONFICTION Needs historical, humor, memoir, personal experience, reviews. **Buys 12 mss/year.** Submit complete ms; no SASE. **Pays $40, a certificate and 2 contributor's copies, plus discounts.**

FICTION Needs adventure, ethnic, experimental, fantasy, historical, humorous, mystery, science fiction, slice-of-life vignettes, suspense. "We do not like assignments or formula stories of any kind." **Buys 60 mss/year.** Send complete ms; no SASE. Length: 150-2,500 words. **Pays $40 for stories, a certificate and 2 contributor's copies, plus discounts.**

POETRY Needs avant-garde, free verse. Wants free verse poetry. Does not want rhyming poetry, haiku, or cinquain. Buys 12 poems/year. **Pays $40/poem, a certificate, and 2 contributor's copies, plus discounts.**

LITERARY & LITTLE

AGNI

Boston University, 236 Bay State Rd., Boston MA 02215. (617)353-7135. **E-mail:** agni@bu.edu. **Website:** www.agnimagazine.org. **Contact:** Sven Birkerts, editor. **90%.** Biannual literary magazine. Eclectic literary magazine publishing first-rate poems, essays, translations, and stories. Estab. 1972. Circ. 3,000 in print, plus more than 60,000 distinct readers online per year. Byline given. Pays on publication. Publishes ms an average of 6 months after acceptance. Accepts simultaneous submissions. Responds in 4 months to mss. No queries please. Sample copy: $10 or online. Guidelines online.

NONFICTION Contact: Sven Birkerts, editor. Needs essays, memoir, reviews. Literary only. "We do not publish journalism or academic work." **Buys 20+ mss/year.** Submit online or by regular mail, no more than one essay at a time. E-mailed submissions will not be considered. Include a stamped addressed envelope or your e-mail address if sending by mail. **Pays $10/page up to $150 (higher some years with grant support), plus a one-year subscription, and, for print publication, 2 contributor's copies and 4 gift copies.**

FICTION Contact: Sven Birkerts, editor. Buys short stories. Needs short stories. No genre scifi, horror, mystery, or romance. **Buys 20+ mss/year.** Submit online or by regular mail, no more than one story at a time. E-mailed submissions will not be considered. Include a stamped addressed envelope or your e-mail address if sending by mail. **Pays $10/page up to $150 (higher some years with grant support), plus a one-year subscription, and, for print publication, 2 contributor's copies and 4 gift copies.**

POETRY Contact: Sven Birkerts, editor. Submit online or by regular mail, no more than 5 poems at a time. E-mailed submissions will not be considered. Include a stamped addressed envelope or your e-mail address if sending by mail. Buys 120+ poems/year. Submit maximum 5 poems. **Pays $20/page up to $150 (higher some years with grant support), plus a one-year subscription, and, for print publication, 2 contributor's copies and 4 gift copies.**

ALASKA QUARTERLY REVIEW

University of Alaska Anchorage, 3211 Providence Dr. (ESH 208), Anchorage AK 99508. **Fax:** (907)786-6916. **E-mail:** uaa_aqr@uaa.alaska.edu. **Website:** www.uaa. alaska.edu/aqr. **Contact:** Ronald Spatz, editor in chief. **95% freelance written.** Semiannual magazine publishing fiction, poetry, literary nonfiction, and short plays in traditional and experimental styles. *"Alaska Quarterly Review is a literary journal devoted to contemporary literary art, publishing fiction, short plays, poetry, photo essays, and literary nonfiction in traditional and experimental styles. The editors encourage new and emerging writers, while continuing to publish award-winning and established writers."* Estab. 1982. Circ. 2,700. Byline given. Publishes ms an average of 6 months after acceptance. Accepts queries by mail. Accepts simultaneous submissions. Responds in 4 months to queries; in 6 weeks-4 months to mss. Sample copy: $6. Guidelines online.

NONFICTION Needs essays, literary nonfiction in traditional and experimental styles. Submit complete ms by postal mail. Include cover letter with contact information and SASE for return of ms. Length: up to 50 pages. **Pays contributor's copies and honoraria when funding is available.**

FICTION "Works in *AQR* have certain characteristics: freshness, honesty, and a compelling subject. The voice of the piece must be strong—idiosyncratic enough to create a unique persona. We look for craft, putting it in a form where it becomes emotionally and intellectually complex. Many pieces in *AQR* concern everyday life. We're not asking our writers to go outside themselves and their experiences to the absolute exotic to catch our interest. We look for the experiential and revelatory qualities of the work. We will champion a piece that may be less polished or stylistically sophisticated if it engages me, surprises me, and resonates for me. The joy in reading such a work is in discovering something true. Moreover, in keeping with our mission to publish new writers, we are looking for voices our readers do not know, voices that may not always be reflected in the dominant culture and that, in all instances, have something important to convey." Needs experimental, contemporary, prose poem, novel excerpts, drama: experimental and traditional one-acts. No romance, children's, or inspirational/religious. Submit complete ms by postal mail. Include cover letter with contact information and SASE for return of ms. Length: up to 50 pages. **Pays contributor's copies and honoraria when funding is available.**

POETRY Needs avant-garde, free verse, traditional. Submit poetry by postal mail. Include cover letter with contact information and SASE for return of ms. No light verse. Length: up to 20 pages. **Pays contributor's copies and honoraria when funding is available.**

ALBEDO ONE

8 Bachelor's Walk, Dublin 1 Ireland. **E-mail:** bobn@yellowbrickroad.ie. **Website:** www.albedo1.com. **Contact:** Bob Nielson. "We are always looking for thoughtful, well-written fiction. Our definition of what constitutes science fiction, horror, and fantasy is extremely broad, and we love to see material which pushes at the boundaries or crosses between genres." Estab. 1993. Circ. 900. Pays on publication. Publishes ms 1 year after acceptance. Accepts queries by mail, e-mail. Responds in 3 months to mss. Guidelines on website.

FICTION Needs experimental, fantasy, horror, science fiction, literary. Submit complete ms by mail or e-mail. Length: 2,000-8,000 words. **Pays €6 per 1,000 words, to a maximum of 8,000 words, and 1 contributor's copy.**

ALLEGORY

P.O. Box 2714, Cherry Hill NJ 08034. **E-mail:** submissions@allegoryezine.com. **Website:** www.allegoryezine.com. **Contact:** Ty Drago, editor. Biannual online

magazine specializing in science fiction, fantasy, and horror. "We are an e-zine by writers for writers. Our articles focus on the art, craft, and business of writing. Our links and editorial policy all focus on the needs of fiction authors." Estab. 1998. Circ. *Allegory* receives upwards of 250,000 hits per year. Pays on publication for one-time, electronic rights. Publishes in May and November. Accepts simultaneous submissions. Responds in 8 weeks to mss. Guidelines online.

NONFICTION Length: 1,500 word limit on nonfiction. Must be related to the craft or business of writing. **Pays $15/article.**

FICTION Receives 150 unsolicited mss/month. Accepts 12 mss/issue; 24 mss/year. Agented fiction 5%. Publishes 10 new writers/year. Also publishes literary essays, literary criticism. Often comments on rejected mss. "No media tie-ins (*Star Trek*, *Star Wars*, etc., or space opera, vampires)." "All submissions should be sent by e-mail (no letters or telephone calls) in either text or .rtf format. Please place 'Submission [Title]-[first and last name]' in the subject line. Include the following in both the body of the e-mail and the attachment: your name, name to use on the story (byline) if different, your preferred e-mail address, your mailing address, the story's title, and the story's word count." Length: 1,500-7,500 words; average length: 2,500 words. **Pays $15/story.**

AMERICAN SHORT FICTION

Badgerdog Literary Publishing, P.O. Box 301209, Austin TX 78703. **E-mail:** editors@americanshortfiction.org. **Website:** www.americanshortfiction.org. **Contact:** Rebecca Markovits and Adeena Reitberger, editors. "Issued triannually, *American Short Fiction* publishes work by emerging and established voices: stories that dive into the wreck, that stretch the reader between recognition and surprise, that conjure a particular world with delicate expertise—stories that take a different way home." Estab. 1991. Circ. 2,500. Byline given. Pays on publication. Publishes ms an average of 3 months after acceptance. Accepts queries by online submission form. Accepts simultaneous submissions. Responds in 2 weeks to queries; in 5 months to mss. "Sample copies are available for sale through our publisher's online store." Guidelines online.

FICTION "Open to publishing mystery or speculative fiction if we feel it has literary value." Does not want young adult or genre fiction. **Buys 20-25 mss/year.** *American Short Fiction* seeks "short fiction by some of the finest writers working in contemporary literature, whether they are established, new, or lesser-known authors." Also publishes stories under 2,000 words online. Submit 1 story at a time via online submissions manager ($3 fee). No paper submissions. Length: open. **Writers receive $250-500, 2 contributor's copies, free subscription to the magazine. Additional copies $5.**

THE ANTIGONISH REVIEW

St. Francis Xavier University, P.O. Box 5000, Antigonish NS B2G 2W5 Canada. (902)867-3962. **Fax:** (902)867-5563. **E-mail:** tar@stfx.ca. **Website:** www.antigonishreview.com. **Contact:** Bonnie McIsaac, office manager. **100% freelance written.** Quarterly literary magazine for educated and creative readers. *The Antigonish Review*, published quarterly, tries "to produce the kind of literary and visual mosaic that the modern sensibility requires or would respond to." Estab. 1970. Circ. 850. Byline given. Pays on publication. Offers variable kill fee. Publishes ms an average of 8 months after acceptance. Editorial lead time 4 months. Submit seasonal material 4 months in advance. Accepts queries by mail, fax. Responds in 1 month to queries; in 6 months to mss. Sample copy: $7. Guidelines for #10 SASE or online.

NONFICTION Needs essays, interview, reviews, book reviews/articles. No academic pieces. **Buys 15-20 mss/year.** Query. Length: 1,500-5,000 words **Pays $50 and 2 contributor's copies.**

FICTION Contact: Bonnie McIsaac. Send complete ms. Accepts submissions by fax. Accepts electronic (disk compatible with WordPerfect/IBM and Windows) submissions. Prefers hard copy. Needs novel excerpts, short stories. No erotica. **Buys 35-40 mss/year.** Send complete ms. Length: 500-5,000 words. **Pays $50 and 2 contributor's copies for stories.**

POETRY Contact: Bonnie McIsaac. Open to poetry on any subject written from any point of view and in any form. However, writers should expect their work to be considered within the full context of old and new poetry in English and other languages. Has published poetry by Andy Wainwright, W.J. Keith, Michael Hulse, Jean McNeil, M. Travis Lane, and Douglas Lochhead. Buys 100-125 poems/year. Submit maximum 8 poems. Submit 6-8 poems at a time. A preferable submission would be 3-4 poems. Lines/poem: not over 80, i.e., 2 pages. **Pays $10/page to a maximum of $50 and 2 contributor's copies.**

ARC POETRY MAGAZINE

Arc, Arc Poetry Society, P.O. Box 81060, Ottawa ON K1P 1B1 Canada. **E-mail:** managingeditor@arcpoetry.ca; coordinatingeditor@arcpoetry.ca; arc@arcpoetry.ca. **Website:** www.arcpoetry.ca. **Contact:** Monty Reid, managing editor; Chris Johnson, coordinating editor. Semiannual magazine featuring poetry, poetry-related articles, and criticism. Focus is poetry, and Canadian poetry, although *Arc* publishes also writers from elsewhere. Looking for the best poetry from new and established writers. Often have special issues. Send a SASE for upcoming special issues and contests. Estab. 1978. Circ. 1,500. Byline given. Pays on publication. Publishes mss an average of 6 months after acceptance. Accepts queries by online submission form. Accepts simultaneous submissions. Responds in 4 to 6 months. Arc accepts unsolicited submissions of previously unpublished poems, on any subject, in any form, from September through May. Poets may only submit once each calendar year. Poetry submissions must not exceed 3 poems total. Submissions must be typed and single spaced (double spaces will be interpreted as blank lines). Include your name, e-mail address, and mailing address on each page. Submit each poem in a separate document along with the poet's biography. Your submission will be grouped together in our submission platform. Biographical statements should be two to three sentences or approximately 50 words. Arc will respond to unsolicited submissions of poetry, artwork, and article queries within four to six months. Arc can't promise to respond to inquiries regarding the status of submissions before the completion of an editorial cycle.

NONFICTION Needs essays, interview, reviews, poetry book reviews. Query first. Length: 500-4,000 words. **Pays $40/printed page (Canadian), and 2 copies.**

POETRY Needs contemporary poetry. For over 30 years, Arc has been publishing the best in contemporary poetry. Arc invites submissions from emerging and established poets. Buys 60 poems/year. Submit maximum 3 poems. **Pays $40/printed page (Canadian).**

ARTS & LETTERS JOURNAL OF CONTEMPORARY CULTURE

Georgia College & State University, Milledgeville GA 31061. (478)445-1289. **Website:** al.gcsu.edu. **Contact:** Laura Newbern, editor. *Arts & Letters Journal of Contemporary Culture*, published semiannually, is devoted to contemporary arts and literature, featuring ongoing series such as The World Poetry Translation Series and The Mentors Interview Series. Wants work that is of the highest literary and artistic quality. Estab. 1999. Pays on publication. No kill fee. Accepts simultaneous submissions. Responds in 1-2 months to mss. Guidelines online.

NONFICTION Submit complete ms via online submissions manager. Length: up to 25 pages typed and double-spaced. **Pays $10 per printed page (minimum payment: $50) and 1 contributor's copy.**

FICTION No genre fiction. Submit complete ms via online submissions manager. Length: up to 25 pages typed and double-spaced. **Pays $10 per printed page (minimum payment: $50) and 1 contributor's copy.**

POETRY Submit via online submissions manager. Include cover letter. "Poems are screened, discussed by group of readers. If approved by group, poems are submitted to poetry editor for final approval." Has published poetry by Margaret Gibson, Marilyn Nelson, Stuart Lishan, R.T. Smith, Laurie Lamon, and Miller Williams. No light verse. Submit maximum 6 poems. **Pays $10 per printed page (minimum payment: $50) and 1 contributor's copy.**

THE BALTIMORE REVIEW

6514 Maplewood Rd., Baltimore MD 21212. **E-mail:** editor@baltimorereview.org. **Website:** www.baltimorereview.org. **Contact:** Barbara Westwood Diehl, senior editor. **100% freelance written.** *The Baltimore Review* publishes poetry, fiction, and creative nonfiction from Baltimore and beyond. Submission periods are August 1-November 30 and February 1-May 31. Estab. 1996. Byline given. Pays $40 on publication No kill fee. Publishes ms an average of 6 months after acceptance. Accepts simultaneous submissions. Responds in 3 months or less. Guidelines online.

NONFICTION creative nonfiction. Publishes 2-6 mss per online issue. Length: up to 5,000 words. **Pays $40.**

FICTION literary fiction. Send complete ms using online submission form. Publishes 16-20 mss per online issue. Work published online also published in annual anthology. Length: 100-6,000 words. **Pays $40.**

POETRY Needs avant-garde, free verse, traditional. Submit 1-3 poems. See editor preferences on submission guidelines on website. **Pays $40.**

BARRELHOUSE

E-mail: yobarrelhouse@gmail.com. **Website:** www.barrelhousemag.com. **Contact:** Dave Housley, Mike

Ingram, and Joe Killiany, fiction editors; Tom McAllister, nonfiction editor; Dan Brady, poetry editor. "*Barrelhouse* is a biannual print journal featuring fiction, poetry, interviews, and essays about music, art, and the detritus of popular culture." Estab. 2004. Byline given. No kill fee. Accepts queries by online submission form. Accepts simultaneous submissions. Responds in 2-3 months to mss.

NONFICTION Needs essays. Submit via online submissions manager. DOC or RTF files only. Length: open, but prefers pieces under 8,000 words. **Pays $50 and 2 contributor copies.**

FICTION Needs experimental, humorous, mainstream. Submit complete ms via online submissions manager. DOC or RTF files only. Length: open, but prefers pieces under 8,000. **Pays $50 and 2 contributor copies.**

POETRY Submit up to 5 poems via online submissions manager. DOC or RTF files only. Submit maximum 5 poems. **Pays $50 and 2 contributor's copies.**

$ $ THE BEAR DELUXE MAGAZINE

Orlo, 240 N. Broadway, #112, Portland OR 97227. **E-mail:** bear@orlo.org. **Website:** www.orlo.org. **Contact:** Tom Webb, editor-in-chief; Kristin Rogers Brown, art director. **80% freelance written.** Covers fiction, essay, poetry, other. Do not combine submissions; rather submit poetry, fiction, and essay in separate packages. News essays, on occasion, are assigned if they have a strong element of reporting. Artists contribute to *The Bear Deluxe* in various ways, including: editorial illustration, editorial photography, spot illustration, independent art, cover art, graphic design, and cartoons. "*The Bear Deluxe Magazine* is a national independent environmental arts magazine publishing significant works of reporting, creative nonfiction, literature, visual art, and design. Based in the Pacific Northwest, it reaches across cultural and political divides to engage readers on vital issues effecting the environment. Published twice per year, *The Bear Deluxe* includes a wider array and a higher percentage of visual artwork and design than many other publications. Artwork is included both as editorial support and as standalone or independent art. It has included nationally recognized artists as well as emerging artists. As with any publication, artists are encouraged to review a sample copy for a clearer understanding of the magazine's approach. Unsolicited submissions and samples are accepted and encouraged." Estab. 1993. Circ. 19,000. Byline given. Pays on publication. Offers 25% kill fee. Publishes ms an average of 6 months after acceptance. Editorial lead time 6 months. Submit seasonal material 9 months in advance. Accepts queries by mail, e-mail. Accepts simultaneous submissions. Responds in 3-6 months to mail queries. Only responds to e-mail queries if interested. Sample copy: $5. Guidelines online.

NONFICTION Needs essays, general interest, interview, new product, opinion, personal experience, photo feature, travel. Special issues: Publishes 1 theme every 2 years. **Buys 40 mss/year.** Query with published clips. Length: 750-4,000 words. **Pays $25-400, depending on piece.** Sometimes pays expenses.

COLUMNS Reviews (almost anything), 100-1,000 words; Front of the Book (mix of short news bits, found writing, quirky tidbits), 300-500 words; Portrait of an Artist (artist profiles), 1,200 words; Back of the Book (creative opinion pieces), 650 words. **Buys 16 mss/year.** Query with published clips. **Pays $25-400, depending on piece.**

FICTION "We are most excited by high-quality writing that furthers the magazine's goal of engaging new and divergent readers. We appreciate strong aspects of storytelling and are open to new formats, though we wouldn't call ourselves publishers of 'experimental fiction.'" Needs adventure, condensed novels, historical, horror, humorous, mystery, western. No traditional sci-fi, horror, romance, or crime/action. **Buys 8 mss/year.** Query or send complete ms. Prefers postal mail submissions. Length: up to 4,000 words. **Pays free subscription to the magazine, contributor's copies, and $25-400, depending on piece; additional copies for postage.**

POETRY Needs avant-garde, free verse, haiku, light verse, traditional. Submit 3-5 poems at a time. Poems are reviewed by a committee of 3-5 people. Publishes 1 theme issue per year. Buys 16-20 poems/year. Length: up to 50 lines/poem. **Pays $20, subscription, and contributor's copies.**

FILLERS Needs facts, newsbreaks, short humor. **Buys 10 mss/year.** Length: 100-750 words.

⚫ BEATDOM

Beatdom Books, 42/R Gowrie St., Dundee Scotland DD2 1AF United Kingdom. **E-mail:** editor@beatdom. com. **Website:** www.beatdom.com. **Contact:** David Wills, editor. **75% freelance written.** "We publish studies of Beat texts, figures and legends; we look at

writers and movements related to the Beats; we support writers of the present who take their influence from the Beats." Estab. 2007. Circ. 1,000. Byline given. Pays on publication. No kill fee. Publishes ms 6 months after acceptance. Accepts queries by e-mail. Accepts simultaneous submissions.

NONFICTION Needs essays, interview, profile. **Buys 10 mss/year.** Query. Length: 1,000-5,000 words. **Pays $10-100.**

BIG PULP

Exter Press, P.O. Box 92, Cumberland MD 21501. **E-mail:** editors@bigpulp.com. **Website:** www.bigpulp. com. **Contact:** Bill Olver, editor. Quarterly literary magazine. Submissions accepted by e-mail only. *Big Pulp* defines "pulp fiction" very broadly: It's lively, challenging, thought-provoking, thrilling, and fun, regardless of how many or how few genre elements are packed in. Doesn't subscribe to the theory that genre fiction is disposable; a great deal of literary fiction could easily fall under one of their general categories. Places a higher value on character and story than genre elements. Estab. 2008. Byline given. Pays on publication. Offers 100% kill fee. Publishes ms 1 year after acceptance. Accepts queries by e-mail. Accepts simultaneous submissions. Responds in 2 months to mss. Sample copy: $10; excerpts available online at no cost. Guidelines online.

FICTION Needs adventure, fantasy, horror, mystery, romance, science fiction, suspense, western, superhero. Does not want generic slice-of-life, memoirs, inspirational, political, pastoral odes. **Buys 70 mss/year.** Submit complete ms. Length: up to 10,000 words. **Pays $5-25.**

POETRY Needs avant-garde, free verse, haiku, light verse, traditional. All types of poetry are considered, but poems should have a genre connection. Buys 20 poems/year. Submit maximum 5 poems. Length: up to 100 lines/poem. **Pays $5/poem.**

BLACK LACE

P.O. Box 83912, Los Angeles CA 90083. (310)410-0808. **Fax:** (310)410-9250. **E-mail:** newsroom@blk.com. **Website:** www.blacklace.org. "*Black Lace* seeks stories, articles, photography, models, illustration, and a very limited amount of poetry all related to black women unclothed or in erotic situations." Estab. 1991. Submit seasonal material 6 months in advance. Accepts queries by mail, e-mail, fax. Accepts simultaneous submissions. Responds in 1 month. Guidelines online.

NONFICTION nostalgia and humor pieces, historical articles, and first-person accounts that are black, in the life (ITL), and erotic. "Wants articles that include details on where black women in the life congregate. These can range from the latest local bar to out-of-the-way resorts. Thoroughness and accuracy are the keys to acceptance of these articles." Also wants shorts, 400-700 words, with "fresh, sharply focused erotic ideas." Submit by postal mail (include SASE for return of work), fax, or e-mail. **Pays average of 10¢/word.**

FICTION Needs erotica, ethnic, gay, lesbian. Submit via postal mail (include SASE if you want your work returned), fax, or e-mail. Length: 2,000-4,000 words. **Pays average of 10¢/word.**

POETRY Submit by postal mail (include SASE if you want your work returned), fax, or e-mail.

$ $ BOULEVARD

Opojaz, Inc., 6614 Clayton Rd., Box 325, Richmond Heights MO 63117. **E-mail:** richardburgin@netzero.com; jessicarogen@boulevardmagazine.org. **Website:** www.boulevardmagazine.org; boulevard.submittable.com/submit. **Contact:** Jessica Rogen, editor. **100% freelance written.** "*Boulevard* is a diverse literary magazine presenting original creative work by well-known authors, as well as by writers of exciting promise." Triannual magazine featuring fiction, poetry, and essays. Sometimes comments on rejected mss. *Boulevard* has been called 'one of the half-dozen best literary journals' by Poet Laureate Daniel Hoffman in *The Philadelphia Inquirer.* We strive to publish the finest in poetry, fiction, and nonfiction. We frequently publish writers with previous credits, and we are very interested in publishing less experienced or unpublished writers with exceptional promise. We've published everything from John Ashbery to Donald Hall to a wide variety of styles from new or lesser known poets. We're eclectic. We are interested in original, moving poetry written from the head as well as the heart. It can be about any topic." Estab. 1985. Circ. 11,000. Byline given. Pays on publication. Offers no kill fee. Publishes ms an average of 9 months after acceptance. Accepts queries by mail, online submission form. Accepts simultaneous submissions. Responds in 2 weeks to queries; in 4-5 months to mss. Sample copy: $10. Subscription: $15 for 3 issues, $27 for 6 issues, $30 for 9 issues. Foreign subscribers, please add $10. Make checks payable to Opojaz, Inc. Subscriptions are available online at www.boulevardmagazine.org/subscribe.html. Guidelines online.

NONFICTION Needs book excerpts, essays, interview, opinion, photo feature. **Buys 10 mss/year.** Submit by mail or via Submittable. Accepts multiple submissions. Does not accept mss May 1-October 1. SASE for reply. Length: up to 8,000 words. **Pays $100-300.**

FICTION Submit by mail or via Submittable. Accepts multiple submissions. Does not accept mss May 1-October 1. SASE for reply. Needs ethnic, experimental, mainstream, novel excerpts, short stories, slice-of-life vignettes. "We do not want erotica, science fiction, romance, western, horror, or children's stories." **Buys 20 mss/year.** Length: up to 8,000 words. **Pays $50-500 (sometimes higher) for accepted work.**

POETRY Needs avant-garde, free verse, haiku, traditional. Submit by mail or via Submittable. Accepts multiple submissions. Does not accept poems May 1-October 1. SASE for reply. Does not consider book reviews. "Do not send us light verse." Does not want "poetry that is uninspired, formulaic, self-conscious, unoriginal, insipid." Buys 80 poems/year. Submit maximum 5 poems. Length: up to 200 lines/poem. **Pays $25-250.**

🍁 $ $ BRICK

Brick, P.O. Box 609, Station P, Toronto ON M5S 2Y4 Canada. **E-mail:** info@brickmag.com. **Website:** www.brickmag.com. **Contact:** Liz Johnston, managing editor. **90% freelance written.** Semiannual magazine covering literature and the arts. "We publish literary nonfiction of a very high quality on a range of arts and culture subjects." Estab. 1977. Circ. 3,000. Byline given. Pays on publication. No kill fee. Publishes ms 3-5 months after acceptance. Editorial lead time 5 months. Accepts simultaneous submissions. Responds in 6 months to mss. Sample copy: $16 plus shipping. Guidelines online.

NONFICTION Needs essays, historical, interview, opinion, travel. No fiction, poetry, personal memoir, or art. **Buys 30-40 mss/year.** Send complete ms. Length: 250-3,000 words. **Pays $75-500 (Canadian).**

BURNSIDE REVIEW

P.O. Box 1782, Portland OR 97207. **Website:** www.burnsidereview.org. **Contact:** Sid Miller, founder and editor; Dan Kaplan, managing editor. *Burnside Review,* published every 9 months, prints "the best poetry and short fiction we can get our hands on." Each issue includes 1 featured poet with an interview and new poems. "We tend to publish writing that finds beauty in truly unexpected places; that combines urban and natural imagery; that breaks the heart." Estab. 2004. Pays on publication. Publishes ms 9 months after acceptance. Submit seasonal material 3-6 months in advance. Accepts queries by online submission form. Accepts simultaneous submissions. Responds in 1-6 months. Single copy: $8; subscription: $13.

FICTION "We like bright, engaging fiction that works to surprise and captivate us." Needs experimental, short stories. Submit complete ms via online submissions manager. Length: up to 5,000 words. **Pays $25 and 1 contributor's copy.**

POETRY Needs avant-garde, free verse, traditional. Open to all forms. Translations are encouraged. "We like lyric. We like narrative. We like when the 2 merge. We like whiskey. We like hourglass figures. We like to be surprised. Surprise us." Has published poetry by Linda Bierds, Dorianne Laux, Ed Skoog, Campbell McGrath, Paul Guest, and Larissa Szporluk. Reads submissions year round. "Editors read all work submitted." Seldom comments on rejected work. Submit 3-5 poems via online submissions manager. Submit maximum 5 poems. **Pays $25 and 1 contributor's copy.**

THE CAFE IRREAL

E-mail: editors@cafeirreal.com. **Website:** www.cafeirreal.com. **Contact:** G.S. Evans and Alice Whittenburg, co-editors. **90% freelance written.** Quarterly webzine focusing on short stories and short shorts of an irreal nature. Also publishes literary essays, literary criticism. "Our audience is composed of people who read or write literary fiction with fantastic themes, similar to the work of Franz Kafka, Kobo Abe, or Clarice Lispector. This is a type of fiction (irreal) that has difficulty finding its way into print in the English-speaking world and defies many of the conventions of American literature especially. As a result, ours is a fairly specialized literary publication, and we would strongly recommend that prospective writers look at our current issue and guidelines carefully." Recently published work by Tom Whalen, Venita Blackburn, Agustín Cadena, Michal Ajvaz, Marianne Villanueva, and Eric G. Wilson. Estab. 1998. Circ. 10,000. Byline given. Pays on publication for first electronic rights. Sends galleys to author. No kill fee. Responds in 4 months. Sometimes comments on rejected mss. Sample copy online. Guidelines online.

FICTION Accepts submissions by e-mail. No attachments; include submission in body of e-mail. Include estimated word count. Accepts 6-8 mss/issue; 24-32 mss/year. Needs experimental, fantasy, science fiction. No horror or 'slice-of-life' stories; no genre or mainstream science fiction or fantasy. Length: up to 2,000 words. **Pays 1¢/word, $2 minimum.**

THE CAPILANO REVIEW

281 Industrial Ave., Vancouver BC V6A 2P2 Canada. (604)984-1712. **E-mail:** contact@thecapilanoreview.ca. **Website:** www.thecapilanoreview.ca. **Contact:** Todd Nickel, managing editor. **100% freelance written.** Triannual visual and literary arts magazine that "publishes only what the editors consider to be the very best fiction, poetry, drama, or visual art being produced. *TCR* editors are interested in fresh, original work that stimulates and challenges readers. Over the years, the magazine has developed a reputation for pushing beyond the boundaries of traditional art and writing. We are interested in work that is new in concept and in execution." Estab. 1972. Circ. 800. Byline given. Pays on publication. Publishes ms an average of within 1 year after acceptance. Accepts queries by mail. Responds in 4-6 months to mss. Sample copy: $10 (outside of Canada, USD). Guidelines with #10 SASE with IRC or Canadian stamps.

FICTION Needs experimental, literary. No traditional, conventional fiction. Wants to see more innovative, genre-blurring work. **Buys 10-15 mss/year.** Send complete ms with SASE and Canadian postage or IRCs. Does not accept submissions through e-mail or on disks. Length: up to 5,000 words **Pays $50-300.**

POETRY Needs avant-garde, free verse, previously unpublished poetry. Submit up to 8 pages of poetry. Buys 40 poems/year. Submit maximum 8 poems. **Pays $50-300.**

THE CINCINNATI REVIEW

P.O. Box 210069, Cincinnati OH 45221-0069. (513)556-3954. **E-mail:** editors@cincinnatireview.com. **Website:** www.cincinnatireview.com. **Contact:** Michael Griffith, fiction editor; Don Bogen, poetry editor. **100% freelance written.** Semiannual magazine containing new literary fiction, creative nonfiction, poetry, book reviews, essays, and interviews. A journal devoted to publishing the best new literary fiction, creative nonfiction, and poetry, as well as book reviews, essays, and interviews. Estab. 2003. Byline given. Pays on publication. No kill fee. Publishes ms an average of 6 months after acceptance. Accepts queries by online submission form. Accepts simultaneous submissions. Responds in 4 months to mss. Always sends prepublication galleys. Sample copy: $7 (back issue). Single copy: $9 (current issue). Subscription: $15. Guidelines available on website.

NONFICTION Submit complete ms via online submissions manager only. Length: up to 40 double-spaced pages. **Pays $25/page.**

FICTION Needs short stories. Does not want genre fiction. **Buys 13 mss/year.** Submit complete ms via online submissions manager only. Length: up to 40 double-spaced pages. **Pays $25/page.**

POETRY Needs avant-garde, free verse, traditional. Submit up to 10 pages of poetry at a time via submission manager only. Buys 120 poems/year. **Pays $30/page.**

$ COLORADO REVIEW

Center for Literary Publishing, Colorado State University, 9105 Campus Delivery, Fort Collins CO 80523. (970)491-5449. **E-mail:** creview@colostate.edu. **Website:** coloradoreview.colostate.edu. **Contact:** Stephanie G'Schwind, editor in chief and nonfiction editor; Steven Schwartz, fiction editor; Don Revell, Sasha Steensen, and Matthew Cooperman, poetry editors; Dan Beachy-Quick, book review editor. Literary magazine published 3 times/year. Estab. 1956. Circ. 1,000. Byline given. Pays on publication. No kill fee. Publishes ms an average of 6 months after acceptance. Editorial lead time 1 year. Accepts simultaneous submissions. Responds in 2 months to mss. Sample copy: $10. Guidelines online.

NONFICTION Needs essays, memoir, personal experience. **Buys 6-9 mss/year.** Mss for nonfiction stories are read year round. Send no more than 1 story at a time. Length: up to 10,000 words. **Pays $200 for essays.**

FICTION Needs experimental, literary short fiction. No genre fiction. **Buys 12 mss/year.** Send complete ms. Fiction mss are read August 1-April 30. Mss received May 1-July 31 will be returned unread. Length: up to 10,000 words. **Pays $200.**

POETRY Considers poetry of any style. Poetry mss are read August 1-April 30. Mss received May 1-July 31 will be returned unread. Has published poetry by Sherman Alexie, Laynie Browne, John Gallaher, Mathias Svalina, Craig Morgan Teicher, Pam Rehm,

Elizabeth Robinson, Elizabeth Willis, and Rosmarie Waldrop. Buys 60-100 poems/year. Submit maximum 5 poems. **Pays minimum of $30 or $10/page for poetry.**

$ $ CONFRONTATION

English Department, LIU Post, Brookville NY 11548. (516)299-2963. **E-mail:** confrontationmag@gmail.com. **Website:** www.confrontationmagazine.org. Terry Kattleman, publicity director/production editor. **Contact:** Jonna Semeiks, editor in chief; Belinda Kremer, poetry editor. **75% freelance written.** Semi-annual magazine comprising all forms and genres of stories, poems, essays, memoirs, and plays. A special section contains book reviews. "We also publish the work of 1 visual artist per issue, selected by the editors." "*Confrontation* has been in continuous publication since 1968. Our taste and our magazine is eclectic, but we always look for excellence in style, an important theme, a memorable voice. We enjoy discovering and fostering new talent. Each issue contains work by both well-established and new writers. We read August 16-April 15. Do not send mss or e-mail submissions between April 16 and August 15." Estab. 1968. Circ. 2,000. Byline given. Pays on publication. Offers kill fee. Publishes work in the first or second issue after acceptance. Accepts simultaneous submissions. Responds in 10 weeks to mss. "We prefer single submissions. Clear copy. **No e-mail submissions unless writer resides outside the U.S.** Mail submissions with a SASE."

NONFICTION Needs essays, personal experience. Special issues: "We publish personal, cultural, political, and other kinds of essays as well as self-contained sections of memoirs." **Buys 5-10 mss/year.** Send complete ms. Length: 1,500-5,000 words. **Pays $100-150; more for commissioned work.**

FICTION "We judge on quality of writing and thought or imagination, so we will accept genre fiction. However, it must have literary merit or must transcend or challenge genre." Needs experimental as well as more traditional fiction, self-contained novel excerpts, slice-of-life vignettes, lyrical or philosophical fiction. No "proselytizing" literature or conventional genre fiction. **Buys 10-15 mss/year.** Send complete ms. Length: up to 7,200 words. **Pays $175-250; more for commissioned work.**

POETRY Needs avant-garde or experimental as well as traditional poems (and forms), lyric poems, dramatic monologues, satiric or philosophical poems. In short, a wide range of verse. "*Confrontation* is interested in all poetic forms. Our only criterion is high literary merit. We think of our audience as an educated, lay group of intelligent readers." Has published poetry by David Ray, T. Alan Broughton, David Ignatow, Philip Appleman, Jane Mayhall, and Joseph Brodsky. Submit no more than 12 pages at a time (up to 6 poems). *Confrontation* also offers the annual Confrontation Poetry Prize. No sentimental verse. No previously published poems. Buys 20 poems/year. Length: up to 2 pages. **Pays $75-100; more for commissioned work.**

$ CONTRARY

P.O. Box 806363, Chicago IL 60616-3299. **E-mail:** chicago@contrarymagazine.com. **Website:** www.contrarymagazine.com. **Contact:** Jeff McMahon, editor; Frances Badgett, fiction editor; Shaindel Beers, poetry editor. **100.** *Contrary* publishes fiction, poetry, and literary commentary, and prefers work that combines the virtues of all those categories. Founded at the University of Chicago, it now operates independently and not-for-profit on the South Side of Chicago. "We like work that is not only contrary in content, but contrary in its evasion of the expectations established by its genre. Our fiction defies traditional story form. For example, a story may bring us to closure without ever delivering an ending. We don't insist on the ending, but we do insist on the closure. And we value fiction as poetic as any poem." Quarterly. Member CLMP. Estab. 2003. Circ. 38,000. Byline given. Pays on publication and receipt of invoice. Mss published 21 days after acceptance. Editorial lead time 3 months. Accepts queries by online submission form. Accepts simultaneous submissions. Responds to queries in 2 weeks; in 3 months to mss. Rarely comments on/critiques rejected mss. Guidelines online.

NONFICTION Needs book excerpts, essays, general interest, humor, memoir, opinion, personal experience, reviews, Accepts lyrical, literary nonfiction. Does not expository or argumentative nonfiction. **Buys 4-6 mss/year.** Accepts submissions through website only: www.contrarymagazine.com/Contrary/Submissions.html. Include estimated word count, brief bio, list of publications.

FICTION Receives 650 mss/month. Accepts 6 mss/issue; 24 mss/year. Publishes 14 new writers/year. Has published Sherman Alexie, Andrew Coburn, Amy Reed, Clare Kirwan, Stephanie Johnson, Laurence Davies, and Edward McWhinney. Needs experimental, mainstream, religious, short stories, slice-of-life vignettes, literary. **Buys 8-12 mss/year.** Accepts submissions through website only: www.contrarymagazine.com/Contrary/Submissions.html. Include estimated word count, brief bio, list of publications. Length: up to 2,000 words. Average length: 750 words. Publishes short shorts. Average length of short shorts: 750 words. **Pays $20-60.**

POETRY Accepts submissions through website only: www.contrarymagazine.com/Contrary/Submissions.html. Include estimated word count, brief bio, list of publications.Often comments on rejected poems. Submit maximum 3 poems. **Pays $20 per byline, $60 for featured work.**

$ CREATIVE NONFICTION

Creative Nonfiction Foundation, 5501 Walnut St., Suite 202, Pittsburgh PA 15232. (412)688-0304. **Fax:** (412)688-0262. **E-mail:** information@creativenonfiction.org. **Website:** www.creativenonfiction.org. **100% freelance written.** Magazine published 4 times/year covering nonfiction—personal essay, memoir, literary journalism. "*Creative Nonfiction* is the voice of the genre. It publishes personal essays, memoirs, and literary journalism on a broad range of subjects. Interviews with prominent writers, reviews, and commentary about the genre also appear in its pages." Estab. 1993. Circ. 7,000. Byline given. Pays on publication. No kill fee. Publishes ms an average of 1 year after acceptance. Editorial lead time 6 months. Accepts queries by mail, online submission form. Accepts simultaneous submissions. Responds in 6 months to mss. Sample copy: $10. Guidelines online.

NONFICTION Needs essays, interview, memoir, personal experience, narrative journalism. No poetry or fiction. Send complete ms. Length: up to 4,000 words. **Pays $50, plus $10/page—sometimes more for theme issues.**

COLUMNS Contact: Hattie Fletcher. "Have an idea for a literary timeline? An opinion on essential texts for readers and/or writers? An in-depth, working knowledge of a specific type of nonfiction? Pitch us your ideas." Complete guidelines found at www.creativenonfiction.org/submissions/pitch-us-column.

$ THE DARK

311 Fairbanks Ave., Northfield NJ 08225. **E-mail:** thedarkmagazine@gmail.com. **Website:** www.the-

darkmagazine.com. **Contact:** Jack Fisher and Sean Wallace, editors. **100% freelance written.** Quarterly electronic magazine publishing horror and dark fantasy. Estab. 2013. Byline given. Pays on acceptance. No kill fee. Publishes ms an average of 6 months after acceptance. Editorial lead time 1 month. Accepts queries by e-mail. Responds in 1-2 weeks to mss. Always sends prepublication galleys. Sample: $2.99 (back issue). Guidelines available on website.

FICTION Needs fantasy, horror, suspense, strange, magic realism, dark fantasy. "Don't be afraid to experiment or to deviate from the ordinary; be different—try us with fiction that may fall out of 'regular' categories. However, it is also important to understand that despite the name, *The Dark* is not a market for graphic, violent horror." **Buys 12-16 mss/year.** Send complete ms by e-mail attached in Microsoft Word DOC only. No multiple submissions. Length: 1,000-6,000 words. **Pays 3¢/word.**

$ DECEMBER

A Literary Legacy Since 1958, December Publishing, P.O. Box 16130, St. Louis MO 63105-0830. (314)301-9980. **E-mail:** editor@decembermag.org. **Website:** decembermag.org. **Contact:** Gianna Jacobson, editor; Jennifer Goldring, managing editor. Committed to distributing the work of emerging writers and artists, and celebrating more seasoned voices through a semiannual nonprofit literary magazine featuring fiction, poetry, creative nonfiction, and visual art. Estab. 1958. Circ. 500. Byline given. Pays on publication. Editorial lead time 5 months. Accepts queries by mail, e-mail. Responds in 2 months to mss. Sample copy: $12. Guidelines online.

NONFICTION Needs essays, general interest, humor, memoir, opinion, personal experience, literary journalism. Not interested in straight journalism (news or features). **Buys 2-10 mss/year.** Submit complete ms. Length: 25-6,000 words. **Pays $10/page (minimum $40; maximum $200).**

FICTION Needs experimental, humorous, novel excerpts, short stories, slice-of-life vignettes, literary fiction, flash fiction. Does not want genre fiction. **Buys 10-20 mss/year.** Send complete ms. Length: up to 10,000 words. **Pays $10/page (minimum $40; maximum $200).**

POETRY Needs avant-garde, free verse, traditional. Buys 100-150 poems/year. Submit maximum 5-7 poems. No length requirements. **Pays $10/page (minimum $40; maximum $200).**

$$$ DELAWARE BEACH LIFE

Endeavours LLC, Endeavours, LLC, P.O. Box 417, Rehoboth Beach DE 19971. (302)227-9499. **E-mail:** info@delawarebeachlife.com. **Website:** www.delawarebeachlife.com. **Contact:** Terry Plowman, publisher/editor. Magazine published 8 times/year covering coastal Delaware. "*Delaware Beach Life* focuses on coastal Delaware: Fenwick to Lewes. You can go slightly inland as long as there's water and a natural connection to the coast, e.g., Angola or Long Neck." Estab. 2002. Circ. 15,000. Byline given. Pays on acceptance. 50% kill fee. Publishes ms 4 months after acceptance. Editorial lead time 6 months. Submit seasonal material 1 year in advance. Accepts queries by e-mail. Reports in 2 months to queries; in 6 months to mss. Sample copy available online at website. Guidelines free and by e-mail.

NONFICTION Needs book excerpts, essays, general interest, humor, interview, opinion, photo feature. Does not want anything not focused on coastal Delaware. Query with published clips. Length: 1,200-3,000 words. **Pays $400-1,000 for assigned articles.**

COLUMNS Profiles, History, and Opinion (focused on coastal DE), all 1,200 words. **Buys 32 mss/year.** Query with published clips. **Pays $150-350.**

FICTION Needs adventure, condensed novels, historical, humorous, novel excerpts, Must have coastal theme. Does not want anything not coastal. **Buys 3 mss/year.** Query with published clips. Length: 1,000-2,000 words.

POETRY Needs avant-garde, free verse, haiku, light verse, traditional. Does not want anything not coastal. No erotic poetry. Buys 6 poems/year. Submit maximum 3 poems. Length: 6-15 lines/poem. **Pays up to $50.**

$ DENVER QUARTERLY

University of Denver, 2000 E. Asbury, Denver CO 80208. (303)871-2892. **E-mail:** denverquarterly@gmail.com. **Website:** www.du.edu/denverquarterly. **Contact:** Laird Hunt, editor. Publishes fiction, articles, and poetry for a generally well-educated audience, primarily interested in literature and the literary experience. Audience reads *DQ* to find something a little different from a strictly academic quarterly or a creative writing outlet. Quarterly. Reads September

15-May 15. Estab. 1965. Circ. 2,000. Publishes ms 1 year after acceptance. Accepts queries by mail, online submission form. Accepts simultaneous submissions. Responds in 3 months. Sample copy: $10.

NONFICTION Needs essays, interview, reviews, critical engagements. Submit by postal mail or online submissions manager. Length: up to 15 pages. **Pays $5/page for fiction and 2 contributor's copies.**

FICTION "We are interested in experimental fiction (minimalism, magic realism, etc.) as well as in realistic fiction and in writing about fiction. No sentimental, science fiction, romance, or spy thrillers." Needs experimental. Submit by postal mail or online submissions manager. Length: up to 15 pages. **Pays $5/page and 2 contributor's copies.**

POETRY Submit 3-5 poems by postal mail or online submissions manager. **Pays $5/page and 2 contributor's copies.**

$ ELLIPSIS

Westminster College, 1840 S. 1300 E., Salt Lake City UT 84105. (801)832-2321. **E-mail:** ellipsis@westminstercollege.edu. **Website:** www.westminstercollege.edu/ellipsis. *Ellipsis*, published annually in April, needs good literary poetry, fiction, essays, plays, and visual art. Estab. 1965. Circ. 2,500. Byline given. Pays on publication. No kill fee. Publishes ms an average of 3 months after acceptance. Accepts queries by mail. Accepts simultaneous submissions. Responds in 6 months to mss. Sample copy: $7.50. Guidelines online.

NONFICTION Needs essays, creative nonfiction. Submit complete ms via online submissions manager. Include cover letter. **Pays $50 and 2 contributor's copies.**

FICTION literary fiction, plays. Submit complete ms via online submissions manager. Include cover letter. Length: up to 6,000 words. **Pays $50 and 2 contributor's copies.**

POETRY Submit poems via online submissions manager. Include cover letter. Has published poetry by Allison Joseph, Molly McQuade, Virgil Suaárez, Maurice Kilwein-Guevara, Richard Cecil, and Ron Carlson. Submit maximum 5 poems. **Pays $10/poem and 2 contributor's copies.**

$ EPOCH

251 Goldwin Smith Hall, Cornell University, Ithaca NY 14853-3201. (607)255-3385. **Website:** english.arts.cornell.edu/publications/epoch. **Contact:** Michael Koch, editor; Heidi E. Marschner, managing editor. **100% freelance written.** Literary magazine published 3 times/year. Looking for well-written literary fiction, poetry, personal essays. Newcomers welcome. Open to mainstream and avant-garde writing. Estab. 1947. Circ. 1,000. Byline given. Pays on publication. Offers 100% kill fee. Publishes ms an average of 6 months after acceptance. Editorial lead time 6 months. Submit seasonal material 8 months in advance. Accepts queries by mail. Responds in 2 weeks to queries; in 6 weeks to mss. Sometimes comments on rejected mss. Sample copy: $5. Guidelines online and for #10 SASE.

NONFICTION Needs essays, interview. No inspirational. **Buys 6-8 mss/year.** Send complete ms. **Pay varies; pays up to $150/unsolicited piece.**

FICTION Needs ethnic, experimental, mainstream, literary short stories. No genre fiction. Would like to see more Southern fiction (Southern U.S.). **Buys 25-30 mss/year.** Send complete ms. Considers fiction in all forms, short short to novella length. **Pay varies; pays up to $150/unsolicited piece.**

POETRY Needs avant-garde, free verse, haiku, light verse, traditional. Mss not accompanied by SASE will be discarded unread. Occasionally provides criticism on poems. Considers poetry in all forms. Buys 30-75 poems/year. Submit maximum 5 poems. **Pay varies; pays $50 minimum/poem.**

TIPS "Tell your story, speak your poem, straight from the heart. We are attracted to language and to good writing, but we are most interested in what the good writing leads us to, or where."

🍁 $ $ EVENT

Douglas College, P.O. Box 2503, New Westminster British Columbia V3L 5B2 Canada. (604)527-5293. **Fax:** (604)527-5095. **E-mail:** event@douglascollege.ca. **Website:** www.eventmags.com. **100% freelance written.** Magazine published 3 times/year containing fiction, poetry, creative nonfiction, notes on writing, and reviews. "We are eclectic and always open to content that invites involvement. Generally, we like strong narrative." Estab. 1971. Circ. 1,000. Byline given. Pays on publication. Publishes ms an average of 8 months after acceptance. Accepts queries by mail. Accepts simultaneous submissions. Responds in 1 month to queries. Responds in 6 months to mss. Guidelines online.

FICTION "We look for readability, style, and writing that invites involvement." Submit maximum 2 stories. , contemporary. No technically poor or unoriginal pieces. **Buys 12-15 mss/year.** Send complete ms. Length: 5,000 words maximum. **Pays $25/page up to $500.**

POETRY Needs free verse. "We tend to appreciate the narrative and sometimes the confessional modes." No light verse. Buys 30-40 poems/year. Submit maximum 10 poems. **Pays $25-500.**

$ FICTION

Department of English, The City College of New York, 138th St. & Convent Ave., New York NY 10031. **Website:** www.fictioninc.com. **Contact:** Mark J. Mirsky, editor. "As the name implies, we publish only fiction; we are looking for the best new writing available, leaning toward the unconventional. *Fiction* has traditionally attempted to make accessible the inaccessible, to bring the experimental to a broader audience." Reading period for unsolicited mss is September 15-June 15. Estab. 1972. Circ. 4,000. No kill fee. Publishes ms an average of 1 year after acceptance. Accepts simultaneous submissions. Responds in 3-6 months to mss. Sample: $7. Guidelines online.

FICTION Needs experimental, short stories, Also needs contemporary, literary, translations. No romance, science fiction, etc. Submit complete ms via online submissions manager. Length: reads any length, but encourages lengths under 5,000 words.

○$ THE FIDDLEHEAD

University of New Brunswick, Campus House, 11 Garland Court, Box 4400, Fredericton NB E3B 5A3 Canada. (506)453-3501. **Fax:** (506)453-5069. **E-mail:** fiddlehd@unb.ca. **Website:** www.thefiddlehead.ca. **Contact:** Kathryn Taglia, managing editor; Ross Leckie, editor; Mark Anthony Jarman and Gerard Beirne, fiction editors; Phillip Crymble, Ian LeTourneau, and Rebecca Salazar, poetry editors; Sabine Campbell and Ross Leckie, reviews editors. Covers feature artwork from New Brunswick artists and museums. "Canada's longest living literary journal, *The Fiddlehead* is published 4 times/year at the University of New Brunswick, with the generous assistance of the University of New Brunswick, the Canada Council for the Arts, and the Province of New Brunswick. It is experienced, wise enough to recognize excellence, and always looking for freshness and surprise. *The Fiddlehead* publishes short stories, poems, book reviews, and a small number of personal essays. Our full-color covers have become collectors' items and feature work by New Brunswick artists and from New Brunswick museums and art galleries. The journal is open to good writing in English from all over the world, looking always for freshness and surprise. Our editors are always happy to see new unsolicited works in fiction and poetry. Work is read on an ongoing basis; the acceptance rate is around 1-2%. Apart from our annual contest, we have no deadlines for submissions." Estab. 1945. Circ. 1,500. Pays on publication. Accepts simultaneous submissions. Responds in 3-9 months to mss. Occasionally comments on rejected mss. Sample copy: $15 U.S. Writer's guidelines online at www.thefiddlehead.ca/submissions.html.

NONFICTION *The Fiddlehead* occasionally publishes creative nonfiction pieces. **Pays up to $40 (Canadian)/published page and 2 contributor's copies.**

FICTION Receives 100-150 unsolicited mss/month. Accepts 4-5 mss/issue; 20-40 mss/year. Agented fiction: small percentage. Publishes high percentage of new writers/year. , *The Fiddlehead* publishes literary short fiction, more rarely literary novel excerpts. Send SASE and *Canadian* stamps or IRCs for return of mss. No e-mail, fax, or disc submissions. Simultaneous submissions only if stated on cover letter; must contact immediately if accepted elsewhere. Length: up to 6,000 words. Also publishes short shorts. **Pays up to $40 (Canadian)/published page and 2 contributor's copies.**

POETRY Send SASE and *Canadian* stamps or IRCs for return of mss. No e-mail, fax, or disc submissions. Simultaneous submissions only if stated on cover letter; must contact immediately if accepted elsewhere. Submit maximum 10 poems. **Pays up to $40 (Canadian)/published page and 2 contributor's copies.**

THE FIRST LINE

Blue Cubicle Press, LLC, P.O. Box 250382, Plano TX 75025. (972)824-0646. **E-mail:** submission@thefirstline.com. **Website:** www.thefirstline.com. **Contact:** Robin LaBounty, manuscript coordinator. **100% freelance written.** "*The First Line* is an exercise in creativity for writers and a chance for readers to see how many different directions we can take when we start from the same place. The purpose of *The First Line* is to jumpstart the imagination—to help writers break through the block that is the blank page. Each issue contains short stories that stem from a common first line; it also provides a forum for discussing favorite first lines in literature." Estab. 1999.

Circ. 2,750. Byline given. Pays on acceptance. Publishes ms 1 month after acceptance. Accepts queries by mail, e-mail. Responds 3 weeks after submission time closes. Sample copy and guidelines online. All stories must be written with the first line provided. The line cannot be altered in any way, unless otherwise noted by the editors. The story should be between 300 and 5,000 words (this is more like a guideline and not a hard-and-fast rule; going over or under the word count won't get your story tossed from the slush pile). The sentences can be found on the home page of *The First Line*'s website, as well as in the prior issue. Note: We are open to all genres. We try to make *TFL* as eclectic as possible.

NONFICTION Needs essays. **Buys 4 mss/year.** Submit complete ms. Length: 300-600 words. **Pays $25.**

FICTION "We only publish stories that start with the first line provided. We are a collection of tales—of different directions writers can take when they start from the same place. " Needs adventure, ethnic, experimental, fantasy, historical, horror, humorous, mainstream, mystery, religious, romance, science fiction, short stories, suspense, western, "No stories that do not start with our first line." **Buys 35-50 mss/year.** Submit complete ms. Length: 300-5,000 words. **Pays $25-50.**

☁ FREEFALL MAGAZINE

Freefall Literary Society of Calgary, 922 Ninth Ave. SE, Calgary AB T2G 0S4 Canada. **E-mail:** editors@freefallmagazine.ca. **Website:** www.freefallmagazine.ca. **Contact:** Ryan Stromquist, managing editor. **100% freelance written.** "Magazine published triannually containing fiction, poetry, creative nonfiction, essays on writing, interviews, and reviews. We are looking for exquisite writing with a strong narrative." Estab. 1990. Circ. 1,000. Pays on publication. Accepts queries by e-mail. Accepts simultaneous submissions. Guidelines and submission forms on website.

NONFICTION Needs essays, interview, creative nonfiction. Submit complete ms via website. Attach submission file (file name format is lastname_firstname_storytitle.doc or .docx or .pdf). Length: up to 4,000 words. **Pays $10/printed page in the magazine, to a maximum of $100, and 1 contributor's copy.**

FICTION Needs short stories, slice-of-life vignettes. Submit via website form. Attach submission file (file name format is lastname_firstname_storytitle.doc or .docx or .pdf). Length: up to 4,000 words. **Pays $10/printed page in the magazine, to a maximum of $100, and 1 contributor's copy.**

POETRY Submit 2-5 poems via website. Attach submission file (file name format is lastname_firstname_storytitle.doc or .docx or .pdf). Accepts any style of poetry. Length: up to 6 pages. **Pays $25/poem and 1 contributor's copy.**

💲 THE GEORGIA REVIEW

The University of Georgia, Main Library, Room 706A, 320 S. Jackson St., Athens GA 30602. (706)542-3481. **Fax:** (706)542-0047. **E-mail:** garev@uga.edu. **Website:** thegeorgiareview.com. **Contact:** Stephen Corey, editor. **99% freelance written.** Quarterly journal. "Our readers are inquisitive people and avid consumers of art and literature. All work submitted should be marked by singularity of vision, exceptional skillfulness of craft, and thoughtful engagement with the contemporary world." Electronic submissions available for $3 fee. Reading period: August 15-May 15. Estab. 1947. Circ. 3,500. Byline given. Pays on publication. No kill fee. Publishes ms an average of 6 months after acceptance. Accepts queries by mail. Responds in 2 weeks to queries; in 2-3 months to mss. Sample copy: $10. Guidelines online.

NONFICTION Needs essays. **Buys 12-20 mss/year.** "We generally avoid publishing scholarly articles that are narrow in focus and/or overly burdened with footnotes. *The Georgia Review* is interested in provocative, thesis-oriented essays that can engage both the intelligent general reader and the specialist, as well as those that are experimental or lyrical in approach but accessible to a range of readers." **Pays $50/published page.**

FICTION "We seek original, excellent short fiction not bound by type. Ordinarily we do not publish novel excerpts or works translated into English, and we discourage authors from submitting these." **Buys 12-20 mss/year.** Send complete ms via online submissions manager or postal mail. **Pays $50/published page.**

POETRY "We seek original, excellent poetry." Submit 3-5 poems at a time. Buys 60-75 poems/year. **Pays $4/line.**

💲 THE GETTYSBURG REVIEW

Gettysburg College, Gettysburg College, 300 N. Washington St., Gettysburg PA 17325. (717)337-6770. **Fax:** (717)337-6775. **E-mail:** mdrew@gettysburg.edu. **Website:** www.gettysburgreview.com. **Contact:** Mark

Drew, editor; Ellen Hathaway, managing editor. Published quarterly, *The Gettysburg Review* considers unsolicited submissions of poetry, fiction, and essays. "Our concern is quality. Mss submitted here should be extremely well written." Reading period September 1-May 31. Estab. 1988. Circ. 2,000. Byline given. Pays on publication. Publishes ms an average of 6 months after acceptance. Editorial lead time 1 year. Submit seasonal material 9 months in advance. Accepts queries by mail, fax. Accepts simultaneous submissions. Responds in 1 month to queries; in 3-5 months to mss. Sample: $15. Guidelines online.

NONFICTION Needs book excerpts, essays, general interest, humor, memoir, personal experience, reviews. **Buys 20 mss/year.** Send complete ms. Length: up to 25 pages. **Pays $15/printed page, a one-year subscription, and 1 contributor's copy.**

FICTION Wants high-quality literary fiction. Needs experimental, historical, humorous, mainstream, novel excerpts, short stories, slice-of-life vignettes, literary, contemporary. "We require that fiction be intelligent and esthetically written." No genre fiction. **Buys 20 mss/year.** Send complete ms with SASE. Length: 2,000-7,000 words. **Pays $15/printed page, a one-year subscription, and 1 contributor's copy.**

POETRY Considers "well-written poems of all kinds on all subjects." Has published poetry by Rita Dove, Alice Friman, Philip Schultz, Michelle Boisseau, Bob Hicok, Linda Pastan, and G.C. Waldrep. Does not want sentimental, clichéd verse. Buys 50 poems/year. Submit maximum 5 poems. **Pays $2/line, a one-year subscription, and 1 contributor's copy.**

GLIMMER TRAIN STORIES

Glimmer Train Press, Inc., P.O. Box 80430, Portland OR 97280. **Fax:** (503)221-0837. **E-mail:** eds@glimmertrain.org. **Website:** www.glimmertrain.org. **100% freelance written.** Triannual magazine of literary short fiction. "We are interested in literary short stories, particularly by new and emerging writers." Estab. 1991. Circ. 12,000. Byline given. Pays on acceptance. Publishes ms an average of 15 months after acceptance. Accepts simultaneous submissions. Responds in 2 months to mss. Sometimes comments on rejected mss. Sample: $15 on website. For guidelines and to submit online: www.glimmertrain.org.

FICTION Submit via the website at www.glimmertrain.org. "In a pinch, send a hard copy and include SASE for response." Receives 36,000 unsolicited mss/year. Accepts 15 mss/issue; 45 mss/year. Agented fiction 2%. Publishes 20 new writers/year. Length: 1,200-12,000 words. **Pays $700 for standard submissions, up to $2,500 for contest-winning stories.**

GRAIN

P.O. Box 3986, Regina SK S4P 3R9 Canada. (306)791-7749. **Fax:** (306)565-8554. **E-mail:** grainmag@skwriter.com. **Website:** www.grainmagazine.ca. Quarterly magazine covering poetry, fiction, creative nonfiction. "*Grain, The Journal of Eclectic Writing* is a literary quarterly that publishes engaging, diverse, and challenging writing and art by some of the best Canadian and international writers and artists. Every issue features superb new writing from both developing and established writers. Each issue also highlights the unique artwork of a different visual artist. *Grain* has garnered national and international recognition for its distinctive, cutting-edge content and design." Estab. 1973. Circ. 1,600. Byline given. Pays on publication. Accepts queries by mail. Responds in 6 months to mss. Sample: $13 CAD. Subscription: $35 CAD/year, $55 CAD for 2 years. (See website for U.S. and foreign postage fees.). Guidelines online.

NONFICTION Needs essays. No academic papers or reportage. Postal submissions only. Send typed, unpublished material only (considers work published online to be previously published). Please only submit work in 1 genre at a time. Length: up to 3,500 words. **Pays $50/page ($250 maximum) and 3 contributor's copies.**

FICTION Needs short stories. No romance, confession, science fiction, vignettes, mystery. Postal submissions only. Send typed, unpublished material only (considers work published online to be previously published). Please only submit work in 1 genre at a time. Length: up to 3,500 words. **Pays $50/page ($250 maximum) and 3 contributor's copies.**

POETRY Needs individual poems, sequences, suites. Wants "high-quality, imaginative, well-crafted poetry." Postal submissions only. Send typed, unpublished material only (considers work published online to be previously published). Has published poetry by Lorna Crozier, Don Domanski, Cornelia Haeussler, Patrick Lane, Karen Solie, and Monty Reid. Length: up to 6 pages. **Pays $50/page ($250 maximum) and 3 contributor's copies.**

GRASSLIMB

P.O. Box 420816, San Diego CA 92142. **E-mail:** editor@grasslimb.com. **Website:** www.grasslimb.com. **Contact:** Valerie Polichar, editor. "*Grasslimb* publishes literary prose, poetry, and art. Fiction is best when it is short and avant-garde or otherwise experimental." Estab. 2002. Circ. 200. Accepts simultaneous submissions. Responds in 4 months to mss. Rarely comments on rejected mss. Sample copy: $3. Guidelines for SASE, e-mail, or on website.

FICTION "Fiction in an experimental, avant-garde, or surreal mode is often more interesting to us than a traditional story." Needs experimental. "Although general topics are welcome, we're less likely to select work regarding romance, sex, aging, and children." Send complete ms via e-mail or postal mail with SASE. Length: up to 2,500 words; average length: 1,500 words. **Pays $10-70 and 2 contributor's copies.**

POETRY Submit poems via e-mail or postal mail with SASE. Submit maximum 5 poems. **Pays $5-20/ poem.**

🌀 GULF COAST: A JOURNAL OF LITERATURE AND FINE ARTS

4800 Calhoun Rd., Houston TX 77204-3013. (713)743-3223. **E-mail:** editors@gulfcoastmag.org. **Website:** www.gulfcoastmag.org. **Contact:** Adrienne Perry, editor; Martin Rock, managing editor; Carlos Hernandez, digital editor; Henk Rossouw, Luisa Muradyan, and Erika Jo Brown, poetry editors; Jennifer McFarland, Dino Piacentini, and Joshua Foster, fiction editors; Georgia Pearle and Nathan Stabenfeldt, nonfiction editors; Matthew Salesses, online fiction editor; Christopher Murray, online poetry editor; Melanie Brkich, online nonfiction editor. Biannual print magazine covering innovative fiction, nonfiction, poetry, visual art, and critical art writing. GC Online is the companion online journal and publishes unique content. Estab. 1986. Circ. 3,000. No kill fee. Publishes ms 6 months-1 year after acceptance. Accepts queries by mail, e-mail, phone. Accepts simultaneous submissions. Responds in 4-6 months to mss. Sometimes comments on rejected mss. Back issue: $8, plus 7x10 SASE with 4 first-class stamps. Writer's guidelines for #10 SASE or on website.

NONFICTION Needs interview, reviews. *Gulf Coast* reads general submissions, submitted by post or through the online submissions manager, September 1-March 1. Submissions e-mailed directly to the editors or postmarked March 1-September 1 will not be read or responded to. "Please visit our contest page for contest submission guidelines." **Pays $100 per review and $200 per interview.**

FICTION "Please do not send multiple submissions; we will read only 1 submission per author at a given time, except in the case of our annual contests." Needs ethnic, multicultural, literary, regional, translations, contemporary. No children's, genre, religious/inspirational. *Gulf Coast* reads general submissions, submitted by post or through the online submissions manager, September 1-March 1. Submissions e-mailed directly to the editors or postmarked March 1-September 1 will not be read or responded to. "Please visit our contest page for contest submission guidelines." Receives 500 unsolicited mss/month. Accepts 6-8 mss/issue; 12-16 mss/year. Agented fiction: 5%. Publishes 2-8 new writers/year. Recently published work by Alan Heathcock, Anne Carson, Bret Anthony Johnston, John D'Agata, Lucie Brock-Broido, Clancy Martin, Steve Almond, Sam Lipsyte, Carl Phillips, Dean Young, and Eula Biss. Publishes short shorts. **Pays $50/page.**

POETRY Submit up to 5 poems at a time. Considers simultaneous submissions with notification; no previously published poems. Cover letter is required. List previous publications and include a brief bio. Reads submissions September-April. **Pays $50/page.**

HUBBUB

5344 SE 38th Ave., Portland OR 97202. (503)775-0370. **E-mail:** lisa.steinman@reed.edu. **Website:** www.reed.edu/hubbub. J. Shugrue and Lisa M. Steinman, co-editors. *Hubbub*, published once/year, is designed "to feature a multitude of voices from interesting, contemporary American poets." Wants "poems that are well crafted, with something to say. We have no single style, subject, or length requirement and in particular will consider long poems." Estab. 1983. Pays on publication. Publishes poems 1-12 months (usually) after acceptance. Accepts queries by mail, e-mail. Responds in 4 months. Sample: $3.35 (back issues), $7 (current issue). Subscription: $7/year. Guidelines available for SASE or online.

POETRY Submit 3-6 typed poems at a time. Include SASE. "We review 2-4 poetry books/year in short (three-page) reviews; all reviews are solicited. We do, however, list books received/recommended." Send materials for review consideration. Has published poetry by Madeline DeFrees, Cecil Giscombe, Carolyn Kizer, Primus St. John, Shara McCallum, and Alice Fulton. Does not want light verse. Buys 40-50 poems/year. Submit maximum 6 poems. No length requirements. **Pays $20/poem.**

$ HUNGER MOUNTAIN

Vermont College of Fine Arts, 36 College St., Montpelier VT 05602. (802)828-8517. **E-mail:** hungermtn@vcfa.edu. **Website:** www.hungermtn.org. **Contact:** Samantha Kolber, managing editor. Monthly online publication and annual perfect-bound journal covering high-quality fiction, poetry, creative nonfiction, craft essays, writing for children, and artwork. Accepts high-quality work from unknown, emerging, or successful writers. Publishing fiction, creative nonfiction, poetry, and young adult & children's writing. Four writing contests annually. Estab. 2002. Circ. 1,000. Byline given. Pays on publication. No kill fee. Publishes ms an average of 1 year after acceptance. Submit between May 1 and October 1. Accepts queries by online submission form. Accepts simultaneous submissions. Responds in 4 months to mss. Single issue: $12; subscription: $18 for 2 issues/2 years; back issue: $8. Checks payable to Vermont College of Fine Arts, or purchase online http://hungermtn.org/subscribe. Guidelines online at http://hungermtn.org/submit.

NONFICTION "We welcome an array of traditional and experimental work, including, but not limited to, personal, lyrical, and meditative essays, memoirs, collages, rants, and humor. The only requirements are recognition of truth, a unique voice with a firm command of language, and an engaging story with multiple pressure points." No informative or instructive articles, no interviews, and no book reviews please. Payment varies. Submit complete ms using online submissions manager at Submittable: https://hungermtn.submittable.com/submit Length: up to 10,000 words. Pays **$50 for general fiction or creative nonfiction, for both children's lit and general adult lit; $50 for general fiction or creative nonfiction, for both children's lit and general adult lit; $50 for general fiction or creative nonfiction, for both children's lit and general adult lit.**

FICTION "We look for work that is beautifully crafted and tells a good story, with characters that are alive and kicking, storylines that stay with us long after we've finished reading, and sentences that slay us with their precision." Needs experimental, humorous, novel excerpts, short stories, slice-of-life vignettes. No genre fiction, meaning science fiction, fantasy, horror, detective, erotic, etc. Submit ms using online submissions manager. Length: up to 10,000 words. **$50 for general fiction.**

POETRY Needs avant-garde, free verse, traditional. Submit 1-5 poems at a time. "We are looking for truly original poems that run the aesthetic gamut: lively engagement with language in the act of pursuit. Some poems remind us in a fresh way of our own best thoughts; some poems bring us to a place beyond language for which there aren't quite words; some poems take us on a complicated language ride that is, itself, its own aim. Complex poem-architectures thrill us and still-points in the turning world do, too. Send us the best of what you have." Submit using online submissions manager. No light verse, humor/quirky/catchy verse, greeting card verse. Submit maximum 5 poems. **$25 for poetry up to two poems (plus $5 per poem for additional poems); $25 for poetry up to two poems (plus $5 per poem for additional poems).**

ICONOCLAST

1675 Amazon Rd., Mohegan Lake NY 10547-1804. **Website:** www.iconoclastliterarymagazine.com. **Contact:** Phil Wagner, editor and publisher. *Iconoclast* seeks and chooses the best new writing and poetry available—of all genres and styles and entertainment levels. Its mission is to provide a serious publishing opportunity for unheralded, unknown, but deserving creators, whose work is often overlooked or trampled in the commercial, university, or Internet marketplace. Estab. 1992. Pays on publication. Accepts queries by mail. Responds in 6 weeks to mss. Sample copy: $4. Subscription: $20 for 6 issues.

FICTION "Subjects and styles are completely open (within the standards of generally accepted taste—though exceptions, as always, can be made for unique and visionary works)." Needs adventure, experimental, fantasy, mainstream, short stories. No slice-of-life stories, stories containing alcoholism, incest, and domestic or public violence. Accepts most genres, "with the exception of mysteries." Submit by postal mail; include SASE. Cover letter not necessary. **Pays 1¢/word and 2 contributor's copies. Contributors get 40% discount on extra copies.**

POETRY "Try for originality; if not in thought than expression. No greeting card verse or noble religious sentiments. Look for the unusual in the usual, parallels in opposites, the capturing of what is unique or often unnoticed in an ordinary or extraordinary moment. What makes us human—and the resultant glories and agonies. The universal usually wins out over the personal. Rhyme isn't as easy as it looks—especially for those unversed in its study." Submit by postal mail; include SASE. Cover letter not necessary. Length: up to 2 pages. **Pays $2-6/poem and 1 contributor's copy per page or work. Contributors get 40% discount on extra copies.**

THE IDAHO REVIEW

Boise State University, 1910 University Dr., Boise ID 83725. **E-mail:** mwieland@boisestate.edu. **Website:** idahoreview.org. **Contact:** Mitch Wieland, editor. *The Idaho Review* is the literary journal of Boise State University. Estab. 1998. Pays on publication. Publishes ms 1 year after acceptance. Accepts queries by mail, online submission form. Accepts simultaneous submissions. Responds in 3-5 months. Guidelines online.

NONFICTION Special issues: "Although we do not regularly publish creative nonfiction, we are open to reading CNF submissions."

FICTION Needs experimental, literary. No genre fiction of any type. Prefers submissions using online submissions manager, but will accept submissions by postal mail. Length: up to 25 double-spaced pages. **Pays $100/story and contributor's copies.**

POETRY Submit up to 5 poems. Prefers submissions using online submissions manager, but will accept submissions by postal mail. Submit maximum 5 poems.

$ ILLUMEN

Alban Lake Publishing, P.O. Box 782, Cedar Rapids IA 52406-0782. **E-mail:** illumensdp@yahoo.com. **Website:** albanlake.com. **Contact:** Terrie Leigh Relf, editor. **100% freelance written.** "*Illumen* is a print magazine of speculative poetry. It is published biannually on 1 April and 1 October in perfect-bound digest format. It contains speculative poetry, illustrations, articles, and reviews." Estab. 2004. Byline given. Offers 100% kill fee. Submit seasonal material 6 months in advance. Accepts queries by e-mail. Accepts simultaneous submissions. Responds in 4 months. Guidelines online.

NONFICTION Special issues: Wants articles that address some aspect of speculative poetry. Send complete ms by e-mail. Length: 800-2,000 words. **Pays $12 and 1 contributor's copy.**

REPRINTS Pays $3 for reprints.

POETRY Needs avant-garde, free verse, haiku, light verse, traditional. "Speculative poetry is 1 result of the application of imagination to reality. In speculative poetry, one's 'vision' often is taken from a different angle, from another perspective, perhaps even from another time and place. Speculative poetry is usually tinged with 1 or more of the genres. Thus, in speculative poetry you find hints of science fiction, fantasy, folklore, myth, the surreal ... and yes, even horror. Good speculative poetry will awaken a sense of adventure in the reader. That's what we're looking for: good, original speculative poetry." Submit poetry by e-mail. "Speculative horror poetry evokes moods, often dark and spooky ones. It should not make you upchuck. Remember: twisted is an attitude, not an action." Buys 40-50 poems/year. Submit maximum 3 poems. Length: up to 100 lines/poem. **Pays 2¢/word, minimum $3.**

IMAGE

3307 Third Ave. W., Seattle WA 98119. (206)281-2988. **Fax:** (206)281-2979. **E-mail:** image@imagejournal.org. **Website:** www.imagejournal.org. **Contact:** Gregory Wolfe, publisher and editor. **50% freelance written.** Quarterly magazine covering the intersection between art and faith. "*Image* is a unique forum for the best writing and artwork that is informed by—or grapples with—religious faith. We have never been interested in art that merely regurgitates dogma or falls back on easy answers or didacticism. Instead, our focus has been on writing and visual artwork that embody a spiritual struggle, that seek to strike a balance between tradition and a profound openness to the world. Each issue explores this relationship through outstanding fiction, poetry, painting, sculpture, architecture, film, music, interviews, and dance. *Image* also features 4-color reproductions of visual art." Estab. 1989. Circ. 4,500. Byline given. Pays on acceptance. No kill fee. Publishes ms an average of 8 months after acceptance. Accepts queries by mail, e-mail. Accepts simultaneous submissions. Responds in 1 month to queries; in 5 months to mss. Sample copy: $16 or available online. Guidelines online.

NONFICTION Needs essays, interview, profile, religious. "No sentimental, preachy, moralistic, or obvious essays." **Buys 10 mss/year.** Send complete ms by postal mail (with SASE for reply or return of ms) or online submissions manager, or query Mary Mitchell (mkenagy@imagejournal.org). Does not accept e-mail submissions. Length: 3,000-6,000 words. **Pays $10/page ($150 maximum) and 4 contributor's copies.**

FICTION Needs religious, short stories. "No sentimental, preachy, moralistic, obvious stories, or genre stories (unless they manage to transcend their genre)." **Buys 8 mss/year.** Send complete ms by postal mail (with SASE for reply or return of ms) or online submissions manager. Does not accept e-mail submissions. Length: 3,000-6,000 words. **Pays $10/page ($150 maximum) and 4 contributor's copies.**

POETRY Wants poems that grapple with religious faith, usually Judeo-Christian. Send up to 5 poems by postal mail (with SASE for reply or return of ms) or online submissions manager. Does not accept e-mail submissions. Submit maximum 5 poems. Length: up to 10 pages. **Pays $2/line ($150 maximum) and 4 contributor's copies.**

🅢 INDIANA REVIEW

Ballantine Hall 529, 1020 E. Kirkwood Ave., Indiana University, Bloomington IN 47405. **E-mail:** inreview@indiana.edu. **Website:** indianareview.org. **Contact:** See masthead for current editorial staff. **100% freelance written.** Biannual magazine. "*Indiana Review*, a nonprofit organization run by IU graduate students, is a journal of innovative fiction, nonfiction, and poetry. We're interested in energy, originality, and careful attention to craft. While we publish many well-known writers, we also welcome new and emerging poets and fiction writers." Estab. 1976. Circ. 5,000. Byline given. Pays on publication. Publishes ms an average of 3-6 months after acceptance. Accepts queries by online submission form. Accepts simultaneous submissions. Responds in 4 or more months to mss. Sample copy: $12. Guidelines online. "We no longer accept hard-copy submissions. All submissions must be made online."

NONFICTION Needs essays, interview. No coming-of-age/slice-of-life pieces or book reviews. **Buys 5-7 mss/year.** Submit complete ms through online submissions manager. Length: up to 8,000 words. **Pays $5/page ($10 minimum), plus 2 contributor's copies.**

FICTION "We look for daring stories which integrate theme, language, character, and form. We like polished writing, humor, and fiction which has conse-

quence beyond the world of its narrator." Needs ethnic, experimental, mainstream, literary, short fictions, translations. No genre fiction. **Buys 14-18 mss/year.** Submit via online submissions manager. Length: up to 8,000 words. **Pays $5/page ($10 minimum), plus 2 contributor's copies.**

POETRY "We look for poems that are skillful and bold, exhibiting an inventiveness of language with attention to voice and sonics." Wants experimental, free verse, prose poem, traditional form, lyrical, narrative. Submit poetry via online submissions manager. Buys 80 poems/year. Submit maximum 6 poems. **Pays $5/page ($10 minimum), plus 2 contributor's copies.**

🅢 THE IOWA REVIEW

308 EPB, The University of Iowa, Iowa City IA 52242. (319)335-0462. **E-mail:** iowa-review@uiowa.edu. **Website:** www.iowareview.org. Lynne Nugent, managing editor. **Contact:** Harilaos Stecopoulos. Triannual magazine covering stories, essays, and poems for a general readership interested in contemporary literature. *The Iowa Review*, published 3 times/year, prints fiction, poetry, essays, reviews, and, occasionally, interviews. Receives about 5,000 submissions/year, accepts up to 100. Press run is 2,900; 1,500 distributed to stores. Estab. 1970. Circ. 3,500. Pays on publication. Publishes ms an average of 12-18 months after acceptance. Accepts queries by mail, online submission form. Accepts simultaneous submissions. Responds to mss in 4 months. Sample: $8.95 and online. Subscription: $20. Guidelines online.

NONFICTION Needs essays, interview. Send complete ms with cover letter. Don't bother with queries. SASE for return of ms. Accepts mss by snail mail (SASE required for response) and online submission form at iowareview.submittable.com/submit; no e-mail submissions. **Pays 8¢/word ($100 minimum), plus 2 contributor's copies.**

FICTION "We are open to a range of styles and voices and always hope to be surprised by work we then feel we need." Receives 600 unsolicited mss/month. Accepts 4-6 mss/issue; 12-18 mss/year. Does not read mss January-August. Publishes ms an average of 12-18 months after acceptance. Agented fiction less than 2%. **Publishes some new writers/year.** Recently published work by Johanna Hunting, Bennett Sims, and Pedro Mairal. Needs experimental, mainstream, novel excerpts, short stories. Send complete ms with cover letter. Don't bother with queries. SASE for return of ms. Accepts mss by snail mail (SASE required for response) and online submission form at iowareview.submittable.com/submit; no e-mail submissions. **Pays 8¢/word ($100 minimum), plus 2 contributor's copies.**

POETRY Submit up to 8 pages at a time. Online submissions accepted, but no e-mail submissions. Cover letter (with title of work and genre) is encouraged. SASE required. Reads submissions "only during the fall semester, September through November, and then contest entries in the spring." Occasionally comments on rejected poems or offers suggestions on accepted poems. "We simply look for poems that, at the time we read and choose, we find we admire. No specifications as to form, length, style, subject matter, or purpose. Though we print work from established writers, we're always delighted when we discover new talent." **Pays $1.50/line, $40 minimum.**

ISLAND

P.O. Box 4703, Hobart Tasmania 7000 Australia. **E-mail:** admin@islandmag.com. **Website:** www.islandmag.com. **Contact:** Geordie Williamson, editor at large. Quarterly magazine. *Island* seeks quality fiction, poetry, and essays. It is "one of Australia's leading literary magazines, tracing the contours of our national, and international, culture while still retaining a uniquely Tasmanian perspective." Estab. 1979. Circ. 1,500. Accepts queries by online submission form. Accepts simultaneous submissions. Subscriptions and sample copies available for purchase online. Guidelines online.

NONFICTION Needs essays. Query first with brief overview of essay and description of why it is suitable for *Island*. **Pay varies.**

FICTION Submit 1 piece via online submissions manager. **Pay varies.**

POETRY Submit via online submissions manager. Submit maximum 3 poems. **Pay varies.**

KANSAS CITY VOICES

Whispering Prairie Press, P.O. Box 410661, Kansas City MO 64141. **E-mail:** info@wppress.org. **Website:** www.wppress.org/kansas-city-voices. **Contact:** Jessica Conoley, managing editor. **100% freelance written.** *Kansas City Voices*, published annually, features an eclectic mix of fiction, poetry, and art. "We seek exceptional written and visual creations from established and emerging voices." Estab. 2003. Circ. 1,000. Byline given. Pays on publication. Publishes ms an average of 6 months after acceptance. Accepts queries by online submission form. Accepts simultaneous submissions. Sample copy online. Guidelines online.

FICTION Needs short stories. Submit up to 2 complete mss via online submissions manager. Length: up to 2,500 words. **Pays small honorarium and 1 contributor's copy.**

POETRY Needs avant-garde, free verse, light verse, traditional. Submit maximum 3 poems. Length: up to 35 lines/poem. **Pays small honorarium and 1 contributor's copy.**

KASMA MAGAZINE

Kasma Publications, **E-mail:** editors@kasmamagazine.com. **Website:** www.kasmamagazine.com. **Contact:** Alex Korovessis, editor. Online magazine. "We publish the best science fiction, from promising new and established writers. Our aim is to provide stories that are well written, original and thought provoking." Estab. 2009. Pays on publication. Publishes mss 2-3 months after acceptance. Editorial lead time 2 months. Submit seasonal material 1 month in advance. Accepts queries by e-mail. Accepts simultaneous submissions. Responds in 1 week to queries; in 3 months to mss. Sample copy available online and by e-mail. Guidelines online.

FICTION Needs science fiction. No erotica, excessive violence/language. Submit complete ms via e-mail. Length: 1,000-5,000 words. **Pays 2¢/word (Canadian).**

THE KENYON REVIEW

Finn House, 102 W. Wiggin, Gambier OH 43022. (740)427-5208. **Fax:** (740)427-5417. **E-mail:** kenyonreview@kenyon.edu. **Website:** www.kenyonreview.org. **Contact:** Alicia Misarti. **100% freelance written.** Bimonthly magazine covering contemporary literature and criticism. "An international journal of literature, culture, and the arts, dedicated to an inclusive representation of the best in new writing (fiction, poetry, essays, interviews, criticism) from established and emerging writers." Estab. 1939. Circ. 6,000. Byline given. Pays on publication. No kill fee. Publishes ms an average of 1 year after acceptance. Editorial lead time 1 year. Submit seasonal material 1 year in advance. Accepts simultaneous submissions. Responds in 4 months to mss. Sample copy: $10; includes postage and handling. Call or e-mail to order. Guidelines online.

NONFICTION Needs essays, interview, criticism. Only accepts mss via online submissions program;

visit website for instructions. Do not submit via e-mail or snail mail. Receives 130 unsolicited mss/month. Unsolicited mss accepted September 15-December 15 only. Length: 3-15 typeset pages preferred. **Pays 8¢/published word of prose (minimum payment $80; maximum payment $450); word count does not include title, notes, or citations.**

FICTION Receives 800 unsolicited mss/month. Unsolicited mss accepted September 15-December 15 only. Recently published work by Alice Hoffman, Beth Ann Fennelly, Romulus Linney, John Koethe, Albert Goldbarth, Erin McGraw. Needs condensed novels, ethnic, experimental, historical, humorous, mainstream, novel excerpts, short stories, contemporary, excerpts from novels, gay/lesbian, literary, translations. Only accepts mss via online submissions program; visit website for instructions. Do not submit via e-mail or snail mail. Length: 3-15 typeset pages preferred. **Pays 8¢/published word of prose (minimum payment $80; maximum payment $450); word count does not include title, notes, or citations.**

POETRY Features all styles, forms, lengths, and subject matters. Considers translations. Has published poetry by Billy Collins, D.A. Powell, Jamaal May, Rachel Zucker, Diane di Prima, and Seamus Heaney. Submit maximum 6 poems. Submit up to 6 poems at a time. No previously published poems. Only accepts mss via online submissions program; visit website for instructions. Do not submit via e-mail or snail mail. Accepts submissions September 15-December 15. **Pays 16¢/published word of poetry (minimum payment $40; maximum payment $200); word count does not include title, notes, or citations.**

LADY CHURCHILL'S ROSEBUD WRISTLET

150 Pleasant St., #306, Easthampton MA 01027. **E-mail:** smallbeerpress@gmail.com. **Website:** www.smallbeerpress.com/lcrw. **Contact:** Gavin Grant, editor. *Lady Churchill's Rosebud Wristlet* accepts fiction, nonfiction, poetry, and b&w art. "The fiction we publish tends toward, but is not limited to, the speculative. This does not mean only quietly desperate stories. We will consider items that fall out with regular categories. We do not accept multiple submissions." Estab. 1996. Circ. 1,000. Yes. Pays on publication. Publishes ms 6-12 months after acceptance. Accepts queries by mail. Responds in 6 months to mss. Sometimes comments on rejected mss. Sample copy: $5. Guidelines online.

NONFICTION Needs essays. Send complete ms with a cover letter. Include estimated word count. Send SASE (or IRC) for return of ms, or send a disposable copy of ms and #10 SASE for reply only. **Pays $25.**

FICTION Receives 100 unsolicited mss/month. Accepts 4-6 mss/issue; 8-12 mss/year. Publishes 2-4 new writers/year. Also publishes literary essays, poetry. Has published work by Ted Chiang, Gwenda Bond, Alissa Nutting, and Charlie Anders. Needs short stories. "We do not publish gore, sword and sorcery, or pornography. We can discuss these terms if you like. There are places for them all; this is not one of them." Send complete ms with a cover letter. Include estimated word count. Send SASE (or IRC) for return of ms, or send a disposable copy of ms and #10 SASE for reply only. Length: 200-7,000 words. **Pays $25.**

POETRY Send complete ms with a cover letter. Include estimated word count. Send SASE (or IRC) for return of ms, or send a disposable copy of ms and #10 SASE for reply only. **Pays $5/poem.**

[C] $ LINE

West Coast Review Publishing Society, Line, 6079 Academic Quadrangle, 8888 University Drive, Simon Fraser University, Burnaby BC V5A 1S6 Canada. **E-mail:** wcl@sfu.ca. **Website:** linejournal.tumblr.com/about. Triannual magazine of literature and criticism. Estab. 1990. Circ. 500. Pays on publication. No kill fee. Editorial lead time 4 months. Accepts queries by mail, e-mail. Accepts simultaneous submissions. Responds in up to 6 months to queries. Responds in up to 6 months to mss. Sample copy for $15 CAD, $20 U.S. Guidelines for SASE (U.S. must include IRC).

NONFICTION Needs essays, experimental prose. No journalistic articles or articles dealing with nonliterary material. **Buys 8-10 mss/year.** Send complete ms. Length: 1,000-5,000 words. **Pays $8/page, 2 contributor's copies and a 1-year subscription.**

FICTION Needs experimental. **Buys 3-6 mss/year.** Send complete ms. Length: 1,000-7,000 words. **Pays $8/page.**

POETRY Needs avant-garde. No light verse, traditional. Buys 10-15 poems/year. Submit maximum 5-6 poems. **Pays $8/page.**

[C] $ THE MALAHAT REVIEW

The University of Victoria, P.O. Box 1700, STN CSC, Victoria BC V8W 2Y2 Canada. (250)721-8524. **E-mail:** malahat@uvic.ca (for queries only). **Website:** www.malahatreview.ca. **Contact:** John Barton, editor. **100% freelance written. Eager to work with new/unpublished writers.** Quarterly magazine covering

CONSUMER MAGAZINES

poetry, fiction, creative nonfiction, and reviews. "We try to achieve a balance of views and styles in each issue. We strive for a mix of the best writing by both established and new writers." Estab. 1967. Circ. 2,000. Byline given. Pays on acceptance. No kill fee. Publishes ms an average of 6 months after acceptance. Accepts queries by online submission form. Accepts simultaneous submissions. Responds in 2 weeks to queries; in 3-10 months to mss. Sample: $16.95 (US). Guidelines online.

NONFICTION Submit via online submissions manager: malahatreview.ca/submission_guidelines.html#submittable. Length: 1,000-3,500 words. **Pays $50/magazine page.**

FICTION Buys 12-14 mss/year. Submit via online submissions manager: malahatreview.ca/submission_guidelines.html#submittable. Length: up to 8,000 words. **Pays $50/magazine page.**

POETRY Needs avant-garde, free verse, traditional. Submit 3-5 poems via online submissions manager: malahatreview.ca/submission_guidelines.html#submittable. Buys 100 poems/year. Length: up to 6 pages. **Pays $50/magazine page.**

$$ MĀNOA: A PACIFIC JOURNAL OF INTERNATIONAL WRITING

English Department, University of Hawaii, Honolulu HI 96822. (808)956-3070. **Fax:** (808)956-3083. **E-mail:** mjournal-l@lists.hawaii.edu. **Website:** manoajournal.hawaii.edu. **Contact:** Frank Stewart, editor. Semiannual magazine. *Mānoa* is seeking "high-quality literary fiction, poetry, essays, and translations. In general, each issue is devoted to new work from Pacific and Asian areas. Our audience is international. US writing need not be confined to Pacific settings or subjects. Please note that we seldom publish unsolicited work; you may query us at our website." Estab. 1989. Circ. 1,000 print, 10,000 digital. Byline given. Pays on publication. Editorial lead time 9 months. Accepts queries by online submission form. Accepts simultaneous submissions. Responds in 3 weeks to queries. Sample: $15 (US). Guidelines online.

NONFICTION No Pacific exotica. Query first. Length: 1,000-5,000 words. **Pays $25/printed page.**

FICTION Query first. Needs mainstream, contemporary, excerpted novel. No Pacific exotica. **Buys 1-2 mss/year.** Send complete ms. Length: 1,000-7,500 words. **Pays $100-500 ($25/printed page).**

POETRY No light verse. Buys 10-20 poems/year. Submit maximum 5-6 poems. **Pays $25/poem.**

$ THE MASSACHUSETTS REVIEW

University of Massachusetts, Photo Lab 309, Amherst MA 01003. (413)545-2689. **E-mail:** massrev@external.umass.edu. **Website:** www.massreview.org. **Contact:** Emily Wojcik, managing editor. Quarterly magazine. Seeks a balance between established writers and promising new ones. Interested in material of variety and vitality relevant to the intellectual and aesthetic questions of our time. Aspire to have a broad appeal. Estab. 1959. Circ. 1,200. Pays on publication. Publishes ms an average of 18 months after acceptance. Accepts queries by mail. Responds in 2-6 months to mss. Sample copy: $8 for back issue, $10 for current issue. Guidelines online.

NONFICTION No reviews of single books. Articles and essays of breadth and depth are considered, as well as discussions of leading writers; of art, music, and drama; analyses of trends in literature, science, philosophy, and public affairs. Include name and contact information on the first page. Encourages page numbers. Send complete ms or query with SASE. Length: up to 6,500 words. **Pays $50 and 2 contributor's copies.**

FICTION Wants short stories. Accepts 1 short story per submission. Include name and contact information on the first page. Encourages page numbers. Has published work by Ahdaf Soueif, Elizabeth Denton, and Nicholas Montemarano. **Buys 30-40 mss/year.** Send complete ms. Length: up to 30 pages or 8,000 words. **Pays $50 and 2 contributor's copies.**

POETRY Has published poetry by Catherine Barnett, Billy Collins, and Dara Wier. Include your name and contact on every page. Submit maximum 6 poems. Length: There are no restrictions for length, but generally poems are less than 100 lines. **Pays $50/publication and 2 contributor's copies.**

$ MICHIGAN QUARTERLY REVIEW

0576 Rackham Bldg., 915 E. Washington, Ann Arbor MI 48109-1070. (734)764-9265. **E-mail:** mqr@umich.edu. **Website:** www.michiganquarterlyreview.com. **Contact:** Jonathan Freedman, editor; Vicki Lawrence, managing editor. **75% freelance written.** Quarterly journal of literature and the humanities publishing literary essays, fiction, poetry, creative nonfiction, memoir, interviews, and book reviews. *Michi-*

gan Quarterly Review is an eclectic interdisciplinary journal of arts and culture that seeks to combine the best of poetry, fiction, and creative nonfiction with outstanding critical essays on literary, cultural, social, and political matters. The flagship journal of the University of Michigan, *MQR* draws on lively minds here and elsewhere, seeking to present accessible work of all varieties for sophisticated readers from within and without the academy. Estab. 1962. Circ. 1,000. Byline given. Pays on publication. No kill fee. Publishes ms an average of 1 year after acceptance. Accepts queries by mail. Accepts simultaneous submissions. Responds in 2 months to queries and mss. Sample: $4. Guidelines online.

NONFICTION Needs essays. Special issues: Publishes theme issues. Upcoming themes available in magazine and on website. **Buys 35 mss/year.** Query. Length: 1,500-7,000 words, 5,000 words average. **Payment varies but is usually in the range of $50 -$150.**

FICTION Contact: Fiction editor. "No restrictions on subject matter or language. We are very selective. We like stories that are unusual in tone and structure, and innovative in language. No genre fiction written for a market. Would like to see more fiction about social, political, and cultural matters, not just centered on a love relationship or dysfunctional family." Receives 300 unsolicited mss/month. Accepts 3-4 mss/issue; 12-16 mss/year. Publishes 1-2 new writers/year. Has published work by Rebecca Makkai, Peter Ho Davies, Laura Kasischke, Gerald Shapiro, and Alan Cheuse. **Buys 10 mss/year.** Send complete ms. Length: 1,500-7,000 words; average length: 5,000 words. **Payment varies but is usually in the range of $50-$150.**

POETRY No previously published poems. No e-mail submissions. Cover letter is preferred. "It puts a human face on the ms. A few sentences of biography is all I want, nothing lengthy or defensive." Prefers typed mss. Reviews books of poetry. "All reviews are commissioned." Length: should not exceed 8-12 pages. **Pays $8-12/published page.**

🌀 MID-AMERICAN REVIEW

Bowling Green State University, Dept. of English, Bowling Green OH 43403. (419)372-2725. **E-mail:** mar@bgsu.edu; marsubmissions.bgsu.edu. **Website:** www.bgsu.edu/midamericanreview. **Contact:** Abigail Cloud, editor in chief; Lydia Munnell, fiction editor. Semiannual magazine of the highest-quality fiction, poetry, and translations of contemporary poetry and fiction. Also publishes creative nonfiction and book reviews of contemporary literature. Reads mss year round. Publishes new and established writers. "We aim to put the best possible work in front of the biggest possible audience. We publish contemporary fiction, poetry, creative nonfiction, translations, and book reviews." Estab. 1981. Circ. 1,500. Byline given. No kill fee. Publishes mss an average of 6 months after acceptance. Accepts queries by online submission form. Accepts simultaneous submissions. Responds in 5 months to mss. Sample copy: $9 (current issue), $5 (back issue), $10 (rare back issues). Guidelines online.

NONFICTION Submit ms by post with SASE or with online submission manager.

FICTION Publishes traditional, character-oriented, literary, experimental, prose poem, and short-short stories. No genre fiction. Submit ms by post with SASE or with online submission manager. Agented fiction 5%. Recently published work by Mollie Ficek and J. David Stevens. Length: 6,000 words maximum.

POETRY Submit by mail with SASE or with online submission manager. Publishes poems with "textured, evocative images, an awareness of how words sound and mean, and a definite sense of voice. Each line should help carry the poem, and an individual vision must be evident." Recently published work by Mary Ann Samyn, G.C. Waldrep, and Daniel Bourne. Submit maximum 6 poems.

MISSISSIPPI REVIEW

University of Southern Mississippi, 118 College Dr., #5144, Hattiesburg MS 39406-0001. (601)266-4321. **Fax:** (601)266-5757. **E-mail:** msreview@usm.edu. **Website:** www.usm.edu/mississippi-review. **Contact:** Andrew Malan Milward, editor in chief; Caleb Tankersley and Allison Campbell, associate editors. Semiannual literary magazine. *Mississippi Review* "is one of the most respected literary journals in the country. Raymond Carver, an early contributor to the magazine, once said that *Mississippi Review* 'is one of the most remarkable and indispensable literary journals of our time.' Well-known and established writers have appeared in the pages of the magazine, including Pulitzer and Nobel Prize winners, as well as new and emerging writers who have gone on to publish books and to receive awards." Estab. 1972. Circ. 1,500. No kill fee. Accepts simultaneous submissions. Sample copy for $10. "We do not accept unsolicited manuscripts except under the rules and guidelines of the

Mississippi Review Prize Competition. See website for guidelines."

FICTION Needs experimental, fantasy, humorous, contemporary, avant-garde, art fiction. No juvenile or genre fiction. Length: 30 pages maximum.

⑨ THE MISSOURI REVIEW

357 McReynolds Hall, University of Missouri, Columbia MO 65211. (573)882-4474. **Fax:** (573)884-4671. **E-mail:** mutmrquestion@moreview.com. **Website:** www.missourireview.com. **Contact:** Speer Morgan, editor; Kate McIntyre, managing editor, Evelyn Somers, associate editor; Chun Ye, poetry editor. **90% freelance written.** Quarterly magazine. Publishes contemporary fiction, poetry, interviews, personal essays, cartoons, special features—such as History as Literature series, Found Text series, and Curio Cabinet art features—for the literary and the general reader interested in a wide range of subjects. Estab. 1978. Circ. 6,500. Byline given. Offers signed contract. Editorial lead time 4-6 months. Accepts queries by mail. Accepts simultaneous submissions. Responds in 2 weeks to queries; in 10-12 weeks to mss. Sample copy: $10 or online. Guidelines online.

NONFICTION Needs book excerpts, essays. No literary criticism. **Buys 10 mss/year.** Send complete ms. **Pays $40/printed page.**

FICTION Contact: Speer Morgan, editor. Needs ethnic, humorous, mainstream, literary. No genre or flash fiction. **Buys 25 mss/year.** Send complete ms. Length: 15-25 pp. average **Pays $40/printed page.**

POETRY *TMR* publishes poetry features only—6-14 pages of poems by each of 3-5 poets per issue. Keep in mind the length of features when submitting poems. Typically, successful submissions include 8-20 pages of unpublished poetry. (Note: Do not send complete mss—published or unpublished—for consideration.) No inspirational verse. **Pays $40/printed page and 3 contributor's copies.**

⑨ MODERN HAIKU

P.O. Box 930, Portsmouth RI 02871. **E-mail:** modernhaiku@gmail.com. **Website:** modernhaiku.org. **Contact:** Paul Miller, editor. **85% freelance written.** Magazine published 3 times/year in February, June, and October covering haiku poetry. *Modern Haiku* is the foremost international journal of English-language haiku and criticism and publishes high-quality material only. Haiku and related genres, articles on haiku, haiku book reviews, and translations comprise its contents. It has an international circulation; subscribers include many university, school, and public libraries. Estab. 1969. Circ. 650. Byline given. No kill fee. Publishes ms an average of 6 months after acceptance. Editorial lead time 4 months. Accepts queries by mail, e-mail. Responds in 1 week to queries; in 6-8 weeks to mss. Sample copy: $15 in North America, $16 in Canada, $20 in Mexico, $22 overseas. Subscription: $35 ppd by regular mail in the U.S. Payment possible by PayPal on the *Modern Haiku* website. Guidelines available for SASE or on website.

NONFICTION Needs essays. Send complete ms. **Pays $5/page.**

COLUMNS Haiku & Senryu; Haibun; Essays (on haiku and related genres); Reviews (books of haiku or related genres). **Buys 40 mss/year.** Send complete ms. **Pays $5/page.**

POETRY Needs haiku, senryu, haibun, haiga. Postal submissions: "Send 5-15 haiku on 1 or 2 letter-sized sheets. Put name and address at the top of each sheet. Include SASE." E-mail submissions: "May be attachments (recommended) or pasted in body of message. Subject line must read: MH Submission. Adhere to guidelines on the website." Publishes 750 poems/year. Has published haiku by Roberta Beary, Billy Collins, Lawrence Ferlinghetti, Carolyn Hall, Sharon Olds, Gary Snyder, John Stevenson, George Swede, and Cor van den Heuvel. Does not want "general poetry, tanka, renku, linked-verse forms. No special consideration given to work by children and teens." **Offers no payment.**

NARRATIVE MAGAZINE

2443 Fillmore St. #214, San Francisco CA 94115. **E-mail:** contact@narrativemagazine.com. **Website:** www.narrativemagazine.com. **Contact:** Michael Croft, senior editor; Mimi Kusch, managing editor; Michael Wiegers, poetry editor. **100% freelance written.** Online literary journal that publishes American and international literature 3 times/year. "*Narrative* publishes high-quality contemporary literature in a full range of styles, forms, and lengths. Submit poetry, fiction, and nonfiction, including stories, short shorts, novels, novel excerpts, novellas, personal essays, humor, sketches, memoirs, literary biographies, commentary, reportage, interviews, and short audio recordings of short-short stories and poems. We welcome submissions of previously unpublished mss of all lengths, ranging from short-short stories to complete book-length works for serialization. In addition to submissions for issues of *Narrative* itself, we also encourage submissions for our Story of the Week, literary contests, and Readers' Narratives. Please read our Submission Guidelines for all information on mss formatting, word lengths, author payment, and other policies. We accept submissions only through our electronic submission system. We do not accept submissions through postal services or e-mail. You may send us mss for the following submission categories: General Submissions, Narrative Prize, Story of the Week, Readers' Narrative, iPoem, iStory, Six-Word Story, or a specific Contest. Your ms must be in one of the following file forms: .doc, .rtf, .pdf, .docx, .txt, .wpd, .odf, .mp3, .mp4, .mov, or .flv." Estab. 2003. Circ. 210,000. Byline given. Accepts queries by e-mail. Accepts simultaneous submissions. Responds in 4-14 weeks to queries. Guidelines online. Charges $23 reading fee except for 2 weeks in April.

NONFICTION Needs book excerpts, essays, general interest, humor, interview, memoir, personal experience, photo feature, travel. Send complete ms.

FICTION Has published work by Alice Munro, Tobias Wolff, Marvin Bell, Jane Smiley, Joyce Carol Oates, E.L. Doctorow, Min Jin Lee, and Alice Munro. Publishes new and emerging writers. , fiction, cartoons, graphic art, and multimedia content "to entertain, inspire, and engage." Send complete ms. **Pays on publication between $150-1,000, $1,000-5,000 for book length, plus annual prizes of more than $32,000 awarded.**

POETRY **Contact:** Michael Wiegers, poetry editor. Needs poetry of all forms.

NEON MAGAZINE

UK. **E-mail:** info@neonmagazine.co.uk. **Website:** www.neonmagazine.co.uk. **Contact:** Krishan Coupland. Quarterly website and print magazine covering alternative work of any form of poetry and prose, short stories, flash fiction, artwork and reviews. "Genre work is welcome. Experimentation is encouraged. We like stark poetry and weird prose. We seek work that is beautiful, shocking, intense, and memorable. Darker pieces are generally favored over humorous ones." No kill fee. Accepts queries by e-mail. Accepts simultaneous submissions. Responds in 2 months. Query if you have received no reply after 10 weeks. Guidelines online.

NONFICTION Needs reviews. No word limit.

FICTION Needs experimental, horror, humorous, science fiction, suspense. "No nonsensical prose; we are not appreciative of sentimentality." **Buys 8-12 mss/year.** No word limit. **Pays royalties.**

POETRY "No nonsensical poetry; we are not appreciative of sentimentality. Rhyming poetry is discouraged." Buys 24-30 poems/year. No word limit. **Pays royalties.**

$ NEW ENGLAND REVIEW

Middlebury College, Middlebury VT 05753. (802)443-5075. **E-mail:** nereview@middlebury.edu. **Website:** www.nereview.com. **Contact:** Marcia Parlow, managing editor. Quarterly literary magazine. *New England Review* is a prestigious, nationally distributed literary journal. Reads September 1 through May 31 (postmarked dates). Estab. 1978. Circ. 2,000. Byline given. Pays on publication. No kill fee. Publishes ms an average of 6 months after acceptance. Accepts simultaneous submissions. Responds in 2 weeks to queries; in 3 months to mss. Sometimes comments on rejected mss. Sample copy: $10 (add $5 for overseas). Subscription: $30. Overseas shipping fees add $25 for subscription, $12 for Canada. Guidelines online.

NONFICTION **Buys 20-25 mss/year.** Send complete ms via online submission manager. No e-mail submissions. Length: up to 7,500 words, though exceptions may be made. **Pays $20/page ($20 minimum) and 2 contributor's copies.**

FICTION Send 1 story at a time, unless it is very short. Serious literary only, novel excerpts. Publishes approximately 10 new writers/year. Has published work by Steve Almond, Christine Sneed, Roy Kesey, Thomas Gough, Norman Lock, Brock Clarke, Carl Phillips, Lucia Perillo, Linda Gregerson, and Natasha Trethewey. **Buys 25 mss/year.** Send complete ms via online submission manager. No e-mail submissions. "Will consider simultaneous submissions, but must be stated as such and you must notify us immediately if the ms accepted for publication elsewhere." Length: not strict on word count. **Pays $20/page ($20 minimum), and 2 contributor's copies.**

POETRY Submit up to 6 poems at a time. No previously published or simultaneous submissions for poetry. Accepts submissions by online submission manager only; accepts questions by e-mail. "Cover letters are useful." Address submissions to "Poetry Editor." Buys 75-90 poems/year. Submit maximum 6 poems. **Pays $20/page ($20 minimum), and 2 contributor's copies.**

💲 NEW LETTERS

University of Missouri-Kansas City, 5101 Rockhill Rd., Kansas City MO 64110. (816)235-1168. **Fax:** (816)235-2611. **E-mail:** newletters@umkc.edu. **Website:** www.newletters.org. **Contact:** Robert Stewart, editor in chief. **100% freelance written.** Quarterly magazine. "*New Letters* continues to seek the best new writing, whether from established writers or those ready and waiting to be discovered. In addition, it supports those writers, readers, and listeners who want to experience the joy of writing that can both surprise and inspire us all." Estab. 1934. Circ. 5,000. Byline given. Pays on publication. No kill fee. Publishes ms an average of 6 months after acceptance. Editorial lead time 6 months. Submit seasonal material 6 months in advance. Accepts queries by mail. Accepts simultaneous submissions. Responds in 1 month to queries; in 5 months to mss. Sample copy: $10 or sample articles on website. Guidelines online.

NONFICTION Needs essays. No self-help, how-to, or nonliterary work. **Buys 8-10 mss/year.** Send complete ms. Length: up to 5,000 words. **Pays $40-100.**

FICTION Needs ethnic, experimental, humorous, mainstream, contemporary. No genre fiction. **Buys 15-20 mss/year.** Send complete ms. Length: up to 5,000 words. **Pays $30-75.**

POETRY Needs avant-garde, free verse, haiku, traditional. No light verse. Buys 40-50 poems/year. Submit maximum 6 poems. Length: open. **Pays $10-25.**

💲 NEW ORLEANS REVIEW

Box 195, Loyola University, New Orleans LA 70118. (504)865-2295. **E-mail:** noreview@loyno.edu. **Website:** neworleansreview.org. **Contact:** Heidi Braden, managing editor. *New Orleans Review* is an annual journal of contemporary literature and culture, publishing new poetry, fiction, nonfiction, art, photography, film and book reviews. Estab. 1968. Circ. 1,500. Pays on publication. No kill fee. Accepts queries by online submission form. Accepts simultaneous submissions. Responds in 4 months to mss.

FICTION Contact: Mark Yakich, editor. , "good writing, from conventional to experimental." "We are now using an online submission system and require a $3 fee." See website for details. Length: up to 6,500 words. **Pays $25-50 and 2 contributor's copies.**

POETRY Submit maximum 3-6 poems.

♻️😊💲 THE NEW QUARTERLY

St. Jerome's University, 290 Westmount Rd. N., Waterloo ON N2L 3G3 Canada. (519)884-8111, ext. 28290. **E-mail:** editor@tnq.ca; info@tnq.ca. **Website:** www.tnq.ca. **95% freelance written.** Quarterly book covering Canadian fiction and poetry. "Emphasis on emerging writers and genres, but we publish more traditional work as well if the language and narrative structure are fresh." Estab. 1981. Circ. 1,000. Byline given. Pays on publication. No kill fee. Editorial lead time 6 months. Accepts queries by mail. Accepts simultaneous submissions. Responds in early January to submissions received March 1-August 31; in early June to submissions received September 1-February 28. Sample copy: $16.95 (cover price, plus mailing). Guidelines online.

NONFICTION Needs essays. Query with a proposal.

FICTION "*Canadian work only.* We are not interested in genre fiction. We are looking for innovative, beautifully crafted, deeply felt literary fiction." , literary. **Buys 20-25 mss/year.** Send complete ms with submission cover sheet and bio. Does not accept submissions by e-mail. Accepts simultaneoues submissions if indicated in cover letter. **Pays $250/story.**

POETRY Needs avant-garde, free verse, traditional. *Canadian work only.* Send with submission cover sheet and bio. Does not accept submissions by e-mail. Accepts simultaneoues submissions if indicated in cover letter. Submit maximum 3 poems. **Pays $40/poem.**

NINTH LETTER

Department of English, University of Illinois, 608 S. Wright St., Urbana IL 61801. (217)300-4315. **E-mail:** info@ninthletter.com; editor@ninthletter.com. **Website:** www.ninthletter.com. **Contact:** Jodee Stanley, editor. "*Ninth Letter* accepts submissions of fiction, poetry, and essays from September 1-February 28 (postmark dates). *Ninth Letter* is published semiannually at the University of Illinois, Urbana-Champaign. We are interested in prose and poetry that experiment with form, narrative, and nontraditional subject matter, as well as more traditional literary work." Pays on publication. Accepts queries by mail, online submission form. Accepts simultaneous submissions.

NONFICTION Contact: nonfiction@ninthletter.com. "Please send only 1 essay at a time. All mailed submissions must include an SASE for reply." Length:

up to 8,000 words. **Pays $25 per printed page and 2 contributor's copies.**

FICTION Contact: fiction@ninthpoetry.com. "Please send only 1 story at a time. All mailed submissions must include an SASE for reply." Length: up to 8,000 words. **Pays $25 per printed page and 2 contributor's copies.**

POETRY Contact: poetry@ninthletter.com. Submit 3-6 poems (no more than 10 pages) at a time. "All mailed submissions must include an SASE for reply." **Pays $25 per printed page and 2 contributor's copies.**

ⓢ NORTH CAROLINA LITERARY REVIEW

East Carolina University, Mailstop 555 English, Greenville NC 27858-4353. (252)328-1537. **Fax:** (252)328-4889. **E-mail:** nclrsubmissions@ecu.edu; bauerm@ecu.edu. **Website:** www.nclr.ecu.edu. **Contact:** Margaret Bauer. Biannual magazine published online in the winter and in print in the summer covering North Carolina writers, literature, culture, history. "Articles should have a North Carolina slant. Fiction, creative nonfiction, and poetry accepted through yearly contests. First consideration is always for quality of work. Although we treat academic and scholarly subjects, we do not wish to see jargon-laden prose; our readers, we hope, are found as often in bookstores and libraries as in academia. We seek to combine the best elements of a magazine for serious readers with the best of a scholarly journal." Estab. 1992. Circ. 750. Byline given. No kill fee. Publishes ms an average of 1 year after acceptance. Editorial lead time 6 months. Accepts simultaneous submissions. Responds in 1 month to queries; in 6 months to mss. Sample copy: $5-25. Guidelines online.

NONFICTION Submit creative nonfiction for Alex Albright Creative Nonfiction Prize competition via Submittable. Length: up to 7,500 words. **Published writers paid in copies of the journal. First-place winners of contests receive a prize of $250.**

FICTION Submit fiction for the Doris Betts Fiction Prize competition via Submittable. Length: up to 6,000 words. **First-place winners of contests receive a prize of $250. Other writers whose stories are selected for publication receive comp copies.**

POETRY Submit poetry for the James Applewhite Poetry Prize competition via Submittable. Only subscribers can submit, and all poets must have a North Carolina connection. Submit up to 3 poems with a 1-year subscription ($15) or up to 5 poems with a 2-year subscription ($25). **First-place winners of contests receive a prize of $250. Other poets whose poems are selected for publication receive comp copies of the issue.**

FILLERS Buys 2-5 mss/year.

NOW & THEN: THE APPALACHIAN MAGAZINE

East Tennessee State University, Box 70556, Johnson City TN 37614-1707. (423)439-5348. **Fax:** (423)439-6340. **E-mail:** nowandthen@etsu.edu. **E-mail:** sandersr@etsu.edu. **Website:** www.etsu.edu/cass/nowandthen. **Contact:** Randy Sanders, managing editor; Wayne Winkler, music editor; Charlie Warden, photo editor. Literary magazine published twice/year. "*Now & Then* accepts a variety of writing genres: fiction, poetry, nonfiction, essays, interviews, memoirs, and book reviews. All submissions must relate to Appalachia and to the issue's specific theme. Our readership is educated and interested in the region." Estab. 1984. Circ. 1,000. Accepts simultaneous submissions. Responds in 5 months to queries; 5 months to mss. Sample copy: $8 plus $3 shipping. Guidelines and upcoming themes available on website.

FICTION "Absolutely has to relate to Appalachian theme. Can be about adjustment to new environment, themes of leaving and returning, for instance. Nothing unrelated to region." Accepts 1-2 mss/issue. Publishes ms 4 months after acceptance. Publishes some new writers/year. Send complete ms. Accepts submissions by mail, e-mail, with a strong preference for e-mail. Include "information we can use for contributor's note." SASE (or IRC). Rarely accepts simultaneous submissions. Reviews fiction. Length: 1,000-1,500 words. **Pays $50 for each accepted article. Pays on publication.**

POETRY Submit up to 5 poems, with SASE and cover letter including "a few lines about yourself for a contributor's note and whether the work has been published or accepted elsewhere." Will consider simultaneous submissions; occasionally accepts previously published poems. Put name, address, and phone number on every poem. Deadlines: last workday in February (spring/summer issue) and August 31 (fall/winter issues). Publishes theme issues. **Pays $25 for each accepted poem. Pays on publication.**

OVERTIME

Blue Cubicle Press, LLC, P.O. Box 250382, Plano TX 75025. **E-mail:** overtime@workerswritejournal.com.

Website: www.workerswritejournal.com/overtime. htm. **Contact:** David LaBounty, editor. **100% freelance written.** Quarterly saddle-stitched chapbook covering working-class literature. Estab. 2006. Circ. 725. Byline given. Pays on acceptance of ms. Publishes ms 6 months after acceptance. Accepts queries by mail, e-mail. Accepts simultaneous submissions. Responds in 1 week to queries; 1 month to mss. Sample copy and writer's guidelines available online at website.

FICTION Needs adventure, condensed novels, ethnic, experimental, historical, humorous, mainstream, novel excerpts, short stories, slice-of-life vignettes, working-class literature. **Buys 4 mss/year.** Query; send complete ms. Length: 5,000-12,000 words. **Pays $35-50.**

⊕⊕⊕⊕ PAKN TREGER

National Yiddish Book Center, 1021 West St., Amherst MA 01002. (413)256-4900. **E-mail:** aatherley@ bikher.org; pt@bikher.org;. **Website:** www.yiddishbookcenter.org. **Contact:** Anne Atherley, editor's assistant. **50% freelance written.** Literary magazine published 3 times/year; focuses on modern and contemporary Jewish and Yiddish culture. Estab. 1980. Circ. 20,000. Byline given. Pays on publication. Publishes ms an average of 3 months after acceptance. Editorial lead time 4 months. Submit seasonal material 3 months in advance. Accepts queries by mail, e-mail, fax. Accepts simultaneous submissions. Responds in 4 weeks to queries. Responds in 3 months to mss. Sample copy online. Guidelines by e-mail.

NONFICTION Needs essays, humor, interview. Does not want personal memoirs, fiction, or poetry. **Buys 6-10 mss/year.** Query. Length: 1,200-4,000 words. **Pays $800-2,000 for assigned articles. Pays $350-1,000 for unsolicited articles.**

COLUMNS Let's Learn Yiddish (Yiddish lesson), 1 page Yid/English; Translations (Yiddish-English), 1,200-2,500 words. **Pays $350-1,000.**

PANK

PANK, Department of Humanities, 1400 Townsend Dr., Houghton MI 49931-1200. **E-mail:** mbartley@pankmagazine.com. **Website:** www.pankmagazine.com. **Contact:** M. Bartley Seigel, editor. **100% freelance written.** Annual literary magazine. "*PANK* Magazine fosters access to emerging and experimental poetry and prose, publishing the brightest and most promising writers for the most adventurous readers. To the end of the road, up country, a far shore, the edge of

things, to a place of amalgamation and unplumbed depths, where the known is made and unmade, and where unimagined futures are born, a place inhabited by contradictions, a place of quirk and startling anomaly. *PANK*, no soft pink hands allowed." Estab. 2006. Circ. 1,000/print; 18,000/online. Publishes ms and average of 3-12 months after acceptance. Accepts queries by online submission form. Accepts simultaneous submissions. Guidelines available on website.

NONFICTION Needs essays, general interest, historical, humor, nostalgic, opinion. Send complete ms through online submissions manager. **Pays $20, a one-year subscription, and a** *PANK* **t-shirt.**

FICTION "Bright, new, energetic, passionate writing, writing that pushes our tender little buttons and gets us excited. Push our tender buttons, excite us, and we'll publish you." Send complete ms through online submissions manager. **Pays $20, a one-year subscription, and a** *PANK* **t-shirt.**

POETRY Submit through online submissions manager. **Pays $20, a one-year subscription, and a** *PANK* **t-shirt.**

⊕⊕⊕ THE PARIS REVIEW

544 West 27th St., New York NY 10001. (212)343-1333. **E-mail:** queries@theparisreview.org. **Website:** www.theparisreview.org. **Contact:** Lorin Stein, editor; Robyn Creswell, poetry editor. Quarterly magazine. *The Paris Review* publishes "fiction and poetry of superlative quality, whatever the genre, style, or mode. Our contributors include prominent, as well as less well-known and previously unpublished writers. The Writers at Work interview series includes important contemporary writers discussing their own work and the craft of writing." Pays on publication. No kill fee. Accepts queries by mail. Accepts simultaneous submissions. Responds in 4 months to mss. Guidelines online.

FICTION Study the publication. Annual Plimpton Prize award of $10,000 given to a new voice published in the magazine. Recently published work by Ottessa Moshfegh, John Jeremiah Sullivan, and Lydia Davis. Send complete ms. Length: no limit. **Pays $1,000-3,000.**

POETRY Contact: Robyn Creswell, poetry editor. Submit no more than 6 poems at a time. Poetry can be sent to the poetry editor (please include a self-addressed, stamped envelope). **Poets receive $100/poem.**

⊕⊕ PARNASSUS: POETRY IN REVIEW

Poetry in Review Foundation, 205 W. 89th St., No. 8F, New York NY 10024. (212)787-3569. **E-mail:** poetryinreview@gmail.com. **Website:** www.parnassusreview.com. **Contact:** Herbert Leibowitz, editor and publisher. Annual magazine covering poetry and criticism. "We now publish 1 double issue/year." *Parnassus: Poetry in Review* provides "a forum where poets, novelists, and critics of all persuasions can gather to review new books of poetry, including translations—international poetries have occupied center stage from our very first issue—with an amplitude and reflectiveness that Sunday book supplements and even the literary quarterlies could not afford. Our editorial philosophy is based on the assumption that reviewing is a complex art. Like a poem or a short story, a review essay requires imagination, scrupulous attention to rhythm, pacing, and supple syntax; space in which to build a persuasive, detailed argument; analytical precision and intuitive gambits; verbal play, wit, and metaphor. We welcome and vigorously seek out voices that break aesthetic molds and disturb xenophobic habits." Estab. 1972. Circ. 1,800. Byline given. Pays on publication. No kill fee. Publishes ms an average of 12-14 months after acceptance. Accepts queries by mail. Accepts simultaneous submissions. Responds in 2 months to mss. Sample copy: $15.

NONFICTION Needs essays, reviews. **Buys 30 mss/year.** Query with published clips. Length: 1,500-7,500 words. **Pays $200-1,000.**

POETRY Needs avant garde, free verse, traditional. Accepts most types of poetry. Buys 3-4 unsolicited poems/year.

POEMELEON: A JOURNAL OF POETRY

Riverside CA **E-mail:** editor@poemeleon.org. **Website:** www.poemeleon.org. **Contact:** Cati Porter, editor. Each issue of *Poemeleon* is devoted to a specific kind of poetry. Previous emphases include: poetry of place, ekphrastic poetry, poems in form, prose poems, persona poems, humor, gender, and collaboration. Estab. 2005. Accepts queries by online submission form. Accepts simultaneous submissions. Responds in 1-3 months after close of submissions. Guidelines online.

NONFICTION Submit 1 craft essay or 1 book review using online subvmission form. Include a brief third-person bio in cover letter.

POETRY Submit 1-5 poems using online submission manager. Include a brief third-person bio in cover letter. Submit maximum 5 poems.

POETRY

The Poetry Foundation, 61 W. Superior St., Chicago IL 60654. (312)787-7070. **Fax:** (312)787-6650. **E-mail:** editors@poetrymagazine.org. **Website:** www.poetry-magazine.org. Don Share, editor. **Contact:** Don Share, editor. **100% freelance written.** Monthly magazine. *Poetry*, published monthly by The Poetry Foundation, "has no special ms needs and no special requirements as to form: We examine in turn all work received and accept that which seems best." Has published poetry by the major voices of our time as well as new talent. Estab. 1912. Circ. 32,500. Byline given. Pays on publication. No kill fee. Publishes ms an average of 9 months after acceptance. Accepts simultaneous submissions. Responds in 2 months to mss and queries. Guidelines online.

NONFICTION Buys 14 mss/year. Query. No length requirements. **Pays $150/page.**

POETRY Accepts all styles and subject matter. Submit up to 4 poems via online submissions manager. Reviews books of poetry in multibook formats of varying lengths. Does not accept unsolicited reviews. Buys 180-250 poems/year. Length: up to 10 pages total. **Pays $10 line (minimum payment of $300).**

POETRY IRELAND REVIEW

Poetry Ireland, 32 Kildare Street, Dublin 2 Ireland. 01-4789974. **Fax:** 01-6789815. **E-mail:** publications@poetryireland.ie. **Website:** www.poetryireland.ie. Quarterly poetry, reviews, and essays magazine in book form. Estab. 1978. Circ. 2,000. Pays on publication. No kill fee. Accepts queries by mail, e-mail, fax, phone. Accepts simultaneous submissions. Responds in 1 week to queries. Responds in 3 months to mss. Guidelines available on website: www.poetryireland.ie/writers/submission-to-pir/.

POETRY Needs avant-garde, free verse, haiku, traditional. Buys 150 poems/year. Submit maximum 6 poems. **Pays $32/submission.**

THE PRAIRIE JOURNAL

P.O. Box 68073, 28 Crowfoot Terrace NW, Calgary AB Y3G 3N8 Canada. **E-mail:** editor@prairiejournal.org (queries only); prairiejournal@yahoo.com. **Website:** www.prairiejournal.org. **Contact:** A.E. Burke, literary editor. **100% freelance written.** Semiannual magazine publishing quality poetry, short fiction, drama, literary criticism, reviews, bibliography, interviews, profiles, and artwork. "The audience is literary, university, library, scholarly, and creative readers/writers." Estab. 1983. Circ. 650-750. Byline given. Pays on publication. No kill fee. Publishes ms an average of 4-6 months after acceptance. Editorial lead time 2-6 months. Accepts queries by mail, e-mail. Responds in 2 weeks to queries; 2-6 months to mss. Sample copy: $5. Guidelines online.

NONFICTION Needs essays, humor, interview, literary. No inspirational, news, religious, or travel. **Buys 25-40 mss/year.** Query with published clips. Length: 100-3,000 words. **Pays $50-100, plus contributor's copy.**

COLUMNS Reviews (books from small presses publishing poetry, short fiction, essays, and criticism), 200-1,000 words. **Buys 5 mss/year.** Query with published clips. **Pays $10-50.**

FICTION Needs mainstream. No genre (romance, horror, western—sagebrush or cowboys), erotic, science fiction, or mystery. **Buys 6 mss/year.** Send complete ms. No e-mail submissions. Length: 100-3,000 words. **Pays $10-75.**

POETRY Needs avant-garde, free verse, haiku. Seeks poetry "of any length; free verse, contemporary themes (feminist, nature, urban, nonpolitical), aesthetic value, a poet's poetry." Does not want to see "most rhymed verse, sentimentality, egotistical ravings. No cowboys or sage brush." Has published poetry by Liliane Welch, Cornelia Hoogland, Sheila Hyland, Zoe Lendale, and Chad Norman. Receives about 1,000 poems/year, accepts 10%. No heroic couplets or greeting card verse. Buys 25-35 poems/year. Submit maximum 6-8 poems. Length: 3-50 lines. **Pays $5-50.**

🍁 $ PRISM INTERNATIONAL

Dept. of Creative Writing, Buch E462, 1866 Main Mall, University of British Columbia, Vancouver British Columbia V6T 1Z1 Canada. (604)822-2514. **Fax:** (604)822-3616. **E-mail:** prismcirculation@gmail.com. **Website:** www.prismmagazine.ca. **100% freelance written. Works with new/unpublished writers.** A quarterly international journal of contemporary writing—fiction, poetry, drama, creative nonfiction and translation. *PRISM international* is 80 pages, digest-sized, elegantly printed, flat-spined, with original color artwork on a glossy card cover. Readership: public and university libraries, individual subscriptions, bookstores—a world-wide audience concerned with the contemporary in literature. "We have no thematic or stylistic allegiances: Excellence is our main criterion for acceptance of manuscripts." Receives 1,000 submissions/year, accepts about 80. Circulation is for 1,200 subscribers. Subscription: $35/year for Canadian subscriptions, $40/year for US subscriptions, $45/year for international. Sample: $13. Estab. 1959. Circ. 1,200. Pays on publication. No kill fee. Publishes ms an average of 4 months after acceptance. Accepts simultaneous submissions. Responds in 4 months to queries. Responds in 3-6 months to mss. Sample copy for $13, more info online. Guidelines online.

NONFICTION No reviews, tracts, or scholarly essays. **Pays $20/printed page, and 2 copies of issue.**

FICTION For Drama: one-acts/excerpts of no more than 1500 words preferred. Also interested in seeing dramatic monologues. Needs experimental, traditional. "New writing that is contemporary and literary. Short stories and self-contained novel excerpts. Works of translation are eagerly sought and should be accompanied by a copy of the original. Would like to see more translations. No gothic, confession, religious, romance, pornography, or science fiction." **Buys 12-16 mss/year.** Send complete ms. 25 pages maximum **Pays $20/printed page, and 2 copies of issue.**

POETRY Needs avant-garde, traditional. Wants "fresh, distinctive poetry that shows an awareness of traditions old and new. We read everything." Considers poetry by children and teens. "Excellence is the only criterion." Has published poetry by Margaret Avison, Elizabeth Bachinsky, John Pass, Warren Heiti, Don McKay, Bill Bissett, and Stephanie Bolster. Submit maximum up to 6 poems. **Pays $40/printed page, and 2 copies of issue.**

🍁 $ $ QUEEN'S QUARTERLY

144 Barrie St., Queen's University, Kingston ON K7L 3N6 Canada. (613)533-2667. **E-mail:** queens.quarterly@queensu.ca. **Website:** www.queensu.ca/quarterly. **Contact:** Joan Harcourt, literary editor (fiction and poetry); Boris Castel, nonfiction editor (articles, essays and reviews). **95% freelance written.** Quartlery literary magazine. *Queen's Quarterly* is "a general interest intellectual review featuring articles on science, politics, humanities, arts and letters, extensive book reviews, and some poetry and fiction." Estab. 1893. Circ. 3,000. Byline given. Pays on publication. Sends galleys to author. Publishes ms on average 6-12 months after acceptance. Accepts queries by e-mail. Responds in 2-3 months to queries; 1-2 months to ms. Sample copy: $6.50. U.S. Subscription: $20 for Canada, $25 for U.S. and foreign subscribers. Guidelines available on website.

NONFICTION Send complete ms with SASE and/or IRC. No reply with insufficient postage. Length:

up to 3,000 words. **"Payment to new writers will be determined at time of acceptance."**

FICTION Send complete ms with SASE and/or IRC. No reply with insufficient postage. Accepts 2 mss/issue; 8 mss/year. Publishes 5 new writers/year. Length: 2,500-3,000 words. "Submissions over 3,000 words shall not be accepted." **"Payment to new writers will be determined at time of acceptance."**

POETRY Receives about 400 submissions of poetry/year, accepts 40. Submissions can be sent on hard copy with a SASE (no replies/returns for foreign submissions unless accompanied by an IRC) or by e-mail and will be responded to by same. "We are especially interested in poetry by Canadian writers. Shorter poems preferred." Has published poetry by Evelyn Lau, Sue Nevill, and Raymond Souster. Each issue contains about 12 pages of poetry. Buys 25 poems/year. Submit maximum 6 poems. **Usually pays $50 (Canadian)/poem (but it varies), plus 2 copies.**

THE RAG

P.O. Box 17463, Portland OR 97217. **E-mail:** submissions@raglitmag.com. **Website:** raglitmag.com. **Contact:** Seth Porter, editor; Dan Reilly, editor. **90% freelance written.** *The Rag* focuses on the grittier genres that tend to fall by the wayside at more traditional literary magazines. *The Rag's* ultimate goal is to put the literary magazine back into the entertainment market while rekindling the social and cultural value short fiction once held in North American literature. Estab. 2011. Byline given. Pays prior to publication. Editorial lead time 1-2 months. Accepts queries by e-mail. Accepts simultaneous submissions. Responds in 1 month or less for queries; in 1-2 months for mss. Guidelines online.

FICTION Accepts all styles and themes. Needs humorous, transgressive. **Buys 12 mss/year.** Send complete ms. Length: up to 10,000 words. **Pays 5¢/word, the average being $250/story.**

FILLERS Length: 150-1,000 words. **Pays $20-100.**

RALEIGH REVIEW LITERARY & ARTS MAGAZINE

Box 6725, Raleigh NC 27628-6725. **E-mail:** info@raleighreview.org. **Website:** www.raleighreview.org. Rob Greene, editor. **Contact:** Rob Greene, editor; Landon Houle, fiction editor; Bryce Emley, poetry editor. **90% freelance written.** Semiannual literary magazine. "*Raleigh Review* is a national nonprofit magazine of poetry, short fiction (including flash), and art. We believe that great literature inspires empathy by allowing us to see the world through the eyes of our neighbors, whether across the street or across the globe. Our mission is to foster the creation and availability of accessible yet provocative contemporary literature. We look for work that is emotionally and intellectually complex. Estab. 2010. Pays on publication. Publishes ms 3-6 months after acceptance. Accepts simultaneous submissions. Responds typically in 1-3 months, though sometimes up to 3-6 months. "Poetry and fiction submissions through Tell It Slant online system; no prior query required." Sample copy: $13.50 hardcopy or $4.95 on Kindle. "Sample work also online at website." Guidelines online.

FICTION Needs confessions, ethnic, mainstream, novel excerpts, slice-of-life vignettes. "We prefer work that is physically grounded and accessible, though complex and rich in emotional or intellectual power. We delight in stories from unique voices and perspectives. Any fiction that is born from a relatively unknown place grabs our attention. We are not opposed to genre fiction, so long as it has real, human characters and is executed artfully." **Buys 10-15 mss/year.** Submit complete ms. Length: 250-7,500 words. "While we accept fiction up to 7,500 words, we are more likely to publish work in the 4,500- to 5,000-word range." **Pays $10 maximum.**

POETRY Needs free verse, traditional, lyric, narrative poems of experience. Submit up to 5 poems. "If you think your poems will make a perfect stranger's toes tingle, heart leap, or brain sizzle, then send them our way. We typically do not publish avant garde, experimental, or language poetry. We *do* like a poem that causes—for a wide audience—a visceral reaction to intellectually and emotionally rich material." Buys 30-40 poems/year. Submit maximum 5 poems. Length: open. **Pays $10 maximum.**

RATTLE

12411 Ventura Blvd., Studio City CA 91604. (818)505-6777. **E-mail:** tim@rattle.com. **Website:** www.rattle.com. **Contact:** Timothy Green, editor. Published quarterly in March, June, September, and October. *RATTLE* "includes poems, essays, and interviews with poets, and tribute features dedicated to a specific ethnic or vocational group." Estab. 1994. Accepts simultaneous submissions. Responds in 1-3 months. Guidelines online.

NONFICTION "Welcomes essays on poetry or the writing process."

POETRY Wants "meaningful poetry in any form." Submit up to 5 poems at a time. Accepts e-mail submissions (pasted into body of message). Cover letter is required (with e-mail address, if possible). Submit maximum 5 poems. **Pays $100/poem and a 1-year subscription for print contributors; $50/poem for online contributors.**

◓ THE RIALTO

P.O. Box 309, Alysham, Norwich NR11 6LN England. **E-mail:** info@therialto.co.uk. **Website:** www.therialto.co.uk. **Contact:** Michael Mackmin, editor. *The Rialto*, published 3 times/year, seeks to publish the best new poems by established and beginning poets. Seeks excellence and originality. Has published poetry by Alice Fulton, Jenny Joseph, Les Murray, George Szirtes, Philip Gross, and Ruth Padel. Estab. 1984. Payment on publication. Publishes ms 5 months after acceptance. Accepts simultaneous submissions. Responds in 3-4 months. Submission guidelines can be found on the website. We now accept online submissions via Submittable. Details on website. Postal submissions still very welcome. We respond by e-mail to postal submissions from outside of the UK.

POETRY Submit up to 6 poems at a time with a SASE. E-mail submissions via Submittable now welcome, details on website. **Pays £20/poem on publication.**

◒ ROOM

West Coast Feminist Literary Magazine Society, P.O. Box 46160, Station D, Vancouver BC V6J 5G5 Canada. **E-mail:** contactus@roommagazine.com. **Website:** www.roommagazine.com. "*Room* is Canada's oldest feminist literary journal. Published quarterly by a collective based in Vancouver, *Room* showcases fiction, poetry, reviews, art work, interviews, and profiles by writers and artists who identify as women or genderqueer. Many of our contributors are at the beginning of their writing careers, looking for an opportunity to get published for the first time. Some later go on to great acclaim. *Room* is a space where women can speak, connect, and showcase their creativity. Each quarter we publish original, thought-provoking works that reflect women's strength, sensuality, vulnerability, and wit." Estab. 1975. Circ. 1,400. Byline given. Pays on publication. Yes, if work is accepted but cannot be published Accepts queries by online submission form. Accepts simultaneous submissions. Responds in 6 months. Sample copy: $12 or online at website.

NONFICTION Buys 1-2 mss/year. Submit complete ms via online submissions manager. Length: up to 3,500 words. **Pays $50-120 (Canadian), 2 contributor's copies, and a one-year subscription.**

FICTION Accepts literature that illustrates the female experience—short stories, creative nonfiction, poetry—by, for and about women. Submit complete ms via online submissions manager. **Pays $50-120 (Canadian), 2 contributor's copies, and a one-year subscription.**

POETRY *Room* uses "poetry by women, including trans* and genderqueer writers, written from a feminist perspective. Nothing simplistic, clichéd. We prefer to receive up to 5 poems at a time, so we can select a pair or group." Submit via online submissions manager. Pays $50-120 (Canadian), 2 contributor's copies, and a one-year subscription.

SALT HILL JOURNAL

Creative Writing Program, Syracuse University, English Deptartment, 401 Hall of Languages, Syracuse University, Syracuse NY 13244. **Website:** salthilljournal.net. **Contact:** Emma DeMilta and Jessica Poli, editors. "*Salt Hill* is published through Syracuse University's Creative Writing MFA program. We strive to publish a mix of the best contemporary and emerging talent in poetry, fiction, and nonfiction. Your work, if accepted, would appear in a long tradition of exceptional contributors, including Steve Almond, Mary Caponegro, Kim Chinquee, Edwidge Danticat, Denise Duhamel, Brian Evenson, B.H. Fairchild, Mary Gaitskill, Terrance Hayes, Bob Hicok, Laura Kasischke, Etgar Keret, Phil Lamarche, Dorianne Laux, Maurice Manning, Karyna McGlynn, Ander Monson, David Ohle, Lucia Perillo, Tomaž Šalamun, Zachary Schomburg, Christine Schutt, David Shields, Charles Simic, Patricia Smith, Dara Wier, and Raúl Zurita among many others." Byline given. No kill fee. Accepts queries by online submission form. Accepts simultaneous submissions. Guidelines online.

NONFICTION Contact: salthillnonfiction@gmail.com. Needs essays, interview, reviews. Special issues: "We accept a wide-range of creative nonfictions. Currently, we are especially interested in memoir and essay forms." Does not want articles or reports. Submit via online submissions manager; contact nonfiction editor via e-mail for retractions and queries only. Length: up to 30 pages.

FICTION Contact: salthillfiction@gmail.com. Submit via online submissions manager; contact fiction editor via e-mail for retractions and queries only. Length: up to 30 pages.

POETRY Contact: salthillpoetry@gmail.com. Submit up to 5 poems via online submissions manager; contact poetry editor via e-mail for retractions and queries only.

⦿⑨ THE SAVAGE KICK LITERARY MAGAZINE

Murder Slim Press, 29 Alpha Rd., Gorleston Norfolk NR31 0EQ United Kingdom. **E-mail:** moonshine@ murderslim.com. **Website:** www.murderslim.com. **100% freelance written.** Semiannual magazine. "*Savage Kick* primarily deals with viewpoints outside the mainstream: honest emotions told in a raw, simplistic way. It is recommended that you are very familiar with the *SK* style before submitting. Ensure you have a distinctive voice and story to tell." Estab. 2005. Circ. 500+. Byline given. Pays on acceptance. Publishes ms an average of up to 2 months after acceptance. Accepts queries by mail, e-mail. Accepts simultaneous submissions. Responds in 7-10 days to queries. Guidelines free.

NONFICTION Needs interview, personal experience. **Buys 10-20 mss/year.** Send complete ms. Length: 500-3,000 words. **Pays $25-35.**

COLUMNS Buys up to 4 mss/year. Query. **Pays $25-35.**

FICTION Needs mystery, slice-of-life vignettes, crime. "Real-life stories are preferred, unless the work is distinctively extreme within the crime genre. No poetry of any kind, no mainstream fiction, Oprah-style fiction, Internet/chat language, teen issues, excessive Shakespearean language, surrealism, overworked irony, or genre fiction (horror, fantasy, science fiction, western, erotica, etc.)." **Buys 10-25 mss/year.** Send complete ms. Length: 500-6,000 words. **Pays $35.**

SENECA REVIEW

Hobart and William Smith Colleges, Geneva NY 14456. (315)781-3392. **Fax:** (315)781-3348. **E-mail:** senecareview@hws.edu. **Website:** www.hws.edu/academics/senecareview/index.aspx. Semiannual magazine publishing mss of poetry, translations, essays on contemporary poetry, and lyric essays (creative nonfiction that borders on poetry). The editors have special interest in translations of contemporary poetry from around the world. Publisher of numerous laureates and award-winning poets, *Seneca Review* also publishes emerging writers and is always open to new, innovative work. Poems from *SR* are regularly honored by inclusion in *The Best American Poetry* and *Pushcart Prize* anthologies. Distributed internationally. No kill fee. Accepts queries by mail or via Submittable. Accepts simultaneous submissions. Responds in 3 months. Guidelines online. E-mail questions to senecareview@hws.edu.

NONFICTION Needs essays, translation. Special issues: Past special features include Irish women's poetry; Israeli women's poetry; Polish, Catalan, and Albanian poetry; excerpts from the notebooks of 32 contemporary American poets, an issue of essays devoted to Hayden Carruth; an issue dedicated to editor Deborah Tall; The Lyric Body, Anthology of Poets, Essayists and Artists Intimately Address Difference and Disability. Length: up to 20 pages.

POETRY Submit maximum 3-5 poems.

SEQUESTRUM

Sequestrum Publishing, 1023 Garfield Ave., Ames IA 50014. **E-mail:** sequr.info@gmail.com. **Website:** www.sequestrum.org. **Contact:** R.M. Cooper, managing editor. Biweekly literary magazine in tabloid and online formats. All publications are paired with a unique visual component. Regularly holds contests and features well-known authors, as well as promising new and emerging voices. Estab. 2014. Circ. 1,200 monthly. Byline given. Pays on acceptance. 100% kill fee. Publishes ms 2-6 months after acceptance. Editorial lead time: 3 months. Accepts queries by online submission form. Accepts simultaneous submissions. Sample copy available for free online. Guidelines available for free online.

NONFICTION Needs book excerpts, essays, general interest, humor, memoir, opinion, personal experience, photo feature, narrative, experimental. Special issues: Two contests yearly: Editor's Reprint Award (for previously published material) and New Writer Awards (for writers yet to publish a book-length manuscript). **Buys 3-5 mss/year.** Submit complete ms via online submissions manager. Length: 500-5,000 words. **Pays $10/article.**

FICTION Needs adventure, confessions, experimental, fantasy, horror, humorous, mainstream, mystery, novel excerpts, science fiction, short stories, suspense, western, Slipstream. **Buys 11-15 mss/year.** Submit complete ms via online submissions manager. Length: 5,000 words max. **Pays $10-15/story.**

POETRY Needs avant-garde, free verse, haiku, light verse, traditional, cross-genre. Buys 20 poems/year. Submit maximum 4 poems. Length: 35 lines max. **Pays $10/set of poems.**

THE SEWANEE REVIEW

University of the South, 735 University Ave., Sewanee TN 37383-1000. (931)598-1000. **E-mail:** sreview@sewanee.edu. **Website:** review.sewanee.edu. **Contact:** George Core, editor. *The Sewanee Review* is America's oldest continuously published literary quarterly. Publishes original fiction, poetry, essays on literary and related subjects, and book reviews for well-educated readers who appreciate good American and English literature. Only erudite work representing depth of knowledge and skill of expression is published. Estab. 1892. Circ. 2,200. Pays on publication. Responds in 6-8 weeks to mss. Sample copy: $8.50 ($9.50 outside U.S.). Guidelines online. Submit complete ms by mail; no electronic submissions. Queries accepted but not preferred. Rarely accepts unsolicited reviews.

NONFICTION Submit complete ms by mail; no electronic submissions. Queries accepted but not preferred. Rarely accepts unsolicited reviews. Length: up to 7,500 words. **Pays $10-12/printed page, plus 2 contributor's copies.**

FICTION literary, contemporary. No erotica, science fiction, fantasy, or excessively violent or profane material. **Buys 10-15 mss/year.** Submit complete ms by mail; no electronic submissions. Length: 3,500-7,500 words. No short-short stories. **Pays $10-12/printed page, plus 2 contributor's copies.**

POETRY Submit up to 6 poems by postal mail. Keep in mind that for each poem published in *The Sewanee Review*, approximately 250 poems are considered. Length: up to 40 lines/poem. **Pays $2.50/line, plus 2 contributor's copies (and reduced price for additional copies).**

SLIPSTREAM

P.O. Box 2071, Dept. W-1, Niagara Falls NY 14301. **E-mail:** editors@slipstreampress.org. **Website:** www.slipstreampress.org/index.html. **Contact:** Dan Sicoli, co-editor. Annual magazine covering poetry only, b&w photos, drawings, and illustrations; a yearly anthology of some of the best poetry and fiction you'll find today in the American small press. Estab. 1980.

No kill fee. Accepts queries by mail. Accepts simultaneous submissions. Guidelines online.

POETRY Submit poetry via mail or online submission manager, Submittable. Prefers contemporary urban themes—writing from the grit that is not afraid to bark or bite. Shies away from pastoral, religious, and rhyming verse. **Chapbook Contest prize is $1,000 plus 50 professionally printed copies of your chapbook.**

SMITHS KNOLL

Goldings, Golding Lane, Leiston, Suffolk England IP16 4EB UK. **E-mail:** michael@klaskey.orangehome.co.uk. **Website:** www.michael-laskey.co.uk/smiths_knoll.php. **Contact:** Michael Laskey and Joanna Cutt, co-editors. Magazine covering contemporary poetry. "We are open to new voices. We like to work with poets too on poems that appeal to us but that we think aren't quite there yet, asking questions, maybe making suggestions if it seems helpful. Then we care a lot about the look of the poems: we print them on good quality paper; and give them space, don't cram them in." Estab. 1991. Circ. 500. Pays on publication. No kill fee. Publishes ms an average of 2 weeks after acceptance. Accepts queries by mail. Accepts simultaneous submissions. Responds in 1 week to mss. Free if you live in the UK. Guidelines online.

POETRY Submit maximum 4-6 poems.

TIPS We're neurotic about proofreading.

THE SOCIETY OF CLASSICAL POETS JOURNAL

The Society of Classical Poets, 11 Heather Lane, Mount Hope NY 10940. **E-mail:** submissions@classicalpoets.org. **Website:** www.classicalpoets.org. **Contact:** Evan Mantyk, president. **10% freelance written.** Annual literary magazine, published in a book format, that features poetry, essays, and artwork. Interested in poetry with rhyme and meter (or syllable counting). Believes in reviving classical poetry and classical arts. Estab. 2012. Circ. 1,000. Byline given. Publishes ms an average of 6 months after acceptance. Editorial lead time is 2 months. Accepts queries by e-mail. Accepts simultaneous submissions. Responds in 1 weeks to queries and 1 month to mss. Guidelines available for SASE.

NONFICTION Needs essays, expose, opinion.

POETRY Needs traditional. Some type of meter, such as iambic pentameter, (or syllable counting) is preferred but not absolutely required. If you want feedback on your submission, indicate it on the submission. Accepts poetry only on 5 themes (generally): beauty (in human nature, culture, the natural world, classical art forms, and the divine), great culture (good figures, stories, and other elements from classical history and literature), persecution of Falun Dafa practitioners in China (and plight of Chinese people under communism in general), and humor (clean humor only, includes riddles), and translations. Also will consider short stories, essays, art, news, and videos on the above themes. Does not want love poetry, free verse, or any dark poetry. Submit maximum 5 poems. **Does not offer payment.**

SOUNDINGS EAST

English Department - MH249 Salem State University, 352 Lafayette St., Salem MA 01970. (978)542-6000. **E-mail:** soundingseast@salemstate.edu. **Website:** www.salemstate.edu/soundingseast/. Annual magazine dedicated to publishing high quality literature covering poetry, fiction, and creative nonfiction. *Soundings East* is the literary journal of Salem State University, published annually with support from the Center for Creative and Performing Arts. Estab. 1973. Circ. 750. No kill fee. Accepts queries by mail, online submission form. Accepts simultaneous submissions. Prose submissions (fiction and nonfiction) should not exceed 10,000 words. Poetry of any style is welcomed; please limit prose submission to 2 pieces and poetry to 5 poems. Include a brief bio. All publication rights revert to authors.

SOUTHERN HUMANITIES REVIEW

Auburn University, 9088 Haley Center, Auburn University AL 36849. (334)844-9088. **Fax:** (334)844-9027. **E-mail:** shr@auburn.edu. **Website:** www.southernhumanitiesreview.com. **Contact:** Aaron Alford, managing editor. *Southern Humanities Review* publishes fiction, nonfiction, and poetry. Estab. 1967. Circ. approximately 800. Accepts simultaneous submissions. Sample copy: $5 U.S., $8 international. Guidelines online.

ⓢ SOUTHERN OCEAN REVIEW

P.O. Box 2143, Dunedin New Zealand. **E-mail:** treeves@es.co.nz. **Website:** homepages.ihug.co.nz/~Streeves/guidline.htm. Quarterly magazine including fiction, poetry, criticism, commentary, essays, and articles on visual arts and music. *Southern*

Ocean Review welcomes submissions from across the globe. Estab. 1996. No kill fee. Accepts queries by mail, e-mail. Accepts simultaneous submissions. Guidelines online.

ⓢ THE SOUTHERN REVIEW

338 Johnston Hall, Louisiana State University, Baton Rouge LA 70803. (225)578-5104. **Fax:** (225)578-6461. **E-mail:** southernreview@lsu.edu. **Website:** thesouthernreview.org. **Contact:** Jessica Faust, co-editor and poetry editor; Emily Nemens, co-editor and prose editor. **100% freelance written. Works with a moderate number of new/unpublished writers each year; reads unsolicited mss.** Quarterly magazine with emphasis on contemporary literature in the U.S. and abroad. "*The Southern Review* is one of the nation's premiere literary journals. Hailed by *Time* as 'superior to any other journal in the English language,' we have made literary history since our founding in 1935. We publish a diverse array of fiction, nonfiction, and poetry by the country's—and the world's—most respected contemporary writers." Reading period: September 1 through December 1 (prose); September 1 through February 1 (poetry). All mss submitted during outside the reading period will be recycled. Estab. 1935. Circ. 2,900. Byline given. Pays on publication. No kill fee. Publishes ms an average of 6 months after acceptance. Accepts queries by mail, online submission form. Accepts simultaneous submissions. Responds in 6 months. Sample copy: $12. Guidelines available online at thesouthernreview.org/submissions.

NONFICTION Needs essays. **Buys 15 mss/year.** Submit ms by mail or through online submission form. Length: up to 8,000 words. **Pays $25/printed page (max $200), 2 contributor's copies, and 1-year subscription.**

FICTION Wants short stories of lasting literary merit, with emphasis on style and technique; novel excerpts. "We emphasize style and substantial content. No mystery, fantasy, or religious mss." **Buys 30 mss/year.** Submit 1 ms at a time by mail or through online submission form. "We rarely publish work that is longer than 8,000 words. We consider novel excerpts if they stand alone." Length: up to 8,000 words. **Pays $25/printed page (max $200), 2 contributor's copies, and 1-year subscription.**

POETRY Submit poems by mail. Submit maximum 5 poems. **Pays $25/printed page (max $200); 2 contributor's copies, and 1-year subscription.**

⊘⊗ STAND MAGAZINE

School of English, Leeds LS2 9JT United Kingdom. (44)(113)233-4794. **E-mail:** stand@leeds.ac.uk. **Website:** www.standmagazine.org. North American submissions: David Latané, Stand Magazine, Dept. of English, Virginia Commonwealth University, Richmond VA 23284. **Contact:** Jon Glover, managing editor. *Stand Magazine* is concerned with what happens when cultures and literatures meet, with translation in its many guises, with the mechanics of language, with the processes by which the policy receives or disables its cultural makers. *Stand* promotes debate of issues that are of radical concern to the intellectual community worldwide. U.S. submissions can be made through the Virginia office (see separate listing). Estab. 1952. Publishes ms an average of 1 year to 18 months after acceptance. Accepts queries by mail. Guidelines online.

FICTION Does not want genre fiction. Length: up to 3,000 words.

POETRY Submit through postal mail only. Include SASE.

STIRRING: A LITERARY COLLECTION

Sundress Publications, **E-mail:** stirring@sundresspublications.com. **E-mail:** stirring.fiction@gmail.com; stirring.poetry@gmail.com; stirring.nonfiction@gmail.com. **Website:** www.sundresspublications.com/stirring. **Contact:** Luci Brown, Managing Editor; Andrew Koch, Managing Editor; Sarah Einstein, Managing Editor. "*Stirring* is one of the oldest continually-published literary journals on the web. *Stirring* is a monthly literary magazine that publishes poetry, short fiction, creative nonfiction, and photography by established and emerging writers." Estab. 1999. Circ. 2500/month. Publishes ms 1-2 weeks after acceptance. Accepts queries by e-mail. Accepts simultaneous submissions. Responds in 3-6 months. Visit our website for guidelines.

NONFICTION Needs essays, memoir, reviews. Submit complete ms by e-mail to stirring.nonfiction@gmail.com. Length: up to 5,000 words.

FICTION Needs literary. Submit complete ms by e-mail to stirring.fiction@gmail.com Length: up to 5,000 words.

POETRY Wants free verse, formal poetry, etc. Doesn't want religious verse or children's verse. Has published poetry by Dorianne Laux, Sharon Olds, Patricia Smith, Chad Davidson. Receives about 1,500 poems/year, accepts 60. Submit up to 5 poems by e-mail to stirring.poetry@gmail.com. Length: 1-6 pages (most often accepts half- to full-page poems).

⊘ STORIE

Via Suor Celestina Donati 13/E, Rome 00167 Italy. (+39)06-454-33670. **Fax:** (+39)06-454-33670. **E-mail:** info@storie.it. **Website:** www.storie.it/english. "*Storie* is one of Italy's leading cultural and literary magazines. Committed to a truly crossover vision of writing, the bilingual (Italian/English) review publishes high-quality fiction and poetry, interspersed with the work of alternative wordsmiths such as filmmakers and musicians. Through writings bordering on narratives and interviews with important contemporary writers, it explores the culture and craft of writing." Estab. 1986.

FICTION "Manuscripts may be submitted directly by regular post without querying first; however, we do not accept unsolicited manuscripts via e-mail. Please query via e-mail first. We only contact writers if their work has been accepted. We also arrange for and oversee a high-quality, professional translation of the piece." **Pays $30-600 and 2 contributor's copies.**

TIPS "More than erudite references or a virtuoso performance, we're interested in a style merging news writing with literary techniques in the manner of new journalism. *Storie* reserves the right to include a brief review of interesting submissions not selected for publication in a special column of the magazine."

STORYSOUTH

3302 MHRA Building, UNCG, Greensboro NC 27412 USA. **E-mail:** terry@storysouth.com. **Website:** www.storysouth.com. **Contact:** Terry Kennedy, editor; Cynthia Nearman, creative nonfiction editor; Drew Perry, fiction editor; Luke Johnson, poetry editor. Covers experimental, literary, regional (South), poetry, translations. "*storySouth* accepts unsolicited submissions of fiction, poetry, and creative nonfiction during 2 submission periods annually: May 15-July 1 and November 15-January 1. Long pieces are encouraged. Please make only 1 submission in a single genre per reading period." Estab. 2001. Publishes ms 1 month after acceptance. Accepts queries by online submission form. Accepts simultaneous submissions. Responds in 2-6 months to mss. Guidelines online.

NONFICTION **Contact:** Cynthia Nearman, creative nonfiction editor. Needs translations. Submit 1 essay via online submissions manager. No word limit.

FICTION Contact: Drew Perry, fiction editor. Submit 1 story via online submissions manager. No word limit.

POETRY Contact: Luke Johnson, poetry editor. Needs experimental, literary, regional (South), translations. Submit 3-5 poems via online submissions manager. No word/line limit.

STUDIO ONE

Murray Hall 170, College of St. Benedict, 37 S. College Ave., St. Joseph MN 56374. **E-mail:** studio1@csbsju. edu. **Website:** digitalcommons.csbsju.edu/studio_ one/. **Contact:** William Harren, Lucas Giese, editors in chief. *Studio One* is a literary and visual arts magazine published each spring by the College of Saint Benedict/Saint John's University. Its mission is to give new and established writers alike a forum in which to present their works. The magazine's focus is poetry, short fiction, essays, and all forms of reproducible visual art works. *Studio One* is student-run, and the student editors change yearly. Submissions are open to all students on either Saint John's or Saint Benedict's campuses and to the general public regardless of regional, national, or international location. Estab. 1976. Accepts simultaneous submissions. Sample copy can be obtained by sending a self-addressed, stamped manila envelope and $6.

FICTION Length: no more than 2,000 words.

POETRY Considers simultaneous submissions; no previously published poems. Accepts e-mail submissions (pasted into body of message); "clearly show page breaks and indentations." Seldom comments on rejected poems. Submit maximum 5 poems. Lines/poem: "poetry no more than 2 pages stands a better chance of publication."

☯☺ SUBTERRAIN

Strong Words for a Polite Nation, P.O. Box 3008, MPO, Vancouver BC V6B 3X5 Canada. (604)876-8710. **Fax:** (604)879-2667. **E-mail:** subter@portal.ca. **Website:** www.subterrain.ca. Natasha Sanders-Kay, managing editor. **Contact:** Brian Kaufman, editor in chief. "*subTerrain* magazine is published 3 times/year from modest offices just off of Main Street in Vancouver, BC. We strive to produce a stimulating fusion of fiction, poetry, photography, and graphic illustration from uprising Canadian, U.S., and international writers and artists." Estab. 1988. Circ. 3,500. Pays on publication for first North American serial rights.

Publishes ms 4-9 months after acceptance. Accepts queries by mail, online submission form. Accepts simultaneous submissions. Responds in 6-9 months to mss. Rarely comments on rejected mss. Sample copy: $5 (subterrain.ca/subscriptions). Writer's guidelines online (subterrain.ca/about/35/sub-terrain-writer-s-guidelines).

NONFICTION Needs book excerpts, essays, expose, general interest, humor, memoir, nostalgic, opinion, personal experience, travel, literary essays, literary criticism. Send complete ms. Include disposable copy of the ms and SASE for reply only. Accepts multiple submissions. Receives 100 unsolicited mss/month. Accepts 4 mss/issue; 10-15 mss/year. **Pays $50/page for prose & $50 per poem**

FICTION Receives 100 unsolicited mss/month. Accepts 4 mss/issue; 10-15 mss/year. Recently published work by J.O. Bruday, Lisa Pike, and Peter Babiak. Needs confessions, erotica, ethnic, experimental, humorous, novel excerpts, short stories, slice-of-life vignettes. Does not want genre fiction or children's fiction. Send complete ms. Include disposable copy of the ms and SASE for reply only. Accepts multiple submissions. **3,000 words max. Pays $50/page for prose.**

POETRY "We accept poetry, but we no longer accept unsolicited submissions, except when related to 1 of our theme issues." "We no longer accept unsolicited poetry submissions (unless specifically related to one of our theme issues)." Poems unrelated to any theme issues may be submitted to the annual "General" issue (usually the summer/fall issue). **Pays $50/poem.**

SYCAMORE REVIEW

Purdue University Department of English, 500 Oval Dr., West Lafayette IN 47907. (765) 494-3783. **Fax:** (765) 494-3780. **E-mail:** sycamore@purdue.edu. **Website:** www.sycamorereview.com. **Contact:** Anthony Sutton, editor in chief; Bess Cooley, managing editor. Semiannual magazine publishing poetry, fiction and nonfiction, books reviews, and art. *Sycamore Review* is Purdue University's internationally acclaimed literary journal, affiliated with Purdue's College of Liberal Arts and the Dept. of English. Strives to publish the best writing by new and established writers. Looks for well-crafted and engaging work, works that illuminate our lives in the collective human search for meaning. Would like to publish more work that takes a reflective look at national identity and how we are perceived by the world. Looks for diversity of voice, pluralistic worldviews, and political and social context. No kill fee. Accepts queries by online submission form. Accepts simultaneous submissions.

NONFICTION Needs essays, humor. No outside interviews, previously published work (except translations). No scholarly articles or journalistic pieces. Submit complete ms via online submissions manager. No mail or e-mail submissions. **Pays in contributor copies and $50/nonfiction piece.**

FICTION No genre fiction. Needs experimental, humorous, mainstream. Submit complete ms via online submissions manager. **Pays in contributor's copies and $50/short story.**

POETRY Submi via online submissions manager. Does not publish creative work by any student currently attending Purdue University. Former students should wait 1 year before submitting. **Pays $25/poem.**

TAB: THE JOURNAL OF POETRY & POETICS

Chapman University, *TAB: The Journal of Poetry & Poetics*, Dept. of English, One University Dr., Orange CA 92866. (714)628-7389. **E-mail:** poetry@chapman. edu; leahy@chapman.edu. **Website:** journals.chapman.edu/ojs/index.php/TAB-journal. **Contact:** Anna Leahy, editor; Claudine Jaenichen, creative director. **100% freelance written.** Publishes monthly electronic issues; 1 special print issue annually. *TAB: A Journal of Poetry & Poetics* is a national and international journal of creative and critical writing. This literary journal's mission is to discover, support, and publish the contemporary poetry and writing about poetry; to provide a forum in which the poetic tradition is practiced, extended, challenged, and discussed by emerging and established voices; and to encourage wide appreciation of poetry and expand the audience for poems and writing about poetry. Welcomes submissions of poems from established and emerging poets as well as critical essays, creative nonfiction, interviews, and reviews. *TAB* will reach audience of poets, poetry readers and appreciators, poetry scholars and critics, and students of poetry. Estab. 2012. Byline given. Pays on publication. Publishes ms 2-6 months after acceptance. Accepts simultaneous submissions. Response time varies. Sample copy for $4 s&h or online at website. Guidelines online.

NONFICTION Needs essays, how-to, interview, photo feature, profile, book reviews, interviews, essays related to poetry or poetics. Do not submit any nonfiction that is not related to poetry or poetics. Sub-

mit complete ms. Length: 3,000-8,000 words, depending on subject of essay. All contributors are awarded Tabula Poetica membership at the Sonnet level ($50 equivalent) and receive 2 copies of the annual print issue, if the work appears in that issue or if copies are available.

POETRY Needs Avant-garde, free verse, haiku, light verse, traditional. No greeting card poetry. No work by writers under 18 years of age. No work by students, faculty, or staff of Chapman University. Buys 50 poems/year. Submit maximum 5 poems. No length restrictions.

TAKAHĒ

P.O. Box 13-335, Christchurch 8141 New Zealand. **E-mail:** admin@takahe.org.nz. **Website:** www.takahe. org.nz. The Takahē Collective Trust is a nonprofit organization that aims to support emerging and published writers, poets, artists, and cultural commentators. Byline given. Pays on publication. Accepts queries by mail, e-mail. Responds in 4 months. Guidelines available online at www.takahe.org.nz.

NONFICTION Contact: essays@takahe.org.nz. Needs essays, Preference will be given to essays, creative nonfiction, and works of cultural criticism that critically engage with or analyze culture or cultural practice in New Zealand and the South Pacific. E-mail submissions are preferred (essays@takahe.org.nz). Overseas submissions are only accepted by e-mail. **Pays small honorarium to New Zealand authors, or one-year subscription to overseas writers.**

FICTION Contact: fiction@takahe.org.nz. "We look for stories that have something special about them: an original idea, a new perspective, an interesting narrative style or use of language, an ability to evoke character and/or atmosphere. Above all, we like some depth, an extra layer of meaning, an insight—something more than just an anecdote or a straightforward narration of events." Needs short stories. E-mail submissions are preferred (fiction@takahe.org.nz). Overseas submissions are only accepted by e-mail. Length: 1,500-3,000 words, "although we do occasionally accept flash fiction, or longer work, up to 5,000 words, for online issues only." **Pays small honorarium to New Zealand authors, or one-year subscription to overseas writers.**

POETRY Contact: poetry@takahe.org.nz. E-mail submissions preferred (poetry@takahe.org.nz). Overseas submissions are only accepted by e-mail. Accepts a maximum of 6 poems per submission and no more than 3 submissions a year. "Please be aware that we publish only a handful of overseas poets each year." Long work (multiple pages) is unlikely to be accepted. **Pays small honorarium to New Zealand authors, or one-year subscription to overseas writers.**

TAMPA REVIEW

University of Tampa Press, 401 W. Kennedy Blvd., Tampa FL 33606. (813)253-6266. **Fax:** (813)258-7593. **E-mail:** utpress@ut.edu. **Website:** www.ut.edu/tampareview. **Contact:** Richard Mathews, editor; Elizabeth Winston and Daniel Dooghan, nonfiction editors; Yuly Restrepo and Andrew Plattner, fiction editors; Erica Dawson, poetry editor. Semiannual magazine published in hardback format. An international literary journal publishing art and literature from Florida and Tampa Bay as well as new work and translations from throughout the world. Estab. 1988. Circ. 700. Byline given. Pays on publication. No kill fee. Publishes ms an average of 10 months after acceptance. Editorial lead time 18 months. Accepts queries by mail. Accepts simultaneous submissions. Responds in 3-4 months to mss. Sample copy: $12. Guidelines online.

NONFICTION Contact: Elizabeth Winston and Daniel Dooghan, nonfiction editors. Needs general interest, interview, personal experience, creative nonfiction. No how-to articles, fads, journalistic reprise, etc. **Buys 6 mss/year.** Send complete ms by mail or online submissions manager. Length: up to 5,000 words. **Pays $10/printed page, 1 contributor's copy, and offers 40% discount on additional copies.**

FICTION Contact: Yuly Restrepo and Andrew Plattner, fiction editors. Needs ethnic, experimental, fantasy, historical, mainstream, literary. "We are far more interested in quality than in genre. Nothing sentimental as opposed to genuinely moving, nor self-conscious style at the expense of human truth." **Buys 6 mss/year.** Send complete ms via mail or online submissions manager. Length: up to 5,000 words. **Pays $10/printed page, 1 contributor's copy, and offers 40% discount on additional copies.**

POETRY Contact: Erica Dawson, poetry editor. Needs avant-garde, free verse, haiku, light verse, traditional. No greeting card verse, hackneyed, singsong, rhyme-for-the-sake-of-rhyme. Buys 45 poems/year. Submit maximum 6 poems. Length: 2-225 lines. **Pays $10/printed page, 1 contributor's copy, and offers 40% discount on additional copies.**

THAT'S LIFE! FAST FICTION

Pacific Magazines, 35-51 Mitchell St., McMahons Point NSW 2060 Australia. **E-mail:** fastfiction@pacificmags.com.au. Quarterly magazine packed with romantic stories, spine-tinglers, humorous reads, tales with a twist, and more. Pays on publication. Accepts simultaneous submissions. Responds in 90 days only if submission is accepted. Guidelines online.

FICTION Submit 1-page for weekly edition or 600-2,600 word story for quarterly *Fast Fiction*. "That's Life! Fast Fiction is looking for humorous, positive contemporary stories with a strong and easy-to-follow plot. If the story has a twist it should arise from the story, rather than from a detail kept from the reader. To check your twist, imagine your story were being made into a film - would the surprise still work?" Needs adventure, horror, humorous, mystery, romance, suspense. "Please avoid straightforward romance i.e., boy meets girl and they live happily ever after. Avoid sci-fi and stories narrated by animals or babies." *That's Life!* is a family magazine so graphic murders, sex crimes and domestic violence are not acceptable. We normally write in chronological order, so please keep events in sequence and avoid "jumping" around time slots, as this can be confusing. Also, please bear in mind that if your story is themed then it needs to be sent to us about 3 months in advance of the magazine in which it needs to appear. For example, a Christmas story would need to reach us no later than September. **weekly magazine (1-page story), $300.** *Flash Fiction* **quarterly, $200-500.**

THEMA

Thema Literary Society, P.O. Box 8747, Metairie LA 70011-8747. **E-mail:** thema@cox.net. **Website:** http://themaliterarysociety.com. **Contact:** Gail Howard, poetry editor. **100% freelance written.** *"THEMA* is designed to stimulate creative thinking by challenging writers with unusual themes, such as 'Golden Isn't Silent' and 'Lost in the Zoo.' Appeals to writers, teachers of creative writing, and general reading audience." Estab. 1988. Byline given. Pays on acceptance. No kill fee. Publishes ms, on average, within 6 months after acceptance. Accepts queries by mail, e-mail. Accepts simultaneous submissions. Responds in 1 week to queries. Responds in 5 months to mss. Sample $15 U.S./$25 foreign. Upcoming themes and guidelines available in magazine, for SASE, by e-mail, or on website.

NONFICTION Contact: Virginia Howard, Editor. Needs book excerpts, essays, personal experience, Nonfiction story/essay must relate to one of *THEMA*'s upcoming themes (indicate the target theme on submission of photo). See website for themes. salacious subject matter **Buys very few mss/year.** from 300 to 6,000 words (one to twenty double-spaced pages) **$10 for under 1,000 words; $25 for articles over 1,000 words**

FICTION All stories must relate to one of *THEMA*'s upcoming themes (**indicate the target theme on submission of manuscript**). See website for themes. Needs adventure, ethnic, experimental, fantasy, historical, humorous, mainstream, mystery, religious, science fiction, short stories, slice-of-life vignettes, suspense. No erotica. Send complete ms with SASE, cover letter; include "name and address, brief introduction, **specifying the intended target issue for the mss.**" SASE. Accepts simultaneous, multiple submissions, and reprints. Does not accept e-mailed submissions except from non-USA addresses. from 300 to 6,000 words (one to twenty double-spaced pages) **$10 for under 1,000 words; $25 for stories over 1,000 words, plus one contributor copy.**

POETRY Submit up to 3 poems at a time. Include SASE. "All submissions should be typewritten on standard 8x11 paper. Submissions are accepted all year, but evaluated after specified deadlines." Specify target theme. Editor comments on submissions. "Each issue is based on an unusual premise. Please send SASE for guidelines before submitting poetry to find out the upcoming themes." Does not want "scatologic language, explicit love poetry." Buys 24 published out of 250 submitted poems/year. Submit maximum 3 poems. 1 - 3 pages **Pays $10/poem and 1 contributor's copy.**

THICK WITH CONVICTION

E-mail: twczine@gmail.com. **Website:** twczine. blogspot.com/. **Contact:** Danielle Masters, Sara Blanton-Allison, Kristina Marie Blanton. Covers all genres of poetry. Considers poetry by teens. *Thick With Conviction*, published biannually online, is "looking for fresh and exciting voices in poetry. I don't want to take a nap while I'm reading, so grab my attention, make me sit up and catch my breath." Wants all genres of poetry, "poems that make me exhale a deep sigh after reading them. Basically, if I can't feel the words in front of me, I'm not going to be happy. I'd like to see new

and cutting-edge poets who think outside the box, but still know how to keep things from getting too strange and inaccessible." Does not want "teen angst poems, religious poems, or greeting card tripe." Has published poetry by Kendall A. Bell, April Michelle Bratten, Kristina Marie Darling, James H. Duncan, Paul Hostovsky, and Kelsey Upward. Receives about 300 poems/year, accepts about 15%. Never comments on rejected poems. Publishes ms 3 months after acceptance. Submit seasonal poems 3 months in advance. Accepts simultaneous submissions. Responds in "roughly 2-3 months." Guidelines available on website.

POETRY Submit 3-5 poems at a time. Lines/poem: no limit. Considers previously published poems; no simultaneous submissions. Accepts e-mail submissions (pasted into body of message; "any attachments will be deleted"); no disk submissions. Cover letter and bio is required. Reads submissions year round.

THIN AIR

Department of English, Building 18, LA Room 133, P.O. Box 6032, Flagstaff AZ 86011. **Website:** thinairmagazine.org. Publishes contemporary voices for a literary-minded audience. Estab. 1995. Circ. 500. No kill fee. Publishes ms an average of 6-9 months after acceptance. Accepts queries by mail, e-mail. Accepts simultaneous submissions. Responds in 3 months to ms. Sample copy $8. Guidelines online.

NONFICTION "Submissions should be 1 short essay (in any form) or up to 3 pieces each under 750 words." Length: up to 3,500 words.

FICTION Needs ethnic, experimental, mainstream. No children's/juvenile, horror, romance, erotica. We would like to see more intelligent comedy. "Submissions should be 1 short story or up to 3 flash pieces each under 750 words. Novel excerpts are OK if self-contained. Stories that contain visuals or art are welcome as long as you own the copyrights. However, we reserve the right to accept stories with or without accepting the art. Please include word count at the top of your manuscript." Length: up to 3,500 words.

POETRY "At *Thin Air*, we're looking for poems that resonate with readers by vibrating along their own emotional frequency. Send us poems that sing their own song, whether through strong imagery, sensory detail, a moving progression, intensive attention to language, or a combination of all these." Submit maximum 3 poems. Length: up to 5 pages per overall submission.

⊕⊛ THE THREEPENNY REVIEW

P.O. Box 9131, Berkeley CA 94709. (510)849-4545. **E-mail:** wlesser@threepennyreview.com. **Website:** www.threepennyreview.com. **Contact:** Wendy Lesser, editor. **100% freelance written. Works with small number of new/unpublished writers each year.** Quarterly tabloid. "We are a general-interest, national literary magazine with coverage of politics, the visual arts, and the performing arts." Reading period: January 1-June 30. Estab. 1980. Circ. 6,000-9,000. Byline given. Pays on acceptance. Publishes ms an average of 1 year after acceptance. Accepts queries by mail, online submission form. Responds in 1 month to queries; in 2 months to mss. Sample copy: $12, or online. Guidelines online.

NONFICTION Needs essays, historical, memoir, personal experience, reviews, book, film, theater, dance, music, and art reviews. **Buys 40 mss/year.** Send complete ms. Length: 1,500-4,000 words. **Pays $400.**

FICTION No fragmentary, sentimental fiction. **Buys 8 mss/year.** Send complete ms. Length: 800-4,000 words. **Pays $400.**

POETRY Needs free verse, traditional. No poems without capital letters or poems without a discernible subject. Buys 30 poems/year. Submit maximum 5 poems. Length: up to 100 lines/poem. **Pays $200.**

TORCH LITERARY ARTS

TORCH: Creative Writing by Black Women, 3720 Gattis School Rd., Suite 800, Round Rock TX 78664. **E-mail:** torchliteraryarts@gmail.com. **E-mail:** torchliteraryarts@gmail.com. **Website:** www.torchliteraryarts.org. **Contact:** Amanda Johnston, founder/editor. *TORCH: Creative Writing by Black Women* , published semiannually online, provides "a place to publish contemporary poetry, prose, and short stories by experienced and emerging writers alike. We prefer our contributors to take risks, and offer a diverse body of work that examines and challenges preconceived notions regarding race, ethnicity, gender roles, and identity." Has published poetry by Sharon Bridgforth, Patricia Smith, Crystal Wilkinson, Tayari Jones, and Natasha Trethewey. Reads submissions April 15-August 31 only. Sometimes comments on rejected poems. Always sends prepublication galleys. No payment. "Within *TORCH*, we offer a special section called Flame that features an interview, biography, and work sample by an established writer as well as an introduction to their Spark—an emerging writer who inspires them and adds to the boundless voice of creative writing by Black women." A free online newsletter is available; see website. Estab. 2006. Publishes ms 2-7 months after acceptance. Accepts queries by e-mail. Accepts simultaneous submissions. Guidelines available on website.

POETRY Submit maximum 3 poems.

TRIQUARTERLY

School of Professional Studies, Northwestern University, 339 E. Chicago Ave., Chicago IL 60611. **E-mail:** triquarterly@northwestern.edu. **Website:** www.triquarterly.org. **Contact:** Adrienne Gunn, managing editor. *TriQuarterly*, the literary magazine of Northwestern University, welcomes submissions of fiction, creative nonfiction, poetry, short drama, and hybrid work. "We also welcome short-short prose pieces." Reading period: October 15-May 1. Estab. 1964. Accepts queries by online submission form. Accepts simultaneous submissions.

NONFICTION Submit complete ms via online submissions manager. Length: up to 5,000 words. **Pays honoraria.**

FICTION Submit complete ms via online submissions manager. Length: up to 5,000 words. **Pays honoraria.**

POETRY Submit up to 6 poems via online submissions manager. **Pays honoraria.**

⊕ VALLUM: CONTEMPORARY POETRY

5038 Sherbrooke West, P.O. Box 23077, CP Vendome, Montreal Quebec H4A 1T0 Canada. **E-mail:** info@vallummag.com; editors@vallummag.com. **Website:** www.vallummag.com. **Contact:** Joshua Auerbach and Eleni Zisimatos, editors. Poetry/fine arts magazine published twice/year. Publishes exciting interplay of poets and artists. Content for magazine is selected according to themes listed on website. Material is not filed but is returned upon request by SASE. E-mail response is preferred. Seeking exciting, unpublished, traditional or avant-garde poetry that reflects contemporary experience. Estab. 2000. Pays on publication. Sample copy online. Guidelines available on website.

NONFICTION Also publishes reviews, interviews, essays and letters to the editor. Please send queries to editors@vallummag.com before submitting. **Pays $85 for accepted reviews or essays on poetry.**

POETRY Pays honorarium for accepted poems.

🌑 VERANDAH LITERARY & ART JOURNAL

Faculty of Arts, Deakin University, 221 Burwood Hwy., Burwood, Victoria 3125 Australia. (61)(3)9251-7134. **E-mail:** verandah@deakin.edu.au. **Website:** verandahjournal.wordpress.com/. *Verandah*, published annually in August, is a high-quality literary journal edited by professional writing students. It aims to give voice to new and innovative writers and artists. Estab. 1985. Accepts simultaneous submissions. Sample: $20 AUD. Guidelines available on website.

NONFICTION Submit by mail or e-mail. However, electronic version of work must be available if accepted by *Verandah*. Do not submit work without the required submission form (available for download on website). Reads submissions by June 5 deadline (postmark). Length: 350-2,500 words. **Pays 1 contributor's copy, "with prizes awarded accordingly."**

FICTION Submit by mail or e-mail. However, electronic version of work must be available if accepted by *Verandah*. Do not submit work without the required submission form (available for download on website). Reads submissions by June 5 deadline (postmark). Length: 350-2,500 words. **Pays 1 contributor's copy, "with prizes awarded accordingly."**

POETRY Submit by mail or e-mail. However, electronic version of work must be available if accepted by *Verandah*. Do not submit work without the required submission form (available for download on website). Reads submissions by June 5 deadline (postmark). Length: 100 lines maximum. **Pays 1 contributor's copy, "with prizes awarded accordingly."**

VERSE

English Department, University of Richmond, Richmond VA 23173. **Website:** versemag.blogspot.com. **Contact:** Brian Henry, co-editor; Andrew Zawacki, co-editor. *Verse*, published 3 times/year, is an international poetry journal which also publishes interviews with poets, essays on poetry, and book reviews. Wants no specific kind; looks for high-quality, innovative poetry. Focus is not only on American poetry, but on all poetry written in English, as well as translations. Has published poetry by James Tate, John Ashbery, Barbara Guest, Gustaf Sobin, and Rae Armantrout. Estab. 1984. Accepts simultaneous submissions. Guidelines online.

NONFICTION Interested in any nonfiction, plus translations, criticisms, interviews, journals/note-books, etc. Submissions should be chapbook-length (20-40 pages). **Pays $10/page, $250 minimum.**

FICTION Interested in any genre. Submissions should be chapbook-length (20-40 pages). **Pays $10/page, $250 minimum.**

POETRY Submissions should be chapbook-length (20-40 pages). **Pays $10/page, $250 minimum.**

💲💲 VESTAL REVIEW

127 Kilsyth Road, Apt. 3, Brighton MA 02135. **E-mail:** submissions@vestalreview.net. **Website:** www.vestalreview.org. Semi-annual print magazine specializing in flash fiction. Circ. 1,500. Pays on publication. No kill fee. Publishes ms an average of 6 months after acceptance. Accepts queries by e-mail. Accepts simultaneous submissions. Responds in 1 week to queries; in 6 months to mss. Guidelines online.

FICTION Needs ethnic, fantasy, horror, humorous, mainstream. No porn, racial slurs, excessive gore, or obscenity. No children's or preachy stories. Publishes flash fiction. "We accept submissions only through our submission manager." Length: 50-500 words. **Pays 3-10¢/word and 1 contributor's copy; additional copies for $10 (plus postage).**

THE VIRGINIA QUARTERLY REVIEW

VQR, P.O. Box 400223, Charlottesville VA 22904. **E-mail:** editors@vqronline.org. **Website:** www.vqronline.org. **Contact:** Allison Wright, managing editor. "*VQR*'s primary mission has been to sustain and strengthen Jefferson's bulwark, long describing itself as 'A National Journal of Literature and Discussion.' And for good reason. From its inception in prohibition, through depression and war, in prosperity and peace, *The Virginia Quarterly Review* has been a haven—and home—for the best essayists, fiction writers, and poets, seeking contributors from every section of the United States and abroad. It has not limited itself to any special field. No topic has been alien: literary, public affairs, the arts, history, the economy. If it could be approached through essay or discussion, poetry or prose, *VQR* has covered it." Press run is 4,000. Estab. 1925. Accepts queries by online submission form. Responds in 3 months to mss. Guidelines available on website.

NONFICTION "We publish literary, art, and cultural criticism; reportage; historical and political analysis; and travel essays. We publish few author interviews or memoirs. In general, we are looking for nonfiction that looks out on the world, rather than within the self." Accepts online submissions only at virginiaquarterlyreview.submittable.com/submit. You can also query via this site. Length: 3,500-10,000 words. **Pays $500 for book reviews; $1,000-3,000 for essays, memoir, criticism, and reportage.**

FICTION "We are generally not interested in genre fiction (such as romance, science fiction, or fantasy)." Accepts online submissions only at virginiaquarterlyreview.submittable.com/submit. Length: 2,000-10,000 words. **Pays $1,000-2,500 for short stories; $1,000-4,000 for novellas and novel excerpts.**

POETRY *The Virginia Quarterly Review* prints approximately 12 pages of poetry in each issue. No length or subject restrictions. Issues have largely included lyric and narrative free verse, most of which features a strong message or powerful voice. Accepts online submissions only at virginiaquarterlyreview.submittable.com/submit. Submit maximum 5 poems. **Pays $200/poem.**

💲 VIRTUE IN THE ARTS

Randy Mate, P.O. Box 11081, Glendale CA 91226. **E-mail:** info@virtueinthearts.com. **Website:** www.virtueinthearts.com. **50% freelance written.** Semiannual magazine covering virtues. Each publication features short stories, articles, poetry and artwork relating to a different virtue each time (such as honesty, compassion, trustworthiness, etc.). Estab. 2006. Byline given. Pays on publication. Publishes ms an average of 6 months after acceptance. Editorial lead time 6 months. Submit seasonal material 1 month in advance. Accepts queries by mail, e-mail. Accepts simultaneous submissions. Responds in 6 months to mss. Guidelines available for SASE and by e-mail.

NONFICTION Needs essays. Special issues: Each issue has a theme. See writer's guidelines for the current theme. Does not want articles that show the virtue in a negative light. **Buys 2 mss/year.** Send complete ms. Length: 100-400 words. **Pays $7.**

FICTION Fiction shedding a positive light on the current theme (a virtue) in an entertaining way. **Buys 2 mss/year.** Send complete ms. Length: 300-1,500 words. **Pays $7.**

POETRY Needs avant-garde, free verse, haiku, light verse, traditional. Poetry needs to reflect the current theme (virtue). Submit maximum 5 poems. Length: 4-32 lines. **Pays $7.**

💲 VISIONS-INTERNATIONAL

Black Buzzard Press, 3503 Ferguson Lane, Austin TX 78754. **E-mail:** vias.poetry@gmail.com. **Website:** visions2010.wordpress.com. **95% freelance written.** Magazine published 2 times/year featuring poetry and translations. Estab. 1979. Circ. 750. Byline given. Pays on publication. No kill fee. Publishes ms an average of 6 months after acceptance. Editorial lead time 1 month. Accepts queries by mail. Accepts simultaneous submissions. Responds in 3 weeks to queries. Responds in 2 months to mss. Sample copy: $5.50. Guidelines online.

NONFICTION Needs essays.

POETRY Needs avant-garde, free verse, traditional. "Send 3-5 unpublished poems not sent elsewhere." "Please no self-centered workshop ramblings; no perfect form without meaningful content; no questionable language used purely for shock value." Buys 110 poems/year. Length: 2-120 lines.

💲 VOICES ISRAEL

P.O. Box 21, Metulla 10292 Israel. **E-mail:** voicesisraelpoetryanthology@gmail.com. **Website:** www.voicesisrael.com. **Contact:** Dina Yehuda, editor. *Voices Israel*, published annually by The Voices Israel Group of Poets, is "an anthology of poetry in English, with worldwide contributions. We consider all kinds of poetry." Poems must be in English; translations must be accompanied by the original poem. Estab. 1972. Accepts simultaneous submissions. Single copy: $25 for nonmembers. Sample: $15 (back issue). "Members receive the anthology with annual dues ($35)."

POETRY Submit up to 3 poems/year via online submissions manager. "We do not guarantee publication of any poem. In poems we publish, we reserve the right to correct obviously unintentional errors in spelling, punctuation, etc." Length: 40 lines or 400 words maximum.

THE WALLACE STEVENS JOURNAL

University of Antwerp, Prinsstraat 13, 2000 Antwerp Belgium. **E-mail:** bart.eeckhout@uantwerp.be; jforjames@aol.com. **Website:** www.press.jhu.edu/journals/wallace_stevens_journal. **Contact:** Bart Eeckhout, editor; James Finnegan, poetry editor. *The Wallace Stevens Journal*, published semiannually by the Wallace Stevens Society, welcomes submissions on all aspects of Wallace Stevens's poetry and life. Estab. 1977. Accepts simultaneous submissions. Subscription: $30 (includes membership in the Wallace Stevens Society).

NONFICTION Needs interpretive criticism of Wallce Stevens's poetry and essays. Submit by e-mail attachment to bart.eeckhout@uantwerp.be.

POETRY Has published poetry by David Athey, Jacqueline Marcus, Charles Wright, X.J. Kennedy, A.M. Juster, and Robert Creeley. Submit poems to James Finnegan at jforjames@aol.com.

WASHINGTON SQUARE

Creative Writing Program, New York University, 58 West 10th St., New York NY 10011. **E-mail:** washingtonsquarereview@gmail.com. **Website:** www.washingtonsquarereview.com. Semiannual magazine covering fiction and poetry by emerging and established writers. *Washington Square* is a nonprofit, innovative, nationally-distributed literary journal edited and produced by students of the NYU Graduate Creative Writing Program. It is published semiannually and features fiction and poetry by emerging and established writers. *Washington Square* also includes interviews and an artist portfolio. There is no submission fee. It accepts simultaneous submissions and queries by mail. It does not offer monetary compensation, other than its $500 prize for annual competitions in poetry, fiction, and flash fiction. No kill fee. Accepts queries by mail. Accepts simultaneous submissions.

NONFICTION Needs interview, translation.

FICTION Length: 1 short story up to 20 pages.

POETRY Submit maximum 5 poems. Length: 5-10 pages total.

WEBER: THE CONTEMPORARY WEST

Weber State University, 1395 Edvalson St., Dept. 1405, Ogden UT 84408-1405. **Website:** www.weber.edu/weberjournal. *Weber: The Contemporary West*, published 2 times/year, "spotlights personal narrative, commentary, fiction, nonfiction, and poetry that speaks to the environment and culture of the American West and beyond." Estab. 1983. Publishes ms 15 months after acceptance. Accepts simultaneous submissions. Responds in 6 months. Sample: $10 (back issue). Subscription: $20 ($30 for institutions); $40 for outside the U.S. Themes and guidelines available in magazine, for SASE, by e-mail, or on website.

POETRY Submit 3-4 poems at a time, 2 copies of each (one without name). "We publish multiple poems from a poet." Cover letter is preferred. Poems are selected by anonymous (blind) evaluation. Always sends prepublication galleys. Has published poetry by Naomi Shihab Nye, Carolyn Forche, Stephen Dunn, Billy Collins, William Kloefkorn, David Lee, Gary Gildner, and Robert Dana. Does not want "poems that are flippant, prurient, sing-song, or preachy." **Pays 2 contributor's copies, one-year subscription, and a small honorarium ($100-300) depending on fluctuating grant monies.**

$ WEST BRANCH

Stadler Center for Poetry, Bucknell University, Lewisburg PA 17837-2029. (570)577-1853. **Fax:** (570)577-1885. **E-mail:** westbranch@bucknell.edu. **Website:** www.bucknell.edu/westbranch. **Contact:** G.C. Waldrep, editor. Semiannual literary magazine. *West Branch* publishes poetry, fiction, and nonfiction in both traditional and innovative styles. Byline given. Pays on publication. No kill fee. Accepts queries by online submission form. Accepts simultaneous submissions. Sample copy for $3. Guidelines online.

NONFICTION Needs essays, general interest, literary. **Buys 4-5 mss/year.** Send complete ms. Length: no more than 30 pages. **Pays 5¢/word, with a maximum of $100.**

FICTION Needs novel excerpts, short stories. No genre fiction. **Buys 10-12 mss/year.** Send complete ms. Length: no more than 30 pages. **Pays 5¢/word, with a maximum of $100.**

POETRY Needs free and formal verse. Buys 30-40 poems/year. Submit maximum 6 poems. **Pays $50/submission.**

🌐 WESTERLY

University of Western Australia, The Westerly Centre (M202), Crawley WA 6009 Australia. (61)(8)6488-3403. **Fax:** (61)(8)6488-1030. **E-mail:** westerly@uwa.edu.au. **Website:** westerlymag.com.au. **Contact:** Catherine Noske, editor. *Westerly*, published in July and November, prints quality short fiction, poetry, literary criticism, socio-historical articles, and book reviews with special attention given to Australia, Asia, and the Indian Ocean region. "We assume a reasonably well-read, intelligent audience. Past issues of *Westerly* provide the best guides. Not consciously an academic magazine." Estab. 1956. Time between acceptance and publication may be up to 1 year, depending on when work is submitted. "Please wait for a response before forwarding any additional submissions for consideration."

NONFICTION Submit complete ms by postal mail, e-mail, or online submissions form. Length: up to 5,000 words for essays; up to 3,500 words for creative nonfiction. **Pays $150 and contributor's copies.**

FICTION Submit complete ms by mail, e-mail, or online submissions form. Length: up to 3,500 words. **Pays $150 and contributor's copies.**

POETRY "We don't dictate to writers on rhyme, style, experimentation, or anything else. We are willing to publish short or long poems." Submit up to 3 poems by mail, e-mail, or online submissions form. **Pays $75 for 1 page or 1 poem, or $100 for 2 or more pages/ poems, and contributor's copies.**

🟢 WESTERN HUMANITIES REVIEW

University of Utah, English Department, 255 S. Central Campus Dr., Salt Lake City UT 84112-0494. (801)581-6070. **Fax:** (801)585-5167. **E-mail:** whr@ mail.hum.utah.edu. **Website:** ourworld.info/whrweb/. **Contact:** Barry Weller, editor; Nate Liederbach, managing editor. A tri-annual magazine for educated readers. *Western Humanities Review* is a journal of contemporary literature and culture housed in the University of Utah English Department. Publishes poetry, fiction, nonfiction essays, artwork, and work that resists categorization. Estab. 1947. Circ. 1,000. Pays in contributor copies. Publishes ms an average of 1 year after acceptance. Accepts simultaneous submissions. Responds in 3-5 months. Sample copy: $10. Guidelines online.

NONFICTION Contact: Stuart Culver, nonfiction editor. **Buys 6-8 unsolicited mss/year.** Send complete ms. **Pays $5/published page (when funds available).**

FICTION Contact: Michael Mejia, fiction editor. Needs experimental, innovative voices. Does not want genre (romance, science fiction, etc.). **Buys 5-8 mss/ year.** Send complete ms. Length: 5,000 words. **Pays $5/published page (when funds available).**

POETRY Contact: Poetry editors: Craig Dworkin, Paisley Rekdal, Tom Stillinger. Considers simultaneous submissions but no more than 5 poems or 25 pages per reading period. No fax or e-mail submissions. Reads submissions October 1 through April 1 only. Wants quality poetry of any form, including translations. Has published poetry by Charles Simic, Olena Kalytiak Davis, Ravi Shankar, Karen Volkman, Dan Beachy-Quick, Lucie Brock-Broido, Christine Hume, and Dan Chiasson. Innovative prose poems may be submitted as fiction or nonfiction to the appropriate editor. **Pays 2 contributor's copies.**

WILLOW SPRINGS

668 N. Riverpoint Blvd. 2 RPT - #259, Spokane WA 99202. (509)359-7435. **E-mail:** willowspringsewu@ gmail.com. **Website:** willowsprings.ewu.edu. **Contact:** Samuel Ligon, editor. **95% freelance written.** *Willow Springs* is a semiannual magazine covering poetry, fiction, literary nonfiction and interviews of notable writers. Published twice a year, in spring and fall. Estab. 1977. Circ. 1,200. Byline given. Publishes ms an average of 3 months after acceptance. Accepts queries by e-mail, online submission form. Accepts simultaneous submissions. Responds in 2 months to mss. Sample copy: $10. Guidelines online.

NONFICTION Needs book excerpts, essays, general interest, humor, personal experience. **Buys 2-6 mss/ year.** Submit via online submissions manager. **Pays $100 and 2 contributor's copies.**

FICTION "We accept any good piece of literary fiction. Buy a sample copy." Needs adventure, ethnic, experimental, historical, mainstream, mystery, slice-of-life vignettes, suspense, western. Does not want to see genre fiction that does not transcend its subject matter. **Buys 10-15 mss/year.** Submit via online submissions manager. Length: open for short stories; up to 750 words for short shorts. **Pays $100 and 2 contributor's copies for short stories; $40 and 2 contributor's copies for short shorts.**

POETRY Needs avant-garde, free verse, haiku, traditional. "Buy a sample copy to learn our tastes. Our aesthetic is very open." Submit only 3-5 poems at a time. Buys 50-60 poems/year. **Pays $20/poem and 2 contributor's copies.**

WORKERS WRITE!

Blue Cubicle Press, LLC, P.O. Box 250382, Plano TX 75025. **E-mail:** info@workerswritejournal.com. **Website:** www.workerswritejournal.com. **Contact:** David LaBounty, managing editor. **100% freelance written.** Covers working-class literature. "*Workers Write!* is an annual print journal published by Blue Cubicle Press, an independent publisher dedicated to giving voice to writers trapped in the daily grind. Each issue focuses on a particular workplace; check website for details. Submit your stories via e-mail or send a hard copy." Estab. 2005. Circ. 750. Byline given. Pays on acceptance. Publishes mss 6 months after acceptance. Accepts queries by mail, e-mail. Accepts simultaneous submissions. Responds in 1 week to queries; in 3 months to mss. Sample copy available on website. Writer's guidelines free for #10 SASE and on website.

FICTION "We need your stories (5,000-12,000 words) about the workplace from our Overtime series. Every 3 months, we'll release a chapbook containing 1 story that centers on work." Needs experimental, historical, humorous, mainstream, short stories, slice-of-life vignettes. **Buys 10-12 mss/year.** Send complete ms. Length: 500-5,000 words. **Payment: $5-50 (depending on length and rights requested).**

POETRY Needs free verse and traditional. Buys 3-5 poems/year. **Pays $5-10.**

WORLD LITERATURE TODAY

630 Parrington Oval, Suite 110, Norman OK 73019-4033. (405)325-4531. **E-mail:** dsimon@ou.edu; mfjohnson@ou.edu. **Website:** www.worldliteratureto-day.com. Bimonthly website covering contemporary literature, culture, topics addressing any geographic region or language area. We prefer essays in the tradition of clear and lively discussion intended for a broad audience, with a minimum of scholarly apparatus. We offer a window to world culture for enlightened readers everywhere. To get an idea of the range of our coverage, see recent issues from our home page. Sponsors The Neustadt International Prize for Literature. Estab. 1927. No kill fee. Accepts simultaneous submissions. Responds in 6 weeks to mss. Guidelines online.

NONFICTION Needs essays, book reviews, author interviews. Length: up to 2,500 words.

THE YALE REVIEW

Yale University, P.O. Box 208243, New Haven CT 06520-8243. (203)432-0499. **Fax:** (203)432-0510. **Website:** www.yale.edu/yalereview. **Contact:** J.D. McClatchy, editor. **20% freelance written.** Quarterly magazine. "Like Yale's schools of music, drama, and architecture, like its libraries and art galleries, *The Yale Review* has helped give the University its leading place in American education. In a land of quick fixes and short view and in a time of increasingly commercial publishing, the journal has an authority that derives from its commitment to bold established writers and promising newcomers, to both challenging literary work and a range of essays and reviews that can explore the connections between academic disciplines and the broader movements in American society, thought, and culture. With independence and boldness, with a concern for issues and ideas, with

a respect for the mind's capacity to be surprised by speculation and delighted by elegance, *The Yale Review* proudly continues into its third century." Estab. 1911. Circ. 7,000. Pays prior to publication. No kill fee. Publishes ms an average of 6 months after acceptance. Accepts simultaneous submissions. Responds in 1-3 months to mss. Sample copy online. Guidelines online.

NONFICTION Send complete ms with cover letter and SASE. **Pays $400-500.**

FICTION Submit complete ms with SASE. All submissions should be sent to the editorial office. **Pays $400-500.**

POETRY Submit with SASE. All submissions should be sent to the editorial office. **Pays $100-250.**

THE YALOBUSHA REVIEW

University of Mississippi, **E-mail:** yreditors@gmail.com. **Website:** yr.olemiss.edu. **Contact:** Maggie Woodward and Marty Cain, senior editors. Annual literary journal seeking quality submissions from around the globe. Estab. 1995. Circ. 500. Accepts queries by online submission form. Accepts simultaneous submissions. Responds in 2-4 months to mss.

NONFICTION Needs reviews.

FICTION Needs experimental. **Buys 3-6 mss/year.** Submit 1 short story or up to 3 pieces of flash fiction via online submissions manager. Length: up to 5,000 words for short stories; up to 1,000 words for flash fiction.

POETRY Needs Experimental. Submit 3-5 poems via online submissions manager.

ZEEK: A JEWISH JOURNAL OF THOUGHT AND CULTURE

125 Maiden Ln., 8th Floor, New York NY 10038. (212)453-9435. **E-mail:** zeek@zeek.net. **Website:** www.zeek.net. **Contact:** Erica Brody, editor in chief. *ZEEK* "relaunched in late February 2013 as a hub for the domestic Jewish social justice movement, one that showcases the people, ideas, and conversations driving an inclusive and diverse progressive Jewish community. At the same time, we've reaffirmed our commitment to building on *ZEEK*'s reputation for original, ahead-of-the-curve Jewish writing and arts, culture and spirituality content, incubating emerging voices and artists, as well as established ones." *ZEEK* seeks "great writing in a variety of styles and voices, original thinking, and accessible content. That means

we're interested in hearing your ideas for first-person essays, reflections and commentary, reporting, profiles, Q&As, analysis, infographics, and more. For the near future, *ZEEK* will focus on domestic issues. Our discourse will be civil." Estab. 2001. Accepts queries by e-mail. Accepts simultaneous submissions. Responds in 6 weeks to queries.

NONFICTION "Pitches should be sent to zeek@zeek.net, with 'submission' or 'pitch' in the subject line. And please include a little bit about yourself and why you think your pitch is a good fit for *ZEEK*'s readers."

FICTION "Calls for fiction submissions are issued periodically. Follow *ZEEK* on Twitter @ZEEKMag for announcements and details."

POETRY "Pitches should be sent to zeek@zeek.net, with 'submission' or 'pitch' in the subject line. And please include a little bit about yourself and why you think your pitch is a good fit for *ZEEK*."

🟢🟢🟢 ZOETROPE: ALL-STORY

Zoetrope: All-Story, The Sentinel Bldg., 916 Kearny St., San Francisco CA 94133. (415)788-7500. **Website:** www.all-story.com. **Contact:** fiction editor. Quarterly magazine specializing in the best of contemporary short fiction. *Zoetrope: All Story* presents a new generation of classic stories. Estab. 1997. Circ. 20,000. Byline given. No kill fee. Publishes ms an average of 5 months after acceptance. Accepts queries by mail. Accepts simultaneous submissions. Responds in 8 months (if SASE included). Sample copy: $8. Guidelines online.

FICTION Buys 25-35 mss/year. "Writers should submit only 1 story at a time and no more than 2 stories a year. We do not accept artwork or design submissions. We do not accept unsolicited revisions nor respond to writers who don't include an SASE." Send complete ms by mail. Length: up to 7,000 words. "Excerpts from larger works, screenplays, treatments, and poetry will be returned unread." **Pays up to $1,000.**

🟢 ZYZZYVA

57 Post St., Suite 604, San Francisco CA 94104. (415)757-0465. **E-mail:** editor@zyzzyva.org. **Website:** www.zyzzyva.org. **Contact:** Laura Cogan, editor; Oscar Villalon, managing editor. **100% freelance written. Works with a small number of new/unpublished writers each year.** "Every issue is a vibrant mix of established talents and new voices, providing an elegantly curated overview of contemporary arts and letters with a distinctly San Francisco perspective." Estab. 1985. Circ. 2,500. Byline given. Pays on acceptance. No kill fee. Publishes ms an average of 3 months after acceptance. Accepts queries by mail. Accepts simultaneous submissions. Responds in 1 week to queries; in 1 month to mss. Sample copy: $12. Guidelines online.

NONFICTION Needs book excerpts, general interest, historical, humor, personal experience. **Buys 50 mss/year.** Submit by mail. Include SASE and contact information. Length: no limit. **Pays $50.**

FICTION Needs ethnic, experimental, humorous, mainstream. **Buys 60 mss/year.** Send complete ms by mail. Include SASE and contact information. Length: no limit. **Pays $50.**

POETRY Submit by mail. Include SASE and contact information. Buys 20 poems/year. Submit maximum 5 poems. Length: no limit. **Pays $50.**

MEN'S

🟢🟢🟢🟢 ESQUIRE

Hearst Media, 300 W. 57th St., New York NY 10019. (212)649-4158. **E-mail:** editor@esquire.com. **Website:** www.esquire.com. Monthly magazine covering the ever-changing trends in American culture. *Esquire* is geared toward smart, well-off men. General readership is college educated and sophisticated, between ages 30 and 45. Written mostly by contributing editors on contract. Rarely accepts unsolicited mss. Estab. 1933. Circ. 720,000. Publishes ms an average of 2-6 months after acceptance. Editorial lead time at least 2 months. Accepts queries by mail, e-mail. Accepts simultaneous submissions. Guidelines on website.

NONFICTION Query. Length: 5,000 words average. **Payment varies.**

GQ

Condé Nast, 1 World Trade Center, New York NY 10007. (212)286-2860. **E-mail:** letters@gq.com. **Website:** www.gq.com. Monthly magazine covering subjects ranging from finance, food, entertainment, technology, celebrity profiles, sports, and fashion. *Gentleman's Quarterly* is devoted to men's personal style and taste, from what he wears to the way he lives his life. Estab. 1957. Circ. 964,264. No kill fee. Accepts queries by e-mail. Accepts simultaneous submissions.

NONFICTION Needs interview.

MAXIM

Alpha Media Group, 1040 Avenue of the Americas, 16th Floor, New York NY 10018-3703. (212)302-2626. **Fax:** (212)302-2635. **E-mail:** editors@maximmag.com. **Website:** www.maximonline.com. Monthly magazine covering relationships, sex, women, careers and sports. Written for young, professional men interested in fun and informative articles. Circ. 2.5 million. No kill fee. Editorial lead time 5 months. Accepts simultaneous submissions. Sample copy for $3.99 at newstands.

MEN'S HEALTH

Rodale, Inc., 400 S. 10th St., Emmaus PA 18098. (212)697-2040. **E-mail:** mhonline@rodale.com. **Website:** www.menshealth.com. **Contact:** Kevin Donahue, senior managing editor. Covers various men's lifestyles topics, such as fitness, nutrition, fashion, and sexuality. The world's largest men's magazine brand, with 40 editions in 47 countries. Estab. 1987. Circ. 1,918,387. Accepts simultaneous submissions.

MEN'S JOURNAL

Wenner Media, Inc., 1290 Avenue of the Americas, 2nd Floor, New York NY 10104-0295. (212)484-1616. **Fax:** (212)484-3434. **E-mail:** letters@mensjournal.com. **Website:** www.mensjournal.com. Monthly magazine covering general lifestyle for men, ages 25-49. *Men's Journal* is for active men with an interest in participatory sports, travel, fitness, and adventure. It provides practical, informative articles on how to spend quality leisure time. Estab. 1992. Circ. 650,000. No kill fee. Accepts queries by mail, fax. Accepts simultaneous submissions.

NONFICTION Needs book excerpts, essays, expose, general interest, historical, how-to, humor, new product, personal experience, photo feature, travel. Query with SASE. **Payment varies.**

MILITARY

🍁 $ $ AIRFORCE

Royal Canadian Air Force Association, P.O Box 2460, Station D, Ottawa ON K1P 5W6 Canada. (613)232-2303. **Fax:** (613)232-2156. **E-mail:** editor@airforce.ca. **Website:** rcafassociation.ca. **5% freelance written.** Quarterly magazine covering Canada's air force heritage. Stories center on Canadian military aviation—past, present, and future. Estab. 1977. Circ. 16,000. Byline given. Pays on publication. Publishes ms an average of 6 months after acceptance. Editorial lead time 3 months. Submit seasonal material 3 months in advance. Accepts queries by mail, e-mail. Accepts simultaneous submissions. Responds in 2 weeks to queries; in 1 month to mss. Sample copy free. Guidelines by e-mail.

NONFICTION Needs historical, interview, personal experience, photo feature. **Buys 2 mss/year.** Query with published clips. Length: 1,500-3,500 words. Limit agreed upon in advance.

FILLERS Needs anecdotes, facts. Length: about 800 words. **Pay negotiable.**

$ $ ARMY MAGAZINE

Association of the US Army, 2425 Wilson Blvd., Arlington VA 22201. (800)336-4570. **E-mail:** armymag@ausa.org. **Website:** www.ausa.org/publications/armymagazine. **Contact:** Rick Maze, editor in chief. **70% freelance written. Prefers to work with published/established writers.** Monthly magazine emphasizing Army interests. Estab. 1950. Circ. 65,000. Byline given. Pays on publication. Publishes ms an average of 5 months after acceptance. Submit seasonal material 3 months in advance. Accepts queries by mail. Accepts simultaneous submissions. Responds to queries within a week. Sample copy for 9x12 SAE with $1 postage, or online. Guidelines available online: www.ausa.org/publications/armymagazine/aboutarmy/Pages/ARMYMagazine'sWriter_sGuidelines.aspx.

NONFICTION Needs essays, historical, interview, photo feature, technical. Special issues: "We would like to see more pieces about little-known episodes involving interesting military personalities. We especially want material lending itself to heavy, contributor-supplied photographic treatment. The first thing a contributor should recognize is that our readership is very savvy militarily. 'Gee-whiz' personal reminiscences get short shrift, unless they hold their own in a company in which long military service, heroism, and unusual experiences are commonplace. At the same time, *ARMY* readers like a well-written story with a fresh slant, whether it is about an experience in a foxhole or the fortunes of a corps in battle." No rehashed history. No unsolicited book reviews. **Buys 40 mss/year.** Submit via e-mail to armymag@ausa.org. Length: 1,000-1,500 words for op-eds and opinion, 1,200-1,800 for features. **Pays 15-20¢/word for**

articles, more for cover stories. Expenses paid only with prior approval.

❸❸❸ MILITARY OFFICER

201 N. Washington St., Alexandria VA 22314-2539. **E-mail:** editor@moaa.org. **Website:** www.moaa.org. **60% freelance written. Prefers to work with published/established writers.** Monthly magazine for officers of the 7 uniformed services and their families. Estab. 1945. Circ. 325,000. Byline given. Pays on acceptance. Publishes ms an average of 1 year after acceptance. Accepts queries by e-mail. Accepts simultaneous submissions. Responds in 3 months to queries. Sample copy and guidelines online.

NONFICTION "We rarely accept unsolicited mss." **Buys 50 mss/year.** Query with résumé, sample clips. Length: 1,000-2,000 words (features). **Pays 80¢/word (features).**

❸ PARAMETERS

U.S. Army War College, 47 Ashburn Dr., Carlisle PA 17013-5010. (717)245-4943. **E-mail:** usarmy.carlisle. awc.mbx.parameters@mail.mil. **Website:** www.car-lisle.army.mil/usawc/parameters. **100% freelance written. Prefers to work with published/established writers or experts in the field.** Readership consists of senior leaders of US defense establishment, both uniformed and civilian, plus members of the media, government, industry and academia. Subjects include national and international security affairs, military strategy, military leadership and management, art and science of warfare, and military history with contemporary relevance. Estab. 1971. Circ. 13,500. Byline given. Pays on publication. No kill fee. Publishes ms an average of 6 months after acceptance. Accepts queries by mail, e-mail, phone. Accepts simultaneous submissions. Responds in 6 weeks to queries. Sample copy free or online. Guidelines online.

NONFICTION Send complete ms. Length: 4,500-5,000 words.

MUSIC CONSUMER

GUITAR WORLD

NewBay Media, LLC, 28 E. 28th St., 12th Floor, New York NY 10016. (212)378-0400. **Fax:** (212)281-4704. **E-mail:** soundingboard@guitarworld.com. **Website:** www.guitarworld.com. Monthly magazine for guitarists. Written for guitar players categorized as either professionals, semi-professionals or amateur players.

Every issue offers broad-ranging interviews that cover technique, instruments, and lifestyles. Circ. 150,000. No kill fee. Editorial lead time 2 months. Accepts simultaneous submissions.

RELIX MAGAZINE

104 W. 29th St., 11th Floor, New York NY 10001. (646)230-0100. **E-mail:** dean@relix.com; mike@re-lix.com. **Website:** www.relix.com. **Contact:** Dean Budnick and Mike Greenhaus, editors in chief. **30% freelance written.** Magazine published 8 times/year focusing on new and independent bands, classic rock, lifestyles, and music alternatives such as roots, improvisational music, psychedelia, and jambands. Estab. 1974. Circ. 100,000. Byline given. Pays on publication. Publishes ms an average of 4 months after acceptance. Accepts queries by mail, e-mail. Accepts simultaneous submissions. Responds in 3 months to queries. Sample copy for $5. Guidelines online.

NONFICTION Needs historical, humor, interview, photo feature, technical, live reviews, new artists, hippy lifestyles, food, mixed media, books. Query with published clips. Length: 300-1,500 words. **Pays variable rates.**

COLUMNS Query with published clips or send complete ms. **Pays variable rates**

ROLLING STONE

Wenner Media, 1290 Avenue of the Americas, New York NY 10104. (212)484-1616. **Fax:** (212)484-1664. **E-mail:** rseditors@rollingstone.com. **Website:** www. rollingstone.com. **Contact:** Caryn Ganz, editorial director. Biweekly magazine geared towards young adults interested in news of popular music, entertainment, and the arts; current news events; politics; and American culture. Circ. 1.46 million. No kill fee. Editorial lead time 1 month. Accepts simultaneous submissions.

❸❸❸ SYMPHONY

League of American Orchestras, 33 W. 60th St., 5th Floor, New York NY 10023. (212)262-5161. **Fax:** (212)262-5198. **E-mail:** clane@americanorches-tras.org; jmelick@americanorchestras.org; editor@ americanorchestras.org. **Website:** www.symphony. org. **Contact:** Chester Lane, senior editor; Jennifer Melick, managing editor. **50% freelance written.** Quarterly magazine for the orchestra industry and classical music enthusiasts covering classical music, orchestra industry, musicians. *Symphony*, the quarterly magazine of the League of American Orchestras, reports on the critical issues, trends, personalities, and developments of the orchestra world. Every issue includes news, provocative essays, in-depth articles, and cutting-edge research relevant to the entire orchestra field. *Symphony* profiles take readers behind the scenes to meet the people who are making a difference in the orchestra world, while wide-ranging survey articles reveal the strategies and tactics that are helping orchestras meet the challenges of the 21st century. *Symphony* is a matchless source of meaningful information about orchestras and serves as an advocate and connector for the orchestra field. Circ. 18,000. Byline given. Pays on acceptance. No kill fee. Publishes ms an average of 10 weeks after acceptance. Editorial lead time 6 months. Submit seasonal material 8 months in advance. Accepts queries by mail, e-mail. Accepts simultaneous submissions. Guidelines online.

NONFICTION Needs book excerpts, essays, inspirational, interview, opinion, personal experience, photo feature. Does not want to see reviews, interviews. **Buys 30 mss/year.** Query with published clips. Length: 1,500-3,500 words. **Pays $500-900.**

COLUMNS Repertoire (orchestral music—essays); Comment (personal views and opinions); Currents (electronic media developments); In Print (books); On Record (CD, DVD, video), all 1,000-2,500 words. **Buys 12 mss/year.** Query with published clips.

MYSTERY

$ THE DEADLY QUILL

E-mail: lorne@deadlyquill.com. **E-mail:** submissions@deadlyquill.com. **Website:** deadlyquill.com. **Contact:** Lorne McMillan. "We are looking to give an outlet for writers of short fiction in the tradition of The Twilight Zone, Alfred Hitchcock, and The Outer Limits. Make the story grab you and not let go until the very end." Estab. 2015. Byline given. Pays on publication. No kill fee. Publishes ms 3-6 months after acceptance. Editorial lead time 3-6 months. Accepts queries by e-mail. Accepts simultaneous submissions. Responds in 1-3 months. Guidelines online.

FICTION The stories should take the reader by the throat and not let go. Needs fantasy, horror, mystery, science fiction, short stories, suspense. Does not want anything that doesn't grab you. No violence for the sake of violence. Length: 2,000-5,000 words. **Pays $0.03 per word.**

$ ELLERY QUEEN'S MYSTERY MAGAZINE

44 Wall St., Suite 904, New York NY 10005-2401. **E-mail:** elleryqueenmm@dellmagazines.com. **Website:** www.themysteryplace.com/eqmm. **100% freelance written.** "*Ellery Queen's Mystery Magazine* welcomes submissions from both new and established writers. We publish every kind of mystery short story: the psychological suspense tale, the deductive puzzle, the private eye case—the gamut of crime and detection from the realistic (including the policeman's lot and stories of police procedure) to the more imaginative (including 'locked rooms' and 'impossible crimes'). We look for strong writing, an original and exciting plot, and professional craftsmanship. We encourage writers whose work meets these general criteria to read an issue of *EQMM* before making a submission." Estab. 1941. Circ. 100,000. Byline given. Pays on acceptance. No kill fee. Publishes ms an average of 6-12 months after acceptance. Accepts queries by online submission form. Accepts simultaneous submissions. Responds in 3 months to mss. Sample copy: $6.50. Make out check to *Ellery Queen Mystery Magazine*, and send to *Ellery Queen Mystery Magazine*, Attn: Sandy Marlowe, 6 Prowitt St., Norwalk CT 06855. Guidelines online.

FICTION "We always need detective stories. Special consideration given to anything timely and original." Publishes ms 6-12 months after acceptance. Agented fiction 50%. **Publishes 10 new writers/year.** Recently published work by Jeffery Deaver, Joyce Carol Oates, and Margaret Maron. Sometimes comments on rejected mss. Needs mystery, suspense. No explicit sex or violence, no gore or horror. Seldom publishes parodies or pastiches. "We do not want true detective or crime stories." **Buys up to 120 mss/year.** "*EQMM* uses an online submission system (eqmm.magazinesubmissions.com) that has been designed to streamline our process and improve communication with authors. We ask that all submissions be made electronically, using this system, rather than on paper. All stories should be in standard ms format and submitted in .DOC format. We cannot accept .DOCX, .RTF, or .TXT files at this time." Length: 2,500-8,000 words, but occasionally accepts longer and shorter submissions—including minute mysteries of 250 words, stories up to 12,000 words, and novellas of up to 20,000 words from established authors. **Pays 5-8¢/word; occasionally higher for established authors.**

ALFRED HITCHCOCK'S MYSTERY MAGAZINE

Dell Magazines, 44 Wall St., Suite 904, New York NY 10005. **E-mail:** alfredhitchcockmm@dellmagazines.com. **Website:** www.themysteryplace.com/ahmm. **100% freelance written.** Monthly magazine featuring new mystery short stories. Estab. 1956. Circ. 90,000. Byline given. Pays on publication. No kill fee. Submit seasonal material 7 months in advance. Accepts queries by mail, online submission form. Responds in 3-5 months to mss. Sample copy: $5. Guidelines for SASE or on website.

FICTION Wants "original and well-written mystery and crime fiction. Because this is a mystery magazine, the stories we buy must fall into that genre in some sense or another. We are interested in nearly every kind of mystery: stories of detection of the classic kind, police procedurals, private eye tales, suspense, courtroom dramas, stories of espionage, and so on. We ask only that the story be about crime (or the threat or fear of one). We sometimes accept ghost stories or supernatural tales, but those also should involve a crime." Needs mystery, suspense. No sensationalism. Send complete ms. Length: up to 12,000 words. **Payment varies.**

SUSPENSE MAGAZINE

Suspense Publishing, 26500 W. Agoura Rd., Suite 102-474, Calabasas CA 91302. **Fax:** (310)626-9670. **E-mail:** editor@suspensemagazine.com; john@suspensemagazine.com. **E-mail:** stories@suspensemagazine.com. **Website:** www.suspensemagazine.com. **Contact:** John Raab, publisher/CEO/editor in chief. **100% freelance written.** Monthly consumer magazine covering suspense, mystery, thriller, and horror genres. Estab. 2007. Pays on acceptance. Pays 100% kill fee. Publishes ms 6-9 months after acceptance. Editorial lead time is 6-9 months. Accepts queries by e-mail. Accepts simultaneous submissions. Responds in 1-2 weeks to queries; 2-3 months to mss.

NONFICTION Query. Length: 1,000-3,000 words. **Pays commissions only, by assignment only.**

COLUMNS Book Reviews (reviews for newly released fiction); Graphic Novel Reviews (reviews for comic books/graphic novels), 250-1,000 words. **Buys 6-12 mss/year mss/year.** Query. **Pays by assignment only.**

FICTION Needs horror, mystery, suspense, thrillers. No explicit scenes. **Buys 15-30 mss/year.** Submit story in body of e-mail. "Attachments will not be opened." Length: 1,500-5,000 words.

NATURE, CONSERVATION & ECOLOGY

🍁 $ ALTERNATIVES JOURNAL

195 King Street West, Kitchener ON N2G 1B1 Canada. (519)888-4505. **E-mail:** megan@alternativesjournal.ca; david@alternativesjournal.ca. **Website:** www.alternativesjournal.ca. **Contact:** Megan Nourse, editorial manager, David McConnachie, publisher. **90% freelance written.** Magazine published 4 times/year with special issue(s) covering international environmental issues. "*Alternatives Journal*, Canada's national environmental magazine, delivers thoughtful analysis and intelligent debate on Canadian and world environmental issues, the latest news and ideas, as well as profiles of environmental leaders who are making a difference. *A/J* is a quarterly+ magazine featuring bright, lively writing by the nation's foremost environmental thinkers and researchers. *A/J* offers a vision of a more sustainable future as well as the tools needed to take us there." Estab. 1971. Circ. 5,000. Byline given. Pays on publication. Offers 50% kill fee. Publishes ms an average of 5 months after acceptance. Editorial lead time 7 months. Submit seasonal material 5 months in advance. Accepts queries by e-mail, online submission form. Accepts simultaneous submissions. Sample copy free for Canadian writers only. Guidelines available on website.

NONFICTION Needs book excerpts, essays, expose, how-to, humor, interview, opinion, photo feature, profile, reviews, technical, we accept the above categories. We prefer that you pitch a story rather than sending a full unsolicited article. **Buys 50 mss/year.** Query with published clips. Length: 800-3,000 words. **Pays $.10/word (Canadian).**

ARIZONA WILDLIFE VIEWS

5000 W. Carefree Hwy., Phoenix AZ 85086. (800)777-0015. **E-mail:** awv@azgfd.gov; hrayment@azgfd.gov. **Website:** www.azgfd.gov/magazine. **Contact:** Heidi Rayment. **50% freelance written.** Bimonthly magazine covering Arizona wildlife, wildlife management, and outdoor recreation (specifically hunting, fishing, wildlife watching, boating and off-highway vehicle recreation). "*Arizona Wildlife Views* is a general interest magazine about Arizona wildlife, wildlife management and outdoor recreation. We publish material that conforms to the mission and policies of the Arizona Game and Fish Department. In addition to Arizona wildlife and wildlife management, topics include habitat issues, outdoor recreation involving wildlife, boating, fishing, hunting, bird-watching, animal observation, off-highway vehicle use, etc., and historical articles about wildlife and wildlife management." Circ. 22,000. Byline given. Pays on publication. No kill fee. Publishes ms an average of 10 months after acceptance. Editorial lead time 1 year. Submit seasonal material 2 months in advance. Accepts queries by mail. Accepts simultaneous submissions. Responds in 1 month to queries. Responds in 2 months to mss. Sample copy free. Guidelines online.

NONFICTION Needs general interest, historical, how-to, interview, photo feature, technical. Does not want "Me and Joe" articles, anthropomorphism of wildlife, or opinionated pieces not based on confirmable facts. **Buys 20 mss/year.** Query. Length: 1,000-2,500 words. **Pays $450-800.**

○ ❸ ❸ ❸ THE ATLANTIC SALMON JOURNAL

The Atlantic Salmon Federation, P.O. Box 5200, St. Andrews NB E5B 3S8 Canada. (514)457-8737. **Fax:** (506)529-1070. **E-mail:** savesalmon@asf.ca; martinsilverstone@videotron.ca. **Website:** www.asf.ca. **Contact:** Martin Silverstone, editor. **50-68% freelance written.** Quarterly magazine covering conservation efforts for the Atlantic salmon, catering to the dedicated angler and conservationist. Circ. 11,000. Byline given. Pays on publication. No kill fee. Publishes ms an average of 6 months after acceptance. Submit seasonal material 3 months in advance. Accepts simultaneous submissions. Responds in 2 months to queries. Sample copy for 9x12 SAE with $1 (Canadian), or IRC. Guidelines free.

NONFICTION Needs historical, how-to, humor, interview, new product, opinion, personal experience, photo feature, technical. **Buys 15-20 mss/year.** Query with published clips. Length: 2,000 words. **Pays $400-800 for articles with photos.**

COLUMNS Fit To Be Tied (conservation issues and salmon research; the design, construction, and suc-

cess of specific flies); interesting characters in the sport and opinion pieces by knowledgeable writers, 900 words; Casting Around (short, informative, entertaining reports, book reviews, and quotes from the world of Atlantic salmon angling and conservation). Query. **Pays $50-300.**

BIRD WATCHER'S DIGEST

P.O. Box 110, Marietta OH 45750. (740)373-5285; (800)879-2473. **E-mail:** editor@birdwatchersdigest.com; submissions@birdwatchersdigest.com. **Website:** www.birdwatchersdigest.com. **Contact:** Bill Thompson III, editor. **60% freelance written.** Bimonthly, digest-sized magazine covering birds, bird watching, travel for birding and natural history. *BWD* is a nontechnical magazine interpreting ornithological material for amateur observers, including the knowledgeable birder, the serious novice and the backyard bird watcher; strives to provide good reading and good ornithology. Works with a small number of new/unpublished writers each year. Estab. 1978. Circ. 42,000. Byline given. Pays after publication. Publishes ms an average of 2 years after acceptance. Submit seasonal material 6 months in advance. Accepts simultaneous submissions. Responds within 4 weeks to queries. Sample copy for $4.99 plus shipping or access online. Guidelines online.

NONFICTION Needs book excerpts, how-to, humor, personal experience, travel. No articles on domestic, pet or caged birds, or raising a baby bird. **Buys 30-40 mss/year.** "We gladly accept e-mail queries and ms submissions. When submitting by e-mail, please use the subject line 'Submission—[your topic].' Attach your submission to your e-mail in either MS Word (.doc) or RichText Format (.rtf). Please include full contact information on every page. Decision within 4 months." Length: 600-2,500 words. **Pays up to $200.**

❸ ❸ BIRDWATCHING

Madavor Media, LLC, *BirdWatching* Editorial Dept., 25 Braintree Hill Office Park, Suite 404, Braintree MA 02184. **E-mail:** mail@birdwatchingdaily.com. **Website:** www.birdwatchingdaily.com. Bimonthly magazine for birdwatchers who actively look for wild birds in the field. "*BirdWatching* concentrates on where to find, how to attract, and how to identify wild birds, and on how to understand what they do." Estab. 1987. Circ. 40,000. Byline given. Pays on publication. Accepts queries by mail, e-mail. Accepts simultaneous submissions. Guidelines online.

NONFICTION Needs book excerpts, essays, how-to, interview, personal experience, photo feature, travel. No poetry, fiction, or puzzles. **Buys 12 mss/year.** Query by mail or e-mail with published clips. Length: 500-2,400 words. **Pays $200-400.**

⬤⬤ EARTH ISLAND JOURNAL

Earth Island Institute, 2150 Allston Way, Suite 460, Berkeley CA 94704. **E-mail:** submissions@earthisland.org. **Website:** www.earthislandjournal.org. **80% freelance written.** Quarterly magazine covering the environment/ecology. *Earth Island Journal*, published quarterly, "combines investigative journalism and thought-provoking essays that make the subtle but profound connections between the environment and other contemporary issues." Estab. 1985. Circ. 10,000. Byline given. Pays on publication. Publishes ms an average of 4 months after acceptance. Editorial lead time 4 months. Submit seasonal material 4 months in advance. Accepts queries by mail, e-mail. Accepts simultaneous submissions. Responds in 1 month to queries and mss. Sample copy online. Guidelines online.

NONFICTION Needs book excerpts, essays, expose, general interest, interview, opinion, personal experience, photo feature. "We do not want product pitches, services, or company news." **Buys 20 mss/year.** Query with published clips. Length: 750-4,000 words. **Pays 25¢/word.**

COLUMNS Voices (first-person reflection about the environment in a person's life), 750 words. **Buys 4 mss/year.** Query. **Pays $50.**

⬤⬤ HIGH COUNTRY NEWS

119 Grand Ave., P.O. Box 1090, Paonia CO 81428. (970)527-4898. **E-mail:** brianc@hcn.org; cindy@hcn.org. **E-mail:** editor@hcn.org; photos@hcn.org. **Website:** www.hcn.org. **Contact:** Brian Calvert, managing editor; Cindy Wehling, art director. **70% freelance written.** Biweekly nonprofit magazine covering environment, rural communities, and natural resource issues in 11 western states for environmentalists, politicians, companies, college classes, government agencies, grass roots activists, public land managers, etc. Estab. 1970. Circ. 25,000. Byline given. Pays on publication. Offers kill fee of 1/3 of agreed rate. Publishes ms an average of 2 months after acceptance. Accepts queries by e-mail. Accepts simultaneous submissions. Responds in 2 weeks to queries. Sample copy online. Guidelines online.

NONFICTION Buys 100 mss/year. Query. Length: up to 2,400 words. **Pays 50¢-$1.50/word.**

COLUMNS Back-Page Essay, 700-900 words; Writers on the Range (taut and pithy opinion pieces). Submit back-page essay queries to Michelle Nijhuis (michelle@hcn.org); submit Writers on the Range pieces to Betsy Marston (betsym@hsn.org).

⬤⬤⬤ MINNESOTA CONSERVATION VOLUNTEER

Minnesota Department of Natural Resources, 500 Lafeyette Rd., St. Paul MN 55155-4046. **Website:** www.dnr.state.mn.us/magazine. **50% freelance written.** Bimonthly magazine covering Minnesota natural resources, wildlife, natural history, outdoor recreation, and land use. *"Minnesota Conservation Volunteer* is a donor-supported magazine advocating conservation and careful use of Minnesota's natural resources. Material must reflect an appreciation of nature and an ethic of care for the environment. We rely on a variety of sources in our reporting. More than 130,000 Minnesota households, businesses, schools, and other groups subscribe to this conservation magazine." Estab. 1940. Circ. 131,000. Byline given. Pays on acceptance. Offers 30% kill fee. Publishes ms an average of 2 months after acceptance. Editorial lead time 9 months. Submit seasonal material 9 months in advance. Accepts queries by mail, e-mail. Accepts simultaneous submissions. Responds in 1 month to queries. Responds in 2 months to mss. Sample copy free or on website. Guidelines online.

NONFICTION Needs essays, expose, general interest, historical, humor, interview, opinion, personal experience, photo feature, Young Naturalists for children. Rarely publishes poetry or uncritical advocacy. **Buys 12 mss/year.** Query with published clips for features and Field Notes; send full ms for essays. Length: 300-1,800 words. **Pays 50¢/word for features and essays.**

COLUMNS Close Encounters (unusual, exciting, or humorous personal wildlife experience in Minnesota), up to 1,500 words; Sense of Place (first- or third-person essay developing character of a Minnesota place), up to 1,500 words; Viewpoint (well-researched and well-reasoned opinion piece), up to 1,500 words; Minnesota Profile (concise description of emblematic state species or geographic feature), 400 words. **Buys 12 mss/year.** Query with published clips. **Pays 50¢/word.**

NATURE

Nature Publishing Group, The Macmillan Building, 4 Crinan St., London N1 9XW United Kingdom. (44)(207)833-4000. **Fax:** (44)(207)843-4596. **E-mail:** nature@nature.com. **Website:** www.nature.com/nature. **5% freelance written.** Weekly magazine covering multidisplinary science. *Nature* is the number one multidisciplinary journal of science, publishing News, Views, Commentary, Reviews, and ground-breaking research. Estab. 1869. Circ. 60,000. Byline given. No kill fee. Publishes ms an average of 2 months after acceptance. Accepts simultaneous submissions. Responds to ms in 1 week. Guidelines online.

NORTHERN WOODLANDS MAGAZINE

Center for Woodlands Education, Inc., 1776 Center Rd., P.O. Box 471, Corinth VT 05039-0471. (802)439-6292; (800)290-5232. **Fax:** (802)368-1053. **E-mail:** dave@northernwoodlands.org; mail@northernwoodlands.org. **Website:** www.northernwoodlands.org. **40-60% freelance written.** Quarterly magazine covering natural history, conservation, and forest management in the Northeast. "*Northern Woodlands* strives to inspire landowners' sense of stewardship by increasing their awareness of the natural history and the principles of conservation and forestry that are directly related to their land. We also hope to increase the public's awareness of the social, economic, and environmental benefits of a working forest." Estab. 1994. Circ. 15,000. Byline given. Pays 1 month prior to publication. Publishes ms an average of 6 months after acceptance. Editorial lead time 6 months. Submit seasonal material 6 months in advance. Accepts queries by mail, e-mail. Accepts simultaneous submissions. Responds in 1 month to queries. Responds in 1-2 months to mss. Sample copy and guidelines online.

NONFICTION No product reviews, first-person travelogues, "cute" animal stories, opinion, or advocacy pieces. **Buys 15-20 mss/year.** Query with published clips. Length: 500-3,000 words. **Pay varies per piece.**

SIERRA

85 Second St., 2nd Floor, San Francisco CA 94105. **Website:** www.sierraclub.org. Estab. 1893. Accepts queries by e-mail. Accepts simultaneous submissions. Responds in 6-8 weeks. Sample copy for $5 and SASE, or on. Guidelines online.

NONFICTION "*Sierra* is looking for strong, well-researched, literate nonfiction storytelling about significant environmental and conservation issues, adventure travel, nature, self-propelled sports, and trends in green living. Writers should look for ways to cast new light on well-established issues. We look for stories of national or international significance; local issues, while sometimes useful as examples of broader trends, are seldom of interest in themselves. We are always looking for adventure-travel pieces that weave events, discoveries, and environmental insights into the narrative. We are more interested in showcasing environmental solutions than adding to the list of environmental problems. We publish dramatic investigative stories that have the potential to reach a broad audience. Nonfiction essays on the natural world are welcome too. Features often focus on aspects of the Sierra Club's work, but few subjects are taboo. For more information about the Club's current campaigns, visit sierraclub.org. We do not want descriptive wildlife articles unless larger conservation issues figure strongly in the story. We are not interested in editorials, general essays about environmentalism, or highly technical writing. We do not publish unsolicited cartoons, poetry, or fiction; please do not submit works in these genres." **Buys 30-36 mss/year.** Well-researched, tightly focused queries should be submitted to **Submissions.Sierra@sierraclub.org.** Phone calls are strongly discouraged. "Please do not send slides, prints, or other artwork. If photos or illustrations are required for your submission, we will request them when your work is accepted for publication." Length: 500-4,000 words. **Features: "Feature lengths range from 500 words to (rarely) 4,000 words or more with payment starting at about 75 cents a word and rising to considerably more for well-known writers with crackerjack credentials." Departments: "Articles are 100 to 1,500 words in length; payment is $50 to $1,000 unless otherwise noted. Payment for all articles is on acceptance, which is contingent on a favorable review of the manuscript by our editorial staff, and by knowledgeable outside reviewers, where appropriate. Kill fees are negotiated when a story is assigned."**

TERRAIN.ORG: A JOURNAL OF THE BUILT + NATURAL ENVIROMENTS

Terrain.org, P.O. Box 19161, Tucson AZ 85731-9161. **E-mail:** contact2@terrain.org. **Website:** www.terrain.org. Reviews Editor address: P.O. Box 51332, Irvine CA 92619-1332. **Contact:** Simmons B. Buntin, editor in chief. Covers how environment influences us. Also publishes literary essays, literary criticism, book reviews, poetry, articles, and artwork. *Terrain. org* is based on, and thus welcomes quality submissions from, new and experienced authors and artists alike. Our online journal accepts only the finest poetry, essays, fiction, articles, artwork, and other contributions' material that reaches deep into the earth's fiery core, or humanity's incalculable core, and brings forth new insights and wisdom. *Terrain.org* is searching for that interface—the integration among the built and natural environments, that might be called the soul of place. The works contained within *Terrain.org* ultimately examine the physical realm around us and how those environments influence us and each other physically, mentally, emotionally, and spiritually." Publishes mss 5 weeks-18 months after acceptance. Accepts queries by online submission form. Accepts simultaneous submissions. Responds in 2 weeks to queries; in 4 months to mss. Sometimes comments on/critiques rejected mss. Guidelines online.

NONFICTION Does not want erotica. Accepts submissions online at sub.terrain.org. Include brief bio. Send complete ms with cover letter. Length: 1,500-6,000 words. Average length: 5,000 words.

FICTION Needs adventure, experimental, historical, horror, humorous, science fiction, suspense. Does not want erotica. Accepts submissions online at sub. terrain.org. Include brief bio. Send complete ms with cover letter. Reads September 1-May 30 for regular submissions; contest submissions open year round. Length: up to 6,000 words. Average length: 5,000 words. Publishes short shorts. Average length of short shorts: 750 words.

POETRY Accepts submissions online at sub.terrain. org. Include brief bio. Send complete ms with cover letter. No erotica. Submit maximum 2-6 poems. Length: open.

PERSONAL COMPUTERS

PC GAMER

Future Network USA, 1 Lombard St., Suite 200, San Francisco CA 94111. **E-mail:** wesley@pcgamer; tyler@ pcgamer. **Website:** www.pcgamer.com. "*PC Gamer* is the global authority on PC games. For more than 20 years we have delivered unrivaled coverage, in print and online, of every aspect of PC gaming." No kill fee. Accepts queries by e-mail. Accepts simultaneous submissions.

NONFICTION Needs general interest, new product. Query.

TEKKA

134 Main St., Watertown MA 02472. (617)924-9044. **E-mail:** editor@tekka.net. **E-mail:** bernstein@eastgate.com. **Website:** www.tekka.net. **Contact:** Mark Bernstein, publisher. "*Tekka* takes a close look at serious ideas that intertwingle computing and expression: hypertext, new media, software aesthetics, and the changing world that lies beyond the new economy. *Tekka* is always seeking new writers who can enhance our understanding, tempt our palate, and help explore new worlds and advance the state of the art. We welcome proposals for incisive, original features, reviews, and profiles from freelance writers. Our rates vary by length, department, and editorial requirements but are generally in line with the best Web magazines. We welcome proposals from scholars as well. We also publish short hypertext fiction, as well as fiction that explores the future of reading, writing, media, and computing. Estab. 2003. Accepts queries by e-mail. Accepts simultaneous submissions.

NONFICTION Needs reviews. Query. **Pay rates vary.**

FICTION hypertext, fiction that explores the future of reading, writing, media, and computing. Query. **Pay rates vary.**

WIRED

Condé Nast Publications, 520 Third St., 3rd Floor, San Francisco CA 94107-1815. **E-mail:** submit@wired. com. **Website:** www.wired.com. **Contact:** Joe Brown, executive editor. **95% freelance written.** Monthly magazine covering technology and digital culture. Covers the digital revolution and related advances in computers, communications, and lifestyles. Estab. 1993. Circ. 500,000. Byline given. Pays on publication. Offers 25% kill fee. Publishes ms an average of 3 months after acceptance. Editorial lead time 3 months. Accepts queries by e-mail. Accepts simultaneous submissions. Responds in 3 weeks to queries. Sample copy: $4.95. Guidelines by e-mail.

NONFICTION Needs essays, interview, opinion. No poetry or trade articles. Query.

PHOTOGRAPHY

APOGEE PHOTO MAGAZINE

Prescott AZ (928) 515-1729. **E-mail:** editor.sales@apogeephoto.com. **E-mail:** editor.sales@apogeephoto.com. **Website:** apogeephoto.com. **Contact:** Marla Meier, Owner. "A free online magazine designed to inspire, educate and inform photographers of all ages and levels. Hundreds of articles, columns and tips covering a wide range of photo topics. Find listings of photo workshops and tours, camera clubs, and books. Submit your articles for publication." Accepts queries by e-mail. Accepts simultaneous submissions.

NONFICTION Needs essays, general interest, how-to, inspirational, interview, new product, photo feature, profile, reviews, technical, travel. Accepts well-written articles with 600-1,200 words on any photography related subject geared towards the beginner to advanced photographer. Articles must be accompanied by a minimum of 6 high quality photographs. Format and photo details will be given via e-mail upon acceptance of terms.

PHOTOGRAPHER'S FORUM MAGAZINE

813 Reddick St., Santa Barbara CA 93103. (805)963-0439, ext. 240. **Fax:** (805)965-0496. **E-mail:** julie@serbin.com. **Website:** www.pfmagazine.com. **Contact:** Julie Simpson, managing editor. Quarterly magazine for the serious student and emerging professional photographer. Includes feature articles on historic and contemporary photographers, interviews, book reviews, workshop listings, and new products. Accepts queries by mail, e-mail. Accepts simultaneous submissions.

NONFICTION Needs historical, interview, new product, photo feature, profile, reviews.

POPULAR PHOTOGRAPHY & IMAGING

Bonnier Corporation, 460 N. Orlando Ave., Suite 200, Winter Park FL 32789. (407)628-4802. **Fax:** (407)628-7061. **E-mail:** mleuchter@hfmus.com; popeditor@hfmus.com. **Website:** www.popularphotography.com. **Contact:** Miriam Leuchter, managing editor. Monthly magazine edited for amateur to professional photographers. Provides incisive instructional articles, authoritative tests of photographic equipment; covers still and digital imaging; travel, color, nature, and large-format columns, plus up-to-date industry information. Estab. 1937. Circ. 450,000. No kill fee.

Editorial lead time 2 months. Accepts simultaneous submissions.

💲💲 VIDEOMAKER

Videomaker, Inc., York Publishing, 645 Mangrove Ave, Chico CA 95926-3946. (530)891-8410. **Fax:** (530)891-8443. **E-mail:** editor@videomaker.com. **Website:** www.videomaker.com. Monthly magazine covering audio and video production, camcorders, editing, computer video, DVDs. Estab. 1985. Circ. 57,814. Byline given. Pays on publication. No kill fee. Publishes ms an average of 4 months after acceptance. Editorial lead time 5 months. Submit seasonal material 5 months in advance. Accepts queries by mail, e-mail. Accepts simultaneous submissions. Responds in 3 weeks to queries. Sample copy and writer's Guidelines online.

NONFICTION Needs how-to, technical. Special issues: Annual Buyer's Guide in October (13th issue of the year). **Buys 34 mss/year.** Query. Length: 900-2,000 words. **Pays $100-300.** Limit agreed upon in advance.

POLITICS & WORLD AFFAIRS

💲 COMMONWEAL

Commonweal Foundation, 475 Riverside Dr., Room 405, New York NY 10115. (212)662-4200. **Fax:** (212)662-4183. **E-mail:** editors@commonwealmagazine.org. **Website:** www.commonwealmagazine.org. **Contact:** Paul Baumann, editor; Tiina Aleman, production editor. Biweekly journal of opinion edited by Catholic lay people, dealing with topical issues of the day on public affairs, religion, literature, and the arts. Estab. 1924. Circ. 20,000. Byline given. Pays on publication. No kill fee. Submit seasonal material 4 months in advance. Accepts simultaneous submissions. Responds in 2 months to queries. Sample copy free. Guidelines online.

NONFICTION Needs essays, general interest, interview, personal experience, religious. **Buys 30 mss/year.** Query with published clips. *Commonweal* welcomes original manuscripts dealing with topical issues of the day on public affairs, religion, literature, and the arts. Looks for articles that are timely, accurate, and well written. Length: 2,000-3,000 words for features. **Pays $200-300 for longer mss; $100-200 for shorter pieces.**

COLUMNS Upfronts: (750-1,000 words) brief, newsy reportorials, giving facts, information and some interpretation behind the headlines of the day; Last Word: (750 words) usually of a personal nature, on some aspect of the human condition: spiritual, individual, political, or social.

POETRY Needs free verse, traditional. *Commonweal*, published every 2 weeks, is a Catholic general interest magazine for college-educated readers. Does not publish inspirational poems. Buys 20 poems/year. Length: no more than 75 lines. **Pays 75¢/line plus 2 contributor's copies. Acquires all rights. Returns rights when requested by the author.**

💲💲 THE FREEMAN: IDEAS ON LIBERTY

1718 Peachtree Street NW, Suite 1048, Atlanta GA 30309 United States. (404)554-9980. **Fax:** (404)393-3142. **E-mail:** freeman@fee.org. **E-mail:** editor@fee.org. **Website:** fee.org. James Anderson, deputy publisher. **Contact:** B.K. Marcus, editor. **85% freelance written.** Monthly publication for the layman and fairly advanced students of liberty. Estab. 1946. Byline given. Pays on publication. No kill fee. Publishes online within weeks. Some online articles are also published in the quarterly print edition. Accepts queries by e-mail. Guidelines available on website.

NONFICTION Buys 100 mss/year. Query with SASE. Length: 3,500 words. **Pays 10¢/word.**

THE NATION

33 Irving Place, 8th Floor, New York NY 10003. **E-mail:** submissions@thenation.com. **Website:** www.thenation.com. Steven Brower, art director. **Contact:** Roane Carey, managing editory; Ange Mlinko, poetry editor. *The Nation*, published weekly, is a journal of left/liberal opinion, with arts coverage that includes poetry. The only requirement for poetry is excellence. Estab. 1865. Circ. 100,000. Guidelines online.

NONFICTION civil liberties, civil rights, labor, economics, environmental, feminist issues, politics, the arts. Queries accepted via online form. Length: 750-2,500 words. **Pays $150-500, depending on length.**

POETRY Contact: Ange Mliko, poetry editor. "Please e-mail poems in a single PDF attachment to PoemNationSubmit@gmail.com. Submissions are not accepted from June 1-September 15." Buys 6 poems/year. Submit maximum 3 poems.

💲💲 THE PROGRESSIVE

30 W. Mifflin Street, Suite 703, Madison WI 53703. (608)257-4626. **E-mail:** editorial@progressive.org. **Website:** www.progressive.org. **Contact:** Elizabeth Kunze, Office Manager. **75% freelance written.** Monthly magazine of investigative reporting, political commentary, cultural coverage, activism, interviews, poetry, and humor. It steadfastly stands against militarism, the concentration of power in corporate hands, and the disenfranchisement of the citizenry. It champions peace, social and economic justice, civil rights, civil liberties, human rights, a preserved environment, and a reinvigorated democracy. Its bedrock values are nonviolence and freedom of speech. Estab. 1909. Byline given. Pays on publication. Publishes ms an average of 6 weeks after acceptance. Accepts queries by e-mail. Accepts simultaneous submissions. Responds in 1 month to queries. Sample copy for 9x12 SASE with 4 first-class stamps or sample articles online. Guidelines online.

NONFICTION Query. Length: 500-4,000 words. **Pays $500-1,300.**

POETRY Publishes 1 original poem a month. "We prefer poems that connect up—in 1 fashion or another, however obliquely—with political concerns." **Pays $150.**

💲💲💲💲 REASON

Reason Foundation, 5737 Mesmer Ave., Los Angeles CA 90230. (310)391-2245. **Fax:** (310)390-8986. **E-mail:** bdoherty@reason.com. **Website:** www.reason.com. **30% freelance written.** Monthly magazine covering politics, current events, culture, ideas. *Reason* covers politics, culture and ideas from a dynamic libertarian perspective. It features reported works, opinion pieces, and book reviews. Estab. 1968. Circ. 55,000. Byline given. Pays on publication. Offers kill fee. Editorial lead time 2 months. Submit seasonal material 3 months in advance. Accepts queries by mail, e-mail. Accepts simultaneous submissions. Responds in 6 weeks to queries. Responds in 2 months to mss. Sample copy for $4. Guidelines online.

NONFICTION Needs book excerpts, essays, expose, general interest, humor, interview, opinion. No products, personal experience, how-to, travel. **Buys 50-60 mss/year.** Query with published clips. Length: 850-5,000 words. **Payment varies.**

CONSUMER MAGAZINES

🅢🅢 WASHINGTON MONTHLY

The Washington Monthly Co., 1200 18th St. NW, Suite 330, Washington DC 20036. **E-mail:** editors@washingtonmonthly.com. **Website:** www.washingtonmonthly.com. **50% freelance written.** Monthly magazine covering politics, policy, media. We are a neo-liberal publication with a long history and specific views—please read our magazine before submitting. Estab. 1969. Circ. 28,000. Byline given. Pays on publication. No kill fee. Publishes ms an average of 2 months after acceptance. Editorial lead time 2 months. Submit seasonal material 4 months in advance. Accepts queries by mail, e-mail, fax, phone. Accepts simultaneous submissions. Responds in 3 weeks to queries. Responds in 2 months to mss. Sample copy for 11×17 SAE with 5 first-class stamps or by e-mail. Guidelines online.

NONFICTION Needs book excerpts, essays, expose, general interest, historical, interview, opinion, personal experience, technical, first-person political. No humor, how-to, or generalized articles. **Buys 20 mss/year.** Send complete ms. Length: 1,500-5,000 words. **Pays 10¢/word.**

COLUMNS 10 Miles Square (about DC); On Political Books, Booknotes (both reviews of current political books), 1,500-3,000 words. **Buys 10 mss/year.** Query with published clips or send complete ms. **Pays 10¢/word.**

REGIONAL

ALABAMA

🅢🅢 ALABAMA HERITAGE

University of Alabama, Box 870342, Tuscaloosa AL 35487-0342. (205)348-7467. **Fax:** (205)348-7473. **E-mail:** reyno031@bama.ua.edu. **Website:** www.alabamaheritage.com. **Contact:** Susan Reynolds, associate editor. **90% freelance written.** *Alabama Heritage* is a nonprofit historical quarterly published by the University of Alabama and the Alabama Department of Archives and History for the intelligent lay reader. "We are interested in lively, well-written, and thoroughly researched articles on Alabama/Southern history and culture. Readability and accuracy are essential." Estab. 1986. Byline given. Pays on publication. No kill fee. Accepts queries by mail, e-mail. Accepts simultaneous submissions. Guidelines online.

NONFICTION "We do not publish fiction, poetry, articles on current events or living artists, and personal/family reminiscences." Query. Length: 750-4,000 words. **Pays $50-350.**

🅢 ALABAMA LIVING

Alabama Rural Electric Association, 340 TechnaCenter Dr., Montgomery AL 36117. (800)410-2737. **Website:** www.alabamaliving.com. **Contact:** Lenore Vickrey, editor; Michael Cornelison, art director. **80% freelance written.** Monthly magazine covering topics of interest to rural and suburban Alabamians. "Our magazine is an editorially balanced, informational and educational service to members of rural electric cooperatives. Our mix regularly includes Alabama history, Alabama features, gardening, outdoor, and consumer pieces." Estab. 1948. Circ. 400,000. Byline given. Pays on acceptance. No kill fee. Editorial lead time 4 months. Submit seasonal material 4 months in advance. Accepts queries by mail, e-mail. Accepts simultaneous submissions. Responds in 1 month to queries. Sample copy free.

NONFICTION Needs historical. Special issues: Gardening (March); Travel (April); Home Improvement (May); Holiday Recipes (December). **Buys 20 mss/year.** Send complete ms. Length: 500-750 words. **Pays $250 minimum for assigned articles. Pays $150 minimum for unsolicited articles.**

MOBILE BAY MONTHLY

PMT Publishing, P.O. Box 66200, Mobile AL 36660. (251)473-6269. **Fax:** (251)479-8822. **E-mail:** careers@pmtpublishing.com. **Website:** www.mobilebaymonthly.com. **Contact:** Mallory Boykin, assistant editor. **25% freelance written.** *Mobile Bay Monthly* is a monthly lifestyle magazine for the South Alabama/Gulf Coast region focusing on the people, ideas, issues, arts, homes, food, culture, and businesses that make Mobile Bay an interesting place. Estab. 1990. Circ. 10,000. Byline given. Pays on publication. No kill fee. Publishes ms an average of 4 months after acceptance. Editorial lead time 4 months. Submit seasonal material 6 months in advance. Accepts queries by mail, e-mail, fax. Accepts simultaneous submissions. Guidelines online.

NONFICTION Needs general interest, historical, how-to, interview, personal experience, photo feature, travel. Query with résumé, cover letter, and published clips. Stories must be about something along the Gulf Coast. Length: 1,200-3,000 words.

ALASKA

💲💲 ALASKA

301 Arctic Slope Ave., Suite 300, Anchorage AK 99518-3035. **E-mail:** editor@alaskamagazine.com. **Website:** www.alaskamagazine.com. **Contact:** Michelle Theall, editor; Corrynn Cochran, photo editor. **70% freelance written. Eager to work with new/unpublished writers.** Magazine published 10 times/year covering topics uniquely Alaskan. Estab. 1935. Circ. 180,000. Byline given. Pays on publication. No kill fee. Publishes ms an average of 6 months after acceptance. Submit seasonal material 1 year in advance. Accepts queries by mail, e-mail. Accepts simultaneous submissions. Responds in 2 months to queries and to mss. Sample copy: $4.99 and 9x12 SASE with 7 first-class stamps. Guidelines online.

NONFICTION Needs historical, humor, interview, personal experience, photo feature. No fiction or poetry. **Buys 40 mss/year.** Query. Length: 700-2,000 words **Pays $100-1,250**

COLUMNS Escape (gives readers a reason to get out and explore the Last Frontier); Outdoors (features a variety of Alaska outdoor subjects, including fishing, hunting, hiking, camping, birding, adventure sports, and extreme activities); Alaska History; Alaska Native Culture; all 800-1,000 words. Query.

ARIZONA

💲💲 TRENDS MAGAZINE

Trends Publishing, 5685 N. Scottsdale Rd., Suite E160, Scottsdale AZ 85250. (480)990-9007. **Fax:** (480)990-0048. **E-mail:** editor@trendspublishing.com. **Website:** www.trendspublishing.com. **Contact:** Bill Dougherty, publisher. **20% freelance written.** Monthly magazine covering society, affluent lifestyle, luxury goods and services. *Trends Magazine* has a focus on the affluent community, especially in Arizona. Estab. 1982. Circ. 45,000. Byline given. Offers 100% kill fee. Editorial lead time 2-3 months. Submit seasonal material 2-3 months in advance. Accepts queries by mail, e-mail, fax, phone. Accepts simultaneous submissions. Responds in 1 month. Sample copy free. Guidelines by e-mail.

NONFICTION Needs general interest, humor, interview, travel. Does not want technical, religious, or political. Query with published clips. Length: 700-1,200 words. **Pays $350-600.**

💲💲 TUCSON LIFESTYLE

Conley Publishing Group, Ltd., Suite 12, 7000 E. Tanque Verde Rd., Tucson AZ 85715-5318. (520)721-2929. **Fax:** (520)721-8665. **E-mail:** scott@tucsonlifestyle.com. **Website:** www.tucsonlifestyle.com. **Contact:** Scott Barker, executive editor. **90% freelance written. Prefers to work with published/established writers.** Monthly magazine covering Southern Arizona-related events and topics. Estab. 1982. Circ. 32,000. Byline given. Pays on acceptance. No kill fee. Publishes ms an average of 6 months after acceptance. Submit seasonal material 1 year in advance. Accepts queries by mail, e-mail. Accepts simultaneous submissions. Responds in 2 months to queries; in 3 months to mss. Sample copy: $3.99, plus $3 postage. Guidelines free.

NONFICTION "Avoid obvious tourist attractions and information that most residents of the Southwest are likely to know. No anecdotes masquerading as articles. Not interested in fish-out-of-water, Easterner-visiting-the-Old-West pieces." **Buys 20 mss/year. Pays $50-500.**

CALIFORNIA

💲💲 CARLSBAD MAGAZINE

Wheelhouse Media, P.O. Box 2089, Carlsbad CA 92018. (760)729-9099. **Fax:** (760)729-9011. **E-mail:** tim@wheelhousemedia.com. **Website:** www.clickoncarlsbad.com. **Contact:** Tim Wrisley. **80% freelance written.** Bimonthly magazine covering people, places, events, arts in Carlsbad, California. "We are a regional magazine highlighting all things pertaining specifically to Carlsbad. We focus on history, events, people, and places that make Carlsbad interesting and unique. Our audience is both Carlsbad residents and visitors or anyone interested in learning more about Carlsbad. We favor a conversational tone that still adheres to standard rules of writing." Estab. 2004. Circ. 35,000. Byline given. Pays on publication. Publishes ms an average of 6 months after acceptance. Editorial lead time 4 months. Submit seasonal material 6-12 months in advance. Accepts queries by mail, e-mail. Accepts simultaneous submissions. Responds in 2 months to queries and mss. Sample copy: $2.31. Guidelines by e-mail.

NONFICTION Needs historical, interview. Does not want self-promoting articles for individuals or businesses, real estate how-tos, advertorials. **Buys 3 mss/year.** Query with published clips. Length: 300-2,700 words. **Pays 20-30¢/word for assigned articles. Pays 20¢/word for unsolicited articles.**

COLUMNS Carlsbad Arts (people, places, or things related to cultural arts in Carlsbad); Happenings (events that take place in Carlsbad); Carlsbad Character (unique Carlsbad residents who have contributed to Carlsbad's character); Commerce (Carlsbad business profiles); Surf Scene (subjects pertaining to the beach/surf in Carlsbad), all 500-700 words. Garden (Carlsbad garden feature); Home (Carlsbad home feature), both 700-1,200 words. **Buys 60 mss/year.** Query with published clips. **Pays $50 flat fee or 20¢/word.**

⊗⊗ THE EAST BAY MONTHLY

Telegraph Media, 1305 Franklin St., Suite 501, Oakland CA 94612. (510)238-9101. **Fax:** (510)238-9163. **Website:** www.themonthly.com. Andreas Jones, art director. **95% freelance written.** Monthly general interest tabloid covering the San Francisco Bay Area. "We feature distinctive, intelligent articles of interest to *East Bay* readers." Estab. 1970. Circ. 62,000. Byline given. Pays on publication. No kill fee. Editorial lead time 2+ months. Submit seasonal material 3 months in advance. Accepts queries by mail, e-mail. Accepts simultaneous submissions. Responds in 1 month to queries. Responds in 1 month to mss. Sample copy for $3. Writer's guidelines for #10 SASE or by e-mail.

NONFICTION No fiction or poetry. Query with published clips. Length: 1,000-3,000 words. **Pays $100-500.**

COLUMNS First Person, 2,000 words. Query with published clips.

⊗⊗ GUESTLIFE

Desert Publications, Inc., 303 N. Indian Canyon Dr., Palm Springs CA 92262. (760)325-2333. **Fax:** (760)325-7008. **Website:** www.guestlife.com. **95% freelance written.** Annual prestige hotel room magazine covering history, highlights, and activities of the area named (i.e., *Monterey Bay GuestLife*). *GuestLife* focuses on its respective area and is placed in hotel rooms in that area for the affluent vacationer. Estab. 1979. Byline given. Pays on publication. Offers negotiable kill fee. Publishes ms an average of 9 months after acceptance. Editorial lead time 6 months. Submit seasonal material 8 months

in advance. Accepts queries by e-mail. Accepts simultaneous submissions. Responds in 1 month to queries; in 1 month to mss. Sample copy: $10.

NONFICTION Needs general interest, historical, photo feature, travel. **Buys 3 mss/year.** Query with published clips. Length: 300-1,500 words. **Pays $100-500.**

FILLERS Needs facts. **Buys 3 mss/year.** Length: 50-100 words. **Pays $50-100.**

⊗ NOB HILL GAZETTE

Nob Hill Gazette, Inc., 950 Mason St., Mezzanine Level, San Francisco CA 94108. (415)227-0190. **E-mail:** fred@nobhillgazette.com. **Website:** www.nobhillgazette.com. **Contact:** Fred Albert, editor. **95% freelance written.** Monthly magazine covering upscale lifestyles in the Bay Area. "The *Gazette* caters to the tastes and lifestyle of an upscale audience. Our main purpose is to publicize events that raise millions of dollars for local cultural programs and charities, and to recognize the dedicated volunteers who work behind the scenes. With publisher Lois Lehrman at the helm, each trendsetting issue of our monthly magazine includes about 150 photos and 15 or more local interest stories. Our features, often 'tongue-in-chic,' cover fashion, beauty, food, wine, finance, arts, travel, health, history, interiors, profiles, and much, much more." Estab. 1978. Circ. 64,000. Byline given. Pays on 15th of month following publication. Offers $50 kill fee. Publishes ms an average of 2 months after acceptance. Editorial lead time 1-2 months. Submit seasonal material 1-2 months in advance. Accepts queries by e-mail. Accepts simultaneous submissions. Responds in 2 weeks to queries; 2 months to mss. Sample copy online. Guidelines free.

NONFICTION Needs general interest, historical, interview, opinion. Does not want anything commercial (from a business or with a product to sell), profiles of people not active in the community, anything technical, anything on people or events not in the Bay Area. **Buys 75 mss/year.** Query with published clips. Length: 800-1,000 words. **Pays $150.**

COLUMNS "All our columnists are freelancers, but they write for us regularly, so we don't take other submissions relating to their topics."

⊗⊗ PALM SPRINGS LIFE

Desert Publications, Inc., 303 N. Indian Canyon, Palm Springs CA 92262. (760)325-2333. **Fax:**

(760)325-7008. **Website:** www.palmspringslife.com. **Contact:** Olga Reyes, managing editor. **80% freelance written.** Monthly magazine covering affluent Palm Springs-area desert resort communities. *Palm Springs Life* celebrates the good life. Estab. 1958. Circ. 20,000. Byline given. Pays on publication. Offers negotiable kill fee. Publishes ms an average of 3 months after acceptance. Submit seasonal material 6 months in advance. Accepts simultaneous submissions. Responds in 4-6 weeks to queries. Guidelines online.

NONFICTION Needs book excerpts, essays, interview, feature stories, celebrity, fashion, spa, epicurean. Query with published clips. Length: 500-2,500 words. **Pays $100-500.**

COLUMNS The Good Life (art, fashion, fine dining, philanthropy, entertainment, luxury living, luxury auto, architecture), 250-750 words. **Buys 12 mss/year.** Query with or without published clips. **Pays $200-350.**

🟡🟡🟡 SACRAMENTO MAGAZINE

Sacramento Magazines Corp., 231 Lathrop Way, Suite A, Sacramento CA 95815. (916)426-1720. **Website:** www.sacmag.com. Publisher: Joe Chiodo. **80% freelance written. Works with a small number of new/unpublished writers each year.** Monthly magazine with a strictly local angle on local issues, human interest and consumer items for readers in the middle to high income brackets. Prefers to work with writers local to Sacramento area. Estab. 1975. Circ. 50,000. Pays on publication. No kill fee. Publishes ms an average of 3 months after acceptance. Accepts queries by mail. Accepts simultaneous submissions. Responds in 3 months.

NONFICTION Buys 5 unsolicited features mss/year. Query. 1,500-3,000 words, depending on author, subject matter and treatment. **Pays $400 and up.**

COLUMNS Business, home and garden, first person essays, regional travel, gourmet, profile, sports, city arts, health, home and garden, profiles of local people (1,000-1,800 words); UpFront (250-300 words). **Pays $600-800.**

🟡🟡 SAN DIEGO MAGAZINE

San Diego Magazine Publishing Co., 707 Broadway, Suite 1100, San Diego CA 92101-7901. (619)230-9292. **Fax:** (619)230-0490. **E-mail:** erin@sandiegomagazine.com. **Website:** www.sandiegomagazine.com. **Contact:** Erin Chambers Smith, editor. **30% freelance written.**

Monthly magazine covering San Diego. "We produce informative and entertaining features and investigative reports about politics; community and neighborhood issues; lifestyle; sports; design; dining; arts; and other facets of life in San Diego." Estab. 1948. Circ. 55,000. Byline given. Pays on publication. Offers 25% kill fee. Publishes ms an average of 2 months after acceptance. Editorial lead time 2 months. Submit seasonal material 4 months in advance. Accepts simultaneous submissions.

NONFICTION Needs expose, general interest, historical, how-to, interview, travel, lifestyle. **Buys 12-24 mss/year.** Send complete ms. Length: 1,000-3,000 words. **Pays $250-750.**

PHOTOS State availability. Offers no additional payment for photos accepted with ms. Buys one time rights.

🟡🟡🟡🟡 SAN FRANCISCO

Modern Luxury, 55 Francisco St., Suite 100, San Francisco CA 94133. (415)398-2800. **E-mail:** preulbach@modernluxury.com. **Website:** modernluxury.com/san-francisco. **Contact:** Paul Reulbach. **50% freelance written. Prefers to work with published/established writers.** Monthly city/regional magazine. Estab. 1968. Circ. 180,000. Byline given. Pays on publication. Offers 25% kill fee. Publishes ms an average of 2 months after acceptance. Submit seasonal material 5 months in advance. Accepts simultaneous submissions. Responds in 2 months.

NONFICTION Needs interview, travel. Query with published clips. Length: 200-4,000 words. **Pays $100-2,000 and some expenses.**

CANADA/ INTERNATIONAL

🟡🟡🟡🟡 CANADA'S HISTORY

Bryce Hall, Main Floor, 515 Portage Ave., Winnipeg MB R3B 2E9 Canada. (204)988-9300, ext. 219. **Fax:** (204)988-9309. **E-mail:** editors@canadashistory.ca. **Website:** www.canadashistory.ca. **50% freelance written.** Bimonthly magazine covering Canadian history. Estab. 1920. Circ. 46,000. Byline given. Pays on acceptance. Offers $200 kill fee. Editorial lead time 4 months. Submit seasonal material 8 months in advance. Accepts queries by mail, e-mail. Accepts simultaneous submissions. Responds in 6 weeks to queries; in 2 months to mss. Guidelines online.

NONFICTION Subject matter covers the whole range of Canadian history, with emphasis on social history, politics, exploration, discovery and settlement, aboriginal peoples, business & trade, war, culture, and sport. Does not want anything unrelated to Canadian history. No memoirs. **Buys 30 mss/year.** Query with the word *query* in the subject line if using e-mail; include published clips, SASE if using postal mail. Length: 600-3,500 words. **Pays 50¢/word for major features.**

COLUMNS Currents (news items that alert readers to history-related events, community action, exhibits, trends, websites, historical research and the like), 400 words; Getaway (a history weekend getaway with 3-5 history-linked attractions), 600 words; Moment (features a singular event or incident that can be pinpointed to a day, ideally even the time of day, presented as a snapshot in time), 500 words; Your Story (readers' firsthand experiences with an historic event or personage), 1,000 words. **Buys 15 mss/year.** Query. **Pays $125.**

THE CANADIAN CO-OPERATOR

LE COOPÉRATEUR, Atlantic Co-operative Publishers, 500 St. George St., Moncton NB E1C 1Y3 Canada. **E-mail:** editor@theatlanticco-operator.coop. **Website:** www.creativecoop.ca. **Contact:** Rayanne Brennan, editor in chief. **95% freelance written.** Bimonthly, bilingual, and national online and print magazine covering co-operatives. Estab. 1933. Byline given. Pays on publication. No kill fee. Publishes ms an average of 2 months after acceptance. Editorial lead time 2 months. Submit seasonal material 2 months in advance. Accepts queries by mail, e-mail, fax. Accepts simultaneous submissions. Responds in 3 weeks to queries.

NONFICTION Needs expose, general interest, historical, interview. No political stories, economical stories, sports. **Buys 90 mss/year.** Query with published clips. Length: 500-2,000 words. **Pays 22¢/word.**

COLUMNS Health and Lifestyle (anything from recipes to travel), 800 words; International Page (co-operatives in developing countries, good ideas from around the world). **Buys 10 mss/year.** Query with published clips.

CANADIAN GEOGRAPHIC

1155 Lola St., Suite 200, Ottawa ON K1K 4C1 Canada. (613)745-4629. **E-mail:** editor@canadiangeographic. ca. **Website:** www.canadiangeographic.ca. **90% freelance written. Works with a small number of new/unpublished writers each year.** Bimonthly magazine covering Canada. "*Canadian Geographic*'s colorful portraits of our ever-changing population show readers just how important the relationship between the people and the land really is." Estab. 1930. Circ. 240,000. Pays on acceptance. Publishes ms an average of 3 months after acceptance. Submit seasonal materials 1 year in advance. Accepts queries by e-mail. Accepts simultaneous submissions. Responds in 1 month to queries.

NONFICTION Needs photo feature, profile, travel. **Buys 30 mss/year.** Query. Length: 1,500-3,000 words. **Pays 80¢/word minimum.**

DEVON LIFE

Archant South West, Newberry House, Fair Oak Close, Exeter Airport Business Park, Clyst Honiton Exeter EX5 2UL United Kingdom. (01)(3)9288-8413. **E-mail:** andy.cooper@archant.co.uk. **Website:** www.devonlife.co.uk. **Contact:** Andy Cooper, editor. "*Devon Life* is the county's number one magazine, and celebrates the best of Devon. We cover everything from food and drink and businesses to art and fashion, and everything in between, ensuring everything has a local angle." No kill fee. Accepts queries by mail, e-mail. Accepts simultaneous submissions. Sample copy online. Guidelines by e-mail.

NONFICTION Length: 500-750 words/single-page articles; 1,000-1,200 words/two-page articles. **Pays £60-75/up to 1,200 words; £40-50/up to 750 words.**

EDGE YK

Verge Communications Ltd., P.O. Box 2451, Yellowknife NT X1A 2P8 Canada. (867)445-8360. **E-mail:** editor@edgeyk.ca. **Website:** www.edgeyk.ca. **Contact:** Laurie Sarkadi, editor. Magazine published 6 times/year covering life in Yellowknife, NT, Canada. "*EDGE YK* magazine is a free publication dedicated to showcasing some of the vast creative talent within Yellowknife, Northwest Territories. We're interested in well-told first-person narrative stories, as well as pieces on the issues, ideas, and people affecting the city's past, present, and future." Estab. 2011. Circ. 5,000. Byline given. Pays on publication. Offers 50% kill fee. Publishes ms 1 month after acceptance. Editorial lead time 3 months. Submit seasonal material 3 months in advance. Accepts queries by mail, e-mail. Accepts simultaneous submissions. Responds in 1 month to queries; in 2 months to mss. Sample copy and guidelines online.

NONFICTION Needs book excerpts, essays, general interest, historical, how-to, humor, interview, nostalgic, opinion, personal experience, photo feature, profile, travel. No fiction. Query. Length: 300-2,000 words. **Pays minimum of $100 for assigned and unsolicited articles.**

COLUMNS On EDGE Opinion, any topic/slant, approximately 400-600 words. Query. **Pays $100.**

FICTION "We rarely publish fiction."

POETRY Needs free verse. "We rarely publish poetry submissions." Buys 4 poems/year. Submit maximum 1 poems. No minimum or maximum.

◐ $ $ $ $ HAMILTON MAGAZINE

Town Media, a division of Sun Media, 940 Main St. W., Hamilton ON L8S 1B1 Canada. (905)522-6117. **Fax:** (905)769-1105. **E-mail:** marc.skulnick@sunmedia.ca; erin.stanley@sunmedia.ca. **Website:** www.hamilton-magazine.com. **Contact:** Marc Skulnick, editor; Erin Stanley, deesign. **50% freelance written.** Quarterly magazine devoted to the Greater Hamilton and Golden Horseshoe area (Ontario, Canada). "Our mandate: to entertain and inform by spotlighting the best of what our city and region has to offer. We invite readers to take part in a vibrant community by supplying them with authoritative and dynamic coverage of local culture, food, fashion, and design. Each story strives to expand your view of the area, every issue an essential resource for exploring, understanding, and unlocking the region. Packed with insight, intrigue, and suspense, *Hamilton Magazine* delivers the city to your doorstep." Estab. 1978. Byline given. Pays on publication. Offers 50% kill fee. Editorial lead time 2-3 months. Submit seasonal material 2-3 months in advance. Accepts queries by e-mail. Responds in 1 week to queries and mss. Sample copy with #10 SASE. Guidelines by e-mail.

NONFICTION Needs book excerpts, essays, expose, historical, how-to, humor, inspirational, interview, personal experience, photo feature, religious, travel. Does not want generic articles that could appear in any mass-market publication. Send complete ms. Length: 800-2,000 words. **Pays $200-1,600 for assigned articles; $100-800 for unsolicited articles.**

COLUMNS A&E Art, 1,200-2,000 words; A&E Music, 1,200-2,000 words; A&E Books, 1,200-1,400 words. **Buys 12 mss/year.** Send complete ms. **Pays $200-400.**

◐ $ $ $ ∅ OUTDOOR CANADA MAGAZINE

54 St. Patrick St., Toronto Ontario M5T 1V1 Canada. (416)599-2000. **E-mail:** editorial@outdoorcanada.ca. **Website:** www.outdoorcanada.ca. **70% freelance written. Works with a small number of new/unpublished writers each year.** Estab. 1972. Circ. 90,000. Byline given. Pays on publication. Publishes ms an average of 8 months after acceptance. Submit seasonal ideas 1 year in advance. Accepts queries by mail, e-mail. Accepts simultaneous submissions. Responds in 1 month to queries. Guidelines online.

NONFICTION Needs how-to, fishing, hunting, outdoor issues, outdoor destinations in Canada. **Buys 35-40 mss/year.** Does not accept unsolicited mss. 2,500 words **Pays 75¢ to ¢1 per word.**

FILLERS Buys 30-40 mss/year. Length: 100-500 words.

◐ UP HERE

P.O. Box 1350, Yellowknife NT X1A 2N9 Canada. (867)766-6710. **Fax:** (867)873-9876. **E-mail:** editor@uphere.ca; photo@uphere.ca. **Website:** www.uphere.ca. **50% freelance written.** Magazine published 8 times/year covering general interest about Canada's Far North. We publish features, columns, and shorts about people, wildlife, native cultures, travel, and adventure in Yukon, Northwest Territories, and Nunavut. Be informative, but entertaining. Estab. 1984. Circ. 22,000. Byline given. Pays on publication. Offers 50% kill fee. Editorial lead time 6 months. Accepts queries by e-mail. Accepts simultaneous submissions. Sample copy for $4.95 (Canadian) and 9x12 SASE.

NONFICTION Needs essays, general interest, how-to, humor, interview, personal experience, photo feature, technical, travel, lifestyle/culture, historical. **Buys 25-30 mss/year.** Query. Length: 1,500-3,000 words. **Fees are negotiable.**

COLUMNS Write for updated guidelines, visit website, or e-mail. **Buys 25-30 mss/year.** Query with published clips.

COLORADO

TELLURIDE MAGAZINE

Big Earth Publishing, Inc., P.O. Box 888, Telluride CO 81435. (970)728-4245. **Fax:** (866)936-8406. **E-mail:** deb@telluridemagazine.com. **Website:** www.

telluridemagazine.com. **Contact:** Deb Dion Kees, editor in chief. **75% freelance written.** Telluride: community, events, recreation, ski resort, surrounding region, San Juan Mountains, history, tourism, mountain living. "*Telluride Magazine* speaks specifically to Telluride and the surrounding mountain environment. Telluride is a resort town supported by the ski industry in winter, festivals in summer, outdoor recreation year round, and the unique lifestyle all of that affords. As a National Historic Landmark District with a colorful mining history, it weaves a tale that readers seek out. The local/visitor interaction is key to Telluride's success in making profiles an important part of the content. Telluriders are an environmentally minded and progressive bunch who appreciate efforts toward sustainability and protecting the natural landscape and wilderness that are the region's number one draw." Estab. 1982. Circ. 70,000. Byline given. Pays 60 days from publication. Editorial lead time and advance on seasonal submissions is 6 months. Accepts queries by e-mail. Accepts simultaneous submissions. Responds in 2 weeks to queries; in 2 months to mss. Sample copy online at website. Guidelines by e-mail.

NONFICTION Needs historical, humor, personal experience, photo feature. No articles about places or adventures other than Telluride. **Buys 10 mss/year.** Query with published clips. Length: 1,000-2,000 words. **Pays $200-700 for assigned articles; $100-700 for unsolicited articles.**

COLUMNS Telluride Turns (news and current topics); Mountain Health (health issues related to mountain sports and living at altitude); Nature Notes (explores the flora, fauna, geology, and climate of San Juan Mountains); Green Bytes (sustainable and environmentally sound ideas and products for home building), all 500 words. **Buys 40 mss/year.** Query. **Pays $50-200.**

FICTION "Please contact us; we are very specific about what we will accept." Needs adventure, historical, humorous, western. **Buys 2 mss/year.** Query with published clips. Length: 800-1,200 words.

POETRY Needs Any poetry must reflect mountains or mountain living. Buys 1 poems/year. Length: 3 lines minimum. **Pays up to to $100.**

FILLERS Wants anecdotes, facts, short humor. Seldom buys fillers. Length: 300-1,000 words. **Pays up to $500.**

💲💲 **VAIL-BEAVER CREEK MAGAZINE**

Rocky Mountain Media, LLC, P.O. Box 1397, Avon CO 81620. (970)476-6600. **Fax:** (970)845-0069. **E-mail:** tkatauskas@vailmag.com. **Website:** www.vail-beavercreekmag.com. Editor: Ted Katauskas. **80% freelance written.** Semiannual magazine showcasing the lifestyles and history of the Vail Valley. "We are particularly interested in personality profiles, home and design features, the arts, winter and summer recreation/adventure stories, and environmental articles." Estab. 1975. Circ. 30,000. Byline given. Pays on acceptance. Offers 100% kill fee. Publishes ms an average of 6 months after acceptance. Editorial lead time 1 year. Submit seasonal material 1 year in advance. Accepts queries by mail, e-mail. Accepts simultaneous submissions. Responds in 1 month to queries; 2 months to mss. Guidelines free.

NONFICTION Needs essays, general interest, historical, humor, interview, personal experience, photo feature. **Buys 20-25 mss/year.** Query with published clips. Length: 500-3,000 words. **Pays 20-30¢/word.**

DELAWARE

💲💲 **DELAWARE TODAY**

Today Media, 3301 Lancaster Pike, Suite 5C, Wilmington DE 19805. (302)656-1809. **Website:** www.delawaretoday.com. **Contact:** Drew Ostroski, managing editor. **50% freelance written.** Monthly magazine geared toward Delaware people, places, and issues. "For more than 50 years, *Delaware Today* has been the lifestyle authority in the First State. The publication boasts various awards for thoughtful commentary and stunning full-color design. As the state's premier magazine, *Delaware Today* helps readers make informed decisions to enhance their lives." Estab. 1962. Circ. 25,000. Byline given. Pays on publication. Offers 50% kill fee. Publishes ms an average of 4 months after acceptance. Editorial lead time 3 months. Submit seasonal material 6 months in advance. Accepts queries by mail, e-mail. Accepts simultaneous submissions. Responds in 2 months to queries.

NONFICTION Needs historical, interview, photo feature, lifestyles, issues. Special issues: Newcomer's Guide to Delaware. **Buys 40 mss/year.** Query with published clips. Length: 100-3,000 words. **Pays $50-750.**

COLUMNS Business, Health, History, People, all 1,500 words. **Buys 24 mss/year.** Query with published clips. **Pays $150-250.**

FILLERS Needs anecdotes, newsbreaks, short humor. **Buys 10 mss/year.** Length: 100-200 words. **Pays $50-75.**

DISTRICT OF COLUMBIA

💲💲 WASHINGTON CITY PAPER

1400 Eye St. NW, Suite 900, Washington DC 20005. (202)332-2100. **Fax:** (202)332-8500. **E-mail:** mail@washingtoncitypaper.com; listings@washingtoncitypaper.com; contact@washingtoncitypaper.com; ccauterucci@washingtoncitypaper.com. **E-mail:** editor@washingtoncitypaper.com. **Website:** www.washingtoncitypaper.com. **50% freelance written.** Relentlessly local alternative weekly in nation's capital covering city and regional politics, media and arts. No national stories. Estab. 1981. Circ. 95,000. Byline given. Pays on publication. Offers kill fee. Offers 10% kill fee for assigned stories. Publishes ms an average of 6 weeks after acceptance. Editorial lead time 7-10 days. Accepts simultaneous submissions. Responds in 1 month to queries. Guidelines online.

NONFICTION Buys 100 mss/year. District Line: 800-1,500 words; Covers: 2,500-10,000 words. **Pays 10-40¢/word.**

COLUMNS Music Writing (eclectic). **Buys 100 mss/year.** Query with published clips or send complete ms. **Pays 10-40¢/word.**

💲💲💲 THE WASHINGTONIAN

1828 L St. NW, Suite 200, Washington DC 20036. (202)296-3600. **E-mail:** editorial@washingtonian.com. **Website:** www.washingtonian.com. **20-25% freelance written.** Monthly magazine. "Writers should keep in mind that we are a general interest city-and-regional magazine. Nearly all our articles have a hard Washington connection. And, please, no political satire." Estab. 1965. Circ. 160,000. Byline given. Pays on publication. No kill fee. Publishes ms an average of 3 months after acceptance. Editorial lead time 10 weeks. Accepts queries by mail, fax. Accepts simultaneous submissions. Guidelines online.

NONFICTION Needs book excerpts, expose, general interest, historical, interview, personal experience, photo feature, travel. **Buys 15-30 mss/year.** Query with published clips. **Pays 50¢/word.**

COLUMNS First Person (personal experience that somehow illuminates life in Washington area), 650-700 words. **Buys 9-12 mss/year.** Query. **Pays $325.**

FLORIDA

💲💲 EMERALD COAST MAGAZINE

Rowland Publishing, Inc., 1932 Miccosukee Rd., Tallahassee FL 32308. (850) 878-0554. **Fax:** (850) 656-1871. **E-mail:** zwolfgram@rowlandpublishing.com. **Website:** www.emeraldcoastmagazine.com. **60% freelance written.** Bimonthly lifestyle publication celebrating life on Florida's Emerald Coast. All content has an Emerald Coast (Northwest Florida) connection. This includes communities between Pensacola to Panama City. Estab. 2000. Circ. 22,000. Byline given. Pays on acceptance. No kill fee. Publishes ms an average of 3 months after acceptance. Editorial lead time 4 months. Submit seasonal material 6 months in advance. Accepts queries by mail, e-mail. Accepts simultaneous submissions. Responds in 3 months. Guidelines by e-mail.

NONFICTION Needs essays, historical, inspirational, interview, new product, personal experience, photo feature. No fiction, poetry, or travel. No general interest—be Northwest Florida specific. **Buys 5 mss/year.** Query with published clips. Length: 500-2,000 words. **Pays $100-350.**

💲 FT.MYERS MAGAZINE

And Pat llc, 52 Park Avenue E., Merrick NY 11566 United States of America. (516)652-6072. **E-mail:** ftmyers@optonline.net. **E-mail:** ftmyers@optonline.net. **Website:** www.ftmyersmagazine.com. **Contact:** Andrew Elias. **90% freelance written.** Bimonthly magazine covering regional arts and living for educated, active, successful and creative residents of Lee & Collier counties (FL) and guests at resorts and hotels in Lee County. "Content: Arts, entertainment, media, culture, travel, sports, health, home, garden, environmental issues." Estab. 2001. Circ. 20,000. Byline given. 30 days after publication. No kill fee. Publishes ms an average of 2-6 months after acceptance. Editorial lead time 2-6 months. Submit seasonal material 2-6 months in advance. Accepts queries by e-mail. Accepts simultaneous submissions. Responds in 3 months to queries and to mss. Guidelines available online on 'Contact Us' page of website.

NONFICTION Needs essays, general interest, historical, how-to, humor, interview, personal experience, travel, reviews, previews, news, informational. **Buys 10-25 mss/year.** Send complete ms. Length: 750-1,500 words. **Pays $50-150 or approximately 10¢/word.**

⬤⬤⬤ GULFSHORE LIFE

Open Sky Media, 1421 Pine Ridge Rd., Suite 100, Naples FL 34109. (239)449-4111. **Fax:** (239)431-8420. **E-mail:** dsendler@gulfshorelifemag.com. **Website:** www.gulfshorelife.com. **Contact:** David Sendler, editor in chief. **75% freelance written.** Magazine published 10 times/year for southwest Florida. Covers the workings of its natural systems, its history, personalities, culture, and lifestyle. Estab. 1970. Circ. 35,000. Byline given. Pays on publication. Publishes ms an average of 4 months after acceptance. Submit seasonal material 8 months in advance. Accepts queries by mail, e-mail, fax. Accepts simultaneous submissions.

NONFICTION Needs historical, interview. **Buys 100 mss/year.** Query with published clips. Length: 500-3,000 words. **Pays $100-1,000.**

⬤⬤ JACKSONVILLE

1261 King St., Jacksonville FL 32204. (904)389-3622. **Fax:** (904)389-3628. **E-mail:** virginia@jacksonvillemag.com. **Website:** www.jacksonvillemag.com. **Contact:** Virginia Chamlee, managing editor. **50% freelance written.** Monthly magazine covering life and business in northeast Florida for upwardly mobile residents of Jacksonville and the Beaches, Orange Park, St. Augustine and Amelia Island, Florida. Estab. 1985. Circ. 25,000. Byline given. Pays on publication. Offers kill fee. Offers 25-33% kill fee to writers on assignment. Editorial lead time 3 months. Submit seasonal material 4 months in advance. Accepts queries by e-mail. Accepts simultaneous submissions. Responds in 6 weeks to queries; in 1 month to mss. Sample copy: $5 (includes postage). Guidelines online.

NONFICTION Needs book excerpts, expose, general interest, historical, how-to, humor, interview, personal experience, photo feature, travel, commentary. **Buys 50 mss/year.** Query with published clips. Length: 1,200-3,000 words. **Pays $50-500 for feature length pieces.**

COLUMNS Business (trends, success stories, personalities), 1,000-1,200 words; Health (trends, emphasis on people, hopeful outlooks), 1,000-1,200 words;

Money (practical personal financial advice using local people, anecdotes, and examples), 1,000-1,200 words; Real Estate/Home (service, trends, home photo features), 1,000-1,200 words; Travel (weekends, daytrips, excursions locally and regionally), 1,000-1,200 words; occasional departments and columns covering local history, sports, family issues, etc. **Buys 40 mss/year. Pays $150-250.**

⬤⬤ PENSACOLA MAGAZINE

Ballinger Publishing, 41 N. Jefferson St., Suite 402, Pensacola FL 32502. **E-mail:** kelly@ballingerpublishing.com. **Website:** www.ballingerpublishing.com. Executive Editor: Kelly Oden. **75% freelance written.** Monthly magazine. *Pensacola Magazine*'s articles are written in a casual, conversational tone. We cover a broad range of topics that citizens of Pensacola relate to. Most of our freelance work is assigned, so it is best to send a résumé, cover letter and 3 clips to the above e-mail address. Estab. 1987. Circ. 10,000. Byline given. Pays at end of shelf life. Offers 20% kill fee. Editorial lead time 1 month. Submit seasonal material 6 months in advance. Accepts queries by e-mail. Accepts simultaneous submissions. Responds in 2 weeks to queries. Sample copy for $1, SASE and 1 First-Class stamp. Guidelines online.

NONFICTION Special issues: Wedding (February); Home & Garden (May). Query with published clips. Length: 700-2,100 words. **Pays 10-15¢/word.**

⬤⬤ TALLAHASSEE MAGAZINE

Rowland Publishing, Inc., 1932 Miccosukee Rd., Tallahassee FL 32308. **Website:** www.tallahasseemagazine.com. **20% freelance written.** Bimonthly magazine covering life in Florida's Capital Region. All content has a Tallahassee, Florida connection. Estab. 1978. Circ. 18,000. Byline given. Pays on acceptance. No kill fee. Publishes ms an average of 2 months after acceptance. Editorial lead time 4 months. Submit seasonal material 6 months in advance. Accepts queries by mail, e-mail. Accepts simultaneous submissions. Responds in 3 months to queries & mss. Sample copy: $4. Guidelines available by e-mail.

NONFICTION Needs book excerpts, essays, historical, inspirational, interview, new product, personal experience, photo feature, travel, sports, business, Calendar items. No fiction, poetry, or travel. No general interest. **Buys 15 mss/year.** Query with published clips. Length: 500-2,500 words. **Pays $100-350.**

GENERAL REGIONAL

⑨⑨ BLUE RIDGE COUNTRY

Leisure Media360, 3424 Brambleton Ave., Roanoke VA 24018. (540)989-6138. **Fax:** (540)989-7603. **E-mail:** krheinheimer@leisuremedia360.com. **Website:** www.blueridgecountry.com. **Contact:** Kurt Rheinheimer, editor. **90% freelance written.** Bimonthly, full-color magazine covering the Blue Ridge region. "The magazine is designed to celebrate the history, heritage and beauty of the Blue Ridge region. It is aimed at adult, upscale readers who enjoy living or traveling in the mountain regions of Virginia, North Carolina, West Virginia, Maryland, Kentucky, Tennessee, South Carolina, Alabama, and Georgia." Estab. 1988. Circ. 325,000. Byline given. Pays on publication. Offers kill fee. Offers $50 kill fee for commissioned pieces only. Publishes ms an average of 8 months after acceptance. Submit seasonal material 6 months in advance. Accepts queries by mail, e-mail. Accepts simultaneous submissions. Responds in 3-4 months to queries. Responds in 2 months to mss. Sample copy with 9x12 SASE with 6 first-class stamps. Guidelines online.

NONFICTION Needs historical, personal experience, photo feature, travel. Special issues: "The photo essay will continue to be part of each issue, but for the foreseeable future will be a combination of book and gallery/museum exhibit previews, and also essays of work by talented individual photographers—though we cannot pay, this is a good option for those who are interested in editorial coverage of their work. Those essays will include short profile, web link and contact information, with the idea of getting them, their work and their business directly in front of 425,000 readers' eyes." **Buys 25-30 mss/year.** Send complete ms. Length: 200-1,500 words. **Pays $50-250.**

COLUMNS Inns and Getaways (reviews of inns); Mountain Delicacies (cookbooks and recipes); Country Roads (shorts on regional news, people, destinations, events, history, antiques, books); Inns and Getaways (reviews of inns); On the Mountainside (first-person outdoor recreation pieces excluding hikes). **Buys 30-42 mss/year.** Query. **Pays $25-125.**

⑨ MIDWEST LIVING

Meredith Corp., 1716 Locust St., Des Moines IA 50309. **E-mail:** midwestliving@meredith.com. **Website:** www.midwestliving.com. **Contact:** Query Editor. Bimonthly magazine covering Midwestern families. Regional service magazine that celebrates the interest, values, and lifestyles of Midwestern families. Estab. 1987. Circ. 925,000. Pays 2-3 weeks after acceptance. No kill fee. Editorial lead time 1 year. Accepts queries by mail. Accepts simultaneous submissions. Sample copy: $3.95. Guidelines online.

NONFICTION Needs general interest, historical, interview, travel. Does not want personal essays, stories about vacations, humor, nostalgia/reminiscent pieces, celebrity profiles, routine pieces on familiar destinations such as the dells, the Black Hills, or Navy Pier. Query with published clips.

SOUTHERN LIVING

Time Inc. Lifestyle Group, 4100 Old Montgomery Hwy., Birmingham AL 35209. (205)445-6000. **Fax:** (205)445-6700. **E-mail:** sl_online@timeinc.com; southernliving@customersvc.com. **Website:** www.southernliving.com. **Contact:** Claire Machamer, online editor. Monthly magazine covering southern lifestyle. Publication addressing the tastes and interest of contemporary southerners. Estab. 1966. Circ. 2.54 million. No kill fee. Editorial lead time 3 months. Accepts queries by mail. Accepts simultaneous submissions. Sample copy for $4.99 at newsstands. Guidelines by e-mail.

NONFICTION Needs essays. Send ms (typed, double-spaced) by postal mail. *Southern Living* column: Above all, it must be southern. Need comments on life in this region, written from the standpoint of a person who is intimately familiar with this part of the world. It's personal, almost always involving something that happened to the writer or someone he or she knows very well. Takes special note of stories that are contemporary in their point of view. Length: 500-600 words.

⑨⑨⑨⑨ SUNSET MAGAZINE

Sunset Publishing Corp., 80 Willow Rd., Menlo Park CA 94025. (510)858-3400. **Fax:** (650)327-7537. **E-mail:** readerletters@sunset.com. **Website:** www.sunset.com. Monthly magazine covering the lifestyle of the Western states. *Sunset* is a Western lifestyle publication for educated, active consumers. Editorial provides localized information on gardening and travel, food and entertainment, home building and remodeling. Byline given. Pays on acceptance. No kill fee. Accepts simultaneous submissions. Guidelines online.

NONFICTION Needs travel. **Buys 50-75 mss/year.** Query before submitting. Freelance articles should be timely and only about the 13 Western states. Garden section accepts queries by mail. Travel section prefers queries by e-mail. Length: 550-750 words. **Pays $1/word.**

COLUMNS Building & Crafts, Food, Garden, Travel. Travel Guide length: 300-350 words. Direct queries to specific editorial department.

YANKEE

Yankee Publishing, Inc., P.O. Box 520, Dublin NH 03444-0520. (603)563-8111. **Fax:** (603)563-8298. **E-mail:** editors@yankeepub.com. **Website:** www.yankeemagazine.com. **Contact:** Joe Bills, associate editor; Heather Marcus, photo editor. **60% freelance written.** Monthly magazine covering the New England states of Connecticut, Massachusetts, Maine, New Hampshire, Rhode Island, and Vermont. "Our feature articles, as well as the departments of Home, Food, and Travel, reflect what is happening currently in these New England states. Our mission is to express and perhaps, indirectly, preserve the New England culture—and to do so in an entertaining way. Our audience is national and has one thing in common—it loves New England." Estab. 1935. Circ. 317,000. Byline given. Pays on acceptance. Offers kill fee. Editorial lead time 12 months. Submit seasonal material 1 year in advance. Accepts simultaneous submissions. Responds in 2 months to queries. Guidelines online.

NONFICTION Needs essays, general interest, interview. Does not want "good old days" pieces or dialect, humor, or anything outside New England. **Buys 30 mss/year.** Query or submit complete ms with published clips and SASE. Length: up to 2,500 words. **Pays per assignment.** Pays expenses of writers on assignment when appropriate.

GEORGIA

💲💲 GEORGIA MAGAZINE

Georgia Electric Membership Corp., P.O. Box 1707, 2100 E. Exchange Place, Tucker GA 30085. (770)270-6500. **E-mail:** laurel.george@georgiaemc.com. **Website:** www.georgiamagazine.org. **Contact:** Laurel George, editor. **50% freelance written.** "We are a monthly magazine for and about Georgians, with a friendly, conversational tone and human interest topics." Estab. 1945. Circ. 500,000. Byline given. Pays on

acceptance. No kill fee. Publishes ms an average of 6 months after acceptance. Editorial lead time 2 months. Submit seasonal material 6 months in advance. Accepts queries by mail, e-mail. Accepts simultaneous submissions. Responds in 1 month to subjects of interest. Sample copy: $2. Guidelines for #10 SASE, or by e-mail.

NONFICTION Needs general interest, historical, how-to, humor, inspirational, interview, photo feature, travel. Query with published clips. Length: 1,000-1,200 words; 800 words for smaller features and departments. **Pays $350-500.**

💲💲 KNOWATLANTA MAGAZINE

New South Publishing, Inc., 9040 Roswell Rd., Suite 210, Atlanta GA 30350. (770)650-1102. **Fax:** (770)650-2848. **E-mail:** lindsay@knowatlanta.com. **Website:** www.knowatlanta.com. **Contact:** Lindsay Penticuff, editor. **80% freelance written.** Quarterly magazine covering the Atlanta area. *KNOWAtlanta* is metro Atlanta's premier relocation guide. The magazine provides valuable information to people relocating to the area with articles on homes, healthcare, jobs, finances, temporary housing, apartments, education, county-by-county guides, and so much more. *KNOWAtlanta* puts Atlanta at its readers' fingertips. The magazine is used by executives relocating their companies, realtors working with future Atlantans, and individuals moving to the "capital of the Southeast." Estab. 1986. Circ. 192,000. Byline given. Pays on publication. Offers 100% kill fee. Editorial lead time 2 months. Submit seasonal material 2 months in advance. Accepts queries by e-mail. Accepts simultaneous submissions. Sample copy free.

NONFICTION Needs general interest, how-to, interview, personal experience, photo feature. No fiction. **Buys 20 mss/year.** Query with published clips. Length: 800-1,500 words. **Pays $100-500 for assigned articles. Pays $100-300 for unsolicited articles.**

💲💲 SAVANNAH MAGAZINE

Morris Publishing Group, P.O. Box 1088, Savannah GA 31402. **Fax:** (912)525-0611. **E-mail:** editor@savannahmagazine.com. **Website:** www.savannahmagazine.com. **Contact:** Annabelle Carr, editor; Amy Paige Condon, associate and digital editor. **95% freelance written.** Bimonthly magazine focusing on homes and entertaining covering coastal lifestyle of Savannah and South Carolina area. "*Savannah Magazine* publishes articles about people, places, and events of interest to the residents of the greater Savannah areas, as well as coastal Georgia and the South Carolina low country. We strive to provide our readers with information that is both useful and entertaining—written in a lively, readable style." Estab. 1990. Circ. 16,000. Byline given. Pays on publication. Offers 20% kill fee. Publishes ms an average of 2 months after acceptance. Editorial lead time 2 months. Submit seasonal material 4 months in advance. Accepts queries by mail, e-mail, fax. Accepts simultaneous submissions. Responds in 4 weeks to queries; 6 weeks to mss. Sample copy free. Guidelines by e-mail.

NONFICTION Needs general interest, historical, humor, interview, travel. Does not want fiction or poetry. Query with published clips. Length: 500-750 words. **Pays $250-450.**

HAWAII

❸❸❸ HONOLULU MAGAZINE

PacificBasin Communications, 1000 Bishop St., Suite 405, Honolulu HI 96813. (808)537-9500. **Fax:** (808)537-6455. **E-mail:** kristinl@honolulumagazine.com. **Website:** www.honolulumagazine.com. Michael Keany, managing editor. **Contact:** Kristin Lipman, senior art director. **Prefers to work with published/established writers.** Monthly magazine covering general interest topics relating to Hawaii residents. Estab. 1888. Circ. 30,000. Byline given. Pays about 30 days after publication. Where appropriate, kill fee of half of assignment fee. Accepts queries by mail, e-mail. Accepts simultaneous submissions. Guidelines online.

NONFICTION Needs historical, interview, sports, politics, lifestyle trends, all Hawaii-related. "We write for Hawaii residents, so travel articles about Hawaii are not appropriate." Send complete ms. determined when assignments discussed. **Pays $250-1,200.**

COLUMNS Length determined when assignments discussed. Query with published clips or send complete ms. **Pays $100-300.**

IDAHO

❸❸ SUN VALLEY MAGAZINE

Valley Publishing, LLC, 313 N. Main St., Hailey ID 83333. (208)788-0770. **Fax:** (208)788-3881. **E-mail:** adam@sunvalleymag.com; julie@sunvalleymag.com. **Website:** www.sunvalleymag.com. **Contact:** Adam Tanous, managing editor; Julie Molema, art director. **95% freelance written.** Quarterly magazine covering the lifestyle of the Sun Valley area. *Sun Valley Magazine* presents the lifestyle of the Sun Valley area and the Wood River Valley, including recreation, culture, profiles, history and the arts. Estab. 1973. Circ. 17,000. Byline given. Pays on publication. No kill fee. Publishes ms an average of 5 months after acceptance. Editorial lead time 1 year. Submit seasonal material 14 months in advance. Accepts queries by mail. Accepts simultaneous submissions. Responds in 5 weeks to queries. Responds in 2 months to mss. Sample copy for $4.95 and $3 postage. Guidelines for #10 SASE.

NONFICTION Needs historical, interview, photo feature, travel. Special issues: Sun Valley home design and architecture (spring); Sun Valley weddings/wedding planner (summer). Query with published clips. **Pays $40-500.**

COLUMNS Conservation issues, winter/summer sports, health and wellness, mountain-related activities and subjects, home (interior design), garden. All columns must have a local slant. Query with published clips. **Pays $40-300.**

ILLINOIS

❸ ILLINOIS ENTERTAINER

4223 W. Lake St., Suite 490, Chicago IL 60624. (773)717-5665. **Fax:** (773)717-5666. **E-mail:** service@illinoisentertainer.com. **Website:** www.illinoisentertainer.com. **80% freelance written.** Monthly free magazine covering popular and alternative music, as well as other entertainment (film, media) in Illinois. Estab. 1974. Circ. 55,000. Byline given. Pays on publication. Offers 50% kill fee. Publishes ms an average of 2 months after acceptance. Editorial lead time 2 months. Submit seasonal material 2 months in advance. Accepts queries by mail. Accepts simultaneous submissions. Responds in 2 months to queries. Sample copy: $5.

NONFICTION Needs expose, how-to, humor, interview, new product, reviews. No personal, confessional, or inspirational articles. **Buys 75 mss/year.** Query with published clips. Length: 600-2,600 words. **Pays $15-160.**

COLUMNS Spins (LP reviews), 100-400 words. **Buys 200-300 mss/year.** Query with published clips. **Pays $8-25.**

$ MIDWESTERN FAMILY MAGAZINE

1100 E. Corrington Ave., Peoria IL 61603. **E-mail:** jrudd@midwesternfamily.com. **Website:** www.mid-westernfamily.com. **90% freelance written.** Bimonthly magazine covering family living in Central Illinois. *Midwestern Family* is a comprehensive guide to fun, health, and happiness for Central Illinois families. Estab. 2003. Circ. 23,000. Byline given. Pays on publication. No kill fee. Publishes ms an average of 2 months after acceptance. Editorial lead time 4-6 weeks. Submit seasonal material 4-6 weeks in advance. Accepts queries by e-mail, online submission form. Accepts simultaneous submissions. Responds in 2 weeks to queries; in 4 months to mss. Sample: $1.50. Guidelines by e-mail.

NONFICTION Query. Length: 1,000-1,500 words. **Pays $50.**

COLUMNS Home; Fun; Life; Food; Health; Discovery, all 1,000-1,250 words. **Buys 40 mss/year.** Query. **Pays $100.**

$ $ NORTHWEST QUARTERLY MAGAZINE

Hughes Media Corp., 222 Seventh St., Rockford IL 61104. (815)316-2300. **E-mail:** clinden@northwest-quarterly.com. **Website:** www.northwestquarterly.com. **Contact:** Chris Linden, editor. **20% freelance written.** Quarterly magazine covering regional lifestyle of Northern Illinois and Southern Wisconsin, and also Kane and McHenry counties (Chicago collar counties), highlighting strengths of living and doing business in the area. Estab. 2004. Circ. 42,000. Byline given. Pays on publication. Publishes ms an average of 4-6 months after acceptance. Editorial lead time 6 months. Submit seasonal material 6 months in advance. Accepts queries by mail, e-mail. Accepts simultaneous submissions. Responds in 2 weeks to queries; in 2 months to mss. Sample copy and guidelines available by e-mail.

NONFICTION Needs historical, interview, photo feature, regional features. Does not want opinion, fiction, or "anything unrelated to our geographic region." **Buys 150 mss/year.** Query. Length: 700-2,500 words. **Pays $25-500.**

COLUMNS Health & Fitness, 1,000-2,000 words; Home & Garden, 1,500 words; Destinations & Recreation, 1,000-2,000 words; Environment & Nature, 2,000-3,000 words. **Buys 120 mss/year.** Query. **Pays $100-500.**

FILLERS Needs Short humor. **Buys 24 mss/year.** Length: 100-200 words. **Pays $30-50.**

INDIANA

$ $ EVANSVILLE LIVING

Tucker Publishing Group, 223 NW Second St., Suite 200, Evansville IN 47708. (812)426-2115. **E-mail:** ktucker@evansvilleliving.com. **Website:** www.evansvilleliving.com. **Contact:** Kristen Tucker, publisher and editor. **80-100% freelance written.** Bimonthly magazine covering Evansville, Indiana, and the greater area. *Evansville Living* is the only full-color, glossy, 100+ page city magazine for the Evansville, Indiana, area. Regular departments include: Home Style, Garden Style, Day Tripping, Sporting Life, and Local Flavor (menus). Estab. 2000. Circ. 50,000. Byline given. Pays on acceptance. No kill fee. Publishes ms an average of 3 months after acceptance. Editorial lead time 6 months. Submit seasonal material 6 months in advance. Accepts queries by mail, e-mail. Accepts simultaneous submissions. Sample copy for $5 or online. Guidelines by e-mail.

NONFICTION Needs essays, general interest, historical, photo feature, travel. **Buys 60-80 mss/year.** Query with published clips. Length: 200-2,000 words. **Pays $100-300.**

COLUMNS Home Style (home); Garden Style (garden); Sporting Life (sports); Local Flavor (menus), all 1,500 words. Query with published clips. **Pays $100-300.**

$ $ $ INDIANAPOLIS MONTHLY

Emmis Communications, 1 Emmis Plaza, 40 Monument Circle, Suite 100, Indianapolis IN 46204. (317)237-9288. **Fax:** (317)684-2080. **Website:** www.indianapolismonthly.com. **Contact:** Amanda Heckert, editor in chief. **30% freelance written. Prefers to work with published/established writers.** *Indianapolis Monthly* attracts and enlightens its upscale, well-educated readership with bright, lively editorial on subjects ranging from personalities to social issues, fashion to food. Its diverse content and attention to service make it the ultimate source by which the Indianapolis area lives. Estab. 1977. Circ. 50,000. Byline given. Pays on publication. Offers negotiable kill fee. Publishes ms an average of 2 months after acceptance. Editorial lead time 3 months. Submit seasonal material 3 months in advance. Accepts queries by mail. Accepts simultaneous submissions. Responds in 6 weeks to queries. Sample copy: $6.10.

NONFICTION Needs essays, expose, general interest, interview, photo feature. "No poetry, fiction, or domestic humor; no 'How Indy Has Changed Since I Left Town,' 'An Outsider's View of the 500,' or generic material with no or little tie to Indianapolis/Indiana." **Buys 35 mss/year.** Query by mail with published clips. Length: 200-3,000 words. **Pays $50-1,000.**

IOWA

$ $ THE IOWAN

Pioneer Communications, Inc., 300 Walnut St., Suite 6, Des Moines IA 50309. (515)246-0402. **E-mail:** editor@iowan.com. **Website:** www.iowan.com. **Contact:** Dan Weeks, editor. **75% freelance written.** Bimonthly magazine covering the state of Iowa. *The Iowan* is a bimonthly magazine exploring everything Iowa has to offer. Each issue travels into diverse pockets of the state to discover the sights, meet the people, learn the history, taste the cuisine, and experience the culture. Estab. 1952. Circ. 20,000. Byline given. Pays 60 days from invoice approval or publication date, whichever comes first. Offers $100 kill fee. Publishes ms an average of 3 months after acceptance. Editorial lead time 9-10 months. Submit seasonal material 6-12 months in advance. Accepts queries by mail, e-mail. Accepts simultaneous submissions. Sample copy for $4.95, plus s&h. Guidelines online.

NONFICTION Needs essays, general interest, historical, interview, photo feature, travel. Special issues: Each issue offers readers a collection of "shorts" that cover timely issues, current trends, interesting people, noteworthy work, enticing food, historical and historic moments, captivating arts and culture, beckoning recreational opportunities, and more. Features cover every topic imaginable with only 2 primary rules: (1) solid storytelling and (2) great photography potential. **Buys 30 mss/year.** Query with published clips. Length: 500-750 words for "shorts"; 1,000-1,500 words for features. **Pays $150-450.**

COLUMNS Last Word (essay), 800 words. **Buys 6 mss/year.** Query with published clips. **Pays $100.**

KANSAS

$ $ KANSAS!

1020 S. Kansas Ave, Suite 200, Topeka KS 66612-1354. (785)296-8478. **Fax:** (785)296-6988. **E-mail:** ksmagazine@sunflowerpub.com. **Website:** www.travelks.com/ks-mag. **Contact:** Andrea Etzel, editor. **90% freelance written.** Quarterly magazine emphasizing Kansas travel attractions and events. Estab. 1945. Circ. 45,000. Byline and courtesy bylines are given to all content. Pays on acceptance. No kill fee. Publishes ms an average of 1 year after acceptance. Submit seasonal material 8 months in advance. Accepts queries by mail, e-mail. Accepts simultaneous submissions. Responds in 2 months to queries. Guidelines available on website.

NONFICTION Needs general interest, photo feature, travel. Query. Length: 750-1,250 words. **Pays $200-350.** Mileage reimbursement is available for writers on assignment in the state of Kansas, TBD by assignment editor.

KENTUCKY

$ $ KENTUCKY LIVING

Kentucky Association of Electric Co-Ops, P.O. Box 32170, Louisville KY 40232. (502)451-2430. **Fax:** (502)459-1611. **E-mail:** e-mail@kentuckyliving.com. **Website:** www.kentuckyliving.com. **Contact:** Anita Travis Richter, editor. **Mostly freelance written. Prefers to work with published/established writers.** Monthly feature magazine primarily for Kentucky residents. Estab. 1948. Circ. 500,000. Byline given. Pays on acceptance. No kill fee. Publishes ms an average of 12 months after acceptance. Submit seasonal material at least 6 months in advance. Accepts queries by e-mail, online submission form. Accepts simultaneous submissions. Responds in 1 month to queries. Sample copy with SASE (9x12 envelope and 4 first-class stamps). Guidelines online.

NONFICTION Needs general interest, historical, profile. Special issues: Stories of interest include: Kentucky-related profiles (people, places, or events), business and social trends, history, biography, recreation, travel, leisure or lifestyle articles/book excerpts, articles on contemporary subjects of general public interest, and general consumer-related features. **Buys 18-24 mss/year.** Prefers queries rather than submissions. Length: 500-1,500 words. **Pays $75-935**

COLUMNS Accepts queries for Worth the Trip column. Other columns have established columnists.

$ $ KENTUCKY MONTHLY

P.O. Box 559, Frankfort KY 40602-0559. (502)227-0053; (888)329-0053. **Fax:** (502)227-5009. **E-mail:** ky-monthly@kentuckymonthly.com; steve@kentucky-monthly.com. **Website:** www.kentuckymonthly.com. **Contact:** Stephen Vest, editor. **50% freelance written.** Monthly magazine. "We publish stories about Kentucky and by Kentuckians, including stories written by those who live elsewhere." Estab. 1998. Circ. 40,000. Byline given. Pays within 3 months of publication. Yes. Publishes ms an average of 3 months after acceptance. Editorial lead time 4-12 months. Submit seasonal material 4-10 months in advance. Accepts queries by e-mail. Accepts simultaneous submissions. Responds in 1-3 months to queries; in 1 month to mss. Sample copy and writer's guidelines online.

NONFICTION Needs book excerpts, general interest, historical, humor, interview, photo feature, religious, travel, All pieces should have a Kentucky angle. **Buys 50 mss/year.** Query. Length: 300-2,000 words. **Pays $45-300 for assigned articles. Pays $50-200 for unsolicited articles.**

FICTION We publish stories about Kentucky and by Kentuckians, including stories written by those who live elsewhere." Needs adventure, historical, mainstream, Wants Kentucky-related stories. **Buys 30 mss/year.** Query with published clips. Accepts submissions by e-mail. Length: 1,000-5,000 words. **Pays $50-500.**

MAINE

$ DISCOVER MAINE MAGAZINE

10 Exchange St., Suite 208, Portland ME 04101. (207)874-7720. **E-mail:** info@discovermainemagazine.com. **Website:** www.discovermainemagazine.com. **Contact:** Jim Burch, editor and publisher. **100% freelance written.** Monthly magazine covering Maine history and nostalgia. Sports and hunting/fishing topics are also included. "*Discover Maine Magazine* is dedicated to bringing the amazing history of the great state of Maine to readers in every corner of the state and to those from away who love the rich heritage and traditions of Maine. From the history of Maine's mill towns, to the traditions of family farming and coastal fishing, 9 times a year *Discover Maine*'s stories tell of life in the cities and towns across Maine as it was years ago." Estab. 1992. Circ. 12,000. Byline given. Pays on publication. No kill fee. Publishes ms an average of 2-3 months after acceptance. Editorial lead time 3 months. Submit seasonal material 3 months in advance. Accepts queries by mail, e-mail. Accepts simultaneous submissions. Responds in 2 weeks to queries; in 1 month to mss.

NONFICTION Needs historical. Does not want poetry. **Buys 200 mss/year.** Send complete ms. Length: 500-2,000 words. **Pays $20-30.**

MARYLAND

$$ BALTIMORE

1000 Lancaster St., Suite 400, Baltimore MD 21202. (443)873-3900. **E-mail:** wmax@baltimoremagazine.net; mjane@baltimoremagazine.net; blauren@baltimoremagazine.net; iken@baltimoremagazine.net; cron@baltimoremagazine.net; wlydia@baltimoremagazine.net. **Website:** www.baltimoremagazine.net. **Contact:** Send correspondence to the appropriate editor: Max Weiss (lifestyle, film, pop culture, general inquiries); Jane Marion (food, travel); Lauren Bell (style, home, beauty, wellness); Ken Iglehart (business, special editions); Ron Cassie (politics, environment, health, sports); Lydia Woolever (calendar, events, party pages). **50-60% freelance written.** Monthly city magazine featuring news, profiles, and service articles. Estab. 1907. Circ. 70,000. Byline given. Pays within 1 month of publication. Offers kill fee in some cases. Submit seasonal material 4 months in advance. Accepts queries by mail, e-mail. Accepts simultaneous submissions. Sample copy: $4.99. Guidelines online.

NONFICTION Needs book excerpts, essays, general interest, historical, humor, new product, personal experience, photo feature, travel. Does not want anything "that lacks a strong Baltimore focus or angle. Unsolicited personal essays are almost never accepted. We've printed only 2 over the past few years; the last was by a 19-year veteran city judge reminiscing on his time on the bench and the odd stories and situations he encountered there. Unsolicited food and restaurant reviews, whether positive or negative, are likewise never accepted." Query appropriate subject editor by e-mail (preferred), or mail query with published clips. Length: 1,600-2,500 words. **Pays 30-40¢/word.** Sometimes pays expenses.

COLUMNS "The shorter pieces are the best places to break into the magazine." Up Front, 300-700 words; Hot Shots and Cameo, 800-2,000 words. Query with published clips.

MASSACHUSETTS

💲💲 CAPE COD LIFE PUBLICATIONS

Cape Cod HOME, Cape Cod ART, 13 Steeple St., Suite 204, P.O. Box 1439, Mashpee MA 02649. (508)419-7381. **Fax:** (508)477-1225. **Website:** www.capecodlife.com. **Contact.** Jen Dow, art director, Matthew Gill, editor. **80% freelance written.** Cape Cod LIFE Magazine published 7 times/year focusing on area lifestyle, history and culture, people and places, business and industry, and issues and answers for year-round and summer residents of Cape Cod, Nantucket, and Martha's Vineyard as well as nonresidents who spend their leisure time here. Cape Cod Life Magazine has become the premier lifestyle magazine for the Cape & Islands, featuring topics ranging from arts and events, history and heritage, beaches and boating as well as a comprehensive resource for planning the perfect vacation.

NONFICTION Needs book excerpts, general interest, historical, interview, photo feature, travel, outdoors, gardening, nautical, nature, arts, antiques, history, housing. **Buys 20 mss/year.** Query. Length: 800-1,500 words. **Pays $200-400.**

💲💲 CAPE COD MAGAZINE

Lighthouse Media Solutions, 396 Main St., Hyannis MA 02601. (508)534-9291. **E-mail:** editor@capecodmagazine.com. **Website:** www.capecodmagazine.com. **80% freelance written.** Magazine published 9 times/year covering Cape Cod lifestyle. "*Cape Cod Magazine* showcases the people, architecture, history, arts, and entertainment that make living and visiting Cape Cod a rich and rewarding experience. *Cape Cod Magazine* and capecodmagazine.com deliver readers the best dining experiences, most beautiful homes, enriching arts, and cultural experiences daily in a multiplatform experience that brings Cape Cod to life." Estab. 1996. Circ. 16,000. Byline given. Pays 30 days after publication. Offers 25% kill fee. Publishes ms an average of 3 months after acceptance. Editorial lead time 6 months. Submit seasonal material 1 year in advance. Accepts queries by mail, e-mail. Accepts simultaneous submissions. Responds in 3 weeks to queries; in 2 months to mss. Sample copy: $5. Guidelines by e-mail.

NONFICTION Needs book excerpts, essays, general interest, historical, humor, personal experience.

Does not want clichéd pieces, interviews, and puff features. **Buys 3 mss/year.** Send complete ms. Length: 800-2,500 words. **Pays $300-500 for assigned articles. Pays $100-300 for unsolicited articles.**

COLUMNS Last Word (personal observations in typical back-page format), 700 words. **Buys 4 mss/year.** Query with or without published clips or send complete ms. **Pays $150-300.**

💲💲 WORCESTER MAGAZINE

72 Shrewbury St., Worcester MA 01604. (508)749-3166. **E-mail:** editor@worcestermag.com; wbird@worcestermag.com. **Website:** www.worcestermag.com. **Contact:** Walter Bird, Jr., editor; Kathy Real, publisher. **10% freelance written.** Weekly tabloid emphasizing the central Massachusetts region, especially the city of Worcester. Estab. 1976. Circ. 40,000. Byline given. Pays on publication. No kill fee. Publishes ms an average of 3 weeks after acceptance. Submit seasonal material 2 months in advance. Accepts queries by mail, e-mail, fax. Accepts simultaneous submissions.

NONFICTION Needs essays, expose, general interest, historical, humor, opinion, personal experience, photo feature. **Buys less than 75 mss/year.** Length: 500-1,500 words. **Pays 10¢/word.**

MICHIGAN

💲💲 GRAND RAPIDS MAGAZINE

Gemini Publications, 549 Ottawa Ave. NW, Suite 201, Grand Rapids MI 49503. (616)459-4545. **Fax:** (616)459-4800. **E-mail:** cvalade@geminipub.com; info@geminipub.com. **Website:** www.grmag.com. *Grand Rapids* is a general interest life and style magazine designed for those who live in the Grand Rapids metropolitan area or desire to maintain contact with the community. Estab. 1964. Circ. 20,000. Byline given. Pays on publication. No kill fee. Editorial lead time 2 months. Submit seasonal material 2 months in advance. Accepts simultaneous submissions. Sample copy for $2 and SASE with $1.50 postage. Guidelines with #10 SASE.

NONFICTION Query. **Pays $25-500.**

💲💲 MICHIGAN HISTORY

The Historical Society of Michigan, 5815 Executive Dr., Lansing MI 48911. (517)332-1828. **Fax:** (517)324-4370. **E-mail:** mhmeditor@hsmichigan.org; hsm@hsmichigan.org. **E-mail:** majher@hsmichigan.org. **Website:**

www.hsmichigan.org. **Contact:** Patricia Majher, editor. Covers exciting stories of Michigan people and their impact on their communities, the nation and the world. *Michigan History* overflows with intriguing feature articles, bold illustrations and departments highlighting history-related books, travel and events 6 times each year. Bimonthly magazine, 64 colorful pages. "A thoroughly entertaining read, *Michigan History* specializes in stories from Michigan's colorful past. Within its pages, you'll learn about logging, mining, manufacturing, and military history as well as art and architecture, music, sports, shipwrecks, and more. Requires idea queries first." In addition to payment, authors receive 5 free copies of issues in which their work appears. Estab. 1917. Circ. 22,000. Byline given. Pays on publication. Publishes ms 6 months after acceptance. Editorial lead time 1 year. Accepts queries by mail, e-mail. Accepts simultaneous submissions. Guidelines for authors at www.hsmichigan.org/michiganhistory/contribute.

NONFICTION Remember the Time features (first-person, factual, personal experiences that happened in Michigan—750 words) pay $100. Other features pay $200-$400, depending on word length and cooperation in gathering photos. "We are not a scholarly journal and do not accept academic papers." **Buys 50-55/mss/year mss/year.** "When you are ready to submit a manuscript, please provide a digital copy of the text, and also list your research sources for fact-checking purposes. Include with your ms a summary of your writing experience and "in the interest of full disclosure" any relationship you have to your subject. You are expected to gather your own graphics (provided digitally and with captions, if possible) or at least suggest possible graphics." Length: 1,500-2,500 words. **Pays $150-400.**

MINNESOTA

$$ LAKE SUPERIOR MAGAZINE

Lake Superior Port Cities, Inc., P.O. Box 16417, Duluth MN 55816-0417. (218)722-5002. **Fax:** (218)722-4096. **E-mail:** edit@lakesuperior.com. **Website:** www.lakesuperior.com. **Contact:** Konnie LeMay, editor. **40% freelance written. Works with a small number of new/unpublished writers each year. Please include phone number and address with e-mail queries.** Bimonthly magazine covering contemporary and historic people, places, and current events around Lake Superior. Estab. 1979. Circ. 20,000. Byline given. Pays on publication. No kill fee. Publishes ms an average of 10 months after acceptance. Submit seasonal material 1 year in advance. Accepts queries by mail, e-mail. Accepts simultaneous submissions. Responds in 3 months to queries. Sample copy: $4.95 plus 6 first-class stamps. Guidelines online.

NONFICTION Needs book excerpts, general interest, historical, humor, interview, personal experience, photo feature, travel, city profiles, regional business, some investigative. **Buys 15 mss/year.** Prefers mss, but accepts short queries via mail or e-mail. Length: 1,600-2,000 words for features. **Pays $200-400.**

COLUMNS Shorter articles on specific topics of interest: Homes, Health & Wellness, Lake Superior Journal, Wild Superior, Heritage, Destinations, Profile, all 800-1,200 words. **Buys 20 mss/year.** Query with published clips. **Pays $75-200.**

FICTION Must be targeted regionally. Needs historical, humorous, mainstream, novel excerpts. Wants stories that are Lake Superior related. Rarely uses fiction stories. **Buys 2-3 mss/year.** Query with published clips. Length: 300-2,500 words. **Pays $50-125.**

$$$ MPLS. ST. PAUL MAGAZINE

MSP Communications, 220 S. Sixth St., Suite 500, Minneapolis MN 55402. **E-mail:** edit@mspmag.com. **Website:** www.mspmag.com. **Contact:** Kelly Ryan Kegans, executive editor. Monthly magazine covering the Minneapolis-St. Paul area. *Mpls. St. Paul Magazine* is a city magazine serving upscale readers in the Minneapolis-St. Paul metro area. Circ. 80,000. Pays on publication. Editorial lead time 3 months. Accepts queries by mail, e-mail. Accepts simultaneous submissions. Sample copy: $10.

NONFICTION Needs book excerpts, essays, general interest, historical, interview, personal experience, photo feature, travel. **Buys 150 mss/year.** Query with published clips. Length: 500-4,000 words. **Pays 50-75¢/word for assigned articles.**

MISSISSIPPI

$$ MISSISSIPPI MAGAZINE

Downhome Publications, 5 Lakeland Circle, Jackson MS 39216. (601)982-8418. **Fax:** (601)982-8447. **E-mail:** editor@mismag.com. **Website:** www.mississippimagazine.com. **Contact:** Melanie M. Ward, editor. **90% freelance written.** Bimonthly magazine covering Mississippi—the state and its lifestyles. "We are interested in positive stories reflecting Mississippi's rich traditions and heritage and focusing on the contributions the state and its natives have made to the arts, literature, and culture. In each issue we showcase homes and gardens, in-state travel, food, design, art, and more." Estab. 1982. Circ. 40,000. Byline given. Pays on publication. Offers 25% kill fee. Publishes ms an average of 6 months after acceptance. Editorial lead time 6 months. Submit seasonal material 1 year in advance. Accepts queries by mail, fax. Responds in 2 months to queries. Guidelines for #10 SASE or online.

NONFICTION Needs general interest, historical, how-to, interview, personal experience, travel. No opinion, political, sports, expose. **Buys 15 mss/year.** Query. Length: 100-1,200 words. **Pays $25-350.**

COLUMNS Southern Scrapbook (see recent issues for example), 100-600 words; Gardening (short informative article on a specific plant or gardening technique), 800-1,200 words; Culture Center (story about an event or person relating to Mississippi's art, music, theatre, or literature), 800-1,200 words; On Being Southern (personal essay about life in Mississippi; only ms submissions accepted), 750 words. **Buys 6 mss/year.** Query. **Pays $25-250.**

MISSOURI

KC MAGAZINE

Anthem Publishing, 4303 W. 119th St., Leawood KS 66209. (913)894-6923. **Website:** www.kcmag.com. **75% freelance written.** Monthly magazine covering life in Kansas City, Kansas. "Our mission is to celebrate living in Kansas City. We are a consumer lifestyle/general-interest magazine focused on Kansas City, its people, and places." Estab. 1994. Circ. 31,000. Byline given. Pays on acceptance. Offers 10% kill fee. Publishes ms an average of 3 months after acceptance. Editorial lead time 4 months. Submit seasonal material 6 months in advance. Accepts queries by mail, e-mail. Accepts simultaneous submissions. Sample copy for 8.5x11 SAE or online.

NONFICTION Needs general interest, interview, photo feature. **Buys 15-20 mss/year.** Query with published clips. Length: 250-3,000 words.

COLUMNS Entertainment (Kansas City only), 1,000 words; Food (Kansas City food and restaurants only), 1,000 words. **Buys 12 mss/year.** Query with published clips.

⊗⊗ MISSOURI LIFE

501 High St., Suite A, Boonville MO 65233. (660)882-9898. **Fax:** (660)882-9899. **E-mail:** dcawthon@missourilife.com. **Website:** www.missourilife.com. **Contact:** David Cawthon, associate editor. **85% freelance written.** Bimonthly magazine covering the state of Missouri. "*Missouri Life's* readers are mostly college-educated people with a wide range of travel and lifestyle interests. Our magazine discovers the people, places, and events—both past and present—that make Missouri a great place to live and/or visit." Estab. 1973. Circ. 96,800. Byline given. Pays on publication. Editorial lead time 6 months. Submit seasonal material 6 months in advance. Accepts queries by mail, e-mail, fax. Accepts simultaneous submissions. Responds in approximately 2 months to queries. Sample copy available for $4.95 and SASE with $2.44 first-class postage (or a digital version can be purchased online). Guidelines online.

NONFICTION Needs general interest, historical, travel, all Missouri related. Length: 300-2,000 words. **No set amount per word.**

COLUMNS "All Around Missouri (people and places, past and present, written in an almanac style); Missouri Artist (features a Missouri artist), 500 words; Made in Missouri (products and businesses native to Missouri), 500 words. Contact assistant manager for restaurant review queries.

⊗⊗ RELOCATING TO THE LAKE OF THE OZARKS

Showcase Publishing, 2820 Bagnell Dam Blvd., #1B, Lake Ozark MO 65049. (573)365-2323, ext. 301. **Fax:** (573)365-2351. **E-mail:** spublishingco@msn.com. **Website:** www.relocatingtothelakeoftheozarks.com. **Contact:** Dave Leathers, publisher. Semi-annual relocation guide; free for people moving to the area. Circ. 12,000. Byline given. Pays on publication. No kill fee. Publishes ms an average of 6 months after acceptance. Accepts queries by e-mail. Accepts simultaneous submissions. Sample copy for $8.95.

NONFICTION Needs historical. Length: 600-1,000 words.

MONTANA

⊗⊗ MONTANA MAGAZINE

Lee Enterprises, P.O. Box 8689, Missoula MT 59807. **E-mail:** editor@montanamagazine.com. **Website:**

www.montanamagazine.com. **90% freelance written.** Strictly Montana-oriented magazine, published bimonthly, that features community profiles, contemporary issues, wildlife and natural history, and travel pieces. Estab. 1970. Circ. 20,000. Byline given. Pays on publication. No kill fee. Publishes ms an average of 1 year after acceptance. Submit seasonal material 1 year in advance. Accepts queries by e-mail. Accepts simultaneous submissions. Responds in 6 months to queries. Sample copy for $5 or online. Guidelines online.

NONFICTION Needs essays, general interest, interview, photo feature, travel. Special issues: Special features on summer and winter destination points. No "me and Joe" hiking and hunting tales; no blood-and-guts hunting stories; no poetry; no fiction; no sentimental essays. **Buys 30 mss/year.** Query with samples and SASE. Length: 1,000-1,500 words. **Pays negotiable rate.**

COLUMNS Memories (reminisces of early-day Montana life), 800-1,000 words; Outdoor Recreation, 1,500-2,000 words; Community Festivals, 500 words, plus b&w or color photo; Montana-Specific Humor, 800-1,000 words. Query with samples.

NEVADA

🟢🟢 NEVADA MAGAZINE

401 N. Carson St., Carson City NV 89701. (775)687-0602. **Fax:** (775)687-6159. **E-mail:** editor@nevadamagazine.com. **Website:** www.nevadamagazine.com. **25% freelance written. Works with a small number of new/unpublished writers each year.** Bimonthly magazine published by the state of Nevada to promote tourism. Estab. 1936. Circ. 20,000. Byline given. Pays on publication. No kill fee. Publishes ms an average of 6 months after acceptance. Submit seasonal material 6 months in advance. Accepts simultaneous submissions. Responds in 1 month to queries. Sample copy available by request. Guidelines online.

NONFICTION Prefers a well-written query or outline with specific story elements before receiving the actual story. Write, e-mail, or call if you have a story that might work. Length: 500-1,500 words. **Pays flat rate of $250 or less. For web stories, pays $100 or $200 depending on the assignment.**

COLUMNS Columns include: Up Front (the latest Nevada news), Visions (emphasizes outstanding photography with extended captions), City Limits

(features destination stories for Nevada's larger cities), Wide Open (features destination stories for Nevada's rural towns and regions), Cravings (stories centered on food and drink), Travels (people traveling Nevada, sharing their adventures), History, and Events & Shows.

NEW HAMPSHIRE

🟢🟢 NEW HAMPSHIRE MAGAZINE

McLean Communications, Inc., 150 Dow St., Manchester NH 03101. (603)624-1442. **E-mail:** editor@nhmagazine.com; bcoles@nhmagazine.com; callen@nhmagazine.com. **Website:** www.nhmagazine.com. **Contact:** Rick Broussard, executive editor; Barbara Coles, managing editor; Chip Allen, creative director. **50% freelance written.** Monthly magazine devoted to New Hampshire. "We want stories written for, by, and about the people of New Hampshire with emphasis on qualities that set us apart from other states. We feature lifestyle, adventure, and home-related stories with a unique local angle." Estab. 1986. Circ. 32,000. Byline given. Pays on publication. Offers 40% kill fee. Editorial lead time 3 months. Submit seasonal material 1 year in advance. Accepts queries by mail, e-mail, fax. Accepts simultaneous submissions. Responds in 2 months to queries. Responds in 3 months to mss. Guidelines online.

NONFICTION Needs essays, general interest, historical, photo feature, business. **Buys 30 mss/year.** Send ms or query via e-mail. Length: 300-2,000 words. **Payment varies.**

FILLERS Length: 200-400 words.

NEW JERSEY

🟢🟢🟢🟢 NEW JERSEY MONTHLY

55 Park Place, P.O. Box 920, Morristown NJ 07963-0920. (973)539-8230. **Fax:** (973)538-2953. **E-mail:** kschlager@njmonthly.com. **Website:** www.njmonthly.com. **Contact:** Ken Schlager, editor. **75-80% freelance written.** Monthly magazine covering just about anything to do with New Jersey, from news, politics, and sports to decorating trends and lifestyle issues. Our readership is well-educated, affluent, and on average our readers have lived in New Jersey 20 years or more. Estab. 1976. Circ. 92,000. Byline given. Pays on completion of fact-checking. Offers

20% kill fee. Publishes ms an average of 3 months after acceptance. Editorial lead time 3 months. Submit seasonal material 6 months in advance. Accepts queries by mail, e-mail, fax, phone. Accepts simultaneous submissions. Responds in 2-3 months to queries. Guidelines online.

NONFICTION Needs book excerpts, essays, expose, general interest, historical, humor, interview, personal experience, photo feature, travel, arts, sports, politics. No experience pieces from people who used to live in New Jersey or general pieces that have no New Jersey angle. **Buys 90-100 mss/year.** Query with published magazine clips via e-mail. Length: 250-3,000 words. **Payment varies.** Pays reasonable expenses of writers on assignment with prior approval.

COLUMNS Exit Ramp (back page essay usually originating from personal experience but written in a way that tells a broader story of statewide interest), 500 words; front-of-the-book Garden Variety (brief profiles or articles on local life, 250-350 words; restaurant reviews. **Buys 12 mss/year.** Query with published clips. **Payment varies.**

FILLERS Needs anecdotes, for front-of-book. **Buys 12-15 mss/year.** Length: 200-250 words. **Payment varies.**

💲💲 THE SANDPAPER

The SandPaper, Inc., 1816 Long Beach Blvd., Surf City NJ 08008. (609)494-5900. **Fax:** (609)494-1437. **E-mail:** jaymann@thesandpaper.net; letters@thesandpaper.net; photo@thesandpaper.net. **Website:** www.thesandpaper.net. **Contact:** Jay Mann, managing editor; Gail Travers, executive editor; Ryan Morrill, photography editor. Weekly tabloid covering subjects of interest to Long Island Beach area residents and visitors. Each issue includes a mix of news, human interest features, opinion columns, and entertainment/calendar listings. Estab. 1976. Circ. 30,000. Byline given. Pays on publication. Offers 100% kill fee. Publishes ms an average of 1 month after acceptance. Submit seasonal material 3 months in advance. Accepts queries by mail, e-mail, fax, phone. Accepts simultaneous submissions. Responds in 1 month to queries.

COLUMNS Speakeasy (opinion and slice-of-life, often humorous); Commentary (forum for social science perspectives); both 1,000-1,500 words, preferably with local or Jersey Shore angle. **Buys 50 mss/year.** Send complete ms. **Pays $40.**

NEW MEXICO

💲💲 NEW MEXICO MAGAZINE

Lew Wallace Bldg., 495 Old Santa Fe Trail, Santa Fe NM 87501-2750. (505)827-7447. **E-mail:** artdirector@nmmagazine.com. **Website:** www.nmmagazine.com. **70% freelance written.** Covers areas throughout the state. "We want to publish a lively editorial mix, covering both the down-home (like a diner in Tucumcari) and the upscale (a new bistro in world-class Santa Fe)." Explore the gamut of the Old West and the New Age. "Our magazine is about the power of place—in particular more than 120,000 square miles of mountains, desert, grasslands, and forest inhabited by a culturally rich mix of individuals. It is an enterprise of the New Mexico Tourism Department, which strives to make potential visitors aware of our state's multicultural heritage, climate, environment, and uniqueness." Estab. 1923. Circ. 100,000. Pays on acceptance. 20% kill fee. Publishes ms an average of 3 months after acceptance. Submit seasonal material 1 year in advance. Accepts queries by mail. Accepts simultaneous submissions. Responds to queries if interested. Sample copy for $5. Guidelines online.

NONFICTION Submit story idea along with a working head and subhead and a paragraph synopsis. Include published clips and a short sum-up about your strengths as a writer. Considers proposal as well as writer's potential to write the conceptualized stories.

NEW YORK

💲💲 ADIRONDACK LIFE

P.O. Box 410, Rt. 9N, Jay NY 12941-0410. (518)946-2191. **Fax:** (518)946-7461. **E-mail:** aledit@adirondacklife.com; khofschneider@adirondacklife.com. **Website:** adirondacklifemag.com. **Contact:** Annie Stoltie, editor; Kelly Hofschneider, photo editor. **70% freelance written. Prefers to work with published/established writers.** Magazine, published bimonthly, that emphasizes the Adirondack region and the North Country of New York State in articles covering outdoor activities, history, and natural history directly related to the Adirondacks. Estab. 1970. Circ. 50,000. Byline given. Pays 30 days after publication. No kill fee. Publishes ms an average of 10 months after acceptance. Submit seasonal material 1 year in advance. Accepts queries by mail, e-mail. Accepts simultaneous submissions. Responds in 1 month to queries. Sample copy for $3 and 9x12 SAE. Guidelines online.

NONFICTION Special issues: Special issues: Annual Guide to the Great Outdoors (how-to and where-to articles that offer in-depth information about recreational offerings in the park); At Home in the Adirondacks (focuses on the region's signature style). Does not want poetry, fiction, or editorial cartoons. **Buys 20-25 unsolicited mss/year.** Query with published clips. Accepts queries, but not unsolicited mss, via e-mail. Length: 1,500-3,000 words. **Pays 30¢/word.**

COLUMNS Short Carries; Northern Lights; Special Places (unique spots in the Adirondack Park); Skills; Working (careers in the Adirondacks); The Scene; Back Page. Length: 1,000-1,800 words. Query with published clips. **Pays 30¢/word.**

FICTION Considers first-serial novel excerpts in its subject matter and region.

CITY LIMITS

Community Service Society of New York, 31 E. 32nd St., 3rd Floor, New York NY 10016. (212)481-8484, ext. 313. **E-mail:** editor@citylimits.org. **Website:** www.citylimits.org. **Contact:** Jarrett Murphy, executive editor and publisher. **50% freelance written.** Monthly magazine covering urban politics and policy in New York City. *City Limits* is a nonprofit online magazine focusing on issues facing New York City and its neighborhoods, particularly low-income communities. The magazine is strongly committed to investigative journalism, in-depth policy analysis, hard-hitting profiles, and investigation of pressing civic issues in New York City. Driven by a mission to inform public discourse, the magazine provides the factual reporting, human faces, data, history, and breadth of knowledge necessary to understanding the nuances, complexities, and hard truths of the city, its politics, and its people. Estab. 1976. Byline given. Pays on publication. Offers 50% kill fee. Publishes ms an average of 3 months after acceptance. Editorial lead time 2 months. Accepts queries by mail, e-mail, fax. Accepts simultaneous submissions. Responds in 1 month. Sample copy for $2.95. Guidelines free.

NONFICTION Needs book excerpts, humor, interview, opinion, photo feature. No essays, polemics. **Buys 25 mss/year.** Query with published clips. Length: 400-3,500 words. **Pays $150-2,000 for assigned articles. Pays $100-800 for unsolicited articles.**

COLUMNS Making Change (nonprofit business), Big Idea (policy news), Book Review—all 800 words; Urban Legend (profile), First Hand (Q&A)—both 350 words. **Buys 15 mss/year.** Query with published clips.

🌑🌑🌑🌑 NEW YORK MAGAZINE

New York Media, Editorial Submissions, 75 Varick St., New York NY 10013. **E-mail:** nyletters@nymag.com. **E-mail:** editorialsubmissions@nymag.com. **Website:** nymag.com. **25% freelance written.** Weekly magazine focusing on current events in the New York metropolitan area. Circ. 405,149. Pays on acceptance. Offers 25% kill fee. Submit seasonal material 2 months in advance. Accepts simultaneous submissions. Responds in 1 month to queries. Sample copy: $6.99 or on website.

NONFICTION Query by e-mail or mail. **Pays $1/word.**

🌑🌑🌑 WESTCHESTER MAGAZINE

Today Media, 2 Clinton Ave., Rye NY 10580. (914)345-0601. **Website:** www.westchestermagazine.com. **35% freelance written.** Monthly magazine covering culture and lifestyle of Westchester County, New York. *Westchester Magazine* is an upscale, high-end regional lifestyle publication covering issues specific to Westchester County, New York. All stories must have a local slant. Estab. 2001. Circ. 65,475. Byline given. Pays on publication. Offers 25% kill fee. Publishes ms an average of 5 months after acceptance. Editorial lead time 3 months. Submit seasonal material 3 months in advance. Accepts queries by mail. Accepts simultaneous submissions. Sample copy online.

NONFICTION Needs expose, general interest, interview, local service. Does not want personal essays, reviews, stories not specific to Westchester. **Buys 36 mss/year.** Query with published clips. Length: 150-5,000 words. **Pays $50-900.**

COLUMNS Our Neighbor (profile of a local celebrity), 500 words; Westchester Chronicles (short items of local interest), 300 words; County Golf (articles about the local golf scene), 500 words. **Buys 36 mss/year.** Query with published clips. **Pays $30-200.**

NORTH CAROLINA

🌑🌑 CARY MAGAZINE

Cherokee Media Group, 301 Cascade Pointe Lane, Cary NC 27513. (919)674-6020. **Fax:** (919)674-6027.

E-mail: editor@carymagazine.com. **Website:** www.carymagazine.com. **Contact:** Nancy Pardue and Amber Keister, editors. **40% freelance written.** "Lifestyle publication for the affluent communities of Cary, Apex, Morrisville, Holly Springs, and Fuquay-Varina. Our editorial objective is to entertain, enlighten, and inform our readers with unique and engaging editorial and vivid photography." Publishes 8 times/year. Estab. 2004. Circ. 18,000. Byline given. Kill fee negotiated. Editorial lead time 3 months. Submit seasonal material 3 months in advance. Accepts queries by mail, e-mail. Accepts simultaneous submissions. Responds in 2-4 weeks to queries; in 1 month to mss. Sample copy: $4.95. Guidelines free.

NONFICTION Needs historical, inspirational, interview, personal experience. Don't submit articles with no local connection. **Buys 2 mss/year.** Query with published clips.

💲💲 CHARLOTTE MAGAZINE

Morris Visitor Publications, 214 W. Tremont Ave., Suite 303, Charlotte NC 28203. (704)335-7181. **Fax:** (704)335-3757. **E-mail:** richard.thurmond@charlottemagazine.com. **Website:** www.charlottemagazine.com. **Contact:** Richard Thurmond, publisher. **75% freelance written.** Monthly magazine covering Charlotte life. This magazine tells its readers things they didn't know about Charlotte in an interesting, entertaining, and sometimes provocative style. Circ. 40,000. Byline given. Pays within 30 days of acceptance. Offers 25% kill fee. Publishes ms an average of 3 months after acceptance. Editorial lead time 3 months. Submit seasonal material 6 months in advance. Accepts queries by mail, e-mail. Accepts simultaneous submissions. Responds in 6 months to mss. Sample copy for $6.

NONFICTION Needs book excerpts, expose, general interest, interview, photo feature, travel. **Buys 35-50 mss/year.** Query with published clips. Length: 200-3,000 words. **Pays 20-40¢/word.**

COLUMNS Buys 35-50 mss/year. Pays 20-40¢/word

💲💲 GO MAGAZINE

AAA Carolinas, 6600 AAA Dr., Charlotte NC 28212. **Fax:** (704)569-7815. **E-mail:** regreene@mailaaa.com. **Website:** carolinas.aaa.com/sites/gomagazine. **Contact:** Rebecca Greene, editor. **20% freelance written.** "*Go Magazine* is a bimonthly lifestyle and travel-focused magazine written and distributed exclusively to AAA members in the Carolinas. Every issue of *Go Magazine* includes features on domestic and international traveldestinations, events throughout the Carolinas, and consumer information regarding automobiles, insurance, safety, and health." Estab. 1922. Circ. 1.9 million. Byline given. Pays on publication. No kill fee. Editorial lead time 2 months. Accepts queries by mail, e-mail. Accepts simultaneous submissions. Responds in 4-6 weeks. Sample copy online. Writer's guidelines by e-mail.

NONFICTION Query. Length: 750-1,000 words.

💲💲 WAKE LIVING

Weiss and Hughes Publishing, 189 Wind Chime Ct., Suite 104, Raleigh NC 27615. (919)870-1722. **Fax:** (919)719-5260. **Website:** www.wakeliving.com. **Contact:** Stuart Weiss, president and publisher. **50% freelance written.** Quarterly magazine covering lifestyle issues in Wake County, North Carolina. "We cover issues important to residents of Wake County. We are committed to improving our readers' overall quality of life and keeping them informed of the lifestyle amenities here." Estab. 2003. Circ. 40,000. Byline given. Pays within 30 days of publication. Offers 25% kill fee. Publishes ms an average of 2 months after acceptance. Editorial lead time 2-3 months. Submit seasonal material 6 months in advance. Accepts queries by mail, e-mail. Accepts simultaneous submissions. Responds in 2-4 weeks to queries. Sample copy online. Guidelines online.

NONFICTION Needs general interest, historical, how-to, inspirational, interview, personal experience, photo feature, technical, travel. Does not want opinion pieces, political topics, religious articles. Query. Length: 600-1,200 words. **Pays 35¢/word. Pay is per article and varies by complexity of assignment.**

COLUMNS Around Town (local lifestyle topics); Hometown Stories, 600 words; Travel (around North Carolina); Home Interiors/Landscaping, all 1,000 words. Restaurants (local restaurants, fine dining), 600-1,000 words. **Buys 20-25 mss/year.** Query. **Pays 35¢/word. Pay is per article and varies by complexity of assignment.**

OHIO

💲💲 AKRON LIFE

Baker Media Group, 1653 Merriman Rd., Suite 116, Akron OH 44313. (330)253-0056. **Fax:** (330)253-5868. **E-mail:** info@bakermediagroup.com; editor@bakermediagroup.com; acymerman@bakermediagroup.com. **Website:** www.akronlife.com. **Contact:** Abby Cymerman, managing editor. **10% freelance written.** Monthly regional magazine covering Summit, Stark, Portage and Medina counties. "*Akron Life* is a monthly lifestyles publication committed to providing information that enhances and enriches the experience of living in or visiting Akron and the surrounding region of Summit, Portage, Medina and Stark counties. Each colorful, thoughtfully designed issue profiles interesting places, personalities and events in the arts, sports, entertainment, business, politics and social scene. We cover issues important to the Greater Akron area and significant trends affecting the lives of those who live here." Estab. 2002. Circ. 15,000. Byline given. Pays on publication. Offers 50% kill fee. Publishes ms an average of 4-6 months after acceptance. Editorial lead time 2+ months. Submit seasonal material 6 months in advance. Accepts queries by mail, e-mail, fax. Accepts simultaneous submissions. Sample copy free. Guidelines free.

NONFICTION Needs essays, general interest, historical, how-to, humor, interview, photo feature, travel. Query with published clips. Length: 300-2,000 words. **Pays $0.10 max/word for assigned and unsolicited articles.**

💲💲💲 CINCINNATI MAGAZINE

Emmis Publishing Corp., 441 Vine St., Suite 200, Cincinnati OH 45202-2039. (513)421-4300. **Fax:** (513)562-2746. **E-mail:** rjsmith@cincinnatimagazine.com; jwilliams@cincinnatimagazine.com; amanda@cincinnatimagazine.com; akonermann@cincinnatimagazine.com. **Website:** www.cincinnatimagazine.com. **Contact:** Jay Stowe, editor in chief; Amanda Boyd Walters, director of editorial operations. Monthly magazine emphasizing Cincinnati living. Circ. 38,000. Byline given. Pays on publication. Offers kill fee only on assigned pieces. Accepts queries by mail, e-mail. Accepts simultaneous submissions. Send SASE for writer's guidelines; view content on magazine website.

NONFICTION Buys 12 mss/year. Query. Length: 2,500-3,500 words. **Pays $500-1,000.**

COLUMNS Cincinnati media, arts and entertainment, people, politics, sports, business, regional. Length: 1,500-2,000 words. **Buys 10-15 mss/year.** Query. **Pays $300-$400.**

💲💲💲 CLEVELAND MAGAZINE

City Magazines, Inc., 1422 Euclid Ave., Suite 730, Cleveland OH 44115. (216)771-2833. **Fax:** (216)781-6318. **E-mail:** gleydura@clevelandmagazine.com; miller@clevelandmagazine.com. **Website:** www.clevelandmagazine.com. **Contact:** Kristen Miller, design director; Steve Gleydura, editor. **60% freelance written. Mostly by assignment.** Monthly magazine with a strong Cleveland/Northeast Ohio angle. Estab. 1972. Circ. 50,000. Byline given. Pays on publication. No kill fee. Publishes ms an average of 3 months after acceptance. Editorial lead time 6 months. Submit seasonal material 8 months in advance. Accepts queries by mail, e-mail, fax. Accepts simultaneous submissions. Responds in 2 months to queries.

NONFICTION Needs general interest, historical, humor, interview, travel, home and garden. Query with published clips. Length: 800-4,000 words. **Pays $250-1,200.**

COLUMNS Talking Points (opinion or observation-driven essay), approximately 1,000 words. Query with published clips. **Pays $300.**

💲💲💲 OHIO MAGAZINE

Great Lakes Publishing Co., 1422 Euclid Ave., Suite 730, Cleveland OH 44115. (216)771-2833. **E-mail:** jvickers@ohiomagazine.com. **Website:** www.ohiomagazine.com. **Contact:** Jim Vickers, editor. **50% freelance written.** "*Ohio Magazine* serves energetic and involved Ohioans by providing award-winning stories and pictures of Ohio's most interesting people, arts, entertainment, history, homes, dining, family life, festivals, and regional travel. We capture the beauty, the adventure, and the fun of life in the Buckeye State." Estab. 1978. Circ. 40,000. Byline given. Pays on publication. 20% kill fee. Publishes ms an average of 6 months after acceptance. Submit seasonal material 6 months in advance. Accepts queries by mail, e-mail. Accepts simultaneous submissions. Responds in 3 months to queries; in 3 months to mss. Sample copy: $3.95 and 9x12 SAE or online. Guidelines online.

NONFICTION Query with résumé and at least 3 published clips. Length: 1,000-3,000 words. **Pays $300-1,200.**

OKLAHOMA

💲💲 INTERMISSION

Langdon Publishing, 1603 S. Boulder, Tulsa OK 74119. **E-mail:** nbizjack@cityoftulsa.org. **Website:** www.tulsapac.com. **Contact:** Nancy Bizjack, editor. **30% free-**

lance written. Monthly magazine covering events held at the Tulsa Performing Arts Center. "We feature profiles of entertainers appearing at our center, Q&As, stories on the events, and entertainers slated for the Tulsa PAC." Byline given. Pays on publication. Offers 50% kill fee. Publishes ms an average of 1 month after acceptance. Editorial lead time 2 months. Submit seasonal material 2 months in advance. Accepts queries by mail, e-mail. Accepts simultaneous submissions. Responds in 2 weeks to queries. Sample copy online. Guidelines by e-mail.

NONFICTION Needs general interest, interview. Does not want personal experience articles. **Buys 35 mss/year.** Query with published clips. Length: 600-1,400 words. **Pays $100-200.**

✪$ OKLAHOMA TODAY

P.O. Box 1468, Oklahoma City OK 73101-1468. (405)230-8450. **Fax:** (405)230-8650. **E-mail:** editorial@travelok.com. **Website:** www.oklahomatoday.com. **Contact:** Nathan Gunter, managing editor; Megan Rossman, photography editor. **80% freelance written. Works with approximately 25 new/unpublished writers each year.** Bimonthly magazine covering people, places, and things of Oklahoma. "We are interested in showing off the best Oklahoma has to offer; we're pretty serious about our travel slant but regularly run history, nature, and personality profiles." Estab. 1956. Circ. 35,000. Byline given. Pays on publication. No kill fee. Publishes ms an average of 6 months after acceptance. Submit seasonal material 1 year in advance. Accepts queries by mail, e-mail. Accepts simultaneous submissions. Responds in 4 months to queries. Sample copy for $4.95 and 9x12 SASE or online.

NONFICTION Needs book excerpts, essays, general interest, historical, interview, photo feature, profile, travel. Special issues: Annual food issue, annual western heritage issue (featuring Native American and cowboy topics). No phone queries. **Buys 20-40 mss/year.** Query with published clips. Length: 250-3,000 words. **Pays $25-750.**

OREGON

✪$ OREGON COAST

4969 Hwy. 101 N, Suite 2, Florence OR 97439. (800)348-8401. **E-mail:** alispooner@gmail.com. **Website:** www.northwestmagazines.com. **Contact:** Alicia Spooner. **65% freelance written.** Bimonthly magazine cover-

ing the Oregon Coast. Estab. 1982. Circ. 50,000. Byline given. Pays after publication. Offers 33% (on assigned stories only, not on stories accepted on spec) kill fee. Publishes ms an average of up to 1 year after acceptance. Submit seasonal material 6 months in advance. Accepts queries by mail, e-mail. Accepts simultaneous submissions. Responds in 3 months to queries. Sample copy for $4.50. Guidelines available on website.

NONFICTION Buys 55 mss/year. Query with published clips. Length: 500-1,500 words. **Pays $75-350, plus 2 contributor copies.**

PENNSYLVANIA

✪$ MAIN LINE TODAY

Today Media, Inc., 4645 West Chester Pike, Newtown Square PA 19073. (610)325-4630. **Fax:** (610)325-4636. **E-mail:** hrowland@mainlinetoday.com; tbehan@mainlinetoday.com; ilynch@mainlinetoday.com. **Website:** www.mainlinetoday.com. **Contact:** Hobart Rowland, editor in chief; Tara Behan, senior editor; Ingrid Lynch, art director. **60% freelance written.** Monthly magazine serving Philadelphia's main line and western suburbs. *Main Line Today*'s high-quality print and electronic media provide authoritative, current and entertaining information on local lifestyle trends, while examining the people, issues and institutions that shape life in Philadelphia's western suburbs. Estab. 1996. Circ. 20,000. Byline given. Pays on publication. Offers 25% kill fee. Publishes ms an average of 3 months after acceptance. Editorial lead time 5 months. Submit seasonal material 5 months in advance. Accepts queries by fax. Accepts simultaneous submissions. Responds in 2 weeks to queries. Responds in 1 month to mss. Sample copy free. Guidelines free.

NONFICTION Needs book excerpts, historical, how-to, humor, interview, opinion, photo feature, travel. Special issues: Health & Wellness Guide (September and March). Query with published clips. Length: 400-3,000 words. **Pays $125-650.**

COLUMNS Profile (local personality); Neighborhood (local people/issues); End of the Line (essay/humor); Living Well (health/wellness), all 1,600 words. **Buys 50 mss/year.** Query with published clips. **Pays $125-350.**

✪$ PENNSYLVANIA

Pennsylvania Magazine Co., P.O. Box 755, Camp Hill PA 17001-0755. (717)697-4660. **E-mail:** editor@pa-mag.com. **Website:** www.pa-mag.com. **Contact:** Matt Holliday, editor. **90% freelance written.** Bimonthly magazine covering people, places, events, and history in Pennsylvania. Estab. 1981. Circ. 30,000. Byline given. Pays on acceptance except for articles (by authors unknown to us) sent on speculation. Offers 25% kill fee for assigned articles. Publishes ms an average of 9 months after acceptance. Submit seasonal material at least 9 months in advance. Accepts queries by mail, e-mail. Accepts simultaneous submissions. Responds in 4-6 weeks to queries. Sample copy free. Guidelines for #10 SASE or by e-mail.

NONFICTION Needs essays, general interest, historical, photo feature, profile, travel. Nothing on Amish topics, hunting, or skiing. **Buys 75-120 mss/year.** Query. Length: 750-2,500 words. **Pays 15¢/word.**

COLUMNS Round Up (short items about people, unusual events, museums, historical topics/events, family and individually owned consumer-related businesses), 250-1,300 words; Town and Country (items about people or events illustrated with photos or commissioned art), 500 words. Include SASE. Query. **Pays 15¢/word.**

🟢🟢 PENNSYLVANIA HERITAGE

The Pennsylvania Heritage Foundation, Commonwealth Keystone Bldg., Plaza Level, 400 North St., Harrisburg PA 17120. (717)787-2407. **Fax:** (717)346-9099. **Website:** www.paheritage.org. **Contact:** Kyle Weaver, editor. **75% freelance written. Prefers to work with published/established writers.** Quarterly magazine covering history and culture in Pennsylvania. *Pennsylvania Heritage* introduces readers to Pennsylvania's rich culture and historic legacy; educates and sensitizes them to the value of preserving that heritage; and entertains and involves them in such a way as to ensure that Pennsylvania's past has a future. The magazine is intended for intelligent lay readers. Estab. 1974. Circ. 10,000. Byline given. Pays on publication. Publishes ms an average of 1 year after acceptance. Accepts queries by mail, e-mail. Accepts simultaneous submissions. Responds in 10 weeks to queries. Responds in 8 months to mss. Sample copy for $5 and 9x12 SAE or online. Guidelines for #10 SASE.

NONFICTION No articles that do not relate to Pennsylvania history or culture. **Buys 20-24 mss/year.** Prefers to see mss with suggested illustrations. Considers freelance submissions that are shorter in length; pictorial/photographic essays; biographies of famous (and not-so-famous) Pennsylvanians; and interviews with individuals who have helped shape, make, and preserve the Keystone State's history and heritage. Length: 2,000-3,500 words. **Pays $100-500.**

🟢 SUSQUEHANNA LIFE MAGAZINE

217 Market St., Lewisburg PA 17837 USA. (800)232-1670. **Fax:** (570)524-7796. **E-mail:** susquehannalife@gmail.com. **Website:** www.susquehannalife.com. **80% freelance written.** Quarterly magazine covering Central Pennsylvania lifestyle. Estab. 1993. Circ. 45,000. Byline given. Within two weeks after publication. Offers 50% kill fee. Publishes ms an average of 6-9 months after acceptance. Editorial lead time 3-6 months. Submit seasonal material 4-6 months in advance. Accepts queries by e-mail. Responds in 4-6 weeks to queries. Responds in 1-3 months to mss. Sample copy for $4.95, plus 5 first-class stamps. Guidelines available for #10 SASE.

NONFICTION Needs book excerpts, essays, general interest, historical, how-to, inspirational, interview, nostalgic, photo feature, travel. Does not want fiction. **Buys 30-40 mss/year.** Query or send complete ms. Length: 800 words. **Pays $75-125.**

POETRY Must have a Central Pennsylvania angle.

SOUTH CAROLINA

CHARLESTON MAGAZINE

P.O. Box 1794, Mt. Pleasant SC 29465. (843)971-9811 or (888)242-7624. **E-mail:** dshankland@charlestonmag.com; anna@charlestonmag.com. **Website:** www.charlestonmag.com. **Contact:** Darcy Shankland, editor in chief; Anna Evans, managing editor. **80% freelance written.** Monthly magazine covering current issues, events, arts and culture, leisure pursuits, travel, and personalities, as they pertain to the city of Charleston and surrounding areas. Estab. 1972. Circ. 25,000. Byline given. Pays 1 month after publication. No kill fee. Submit seasonal material 4 months in advance. Accepts queries by mail, e-mail, fax. Accepts simultaneous submissions. Sample copies may be ordered at cover price from office. Guidelines for #10 SASE.

NONFICTION Needs general interest, humor, interview, opinion, photo feature, travel, food, architecture, sports, current events/issues, art. Not interested in "Southern nostalgia" articles or gratuitous history pieces. **Buys 40 mss/year.** Query with published clips and SASE. Length: 150-1,500 words. **Payment negotiated.**

COLUMNS Channel Markers (general local interest), 50-400 words; Local Seen (profile of local interest), 500 words; In Good Taste (restaurants and culinary trends in the city), 1,000-1,200 words, plus recipes; Chef at Home (profile of local chefs), 1,200 words, plus recipes; On the Road (travel opportunities near Charleston), 1,000-1,200 words; Southern View (personal experience about Charleston life), 750 words; Doing Business (profiles of exceptional local businesses and entrepreneurs), 1,000-1,200 words; Native Talent (local profiles), 1,000-1,200 words; Top of the Shelf (reviews of books with Southern content or by a Southern author), 750 words.

💲💲 HILTON HEAD MONTHLY

Monthly Media LLC, P.O. Box 5926, Hilton Head Island SC 29938. (843)842-6988, ext. 230. **E-mail:** lance@hiltonheadmonthly.com. **Website:** www.hiltonheadmonthly.com. **Contact:** Lance Hanlin, editor in chief. **75% freelance written.** Monthly magazine covering the people, business, community, environment, and lifestyle of Hilton Head, SC, and the surrounding Lowcountry. "Our mission is to offer lively, fresh writing about Hilton Head Island, an upscale, environmentally conscious, and intensely proactive resort community on the coast of South Carolina." Circ. 35,000. Byline given. Pays on publication. Offers 50% kill fee. Publishes ms an average of 6 months after acceptance. Editorial lead time 3 months. Submit seasonal material 4 months in advance. Accepts queries by mail, e-mail. Accepts simultaneous submissions. Responds in 1 week to queries; in 4 months to mss. Sample copy: $3.

NONFICTION Needs general interest, how-to, humor, opinion, personal experience, travel. "Everything is local, local, local, so we're especially interested in profiles of notable residents (or those with Lowcountry ties) and original takes on home design/maintenance, environmental issues, entrepreneurship, health, sports, arts and entertainment, humor, travel, and volunteerism. We like to see how national trends/issues play out on a local level." **Buys 225-250 mss/year.** Query with published clips.

COLUMNS News; Business; Lifestyles (hobbies, health, sports, etc.); Home; Around Town (local events, charities, and personalities); People (profiles, weddings, etc.). Query with synopsis. **Pays 20¢/word.**

TENNESSEE

💲💲 MEMPHIS

Contemporary Media, 460 Tennessee St., Suite 200, Memphis TN 38103. (901)521-9000. **Fax:** (901)521-0129. **E-mail:** murtaugh@memphismagazine.com. **Website:** www.memphismagazine.com. **Contact:** Frank Murtaugh, managing editor. **30% freelance written. Works with a small number of new/unpublished writers.** Monthly magazine covering Memphis and the local region. Our mission is to provide Memphis with a colorful and informative look at the people, places, lifestyles and businesses that make the Bluff City unique. Estab. 1976. Circ. 24,000. No byline given. Pays on publication. Submit seasonal material 3 months in advance. Accepts queries by mail, e-mail, fax. Accepts simultaneous submissions.

NONFICTION Needs essays, general interest, historical, interview, photo feature, travel, Interiors/exteriors, local issues and events. Special issues: Restaurant Guide and City Guide. **Buys 20 mss/year.** Query with published clips. Length: 500-3,000 words. **Pays 10-30¢/word.**

FICTION One story published annually as part of contest. Open only to those within 150 miles of Memphis. See website for details.

💲💲 MEMPHIS DOWNTOWNER MAGAZINE

Downtown Productions, Inc., 408 S. Front St., Suite 109, Memphis TN 38103. (901)525-7118. **Fax:** (901)525-7128. **E-mail:** editor@memphisdowntowner.com. **Website:** www.memphisdowntowner.com. **Contact:** Terre Gorham, editor. **50% freelance written.** Monthly magazine covering features on positive aspects with a Memphis tie-in, especially to downtown. "We feature people, companies, nonprofits, and other issues that the general Memphis public would find interesting, entertaining, and informative. All editorial focuses on the positives Memphis has. No negative commentary or personal judgements. Controversial subjects should be treated fairly and balanced without bias." Estab. 1991. Circ. 30,000. Byline given. Pays on 15th of month in which assignment is published. Offers 25% kill fee. Publishes ms an average of 2-6 months after acceptance. Editorial lead time 3-6 months. Submit seasonal material 3-6 months in advance. Accepts queries by mail, e-mail. Responds in 2 weeks to queries. Guidelines by e-mail.

CONSUMER MAGAZINES

NONFICTION Needs general interest, historical, how-to, humor, interview, personal experience, photo feature. **Buys 40-50 mss/year.** Query with published clips. Length: 600-2,000 words. **Pays scales vary depending on scope of assignment, but typically runs 15¢/word.**

COLUMNS So It Goes (G-rated humor), 600-800 words; Discovery 901 (Memphis one-of-a-kinds), 1,000-1,200 words. **Buys 6 mss/year.** Query with published clips. **Pays $100-150.**

FILLERS "Unusual, interesting, or how-to or what to look for appealing to a large, general audience."

TEXAS

$ HILL COUNTRY SUN

TD Austin Lane, Inc., 100 Commons Rd., Suite 7, #319, Dripping Springs TX 78620. (512)484-9716. **E-mail:** melissa@hillcountrysun.com. **Website:** www.hillcountrysun.com. **Contact:** Melissa Maxwell Ball, editor. **75% freelance written.** Monthly tabloid covering traveling in the Central Texas Hill Country. Publishes stories of interesting people, places, and events in the Central Texas Hill Country. Estab. 1990. Circ. 34,000. Byline given. Pays on acceptance. Publishes ms an average of 2 months after acceptance. Editorial lead time 1 month. Submit seasonal material 2 months in advance. Accepts queries by e-mail. Accepts simultaneous submissions. Responds in 1 week to queries. Sample copy free. Guidelines online.

NONFICTION Needs interview, travel. No first-person articles. **Buys 50 mss/year.** Query. Length: 600-800 words. **Pays $60 minimum.**

$$$ TEXAS HIGHWAYS

P.O. Box 141009, Austin TX 78714-1009. (800)839-4997. **E-mail:** letters05@texashighways.com. **Website:** www.texashighways.com. **70% freelance written.** Monthly magazine encourages travel within the state and tells the Texas story to readers around the world. Estab. 1974. Circ. 250,000. Pays on acceptance. No kill fee. Publishes ms an average of 1 year after acceptance. Accepts queries by mail. Accepts simultaneous submissions. Responds in 2 months to queries. Guidelines online.

NONFICTION Query with description, published clips, additional background materials (charts, maps, etc.) and SASE. Length: 1,200-1,500 words. **Pays 40-50¢/word.**

$$$$ TEXAS MONTHLY

Emmis Publishing LP, P.O. Box 1569, Austin TX 78767. (512)320-6900. **Fax:** (512)476-9007. **E-mail:** bsweany@texasmonthly.com. **Website:** www.texasmonthly.com. **Contact:** Brian D. Sweany, editor; Leslie Baldwin, photo editor; Stacy Hollister, director of editorial operations. **10% freelance written.** Monthly magazine covering Texas. Estab. 1973. Circ. 300,000. Byline given. Pays on acceptance, $1/word and writer's expenses. Publishes ms an average of 1-3 months after acceptance. Editorial lead time 2 months. Submit seasonal material 3 months in advance. Accepts queries by mail, e-mail, fax, online submission form. Responds in 6-8 weeks to queries and mss. Guidelines online.

NONFICTION Contact: John Broders, associate editor (jbroders@texasmonthly.com). Needs book excerpts, essays, expose, general interest, interview, personal experience, photo feature, travel. Does not want articles without a Texas connection. Query. Length: 2,000-5,000 words.

$$ TEXAS PARKS & WILDLIFE

4200 Smith School Rd., Bldg. D, Austin TX 78744. (800)937-9393. **Fax:** (512)389-8397. **E-mail:** magazine@tpwd.texas.gov. **Website:** www.tpwmagazine.com. **20% freelance written.** Monthly magazine featuring articles about "Texas hunting, fishing, birding, outdoor recreation, game and nongame wildlife, state parks, environmental issues." All articles must be about Texas. Estab. 1942. Circ. 150,000. Byline given. Pays on acceptance. Offers kill fee. Negotiable. Publishes ms an average of 4 months after acceptance. Accepts queries by e-mail. Accepts simultaneous submissions. Responds in 1 month to queries; 3 months to mss. Sample copy and guidelines online.

NONFICTION Needs how-to, photo feature, travel. **Buys 20 mss/year.** Query with published clips; follow up by e-mail 1 month after submitting query. Length: 500-2,500 words. **Pays per article content.**

VERMONT

$$ VERMONT LIFE MAGAZINE

One National Life Dr., 6th Floor, Montpelier VT 05620. (802)828-3241. **Fax:** (802)828-3366. **E-mail:** editors@vtlife.com. **Website:** www.vermontlife.com. **Contact:** Bill Anderson, managing editor. **90% free-**

lance written. **Prefers to work with published/established writers.** Quarterly magazine. "We read all story ideas submitted, but we cannot reply individually to each one. If we want to pursue a given manuscript or idea, we will contact you within 30 days of receiving it. Please bear in mind that *Vermont Life* produces pages as much as 6 months in advance of publication and may require photographs to be taken a year ahead of publication. We seek stories that have to do with contemporary Vermont culture and the Vermont way of life. As the state magazine, we are most interested in ideas that present positive aspects of life in Vermont. However, while we are nonpartisan, we have no rules about avoiding controversy when the presentation of the subject can illustrate some aspect of Vermont's unique character. We prefer reporting and journalism built around original ideas and insights, emerging trends, and thought-provoking connections in a Vermont context." Estab. 1946. Circ. 53,000. Byline given. Publishes ms an average of 9 months after acceptance. Submit seasonal material 1 year in advance. Accepts simultaneous submissions. Responds in 1 month to queries. "Read online guidelines before submitting: www.vermontlife.com/guidelines-for-contributors."

VIRGINIA

💲💲 THE ROANOKER

Leisure Publishing Co., 3424 Brambleton Ave., Roanoke VA 24018. (540)989-6138; (800)548-1672. **Fax:** (540)989-7603. **E-mail:** jwood@leisurepublishing.com; krheinheimer@leisurepublishing.com. **Website:** www.theroanoker.com. **Contact:** Kurt Rheinheimer, editor; Austin Clark, creative director; Patty Jackson, production director. **75% freelance written. Works with a small number of new/unpublished writers each year.** Magazine published 6 times/year. "*The Roanoker* is a general interest city magazine for the people of Roanoke, Virginia and the surrounding area. Our readers are primarily upper-income, well-educated professionals between the ages of 35 and 60. Coverage ranges from hard news and consumer information to restaurant reviews and local history." Estab. 1974. Circ. 10,000. Byline given. Pays on publication. No kill fee. Publishes ms an average of 4 months after acceptance. Submit seasonal material 4 months in advance. Accepts queries by mail, e-mail, fax. Accepts simultaneous submissions. Responds in 2 months to queries. Sample copy for $2 with 9x12 SASE and 5 first-class stamps or online.

NONFICTION Needs historical, how-to, interview, photo feature, travel, periodic special sections on fashion, real estate, media, banking, investing. **Buys 30 mss/year.** Send complete ms. 1,400 words maximum. **Pays $35-200.**

COLUMNS Skinny (shorts on people, Roanoke-related books, local issues, events, arts and culture).

💲💲 VIRGINIA LIVING

Cape Fear Publishing, 109 E. Cary St., Richmond VA 23219. **E-mail:** erinparkhurst@capefear.com, taylorpilkington@capefear.com. **Website:** www.virginialiving.com. **Contact:** Erin Parkhurst, editor; Taylor Pilkington, associate editor. **80% freelance written.** Bimonthly magazine covering life and lifestyle in Virginia. "We are a large-format (10x13) glossy magazine covering life in Virginia, from food, architecture, and gardening to issues, profiles, and travel." Estab. 2002. Circ. 70,000. Byline given. Pays on publication. Publishes ms an average of 4-6 months after acceptance. Editorial lead time 2-6 months. Submit seasonal material 1 year in advance. Accepts queries by mail. Accepts simultaneous submissions. Responds in 1-3 month to queries. Sample copy: $5.95.

NONFICTION Needs book excerpts, essays, general interest, historical, interview, new product, personal experience, photo feature. No fiction, poetry, previously published articles, or stories with a firm grasp of the obvious. **Buys 180 mss/year.** Query with published clips or send complete ms. Length: 300-3,000 words. **Pays 50¢/word.**

COLUMNS Beauty; Travel; Books; Events; Sports (all with a unique Virginia slant), all 1,000-1,500 words. **Buys 50 mss/year.** Send complete ms. **Pays $120-200.**

WASHINGTON

💲💲💲 SEATTLE WEEKLY

307 Third Ave. S., 2nd Floor, Seattle WA 98104. (206)623-0500. **Fax:** (206)467-4338. **E-mail:** editorial@seattleweekly.com; mbaumgarten@seattleweekly.com. **Website:** www.seattleweekly.com. **Contact:** Matt Baumgarten, editor in chief. **20% freelance written.** Weekly tabloid covering arts, politics, food, business and books with local and regional emphasis. The *Seattle Weekly* publishes stories on Northwest politics and art, usually written by regional and local writers,

for a mostly upscale, urban audience; writing is high-quality magazine style. Estab. 1976. Circ. 105,000. Byline given. Pays on publication. Offers variable kill fee. Publishes ms an average of 1 month after acceptance. Submit seasonal material 2 months in advance. Accepts simultaneous submissions. Responds in 1 month to queries. Sample copy for $3.

NONFICTION Needs book excerpts, expose, general interest, historical, humor, interview, opinion. **Buys 6-8 mss/year.** Query with cover letter, résumé, published clips, and SASE. Length: 300-4,000 words. **Pays $50-800.**

WISCONSIN

🖥️💲 MADISON MAGAZINE

Morgan Murphy Media, 7025 Raymond Rd., Madison WI 53719. (608)270-3600. **Fax:** (608)270-3636. **E-mail:** kmichel@madisonmagazine.com. **Website:** www.madisonmagazine.com. **Contact:** Karen Lincoln Michel, editor. **75% freelance written.** Monthly magazine covering life in the greater Madison, Wisconsin, area. Estab. 1978. Byline given. Pays on publication. Offers 33% kill fee. Publishes ms an average of 2 months after acceptance. Editorial lead time 3 months. Submit seasonal material 3-4 months in advance. Accepts queries by mail, e-mail. Accepts simultaneous submissions. Responds in 3 weeks to queries. Responds in 3 weeks to mss. Sample copy free. Guidelines available via e-mail.

NONFICTION Needs book excerpts, essays, expose, general interest, historical, how-to, humor, inspirational, interview, new product, opinion, personal experience, photo feature, religious, technical, travel.

COLUMNS Columns: Your Town (local events) and OverTones (local arts/entertainment), both 300 words; Habitat (local house/garden) and Business (local business), both 800 words. **Buys 120 mss/year.** Query with published clips. **Pays variable amount.**

FILLERS Needs anecdotes, facts, gags, newsbreaks, short humor. Length: 100 words. **Pays 20-30¢/word.**

💲💲💲💲 MILWAUKEE MAGAZINE

126 N. Jefferson St., Suite 100, Milwaukee WI 53202. (414)273-1101. **Fax:** (414)273-0016. **Website:** www.milwaukeemag.com. **Contact:** E-mail appropriate editor (see website). **40% freelance written.** Monthly magazine covering the people, issues, and places of the Milwaukee, Wisconsin, area. "We publish stories about Milwaukee, of service to Milwaukee-area resi-

dents and exploring the area's changing lifestyle, business, arts, politics, and dining. Our goal has always been to create an informative, literate and entertaining magazine that will challenge Milwaukeeans with in-depth reporting and analysis of issues of the day, provide useful service features, and enlighten readers with thoughtful stories, essays and columns. Underlying this mission is the desire to discover what is unique about Wisconsin and its people, to challenge conventional wisdom when necessary, criticize when warranted, heap praise when deserved, and season all with affection and concern for the place we call home." Circ. 35,000. Byline given. Pays on publication. Offers 20% kill fee. Publishes ms an average of 2 months after acceptance. Submit seasonal material 6 months in advance. Accepts queries by e-mail. Accepts simultaneous submissions. Responds in 6 weeks to queries. Sample copy for $6. Guidelines online.

NONFICTION Needs essays, expose, general interest, historical, interview, photo feature, travel, food and dining, and other services. No articles without a strong Milwaukee or Wisconsin angle. **Buys 30-50 mss/year.** Query with published clips. Length: 2,500-5,000 words for full-length features; 800 words for 2-page breaker features (short on copy, long on visuals). **Payment varies.**

COLUMNS Insider (inside information on Milwaukee, exposé, slice-of-life, unconventional angles on current scene), up to 500 words; Mini Reviews for Insider, 125 words. Query with published clips.

WISCONSIN NATURAL RESOURCES

Wisconsin Department of Natural Resources, P.O. Box 7921, Madison WI 53707-7921. (608)261-8446. **E-mail:** natasha.kassulke@wisconsin.gov. **E-mail:** Natasha Kassulke. **Website:** www.wnrmag.com. **30% freelance written.** Bimonthly magazine covering environment, natural resource management, and outdoor skills. "We cover current issues in Wisconsin aimed to educate and advocate for resource conservation, outdoor recreation, and wise land use." Estab. 1931. Circ. 88,000. Byline given. Publishes ms an average of 8 months after acceptance. Editorial lead time 6 months. Submit seasonal material 1 year in advance. Accepts queries by mail, e-mail. Accepts simultaneous submissions. Responds in 3 weeks to queries; in 6 months to mss. Sample copy free. Guidelines online.

NONFICTION Needs essays, how-to, photo feature, features on current outdoor issues and environmental issues. Does not want animal rights pieces, poetry, or fiction. Query. Length: 500-2,500 words.

💲💲 WISCONSIN TRAILS

333 W. State St., Milwaukee WI 53201. **Fax:** (414)647-4723. **E-mail:** clewis@jrn.com. **Website:** www.wisconsintrails.com. **Contact:** Chelsey Lewis, assistant editor. **40% freelance written.** Bimonthly magazine for readers interested in Wisconsin and its contemporary issues, personalities, recreation, history, natural beauty, and arts. Estab. 1960. Circ. 55,000. Byline given. Pays 1 month from publication. 20% kill fee, up to $75. Publishes ms an average of 6 months after acceptance. Submit seasonal material 1 year in advance. Accepts queries by mail, e-mail, fax. Accepts simultaneous submissions. Responds in 2-3 months to queries. Sample copy: $4.95. Guidelines for #10 SASE or online.

NONFICTION Does not accept unsolicited mss. Query or send a story idea via e-mail. Length: 250-1,500 words. **Pays 25¢/word.**

WYOMING

💲 WYOMING RURAL ELECTRIC NEWS (WREN)

2710 Thomas Ave., Cheyenne WY 82001. (307)772-1986. **Fax:** (307)634-0728. **E-mail:** wren@wyomingrea.org. **Website:** www.wyomingrea.org/community/wren-magazine.php. **40% freelance written.** Monthly magazine (except in January) for audience of rural residents, vacation-home owners, farmers, ranchers and business owners in Wyoming. Estab. 1954. Circ. 39,100. Byline given. Pays on publication. No kill fee. Publishes ms an average of 2 months after acceptance. At least 3 months. Submit seasonal material 2 months in advance. Accepts queries by mail, e-mail. Accepts simultaneous submissions. Responds in 1 month to queries. Sample copy for $2.50 and 9x12 SASE. Guidelines for #10 SASE.

NONFICTION No nostalgia, sarcasm, or tongue-in-cheek. **Buys 4-10 mss/year.** Send complete ms. Length: 600-800 words. **Pays up to $150, plus 3 copies.**

RELIGIOUS

ALIVE NOW

1908 Grand Ave., P.O. Box 340004, Nashville TN 37203. (615)340-7254. **E-mail:** alivenow@upperroom.org. **Website:** www.alivenow.org; alivenow.up-

perroom.org. **Contact:** Beth A. Richardson, editor. *Alive Now*, published bimonthly, is a devotional magazine that invites readers to enter an ever-deepening relationship with God. "*Alive Now* seeks to nourish people who are hungry for a sacred way of living. Submissions should invite readers to see God in the midst of daily life by exploring how contemporary issues impact their faith lives. Each word must be vivid and dynamic and contribute to the whole. We make selections based on a list of upcoming themes. Mss which do not fit a theme will be returned." Estab. 1971. Circ. 70,000. Pays on acceptance. Accepts queries by mail, e-mail. Accepts simultaneous submissions. Subscription: $17.95/year (6 issues); $26.95 for 2 years (12 issues). Additional subscription information, including foreign rates, available on website. Guidelines online.

NONFICTION Needs meditations. Prefers electronic submissions attached as Word document. Postal submissions should include SASE. Include name, address, theme on each sheet. Length: 400-500 words. **Pays $35 minimum.**

FICTION Needs religious. Prefers electronic submissions attached as Word document. Postal submissions should include SASE. Include name, address, theme on each sheet. Length: 400-500 words. **Pays $35 minimum.**

POETRY Prefers electronic submissions attached as Word document. Postal submissions should include SASE. Include name, address, theme on each sheet. **Pays $35 minimum.**

💲💲 AMERICA

106 W. 56th St., New York NY 10019. **E-mail:** zdavis@americamedia.org. **Website:** www.americamagazine.org. **Contact:** Zac Davis, editorial assistant. "Published weekly for adult, educated, largely Roman Catholic audience. Founded by the Jesuit order and directed today by Jesuits and lay colleagues, *America* is a resource for spiritual renewal and social analysis guided by the spirit of charity. The print and Web editions of *America* feature timely and thought-provoking articles written by prestigious writers and theologians, and incisive book, film, and art reviews." Estab. 1909. Byline given. Pays on acceptance. No kill fee. Guidelines online.

NONFICTION Needs essays, religious. Submit via online submissions manager. No e-mail submissions. Length: up to 2,500 words for features; 800-1,500 words for "Faith in Focus" personal essays. **Pays competitive rate.**

POETRY "Many poems we publish address matters of faith and spirituality, but this is not a requirement for publication. We are looking for authentic, truthful, good poetry." Submit via online submissions manager. Submit maximum 3 poems. Length: up to 30 lines/poem. **Pays competitive rate.**

ANCIENT PATHS

E-mail: skylarburris@yahoo.com. **Website:** www.editorskylar.com/magazine/table.html. **Contact:** Skylar H. Burris, editor. **100% freelance written.** *Ancient Paths* provides "a forum for quality spiritual poetry and short fiction. We consider works from writers of all religions, but poets and authors should be comfortable appearing in a predominantly Christian publication. Works published in *Ancient Paths* explore themes such as redemption, sin, forgiveness, doubt, faith, gratitude for the ordinary blessings of life, spiritual struggle, and spiritual growth. Please, no overly didactic works. Subtlety is preferred." Estab. 1998. Byline given. Pays on publication. Time between acceptance and publication 1-4 months. Accepts queries by e-mail. Accepts simultaneous submissions. Responds in 8 weeks, usually sooner. Sample copy of a past printed issue: $9. Purchase online. Guidelines available on website.

FICTION E-mail submissions only. Paste short fiction directly in the e-mail message. Use the subject heading "AP Online Submission (title of your work)." Include name and e-mail address at top of e-mail. Previously published works accepted, provided they are not currently available online. Please indicate if your work has been published elsewhere. Needs humorous, mainstream, novel excerpts, religious, short stories, slice-of-life vignettes, All fiction submissions should be under 2,500 words. Very short submission of under 800 words have a better chance of acceptance. Length: under 800 words preferred; up to 2,500 words. **Pays $1.25 per work published. Published authors also receive discount code for $3 off 2 past printed issues.**

POETRY Needs formal verse or free verse on spiritual themes. E-mail all submissions. Paste poems in e-mail message. Use the subject heading "AP Online Submission (title of your work)." Include your name and e-mail address at the top of your e-mail. Poems may be rhymed, unrhymed, free verse, or formal and should have a spiritual theme, which may be explicit or implicit, but which should not be overly didactic. No "preachy" poetry; avoid inconsistent meter and forced rhyme; no stream-of-consciousness or avant-garde work; no esoteric academic poetry; no concrete (shape) poetry; no use of the lowercase "i" for the personal pronoun; do not center poetry. Buys 52 poems/year. Submit maximum 5 poems. Length: 8-60 lines. **Pays $1.25 per poem. Published poets also receive discount code for $3 off 2 past printed issues.**

$ BIBLE ADVOCATE

Church of God (Seventh Day), P.O. Box 33677, Denver CO 80233. (303)452-7973. **E-mail:** bibleadvocate@cog7.org. **Website:** baonline.org. **Contact:** Sherri Langton, associate editor. **25% freelance written.** Religious magazine published 6 times/year. "Our purpose is to advocate the Bible and represent the Church of God (Seventh Day) to a Christian audience." Estab. 1863. Circ. 13,500. Byline given. Pays on publication. No kill fee. Publishes ms an average of 3-9 months after acceptance. Editorial lead time 3 months. Submit seasonal material 6 months in advance. Accepts queries by mail, e-mail. Accepts simultaneous submissions. Responds in 2 months to queries. Sample copy for SAE with 9x12 envelope and 3 first-class stamps. Guidelines online.

NONFICTION Contact: Sherri Langton, associate editor. Needs inspirational, personal experience, religious, Biblical studies. No articles on Christmas or Easter. **Buys 10-20 mss/year.** Send complete ms by e-mail, preferably. Length: 600-1,200 words. **Pays $25-65.**

POETRY Contact: Sherri Langton, associate editor. Needs Wants free verse, traditional, Christian/Bible themes. Seldom comments on rejected poems. No avant-garde. Buys 10-12 poems/year. Submit maximum 5 poems. Length: 5-20 lines. **Pays $20 and 2 contributor's copies.**

$$ CATHOLIC DIGEST

P.O. Box 6015, New London CT 06320. (800)321-0411. **Fax:** (860)457-3013. **E-mail:** queries@catholicdigest.com. **Website:** www.catholicdigest.com. **80% freelance written.** Magazine published 9 times/year on Catholic lifestyle and faith. Publishes features and advice on topics ranging from health, psychology, humor, adventure, and family to ethics, spirituality, and Catholics, from modern-day heroes to saints through the ages. Helpful and relevant reading culled from secular and religious periodicals. Estab. 1936. Circ.

275,000. Byline given. Pays on publication. No kill fee. Editorial lead time 3 months. Submit seasonal material 6 months in advance. Accepts queries by e-mail. Accepts simultaneous submissions. Does not respond to unsolicited ms. Guidelines available on website.

NONFICTION Needs book excerpts, essays, general interest, historical, how-to, humor, inspirational, interview, personal experience, religious, travel. Special issues: Accepts features on the following topics: Marriage, Practical Spirituality, Parish/Work, Parenting, Grandparenting, Homemaking, Relationships, Good Looks. Does not accept unsolicited submissions. Query with 1-2 relevant writing samples. Length: 350-1,500 words. **Pays $100-$500.**

FILLERS Open Door (statements of true incidents through which people are brought into the Catholic faith, or recover the Catholic faith they had lost), 350-600 words, send to opendoor@catholicdigest.com; Last Word (back page, personal, inspirational, reflective essay), 550-700 words, send to queries@catholicdigest.com. Query with 1-2 relevant writing samples.

💲💲 CELEBRATE LIFE MAGAZINE

American Life League, P.O. Box 1350, Stafford VA 22555. (540)659-4171. **Fax:** (540)659-2586. **E-mail:** clmag@all.org. **Website:** www.clmagazine.org. **Contact:** William Mahoney, PhD, editor. **50% freelance written.** Quarterly magazine "publishing educational articles and human-interest stories on the right to life and dignity of all human beings." Estab. 1979. Circ. 30,000. Byline given. Pays on publication. Submit seasonal material 4 months in advance. Accepts queries by mail, e-mail. Responds in 3 months to mss. For sample copy, send 9x12 SAE and 4 first-class stamps. Guidelines available on website.

NONFICTION "Nonfiction only; no fiction, poetry, songs, music, allegory, or devotionals." Does not publish reprints. Query with published clips or send complete ms. Length: 600-1,800 words.

💲💲💲 CHARISMA

Charisma Media, 600 Rinehart Rd., Lake Mary FL 32746. (407)333-0600. **Fax:** (407)333-7100. **E-mail:** charisma@charismamedia.com. **Website:** www. charismamag.com. **Contact:** Jennifer LeClaire, senior editor. **80% freelance written.** Monthly magazine covering items of interest to the Pentecostal or independent charismatic reader. Now also online. "More than half of our readers are Christians who belong to Pentecostal or independent charismatic churches, and numerous others participate in the charismatic renewal in mainline denominations." Estab. 1975. Circ. 250,000. Byline given. Pays on publication. Offers $50 kill fee. Publishes ms an average of 3 months after acceptance. Editorial lead time 4 months. Submit seasonal material 5 months in advance. Accepts queries by mail, e-mail. Accepts simultaneous submissions. Sample copy: $4. Guidelines by e-mail and online.

NONFICTION Needs book excerpts, expose, general interest, interview, religious. No essays, editorials, sermons, book reviews, or works of fiction and poetry. **Buys 40 mss/year.** Query through online submission form. Length: up to 2,600 words.

COLUMNS Inspire (reflections on the work of a particular ministry, Christian author or artist), 700 words. Query through online submission form.

💲💲 THE CHRISTIAN CENTURY

104 S. Michigan Ave., Suite 1100, Chicago IL 60603-5901. (312)263-7510. **Fax:** (312)263-7540. **E-mail:** main@christiancentury.org. **E-mail:** submissions@ christiancentury.org; poetry@christiancentury.org. **Website:** www.christiancentury.org. **Contact:** Jill Peláez Baumgaertner, poetry editor. **90% freelance written. Works with new/unpublished writers.** Biweekly magazine for ecumenically minded, progressive Protestants, both clergy and lay. "We seek mss that articulate the public meaning of faith, bringing the resources of religious tradition to bear on such topics as poverty, human rights, economic justice, international relations, national priorities, and popular culture. We are also interested in pieces that examine or critique the theology and ethos of individual religious communities. We welcome articles that find fresh meaning in old traditions and that adapt or apply religious traditions to new circumstances. Authors should assume that readers are familiar with main themes in Christian history and theology, are accustomed to the historical-critical study of the Bible and are already engaged in relating faith to social and political issues. Many of our readers are ministers or teachers of religion at the college level. Book reviews are solicited by our books editor. Please note that submissions via e-mail will not be considered. If you are interested in becoming a reviewer for *The Christian Century*, please send your résumé and a list of subjects of interest to "Attn: Book reviews." Authors must have

a critical and analytical perspective on the church and be familiar with contemporary theological discussion." Estab. 1884. Circ. 37,000. Byline given. Pays on publication. No kill fee. Editorial lead time 1 month. Submit seasonal material 4 months in advance. Accepts queries by mail, e-mail. Accepts simultaneous submissions. Responds in 4-6 weeks to queries; in 2 months to mss. Sample copy: $3.50. Guidelines online.

NONFICTION Needs essays, humor, interview, opinion, religious. Does not want inspirational. **Buys 150 mss/year.** Send complete ms; query appreciated but not essential. Length: 1,000-3,000 words. **Pays variable amount for assigned articles. Pays $100-300 for unsolicited articles.**

COLUMNS "We do not accept unsolicited submissions for our regular columns."

POETRY Contact: Jill Pelàez Baumgaertner, poetry editor. Needs free verse, traditional. Wants "poems that are not statements but experiences, that do not talk about the world but show it. We want to publish poems that are grounded in images and that reveal an awareness of the sounds of language and the forms of poetry even when the poems are written in free verse." Submissions without SASE (or SAE and IRCs) will not be returned. Submit poems typed, double-spaced, 1 poem/page. Include name, address, and phone number on each page. Please submit poetry to poetry@christiancentury.org. Has published poetry by Jeanne Murray Walker, Ida Fasel, Kathleen Norris, Luci Shaw, J. Barrie Shepherd, and Wendell Berry. Prefers shorter poems. Inquire about reprint permission. Does not want "pietistic or sentimental doggerel." Buys 50 poems/year. Length: up to 20 lines/poem. **Usually pays $50/poem plus 1 contributor's copy and discount on additional copies. Acquires all rights.**

CONSCIENCE

Catholics for Choice, 1436 U St. NW, Suite 301, Washington DC 20009. (202)986-6093. **E-mail:** conscience@catholicsforchoice.org. **Website:** www.catholicsforchoice.org. **Contact:** Jon O'Brien, executive editor. **80% written by nonstaff writers. Publishes 40 freelance submissions yearly; 10% by unpublished writers, 50% by authors who are new to the magazine, 70% by experts.** "Conscience offers in-depth coverage of a range of topics, including contemporary politics, Catholicism, women's rights in society and in religions, U.S. politics, reproductive rights, sexuality and gender, ethics and bioethics, feminist theology, social justice, church and state issues, and the role of religion in formulating public policy." Estab. 1980. Circ. 12,000. Byline given. Pays on publication. No kill fee. Publishes ms an average of 2 months after acceptance. Accepts queries by mail, e-mail. Accepts simultaneous submissions. Responds in 4 months to queries. Sample copy free with 9x12 envelope and $1.85 postage. Guidelines with #10 SASE.

NONFICTION Needs book excerpts, interview, opinion, personal experience, issue analysis. **Buys 4-8 mss/year.** Send complete ms. Length: 1,500-3,500 words. **Pays $200 negotiable.**

COLUMNS Book Reviews, 600-1,200 words. **Buys 4-8 mss/year. Pays $75.**

$$ DECISION

Billy Graham Evangelistic Association, P.O. Box 668886, Charlotte NC 28266. (704)401-2432. **Fax:** (704)401-3009. **E-mail:** submissions@bgea.org. **Website:** www.decisionmag.org. **Contact:** Bob Paulson, editor. **5% freelance written. Works each year with small number of new/unpublished writers.** "Magazine published 11 times/year with a mission to extend the ministry of Billy Graham Evangelistic Association; to communicate the Good News of Jesus Christ in such a way that readers will be drawn to make a commitment to Christ; and to encourage, strengthen and equip Christians in evangelism and discipleship." Estab. 1960. Circ. 400,000. Byline given. Pays on publication. Publishes ms up to 18 months after acceptance. Editorial lead time 6 months. Submit seasonal material 6 months in advance. Accepts queries by mail, e-mail. Accepts simultaneous submissions. Sample copy for sae with 9x12 envelope and 4 first-class stamps. Guidelines online.

NONFICTION Needs personal experience, testimony. **Buys approximately 8 mss/year.** Send complete ms. Length: 400-1,500 words. **Pays $200-400.**

COLUMNS Finding Jesus (people who have become Christians through Billy Graham Ministries), 500-900 words. **Buys 11 mss/year.** Send complete ms. **Pays $200.**

$$ EFCA TODAY

Evangelical Free Church of America, 418 Fourth St., NE, Charlottesville VA 22902. **E-mail:** editor@efca.org. **Website:** efcatoday.org. **Contact:** Diane J. McDougall, editor. **30% freelance written.** Quarterly digital magazine. "*EFCA Today*'s purpose is to unify church leaders around the overall mission of the EFCA by bringing its stories and vision to life, and to sharpen those leaders by generating conversations over topics pertinent to faith and life in the 21st century." Estab. 1931. Byline given. Pays on acceptance. Offers 50% kill fee. Publishes ms an average of 3 months after acceptance. Editorial lead time 5 months. Submit seasonal material 6 months in advance. Accepts queries by e-mail. Accepts simultaneous submissions. Responds in 6 weeks. Sample available online. Guidelines online.

NONFICTION articles related to *EFCA* themes, book reviews, blog posts. Special issues: "Each *EFCA Today* is devoted to a topic designed to stimulate thoughtful dialogue and leadership growth, and to highlight how EFCA leaders are already involved in living out that theme. Examples of themes are: new paradigms for 'doing church,' church planting, and rural/small-town churches. These articles focus on an issue rather than on an individual, although individuals indeed illustrate each theme." Query with published clips. Length: 500-2,000 words for articles. **Pays 23¢/word.**

$$ ENRICHMENT

The General Council of the Assemblies of God, 1445 N. Boonville Ave., Springfield MO 65802. (417)862-2781, ext. 4095. **E-mail:** enrichmentjournal@ag.org; rknoth@ag.org. **Website:** www.enrichmentjournal.ag.org. **Contact:** Rick Knoth, managing editor. **15% freelance written.** Quarterly journal covering church leadership and ministry. "*Enrichment* offers enriching and encouraging information to equip and empower spirit-filled leaders." Circ. 33,000. Byline given. Pays on publication. Offers 50% kill fee. Publishes ms an average of 1 year after acceptance. Editorial lead time 18 months. Submit seasonal material 18 months in advance. Accepts queries by mail, e-mail. Accepts simultaneous submissions. Sample copy: $7. Guidelines free.

NONFICTION Needs religious. Send complete ms. Length: 1,000-3,000 words. **Pays up to 15¢/word.**

$ EVANGELICAL MISSIONS QUARTERLY

Billy Graham Center at Wheaton College, P.O. Box 794, Wheaton IL 60187. (630)752-7158. **E-mail:** emq@wheaton.edu. **Website:** www.emqonline.com. **Contact:** Laurie Fortunak Nichols, managing editor; A. Scott Moreau, editor. **67% freelance written.** Quarterly magazine covering evangelical missions. *Evangelical Missions Quarterly* is a professional journal serving the worldwide missions community. *EMQ* articles reflect missionary life, thought, and practice. Each issue includes articles, book reviews, editorials, and letters. Subjects are related to worldwide mission and evangelism efforts and include successful ministries, practical ideas, new tactics and strategies, trends in world evangelization, church planting and discipleship, health and medicine, literature and media, education and training, relief and development, missionary family life, and much more. Estab. 1964. Circ. 7,000. Byline given. Pays on publication. Offers negotiable kill fee. Publishes ms an average of 18 months after acceptance. Editorial lead time 1 year. Accepts queries by e-mail. Accepts simultaneous submissions. Responds in 2 weeks to queries. Sample copy free. Guidelines online.

NONFICTION Needs interview, opinion, personal experience, religious. No sermons, poetry, or straight news. **Buys 24 mss/year.** Query. Length: 3,000 words. **Pays $25-100.**

COLUMNS In the Workshop (practical how tos), 800-2,000 words; Perspectives (opinion), 800 words. **Buys 8 mss/year.** Query. **Pays $50-100.**

🍁$$ FAITH TODAY

Evangelical Fellowship of Canada, P.O. Box 5885, West Beaver Creek Post Office, Richmond Hill ON L4B 0B8 Canada. (905)479-5885. **Fax:** (905)479-4742. **Website:** www.faithtoday.ca. Bimonthly magazine. "*Faith Today* is the magazine of an association of more than 40 evangelical denominations but serves evangelicals in all denominations. It focuses on church issues, social issues, and personal faith as they are tied to the Canadian context. Writing should explicitly acknowledge that Canadian evangelical context." Estab. 1983. Circ. 20,000. Byline given. Pays on publication. Offers 30-50% kill fee. Publishes ms an average of 4 months after acceptance. Editorial lead time 4 months. Accepts queries by mail, e-mail, fax. Accepts simultaneous submissions. Responds in 6 weeks to queries. Sample copy for SASE in Canadian postage. Guidelines available online at www.faithtoday.ca/writers. "View complete back issues at www.faithtoday.ca/digital. Or download 1 of our free apps from www.faithtoday.ca/mobile."

NONFICTION Needs book excerpts, essays, general interest, how-to, interview, opinion, religious, news feature. **Buys 75 mss/year.** Query. Length: 400-2,000 words. **Pays $100-500 Canadian.**

GUIDE

Pacific Press Publishing Association, P.O. Box 5353, Nampa ID 83653. (208)465-2579. **E-mail:** guide@pacificpress.com. **Website:** www.guidemagazine.org. **Contact:** Randy Fishell, editor; Brandon Reese, designer. *Guide* is a Christian story magazine for young people ages 10-14. The 32-page, 4-color publication is published weekly by the Pacific Press. Their mission is to show readers, through stories that illustrate Bible truth, how to walk with God now and forever. Estab. 1953. Byline given. Pays on acceptance. Accepts queries by mail, e-mail. Accepts simultaneous submissions. Responds in 6 weeks to mss. Sample copy free with 6x9 SAE and 2 first-class stamps. Guidelines available on website.

NONFICTION Needs humor, personal experience, religious. Send complete ms. "Each issue includes 3-4 true stories. *Guide* does not publish fiction, poetry, or articles (devotionals, how-to, profiles, etc.). However, we sometimes accept quizzes and other unique nonstory formats. Each piece should include a clear spiritual element." Looking for pieces on adventure, personal growth, Christian humor, inspiration, biography, story series, and nature. Length: 1,000-1,200 words. **Pays 7-10¢/word.**

FILLERS Needs games and puzzles. Send complete ms. **Pays $25-40.**

⬤⬤ GUIDEPOSTS

110 William St., Suite 901, New York NY 10038. **E-mail:** submissions@guidepostsmag.com. **Website:** www.guideposts.com. **Contact:** Edward Grinnan, editor. **40% freelance written. Works with a small number of new/unpublished writers each year.** Monthly magazine featuring personal inspirational stories. *Guideposts* is an inspirational monthly magazine for people of all faiths, in which men and women from all walks of life tell true, first-person narratives of how they overcame obstacles, rose above failures, handled sorrow, gained new spiritual insight, and became more effective people through faith in God. Estab. 1945. Pays on publication. Offers kill fee. Offers 20% kill fee on assigned stories, but not to first-time freelancers. Publishes ms an average of several months after acceptance. Accepts queries by online submission form. Accepts simultaneous submissions. Guidelines online.

NONFICTION Needs personal experience. Does not want essays, sermons, or fiction. **Buys 40-60 unsolic-ited mss/year.** Submit complete ms via online submission form. Length: up to 1,500 words. **Pays $100-500.**

HIGHWAY NEWS AND GOOD NEWS

Transport for Christ, P.O. Box 117, 1525 River Rd., Marietta PA 17547. (717)426-9977. **Fax:** (717)426-9980. **E-mail:** editor@transportforchrist.org. **Website:** www.transportforchrist.org. **Contact:** Inge Koenig. **50% freelance written.** Monthly magazine covering trucking and Christianity. "We publish human interest stories, testimonials, and teachings that have a foundation in Biblical/Christian values. Since truck drivers and their families are our primary readers, we publish works that they will find edifying and helpful." Estab. 1957. Circ. 20,000. Byline given. Publishes ms an average of 1 year after acceptance. Submit seasonal material 1 year in advance. Accepts queries by mail, e-mail, fax. Accepts simultaneous submissions. Only responds to unsolicited submissions when they are due for publishing. Sample copy free. Writer's guidelines by e-mail.

NONFICTION Needs general interest, inspirational, interview, personal experience, photo feature. Does not want anything of a political nature. Send complete ms. Length: 600-800 words.

COLUMNS From the Road (stories by truckers on the road), 600 words. Send complete ms.

INSIGHTS TO A CHANGING WORLD

Franklin Publishing Company, 2723 Steamboat Circle, Arlington TX 76006. (817)548-1124. **E-mail:** ludwigotto@sbcglobal.net. **E-mail:** ludwigotto@sbcglobal.net. **Website:** www.franklinpublishing.net; www.londonpress.us. **Contact:** Dr. Ludwig Otto. **59% freelance written.** Monthly journal covering positive responses to the problems in life. Estab. 1983. Circ. 1,000. Byline given. Does not pay, but offers 25% discount on issues purchased and one-year free membership in the International Association of Professionals. No kill fee. Publishes ms an average of 1 month after acceptance. Editorial lead time 1 month. Submit seasonal material 1 month in advance. Accepts queries by e-mail. Accepts simultaneous submissions. Responds in 1 week to queries and mss. Guidelines online.

NONFICTION Needs book excerpts, essays, expose, general interest, historical, how-to, humor, inspirational, interview, memoir, new product, opinion, personal experience, religious, reviews, technical, travel. Send complete ms. Length: 750-86,000 words.

FICTION Needs adventure, condensed novels, ethnic, horror, humorous, mainstream, mystery, religious, science fiction, suspense, western. Send complete ms.

POETRY Needs avant-garde, free verse, haiku, light verse, traditional.

FILLERS Needs anecdotes, facts, gags.

JEWISH ACTION

Orthodox Union, 11 Broadway, New York NY 10004. (212)563-4000. **E-mail:** ja@ou.org. **Website:** www.ou.org/jewish_action. **Contact:** Nechama Carmel, editor; Rashel Zywica, assistant editor. **80% freelance written.** Quarterly magazine covering a vibrant approach to Jewish issues, Orthodox lifestyle, and values. "*Jewish Action*, the quarterly magazine publication of the Orthodox Union, serves as a forum for a diversity of legitimate opinions within the spectrum of Orthodox Judaism. Our goal is to produce a high-quality, intellectually sophisticated, and relevant publication that conveys Orthodox Jewish values and concerns in a way that will enlighten, educate, and inspire our readers. We aim to attract the best writers and thinkers in the Orthodox Jewish world and to provide lively and thought-provoking articles about issues that affect Orthodox Jewish life today." Estab. 1986. Circ. 40,000. Byline given. Pays 2 months after publication. Submit seasonal material 4 months in advance. Accepts queries by mail, e-mail. Accepts simultaneous submissions. Responds in 3 months to mss. Sample copy online. Guidelines online.

NONFICTION Needs essays, historical, humor, reviews, articles related to current ongoing issues of Jewish life and experience, human-interest features. "We are not looking for Holocaust accounts. We welcome essays about responses to personal or societal challenges." **Buys 30-40 mss/year.** Submit complete ms. E-mailed submissions preferred. Length: 1,000-3,000 words. **Pays $100-400 for assigned articles. Pays $75-150 for unsolicited articles.**

COLUMNS Just Between Us (personal opinion on current Jewish life and issues), 1,000 words. **Buys 4 mss/year.**

POETRY Buys limited number of poems/year. **Pays $25-75.**

LIGHT AND LIFE MAGAZINE

Free Methodist Church–USA, 770 N. High School Rd., Indianapolis IN 46214. (317)616-4776. **Fax:** (317)244-1247. **E-mail:** jeff.finley@fmcusa.org. **Website:** lightandlifemagazine.com. **Contact:** Jeff Finley, managing editor. **50% freelance written.** *Light and Life Magazine* is a monthly magazine published by Light + Life Communications, the publishing arm of the Free Methodist Church–USA. Each issue focuses on a specific theme with a cohesive approach in which the articles complement each other. The magazine has a flip format with articles in English and Spanish." Estab. 1868. Circ. 38,000. Byline given. Pays on publication. No kill fee. Accepts queries by e-mail. Accepts simultaneous submissions. Responds in 2 months. Guidelines available at fmcusa.org/lightandlifemag/writers.

NONFICTION Needs religious. Query. Length: 2,100 words for feature articles, 800 words for print discipleship articles, 500-1,000 words for online discipleship articles, 500-1,000 words for online articles not published in the magazine. **Pays $100/article, $200/feature, $50/discipleship article.**

LIVE

Gospel Publishing House, 1445 N. Boonville Ave., Springfield MO 65802-1894. (417)862-1447. **E-mail:** rl-live@gph.org. **Website:** www.gospelpublishing.com. **100% freelance written.** Weekly magazine for weekly distribution covering practical Christian living. "*LIVE* is a take-home paper distributed weekly in young adult and adult Sunday school classes. We seek to encourage Christians in living for God through fiction and true stories which apply Biblical principles to everyday problems." Estab. 1928. Circ. 35,000. Byline given. Pays on acceptance. No kill fee. Publishes ms an average of 18 months after acceptance. Editorial lead time 12 months. Submit seasonal material 18 months in advance. Accepts queries by mail, e-mail. Accepts simultaneous submissions. Responds in 2 weeks to queries; in 8 weeks to mss. Sample copy for #10 SASE. Guidelines for #10 SASE or on website.

NONFICTION Needs inspirational, religious. No preachy articles or stories that refer to religious myths (e.g., Santa Claus, Easter Bunny, etc.). **Buys 50-100 mss/year.** Send complete ms. Length: 450-1,100 words. **Pays 7-10¢/word.**

FICTION Contact: Wade Quick, editor. Needs religious, inspirational, prose poem. No preachy fiction, fiction about Bible characters, or stories that refer to religious myths (e.g., Santa Claus, Easter Bunny, etc.). No science or Bible fiction. No controversial stories about such subjects as feminism, war, or capital punishment. **Buys 20-50 mss/year.** Send complete ms. Length: 800-1,200 words. **Pays 7-10¢/word.**

POETRY Needs free verse, haiku, light verse, traditional. Buys 15-24 poems/year. Submit maximum 3 poems. Length: 12-25 lines. **Pays $35-60.**

💲💲 THE LOOKOUT

Standard Publishing, 8805 Governor's Hill Dr., Suite 400, Cincinnati OH 45249. (513)931-4050. **Fax:** (513)931-0950. **E-mail:** lookout@standardpub.com. **Website:** www.lookoutmag.com. **Contact:** Kelly Carr, editor. **70% freelance written.** Weekly magazine for Christian adults, with emphasis on spiritual growth, family life, and topical issues. "Our purpose is to provide Christian adults with practical, Biblical teaching and current information that will help them mature as believers." Estab. 1894. Circ. 35,000. Byline given. Pays on acceptance. Offers 33% kill fee. Publishes ms an average of 1 year after acceptance. Editorial lead time 9 months. Submit seasonal material 1 year in advance. Accepts queries by mail, e-mail. Accepts simultaneous submissions. Responds in 10 weeks to queries. Sample copy for $1, or on website. Guidelines by e-mail or online.

NONFICTION Needs inspirational, interview, opinion, personal experience, religious. No fiction or poetry. **Buys 100 mss/year.** Query article first. Length: 1,200-1,400 words. **Pays 11-17¢/word.**

💲 THE LUTHERAN DIGEST

The Lutheran Digest, Inc., 6160 Carmen Ave., Inver Grove Heights MN 55076. (651)451-9945. **E-mail:** editor@lutherandigest.com. **Website:** www.lutherandigest.com. **Contact:** Nick Skapyak, editor. **95% freelance written.** Quarterly magazine covering Christianity from a Lutheran perspective. Publishes articles, humor, and poetry. Articles frequently reflect a Lutheran Christian perspective but are not intended to be sermonettes. Popular stories show how God has intervened in a person's life to help solve a problem. Estab. 1953. Circ. 20,000. No byline given. Pays on publication. No kill fee. Publishes ms an average of 6 months after acceptance. Editorial lead time 9 months. Submit seasonal material 9 months in advance. "No queries, please." Accepts simultaneous submissions. Responds in 4 months to mss. No response to e-mailed mss unless selected for publication. Sample copy: $3.50. Subscription: $16/year, $22 for 2 years. Guidelines online.

NONFICTION Needs general interest, historical, how-to, humor, inspirational, personal experience. Does not want to see personal tributes to deceased relatives or friends. These are seldom used unless the subject of the article is well known. Avoids articles about the moment a person finds Christ as his or her personal savior. **Buys 50-60 mss/year.** Send complete ms. Length: up to 1,500 words. **Pays $25-50.**

POETRY Submit up to 3 poems at a time. Prefers e-mail submissions but also accepts mailed submissions. Cover letter is preferred. Include SASE only if return is desired. Poems are selected by editor and reviewed by publication panel. Length: up to 25 lines/poem. **Pays 1 contributor's copy.**

THE MENNONITE

718 N. Main St., Newton KS 67114-1703. (866)866-2872, ext. 34398. **Fax:** (316)283-0454. **E-mail:** gordonh@themennonite.org. **Website:** www.themennonite.org. **Contact:** Gordon Houser, editor. *The Mennonite*, published monthly, seeks "to help readers glorify God, grow in faith, and become agents of healing and hope in the world. Our readers are primarily people in Mennonite churches." Estab. 1998. Circ. 6,700. Publishes ms up to 1 year after acceptance. Accepts queries by e-mail. Accepts simultaneous submissions. Responds in 2 weeks. Single copy: $4. Subscription: $46. Guidelines online.

NONFICTION Needs general interest. Query via e-mail (preferred). Include name, address, phone number, one-sentence summary of the article and 3 catchy, creative titles. Illustrations, charts, graphs, and photos (in color) to go with the article are welcome. If sending by regular mail, also include SASE. Length: 1,200-1,500 words. **Payment varies. "We only pay for solicited articles."**

💲💲 MESSAGE MAGAZINE

Review and Herald Publishing Association, 12501 Old Columbia Pike, Silver Spring MD 20904. (301)680-6598. **Fax:** (301)393-4103. **E-mail:** ccrawford@rhpa.org; pat.harris@nad.adventist.org. **Website:** www.messagemagazine.org. **Contact:** Carmela Monk Crawford, editor. **10-20% freelance written.** Bimonthly magazine. "*Message* is the oldest religious journal addressing ethnic issues in the country. Our audience is predominantly Black and Seventh-day Adventist; however, *Message* is an outreach magazine for the churched and un-churched across cultural lines." Estab. 1898. Circ. 110,000. Byline given.

Pays on acceptance. No kill fee. Publishes ms an average of 12 months after acceptance. Editorial lead time 6 months. Submit seasonal material 6 months in advance. Accepts simultaneous submissions. Responds in 9 months to queries. Sample copy by e-mail. Guidelines by e-mail and online.

NONFICTION Send complete ms. Length: 300-900 words. **Pays $75-300 for features.**

COLUMNS Eye On the Times: religious liberty, public affairs, human rights and news (300 words); Optimal Health: health news, how-tos and healthy habits (550 words). **Pays $75-150.**

MESSAGE OF THE OPEN BIBLE

Open Bible Churches, 2020 Bell Ave., Des Moines IA 50315-1096. (515)288-6761. **E-mail:** andrea@openbible.org. **Website:** www.openbible.org. **5% freelance written.** "*The Message of the Open Bible* is the official bimonthly publication of Open Bible Churches. Its readership consists mostly of people affiliated with Open Bible." Estab. 1932. Circ. 2,700. Byline given. No kill fee. Publishes ms an average of 4-6 months after acceptance. Editorial lead time 6 months. Submit seasonal material 6 months in advance. Accepts queries by mail, e-mail. Accepts simultaneous submissions. Responds in 1 month to queries. Responds in 2 months to mss. Sample copy for SAE with 9x12 envelope and 3 first-class stamps. Writer's guidelines for #10 SASE or by e-mail (message@openbible.org).

NONFICTION Needs inspirational, interview, personal experience, religious. No sermons. Send complete ms. Length: 650 words maximum.

💲💲 ONE

Catholic Near East Welfare Association, 1011 First Ave., New York NY 10022-4195. (212)826-1480. **Fax:** (212)838-1344. **E-mail:** cnewa@cnewa.org. **Website:** www.cnewa.org. **Contact:** Deacon Greg Kandra, executive editor. **75% freelance written.** Bimonthly magazine for a Catholic audience with interest in the Near East, particularly its current religious, cultural, and political aspects. Estab. 1974. Circ. 100,000. Byline given. Pays on publication. No kill fee. Publishes ms an average of 6 months after acceptance. Accepts queries by mail, fax. Accepts simultaneous submissions. Responds in 1 month to queries. Sample copy and writer's guidelines for 7½×10½ SAE with 2 first-class stamps.

NONFICTION Query. Length: 1,200-1,800 words. **Pays 20¢/edited word.**

💲💲 PENTECOSTAL EVANGEL

The General Council of the Assemblies of God, 1445 N. Boonville Ave., Springfield MO 65802. (417)862-2781. **Fax:** (417)862-0416. **E-mail:** pe@ag.org. **Website:** pe.ag.org. **Contact:** Ken Horn, editor. **5-10% freelance written.** Weekly magazine emphasizing news of the Assemblies of God for members of the Assemblies and other Pentecostal and charismatic Christians. "Articles should be inspirational without being preachy. Any devotional writing should take a literal approach to the Bible. A variety of general topics and personal experience accepted with inspirational tie-in." Estab. 1913. Circ. 180,000. Byline given. Pays on acceptance. Offers 100% kill fee. Publishes ms an average of 6 months or more after acceptance. Editorial lead time 3 months. Submit seasonal material 6 months in advance. Accepts queries by e-mail. Accepts simultaneous submissions. Responds in 2 weeks to queries. Responds in 2 months to mss. Sample copy free. Guidelines online.

NONFICTION Needs book excerpts, general interest, inspirational, personal experience, religious. Does not want poetry, fiction, self-promotional. **Buys 10-15 mss/year.** Send complete ms. Length: 500-1,200 words. **Pays 6 ¢/word and contributor's copies.**

PERSPECTIVES

c/o Jason Lief, Dordt College, 498 4th Ave. NE, Sioux Center, Sioux Center IA 51250. **E-mail:** submissions@perspectivesjournal.org. **Website:** perspectivesjournal.org. Malcolm McBryde. **Contact:** Jason Lief. "*Perspectives* is a journal of theology in the broad Reformed tradition. We seek to express the Reformed faith theologically; to engage issues that Reformed Christians meet in personal, ecclesiastical, and societal life; and thus to contribute to the mission of the church of Jesus Christ. The editors are interested in submissions that contribute to a contemporary Reformed theological discussion. Our readers tend to be affiliated with the Presbyterian Church (USA), the Reformed Church in America, and the Christian Reformed Church. Some of our subscribers are academics or pastors, but we also gear our articles to thoughtful, literate laypeople who want to engage in Reformed theological reflection on faith and culture." Time between acceptance and publication is 3-12 months. Accepts queries by e-mail. Responds in 3-6 months. Sample: $3.50. Subscription: $20.

NONFICTION scholarly, general interest, spiritual autobiography, editorial commentary, book and film reviews. Submit complete ms. Length: up to 3,000 words for general interest and spiritual autobiography; up to 1,500 words for editorial commentary; up to 1,200 words for book and film reviews.

COLUMNS Inside Out (brief Biblical reflection/commentary), up to 600 words; As We See It (reflections on faith/culture), 500-750 words.

FICTION Needs religious. Submit complete ms by e-mail. Length: up to 3,000 words.

POETRY Wants "poems excellent in craft and significant in subject, both traditional and free in form. We publish 1-2 poems every other issue." Has published poetry by Ann Hostetler, Paul Willis, and Priscilla Atkins. Submit poems via e-mail. **Pays 5 contributor's copies.**

⊘⊜ POINT

Converge (Baptist General Conference), Mail Code 200, 11002 Lake Hart Dr., Orlando FL 32832. **Fax:** (866)990-8980. **E-mail:** bob.putman@converge.org. **Website:** www.converge.org. **Contact:** Editor Bob Putman. **15% freelance written.** Nonprofit, religious, evangelical Christian magazine published 4 times/year covering Converge. *Point* is the official magazine of Converge (BCG). Almost exclusively uses articles related to Converge, their churches, or by/about Converge people. Circ. 43,000. Byline given. Pays on publication. Offers 50% kill fee. Editorial lead time 6 months. Submit seasonal material 6 months in advance. Accepts queries by e-mail. Accepts simultaneous submissions. Responds in 1 month to queries; in 3 months to mss. Sample upon request. Guidelines available free.

NONFICTION Buys 6-8 mss/year. Query with published clips. Wants "articles about our people, churches, missions. View online at: www.converge.org. before sending anything." Length: 300-1,500 words. **Pays $60-280.**

COLUMNS Converge Connection (blurbs of news happening in Converge Worldwide), 50-150 words. Send complete ms and photos. **Pays $30.**

◐⊜ PRAIRIE MESSENGER

Benedictine Monks of St. Peter's Abbey, P.O. Box 190, 100 College Drive, Muenster Saskatchewan S0K 2Y0 Canada. (306)682-1772. **Fax:** (306)682-5285. **E-mail:** pm.canadian@stpeterspress.ca. **Website:** www.prairiemessenger.ca. **Contact:** Maureen Weber, associate editor. **30% Freelance written.** Weekly Catholic pub-

lication published by the Benedictine Monks of St. Peter's Abbey. Has a strong focus on ecumenism, social justice, interfaith relations, aboriginal issues, arts and culture. Estab. 1904. Circ. 4,000. Byline given. Pays on publication. No kill fee. Publishes ms an average of 4 months after acceptance. Submit seasonal material 3 months in advance. Accepts queries by mail, e-mail, fax, phone. Accepts simultaneous submissions. Responds only if interested; send nonreturnable samples. Sample copy for 9x12 SASE with $1 Canadian postage or IRCs. Guidelines online. "Because of government subsidy regulations, we are no longer able to accept non-Canadian freelance material."

NONFICTION Needs book excerpts, essays, interview, opinion, religious. **Buys 15 mss/year.** Send complete ms. Length: 500-800 words. **Pays $60/article.**

POETRY Buys We publish 45 poems per year. poems/year. Up to 35 lines **$30 per published poem.**

⊘⊜ PRESBYTERIANS TODAY

Presbyterian Church (U.S.A.), 100 Witherspoon St., Louisville KY 40202-1396. (502)569-5627. **Fax:** (502)569-8887. **E-mail:** editor@pcusa.org. **Website:** www.pcusa.org/today. **Contact:** Patrick David Heery, editor. **25% freelance written. Prefers to work with published/established writers.** Denominational magazine published 6 times/year covering religion, denominational activities, and public issues for members of the Presbyterian Church (U.S.A.). "The magazine's purpose is to increase understanding and appreciation of what the church and its members are doing to live out their Christian faith." Estab. 1867. Circ. 30,000. Byline given. Pays on acceptance. Publishes ms an average of 6 months after acceptance. Editorial lead time 3 months. Submit seasonal material 3 months in advance. Accepts queries by e-mail. Accepts simultaneous submissions. Responds in 2 weeks to queries. Sample copy free. Guidelines online.

NONFICTION Buys 20 mss/year. Send complete ms. Length: 1,000-1,800 words. **Pays $300 maximum for assigned articles; $75-300 for unsolicited articles.**

⊜ PURPOSE

718 N. Main St., Newton KS 67114. **E-mail:** PurposeEditor@MennoMedia.org. **Website:** www.mennomedia.org/purpose. **20% freelance written.** Magazine focuses on Christian discipleship—how to be a faithful Christian in the midst of everyday life situ-

ations. Uses personal story form to present models and examples to encourage Christians in living a life of faithful discipleship. Each issue follows a designated theme. *Purpose* is published monthly by Mennomedia, the publisher for Mennonite Church Canada and Mennonite Church USA. It is a faith-based adult monthly magazine that focuses on discipleship-living, simplicity, and the Christian faith. Estab. 1968. Circ. 4,400. Pays upon publication. No kill fee. Submit material according to writer guidelines and theme deadlines posted on the website. Accepts queries by e-mail. Guidelines available online at www.mennomedia.org/purpose.

NONFICTION Buys 140 mss/year. E-mail submissions preferred. Length: 400-650 words. **Pays $25-50/ story.**

POETRY Needs free verse, light verse, traditional. Poetry must address monthly themes. Buys 12 poems/year. Length: 12 lines maximum. **Pays $10-20/poem.**

💲💲 RELEVANT

Relevant Media Group, 900 N. Orange Ave., Winter Park FL 32789. (407)660-1411. **Fax:** (407)660-8555. **E-mail:** ryan@relevantmediagroup.com; alyce@relevantmediagroup.com. **E-mail:** submissions@relevantmediagroup.com. **Website:** www.relevantmagazine.com. **Contact:** Ryan Hamm, managing editor; Alyca Giligan, associate editor. **80% freelance written.** Bimonthly magazine covering God, life, and progressive culture. *Relevant* is a lifestyle magazine for Christians in their 20s and 30s. Estab. 2002. Circ. 83,000. Byline given. Pays 45 days after publication. Offers 50% kill fee. Publishes ms an average of 6 months after acceptance. Editorial lead time 4 months. Submit seasonal material 5 months in advance. Accepts queries by e-mail. Accepts simultaneous submissions. Responds in 6 weeks to queries. Responds in 3 months to mss. Sample copy online. Guidelines online.

NONFICTION Needs general interest, how-to, inspirational, interview, new product, personal experience, religious. Don't submit anything that doesn't target ages 18-34. Query with published clips. Length: 750-1,000 words. **Payment varies.**

💲 THE SECRET PLACE

P.O. Box 851, Valley Forge PA 19482. (610)768-2434. **Fax:** (610)768-2441. **E-mail:** thesecretplace@abc-usa.org. **Website:** www.judsonpress.com/catalog_secretplace.cfm. **100% freelance written.** Quarterly devo-

tional covering Christian daily devotions. Estab. 1937. Circ. 250,000. Byline given. Pays on acceptance. No kill fee. Editorial lead time 1 year. Submit seasonal material 9 months in advance. Accepts simultaneous submissions. Guidelines online.

NONFICTION Needs inspirational. **Buys about 400 mss/year.** Send complete ms. Length: 100 200 words. **Pays $20.**

POETRY Needs avant-garde, free verse, light verse, traditional. Submit up to 6 poems by mail or e-mail. E-mail preferred. Buys 12-15 poems/year. Submit maximum 6 poems. Length: 4-30 lines/poem. **Pays $20.**

💲 SEEK

Standard Publishing, 4050 Lee Vance View Dr., Colorado Springs CO 80918. (800)323-7543. **E-mail:** seek@standardpublishing.com. **Website:** www.standardpub.com. "Inspirational stories of faith-in-action for Christian adults; a Sunday School take-home paper." Quarterly. Estab. 1970. Circ. 27,000. Byline given. Pays on acceptance. No kill fee. Acceptance to publishing time is 1 year. Accepts queries by e-mail. Accepts simultaneous submissions. Guidelines online.

NONFICTION Send complete ms. Length: 850-1,000 words. **Pays 7¢/word for first rights; 5¢/word for reprint rights.**

FICTION List of upcoming themes available online. Accepts 150 mss/year. Send complete ms. Prefers submissions by e-mail. "*SEEK* corresponds to the topics of Standard Publishing's adult curriculum line and is designed to further apply these topics to everyday life." Unsolicited mss must be written to a theme list. Does not want poetry. Send complete ms. Prefers submissions by e-mail. Length: 850-1,000 words. **Pays 7¢/word.**

💲💲 ST. ANTHONY MESSENGER

Franciscan Media, 28 W. Liberty St., Cincinnati OH 45202-6498. (513)241-5615. **Fax:** (513)241-0399. **E-mail:** magazineeditors@franciscanmedia.org. **Website:** www.stanthonymessenger.org. **Contact:** John Feister, editor-in-chief. **55% freelance written.** Monthly general-interest magazine for a national readership of Catholic families, most of which have children or grandchildren in grade school, high school, or college. *St. Anthony Messenger* is a Catholic family magazine which aims to help its readers lead more fully human and Christian lives. "We publish articles that report on a changing church and world, opinion pieces written from the perspective of Christian faith and values, personality profiles, and fiction which entertains and informs." Estab. 1893. Circ. 105,000. Byline given. Pays on acceptance. No kill fee. Publishes ms within an average of 1 year after acceptance. Submit seasonal material 6 months in advance. Accepts queries by mail, e-mail, fax. Responds in 3 weeks to queries. Responds in 2 months to mss. Sample copy for 9x12 SAE with 4 first-class stamps. Please study writer's guidelines at StAnthonyMessenger.org.

NONFICTION Needs how-to, humor, inspirational, interview, opinion, personal experience. **Buys 35-50 mss/year.** Query with published clips. Length: 2,000-2,500 words. **Pays 20¢/word.**

FICTION Needs mainstream. "We do not want mawkishly sentimental or preachy fiction. Stories are most often rejected for poor plotting and characterization, bad dialogue (listen to how people talk), and inadequate motivation. Many stories say nothing, are 'happenings' rather than stories. No fetal journals, no rewritten Bible stories." **Buys 12 mss/year.** Send complete ms. Length: 2,000-2,500 words. **Pays 20¢/word maximum and 2 contributor's copies; $1 charge for extras.**

POETRY Submit a few poems at a time. "Please include your phone number and a SASE with your submission. Do not send us your entire collection of poetry. Poems must be original." Submit seasonal poems several months in advance. "Our poetry needs are very limited." Submit maximum 4-5 poems. Length: up to 20-25 lines; "the shorter, the better." **Pays $2/line; $20 minimum.**

🌕🌑 THE UPPER ROOM

1908 Grand Ave., P.O. Box 340004, Nashville TN 37203. (615)340-7252. **Fax:** (615)340-7267. **E-mail:** theupperroommagazine@upperroom.org. **Website:** submissions.upperroom.org. **95% freelance written. Eager to work with new/unpublished writers.** Bimonthly magazine offering a daily inspirational message, which includes a Bible reading, text, prayer, "Thought for the Day," and suggestion for further prayer. Each day's meditation is written by a different person and is usually a personal witness about discovering meaning and power for Christian living through scripture study which illuminates daily life. Circ. 2.2 million (US); 385,000 outside US. Byline given. Pays on publication. No kill fee. Publishes ms an average of 1 year after acceptance. Submit seasonal material 14 months in advance. Accepts queries by online submission form. Accepts simultaneous submissions. Sample copy and writer's guidelines with a 4x6 SAE and 2 first-class stamps. Guidelines only for #10 SASE or online, submissions.upperroom.org/guidelines.

NONFICTION Needs inspirational, personal experience, Bible-study insights. Special issues: Lent and Easter; Advent. No poetry or lengthy spiritual journey stories. **Buys 365 unsolicited mss/year.** Send complete ms by mail or use online submission form, submissions.upperroom.org. Length: 300-400 words. **Pays $30/meditation.**

🌑🌕 THE WAR CRY

The Salvation Army, 615 Slaters Lane, Alexandria VA 22314. (703)684-4128. **Fax:** (703)684-5539. **E-mail:** war.cry@usn.salvationarmy.org. **Website:** publications.salvationarmyusa.org. **10% freelance written.** "Inspirational magazine with evangelical emphasis and portrayals that express the mission of the Salvation Army. Twelve issues published per year, including special Easter and Christmas issues." Estab. 1881. Circ. 200,000 monthly; 1.7 million Christmas; 1.1 million Easter. Byline given. Pays on acceptance. No kill fee. Publishes ms an average of 2 months to 1 year after acceptance. Editorial lead time 2 months before issue date; Christmas and Easter issues 6 months before issue date. Submit Christmas and Easter material 6 months in advance. Accepts simultaneous submissions. Responds in 3-4 weeks to mss. Sample copy, theme list, and writer's guidelines free with #10 SASE or online.

NONFICTION "*The War Cry* represents The Salvation Army's mission through features, news, profiles, commentaries, and stories. It seeks to bring people to Christ, help believers grow in faith and character, and promote redemptive cultural practices from the perspective of The Salvation Army programs, minisitries, and doctrines." No missionary stories, confessions. **Buys 30 mss/year.** Complete mss and reprints accepted through website at publications.salvationarmyusa.org/writers-submissions. Submissions strengthened when photos included where appropriate. **Pays 35¢/word.**

FICTION Short stories that do not expound on dogma but depict how faith and life intersect.

POETRY Purchases limited poetry (10 per year maximum).

FILLERS Needs anecdotes, religious news, statistical analysis of trends, and vignettes. **Buys 10-20 mss/year.** Length: 100-400 words. **Pays 35¢/word.**

💲 WESLEYAN LIFE

The Wesleyan Publishing House, P.O. Box 50434, Indianapolis IN 46250. (317)774-7909. **Fax:** (317)774-3924. **E-mail:** communications@wesleyan.org; macbethw@wesleyan.org; rifet@wesleyan.org. **Website:** www.wesleyanlifeonline.com. **Contact:** Wayne MacBeth, executive editor; Kerry Kind, editor; Tricia Rife, assistant editor. Quarterly magazine of The Wesleyan Church. Estab. 1842. Circ. 40,000+ print plus digital (ePub). Byline given. No honoraria or expenses paid. Accepts simultaneous submissions.

NONFICTION Needs inspirational, religious. Length: 250-1,000 words.

🌐💲 WOMAN ALIVE

Christian Publishing and Outreach, Garcia Estate, Canterbury Rd., Worthing West Sussex BN13 1BW United Kingdom. (44)(1903) 60-4352. **E-mail:** womanalive@cpo.org.uk. **Website:** www.womanalive.co.uk. **Contact:** Jackie Harris, editor; Wendy Longhurst, editorial assistant. *Woman Alive* is a Christian magazine geared specifically toward women. It covers all denominations and seeks to inspire, encourage, and provide resources to women in their faith, helping them to grow in their relationship with God and providing practical help and biblical perspective on the issues impacting their lives. Pays on publication. No kill fee. Accepts queries by mail, e-mail. Accepts simultaneous submissions. Sample copy for £1.50, plus postage. Guidelines available on website.

NONFICTION Needs how-to, personal experience. Submit clips, bio, article summary, ms, SASE. Length: 750-850 words/1-page article; 1,200-1,500 words/2-page article; 1,600-1,800 words/3-page article. **Pays £75/1-page article; £100/2-page article; £130/3-page article.**

RETIREMENT

AARP BULLETIN

AARP, c/o Editorial Submissions, 601 E. Street NW, Washington DC 20049. **E-mail:** member@aarp.org. **Website:** www.aarp.org/bulletin. *AARP Bulletin* provides timely insights and news on health, healthy policy, Social Security, consumer protection, and more from an award-winning source. Accepts simultaneous submissions.

NONFICTION Needs essays, general interest, personal experience.

💲💲💲💲 AARP THE MAGAZINE

AARP, c/o Editorial Submissions, 601 E. St. NW, Washington DC 20049. **E-mail:** aarpmagazine@aarp.org. **Website:** www.aarp.org/magazine. **50% freelance written. Prefers to work with published/established writers.** Bimonthly magazine covering issues that affect people over the age of 50. *AARP The Magazine* is devoted to the varied needs and active life interests of AARP members, age 50 and over, covering such topics as financial planning, travel, health, careers, retirement, relationships, and social and cultural change. Its editorial content serves the mission of AARP seeking through education, advocacy, and service to enhance the quality of life for all by promoting independence, dignity, and purpose. Circ. 22,721,661. Byline given. Pays on acceptance. Offers 25% kill fee. Publishes ms an average of 6 months after acceptance. Submit seasonal material 6 months in advance. Accepts queries by mail. Accepts simultaneous submissions. Responds in 3 months to queries. Sample copy free. Guidelines online.

NONFICTION No previously published articles. Query for features, or submit complete ms for personal essays. Submit queries and mss via e-mail or postal mail. "Story pitches for specific features and departments should be 1 page in length and accompanied by recent writing samples. The pitch should explain the idea for the piece, tell how you would approach it as a writer, give some sense of your writing style, and mention the section of the magazine for which the piece is intended. Your samples should not include the actual story that you are proposing, except in the case of personal essays, which should be submitted in full. Features and departments cover the following categories: Money (investments, savings, retirement, and work issues); Health and Fitness (tips, trends, studies); Food and Nutrition (recipes, emphasis on healthy eating); Travel (tips and trends on how and where to travel); Consumerism (practical information and advice); General interest (new thinking, research, information on timely topics, trends); Relationships (family matters, caregiving, living arrangements, grandparents); Personal Essay (thoughtful, timely, new takes on matters of importance to people over 50); Personal Best (first-person essays on leisure-time pursuits). Length: up to 2,000 words. **Pays $1/word.**

🌑 CHRISTIAN LIVING IN THE MATURE YEARS

The United Methodist Publishing House, 2222 Rosa L. Parks Blvd., P.O. Box 17890, Nashville TN 37228-7890. (615)749-6474. **Fax:** (615)749-6512. **E-mail:** matureyears@umpublishing.org. **80% freelance written. Prefers to work with published/established writers.** Quarterly magazine designed to help persons in and nearing the retirement years understand and appropriate the resources of the Christian faith in dealing with specific problems and opportunities related to aging. Estab. 1954. Circ. 35,000. Pays on acceptance. No kill fee. Publishes ms an average of 1 year after acceptance. Submit seasonal material 14 months in advance. Accepts queries by e-mail. Responds in 6-7 months to mss. Sample copy: $6, plus 9x12 SAE. Writer's guidelines for #10 SASE or by e-mail.

NONFICTION Needs how-to, inspirational, religious, travel, older adult health, life, faith, travel, finance issues. **Buys 75-80 mss/year.** Send complete ms; e-mail submissions preferred. Length: 900-2,000 words. **Pays 7¢/word.**

COLUMNS Health Hints (retirement, health), 900-1,500 words; Going Places (travel, pilgrimage), 1,000-1,500 words; Fragments of Life (personal inspiration), 250-600 words; Modern Revelations religious/inspirational), 900-1,500 words; Money Matters (personal finance), 1,200-1,800 words; Merry-Go-Round (cartoons, jokes, 4- to 6-line humorous verse); Puzzle Time (religious puzzles, crosswords). **Buys 4 mss/year.** Send complete ms. **Pays 7-10¢/word.**

POETRY Needs free verse, haiku, light verse, traditional. Wants upbeat poetry. Must express hope; strong imagery preferred. Buys 24 poems/year. Submit maximum 6 poems. Length: 3-16 lines; up to 50 characters maximum. **Pays $5-20/poem.**

🌑 MATURE LIVING

Lifeway Christian Resources, 1 Lifeway Plaza, Nashville TN 37234. (615)251-2000. **E-mail:** matureliving@lifeway.com. **Website:** www.lifeway.com. **Contact:** Mike Glenn, executive editor. **90% freelance written.** "Monthly leisure reading magazine for senior adults 55 and older. *Mature Living* is Christian in content, and the material required is what would appeal to the 55-and-over age group: inspirational, informational, nostalgic, humorous. Our magazine is distributed mainly through churches (especially Southern Baptist churches) that buy the magazine in bulk and distribute it to members in this age group." Estab. 1977. Circ. 320,000. Byline given. Pays on acceptance. No kill fee. Publishes ms an average of 7-8 weeks after acceptance. Submit seasonal material 1 year in advance. Accepts queries by mail, e-mail. Accepts simultaneous submissions. Responds in 3 months to mss. Sample copy: $4. Guidelines for #10 SASE.

NONFICTION Needs historical, how-to, humor, inspirational, interview, personal experience, travel. No pornography, profanity, occult, liquor, dancing, drugs, gambling. **Buys 100 mss/year.** Query. Length: 600-1,200 words. **Pays $85-115**

COLUMNS Cracker Barrel (brief, humorous, original quips and verses); Grandparents' Brag Board (something humorous or insightful said or done by your grandchild or great-grandchild); Inspirational (devotional items); Food (introduction and 4-6 recipes); Over the Garden Fence (vegetable or flower gardening); Crafts (step-by-step procedures); Game Page (crossword or word-search puzzles and quizzes). **Pays $15-40.**

RURAL

🌑🌑 BACKWOODS HOME MAGAZINE

P.O. Box 712, Gold Beach OR 97444. (541)247-8900. **Fax:** (541)247-8600. **E-mail:** lisa@backwoodshome.com. **E-mail:** article-submission@backwoodshome.com. **Website:** www.backwoodshome.com. **Contact:** Lisa Nourse, editorial coordinator. **90% freelance written.** Bimonthly magazine covering self-reliance. *Backwoods Home Magazine* is written for people who have a desire to pursue personal independence, self-sufficiency, and their dreams. Offers how-to articles on self-reliance. Estab. 1989. Circ. 38,000. Byline given. Pays on acceptance. Editorial lead time 4-6 months. Submit seasonal material 4-6 months in advance. Accepts queries by mail, e-mail. Sample copy for 9x10 SAE and 6 first-class stamps. Guidelines online.

NONFICTION Needs general interest, how-to, humor, personal experience, technical. **Buys 120 mss/year.** Send complete ms via e-mail (no attachments) or postal mail. Looking for straightforward, clear writing similar to what you would find in a good newspaper. Length: 500 words. **Pays $40-200.**

COUNTRY WOMAN

Reiman Publications, 5400 S. 60th St., Greendale WI 53129. (414)423-0100. **E-mail:** editors@country-womanmagazine.com. **Website:** http://www.lovethe-country.com/. **Contact:** Lori Lau Grzybowski, editor. **75-85% freelance written.** Bimonthly magazine. *Country Woman* is for contemporary rural women of all ages and backgrounds and from all over the U.S. and Canada. It includes a sampling of the diversity that makes up rural women's lives—love of home, family, farm, ranch, community, hobbies, enduring values, humor, attaining new skills and appreciating present, past and future all within the context of the lifestyle that surrounds country living. Estab. 1970. Byline given. Pays on acceptance. No kill fee. Submit seasonal material 5 months in advance. Accepts queries by mail. Accepts simultaneous submissions. Responds in 2 months to queries. Responds in 3 months to mss. Sample copy for $2 and SASE. Guidelines with #10 SASE.

NONFICTION Needs general interest, historical, how-to, humor, inspirational, interview, personal experience, photo feature. Query. 1,000 words maximum.

COLUMNS Why Farm Wives Age Fast (humor), I Remember When (nostalgia), and Country Decorating. Length: 500-1,000 words. **Buys 10-12 mss/year.** Query or send ms.

FICTION Contact: Kathleen Anderson, managing editor. Main character *must* be a country woman. All fiction must have a country setting. Fiction must have a positive, upbeat message. Includes fiction in every issue. Would buy more fiction if stories suitable for our audience were sent our way. No contemporary, urban pieces that deal with divorce, drugs, etc. Send complete ms. Length: 750-1,000 words.

POETRY Needs light verse, traditional. Poetry must have rhythm and rhyme. It must be country-related, positive, and upbeat. Always looking for seasonal poetry. Buys 6-12 poems/year. Submit maximum 6 poems. Length: 4-24 lines. **Pays $10-25/poem plus one contribtor's copy.**

💲💲 FARM & RANCH LIVING

RDA Enthusiast Brands, LLC, 1610 N. Second St., Suite 102, Milwaukee WI 53212-3906. (414)423-0100. **Fax:** (414)423-8463. **E-mail:** submissions@farmandranchliving.com. **Website:** lovethecountry.com. **30% freelance written. Eager to work with new/**

unpublished writers. Bimonthly magazine aimed at families that live on, work on, or have ties to a farm or ranch. "*F&RL* is *not* a 'how-to' magazine—it focuses on people who celebrate the pleasures of living off the land rather than production and profits." Estab. 1978. Circ. 400,000. Byline given. Pays on publication. No kill fee. Publishes ms an average of 6 months after acceptance. Submit seasonal material 6 months in advance. Accepts simultaneous submissions. "We are unable to respond to queries."

NONFICTION Needs humor, inspirational, interview, personal experience, photo feature, nostalgia, prettiest place in the country (photo/text tour of ranch or farm). No issue-oriented stories (pollution, animal rights, etc.). **Buys 30 mss/year.** Send complete ms. Length: 600-1,200 words. **Pays up to $400 for text/photo package.**

💲💲 HOBBY FARMS

I-5 Publishing, 470 Conway Court, Suite B6, Lexington KY 40511. **E-mail:** hobbyfarms@i5publishing.com. **Website:** www.hobbyfarms.com. **85% freelance written.** Bimonthly magazine covering small farms and rural lifestyle. "*Hobby Farms* is the magazine for rural enthusiasts. Whether you have a small garden or 100 acres, there is something in *Hobby Farms* to educate, enlighten, or inspire you." Estab. 2001. Circ. 252,801. Byline given. Pays on publication. Publishes ms an average of 6 months after acceptance. Editorial lead time 4 months. Submit seasonal material 6 months in advance. Accepts queries by mail, e-mail. Accepts simultaneous submissions. Responds in 2 months to queries and mss. Guidelines free.

NONFICTION Needs historical, how-to, interview, personal experience, technical, breed or crop profiles. **Buys 10 mss/year.** Send complete ms. Length: 1,000-1,500 words. Limit agreed upon in advance.

MONADNOCK TABLE: THE GUIDE TO OUR REGION'S FOOD, FARMS & COMMUNITY

60 West St., Keene NH 03431. (603)369-2525. **E-mail:** marcia@monadnocktable.com. **Website:** www.monadnocktable.com. **Contact:** Marcia Passos Duffy, editor. Quarterly magazine for local food/farms in the Monadnock Region of New Hampshire. Estab. 2010. Circ. 10,000. Byline given. Pays on publication. Offers 25% kill fee. Publishes ms 3 months after acceptance. Editorial lead time 3 months. Submit seasonal material 3 months in advance. Accepts queries by e-mail. Accepts simultaneous submissions. Responds

in 1 month to queries and mss. Sample copy online. Guidelines online.

NONFICTION Needs book excerpts, essays, how-to, interview, opinion, personal experience. Query. Length: 500-1,200 words. **Pays $75-125.**

COLUMNS Local Farmer (profile of local farmer in Monadnock Region), up to 600 words; Local Eats (profile of local chef and/or restaurant using local food), up to 600 words; Feature (how-to or "think" piece about local foods), up to 1,000 words; Books/Opinion/Commentary (review of books, book excerpt, commentary, opinion pieces about local food), up to 500 words. **Buys 10 mss/year.** Query.

$ MOTHER EARTH NEWS

Ogden Publications, 1503 SW 42nd St., Topeka KS 66609-1265. (785)274-4300. **E-mail:** letters@motherearthnews.com. **Website:** www.motherearthnews.com. **Contact:** Oscar "Hank" Will III, editor; Rebecca Martin, managing editor. **Mostly written by staff and team of established freelancers.** Bimonthly magazine emphasizing country living, country skills, natural health, and sustainable technologies for both long-time and would-be ruralists. "*Mother Earth News* promotes self-sufficient, financially independent, and environmentally aware lifestyles. Many of our feature articles are written by our Contributing Editors, but we also assign articles to freelance writers, particularly those who have experience with our subject matter (both firsthand and writing experience)." Circ. 350,000. Byline given. Pays on publication. No kill fee. Submit seasonal material 5 months in advance. Accepts queries by mail, e-mail. Accepts simultaneous submissions. Responds in 6 months to mss. Sample copy: $5. Guidelines online.

NONFICTION Needs how-to, green building, do-it-yourself, organic gardening, whole foods and cooking, natural health, livestock and sustainable farming, renewable energy, 21st-century homesteading, nature-environment-community, green transportation. No fiction, please. **Buys 35-50 mss/year.** "Query. Please send a short synopsis of the idea, a one-page outline, and any relevant digital photos and samples. If available, please send us copies of 1 or 2 published articles, or tell us where to find them online." **Pays $25-150.**

COLUMNS Country Lore (helpful how-to tips); 100-300 words; Firsthand Reports (first-person stories about sustainable lifestyles of all sorts), 1,500-2,000 words.

$$ RANGE

Purple Coyote Corp., 106 E. Adams St., Suite 201, Carson City NV 89706. (775)884-2200. **Fax:** (775)884-2213. **E-mail:** edit@rangemagazine.com. **Website:** www.rangemagazine.com. **Contact:** C.J. Hadley, editor/publisher. **70% freelance written.** *RANGE* covers ranching, farming, and the issues that affect agriculture. *RANGE* magazine is devoted to the issues that threaten the West, its people, lifestyles, lands, and wildlife. No stranger to controversy, *RANGE* is the leading forum for opposing viewpoints in the search for solutions that will halt the depletion of a national resource, the American rancher. Estab. 1991. Pays on publication. Publishes ms an average of 3-6 months after acceptance. Accepts queries by e-mail. Accepts simultaneous submissions. Responds in 1-2 months to queries; in 1-4 months to mss. Sample copy: $2. Guidelines online.

NONFICTION **Contact:** C.J. Hadley, editor, edit@rangemagazine.com. Needs expose, historical, humor, nostalgic, photo feature, profile. No sports or events. No book reviews. Writer must be familiar with *RANGE*. Query. Length: 500-2,000 words. **Pays $50-500.**

$ RURAL HERITAGE

P.O. Box 2067, Cedar Rapids IA 52406. (319)362-3027. **E-mail:** info@ruralheritage.com. **Website:** www.ruralheritage.com. **Contact:** Joe Mischka, editor. **98% freelance written. Willing to work with a small number of new/unpublished writers.** Bimonthly magazine devoted to the training and care of draft animals. Estab. 1976. Circ. 9,500. Byline given. Pays on publication. No kill fee. Publishes ms an average of 6 months after acceptance. Submit seasonal material 6 months in advance. Accepts queries by mail, e-mail. Accepts simultaneous submissions. Responds in 3 months to queries. Sample copy for $8. Guidelines online.

NONFICTION Needs how-to, interview, photo feature. No articles on *mechanized* farming. **Buys 200 mss/year.** Query or send complete ms. Length: 1,200-1,500 words. **Pays 5¢/word.**

POETRY Needs traditional. **Pays $5-25.**

SCIENCE

$$ AD ASTRA

To the Stars, National Space Society, P.O. Box 98106, Washington DC 20090. (202)429-1600. **Fax:** (703)435-

4390. **E-mail:** adastra@nss.org. **Website:** www.nss.org/adastra. **Contact:** Katherine Brick, Editor. **90% freelance written.** *Ad Astra* ("to the stars") is the award-winning magazine of the National Space Society, featuring the latest news in space exploration and stunning full-color photography. Published quarterly. "We publish non-technical, lively articles about all aspects of international space programs, from shuttle missions to planetary probes to plans for the future and commercial space." Estab. 1989. Circ. 25,000. Byline given. Pays on publication. No kill fee. Publishes ms 3-6 months after acceptance. Accepts queries by e-mail. Accepts simultaneous submissions. Responds only when interested. Sample copy for 9x12 SASE.

NONFICTION Needs book excerpts, essays, general interest, interview, opinion, photo feature, technical. No science fiction or UFO stories. Query with published clips. Length: 1,000-4,000 words with 2-8 full-size (8.5x11) color images at 300 dpi; 100-600 words for sidebars; 600-750 words for book reviews. **Pays 25¢/word.**

PHOTOS State availability. Identification of subjects required. Reviews color prints, digital, JPEG-IS, GISS. Negotiates pay. Buys one-time rights.

TIPS "We require mss to be in Word or text file formats. Know the field of space technology, programs, and policy. Know the players. Look for fresh angles. And, please, know how to write!"

🄢🄢🄢🄢 AMERICAN ARCHAEOLOGY

The Archaeological Conservancy, 1717 Girard Blvd., NE, Albuquerque NM 87106. (505)266-9668. **Fax:** (505)266-0311. **E-mail:** tacmag@nm.net. **Website:** www.americanarchaeology.org. **Contact:** Michael Bawaya, editor; Vicki Singer, art director. **60% freelance written.** Quarterly magazine. "We're a popular archaeology magazine. Our readers are very interested in this science. Our features cover important digs, prominent archaeologists, and most any aspect of the science. We only cover North America." Estab. 1997. Circ. 35,000. Byline given. Pays on acceptance. Offers 20% kill fee. Publishes ms an average of 3 months after acceptance. Editorial lead time 3 months. Accepts queries by mail, e-mail, fax. Accepts simultaneous submissions. Responds in 3 weeks to queries; in 1 month to mss.

NONFICTION No fiction, poetry, humor. **Buys 15 mss/year.** Query with published clips. Length: 1,500-3,000 words. **Pays $1,000-2,000.**

PHOTOS State availability. Identification of subjects required. Reviews transparencies, prints. Pays $50 and up for occasional stock images; assigns work by project (pay varies); negotiable. **Pays on acceptance.** Credit line given. Buys one-time rights. Offers $400-600/photo shoot. Negotiates payment individually. Buys one-time rights.

TIPS "Read the magazine. Features must have a considerable amount of archaeological detail."

🄢🄢🄢🄢 ARCHAEOLOGY

Archaeological Institute of America, 36-36 33rd St., Long Island NY 11106. (718)472-3050. **Fax:** (718)472-3051. **E-mail:** cvalentino@archaeology.org; editorial@archaeology.org. **Website:** www.archaeology.org. **Contact:** Editor-in-chief. **50% freelance written.** *ARCHAEOLOGY* combines worldwide archaeological findings with photography, specially rendered maps, drawings, and charts. Covers current excavations and recent discoveries, and includes personality profiles, technology updates, adventure, travel and studies of ancient cultures. "*ARCHAEOLOGY* magazine is a publication of the Archaeological Institute of America, a 130-year-old nonprofit organization. The magazine has been published continuously for more than 60 years. We have a total audience of nearly 750,000, mostly in the United States and Canada. Our readership is a combination of the general public, enthusiastic amateurs, and scholars in the field. Publishing bi-monthly, we bring our readers all the exciting aspects of archaeology: adventure, discovery, culture, history, technology, and travel. Authors include both professional journalists and professional archaeologists. If you are a scientist interested in writing about your research for *ARCHAEOLOGY*, see tips and suggestions on writing for a general audience online." Estab. 1948. Circ. 750,000. Byline given. Pays on acceptance. Offers 25% kill fee. Submit seasonal material 6 months in advance. Accepts queries by mail, e-mail, fax. Accepts simultaneous submissions. Sample copy and writer's guidelines free. Guidelines online. Request photographer's sample copy for $6 through paypal to scribblesbyshannon@yahoo.com.

NONFICTION Needs essays. **Buys 6 mss/year.** Query preferred. "Preliminary queries should be no more than 1 or 2 pages (500 words max.) in length and may be sent to the Editor-in-Chief by mail or via e-mail to editorial@archaeology.org. We do not accept telephone queries. Check our online index and search to make sure that we have not already published a similar article. Your query should tell us the following: who you are, why you are qualified to cover the subject, how you will cover the subject (with an emphasis on narrative structure, new knowledge, etc.), and why our readers would be interested in the subject." Length: 1,000-3,000 words. **Pays $2,000 maximum.**

COLUMNS Insider is a piece of about 2,500 words dealing with subject matter with which the author has an intimate, personal interest. **Conversation** is a one-page interview in a Q&A format with someone who has made a considerable impact on the field of archaeology or has done something unusual or intriguing. **Letter From.** is an account of a personal experience involving a particular topic or site. "Letters" have included a visit to an alien-archaeology theme park, the account of an archaeologist caught in a civil war, and an overnight stay with the guards at Angkor Wat. "Letters" are usually about 2,500 to 3,000 words in length. **Artifact** is the last editorial page of the magazine. Its purpose is to introduce the reader to a single artifact that reveals something surprising about a site or an historical event. Unusual artifacts recently excavated are preferred and visuals must be of the highest quality. The writer must explain the archaeological context, date, site found, etc., as well as summarize the artifact's importance in about 200 words or less. First person accounts by the actual excavators or specialists are preferred, although exceptions are be made.

$$ ASTRONOMY

Kalmbach Publishing, 21027 Crossroads Circle, P.O. Box 1612, Waukesha WI 53187-1612. (800)533-6644. **Fax:** (262)798-6468. **Website:** www.astronomy.com. **Contact:** David J. Eicher, editor; LuAnn Williams Belter, art director (for art and photography). **50% of articles submitted and written by science writers; includes commissioned and unsolicited.** Monthly magazine covering the science and hobby of astronomy. "Half of our magazine is for hobbyists (who are active observers of the sky); the other half is directed toward armchair astronomers who are intrigued by the science." Estab. 1973. Circ. 108,000. Byline given. Pays on acceptance. Does pay a kill fee, although rarely used. Accepts simultaneous submissions. Responds in 1 month to queries. Responds in 3 months to mss. on website.

NONFICTION Needs book excerpts, new product, photo feature, technical, space, astronomy. **Buys 75 mss/year.** Please query on all article ideas Length: 500-3,000 words. **Pays $100-1,000.**

$$$ CHEMICAL HERITAGE

Chemical Heritage Foundation (CHF), 315 Chestnut St., Philadelphia PA 19106. (215)925-2222. **E-mail:** editor@chemheritage.org. **Website:** www.chemheritage.org. **40% freelance written.** Published 3 times/year. *Chemical Heritage* reports on the history of the chemical and molecular sciences and industries, on Chemical Heritage Foundation activities, and on other activities of interest to our readers. Estab. 1982. Circ. 17,000. Byline given. Pays on acceptance. Publishes ms an average of 6-12 months after acceptance. Editorial lead time 4 months. Accepts queries by e-mail. Accepts simultaneous submissions. Responds in 1 month to queries and mss. Sample copy free.

NONFICTION Needs book excerpts, essays, historical, interview. "No exposés or excessively technical material. Many of our readers are highly educated professionals, but they may not be familiar with, for example, specific chemical processes." **Buys 3-5 mss/year.** Query. Length: 1,000-3,500 words. **Pays 50¢-$1/word.**

COLUMNS Book reviews: 200 or 750 words; CHF collections: 300-500 words; policy: 1,000 words; personal remembrances: 750 words; profiles of CHF awardees and oral history subjects: 600-900 words: buys 3-5 mms/year. **Buys 10 mss/year.** Query.

$$$ CHEMMATTERS

American Chemical Society, Education Division, 1155 16th St., NW, Washington DC 20036. (202)872-6164. **Fax:** (202)872-8068. **E-mail:** chemmatters@acs.org. **Website:** www.acs.org/chemmatters. **Contact:** Patrice Pages, editor; Cornithia Harris, art director. **100% freelance written.** Covers topics of interest to teenagers and that can be explained with chemistry. *ChemMatters*, published 4 times/year, is a magazine that helps high school students find connections between chemistry and the world around them. Estab. 1983. Circ. 30,000. Byline given. Pays on acceptance. Publishes ms 6 months after acceptance. Accepts queries by mail, e-mail. Accepts simultaneous submissions. Responds in 4 weeks to queries and mss. Sample copies and writer's guidelines free (available as e-mail attachment upon request).

NONFICTION Query with published clips. **Pays $700-1,000 for article.**

$$$$ INVENTORS DIGEST

520 Elliot St., Suite 200, Charlotte NC 28202. (800)838-8808. **Fax:** (704)333-5115. **E-mail:** info@inventorsdigest.com. **Website:** www.inventorsdigest.com. **50% freelance written.** Monthly magazine covering inventions, technology, engineering, intellectual property issues. *Inventors Digest* is committed to educating and inspiring entry- and enterprise-level inventors and professional innovators. As the leading print and online publication for the innovation culture, *Inventors Digest* delivers useful, entertaining, and cutting-edge information to help its readers succeed. Estab. 1983. Circ. 40,000. Byline given. Pays on publication. Offers 40% kill fee. Publishes ms an average of 2 months after acceptance. Editorial lead time 2 months. Submit seasonal material 4 months in advance. Accepts queries by mail, e-mail. Accepts simultaneous submissions. Responds in 3 weeks to queries; in 1 month to mss. Sample copy online. Guidelines free.

NONFICTION Needs book excerpts, historical, how-to, inspirational, interview, new product, opinion, personal experience, technical. Special issues: Editorial calendar available online. "We don't want poetry. No stories that talk about readers—stay away from 'one should do X' construction. Nothing that duplicates what you can read elsewhere." **Buys 4 mss/year.** Query. Length varies. For any piece more than 2,000 words, send a 300-word synopsis first. **Payment varies, usually at least $50 for both requested and unsolicited articles.**

COLUMNS Cover (the most important package—puts a key topic in compelling context), 2,000-3,000 words; Radar (news/product snippets), 1,200 words; Bookshelf (book reviews), 700 words; Pro Bono (legal issues), 850 words; Profile (human-interest stories on inventors and innovators), 1,000 words; BrainChild (celebration of young inventors and innovators), 1,000 words; FirstPerson (inventors show how they've overcome hurdles), 1,000; MeetingRoom (learn secrets to success of best inventor groups in the country), 900 words; TalkBack (Q&A with manufacturers, retailers, etc. in the innovation industry), 800 words; Five Questions With . (a conversation with some of the brightest and most controversial minds in Technology, manufacturing, academia and other fields), 800 words. **Buys 4 mss/year.** Query. **Pays $20.**

$$$$ SCIENTIFIC AMERICAN

75 Varick St., 9th Floor, New York NY 10013-1917. (212)451-8200. **E-mail:** editors@sciam.com. **Website:** www.sciam.com. **Contact:** Mariette DiChristina, editor-in-chief. Monthly magazine covering developments and topics of interest in the world of science. "*Scientific American* brings its readers directly to the wellspring of exploration and technological innovation. The magazine specializes in first-hand accounts by the people who actually do the work. Their personal experience provides an authoritative perspective on future growth. Over 100 of our authors have won Nobel Prizes. Complementing those articles are regular departments written by *Scientific American*'s staff of professional journalists, all specialists in their fields. *Scientific American* is the authoritative source of advance information. Authors are the first to report on important breakthroughs, because they're the people who make them. It all goes back to *Scientific American*'s corporate mission: to link those who use knowledge with those who create it." Estab. 1845. Circ. 710,000. Byline given. Pays on publication. No kill fee. Accepts simultaneous submissions. Guidelines available on website.

NONFICTION Query before submitting. **Pays $1/word average.**

$$ SKY & TELESCOPE

F+W, A Content and Ecommerce Company, 90 Sherman St., Cambridge MA 02140. (617)864-7360. **Fax:** (617)864-6117. **E-mail:** ptyson@skyandtelescope.com. **Website:** skyandtelescope.com. **Contact:** Peter Tyson, editor in chief. **15% freelance written.** Monthly magazine covering astronomy. "*Sky & Telescope* is the magazine of record for astronomy. We cover amateur activities, research news, equipment, book, and software reviews. Our audience is the amateur astronomer who wants to learn more about the night sky." Estab. 1941. Circ. 65,000. Byline given. Pays on publication. 20% kill fee. Publishes ms an average of 6 months after acceptance. Editorial lead time 4 months. Submit seasonal material 1 year in advance. Accepts queries by mail, e-mail, fax. Accepts simultaneous submissions. Responds in 3 weeks to queries; in 1 month to mss. Sample copy: $6.99. Guidelines online.

NONFICTION Needs essays, historical, how-to, opinion, personal experience, photo feature, technical. No poetry, crosswords, New Age, or alternative cosmologies. **Buys 10 mss/year.** Query. Length: 1,000-2,400 words. **Pays at least 25¢/word.**

COLUMNS Focal Point (opinion), 550 words. **Buys 12 mss/year.** Query. **Pays 25¢/word.**

$$ WEATHERWISE

Taylor & Francis Group, 530 Walnut Str., Suite 850, Philadelphia PA 19106. (215)625-8900. **E-mail:** margaret.benner@taylorandfrancis.com. **Website:** www.weatherwise.org. **Contact:** Margaret Benner Smidt, editor in chief. **75% freelance written.** Bimonthly magazine covering weather and meteorology. "*Weatherwise* is America's only magazine about the weather. Our readers range from professional weathercasters and scientists to basement-bound hobbyists, but all share a common interest in craving information about weather as it relates to the atmospheric sciences, technology, history, culture, society, art, etc." Estab. 1948. Circ. 11,000. Byline given. Pays on publication. No kill fee. Publishes ms an average of 6 months after acceptance. Editorial lead time 6-9 months. Submit seasonal material 9 months in advance. Accepts queries by mail, e-mail, fax, phone. Accepts simultaneous submissions. Responds in 2 months to queries. Guidelines online.

NONFICTION Needs book excerpts, essays, general interest, historical, how-to, interview, new product, opinion, personal experience, photo feature, technical, travel. Special issues: Photo Contest (September/October deadline June 2). No blow-by-blow accounts of the biggest storm to ever hit your backyard. **Buys 15-18 mss/year.** Query with published clips. Length: 2,000-3,000 words. **Pays $200-500 for assigned articles. Pays $0-300 for unsolicited articles.**

COLUMNS Weather Front (news, trends), 300-400 words; Weather Talk (folklore and humor), 650-1,000 words. **Buys 12-15 mss/year.** Query with published clips. **Pays $0-200.**

SCIENCE FICTION, FANTASY & HORROR

ANALOG SCIENCE FICTION & FACT

Dell Magazines, 44 Wall St., Suite 904, New York NY 10005-2401. **E-mail:** analog@dellmagazines.com. **Website:** www.analogsf.com. **Contact:** Trevor Quachri, editor. **100% freelance written. Eager to work with new/unpublished writers.** *Analog* seeks "solidly entertaining stories exploring solidly thought-out speculative ideas. But the ideas, and consequently the stories, are always new. Real science and technology have always been important in *ASF,* not only as the foundation of its fiction but as the subject of articles about real research with big implications for the future." Estab. 1930. Circ. 50,000. Byline given. Pays on acceptance. No kill fee. Publishes ms an average of 10 months after acceptance. Accepts queries by mail, online submission form. Accepts simultaneous submissions. Responds in 2-3 months to mss. Sample copy: $5 and SASE. Guidelines online.

NONFICTION Special issues: Articles should deal with subjects of not only current but future interest, i.e., with topics at the present frontiers of research whose likely future developments have implications of wide interest. **Buys 11 mss/year.** Send complete ms via online submissions manager (preferred) or postal mail. Does not accept e-mail submissions. Length: up to 4,000 words. **Pays 9¢/word.**

FICTION "Basically, we publish science fiction stories. That is, stories in which some aspect of future science or technology is so integral to the plot that, if that aspect were removed, the story would collapse. The science can be physical, sociological, psychological. The technology can be anything from electronic engineering to biogenetic engineering. But the stories must be strong and realistic, with believable people (who needn't be human) doing believable things—no matter how fantastic the background might be." Needs science fiction. No fantasy or stories in which the scientific background is implausible or plays no essential role. Send complete ms via online submissions manager (preferred) or postal mail. Does not accept e-mail submissions. Length: 2,000-7,000 words for short stories, 10,000-20,000 words for novelettes and novellas, and 40,000-80,000 for serials. **Analog pays 8-10¢/word for short stories up to 7,500 words, 8-8.5¢ for longer material, 6¢/word for serials.**

POETRY Send poems via online submissions manager (preferred) or postal mail. Does not accept e-mail submissions. Length: up to 40 lines/poem. **Pays $1/line.**

$ APEX MAGAZINE

Apex Publications, LLC, P.O. Box 24323, Lexington KY 40524. **E-mail:** lesley@apex-magazine.com. **Website:** www.apexbookcompany.com. **Contact:** Lesley Conner, managing editor. **100% freelance written.**

Monthly e-zine publishing dark speculative fiction. "An elite repository for new and seasoned authors with an other-worldly interest in the unquestioned and slightly bizarre parts of the universe." Estab. 2004. Circ. 28,000 unique visits per month. Byline given. Pays 30 days after publication. Offers 30% kill fee. Publishes mss an average of 6 months after acceptance. Editorial lead time 2 weeks. Submit seasonal material 6 months in advance. Accepts queries by e-mail. Responds in 20-30 days to queries and mss. Sample content available online. Guidelines online.

NONFICTION Buys 36 mss/year. Send complete ms. Length: 100-7,500 words. **Pays 6¢/word.**

FICTION Needs fantasy, horror, science fiction, short stories. **Buys 36 mss/year.** Send complete ms. Length: 100-7,500 words. **Pays 6¢/word.**

POETRY Submit up to 5 poems. Length: up to 200 lines/poem. **Pays 25¢/line.**

⑤ ASIMOV'S SCIENCE FICTION

Dell Magazines, 44 Wall St., Suite 904, New York NY 10005. **E-mail:** asimovs@dellmagazines.com. **Website:** www.asimovs.com. **Contact:** Sheila Williams, editor; Victoria Green, senior art director. **98% freelance written. Works with a small number of new/unpublished writers each year.** *Asimov's*, published 10 times/year, including 2 double issues, is 5.875x8.625 (trim size); 112 pages; 30 lb. newspaper; 70 lb. to 8 pt. C1S cover stock; illustrations; rarely has photos. "Magazine consists of science fiction and fantasy stories for adults and young adults. Publishes the best short science fiction available." Estab. 1977. Circ. 50,000. Pays on acceptance. No kill fee. Publishes ms an average of 6-12 months after acceptance. Accepts queries by mail. Responds in 2 months to queries; in 3 months to mss. Sample copy: $5. Guidelines online or for #10 SASE.

FICTION Wants "science fiction primarily. Some fantasy and humor. It is best to read a great deal of material in the genre to avoid the use of some very old ideas." Submit ms via online submissions manager or postal mail; no e-mail submissions. Needs fantasy, science fiction. No horror or psychic/supernatural, sword and sorcery, explicit sex or violence that isn't integral to the story. Would like to see more hard science fiction. Length: 750-15,000 words. **Pays 8-10¢/word for short stories up to 7,500 words; 8-8.5¢/word for longer material. Works between 7,500-10,000 words by authors who make more than 8¢/word for short**

stories will receive a flat rate that will be no less than the payment would be for a shorter story.

BEYOND CENTAURI

White Cat Publications, LLC, 33080 Industrial Rd., Suite 101, Livonia MI 48150. (734)237-8522. **Fax:** (313)557-5162. **E-mail:** beyondcentauri@whitecat-publications.com. **Website:** www.whitecatpublications.com/guidelines/beyond-centauri. *Beyond Centauri*, published quarterly, contains fantasy, science fiction, sword and sorcery, very mild horror short stories, poetry, and illustrations for readers ages 10 and up. Estab. 2003. Publishes ms 1-2 months after acceptance. Accepts queries by e-mail. Accepts simultaneous submissions. Responds in 2-3 months. Single copy: $7.

NONFICTION Needs opinion, reviews, short articles about space exploration, science, and technology. Send complete ms in the body of an e-mail, or as an RTF attachment. Length: up to 1,500 words. **Pays $7/piece and 1 contributor's copy.**

FICTION Looks for themes of science fiction or fantasy. "Science fiction and especially stories that take place in outer space will find great favor with us." Needs fantasy, horror, science fiction, short stories. Submit in the body of an e-mail, or as an RTF attachment. Length: up to 2,500 words. **Pays $6/story, $3/reprints, and $2/flash fiction (under 1,000 words), plus 1 contributor's copy.**

POETRY Wants fantasy, science fiction, spooky horror, and speculative poetry for younger readers. Considers poetry by children and teens. Has published poetry by Bruce Boston, Bobbi Sinha-Morey, Debbie Feo, Dorothy Imm, Cythera, and Terrie Leigh Relf. Looks for themes of science fiction and fantasy. Poetry should be submitted in the body of an e-mail, or as an RTF attachment. Does not want horror with excessive blood and gore. Length: up to 50 lines/poem. **Pays $2/original poem, $1/reprints, $1/scifaiku and related form, plus 1 contributor's copy.**

⑤ DARK TALES

Dark Tales, 7 Offley St., Worcester WR3 8BH United Kingdom. **Website:** www.darktales.co.uk. **Contact:** Sean Jeffery, editor. "We publish horror and speculative short fiction from anybody, anywhere. The publication is professionally illustrated throughout." Estab. 2003. Circ. 350+. Pays on publication. Accepts simultaneous submissions. Responds in 1 week to queries;

in 3 months to mss. Sometimes comments on rejected mss. Sample copy: $3. Guidelines available on website.

FICTION Needs fantasy, science fiction, short stories, horror (dark fantasy, futuristic, psychological, supernatural), science fiction (soft/sociological). Currently only publishing from our monthly contest—please see www.darktales.co.uk for details. Length: 500-3,500 words. Average length: 2,500 words. Publishes short shorts. Average length of short shorts: 500 words. **Pays £100.**

$$ HELIOTROPE

E-mail: heliotropeditor@gmail.com. **Website:** www.heliotropemag.com. *Heliotrope* is a quarterly e-zine that publishes fiction, articles, and poetry. Estab. 2006. Pays on publication. No kill fee. Accepts queries by e-mail. Responds in 1 month to mss. Guidelines online.

NONFICTION Needs opinion. Submit complete ms via e-mail. Length: 2,000 words minimum. **Pays $90.**

FICTION "If your story is something we can't label, we're interested in that, too." Needs fantasy, horror, mystery, science fiction. Submit complete ms via e-mail. Length: up to 5,000 words. **Pays 10¢/word.**

POETRY Submit via e-mail. **Pays $50.**

$ LEADING EDGE MAGAZINE

4087 JKB, Provo UT 84602. **E-mail:** editor@leadingedgemagazine.com; fiction@leadingedgemagazine.com; art@leadingedgemagazine.com; poetry@leadingedgemagazine.com; nonfiction@leadingedgemagazine.com. **Website:** www.leadingedgemagazine.com. **Contact:** Leah Welker, editor in chief. **90% freelance written.** Semiannual magazine covering science fiction and fantasy. "*Leading Edge* is a magazine dedicated to new and upcoming talent in the fields of science fiction and fantasy. We strive to encourage developing and established talent and provide high-quality speculative fiction to our readers." Does not accept mss with sex, excessive violence, or profanity. Estab. 1981. Circ. 200. Byline given. Pays on publication. No kill fee. Publishes ms an average of 2-4 months after acceptance. Accepts queries by mail, e-mail. Responds within 12 months to mss. Single copy: $5.95. "We no longer provide subscriptions, but *Leading Edge* is now available on Amazon Kindle, as well as print-on-demand." Guidelines online.

NONFICTION Needs essays, expose, interview, reviews. Send complete ms with cover letter and SASE. Include estimated word count. Length: up to 15,000 words. **Pays 1¢/word; $50 maximum.**

FICTION Needs fantasy, science fiction. **Buys 14-16 mss/year.** Send complete ms with cover letter and SASE. Include estimated word count. Length: up to 15,000 words. **Pays 1¢/word; $50 maximum.**

POETRY Needs avant-garde, haiku, light verse, traditional. Publishes 2-4 poems per issue. "Poetry should reflect both literary value and popular appeal and should deal with science fiction- or fantasy-related themes." No e-mail submissions. Cover letter is preferred. Include name, address, phone number, length of poem, title, and type of poem at the top of each page. Please include SASE with every submission." Submit maximum 10 poems. Pays $10 for first 4 pages; $1.50/each subsequent page.

THE MAGAZINE OF FANTASY & SCIENCE FICTION

P.O. Box 3447, Hoboken NJ 07030. (201) 876-2551. **E-mail:** fandsf@aol.com. **Website:** www.fandsf.com; submissions.ccfinlay.com/fsf. **Contact:** C.C. Finlay, editor. **100% freelance written.** "*The Magazine of Fantasy and Science Fiction* publishes various types of science fiction and fantasy short stories and novellas, making up about 80% of each issue. The balance of each issue is devoted to articles about science fiction, a science column, book and film reviews, cartoons, and competitions." Bimonthly. Estab. 1949. Circ. 40,000. Byline given. Pays on acceptance. No kill fee. Publishes ms an average of 9-12 months after acceptance. Submit seasonal material 8 months in advance. Accepts queries by mail, e-mail. Accepts simultaneous submissions. Responds in 2 months to queries. Sample: $7 US, $15.00 international. Guidelines for SASE, by e-mail, or on website at www.sfsite.com/fsf/glines.htm.

NONFICTION Needs memoir. Send complete ms.

COLUMNS Curiosities (reviews of odd and obscure books), up to 270 words. Accepts 6 mss/year. Query. **Pays $75.**

FICTION "Prefers character-oriented stories. We receive a lot of fantasy fiction but never enough science fiction." Needs adventure, fantasy, horror, humorous, science fiction, short stories, space fantasy, sword & sorcery, dark fantasy, futuristic, psychological, supernatural, science fiction, hard science/technological, soft/sociological. **Buys 60-90 mss/year.** Send complete ms. Length: up to 25,000 words. **Pays 7-12¢/word.**

POETRY Wants only poetry that deals with the fantastic or the science fictional. Has published poetry by Rebecca Kavaler, Elizabeth Bear, Sophie M. White, and Robert Frazier. **Pays $50/poem and 2 contributor's copies.**

SCIFAIKUEST

P.O. Box 782, Cedar Rapids IA 52406. **E-mail:** gatrix65@yahoo.com. **Website:** albanlake.com/scifaikuest. **Contact:** Tyree Campbell, managing editor; Teri Santitoro, editor. *Scifaikuest*, published quarterly both online and in print, features "science fiction/fantasy/horror minimalist poetry, especially scifaiku, and related forms. We also publish articles about various poetic forms and reviews of poetry collections. The online and print versions of *Scifaikuest* are different." Estab. 2003. Time between acceptance and publication is 1-2 months. Submit seasonal poems 6 months in advance. Responds in 6-8 weeks. Single copy: $7; subscription: $20/year, $37 for 2 years. Make checks payable to Tyree Campbell/Alban Lake Publishing. Guidelines available on website.

NONFICTION "We're looking for articles related in some way to one or more of the poetry forms we publish, or related to similar forms such as sijo." Length: under 1,000 words but considers longer essays. **Pays $6/article and 1 contributor's copy.**

POETRY Wants "artwork, scifaiku, and speculative minimalist forms such as tanka, haibun, ghazals, senryu. Submit 10 poems at a time. Accepts e-mail submissions (pasted into body of message). No disk submissions; artwork as e-mail attachment or inserted body of e-mail. "Submission should include snail-mail address and a short (1-2 lines) bio." Reads submissions year round. "Editor Teri Santitoro makes all decisions regarding acceptances." Often comments on rejected poems. Has published poetry by Tom Brinck, Oino Sakai, Deborah P. Kolodji, Aurelio Rico Lopez III, Joanne Morcom, and John Dunphy. "No 'traditional' poetry." Length: varies, depending on poem type. **Pays $1/poem, $6/review or article, and 1 contributor's copy.**

SCREEM MAGAZINE

41 Mayer St., Wilkes Barre PA 18702. **E-mail:** screemagazine@msn.com. **Website:** www.screemag.com. Magazine covering everything related to horror. Accepts simultaneous submissions. Sample copy online at website. Back copies between $7.95 and $20.

NONFICTION Query first.

SPACE AND TIME

458 Elizabeth Ave., Somerset NJ 08873. **Website:** www.spaceandtimemagazine.com. **Contact:** Hildy Silverman, publisher. **100% freelance written.** *Space and Time* is the longest continually published small-press genre fiction magazine still in print. We pride ourselves in having published the first stories of some of the great writers in science fiction, fantasy, and horror. Estab. 1966. Circ. 2,000. Byline given. Pays on publication. No kill fee. Publishes stories/poems 6-12 months after acceptance. Accepts queries by e-mail. Sample copy: $6. Guidelines available only on website. Only opens periodically—announcements of open reading periods appear on Facebook page and website. No fiction or poetry considered outside of open reading periods.

FICTION Contact: Gerard Houarner. "We are looking for creative blends of science fiction, fantasy, and/or horror." Needs fantasy, horror, science fiction, short stories. "Do not send children's stories." Submit electronically as a Word doc or .rtf attachment ONLY during open reading periods. Anything sent outside those period will be rejected out of hand. Length: 1,000-10,000 words. Average length: 6,500 words. Average length of short shorts: 1,000 words. **Pays 1¢/word.**

POETRY Contact: Linda Addison. Needs speculative nature—science fiction, fantasy, horror themes and imagery. "Multiple submissions are okay within reason (no more than 3 at a time). Submit embedded in an e-mail, a Word doc, or .rtf attachment. ONLY submit during open poetry reading periods, which are announced via the Facebook page and on the website. All other poetry submitted outside these reading periods will be rejected out of hand." Poetry without any sort of genre or speculative element. Buys Publish an average of 15 per year poems/year. Submit maximum 3 poems. No longer than a single standard page. **Pays $5/poem.**

STAR*LINE

Science Fiction Poetry Association, W5679 State Rd. 60, Poynette WI 53955. **E-mail:** starlineeditor@gmail.com. **Website:** www.sfpoetry.com. **Contact:** F.J. Bergmann, editor. *Star*Line*, published quarterly in print and .pdf format by the Science Fiction Poetry Association (see separate listing in Organizations), is a speculative poetry magazine. "Open to all forms as long as your poetry uses speculative motifs: science fiction, fantasy, or horror." Estab. 1978. Accepts queries by e-mail. Accepts simultaneous submissions. Responds in 3 days. Guidelines online.

POETRY Submit 3-5 poems at a time. Accepts e-mail submissions (preferred; pasted into body of message, no attachments). **Pays 3¢/word rounded to the next dollar; minimum $3, maximum $25.**

🖐 VAMPIRES 2 MAGAZINE

Man's Story 2 Publishing Co., 1321 Snapfinger Rd., Decatur GA 30032. **E-mail:** vampires2com2@aol. com. **Website:** www.vampires2.us. **Contact:** Carlos Dunn, founder and editor. **80% freelance written.** "Online e-zine that strives to re-create vampire romance in the pulp fiction style of the 1920s through the 1970s with strong emphasis on 3D graphic art." Also features illustrated stories, online magazine, online photo galleries, and more. Estab. 1999. Circ. 2,500. Pays on publication. Publishes ms an average of 1-6 months after acceptance. Accepts queries by e-mail. Accepts simultaneous submissions. Guidelines online.

FICTION Needs adventure, fantasy, horror, suspense, pulp fiction involving vampires. Send complete ms via e-mail as a .doc attachment. Include short summary of story. Length: up to 3,500 words or up to 10,000 words (two options offered; see website for details).

SEX

🖐🖐 EXOTIC MAGAZINE

XMAG, LLC, 818 SW Third Ave., Suite 1324, Portland OR 97204. (503)241-4317. **Fax:** (503)914-0439. **E-mail:** editorial@xmag.com; info@xmag.com. **Website:** www.xmag.com. **Contact:** John R. Voge, editor. Monthly magazine covering adult entertainment and sexuality. "*Exotic* is pro-sex, informative, amusing, mature, and intelligent. Our readers rent and/or buy adult videos, visit strip clubs, and are interested in topics related to the adult entertainment industry and sexuality/culture. Don't talk down to them or fire too far over their heads. Many readers are computer literate and well-traveled. We're also interested in insightful fetish material. We are not a 'hard core' publication." Estab. 1993. Circ. 75,000. Byline given. Pays 30 days after publication. No kill fee. Accepts queries by e-mail. Accepts simultaneous submissions. Responds in 2 weeks to queries; in 2 months to mss. Sample copy for SAE with 9x12 envelope and 5 first-class stamps. Guidelines for #10 SASE.

NONFICTION Needs expose, general interest, historical, how-to, humor, interview. No men writing as women, articles about being a "horny guy," or opinion pieces pretending to be fact pieces. **Buys 36 mss/year.** Send complete ms. Length: 1,000-1,800 words. **Pays 10¢/word, up to $150.**

FICTION "We are currently overwhelmed with fiction submissions. Please only send fiction if it's really amazing." Needs erotica, slice-of-life vignettes. Send complete ms. Length: 1,000-1,800 words. **Pays 10¢/word, up to $150.**

🖐 M.I.P. COMPANY

P.O. Box 27484, Minneapolis MN 55427. **Website:** www.mipco.com. **Contact:** Michael Peltsman, editor. Specializes in Russian erotic prose and poetry. The publisher of controversial Russian literature (erotic prose and poetry). Estab. 1984. Accepts simultaneous submissions. Responds in 1 month to queries. Seldom comments on rejected poems.

POETRY Considers simultaneous submissions; no previously published poems.

🖐🖐🖐🖐🖐 PENTHOUSE

General Media Communications, 2 Penn Plaza, 11th Floor, New York NY 10121. (212)702-6000. **Fax:** (212)702-6279. **E-mail:** pbloch@pmgi.com. **Website:** www.penthouse.com. Monthly magazine. *Penthouse* is for the sophisticated male. Its editorial scope ranges from outspoken contemporary comment to photography essays of beautiful women. *Penthouse* features interviews with personalities, sociological studies, humor, travel, food and wine, and fashion and grooming for men. Estab. 1969. Circ. 640,000. Byline given. Pays 2 months after acceptance. Offers 25% kill fee. Editorial lead time 3 months. Accepts simultaneous submissions. Guidelines for #10 SASE.

NONFICTION Needs expose, general interest, interview. **Buys 50 mss/year.** Send complete ms. Length: 4,000-6,000 words. **Pays $3,000.**

COLUMNS Length: 1,000 words. **Buys 25 mss/year.** Query with published clips or send complete ms. **Pays $500.**

PLAYBOY MAGAZINE

9346 Civic Center Dr., #200, Beverly Hills CA 90210. **Fax:** (310)786-7440. **Website:** www.playboy.com. Monthly magazine. The preeminent entertainment magazine for the sophisticated urban male. This legendary brand continues to produce top-tier literature and journalism while maintaining its legacy as the industry's most artful and provocative image maker. Estab. 1953. Accepts simultaneous submissions.

VANILLEROTICA LITERARY EZINE

Cleveland OH 44102. (216)799-9775. **E-mail:** talentdripseroticpublishing@yahoo.com. **Website:** eroticatalentdrips.wordpress.com. **Contact:** Kimberly Steele, founder. *Vanillerotica*, published monthly on line, focuses solely on showcasing new erotic fiction. Estab. 2007. Time between acceptance and publication is 2 months. Accepts queries by e-mail. Accepts simultaneous submissions. Responds to general and submission queries within a week. Guidelines available on website.

FICTION Submit short stories by e-mail to talentdripseroticpublishing@yahoo.com. Stories should be pasted into body of message. Reads submissions during publication months only. Length: 5,000-10,000 words. **Pays $15 for each accepted short story.**

POETRY Needs erotic. Submit by e-mail to talentdripseroticpublishing@yahoo.com. Accepts e-mail pasted into body of message. Reads submissions during publication months only. Submit maximum 2-3 poems. Length: up to 30 lines/poem. **Pays $10 for each accepted poem.**

SPORTS

BASEBALL

🟡 JUNIOR BASEBALL

JSAN Publishing LLC, 14 Woodway Ln., Wilton CT 06897. **E-mail:** publisher@juniorbaseball.com. **Website:** www.juniorbaseball.com. **Contact:** Jim Beecher, editor and publisher. **25% freelance written.** Bimonthly magazine focused on youth baseball players ages 7-17 (including high school) and their parents/coaches. Edited to various reading levels, depending upon age/skill level of feature. Estab. 1996. Circ. 20,000. Byline given. Pays on publication. No kill fee. Publishes ms an average of 4 months after acceptance. Editorial lead time 3 months. Submit seasonal material 4 months in advance. Accepts queries by e-mail. Accepts simultaneous submissions. Responds in 2 weeks to queries; in 1 month to mss. Sample copy: $5 or free online.

NONFICTION "No trite first-person articles about your kid. No fiction or poetry." **Buys 8-12 mss/year.** Query. Length: 500-1,000 words. **Pays $50-100.**

COLUMNS When I Was a Kid (a current Major League Baseball player profile); Parents Feature (topics of interest to parents of youth ball players); all 1,000-1,500 words. In the Spotlight (news, events, new products), 50-100 words; Hot Prospect (written for the 14-and-older competitive player; high school baseball is included, and the focus is on improving the finer points of the game to make the high school team, earn a college scholarship, or attract scouts, written to an adult level), 500-1,000 words. **Buys 8-12 mss/year. Pays $50-100.**

BASKETBALL

WOMEN'S BASKETBALL

4125 Gunn Hwy, Ste. B1, Tampa FL 33618. (813)264-2772. **Fax:** (813)264-2343. **E-mail:** clay@wbmagazine.com. **Website:** www.wbmagazine.com. **Contact:** Clay Kallam, managing editor. Bimonthly magazine covering all aspects of women's basketball from youth to college to WNBA/Olympics. We are the only printed national publication devoted exclusively to girls and women's basketball. Accepts queries by e-mail. Accepts simultaneous submissions.

NONFICTION Needs general interest, how-to, interview. Query with published clips. **Payment based on work being published.**

BICYCLING

🟡🟡🟡 ADVENTURE CYCLIST

Adventure Cycling Association, Box 8308, Missoula MT 59807. (406)721-1776, ext. 222. **Fax:** (406)721-8754. **E-mail:** magazine@adventurecycling.org. **Website:** www.adventurecycling.org/adventure-cyclist. **Contact:** Alex Strickland. **75% freelance written.** Published 9 times/year for Adventure Cycling Association members, emphasizing bicycle tourism and travel. Estab. 1975. Circ. 45,500. Byline given. Pays on publication. Kill fee 25%. Publishes ms 8-12 months after acceptance. Submit seasonal material 12 months in advance. Accepts queries by online submission form. Accepts simultaneous submissions. Sample copy and guidelines for 9x12 SAE with 4 first-class stamps. Guidelines online.

NONFICTION Needs essays, historical, how-to, humor, inspirational, memoir, opinion, personal experience, photo feature, reviews, travel, U.S. or foreign tour accounts. **Buys 20-25 mss/year.** Send complete ms. Length: 1,400-3,500 words. **Inquiries requested prior to complete manuscripts. Pays sliding scale per word.** Expenses must be agreed upon before final contract is signed.

🌑🌑 CYCLE CALIFORNIA! MAGAZINE

1702 Meridian Ave. Suite L , #289, San Jose CA 95125. (408)924-0270. **Fax:** (408)292-3005. **E-mail:** tcorral@cyclecalifornia.com; BMack@cyclecalifornia.com. **E-mail:** tcorral@cyclecalifornia.com. **Website:** www.cyclecalifornia.com. **Contact:** Tracy L. Corral; Bob Mack, publisher. **75% freelance written.** Magazine published 11 times/year covering Northern California bicycling events, races, people. Issues (topics) covered include bicycle commuting, bicycle politics, touring, racing, nostalgia, history—anything at all to do with riding a bike. Magazine published 11 times/year covering Northern California bicycling events, races, people. Issues (topics) covered include bicycle commuting, bicycle politics, touring, racing, nostalgia, history—anything at all to do with riding a bike. Estab. 1995. Circ. 32,000 print; 70,000 digital. Byline given. Pays on publication. No kill fee. Publishes ms an average of 3 months after acceptance. Editorial lead time 6 weeks. Submit seasonal material 8 weeks in advance. Accepts queries by e-mail. Accepts simultaneous submissions. Responds in 1 month to queries. Sample copy with 9x12 SASE and $1.50 first-class postage. Guidelines with #10 SASE.

NONFICTION Needs historical, how-to, humor, interview, memoir, opinion, personal experience, profile, technical, travel. Special issues: Bicycle Tour & Travel (January). No articles about any sport that doesn't relate to bicycling. No product reviews. **Buys 36 mss/year.** Query. Length: 500-1,500 words. **Pays 10-15¢/word.**

COLUMNS Contact: Tracy Corral, tcorral@cyclecalifornia.com. **Buys 2-3 mss/year.** Query with links to published stories. **Pays 10-15¢/word.**

FICTION Needs humorous.

POETRY Contact: Tracy Corral, tcorral@cyclecalifornia.com. Needs Poetry, as it relates to bike riding. Buys 1-2 poems/year.

🌑🌑 VELONEWS

Inside Communications, Inc., Velo News, 3002 Sterling Circle, Suite 100, Boulder CO 80301. (303)440-0601. **Fax:** (303)444-6788. **E-mail:** webletters@competitorgroup.com. **E-mail:** jbradley@competitorgroup.com. **Website:** www.velonews.com. **Contact:** John Bradley, editor in chief. **40% freelance written.** Monthly tabloid covering bicycle racing. Estab. 1972. Circ. 48,000. Byline given. Pays on publication. No kill fee. Publishes ms an average of 1 month after acceptance. Accepts simultaneous submissions. Responds in 3 weeks to queries. Guidelines online.

NONFICTION Buys 80 mss/year. Query. Length: 300-1,200 words. **Pays $100-400.**

BOATING

🌑🌑🌑 CANOE & KAYAK

GrindMedia, LLC, 2052 Corte del Nogal, Carlsbad CA 92011. (425)827-6363. **E-mail:** jeff@canoekayak.com. **Website:** www.canoekayak.com. **Contact:** Jeff Moag. **75% freelance written.** Quarterly magazine covering paddlesports. "*Canoe & Kayak* is North America's No. 1 paddlesports resource. Our readers include flatwater and whitewater canoeists and kayakers of all skill levels. We provide comprehensive information on destinations, technique and equipment. Beyond that, we cover canoe and kayak camping, safety, the environment, and the history of boats and sport." Estab. 1972. Circ. 35,000. Byline given. Pays on or shortly after publication. No kill fee. Publishes ms an average of 6 months after acceptance. Editorial lead time 6 months. Submit seasonal material 8 months in advance. Accepts queries by mail, e-mail. Accepts simultaneous submissions. Responds in 2 months to queries. Sample copy and writer's guidelines for 9x12 SAE with 7 first-class stamps.

NONFICTION Needs historical, how-to, personal experience, photo feature, technical, travel. Special issues: Kayak Fish. No cartoons, poems, stories in which bad judgement is portrayed or 'Me and Molly' articles. **Buys 25 mss/year.** Send complete ms. Length: 400-2,500 words. **Pays $100-800 for assigned articles; $100-500 for unsolicited articles.**

COLUMNS Put In (environment, conservation, events), 500 words; Destinations (canoe and kayak destinations in US, Canada), 1,500 words; Essays, 750 words. **Buys 40 mss/year.** Send complete ms. **Pays $100-350.**

FILLERS Needs anecdotes, facts, newsbreaks. **Buys 20 mss/year.** Length: 200-500 words. **Pays $25-50.**

⊕⊕⊕ CHESAPEAKE BAY MAGAZINE

601 Sixth St, Annapolis MD 21403. (410)263-2662. **Fax:** (410)267-6924. **E-mail:** editor@chesapeakebay-magazine.com. **Website:** www.chesapeakebaymagazine.com. **Contact:** Ann Levelle, managing editor. **60% freelance written.** Monthly magazine covering boating and the Chesapeake Bay. "Our readers are boaters. Our writers should know boats and boating. Read the magazine before submitting." Estab. 1972. Circ. 25,000. Byline given. publication No kill fee. Publishes ms an average of 1 year after acceptance. Editorial lead time 1 year. Submit seasonal material 1 year in advance. Accepts queries by mail, e-mail, fax, phone. Accepts simultaneous submissions. Responds in 2 months to queries. Responds in 3 months to mss. Sample copy for $5.19 prepaid and SASE.

NONFICTION **Buys 30 mss/year.** Query with published clips. Length: 300-3,000 words. **Pays $100-1,000.**

⊕⊕ COAST&KAYAK MAGAZINE

Wild Coast Publishing, P.O. Box 24 Stn. A, Nanaimo BC V9R 5K4 Canada. (360)406-4708; (866)984-6437. **Fax:** (866)654-1937. **E-mail:** editor@coastandkayak.com; kayak@coastandkayak.com. **Website:** www.coastandkayak.com. **Contact:** John Kimantas, editor. **75% freelance written.** Quarterly magazine with a major focus on paddling the Pacific coast. "We promote safe paddling, guide paddlers to useful products and services, and explore coastal environmental issues." Estab. 1991. Circ. 65,000 print and electronic readers. Byline given. Pays on publication. Publishes ms an average of 4 months after acceptance. Editorial lead time 4 months. Submit seasonal material 4 months in advance. Accepts queries by mail, e-mail. Accepts simultaneous submissions. Sample copy and guidelines online.

NONFICTION Needs how-to, humor, new product, personal experience, technical. **Buys 25 mss/year.** Query. Length: 1,000-1,500 words. **Pays $50-75.**

⊕⊕⊕⊕ CRUISING WORLD

The Sailing Co., 55 Hammarlund Way, Middletown RI 02842. (401)845-5100. **Fax:** (401)845-5180. **E-mail:** cw.manuscripts@gmail.com; elaine.lembo@cruising-world.com. **Website:** www.cruisingworld.com. **Contact:** Elaine Lembo, deputy editor. **60% freelance written.** Monthly magazine covering sailing, cruising/adventuring, do-it-yourself boat improvements. "*Cruising World* is a publication by and for sailboat owners who spend time in home waters as well as voyaging the world. Its readership is extremely loyal, savvy, and driven by independent thinking." Estab. 1974. Circ. 91,244. Byline given. **Pays on acceptance for articles;** on publication for photography. No kill fee. Publishes ms an average of 18 months after acceptance. Editorial lead time 3 months. Submit seasonal material 1 year in advance. Accepts queries by mail. Accepts simultaneous submissions. Responds in 2 months to queries. Responds in 4 months to mss. Sample copy free. Guidelines online.

NONFICTION Needs book excerpts, essays, expose, general interest, historical, how-to, humor, interview, new product, opinion, personal experience, photo feature, technical, travel. No travel articles that have nothing to do with cruising aboard sailboats from 20-50 feet in length. **Buys dozens mss/year.** Send complete ms. **Pays $50-1,500 for assigned articles. Pays $50-1,000 for unsolicited articles.**

COLUMNS Underway Shoreline (sailing news, people, and short features; contact Elaine Lembo), 300 words maximum; Hands-on Sailor (refit, voyaging, seamanship, how-to), 1,000-1,500 words. **Buys dozens mss/year.** Query with or without published clips or send complete ms.

GOOD OLD BOAT

Partnership for Excellence, Inc., 7340 Niagara Lane N., Maple Grove MN 55311-2655 United States of America. (701)952-9433. **Fax:** (701)952-9434. **E-mail:** karen@goodoldboat.com. **Website:** www.goodoldboat.com. **Contact:** Karen Larson, editor. **90% freelance written.** Bimonthly magazine covering sailing. *Good Old Boat* magazine focuses on maintaining, upgrading, and loving fiberglass cruising sailboats from the 1960s and well into the 2000s. Readers see themselves as part of a community of sailors who share similar maintenance and replacement concerns not generally addressed in the other sailing publications. Readers do much of the writing about projects they have done on their boats and the joy they receive from sailing them. Estab. 1998. Circ. 30,000. Byline given. Pays 2 months in advance of publication. No kill fee. Publishes ms an average of 12-18 months after acceptance. Editorial lead time 4-6 months. Submit seasonal material 12-15 months in advance. Accepts queries by mail, e-mail. Accepts simultaneous submissions. Responds in 1-2 weeks to queries; in 1-2 months to mss. Guidelines online.

NONFICTION Needs general interest, historical, how-to, interview, personal experience, photo feature, technical. "Articles written by nonsailors serve no purpose for us." **Buys 150 mss/year.** Query or send complete ms. Length: up to 5,000 words. **Payment varies.**

HEARTLAND BOATING

The Waterways Journal, Inc., 319 N. Fourth St., Suite 650, St. Louis MO 63102. (314)241-4310. **Fax:** (314)241-4207. **E-mail:** brad@heartlandboating.com. **Website:** www.heartlandboating.com. **Contact:** Brad Kovach, editor. **75% freelance written.** Magazine published 5 times/year covering recreational boating on the inland waterways of mid-America, from the Great Lakes south to the Gulf of Mexico. "Our writers must have experience with, and a great interest in, boating in mid-America. *Heartland Boating*'s content is both informative and inspirational—describing boating life as the heartland boater knows it. The content reflects the challenge, joy, and excitement of our way of life. We are devoted to both power and sailboating enthusiasts throughout America's inland waterways." Estab. 1989. Circ. 10,000. Byline given. Pays on publication. No kill fee. Editorial lead time 3 months. Accepts queries by mail. Responds only if interested. Sample copy upon request. Guidelines for #10 SASE.

NONFICTION Needs how-to, humor, personal experience, technical. Special issues: Annual houseboat issue in March looks at what is coming out on the houseboat market for the coming year. **Buys 100 mss/year.** Send complete ms. Length: 850-1,500 words. **Pays $150-250.**

COLUMNS Books Aboard (assigned book reviews), 400 words; Handy Hints (boat improvement or safety projects), 1,000 words; Heartland Haunts (waterside restaurants, bars, or B&Bs), 1,000 words. Query with published clips or send complete ms. **Pays $40-180.**

NORTHERN BREEZES, SAILING MAGAZINE

Northern Breezes, Inc., 3949 Winnetka Ave. N, Minneapolis MN 55427. (763)542-9707. **Fax:** (763)542-8998. **E-mail:** info@sailingbreezes.com. **Website:**

www.sailingbreezes.com. **70% freelance written.** Magazine published 8 times/year for the Great Lakes and Midwest sailing community. Focusing on regional cruising, racing, and day sailing. Digital publication only. Estab. 1989. Circ. 22,300. Byline given. Does not offer payment. No kill fee. Editorial lead time 1 month. Submit seasonal material 3 months in advance. Accepts queries by mail, e-mail, fax. Accepts simultaneous submissions. Responds in 1 month to queries. Responds in 2 months to mss.

NONFICTION Needs book excerpts, historical, how-to, humor, inspirational, interview, new product, personal experience, photo feature, technical, travel. **Buys 24 mss/year.** Query with published clips. Length: 300-3,500 words.

COLUMNS This Old Boat (sailboat), 500-1,000 words; Surveyor's Notebook, 500-800 words. **Buys 8 mss/year.** Query with published clips.

PACIFIC YACHTING

OP Publishing, Ltd., 1166 Alberni St., Suite 802, Vancouver British Columbia V6E 3Z3 Canada. (604)428-0259. **Fax:** (604)620-0425. **E-mail:** editor@pacificyachting.com; ayates@oppublishing.com. **Website:** www.pacificyachting.com. **Contact:** Dale Miller, editor; Arran Yates, art director. **90% freelance written.** Monthly magazine covering all aspects of recreational boating in the Pacific Northwest. "The bulk of our writers and photographers not only come from the local boating community, many of them were longtime *PY* readers before coming aboard as a contributor. The *PY* reader buys the magazine to read about new destinations or changes to old haunts on the British Columbia coast and the Pacific Northwest and to learn the latest about boats and gear." Estab. 1968. Circ. 19,000. Byline given. Pays on publication. No kill fee. Publishes ms an average of 6 months after acceptance. Editorial lead time 4 months. Submit seasonal material 6 months in advance. Accepts queries by mail, e-mail, fax. Accepts simultaneous submissions. Sample copy for $6.95, plus postage charged to credit card. Guidelines online.

NONFICTION Needs historical, how-to, humor, interview, personal experience, technical, travel, cruising, and destination on the British Columbia coast. "No articles from writers who are obviously not boaters!" Query. Length: 800-2,000 words. **Pays $150-500. Pays some expenses of writers on assignment for unsolicited articles.**

COLUMNS Currents (current events, trade and people news, boat gatherings, and festivities), 50-250 words. Reflections; Cruising, both 800-1,000 words. Query. **Pay varies.**

💲💲💲 POWER & MOTORYACHT

10 Bokum Rd., Essex CT 06426. (860)767-3200. **E-mail:** gsass@aimmedia.com. **Website:** www.powerandmotoryacht.com. Erin Kenney, creative director. **Contact:** George Sass, editor in chief. **25% freelance written.** Monthly magazine covering powerboats 24 feet and larger with special emphasis on the 35-foot-plus market. "Readers have an average of 33 years experience boating, and we give them accurate advice on how to choose, operate, and maintain their boats as well as what electronics and gear will help them pursue their favorite pastime. In addition, since powerboating is truly a lifestyle and not just a hobby for them, *Power & Motoryacht* reports on a host of other topics that affect their enjoyment of the water: chartering, sportfishing, and the environment, among others. Articles must therefore be clear, concise, and authoritative; knowledge of the marine industry is mandatory. Include personal experience and information for marine industry experts where appropriate." Estab. 1985. Circ. 157,000. Byline given. Pays on acceptance. Offers 33% kill fee. Publishes ms an average of 4-6 months after acceptance. Editorial lead time 4-6 months. Submit seasonal material 4-6 months in advance. Accepts queries by mail, e-mail. Responds in 1 month to queries. Sample copy with 10x12 SASE. Guidelines with #10 SASE or via e-mail.

NONFICTION Needs how-to, interview, personal experience, photo feature, travel. No unsolicited mss or articles about sailboats and/or sailing yachts (including motorsailers or cruise ships). **Buys 20-25 mss/year.** Query with published clips. Length: 800-1,500 words. **Pays $500-1,000 for assigned articles.**

💲💲💲 SAIL

180 Canal St., Suite 301, Boston MA 02114. (860)767-3200. **Fax:** (860)767-1048. **E-mail:** sailmail@sailmagazine.com; pnielsen@sailmagazine.com. **Website:** www.sailmagazine.com. **Contact:** Peter Nielsen, editor in chief. **30% freelance written.** Monthly magazine written and edited for everyone who sails—aboard a coastal or bluewater cruiser, trailerable, one-design or offshore racer, or daysailer. How-to and technical articles concentrate on techniques of sailing and aspects of design and construction, boat systems, and gear; the feature section emphasizes the fun and rewards of sailing in a practical and instructive way. Estab. 1970. Circ. 180,000. Byline given. Pays on acceptance. No kill fee. Publishes ms an average of 1 year after acceptance. Accepts queries by mail, e-mail, fax. Accepts simultaneous submissions. Responds in 3 months to queries. Guidelines with SASE or available online.

NONFICTION Needs how-to, personal experience, technical, distance cruising, destinations. Special issues: Cruising, chartering, commissioning, fitting-out, special race (e.g., America's Cup), Top 10 Boats. **Buys 50 mss/year.** Query. Length: 1,500-3,000 words. **Pays $200-800.**

COLUMNS Sailing Memories (short essay); Sailing News (cruising, racing, legal, political, environmental); Under Sail (human interest). Query. **Pays $50-400.**

💲💲💲 SAILING MAGAZINE

125 E. Main St., P.O. Box 249, Port Washington WI 53074. (262)284-3494. **Fax:** (262)284-7764. **E-mail:** editorial@sailingmagazine.net. **Website:** www.sailingmagazine.net. **Contact:** Greta Schanen, managing editor. Monthly magazine for the experienced sailor. Covers all aspects of sailing, from learning how to sail in a dinghy to crossing the ocean on a large cruiser to racing around the buoys against the best sailors in the world. Typically focuses on sailing in places that are realistic destinations for readers, but will occasionally feature an outstanding and unique sailing destination. Estab. 1966. Circ. 45,000. Pays after publication. No kill fee. Accepts queries by mail, e-mail. Accepts simultaneous submissions. Responds in 3 months to unsolicited submission.

NONFICTION Needs book excerpts, how-to, interview, personal experience. **Buys 15-20 mss/year.** Send complete ms in Word as an attachment, or send via mail. Length: 1,000-3,000 words. **Pays $50-500.**

COLUMNS Splashes, short news stories (100-500 words).

💲💲 SAILING WORLD

Bonnier Corporation, 55 Hammarlund Way, Middletown RI 02842. (401)845-5100. **Fax:** (401)845-5180. **E-mail:** editor@sailingworld.com; dave.reed@sailingworld.com. **Website:** www.sailingworld.com. **Contact:** Dave Reed, editor. **40% freelance written.** Magazine published 8 times/year covering performance sailing. Estab. 1962. Circ. 65,000. Byline given. Pays on publication. No kill fee. Publishes ms an average of 4 months after acceptance. Accepts queries by e-mail. Accepts simultaneous submissions. Responds in 1 month to queries. Sample copy: $7. Guidelines online.

NONFICTION Needs interview. Special issues: "The emphasis here is on performance sailing: Keep in mind that the *Sailing World* readership is relatively educated about the sport. Unless you are dealing with a totally new aspect of sailing, you can and should discuss ideas on an advanced technical level; however, extensive formulae and graphs don't play well to our audience. When in doubt as to the suitability of an article or idea, submit a written query before time and energy are misdirected." No travelogs. **Buys 5-10 unsolicited mss/year.** Query unsolicited articles to dave.reed@sailingworld.com. No phone queries. Length: up to 2,000 words. **Pays $400 for up to 2,000 words.** Does not pay expenses of writers on assignment unless pre-approved.

SEA MAGAZINE

17782 Cowan, Suite C, Irvine CA 92614. (949)660-6150. **Fax:** (949)660-6172. **Website:** www.seamag.com. **Contact:** Mike Werling, managing editor. Monthly magazine covering West Coast power boating. Estab. 1908. Circ. 55,000. Byline given. Pays on publication. Publishes ms an average of 6 months after acceptance. Editorial lead time 3 months. Submit seasonal material 6 months in advance. Accepts simultaneous submissions. Responds in 3 months to queries.

NONFICTION Needs how-to, new product, personal experience, technical, travel. **Buys 36 mss/year.** Send complete ms. Length: 1,000-1,500 words. **Payment varies.**

🌐$$$$ SHOWBOATS INTERNATIONAL

Boat International Media, 41-47 Hartfield Rd., London SW19 3RQ United Kingdom. (954)522-2628 (US number). **Fax:** (954)522-2240. **E-mail:** kate.lardy@showboats.com. **Website:** www.boatinternational.com. **Contact:** Marilyn Mower, editorial director. **70% freelance written.** Magazine published 11 times/year covering luxury superyacht industry. Estab. 1995. Circ. 46,000. Byline given. Pays on publication. Offers 30% kill fee. Editorial lead time 2 months. Submit seasonal material 4 months in advance. Accepts queries by e-mail. Accepts simultaneous submissions. Responds in 2 months to mss. Sample copy for $6.00. Guidelines free.

NONFICTION Contact: kate.lardy@showboats.com. Needs profile, travel, Travel/destination pieces that are superyacht related. **Buys 10/year mss/year.** Query. Length: 300-2,000 words. **Pays $300 minimum, $2,000 maximum for assigned articles.**

$$ SOUTHERN BOATING

Southern Boating & Yachting, Inc., 330 N. Andrews Ave., Suite 200, Ft. Lauderdale FL 33301 USA. (954)522-5515. **Fax:** (954)522-2260. **E-mail:** liz@southernboating.com; john@southernboating.com. **Website:** www.southernboating.com. **Contact:** Liz Pasch, editorial director; John Lambert, art director. **75% freelance written.** Monthly boating magazine. Upscale monthly yachting magazine focusing on the Southeast US, Bahamas, Caribbean, and Gulf of Mexico. Estab. 1972. Circ. 40,000. Byline given Pays 30 days after publication. Publishes ms an average of 3 months after acceptance. Editorial lead time 3 months. Submit seasonal material 6 months in advance. Accepts queries by e-mail. Accepts simultaneous submissions.

NONFICTION Needs how-to, new product, profile, reviews, technical, travel. Query. Length: 900-1,200 words. **Pays $400-600 with art.**

COLUMNS DIY (how-to/maintenance), 900 words; What's New in Electronics (electronics), 900 words; Engine Room (new developments), 900 words. **Buys 24 mss/year.** Query first; see media kit for special issue focus.

$ WATERFRONT TIMES

Storyboard Media Inc., 2787 E. Oakland Park Blvd., Suite 205, Ft. Lauderdale FL 33306. (954)524-9450. **Fax:** (954)524-9464. **E-mail:** editor@waterfronttimes.com. **Website:** www.waterfronttimes.com. **Contact:** Jennifer Heit, editor. **20% freelance written.** Monthly tabloid covering marine and boating topics for the Greater Ft. Lauderdale waterfront community. Estab. 1984. Circ. 20,000. Byline given. Pays on publication. No kill fee. Publishes ms an average of 2 months after acceptance. Submit seasonal material 3 months in advance. Accepts simultaneous submissions. Responds in 1 month to queries. Sample copy for SAE with 9x12 envelope and 4 first-class stamps.

NONFICTION Length: 500-1,000 words. **Pays $100-125 for assigned articles.**

$$ WATERWAY GUIDE

P.O. Box 1125, 16273 General Puller Hwy., Deltaville VA 23043. (804)776-8999. **Fax:** (804)776-6111. **Website:** www.waterwayguide.com. **Contact:** Jani Parker, managing editor. **90% freelance written.** Annual magazine covering intracoastal waterway travel for recreational boats. Six editions cover coastal waters from Maine to Florida, the Bahamas, the Gulf of Mexico, the Great Lakes, and the Great Loop Cruise of America's inland waterways. "Writer must be knowledgeable about navigation and the areas covered by the guide." Estab. 1947. Circ. 30,000. Byline given. Pays on publication. No kill fee. Publishes ms an average of 3 months after acceptance. Editorial lead time 4 months. Submit seasonal material 3 months in advance. Accepts queries by mail, phone. Accepts simultaneous submissions. Responds in 6 weeks to queries. Responds in 2 months to mss. Sample copy: $39.95 with $3 postage and available online.

NONFICTION Needs essays, historical, how-to, photo feature, technical, travel. **Buys 6 mss/year.** Send complete ms. Length: 250-5,000 words. **Pays $50-500.**

🌐 WATERWAYS WORLD

Waterways World, Ltd, 151 Station St., Burton-on-Trent Staffordshire DE14 1BG United Kingdom. 01283 742950. **E-mail:** editorial@waterwaysworld.com. **Website:** www.waterwaysworld.com. **Contact:** Bobby Cowling, editor. Monthly magazine publishing news, photographs, and illustrated articles on all aspects of inland waterways in Britain and on limited aspects of waterways abroad. Estab. 1972. Pays on publication. No kill fee. Editorial lead time 2 months. Accepts queries by mail, e-mail. Guidelines available by e-mail.

NONFICTION Does not want poetry or fiction. Submit query letter or complete ms with SAE.

$$ WOODENBOAT MAGAZINE

WoodenBoat Publications, Inc., P.O. Box 78, Brookline ME 04616. (207)359-4651. **Website:** www.woodenboat.com. **Contact:** Matthew P. Murphy, editor. **50% freelance written.** Bimonthly magazine for wooden boat owners, builders, and designers. "We are devoted exclusively to the design, building, care, preservation, and use of wooden boats, both commercial and pleasure, old and new, sail and power. We work to convey quality, integrity, and involvement in the creation and care of these craft, to entertain, inform, inspire, and to provide our varied readers with access to individuals who are deeply experienced in the world of wooden boats." Estab. 1974. Circ. 90,000. Byline given. Pays on publication. Offers variable kill fee. Publishes ms an average of 1 year after acceptance. Accepts queries by online submission form. Accepts simultaneous submissions. Responds in 2 months to queries and mss. Sample copy: $5.99. Guidelines online.

NONFICTION Needs technical. No poetry, fiction. **Buys 50 mss/year.** Query with published clips. Length: 1,500-5,000 words. **Pays $300/1,000 words.**

COLUMNS Currents pays for information on wooden boat-related events, projects, boatshop activities, etc. Uses same columnists for each issue. Length: 250-1,000 words. Send complete information. **Pays $5-50.**

$$$ YACHTING

Bonnier Corporation, 55 Hammarlund Way, Middletown RI 02842. **Website:** www.yachtingmagazine.com. **30% freelance written.** Monthly magazine covering yachts, boats. Monthly magazine written and edited for experienced, knowledgeable yachtsmen. Estab. 1907. Circ. 132,000. Byline given. Pays on acceptance. No kill fee. Editorial lead time 2 months. Submit seasonal material 6 months in advance. Accepts queries by mail, e-mail, fax. Accepts simultaneous submissions. Responds in 1 month to queries. Responds in 3 months to mss. Sample copy free.

NONFICTION Needs personal experience, technical. **Buys 50 mss/year.** Query with published clips. Length: 750-800 words. **Pays $150-1,500.**

🌐 YACHTING MONTHLY

IPC Media Ltd, Room 2215, King's Reach Tower, Stamford Street, London England SE1 9LS United Kingdom. **E-mail:** dick_durham@ipcmedia.com. Monthly magazine covering practical and technical articles on all aspects of seamanship, navigation, and the handling of small craft and their design, construction , and equipment. Also accepts cruising narratives about sailing almost anywhere in the world and carefully researched pilotage articles on anchorages and cruising areas. No kill fee. Accepts queries by mail, e-mail. Accepts simultaneous submissions. Guidelines online.

NONFICTION Needs humor, technical, cruising narratives, lessons learned from mistakes/mishaps.

Submit 150-word synopsis or complete ms. Length: 450-1,800 words. **Fees are quoted on acceptance.**

GENERAL INTEREST

ESPN THE MAGAZINE

ESPN Inc. (The Walt Disney Company/Hearst Corporation), 19 E. 34th St., New York NY 10016. **E-mail:** post@espnmag.com. **Website:** www.espn.go.com/magazine. **Contact:** Craig Winston, managing editor. Bi-weekly sports magazine published by ESPN. *ESPN The Magazine* covers Major League Baseball, National Basketball Association, National Football League, National Hockey League, college basketball, and college football. The magazine typically takes a more lighthearted and humorous approach to sporting news. Estab. 1998. Circ. 2.1 million. Accepts simultaneous submissions.

SPORTS ILLUSTRATED

Time, Inc., 1271 Avenue of the Americas, New York NY 10020. (212)522-1212. **E-mail:** story_queries@simail.com. **Website:** www.si.com. Weekly magazine covering sports. *Sports Illustrated* reports and interprets the world of sport, recreation, and active leisure. It previews, analyzes, and comments upon major games and events, as well as those noteworthy for character and spirit alone. It features individuals connected to sport and evaluates trends concerning the part sport plays in contemporary life. In addition, the magazine has articles on such subjects as sports gear and swim suits. Special departments deal with sports equipment, books, and statistics. Estab. 1954. Circ. 3.3 million. No kill fee. Accepts queries by mail. Accepts simultaneous submissions. Responds in 4-6 weeks to queries.

NONFICTION Query.

GOLF

🌀🌀 AFRICAN AMERICAN GOLFER'S DIGEST

80 Wall St., Suite 720, New York NY 10005. (212)571-6559. **E-mail:** debertcook@aol.com. **Website:** www.africanamericangolfersdigest.com. **Contact:** Debert Cook, managing editor. **100% freelance written.** Quarterly. Covering golf lifestyle, health, travel destinations and reviews, golf equipment, golfer profiles. "Editorial should focus on interests of our market demographic of African Americans with historical, artistic, musical, educational (higher learning), automotive, sports, fashion, entertainment, and other categories of high interest to them." Estab. 2003. Circ. 20,000. Byline given. No kill fee. Publishes ms an average of 3 months after acceptance. Editorial lead time 3-6 months. Submit seasonal material 3-6 months in advance. Accepts queries by e-mail. Accepts simultaneous submissions. Responds in 3 weeks to queries; 3 months to mss. Sample copy for $8. Guidelines by e-mail.

NONFICTION Needs how-to, interview, new product, opinion, personal experience, photo feature, reviews, technical, travel, golf-related. **Buys 3 mss/year.** Query. Length: 250-1,500 words. **Pays 0.03-0.5¢/word.**

COLUMNS Profiles (celebrities, national leaders, entertainers, corporate leaders, etc., who golf); Travel (destination/golf course reviews); Golf Fashion (jewelry, clothing, accessories). **Buys 3 mss/year.** Query. **Pays 10-50¢/word.**

FILLERS Needs anecdotes, facts, gags, newsbreaks, short humor. **Buys 3 mss/year. mss/year.** Length: 20-125 words. **Pays 10-50¢/word.**

🌀🌀💲💲💲 GOLF CANADA

Chill Media Inc., 482 S. Service Rd. E., Suite 100, Oakville ON L6J 2X6 Canada. (905)337-1886. **E-mail:** scotty@ichill.ca; david@ichill.ca. **Website:** www.golfcanada.ca. **Contact:** Scott Stevenson, publisher; David McPherson, managing editor. **80% freelance written.** Magazine published 4 times/year covering Canadian golf. *Golf Canada* is the official magazine of the Royal Canadian Golf Association, published to entertain and enlighten members about RCGA-related activities and to generally support and promote amateur golf in Canada. Estab. 1994. Circ. 159,000. Byline given. Pays 30 days after publication. Offers 25% kill fee. Editorial lead time 3 months. Submit seasonal material 6 months in advance. Accepts queries by mail, e-mail, phone. Accepts simultaneous submissions. Sample copy free.

NONFICTION Needs historical, interview, new product, opinion, photo feature, travel. Query with published clips. Length varies. **Rates negotiated upon agreement.**

COLUMNS Guest Column (focus on issues surrounding the Canadian golf community), 700 words. Query. **Rates negotiated upon agreement.**

GOLF DIGEST

Condé Nast, 1 World Trade Center, New York NY 10007. (212)286-2860. **Fax:** (212)286-3147. **E-mail:** contact@golfdigest.com. **Website:** www.golfdigest.com. **Contact:** Jerry Tarde, editor in chief. Monthly magazine covering the sport of golf. Written for all golf enthusiasts, whether recreational, amateur, or professional. Estab. 1950. Circ. 1.6 million. No kill fee. Editorial lead time 6 months. Accepts queries by mail. Accepts simultaneous submissions. Sample copy: $3.95.

NONFICTION Query.

$$ THE GOLFER

59 E. 72nd St., New York NY 10021. **E-mail:** info@thegolferinc.com. **Website:** www.thegolferinc.com. **40% freelance written.** Bimonthly magazine covering golf. A sophisticated tone for a lifestyle-oriented magazine. "The Golfer Inc. is an international luxury brand, a new media company that is a driving force in the game. Its website is the source for those who want the best the game has to offer—the classic courses, great destinations, finest accoutrements, most intriguing personalities, and latest trends on and off the course.The magazine has distinguished itself as the highest quality, most innovative in its field. It is written for the top of the market—those who live a lifestyle shaped by their passion for the game. With its stunning photography, elegant design and evocative writing, *The Golfer* speaks to its affluent readers with a sense of style and sophistication—it is a world-class publication with an international flair, celebrating the lifestyle of the game." Estab. 1994. Circ. 253,000. Byline given. Pays on publication. Offers negotiable kill fee. Publishes ms an average of 2 months after acceptance. Editorial lead time 2 months. Submit seasonal material 4 months in advance. Accepts queries by mail, e-mail. Accepts simultaneous submissions. Sample copy free.

NONFICTION Needs book excerpts, essays, general interest, historical, how-to, humor, inspirational, interview, new product, opinion, personal experience, photo feature, technical, travel. Send complete ms. Length: 300-2,000 words. **Pays $150-600.**

$$$ GOLFING MAGAZINE

Golfer Magazine, Inc., 449 Silas Deane Hwy., Suite 3E, Wethersfield CT 06109. (860)563-1633. **E-mail:** editor@golfingmagazine.net. **Website:** www.golfingmagazineonline.com. **Contact:** John Torsiello, editor. **30% freelance written.** Bimonthly magazine covering golf, including travel, products, player profiles, and company profiles. Estab. 1999. Circ. 175,000. Byline given. Pays on publication. Offers negotiable kill fee. Editorial lead time 2 months. Submit seasonal material 2 months in advance. Accepts queries by mail, e-mail. Accepts simultaneous submissions. Sample copy free.

NONFICTION Needs book excerpts, new product, photo feature, travel. **Buys 4-5 mss/year.** Query. Length: 700-2,500 words. **Pays $250-1,000 for assigned articles. Pays $100-500 for unsolicited articles.**

FILLERS Needs facts, gags. **Buys 2-3 mss/year. Payment individually determined.**

$$$ GOLF TIPS

Madavor Media, 25 Braintree Hill Office Park, Suite 404, Braintree MA 02184. (617)706-9110. **Fax:** (617)536-0102. **E-mail:** editors@golftipsmag.com. **Website:** www.golftipsmag.com. **95% freelance written.** Magazine published 9 times/year covering golf instruction and equipment. "We provide mostly concise, very clear golf instruction pieces for the serious golfer." Estab. 1986. Circ. 300,000. Byline given. Pays on publication. Offers 33% kill fee. Publishes ms an average of 2 months after acceptance. Editorial lead time 3 months. Submit seasonal material 4 months in advance. Accepts queries by e-mail. Accepts simultaneous submissions. Responds in 1 month to queries. Sample copy free. Guidelines on website.

NONFICTION Needs book excerpts, how-to, interview, new product, photo feature, technical. "Generally, golf essays rarely make it." **Buys 125 mss/year.** Query. Length: 250-2,000 words. **Pays $300-1,000 for assigned articles. Pays $300-800 for unsolicited articles.**

COLUMNS Stroke Saver (very clear, concise instruction), 350 words; Lesson Library (book excerpts—usually in a series), 1,000 words; Travel Tips (formatted golf travel), 2,500 words. **Buys 40 mss/year.** Query. **Pays $300-850.**

$$$ MINNESOTA GOLFER

Minnesota Golf Association, 6550 York Ave. S., Suite 211, Edina MN 55435. (952)927-4643. **Fax:** (952)927-9642. **E-mail:** wp@mngolf.org; editor@mngolf.org; info@mngolf.org. **Website:** www.www.mngolf.org/magazine. **Contact:** W.P. Ryan, editor. **75% freelance**

written. Bimonthly magazine covering golf in Minnesota; the official publication of the Minnesota Golf Association. Estab. 1975. Circ. 66,000. Byline given. Pays on acceptance or publication. No kill fee. Editorial lead time 3 months. Accepts queries by mail, e-mail, fax.

NONFICTION Needs historical, interview, new product. Query with published clips. Length: 400-2,000 words. **Pays $50-750.**

COLUMNS Punch shots (golf news and notes); Q School (news and information targeted to beginners, junior golfers and women); Great Drives (featuring noteworthy golf holes in Minnesota); Instruction.

💲💲 TEXAS GOLFER MAGAZINE

Texas Golder Media, 15721 Park Row, Suite 100, Houston TX 77084. (888)863-9899. **E-mail:** zane@texasgolfermagazine.com. **Website:** www.texasgolfermagazine.com. **Contact:** Zane Russell, CEO/publisher. **10% freelance written.** Bi-monthly magazine covering golf in Texas. Estab. 1984. Circ. 50,000. Byline given. Pays 10 days after publication. No kill fee. Publishes ms an average of 2 months after acceptance. Editorial lead time 2 months. Submit seasonal material 3 months in advance. Accepts simultaneous submissions. Responds in 2 weeks to queries; 1 month to mss. Sample copy free. Prefers direct phone discussion for writer's guidelines.

NONFICTION Needs book excerpts, humor, personal experience, all golf-related. Travel pieces accepted about golf outside of Texas. **Buys 20 mss/year.** Query. **Pays 25-40¢/word.**

💲💲 VIRGINIA GOLFER

Touchpoint Publishing, Inc., Virginia Golfer, 2400 Dovercourt Dr., Midlothian VA 23113. (804)378-2300, ext. 12. **Fax:** (804)378-2369. **Website:** www.vsga.org. **Contact:** Chris Lang, editor. **65% freelance written.** Bimonthly magazine covering golf in Virginia, the official publication of the Virginia State Golf Association. Estab. 1983. Circ. 45,000. Byline given. Pays on publication. No kill fee. Editorial lead time 6 months. Submit seasonal material 3 months in advance. Accepts queries by mail, e-mail. Accepts simultaneous submissions. Sample copy and writer's guidelines free.

NONFICTION Needs book excerpts, essays, historical, how-to, humor, inspirational, interview, personal experience, photo feature, technical, where to play, golf business. **Buys 30-40 mss/year.** Send complete ms. Length: 500-2,500 words. **Pays $50-200.**

COLUMNS Chip ins & Three Putts (news notes), Rules Corner (golf rules explanations and discussion), Your Game, Golf Travel (where to play), Great Holes, Q&A, Golf Business (what's happening?), Fashion. Query.

GUNS

💲💲 GUN DIGEST THE MAGAZINE

F+W, a Content and eCommerce Company, 700 E. State St., Iola WI 54990. (715)445-2214. **Fax:** (715)445-2164. **E-mail:** gundigestonline@fwmedia.com. **Website:** www.gundigest.com. **90% freelance written.** Bimonthly magazine covering firearms. "*Gun Digest the Magazine* covers all aspects of the firearms community, from collectible guns to tactical gear to reloading and accessories. We also publish gun reviews and tests of new and collectible firearms and news features about firearms legislation. We are 100% pro-gun, fully support the NRA, and make no bones about our support of Constitutional freedoms." Byline given. Pays on publication. Publishes ms 2 months after acceptance. Editorial lead time 3 months. Accepts queries by e-mail. Accepts simultaneous submissions. Responds in 3 weeks to queries; in 1 month to mss. Free sample copy. Guidelines available via e-mail.

NONFICTION Needs historical, how-to, interview, new product, nostalgic, profile, technical. Special issues: All submissions must focus on firearms, accessories, or the firearms industry and legislation. Stories that include hunting reference must have as their focus the firearms or ammunition used. The hunting should be secondary. *Gun Digest* also publishes an annual gear guide. "We do not publish 'Me and Joe' hunting stories." **Buys 50-75 mss/year.** Query. Length: 500-3,500 words. **Pays $175-500 for assigned and for unsolicited articles. Does not pay in contributor copies.**

💲 GUNS AUSTRALIA

Yaffa Media, Australia. (02)9213-8258. **E-mail:** marcusodean@yaffa.com.au. **Website:** www.yaffa.com.au/consumer/guns-australia. **Contact:** Marcus O'Dean, editor. Quarterly magazine delivering comprehensive reviews and articles on the enjoyment of shooting and collecting. "The readers of *Guns Australia* are committed to gun ownership and collecting, target shooting, and hunting in Australia." Accepts queries by e-mail. Accepts simultaneous submissions.

NONFICTION Needs general interest, how-to, interview, new product. Query.

💲💲 MUZZLE BLASTS

National Muzzle Loading Rifle Association, P.O. Box 67, Friendship IN 47021. (812)667-5131. **Fax:** (812)667-5136. **E-mail:** ttrowbridge@nmlra.org. **E-mail:** ttrowbridge@nmlra.org. **Website:** www.nmlra.org. **Contact:** Terri Trowbridge. **65% freelance written.** Monthly magazine. "Articles must relate to muzzleloading or the muzzleloading era of American history." Estab. 1939. Circ. 17,500. Byline given. Pays on publication. Offers $50 kill fee. Publishes ms an average of 6 months after acceptance. Editorial lead time 4 months. Submit seasonal material 6 months in advance. Accepts queries by mail, e-mail. Responds in 1 month to mss. Sample copy and writer's guidelines free.

NONFICTION Needs general interest, historical, how-to, humor, interview, new product, personal experience, photo feature, technical, travel. No subjects that do not pertain to muzzleloading. **Buys 80 mss/year.** Query. Length: 2,000-2,500 words. **Pays $150 minimum for assigned articles. Pays $50 minimum for unsolicited articles.**

COLUMNS Buys 96 mss/year. Query. **Pays $50-200.**

FICTION Must pertain to muzzleloading. Needs adventure, historical, humorous. **Buys 6 mss/year.** Query. Length: 2,500 words. **Pays $50-300.**

FILLERS Needs facts. **Pays $50.**

💲💲 SHOTGUN SPORTS MAGAZINE

P.O. Box 6810, Auburn CA 95604. (530)889-2220. **Fax:** (530)889-9106. **E-mail:** shotgun@shotgunsportsmagazine.com. **Website:** www.shotgunsportsmagazine.com. **Contact:** Johnny Cantu, editor in chief. **50% freelance written. Welcomes new writers.** Monthly magazine covering all the shotgun sports and shotgun hunting—sporting clays, trap, skeet, hunting, gunsmithing, shotshell patterning, shotsell reloading, mental training for the shotgun sports, shotgun tests, anything shotgun. Pays on publication. No kill fee. Publishes ms an average of 1-6 months after acceptance. Accepts simultaneous submissions. Responds within 3 weeks. Sample copy and writer's guidelines available on the website. Subscription: $32.95 (U.S.); $49.95 (Canada); $79.95 (foreign).

NONFICTION Currently needs anything with a "shotgun" subject. Think pieces, roundups, historical, interviews, etc. No articles promoting a specific club or sponsored hunting trip, etc. Submit complete ms with photos by mail with SASE. Can submit by e-mail. Length: 1,500-3,000 words. **Pays $50-150.**

HIKING & BACKPACKING

💲💲 A.T. JOURNEYS

Appalachian Trail Conservancy, P.O. Box 807, 799 Washington St., Harpers Ferry WV 25425-0807. (304)535-6331. **Fax:** (304)535-2667. **E-mail:** editor@appalachiantrail.org. **Website:** www.appalachiantrail.org. **30% freelance written.** *A.T. Journeys*, published 4 times/year, features "the people, places, and events that make up the Appalachian Trail community." Estab. 1925. Byline given. Pays on publication. No kill fee. Accepts queries by mail, e-mail. Accepts simultaneous submissions. Responds in 2 months to queries. Guidelines online.

NONFICTION Needs general interest, historical, how-to, interview, profile, travel. **Buys 5-10 mss/year.** Query with or without published clips, or send complete ms. Prefers e-mail queries. Length: 250-3,000 words. **Pays $25-300.**

REPRINTS Send photocopy with rights for sale noted and information about when and where the material previously appeared.

💲💲💲💲 BACKPACKER MAGAZINE

Cruz Bay Publishing, Inc., Active Interest Media Co., 5720 Flatiron Pkwy., Boulder CO 80301. **E-mail:** dlewon@backpacker.com; mhorjus@aimmedia.com; caseylyons@aimmedia.com; khostetter1@gmail.com. **Website:** www.backpacker.com. **Contact:** Dennis Lewon, editor in chief; Casey Lyons, senior editor; Maren Horjus, assistant editor; Kristin Hostetter, gear editor. **50% freelance written.** Magazine published 9 times/year covering wilderness travel for backpackers. "*Backpacker* is the source for backpacking gear reviews, outdoor skills information and advice, and destinations for backpacking, camping, and hiking." Estab. 1973. Circ. 340,000. Byline given. Pays on acceptance. Offers 25% kill fee. Editorial lead time 6 months. Accepts queries by e-mail. Accepts simultaneous submissions. Responds in 2-4 weeks to queries. Sample copy free. Guidelines online.

NONFICTION Needs inspirational, interview, new product, personal experience, technical. "Features usually fall into 1 of several distinct categories: destinations, personality, skills, or gear. Gear features are generally staff written. In order to make the grade, a potential feature needs an unusual hook, a compelling story, a passionate sense of place, or unique individuals finding unique ways to improve or enjoy the wilderness." Special issues: See website for upcoming issue themes. "Journal-style articles are generally unacceptable." Query with published clips before sending complete ms. Length: 1,500-5,000 words. **Pays 10¢-$1/word.**

COLUMNS Life List (personal essay telling a story about a premier wilderness destination or experience), 300-400 words; Done in a Day (a hike that can be finished in a day), 500 words; Weekend (a trip of 1-2 nights, 6-10 miles/day, within striking distance of a major city, and seasonally appropriate for the month in which they run); Skills (the advice source for all essential hiking and adventure skills, with information targeted to help both beginners and experts); Gear (short reviews of gear that has been field-tested; unlike other departments, Gear is done by assignment only). **Buys 50-75 mss/year.** Query with published clips. **Pays 10¢-$1/word.**

HOCKEY

💲💲 MINNESOTA HOCKEY JOURNAL

Touchpoint Sports, 505 N. Hwy 169, Ste. 465, Minneapolis MN 55441. (763)595-0808. **Fax:** (763)595-0016. **E-mail:** contactus@minnesotahockeyjournal.com. **E-mail:** aaron@touchpointmedia.com. **Website:** www.minnesotahockeyjournal.com. **Contact:** Aaron Paitich, editor. **50% freelance written.** Journal published 4 times/year covering Minnesota hockey. Estab. 2000. Circ. 40,000. Byline given. Pays on publication. No kill fee. Editorial lead time 6 months. Submit seasonal material 4 months in advance. Accepts simultaneous submissions. Sample copy and writer's guidelines free.

NONFICTION Needs essays, general interest, historical, how-to, humor, inspirational, interview, new product, opinion, personal experience, photo feature. **Buys 3-5 mss/year.** Query. Length: 500-1,500 words. **Pays $100-300.**

HORSE RACING

AMERICAN TURF MONTHLY

747 Middle Neck Rd., Great Neck NY 11024. (516)773-4075. **Fax:** (516)773-2944. **E-mail:** jcorbett@ameri-

canturf.com; editor@americanturf.com. **Website:** www.americanturf.com. **Contact:** Joe Girardi, editor. **90% freelance written.** Monthly magazine squarely focused on Thoroughbred racing, handicapping and wagering. *ATM* is a magazine for horseplayers, not owners, breeders, or 12-year-old girls enthralled with ponies. Estab. 1946. Circ. 30,000. Byline given. Pays on publication. No kill fee. Publishes ms an average of 4 months after acceptance. Editorial lead time 2 months. Submit seasonal material 2 months in advance. Accepts queries by mail, e-mail. Accepts simultaneous submissions. Responds in 1 month to queries. Sample copy and writer's guidelines free.

NONFICTION No historical essays, bilious 'guest editorials,' saccharine poetry, fiction. Special issues: Triple Crown/Kentucky Derby (May); Saratoga/Del Mar (August); Breeder's Cup (November). **Buys Length: 800-2,000 words. Pays $75-300 for assigned articles. Pays $100-500 for unsolicited articles. mss/year.** Query. Length: 800-2,000 words. **Pays $75-300 for assigned articles. Pays $100-500 for unsolicited articles.** No.

FILLERS newsbreaks, short humor Needs newsbreaks, short humor. **Buys 5 mss/year.** Length: 400 words. **Pays $25.**

💲💲 HOOF BEATS

6130 S. Sunbury Rd., Westerville OH 43081-9309. **E-mail:** hoofbeats@ustrotting.com. **Website:** www.hoofbeatsmagazine.com. **Contact:** T.J. Burkett. **60% freelance written.** Monthly magazine covering harness racing and standardbred horses. "Articles and photos must relate to harness racing or Standardbreds. We do not accept any topics that do not touch on these subjects." Estab. 1933. Circ. 8,000. Byline given. Pays on publication. Offers 25% kill fee. Publishes ms an average of 2-4 months after acceptance. Editorial lead time 6 months. Submit seasonal material 6 months in advance. Accepts queries by mail, e-mail, fax. Accepts simultaneous submissions. Responds in 2 weeks to queries. Responds in 1 month to mss. Sample copy online. Guidelines free.

NONFICTION Needs general interest, how-to, interview, personal experience, photo feature, technical. "We do not want any fiction or poetry." **Buys 48-72 mss/year.** Query. Length: 750-3,000 words. **Pays $100-500. Pays $100-500 for unsolicited articles.**

COLUMNS Equine Clinic (Standardbreds who overcame major health issues), 900-1,200 words; Profiles (short profiles on people or horses in harness racing), 600-1,000 words; Industry Trends (issues impacting Standardbreds & harness racing), 1,000-2,000 words. **Buys 60 mss/year mss/year.** Query. **Pays $100-500.**

HUNTING & FISHING

⊘⊛ ALABAMA GAME & FISH

Game & Fish, 3330 Chastain Meadows Pkwy, NW, Suite 200, Kennesaw GA 30144. (770)953-9222. **Fax:** (678)279-7512. **E-mail:** ken.dunwoody@imoutdoors. com. **Website:** www.alabamagameandfish.com. **Contact:** Ken Dunwoody, editorial director; Paul Rackley, editor. Covers fishing and hunting opportunities in Alabama. See listing for *Game & Fish* for more information. Accepts simultaneous submissions.

⊘⊛ AMERICAN ANGLER

Morris Communications Company, LLC, 735 Broad St., Augusta GA 30904. (706)828-3971. **E-mail:** editor@americanangler.com. **Website:** www.americanangler.com. **Contact:** Ben Romans, editor; Wayne Knight, art director. **95% freelance written.** Bimonthly magazine covering fly fishing. "*American Angler* is devoted exclusively to fly fishing. We focus mainly on coldwater fly fishing for trout, steelhead, and salmon, but we also run articles about warmwater and saltwater fly fishing. Our mission is to supply our readers with well-written, accurate articles on every aspect of the sport—angling techniques and methods, reading water, finding fish, selecting flies, tying flies, fish behavior, places to fish, casting, managing line, rigging, tackle, accessories, entomology, and any other relevant topics. Each submission should present specific, useful information that will increase our readers' enjoyment of the sport and help them catch more fish." Estab. 1976. Circ. 32,000. Byline given. Pays on publication. No kill fee. Publishes ms an average of 6 months after acceptance. Editorial lead time 3 months. Submit seasonal material 5 months in advance. Accepts queries by e-mail. Accepts simultaneous submissions. Responds in 6 weeks to queries; in 2 months to mss.

NONFICTION Needs general interest, historical, how-to, interview, personal experience, photo feature, profile, technical, travel. "No superficial, broad-brush coverage of subjects. We're interested in queries created with the magazine in mind; not shotgunned ideas. The more specific and unique, the better. Not

interested in concepts that don't have a solid structure or are one-sided opinions. The more journalistic the approach (the inclusion of interviews, data, or other supporting evidence and information), the better. We're interested in someone who's willing to chase a story angle, beat the pavement, and put together a strong package more than we're interested in how well you can write a sentence." **Buys 45-60 mss/year.** Query with published clips. Length: 800-2,200 words. **Pays $200-600.**

COLUMNS One-page shorts (problem solvers), 350-750 words. Query with published clips. **Pays $100-300.**

⊛⊛⊛ AMERICAN HUNTER

National Rifle Association of America, 11250 Waples Mill Rd., Fairfax VA 22030-9400. (800)672-3888. **E-mail:** Publications@nrahq.org; americanhunter@nrahq.org; EmediaHunter@nrahq.org. **Website:** www.americanhunter.org. **Contact:** Editor-in-Chief. Monthly magazine for hunters who are members of the National Rifle Association (NRA). *American Hunter*, the official journal of the National Rifle Association, contains articles dealing with various sport hunting and related activities both at home and abroad. With the encouragement of the sport as a prime game management tool, emphasis is on technique, sportsmanship, and safety. In each issue, hunting equipment and firearms are evaluated, legislative happenings affecting the sport are reported, lore and legend are retold, and the business of the Association is recorded in the Official Journal section. Circ. 1,000,000. Byline given. Pays on publication. No kill fee. Accepts queries by mail, e-mail. Accepts simultaneous submissions. Responds in 6 months to queries. Guidelines online at www.professionaloutdoormedia.org/sites/all/downloads/American%20Hunter%20Writer%27s%20Guidelines.pdf.

NONFICTION Special issues: Special issues: pheasants, whitetail tactics, black bear feed areas, mule deer, duck hunters' transport by land and sea, tech topics to be decided, rut strategies, muzzleloader moose and elk, fall turkeys, staying warm, goose talk, long-range muzzleloading. Not interested in material on fishing, camping, or firearms knowledge. Query (preferred) or submit complete ms by mail or e-mail. Length: 2,000-3,000 words. **Pays up to $1,500 for full-length features with complete photo packages.**

COLUMNS Build Your Skills (technical how-to column on hunting-related procedure); Hardware (covers new firearms, ammunition, and optics used for hunting), 800-1,200 words. **Pays $500-1,000.**

● BACON BUSTERS

Yaffa Publishing, 17-21 Bellevue St., Surry Hills NSW 2010 Australia. (02)9213-8258. **E-mail:** marcusodean@yaffa.com.au. **Website:** www.yaffa.com.au. **Contact:** Marcus O'Dean, editor. Bimonthly magazine covering the hog hunting scene in Australia. "*Bacon Busters* content includes readers' short stories, how-to articles, pig hunting features, technical advice, pig dog profiles, and Australia's biggest collection of pig hunting photos. Not to mention the famous Babes & Boars section!" Estab. 1995. Accepts queries by e-mail. Accepts simultaneous submissions.

NONFICTION Needs expose, general interest, how-to, interview. Query by e-mail with image, short bio, and contact info.

○●● BC OUTDOORS HUNTING AND SHOOTING

Outdoor Group Media, 7261 River Place, 201a, Mission British Columbia V4S 0A2 Canada. (604)820-3400; (800)898-8811. **Fax:** (604)820-3477. **E-mail:** info@outdoorgroupmedia.com; mmitchell@outdoorgroupmedia.com; production@outdoorgroupmedia.com; bcoutdoors@cdsglobal.ca; mmitchell@outdoorgroupmedia.com. **Website:** www.bcoutdoorsmagazine.com. **Contact:** Mike Mitchell, editor. **80% freelance written.** Biannual magazine covering hunting, shooting, camping, and backroads in British Columbia, Canada. *BC Outdoors Magazine* publishes 7 sport fishing issues a year with 2 hunting and shooting supplement issues each summer and fall. "Our magazine is about the best outdoor experiences in BC. Whether you're camping on an ocean shore, hiking into your favorite lake, or learning how to fly-fish on your favourite river, we want to showcase what our province has to offer to sport fishing and outdoor enthusiasts. *BC Outdoors Hunting and Shooting* provides trusted editorial for trapping, deer hunting, big buck, bowhunting, bag limits, baitling, decoys, calling, camouflage, tracking, trophy hunting, pheasant hunting, goose hunting, hunting regulations, duck hunting, whitetail hunting, hunting regulations, hunting trips, and mule deer hunting." Estab. 1945. Circ. 30,000. Byline given. Pays on publication. Offers kill fee. Publishes ms an average of 3 months after acceptance. Accepts queries by e-mail. Accepts

simultaneous submissions. Guidelines for 8x10 SASE with 7 Canadian first-class stamps.

NONFICTION Needs how-to, personal experience. **Buys 50 mss/year.** Query the publication before submitting. Do not send unsolicited mss or photos. Submit no more than 100-words outlining exactly what your story will be. "You should be able to encapsulate the essence of your story and show us why our readers would be interested in reading or knowing what you are writing about. Queries need to be clear, succinct and straight to the point. Show us why we should publish your article in 150 words or less." Length: 1,700-2,000 words. **Pays $300-500.**

COLUMNS Column needs basically supplied in-house.

●● THE BIG GAME FISHING JOURNAL

Open Ocean Publications, LLC, 308 S. Main St., Suite 2, Forked River NJ 08731. **Website:** www.biggamefishingjournal.com. **90% freelance written.** Bimonthly magazine covering big game fishing. Estab. 1994. Circ. 45,000. Byline given. Pays on publication. Offers 50% kill fee. Editorial lead time 3 months. Submit seasonal material 3 months in advance. Accepts queries by mail. Accepts simultaneous submissions. Responds in 2 weeks to queries; in 1 month to mss. Guidelines free.

NONFICTION Needs how-to, interview, technical. **Buys 50-70 mss/year.** Send complete ms. Length: 2,000-3,000 words.

●● BOWHUNTER

InterMedia Outdoors, 6385 Flank Dr., Suite 800, Harrisburg PA 17112. (717)695-8085. **Fax:** (717)545-2527. **E-mail:** curt.wells@imoutdoors.com. **Website:** www.bowhunter.com. Mark Olszewski, art director; Jeff Waring, publisher. **Contact:** Curt Wells, editor. **50% freelance written.** Bimonthly magazine covering hunting big and small game with bow and arrow. "We are a special-interest publication, produced by bowhunters for bowhunters, covering all aspects of the sport. Material included in each issue is designed to entertain and inform readers, making them better bowhunters." Estab. 1971. Circ. 126,480. Byline given. Pays on acceptance. No kill fee. Submit seasonal material 8 months in advance. Accepts queries by mail, e-mail, fax. Accepts simultaneous submissions. Responds in 1 month to queries. Responds in 2 months to mss. Sample copy for $2 and 8 1/2x11

SASE with appropriate postage. Guidelines for #10 SASE or on website.

NONFICTION Needs general interest, how-to, interview, opinion, personal experience, photo feature. **Buys 60-plus mss/year.** Query. Length: 250-2,000 words. **Pays $500 maximum for assigned articles. Pays $100-400 for unsolicited articles.**

💲💲 BOWHUNTING WORLD

Grand View Media Group, 6121 Baker Rd., Suite 101, Minnetonka MN 55345. (888)431-2877. **E-mail:** molis@grandviewmedia.com. **Website:** www.bowhuntingworld.com. **Contact:** Mark Olis. **50% freelance written.** Bimonthly magazine with 3 additional issues for bowhunting and archery enthusiasts who participate in the sport year-round. Estab. 1952. Circ. 95,000. Byline given. Pays on acceptance. No kill fee. Publishes ms an average of 5 months after acceptance. Accepts simultaneous submissions. Responds in 1 week (e-mail queries). Responds in 6 weeks to mss. Sample copy for $3 and 9x12 SASE with 10 first-class stamps. Guidelines with #10 SASE.

NONFICTION Buys 60 mss/year. Send complete ms. Length: 1,500-2,500 words. **Pays $350-600.**

💲💲 CALIFORNIA GAME & FISH

Outdoor Sportsman Group, 3330 Chastain Meadows Pkwy. NW, Suite 200, Kennesaw GA 30144. (770)953-9222. **Fax:** (678)279-7512. **E-mail:** ken.dunwoody@imoutdoors.com. **Website:** www.californiagameandfish.com. Covers fishing and hunting opportunities in California. See listing for *Game & Fish* for more information. Accepts simultaneous submissions.

💲💲 DEER & DEER HUNTING

F+W, a Content + eCommerce Company, 700 E. State St., Iola WI 54990. **Website:** www.deeranddeerhunting.com. **Contact:** Daniel E. Schmidt, editor. **95% freelance written.** Magazine published 10 times/year covering white-tailed deer. "Readers include a cross section of the deer hunting population—individuals who hunt with bow, gun, or camera. The editorial content of the magazine focuses on white-tailed deer biology and behavior, management principle and practices, habitat requirements, natural history of deer, hunting techniques, and hunting ethics. We also publish a wide range of how-to articles designed to help hunters locate and get close to deer at all times of the year. The majority of our readership consists of two-season hunters (bow & gun) and approximately one-third

camera hunt." Estab. 1977. Circ. 200,000. Byline given. Pays on acceptance. No kill fee. Publishes ms an average of 18 months after acceptance. Editorial lead time 6 months. Submit seasonal material 12 months in advance. Accepts queries by mail, e-mail. Accepts simultaneous submissions. Responds in 1 month to queries; in 2 months to mss. Sample copy for 9x12 SASE. Guidelines available on website.

NONFICTION Needs general interest, historical, how-to, photo feature, technical. No "Joe and me" articles. **Buys 100 mss/year.** Send complete ms. Length: 1,000-2,000 words. **Pays $150-600 for assigned articles.**

COLUMNS Browse (odd occurrences), 200-500 words. **Buys 10 mss/year.** Query. **Pays $25-250.**

💲💲 THE DRAKE MAGAZINE

P.O. Box 11546, Denver CO 80211. (720)638-3114. **E-mail:** info@drakemag.com. **Website:** www.drakemag.com. Dawn Wieber. **70% freelance written.** Quarterly magazine for people who love flyfishing. Estab. 1998. Byline given. Pays 1 month after publication. No kill fee. Publishes ms an average of 1 year after acceptance. Editorial lead time 1 year. Submit seasonal material 1 year in advance. Accepts queries by e-mail. Accepts simultaneous submissions. Responds in 6 months to mss. Guidelines online.

NONFICTION Buys 20-30 mss/year. Query. Length: 650-2,000 words. **Pays 25¢/word, "depending on the amount of work we have to put into the piece."**

💲💲💲 FIELD & STREAM

2 Park Ave., New York NY 10016. (212)779-5296. **Fax:** (212)779-5114. **E-mail:** fsletters@bonniercorp.com. **Website:** www.fieldandstream.com. **50% freelance written.** Broad-based monthly service magazine for the hunter and fisherman. Editorial content consists of articles of penetrating depth about national hunting, fishing, and related activities. Also humor, personal essays, profiles on outdoor people, conservation, sportsmen's insider secrets, tactics and techniques, and adventures. Estab. 1895. Circ. 1,500,000. Byline given. Pays on acceptance for most articles. No kill fee. Accepts queries by mail. Accepts simultaneous submissions. Responds in 1 month to queries. Guidelines online.

💲💲 FLORIDA SPORTSMAN

Wickstrom Communications, Intermedia Outdoors, 2700 S. Kanner Hwy., Stuart FL 34994. (772)219-

7400. **Fax:** (772)219-6900. **E-mail:** editor@florida-sportsman.com. **Website:** www.floridasportsman.com. **Contact:** Jeff Weakley, executive editor. **30% freelance written.** Monthly magazine covering fishing, boating, hunting, and related sports—Florida and Caribbean only. Edited for the boat owner and offshore, coastal, and fresh water fisherman. It provides a how, when, and where approach in its articles, which also includes occasional camping, diving, and hunting stories—plus ecology (in-depth articles and editorials attempting to protect Florida's wilderness, wetlands, and natural beauty). Circ. 115,000. Byline given. Pays on acceptance. No kill fee. Publishes ms an average of 6 months after acceptance. Submit seasonal material 6 months in advance. Accepts queries by mail, e-mail. Accepts simultaneous submissions. Responds in 1 month to queries. Sample copy free. E-mail editor for submission guidelines.

NONFICTION Buys 20-40 mss/year. Query. Length: 1,500-2,500 words. **Pays $475.**

💲💲 FUR-FISH-GAME

2878 E. Main St., Columbus OH 43209-9947. **E-mail:** ffgcox@ameritech.net. **Website:** www.furfishgame.com. **Contact:** Mitch Cox, editor. **65% freelance written.** Monthly magazine for outdoorsmen of all ages who are interested in hunting, fishing, trapping, dogs, camping, conservation, and related topics. Estab. 1900. Circ. 118,000. Byline given. Pays on acceptance. No kill fee. Publishes ms an average of 4 months after acceptance. Accepts simultaneous submissions. Responds in 2 months to queries. Sample copy for $1 and 9x12 SASE. Guidelines with #10 SASE.

NONFICTION Query. Length: 500-3,000 words. **Pays $50-250 or more for features depending upon quality, photo support, and importance to magazine.**

💲💲 GAME & FISH

3330 Chastain Meadows Pkwy. NW, Suite 200, Kennesaw GA 30144. (770)953-9222. **Fax:** (678)279-7512. **E-mail:** ken.dunwoody@imoutdoors.com. **Website:** www.gameandfishmag.com. **Contact:** Ken Dunwoody, editorial director; Ron Sinfelt, photo editor; Allen Hansen, graphic artist. **90% freelance written.** Publishes 28 different monthly outdoor magazines, each covering the fishing and hunting opportunities in a particular state or region (see individual titles to contact editors). Estab. 1975. Circ. 570,000 for 28 state-specific magazines. Byline given. Pays 3 months prior to cover date of issue. Offers negotiable kill fee.

Publishes ms an average of 7 months after acceptance. Submit seasonal material 8 months in advance. Accepts queries by mail, e-mail, fax. Accepts simultaneous submissions. Responds in 3 months to queries. Sample copy for $3.50 and 9x12 SASE. Guidelines for #10 SASE.

NONFICTION Length: 1,500-2,400 words. **Pays $150-300; additional payment made for electronic rights.**

💲💲 GEORGIA SPORTSMAN

Game & Fish, 3330 Chastain Meadows Pkwy. NW, Suite 200, Kennesaw GA 30144. (770)953-9222. **Fax:** (678)279-7512. **E-mail:** ken.dunwoody@imoutdoors.com. **Website:** www.georgiasportsmanmag.com. **Contact:** Ken Dunwoody, editorial director; Paul Rackley, editor. Covers fishing and hunting opportunities in Georgia. See listing for *Game & Fish* for more information. Accepts simultaneous submissions.

💲💲💲 GRAY'S SPORTING JOURNAL

735 Broad St., Augusta GA 30901. **E-mail:** steve.walburn@morris.com; wayne.knight@morris.com. **Website:** www.grayssportingjournal.com. **Contact:** Steve Walburn, editor in chief; Wayne Knight, art director. **75% freelance written.** "*Gray's Hunting Journal* is published 7 times/year. Because 90% of our readers are bird hunters, 85% are fly fishers, and 67% hunt big game, we're always looking for good upland-bird-hunting, fly-fishing, and big-game mss throughout the year, but don't confine yourself to these themes. Other subjects of interest include waterfowl, turkeys, small game, unusual quarry (feral hogs, etc.), sporting adventures in exciting locales (foreign and domestic) and yarns (tall tales or true)." Estab. 1975. Circ. 32,000. Byline given. Pays on publication. No kill fee. Publishes ms an average of 1 year after acceptance. Editorial lead time 14 months. Submit seasonal material 16 months in advance. Accepts queries by e-mail. Accepts simultaneous submissions. Responds in 3 months to mss. Guidelines online.

NONFICTION Needs essays, historical, humor, personal experience, photo feature, travel. Special issues: Publishes 4 themed issues: the Fly Fishing Edition (March/April), the Upland Bird Hunting Edition (August), the Big Game Edition (September/October), and the Expeditions and Guides Annual (December). Does not want how-to articles. **Buys 20-30 mss/year.** Send complete ms via e-mail with "Gray's Manuscript" in subject line. Length: 1,500-12,000 words. **Pays $600-1,250 (based on quality, not length).**

FICTION Accepts quality fiction with some aspect of hunting or fishing at the core. Needs adventure, experimental, historical, humorous, slice-of-life vignettes. If some aspect of hunting or fishing isn't at the core of the story, it has zero chance of interesting *Gray's*. **Buys 20 mss/year.** Send complete ms. Length: 750-1,500 words. **Pays $600.**

POETRY Needs avant-garde, haiku, light verse, traditional. Buys 7 poems/year. Submit maximum 1 poems. Length: up to 1,000 words. **Pays $100.**

💲💲 ILLINOIS GAME & FISH

Game & Fish, 3330 Chastain Meadows Pkwy. NW, Suite 200, Kennesaw GA 30144. (770)953-9222. **Fax:** (678)279-7512. **E-mail:** ken.dunwoody@imoutdoors. com. **Website:** www.illinoisgameandfish.com. **Contact:** Ken Dunwoody, editorial director; Shaun Epperson, editor. Covers fishing and hunting opportunities in Illinois. See listing for *Game & Fish* for more information. Accepts simultaneous submissions.

💲💲 IOWA GAME & FISH

Game & Fish, 3330 Chastain Meadows Pkwy. NW, Suite 200, Kennesaw GA 30144. (770)953-9222. **Fax:** (678)279-7512. **E-mail:** ken.dunwoody@imoutdoors. com. **Website:** www.iowagameandfish.com. **Contact:** Ken Dunwoody, editorial director; Shaun Epperson, editor. Covers fishing and hunting opportunities in Iowa. See listing for *Game & Fish* for more information. Accepts simultaneous submissions.

💲💲 KENTUCKY GAME & FISH

Game & Fish, 3330 Chastain Meadows Pkwy. NW, Suite 200, Kennesaw GA 30144. (770)953-9222. **Fax:** (678)279-7512. **E-mail:** ken.dunwoody@imoutdoors. com. **Website:** www.kentuckygameandfish.com. **Contact:** Ken Dunwoody, editorial director; Paul Rackley, editor. Covers fishing and hunting opportunities in Kentucky. See listing for *Game & Fish*. Accepts simultaneous submissions.

💲💲 THE MAINE SPORTSMAN

183 State St., Augusta ME 04330. (207)622-4242. **Fax:** (207)622-4255. **E-mail:** will.sportster@yahoo.com. **Website:** www.mainesportsman.com. **80% freelance written.** Monthly tabloid covering Maine's outdoors. "Eager to work with new/unpublished writers, but because we run over 30 regular columns, it's hard to get into *The Maine Sportsman* as a beginner." Estab. 1972. Circ. 30,000. Byline given. Pays during month of publication. No kill fee. Publishes ms an average of 3 months after acceptance. Accepts queries by mail, e-mail. Accepts simultaneous submissions. Responds in 2 weeks to queries.

NONFICTION Buys 25-40 mss/year. Send complete ms. Length: 200-2,000 words. **Pays $20-300.**

💲💲 MARLIN

460 North Orlando Ave., Suite 200, Winter Park FL 32789. (407)628-4802. **Fax:** (407)628-7061. **E-mail:** editor@marlinmag.com. **Website:** www.marlinmag.com. **90% freelance written.** Magazine published 8 times/year covering the sport of big game fishing (billfish, tuna, dorado, and wahoo). "Our readers are sophisticated, affluent, and serious about their sport—they expect a high-class, well-written magazine that provides information and practical advice." Estab. 1982. Circ. 50,000. Byline given. Pays on acceptance. No kill fee. Publishes ms an average of 3 months after acceptance. Submit seasonal material 3 months in advance. Accepts simultaneous submissions. Sample copy free with SASE.

NONFICTION Needs general interest, how-to, new product, personal experience, photo feature, technical, travel. No freshwater fishing stories. No "Me & Joe went fishing'" stories. **Buys 30-50 mss/year.** Query with published clips. Length: 800-3,000 words. **Pays $250-500.**

COLUMNS Tournament Reports (reports on winners of major big game fishing tournaments), 200-400 words; Blue Water Currents (news features), 100-400 words. **Buys 25 mss/year.** Query. **Pays $75-250.**

💲 MICHIGAN OUT-OF-DOORS

P.O. Box 30235, Lansing MI 48912. (517)371-1041. **Fax:** (517)371-1505. **E-mail:** thansen@mucc.org; magazine@mucc.org. **Website:** www.michiganoutofdoors. com. **Contact:** Tony Hansen, editor. **75% freelance written.** Monthly magazine emphasizing Michigan hunting and fishing with associated conservation issues. Estab. 1947. Circ. 40,000. Byline given. Pays on acceptance. No kill fee. Publishes ms an average of 6 months after acceptance. Submit seasonal material 6 months in advance. Accepts simultaneous submissions. Responds in 1 month to queries. Sample copy for $3.50. Guidelines for free.

NONFICTION Needs expose, historical, how-to, interview, opinion, personal experience. Special issues:

Archery Deer and Small Game Hunting (October); Firearm Deer Hunting (November); Cross-country Skiing and Early-ice Lake Fishing (December or January); Camping/Hiking (May); Family Fishing (June). No humor or poetry. **Buys 96 mss/year.** Send complete ms. Length: 1,000-2,000 words. **Pays $150 minimum for feature stories. Photos must be included with story.**

💲💲 MICHIGAN SPORTSMAN

Game & Fish, 3330 Chastain Meadows Pkwy. N.W., Suite 200, Kennesaw GA 30144. (770)953-9222. **Fax:** (678)279-7512. **E-mail:** ken.dunwoody@outdoorsg. com. **Website:** www.michigansportsmanmag.com. **Contact:** Ken Dunwoody, editorial director; Nick Gilmore, editor. Covers fishing and hunting opportunities in Michigan. See listing for *Game & Fish*. Accepts simultaneous submissions.

💲 MIDWEST OUTDOORS

MidWest Outdoors, Ltd., 111 Shore Dr., Burr Ridge IL 60527. (630)887-7722. **Fax:** (630)887-1958. **Website:** www.midwestoutdoors.com. **100% freelance written.** Monthly tabloid emphasizing fishing, hunting, camping, and boating. Estab. 1967. Byline given. Pays on publication. No kill fee. Publishes ms an average of 3 months after acceptance. Submit seasonal material 2 months in advance. Accepts simultaneous submissions. Responds in 3 weeks to queries. Sample copy for $1 or online. Guidelines online.

NONFICTION Needs how-to. "We do not want to see any articles on 'my first fishing, hunting, or camping experiences,' 'cleaning my tackle box,' 'tackle tune-up,' 'making fishing fun for kids,' or 'catch and release.'" **Buys 1,800 unsolicited mss/year.** Send complete ms. Submissions should be submitted via website's online form as a Microsoft Word doc. Length: 600-1,500 words. **Pays $15-30.**

COLUMNS Fishing; Hunting. Send complete ms. **Pays $30.**

💲💲 MINNESOTA SPORTSMAN

Game & Fish, 3330 Chastain Meadows Pkwy. N.W., Suite 200, Kennesaw GA 30144. (770)953-9222. **Fax:** (678)279-7512. **E-mail:** ken.dunwoody@outdoorsg. com. **Website:** www.minnesotasportsmanmag.com. **Contact:** Ken Dunwoody, editorial director; Nick Gilmore, editor. Covers fishing and hunting opportunities in Minnesota. See listing for *Game & Fish*. Pays a kill fee. Accepts simultaneous submissions.

💲💲 MISSISSIPPI/LOUISIANA GAME & FISH

Game & Fish, 3330 Chastain Meadows Pkwy. N.W., Suite 200, Kennesaw GA 30144. (770)953-9222. **Fax:** (678)279-7512. **E-mail:** ken.dunwoody@outdoorsg. com. **Website:** www.mississippigameandfish.com; www.lagameandfish.com. Jimmy Jacobs, editor. **Contact:** Ken Dunwoody, editorial director. Covers fishing and hunting opportunities in Mississippi and Louisiana. See listing for *Game & Fish* for more information. Accepts simultaneous submissions.

💲💲 MUSKY HUNTER MAGAZINE

P.O. Box 340, 7978 Hwy. 70 E., St. Germain WI 54558. (715)477-2178. **Fax:** (715)477-8858. **E-mail:** editor@ muskyhunter.com. **Website:** www.muskyhunter.com. **Contact:** Jim Saric, editor. **90% freelance written.** Bimonthly magazine on musky fishing. Serves the vertical market of musky fishing enthusiasts. "We're interested in how-to, where-to articles." Estab. 1988. Circ. 37,000. Byline given. Pays on publication. No kill fee. Publishes ms an average of 4 months after acceptance. Submit seasonal material 4 months in advance. Accepts simultaneous submissions. Responds in 2 months to queries. Sample copy for 9x12 SASE and $2.79 postage. Guidelines for #10 SASE.

NONFICTION Needs historical, how-to, travel. **Buys 50 mss/year.** Send complete ms. Length: 1,000-2,500 words. **Pays $100-300 for assigned articles. Pays $50-300 for unsolicited articles.**

💲💲 NEW ENGLAND GAME & FISH

Game & Fish, 3330 Chastain Meadows Pkwy. N.W., Suite 200, Kennesaw GA 30144. (770)953-9222. **Fax:** (678)279-7512. **E-mail:** ken.dunwoody@outdoorsg. com. **Website:** www.newenglandgameandfish.com. **Contact:** Ken Dunwoody, editorial director; David Johnson, editor. Covers fishing and hunting opportunities in New England region (Connecticut, Maine, Massachusetts, New Hampshire, Rhode Island, and Vermont). See listing for *Game & Fish* for more information. Accepts simultaneous submissions.

💲💲 NEW YORK GAME & FISH

Game & Fish, 3330 Chastain Meadows Pkwy. N.W., Suite 200, Kennesaw GA 30144. (770)953-9222. **Fax:** (678)279-7512. **E-mail:** ken.dunwoody@outdoorsg. com. **Website:** www.newyorkgameandfish.com. **Contact:** Ken Dunwoody, editorial director; David Johnson, editor. Covers fishing and hunting opportunities in New York. See listing for *Game & Fish* for more information. Accepts simultaneous submissions.

🟡🟢 OHIO GAME & FISH

Game & Fish, 3330 Chastain Meadows Pkwy. N.W., Suite 200, Kennesaw GA 30144. (770)953-9222. **Fax:** (678)279-7512. **E-mail:** ken.dunwoody@outdoorsg. com. **Website:** www.ohiogameandfish.com. **Contact:** Ken Dunwoody, editorial director; David Johnson, editor. Covers fishing and hunting opportunities in Ohio. See listing for *Game & Fish* for more information. Accepts simultaneous submissions.

🟡🟢 OKLAHOMA GAME & FISH

Game & Fish, 3330 Chastain Meadows Pkwy. N.W., Suite 200, Kennesaw GA 30144. (770)953-9222. **Fax:** (678)279-7512. **E-mail:** ken.dunwoody@outdoorsg. com. **Website:** www.oklahomagameandfish.com. **Contact:** Ken Dunwoody, editorial director; Nick Gilmore, editor. Covers fishing and hunting opportunities in Oklahoma. See listing for *Game & Fish* for more information. Accepts simultaneous submissions.

🟡🟢⊘ PENNSYLVANIA ANGLER & BOATER

Pennsylvania Fish & Boat Commission, P.O. Box 67000, Harrisburg PA 17106-7000. (717)705-7835. **E-mail:** ra-pfbcmagazine@state.pa.us. **Website:** www. fish.state.pa.us. **80% freelance written.** Bimonthly magazine covering fishing, boating, and related conservation topics in Pennsylvania. Circ. 28,000. Byline given. Pays 2 months after acceptance. Publishes ms an average of 8 months after acceptance. Submit seasonal material 8 months in advance. Accepts simultaneous submissions. Responds in 1 month to queries. Responds in 2 months to mss. Sample copy for 9x12 SAE with 9 first-class stamps. Guidelines online.

NONFICTION Needs how-to, technical. No saltwater or hunting material. **Buys 75 mss/year.** Query. Length: 600-2,500 words. **Payment varies.**

🟡🟢 PENNSYLVANIA GAME & FISH

Game & Fish, 3330 Chastain Meadows Pkwy. N.W., Suite 200, Kennesaw GA 30144. (770)953-9222. **Fax:** (678)279-7512. **E-mail:** ken.dunwoody@outdoorsg. com. **Website:** www.pagameandfish.com. **Contact:** Ken Dunwoody, editorial director; David Johnson, editor. Covers fishing and hunting opportunities in Pennsylvania. See listing for *Game & Fish* for more information. Accepts simultaneous submissions.

PETERSEN'S BOWHUNTING

Outdoor Sportsman Group, P.O. Box 37539, Boone IA 50037-0539. (218)824-2549. **Fax:** (218)829-2371. **E-mail:** christian.berg@outdoorsg.com. **Website:** www. bowhuntingmag.com. **Contact:** Christian Berg, editor. **70% freelance written.** Magazine published 9 times/year covering bowhunting. Very equipment oriented. Our readers are "superenthusiasts," therefore our writers must have an advanced knowledge of hunting archery. Circ. 175,000. Byline given. Pays on acceptance. No kill fee. Editorial lead time 6 months. Submit seasonal material 6 months in advance. Accepts queries by mail. Accepts simultaneous submissions. Responds in 1 month to queries. Guidelines free.

NONFICTION Needs how-to, humor, interview, new product, opinion, personal experience, photo feature. **Buys 50 mss/year.** Query.

COLUMNS Query.

PETERSEN'S HUNTING

Outdoor Sportsman Group, 6420 Wilshire Blvd., Los Angeles CA 90048. (323)782-2563. **Fax:** (323)782-2477. **Website:** www.huntingmag.com. **10% freelance written.** Magazine published 10 times/year covering sport hunting. We are a how-to magazine devoted to all facets of sport hunting, with the intent to make our readers more knowledgeable, more successful and safer hunters. Circ. 207,000. Byline given. Pays on scheduling. No kill fee. Publishes ms an average of 9 months after acceptance. Accepts simultaneous submissions. Writer's guidelines on request.

NONFICTION Needs general interest, how-to, travel. Query.

🟡🟢 RACK MAGAZINE

Buckmasters, Ltd., 10350 U.S. Hwy. 80 E., PO Box 244022, Montgomery AL 36117 US. (800)240-3337. **Fax:** (334)215-3535. **E-mail:** mhandley@buckmasters. com, loconnor@buckmasters.com. **Website:** www. buckmasters.com. **Contact:** mhandley@buckmasters.com. **75% freelance written.** 6X year (February, April, June, August, October, December) magazine covering big game hunting. "All features are either first- or third-person narratives detailing the successful hunts for world-class, big game animals—mostly white-tailed deer and other North American species." Estab. 1998. Circ. 75,000. Byline given. Pays on publication. No kill fee. Publishes ms an average of 9 months after acceptance. Editorial lead time 9-12 months. Submit seasonal material 9 months in advance. Accepts queries by mail, e-mail. Accepts simultaneous submissions. Responds in 1 month to queries; in 2 months to mss.

NONFICTION Needs personal experience. "We're interested only in articles chronicling successful hunts." **Buys 40-50 mss/year.** Query. Length: 1,000 words. **Pays $100-325 for assigned and unsolicited articles.**

SALT WATER SPORTSMAN

Bonnier Corporation, 460 N. Orlando Ave., Suite 200, Winter Park FL 32789. (407)628-4802. **E-mail:** editor@saltwatersportsman.com. **Website:** www.saltwatersportsman.com. **Contact:** Glenn Law, editor-in-chief. **85% freelance written.** Monthly magazine covering saltwater sport fishing. *Salt Water Sportsman* is edited for serious marine sport fishermen whose lifestyle includes the pursuit of game fish in U.S. waters and around the world. It provides information on fishing trends, techniques, and destinations, both local and international. Each issue reviews offshore and inshore fishing boats, high-tech electronics, innovative tackle, engines, and other new products. Coverage also focuses on sound fisheries management and conservation. Circ. 170,000. Byline given. Pays on acceptance. Offers kill fee. Publishes ms an average of 5 months after acceptance. Submit seasonal material 8 months in advance. Accepts queries by mail, e-mail. Accepts simultaneous submissions. Responds in 1 month to queries. Guidelines available by request.

NONFICTION Needs how-to, personal experience, photo feature, technical, travel. **Buys 100 mss/year.** Query. Length: 900-1,200 words. **Pay for feature/photo package starts at $750.**

COLUMNS Sportsman's Tips (short, how-to tips and techniques on salt water fishing; emphasis is on building, repairing, or reconditioning specific items or gear). Send complete ms.

SOUTH CAROLINA GAME & FISH

Game & Fish, 3330 Chastain Meadows Pkwy. N.W., Suite 200, Kennesaw GA 30144. (770)953-9222. **Fax:** (678)279-7512. **E-mail:** ken.dunwoody@outdoorsg.com. **Website:** www.scgameandfish.com. **Contact:** Ken Dunwoody, editorial director; David Johnson, editor. Covers fishing and hunting opportunities in South Carolina. See listing for *Game & Fish* for more information. Accepts simultaneous submissions.

SPORT FISHING

Bonnier Corporation, 460 N. Orlando Ave., Suite 200, Winter Park FL 32789. (407)628-4802. **Fax:** (407)628-7061. **E-mail:** Editor@sportfishingmag.com. **Website:** www.sportfishingmag.com. **Contact:** Stephanie Pancratz, Senior Managing Editor. **50% freelance written.** Magazine published 10 times/year covering saltwater angling, saltwater fish and fisheries. "*Sport Fishing*'s readers are middle-aged, affluent, mostly male, who are generally proficient in and very educated to their sport. We are about fishing from boats, not from surf or jetties." Estab. 1985. Circ. 85,0000. Byline given. Pays on acceptance. Offers 25% kill fee. Publishes ms an average of 6-12 months after acceptance. Editorial lead time 2-12 months. Submit seasonal material 1 year in advance. Accepts queries by e-mail. Accepts simultaneous submissions. Responds in 1 week to queries. Responds in 1 month to mss. Sample copy with #10 SASE. Guidelines online.

NONFICTION Needs general interest, how-to. Query. Length: 2,500-3,000 words. **Pays $500-750 for text only; $1,500+ possible for complete package with photos.**

SPORTS AFIELD

Field Sports Publishing, 15621 Chemical Lane, Huntington Beach CA 92649. (714)373-4910. **E-mail:** letters@sportsafield.com. **Website:** www.sportsafield.com. **Contact:** Jerry Gutierrez, art director. **60% freelance written.** Magazine published 6 times/year covering big game hunting. "We cater to the upscale hunting market, especially hunters who travel to exotic destinations like Alaska and Africa. We are not a deer hunting magazine, and we do not cover fishing." Estab. 1887. Circ. 50,000. Byline given. Pays 1 month prior to publication. Publishes ms an average of 6 months after acceptance. Editorial lead time 4 months. Submit seasonal material 5 months in advance. Accepts queries by mail, e-mail. Accepts simultaneous submissions. Responds in 2 months to queries and to mss Sample copy for $7.99. Guidelines online.

NONFICTION Needs personal experience, travel. **Buys 6-8 mss/year.** Query. Length: 1,500-2,500 words. **Pays $500-800.**

FILLERS Needs newsbreaks. **Buys 30 mss/year.** Length: 200-500 words. **Pays $75-150.**

⊛⊛ TENNESSEE SPORTSMAN

Game & Fish, 3330 Chastain Meadows Pkwy. N.W., Suite 200, Kennesaw GA 30144. (770)953-9222. **Fax:** (678)279-7512. **E-mail:** ken.dunwoody@outdoorsg. com. **Website:** www.tennesseesportsmanmag.com. **Contact:** Ken Dunwoody, editorial director; Paul Rackley, editor. Covers fishing and hunting opportunities in Tennessee. See listing for *Game & Fish*. Accepts simultaneous submissions.

⊛⊛ TEXAS SPORTSMAN

Game & Fish, 3330 Chastain Meadows Pkwy. N.W., Suite 200, Kennesaw GA 30144. (770)953-9222. **Fax:** (678)279-7512. **E-mail:** ken.dunwoody@outdoorsg. com. **Website:** www.texassportsmanmag.com. **Contact:** Ken Dunwoody, editorial director; Nick Gilmore, editor. Covers fishing and hunting opportunities in Texas. See listing for *Game & Fish* for more information. Accepts simultaneous submissions.

⊛⊛ TURKEY COUNTRY

National Wild Turkey Federation, P.O. Box 530, Edgefield SC 29824-0530. (803)637-3106. **E-mail:** turkeycountry@nwtf.net; mjones@nwtf.net. **Website:** www. nwtf.org. **Contact:** Matt Lindler, editor; Michelle Jones, publishing assistant. **50-60% freelance written.** Bimonthly educational magazine for members of the National Wild Turkey Federation. Topics covered include hunting, history, restoration, management, biology, and distribution of wild turkey. Estab. 1973. Circ. 180,000. Byline given. Pays on acceptance. 20% kill fee. Publishes ms an average of 6 months after acceptance. Editorial lead time 1 year. Accepts queries by mail, e-mail. Accepts simultaneous submissions. Responds in 2 months to queries Sample copy: $5 and 9x12 SAE. Guidelines online.

NONFICTION Query (preferred) or send complete ms. Length: 500-1,200 words. **Pays $350-450.**

COLUMNS Acquires for various departments, all 500-1,000 words. Query. **Pays $350.**

⊛⊛ WASHINGTON-OREGON GAME & FISH

Game & Fish, 2250 Newmarket Pkwy., Suite 110, Marietta GA 30067. (770)953-9222. **E-mail:** ken.dunwoody@imoutdoors.com. **Website:** www.wogameandfish.com. Daniel McElrath, editor. **Contact:** Ken Dunwoody, editorial director. See *Game & Fish*. Pays a kill fee. Accepts simultaneous submissions.

☼ WESTERN SPORTSMAN

202-9644 54 Ave., Edmonton AB T6E 5V1 Canada. (780)643-3963. **Fax:** (780)643-3960. **E-mail:** editorial@outdoorgroupmedia.com. **E-mail:** editor@westernsportsman.com. **Website:** www.westernsportsman.com. **90% freelance written.** Bimonthly magazine for anglers and hunters. Main coverage area is Alberta, Saskatchewan, Manitoba, and the Northern Territories. Occasionally publishes adventure destination stories that cover parts of the country as well. Short news items pertaining to all provinces/territories are also accepted. Tries to include as much information as possible on all subjects in each edition. Estab. 1968. Circ. 35,000. Byline given. Pays on publication. No kill fee. Accepts queries by e-mail. Accepts simultaneous submissions. Responds in 1 month to queries. Guidelines available online or by e-mail.

NONFICTION Buys 60 mss/year. Length: 1,500-2,000 words for features; 600-1,000 words for columns; 150-300 words for news items. **Payment is negotiable.**

⊛⊛ WEST VIRGINIA GAME & FISH

Game & Fish, 3330 Chastain Meadows Pkwy. N.W., Suite 200, Kennesaw GA 30144. (770)953-9222. **Fax:** (678)279-7512. **Website:** www.wvgameandfish.com. **Contact:** Ken Dunwoody, editorial director; Paul Rackley, editor. Covers fishing and hunting opportunities in West Virginia. See listing for *Game & Fish* for more information. Accepts simultaneous submissions.

⊛⊛ WISCONSIN SPORTSMAN

Game & Fish, 3330 Chastain Meadows Pkwy. N.W., Suite 200, Kennesaw GA 30144. (770)953-9222. **Fax:** (678)279-7512. **E-mail:** ken.dunwoody@imoutdoors. com. **Website:** www.wisconsinsportsmanmag.com. **Contact:** Ken Dunwoody, editorial director; Nick Gilmore, editor. Covers fishing and hunting opportunities in Wisconsin. See listing for *Game & Fish* for more information. Accepts simultaneous submissions.

MARTIAL ARTS

↻ BLITZ AUSTRALASIAN MARTIAL ARTS MAGAZINE

Blitz Publications, P.O. Box 4075, Mulgrave VIC 3170 Australia. (61)(3)9574-8999. **Fax:** (61)(3)9574-8899. **E-**

mail: ben@blitzmag.com.au. **Website:** www.blitzmag. net. "*Blitz Australasian Martial Arts* monthly magazine features interviews and articles on the world's best martial arts and combat sports personalities, unique styles, technique and fitness tips, health and self-defense strategies, combat psychology, as well as unrivaled coverage of local fight news and events." Accepts simultaneous submissions.

NONFICTION Needs general interest, how-to. Query.

● BLITZ AUSTRALASIAN MARTIAL ARTS MAGAZINE

Blitz Publications, 1 Miles St., P.O. Box 4075, Mulgrave VIC 3170 Australia. (3)9574-8999. **Fax:** (3)9574-8899. **E-mail:** ben@blitzmag.com.au. **Website:** www. blitzpublications.com.au. **Contact:** Ben Stone, editor. "*Blitz Australasian Martial Arts Magazine* has become the leading martial arts publication in Australia and the Southern Hemisphere. On a monthly basis, *Blitz* covers both the domestic and international scene, self-defense strategies, training and fitness advice, combat psychology, and the ever-popular action entertainment genre." Estab. 1987. Accepts queries by e-mail. Accepts simultaneous submissions.

NONFICTION Needs general interest, how-to, interview, new product. Query.

● KUNG FU TAI CHI

TC Media International, 40748 Encyclopedia Circle, Fremont CA 94538. (510)656-5100. **Fax:** (510)656-8844. **E-mail:** gene@kungfumagazine.com. **Website:** www.kungfumagazine.com. **Contact:** Gene Ching. **70% freelance written.** Bimonthly magazine covering Chinese martial arts and culture. *Kung Fu Tai Chi* covers the full range of Kung Fu culture, including healing, philosophy, meditation, Fengshui, Buddhism, Taoism, history, and the latest events in art and culture, plus insightful features on the martial arts. Estab. 1992. Circ. 10,000. Byline given. Pays on publication. No kill fee. Publishes ms 3 or more months after acceptance. Editorial lead time 4 months. Submit seasonal material 4 months in advance. Accepts queries by mail, e-mail, fax, phone. Accepts simultaneous submissions. Responds in 2 months to queries; in 3 months to mss. Sample copy for $4.99 or online. Guidelines online.

NONFICTION Needs general interest, historical, interview, personal experience, religious, technical, travel, cultural perspectives. No poetry or fiction.

Buys 70 mss/year. Query. Length: 500-2,500 words. **Pays $35-125.**

● ● T'AI CHI

Wayfarer Publications, P.O. Box 39938, Los Angeles CA 90039. (323)665-7773. **Fax:** (323)665-1627. **E-mail:** taichi@tai-chi.com. **Website:** www.tai-chi.com. **Contact:** Marvin Smalheiser, editor. **90% freelance written.** Quarterly magazine covering T'ai Chi Ch'uan as a martial art and for health and fitness. "Covers T'ai Chi Ch'uan and other internal martial arts, plus qigong and Chinese health, nutrition, and philosophical disciplines. Readers are practitioners or laymen interested in developing skills and insight for self-defense, health, and self-improvement." Estab. 1977. Circ. 50,000. Byline given. Pays on publication. No kill fee. Publishes ms an average of 3 months after acceptance. Editorial lead time 3 months. Submit seasonal material 6 months in advance. Accepts queries by mail, e-mail, fax. Accepts simultaneous submissions. Responds in 3 weeks to queries. Responds in 3 months to mss. Sample copy: $5.99. Guidelines online.

NONFICTION Needs essays, how-to, interview, personal experience. "Do not want articles promoting an individual, system, or school." Send complete ms. Length: 1,200-4,500 words. **Pays $75-500.**

MISCELLANEOUS SPORTS

● ● CLIMBING

Cruz Bay Publishing, Inc., 2520 55th St., Suite 210, Boulder CO 80302. (303)625-1600. **Fax:** (303)440-3618. **E-mail:** sdavis@climbing.com. **E-mail:** contribute@climbing.com. **Website:** www.climbing. com. Magazine published 9 times/year covering climbing and mountaineering. Provides features on rock climbing and mountaineering worldwide. Estab. 1970. Circ. 51,000. Pays on publication. No kill fee. Editorial lead time 6 weeks. Accepts queries by e-mail. Accepts simultaneous submissions. Sample copy for $4.99. Guidelines online.

NONFICTION Needs interview, personal experience. Query. Length: 1,500-3,500 words. **Pays 35¢/word.**

COLUMNS Query. **Payment varies.**

● LACROSSE MAGAZINE

113 W. University Pkwy., Baltimore MD 21210. (410)235-6882. **Fax:** (410)366-6735. **E-mail:** feed-

back@laxmagazine.com; mdasilva@uslacrosse.org. **Website:** www.laxmagazine.com; www.uslacrosse.org. **Contact:** Matt DaSilva, editor; Gabriella O'Brien, art director. **60% freelance written.** Monthly magazine covering the sport of lacrosse. "*Lacrosse* is the only national feature publication devoted to the sport of lacrosse. It is a benefit of membership in U.S. Lacrosse, a nonprofit organization devoted to promoting the growth of lacrosse and preserving its history. U.S. Lacrosse maintains *Lacrosse Magazine Online* (*LMO*) at www.laxmagazine.com. *LMO* features daily lacrosse news and scores directly from lacrosse-playing colleges. *LMO* also includes originally produced features and news briefs covering all levels of play. Occasional feature articles printed in *Lacrosse* are republished at *LMO*, and vice versa. The online component of *Lacrosse* does things that a printed publication can't—provide news, scores, and information in a timely manner." Estab. 1978. Circ. 235,000. Byline given. Pays on publication. No kill fee. Publishes ms an average of 2 months after acceptance. Editorial lead time 2 months. Submit seasonal material 2 months in advance. Accepts simultaneous submissions. Sample copy free.

NONFICTION Needs book excerpts, general interest, historical, how-to, interview, new product, opinion, personal experience, photo feature, technical. **Buys 30-40 mss/year.** Length: 500-1,750 words. **Payment negotiable.**

COLUMNS First Person (personal experience), 1,000 words; Fitness (conditioning/strength/exercise), 500-1,000 words; How-to, 500-1,000 words. **Buys 10-15 mss/year. Payment negotiable.**

⊛⊛ MUSHING MAGAZINE

P.O. Box 1195, Willow AK 99688. (907)495-2468. **E-mail:** editor@mushing.com. **Website:** www.mushing.com. **Contact:** Greg Sellentin, publisher and executive editor. Bimonthly magazine covering "all aspects of the growing sports of dogsledding, skijoring, carting, dog packing, and weight pulling. *Mushing* promotes responsible dog care through feature articles and updates on working animal health care, safety, nutrition, and training." Estab. 1987. Circ. 10,000. Byline given. Pays within 3 months of publication. No kill fee. Publishes ms an average of 4 months after acceptance. Submit seasonal material 4 months in advance. Accepts queries by mail, e-mail, fax, phone. Accepts simultaneous submissions. Responds in 8 months to queries. Sample copy: $5 ($6 U.S. to Canada). Guidelines online.

NONFICTION Needs historical, how-to. Special issues: Iditarod (January/February); Skijor/Sprint/Peak of Season (March/April); Health and Nutrition (May/June); Meet the Mushers/Tour Business Directory (July/August); Equipment (September/October); Races and Places/Sled Dog Events Calendar (November/December). See website for current editorial calendar. Query with or without published clips. "We prefer detailed queries but also consider unsolicited mss. Please make proposals informative yet to the point. Spell out your qualifications for handling the topic. We like to see clips of previously published material but are eager to work with new and unpublished authors, too." Considers complete ms by postal mail (with SASE) or e-mail (as attachment or part of message). Also accepts disk submissions. Length: 1,000-2,500 words. **Pays $50-250.**

COLUMNS Query with or without published clips or send complete ms. Length: 150-500 words.

FILLERS Needs anecdotes, facts, newsbreaks, short humor, cartoons, puzzles. Length: 100-250 words. **Pays $20-35.**

TENNIS MAGAZINE

Miller Sports Group LLC, 48 West 21st St., 6th Floor, New York NY 10010. (212)636-2700. **Fax:** (212)636-2720. **E-mail:** emcgrogan@tennis.com; nina@10TenMedia.com. **Website:** www.tennis.com. **Contact:** James Martin, editor in chief. Magazine published 10 times/year covering the sport of tennis. "Featuring in-depth reporting, exclusive player interviews and highly regarded instruction articles, as well as expert advice on tennis equipment, health, fitness, and tennis-specific travel, *TENNIS* enjoys a loyal audience of affluent and energetic players and fans." Estab. 1965. Circ. 600,000. No kill fee. Accepts simultaneous submissions.

NONFICTION Query with published clips.

VOLLEYBALL MAGAZINE

Volleyball Magazine, Madavor Media LLC, 25 Braintree Hill Office Park, Suite 404, Braintree MA 02184. **E-mail:** mkaplon@madavor.com. **Website:** www.volleyballmag.com. Only printed monthly publication devoted exclusively to all aspects of the sport of volleyball. We cover anything volleyball-related from the expanding juniors scene, to the college, professional and Olympic-International levels, both indoor and outdoor. Accepts queries by e-mail. Accepts simultaneous submissions.

NONFICTION Needs general interest, how-to, interview. Query with published clips. **Payment based on work being published.**

MOTOR SPORTS

💲⊘ AUTO ACTION

Bauer Media, 54-58 Park St., Sydney NSW 2000 Australia. **E-mail:** autoaction@bauer-media.com.au. **Website:** autoaction.com.au. Weekly magazine covering motorsports. "*Auto Action* features a diverse coverage, ensuring there is something of interest to everyone. We cover an extensive range of international, national, and local events and series, including V8 Supercars, Formula One, Champ Car, IRL, WRC and ARC, Formula Ford, F3, F4000, Carrera Cup, Speedway, Drag racing, and more. If it happens in motor sport, *Auto Action* covers it. This coverage is provided in the form of news, features, race report, and technical articles. Issues are planned well in advance." Circ. 11,667. Accepts queries by e-mail. Accepts simultaneous submissions.

NONFICTION Needs general interest, interview, race results. Query.

💲 DIRT RIDER

Bonnier Corp., 15215 Alton Pkwy., Suite 100, Irvine CA 92618. (760)707-0100. **E-mail:** drmail@bonniercorp.com. **Website:** www.dirtrider.com. Monthly magazine devoted to the sport of off-road motorcycle riding that showcases the many ways enthusiasts can enjoy dirt bikes. Circ. 200,000. No kill fee. Accepts queries by mail, e-mail.

NONFICTION Query before submitting.

💲💲 SAND SPORTS MAGAZINE

Wright Publishing Co., Inc., 3176 Pullman, Suite 107, Costa Mesa CA 92626. (714)979-2560, ext. 107. **E-mail:** info@sandsports.net. **Website:** www.sandsports.net. **Contact:** Michael Sommer, editor. **20% freelance written.** Bimonthly magazine covering vehicles for off-road and sand dunes. Estab. 1995. Circ. 35,000. Byline given. Pays on publication. Editorial lead time 3 months. Submit seasonal material 6 months in advance. Accepts queries by mail. Accepts simultaneous submissions. Sample copy and writer's guidelines free.

NONFICTION Needs how-to, photo feature, technical. **Buys 20 mss/year.** Query. Length: 1,500 words minimum. **Pays $175/page.**

RUNNING

💲 INSIDE TEXAS RUNNING

P.O. Box 19909, Houston TX 77224. (713)935-0555. **Fax:** (713)935-0559. **Website:** www.insidetexasrunning.com. **Contact:** Lance Phegley, editor. **70% freelance written.** Monthly (except June and August) tabloid covering running and running-related events. "Our audience is made up of Texas runners who may also be interested in cross training." Estab. 1977. Circ. 10,000. Byline given. Pays on publication. No kill fee. Publishes ms an average of 2 months after acceptance. Submit seasonal material 2 months in advance. Accepts simultaneous submissions. Responds in 1 month to mss. Sample copy: $4.95. Guidelines for #10 SASE.

NONFICTION Special issues: Shoe Review (March); Fall Race Review (September); Marathon Focus (October); Resource Guide (December). **Buys 20 mss/year.** Send complete ms. Length: 500-1,500 words. **Pays $100 maximum for assigned articles. Pays $50 maximum for unsolicited articles.**

REPRINTS Send tearsheet, photocopy, or typed ms with rights for sale noted and information about when and where the material previously appeared.

💲💲 RUNNING TIMES

Rodale, Inc., 400 S. 10th St., Emmaus PA 18098-0099. (610)967-5171. **Fax:** (610)967-8964. **E-mail:** editor@runningtimes.com. **Website:** www.runningtimes.com. **Contact:** Jonathan Beverly, editor-in-chief. **40% freelance written.** Magazine published 10 times/year covering distance running and racing. "*Running Times* is the national magazine for the experienced running participant and fan. Our audience is knowledgeable about the sport and active in running and racing. All editorial relates specifically to running: improving performance, enhancing enjoyment, or exploring events, places, and people in the sport." Estab. 1977. Circ. 125,000. Byline given. Pays on publication. No kill fee. Publishes ms an average of 3 months after acceptance. Editorial lead time 4-6 months. Submit seasonal material 6 months in advance. Accepts queries by mail, e-mail. Accepts simultaneous submissions. Responds in 1 month to queries. Responds in 2 months to mss. Sample copy for $8. Guidelines online.

NONFICTION Needs book excerpts, essays, historical, how-to, humor, inspirational, interview, new product, opinion, personal experience, photo feature, news, reports. No basic, beginner how-to, generic fitness/nutrition, or generic first-person accounts. **Buys 35 mss/year.** Query. Length: 1,500-3,000 words. **Pays $600-2,500 for assigned articles. Pays $500-2,000 for unsolicited articles.**

COLUMNS Training (short topics related to enhancing performance), 1,000 words; Sports-Med (application of medical knowledge to running), 1,000 words; Nutrition (application of nutritional principles to running performance), 1,000 words. **Buys 10 mss/year.** Query. **Pays $200-400.**

FICTION Any genre, with running-related theme or characters. Buys 1 ms/year. Send complete ms. Length: 1,500-3,000 words. **Pays $100-500.**

💲💲 TRAIL RUNNER

Big Stone Publishing, 2567 Dolores Way, Carbondale CO 81623. (970)704-1442. **Fax:** (970)963-4965. **E-mail:** pcunobooth@bigstonepub; mbenge@bigstonepub.com. **Website:** www.trailrunnermag.com. **Contact:** Michael Benge, editor; Yitka Winn, associate editor. **80% freelance written.** Magazine published 8x year, covering trail runing, ultratanning, fastpacking, adventure racing, and snowshoeing. Covers all aspects of off-road running. "North America's only magazine dedicated to trail running. In-depth editorial and compelling photography informs, entertains and inspires readers of all ages and abilities to enjoy the outdoors and to improve their health and fitness through the sport of trail running." Estab. 1999. Circ. 31,000. Byline given. Pays 30 days post-publication Publishes ms an average of 2 months after acceptance. Editorial lead time is 3 months. Submit seasonal material 5 months in advance. Accepts queries by e-mail. Accepts simultaneous submissions. Responds in 4 weeks to queries. Sample copy for $5. Guidelines online.

NONFICTION Needs expose, historical, how-to, humor, inspirational, interview, personal experience, technical, travel, racing. Does not want "My first trail race." **Buys 30-40 mss/year.** Query with one or two writing samples (preferably previously published articles), including your name, phone number and e-mail address. Identify which department your story would be best suited for. **Pays 25¢/word for assigned and unsolicited articles.**

COLUMNS Contact: Michael Benge, editor, or Yitka Winn, associate editor. Making Tracks (news, race reports, athlete Q&A), 300-800 words; Trail Tips, Training, Trail Rx (injury prevention/treatment, recovery), Take Your Mark (race previews); Nutrition (sports nutrition, health news), 800-1,000 words; Adventure, Great Escapes (running destinations/trails), Faces (athlete profiles), 1,200 words **Buys 40 mss/year. mss/year.** Query with published clips. **Pays 25 cents/word.**

FILLERS Needs anecdotes, facts, newsbreaks, short humor. **Buys 10 mss/year. mss/year.** Length: 75-400 words. **Pays 30 cents/word.**

SKIING & SNOW SPORTS

💲💲💲⊘ SKIING MAGAZINE

Bonnier Corp., 5720 Flatiron Pkwy., Boulder CO 80301. (303)253-6300. **Fax:** (303)448-7638. **E-mail:** editor@skiingmag.com. **Website:** www.skinet.com/skiing. **60% freelance written.** Magazine published 8 times/year. *Skiing Magazine* is an online ski-lifestyle publication written and edited for recreational skiers. Its content is intended to help them ski better (technique), buy better (equipment and skiwear), and introduce them to new experiences, people, and adventures. Estab. 1936. Circ. 430,000. Byline given. Pays on acceptance. Offers 15% kill fee. Publishes ms an average of 3 months after acceptance. Submit seasonal material 8 months in advance. Accepts queries by mail, e-mail. Accepts simultaneous submissions. Sample copy with 9 x 12 SASE and 5 first-class stamps.

NONFICTION Needs essays, historical, how-to, humor, interview, personal experience. **Buys 5-10 mss/year.** Send complete ms. Length: 1,000-3,500 words. **Pays $500-1,000 for assigned articles. Pays $300-700 for unsolicited articles.**

FILLERS Needs facts, short humor. **Buys 10 mss/year.** Length: 60-75 words. **Pays $50-75.**

⊘ SNOWBOARDER

The Enthusiast Network, 2052 Corte Del Nogal, Suite 100, Carlsbad CA 92011. **Website:** www.snowboardermag.com. Magazine published 8 times/year edited primarily for male youths who are snowboard enthusiasts. Circ. 137,800. No kill fee. Editorial lead time 3 months. Accepts queries by online submission form. Accepts simultaneous submissions.

WATER SPORTS

⊕$ DIVER

216 E. Esplanade St., North Vancouver BC V7L 1A3 Canada. (604)988-0711. **E-mail:** editor@divermag.com. **Website:** www.divermag.com. Magazine published 8 times/year emphasizing sport SCUBA diving, ocean science, and technology for a well-educated, active readership across North America and around the world. Circ. 30,000. No kill fee. Accepts queries by mail, e-mail. Accepts simultaneous submissions.

NONFICTION Query. Length: 500-3,000 words. **Pays 12.5¢/word.**

SCUBA DIVING

Bonnier Corporation, 460 N. Orlando Ave., Suite 200, Winter Park FL 32789. **E-mail:** edit@scubadiving.com; ashley.annin@bonniercorp.com. **Website:** www.scubadiving.com. **Contact:** Ashley Annin, managing editor. Monthly magazine covering scuba diving. "*Scuba Diving* magazine is the ultimate resource for passionate scuba divers to get the latest information on gear, training and destinations." Estab. 1992. Accepts queries by mail, e-mail, fax, phone. Accepts simultaneous submissions. Guidelines by e-mail.

NONFICTION Query.

COLUMNS Query.

$⊘ SURFER MAGAZINE

Source Interlink, 2052 Corte Del Nogal, Suite 100, Carlsbad CA 92011. (949)325-6212. **E-mail:** brendon@surfermag.com; janna@surfermag.com. **Website:** www.surfermag.com. **Contact:** Brendon Thomas, editor; Janna Irons, managing editor. Monthly magazine edited for the avid surfers and those who follow the beach, wave riding scene. Circ. 118,570. No kill fee. Editorial lead time 10 weeks. Accepts simultaneous submissions.

$$ SWIMMING WORLD MAGAZINE

Sports Publications International, 2744 East Glenrosa, Phoenix AZ 85016. (928)284-4005. **Fax:** (928)284-2477. **E-mail:** editorial@swimmingworld.com. **Website:** www.swimmingworldmagazine.com. **Contact:** Jason Marsteller, managing editor. **30% freelance written.** Bimonthly magazine about competitive swimming. Readers are fitness-oriented adults from varied social and professional backgrounds who share swimming as part of their lifestyle. Estab. 1960. Circ. 50,000. Byline given. Pays on publication. Editorial lead time 2 months. Submit seasonal material 3 months in advance. Accepts queries by mail, e-mail, fax. Accepts simultaneous submissions. Responds in 1 month to queries. Guidelines online.

NONFICTION Needs book excerpts, essays, expose, general interest, historical, how-to, humor, inspirational, interview, new product, personal experience, photo feature, technical, travel, general health. **Buys 30 mss/year.** Query with a 250-word synopsis of article. Length: 250-2,500 words. **Pays $75-400.**

◐ TRACKS MAGAZINE

Wolseley Media, Level 6, Building A, 207 Pacific Highway, St. Leonards NSW 2065 Australia. 02 9901 6170. **Fax:** 02 9901 6116. **E-mail:** lkennedy@tracksmag.com.au. **Website:** www.tracksmag.com/#. **Contact:** Luke Kennedy, editor. Monthly magazine covering surfing. "*Tracks* is innovation in surfing. It is hero-driven, irreverent & fashionable." Circ. 30,000. Accepts simultaneous submissions.

NONFICTION Needs general interest, how-to, interview, new product. Query.

WAKE BOARDING MAGAZINE

460 N. Orlando Ave., Suite 200, Winter Park FL 32789. **E-mail:** shawn.perry@wakeboardingmag.com. **Website:** www.wakeboardingmag.com. **10% freelance written.** Magazine published 9 times/year covering wakeboarding. *Wake Boarding Magazine* is the leading publication for wakeboarding in the world. Articles must focus on good riding, first and foremost, then good fun and good times. Covers competition, travel, instruction, personalities, and humor. Estab. 1994. Circ. 60,000. Byline given. Pays on publication. No kill fee. Publishes ms an average of 3 months after acceptance. Editorial lead time 4 months. Submit seasonal material 4 months in advance. Accepts queries by mail, e-mail. Accepts simultaneous submissions. Responds in 1 week to queries. Responds in 1 month to mss. Sample copy and writer's guidelines free.

NONFICTION Needs general interest, how-to, humor, interview, new product, photo feature, travel. No Weekend Wallys having fun on the lake. Serious riders only. Nothing to do with waterskiing or barefooting. Send complete ms. Length: 1,000-2,500 words.

$ THE WATER SKIER

1251 Holy Cow Rd., Polk City FL 33868. (863)324-4341. **Fax:** (863)325-8259. **E-mail:** satkinson@usawaterski.org. **Website:** www.usawaterski.org. **Contact:** Scott Atkinson, editor. **10-20% freelance written.** Magazine published 6 times/year. *The Water Skier* is the membership magazine of USA Water Ski, the national governing body for organized water skiing in the United States. The magazine has a controlled circulation and is available only to USA Water Ski's membership, which is made up of 17,000 active competitive water skiers. The editorial content of the magazine features distinctive and informative writing about the sport of water skiing and wakeboarding. Estab. 1951. Circ. 20,000. Byline given. Editorial lead time 4 months. Submit seasonal material 6 months in advance. Accepts simultaneous submissions. Responds in 2 weeks to queries. Sample copy: $3.50. Guidelines available with #10 SASE.

NONFICTION **Buys 10-15 mss/year.** Query. Length: 1,500-3,000 words. **Pays $100-150.**

COLUMNS The Water Skier News (small news items about people and events in the sport), 400-500 words. Other topics include safety, training (3-event, barefoot, disabled, show ski, ski race, kneeboard, and wakeboard); champions on their way; new products. Query. **Pays $50-100.**

WATERSKI MAGAZINE

Bonnier Corporation, 460 N. Orlando Ave., Suite 200, Winter Park FL 32703. **E-mail:** todd.ristorcelli@bonniercorp.com. **Website:** www.waterskimag.com. **25% freelance written.** Magazine published 9 times/year for water skiing and related watersports. *WaterSki* instructs, advises, enlightens, informs and creates an open forum for skiers around the world. It provides definitive information on instruction, products, people and travel destinations. Estab. 1978. Circ. 105,000. Pays on acceptance. Publishes ms an average of 4 months after acceptance. Editorial lead time 2 months. Submit seasonal material 2 months in advance. Accepts simultaneous submissions. Responds in 1 month to queries. Responds in 2 months to mss. Sample copy for SAE with 8 1/2 x 11 envelope and 4 first-class stamps. Guidelines for #10 SASE.

NONFICTION Needs general interest, historical, how-to, interview, new product, photo feature, technical, travel. Nothing unrelated to water skiing. **Buys 10 mss/year.** Query with published clips. Length: 800-2,000 words. **Pays negotiable amount.**

COLUMNS Shortline (interesting news of the sport), 300 words. Query with published clips.

FILLERS Needs anecdotes, facts, gags, newsbreaks, short humor. Length: 200-500 words.

TEEN & YOUNG ADULT

🪙🪙 CICADA

Cricket Media, Inc., **E-mail:** cicada@cicadamag.com **Website:** www.cricketmag.com/cicada. "*Cicada* is a YA lit/comics magazine fascinated with the lyric and strange and committed to work that speaks to teens' truths. We publish poetry, realistic and genre fiction, essay, and comics by adults and teens. (We are also inordinately fond of Viking jokes.) Our readers are smart and curious; submissions are invited but not required to engage young adult themes." Bimonthly literary magazine for ages 14 and up. Publishes 6 issues/year. Estab. 1998. Circ. 6,000. Pays after publication. Accepts queries by online submission form. Accepts simultaneous submissions. Responds in 3-6 months to mss. Sample copy online. Guidelines online.

NONFICTION narrative nonfiction (especially teen-written), essays on literature, culture, and the arts. Submit complete ms via online submissions manager (cricketmag.submittable.com). Length: up to 5,000 words. **Pays up to 25¢/word.**

FICTION realism, science fiction, fantasy, historical fiction. Wants everything from flash fiction to novellas. Length: up to 9,000 words. **Pays up to 25¢/word.**

POETRY Needs free verse, light verse, traditional. Reviews serious, humorous, free verse, rhyming. Length: no limit. **Pays up to $3/line ($25 minimum).**

🅐 SEVENTEEN MAGAZINE

300 W. 57th St., 17th Floor, New York NY 10019. (917)934-6500. **Fax:** (917)934-6574. **E-mail:** mail@seventeen.com. **Website:** www.seventeen.com. **Contact:** Consult masthead to contact appropriate editor. Monthly magazine covering topics geared toward young adult American women. "We reach 14.5 million girls each month. Over the past 6 decades, *Seventeen* has helped shape teenage life in America. We represent an important rite of passage, helping to define, socialize, and empower young women. We create notions of beauty and style, proclaim what's hot in popular culture, and identify social issues." Estab. 1944. Circ. 2,000,000. Byline sometimes given. Pays on publication. Accepts queries by mail. Accepts simultaneous submissions. Writer's guidelines for SASE.

NONFICTION Buys 7-12 mss/year. Query by mail. Consult masthead to pitch appropriate editor. Length: 200-2,000 words.

TEEN VOGUE

Conde Nast Publications, 4 Times Square, 10th Floor, New York NY 10036. (212)286-2860. **Fax:** (212)286-2378. **Website:** www.teenvogue.com. Magazine published 10 times/year. Written for sophisticated teenage girls age 12-17 years old. Circ. 450,000. No kill fee. Editorial lead time 2 months. Accepts simultaneous submissions.

💲💲 YOUNG SALVATIONIST

The Salvation Army, P.O. Box 269, Alexandria VA 22313-0269. (703)684-5500. **Fax:** (703)684-5539. **E-mail:** ys@usn.salvationarmy.org. **Website:** www.youngsalvationist.org. **Contact:** Captain Pamela Maynor, editor. **10% freelance written.** Monthly magazine for teens and early college youth. "*Young Salvationist* provides young people with biblically based inspiration and resources to develop their spirituality within the context of the Salvation Army." Circ. 40,000. Byline given. Pays on acceptance. No kill fee. Publishes ms an average of 6 months after acceptance. Submit special issues material 6 months in advance. Accepts simultaneous submissions. Responds in 2 months to mss. Sample copy and theme list free with #10 SASE or online.

NONFICTION Needs how-to, humor, inspirational, interview, personal experience, photo feature, religious. **Buys 10 mss/year.** Send complete ms through website at publications.salvationarmyusa.org/writers-submissions. Length: 700-900 words. **Pays 35¢/word.**

TRAVEL, CAMPING & TRAILER

💲💲 AAA MIDWEST TRAVELER

AAA Auto Club of Missouri, 12901 N. 40 Dr., St. Louis MO 63141. (314)523-7350, ext. 6301. **Fax:** (314)523-6982. **E-mail:** dreinhardt@aaamissouri.com. **Website:** www.aaa.com/traveler. **Contact:** Deborah Reinhardt, managing editor. **80% freelance written.** Bimonthly magazine covering travel and automotive safety. "We provide members with useful information on travel, auto safety and related topics." Estab. 1901. Circ. 500,000. Byline given. Pays on acceptance. Of-

fers $50 kill fee. Editorial lead time 1 year. Submit seasonal material 6 months in advance. Accepts queries by mail, e-mail, fax. Accepts simultaneous submissions. Responds in 1 month to queries. Responds in 1 month to mss. Sample copy with 10x13 SASE and 4 First-Class stamps. Guidelines with #10 SASE.

NONFICTION Needs travel. No humor, fiction, poetry or cartoons. **Buys 20-30 mss/year.** Query; query with published clips the first time. Length: 800-1,200 words. **Pays $400.**

BACKROADS

P.O. Box 317, Branchville NJ 07826. (973)948-4176. **Fax:** (973)948-0823. **E-mail:** editor@backroadsusa.com. **Website:** www.backroadsusa.com. **50% freelance written.** Monthly tabloid covering motorcycle touring. "*Backroads* is a motorcycle tour magazine geared toward getting motorcyclists on the road and traveling. We provide interesting destinations, unique roadside attractions and eateries, plus Rip & Ride Route Sheets. We cater to all brands. Although *Backroads* is geared towards the motorcycling population, it is not by any means limited to just motorcycle riders. Non-motorcyclists enjoy great destinations, too. As time has gone by, *Backroads* has developed more and more into a cutting-edge touring publication. We like to see submissions that give the reader the distinct impression of being part of the ride they're reading. Words describing the feelings and emotions brought on by partaking in this great and exciting lifestyle are encouraged." Estab. 1995. Circ. 50,000. Byline given. Pays 1 month after publication. Editorial lead time 1 month. Submit seasonal material 3 months in advance. Accepts queries by mail, e-mail. Responds in 1 month. Sample copy: $4. Guidelines online.

NONFICTION "What *Backroads* does not want is any 'us vs. them' submissions. We are decidedly non-political and secular. *Backroads* is about getting out and riding, not getting down on any particular group, nor do we feel this paper should be a pulpit for a writer's beliefs . be they religious, political, or personal." Query. Needs travel features: "This type of story offers a good opportunity for prospective contributors. They must feature spectacular photography, color preferably, and may be used as a cover story, if of acceptable quality. **All submissions must be accompanied by images**, with an SASE of adequate size (10x13) to return all material sent, as well as a copy of the issue in which they were published, and a hard copy printout of the article, including your name, address, and phone number. If none is enclosed, the materials will not be returned. Text submissions are accepted via U.S. mail or e-mail. We can usually convert most file types, although it is easier to submit in plain text format, sometimes called ASCII." **Pays $75 and up; varies.**

COLUMNS We're Outta Here (weekend destinations), 500-750 words; Great All-American Diner Run (good eateries with great location), 500-750 words; Thoughts from the Road (personal opinion/insights), 400-600 words; Mysterious America (unique and obscure sights), 500-750 words; Big City Getaway (day trips), 500-750 words. **Buys 20-24 mss/year.** Query. **Pays $75/article.**

$ CAMPING TODAY

Family Campers and RVers, 4804 Transit Rd., Bldg. 2, Depew NY 14043. (716)668-6242; (800)245-9755. **E-mail:** d_johnston01@msn.com. **Website:** www.fcrv.org/news/camping-today. **Contact:** DeWayne Johnston, editor. *Camping Today* is the member magazine for Family Campers & RVers, a nonprofit camping and RV organization with over 4,000 families in the U.S. and Canada. Many of the members are retired. Some take grandchildren camping. Working families with kids travel and camp when time permits. FCRV has local clubs or chapters in almost every state and province. Seventy percent of the magazine's content is member activities, including promotion for FCRV's 2 biggest annual events, the National Campvention (rally) in July, which moves to a different location each year, and the Retiree Rally in March in the sun belt. Estab. 1983. Byline given. Pays on publication. Submit seasonal material 3 months in advance. Accepts simultaneous submissions. Responds in 2 months. Sample copy for 3 first-class stamps. E-mail editor for guidelines.

NONFICTION Needs humor, interview, new product, technical, travel. Query by mail or e-mail or send complete ms with photos. E-mail photos separate from text, or mail copy and prints with SASE. Length: 700-2,000 words. **Pays $50-150.**

CONDE NAST TRAVELER

4 Times Square, 14th Floor, New York NY 10036. (212)286-2860. **Fax:** (212)286-2258. **E-mail:** web@condenasttraveler.com; letters@condenasttraveler.com. **Website:** www.cntraveler.com. **Contact:** Laura Garvey and Maeve Nicholson, editorial assistants; Greg Ferro, managing editor. Monthly magazine. Conde Nast Traveler is a luxury and lifestyle magazine. Estab. 1987. Circ. 800,000.

ESCAPEES

Sharing the RV Lifestyle, Roving Press, 100 Rainbow Dr., Livingston TX 77351. (888)757-2582. **Fax:** (409)327-4388. **E-mail:** editor@escapees.com. **Website:** escapees.com. **Contact:** Kelly-Evans Hill, editorial assistant. *Escapees* magazine's contributors are RVers interested in sharing the RV lifestyle. Audience includes full-time RVers, snowbirds, and those looking forward to traveling extensively. *Escapees* members have varying levels of experience; therefore, the magazine looks for a wide variety of material, beyond what is found in conventional RV magazines, and welcomes submissions on all phases of RV life, especially relevant mechanical/technical information. About 85% of the club members are retired, over 98% travel without children, and about 50% live in their motorhomes, fifth-wheels, or travel trailers on a full-time basis. A bimonthly magazine that provides a total support network to RVers and shares the RV lifestyle. Estab. 1979. Circ. 25,000. Byline given. Pays on publication. Publishes ms an average of 3-6 months after acceptance. Editorial lead time 3 months. Submit seasonal material 6 months in advance. Accepts simultaneous submissions. Responds in 2 weeks to queries; in 3 months to mss. Sample copy available free online. Guidelines available online and by e-mail at departmentseditor@escapees.com. Editor does not accept articles based on queries alone. Decisions for use of material are based on the full article with any accompanying photos, graphics, or diagrams. Only complete articles are considered.

NONFICTION Needs general interest, historical, how-to, humor, inspirational, interview, nostalgic, personal experience, photo feature, profile, technical, travel. Do not send anything religious, political, or unrelated to RVs. Submit complete ms. When submitting an article via e-mail as an attachment, please include the text in the body of the e-mail. Length: 300-1,400 words. Please include word count on first page of article. **Pays $50-150 for unsolicited articles.** Publication sometimes "pays" writers with contributor copies rather than a cash payment, often in exchange for company bio/company product-themed photos.

COLUMNS **Contact:** Megan Swander, editorial assistant. SKP Stops (short blurbs with photos on unique travel destination stops for RVers), 300-500 words. **Buys 10-15 mss/year.** Submit complete ms. **Pays $25-75.**

⊘⊘ FAMILY MOTOR COACHING

Family Motor Coach Association, 8291 Clough Pike, Cincinnati OH 45244. (513)474-3622; (800)543-3622. **Fax:** (513) 474-2332. **E-mail:** rgould@fmca.com. **E-mail:** magazine@fmca.com. **Website:** www.fmca.com. **Contact:** Robbin Gould, editor. **80% freelance written. "We prefer that writers be experienced RVers."** Monthly magazine emphasizing travel by motorhome, motorhome mechanics, maintenance, and other technical information. *Family Motor Coaching* is the official publication of Family Motor Coach Association, an international organization serving motorhome owners and enthusiasts. The magazine is distributed to association members who own motorhomes as a requirement of membership—specifically, self-contained, motorized recreation vehicles—and is also read by prospective members who may or may not already own a motorhome. Articles focus on RV travel, recreation, and related lifestyle topics; association news and activities; motorhome maintenance, repair, and DIY projects; new motorhome models; and related components and accessories. Approximately one-third of editorial content is devoted to travel and entertainment; one-third to association news; and one-third to new products, industry news, and motorhome maintenance/technical topics. Estab. 1963. Circ. 75,000. Byline given. Pays on acceptance. Publishes ms an average of 8 months after acceptance. Submit seasonal material 4-6 months in advance. Accepts queries by mail, e-mail, fax. Responds in 3 months to queries. Sample copy: $3.99; $5 if paying by credit card. Guidelines with #10 SASE or request PDF by e-mail.

NONFICTION Needs how-to, humor, interview, new product, nostalgic, profile, technical, travel, motorhome travel (various areas of North America accessible by motorhome), bus conversions, nostalgia. **Buys 50-75 mss/year.** Query with published clips. Length: 1,000-2,000 words. **Pays $100-500, depending on article category.** Expenses paid in select cases if discussed in advance.

⊘⊘ HIGHROADS

AAA Arizona, 2375 E. Camelback Rd., Suite 500, Phoenix AZ 85016. (602)650-2732. **Fax:** (602)241-2917.

E-mail: highroads@arizona.aaa.com. **Website:** highroads.az.aaa.com. **50% freelance written.** *Highroads*, the AAA Arizona member magazine, offers inspiring travel articles about destinations throughout Arizona and around the world, automotive news and reviews, and educational resources on insurance and finance. The print edition is published bimonthly and has been honored for writing and design with Communicator Awards, Davey Awards, and Maggie Awards. Byline given. Pays on publication. Offers 30% kill fee. Editorial lead time 1 year. Submit seasonal material 6 months in advance. Accepts queries by e-mail. Accepts simultaneous submissions. Sample copy online. Guidelines online.

NONFICTION Needs reviews, travel. Does not want fiction, humor, poetry, or pitches for new columns. **Buys 21 mss/year.** Query with published clips. Length: 1,200 words. **Pays 25-40¢/word.**

COLUMNS Weekender (a short getaway you can travel to from Arizona), 400 words; Road Trip (driving directions about attractions along a specific stretch of road reachable from Arizona), 800 words; Talk of the Town (an Arizona town with a unique hidden attraction), 400 words. **Buys 10 mss/year. Pays 25-40¢/word.**

⊘⊘ HIGHWAYS

Affinity Group, Inc., 2575 Vista Del Mar Dr., Ventura CA 93001. (805)667-4100. **E-mail:** highways@goodsamclub.com. **Website:** www.goodsamclub.com/highways. Monthly magazine covering recreational vehicle lifestyle. "All of our readers own some type of RV—a motorhome, trailer, pop-up, tent—so our stories need to include places that you can go with large vehicles, and campgrounds in and around the area where they can spend the night." Estab. 1966. Circ. 975,000. Byline given. Pays on acceptance. Offers 50% kill fee. Publishes ms an average of 6 months after acceptance. Accepts queries by e-mail. Accepts simultaneous submissions. Responds in 2 weeks to queries. Sample copy and writer's guidelines free or online.

NONFICTION Needs how-to, humor, technical, travel. **Buys 15-20 mss/year.** Query. Length: 800-1,100 words.

COLUMNS On the Road (issue related); RV Insight (for people new to the RV lifestyle); Action Line (consumer help); Tech Topics (tech Q&A); Camp Cuisine (cooking in an RV); Product Previews (new products). No plans on adding new columns/departments.

◐⊖⊗ INNS MAGAZINE

Harworth Publishing Inc., 521 Woolwich St., Guelph ON N1H 3X9 Canada. (519)767-6059. **E-mail:** mary@innsmagazine.com. **Website:** www.innsmagazine.com. **Contact:** Mary Hughes, editor. *Inns* is a national publication for travel, dining, and pastimes. It focuses on inns, beds and breakfasts, resorts, and travel in North America. The magazine is targeted to travelers looking for exquisite getaways. Accepts queries by e-mail. Accepts simultaneous submissions. Guidelines by e-mail.

NONFICTION Needs general interest, interview, new product, opinion, personal experience, travel. Query. Length: 300-600 words. **Pays $175-250 (Canadian).**

FILLERS Short quips or nominations, 75 words. All stories submitted must have accompany photos. **Pays $25.**

⚫⊖⊗ INTERNATIONAL LIVING

International Living Publishing, Ltd., Elysium House, Ballytruckle, Waterford Ireland (800)643-2479. **Fax:** 353-51-304-561. **E-mail:** submissions@internationalliving.com. **Website:** www.internationalliving.com. **Contact:** Eoin Bassett, editorial director. **50% freelance written.** "*International Living* magazine aims at providing a scope and depth of information about global travel, living, retiring, investing, and real estate that is not available anywhere else at any price." Estab. 1981. Circ. 500,000. Byline given. Pays on publication. Offers 25-50% kill fee. Publishes ms an average of 3 months after acceptance. Editorial lead time 2 months. Submit seasonal material 3 months in advance. Accepts queries by e-mail. Accepts simultaneous submissions. Responds in 2 months to mss. Sample copy online. Guidelines online.

NONFICTION Needs how-to, interview, new product, personal experience, travel, health care. No descriptive, run-of-the-mill travel articles. **Buys 100 mss/year.** Query. Length: 840-1,400 words. **Pays $250-400.**

⊗⊗⊗⊗ ISLANDS

Bonnier Corp., 460 N. Orlando Ave., Suite 200, Winter Park FL 32789. **E-mail:** editor@islands.com. **Website:** www.islands.com. **80% freelance written.** Magazine published 8 times/year. "We cover accessible and once-in-a-lifetime islands from many different perspectives: travel, culture, lifestyle. We ask our authors to give us the essence of the island and do it with literary flair." Estab. 1981. Circ. 250,000. Byline given. Pays on publication. Offers 25% kill fee. Publishes ms an average of 8 months after acceptance. Accepts queries by mail, e-mail. Accepts simultaneous submissions. Responds in 2 months to queries; in 6 weeks to mss. Sample copy: $6. Writer's guidelines by e-mail.

NONFICTION Needs book excerpts, essays, general interest, interview, photo feature, travel, service shorts, island-related material. **Buys 25 feature mss/year.** Send complete ms. Length: 2,000-4,000 words. **Pays $750-2,500.**

COLUMNS Discovers section (island related news), 100-250 words; Taste (island cuisine), 900-1,000 words; Travel Tales (personal essay), 900-1,100 words; Live the Life (island expat Q&A). Query with published clips. **Pays $25-1,000.**

⊖⊗ MOTORHOME

2750 Park View Court, Suite 240, Oxnard CA 93036. **E-mail:** info@motorhomemagazine.com. **Website:** www.motorhomemagazine.com. **Contact:** Eileen Hubbard, editor. **60% freelance written.** Monthly magazine covering topics for RV enthusiasts. "*MotorHome* is a magazine for owners and prospective buyers of motorized recreational vehicles who are active outdoorsmen and wide-ranging travelers. We cover all aspects of the RV lifestyle; editorial material is both technical and nontechnical in nature. Regular features include tests and descriptions of various models of motorhomes, travel adventures, and hobbies pursued in such vehicles, objective analysis of equipment and supplies for such vehicles, and do-it-yourself articles. Guides within the magazine provide listings of manufacturers, rentals, and other sources of equipment and accessories of interest to enthusiasts. Articles must have an RV slant and excellent photography accompanying text." Estab. 1968. Circ. 150,000. Byline given. Pays on acceptance. Offers 30% kill fee. Publishes ms an average of 1 year after acceptance. Editorial lead time 4 months. Submit seasonal material 6 months in advance. Accepts queries by mail, fax. Accepts simultaneous submissions. Responds in 1 month to queries; in 2 months to mss. Sample copy free. Guidelines online.

NONFICTION Needs general interest, historical, how-to, humor, interview, new product, personal experience, photo feature, technical. No diaries of RV trips or negative RV experiences. **Buys 120 mss/year.**

Query with published clips. Length: 800-2,500 words. **Pays $400-900.**

COLUMNS Crossroads (offbeat briefs of people, places, and events of interest to travelers), 100-200 words; Keepers (tips, resources). Query with published clips, or send complete ms. **Pays $100.**

💲 PATHFINDERS

6325 Germantown Ave., Philadelphia PA 19144. (215)438-2140. **Fax:** (215)438-2144. **E-mail:** editors@pathfinderstravel.com; info@pathfinderstravel.com. **Website:** www.pathfinderstravel.com. **75% freelance written.** Bimonthly magazine covering travel for people of color, primarily African-Americans. We look for lively, original, well-written stories that provide a good sense of place, with useful information and fresh ideas about travel and the travel industry. Our main audience is African-Americans, though we do look for articles relating to other persons of color: Native Americans, Hispanics and Asians. Pathfinders Travel Magazine for People of Color is is published quarterly. The magazine, which enjoys a circulation of 100,000 copies, reaches an affluent audience of African American travelers interested in enjoying the good life. Pathfinders tells readers where to go, what to do, where to dine and how to `get there from a cultural perspective. Pathfinders covers domestic and international destinations. The slick, glossy, color magazine is available nationally in Barnes & Nobel, Crown, Borders, Hastings and other independent book stores. Estab. 1997. Circ. 100,000. Byline given. Pays on publication. Accepts queries by mail, e-mail. Accepts simultaneous submissions. Responds in 1 month to queries. Responds in 2 months to mss. Sample copy at bookstores (Barnes & Noble). Guidelines online.

NONFICTION Needs essays, historical, how-to, personal experience, photo feature, travel. "No more pitches on Jamaica. We get these all the time." **Buys 16-20 mss/year.** Send complete ms. Length: 800-1,000 words for features. **Pays $150.**

COLUMNS Chef's Table, Post Cards from Home; Looking Back; City of the Month, 500-600 words. Send complete ms. **Pays $150.**

💲💲 RECREATION NEWS

Official Publication of the GovEmployee.com, 1607 Sailaway Circle, Baltimore MD 21221. (410)944-4852. **Fax:** (410)638-6902. **E-mail:** editor@recreationnews.com. **Website:** www.recreationnews.com. **Contact:** Marvin Bond, editor. **75% freelance written.** Monthly guide to leisure-time activities for federal and private industry workers covering Mid-Atlantic travel destinations, outdoor recreation, and cultural activities. Estab. 1982. Circ. 115,000. Byline given. Pays on publication. No kill fee. Publishes ms an average of 3 months after acceptance. Submit seasonal material 10 months in advance. Accepts queries by mail, e-mail, phone. Accepts simultaneous submissions. Responds in 2 months to queries. See sample copy and writer's guidelines online.

NONFICTION Needs travel. No reviews/critiques or material outside of Mid-Atlantic region. Query with published clips or links. Length: 600-1,000 words. **Pays $50-300.**

🌐💲💲 TIMES OF THE ISLANDS

Times Publications, Ltd., P.O. Box 234, Lucille Lightbourne Bldg., #1, Providenciales Turks & Caicos Islands British West Indies. (649)946-4788. **Fax:** (649)946-4788. **E-mail:** timespub@tciway.tc. **Website:** www.timespub.tc. **60% freelance written.** Quarterly magazine covering the Turks & Caicos Islands. "*Times of the Islands* is used by the public and private sector to inform visitors and potential investors/developers about the Islands. It goes beyond a superficial overview of tourist attractions with in-depth articles about natural history, island heritage, local personalities, new development, offshore finance, sporting activities, visitors' experiences, and Caribbean fiction." Estab. 1988. Circ. 10,000. Byline given. Pays on publication. No kill fee. Publishes ms an average of 6 months after acceptance. Editorial lead time 4 months. Submit seasonal material at least 4 months in advance. Accepts queries by e-mail. Accepts simultaneous submissions. Responds in 6 weeks to queries. Responds in 2 months to mss. Sample copy for $6. Guidelines online.

NONFICTION Needs book excerpts, essays, general interest, historical, humor, inspirational, interview, nostalgic, personal experience, photo feature, profile, technical, travel, book reviews, nature, ecology, business (offshore finance), watersports. **Buys 20 mss/year.** Query. Length: 500-3,000 words. **Pays $150-500.**

COLUMNS On Holiday (unique experiences of visitors to Turks & Caicos), 500-1,500 words. **Buys 4 mss/year. mss./year.** Query. **Pays $150.**

FICTION Needs adventure, ethnic, historical, humorous, novel excerpts, slice-of-life vignettes. **Buys**

1 mss/year. Query. Length: 1,000-3,000 words. **Pays $250-400.**

✪$$ VERGE MAGAZINE

Verge Magazine Inc., P.O. Box 147, Peterborough ON K9J 6Y5 Canada. **E-mail:** contributing@vergemagazine.ca. **Website:** www.vergemagazine.com. **Contact:** Jessica Lockhart, contributing editor. **60% freelance written.** Quarterly magazine. "Each issue takes you around the world, with people who are doing something different and making a difference doing it. This is the magazine resource for those wanting to volunteer, work, study or adventure overseas." "*Verge* is the magazine for people who travel with purpose. It explores ways to get out and see the world by volunteering, working, and studying overseas. Our readers are typically young (17-40 years), or young at heart, active, independent travelers. Editorial content is intended to inform and motivate the reader by profiling unique individuals and experiences that are timely and socially relevant. We look for articles that are issue driven and combine an engaging and well-told story with nuts and bolts how-to information. Wherever possible and applicable, efforts should be made to provide sources where readers can find out more about the subject, or ways in which readers can become involved in the issue covered." Estab. 2002. Circ. 10,000. Byline given. Pays on publication. No kill fee. Publishes ms an average of 6 months after acceptance. Submit seasonal material 8-12 months in advance. Accepts queries by mail, e-mail. Accepts simultaneous submissions. Responds in 8 weeks to queries. Responds in 2 months to mss. Sample copy for $6, plus shipping. Guidelines online.

NONFICTION Needs how-to, humor, interview. "We do not want pure travelogues, predictable tourist experiences, luxury travel, stories highlighting a specific company, or organisation." **Buys 30-40 mss/year.** Send complete ms. Length: 800-2,500 words. **Pays $0.10 (CAD) per word to first-time contributors.**

COLUMNS Buys 20-30 mss/year. Query with published clips. **Pays $0.10 (CAD) per word to first-time contributors.**

WESTERN JOURNEY MAGAZINE

AAA Washington, 1745 114th Ave. SE, Bellevue WA 98004. **E-mail:** robbhatt@aaawin.com; sueboylan@aaawin.com. **Website:** www.washington.aaa.com/journey. Sue Boylan, art director. **Contact:** Rob Bhatt, editor. Bimonthly magazine. "We present engaging, inspiring content on a mix of subjects for AAA members in Washington state and North Idaho. In addition to long-form features and shorter items on regional and international travel, curated specifically for residents of the Pacific Northwest, we also share the latest about research and trends in traffic safety, auto technology, and other AAA-centric topics." Circ. 550,000. Pays on acceptance. Accepts queries by e-mail. Response time varies.

NONFICTION "We assign stories based on writers' proposals and rarely accept completed mss. We look for writers who combine sound research and reporting skills with a strong voice and excellent storytelling ability. We adhere to AP style. Each spring, we create our features calendar for the following calendar year. We encourage you to read several issues of the magazine to familiarize yourself with our publication before you submit article ideas. We run all articles with high-quality photographs and illustrations. If you are a published photographer, let us know—but please do not submit any photos unless requested. To be considered for an assignment, submit a query by e-mail with 3 samples of published work (or links to websites where your work can be found)." Length: 200-1,500 words. **Pay negotiable, based on experience.** Travel expenses must be approved ahead of time.

WOMEN'S

✪$$$$ CHATELAINE

1 Mount Pleasant Rd., 8th Floor, Toronto ON M4Y 2Y5 Canada. (416)764-2000. **Fax:** (416)764-1888. **E-mail:** storyideas@chatelaine.rogers.com; brendan.fisher@chatelaine.rogers.com. **Website:** www.chatelaine.com. **Contact:** Laura Brown, managing editor; Brendan Fisher, deputy art director. Monthly magazine covering Canadian women's lifestyles. "*Chatelaine* is edited for Canadian women ages 25-49, their changing attitudes and lifestyles. Key editorial ingredients include health, finance, social issues, and trends, as well as fashion, beauty, food, and home décor. Regular departments include Health pages, Entertainment, Money, Home, Humour, and How-to." Byline given. Pays on acceptance. Offers 25-50% kill fee. Accepts queries by e-mail. Accepts simultaneous submissions. Responds in 2 months to queries. Guidelines online.

NONFICTION Query with published clips. **Pays $1/word.**

COSMOPOLITAN

Hearst Corp., 300 W. 57th St., New York NY 10019-3791. (212)649-2000. **E-mail:** cosmo@hearst.com; youtellcosmo@hearst.com. **Website:** www.cosmopolitan.com. Monthly magazine that includes articles on women's issues, relationships, sex, health, careers, self-improvement, celebrities, fashion, and beauty. *Cosmopolitan* is an international magazine for women. Estab. 1886. Circ. 3 million. Accepts queries by mail, e-mail. Accepts simultaneous submissions.

NONFICTION *Cosmopolitan* is the largest magazine in the world and does not consider itself a starting point for writers. If you have a good set of published clips and a strong idea that you think would fit in Cosmo, e-mail your query, with "Story Pitch" in the subject line. An editor will then get in touch if they are interested in the idea. Consider using the masthead to get in touch with the editor most appropriate for your query.

MARIE CLAIRE

Hearst Corporation, 300 West 57th St., 34th Floor, New York NY 10019-1497. **Website:** www.marieclaire.com. Monthly women's magazine focusing on women around the world and worldwide issues. Also covers health, beauty, and fashion topics. Estab. 1937. Circ. 950,000. Accepts queries by mail. Accepts simultaneous submissions. Responds in 4-6 weeks. Guidelines online.

NONFICTION Prefers story proposals, rather than completed mss. Send query letter detailing idea via postal mail. If the editors find the subject suitable, they will respond. Enclose clips of previously published materials. Materials will not be returned.

$$$$ ELLE

Hearst Communications, Inc., 300 W. 57th St., 24th Floor, New York NY 10019. (212)903-5000. **E-mail:** editors@elle.com. **Website:** www.elle.com. Monthly magazine. Edited for the modern, sophisticated, affluent, well-traveled woman in her twenties to early thirties. Circ. 1,100,000. No kill fee. Editorial lead time 3 months. Accepts queries by e-mail. Accepts simultaneous submissions.

NONFICTION Query before submitting.

ESSENCE

135 W. 50th St., New York NY 10020. **Website:** www.essence.com. Monthly magazine. *Essence* is the magazine for today's black women. Edited for career-minded, sophisticated, and independent achievers, *Essence*'s editorial is dedicated to helping its readers attain their maximum potential in various lifestyles and roles. The editorial content includes career and educational opportunities, fashion and beauty, investing and money management, health and fitness, parenting, information on home decorating and food, travel, cultural reviews, and profiles of achievers and celebrities. Estab. 1970. Circ. 1 million. Byline given. Pays on acceptance. Offers 25% kill fee. Editorial lead time 6 months. Submit seasonal material 6 months in advance. Accepts queries by mail, fax. Accepts simultaneous submissions. Responds in 2 months to queries; in 2 months to mss. Sample copy: $3.25. Guidelines online.

NONFICTION Needs book excerpts. **Buys 200 mss/year.** Query with published clips. Address to specific editor. Departments include Arts and Entertainment; Books and Poetry; Beauty and Style; Health, Relationships, and Food; Personal Essays; News; Money and Power; Feature Articles/Personal Growth. See online guidelines for specific editors. Length is given upon assignment. **Pays competitive rate.**

$$$$ GLAMOUR

Condé Nast, 4 Times Square, 16th Floor, New York NY 10036. (212)286-2860. **Fax:** (212)286-8336. **Website:** www.glamour.com. **Contact:** Cyndi Leive, editor-in-chief. Monthly magazine covering subjects ranging from fashion, beauty, and health; personal relationships; career; travel; food; and entertainment. *Glamour* is edited for the contemporary woman, and informs her of the trends and recommends how she can adapt them to her needs, and motivates her to take action. Estab. 1939. Circ. 2.3 million. No kill fee. Accepts queries by mail. Accepts simultaneous submissions.

NONFICTION Needs personal experience, travel.

$$ GRACE ORMONDE WEDDING STYLE

Elegant Publishing, Inc., P.O. Box 89, Barrington RI 02806. (401)245-9726. **Fax:** (401)245-5371. **E-mail:** contact@weddingstylemagazine.com. **Website:** www.weddingstylemagazine.com. **Contact:** Director of Accounts. **90% freelance written.** Bi-annual print magazine encompassing real weddings, bridal fashion, destination wedding, lifestyle, jewelry and local vendors. Grace Ormonde Wedding Style is the luxury wedding source for Fashion, Jewelry, Lifestyle and Travel: Wedding Gowns, Eveningwear, Engagement Rings, Bridal Registry and Home Decor, Destination Weddings and Romantic Honeymoons. Estab. 1997. Circ. 350,000. Pays on publication. No kill fee. 4 months after acceptance. Editorial lead time 3-6 months. 3-6 months Accepts queries by e-mail, online submission form. Accepts simultaneous submissions. 2 weeks https://www.weddingstylemagazine.com/submissions. https://www.weddingstylemagazine.com/submissions.

NONFICTION Needs inspirational, new product, photo feature, travel.

$$$$ HARPER'S BAZAAR

Hearst Communications, Inc., 300 W. 57th St., New York NY 10019. (212)903-5000. **E-mail:** editors@harpersbazaar.com. **Website:** www.harpersbazaar.com. **Contact:** Glenda Bailey, editor in chief. *Harper's Bazaar* is a specialist magazine published 10 times/year for women who enjoy fashion and beauty. It is edited for sophisticated women with exceptional taste. *Harper's Bazaar* offers ideas in fashion and beauty, and reports on issues and interests relevant to the lives of modern women. Estab. 1867. Circ. 734,504. Byline given. Pays on publication. Offers 25% kill fee. Accepts queries by e-mail. Accepts simultaneous submissions. Responds in 2 months to queries.

NONFICTION **Buys 36 mss/year.** Query with published clips. Length: 2,000-3,000 words. **Payment negotiable.**

COLUMNS Length: 500-700 words. **Payment negotiable.**

$$ HOPE FOR WOMEN

P.O. Box 3241, Muncie IN 47307. **E-mail:** hope@hopeforwomenmag.org. **Website:** www.hopeforwomenmag.org. **90% freelance written.** Bimonthly lifestyle magazine that offers faith, love, and virtue for the modern Christian Woman. *Hope for Women* presents refreshing, inspirational articles in an engaging and authentic tone to women from various walks of life. The magazine encourages readers and deals with real-world issues—all while adhering to Christian values and principles. Estab. 2005. Circ. 10,000. Byline given. Pays on publication. Publishes ms an average of 4-6 months after acceptance. Editorial lead time 4-6 months. Accepts queries by mail, e-mail. Accepts simultaneous submissions. Guidelines by e-mail.

NONFICTION Needs book excerpts, essays, general interest, how-to, humor, inspirational, interview, new product, opinion, personal experience, photo feature, religious, travel. Query. Length: 500 words minimum. **Pays 10-20¢/word.**

COLUMNS Relationships (nurturing positive relationships—marriage, dating, divorce, single life), 800-1,200 words; Light (reports on issues such as infidelity, homosexuality, addiction, and domestic violence), 500-800 words; Journey (essays on finding your identity with Christ), 500-800 words; Marketplace (finance/money management), 800-1,200 words); E-Spot (book, music, TV, and film reviews), 500-800 words; Family First (parenting encouragement and instruction), 800-1,500 words; Health/Fitness (nutrition/exercise), 800-1,200 words; The Look (fashion/beauty tips), 500-800 words; Home Essentials (home/garden how-to), 500-800 words. Query. **Pays 10-20¢/word.**

INSTYLE

Time, Inc., 1271 Avenue of the Americas, 18th Floor, New York NY 10020. (212)522-1212. **Fax:** (212)522-0867. **E-mail:** letters@instylemag.com. **Website:** www.instyle.com. **Contact:** Ariel Foxman, editorial director. Monthly magazine. Written to be the most trusted style adviser and lifestyle resource for women. Circ. 1,670,000. No kill fee. Editorial lead time 4 months. Accepts simultaneous submissions.

$$$$ LADIES' HOME JOURNAL

Meredith Corp., P.O.Box 37508, Boone IA 50037. 212-499-2087. **E-mail:** lhjcustserv@cdsfulfillment.com. **Website:** www.divinecaroline.com/ladies-home-journal. **50% freelance written.** Monthly magazine focusing on issues of concern to women 30-45. *Ladies' Home Journal* is for active, empowered women who are evolving in new directions. It addresses informational needs with highly focused features and articles on a variety of topics: self, style, family, home, world, health, and food. Estab. 1882. Circ. 4.1 million. Pays on acceptance. Offers 25% kill fee. Publishes ms an average of 4-12 months after acceptance. Editorial lead time 4 months. Accepts queries by mail, e-mail. Accepts simultaneous submissions. Responds in 3 months to queries. Guidelines online.

NONFICTION Send 1-2 page query, SASE, résumé, and clips via mail or e-mail (preferred). Length: 2,000-3,000 words. **Pays $2,000-4,000.**

FICTION Only short stories and novels submitted by an agent or publisher will be considered. No poetry of any kind. **Buys 12 mss/year.** Send complete ms. Length: 2,000-2,500 words.

☯❸❸ LIVE

Canadian Baptist Women of Ontario and Quebec, 100-304 The East Mall, Etobicoke ON M9B 6E2 Canada. (416)651-8967. **E-mail:** rsejames@gmail.com. **Website:** www.baptistwomen.com. **Contact:** Renee James, editor/director of communications. **50% freelance written.** Magazine published 6 times/year designed to help women grow their world, faith, relationships, creativity, and mission vision—evangelical, egalitarian, Canadian. Estab. 1878. Circ. 3,500. Byline given. Pays on publication. No kill fee. Publishes ms an average of 6 months after acceptance. Editorial lead time 2 months. Submit seasonal material 4 months in advance. Accepts simultaneous submissions. Sample copy for 9x12 SAE with 2 first-class Canadian stamps.

NONFICTION Needs inspirational, interview, personal experience, religious. **Buys 30-35 mss/year.** Query first. Unsolicited mss not accepted. Length: 650-800 words. **Pays 5-12¢/word (Canadian).**

MORE

Meredith Corp., 125 Park Ave., New York NY 10017. **E-mail:** more@meredith.com. **Website:** www.more. com. **Contact:** Ila Stanger, managing editor. Magazine published 10 times/year. *More* celebrates women of style and substance. The magazine is the leading voice for the woman who lives in a constant state of possibility. Estab. 1998. Circ. 1.8 million. Byline given. Editorial lead time 4 months. Accepts queries by mail. Accepts simultaneous submissions. Guidelines online.

NONFICTION *More* only accepts queries, before submissions. Keep query brief (1-2 pages), citing lead and describing how you will research and develop story. Be specific, and direct query to the appropriate editor, as listed on the masthead of the magazine. Send published clips, credits, and a résumé. Does not respond unless a SASE is enclosed. Word length is discussed upon assignment. Average story length is 2,000 words. **Payment is discussed upon assignment.**

❸❸ NA'AMAT WOMAN

505 Eighth Ave., Suite 12A04, New York NY 10018. (212)563-5222. **E-mail:** naamat@naamat.org; judith@naamat.org. **Website:** www.naamat.org. **Contact:** Judith Sokoloff, editor. **80% freelance written.** Published three times per year, covering Jewish issues/subjects. "Magazine covering a wide variety of subjects of interest to the Jewish community— including political and social issues, arts, profiles; many articles about Israel and women's issues. Fiction must have a Jewish theme. Readers are the American Jewish community." Estab. 1926. Circ. 10,000. Byline given. Pays on publication. No kill fee. Publishes ms an average of 6 months after acceptance. Submit seasonal material 6 months in advance. Accepts queries by e-mail. Accepts simultaneous submissions. Responds in 4 weeks to queries. Responds in 3 months to mss. Sample copy for $2. Guidelines by e-mail.

NONFICTION Needs book excerpts, essays, historical, interview, personal experience, photo feature, travel, Jewish topics & issues, political & social issues & women's issues. **Buys 16-20 mss/year.** Send complete ms. **Pays 10-20¢/word for assigned and unsolicited articles.**

FICTION "We want serious fiction, with insight, reflection and consciousness." Needs novel excerpts, literary with Jewish content. "We do not want fiction that is mostly dialogue. No corny Jewish humor. No Holocaust fiction." **Buys 1-2 mss/year. mss/year.** Query with published clips or send complete ms. Length: 2,000-3,000 words. **Pays 10-20¢/word for assigned articles and for unsolicited articles.**

O, THE OPRAH MAGAZINE

Hearst Corp., 1700 Broadway, 38th Floor, New York NY 10019-5905. (212)903-5187. **Fax:** (212)977-1947. **Website:** www.oprah.com. Monthly magazine founded by Oprah Winfrey and Hearst Corporation, primarily marketed at women. Circ. 2.4 million. No kill fee. Accepts simultaneous submissions. Guidelines available.

REAL SIMPLE

Time Inc., 1271 Avenue of the Americas, New York NY 10020. (212)522-1212. **Fax:** (212)467-1392. **Website:** www.realsimple.com. *Real Simple* is a monthly women's interest magazine. *Real Simple* features articles and information related to homekeeping, childcare, cooking, and emotional wellbeing. The magazine is distinguished by its clean, uncluttered style of layout and photos. Estab. 2000. Circ. 1.97 million. Accepts simultaneous submissions.

❸❸❸ REDBOOK MAGAZINE

Hearst Corp., Articles Department, Redbook, 300 W. 57th St., 22nd Floor, New York NY 10019. **Website:**

www.redbookmag.com. Monthly magazine covering women's issues. *Redbook* is targeted to women between the ages of 25-45 who define themselves as smart, capable, and happy with their lives. Many, but not all, readers are going through 1 of 2 key life transitions: single to married, and married to mom. Each issue is a provocative mix of features geared to entertain and inform them, including: news stories on contemporary issues that are relevant to the reader's life and experience and that explore the emotional ramifications of cultural and social changes; first-person essays about dramatic pivotal moments in a woman's life; marriage articles with an emphasis on strengthening the relationship; short parenting features on how to deal with universal health and behavioral issues; reporting on exciting trends in women's lives. Estab. 1903. Circ. 2,200,000. Pays on acceptance. No kill fee. Publishes ms an average of 6 months after acceptance. Accepts simultaneous submissions. Responds in 3 months to queries and mss. Guidelines online.

NONFICTION Query with published clips and SASE. Length: 2,500-3,000 words for features; 1,000-1,500 words for short articles.

🍁 RESOURCES FOR FEMINIST RESEARCH

RFR/DRF (Resources for Feminist Research), OISE, University of Toronto, 2-231, 252 Bloor St. W., Toronto ON M5S 1V6 Canada. **E-mail:** rfr@utoronto.ca. **Website:** www.oise.utoronto.ca/rfr. Semiannual academic journal covering feminist research in an interdisciplinary, international perspective. Estab. 1972. Circ. 2,500. Byline given. Publishes ms an average of 1 year after acceptance. Editorial lead time 1 year. Accepts queries by e-mail. Accepts simultaneous submissions. Responds in 2 weeks to queries. Responds in 6-8 months to mss. Guidelines online.

NONFICTION Needs essays, academic articles and book reviews. Does not want nonacademic articles. Send complete ms. Length: up to 10,000 words, including footnotes and endnotes.

$$$$ SELF

Conde Nast, 4 Times Square, New York NY 10036. (212)286-2860. **Fax:** (212)286-6174. **E-mail:** comments@self.com. **Website:** www.self.com. Monthly magazine for women ages 20-45. Self-confidence, self-assurance, and a healthy, happy lifestyle are pivotal to *Self* readers. This healthy lifestyle magazine delivers by addressing real-life issues from the inside out, with unparalleled energy and authority. From beauty, fitness, health and nutrition to personal style, finance, and happiness, the path to total well-being begins with *Self*. Circ. 1.3 million. Byline given on features and most short items. Pays on acceptance. No kill fee. Accepts queries by online submission form. Accepts simultaneous submissions. Responds in 1 month to queries. Guidelines for #10 SASE.

NONFICTION **Buys 40 mss/year.** Query with published clips. Length: 1,500-5,000 words. **Pays $1-2/word.**

COLUMNS Uses short, news-driven items on health, fitness, nutrition, money, jobs, love/sex, psychology and happiness, travel. Length: 300-1,000 words. **Buys 50 mss/year.** Query with published clips. **Pays $1-2/word.**

$$ SKIRT!

Morris Communications, 1 Henrietta St., First Floor, Charleston SC 29403. (843)958-0027. **Fax:** (843)958-0029. **E-mail:** submissions@skirt.com; jenny.dennis@skirt.com. **Website:** www.skirt.com. **Contact:** Jenny Dennis, publisher. **50% freelance written.** Monthly magazine covering women's interest. *Skirt!* is all about women—their work, play, families, creativity, style, health, wealth, bodies, and souls. The magazine's attitude is spirited, independent, outspoken, serious, playful, irreverent, sometimes controversial, and always passionate. Estab. 1994. Circ. 285,000. Byline given. Pays on publication. No kill fee. Publishes ms an average of 2 months after acceptance. Editorial lead time 2-3 months. Submit seasonal material 2-3 months in advance. Accepts simultaneous submissions. Responds in 6-8 weeks to queries. Responds in 1-2 months to mss. Guidelines on website.

NONFICTION Needs essays, humor, personal experience. "Do not send feature articles. We only accept submissions of completed personal essays that will work with our monthly themes available online." **Buys 100+ mss/year.** Send complete ms (preferably as a Rich Text Format attachment) via e-mail. Publishes 2 personal essays every month on topics related to women and women's interests. Length: 800-1,100 words. **Pays $150-200.**

TRUE CONFESSIONS

105 E. 34th St., Box 141, New York NY 10016. **E-mail:** shazell@truerenditionsllc.com. **E-mail:** trueswriters@yahoo.com. **Website:** www.truerenditionsllc.com. **Contact:** Samantha Hazell, editor. "*True Con-*

fessions is a women's magazine featuring true-to-life stories about working-class women and their families. The stories must be in first-person and generally deal with family problems, relationship issues, romances, single moms, abuse, and any other realistic issue women face in our society. The stories we look for are true or at least believable. We look for stories that evoke some sort of emotion, be it happiness or sadness, but in the end there needs to be some sort of moral or lesson learned." Pays on last week of the month after publication. Editorial lead time 3 months. Submit seasonal material 6 months in advance. Guidelines online.

NONFICTION E-mail submissions preferred (trueswriters@yahoo.com). Include contact information and brief synopsis of story. To submit by postal mail, include disk saved in Word, a hard copy, and SASE for return of materials. Length: 3,000-7,000 words. **Pays 3¢/word.**

COLUMNS My Man! (about a special man in your life); That's Incredible! (about an experience in your life that reaffirms your faith); The Life I Live (about an inspirational time in your life); My Moment with God (thoughts during a meditative moment, quiet reflection, or prayer); Phenomenal Woman (about a special woman in your life). E-mail submissions preferred (trueswriters@yahoo.com). Include contact information and brief synopsis of story. To submit by postal mail, include disk saved in Word, a hard copy, and SASE for return of materials. **Pays $65-100.**

FICTION "Stories should be written in first person and past tense. We generally look for more serious stories. The underlying theme is overcoming adversities in life. These are supposed to be 'true' stories—or at least stories that could be true!" E-mail submissions preferred (trueswriters@yahoo.com). Include contact information and brief synopsis of story. To submit by postal mail, include disk saved in Word, a hard copy, and SASE for return of materials. Length: 3,000-7,000 words. **Pays 3¢/word.**

$$$$ VOGUE

Condè Nast, 4 Times Square, 12th Floor, New York NY 10036-6518. (212)286-2860. **Website:** www.vogue.com. Monthly magazine. *Vogue* mirrors the changing roles and concerns of women, covering not only evolutions in fashion, beauty and style, but the important issues and ideas of the arts, health care, politics, and world affairs. Estab. 1892. Circ. 1.1 million. Byline sometimes given. Pays on acceptance. Offers 25% kill fee. Accepts simultaneous submissions. Responds in 3 months to queries. Guidelines for #10 SASE.

NONFICTION Query with published clips. 2,500 words maximum. **Pays $1-2/word.**

W

Fairchild Publications, Inc., 750 3rd Ave., New York NY 10017. (212)630-4900. **Fax:** (212)630-4919. **Website:** www.wmagazine.com. **Contact:** Nina Lawrence. Monthly magazine covering pop culture, fashion, beauty, the arts, celebrities, homes, hotels, and more. "Written for today's contemporary woman whose fashion sensibility and sense of style define her own look, in her own way." Circ. 463,000. No kill fee. Editorial lead time 6 weeks. Accepts simultaneous submissions.

WOMAN'S DAY

Hearst Communications, Inc., 300 W. 57th St., 28th Floor, New York NY 10019. (212)649-2000. **E-mail:** womansday@hearst.com. **Website:** www.womansday.com. **Contact:** Sue Kakstys, managing editor. Monthly magazine. Woman's Day is a women's magazine that covers such topics as homemaking, food, nutrition, physical fitness, physical attractiveness, and fashion. Estab. 1937. Circ. 3.3 million. Accepts queries by e-mail. Accepts simultaneous submissions. Guidelines online.

NONFICTION Editors work almost exclusively with experienced writers who have clips from major national magazines. Accepts unsolicited mss only from writers with such credentials. There are no exceptions. E-mail an idea or mss that might be of interest and include recent, published clips. Will respond only if interested. Does not accept hard copy submissions.

$$ WOMAN'S LIFE

A Publication of Woman's Life Insurance Society, 1338 Military St., P.O. Box 5020, Port Huron MI 48061-5020. (800)521-9292, ext. 181. **Fax:** (810)985-6970. **E-mail:** website@womanslife.org. **Website:** www.womanslife.org. **Contact:** Karen Deschaine, managing editor. **30% freelance written.** Quarterly magazine published for a primarily female membership to help them care for themselves and their families. Estab. 1892. Circ. 32,000. Byline given. Pays on publication. No kill fee. Publishes ms an average of 1 year after acceptance. Submit seasonal material 6 months in advance. Accepts queries by mail, e-mail, fax. Accepts simultaneous submissions. Responds in 1 year to queries and to mss. Sample copy for SAE with 9X12 envelope and 4 first-class Sample copy online. Guidelines for #10 SASE.

NONFICTION Buys 4-10 mss/year. Send complete ms. Length: 1,000-2,000 words. **Pays $150-500.**

💲💲💲 WOMAN'S WORLD

Bauer Publishing, 270 Sylvan Ave., Englewood Cliffs NJ 07632. (201)569-6699. **Fax:** (201)569-3584. **E-mail:** dearww@womansworldmag.com. **Website:** www.womansworldmag.com. Weekly magazine covering human interest and service pieces of interest to family-oriented women across the nation. *Woman's World* is a women's service magazine. It offers a blend of fashion, food, parenting, beauty, and relationship features coupled with the true-life human interest stories. Publishes short romances and mini-mysteries for all women, ages 18-68. Estab. 1980. Circ. 1.6 million. Pays on acceptance. No kill fee. Publishes ms an average of 4 months after acceptance. Submit seasonal material 4 months in advance. Accepts queries by mail. Accepts simultaneous submissions. Responds in 2 months to mss. Guidelines for #10 SASE.

NONFICTION Query.

FICTION Contact: Johnene Granger, fiction editor. Wants romance and mainstream short stories of 800 words and mini-mysteries of 1,000 words. Each of story should have a light romantic theme and can be written from either a masculine or feminine point of view. Women characters may be single, married, or divorced. Plots must be fast moving with vivid dialogue and action. The problems and dilemmas inherent in them should be contemporary and realistic, handled with warmth and feeling. The stories must have a positive resolution. Specify Fiction on envelope. Always enclose SASE. Mini-mysteries may revolve around anything from a theft to murder. Not interested in sordid or grotesque crimes. Emphasis should be on intricacies of plot rather than gratuitous violence. The story must include a resolution that clearly states the villain is getting his or her come-uppance. Submit complete mss. Specify Mini-Mystery on envelope. Needs mystery, romance. Not interested in science fiction, fantasy, historical romance, or foreign locales. No explicit sex, graphic language, or steamy settings. Send complete ms. Romances: 800 words; mysteries: 1,000 words. **Pays $1,000.**

💲 WOMEN IN BUSINESS

American Business Women's Association (The ABWA Co., Inc.), 9820 Metcalf Ave., Suite 110, Overland Park KS 66212. (913)732-5100. **Fax:** (913)660-0101. **E-mail:** abwa@abwa.org; rstreet@abwa.org. **Website:** www.abwa.org. **Contact:** Rene Street, executive director. **30% freelance written.** Bimonthly magazine covering issues affecting working women. "How-to features for career women on business trends, small-business ownership, self-improvement, and retirement issues. Profiles business women." Estab. 1949. Circ. 45,000. Byline given. Pays on acceptance. No kill fee. Publishes ms an average of 3 months after acceptance. Editorial lead time 3 months. Accepts queries by mail, e-mail, fax. Accepts simultaneous submissions. Responds in 3 weeks to queries. Responds in 2 months to mss. Sample copy for SAE with 9x12 envelope and 4 first-class stamps. Guidelines for #10 SASE.

NONFICTION Needs how-to. No fiction or poetry. **Buys 3% of submitted. mss/year.** Query. Length: 500-1,000 words. **Pays $100/500 words.**

COLUMNS Life After Business (concerns of retired business women); It's Your Business (entrepreneurial advice for business owners); Health Spot (health issues that affect women in the work place). Length: 500-750 words. Query. **Pays $100/500 words.**

TRADE JOURNALS

///

Many writers who pick up *Writer's Market* for the first time do so with the hope of selling an article to one of the popular, high-profile consumer magazines found on newsstands and in bookstores. Many of those writers are surprised to find an entire world of magazine publishing exists outside the realm of commercial magazines—trade journals. Writers who *have* discovered trade journals have found a market that offers the chance to publish regularly in subject areas they find interesting, editors who are typically more accessible than their commercial counterparts, and pay rates that rival those of the big-name magazines.

Trade journal is the general term for any publication focusing on a particular occupation or industry. Other terms used to describe the different types of trade publications are business, technical, and professional journals. They are read by truck drivers, bricklayers, farmers, fishermen, heart surgeons, and just about everyone else working in a trade or profession. Trade periodicals are sharply angled to the specifics of the professions on which they report. They offer business-related news, features, and service articles that will foster their readers' professional development.

Writers for trade journals have to either possess knowledge about the field in question or be able to report it accurately from interviews with those who do. Writers who have or can develop a good grasp of a specialized body of knowledge will find trade magazine editors who are eager to hear from them.

An ideal way to begin your foray into trade journals is to write for those that report on your present profession. If you don't have experience in a profession but can demonstrate an ability to understand (and write about) the intricacies and issues of a particular trade that interests you, editors will still be willing to hear from you.

ADVERTISING, MARKETING & PR

💲💲💲 BRAND PACKAGING

BNP Media, 2401 W. Big Beaver Rd., Suite 700, Troy MI 48084. (248)362-3700. **Fax:** (847)362-0317. **E-mail:** zielinskil@bnpmedia.com. **Website:** www.brand-packaging.com. **Contact:** Laura Zielinski, editor-in-chief. **15% freelance written.** Magazine published 10 times/year covering how packaging can be a marketing tool. Publishes strategies and tactics to make products stand out on the shelf. Market is brand managers who are marketers but need to know something about packaging. Estab. 1997. Circ. 33,000. Byline given. Pays on acceptance. Publishes ms an average of 2 months after acceptance. Editorial lead time 3 months. Submit seasonal material 3 months in advance. Accepts queries by mail, fax. Accepts simultaneous submissions. Sample copy free.

NONFICTION Needs how-to, interview, new product. **Buys 10 mss/year.** Send complete ms. Length: 600-2,400 words. **Pays 40-50¢/word.** Pays expenses of writers on assignment.

PHOTOS State availability. Identification of subjects required. Reviews contact sheets, 35mm transparencies, 4x5 prints. Negotiates payment individually. Buys one-time rights.

COLUMNS Emerging Technology (new packaging technology), 600 words. **Buys 10 mss/year.** Query. **Pays $150-300.**

TIPS "Be knowledgeable on marketing techniques and be able to grasp packaging techniques. Be sure you focus on packaging as a marketing tool. Use concrete examples. We are not seeking case histories at this time."

💲 DECA DIRECT

1908 Association Dr., Reston VA 20191. (703)860-5000. **E-mail:** info@deca.org. **E-mail:** christopher_young@deca.org. **Website:** www.decadirect.org. **Contact:** Christopher Young, editor in chief. **30% freelance written.** Quarterly magazine covering marketing, professional development, business, and career training during school year (no issues published May-August). *DECA Direct* is the membership magazine for DECA—The Association of Marketing Students, primarily ages 15-19 in all 50 states, the U.S. territories, Germany, and Canada. The magazine is delivered through the classroom. Students are interested in developing professional, leadership, and career skills. Estab. 1947. Circ. 160,000. Byline given. Pays on publication. No kill fee. Editorial lead time 3 months. Submit seasonal material 4 months in advance. Accepts queries by e-mail. Accepts simultaneous submissions. Sample copy free online.

NONFICTION Needs essays, general interest, how-to, interview, personal experience. **Buys 10 mss/year.** Submit a paragraph description of your article by e-mail. Length: 500-1,000 words. **Pays $125 for assigned articles. Pays $100 for unsolicited articles.** Pays expenses of writers on assignment.

REPRINTS Send typed ms and information about when and where the material previously appeared. Pays 85% of amount paid for an original article.

COLUMNS Professional Development; Leadership, 500-1,000 words. **Buys 6 mss/year.** Send complete ms. **Pays $75-100.**

TIPS "Articles can be theme specific, but we accept a variety of articles that are appropriate for our readership on topics such as community service, leadership development, or professionalism. The primary readership of the magazine is compromised of high school students, and articles should be relevant to their needs and interests. In most cases, articles should not promote the products or services of a specific company or organization; however, you may use examples to convey concepts or principles."

NETWORKING TIMES

Gabriel Media Group, 11418 Kokopeli Place, Chatsworth CA 91311. (818)727-2000. **E-mail:** editors@networkingtimes.com. **Website:** www.networkingtimes.com. **30% freelance written.** "*Networking Times* is an advertisement-free educational journal for professional networkers worldwide, available at major bookstores and by subscription. We don't mention any company names, instead filling the pages with practical information that covers two areas: acquisition of skills and building the right mind-set to be successful in the world of network marketing today." Estab. 2001. Circ. 12,000. Byline given. Pays on publication. Editorial lead time 3 months. Submit seasonal material 3 months in advance. Accepts queries by e-mail. Accepts simultaneous submissions. Sample copy for $7.97 (US), $10.97 (Canada). Guidelines online.

NONFICTION Special issues: "In order for article submissions to be considered, they need to be content-driven and hold value for all readers regardless of whether they will buy your book or program. In other words, the intent and tone is always educational and never promotional." Submit complete ms by e-mail as Word doc attachment. Include short bio and a hi-res JPEG headshot. Length: 950-1,000 words. Pays expenses of writers on assignment.

💲💲 O'DWYER'S PR REPORT

271 Madison Ave., #600, New York NY 10016. (212)679-2471; (866)395-7710. **Fax:** (212)683-2750. **E-mail:** john@odwyerpr.com. **Website:** www.odwyerpr.com. **Contact:** John O'Dwyer, associate publisher/editor. Monthly magazine providing PR articles. *O'Dwyer's* has been covering public relations, marketing communications, and related fields for over 40 years. The company provides the latest news and information about PR firms and professionals, the media, corporations, legal issues, jobs, technology, and much more through its website, weekly newsletter, monthly magazine, directories, and guides. Many of the contributors are PR people publicizing themselves while analyzing something. Byline given. No kill fee. Accepts queries by mail. Accepts simultaneous submissions.

NONFICTION Needs opinion. Query. **Pays $250.** Pays expenses of writers on assignment.

💲 SCREEN MAGAZINE

Screen Enterprises, Inc., 676 N. LaSalle Blvd., #501, Chicago IL 60654. (312)640-0800. **Fax:** (312)640-1928. **E-mail:** editor@screenmag.com. **Website:** www.screenmag.com. **Contact:** Andrew Schneider, editor. **5% freelance written.** Biweekly Chicago-based trade magazine covering advertising and film production in the Midwest and national markets. *Screen* is written for Midwest producers (and other creatives involved) of commercials, AV, features, independent corporate, and multimedia. Estab. 1979. Circ. 15,000. Byline given. Pays on publication. No kill fee. Accepts queries by e-mail. Accepts simultaneous submissions. Responds in 3 weeks to queries. Sample copy online.

NONFICTION Needs interview, new product, technical. No general AV; nothing specific to other markets; no no-brainers or opinion. **Buys 26 mss/year.** Query with published clips. Length: 750-1,500 words. **Pays $50.** Pays expenses of writers on assignment.

PHOTOS Send photos. Captions required. Reviews prints. Offers no additional payment for photos accepted with ms.

TIPS "Our readers want to know facts and figures. They want to know the news about a company or an individual. We provide exclusive news of this market, in as much depth as space allows without being boring, with lots of specific information and details. We write knowledgably about the market we serve. We recognize the film/video-making process is a difficult one because it 1) is often technical, 2) has implications not immediately discerned."

ART, DESIGN & COLLECTIBLES

💲💲 AIRBRUSH ACTION MAGAZINE

Action, Inc., P.O. Box 438, Allenwood NJ 08720. (732)223-7878; (800)876-2472. **E-mail:** ceo@airbrushaction.com. **Website:** www.airbrushaction.com. **Contact:** Cliff Stieglitz, publisher. **80% freelance written.** Bimonthly magazine covering the spectrum of airbrush applications: automotive and custom paint applications, illustration, T-shirt airbrushing, fine art, automotive and sign painting, hobby/craft applications, wall murals, fingernails, temporary tattoos, artist profiles, reviews, and more. Estab. 1985. Circ. 35,000. Byline given. Pays 1 month after publication. Publishes ms an average of 6 months after acceptance. Editorial lead time 6 months. Submit seasonal material 6 months in advance. Accepts queries by mail, e-mail. Accepts simultaneous submissions.

NONFICTION Needs how-to, humor, inspirational, interview, new product, personal experience, technical. Doesn't want anything unrelated to airbrush. Query with published clips. **Pays 15¢/word.** Pays expenses of writers on assignment.

PHOTOS Digital images preferred. Send photos. Captions, identification of subjects, model releases required. Negotiates payment individually. Buys all rights.

COLUMNS Query with published clips.

TIPS "Send bio and writing samples. Send well-written technical information pertaining to airbrush art. We publish a lot of artist profiles—they all sound the same. Looking for new pizzazz!"

💲💲 ANTIQUEWEEK

MidCountry Media, 27 N. Jefferson St., P.O. Box 90, Knightstown IN 46148. (800)876-5133, ext. 188. **Fax:** (800)695-8153. **E-mail:** davidb@antiqueweek.com;

tony@antiqueweek.com. **Website:** www.antiqueweek. com. **Contact:** David Blower, Jr., senior editor; Tony Gregory, publisher. **80% freelance written.** Weekly tabloid covering antiques and collectibles with 3 editions: Eastern, Central, and National, plus the monthly *AntiqueWest. AntiqueWeek* has a wide range of readership from dealers and auctioneers to collectors, both advanced and novice. Readers demand accurate information presented in an entertaining style. Estab. 1968. Circ. 50,000. Byline given. Pays on publication. Offers 10% kill fee or $25. Submit seasonal material 1 month in advance. Accepts queries by mail, e-mail. Accepts simultaneous submissions. Sample copy free. Guidelines by e-mail.

NONFICTION Needs historical, how-to, interview, opinion, personal experience, antique show and auction reports, feature articles on particular types of antiques and collectibles. **Buys 400-500 mss/year.** Query. Length: 1,000-2,000 words. **Pays $50-250.** Pays expenses of writers on assignment.

REPRINTS Send electronic copy with rights for sale noted and information about when and where the material previously appeared.

PHOTOS All material must be submitted electronically via e-mail or on CD. Send photos. Identification of subjects required.

TIPS "Writers should know their topics thoroughly. Feature articles must be well researched and clearly written. An interview and profile article with a knowledgeable collector might be the break for a first-time contributor. We seek a balanced mix of information on traditional antiques and 20th-century collectibles."

💲💲 FAITH + FORM

47 Grandview Terrace, Essex CT 06426. (860)575-4702. **E-mail:** mcrosbie@faithandform.com. **Website:** www.faithandform.com. **Contact:** Michael J. Crosbie, editor-in-chief. **50% freelance written.** Quarterly magazine covering relgious buildings and art. *Faith + Form*, devoted to religious art and architecture, is read by artists, designers, architects, clergy, congregations, and all who care about environments for worship. Writers must be knowledgeable about environments for worship, or able to explain them. Estab. 1967. Circ. 4,500. Byline given. Publishes ms an average of 6 months after acceptance. Editorial lead time 6 months. Submit seasonal material 6 months in advance. Accepts queries by e-mail, online submission form. Accepts simultaneous submissions. Responds

in 2 weeks to queries; 1 month to mss. Sample copy online. Guidelines available.

NONFICTION Needs book excerpts, essays, how-to, inspirational, interview, opinion, personal experience, photo feature, religious, reviews, technical. **Buys 6 mss/year.** Query. Submit via online submission form, in Microsoft Word or Rich Text format. Length: 500-2,500 words.

PHOTOS Photos must be scanned at a size no smaller than 5x7, at 300 dpi. State availability. Captions required. Reviews Photoshop or TIFF files. Offers no additional payment for photos accepted with ms. Buys one-time rights.

COLUMNS News, 250-750 words; Book Reviews, 250-500 words. **Buys 3 mss/year.** Query.

💲💲 PASTEL JOURNAL

F+W, 10151 Carver Rd., Suite 200, Cincinnati OH 45242. (513)531-2690. **Fax:** (513)891-7153. **E-mail:** pjedit@fwcommunity.com. **Website:** www.pasteljournal.com. **Contact:** Anne Hevener, editor; Jessica Canterbury, managing editor. Bimonthly magazine covering pastel art. *Pastel Journal* is the only national magazine devoted to the medium of pastel. Addressing the working professional as well as passionate amateurs, *Pastel Journal* offers inspiration, information, and instruction to our readers. Estab. 1999. Circ. 22,000. Byline given. Pays on acceptance. Offers 25% kill fee. Publishes ms an average of 3-6 months after acceptance. Editorial lead time 6 months. Submit seasonal material 6 months in advance. Accepts queries by mail, e-mail. Accepts simultaneous submissions. Responds in 4-6 weeks to queries. Guidelines online.

NONFICTION Needs how-to, interview, new product, profile. Does not want articles that aren't art-related. Review magazine before submitting. Query with or without published clips. Length: 500-2,000 words. **Payment does not exceed $600.**

PHOTOS State availability of or send photos. Captions required. Reviews transparencies, prints, GIF/JPEG files. Offers no additional payment for photos accepted with ms. Buys all rights.

💲💲💲 PRINT

F+W, a Content + eCommerce Company, 10151 Carver Rd., Suite 200, Blue Ash OH 45242. (513)531-2690. **E-mail:** info@printmag.com. **Website:** www.printmag.com. **Contact:** Zachary Petit, editor. **75% freelance written.** Quarterly magazine covering graphic design and visual culture. *PRINT*'s articles, written by design specialists and cultural critics, focus on the social, political and historical context of graphic design, and on the places where consumer culture and popular culture meet. Aims to produce a general interest magazine for professionals with engagingly written text and lavish illustrations. By covering a broad spectrum of topics, both international and local, *Print* tries to demonstrate the significance of design in the world at large. Estab. 1940. Circ. 45,000. Byline given. Pays on acceptance. Offers 25% kill fee. Publishes ms an average of 2 months after acceptance. Editorial lead time 3 months. Submit seasonal material 3 months in advance. Accepts queries by e-mail. Accepts simultaneous submissions. Responds in 2 weeks to queries. Responds in 1 month to mss.

NONFICTION Needs book excerpts, essays, interview, opinion, photo feature, profile, reviews. **Buys 35-40 mss/year.** Query with published clips. Length: 500-3,500 words. **Pays 50¢/word.**

COLUMNS Query with published clips. **Pays 50¢/word.**

TIPS "Be well versed in issues related to the field of graphic design; don't submit ideas that are too general or geared to nonprofessionals."

TEXAS ARCHITECT

Texas Society of Architects, 500 Chicon St., Austin TX 78702. (512)478-7386. **Fax:** (512)478-0528. **Website:** www.texasarchitect.org. **Contact:** Aaron Seward, editor. **30% freelance written. Mostly written by unpaid members of the professional society.** Bimonthly journal covering architecture and architects of Texas. *Texas Architect* is a highly visually-oriented look at Texas architecture, design, and urban planning. Articles cover varied subtopics within architecture. Readers are mostly architects and related building professionals. Estab. 1951. Circ. 12,500. Byline given. Pays on publication. No kill fee. Publishes ms an average of 3 months after acceptance. Submit seasonal material 4 months in advance. Accepts queries by mail, e-mail. Accepts simultaneous submissions. Responds in 6 weeks to queries. Guidelines online.

NONFICTION Needs interview, photo feature, technical, book reviews. Query with published clips. Length: 100-2,000 words. **Pays $50-100 for assigned articles.**

PHOTOS Send photos. Identification of subjects required. Reviews contact sheets, 35mm or 4x5 trans-

parencies, 4x5 prints. Offers no additional payment for photos accepted with ms. Buys one-time rights.

COLUMNS News (timely reports on architectural issues, projects, and people), 100-500 words. **Buys 10 articles/year mss/year.** Query with published clips. **Pays $50-100.**

WATERCOLOR ARTIST

F+W, a Content + eCommerce Company, 10151 Carver Rd., Suite 200, Blue Ash OH 45242. (513)531-2690. **Fax:** (513)891-7153. **E-mail:** wcamag@fwmedia.com. **Website:** www.watercolorartistmagazine.com. **Contact:** Jennifer Hoffman, art director; Kelly Kane, editor. Bimonthly magazine covering water media arts. Estab. 1984. Circ. 44,000. Byline given. Pays on acceptance. Publishes ms an average of 3-6 months after acceptance. Editorial lead time 6 months. Submit seasonal material 6 months in advance. Accepts queries by mail. Accepts simultaneous submissions. Writer's guidelines available at www.artistsnetwork.com/contactus.

"*Watercolor Artist* is the definitive source of how-to instruction and creative inspiration for artists working in water-based media."

NONFICTION Needs book excerpts, essays, how-to, inspirational, interview, new product, personal experience. Does not want articles that aren't art-related. Review magazine before submitting. **Buys 36 mss/year.** Send query letter with images. Length: 350-2,500 words. **Pays $150-600.** Pays expenses of writers on assignment.

PHOTOS State availability of or send photos. Captions required. Reviews transparencies, prints, slides, GIF/JPEG files. Buys one-time rights.

AUTO & TRUCK

AFTERMARKET BUSINESS WORLD

Advanstar Communications, 24950 Country Club Blvd., Suite 200, North Olmsted OH 44070. (440)891-2617. **Fax:** (440)891-2675. **E-mail:** bruce.adams@advanstar.com. **Website:** www.searchautoparts.com. **Contact:** Bruce Adams, managing editor. The mission of *Aftermarket Business World* (formerly *Aftermarket Business*) involves satisfying the needs of U.S. readers who want to do business here and elsewhere and helping readers in other countries who want to do business with U.S. companies. Editorial material for *Aftermarket Business World* focuses on news, trends, and analysis about the international automotive aftermarket. Written for corporate executives and key decision makers responsible for buying automotive products (parts, accessories, chemicals) and other services sold at retail to consumers and professional installers, it's the oldest continuously published business magazine covering the retail automotive aftermarket, and is the only publication dedicated to the specialized needs of this industry. Estab. 1936. Circ. 120,000. Byline given. "Corporate policy requires all freelancers to sign a print and online usage contract for stories." Pays on publication. Payment is negotiable. Accepts simultaneous submissions. Sample copies available; call (888)527-7008 for rates.

NONFICTION Pays expenses of writers on assignment.

TIPS "We can't stress enough the importance of knowing our audience. We are not a magazine aimed at car dealers or consumers. Our readers are auto parts distributors. Looking through sample issues will show you a lot about what we need."

🟢🟢 AUTOINC.

Automotive Service Association, 8209 Mid Cities Blvd., North Richland Hills TX 76182. (817)514-2900, ext. 119. Direct line: (817)514-2919. **Fax:** (817)514-0770. **E-mail:** editor@asashop.org; leonad@asashop.org. **Website:** www.autoinc.org. **10% freelance written.** The mission of *AutoInc.*, ASA's official publication, is to be the informational authority for ASA and industry members nationwide. Its purpose is to enhance the professionalism of these members through management, technical and legislative articles, researched and written with the highest regard for accuracy, quality, and integrity. Estab. 1952. Circ. 14,000. Byline given. Pays on publication. No kill fee. Publishes ms an average of 3 months after acceptance. Editorial lead time 2 months. Accepts queries by mail, e-mail, fax. Accepts simultaneous submissions. Responds in 6 weeks to queries and in 2 months to mss. Sample copy for $5 or online. Guidelines online.

NONFICTION Needs how-to, technical. No coverage of staff moves or financial reports. **Buys 6 mss/year.** Query with published clips. Length: 1,200 words. **Pays $300.** Pays expenses of writers on assignment. Sometimes pays phone expenses of writers on assignment.

PHOTOS State availability of or send photos. Captions, identification of subjects, model releases re-

quired. Reviews 2×3 transparencies, 3×5 prints, high resolution digital images. Negotiates payment individually. Buys one-time and electronic rights.

TIPS "Learn about the automotive repair industry, specifically the independent shop segment. Understand the high-tech requirements needed to succeed today. We target professional repair shop owners rather than consumers."

🟢 AUTO RESTORER

i5 Publishing, Inc., 3 Burroughs, Irvine CA 92618. (213)385-2222. **Fax:** (213)385-8565. **E-mail:** tkade@i5publishing.com. **Website:** www.autorestorermagazine.com. **Contact:** Ted Kade, editor. **85% freelance written.** Monthly magazine covering auto restoration. "Our readers own old cars, and they work on them. We help our readers by providing as much practical, how-to information as we can about restoration and old cars." Estab. 1989. Circ. 60,000. Pays on publication. Publishes mss 3 months after acceptance. Submit seasonal material 4 months in advance. Accepts queries by mail, e-mail, fax. Accepts simultaneous submissions. Responds in 2 months to queries. Sample copy: $7. Guidelines free.

NONFICTION Needs how-to, new product, photo feature. **Buys 60 mss/year.** Query first. Length: 250-2,000 words. **Pays $150/published page, including photos and illustrations.** Pays expenses of writers on assignment.

PHOTOS Emphasizes restoration of collector cars and trucks. Readers are 98% male, professional/technical/managerial, ages 35-65. Buys 47 photos from freelancers/issue; 564 photos/year. Send photos. Model/property release preferred. Photo captions required; include year, make, and model of car; identification of people in photo. Reviews photos with accompanying ms only. Reviews contact sheets, transparencies, 5x7 prints. Looks for "technically proficient or dramatic photos of various automotive subjects, auto portraits, detail shots, action photos, good angles, composition, and lighting. We're also looking for photos to illustrate how-to articles such as how to repair a damaged fender or how to repair a carburetor." Pays $50 for b&w cover; $35 for b&w inside. Pays on publication. Credit line given. Buys first North American serial rights.

TIPS "Interview the owner of a restored car. Present advice to others on how to do a similar restoration. Seek advice from experts. Go light on history and nonspecific details. Make it something that the magazine regularly uses. Do automotive how-tos."

⊘ WARD'S AUTOWORLD

Primedia Business Magazines and Media, 3000 Town Center, Suite 2750, Southfield MI 48075-1245. **Website:** www.wardsauto.com. Monthly magazine. For personnel involved in the original equipment manufacturing industry. Circ. 101,349. No kill fee. Editorial lead time 1 month. Accepts simultaneous submissions.

○ Query before submitting.

NONFICTION Pays expenses of writers on assignment.

⊘ WARD'S DEALER BUSINESS

Primedia Business Magazines and Media, 3000 Town Center, Suite 2750, Southfield MI 48075-1245. **Website:** www.wardsauto.com. Monthly magazine edited for personnel involved in aftermarket sales. Circ. 30,000. No kill fee. Editorial lead time 1 month. Accepts simultaneous submissions.

○ Query before submitting.

NONFICTION Pays expenses of writers on assignment.

○⊘⊘ WESTERN CANADA HIGHWAY NEWS

Craig Kelman & Associates, 2020 Portage Ave., 3rd Floor, Winnipeg MB R3J 0K4 Canada. (204)985-9785. **Fax:** (204)985-9795. **E-mail:** terry@kelman.ca. **Website:** highwaynews.ca. **Contact:** Terry Ross, editor. **30% freelance written.** Quarterly magazine covering trucking. The official magazine of the Alberta, Saskatchewan, and Manitoba trucking associations. As the official magazine of the trucking associations in Alberta, Saskatchewan and Manitoba, *Western Canada Highway News* is committed to providing leading edge, timely information on business practices, technology, trends, new products/services, legal and legislative issues that affect professionals in Western Canada's trucking industry. Estab. 1995. Circ. 4,500. Byline given. Pays on publication. No kill fee. Publishes ms an average of 2 months after acceptance. Editorial lead time 3 months. Submit seasonal material 3 months in advance. Accepts simultaneous submissions. Responds in 1 month. Sample copy for 10x13 SAE with 1 IRC. Guidelines for #10 SASE.

NONFICTION Needs essays, general interest, how-to, interview, new product, opinion, personal experi-

ence, photo feature, technical, profiles in excellence (bios of trucking or associate firms enjoying success). **Buys 8-10 mss/year.** Query. Length: 500-3,000 words. **Pays 18-25¢/word.** Pays expenses of writers on assignment.

PHOTOS State availability. Identification of subjects required. Reviews 4x6 prints. Buys one-ime rights.

COLUMNS Safety (new safety innovation/products), 500 words; Trade Talk (new products), 300 words. Query. **Pays 18-25¢/word.**

TIPS "Our publication is fairly time sensitive regarding issues affecting the trucking industry in Western Canada. Current 'hot' topics are international trucking, security, driver fatigue, health and safety, emissions control, and national/international highway systems."

AVIATION & SPACE

⊘⊘ AEROSAFETY WORLD MAGAZINE

Flight Safety Foundation, 801 N. Fairfax St., Suite 400, Alexandria VA 22314-1774. (703)739-6700. **Fax:** (703)739-6708. **E-mail:** jackman@flightsafety.org. **Website:** www.flightsafety.org. **Contact:** Frank Jackman, vice president of communications. Monthly newsletter covering safety aspects of airport operations. Full-color monthly magazine offers in-depth analysis of important safety issues facing the industry, with emphasis on timely news coverage in a convenient format and eye-catching contemporary design. Estab. 2006. Pays on publication. Accepts queries by mail, e-mail. Guidelines online.

○ "AeroSafety World continues Flight Safety Foundation's tradition of excellence in aviation safety journalism that stretches back more than 50 years. The new full-color monthly magazine, initially called *Aviation Safety World,* offers in-depth analysis of important safety issues facing the industry, along with several new departments and a greater emphasis on timely news coverage—in a convenient format and eye-catching contemporary design. While *AeroSafety World* has taken the place of the 7 newsletters the Foundation used to produce, including *Airport Operations,* the archives remain active, and back issues of the newsletters are still available."

NONFICTION Needs technical. Query. **Pays $300-1,500.**

PHOTOS Pays $75 for each piece of original art.

TIPS "Few aviation topics are outside its scope."

💲💲 AIRCRAFT MAINTENANCE TECHNOLOGY

SouthComm, 1233 Janesville Ave., Fort Atkinson WI 53538. (920)563-6388. **Website:** www.aviationpros. com/magazine/amt. **Contact:** Barb Zuehlke, senior editor. **10% freelance written.** Magazine published 9 times/year covering aircraft maintenance. *Aircraft Maintenance Technology* provides aircraft mainte- nance professionals worldwide with a curriculum of technical, professional, and managerial develop- ment information that enables them to more efficient- ly and effectively perform their jobs. Estab. 1989. Circ. 41,500 worldwide. Byline given. Pays on publication. No kill fee. Publishes ms an average of 2 months after acceptance. Editorial lead time 3 months. Submit sea- sonal material 6 months in advance. Accepts queries by e-mail, online submission form. Accepts simulta- neous submissions. Responds in 2 weeks to queries; in 1 month to mss. Sample copy free. Guidelines for #10 SASE or by e-mail.

○ "*Aircraft Maintenance Technology* is the source for information for the professional mainte- nance team. We welcome your questions, com- ments, and suggestions regarding our editorial content, as well as ideas for future stories."

NONFICTION Needs how-to, technical, safety. Spe- cial issues: Aviation career issue (August/September). No travel/pilot-oriented pieces. **Buys 10-12 mss/year.** Query with published clips. "Please use the online form to contact us." Length: 600-1,500 words, tech- nical articles 1,500 words. **Payment negotiable.**

PHOTOS State availability. Captions, identification of subjects, model releases required. Offers no addi- tional payment for photos accepted with ms.

COLUMNS Professionalism, 1,000-1,500 words; Safety Matters, 1,000-1,500 words; Human Fac- tors,1,000-1,500 words. **Buys 10-12 mss/year.** Query with published clips.

TIPS "This is a technical magazine approved by the FAA and Transport Canada for recurrency train- ing for technicians. Freelancers should have a strong background in aviation, particularly maintenance, to be considered for technical articles. Columns/ Departments: Freelancers still should have a strong knowledge of aviation to slant professionalism, safety, and human factors pieces to that audience."

💲💲 AVIATION INTERNATIONAL NEWS

AIN Publications, 214 Franklin Ave., Midland Park NJ 07432. (201)444-5075. **Fax:** (201)251-2106. **E-mail:** nmoll@ainonline.com. **E-mail:** nmoll@ainonline. com. **Website:** www.ainonline.com. **Contact:** Nigel Moll, editor. **30% freelance written.** Monthly maga- zine covering business and commercial aviation with news features, special reports, aircraft evaluations and surveys on business aviation worldwide, written for business pilots and industry professionals. Sister print products include daily onsite issues published at 6 conventions and 4 international air shows. Elec- tronic products include four-times-weekly AINalerts, once-weekly AIN Air Transport Perspective and AIN Defense Perspective, and AINonline website. "While the heartbeat of *AIN* is driven by the news it carries, the human touch is not neglected. We pride ourselves on our people stories about the industry's 'movers and shakers' and others in aviation who make a difference." Estab. 1972. Circ. 40,000. Byline given. Pays on ac- ceptance and upon receipt of writer's invoice. Offers variable kill fee. Publishes ms an average of 2 months after acceptance. Editorial lead time 2 months. Submit seasonal material 3 months in advance. Accepts que- ries by mail, e-mail, fax. Accepts simultaneous sub- missions. Responds in 6 weeks to queries; 2 months to mss. Sample copy for $10.

NONFICTION Needs how-to, interview, new prod- uct, opinion, personal experience, photo feature, tech- nical. No place for puff pieces. "Our readers expect serious, real news. We don't pull any punches. *AIN* is not a 'good news' publication; it tells the story, both good and bad." **Buys 150-200 mss/year.** Query with published clips. Do not send mss by e-mail unless re- quested. Length: 200-3,000 words. **Pays 45¢/word to first timers, higher rates to proven *AIN* freelancers.** Pays expenses of writers on assignment.

PHOTOS Send photos. Captions required. Reviews contact sheets, transparencies, prints, TIFF files (300 dpi). Negotiates payment individually. Buys one-time rights.

TIPS "Our core freelancers are professional pilots with good writing skills, or good journalists and re- porters with an interest in aviation (some with pilot certificates) or technical experts in the aviation in- dustry. The ideal *AIN* writer has an intense interest in and strong knowledge of aviation, a talent for writ- ing news stories, and journalistic cussedness. Hit me with a strong news story relating to business aviation that takes me by surprise—something from your local area or area of expertise. Make it readable, fact-filled and in the inverted-pyramid style. Double-check facts and names. Interview the right people. Send me good, clear photos and illustrations. Send me well written, logically ordered copy. Do this for me consistently and we may take you along on our staff to 1 of the conventions in the U.S. or an airshow in Paris, Singapore, London or Dubai."

BEAUTY & SALON

💲💲 ASCP SKIN DEEP

Associated Skin Care Professionals, 25188 Genesee Trail Rd., Suite 200, Golden CO 80401. (800)789-0411. **E-mail:** editor@ascpskincare.com; getconnected@ascpskincare.com. **Website:** www.ascpskincare.com. **Contact:** Mary Abel, editor. **80% freelance written.** Bimonthly member magazine of Associated Skin Care Professionals (ASCP), covering technical, educational, and business information for estheticians with an emphasis on solo practitioners and spa/salon employees or independent contractors. Audience is the U.S. individual skin care practitioner who may work on her own and/or in a spa or salon setting. Magazine keeps her up to date on skin care trends and techniques and ways to earn more income doing waxing, facials, peels, microdermabrasion, body wraps, and other skin treatments. Product-neutral stories may include novel spa treatments within the esthetician scope of practice. Does not cover mass-market retail products, hair care, nail care, physician-only treatments/products, cosmetic surgery, or invasive treatments like colonics or ear candling. Successful stories have included how-tos on paraffin facials, aromatherapy body wraps, waxing tips, how to read ingredient labels, how to improve word-of-mouth advertising, and how to choose an online scheduling software package. Estab. 2003. Circ. 14,000+. Byline given. Pays on acceptance. No kill fee. Publishes ms an average of 4-6 months after acceptance. Editorial lead time 4-5 months. Submit seasonal material 7 months in advance. Accepts queries by e-mail. Accepts simultaneous submissions. Responds in 2-4 weeks to queries. Sample copy online at www.ascpskindeepdigital.com.

NONFICTION Needs how-to. "We don't run general consumer beauty material or products, and very rarely run a new product that is available through retail outlets. 'New' products means introduced in the last 12 months. We do not run industry personnel announcements or stories on individual spas/salons or getaways. We don't cover hair or nails." **Buys 12 mss/year.** Query. Length: 1,200-1,600 words. **Pays $75-300 for assigned articles.** Pays expenses of writers on assignment.

TIPS "Visit website to read previous issues and learn about what we do. Submit a brief query with an idea to determine if you are on the right track. State specifically what value this has to estheticians and their work/income. Please note that we do not publish fashion, nails, hair, or consumer-focused articles."

💲💲 BEAUTY STORE BUSINESS

Creative Age Communications, 7628 Densmore Ave., Van Nuys CA 91406. (818)782-7328, ext. 353 or (800)442-5667. **E-mail:** mbirenbaum@creativeage.com. **Website:** www.beautystorebusiness.com. **Contact:** Marc Birenbaum, executive editor; Shelley Moench-Kelly, managing editor. **50% freelance written.** Monthly magazine covering beauty store business management, news, and beauty products. The primary readers of the publication are owners, managers, and buyers at open-to-the-public beauty stores, including general-market and multicultural market-oriented ones with or without salon services. Secondary readers are those at beauty stores only open to salon industry professionals. Also goes to beauty distributors. Estab. 1994. Circ. 15,000. Byline given. Pays on acceptance. Offers negotiable kill fee. Publishes ms an average of 3 months after acceptance. Editorial lead time 3 months. Submit seasonal material 4 months in advance. Accepts queries by mail, e-mail. Accepts simultaneous submissions. Responds in 2 weeks, if interested. Sample copy free.

NONFICTION Needs how-to, interview. **Buys 20-30 mss/year.** Query. Length: 1,800-2,200 words. **Pays $250-525 for assigned articles.** Pays expenses of writers on assignment.

PHOTOS Do not send computer art electronically. State availability. Captions, identification of subjects required. Reviews transparencies, computer art (artists work on Macs, request 300 dpi, on CD or Zip disk, saved as JPEG, TIFF, or EPS). Negotiates payment individually. Buys all rights.

$$ DAYSPA

Creative Age Publications, 7628 Densmore Ave., Van Nuys CA 91406. (818)782-7328, ext. 301. **Fax:** (818)782-7450. **Website:** www.dayspamagazine.com. **Contact:** Linda Kossoff, executive editor. **50% freelance written.** Monthly magazine covering the business of day spas, multiservice/skincare salons, and resort/hotel spas. *Dayspa* includes only well-targeted business and trend articles directed at the owners and managers. It serves to enrich, enlighten, and empower spa/salon professionals. Estab. 1996. Circ. 31,000. Byline given. Pays on acceptance. No kill fee. Publishes ms an average of 4 months after acceptance. Editorial lead time 4 months. Submit seasonal material 4 months in advance. Accepts queries by online submission form. Accepts simultaneous submissions. Responds in 2 months to queries. Sample copy: $5.

NONFICTION **Buys 40 mss/year.** Query. Length: 1,500-1,800 words. **Pays $150-500.**

PHOTOS Send photos. Identification of subjects, model releases required. Negotiates payment individually. Buys one-time rights.

COLUMNS Legal Pad (legal issues affecting salons/spas); Money Matters (financial issues); Management Workshop (spa management issues); Health Wise (wellness trends), all 1,200-1,500 words. **Buys 20 mss/year.** Query. **Pays $150-400.**

DERMASCOPE MAGAZINE

Aesthetics International Association, 310 E. Interstate 30, Suite B107, Garland TX 75043. (469)429-9300. **Fax:** (469)429-9301. **E-mail:** amanda@dermascope.com. **Website:** www.dermascope.com. **Contact:** Amanda Strunk-Miller, managing editor. Monthly magazine covering aesthetics (skin care) and body and spa therapy. *Dermascope* is a source of practical advice and continuing education for skin care, body, and spa therapy professionals. Main readers are salon, day spa, and destination spa owners, managers, or technicians and aesthetics students. Estab. 1978. Circ. 16,000. No byline given. No kill fee. Publishes ms an average of 6 months after acceptance. Editorial lead time 3 months. Submit seasonal material 6 months in advance. Accepts queries by mail, e-mail, fax. Responds in 4-6 months. Guidelines online.

💬 A copyright waiver must be signed guaranteeing article has not been submitted elsewhere. Does not pay for articles.

NONFICTION Needs book excerpts, general interest, historical, how-to, inspirational, personal experience, photo feature, technical. Submit complete ms with published clips. Include biography, along with contact info for readers; a professional headshot; a 1-2 sentence quote/tease about the article; and 3-5 review questions. Length: 1,500-2,000 words for how-tos, skin therapy, body therapy, diet, nutrition, spa, equipment, medical procedures, makeup, and business articles; 1,800-2,500 words for features. Stories exceeding 2,500 may be printed in part and run in concurrent issues. Pays expenses of writers on assignment.

REPRINTS Does not accept reprints.

PHOTOS Monthly magazine/trade journal, 128 pages, for aestheticians, plastic surgeons, and stylists. Articles should include quality images, graphs, or charts when available. Sample copies and art guidelines available. Accepts disk submissions. Electronic images should be 300 dpi, CMYK, and either JPEG, TIFF, PSD, or EPS format. Photo credits, model releases, and identification of subjects or techniques shown in photos are required. Samples are not filed. Photos will not be returned; do not send original artwork. Responds only if interested. Rights purchased vary according to project. Pays on publication.

$$ MASSAGE MAGAZINE

E-mail: kmenehan@massagemag.com. **E-mail:** kmenehan@massagemag.com. **Website:** www.massagemag.com. **Contact:** Karen Menehan. **20% freelance written.** Magazine about massage and other touch therapies published 10-12 times/year. Readers are professional therapists who have been in practice for several years. About 80% are self-employed; 95% live in the U.S. The techniques they practice include Swedish, sports, and geriatric massage and energy work. Readers work in settings ranging from home-based studios to spas to integrated clinics. Readers care deeply that massage is portrayed in a professional manner. Estab. 1985. Circ. 50,000. Byline given. Pays the month of publication. Offers kill fee. Publishes ms an average of 1-3 months after submission. Editorial lead time 1 month. Advance time 1 month. Accepts queries by e-mail. Responds in 2 weeks to queries. Do not send ms without querying first. Sample copy: $6.95; however; sample articles available via e-mail. Guidelines available by request.

NONFICTION Needs general interest, interview, profile, News: hard news, features and profiles. "We do not publish humorous travel pieces about unusual massage experiences." **Buys 12 mss/year.** Length: 700-1,500 words for news; 1,600 words for features. **Pays $80-200.**

PHOTOS Send photos with submission via e-mail. Identification of subjects. Identification of photographer. Buys one-time rights.

COLUMNS Profiles; News and Current Events; Practice Building (business); Technique; Mind/Body/Spirit. Length: 200-2,500 words. See website for details.

FILLERS Needs facts, newsbreaks.

TIPS "Our readers seek practical information on how to help their clients and make their businesses more successful, as well as feature articles that place massage therapy in a positive or inspiring light. Since most of our readers are professional therapists, we do not publish articles on topics like 'How Massage Can Help You Relax'; nor do we publish humorous essays or travel essays."

💲💲 NAILPRO

Creative Age Publications, 7628 Densmore Ave., Van Nuys CA 91406. (800)442-5667; (818)782-7328. **Fax:** (818)782-7450. **E-mail:** nailpro@creativeage.com. **Website:** www.nailpro.com. **Contact:** Stephanie Lavery, executive editor. **20% freelance written.** Monthly magazine written for manicurists and salon owners working as an independent contractor or in a full-service salon or nails-only salons. Estab. 1989. Circ. 65,000. Byline given. Pays on acceptance. 25% kill fee. Publishes ms an average of 6 months after acceptance. Editorial lead time 3 months. Submit seasonal material 3 months in advance. Accepts queries by e-mail. Accepts simultaneous submissions. Responds in 6 weeks to queries only if interested. Sample copy: $2 and 9x12 SASE.

○   "*Nailpro* is the premiere magazine for the professional nail industry. Content includes nail trends, products and techniques, from simple polishing to elaborate nail art, as well as tips and tricks for running a successful nail business."

NONFICTION Needs book excerpts, how-to, humor, inspirational, interview, personal experience, photo feature, profile, technical. No general interest articles or business articles not geared to the nail-care industry. **Buys 50 mss/year.** Query. Length: 1,000-3,000 words. **Pays $150-450.** Pays expenses of writers on assignment.

PHOTOS Send photos. Identification of subjects, model releases required. Reviews transparencies, prints. Negotiates payment individually. Pays on acceptance. Buys one-time rights for print and web.

COLUMNS Business (articles on building salon business, marketing and advertising, dealing with employees), 1,500-2,500 words; Attitudes (aspects of operating a nail salon and trends in the nail industry), 1,200-2,500 words. **Buys 50 mss/year.** Query. **Pays $250-350.**

💲💲⊘ NAILS

Bobit Business Media, 3520 Challenger St., Torrance CA 90503. (310)533-2457. **Fax:** (310)533-2507. **E-mail:** judy.lessin@bobit.com. **Website:** www.nailsmag.com. **Contact:** Judy Lessin, features editor. **10% freelance written.** Monthly magazine. *NAILS* seeks to educate its readers on new techniques and products, nail anatomy and health, customer relations, working safely and ergonomically, salon sanitation, and the business aspects of running a salon. Estab. 1983. Circ. 55,000. Byline given. Pays on acceptance. No kill fee. Editorial lead time 3 months. Submit seasonal material 4 months in advance. Accepts queries by e-mail. Accepts simultaneous submissions. Responds in 1 month to queries. Visit website to view past issues.

NONFICTION Needs historical, how-to, inspirational, interview, personal experience, photo feature, profile, technical. No articles on one particular product, company profiles, or articles slanted toward a particular company or manufacturer. **Buys 20 mss/year.** Query with published clips. Length: 750-1,600 words. **Pays $100-350.** Pays expenses of writers on assignment.

PHOTOS State availability. Captions, identification of subjects, model releases required. Reviews contact sheets, transparencies, prints (any standard size acceptable). Rarely buys unsolicited photos. Buys all rights.

TIPS "Send clips and query; *do not send unsolicited manuscripts.* We would like to see fresh and unique angles on business, health, or technical topics. Topics must be geared specifically to salon owners and nail technicians. Focus on an innovative business idea or unique point of view. Articles from experts on specific business issues—insurance, handling difficult employees, cultivating clients, navigating social media—are encouraged."

BEVERAGES & BOTTLING

AMERICAN BAR ASSOCIATION JOURNAL

321 N. Clark St., 20th Floor, Chicago IL 60654. (312)988-6018. **Fax:** (312)988-6014. **E-mail:** releases@americanbar.org. **Website:** www.abajournal.com. **Contact:** Molly Mcdonough. Monthly membership magazine of the American Bar Association. Emphasizes law and the legal profession. Readers are lawyers. Estab. 1915. Circ. 330,000. Accepts queries by e-mail, fax. Accepts simultaneous submissions.

NONFICTION Query with résumé and published clips. Pays expenses of writers on assignment.

PHOTOS Contact: Debora Clark, deputy design director (debora.clark@americanbar.org).

🍁 $ $ BAR & BEVERAGE BUSINESS MAGAZINE

Mercury Publications, 1313 Border St., Unit 16, Winnipeg MB R3H 0X4 Canada. (204)954-2085, ext. 213. **Fax:** (204)954-2057. **E-mail:** edufault@mercurypublications.ca. **Website:** www.barandbeverage.com. **Contact:** Elaine Dufault, associate publisher and national account manager. **33% freelance written.** Bimonthly magazine providing information on the latest trends, happenings, and buying/selling of beverages and product merchandising. Estab. 1998. Circ. 15,000+. Byline given. Pays 30-45 days from receipt of invoice. Offers 33% kill fee. Submit seasonal material 3 months in advance. Accepts simultaneous submissions. Sample copy and writer's guidelines free or by e-mail.

💬 Does not accept queries for specific stories. Assigns stories to Canadian writers.

NONFICTION Needs how-to, interview. Does not want industry reports, profiles on companies. Query with published clips. Length: 500-9,000 words. **Pays 25-35¢/word.** Pays expenses of writers on assignment.

PHOTOS State availability. Captions required. Reviews negatives; transparencies; 3x5 prints; JPEG, EPS, or TIFF files. Negotiates payment individually. Buys all rights.

COLUMNS Out There (bar and beverage news in various parts of the country), 100-500 words. Query. **Pays up to $100.**

BREWERS ASSOCIATION

P.O. Box 1679, Boulder CO 80306. (303)447-0816; (888)822-6273. **E-mail:** allison@brewersassociation.org; info@brewersassociation.org. **Website:** www.brewersassociation.org. **Contact:** Jill Redding, editor; Kristi Switzer, publisher; Allison Seymour, art director. The Brewers Association is an organization of brewers, for brewers and by brewers. More than 1,300 US brewery members and 27,000 members of the American Homebrewers Association are joined by members of the allied trade, beer wholesalers, individuals, other associate members and the Brewers Association staff to make up the Brewers Association. Estab. 1978. Accepts simultaneous submissions.

💬 Publishes *The New Brewer*, American Craft Beer Guides, The Brewers Association Guide to Starting Your Own Brewery, Brewers' Resource Directory.

NONFICTION Pays expenses of writers on assignment.

PHOTOS Publishes beer how-to, cooking with beer, trade, hobby, brewing, beer-related books. Photos used for text illustrations, promotional materials, books, magazines. Examples of published magazines: *Zymurgy* (front cover and inside); *The New Brewer* (front cover and inside). Examples of published book titles: *Sacred & Herbal Healing Beers* (front/back covers and inside); *Standards of Brewing* (front/back covers).

$ BREW YOUR OWN

Battenkill Communications, 5515 Main St., Manchester Center VT 05255. (802)362-3981. **Fax:** (802)362-2377. **E-mail:** edit@byo.com; byo@byo.com. **Website:** www.byo.com. **Contact:** Betsy Parker, editor. **85% freelance written.** Magazine published 8 times/year covering home brewing. "Our mission is to provide practical information in an entertaining format. We try to capture the spirit and challenge of brewing while helping our readers brew the best beer they can." Estab. 1995. Circ. 50,000. Byline given. Pays on acceptance. Offers 25% kill fee. Publishes ms an average of 4 months after acceptance. Editorial lead time 3 months. Submit seasonal material 3 months in advance. Accepts queries by mail, e-mail, fax. Accepts simultaneous submissions. Responds in 2 months to queries. Guidelines online.

NONFICTION Needs historical, how-to, humor, interview. **Buys 75 mss/year.** Query with published clips or description of brewing expertise, or submit complete ms. Length: 1,500-3,000 words. **Pays $25-200, depending on length, complexity of article, and**

experience of writer. Pays expenses of writers on assignment.

PHOTOS State availability. Captions required. Reviews contact sheets, transparencies, 5x7 prints, slides, and electronic images. Negotiates payment individually. Buys all rights.

COLUMNS Homebrew Nation (short first-person brewing stories and photos of homemade equipment); Last Call (humorous stories about homebrewing), 600-750 words. **Buys 12 mss/year.** Query with or without published clips. **Pays $75 for Last Call; no payment for Homebrew Nation.**

TIPS "*Brew Your Own* is for anyone who is interested in brewing beer, from beginners to advanced all-grain brewers. We seek articles that are straightforward and factual, not full of esoteric theories or complex calculations. Our readers tend to be intelligent, upscale, and literate."

$$$ SANTÉ MAGAZINE

On-Premise Communications, 160 Benmont Ave., Suite 92, Third Floor, West Wing, Bennington VT 05201. (802)442-6771. **Fax:** (802)442-6859. **E-mail:** mvaughan@santemagazine.com. **Website:** www.isantemagazine.com. **Contact:** Mark Vaughan, editor. **75% freelance written.** Four issues/year magazine covering food, wine, spirits, and management topics for restaurant professionals. Information and specific advice for restaurant professionals on operating a profitable food and beverage program. Writers should "speak" to readers on a professional-to-professional basis. Estab. 1996. Circ. 45,000. Byline given. Pays on publication. Offers 50% kill fee. Publishes ms an average of 2 months after acceptance. Editorial lead time 3 months. Submit seasonal material 6 months in advance. Accepts queries by e-mail. Accepts simultaneous submissions. Responds in 2 weeks to queries. Does not accept mss. Sample copy available. Guidelines by e-mail.

💬 "Articles should be concise and to the point and should closely adhere to the assigned word count. Our readers will only read articles that provide useful information in a readily accessible format. Where possible, articles should be broken into stand-alone sections that can be boxed or otherwise highlighted."

NONFICTION Needs interview, restaurant business news. Does not want consumer-focused pieces. **Buys 20 mss/year.** Query with published clips. Length: 650-1,800 words. Pays expenses of writers on assignment.

PHOTOS State availability. Captions required. Reviews PDF/GIF/JPEG files 500kb-10mb. Offers no additional payment for photos accepted. Buys one-time rights.

COLUMNS Due to a Redesign, 650 words; Bar Tab (focuses on 1 bar's unique strategy for success), 1,000 words; Restaurant Profile (a business-related look at what qualities make 1 restaurant successful), 1,000 words; Maximizing Profits (covers 1 great profit-maximizing strategy per issue from several sources), Signature Dish (highlights 1 chef's background and favorite dish with recipe), Sommeliers Choice (6 top wine managers recommend favorite wines; with brief profiles of each manager), Distillations (6 bar professionals offer their favorite drink for a particular type of spirit; with brief profiles of each manager), 1,500 words; Provisions (like The Goods only longer; an in-depth look at a special ingredient), 1,500 words. **Buys 20 mss/year.** Query with published clips. **Pays $300-800.**

TIPS "Present 2 or 3 of your best ideas via e-mail. Include a brief statement of your qualifications. Attach your resumè and 3 electronic clips. The same format may be used to query via postal mail if necessary."

TEA & COFFEE TRADE JOURNAL

Lockwood Publications, 3743 Crescent St., 2nd Floor, Long Island City NY 11101. (212)391-2060. **Fax:** (212)827-0945. **E-mail:** editor@teaandcoffee.net; v.facenda@teaandcoffee.net. **Website:** www.teaandcoffee.net. **Contact:** Vanessa L. Facenda, editor in chief. Monthly magazine covering tea and coffee industry. This is a comprehensive magazine dedicated to providing in-depth articles on all aspects of the tea & coffee industries. *Tea & Coffee Trade Journal* provides the latest informaton on everything from producing countries to retail trends. Estab. 1901. Byline given. Pays on publication. No kill fee. Publishes ms an average of 3 months after acceptance. Editorial lead time 2 months. Submit seasonal material 6 months in advance. Accepts queries by mail, e-mail. Accepts simultaneous submissions. Responds in days to queries. Responds in days to mss. Sample available online. Guidelines free.

NONFICTION Pays expenses of writers on assignment.

$$$ VINEYARD & WINERY MANAGEMENT

P.O. Box 14459, Santa Rosa CA 95402-6459. (707)577-7700. **Fax:** (707)577-7705. **E-mail:** tcaputo@vwmmedia.com. **Website:** www.vwmmedia.com. **Contact:** Tina Caputo, editor in chief. **80% freelance written.** Bimonthly magazine of professional importance to grape growers, winemakers, and winery sales and business people. Headquartered in Sonoma County, California, *Vineyard & Winery Management* proudly remains a leading independent wine trade magazine serving all of North America. Estab. 1975. Circ. 6,500. Byline given. Pays on publication. 20% kill fee. Accepts queries by e-mail. Accepts simultaneous submissions. Responds in 3 weeks to queries. Responds in 1 month to mss. Sample copy free. Guidelines available by e-mail.

Focuses on the management of people and process in the areas of viticulture, enology, winery marketing and finance. Articles are written with a high degree of technical expertise by a team of wine industry professionals and top-notch journalists. Timely articles and columns keep subscribers poised for excellence and success.

NONFICTION Needs how-to, interview, new product, technical. **Buys 30 mss/year.** Query. Length: 1,500-2,000 words. **Pays approximately $500/feature.** Pays expenses of writers on assignment.

PHOTOS State availability. Captions, identification of subjects required. Digital photos preferred, JPEG or TIFF files 300 pixels/inch resolution at print size. Pays $20/each photo published.

TIPS "We're looking for long-term relationships with authors who know the business and write well. Electronic submissions required; query for formats."

$$ WINES & VINES

Wine Communications Group, 65 Mitchell Blvd., Suite A, San Rafael CA 94903. (415)453-9700; (866)453-9701. **Fax:** (415)453-2517. **E-mail:** edit@winesandvines.com; info@winesandvines.com. **Website:** www.winesandvines.com. **Contact:** Jim Gordon, editor; Kate Lavin, managing editor. **50% freelance written.** Monthly magazine covering the North American winegrape and winemaking industry. "Since 1919, *Wines & Vines Magazine* has been the authoritative voice of the wine and grape industry—from prohibition to phylloxera, we have covered it all. Our paid circulation reaches all 50 states and many foreign countries. Because we are intended for the trade—including growers, winemakers, winery owners, wholesalers, restauranteurs, and serious amateurs—we accept more technical, informative articles. We do not accept wine reviews, wine country tours, or anything of a wine consumer nature." Estab. 1919. Circ. 5,000. Byline given. Pays 30 days after acceptance. No kill fee. Publishes ms an average of 3 months after acceptance. Editorial lead time 2 months. Submit seasonal material 4 months in advance. Accepts queries by e-mail. Accepts simultaneous submissions. Responds in 2-3 weeks to queries. Sample copy: $5. Guidelines free.

NONFICTION Needs interview, new product, technical. "No wine reviews, wine country travelogues, 'lifestyle' pieces, or anything aimed at wine consumers. Our readers are professionals in the field." **Buys 60 mss/year.** Query with published clips. Length: 1,000-2,000 words. **Pays flat fee of $500 for assigned articles.** Pays expenses of writers on assignment.

PHOTOS Prefers JPEG files (JPEG, 300 dpi minimum). Can use high-quality prints. State availability of or send photos. Captions, identification of subjects required. Does not pay for photos submitted by author, but will give photo credit.

BOOK & BOOKSTORE

$$ FOREWORD REVIEWS

FOREWORD MAGAZINE INC., 425 Boardman Ave., Suite B, Traverse City MI 49684. (231)933-3699. **Fax:** (231)933-3899. **E-mail:** howard@forewordreviews.com; victoria@forewordreviews.com. **E-mail:** matt@forewordreviews.com. **Website:** www.forewordreviews.com. Associate Publisher: Jennifer Szunko. Audience Development: Seth Dellon. **Contact:** Matt Sutherland, book review editor; Howard Lovy, executive editor. **75% freelance written.** Quarterly magazine covering reviews of good books independently published. In each issue of the magazine, there are 3 to 4 feature *ForeSight* articles focusing on trends in popular categories. These are in addition to the 100 or more critical reviews of forthcoming titles from independent and university presses in the *Review* section. Look online for review submission guidelines or view editorial calendar. Estab. 1998. Circ. 10,000 (about 80% librarians, 10% bookstores, 10% publishing professionals). Byline given. Pays 1 months after submissions. $20 kill fee. Publishes ms an average of 2-3 months after acceptance. Editorial lead time 2-3 months. Submit seasonal material 5 months in advance. Accepts queries by mail, e-mail. Accepts simultaneous submissions. Responds in 1 month. Sample copy for $5.99 and 8 ½ x11 SASE with $1.50 postage.

NONFICTION Contact: Matt Sutherland. Needs book excerpts, interview, profile. **Buys 4 mss/year.** Query with published clips. All review submissions should be sent to the book review editor. Submissions should include a fact sheet or press release. Length: 400-1,500 words. **Pays $50-250 for assigned articles.**

TIPS "Be knowledgeable about the needs of book-sellers and librarians—remember we are an industry trade journal, not a how-to or consumer publication. We review books prior to publication, so book reviews are always assigned—but send us a note telling subjects you wish to review, as well as a résumé."

THE HORN BOOK MAGAZINE

Media Source, Inc., 300 The Fenway, Palace Road Building, Suite P-311, Boston MA 02115. (617)278-0225. **Fax:** (617)278-6062. **Website:** www.hbook.com. **Contact:** Shoshana Flax, editorial assistant. **75% freelance written. Prefers to work with published/established writers.** Bimonthly magazine covering children's literature for librarians, booksellers, professors, teachers, and students of children's literature. Estab. 1924. Circ. 10,000. Byline given. Pays on publication. No kill fee. Publishes ms an average of 4 months after acceptance. Submit seasonal material 6 months in advance. Accepts queries by mail, e-mail, fax. Accepts simultaneous submissions. Responds in 3 months to queries. Sample copy and writer's guidelines online.

NONFICTION , interviews with children's book authors and illustrators, topics of interest to the children's book world. **Buys 20 mss/year.** Query or send complete ms. Preferred length: 1,000-2,000 words. **Pays honorarium.**

TIPS "Writers have a better chance of breaking into our publication with a query letter on a specific article they want to write."

VIDEO LIBRARIAN

3435 NE Nine Boulder Dr., Poulsbo WA 98370. (360)626-1259. **Fax:** (360)626-1260. **E-mail:** vidlib@videolibrarian.com. **Website:** www.videolibrarian.com. **75% freelance written.** Bimonthly magazine covering DVD/Blu-ray reviews for librarians. "*Video*

Librarian reviews approximately 225 titles in each issue: children's, documentaries, how-to's, movies, TV, music and anime." Estab. 1986. Circ. 2,000. Byline given. Pays on publication. Publishes ms an average of 2 months after acceptance. Editorial lead time 2 months. Accepts queries by e-mail. Accepts simultaneous submissions. Responds in 1 week to queries. Sample copy: $11.

NONFICTION Buys 500+ mss/year. Query with published clips. Length: 200-300 words. **Pays $10-20/review.** Pays expenses of writers on assignment.

TIPS "We are looking for DVD/Blu-ray reviewers with a wide range of interests, good critical eye, and strong writing skills."

BUILDING INTERIORS

💲💲 KITCHEN & BATH DESIGN NEWS

SOLA Group Inc., 724 12th St., Suite 1W, Wilmette IL 60091. (631)581-2029 or (516)605-1426. **E-mail:** anita@solabrands.com; janice@solabrands.com. **Website:** www.kitchenbathdesign.com. **15% freelance written.** Monthly tabloid for kitchen and bath dealers and design professionals, offering design, business, and marketing advice to help readers be more successful. It is not a consumer publication about design, a book for do-it-yourselfers, or a magazine created to showcase pretty pictures of kitchens and baths. Rather, the magazine covers the professional kitchen and bath design industry in depth, looking at the specific challenges facing these professionals, and how they address these challenges. Estab. 1983. Circ. 51,000. Byline given. Pays on publication. Publishes ms an average of 2-3 months after acceptance. Editorial lead time 2 months. Accepts queries by mail, e-mail. Accepts simultaneous submissions. Responds in 2-4 weeks to queries. Sample copy online. Guidelines by e-mail.

NONFICTION Needs how-to, interview. Does not want consumer stories, generic business stories, or "I remodeled my kitchen and it's so beautiful" stories. This is a magazine for trade professionals, so stories need to be both slanted for these professionals, as well as sophisticated enough that people who have been working in the field 30 years can still learn something from them. **Buys 16 mss/year.** Query with published clips. Length: 1,100-3,000 words. **Pays $200-650.** Pays expenses of writers on assignment.

PHOTOS Send photos. Identification of subjects required. Offers no additional payment for photos accepted with ms.

TIPS "This is a trade magazine for kitchen and bath dealers and designers, so trade experience and knowledge of the industry are essential. We look for writers who already know the unique challenges facing this industry, as well as the major players, acronyms, etc. This is not a market for beginners, and the vast majority of our freelancers are either design professionals or experienced in the industry."

💲💲💲💲 REMODELING

HanleyWood, LLC, One Thomas Circle NW, Suite 600, Washington DC 20005. (202)452-0800. **Fax:** (202)785-1974. **E-mail:** cwebb@hanleywood.com. **Website:** www.remodelingmagazine.com. **Contact:** Craig Webb, editor. **10% freelance written.** Monthly magazine covering residential and light commercial remodeling. "We cover the best new ideas in remodeling design, business, construction and products." Estab. 1985. Circ. 80,000. Byline given. Pays on publication. Offers 5¢/word kill fee. Publishes ms an average of 3 months after acceptance. Accepts queries by mail, e-mail, fax. Accepts simultaneous submissions. Sample copy free.

NONFICTION Needs interview, new product, technical, small business trends. **Buys 6 mss/year.** Query with published clips. Length: 250-1,000 words. **Pays $1/word.** Pays expenses of writers on assignment.

PHOTOS State availability. Captions, identification of subjects, model releases required. Reviews 4x5 transparencies, slides, 8x10 prints. Offers $25-125/photo. Buys one-time rights.

TIPS "We specialize in service journalism for remodeling contractors. Knowledge of the industry is essential."

💲💲 WALLS & CEILINGS

2401 W. Big Beaver Rd., Suite 700, Troy MI 48084. **Fax:** (248)362-5103. **E-mail:** wyattj@bnpmedia.com; mark@wwcca.org. **Website:** www.wconline.com. **Contact:** John Wyatt, editor; Mark Fowler, editorial director. **20% freelance written.** Monthly magazine for contractors involved in lathing and plastering, drywall, acoustics, fireproofing, curtain walls, and movable partitions, together with manufacturers, dealers, and architects. Estab. 1938. Circ. 30,000. Byline given. Pays on publication. No kill fee. Publish-

es ms an average of 6 months after acceptance. Submit seasonal material 4 months in advance. Accepts queries by mail, e-mail. Accepts simultaneous submissions. Responds in 6 months to queries. Sample copy for 9x12 SAE with $2 postage. Guidelines for #10 SASE.

NONFICTION Needs how-to, technical. **Buys 20 mss/year.** Query or send complete ms. Length: 1,000-1,500 words. **Pays $50-500.** Pays expenses of writers on assignment.

REPRINTS Send tearsheet or photocopy with rights for sale noted and information about when and where the material previously appeared. Pays 50% of the amount paid for an original article.

PHOTOS Send photos. Captions, identification of subjects required. Reviews contact sheets, negatives, transparencies, prints. Buys one-time rights.

BUSINESS MANAGEMENT

💲💲 CBA RETAILERS+RESOURCES

CBA, the Association for Christian Retail, 1365 Garden of the Gods Rd., Suite 105, Colorado Springs CO 80907. **Fax:** (719)272-3510. **E-mail:** cellis@cbaonline.org; info@cbaonline.org. **Website:** www.cbaonline.org. **Contact:** Cathy Ellis. **80% freelance written.** Monthly magazine covering the Christian products industry. Writers must have knowledge of and direct experience in the Christian products industry. Subject matter must specifically pertain to the Christian products audience. Estab. 1968. Byline given. Pays on publication. No kill fee. Publishes ms an average of 3 months after acceptance. Editorial lead time 3 months. Submit seasonal material 6 months in advance. Accepts queries by e-mail. Accepts simultaneous submissions. Responds in 2 months to queries. Sample copy for $9.50 or online. ⚪ "Please use AP style."

NONFICTION Buys 24 mss/year. Query. Length: 650-1,500 words. **Pays 25¢/word.**

TIPS "Only experts on Christian retail industry, completely familiar with supplier and retail audience and their needs and considerations, should submit a query. Do not submit articles unless requested."

✪ CPA MAGAZINE

Chartered Professional Accountants Canada, 277 Wellington St. W., Toronto ON M5V 3H2 Canada.

(416)977-3222. **Fax:** (416)977-8585. **E-mail:** cpamagazineinfo@cpacanada.ca. **Website:** www.cpacanada.ca. **30% freelance written.** Magazine published 10 times/year covering accounting and finance. *CPA Magazine* is the leading accounting publication in Canada and the preferred information source for chartered accountants and financial executives. It provides a forum for discussion and debate on professional, financial, and other business issues. Estab. 1911. Circ. 90,602. Byline given. Pays on acceptance. Offers 30% kill fee. Publishes ms an average of 3 months after acceptance. Editorial lead time 4 months. Accepts queries by e-mail. Accepts simultaneous submissions. Responds in 1 month to queries. Sample copy and writer's guidelines online.

NONFICTION Needs book excerpts, financial/accounting business. **Buys 30 mss/year.** Query. Length: 2,500-3,500 words. **Pays honorarium for chartered accountants; freelance rate varies. Does not pay business professionals.** Pays expenses of writers on assignment.

💲💲 MAINEBIZ

Mainebiz Publications, Inc., 48 Free St., Portland ME 04101. (207)761-8379. **Fax:** (207)761-0732. **E-mail:** pvanallen@mainebiz.biz; editorial@mainebiz.biz. **Website:** www.mainebiz.biz. **Contact:** Peter Van Allen, editor. **25% freelance written.** Biweekly tabloid covering business in Maine. *Mainebiz* is read by business decision makers across the state. Readers look to the publication for business news and analysis. Estab. 1994. Circ. 13,000. Byline given. Pays on publication. Offers 10% kill fee. Publishes ms an average of 1 month after acceptance. Editorial lead time 1 month. Submit seasonal material 2 months in advance. Accepts queries by mail, e-mail. Accepts simultaneous submissions. Responds in 3 weeks to queries. Sample copy online.

NONFICTION Needs essays, expose, interview, business trends. Special issues: See website for editorial calendar. **Buys 50+ mss/year.** Query with published clips. Length: 500-2,500 words. **Pays $75-350.** Pays expenses of writers on assignment.

PHOTOS State availability. Identification of subjects required. Reviews GIF/JPEG files. Negotiates payment individually. Buys one-time rights.

TIPS "If you wish to contribute, please spend some time familiarizing yourself with *Mainebiz*. Tell us a little about yourself, your experience and background as a writer and qualifications for writing a particular story. If you have clips you can send us via e-mail, or web addresses of pages that contain your work, please send us a representative sampling (no more than 3 or 4, please). Stories should be well thought out with specific relevance to Maine. Arts and culture-related queries are welcome, as long as there is a business angle. We appreciate unusual angles on business stories and regularly work with new freelancers. Send the text of your query or submission in plain text in the body of your e-mail, rather than as an attached file, as we may not be able to read the format of your file. We do our best to respond to all inquiries, but be aware that we are sometimes inundated."

💲💲 RTOHQ: THE MAGAZINE

1504 Robin Hood Trail, Austin TX 78703. (800)204-2776. **Fax:** (512)794-0097. **E-mail:** nferguson@rtohq.org; bkeese@rtohq.org. **Website:** www.rtohq.org. **Contact:** Neil Ferguson, art director; Bill Keese, executive editor. **50% freelance written.** Bimonthly magazine covering the rent-to-own industry. *RTOHQ: The Magazine* is the only publication representing the rent-to-own industry and members of APRO. The magazine covers timely news and features affecting the industry, association activities, and member profiles. Awarded best 4-color magazine by the American Society of Association Executives in 1999. Estab. 1980. Circ. 5,500. Byline given. Pays on acceptance. Offers 25% kill fee. Publishes ms an average of 2 months after acceptance. Editorial lead time 2 months. Submit seasonal material 4 months in advance. Accepts queries by mail, e-mail, fax, phone, online submission form. Accepts simultaneous submissions. Responds in 1 month to queries. Responds in 2 months to mss. Sample copy free.

NONFICTION Needs expose, general interest, how-to, inspirational, interview, technical, industry features. **Buys 12 mss/year.** Query with published clips. Length: 1,200-2,500 words. **Pays $150-700.** Pays expenses of writers on assignment.

💲💲 SECURITY DEALER & INTEGRATOR

Cygnus Business Media, 12735 Morris Rd., Bldg. 200, Suite 180, Alpharetta GA 30004. (800)547-7377, ext 2226. **E-mail:** paul.rothman@cygnus.com. **Website:** www.securityinfowatch.com/magazine. **Contact:** Paul Rothman, editor in chief. **25% freelance written.** Circ. 25,000. Byline sometimes given. Pays 3 weeks after publication. No kill fee. Publishes ms an average of 3 months after acceptance. Accepts queries by e-mail. Accepts simultaneous submissions.

"*Security Dealer & Integrator* magazine is a leading voice for security resellers and the related security service community, covering business intelligence and technology solutions that effectively mitigate a wide variety of security risks faced by commercial, industrial, government, and residential resellers. Content includes vertical market and industry specific needs; new technologies and their impact on the market; business issues including operations, business development, funding, mergers and acquisitions; and in-depth coverage of the market's vendors."

NONFICTION Needs how-to, interview, technical. No consumer pieces. Query by e-mail. Length: 1,000-3,000 words. **Pays $300 for assigned articles; $100-200 for unsolicited articles.** Pays expenses of writers on assignment.

PHOTOS State availability. Captions, identification of subjects required. Reviews contact sheets, transparencies. Offers $25 additional payment for photos accepted with ms.

COLUMNS Closed Circuit TV, Access Control (both on application, installation, new products), 500-1,000 words. **Buys 25 mss/year.** Query by mail only. **Pays $100-150.**

TIPS "The areas of our publication most open to freelancers are technical innovations, trends in the alarm industry, and crime patterns as related to the business as well as business finance and management pieces."

SMART BUSINESS

Smart Business Network, Inc., 835 Sharon Dr., Suite 200, Cleveland OH 44145. (440)250-7000. **Fax:** (440)250-7001. **E-mail:** mscott@sbnonline.com. **Website:** www.sbnonline.com. **Contact:** Mark Scott, senior associate editor. **5% freelance written.** Monthly business magazine with an audience made up of business owners and top decision makers. *Smart Business* is one of the fastest growing national chains of regional management journals for corporate executives. Every issue delves into the minds of the most innovative executives in each of our regions to report on how market leaders got to the top and what strategies they use to stay there. Estab. 1989. Byline given. Pays on publication. Offers 50% kill fee. Publishes ms an average of 2 months after acceptance. Editorial lead time 3 months. Submit seasonal material 3 months in advance. Accepts queries by mail, e-mail. Accepts simultaneous submissions.

Responds in 2 weeks to queries. Responds in 1 month to mss. Sample copy online. Guidelines by e-mail.

Publishes local editions in Dallas, Houston, St. Louis, Northern California, San Diego, Orange County, Tampa Bay/St. Petersburg, Miami, Philadephia, Cincinnati, Detroit, Los Angeles, Broward/Palm Beach, Cleveland, Akron/Canton, Columbus, Pittsburgh, Atlanta, Chicago, and Indianapolis.

NONFICTION Needs how-to, interview. No breaking news or news features. **Buys 10-12 mss/year.** Query with published clips. Length: 1,150-2,000 words. **Pays $200-500.** Pays expenses of writers on assignment.

PHOTOS State availability. Identification of subjects required. Reviews negatives, prints. Offers no additional payment for photos accepted with ms. Buys one-time, reprint, and Web rights.

TIPS "The best way to submit to *Smart Business* is to read us—either online or in print. Remember, our audience is made up of top level business executives and owners."

SUPERVISION MAGAZINE

National Research Bureau, 320 Valley St., Burlington IA 52601. (319)752-5415. **E-mail:** articles@supervisionmagazine.com. **Website:** www.supervisionmagazine.com/. **Contact:** Todd Darnall. **80% freelance written.** Monthly magazine covering management and supervision. *Supervision Magazine* explains complex issues in a clear and understandable format. Articles written by both experts and scholars provide practical and concise answers to issues facing today's supervisors and managers. Estab. 1939. Circ. 500. Byline given. Pays on acceptance. Publishes ms an average of 1 month after acceptance. Editorial lead time 1 month. Submit seasonal material 2 months in advance. Accepts queries by e-mail. Accepts simultaneous submissions. Sample copy free. Guidelines online.

NONFICTION Needs personal experience, "We can use articles dealing with motivation, leadership, human relations and communication." Send complete ms. Length: 1,500-2,000 words. **Pays 4¢/word.** Pays expenses of writers on assignment.

VENECONOMY/VENECONOMA

VenEconomia, Edificio Gran Sabana, Piso 1, Ave. Abraham Lincoln, No. 174, Blvd. de Sabana Grande, Caracas Venezuela. (58)(212)761-8121. **Fax:** (58)

(212)762-8160. **E-mail:** mercadeo@veneconomia.com. **Website:** www.veneconomia.com; www.veneconomy.com. **70% freelance written.** Monthly business magazine covering business, political, and social issues in Venezuela. *VenEconomy*'s subscribers are mostly business people, both Venezuelans and foreigners doing business in Venezuela. Some academics and diplomats also read our magazine. The magazine is published monthly both in English and Spanish. Freelancers may query in either language. Slant is decidedly pro-business, but not dogmatically conservative. Development, human rights, political, and environmental issues are covered from a business-friendly angle. Estab. 1983. Byline given. Pays on publication. Offers 50% kill fee. Publishes ms an average of 1 month after acceptance. Editorial lead time 1-2 months. Submit seasonal material 1 month in advance. Accepts queries by e-mail. Accepts simultaneous submissions. Responds in 2 weeks to queries. Responds in 4 months to mss. Sample copy by e-mail.

NONFICTION Contact: Francisco Toro, political editor. Needs essays, expose, interview, new product, opinion. No first-person stories or travel articles. **Buys 50 mss/year.** Query. Length: 1,100-3,200 words. **Pays 10-15¢/word for assigned articles.** Pays expenses of writers on assignment.

TIPS "A Venezuela tie-in is absolutely indispensable. While most of our readers are business people, *VenEconomy* does not limit itself strictly to business-magazine fare. Our aim is to give our readers a sophisticated understanding of the main issues affecting the country as a whole. Stories about successful Venezuelan companies, or foreign companies doing business successfully with Venezuela, are particularly welcome. Stories about the oil-sector, especially as it relates to Venezuela, are useful. Other promising topics for freelancers outside Venezuela include international trade and trade negotiations, US-Venezuela bilateral diplomatic relations, international investors' perceptions of business prospects in Venezuela, and international organizations' assessments of environmental, human rights, or democracy and development issues in Venezuela, etc. Both straight reportage and somewhat more opinionated pieces are acceptable, articles that straddle the borderline between reportage and opinion are best. Before querying, ask yourself: Would this be of interest to me if I was doing business in or with Venezuela?"

CHURCH ADMINISTRATION & MINISTRY

💲💲 THE JOURNAL OF ADVENTIST EDUCATION

General Conference of SDA, 12501 Old Columbia Pike, Silver Spring MD 20904. (301)680-5069. **Fax:** (301)622-9627. **E-mail:** mcgarrellf@gc.adventist.org; goffc@gc.adventist.org. **Website:** jae.adventist.org. **Contact:** Faith-Ann McGarrell, editor; Chandra Goff, admin assistant. Bimonthly (except skips issue in summer) professional journal covering teachers and administrators in Seventh-Day Adventist school systems. Published 5 times/year in English, 2 times/year in French, Spanish, and Portuguese. Emphasizes procedures, philosophy, and subject matter of Christian education. Estab. 1939. Circ. 14,000 in English; 13,000 in other languages. Byline given. Pays on publication. No kill fee. Publishes ms an average of 1 year after acceptance. Editorial lead time 1 year. Accepts queries by mail, e-mail, fax, phone. Accepts simultaneous submissions. Responds in 6 weeks to queries; 4 months to mss. Sample copy for SAE with 10x12 envelope and 5 first-class stamps. Guidelines online.

NONFICTION Needs book excerpts, essays, how-to, personal experience, photo feature, religious, education. "No brief first-person stories about Sunday Schools." Query. All articles must be submitted in electronic format. Store in Word or .rtf format. If you submit a CD, include a printed copy of the article with the CD. Articles should be 6-8 pages long, with a max of 10 pages, including references. Two-part articles will be considered. Length: 1,000-1,500 words. **Pays $25-300.**

REPRINTS Send tearsheet or photocopy and information about when and where the material previously appeared.

PHOTOS Buys 5-15 photos from freelancers/issue; up to 75 photos/year. Photos of children/teens, multicultural, parents, education, religious, health/fitness, technology/computers with people, committees, offices, school photos of teachers, students, parents, activities at all levels, elementary though graduate school. Reviews photos with or without a ms. Model release preferred. Photo captions preferred. Uses mostly digital color images but also accepts color prints; 35mm,

21/4x21/4, 4x5 transparencies. Send digital photos via ZIP, CD, or DVD (preferred); e-mail as TIFF, GIF, JPEG files at 300 DPI. Do not send large numbers of photos as e-mail attachments. Send query letter with prints, photocopies, transparencies. Provide self-promotion piece to be kept on file for possible future assignments. Responds in 1 month to queries. Simultaneous submissions and previously published work OK. State availability of or send photos. Pays $100-350 for color cover; $50-100 for color inside. Willing to negotiate on electronic usage of photos. Pays on publication. Credit line given. Buys one-time rights for use in magazine and on website.

TIPS "Articles may deal with educational theory or practice, although the *Journal* seeks to emphasize the practical. Articles dealing with the creative and effective use of methods to enhance teaching skills or learning in the classroom are especially welcome. Whether theoretical or practical, such essays should demonstrate the skillful integration of Seventh-day Adventist faith/values and learning."

JOURNAL OF CHURCH AND STATE

Oxford University Press, 2001 Evans Rd., Cary NC 27513. **Website:** www.oxfordjournals.org/our_journals/jcs/. **Contact:** Dr. Jerold Waltman, editor. Journal covering law, social studies, religion, philosophy, and history. "The *Journal of Church and State* is concerned with what has been called the 'greatest subject in the history of the West.' It seeks to stimulate interest, dialogue, research, and publication in the broad area of religion and the state. *JCS* publishes constitutional, historical, philosophical, theological, and sociological studies on religion and the body politic in various countries and cultures of the world, including the U.S. Each issue features, in addition to a timely editorial, 5 or more major articles, and 35-40 reviews of significant books related to church and state. Periodically, important ecclesiastical documents and government texts of legislation and/or court decisions are also published. Regular features include 'Notes on Church State Affairs,' which reports current developments throughout the world, and a list of 'Recent Doctoral Dissertations in Church and State.'" Estab. 1959. Accepts queries by online submission form. Accepts simultaneous submissions. Guidelines online.

NONFICTION Needs essays, historical, religious, law. Submit complete ms via online submissions manager. Length: 6,000-8,000 words, including footnotes. Pays expenses of writers on assignment.

💲💲💲 WORSHIP LEADER MAGAZINE

Worship Leader, 29222 Rancho Viejo, Ste. 215, San Juan Capistrano CA 92675. (949)240-9339. **Fax:** (949)240-0038. **Website:** www.worshipleader.com. **Contact:** Jeremy Armstrong, managing editor. **80% freelance written.** Bimonthly magazine covering all aspects of Christian worship. *Worship Leader Magazine* exists to challenge, serve, equip, and train those involved in leading the 21st-century church in worship. The intended readership is the worship team (all those who plan and lead) of the local church. Estab. 1990. Circ. 40,000. Byline given. Pays on publication. Offers 50% kill fee. Editorial lead time 3 months. Submit seasonal material 6 months in advance. Accepts queries by online submission form. Accepts simultaneous submissions. Responds in 6 weeks to queries. Responds in 3 months to mss. Sample copy: $5.

NONFICTION Needs general interest, how-to, inspirational, interview, opinion. **Buys 15-30 mss/year.** Unsolicited articles are only accepted for the web and should be between 700 and 900 words. Web articles are published on a gratis basis and are often the first step in creating a relationship with *Worship Leader Magazine* and its readers, which could lead to more involvement as a writer. Length: 700-900 words. **Pays $200-800 for assigned articles. Pays $200-500 for unsolicited articles.** Pays expenses of writers on assignment.

PHOTOS State availability. Identification of subjects required. Negotiate payment individually. Buys one-time rights.

TIPS "Our goal has been and is to provide the tools and information pastors, worship leaders, and ministers of music, youth, and the arts need to facilitate and enhance worship in their churches. In achieving this goal, we strive to maintain high journalistic standards, Biblical soundness, and theological neutrality. Our intent is to present the philosophical, scholarly insight on worship, as well as the day-to-day, 'putting it all together' side of worship, while celebrating our unity and diversity."

💲💲 YOUTHWORKER JOURNAL

Salem Publishing/CCM Communications, 402 BNA Dr., Suite 400, Nashville TN 37217-2509. **E-mail:** ALee@SalemPublishing.com. **Website:** www.youthworker.com. **Contact:** Steve Rabey, editor; Amy L. Lee, managing editor. **100% freelance written.** Website and bimonthly magazine covering professional youth ministry in the church and parachurch. Estab. 1984. Circ. 20,000. Byline given. Pays on publication. No kill fee. Publishes ms an average of 3 months after acceptance for print; immediately online. Editorial lead time 6 months for print; immediately online. Submit seasonal material 6 months in advance for print. Accepts queries by e-mail, online submission form. Accepts simultaneous submissions. Responds within 6 weeks to queries. Sample copy for $5. Guidelines online.

NONFICTION Needs essays, new product, personal experience, photo feature, religious. Special issues: See website for themes in upcoming issues. Query. Length: 250-3,000 words. **Pays $15-200.**

PHOTOS Send photos. Reviews GIF/JPEG files. Negotiates payment individually.

TIPS "We exist to help meet the personal and professional needs of career, Christian youth workers in the church and parachurch. Proposals accepted on the posted theme, according to the writer's guidelines on our website. It's not enough to write well—you must know youth ministry."

CLOTHING

💲💲 IMPRESSIONS

Emerald Expositions, 1145 Sanctuary Pkwy., Suite 355, Alpharetta GA 30009-4772. (800)241-9034. **Fax:** (770)777-8733. **E-mail:** mderryberry@impressionsmag.com; jlaster@impressionsmag.com; michelle.havich@emeraldexpo.com. **Website:** www.impressionsmag.com. **Contact:** Marcia Derryberry, editor in chief; Jamar Laster, senior editor; Michelle Havich, managing editor. **30% freelance written.** Magazine, published 13 times/year, covering computerized embroidery and digitizing design. Features authoritative, up-to-date information on screen printing, embroidery, heat-applied graphics, and inkjet-to-garment printing. Readable, practical business and/or technical articles show readers how to succeed in their profession. Estab. 1994. Circ. 20,000. Byline given. Pays on publication. No kill fee. Publishes ms an average of 3 months after acceptance. Editorial lead time 3 months. Submit seasonal material 6 months in advance. Accepts queries by mail, e-mail. Accepts simultaneous submissions. Sample copy: $10.

NONFICTION Needs how-to, interview, new product, photo feature, technical. **Buys 40 mss/year.** Query. Length: 800-2,000 words. **Pays $200 and up for assigned articles.** Pays expenses of writers on assignment.

PHOTOS Send photos. Reviews transparencies, prints. Negotiates payment individually.

TIPS "Show us you have specified knowledge, experience, or contacts in the embroidery industry or a related field."

💲💲 MADE TO MEASURE

The Uniform Magazine, UniformMartket LLC, 633 Skokie Blvd., Suite 490, Northbrook IL 60062. (224)406-8840. **Fax:** (224)406-8850. **E-mail:** news@uniformmarket.com. **Website:** www.madetomeasuremag.com; www.uniformmarketnews.com. **Contact:** Rick Levine, editor. **50% freelance written.** Semi-annual magazine covering uniforms and career apparel. A semi-annual magazine/buyers' reference containing leading sources of supply, equipment, and services of every description related to the Uniform, Career Apparel, and allied trades, throughout the entire US. Estab. 1930. Circ. 25,000. Byline given. Pays on acceptance. No kill fee. Publishes ms an average of 2 months after acceptance. Editorial lead time 4 months. Submit seasonal material 4 months in advance. Accepts queries by mail, e-mail. Accepts simultaneous submissions. Responds in 3 weeks to queries. Sample copy online.

NONFICTION Needs interview, new product, personal experience, photo feature, technical. **Buys 6-8 mss/year.** Query with published clips. Length: 1,000-3,000 words. Pays expenses of writers on assignment.

PHOTOS State availability. Reviews contact sheets, any prints. Negotiates payment individually. Buys one time rights.

TIPS "We look for features about large and small companies who wear uniforms (restaurants, hotels, industrial, medical, public safety, etc.)."

💲 RAGTRADER

Yaffa Publishing, 17-21 Bellevue St., Surry Hills NSW 2010 Australia. (61)(2)9281-2333. **Fax:** (61)(2)9281-2750. **E-mail:** info@yaffa.com.au; assia@yaffa.com.au. **Website:** www.yaffa.com.au. **Contact:** Assia Benmedjdoub, editor. Monthly magazine covering the latest fashion trends for the fashion retail and international runway industry. "*Ragtrader* features all the latest gossip on the local industry along with news, views, directional looks and topical features." Circ. 5,000. Accepts simultaneous submissions.

NONFICTION Needs general interest, new product. Query. Pays expenses of writers on assignment.

CONSTRUCTION & CONTRACTING

💲💲 AUTOMATED BUILDER

CMN Associates, Inc., 2401 Grapevine Dr., Oxnard CA 93036. (805)351-5931. **Fax:** (805)351-5755. **E-mail:** cms03@pacbell.net. **Website:** www.automatedbuilder.com. **Contact:** Don O. Carlson, editor/publisher. **5% freelance written.** "*Automated Builder* covers management, production and marketing information on all 7 segments of home, apartment and commercial construction. These include: (1) production (site) builders, (2) panelized home manufacturers, (3) HUD-code (mobile) home manufacturers, (4) modular home manufacturers, (5) component manufacturers, (6) special unit (commercial) manufacturers, and (7) all types of builders and builders/dealers. The in-plant material is technical in content and covers new machine technologies and improved methods for in-plant building and erecting. Home and commercial buyers will see the latest in homes and commercial structures." Estab. 1964. Circ. 75,000 when printed. Byline given if desired. Pays on acceptance. Publishes ms an average of 2 months after acceptance. Editorial lead time 2 months. Accepts queries by mail, e-mail, fax. Accepts simultaneous submissions. Responds in 2 weeks to queries.

NONFICTION "No fiction and no planned 'dreams.' Housing projects must be built or under construction. Same for commercial structures" **Buys 6-8 mss/year.** Phone queries OK. Length: 500-750 words. **Pays $250 for stories including photos.** Pays expenses of writers on assignment.

PHOTOS Captions are required for each photo. Offers no additional payment for photos accepted with ms. Payment is on acceptance.

TIPS "Stories often are too long, too loose; we prefer 500-750 words plus captions. We prefer a phone query on feature articles. If accepted on query, articles will rarely be rejected later. It is required that every

story and photos are cleared with the source before sending to *Automated Builder*. At-Home segment will contain details and photos of newest residential and commercial buildings sold or ready for sale. At-Home segment also will welcome stories and photos of new units added to existing homes or commercial structures. Ideal layout would be one page of photos with exterior and/or interior photos of the structures and an adjoining page for text."

CAM MAGAZINE

Construction Association of Michigan, 43636 Woodward Ave., Bloomfield Hills MI 48302. (248)972-1000. **Fax:** (248)972-1001. **E-mail:** tackett@cam-online.com. **Website:** www.cam-online.com. **5% freelance written.** Monthly magazine covering all facets of the Michigan construction industry. *CAM Magazine* is devoted to the growth and progress of individuals and companies serving and servicing the industry. It provides a forum on new construction-related technology, products, and services, plus publishes information on industry personnel changes and advancements. Estab. 1980. Circ. 4,500. Byline given. No kill fee. Editorial lead time 2 months. Submit seasonal material 3 months in advance. Accepts queries by mail, e-mail. Accepts simultaneous submissions. Sample copy and editorial subject calendar with query and SASE.

NONFICTION Query with published clips. Length: 1,000-2,000 words for features; will also review short pieces. Pays expenses of writers on assignment.

PHOTOS Digital format preferred. Send photos. Offers no payment for photos accepted with ms.

TIPS "Anyone having current knowledge or expertise on trends and innovations related to commercial construction is welcome to submit articles. Our readers are construction experts."

💲💲💲 THE CONCRETE PRODUCER

Hanley-Wood, LLC, 8725 W. Higgins Rd., Suite 600, Chicago IL 60631. (773)824-2400 or (773)824-2496. **E-mail:** tbagsarian@hanleywood.com; ryelton@hanleywood.com; tcpeditor@hanleywood.com. **Website:** www.theconcreteproducer.com. **Contact:** Tom Bagsarian, group managing editor; Richard Yelton, editor-at-large. **25% freelance written.** Monthly magazine covering concrete production. Audience consists of producers who have succeeded in making concrete the preferred building material through management, operating, quality control, use of the latest technology, or use of superior materials. Estab. 1982. Circ. 18,000.

Byline given. Pays on acceptance. No kill fee. Publishes ms an average of 2 months after acceptance. Editorial lead time 4 months. Accepts queries by mail, e-mail, fax, phone. Accepts simultaneous submissions. Responds in 1 week to queries; in 2 months to mss. Sample copy: $4. Guidelines free.

NONFICTION Needs how-to, new product, technical. **Buys 10 mss/year.** Send complete ms. Length: 500-2,000 words. **Pays $200-1,000.** Pays expenses of writers on assignment.

PHOTOS Scan photos at 300 dpi. State availability. Captions, identification of subjects required. Reviews transparencies, prints. Offers no additional payment for photos accepted with ms.

💲 HARD HAT NEWS

Lee Publications, Inc., P.O. Box 121, Palatine Bridge NY 13428. (518)673-3763 or (800)218-5586. **Fax:** (518)673-2381. **E-mail:** jcasey@leepub.com. **Website:** www.hardhat.com. **Contact:** Jon Casey, editor. **50% freelance written.** Biweekly tabloid covering heavy construction, equipment, road, and bridge work. "Our readers are contractors and heavy construction workers involved in excavation, highways, bridges, utility construction, and underground construction." Estab. 1980. Circ. 15,000. Byline given. No kill fee. Editorial lead time 2 weeks. Submit seasonal material 2 weeks in advance. Accepts queries by mail, e-mail, fax, phone. Sample copy and writer's guidelines free.

NONFICTION Needs interview, new product, opinion, photo feature, technical. Send complete ms. Length: 800-2,000 words. **Pays $2.50/inch.** Pays expenses of writers on assignment.

PHOTOS Send photos. Captions, identification of subjects required. Reviews prints, digital preferred. Offers $15/photo.

COLUMNS Association News; Parts and Repairs; Attachments; Trucks and Trailers; People on the Move.

TIPS "Every issue has a focus—see our editorial calendar. Special consideration is given to a story that coincides with the focus. A color photo is necessary for the front page. Vertical shots work best. We need more writers in the metro New York area. Also, we are expanding our distribution into the Mid-Atlantic states and need writers in New York, Massachusetts, Vermont, Connecticut, and New Hampshire."

💲💲 HOME ENERGY MAGAZINE

1250 Addison St., Suite 211B, Berkeley CA 94702. (510)524-5405. **Fax:** (510)981-1406. **E-mail:** contact@homeenergy.org; jpgunshinan@homeenergy.org. **Website:** www.homeenergy.org. **Contact:** Jim Gunshinan, editor. **10% freelance written.** Bimonthly magazine covering green home building and renovation. Readers are building contractors, energy auditors, and weatherization professionals. They expect technical detail, accuracy, and brevity. Estab. 1984. Circ. 5,000. Byline given. Pays on publication. Offers 10% kill fee. Publishes ms an average of 4 months after acceptance. Editorial lead time 4 months. Accepts queries by e-mail. Accepts simultaneous submissions. Responds in 2 weeks to queries; 2 months to mss. Guidelines online.

NONFICTION Needs interview, technical. Does not want articles for consumers/general public. **Buys 6 mss/year.** Query with published clips. Submit article via e-mail. Length: 400-2,500 words. **Pays 20¢/word; $400 maximum for both assigned and unsolicited articles.**

COLUMNS "Trends" are short stories explaining a single advance or research result (400-1,500 words). "Features" are longer pieces that provide more in-depth information (1,500-2,500 words). "Field Notes" provide readers with first-person testimonials (1,500-2,500 words). "Columns" provide readers with direct answers to their specific questions (400-1,500 words). Submit columns via e-mail. Accepts Word, RTF documents, Text documents, and other common formats.

💲💲 UNDERGROUND CONSTRUCTION

Oildom Publishing Company of Texas, Inc., P.O. Box 941669, Houston TX 77094-8669. (281)558-6930, ext. 220. **Fax:** (281)558-7029. **E-mail:** rcarpenter@oildom.com; efitzpatrick@oildom.com. **Website:** www.undergroundconstructionmagazine.com. **Contact:** Robert Carpenter, editor-in-chief; Oliver Klinger, publisher; Elizabeth Fitzpatrick, art director. **35% freelance written.** Monthly magazine covering underground oil and gas pipeline, water and sewer pipeline, cable construction for contractors, and owning companies. Circ. 40,000. No kill fee. Publishes ms an average of 6 months after acceptance. Accepts queries by mail, e-mail, fax, phone. Accepts simultaneous submissions. Responds in 1 month to mss. Sample copy for SAE.

NONFICTION Needs how-to, job stories and industry issues. Query with published clips. Length: 1,000-

2,000 words. **Pays $3-500.** Pays expenses of writers on assignment.

PHOTOS Send photos. Captions required. Reviews color prints and slides. Buys one-time rights.

EDUCATION & COUNSELING

◑❸ THE ATA MAGAZINE

11010 142nd St. NW, Edmonton AB T5N 2R1 Canada. (780)447-9400. **Fax:** (780)455-6481. **E-mail:** government@teachers.ab.ca. **Website:** www.teachers.ab.ca. Quarterly magazine covering education. Estab. 1920. Circ. 42,100. Byline given. Pays on publication. No kill fee. Publishes ms an average of 4 months after acceptance. Editorial lead time 2 months. Submit seasonal material 2 months in advance. Accepts queries by mail, e-mail, fax, phone. Accepts simultaneous submissions. Responds in 2 months to queries. Previous articles available for viewing online. Guidelines online.

NONFICTION Query with published clips. Length: 500-1,500 words. **Pays $100 (Canadian).** Pays expenses of writers on assignment.

PHOTOS Send photos. Captions required. Reviews 4x6 prints. Negotiates payment individually. Negotiates rights.

❸ EDUCATION TODAY & LEARNING AUCKLAND

Education Today Limited, 141 Barnard Street Wadestown, Wellington 6012 New Zealand. 001164277344756. **E-mail:** production@educationtoday.co.nz. **Website:** www.educationtoday.co.nz. **Contact:** Consulting Editor. **Excellent venue for student writers, thesis insight, education comment, education product and services.** Significant student content via student editorial groups and submitted material. News and issues for schools, students, families and educational professionals. Education magazines in most New Zealand schools and wider education sector Estab. 1989. Circ. 70 per cent of NZ schools, local government, central government, wider education sector. Yes No kill fee. See deadlines Accepts queries by mail, e-mail, phone. Accepts simultaneous submissions. Material helping raise student achievement.

◯   Query before submitting.

◐   Unique position in education sector

NONFICTION Needs book excerpts, essays, expose, general interest, historical, how-to, humor, inspirational, interview, memoir, new product, nostalgic, opinion, personal experience, photo feature, profile, religious, reviews, technical. Submit complete ms with brief bio and headshot. Length: up to 1,200 words. Pays expenses of writers on assignment.

PHOTOS min 300dpi jpeg attachment.

❸ THE FORENSIC TEACHER MAGAZINE

Wide Open Minds Educational Services, P.O. Box 5263, Wilmington DE 19808. **E-mail:** admin@theforensicteacher.com. **Website:** www.theforensicteacher.com. **Contact:** Dr. Mark R. Feil, editor. **70% freelance written.** Quarterly magazine covering forensic education. Readers are middle, high and post-secondary teachers who are looking for better, easier and more engaging ways to teach forensics as well as law enforcement and scientific forensic experts. Writers understand this and are writing from a forensic or educational background, or both. Prefers a first-person writing style. Estab. 2006. Circ. 30,000. Byline given. Pays 60 days after publication. No kill fee. Publishes ms an average of 6 months after acceptance. Editorial lead time 6 months. Submit seasonal material 6 months in advance. Accepts queries by e-mail. Accepts simultaneous submissions. Responds in 2 weeks to queries; 2 months to mss. Sample copy available at website. Guidelines online.

NONFICTION Needs general interest, how-to, personal experience, photo feature, technical, lesson plans. Does not want poetry, fiction or anything unrelated to medicine, law, forensics or teaching. **Buys 18 mss/year.** Send complete ms. Length: 400-3,000 words. **Pays 2¢/word.**

PHOTOS State availability. Captions required. Reviews GIF/JPEG files/pdf. Send photos separately in e-mail, not in the article. Negotiates payment individually. Buys electronic rights.

COLUMNS Needs lesson experiences or ideas, personal or professional experiences with a branch of forensics. "If you've done it in your classroom please share it with us. Also, if you're a professional, please tell our readers how they can duplicate the lesson/demo/experiment in their classrooms. Please share what you know."

FILLERS Needs Needs facts, newsbreaks. **Buys Buys 15 fillers/year. mss/year.** Length: 50-200 words. **Pays 2¢/word.**

TIPS "Your article will benefit forensics teachers and their students. It should inform, entertain and enlighten the teacher and the students. Would you read it if you were a busy forensics teacher? Also, don't send a rèsumè and tell us how much experience you have and ask for an assignment; query via e-mail with an outline of your proposed piece."

🄌🄍 PTO TODAY

PTO Today, Inc., 100 Stonewall Blvd., Suite 3, Wrentham MA 02093. (800)644-3561. **Fax:** (508)384-6108. **E-mail:** editor@ptotoday.com. **Website:** www.ptotoday.com. **Contact:** Craig Bystrynski, editor-in-chief. **50% freelance written.** Magazine published 6 times during the school year covering the work of school parent-teacher groups. Celebrates the work of school parent volunteers and provide resources to help them do that work more effectively. Estab. 1999. Circ. 80,000. Byline given. Pays on acceptance. Offers 30% kill fee. Publishes ms an average of 4-6 months after acceptance. Editorial lead time 4 months. Submit seasonal material 4 months in advance. Accepts queries by e-mail. Accepts simultaneous submissions. Guidelines by e-mail.

NONFICTION Needs general interest, how-to, interview, personal experience. **Buys 20 mss/year.** Query. "We review but do not encourage unsolicited submissions." Features are roughly 1,200-2,200 words. Average assignment is 1,200 words. Department pieces are 600-1,200 words. **Payment depends on the difficulty of the topic and the experience of the writer. "We pay by the assignment, not by the word; our pay scale ranges from $200 to $700 for features and $150 to $400 for departments. We occasionally pay more for high-impact stories and highly experienced writers. We buy all rights, and we pay on acceptance (within 30 days of invoice)."** Pays expenses of writers on assignment.

PHOTOS State availability. Identification of subjects required. Negotiates payment individually. Permission for print and web publishing.

TIPS "It's difficult for us to find talented writers with strong experience with parent groups. This experience is a big plus. Also, it helps to review our writer's guidelines before querying. All queries must have a strong parent group angle."

🄍 SCHOOLARTS MAGAZINE

Davis Art, 50 Portland St., Worcester MA 01608. **E-mail:** lmarkey@schoolartsmagazine.com. **E-mail:** sa-

submissions@davisart.com. **Website:** schoolartsmagazine.com. **Contact:** Lorraine Markey. **85% freelance written.** Monthly magazine (September-July), serving arts and craft education profession, K-12, higher education, and museum education programs written by and for art teachers. Estab. 1901. Pays on publication (honorarium and 6 copies). No kill fee. Publishes ms an average of 24 months after acceptance. Accepts queries by mail. Responds in 2-4 months to queries. Yes. Guidelines online.

○ Each issue of the volume year revolves around a theme that focuses on the human side of the studio art projects, i.e., story, play, meaning. The editor determines which issue/theme is the best fit for articles, so don't worry about fitting a theme. It is more important to be passionate about your lesson, idea, or concept. Look online for upcoming themes.

NONFICTION Query or send complete ms and SASE. E-mail submissions are also accepted. See website for details. Length: 800 words maximum. **Pays $30-150.** Pays expenses of writers on assignment.

TIPS "We prefer articles on actual art projects or techniques done by students in actual classroom situations. Philosophical and theoretical aspects of art and art education are usually handled by our contributing editors. Our articles are reviewed and accepted on merit and each is tailored to meet our needs. Keep in mind that art teachers want practical tips above all—more hands-on information than academic theory. Write your article with the accompanying photographs in hand. The most frequent mistakes made by writers are bad visual material (photographs, drawings) submitted with articles, a lack of complete descriptions of art processes, and no rationale behind programs or activities. Familiarity with the field of art education is essential. Review recent issues of *SchoolArts*."

🄍 SCREEN EDUCATION

P.O. Box 2040, St. Kilda West VIC 3182 Australia. (61)(3)9525-5302. **Fax:** (61)(3)9537-2325. **E-mail:** screen_ed@atom.org.au. **Website:** www.screeneducation.com.au. Quarterly magazine written by and for teachers and students in secondary and primary schools, covering media education across all curriculum areas. Accepts simultaneous submissions. Guidelines online.

NONFICTION Needs general interest, interview, reviews, classroom activities. E-mail proposals or complete article. Length: 1,000-3,000 words. Pays expenses of writers on assignment.

PHOTOS Reviews TIFF/JPEG files.

TEACHERS & WRITERS MAGAZINE

Teachers & Writers Collaborative, 520 Eighth Ave., Suite 2020, New York NY 10018. (212)691-6590. **Fax:** (212)675-0171. **E-mail:** editors@twc.org. **Website.** www.twc.org/magazine. **Contact:** Amy Swauger. **30% freelance written.** *Teachers & Writers Magazine* covers a cross-section of contemporary issues and innovations in education and writing, and engages writers, educators, critics, and students in a conversation on the nature of creativity and the imagination. Estab. 1967. Circ. 6,500. Byline given. Pays on publication. No kill fee. Publishes ms an average of 4-6 months after acceptance. Editorial lead time 2-4 months. Submit seasonal material 4-6 months in advance. Accepts queries by e-mail. Accepts simultaneous submissions. Responds in 1-2 months to queries and submissions. Guidelines available online: www.teachersandwritersmagazine.org/about-us/submission-guidelines.

NONFICTION Needs book excerpts, essays, how-to, interview, opinion, personal experience, creative writing exercises. Length: 500-2,500 words. **Pays $50-150.**

💲 TEACHERS OF VISION

A Publication of Christian Educators Association, P.O. Box 45610, Westlake OH 44145. (888)798-1124. **E-mail:** TOV@ceai.org. **Website:** www.ceai.org. **70% freelance written.** Magazine published 3 times/year for Christians in public education. *Teachers of Vision*'s articles inspire, inform, and equip teachers and administrators in the educational arena. Readers look for teacher tips, integrating faith and work, and general interest education articles. Topics include subject matter, religious expression and activity in public schools, and legal rights of Christian educators. Audience is primarily public school educators. Other readers include teachers in private schools, university professors, school administrators, parents, and school board members. Estab. 1953. Circ. 10,000. Byline given. Pays on publication. No kill fee. Publishes ms an average of 6 months after acceptance. Editorial lead time 4 months. Submit seasonal material 4 months in advance. Accepts queries by mail, e-mail. Accepts simultaneous submissions. Responds in 1 month to queries; 3-4 months to mss. Sample copy

for SAE with 9x12 envelope and 4 first-class stamps. Guidelines online.

NONFICTION Needs how-to, humor, inspirational, interview, opinion, personal experience, religious. No preaching. **Buys 30-50 mss/year.** Query or send complete ms if 2,000 words or less. Length: 1,500 words. **Pays $25-50.** Pays expenses of writers on assignment.

REPRINTS Buys reprints.

PHOTOS State availability of photos. Offers no additional payment for photos accepted with ms. Buys one-time, web, and reprint rights by members for educational purposes.

COLUMNS Query. **Pays $25-50.**

POETRY Will accept poetry if it pertains to education.

FILLERS Send with SASE—must relate to public education.

TIPS "We are looking for material on living out one's faith in appropriate, legal ways in the public school setting."

💲💲 TEACHING THEATRE

Educational Theatre Association, 2343 Auburn Ave., Cincinnati OH 45219-2815. (513)421-3900. **E-mail:** gbossler@schooltheatre.org. **Website:** www.schooltheatre.org. **Contact:** Gregory Bossler, managing editor. **65% freelance written.** Quarterly magazine covering education theater K-12; primary emphasis on middle and secondary level education. Estab. 1989. Circ. 5,000. Byline given. Pays on acceptance. No kill fee. Publishes ms an average of 3 months after acceptance. Editorial lead time 2 months. Accepts queries by mail, e-mail. Accepts simultaneous submissions. Responds in 4-6 weeks to queries. Responds in 3 months to mss. Sample copy online. Guidelines online.

💬 *Teaching Theatre* emphasizes the teaching, theory, philosophy issues that are of concern to teachers at the elementary, secondary, and—as they relate to teaching K-12 theater—college levels. A typical issue includes an article on acting, directing, playwriting, or technical theatre; a profile of an outstanding educational theatre program; a piece on curriculum design, assessment, or teaching methodology; and a report on current trends or issues in the field, such as funding, standards, or certification.

NONFICTION Needs book excerpts, essays, how-to, interview. **Buys 12-15 mss/year.** Query. A typical issue might include: an article on theatre curriculum development; a profile of an exemplary theatre education program; a how-to teach piece on acting, directing, or playwriting; and a news story or 2 about pertinent educational theatre issues and events. Once articles are accepted, authors are asked to supply their work electronically via e-mail. Length: 750-4,000 words. **Pays $150-500.** Pays expenses of writers on assignment.

PHOTOS State availability. Reviews digital images (300 dpi minimum), prints. Unless other arrangements are made, payment for articles includes payment for the photos and illustrations.

TIPS Wants "articles that address the needs of the busy but experienced high school theater educators. Fundamental pieces on the value of theater education are not of value to us—our readers already know that."

⊖⊖⊖⊖ TEACHING TOLERANCE

A Project of The Southern Poverty Law Center, 400 Washington Ave., Montgomery AL 36104. (334)956-8374. **Fax:** (334)956-8488. **E-mail:** editor@tolerance.org. **Website:** www.teachingtolerance.org. **Contact:** Adrienne van der Valk, managing editor. **30% freelance written.** Semiannual magazine. Estab. 1991. Circ. 400,000. Byline given. Pays on acceptance. No kill fee. Editorial lead time 6 months. Submit seasonal material 6 months in advance. Accepts queries by mail, fax, online submission form. Accepts simultaneous submissions. Sample copy avialble online. Guidelines online.

"*Teaching Tolerance* is dedicated to helping K-12 teachers promote tolerance and understanding between widely diverse groups of students. Includes articles, teaching ideas, and reviews of other resources available to educators."

NONFICTION Needs essays, how-to, personal experience, photo feature. No jargon, rhetoric or academic analysis. No theoretical discussions on the pros/cons of multicultural education. **Buys 2-4 mss/year.** Submit outlines or complete mss. Length: 400-1,600 words. **Pays $1/word.** Pays expenses of writers on assignment.

PHOTOS State availability. Captions, identification of subjects required. Reviews contact sheets, transparencies. Buys one-time rights.

COLUMNS Features (stories and issues related to anti-bias education), 800-1,600 words; Why I Teach (personal reflections about life in the classroom), 600 words or less; Story Corner (designed to be read by or to students and must cover topics that are appealing to children), 600 words; Activity Exchange (brief descriptions of classroom lesson plans, special projects or other school activities that can be used by others to promote tolerance), 400 words. **Buys 8-12 mss/year.** Query with published clips. Does not accept unsolicited mss. **Pays $1/ word.**

TIPS "We want lively, simple, concise writing. Be descriptive and reflective, showing the strength of programs dealing successfully with diversity by employing clear descriptions of real scenes and interactions, and by using quotes from teachers and students. Study previous issues of the magazine before submitting. Most open to articles that have a strong classroom focus. We are interested in approaches to teaching tolerance and promoting understanding that really work that we might not have heard of. We want to inform, inspire and encourage our readers. We know what's happening nationally; we want to know what's happening in your neighborhood classroom."

ELECTRONICS & COMMUNICATION

⊖⊖ THE ACUTA JOURNAL

Information Communications Technology in Higher Education, 152 W. Zandale Dr., Suite 200, Lexington KY 40503. (859)278-3338. **Fax:** (859)278-3268. **E-mail:** pscott@acuta.org. **Website:** www.acuta.org. **Contact:** Pat Scott, director of communications. **20% freelance written.** Quarterly professional association journal covering information communications technology (ICT) in higher education. Audience includes, primarily, middle to upper management in the IT/telecommunications department on college/university campuses. They are highly skilled, technology-oriented professionals who provide data, voice, and video communications services for residential and academic purposes. Estab. 1997. Circ. 2,200. Byline given. Pays on publication. No kill fee. Publishes ms an average of 6 months after acceptance. Editorial lead time 6 months. Accepts queries by mail, e-mail, fax, phone. Accepts simultaneous submissions. Responds in 2 weeks to queries. Request a sample copy by calling (859)721-1659. Guidelines free.

NONFICTION Needs how-to, technical, case study, college/university application of technology. **Buys 6-8 mss/year.** Query. Length: 1,200-4,000 words. **Pays 8-10¢/word.** Pays expenses of writers on assignment.

PHOTOS State availability. Captions, model releases required. Reviews prints. Offers no additional payment for photos accepted with ms.

TIPS "Our audience expects every article to be relevant to information communications technology on the college/university campus, whether it is related to technology, facilities, or management. Writers must read back issues to understand this focus and the level of technicality we expect."

SOUND & VISION

TEN: The Enthusiast Network, 6420 Wilshire Blvd., Los Angeles CA 90048-5502. **E-mail:** rsabin@enthusiastnetwork.com. **Website:** www.soundandvision.com. **Contact:** Rob Sabin, editor. Monthly magazine covering audio, video, high-end components, and movies and music. "*Sound and Vision* spreads the gospel of the home theater experience and gives everyone—from the everyday shopper to the hardcore enthusiast—the information and tools they need to put those pieces in place to their own satisfaction, get them working at their best, and press Play." Estab. 1995. Circ. 90,000. No kill fee. Accepts queries by e-mail. Accepts simultaneous submissions. Sample copy: $4.95.

NONFICTION Query with published clips. Pays expenses of writers on assignment.

COLUMNS Query with published clips.

ENERGY & UTILITIES

💲💲 ELECTRICAL APPARATUS

Barks Publications, Inc., Suite 901, 500 N. Michigan Ave., Chicago IL 60611. (312)321-9440. **Fax:** (312)321-1288. **E-mail:** eamagazine@barks.com. **Website:** www.barks.com/eacurr.html. **Contact:** Elizabeth Van Ness, publisher; Kevin N. Jones, senior editor. Monthly magazine for persons working in electrical and electronic maintenance, in industrial plants and service and sales centers, who install and service electric motors, transformers, generators, controls, and related equipment. Contact staff members by telephone for their preferred e-mail addresses. Estab. 1967. Circ. 16,000. Byline given. Pays on publication. No kill fee. Publishes ms an average of 1 month after acceptance. Accepts queries by mail, e-mail, fax. Accepts simultaneous submissions. Responds in 1 week to queries sent by US mail.

NONFICTION Needs technical. Length: 1,500-2,500 words. **Pays $250-500 for assigned articles.** Pays expenses of writers on assignment.

TIPS "We welcome queries re: technical columns on electro-mehanical subjects as pump repari, automation, drives, etc. All feature articles are assigned to staff and contributing editors and correspondents. Professionals interested in appointments as contributing editors and correspondents should submit résumé and article outlines, including illustration suggestions. Writers should be competent with a camera, which should be described in résumé. Technical expertise is absolutely necessary, preferably an E.E. degree, or practical experience. We are also book publishers and some of the material in *EA* is now in book form, bringing the authors royalties. Also publishes an annual directory, subtitled *ElectroMechanical Bench Reference*."

💲💲 PUBLIC POWER

American Public Power Association, 2451 Crystal Dr., Suite 1000, Arlington VA 22202-4804. (202)467-2900. **Fax:** (202)467-2910. **E-mail:** news@publicpower.org; ldalessandro@publicpower.org; rthomas@publicpower.org. **Website:** www.publicpower.org. **Contact:** Laura D'Alessandro, editor; Robert Thomas, art director. **60% freelance written. Prefers to work with published/established writers.** Publication of the American Public Power Association, published 6 times a year. Emphasizes electric power provided by cities, towns, and utility districts. Estab. 1942. Circ. 14,000. Byline given. Pays on acceptance. No kill fee. Publishes ms an average of 3 months after acceptance. Accepts queries by mail, e-mail, fax. Accepts simultaneous submissions. Responds in 6 months to queries. Sample copy and writer's guidelines free.

NONFICTION **Pays $500 and up.** Pays expenses of writers on assignment.

PHOTOS Reviews electronic photos (minimum 300 dpi at reproduction size).

TIPS "We look for writers who are familiar with energy policy issues."

💲💲💲 TEXAS CO-OP POWER

Texas Electric Cooperatives, Inc., 1122 Colorado St., 24th Floor, Austin TX 78701. (512)486-6242. **E-mail:** clohrmann@texas-ec.org; twidlowski@texas-ec.org. **Website:** www.texascooppower.com. **Contact:** Charles Lorhmann, editor; Tom Widlowski, associate editor. **60% freelance written.** Monthly magazine covering rural and suburban Texas life, people, and places. *Texas Co-op Power* provides more than 1 million households and businesses educational and technical information about electric cooperatives in a high-quality and entertaining format to promote the general welfare of cooperatives, their member-owners, and the areas in which they serve. *Texas Co-op Power* is published by your electric cooperative to enhance the quality of life of its member-customers in an educational and entertaining format. Estab. 1948. Circ. 1.3 million. Byline given. Pays upon final acceptance. Kill fee of 1/3 of the contracted amount. Publishes ms an average of 6 months after acceptance. Editorial lead time 6-12 months. Submit seasonal material 6 months in advance. Accepts queries by mail, e-mail, fax, online submission form. Accepts simultaneous submissions. Responds in 1 month to queries. Responds in 3 months to mss. Sample copy online. Guidelines for #10 SASE.

NONFICTION Needs general interest, historical, interview, photo feature, travel. **Buys 30 mss/year.** Query via e-mail with published clips. Length: 800-1,200 words. **Pays $300-1,200.** Pays expenses of writers on assignment.

PHOTOS State availability. Identification of subjects, model releases required. Reviews transparencies, prints. Negotiates payment individually. Buys one-time rights.

TIPS "We're looking for Texas-related, rural-based articles, often first-person, always lively and interesting."

ENGINEERING & TECHNOLOGY

✪⊕⊕⊕ CANADIAN CONSULTING ENGINEER

Business Information Group, 80 Valleybrook Dr., Toronto ON M3B 2S9 Canada. (416)510-5119. **Fax:** (416)510-5134. **E-mail:** bparsons@ccemag.com. **Website:** www.canadianconsultingengineer.com. **Contact:** Bronwen Parsons, M.A., editor. **20% freelance written.** Bimonthly magazine covering consulting engineering in private practice. Estab. 1958. Circ. 8,900. Byline given depending on length of story. Pays on publication. Offers 50% kill fee. Publishes ms an average of 4 months after acceptance. Editorial lead time 6 months. Accepts simultaneous submissions. Responds in 3 months to mss. Sample copy free.

⊕ Canadian content only. Impartial editorial required.

NONFICTION Needs historical, new product. **Buys 8-10 mss/year.** Query with published clips. Length: 300-1,500 words. **Pays $200-1,000 (Canadian).** Pays expenses of writers on assignment.

PHOTOS State availability. Negotiates payment individually. Buys one-time rights.

COLUMNS Export (selling consulting engineering services abroad); Management (managing consulting engineering businesses); On-Line (trends in CAD systems); Employment; Business; Construction and Environmental Law (Canada); all 800 words. **Buys 4 mss/year.** Query with published clips. **Pays $250-400.**

ECN ELECTRONIC COMPONENT NEWS

Advantage Business Media, 100 Enterprise Dr., Suite 600, Rockaway NJ 07866. (973)920-7057. **E-mail:** kasey.panetta@advantagemedia.com. **Website:** www.ecnmag.com. **Contact:** Kasey Panetta, editor. Monthly magazine. Provides design engineers and engineering management in electronics OEM with a monthly update on new products and literature. Circ. 95,000. No kill fee. Editorial lead time 2 months. Accepts queries by e-mail. Accepts simultaneous submissions. Guidelines online.

NONFICTION Query or submit complete ms. Length: 800-1,000 words. Pays expenses of writers on assignment.

⊕⊕⊕ ENTERPRISE MINNESOTA MAGAZINE

Enterprise Minnesota, Inc., 310 Fourth Ave. S., Suite 7050, Minneapolis MN 55415. (612)373-2900. **Fax:** (612)373-2901. **E-mail:** editor@enterpriseminnesota.org. **Website:** www.enterpriseminnesota.org. **90% freelance written.** Magazine published 5 times/year. *Enterprise Minnesota Magazine* is for the owners and top management of Minnesota's technology and manufacturing companies. The magazine covers technology trends and issues, global trade, management techniques, and finance. Profiles new and growing companies, new products, and the innovators and entrepreneurs of Minnesota's technology sector. Estab. 1991. Circ. 16,000. Byline given. Pays on publication. Offers 10% kill fee. Publishes ms an average of 3 months after acceptance. Editorial lead time 1 month. Submit seasonal material 1 year in advance. Accepts queries by mail, e-mail. Accepts simultaneous submissions. Guidelines free.

NONFICTION Needs general interest, how-to, interview. **Buys 60 mss/year.** Query with published clips. **Pays $150-1,000.** Pays expenses of writers on assignment.

COLUMNS Feature Well (Q&A format, provocative ideas from Minnesota business and industry leaders), 2,000 words; Up Front (mini profiles, anecdotal news items), 250-500 words. Query with published clips.

MANUFACTURING BUSINESS TECHNOLOGY

Reed Business Information, 199 East Badger Rd., Suite 101, Madison WI 53713. **E-mail:** jon.minnick@advantagemedia.com. **Website:** www.mbtmag.com. Monthly magazine about the use of information technology to improve productivity in discrete manufacturing and process industries. Estab. 1984. Circ. 97,000. Byline sometimes given. Pays on publication. No kill fee. Publishes ms an average of 3 months after acceptance. Editorial lead time 3 months. Submit seasonal material 4 months in advance. Accepts queries by e-mail. Accepts simultaneous submissions. Sample copy free. Guidelines online.

NONFICTION Needs technical. **Buys 30 mss/year.** Send ms via e-mail. "Each submission should include the author name, title and affiliation. Please include a headshot of the author." Length: up to 1,000 words. Pays expenses of writers on assignment.

PHOTOS Captions required. No additional payment for photos.

💲 TECH DIRECTIONS

Prakken Publications, Inc., P.O. Box 8623, P, Ann Arbor MI 48107-8623. (734)975-2800. **Fax:** (734)975-2787. **E-mail:** vanessa@techdirections.com. **Website:** www.techdirections.com. **Contact:** Susanne Peckham, managing editor. **100% freelance written. Eager to work with new/unpublished writers.** Monthly (except June and July) magazine covering issues, trends, and activities of interest to science, technical, and technology educators at the elementary through post-secondary school levels. Estab. 1934. Circ. 40,000. Byline given. Pays on publication. No kill fee. Publishes ms an average of 1 year after acceptance. Responds in 1 month to queries. Sample copy for $5. Guidelines online.

NONFICTION Needs general interest, how-to, personal experience, technical, think pieces. **Buys 50 unsolicited mss/year.** Length: 2,000 words. **Pays $50-150.** Pays expenses of writers on assignment.

PHOTOS Send photos. Reviews color prints. Payment for photos included in payment for ms. Will accept electronic art as well.

COLUMNS Direct from Washington (education news from Washington, DC); Technology Today (new products under development); Technologies Past (profiles the inventors of last century); Mastering Computers, Technology Concepts (project orientation).

TIPS "We are mostly interested in articles written by technology and science educators about their class projects and their ideas about the field. We need more and more technology-related articles, especially written for the community college level."

💲💲 WOMAN ENGINEER

Equal Opportunity Publications, Inc., 445 Broad Hollow Rd., Suite 425, Melville NY 11747. (631)421-9421. **Fax:** (631)421-1352. **E-mail:** info@eop.com; jwhitcher@eop.com. **Website:** www.eop.com. **Contact:** Joann Whitcher, director, editorial and production. **60% freelance written. Works with a small number of new/unpublished writers each year.** Triannual magazine aimed at advancing the careers of women engineering students and professional women engineers. Estab. 1968. Circ. 16,000. Byline given. Pays on publication. No kill fee. Publishes ms an average of 3 months after acceptance. Editorial lead time 3 months. Accepts queries by mail, e-mail, fax, phone. Accepts simultaneous submissions. Responds in 2 weeks to queries. Responds in 2 months to mss. Sample copy and writer's guidelines free.

NONFICTION Needs how-to, interview, personal experience. Query. Length: 1,500-2,500 words. **Pays $350 for assigned articles.** Pays expenses of writers on assignment.

PHOTOS Captions, identification of subjects required. Reviews color slides but will accept b&w. Buys all rights.

TIPS "We are looking for first-person 'As I See It' personal perspectives. Gear it to our audience."

ENTERTAINMENT & THE ARTS

💲💲💲 AMERICAN CINEMATOGRAPHER

American Society of Cinematographers, 1782 N. Orange Dr., Hollywood CA 90028. (800)448-0145; outside US: (323)969-4333. **Fax:** (323)876-4973. **E-mail:** stephen@ascmag.com. **E-mail:** jon@ascmag.com. **Website:** www.theasc.com. **Contact:** Stephen Pizzello, editor-in-chief and publisher; Jon Witmer, Jon

Witmer, managing editor (jon@ascmag.com). **90% freelance written.** Monthly magazine covering cinematography (motion picture, TV, music video, commercial). "*American Cinematographer* is a trade publication devoted to the art and craft of cinematography. Our readers are predominantly film industry professionals." Estab. 1919. Circ. 40,000. Byline given. Pays on publication. Offers 50% kill fee. Publishes ms an average of 2-3 months after acceptance. Editorial lead time 2 months. Submit seasonal material 3 months in advance. Accepts queries by mail, e-mail, phone. Responds in 2 weeks to queries; 2 months to mss. Sample copy and guidelines free.

NONFICTION Needs interview, new product, technical. No reviews or opinion pieces. **Buys 20-25 mss/year.** Query with published clips. Length: 1,000-4,000 words. **Pays $400-1,500.** Pays expenses of writers on assignment.

TIPS "Familiarity with the technical side of film production and the ability to present that information in an articulate fashion to our audience are crucial."

AMERICAN THEATRE

Theatre Communications Group, 520 Eighth Ave., 24th Floor, New York NY 10018. (212)609-5900. **Fax:** (212)609-5902. **E-mail:** rwkendt@tcg.org. **Website:** www.tcg.org. **Contact:** Rob Weinert-Kendt, editor-in-chief. **60% freelance written.** Monthly magazine covering theatre. Focus is on American regional non-profit theatre. *American Theatre* typically publishes 2-3 features and 4-6 back-of-the-book articles covering trends and events in all types of theatre, as well as economic and legislative developments affecting the arts. *American Theatre* rarely publishes articles about commercial, amateur, or university theatre, nor about works that would widely be classified as dance or opera, except at the editors' discretion. While significant productions may be highlighted in the Critic's Notebook section, *American Theatre* does not review productions (but does review theatre-related books). Estab. 1982. Circ. 100,000. Byline given. Pays on publication. Editorial lead time 2 months. Submit seasonal material 3 months in advance. Accepts queries by mail, e-mail, online submission form. Accepts simultaneous submissions. Responds in 2 months to queries. Sample copy and Guidelines online.

NONFICTION Needs book excerpts, essays, general interest, historical, how-to, humor, inspirational, interview, opinion, personal experience, photo fea-

ture, travel. Special issues: Training (January); International (May/June); Season Preview (October). No unsolicited submissions (rarely accepted). No reviews. Writers wishing to submit articles to *American Theatre* should mail or e-mail a query to editor-in-chief Rob Weinert-Kendt outlining a particular proposal; unsolicited material is rarely accepted. Include a brief résumé and sample clips. Planning of major articles usually occurs at least 3 months in advance of publication. All mss are subject to editing. Length: 200-2,000 words. **"While fees are negotiated per ms, we pay an average of $350 for full-length (2,500-3,500 words) features, and less for shorter pieces."** Pays expenses of writers on assignment.

PHOTOS Contact: Kitty Suen, creative director: atphoto@tcg.com. Send photos. Captions required. Reviews JPEG files. Negotiates payment individually.

TIPS "The main focus is on professional American nonprofit theatre. Don't pitch music or film festivals. Must be about theatre."

DANCE TEACHER

McFadden Performing Arts Media, 333 Seventh Ave., 11th Floor, New York NY 10001. **E-mail:** khildebrand@dancemedia.com; jsullivan@dancemedia.com. **Website:** www.dance-teacher.com. **Contact:** Karen Hildebrand, editor in chief; Joe Sullivan, managing editor. **60% freelance written.** Monthly magazine. Estab. 1979. Circ. 25,000. Byline given. Pays on publication. No kill fee. Publishes ms an average of 3 months after acceptance. Submit seasonal material 6 months in advance. Accepts queries by e-mail. Accepts simultaneous submissions. Responds in 3 months to mss. Sample copy for SAE with 9x12 envelope and 6 first-class stamps. Guidelines available for free.

"Our readers are professional dance educators, business persons, and related professionals in all forms of dance."

NONFICTION Needs how-to. Special issues: Summer Programs (January); Music & More (May); Costumes and Production Preview (November); College/Training Schools (December). No PR or puff pieces. All articles must be well researched. **Buys 50 mss/year.** Query. Length: 700-2,000 words. **Pays $100-300.** Pays expenses of writers on assignment.

PHOTOS Send photos. Reviews contact sheets, negatives, transparencies, prints. Limited photo budget.

TIPS "Read several issues—particularly seasonal. Stay within writer's guidelines."

DRAMATICS MAGAZINE

Educational Theatre Association, 2343 Auburn Ave., Cincinnati OH 45219. (513)421-3900. **E-mail:** dcorathers@schooltheatre.org. **Website:** schooltheatre.org. **Contact:** Don Corathers, editor. *Dramatics* is for students (mainly high school age) and teachers of theater. The magazine wants student readers to grow as theater artists and become a more discerning and appreciative audience. Material is directed to both theater students and their teachers, with strong student slant. Tries to portray the theater community in all its diversity. Estab. 1929. Circ. 45,000. Byline given. Pays on acceptance. Publishes ms 3 months after acceptance. Accepts queries by mail, e-mail. Accepts simultaneous submissions. Sample copy available for 9x12 SAE with 4-ounce first-class postage. Guidelines available for SASE.

NONFICTION Needs how-to, profile, practical articles on acting, directing, design, production, and other facets of theater; career-oriented profiles of working theater professionals. Special issues: College Theater Programs (November); Summer Theater Work and Study Opportunities (January). Does not want academic treatises. **Buys 50 mss/year.** Submit complete ms. Length: 750-3,000 words. **Pays $50-500 for articles.** Pays expenses of writers on assignment.

FICTION Young adults: drama (one-act and full-length plays). "We prefer unpublished scripts that have been produced at least once." Does not want to see plays that show no understanding of the conventions of the theater. No plays for children, no Christmas or didactic "message" plays. Submit complete ms. Buys 5-9 plays/year. Emerging playwrights have better chances with résumé of credits. Length: 10 minutes to full length. **Pays $100-500 for plays.**

TIPS "Obtain our writer's guidelines and look at recent back issues. The best way to break in is to know our audience—drama students, teachers, and others interested in theater—and write for them. Writers who have some practical experience in theater, especially in technical areas, have an advantage, but we'll work with anybody who has a good idea. Some freelancers have become regular contributors."

💲💲💲 EMMY

Television Academy, 5220 Lankershim Blvd., North Hollywood CA 91601. (818)754-2800. **E-mail:** emmymag@emmys.org. **Website:** www.emmymagazine.com; www.emmys.tv/emmy-magazine. **Contact:** Editor. **90% freelance written. Prefers to work with published/established writers.** Bimonthly magazine on television for TV professionals. "From the executive suite to the editing bay, *emmy* magazine goes behind the scenes of television and digital entertainment to cover the people who make the magic happen. *Emmy*'s core readers include the members of the Television Academy and other television industry professionals. Articles must appeal to the television and digital entertainment professional while being understandable to the enthusiast." Circ. 14,000. Byline given. Pays on publication or within 6 months. Offers 25% kill fee. Publishes ms an average of 4 months after acceptance. Accepts queries by mail. Accepts simultaneous submissions. Responds in 1 month to queries. Sample copy for SAE with 9x12 envelope and 6 first-class stamps. Guidelines online.

NONFICTION "We do not run highly technical articles, nor do we accept academic or fan-magazine approaches." Query with published clips. Length: 1,500-2,000 words. **Pays $1,000-1,200.** Pays expenses of writers on assignment.

COLUMNS Mostly written by regular contributors, but newcomers can break in with filler items with In the Mix or short profiles in Labors of Love. Length: 250-500 words, depending on department. Query with published clips. **Pays $250-500.**

TIPS "Demonstrate experience in covering the business of television and your ability to write in a lively and compelling manner about programming trends and new technology. Identify fascinating people behind the scenes, not just in the executive suites, but in all ranks of the industry."

💲💲 MAKE-UP ARTIST MAGAZINE

12808 NE 95th St., Vancouver WA 98682. (360)882-3488. **E-mail:** heatherw@kpgmedia.com. **Website:** www.makeupmag.com; www.makeup411.com; www.imats.net. **Contact:** Heather Wisner, managing editor. **90% freelance written.** Bimonthly magazine covering all types of professional make-up artistry. Audience is a mixture of high-level make-up artists, make-up students, fashion and movie buffs. Writers should be comfortable with technical writing, and should have substantial knowledge of at least one area of make-up, such as effects or fashion. This is an entertainment-industry magazine, so writing should have an element of fun and storytelling. Good interview skills required. Estab. 1996. Circ. 16,000. Byline given. Pays within

30 days of publication. No kill fee. Editorial lead time 6 weeks. Submit seasonal material 2 months in advance. Accepts queries by e-mail. Accepts simultaneous submissions. Sample copy for $7. Guidelines available via e-mail.

NONFICTION "Does not want fluff pieces about consumer beauty products." **Buys 20+ mss/year.** Query with published clips. Length: 500-3,000 words. **Pays 20-50¢/word.** Pays expenses of writers on assignment.

PHOTOS Send photos. Captions, identification of subjects required. Reviews prints, GIF/JPEG files. Negotiates payment individually. Buys all rights.

COLUMNS Lab Tech, how-to advice for effects artists, written by a current make-up artist working in a lab (700 words + photos); Backstage (behind the scenes info on a theatrical production's make-up (700 words + photos): Out of the Kit, written by make-up artists working on sets (700 words + photos); Industry Buzz (industry news), length varies. Query with published clips. .

TIPS "Read books about professional make-up artistry (see http://makeupmag.com/shop). Read online interviews with make-up artists. Read make-up oriented mainstream magazines, such as *Allure*. Read *Cinefex* and other film-industry publications. Meet and talk to make-up artists and make-up students."

FARM

AGRICULTURAL EQUIPMENT

💲 AG WEEKLY

Lee Agri-Media, P.O. Box 918, Bismarck ND 58501. (701)255-4905. **Fax:** (701)255-2312. **E-mail:** editor@theprairiestar.com. **Website:** www.agweekly.com. **40% freelance written.** *Ag Weekly* is an agricultural publication covering production, markets, regulation, politics. Writers need to be familiar with Idaho agricultural commodities. No printed component; website with 6,000 monthly unique visitors; weekly e-mail newsletter with 3,000 subscribers. Byline given. Pays on publication. Publishes ms an average of 1 month after acceptance. Editorial lead time 1 month. Submit seasonal material 1 month in advance. Accepts queries by e-mail. Accepts simultaneous sub-

missions. Responds in 2 weeks to queries. Responds in 1 month to mss. Sample copy online. Guidelines with #10 SASE.

NONFICTION Needs interview, new product, opinion, travel, ag-related. Does not want anything other than local/regional ag-related articles. No cowboy poetry. **Buys 100 mss/year.** Query. Length: 250-700 words. **Pays $40-70.** Pays expenses of writers on assignment.

PHOTOS State availability. Captions required. Reviews GIF/JPEG files. Offers $10/photo. Buys one-time rights.

CROPS AND SOIL MANAGEMENT

💲💲 AMERICAN/WESTERN GROWER

Meister Media Worldwide, 37733 Euclid Ave., Willoughby OH 44094. (290)573-8740. **E-mail:** deddy@meistermedia.com. **Website:** www.fruitgrower.com. **Contact:** David Eddy, editor. **3% freelance written.** Annual magazines covering commercial fruit growing. "Founded in 1880, *American Fruit Grower* and *Western Fruit Grower* magazines reaches producers, shippers, and other influencers who serve the fresh and processing markets for deciduous fruits, citrus, grapes, berries, and nuts. *Western Fruit Grower* has additional reach to producers and others who work with unique varieties and climate and market conditions in the American West." Estab. 1880. Circ. 44,000. Byline given. Pays on publication. No kill fee. Publishes ms an average of 4 months after acceptance. Editorial lead time 2 months. Submit seasonal material 4 months in advance. Accepts queries by mail, e-mail, fax, phone. Accepts simultaneous submissions. Responds in 2 weeks to queries; in 2 months to mss. Sample copy and writer's guidelines free.

NONFICTION Needs how-to. **Buys 6-10 mss/year.** Send complete ms. Length: 800-1,200 words. **Pays $200-250.** Pays expenses of writers on assignment.

PHOTOS Send photos. Reviews prints, slides. Negotiates payment individually. Buys one-time rights.

TIPS "How-to articles are best."

💲💲 COTTON GROWER MAGAZINE

Meister Media Worldwide, Cotton Media Group, 8000 Centerview Pkwy., Suite 114, Cordova TN 38018-4246. (901)756-8822. **E-mail:** mccue@meistermedia.com. **Website:** www.cotton247.com. **Contact:** Mike McCue, editor. **5% freelance written.** Monthly magazine covering cotton production, cotton markets, and related subjects. Circ. 43,000. Byline given. Pays on acceptance. No kill fee. Publishes ms an average of 2 months after acceptance. Editorial lead time 2 months. Submit seasonal material 2 months in advance. Accepts queries by mail, e-mail, fax, phone. Accepts simultaneous submissions. Sample copy free.

○ Readers are mostly cotton producers who seek information on production practices, equipment, and products related to cotton.

NONFICTION Needs interview, new product, photo feature, technical. No fiction or humorous pieces. **Buys 5-10 mss/year.** Query with published clips. Length: 500-800 words. **Pays $200-400.** Pays expenses of writers on assignment.

PHOTOS State availability. Captions, identification of subjects required. Reviews transparencies. Offers no additional payment for photos accepted with ms. Buys all rights.

💲 FRUIT GROWERS NEWS

Great American Publishing, P.O. Box 128, Sparta MI 49345. (616)887-9008. **Fax:** (616)887-2666. **E-mail:** fgnedit@fruitgrowersnews.com. **Website:** www.fruit-growersnews.com. **Contact:** Matt Milkovich, managing editor; Lee Dean, editorial director. **10% freelance written.** Monthly tabloid covering agriculture. "Our objective is to provide commercial fruit growers of all sizes with information to help them succeed." Estab. 1961. Circ. 16,429. Pays on publication. No kill fee. Publishes ms an average of 2 months after acceptance. Editorial lead time 1-2 months. Submit seasonal material 3 months in advance. Accepts queries by mail, e-mail, fax. Accepts simultaneous submissions. Responds in 2 weeks to queries. Responds in 1 month to mss. Sample copy free.

NONFICTION Needs general interest, interview, new product. No advertorials or other puff pieces. **Buys 25 mss/year.** Query with published clips and résumé. Length: 600-1,000 words. **Pays $150-250.** Pays expenses of writers on assignment.

PHOTOS Send photos. Captions required. Reviews prints. Offers $15/photo. Buys one-time rights.

💲💲 GOOD FRUIT GROWER

Washington State Fruit Commission, 105 S. 18th St., Suite 217, Yakima WA 98901. (509)853-3520. **Fax:**

(509)853-3521. **E-mail:** casey.corr@goodfruit.com. **Website:** www.goodfruit.com. **Contact:** O. Casey Corr, managing editor. **10% freelance written.** Semimonthly magazine covering tree fruit/grape growing. Estab. 1946. Circ. 11,000. Byline given. Pays on acceptance. Publishes ms an average of 2 months after acceptance. Accepts queries by mail, e-mail. Accepts simultaneous submissions. Responds in 1 week to queries; in 1 month to mss. Sample copy free. Guidelines free.

NONFICTION **Buys 20 mss/year.** Query. Length: 500-1,500 words. **Pays 40-50¢/word.** Pays expenses of writers on assignment.

PHOTOS **Contact:** Jim Black. Reviews GIF/JPEG files. Negotiates payment individually. Buys one-time rights.

TIPS "We want well-written, accurate information. We deal with our writers honestly and expect the same in return."

💲 GRAIN JOURNAL

Country Journal Publishing Co., 3065 Pershing Court, Decatur IL 62526. (800)728-7511. **E-mail:** ed@grain-net.com. **Website:** www.grainnet.com. **Contact:** Ed Zdrojewski, editor. **5% freelance written.** Bimonthly magazine covering grain handling and merchandising. *Grain Journal* serves the North American grain industry, from the smallest country grain elevators and feed mills to major export terminals. Estab. 1972. Circ. 12,000. Byline sometimes given. Pays on publication. No kill fee. Publishes ms an average of 2 months after acceptance. Editorial lead time 2 months. Submit seasonal material 2 months in advance. Accepts simultaneous submissions. Sample copy free.

NONFICTION Needs how-to, interview, new product, technical. Query. 750 words maximum. **Pays $100.** Pays expenses of writers on assignment.

PHOTOS Send photos. Captions, identification of subjects required. Reviews contact sheets, negatives, transparencies, 3x5 prints, electronic files. Offers $50-100/photo. Buys one time rights.

TIPS "Call with your idea. We'll let you know if it is suitable for our publication."

💲 THE VEGETABLE GROWERS NEWS

Great American Publishing, P.O. Box 128, Sparta MI 49345. (616)887-9008, ext. 102. **Fax:** (616)887-2666. **E-mail:** vgnedit@vegetablegrowersnews.com. **Website:** www.vegetablegrowersnews.com. **Contact:** Matt

Milkovich, managing editor. **10% freelance written.** Monthly tabloid covering agriculture. Estab. 1970. Circ. 16,000. Pays on publication. No kill fee. Publishes ms an average of 2 months after acceptance. Editorial lead time 1-2 months. Submit seasonal material 3 months in advance. Accepts queries by mail, e-mail, fax. Accepts simultaneous submissions. Responds in 2 weeks to queries. Responds in 1 month to mss. Sample copy free.

◯ "Our objective is to provide commercial vegetable growers of all sizes with information to help them succeed."

NONFICTION Needs general interest, interview, new product. No advertorials, other puff pieces. **Buys 25 mss/year.** Query with published clips and résumé. Length: 800-1,200 words. **Pays $100-125.** Pays expenses of writers on assignment.

PHOTOS Send photos. Captions required. Reviews prints. Offers $15/photo. Buys one-time rights.

LIVESTOCK

💲💲 ANGUS BEEF BULLETIN

Angus Productions, Inc., 3201 Frederick Ave., St. Joseph MO 64506-2997. (816)383-5270. **E-mail:** journal@angusjournal.com; shermel@angusjournal.com. **Website:** www.angusbeefbulletin.com. **Contact:** Shauna Rose Hermel, editor. **45% freelance written.** Tabloid published 5 times/year covering commercial cattle industry. The *Angus Beef Bulletin* is mailed free to commercial cattlemen who have purchased an Angus bull and had the registration transferred to them, and to others who sign a request card. Estab. 1985. Circ. 65,000-70,000. Byline given. Pays on publication. No kill fee. Publishes ms an average of 3 months after acceptance. Editorial lead time 3 months. Submit seasonal material 3 months in advance. Accepts queries by mail, e-mail. Accepts simultaneous submissions. Responds in 3 weeks to queries; in 3 months to mss. Sample copy: $5. Guidelines for #10 SASE.

NONFICTION Needs how-to, interview, technical. **Buys 10 mss/year.** Query with published clips. Length: 800-2,500 words. **Pays $50-600.** Pays expenses of writers on assignment.

PHOTOS Send photos. Identification of subjects required. Reviews 5×7 transparencies, 5×7 glossy prints, and digital images. No alterations permitted. Offers $25/photo. Buys all rights.

TIPS "Read the publication and have a firm grasp of the commercial cattle industry and how the Angus breed fits in that industry."

💲💲💲 ANGUS JOURNAL

Angus Productions, Inc., 3201 Frederick Ave., St. Joseph MO 64506-2997. (816)383-5270. **E-mail:** shermel@angusjournal.com. **Website:** www.angusjournal.com. **40% freelance written.** Monthly magazine covering Angus cattle. *Angus Journal* is the official magazine of the American Angus Association. Its primary function as such is to report to the membership association activities and information pertinent to raising Angus cattle. Estab. 1919. Circ. 13,500. Byline given. Pays on publication. No kill fee. Publishes ms an average of 3 months after acceptance. Editorial lead time 2 months. Submit seasonal material 3 months in advance. Accepts queries by mail, e-mail. Accepts simultaneous submissions. Responds in 3 weeks to queries; in 2 months to mss. Sample copy: $5. Guidelines with #10 SASE.

NONFICTION Needs how-to, interview, technical. **Buys 20-30 mss/year.** Query with published clips. Length: 800-3,500 words. **Pays $50-1,000.** Pays expenses of writers on assignment.

PHOTOS Send photos. Identification of subjects required. Reviews 5×7 glossy prints. Offers $25-400/photo. Buys all rights.

TIPS "Have a firm grasp of the cattle industry."

BACKYARD POULTRY

Swift Communications, Inc., 145 Industrial Dr., Medford WI 54451. (715)785-7979. **Fax:** (715)785-7414. **E-mail:** customerservice@backyardpoultrymag.com. **E-mail:** backyardpoultry@swiftcom.com. **Website:** www.backyardpoultrymag.com. **Contact:** Ryan Slabaugh, editor. Bimonthly magazine covering breed selection, housing, management, health and nutrition, and other topics of interest to promote more and better raising of small-scale poultry. Accepts queries by e-mail. Accepts simultaneous submissions. Responds in 9 months to queries. Guidelines online.

NONFICTION Needs essays, how-to, interview. Query or submit complete ms by e-mail. "We like to plan well ahead on our editions, so writers and photographers are encouraged to submit story ideas and pitches up to a year in advance of actual publication. Stories and pitches should be attached as DOC or TXT files. Length: 800-2,000 words. **Payment negotiable.** Pays expenses of writers on assignment.

$$ BEE CULTURE

P.O. Box 706, Medina OH 44256-0706. (330)725-6677; (800)289-7668. **Fax:** (330)725-5624. **E-mail:** kim@beeculture.com; info@beeculture.com. **Website:** www.beeculture.com. **Contact:** Mr. Kim Flottum, editor. **50% freelance written.** Covers the natural science of honey bees. "Monthly magazine for beekeepers and those interested in the natural science of honey bees, with environmentally-oriented articles relating to honey bees or pollination." Estab. 1873. Pays on publication. No kill fee. Publishes ms an average of 4 months after acceptance. Accepts queries by mail, e-mail, fax, phone. Accepts simultaneous submissions. Responds in 1 month to mss. Sample copy with 9x12 SASE and 5 first-class stamps. Guidelines and Sample copy online.

NONFICTION Needs interview, personal experience, photo feature. No "How I Began Beekeeping" articles. Highly advanced, technical, and scientific abstracts accepted for review for quarterly Refered section. Length: 2,000 words average. **Pays $200-250.** Pays expenses of writers on assignment.

REPRINTS Send photocopy and information about when and where the material previously appeared. Pays about the same as for an original article, on negotiation.

PHOTOS Color prints, 5x7 standard, but 3x5 are OK. Electronic images encouraged. Digital JPEG, color only, at 300 dpi best, prints acceptable. Model release required. Photo captions preferred. Pays $50 for cover photos. Photos payment included with article payment. Buys first rights.

TIPS "Do an interview story on commercial beekeepers who are cooperative enough to furnish accurate, factual information on their operations. Frequent mistakes made by writers in completing articles are that they are too general in nature and lack management knowledge."

$$ THE CATTLEMAN

Texas and Southwestern Cattle Raisers Association, 1301 W. Seventh St., Suite 201, Fort Worth TX 76102. (817)332-7064. **Fax:** (817)332-6441. **E-mail:** ehbrisendine@tscra.org. **Website:** www.thecattlemanmagazine.com. **Contact:** Ellen H. Brisendine, editor. **25% freelance written.** Monthly magazine covering the Texas/Oklahoma beef cattle industry. Specializes in in-depth, management-type articles related to range and pasture, beef cattle production, animal health, nutrition, and marketing. Wants "how-to" articles. Estab. 1914. Circ. 15,000. Byline given. Pays on acceptance. No kill fee. Publishes ms an average of 2 months after acceptance. Editorial lead time 2 months. Submit seasonal material 6 months in advance. Accepts queries by mail, e-mail. Accepts simultaneous submissions. Sample copy free. Guidelines online.

NONFICTION Needs how-to, interview, new product, personal experience, technical, agricultural research. Does not want to see anything not specifically related to beef production in the Southwest. **Buys 20 mss/year.** Query with published clips. Length: 1,500-2,000 words. **Pays $350-500 for assigned articles. Pays $100-350 for unsolicited articles.** Pays expenses of writers on assignment.

PHOTOS Identification of subjects required. Reviews digital files. Offers no additional payment for photos accepted with ms. Buys one-time rights.

TIPS "Subscribers said they were most interested in the following topics, in this order: range/pasture, property rights, animal health, water, new innovations, and marketing. *The Cattleman* prefers to work on an assignment basis. However, prospective contributors are urged to write the managing editor of the magazine to inquire of interest on a proposed subject. Occasionally, the editor will return a ms to a potential contributor for cutting, polishing, checking, rewriting, or condensing. Be able to demonstrate background/knowledge in this field. Include tearsheets from similar magazines."

$$ FEED LOT MAGAZINE

Feed Lot Magazine, Inc., P.O. Box 850, Dighton KS 67839. (620)397-2838. **Fax:** (620)397-2839. **E-mail:** feedlot@st-tel.net. **Website:** www.feedlotmagazine.com. Annita Lorimor. **80% freelance written.** Published 8 times/year. Magazine provides readers with the most up-to-date information on the beef industry in concise, easy-to-read articles designed to increase overall awareness among the feedlot community. "The editorial information content fits a dual role: large feedlots and their related cow/calf operations, and large 500+ cow/calf, 100+ stocker operations. The information covers all phases of production from breeding, genetics, animal health, nutrition, equipment design, research through finishing fat cattle. *Feed Lot* publishes a mix of new information and timely articles which directly affect the cattle industry." Estab. 1992. Circ. 12,000. Byline given. Pays on publication. Offers 50% kill fee. Publishes ms an average of 2 months after acceptance. Editorial lead time 2 months. Submit seasonal material 6 months in advance. Accepts queries by mail, e-mail, fax. Accepts simultaneous submissions. Responds in 1 month to queries. Sample copy and writer's guidelines by e-mail.

NONFICTION Needs interview, new product, photo feature. Send complete ms; original material only. Length: 100-700 words. **Pays 30¢/word.** Pays expenses of writers on assignment.

PHOTOS State availability or send photos. Captions, model releases required. Reviews contact sheets. Negotiates payment individually. Buys all rights.

TIPS "Know what you are writing about—have a good knowledge of the subject."

MANAGEMENT

⊙ AG JOURNAL

Gatehouse Media, Inc., 422 Colorado Ave., (P.O. Box 500), La Junta CO 81050. (719)384-1453. **E-mail:** publisher@ljtdmail.com; bcd@ljtdmail.com. **Website:** www.agjournalonline.com. **Contact:** Candi Hill, publisher/editor; Jennifer Justice, assistant editor. **20% freelance written.** Weekly journal covering agriculture. Estab. 1949. Circ. 11,000. Byline given. Pays on publication. No kill fee. Publishes ms an average of 2 weeks after acceptance. Editorial lead time 1 month. Submit seasonal material 1 month in advance. Accepts queries by e-mail. Accepts simultaneous submissions. Responds in 2 weeks to queries. Sample copy and writer's guidelines free.

○ The *Ag Journal* covers people, issues, and events relevant to agriculture producers in a seven-state region (Colorado, Kansas, Oklahoma, Texas, Wyoming, Nebraska, New Mexico).

NONFICTION Needs how-to, interview, new product, opinion, photo feature, technical. Query by e-mail only. **Pays 4¢/word.** Pays expenses of writers on assignment.

PHOTOS State availability. Captions, identification of subjects required. Offers $8/photo. Buys one-time rights.

SMALL FARM TODAY

Missouri Farm Publishing, Inc., Ridge Top Ranch, 3903 W. Ridge Trail Rd., Clark MO 65243-9525. (573)687-3525. **E-mail:** smallfarm@socket.net. **Website:** www.smallfarmtoday.com. Bimonthly magazine

for small farmers and small-acreage landowners interested in diversification, direct marketing, alternative crops, horses, draft animals, small livestock, exotic and minor breeds, home-based businesses, gardening, vegetable and small fruit crops. Estab. 1984 as *Missouri Farm Magazine.* Circ. 12,000. Byline given. Pays 60 days after publication. No kill fee. Publishes ms an average of 6 months to 1 year after acceptance. Submit seasonal material 4 months in advance. Accepts queries by mail, e-mail. Accepts simultaneous submissions. Responds in 3 months to queries. Sample copy for $3. Guidelines online.

NONFICTION Special issues: Poultry (January); Wool & Fiber (March); Aquaculture (July); Equipment (November). Query letters recommended. Length: 1,400-2,600 words. **Pays 3.5¢/word.** Pays expenses of writers on assignment.

REPRINTS Send tearsheet, photocopy or typed ms with rights for sale noted and information about when and where the material previously appeared. Pays 2¢/word of original article.

PHOTOS Send photos. Captions required. Offers $6 for inside photos and $10 for cover photos. Pays $4 for negatives or slides. Buys one-time and nonexclusive reprint rights (for anthologies).

TIPS "We need 'how-to' articles (how to grow, raise, market, build, etc.), as well as articles about small farmers who are experiencing success through diversification, specialty/alternative crops and livestock, and direct marketing. *Small Farm Today* is especially interested in articles that explain how to do something from start to finish citing specific examples involved in the process or operation being discussed. It is important to include data on production costs, budgets, potential profits, etc."

◐⊙ SMALLHOLDER MAGAZINE

Newsquest Media Group, 3 Falmouth Business Park, Bickland Water Rd., Falmouth Cornwall TR11 4SZ United Kingdom. (01)326-213338. **Fax:** (01)326-212084. **E-mail:** elizabeth.perry@packetseries.co.uk. **Website:** www.smallholder.co.uk. **Contact:** Elizabeth Perry, editor. *Smallholder* magazine is the leading monthly publication for the small producer and self-reliant household and has a publishing history spanning more than 100 years. The magazine has a reputation for quality and informed editorial content, and back issues are highly collectable. It is available nationally, through newsagent sales, specialist retail outlets and by subscription. No kill fee. Accepts queries by e-mail. Accepts simultaneous submissions. Sample copy online. Guidelines by e-mail.

O "Copy is required at least 2 months before publication, e.g. 1st April for June. News items may be accepted up until one month before publication. The editor's decision on copy is final and, although every effort will be made to return mss and photos, no responsibility can be accepted."

NONFICTION Length: 700-1,400 words. **Pays 4£/word.** Pays expenses of writers on assignment.

PHOTOS Send photos. Reviews 300 dpi digital images. Pays £5-50.

MISCELLANEOUS FARM

⑨⑨ ACRES U.S.A.

P.O. Box 301209, Austin TX 78703. (512)892-4400. **Fax:** (512)892-4448. **E-mail:** editor@acresusa.com. **Website:** www.acresusa.com. **Contact:** Tara Maxwell. "Monthly trade journal written by people who have a sincere interest in the principles of organic and sustainable agriculture." Estab. 1970. Circ. 20,000. Byline given. Pays on publication. No kill fee. Editorial lead time 3 months. Submit seasonal material 6 months in advance. Accepts queries by mail, e-mail. Accepts simultaneous submissions. Sample copy and writer's guidelines free.

NONFICTION Needs expose, how-to, interview, new product, personal experience, photo feature, profile, technical. Special issues: Seeds (January), Poultry (March), Permaculture (May), Livestock (June), Homesteading (August), Soil Fertility & Testing (October). Does not want poetry, fillers, product profiles, or anything with an overly promotional tone. **Buys about 50 mss/year.** Send complete ms. Length: 500-3,000 words. **Pays 10¢/word** Pays expenses of writers on assignment.

PHOTOS State availability of or send photos. Captions, identification of subjects required. Reviews JPEG/TIF files. Negotiates payment individually. Buys one-time rights.

REGIONAL FARM

⑨⑨ AMERICAN AGRICULTURIST

5227 B Baltimore Pike, Littlestown PA 17340. (717)359-0150. **Fax:** (717)359-0250. **E-mail:** john.vo-gel@penton.com. **Website:** www.farmprogress.com. **Contact:** John Vogel, editor. **20% freelance written.** Monthly magazine covering cutting-edge technology and news to help farmers improve their operations. Publishes cutting-edge technology with ready on-farm application. Estab. 1842. Circ. 32,000. Pays on publication. No kill fee. Publishes ms an average of 3 months after acceptance. Editorial lead time 3 months. Submit seasonal material 3 months in advance. Accepts queries by e-mail, fax. Responds in 2 weeks to queries; in 1 month to mss. Guidelines for #10 SASE.

NONFICTION Needs how-to, humor, inspirational, interview, new product, technical. No stories without a strong tie to Mid-Atlantic farming. **Buys 20 mss/year.** Query. Length: 500-1,000 words. **Pays $250-500.** Pays expenses of writers on assignment.

PHOTOS Send photos. Captions, identification of subjects, model releases required. Reviews transparencies, JPEG files. Offers $75-200/photo. Buys one-time rights.

COLUMNS Country Air (humor, nostalgia, inspirational), 300-400 words. **Buys 12 mss/year.** Send complete ms. **Pays $100.**

⑨ THE LAND

Free Press Co., P.O. Box 3169, Mankato MN 56002-3169. (507)345-4523. **E-mail:** editor@thelandonline. com. **Website:** www.thelandonline.com. **40% freelance written.** Weekly tabloid covering farming and rural life in Minnesota and Northern Iowa. "Although we're not tightly focused on any one type of farming, our articles must be of interest to farmers. In other words, will your article topic have an impact on people who live and work in rural areas?" Prefers to work with Minnesota or Iowa writers. Estab. 1976. Circ. 33,000. Byline given. Pays on acceptance. No kill fee. Publishes ms an average of 2 months after acceptance. Editorial lead time 2 months. Submit seasonal material 2 months in advance. Accepts queries by mail, e-mail. Accepts simultaneous submissions. Responds in 3 weeks to queries; in 2 months to mss. Sample copy free. Guidelines with #10 SASE.

NONFICTION Needs general interest, how-to. **Buys 80 mss/year.** Query. Length: 500-750 words. **Pays $50-70 for assigned articles.** Pays expenses of writers on assignment.

PHOTOS Send photos. Reviews contact sheets. Negotiates payment individually. Buys one-time rights.

COLUMNS Query. **Pays $10-50.**

TIPS "Be enthused about rural Minnesota and Iowa life and agriculture, and be willing to work with our editors. We try to stress relevance. When sending me a query, convince me the story belongs in a Minnesota farm publication."

💲💲 MAINE ORGANIC FARMER & GARDENER

Maine Organic Farmers & Gardeners Association, 662 Slab City Rd., Lincolnville ME 04849. (207)763-3043. **E-mail:** jenglish@tidewater.ne. **Website:** www.mofga.org. **40% freelance written. Prefers to work with published/established local writers.** Quarterly newspaper. "The *MOF&G* promotes and encourages sustainable agriculture and environmentally sound living. Our primary focus is organic farming, gardening, and forestry, but we also deal with local, national, and international agriculture, food, and environmental issues." Estab. 1976. Circ. 10,000. Byline and bio offered. Pays on publication. No kill fee. Publishes ms an average of 8 months after acceptance. Submit seasonal material 1 year in advance. Accepts queries by mail, e-mail. Accepts simultaneous submissions. Responds in 2 months to queries. Sample copy for $2 and SAE with 7 first-class stamps; from MOFGA, P.O. Box 170, Unity ME 04988. Guidelines available at www.mofga.org.

NONFICTION Buys 30 mss/year. Send complete ms. Length: 250-3,000 words. **Pays $25-300.** Pays expenses of writers on assignment.

REPRINTS E-mail manuscript with rights for sale noted and information about when and where the material previously appeared. Pays 50% of amount paid for an original article.

PHOTOS State availability of photos with query. Captions, identification of subjects, model releases required. Buys one time rights. We rarely buy photos without an accompanying article.

TIPS "We are a nonprofit organization. Our publication's primary mission is to inform and educate, but we also want readers to enjoy the articles. Most of our articles are written by our staff or by freelancers who have been associated with the publication for several years."

FINANCE

💲💲💲💲 ADVISOR TODAY

NAIFA, 2901 Telestar Court, Falls Church VA 22042. (703)770-8204. **E-mail:** amseka@naifa.org. **Website:** www.advisortoday.com. **Contact:** Ayo Mseka, editor in chief. **25% freelance written.** Monthly magazine covering life insurance and financial planning. "*Advisor Today* has the largest circulation among insurance and financial planning advising magazines. Founded in 1906 as *Life Association News, Advisor Today* is the official publication of the National Association of Insurance and Financial Advisors. Our mission is to provide practical information, sales ideas, resources, and business strategies to help insurance and financial advisors succeed." Estab. 1906. Circ. 110,000. Pays on acceptance or publication (by mutual agreement with editor). No kill fee. Publishes ms an average of 3 months after acceptance. Editorial lead time: 3 months. Submit seasonal material 6 months in advance. Accepts queries by mail, e-mail, fax, phone. Accepts simultaneous submissions. Sample copy free. Guidelines available online at www.advisortoday.com/about/contribute.cfm.

NONFICTION Buys 8 mss/year. "We prefer e-mail submissions in Microsoft Word format. For other formats and submission methods, please query first. For all articles and queries, contact Ayo Mseka. Web articles should cover the same subject matter covered in the magazine. The articles can be between 300-800 words and should be submitted to Ayo Mseka." Length: 2,300 words for cover articles; 1,000 words for feature articles; 650-700 words for columns and speciality articles; 300-800 words for Web articles. **Pays $800-2,000.** Pays expenses of writers on assignment.

🌐💲💲💲 ADVISOR'S EDGE

Rogers Media, Inc., 333 Bloor St. E., 6th Floor, Toronto ON M4W 1G6 Canada. **E-mail:** melissa.shin@rci.rogers.com. **Website:** www.advisor.ca. **Contact:** Melissa Shin, deputy editor. Monthly magazine covering the financial industry (financial advisors and investment advisors). *Advisor's Edge* focuses on sales and marketing opportunities for the financial advisor (how they can build their business and improve relationships with clients). Estab. 1998. Circ. 36,000. Byline given. Pays on publication. Offers 25% kill fee. Publishes ms an average of 3 months after acceptance. Editorial lead time 3 months. Accepts queries by e-mail. Accepts simultaneous submissions. Sample copy online.

NONFICTION Needs how-to, interview. No articles that aren't relevant to how a financial advisor does his/her job. **Buys 12 mss/year.** Query with published clips.

Length: 1,500-2,000 words. **Pays $900 (Canadian).** Pays expenses of writers on assignment.

☯☉☉☉☉ AFP EXCHANGE

Association for Financial Professionals, 4520 East West Hwy., Suite 750, Bethesda MD 20814. (301)907-2862. **E-mail:** exchange@afponline.org. **Website:** www.afponline.org/exchange. **20% freelance written.** Monthly magazine covering corporate treasury, corporate finance, B2B payments issues, corporate risk management, accounting, and regulatory issues from the perspective of corporations. Welcomes interviews with CFOs and senior-level practitioners. Best practices and practical information for corporate CFOs and treasurers. Tone is professional, intended to appeal to financial professionals on the job. Most accepted articles are written by professional journalists and editors, many featuring high-level AFP members in profile and case studies. Estab. 1979. Circ. 25,000. Byline given. Pays on publication. Offers kill fee. Pays negotiable kill fee in advance. Editorial lead time 2 months. Submit seasonal material 3 months in advance. Accepts queries by e-mail. Accepts simultaneous submissions. Responds in 1 week to queries; in 1 month to mss.

NONFICTION Needs book excerpts, how-to, interview, personal experience, technical. No PR-type articles pointing to any type of product or solution. **Buys 3-4 mss/year.** Query. Length: 1,100-1,800 words. **Pays 75¢-$1/word for assigned articles.** Pays expenses of writers on assignment.

COLUMNS Cash Flow Forecasting (practical tips for treasurers, CFOs); Financial Reporting (insight, practical tips); Risk Management (practical tips for treasurers, CFOs); Corporate Payments (practical tips for treasurers), all 1,000-1,300 words. Professional Development (success stories, career related, about high-level financial professionals), 1,100 words. **Buys 10 mss/year.** Query. **Pays $75¢-$1/word.**

FILLERS Needs anecdotes. Length: 400-700 words. **Pays 75¢/word.**

TIPS "Accepted submissions deal with high-level issues relevant to today's corporate CFO or treasurer, including issues of global trade, global finance, accounting, M&A, risk management, corporate cash management, international regulatory issues, communications issues with corporate boards and shareholders, and especially new issues on the horizon. Preference given to articles by or about corporate

practitioners in the finance function of mid- to large-size corporations in the U.S. or abroad. We also purchase articles by accomplished financial writers. We cannot accept content that points to any product, 'solution,' or that promotes any vendor. We should not be considered a PR outlet. Authors may be required to sign agreement."

☉ THE AUSTRALIAN ECONOMIC REVIEW

Melbourne Institute of Applied Economic and Social Research, The University of Melbourne, Melbourne VIC 3010 Australia. **E-mail:** aer@melbourneinstitute.com. **Website:** www.melbourneinstitute.com. **Contact:** Professor Ross Williams, editor. Quarterly magazine applying economic analysis to a wide range of macroeconomic and microeconomic topics relevant to both economic and social policy issues. Accepts simultaneous submissions. Guidelines online.

NONFICTION Needs essays. Send complete ms. Pays expenses of writers on assignment.

BAI BANKING STRATEGIES ONLINE

Bank Administration Institute (BAI), 115 S. LaSalle St., Suite 3300, Chicago IL 60606. (770)394-8615. **E-mail:** kcline@bai.org. **Website:** www.bai.org/bankingstrategies. **Contact:** Kenneth Cline, managing editor. **70% freelance written.** Online magazine covering banking from a strategic and managerial perspective for its senior financial executive audience. Each issue includes in-depth trend articles and interviews with influential executives. Accepts queries by e-mail. Accepts simultaneous submissions. Responds almost immediately. Guidelines online.

NONFICTION Needs how-to, interview. "No topic queries; we assign stories to freelancers. I'm looking for qualifications as opposed to topic queries. I need experienced writers/reporters." **Buys 30 mss/year.** Query by e-mail with one-page synopsis. Length: 600-2,000 words **Does not pay.** Pays expenses of writers on assignment.

TIPS "Demonstrate ability and financial services expertise. I'm looking for freelancers who can write according to our standards, which are quite high."

☉☉☉ CREDIT TODAY

P.O. Box 20091, Roanoke VA 24018. (540)343-7500. **E-mail:** robl@credittoday.net; editor@credittoday.net. **Website:** www.credittoday.net. **Contact:** Rob Lawson, publisher. **10% freelance written.** Web-based publication covering business or trade credit. Estab. 1997.

No byline given. Pays on acceptance. Publishes ms an average of 1 week after acceptance. Editorial lead time 1-2 months. Accepts queries by e-mail. Sample copy free. Guidelines free.

NONFICTION Needs how-to, interview, technical. Does not want "puff" pieces promoting a particular product or vendor. **Buys 20 mss/year.** Send complete ms. Length: 700-1,800 words. **Pays $200-1,400.** Pays expenses of writers on assignment.

TIPS "Make pieces actionable, personable, and a quick read."

PALMETTO BANKER

South Carolina Bankers Association, P.O. Box 1483, Columbia SC 29202. (803)779-0850. **Fax:** (803)256-8150. **Website:** www.scbankers.org. **Contact:** R. Kevin Dietrich, editor. **15% freelance written.** Quarterly magazine covering Banking in South Carolina, trends & industry. We focus only on banking trends, regulations, laws, news, economic development of SC, technology and education of bankers. Estab. 1967. Circ. 1,600. Byline given. No kill fee. Publishes ms an average of 6 months after acceptance. Editorial lead time 6 months. Submit seasonal material 3 months in advance. Accepts queries by mail, fax. Accepts simultaneous submissions. Sample copy online.

NONFICTION Needs technical. Does not want anything that does not pertain to banking trends, operations or technology. Anything that smacks of product sales. Send complete ms. Length: 600-1,500 words. Pays expenses of writers on assignment.

PHOTOS Send photos. Model releases required. Reviews GIF/JPEG files. Offers no additional payment for photos accepted with ms.

TIPS Recommendations/referrals from other state banking/national banking associations are helpful.

FLORISTS, NURSERIES & LANDSCAPERS

💲💲 DIGGER

Oregon Association of Nurseries, 29751 SW Town Center Loop W., Wilsonville OR 97070. (503)682-5089. **Fax:** (503)682-5099. **E-mail:** ckipp@oan.org; info@oan.org. **Website:** www.diggermagazine.com. **Contact:** Curt Kipp, editor. **50% freelance written.** Monthly magazine covering the nursery and greenhouse industry. *Digger* is a monthly magazine that

focuses on industry trends, regulations, research, marketing, and membership activities. In August the magazine becomes *Digger Farwest Edition*, with all the features of *Digger* plus a complete guide to the annual Farwest Show, one of North America's top-attended nursery industry trade shows. Circ. 8,000. Byline given. Pays on receipt of copy. Offers 100% kill fee. Publishes ms an average of 2 months after acceptance. Editorial lead time 6 weeks. Submit seasonal material 2 months in advance. Accepts queries by mail, e-mail, fax, phone. Accepts simultaneous submissions. Sample copy and writer's guidelines free.

NONFICTION Needs general interest, how-to, interview, personal experience, technical. Special issues: Farwest Edition (August): "This is a triple-size issue that runs in tandem with our annual trade show (14,500 circulation for this issue)." No articles not related or pertinent to nursery and greenhouse industry. **Buys 20-30 mss/year.** Query. Length: 800-2,000 words. **Pays $125-400 for assigned articles. Pays $100-300 for unsolicited articles.** Pays expenses of writers on assignment.

PHOTOS State availability. Captions, identification of subjects required. Reviews high-res digital images sent by e-mail or on CD. Offers $25-150/photo. Buys one-time rights, which includes Web posting.

TIPS "Our best freelancers are familiar with or have experience in the horticultural industry. Some 'green' knowledge is a definite advantage. Our readers are mainly nursery and greenhouse operators and owners who propagate nursery stock/crops, so we write with them in mind."

💲💲💲 EROSION CONTROL

Forester Media Inc., P.O. Box 3100, Santa Barbara CA 93130. (805)679-7629. **E-mail:** asantiago@forester.net. **Website:** www.erosioncontrol.com. **Contact:** Arturo Santiago. **60% freelance written.** Magazine published 7 times/year covering all aspects of erosion prevention and sediment control. *Erosion Control* is a practical, hands-on, how-to professional journal. Readers are civil engineers, landscape architects, builders, developers, public works officials, road and highway construction officials and engineers, soils specialists, farmers, landscape contractors, and others involved with any activity that disturbs significant areas of surface vegetation. Estab. 1994. Circ. 23,000. Byline given. Pays 1 month after acceptance. No kill fee. Publishes ms an average of 3 months after acceptance. Editorial lead time 4 months. Submit seasonal material 4 months in advance. Accepts queries by e-mail, phone. Responds in 3 weeks to queries. Sample copy and writer's guidelines free.

NONFICTION Needs photo feature, technical. **Buys 15 mss/year.** Query with published clips. Length: 2,000-4,000 words. **Pays $700-850.** Pays expenses of writers on assignment.

PHOTOS Send photos. Captions, identification of subjects, model releases required. Reviews transparencies, prints. Offers no additional payment for photos accepted with ms. Buys all rights.

TIPS "Writers should have a good grasp of technology involved and good writing and communication skills. Most of our freelance articles include extensive interviews with engineers, contractors, developers, or project owners, and we often provide contact names for articles we assign."

$$ TREE CARE INDUSTRY MAGAZINE

Tree Care Industry Association, 136 Harvey Rd., Suite 101, Londonderry NH 03053. (800)733-2622 or (603)314-5380. **Fax:** (603)314-5386. **E-mail:** editor@tcia.org. **Website:** www.tcia.org. **Contact:** Don Staruk, editor. **50% freelance written.** Monthly magazine covering tree care and landscape maintenance. Estab. 1990. Circ. 24,000. Byline given. Pays within 1 month of publication. No kill fee. Publishes ms an average of 3 months after acceptance. Editorial lead time 10 weeks. Submit seasonal material 3 months in advance. Accepts queries by e-mail. Accepts simultaneous submissions. Responds within 2 days to queries; 2 months to mss. Sample copies online. Guidelines free.

NONFICTION Needs book excerpts, historical, interview, new product, technical. **Buys 60 mss/year.** Query with published clips. Length: 900-3,500 words. **Pays negotiable rate.**

PHOTOS Send photos with submission by e-mail or FTP site. Captions, identification of subjects required. Reviews prints. Negotiates payment individually. Buys one-time and online rights.

COLUMNS Buys 40 mss/year. Send complete ms. **Pays $100 and up.**

TIPS "Preference is given to writers with background and knowledge of the tree care industry; our focus is relatively narrow."

GOVERNMENT & PUBLIC SERVICE

$$ AMERICAN CITY & COUNTY

Penton Media, 6151 Powers Ferry Rd. NW, Suite 200, Atlanta GA 30339. (770)618-0401. **E-mail:** bill.wolpin@penton.com; derek.prall@penton.com. **Website:** www.americancityandcounty.com. **Contact:** Bill Wolpin, editorial director; Derek Prall, managing editor. **40% freelance written.** Monthly magazine covering local and state government in the U.S. Estab. 1909. Circ. 65,000. Byline given. Pays on publication. Offers 25% kill fee. Publishes ms an average of 2 months after acceptance. Editorial lead time 3 months. Accepts queries by e-mail. Accepts simultaneous submissions. Sample copy online. Guidelines by e-mail.

💬 *American City & County* is received by elected and appointed local and state government officials and public and private engineers. Included in the circulation list are administrators, supervisors, and department heads of municipal, county, township, state, and special district governments. The magazine maintains its leadership position by providing these readers with news, government trends, policy alternatives, and operational solutions.

NONFICTION Needs new product, local and state government news analysis. **Buys 36 mss/year.** Query. Length: 600-2,000 words. **Pays 30¢/published word.** Pays expenses of writers on assignment.

PHOTOS State availability. Captions required. Reviews GIF/JPEG files. Negotiates payment individually. Buys all rights.

COLUMNS Issues & Trends (local and state government news analysis), 500-700 words. **Buys 24 mss/year.** Query. **Pays $150-250.**

TIPS "We use only third-person articles. We do not tell the reader what to do; we offer the facts and assume the reader will make his or her own informed decision. We cover city and county government and state highway departments. We do not cover state legislatures or the federal government, except as they affect local government."

🍁 BLUE LINE MAGAZINE

12A-4981 Hwy. 7 E., Suite 254, Markham ON L3R 1N1 Canada. (905)640-3048. **Fax:** (905)640-7547. **E-mail:** blueline@blueline.ca. **Website:** www.blueline.

ca. Monthly magazine keeping readers on the leading edge of law enforcement information, whether it be case law, training issues or technology trends. Estab. 1989. Circ. 12,000. Accepts simultaneous submissions.

NONFICTION Needs general interest, how-to, interview, new product. Query. Pays expenses of writers on assignment.

EVIDENCE TECHNOLOGY MAGAZINE

Wordsmith Publishing, P.O. Box 555, Kearney MO 64060. **E-mail:** kmayo@evidencemagazine.com. **Website:** www.evidencemagazine.com. **Contact:** Kristi Mayo, editor. Bimonthly magazine providing news and information relating to the collection, processing, and preservation of evidence. This is a business-to-business publication, not a peer reviewed journal. Looks for mainstream pieces. Readers want general crime scenes and forensic science articles. Estab. 2003. Circ. 10,000. Byline given. Accepts queries by e-mail. Sample copy online. Guidelines online.

NONFICTION Needs general interest, how-to, interview, new product, technical. Query. **Pays 2 contributor copies.**

PHOTOS Provide photos and/or illustrations. Reviews JPEG files (300 dpi or larger).

TIPS "Opening a dialogue with the editor will give you the opportunity to get guidelines on length, style, and deadlines."

🌐💲 FIRE CHIEF

Primedia Business, 330 N. Wabash Ave., Suite 2300, Chicago IL 60611. (312)595-1080. **Fax:** (312)595-0295. **E-mail:** lisa@firechief.com; sundee@firechief.com. **Website:** www.firechief.com. **Contact:** Lisa Allegretti, editor; Sundee Koffarnus; art director. **60% freelance written.** Monthly magazine covering the fire chief occupation. "*Fire Chief* is the management magazine of the fire service, addressing the administrative, personnel, training, prevention/education, professional development, and operational issues faced by chiefs and other fire officers, whether in paid, volunteer, or combination departments. We're potentially interested in any article that can help them do their jobs better, whether that's as incident commanders, financial managers, supervisors, leaders, trainers, planners, or ambassadors to municipal officials or the public." Estab. 1956. Circ. 53,000. Byline given. Pays on publication. Offers kill fee. Kill fee negotiable. Publishes ms an average of 6 months after acceptance. Editorial lead time 2 months. Submit seasonal material 4 months in advance. Accepts queries by mail, e-mail, fax. Responds in 1 month to queries. Responds in 2 months to mss. Sample copy and submission guidelines free.

NONFICTION Needs how-to, technical. "We do not publish fiction, poetry, or historical articles. We also aren't interested in straightforward accounts of fires or other incidents, unless there are one or more specific lessons to be drawn from a particular incident, especially lessons that are applicable to a large number of departments." **Buys 50-60 mss/year.** Query first with published clips. Length: 1,000-10,000 words. **Pays $50-400.** Pays expenses of writers on assignment.

PHOTOS State availability. Captions, identification of subjects required. Reviews transparencies, prints. Buys one-time or reprint rights.

COLUMNS Training Perspectives; EMS Viewpoints; Sound Off; Volunteer Voice; all 1,000-1,800 words.

TIPS "Writers who are unfamiliar with the fire service are very unlikely to place anything with us. Many pieces that we reject are either too unfocused or too abstract. We want articles that help keep fire chiefs well informed and effective at their jobs."

FIRE ENGINEERING

PennWell Corporation, 21-00 Rt. 208 S., Fair Lawn NJ 07410-2602. (973)251-5054. **E-mail:** dianer@pennwell.com. **Website:** www.fireengineering.com. **Contact:** Diane Rothschild, executive editor. Monthly magazine covering issues of importance to firefighters. Estab. 1877. Accepts queries by mail, e-mail. Responds in 2-3 months to mss. Guidelines online.

NONFICTION Needs how-to, incident reports, training. Send complete ms. Pays expenses of writers on assignment.

PHOTOS Reviews electronic format only: JPEG/TIFF/EPS files (300 dpi).

COLUMNS Volunteers Corner; Training Notebook; Rescue Company; The Engine Company; The Truck Company; Fire Prevention Bureau; Apparatus; The Shops; Fire Service EMS; Fire Service Court; Speaking of Safety; Fire Commentary; Technology Today; and Innovations: Homegrown. Send complete ms.

FIRERESCUE

4180 La Jolla Village Dr., Suite 260, La Jolla CA 92037. (800)266-5367. **E-mail:** frm.editor@pennwell.com.

Website: www.firefighternation.com. **Contact:** Editor. "FireRescue covers the fire and rescue markets. Our 'Read It Today, Use It Tomorrow' mission weaves through every article and image we publish. Our readers consist of fire chiefs, company officers, training officers, firefighters, and technical rescue personnel." Estab. 1997. Circ. 50,000. Pays on publication. Accepts queries by mail, e-mail. Responds in 1 month to mss. Guidelines online.

NONFICTION Needs general interest, how-to, interview, new product, technical. "All story ideas must be submitted with a cover letter that outlines your qualifications and includes your name, full address, phone, and e-mail address. We accept story submissions in 1 of the following 2 formats: query letters and mss." Length: 800-2,200 words. **Pays $100—$200 for features.** Pays expenses of writers on assignment.

PHOTOS Looks for "photographs that show firefighters in action, using proper techniques and wearing the proper equipment. Submit timely photographs that show the technical aspects of firefighting and rescue. ". Digital images in JPEG, TIFF, or EPS format at 72 dpi for initial review. We require 300 dpi resolution for publication. If you send images as attachments via e-mail, compress your files first.

TIPS "Read back issues of the magazine to learn our style. Research back issues to ensure we haven't covered your topic within the past three years. Read and follow the instructions on our guidelines page."

💲💲 PLANNING

American Planning Association, 205 N. Michigan Ave., Suite 1200, Chicago IL 60601. (312)431-9100. **Fax:** (312)786-6700. **E-mail:** slewis@planning.org; mstromberg@planning.org. **Website:** www.planning.org. **Contact:** Sylvia Lewis, editor; Joan Cairney, art director; Meghan Stromberg, executive editor. **30% freelance written.** Monthly magazine emphasizing urban planning for adult, college-educated readers who are regional and urban planners in city, state, or federal agencies or in private business, or university faculty or students. Estab. 1972. Circ. 44,000. Byline given. Pays on publication. No kill fee. Publishes ms an average of 2 months after acceptance. Accepts queries by mail, e-mail. Accepts simultaneous submissions. Responds in 5 weeks to queries. Guidelines online.

NONFICTION Special issues: Transportation issue. Also needs news stories up to 500 words. **Buys 44 features and 33 news stories mss/year.** Length: 500-3,000 words. **Pays $150-1,500.** Pays expenses of writers on assignment.

PHOTOS "We prefer authors supply their own photos, but we sometimes take our own or arrange for them in other ways." State availability. Captions required. Pays $100 minimum for photos used on inside pages and $300 for cover photos. Buys one-time rights.

💲💲 POLICE AND SECURITY NEWS

DAYS Communications, Inc., 1208 Juniper St., Quakertown PA 18951-1520. (215)538-1240. **Fax:** (215)538-1208. **E-mail:** dyaw@policeandsecuritynews.com. **Website:** www.policeandsecuritynews.com. **Contact:** David Yaw, publisher. **40% freelance written.** Bimonthly periodical on public law enforcement and Homeland Security. "Our publication is designed to provide educational and entertaining information directed toward management level. Technical information written for the expert in a manner the nonexpert can understand." Estab. 1984. Circ. 24,000. Byline given. Pays on publication. No kill fee. Publishes ms an average of 2 months after acceptance. Accepts queries by mail, e-mail, fax, phone, online submission form. Accepts simultaneous submissions. Sample copy and writer's guidelines with 10x13 SASE with $2.53 postage.

NONFICTION Contact: Al Menear, articles editor. Needs historical, how-to, humor, interview, opinion, personal experience, photo feature, technical. **Buys 12 mss/year.** Query. Length: 200-2,500 words. **Pays 10¢/word. Sometimes pays in trade-out of services.** Pays expenses of writers on assignment.

REPRINTS Send tearsheet, photocopy or typed ms with rights for sale noted and information about when and where the material previously appeared.

PHOTOS State availability. Reviews 3x5 prints. Offers $10-50/photo. Buys one-time rights.

FILLERS Needs facts, newsbreaks, short humor. **Buys 6 mss/year.** Length: 200-2,000 words. **10¢/word.**

💲💲💲💲 YOUTH TODAY

Kennesaw State University, 1000 Chastain Rd., MD 2212, Bldg. 22, Kennesaw GA 30144. (678)797-2899. **E-mail:** jfleming@youthtoday.org. **Website:** www.youthtoday.org. **Contact:** John Fleming, editor. **50% freelance written.** Bi-monthly newspaper covering businesses that provide services to youth. Audience is people who run youth programs—mostly nonprofits and government agencies—who want help in providing services and getting funding. Estab. 1994. Circ. 9,000. Byline given. Pays on publication. Offers $200 kill fee for features. Editorial lead time 2 months. Accepts queries by mail. Accepts simultaneous submissions. Responds in 2 weeks to queries. Responds in 1 month to mss. Sample copy for $5. Guidelines available on website.

○ "Our freelance writers work for or have worked for daily newspapers, or have extensive experience writing for newspapers and magazines."

NONFICTION Needs general interest, technical. "No feel-good stories about do-gooders. We examine the business of youth work." **Buys 5 mss/year.** Query. Send rèsumè, short cover letter, clips. Length: 600-2,500 words. **Pays $150-2,000 for assigned articles.** Pays expenses of writers on assignment.

PHOTOS Identification of subjects required. Offers no additional payment for photos accepted with ms. Buys one-time and Internet rights.

COLUMNS "*Youth Today* also publishes 750-word guest columns, called Viewpoints. These pieces can be based on the writer's own experiences or based on research, but they must deal with an issue of interest to our readership and must soundly argue an opinion, or advocate for a change in thinking or action within the youth field."

TIPS "Business writers have the best shot. Focus on evaluations of programs, or why a program succeeds or fails. Please visit online."

GROCERIES & FOOD PRODUCTS

○○○ WESTERN GROCER MAGAZINE

Mercury Publications Ltd., 1313 Border Ave., Unit 16, Winnipeg MB R3H 0X4 Canada. (204)954-2085, ext. 219; (800)337-6372. **Fax:** (204)954-2057. **E-mail:** rbradley@mercurypublications.ca. **Website:** www.westerngrocer.com. **Contact:** Robin Bradley, associate publisher and national account manager. **75% freelance written.** Bimonthly magazine covering the grocery industry. Reports for the Western Canadian grocery, allied non-food and institutional industries. Each issue features a selection of relevant trade news and event coverage from the West and around the world. Feature reports offer market analysis, trend views, and insightful interviews from a wide variety

of industry leaders. *The Western Grocer* target audience is independent retail food stores, supermarkets, manufacturers and food brokers, distributors and wholesalers of food, and allied non-food products, as well as bakers, specialty and health food stores, and convenience outlets. Estab. 1916. Circ. 15,500. Byline given. Pays 30-45 days from receipt of invoice. Offers 33% kill fee. Submit seasonal material 3 months in advance. Sample copy and writer's guidelines free.

○ Assigns stories to Canadian writers based on editorial needs of publication.

NONFICTION Needs how-to, interview. Does not want industry reports and profiles on companies. Query with published clips. Length: 500-9,000 words. **Pays 25-35¢/word.** Pays expenses of writers on assignment.

PHOTOS State availability. Captions required. Reviews negatives, transparencies, 3x5 prints, JPEG, EPS, or TIF files. Negotiates payment individually. Buys all rights.

TIPS "E-mail, fax, or mail a query outlining your experience, interest, and pay expectations. Include clippings."

HOME FURNISHINGS & HOUSEHOLD GOODS

○○○○○ BEDTIMES

International Sleep Products Association, 501 Wythe St., Alexandria VA 22314. (336)500-3816. **E-mail:** mbest@sleepproducts.org. **Website:** www.bedtimesmagazine.com; www.sleepproducts.org. **Contact:** Mary Best, editorial director. **20-40% freelance written.** *BedTimes,* published monthly, focuses on news, trends, and issues of interest to mattress manufacturers and their suppliers, as well as more general business stories. Estab. 1917. Circ. 3,800. Byline given. Pays on acceptance. No kill fee. Publishes ms an average of 3 months after acceptance. Editorial lead time 2 months. Accepts queries by e-mail. Accepts simultaneous submissions. Responds in 1 month to queries. Sample copy: $4. Guidelines by e-mail or online.

○ "We are particularly interested in stories that show mattress manufacturers ways to reduce costs and operate more efficiently. *BedTimes* is not written for retailers or consumers: We do not run stories about how to shop for a mattress or how to lure customers into a bedding store."

NONFICTION Buys 15-25 mss/year. Query with published clips. Length: 500-2,500 words. **Pays 50-$1/word for short features; $2,000 for cover story.**

PHOTOS State availability. Identification of subjects required. Negotiates payment individually. Buys one-time rights.

TIPS "Cover topics have included annual industry forecast, e-commerce, flammability and home furnishings, the risks and rewards of marketing overseas, the evolving family business, the shifting workplace environment, and what do consumers really want? Our news and features are straightforward—we are not a lobbying vehicle for our association. No special slant."

HOME TEXTILES TODAY

Progressive Business Media, 1359 Broadway, Suite 1208, New York NY 10018. (732)204-2012. **E-mail:** jmarks@homeandtextilestoday.com. **Website:** www.hometextilestoday.com. **Contact:** Jennifer Marks, editor in chief. **5% freelance written.** Tabloid published 33 times/year covering home textiles retailers, manufacturers, and importers/exporters. "Our readers are interested in business trends and statistics about business trends related to their niche in the home furnishings market." Estab. 1979. Circ. 7,700. Byline given. Pays on publication. Offers 30% kill fee. Publishes ms an average of 2 weeks after acceptance. Editorial lead time 1-2 weeks. Submit seasonal material 3 weeks in advance. Accepts queries by mail, e-mail, phone. Accepts simultaneous submissions. Responds in 2 weeks to queries and mss. Sample copy free. Guidelines free.

NONFICTION Query. Pays expenses of writers on assignment.

TIPS "Information has to be focused on home textiles business—sheets, towels, bedding, curtains, rugs, table linens, kitchen textiles, curtains. Most of our readers are doing volume business at discount chains, mass market retailers, big box stores, and department stores."

WINDOW FASHION VISION

Grace McNamara, Inc., 4756 Banning Avenue, Suite 206, St. Paul MN 55110. **Fax:** (651)756-8141. **Website:** www.wf-vision.com. **Contact:** Susan Schultz, editorial director; Lynn Thompson, managing editor. **30% freelance written.** Monthly magazine dedicated to the advancement of the window fashions industry, *Window Fashions* provides comprehensive information on design and business principles, window fashion aesthetics, and product applications. The magazine serves the window-treatment and wall-coverings industry, including designers, retailers, dealers, specialty stores, workrooms, manufacturers, fabricators, and others associated with the field of interior design. Writers should be thoroughly knowledgable on the subject, and submissions need to be comprehensive. Estab. 1981. Circ. 30,000. Byline given. Pays on publication. No kill fee. Publishes ms an average of 3 months after acceptance. Editorial lead time 3 months. Submit seasonal material 4 months in advance. Accepts queries by mail, e-mail. Accepts simultaneous submissions. Sample copy online.

NONFICTION Needs how-to, interview, personal experience, specific topics within the field. No broad topics not specific to the window fashions industry. **Buys 24 mss/year.** Query or send complete ms Length: 800-1,000 words. Pays expenses of writers on assignment.

TIPS The most helpful experience is if a writer has knowledge of interior design or, specifically, window treatments. We already have a pool of generalists, although we welcome clips from writers who would like to be considered for assignments. Our style is professional business writing—no flowery prose. Articles tend to be to the point, as our readers are busy professionals who read for information, not for leisure. Most of all we need creative ideas and approaches to topics in the field of window treatments and interior design. A writer needs to be knowledgeable in the field because our readers would know if information was inaccurate.

HOSPITALS, NURSING & NURSING HOMES

ALZHEIMER'S CARE GUIDE

Freiberg Press Inc., P.O. Box 612, Cedar Falls IA 50613. (800)354-3371. **Fax:** (319)553-0644. **E-mail:** kfreiberg@cfu.net. **Website:** www.care4elders.com. **Contact:** Kathy Freiberg. **25% freelance written.** Bimonthly magazine covering Alzheimer's care. Aimed at caregivers of Alzheimer's patients. Interested in either inspirational first-person type stories or features/articles involving authoritative advice or caregiving tips. Estab. 1992. Circ. 10,000. Byline sometimes given. Pays on acceptance. No kill fee. Accepts queries by e-mail. Accepts simultaneous submissions.

💬 Query first. Only pays for assigned articles.

NONFICTION Needs book excerpts, interview, personal experience, technical. **Buys 50 mss/year.** Query. Length: 500-2,000 words. Pays expenses of writers on assignment.

🌐 AUSTRALIAN NURSING AND MIDWIFERY JOURNAL

Level 1, 365 Queen Street, Melbourne VIC 3000 Australia. (61)(3)9602-8500. **Fax:** (61)(3)96502-8567. **E-mail:** anmj@anmf.org.au. **Website:** www.anmf.org.au. Monthly magazine covering nursing issues in Australia. *ANJ* welcomes articles written by nurses for nurses. Please contact the editor first to make sure your article is appropriate for the journal. Publishes ms an average of 3-12 months after acceptance. Accepts simultaneous submissions. Responds in 3 months to queries. Guidelines online.

NONFICTION Needs general interest, how-to, interview, opinion, technical. Query. Length: 400-2,000 words. Pays expenses of writers on assignment.

$ SCHOOL NURSE NEWS

Franklin Communications, Inc., 767 Buena Vista Ave. W., #101, San Francisco CA 94117. (415)670-0436. **Fax:** (415)663-4768. **E-mail:** editor@schoolnursenews.org. **Website:** www.schoolnursenews.org. **Contact:** Deb Ilardi. **10% freelance written.** Magazine published 5 times/year covering school nursing. *School Nurse News* focuses on topics related to the health issues of school-aged children and adolescents (grades K-12), as well as the health and professional issues that concern school nurses. This is an excellent opportunity for both new and experienced writers. *School Nurse News* publishes feature articles as well as news articles and regular departments, such as Asthma & Allergy Watch, Career & Salary Survey, Oral Health, Nursing Currents, and Sights & Sounds. Estab. 1982. Circ. 7,500. Byline given. Pays on publication. Publishes ms an average of 3-6 months after acceptance. Editorial lead time 3-6 months. Submit seasonal material 6 months in advance. Accepts queries by e-mail, fax, phone. Accepts simultaneous submissions. Sample copy free. Guidelines available on website.

NONFICTION Needs how-to, interview, new product, personal experience. **Buys 1-2 mss/year.** Query. Send via e-mail or forward ms with disk. Mss can include case histories, scenarios of health office situations, updates on diseases, reporting of research, and discussion of procedures and techniques, among others. The author is responsible for the accuracy of content. References should be complete, accurate, and in APA format. Tables, charts and photographs are welcome. Authors are responsible for obtaining permission to reproduce any material that has a pre-existing copyright. The feature article, references, tables, and charts should total 8-10 typewritten pages, double-spaced. The author's name should be included only on the top sheet. The top sheet should also include the title of the article, the author's credentials, current position, address, and phone. **Pays $100.** Pays expenses of writers on assignment.

HOTELS, MOTELS, CLUBS, RESORTS & RESTAURANTS

AQUA MAGAZINE

22 E. Mifflin St., Suite 910, Madison WI 53703. (608)249-0186. **E-mail:** scott@aquamagazine.com. **Website:** www.aquamagazine.com. **Contact:** Scott Webb, executive editor; Eric Herman, senior editor; Cailley Hammel, associate editor; Scott Maurer, art director. *AQUA Magazine* is a print and online publication dedicated to the pool and spa industry. AQUA provides the industry's top decision-makers with the timely, critical information they need to be successful in their jobs. Every month thousands of spa and pool professionals turn to the online and print pages of *AQUA* for its valuable mix of editorial. Estab. 1976. Circ. 15,000. Accepts simultaneous submissions.

NONFICTION Pays expenses of writers on assignment.

COLUMNS Columns include: product features, industry issue stories, business columns, reader profiles, industry news.

TIPS Wants to see "visually arresting, architectural images, high- quality, multiple angles, day/night lighting situations. Photos including people are rarely published."

$$ BARTENDER ® MAGAZINE

Foley Publishing, P.O. Box 157, Spring Lake NJ 07762 USA. (732)449-4499. **Fax:** (732)974-8289. **E-mail:** barmag2@gmail.com. **Website:** bartender.

com / mixologist.com. **Contact:** Jackie Foley, editor. **100% freelance written. Prefers to work with published/established writers; eager to work with new/unpublished writers.** Quarterly publication for full-service on-premise establishments able to serve a mixed drink on-premise. Features bartenders, bars, creative cocktails, signature drinks, jokes, cartoons, wine, beer, liquor, new products and those products aligned to the field. Estab. 1979. Circ. 150,000. Byline given. Pays on publication. No kill fee. Publishes ms an average of 3 months after acceptance. Submit seasonal material 3 months in advance. Accepts simultaneous submissions. Responds in 2 months to mss. Sample copy with 9x12 SAE and 4 first-class stamps.

NONFICTION Needs general interest, historical, how-to, humor, new product, opinion, personal experience, photo feature. Special issues: Special issues: Annual Calendar and Daily Cocktail Recipe Guide. Send complete ms and SASE. Length: 100-1,000 words. Pays expenses of writers on assignment.

REPRINTS Send tearsheet and information about when and where the material previously appeared. Pays 25% of amount paid for an original article.

PHOTOS Send photos. Captions, model releases required. Pays $7.50-50 for 8x10 b&w glossy prints; $10-75 for 8x10 color glossy prints.

COLUMNS Bar of the Month; Bartender of the Month; Creative Cocktails; Bar Sports; Quiz; Bar Art; Wine Cellar; Tips from the Top (from prominent figures in the liquor industry); One For the Road (travel); Collectors (bar or liquor-related items); Photo Essays. Length: 200-1,000 words. Query by mail only with SASE. **Pays $50-200.**

FILLERS Needs anecdotes, newsbreaks, short humor, clippings, jokes, gags. Length: 25-100 words. **Pays $5-25.**

TIPS "To break in, absolutely make sure your work will be of interest to all bartenders across the country. Your style of writing should reflect the audience you are addressing. The most frequent mistake made by writers in completing an article for us is using the wrong subject."

🌑🌑 EL RESTAURANTE

P.O. Box 2249, Oak Park IL 60303-2249. (708)267-0023. **E-mail:** kfurore@comcast.net. **Website:** www.restmex.com. **Contact:** Kathleen Furore, editor. Bi-monthly magazine covering Mexican and other Latin cuisines. "*el Restaurante* offers features and business-related articles that are geared specifically to owners and operators of Mexican, Tex-Mex, Southwestern, and Latin cuisine restaurants and other foodservice establishments that want to add that type of cuisine." Estab. 1997. Circ. 25,000. Byline given. Pays on publication. No kill fee. Publishes ms an average of 3 months after acceptance. Accepts simultaneous submissions. Responds in 2 months to queries. Sample copy free.

NONFICTION "No specific knowledge of food or restaurants is needed; the key qualification is to be a good reporter who knows how to slant a story toward the Mexican restaurant operator." **Buys 2-4 mss/year.** Query with published clips. Length: 800-1,200 words. **Pays $250-300.**

TIPS "Query with a story idea, and tell how it pertains to Mexican restaurants."

MASSAGE & BODYWORK

Associated Bodywork & Massage Professionals, 25188 Genesee Trail Rd., Suite 200, Golden CO 80401. (303)674-8478 or (800)458-2267. **Fax:** (303)674-0859. **E-mail:** editor@abmp.com. **Website:** www.massageandbodywork.com. **85% freelance written.** Bi-monthly magazine covering therapeutic massage/bodywork. A trade publication for the massage therapist, and bodyworker. An all-inclusive publication encompassing everything from traditional Swedish massage to energy work to other complementary therapies (i.e., homeopathy, herbs, aromatherapy, etc.). Pays on acceptance. No kill fee. Publishes ms an average of 6 months after acceptance. Editorial lead time 6 months. Submit seasonal material 6 months in advance. Accepts queries by e-mail. Accepts simultaneous submissions. Responds in 45 days to queries. Guidelines online.

NONFICTION Needs how-to, interview, opinion, personal experience, technical. **Buys 60-75 mss/year.** Query with published clips. Length: 1,500-3,500 words. Pays expenses of writers on assignment.

PHOTOS Not interested in photo submissions separate from feature queries. State availability. Captions, identification of subjects, model releases required. Reviews digital images (300 dpi). Negotiates payment individually. Buys one-time rights.

COLUMNS Buys 20 mss/year. mss/year.

TIPS "Know your topic. Offer suggestions for art to accompany your submission. *Massage & Bodywork* looks for interesting, tightly focused stories concerning a particular modality or technique of massage, bodywork, and somatic therapies. The editorial staff welcomes the opportunity to review mss which may be relevant to the field of massage and bodywork in addition to more general pieces pertaining to complementary and alternative medicine. This would include the widely varying modalities of massage and bodywork (from Swedish massage to Polarity therapy), specific technical or ancillary therapies, including such topics as biomagnetics, aromatherapy, and facial rejuvenation. Reference lists relating to technical articles should include the author, title, publisher, and publication date of works cited according to Chicago Manual of Style. Word count: 1,500-3,500 words; longer articles negotiable."

✪❸❺ WESTERN HOTELIER MAGAZINE

Mercury Publications, Ltd., 1313 Border St., Unit 16, Winnipeg MB R3H 0X4 Canada. (800)337-6372 ext. 221. **Fax:** (204)954-2057. **E-mail:** dbastable@mercurypublications.ca. **Website:** www.westernhotelier.com. **Contact:** David Bastable, associate publisher and national accounts manager. **33% freelance written.** Quarterly magazine covering the hotel industry. *Western Hotelier* is dedicated to the accommodation industry in Western Canada and U.S. western border states. *WH* offers the West's best mix of news and feature reports geared to hotel management. Feature reports are written on a sector basis and are created to help generate enhanced profitability and better understanding. Circ. 4,342. Byline given. Pays 30-45 days from receipt of invoice. Offers 33% kill fee. Submit seasonal material 3 months in advance. Accepts queries by mail, fax. Accepts simultaneous submissions. Responds in 2 weeks to queries. Sample copy and writer's guidelines free.

NONFICTION Needs how-to, interview. Industry reports and profiles on companies. Query with published clips. Length: 500-9,000 words. **Pays 25-35¢/word.** Pays expenses of writers on assignment.

PHOTOS State availability. Captions required. Reviews negatives, transparencies, 3x5 prints, JPEG, EPS, or TIF files. Negotiates payment individually. Buys all rights.

TIPS "E-mail, fax, or mail a query outlining your experience, interests, and pay expectations. Include clippings."

✪❸❺ WESTERN RESTAURANT NEWS

Mercury Publications, Ltd., 1313 Border St., Unit 16, Winnipeg MB R3H 0X4 Canada. (800)337-6372 ext. 213. **Fax:** (204)954-2057. **E-mail:** editorial@mercury.mb.ca; edufault@mercurypublications.ca. **Website:** www.westernrestaurantnews.com; www.mercury.mb.ca. **Contact:** Elaine Dufault, associate publisher and national accounts manager. **20% freelance written.** Bimonthly magazine covering the restaurant trade in Western Canada. Reports profiles and industry reports on associations, regional business developments, etc. *Western Restaurant News* is the authoritative voice of the food service industry in Western Canada. Offering a total package to readers, *WRN* delivers concise news articles, new product news, and coverage of the leading trade events in the West, across the country, and around the world. Estab. 1994. Circ. 14,532. Byline given. Pays 30-45 days from receipt of invoice. Offers 33% kill fee. Submit seasonal material 3 months in advance. Accepts queries by mail, fax. Accepts simultaneous submissions. Sample copy and writer's guidelines free.

NONFICTION Needs how-to, interview. Industry reports and profiles on companies. Query with published clips. "E-mail, fax, or mail a query outlining your experience, interests, and pay expectations. Include clippings." Length: 500-9,000 words. **Pays 25-35¢/word.** Pays expenses of writers on assignment.

PHOTOS State availability. Captions required. Reviews negatives, transparencies, 3x5 prints, JPEG, EPS, or TIFF files. Negotiates payment individually. Buys all rights.

INDUSTRIAL OPERATIONS

❸❺ INDUSTRIAL WEIGH & MEASURE

WAM Publishing Company, Inc., P.O. Box 2247, Hendersonville TN 37077. (615)239-8087. **E-mail:** dave.mathieu@comcast.net. **Website:** www.weighproducts.com. **Contact:** David M. Mathieu, publisher and editor. Bimonthly magazine for users of industrial scales; covers material handling and logistics industries. Estab. 1914. Circ. 13,900. Byline given. Pays on acceptance. Offers 20% kill fee. Accepts queries by mail, e-mail, phone. Accepts simultaneous submissions. Responds in 2 weeks to queries. Sample copy online.

NONFICTION Needs general interest, technical. **Buys 15 mss/year.** Query on technical articles; submit complete ms for general interest material. Length:

1,000-2,500 words. **Pays $175-300.** Pays expenses of writers on assignment.

INFORMATION SYSTEMS

ⓈⓈⓈ DESKTOP ENGINEERING

Peerless Media, LLC, 111 Speen St., Suite 200, Framingham MA 01701. **E-mail:** jgooch@deskeng.com. **E-mail:** de-editors@deskeng.com. **Website:** www.deskeng.com. **Contact:** Jamie Gooch, editorial director. **90% freelance written.** Monthly magazine covering computer hardware/software for hands-on design and mechanical engineers, analysis engineers, and engineering management. Ten special supplements/year. Estab. 1995. Circ. 63,000. Byline given. Pays in month of publication. Offers kill fee for assigned story. Publishes ms an average of 2 months after acceptance. Editorial lead time 3 months. Accepts queries by mail, e-mail. Accepts simultaneous submissions. Responds in 2 weeks to queries; in 1 month to mss. Sample copy free with 8x10 SASE. Guidelines available on website.

NONFICTION Needs how-to, new product, reviews, technical, design. No fluff. **Buys 50-70 mss/year.** Query. Submit outline before you write an article. Length: 800-1,200 words for articles (plus artwork) presenting tutorials, application stories, product reviews or other features; 500-700 words for guest commentaries for almost any topic related to desktop engineering. **Pays per project. Pay negotiable for unsolicited articles.** Pays expenses of writers on assignment.

PHOTOS "No matter what type of article you write, it must be supported and enhanced visually. Visual information can include screen shots, photos, schematics, tables, charts, checklists, time lines, reading lists, and program code. The exact mix will depend on your particular article, but each of these items must be accompanied by specific, detailed captions." Send photos. Captions required. Negotiates payment individually.

COLUMNS Product Briefs (new products), 50-100 words; Reviews (software, hardware), 500-1,500 words. Query.

Ⓢ JOURNAL OF INFORMATION ETHICS

McFarland & Co., Inc., Publishers, P.O. Box 611, Jefferson NC 28640. (336)246-4460. **E-mail:** hauptman@stcloudstate.edu. **90% freelance written.** Semiannual scholarly journal covering all of the information sciences. Addresses ethical issues in all of the information sciences with a deliberately interdisciplinary approach. Topics range from electronic mail monitoring to library acquisition of controversial material to archival ethics. The *Journal*'s aim is to present thoughtful considerations of ethical dilemmas that arise in a rapidly evolving system of information exchange and dissemination. Estab. 1992. Byline given. Pays on publication. No kill fee. Publishes ms an average of 2 years after acceptance. Submit seasonal material 8 months in advance. Accepts queries by mail, e-mail, phone. Accepts simultaneous submissions. Sample copy for $30. Guidelines free.

NONFICTION Needs essays, reviews. **Buys 10-12 mss/year.** Send complete ms. Length: 500-3,500 words. **Pays $25-50, depending on length.**

TIPS "Familiarize yourself with the many areas subsumed under the rubric of information ethics, e.g., privacy, scholarly communication, errors, peer review, confidentiality, e-mail, etc. Present a well-rounded discussion of any fresh, current, or evolving ethical topic within the information sciences or involving real-world information collection/exchange."

R & D MAGAZINE

Advantage Business Media, 100 Enterprise Dr., Suite 600, Rockaway NJ 07866. **E-mail:** rdeditors@advantagemedia.com; lindsay.hock@advantagemedia.com. **Website:** www.rdmag.com. **Contact:** Lindsay Hock, editor. Monthly magazine. "*R&D Magazine* and www.rdmag.com informs and educates research scientists, engineers, and technical staff members at laboratories around the world with timely, informative news—and useful technical articles that broaden our readers' knowledge of the research and development industry and improve the quality of their work." Estab. 1959. Circ. 85,000. Byline given. No kill fee. Editorial lead time 2 months. Responds to queries in 1 week. Guidelines online.

NONFICTION Query. **Pays 4 contributor copies upon request.** Pays expenses of writers on assignment.

PHOTOS Contact: Contact: editor in chief. Captions, identification of subjects required. Reviews 2 1/4x2 1/4 transparencies, 6x9 prints, TIFF/EPS files (300 dpi) or 35mm slides.

TIPS "All articles in *R & D Magazine* must be original, accurate, timely, noncommercial, useful to our readers, and exclusive to our magazine."

ⓈⓈⓈⓈ TECHNOLOGY REVIEW

MIT, One Main St., 13th Floor, Cambridge MA 02142. (617)475-8000. **Fax:** (617)475-8042. **E-mail:** jason.

pontin@technologyreview.com; david.rotman@technologyreview.com. **Website:** www.technologyreview.com. **Contact:** Jason Pontin, editor in chief; David Rotman, editor. Magazine published 10 times/year covering information technology, biotech, material science, and nanotechnology. *Technology Review* promotes the understanding of emerging technologies and their impact. Estab. 1899. Circ. 310,000. Byline given. Pays on acceptance. Accepts queries by mail, e-mail. Accepts simultaneous submissions.

NONFICTION Query with a pitch via online contact form. Length: 2,000-4,000 words. **Pays $1-3/word.** Pays expenses of writers on assignment.

FILLERS Short tidbits that relate laboratory prototypes on their way to market in 1-5 years. Length: 150-250 words. **Pays $1-3/word.**

JEWELRY

$ ADORNMENT

Association for the Study of Jewelry & Related Arts, 5070 Bonnie Branch Rd., Ellicott City MD 21043. **E-mail:** elyse@jewelryandrelatedarts.com. **Website:** www.jewelryandrelatedarts.com; www.asjra.net; www.jewelryconference.com. **50% freelance written.** Quarterly magazine covering jewelry—antique to modern. "This magazine is a perk of membership in the Association for the Study of Jewelry & Related Arts. It is not sold as a stand-alone publication. It is delivered electronically." Estab. 2002. Circ. 1,000+. Byline given. Pays on publication. No kill fee. Publishes ms an average of 3 months after acceptance. Editorial lead time 3 months. Accepts queries by mail, e-mail. Accepts simultaneous submissions. Responds in 1-2 weeks to queries; in 1 month to mss. Sample copy free as an e-mailed PDF. Guidelines free.

💬 "Readers are collectors, appraisers, antique jewelry dealers, gemologists, jewelry artists, museum curators—anyone with an interest in jewelry."

NONFICTION Needs book excerpts, interview, exhibition reviews—in-depth articles on jewelry subjects. "We do not want articles about retail jewelry. We write about ancient, antique, period, and unique and studio jewelers." **Buys 12-15 mss/year.** Query with published clips. Length: 1,000-3,000 words. **Pays $125 maximum for assigned articles. Does not pay for unsolicited articles.** Pays expenses of writers on assignment.

PHOTOS "We only want photos that accompany articles. Quality must be professional. We pay $25 flat fee for them; We don't accept articles without accompanying photography. You must obtain permission for the use of photos. We won't publish without written approvals."

TIPS "Know your subject and provide applicable credentials."

$$ THE ENGRAVERS JOURNAL

P.O. Box 318, Brighton MI 48116. (810)229-5725. **Fax:** (810)229-8320. **E-mail:** editor@engraversjournal.com. **Website:** www.engraversjournal.com. **Contact:** Senior editor. **70% freelance written.** Monthly magazine covering the recognition and personalization industry (engraving, marking devices, awards, jewelry, and signage). "We provide practical information for the education and advancement of our readers, mainly retail business owners." Estab. 1975. Byline given. Pays on acceptance. No kill fee. Publishes ms an average of 3-9 months after acceptance. Accepts queries by mail, e-mail, fax. Accepts simultaneous submissions. Responds in 2 weeks to mss. Sample copy free. Guidelines free.

NONFICTION Needs general interest, how-to, technical. No general overviews of the industry. Length: 1,000-5,000 words. **Pays $200 and up.**

REPRINTS Send tearsheet, photocopy, or typed ms with rights for sale noted, and information about when and where the material previously appeared. Pays 50-100% of amount paid for original article.

PHOTOS Send photos. Captions, identification of subjects, model releases required. Pays variable rate.

TIPS "Articles should always be down to earth, practical, and thoroughly cover the subject with authority. We do not want the 'textbook' writing approach, vagueness, or theory—our readers look to us for sound, practical information. We use an educational slant, publishing both trade-oriented articles and general business topics of interest to a small retail-oriented readership."

JOURNALISM & WRITING

$$$$ AMERICAN JOURNALISM REVIEW

University of Maryland Foundation, Knight Hall, University of Maryland, College Park MD 20742.

(301)405-8805. **E-mail:** editor@ajr.org. **Website:** www.ajr.org. **Contact:** Lucy Dalglish, dean and publisher. **80% freelance written.** Bimonthly magazine covering print, broadcast, and online journalism. *American Journalism Review* covers ethical issues, trends in the industry, and coverage that falls short. Circ. 25,000. Byline given. Pays 1 month after publication. Offers 25% kill fee. Publishes ms an average of 2 months after acceptance. Editorial lead time 1 month. Accepts queries by mail, e-mail. Responds in 1 month to queries and unsolicited mss. Sample copy: $4.95 prepaid or online. Guidelines online.

NONFICTION Needs expose. **Buys many mss/year.** Query or send complete ms. Length: 2,000-4,000 words. **Pays $1,500-2,000.** Pays expenses of writers on assignment.

FILLERS Needs anecdotes, facts, short humor, short pieces. Length: 150-1,000 words. **Pays $100-250.**

TIPS "Write a short story for the front-of-the-book section. We prefer queries to completed articles. Include in a page what you'd like to write about, who you'll interview, why it's important, and why you should write it."

AUSTRALIAN AUTHOR

Australian Society of Authors, Suite C1.06, 22-36 Mountain St., Ultimo NSW 2007 Australia. (61)(2)9211-1004. **Fax:** (61)(2)9211-0125. **E-mail:** editor@asauthors.org. **E-mail:** kirsten@asauthors.org. **Website:** australian-author.org. **Contact:** Kirsten Krauth, editor. *Australian Author* is the literary journal of the Australian Society of Authors. The magazine is a vibrant source of discussion and commentary about writing and publishing in Australia. It's the best way to keep up with publishing industry gossip, issues affecting authors, and writers' thoughts on what inspires, concerns, and sustains them. Published twice/year. Accepts simultaneous submissions.

NONFICTION, articles on publishing, e-books, literary agents, grants and funding, pay and financial concerns, indie publishing, intellectual property, the digital environment, marketing, social media, illustration, comics and graphic novels, ghostwriting, and more. Query with published clips. Length: 1,500 words minimum. Pays expenses of writers on assignment.

$ AUTHORSHIP

National Writers Association, 10940 S. Parker Rd., #508, Parker CO 80134. (303)841-0246. **E-mail:** natlwritersassn@hotmail.com. **Website:** www.nationalwriters.com. Quarterly magazine covering writing articles only. "Association magazine targeted to beginning and professional writers. Covers how-to, humor, marketing issues. Disk and e-mail submissions preferred." Estab. 1950s. Circ. 4,000. Byline given. Pays on acceptance. No kill fee. Editorial lead time 3 months. Submit seasonal material 6 months in advance. Accepts queries by mail. Accepts simultaneous submissions. Responds in 2 months to queries. Sample copy for stamped, self-addressed, 8½x11 envelope.

NONFICTION **Buys 25 mss/year.** Query or send complete ms. Length: 1,200 words. **Pays $10, or discount on memberships and copies.** Pays expenses of writers on assignment.

PHOTOS State availability. Identification of subjects, model releases required. Reviews 5x7 prints. Offers no additional payment for photos accepted with ms. Buys one-time rights.

TIPS "Members of National Writers Association are given preference."

$ BOOK DEALERS WORLD

North American Bookdealers Exchange, P.O. Box 606, Cottage Grove OR 97424. (541)942-7455. **E-mail:** nabe@bookmarketingprofits.com. **Website:** www.bookmarketingprofits.com. **50% freelance written.** Magazine covering writing, self-publishing, and marketing books by mail. Publishes 3 issues/year online. Estab. 1980. Circ. 20,000. Byline given. Pays on publication. No kill fee. Publishes ms an average of 3 months after acceptance. Accepts queries by mail, e-mail. Accepts simultaneous submissions. Responds in 1 month to queries. Sample copy online.

NONFICTION Needs book excerpts, how-to, interview, positive articles on self-publishing, new writing angles, marketing. **Buys 10 mss/year.** Send complete ms. Length: 1,000-1,500 words. **Pays $25-50.** Pays expenses of writers on assignment.

REPRINTS Send typed ms with rights for sale noted and information about when and where the material previously appeared. Pays 80% of amount paid for an original article.

COLUMNS Publisher Profile (on successful self-publishers and their marketing strategy), 250-1,000 words. **Buys 20 mss/year.** Send complete ms. **Pays $5-20.**

FILLERS Needs fillers concerning writing, publishing, or books. **Buys 6 mss/year.** Length: 100-250 words. **Pays $3-10.**

TIPS "Query first. Get a sample copy of the magazine online at website."

○$$ CANADIAN SCREENWRITER

Writers Guild of Canada, 366 Adelaide St. W., Suite 401, Toronto ON M5V 1R9 Canada. (416)979-7907. **Fax:** (416)979-9273. **E-mail:** info@wgc.ca. **Website:** www.wgc.ca. **Contact:** Li Robbins, director of communications. **80% freelance written.** Magazine published 3 times/year covering Canadian screenwriting for television, film, and digital media. *Canadian Screenwriter* profiles Canadian screenwriters, provides industry news, and offers practical writing tips for screenwriters. Estab. 1998. Circ. 4,000. Byline given. Pays on acceptance. Offers 50% kill fee. Publishes ms an average of 1 month after acceptance. Editorial lead time 2 months. Submit seasonal material 2 months in advance. Accepts queries by e-mail. Accepts simultaneous submissions. Responds in 1 week to queries; in 1 month to mss. Sample copy free. Guidelines by e-mail.

NONFICTION Needs how-to, humor, interview. Does not want writing on foreign screenwriters; the focus is on Canadian-resident screenwriters. **Buys 12 mss/year.** Query with published clips. Length: 750-2,200 words. **Pays $1/word.** Pays expenses of writers on assignment.

PHOTOS State availability. Identification of subjects required. Reviews GIF/JPEG files. Negotiates payment individually. Buys one-time rights.

TIPS "Read other Canadian film and television publications."

$$$ ECONTENT MAGAZINE

Information Today, Inc., 143 Old Marlton Pike, Medford NJ 08055. (609)654-6266. **Fax:** (609)654-4309. **E-mail:** theresa.cramer@infotoday.com. **Website:** www.econtentmag.com. **Contact:** Theresa Cramer, editor. **90% freelance written.** Monthly magazine covering digital content trends, strategies, etc. *EContent* is a business publication. Readers need to stay on top of industry trends and developments. Estab. 1979. Circ. 12,000. Byline given. Pays within 1 month of publication. No kill fee. Editorial lead time 3-4 months. Accepts simultaneous submissions. Responds in 3 weeks to queries; in 1 month to mss. Sample copy and writer's guidelines online.

NONFICTION Needs expose, how-to, interview, new product, opinion. No academic or straight Q&A. **Buys 48 mss/year.** Query with published clips. Submit electronically as e-mail attachment. Length: 1,000 words. Pays expenses of writers on assignment.

PHOTOS State availability. Captions required. Negotiates payment individually. Buys one-time rights.

COLUMNS Profiles (short profile of unique company, person or product), 1,200 words; New Features (breaking news of content-related topics), up to 500 words. **Buys 40 mss/year.** Query with published clips. **Pays 30-40¢/word.**

TIPS "Take a look at the website. Most of the time, an e-mail query with specific article ideas works well. A general outline of talking points is good, too. State prior experience."

●$ FREELANCE MARKET NEWS

The Writers Bureau Ltd., 8-10 Dutton St., Manchester M3 1LE England. (44)(161)819-9922. **Fax:** (44)(161)819-2842. **E-mail:** fmn@writersbureau.com. **Website:** www.freelancemarketnews.com. **15% freelance written.** Monthly newsletter covering freelance writing. For all writers, established and new, *Freelance Market News* is an excellent source of the most up-to-date information about the publishing world. It is packed with news, views and the latest advice about new publications, plus the trends and developments in established markets, in the UK and around the world. Informs readers about publications that are looking for new writers and even warn about those writers should avoid. Estab. 1968. Byline given. Pays on acceptance. No kill fee. Publishes ms an average of 3 months after acceptance. Editorial lead time 3 months. Submit seasonal material 3 months in advance. Accepts queries by mail, e-mail. Sample copy and Guidelines online.

○ Prefers to receive a complete ms rather than a query.

NONFICTION **Buys 12 mss/year.** Length: 1,00 words. **Pays £50/1,000 words.** Pays expenses of writers on assignment.

COLUMNS New Markets (magazines which have recently been published); Fillers & Letters; Overseas Markets (obviously only English-language publications); Market Notes (established publications accepting articles, fiction, reviews, or poetry). All should be between 40 and 200 words. **Pays £40/1,000 words.**

💲💲 FREELANCE WRITER'S REPORT

CNW Publishing, Inc., 45 Main St., P.O. Box A, North Stratford NH 03590-0167. (603)922-8338. **E-mail:** fwrwm@writers-editors.com. **Website:** www. writers-editors.com. **25% freelance written.** Monthly newsletter covering the business of freelance writing. *FWR* covers the marketing and business/office management aspects of running a freelance writing business. Articles must be of value to the established freelancer; nothing basic. Estab. 1982. Byline given. Pays on publication. No kill fee. Publishes ms an average of 12 months after acceptance. Editorial lead time 2 months. Submit seasonal material 2 months in advance. Accepts simultaneous submissions. Responds in 1 week to queries; 2 weeks to mss. Sample copy for 6x9 SAE with 2 first-class stamps (for back copy); $4 for current copy. Guidelines and Sample copy online.

NONFICTION Needs book excerpts. Does not want articles about the basics of freelancing. **Buys 5 mss/year.** Send complete ms by e-mail. Length: up to 900 words. **Pays 10¢/word.** Pays expenses of writers on assignment.

TIPS "Write in a terse, newsletter style."

💲💲 POETS & WRITERS MAGAZINE

90 Broad St., Suite 2100, New York NY 10004. (212)226-3586. **E-mail:** editor@pw.org. **Website:** www.pw.org/magazine. **Contact:** Kevin Larimer, editor. **95% freelance written.** Bimonthly professional trade journal for poets and fiction writers and creative nonfiction writers. Estab. 1987. Circ. 60,000. Byline given. Pays on publication. Offers 25% kill fee. Publishes ms an average of 4 months after acceptance. Submit seasonal material 4 months in advance. Accepts queries by mail, e-mail. Accepts simultaneous submissions. Responds in 2 months to mss. Sample copy: $5.95. Guidelines online.

🚫 No poetry or fiction submissions.

NONFICTION Needs how-to. **Buys 35 mss/year.** Send complete ms. Length: 700-3,000 words (depending on topic). Pays expenses of writers on assignment.

PHOTOS State availability. Reviews color prints. Offers no additional payment for photos accepted with ms.

COLUMNS Literary and Publishing News, 700-1,000 words; Profiles of Emerging and Established Poets, Fiction Writers and Creative Nonfiction Writers, 2,000-3,000 words; Craft Essays and Publishing Advice, 2,000-2,500 words. Query with published clips or send complete ms. **Pays $225-500.**

TIPS "We typically assign profiles to coincide with an author's forthcoming book publication. We are not looking for the Get Rich Quick or 10 Easy Steps variety of writing and publishing advice."

💲💲 QUILL & SCROLL MAGAZINE

Quill and Scroll International Honorary Society for High School Journalists, University of Iowa, School of Journalism and Mass Communication, 100 Adler Journalism Bldg., Iowa City IA 52242. (319)335-3457. **Fax:** (319)335-3989. **E-mail:** quill-scroll@uiowa.edu. **Website:** www.quillandscroll.org. **Contact:** Vanessa Shelton, executive director. **20% freelance written.** Fall and spring issues covering scholastic journalism-related topics during school year. Primary audience is high school journalism students working on and studying topics related to newspapers, yearbooks, radio, television, and online media; secondary audience is their teachers and others interested in this topic. Invites journalism students and advisers to submit mss about important lessons learned or obstacles overcome. Estab. 1926. Circ. 10,000. Byline given. Pays on acceptance and publication. No kill fee. Publishes ms an average of 4 months after acceptance. Editorial lead time 2 months. Accepts queries by mail, e-mail. Accepts simultaneous submissions. Responds in 2 weeks to queries. Guidelines available.

NONFICTION Needs essays, how-to, humor, interview, new product, opinion, personal experience, photo feature, technical, travel, types on topic. Does not want articles not pertinent to high school student journalists. Query with your submission. Length: 600-1,000 words. **Pays $100-500 for assigned articles. Pays complementary copy and $200 maximum for unsolicited articles.** Pays expenses of writers on assignment.

PHOTOS State availability. Reviews GIF/JPEG files. Offers no additional payment for photos accepted with ms.

💲💲 THE WRITER'S CHRONICLE

Association of Writers & Writing Programs (AWP), Carty House MS 1E3, George Mason University, Fairfax VA 22030-4444. (703)993-4301. **Fax:** (703)993-4302. **E-mail:** chronicle@awpwriter.org. **Website:** www.awpwriter.org. **90% freelance written.** Published 6 times during the academic year; 3 times a semester. Magazine covering the art and craft of writing. "*Writer's Chronicle* strives to: present the best essays on the craft and art of writing poetry, fiction, and nonfiction; help overcome the over-specialization of the literary arts by presenting a public forum for the appreciation, debate, and analysis of contemporary literature; present the diversity of accomplishments and points of view within contemporary literature; provide serious and committed writers and students of writing the best advice on how to manage their professional lives; provide writers who teach with new pedagogical approaches for their classrooms; provide the members and subscribers with a literary community as a compensation for a devotion to a difficult and lonely art; provide information on publishing opportunities, grants, and awards; and promote the good works of AWP, its programs, and its individual members." Estab. 1967. Circ. 35,000. Byline given. Pays on publication. No kill fee. Editorial lead time 3 months. Accepts simultaneous submissions. Responds in 2 weeks to queries. Sample copy free. Guidelines online. Reading period: February 1 through September 30.

NONFICTION Needs essays, interview, opinion. No personal essays. **Buys 15-20 mss/year.** Send complete ms. Length: 2,500-7,000 words. **Pays $18/100 words for assigned articles.**

TIPS "In general, the editors look for articles that demonstrate an excellent working knowledge of literary issues and a generosity of spirit that esteems the arguments of other writers on similar topics. When writing essays on craft, do not use your own work as an example. Keep in mind that 18,000 of our readers are students or just-emerging writers. They must become good readers before they can become good writers, so we expect essays on craft to show exemplary close readings of a variety of contemporary and older works. Essays must embody erudition, generosity, curiosity, and discernment rather than self-involvement. Writers may refer to their own travails and successes if they do so modestly, in small proportion to the other examples. We look for a generosity of spirit—a general love and command of literature as well as an expert, writerly viewpoint."

💲💲💲 WRITER'S DIGEST

F+W Media, Inc., 10151 Carver Rd., Suite #200, Blue Ash OH 45242. (513)531-2690. **E-mail:** wdsubmissions@fwmedia.com. **Website:** www.writersdigest. com. **75% freelance written.** Magazine for those who want to write better, get published, and participate in the vibrant culture of writers. Readers look for specific ideas and tips that will help them succeed, whether success means getting into print, finding personal fulfillment through writing, or building and maintaining a thriving writing career and network. *Writer's Digest*, the No. 1 magazine for writers, celebrates the writing life and what it means to be a writer in today's publishing environment. Estab. 1920. Byline given. Pays on acceptance. Offers 25% kill fee. Publishes ms an average of 4 months after acceptance. Accepts simultaneous submissions. Responds in 1-4 months to queries and mss. Guidelines and editorial calendar available online (writersdigest.com/submission-guidelines).

💭 The magazine does not accept or read e-queries with attachments.

NONFICTION Needs essays; short front-of-book pieces; how-to (writing craft, business of publishing, etc.); humor; inspirational; interviews/profiles (rarely, as those are typically handled in house). Does not accept phone, snail mail, or fax queries, and queries of this nature will receive no response. Does not buy newspaper clippings or reprints of articles previously published in other mainstream media, whether in print or online. Product reviews are handled in-house. **Buys 80 mss/year.** A query should include a thorough outline that introduces your article proposal and highlights each of the points you intend to make. Your query should discuss how the article will benefit readers, why the topic is timely, and why you're the appropriate writer to discuss the topic. Please include your publishing credential related to your topic with your submission. Do not send attachments. Length: 800-2,400 words. **Pays 30-50¢/word.** Pays expenses of writers on assignment.

TIPS "*InkWell* is the best place for new writers to break in. We recommend you consult our editorial calendar before pitching feature-length articles. Check our writer's guidelines for more details."

💲💲💲💲 WRITTEN BY

7000 W. Third St., Los Angeles CA 90048. (323)782-4574. **Fax:** (323)782-4800. **Website:** www.wga.org/writtenby/writtenby.aspx. **40% freelance written.** Magazine published 9 times/year. *Written By* is the premier magazine written by and for America's screen and TV writers. Focuses on the craft of screenwriting and covers all aspects of the entertainment industry from the perspective of the writer. Audience is screenwriters and most entertainment executives. Estab. 1987. Circ. 12,000. Byline given. Pays on acceptance. Offers 10% kill fee. Publishes ms an average of 2 months after acceptance. Editorial lead time 4 months. Submit seasonal material 4 months in advance. Accepts queries by mail, e-mail, fax, phone, online submission form. Accepts simultaneous submissions. Guidelines for #10 SASE or online contact form.

💬 Guidelines are currently being rewritten. Contact via phone or online contact form to pitch a story idea.

NONFICTION Needs book excerpts, essays, historical, humor, interview, opinion, personal experience, photo feature, technical. No beginner pieces on how to break into Hollywood or how to write scripts. **Buys 20 mss/year.** Query with published clips. Length: 500-3,500 words. **Pays $500-3,500 for assigned articles.** Pays expenses of writers on assignment.

PHOTOS State availability. Captions, identification of subjects, model releases required. Reviews transparencies. Offers no additional payment for photos accepted with ms. Buys one-time rights.

COLUMNS **Pays $1,000 maximum.**

TIPS "We are looking for more theoretical essays on screenwriting past and/or present. Also, the writer must always keep in mind that our audience is made up primarily of working writers who are inside the business; therefore all articles need to have an 'insider' feel and not be written for those who are still trying to break in to Hollywood. We prefer a hard copy of submission or e-mail."

LAW

$$$$ ABA JOURNAL

American Bar Association, 321 N. Clark St., 20th Floor, Chicago IL 60654. (312)988-6018. **Fax:** (312)988-6014. **E-mail:** releases@americanbar.org. **Website:** www.abajournal.com. **Contact:** Allen Pusey, editor and publisher. **10% freelance written.** Monthly magazine covering the trends, people, and finances of the legal profession from Wall Street to Main Street to Pennsylvania Avenue. The *ABA Journal* is an independent, thoughtful, and inquiring observer of the law and the legal profession. The magazine is edited for members of the American Bar Association. Circ. 380,000. Byline given. Pays on acceptance. No kill fee. Accepts queries by e-mail, fax. Accepts simultaneous submissions. Sample copy free. Guidelines online.

NONFICTION "We don't want anything that does not have a legal theme. No poetry or fiction." **Buys 5 mss/year.** "We use freelancers with experience reporting for legal or consumer publications; most have law degrees. If you are interested in freelancing for the *Journal*, we urge you to include your résumé and published clips when you contact us with story ideas." Length: 500-3,500 words. **Pays $300-2,000 for assigned articles.** Pays expenses of writers on assignment.

COLUMNS The National Pulse/Ideas from the Front (reports on legal news and trends), 650 words; eReport (reports on legal news and trends), 500-1,500 words. "The *ABA Journal eReport* is our weekly online newsletter sent out to members." **Buys 25 mss/year.** Query with published clips. **Pays $300, regardless of story length.**

$$$$ CALIFORNIA LAWYER

Daily Journal Corp., 44 Montgomery St., Suite 500, San Francisco CA 94104. (415)296-2400. **Fax:** (415)296-2440. **E-mail:** cl_contributingeditor@dailyjournal.com; bo_links@dailyjournal.com. **Website:** www.callawyer.com. **Contact:** Bo Links, legal editor; Marsha Sessa, art director. **30% freelance written.** Monthly magazine of law-related articles and general-interest subjects of appeal to lawyers and judges. Primary mission is to cover the news of the world as it affects the law and lawyers, helping readers better comprehend the issues of the day and to cover changes and trends in the legal profession. Readers are all California lawyers, plus judges, legislators, and corporate executives. Although the magazine focuses on California and the West, they have subscribers in every state. *California Lawyer* is a general interest magazine for people interested in law. Estab. 1981. Circ. 140,000. Byline given. Pays on acceptance. Offers 25% kill fee. Publishes ms an average of 3 months after acceptance. Editorial lead time 3 months. Accepts queries by e-mail. Accepts simultaneous submissions. Guidelines online.

NONFICTION Needs essays, general interest, profile, "We will consider well-researched, in-depth stories on the law, including legal trends of statewide and national significance, thought-provoking legal issues, and profiles of lawyers doing groundbreaking work. We will consider local issues if they have statewide or national implications or if you have a new unique angle to the story." **Buys 12 mss/year.** Query contributing editor: cl_contributingeditor@dailyjournal.com. Please do not send unsolicited mss. Length: 500-5,000 words. **Pays $50-2,000.** Pays expenses of writers on assignment.

PHOTOS Contact: Marsha Sessa, art director. State availability. Identification of subjects, model releases required. Reviews prints.

COLUMNS Expert Advice (specific, practical tips on an area of law or practice management), 650-750 words; Tech (lawyers and technology), up to 1,000 words; First Person (personal experience), 700 words; In House (working as corporate counsel in California), up to 1,000 words. Query appropriate editor (see website submission guidelines). **Pays $50-250.**

$$$ JOURNAL OF COURT REPORTING

National Court Reporters Association, 12030 Sunrise Valley Dr., Suite 400, Reston VA 20191. (703)584-9064. **E-mail:** jschmidt@ncra.org. **Website:** www.ncra.org. **Contact:** Jacqueline Schmidt, editor. **10% freelance written.** Monthly (bimonthly July/August and November/December) magazine. The *Journal of Court Reporting* has 2 complementary purposes: to communicate the activities, goals, and mission of its publisher, the National Court Reporters Association, and, simultaneously, to seek out and publish diverse information and views on matters significantly related to the court reporting and captioning professions. Estab. 1899. Circ. 20,000. Byline sometimes given. Pays on acceptance. No kill fee. Publishes ms an average of 4-5 months after acceptance. Editorial lead time 4 months. Submit seasonal material 4 months in advance. Accepts queries by mail, e-mail. Accepts simultaneous submissions. Sample copy free. Guidelines online.

NONFICTION Needs book excerpts, how-to, interview, technical, legal issues. **Buys 10 mss/year.** Send complete ms. Length: "People often ask how long an article should be; however, length should not be the goal. If you can tell the story in 200 words, that may be right for that story. Other stories may need 1,000 words or more to include the necessary materials on the subject. Just tell the story, and we will edit as needs determine. We contact writers regarding questions or major changes." Pays expenses of writers on assignment.

✪$$$$ NATIONAL

The Canadian Bar Association, 865 Carling Ave., Ottawa ON K1S 5S8 Canada. (613)237-2925. **Fax:** (613)237-0185. **E-mail:** beverleys@cba.org; national@cba.org. **Website:** www.nationalmagazine.ca. **Contact:** Beverley Spencer, editor in chief. **90% freelance written.** Magazine published 8 times/year covering practice trends and business developments in the law, with a focus on technology, innovation, practice management, and client relations. Estab. 1993. Circ. 37,000. Byline given. Pays on acceptance. Offers 50% kill fee. Publishes ms an average of 2 months after acceptance. Editorial lead time 2 months. Accepts queries by e-mail. Accepts simultaneous submissions. Sample copy free.

NONFICTION Buys 25 mss/year. Query with published clips. Length: 1,000-2,500 words. **Pays $1/word.** Pays expenses of writers on assignment.

$$ THE NATIONAL JURIST AND PRE LAW

Cypress Magazines, 7670 Opportunity Rd #105, San Diego CA 92111. (858)300-3201; (800)296-9656. **Fax:** (858)503-7588. **E-mail:** jack@cypressmagazines.com; callahan@cypressmagazines.com. **Website:** www.nationaljurist.com. **Contact:** Jack Crittenden, editor in chief. **25% freelance written.** Bimonthly magazine covering law students and issues of interest to law students. Estab. 1991. Circ. 145,000. Pays on publication. No kill fee. Accepts queries by mail, e-mail. Accepts simultaneous submissions.

NONFICTION Needs general interest, how-to, humor, interview. **Buys 4 mss/year.** Query. Length: 750-3,000 words. **Pays $100-500.** Pays expenses of writers on assignment.

PHOTOS State availability. Reviews contact sheets. Negotiates payment individually.

COLUMNS Pays $100-500.

$ PARALEGAL TODAY

Conexion International Media, Inc., 6030 Marshalee Dr., Elkridge MD 21075-5935. (443)445-3057. **Fax:** (443)445-3257. **E-mail:** pinfanti@connexionmedia.com. **Website:** www.paralegaltoday.com. **Contact:** Patricia E. Infanti, editor in chief; Charles Buckwalter, publisher. Quarterly magazine geared toward all legal assistants/paralegals throughout the U.S. and Canada, regardless of specialty (litigation, corporate, bankruptcy, environmental law, etc.). How-to articles to help paralegals perform their jobs more effectively are most in demand, as are career and salary information, technolgoy tips, and trends pieces.

Estab. 1983. Circ. 8,000. Byline given. Pays on publication. Offers kill fee ($25-50 standard rate). Editorial lead time is 10 weeks. Submit seasonal material 3 months in advance. Accepts queries by mail, e-mail, fax, online submission form. Accepts simultaneous submissions. Responds in 2 months to mss. Sample copy online. Guidelines online.

NONFICTION Needs interview, news (brief, hard news topics regarding paralegals), features (present information to help paralegals advance their careers). Send query letter first; if electronic, send submission as attachment. **Pays $75-300.** Pays expenses of writers on assignment.

PHOTOS Send photos.

TIPS "Query editor first. Features run 1,500-2,500 words with sidebars. Writers must understand our audience. There is some opportunity for investigative journalism as well as the usual features, profiles, and columns. How-to articles are especially desired. If you are a great writer who can interview effectively and really dig into the topic to grab readers' attention, we need you."

THE PUBLIC LAWYER

American Bar Association Government and Public Sector Lawyers Division, ABA Government and Public Sector Lawyers Division, 321 N. Clark St., MS 19.1, Chicago IL 60610. (312)988-5809. **Fax:** (312)932-6471. **E-mail:** katherine.mikkelson@americanbar.org. **Website:** www.governmentlawyer.org. **60% freelance written.** Biannual magazine covering government attorneys and the legal issues that pertain to them. The mission of *The Public Lawyer* is to provide timely, practical information useful to all public lawyers regardless of practice setting. Publishes articles covering topics that are of universal interest to a diverse audience of public lawyers, such as public law office management, dealing with the media, politically motivated personnel decisions, etc. Articles must be national in scope. Estab. 1993. Circ. 6,500. Byline given. Publishes ms an average of 4 months after acceptance. Editorial lead time 6 months. Accepts queries by e-mail. Accepts simultaneous submissions. Responds in 1 month to queries. Responds in 2 months to mss. Sample copy free. Guidelines online.

NONFICTION Needs interview, opinion, personal experience, profile, reviews, technical, book reviews. Does not want "pieces that do not relate to the status of government lawyers or that are not legal issues exclusive to government lawyers." **Buys 6-8 mss/year.** Query. Length: 2,000-5,000 words. **Pays contributor's copies.** Pays expenses of writers on assignment.

PHOTOS State availability. Identification of subjects, model releases required. Reviews GIF/JPEG files. Offers no additional payment for photos accepted with ms. Buys one-time rights.

TIPS "Articles stand a better chance of acceptance if they include one or more sidebars. Examples of sidebars include pieces explaining how government and public sector lawyers could use suggestions from the main article in their own practice, checklists, or other reference sources."

❻❻❻❻ SUPER LAWYERS

Thomson Reuters, 610 Opperman Dr., Eagan MN 55123. (877)787-5290. **Website:** www.superlawyers. com. **Contact:** Erik Lundegaard, editor. **100% freelance written.** Monthly magazine covering law and politics. Publishes glossy magazines in every region of the country; all serve a legal audience and have a storytelling sensibility. Writes profiles of interesting attorneys exclusively. Estab. 1990. Byline given. Pays on acceptance. Offers 25% kill fee. Publishes ms an average of 1 month after acceptance. Editorial lead time 6 months. Submit seasonal material 6 months in advance. Accepts queries by phone, online submission form. Accepts simultaneous submissions. Sample copy free. Guidelines free.

NONFICTION Needs general interest, historical. Query. Length: 500-2,000 words. **Pays 50¢-$1.50/ word.** Pays expenses of writers on assignment.

LUMBER

ALABAMA FORESTS

Alabama Foresty Association, 555 Alabama St., Montgomery AL 36104-4395. **Website:** www.alaforestry. org. **Contact:** Sam Duvall, director of communications. **0-5% freelance written.** Quarterly magazine covering the forest industry in Alabama. Also publishes a bimonthly electronic newsletter. Estab. 1948. Circ. 3,500-4,000. Pays on acceptance. No kill fee. Publishes ms an average of 3-6 months after acceptance. Editorial lead time 6-12 months. Submit seasonal material 3-6 months in advance. Accepts queries by e-mail. Accepts simultaneous submissions. Responds in 2-4 weeks to queries; 3-6 months to mss. Sample copy by e-mail. Guidelines available.

NONFICTION Needs book excerpts, historical, how-to, new product, photo feature. **Buys couple (sometimes) mss/year.** Send complete ms. "If you have something you've already had published that you would like to share with our readers, we might want to do that and give you 5-10 copies for your portfolio and the exposure to our membership, which includes most of the key players in forestry in Alabama (the pulp and paper companies, large and small sawmills, veneer mills, plywood mills, consulting foresters, furniture and other types of secondary wood manufacturers, landowners, etc." Length: 700-1,500 words. Pays expenses of writers on assignment.

PHOTOS Send photos. Captions, identification of subjects required. Reviews GIF/JPEG files (300 dpi at 1-2 MB). Offers no additional payment for photos accepted with ms. Negotiates payment individually. Buys one-time rights.

TIPS "We have a 'New Products & Services' section where we preview new forestry products for our members. I am also interested in insightful and informative stories about hunting and fishing in Alabama. Also, stories that give a new slant to forestry-specific issues and practices. Reading the magazine will help some. I do a lot of the writing of feature/personal interest-type articles myself."

🪙🪙 PALLET ENTERPRISE

Industrial Reporting, Inc., 10244 Timber Ridge Dr., Ashland VA 23005. (804)550-0323. **Fax:** (804)550-2181. **E-mail:** edb@ireporting.com; mbrindleypallet@gmail.com. **Website:** www.palletenterprise. com. **Contact:** Edward C. Brindley, Jr., Ph.D., publisher; Melissa Brindley, editor. **40% freelance written.** Monthly magazine covering lumber and pallet operations. The *Pallet Enterprise* is a monthly trade magazine for the sawmill, pallet, remanufacturing, and wood processing industries. Articles should offer technical, solution-oriented information. Anti-forest articles are not accepted. Articles should focus on machinery and unique ways to improve profitability/make money. Estab. 1981. Circ. 14,500. Pays on publication. Editorial lead time 2 months. Submit seasonal material 2 months in advance. Accepts queries by mail, e-mail, fax, phone. Accepts simultaneous submissions. Sample copy online. Guidelines free.

NONFICTION Needs interview, new product, opinion, technical, industry news, environmental, forests operation/plant features. No lifestyle, humor, general news, etc. **Buys 20 mss/year.** Query with published clips. Length: 1,000-3,000 words. **Pays $200-400 for assigned articles. Pays $100-400 for unsolicited articles.** Pays expenses of writers on assignment.

PHOTOS State availability. Captions, identification of subjects required. Reviews 3x5 prints. Negotiates payment individually. Buys one-time rights and Web rights.

COLUMNS Green Watch (environmental news/opinion affecting US forests), 1,500 words. **Buys 12 mss/year.** Query with published clips. **Pays $200-400.**

TIPS "Provide unique environmental or industry-oriented articles. Many of our freelance articles are company features of sawmills, pallet manufacturers, pallet recyclers, and wood waste processors."

🪙🪙 TIMBERWEST

TimberWest Publications, LLC, P.O. Box 610, Edmonds WA 98020. (425)778-3388. **Fax:** (425)771-3623. **E-mail:** timberwest@forestnet.com; diane@forestnet.com. **Website:** www.forestnet.com. **Contact:** Diane Mettler, managing editor. **75% freelance written.** Monthly magazine covering logging and lumber segment of the forestry industry in the Northwest. Primarily publishes profiles on loggers and their operations—with an emphasis on the machinery—in Washington, Oregon, Idaho, Montana, Northern California, and Alaska. Some timber issues are highly controversial, and although the magazine will report on the issues, this is a pro-logging publication. Does not publish articles with a negative slant on the timber industry. Estab. 1975. Circ. 10,000. Byline given. Pays on acceptance. No kill fee. Editorial lead time 2 months. Accepts queries by mail, fax. Accepts simultaneous submissions. Responds in 3 weeks to queries. Sample copy: $2. Guidelines for #10 SASE.

NONFICTION Needs historical, interview, new product. No articles that put the timber industry in a bad light, such as environmental articles against logging. **Buys 50 mss/year.** Query with published clips. Length: 1,100-1,500 words. **Pays $350.** Pays expenses of writers on assignment.

PHOTOS Send photos. Captions, identification of subjects required. Reviews contact sheets, transparencies, prints, GIF/JPEG files. Offers no additional payment for photos accepted with ms, but does pay $50 if shot is used on cover. Buys first rights.

FILLERS Needs facts, newsbreaks. **Buys 10 mss/year.** Length: 400-800 words. **Pays $100-250.**

TIPS "We are always interested in profiles of loggers and their operations in Alaska, Oregon, Washington, Montana, and Northern California. We also want articles pertaining to current industry topics, such as fire abatement, sustainable forests, or new technology. Read an issue to get a clear idea of the type of material *TimberWest* publishes. The audience is primarily loggers, and topics that focus on an 'evolving' timber industry versus a 'dying' industry will find a place in the magazine. When querying, a clear overview of the article will enhance acceptance."

MACHINERY & METAL

💲💲💲 CUTTING TOOL ENGINEERING

CTE Publications, Inc., 1 Northfield Plaza, Suite 240, Northfield IL 60093. (847)714-0175. **Fax:** (847)559-4444. **E-mail:** alanr@jwr.com. **Website:** www.ctemag.com. **Contact:** Alan Richter, editor. **40% freelance written.** Monthly magazine covering industrial metal cutting tools and metal cutting and grinding operations. *Cutting Tool Engineering* serves owners, managers, and engineers who work in manufacturing, specifically manufacturing that involves cutting or grinding metal or other materials. Writing should be geared toward improving manufacturing processes. Circ. 58,500. Byline given. Pays on publication. Offers 50% kill fee. Publishes ms an average of 2 months after acceptance. Editorial lead time 2 months. Accepts queries by mail, e-mail, phone. Responds in 2 months to mss. Sample copy and guidelines free.

NONFICTION Needs how-to, opinion, personal experience, profile, technical. Does not want fiction or articles that don't relate to manufacturing. **Buys 10 mss/year.** Length: 1,500-2,000 words. **Pays $750-1,100.** Pays expenses of writers on assignment.

PHOTOS State availability. Captions required. Reviews transparencies, prints. Negotiates payment individually. Buys all rights.

TIPS "For queries, write 2 clear paragraphs about how the proposed article will play out. Include sources that would be in the article."

◐💲💲 EQUIPMENT JOURNAL

Pace Publishing, 5160 Explorer Dr., Unit 6, Mississauga ON L4W 4T7 Canada. (416)459-5163. **E-mail:** editor@equipmentjournal.com. **Website:** www.equipmentjournal.com. **Contact:** Nathan Medcalf. **5% freelance written.** Canada's national heavy equipment newspaper. Focuses on the construction, material handling, mining, forestry, and on-highway transportation industries." Estab. 1964. Circ. 23,000. Byline given. Pays on publication. No kill fee. Publishes ms an average of 1-2 months after acceptance. Editorial lead time 2-3 months. Accepts queries by e-mail, phone. Accepts simultaneous submissions. Sample copy and guidelines free.

NONFICTION Needs how-to, interview, new product, photo feature, technical. Does not want "material that falls outside of *Equipment Journal*'s mandate—the Canadian equipment industry." **Buys 15 mss/year.** Send complete ms. "We prefer electronic submissions. We do not accept unsolicited freelance submissions." Length: 400-1,200 words. **Pays 40-50¢/word.** Pays expenses of writers on assignment.

REPRINTS Reprint payment negotiable.

PHOTOS Contact: Nathan Medcalf, editor. State availability. Identification of subjects required. Negotiates payment individually. Buys one-time rights.

COLUMNS Contact: Nathan Medcalf, editor. **Buys 2 mss/year.**

TIPS "Please pitch a story, instead of asking for an assignment. We are looking for stories of construction sites."

💲💲💲 THE FABRICATOR

833 Featherstone Rd., Rockford IL 61107. (815)399-8700. **Fax:** (815)381-1370. **E-mail:** timh@thefabricator.com. **Website:** www.thefabricator.com; www.fma-communications.com. **Contact:** Dan Davis, editor in chief; Tim Heston, senior editor. **15% freelance written.** Monthly magazine covering metal forming and fabricating. Purpose is to disseminate information about modern metal forming and fabricating techniques, machinery, tooling, and management concepts for the metal fabricator. Estab. 1971. Circ. 58,000. Byline given. Pays on publication. No kill fee. Editorial lead time 6 months. Accepts queries by mail, e-mail. Accepts simultaneous submissions. Responds in 2 weeks to queries; in 1 month to mss. Sample copy free.

NONFICTION Needs how-to, technical, company profile. Query with published clips. Length: 1,200-2,000 words. Pays expenses of writers on assignment.

PHOTOS Request guidelines for digital images. State availability. Captions, identification of subjects required. Reviews transparencies, prints. Negotiates payment individually. Rights purchased depends on photographer requirements.

MACHINE DESIGN

Penton Media, Penton Media Bldg., 1300 E. 9th St., Cleveland OH 44114. (216)931-9412. **Fax:** (216)621-8469. **E-mail:** nancy.friedrich@penton.com. **Website:** www.machinedesign.com. **Contact:** Nancy K. Friedrich, editor in chief. Semimonthly magazine covering machine design. Covers the design engineering of manufactured products across the entire spectrum of the industry for people who perform design engineering functions. Circ. 134,000. No kill fee. Editorial lead time 10 weeks. Accepts queries by mail, e-mail. Accepts simultaneous submissions. Guidelines available on website.

NONFICTION Needs how-to, new product, technical. Query. Pays expenses of writers on assignment.

COLUMNS Query with or without published clips, or send complete ms.

🍁➡$$$ MACHINERY & EQUIPMENT MRO

Annex Business Media, 80 Valleybrook Dr., Toronto ON M3B 2S9 Canada. (416)510-6851. **Fax:** (416)510-5134. **E-mail:** rbegg@annexweb.com. **Website:** www.mromagazine.com. **Contact:** Rehana Begg, Editor. **30% freelance written.** Bimonthly magazine looking for informative articles on issues that affect plant floor operations and maintenance. Estab. 1985. Circ. 18,000. Byline given. Pays on publication. No kill fee. Publishes ms an average of 3 months after acceptance. Editorial lead time 4 months. Submit seasonal material 4 months in advance. Accepts simultaneous submissions. Responds in 3 weeks to queries. Responds in 1 month to mss. Sample copy free. Guidelines available.

NONFICTION Needs essays, how-to, new product, technical. **Buys 6 mss/year.** Query with published clips. Length: 750-4,000 words. **Pays $200-1,400 (Canadian).** Pays expenses of writers on assignment.

PHOTOS State availability. Captions required. Reviews transparencies, prints. Negotiates payment individually. Buys one-time rights.

TIPS "Information can be found at our website. Call us for sample issues, ideas, etc."

MACHINERY LUBRICATION MAGAZINE

Noria Corporation, 1328 East 43rd Court, Tulsa OK 74105. (800)597-5460. **Fax:** (918)746-0925. **E-mail:** editor@noria.com. **Website:** noria.com. **Contact:** Jason Sowards, editor in chief. Bimonthly hardcopy magazine and website covering machinery lubrication, oil analysis, tribology. Estab. 2001. Circ. 41,000. Byline given. No kill fee. Publishes ms an average of 3-6 months after acceptance. Editorial lead time 3 months. Accepts queries by e-mail. Accepts simultaneous submissions. Responds in 2 weeks to queries. Responds in 3 months to mss. Sample copy online.

NONFICTION Needs how-to, new product, technical. "No heavy commercial, opinion articles." Query. Length: 1,000-2,000 words. Pays expenses of writers on assignment.

PHOTOS Send photos. Captions, identification of subjects required. Reviews GIF/JPEG files. Offers no additional payment for photos accepted with ms.

TIPS "Please request editorial guidelines by sending e-mail."

$$$ STAMPING JOURNAL

Fabricators & Manufacturers Association (FMA), 833 Featherstone Rd., Rockford IL 61107. (815)399-8700. **Fax:** (815)381-1370. **E-mail:** kateb@thefabricator.com. **Website:** www.thefabricator.com. **Contact:** Dan Davis, editor-in-chief; Kate Bachman, editor. **15% freelance written.** Bimonthly magazine covering metal stamping. Looks for how-to and educational articles—nonpromotional. Estab. 1989. Circ. 35,000. Byline given. Pays on publication. No kill fee. Editorial lead time 6 months. Accepts queries by mail, e-mail, phone. Accepts simultaneous submissions. Responds in 2 weeks to queries. Sample copy and writer's guidelines free.

NONFICTION Pays 40-80¢/word. Pays expenses of writers on assignment.

PHOTOS State availability. Captions, identification of subjects required. Negotiates payment individually. Rights purchased depends on photographer requirements.

TIPS "Articles should be impartial and should not describe the benefits of certain products available from certain companies. They should not be biased toward the author's or against a competitor's products or technologies. The publisher may refuse any article that does not conform to this guideline."

$$$ WELDING DESIGN & FABRICATION

Penton Media, 1300 E. 9th St., Cleveland OH 44114. (216)696-7000. **Fax:** (216)931-9524. **E-mail:** wdeditor@penton.com. **Website:** www.weldingdesign.com. **10% freelance written.** Bimonthly magazine covering all facets of welding and running a welding business. *Welding Design & Fabrication* provides information to the owners and managers of welding shops, including business, technology and trends. We include information on engineering and technological developments that could change the business as it is currently known, and feature stories on how welders are doing business with the goal of helping our readers to be more productive, effecient, and competitive. Welding shops are very local in nature and need to be addressed as small businessmen in a field that is consolidating and becoming more challenging and more global. We do not write about business management theory as much as we write about putting into practice good management techniques that have proved to work at similar businesses. Estab. 1930. Circ. 40,000. Byline given. Pays on publication. Offers 20% kill fee. Publishes ms an average of 1-2 months after acceptance. Editorial lead time 3-6 months. Submit seasonal material 4-6 months in advance. Accepts queries by mail, e-mail, phone. Accepts simultaneous submissions. Responds in 1-2 weeks to queries. Responds in 1 month to mss. Sample copy online.

NONFICTION Needs general interest, how-to, new product, opinion, personal experience, photo feature, technical. Query. Length: 600-2,400 words. **Pays $300-1,200.** Pays expenses of writers on assignment.

PHOTOS State availability. Captions, identification of subjects, model releases required. Reviews GIF/JPEG files (300 dpi). Negotiates payment individually. Buys all rights.

FILLERS Needs anecdotes, facts, gags, newsbreaks, short humor. **Buys 12-18 mss/year.** Length: 50-200 words. **Pays $25-100.**

TIPS Writers should be familiar with welding and/or metalworking and metal joining techniques. With that, calling or e-mailing me directly is the next best approach. We are interested in information that will help to make welding shops more competitive, and a writer should have a very specific idea before approaching me.

⊙⊙ WIRE ROPE NEWS & SLING TECHNOLOGY

Wire Rope News LLC, P.O. Box 871, Clark NJ 07066. (908)486-3221. **Fax:** (732)396-4215. **E-mail:** info@wireropenews.com. **Website:** www.wireropenews.

com. **Contact:** Edward Bluvias III, publisher and editorial director. **100% freelance written.** Bimonthly magazine published for manufacturers and distributors of wire rope, chain, cordage, related hardware, and sling fabricators. Content includes technical articles, news and reports describing the manufacturing and use of wire rope and related products in marine, construction, mining, aircraft and offshore drilling operations. Estab. 1979. Circ. 4,300. Byline sometimes given. Pays on acceptance. No kill fee. Publishes ms an average of 6 months after acceptance. Editorial lead time 2 months. Submit seasonal material 2 months in advance. Accepts queries by mail, fax. Accepts simultaneous submissions.

NONFICTION Needs general interest, historical, interview, photo feature, technical. **Buys 30 mss/year.** Send complete ms. Length: 2,500-5,000 words. **Pays $300-500.** Pays expenses of writers on assignment.

PHOTOS Send photos. Identification of subjects required. Reviews contact sheets, 5x7 prints, digital. Offers no additional payment for photos accepted with ms. Buys all rights.

TIPS We are accepting more submissions and queries by e-mail.

THE WORLD OF WELDING

Hobart Institute of Welding Technology, 400 Trade Square E, Troy OH 45373. (937)332-9500. **Fax:** (937)332-5220. **E-mail:** hiwt@welding.org. **Website:** www.worldofwelding.org. **10% freelance written.** Quarterly magazine covering welding training and education. Estab. 1930. Circ. 6,500. Byline given. Publishes ms an average of 3 months after acceptance. Editorial lead time 3 months. Submit seasonal material 3 months in advance. Accepts queries by mail, e-mail, fax. Accepts simultaneous submissions. Responds in 1 week to queries. Responds in 3 months to mss. Sample copy and guidelines free.

⊙ The content must be educational and must contain welding topic information.

NONFICTION Needs general interest, historical, how-to, interview, personal experience, photo feature. Query with published clips. Pays expenses of writers on assignment.

PHOTOS Send photos. Captions, identification of subjects, model releases required. Reviews GIF/JPEG files. Offers no additional payment for photos accepted with ms.

FILLERS Needs facts, newsbreaks. Query.

TIPS "Writers must be willing to donate material on welding and metallurgy related topics, welded art/sculpture, personal welding experiences. An editorial committee reviews submissions and determines acceptance."

MAINTENANCE & SAFETY

💲💲 AMERICAN WINDOW CLEANER MAGAZINE

12Twelve Publishing Corp., 750-B NW Broad St., Southern Pines NC 28387. (910)693-2644. **Fax:** (910)246-1681. **E-mail:** info@awcmag.com; karen@awcmag.com. **Website:** www.awcmag.com. **Contact:** Karen Grinter, creative director. **20% freelance written.** Bimonthly magazine on window cleaning. Produces articles to help window cleaners become more profitable, safe, professional, and feel good about what they do. Estab. 1986. Circ. 8,000. Byline given. Pays on acceptance. Offers 33% kill fee. Publishes ms an average of 4-8 months after acceptance. Editorial lead time 2 months. Submit seasonal material 3 months in advance. Accepts simultaneous submissions. Responds in 2 weeks to queries; in 1 month to mss. Sample copy free.

NONFICTION Needs how-to, humor, inspirational, interview, personal experience, photo feature. "We do not want PR-driven pieces. We want to educate—not push a particular product." **Buys 20 mss/year.** Query. Length: 500-5,000 words. **Pays $50-250.** Pays expenses of writers on assignment.

PHOTOS State availability. Captions required. Reviews contact sheets, transparencies, 4x6 prints. Offers $10 per photo. Buys one-time rights.

COLUMNS Window Cleaning Tips (tricks of the trade); 1,000-2,000 words; Humor-anecdotes-feel good-abouts (window cleaning industry); Computer High-Tech (tips on new technology), all 1,000 words. **Buys 12 mss/year.** Query. **Pays $50-100.**

TIPS "*American Window Cleaner Magazine* covers an unusual niche that gets people's curiosity. Articles that are technical in nature and emphasize practical tips or safety, and how to work more efficiently, have the best chances of being published. Articles include: window cleaning unusual buildings, landmarks; working for well-known people/celebrities; window cleaning in resorts/casinos/unusual cities; humor or satire about our industry or the public's perception of it. At some point, we make phone contact and chat to see if our interests are compatible."

💲💲 EXECUTIVE HOUSEKEEPING TODAY

The International Executive Housekeepers Association, 1001 Eastwind Dr., Suite 301, Westerville OH 43081-3361. (614)895-7166. **Fax:** (614)895-1248. **E-mail:** editor@ieha.org; excel@ieha.org. **Website:** www.ieha.org. **Contact:** Andi Curry, editor. **50% freelance written.** Digital magazine published bimonthly for nearly 3,500 decision makers responsible for housekeeping management (cleaning, grounds maintenance, laundry, linen, pest control, waste management, regulatory compliance, training) for a variety of institutions: hospitality, healthcare, education, retail, and government. Estab. 1930. Circ. 3,500. Byline given. No kill fee. Publishes ms an average of 6 months after acceptance. Editorial lead time 2 months. Submit seasonal material 3 months in advance. Accepts queries by mail, e-mail. Accepts simultaneous submissions.

NONFICTION Needs general interest, interview, new product, personal experience, technical. **Buys 30 mss/year.** Query with published clips. Length: 800-1,200 words Pays expenses of writers on assignment.

PHOTOS State availability. Identification of subjects required. Offers no additional payment for photos accepted with ms. Buys one-time rights.

COLUMNS Federal Report (OSHA/EPA requirements), 1,000 words; Industry News; Management Perspectives (industry specific), 1,500-2,000 words. Query with published clips.

TIPS "Have a background in the industry or personal experience with any aspect of it."

MANAGEMENT & SUPERVISION

APICS MAGAZINE

APICS The Association for Operations Management, 8430 W. Bryn Mawr Ave., Suite 1000, Chicago IL 60631. (773)867-1777. **E-mail:** editorial@apics.org. **Website:** www.apics.org. **Contact:** Elizabeth Rennie, managing editor. **15% freelance written.** Bimonthly magazine covering operations management, enterprise, supply chain, production and inventory management, warehousing and logistics. *APICS* is an award-winning publication featuring innovative ideas and real-world strategies for inventory, materials, production, and supply chain management; planning and scheduling; purchasing; logistics; warehousing; transportation and logistics; and more. Estab. 1987. Circ. 45,000. Byline given. Pays on acceptance. Offers 50% kill fee. Publishes ms an average of 2 months after acceptance. Editorial lead time 3-4 months. Submit seasonal material 3-4 months in advance. Accepts queries by e-mail. Accepts simultaneous submissions.

NONFICTION Needs technical, general research/reporting. Does not want vendor-driven articles. **Buys 3-5 mss/year.** Submit complete ms. Length: 1,750-2,250 words. Pays expenses of writers on assignment.

⑨⑨ AREA DEVELOPMENT ONLINE

Halcyon Business Publications, Inc., 400 Post Ave., Westbury NY 11590. (516)338-0900, ext. 211. **Fax:** (516)338-0100. **E-mail:** gerri@areadevelopment. com. **Website:** www.areadevelopment.com. **Contact:** Geraldine Gambale, editor. **60% freelance written. Prefers to work with published/established writers.** Quarterly magazine covering corporate facility planning and site selection for industrial chief executives worldwide. Estab. 1965. Circ. 45,000. Byline given. Pays within 90 days. No kill fee. Publishes ms an average of 2 months after acceptance. Editorial lead time 2-3 months. Accepts queries by e-mail. Accepts simultaneous submissions. Responds as soon as possible to queries. Sample copy free. E-mails submission guidelines upon request.

NONFICTION Needs historical, how-to, interview. **Buys 75 mss/year.** Query. Length: 1,500-1,800 words. **Pays 50¢/word.** Pays expenses of writers on assignment.

PHOTOS State availability. Captions, identification of subjects required. Reviews JPEGs of at least 300 dpi. Negotiates payment individually.

⑨⑨ INCENTIVE

Northstar Travel Media LLC, 100 Lighting Way, Secaucus NJ 07094. (646)380-6247; (646)380-6251. **E-mail:** valonzo@ntmllc.com; apalmer@successfulmeetings. com. **Website:** www.incentivemag.com. **Contact:** Vincent Alonzo, editor in chief; Alex Palmer, managing editor. Monthly magazine covering sales promotion and employee motivation: managing and marketing through motivation. Estab. 1905. Circ. 41,000. Byline given. Pays on acceptance. No kill fee. Publishes ms an average of 3 months after acceptance. Accepts queries

by mail, e-mail. Accepts simultaneous submissions. Responds in 1 month to queries; in 2 months to mss. Sample copy for SAE with 9x12 envelope.

NONFICTION Needs general interest, how-to, interview, travel, corporate case studies. **Buys 48 mss/ year.** Query with published clips. Length: 1,000-2,000 words. **Pays $250-700 for assigned articles. Does not pay for unsolicited articles.** Pays expenses of writers on assignment.

REPRINTS Send tearsheet and information about when and where the material previously appeared. Pays 50% of the amount paid for an original article.

PHOTOS Send photos. Identification of subjects required. Reviews contact sheets, transparencies. Offers some additional payment for photos accepted with ms.

TIPS "Read the publication, then query."

MARINE & MARITIME INDUSTRIES

⑨ WORK BOAT WORLD

Baird Maritime, Suite 3, 20 Cato St., Hawthorn East Victoria 3123 Australia. (61)(3)9824-6055. **Fax:** (61)(3)9824-6588. **E-mail:** marinfo@baird.com.au; editor@ baird.com.au. **Website:** www.bairdmaritime.com. **Contact:** Alex Baird, managing director and editor in chief. Monthly magazine covering all types of commercial, military, and government vessels to around 130 meters in length. Maintaining close contact with ship builders, designers, owners and operators, suppliers of vessel equipment and suppliers of services on a worldwide basis, the editors and journalists of *Work Boat World* seek always to be informative. They constantly put themselves in the shoes of readers so as to produce editorial matter that interests, educates, informs, and entertains. Estab. 1982. Accepts simultaneous submissions.

NONFICTION Needs general interest, how-to, interview, new product. Query. See website for info on upcoming editorial material. Pays expenses of writers on assignment.

MEDICAL

⑨ ADVANCE FOR RESPIRATORY CARE & SLEEP MEDICINE

Merion Publications, Inc., 2900 Horizon Dr., King of Prussia PA 19406. (800)355-5627, ext. 1229. **E-mail:**

cholt@advanceweb.com. **Website:** respiratory-care-sleep-medicine.advanceweb.com; www.advanceweb.com. **Contact:** Chuck Holt, editor. **50% freelance written.** Biweekly magazine covering clinical, technical, and business management trends for professionals in pulmonary, respiratory care, and sleep. *ADVANCE for Respiratory Care & Sleep Medicine* welcomes original articles, on speculation, from members of the respiratory care and sleep professions. Once accepted, mss become the property of *ADVANCE for Respiratory Care & Sleep Medicine* and cannot be reproduced elsewhere without permission from the editor. An honorarium is paid for published articles. Estab. 1988. Circ. 45,500. Byline given. Pays on publication. Offers 75% kill fee. Publishes ms an average of 6 months after acceptance. Editorial lead time 1 month. Submit seasonal material 3 months in advance. Accepts queries by mail, e-mail. Accepts simultaneous submissions. Responds in 2 weeks to queries; in 6 months to mss. Sample copy online. Guidelines available online for download.

NONFICTION Needs technical. "We do not want to get general information articles about specific respiratory care related diseases. For example, our audience is all too familiar with cystic fibrosis, asthma, COPD, bronchitis, Alpha 1 Antitrypsin Defiency, pulmonary hypertension and the like." **Buys 2-3 mss/year.** Query. E-mail article and send printout by mail. Length: 1,500-2,000 words; double-spaced, 4-7 pages. **Pays honorarium.** Pays expenses of writers on assignment.

PHOTOS State availability. Captions, identification of subjects, model releases required. Reviews GIF/JPEG files. Negotiates payment individually. Buys all rights.

TIPS "The only way to truly break into the market for this publication on a freelance basis is to have a background in health care. All of our columnists are caregivers; most of our freelancers are caregivers. Any materials that come in of a general nature like 'contact me for freelance writing assignments or photography' are discarded."

⑨ ADVANCE NEWSMAGAZINES

Merion Publications Inc., 2900 Horizon Dr., King of Prussia PA 19406. (800)355-5627, ext. 1229. **Website:** www.advanceweb.com. More than 30 magazines covering allied health fields, nursing, age management, long-term care, and more. Byline given. Pays on pub-

lication. Editorial lead time 3 months. Accepts simultaneous submissions.

NONFICTION Needs interview, new product, personal experience, technical. Query with published clips via online Web form. Include name and phone number for verification. Length: 2,000 words. Pays expenses of writers on assignment.

COLUMNS Phlebotomy Focus, Safety Solutions, Technology Trends, POL Perspectives, Performance in POCT, Eye on Education.

⑨⑨⑨ AHIP COVERAGE

America's Health Insurance Plans, 601 Pennsylvania Ave. NW, South Bldg., Suite 500, Washington DC 20004. (202)778-3200. **Fax:** (202)331-7487. **E-mail:** ahip@ahip.org. **Website:** www.ahip.org. **75% freelance written.** Bimonthly magazine geared toward administrators in America's health insurance companies. Articles should inform and generate interest and discussion about topics on anything from patient care to regulatory issues. Estab. 1990. Circ. 12,000. Byline given. Pays within 30 days of acceptance of article in final form. Offers 30% kill fee. Publishes ms an average of 2 months after acceptance. Editorial lead time 2 months. Submit seasonal material 4 months in advance. Accepts queries by mail, e-mail, fax. Accepts simultaneous submissions. Sample copy free.

NONFICTION Needs book excerpts, how-to, opinion. "We do not accept stories that promote products." Send complete ms. Length: 1,800-2,500 words. **Pays 65¢/word minimum.** Pays expenses of writers on assignment. Pays phone expenses of writers on assignment.

PHOTOS Buys all rights.

TIPS "Look for health plan success stories in your community; we like to include case studies on a variety of topics—including patient care, provider relations, regulatory issues—so that our readers can learn from their colleagues. Our readers are members of our trade association and look for advice and news. Topics relating to the quality of health plans are the ones more frequently assigned to writers, whether a feature or department. We also welcome story ideas. Just send us a letter with the details."

AMERICA'S PHARMACIST

National Community Pharmacists Association, 100 Daingerfield Rd., Suite 205, Alexandria VA 22314-2885. (800)544-7447. **Fax:** (703)683-3619. **E-mail:**

mike.conlan@ncpanet.org; chris.linville@ncpanet.org. **Website:** www.americaspharmacist.net. **Contact:** Michael F. Conlan, vice president; Chris Linville, managing editor. **10% freelance written.** Monthly magazine. *America's Pharmacist* publishes business and management information and personal profiles of independent community pharmacists, the magazine's principal readers. Articles feature the very latest in successful business strategies, specialty pharmacy services, medication safety, consumer advice, continuing education, legislation, and regulation. Estab. 1904. Circ. 25,000. Byline given. Pays on publication. No kill fee. Publishes ms an average of 3 months after acceptance. Editorial lead time 3 months. Submit seasonal material 3 months in advance. Accepts queries by mail, e-mail, fax. Accepts simultaneous submissions. Responds in 1 week to queries; in 2 weeks to mss. Sample copy free.

NONFICTION Needs interview, business information. **Buys 3 mss/year.** Query. Length: 1,500-2,500 words. Pays expenses of writers on assignment.

PHOTOS State availability. Captions, identification of subjects, model releases required. Reviews contact sheets. Negotiates payment individually. Buys one-time rights.

EMERGENCY MEDICINE NEWS

Wolters Kluwer Health, Inc., 333 Seventh Ave., 20th Floor, New York NY 10001. (646)674-6544. **Fax:** (646)674-6500. **E-mail:** emn@lww.com. **Website:** www.em-news.com. **Contact:** Lisa Hoffman, editor. **100% freelance written.** Monthly publication covering emergency medicine only, not emergency nursing, EMTs, PAs. *Emergency Medicine News* provides breaking coverage of advances, trends, and issues within the field, as well as clinical commentary with a CME activity by Editorial Board Chairman James R. Roberts, MD, a leader in the field. Estab. 1978. Circ. 37,000. Byline given. Pays on acceptance. Editorial lead time 2 months. Submit seasonal material 4 months in advance. Accepts queries by e-mail. Accepts simultaneous submissions. Responds in 2 weeks to queries; in 1 month to mss. Sample copy online.

NONFICTION Special issues: "*Emergency Medicine News* welcomes submissions from physicians. Articles may be on any topic relevant to emergency medicine, but timely, original pieces receive preference. Except for opinion pieces, full references are required." Query.

TIPS "The best way to break in is to read the publication online and pitch a unique idea. No queries that merely tout experience or are looking for assignment."

$$ JEMS

PennWell Corporation, 4180 La Jolla Village Dr., Suite 260, San Diego CA 92037. (800)266-5367. **E-mail:** rkelley@pennwell.com. **Website:** www.Jems.com. **Contact:** Ryan Kelley, managing editor. **95% freelance written.** Monthly magazine directed to personnel who serve the prehospital emergency medicine industry: paramedics, EMTs, emergency physicians and nurses, administrators, EMS consultants, etc. Estab. 1980. Circ. 45,000. Byline given. Pays on publication. No kill fee. Publishes ms an average of 6 months after acceptance. Submit seasonal material 6 months in advance. Accepts queries by e-mail. Accepts simultaneous submissions. Responds in 2-3 months to queries. Sample copy free. Guidelines available at www.jems.com/about/author-guidelines.

NONFICTION Needs general interest, how-to, interview, new product, personal experience, photo feature, profile, technical. **Buys 50 mss/year.** Query Ryan Kelley with contact information, suggested title, ms document (can be an outline), a summary, a general ms classification, and photos or figures to be considered with the ms. **Pays $100-350.**

PHOTOS State availability. Identification of subjects, model releases required. Reviews digital images. Offers $25 minimum per photo. Buys one-time rights.

COLUMNS Length: up to 850 words. Query with or without published clips. **Pays $50-250.**

TIPS "Please submit a one-page cover letter with your ms. Your letter should answer these questions: (1) What specifically are you going to tell *JEMS* readers about prehospital medical care? (2) Why do *JEMS* readers need to know this? (3) How will you make your case (i.e., literature review, original research, interviews, personal experience, observation)? Your query should explain your qualifications, as well as include previous writing samples."

JOURNAL OF THE AMERICAN MEDICAL ASSOCIATION (JAMA)

330 N. Wabash Ave., Chicago IL 60611-5885. (312)464-4444 or (312)464-2402. **E-mail:** jamams@jamanetwork.org. **Website:** www.jama.com. **Contact:** Howard Bauchner, editor-in-chief; Phil B. Fontanarosa, executive editor. *JAMA* is an international

peer-reviewed general medical journal published 48 times/year. It is the most widely circulated journal in the world. *JAMA* publishes Original Investigations, Reviews, Brief Reports, Special Communications, Viewpoints, and other categories of articles. Estab. 1883. Publishes mss 1 month after acceptance. Accepts queries by e-mail. Accepts simultaneous submissions. Guidelines online.

💬 Receives about 6,000 mss annually. Publishes 9% of mss.

NONFICTION Mss should be submitted online via submission and review system. Include a cover letter and complete contact information. Include a title page, abstract, text, references, and, as appropriate, figure legends, tables, and figures. Pays expenses of writers on assignment.

POETRY *JAMA* includes a poetry and medicine column, and publishes poetry in some way related to a medical experience, whether from the point of view of a health care worker or patient, or simply an observer. Has published poetry by Jack Coulehan, Floyd Skloot, and Walt McDonald. Length: up to 50 lines/poem.

THE JOURNAL OF URGENT CARE MEDICINE (JUCM)

Urgent Care Association of America (UCAOA), 185 St. Rt. 17 N., Second Floor, Mahwah NJ 07430. **E-mail:** editor@jucm.com. **Contact:** Lee Resnick, MD, editor in chief; Katharine O'Moore-Klopf, ELS, managing editor. **80% freelance written.** Monthly magazine covering clinical and practice management issues relevant to the field of urgent care medicine. "*JUCM* supports the evolution of urgent care medicine by creating content that addresses both the clinical needs and practice management challenges of urgent care clinicians, managers, and owners. Hence, each article must offer practical, concrete ways to improve care offered or management of the business." Estab. 2006. Circ. 11,000. Byline given. No kill fee. Publishes ms an average of 6 months after acceptance. Editorial lead time 2 months. Submit seasonal material 4 months in advance. Accepts queries by e-mail. Accepts simultaneous submissions. Responds in 1 month to queries; in 1-2 months to mss. Sample copy and guidelines free online.

NONFICTION Needs essays, how-to, opinion, clinical and practice-management. **Buys 22 mss/year.** Query. Length: 2,600-3,200 words. Pays expenses of writers on assignment.

$$ LABTALK

P.O. Box 1945, Big Bear Lake CA 92315. (909)547-2234. **E-mail:** cwalker@jobson.com. **Website:** www.labtalkonline.com. **Contact:** Christie Walker, editor. **20% freelance written.** Magazine published 6 times/year for the eye wear industry. Estab. 1970. Accepts queries by mail, e-mail. Accepts simultaneous submissions.

NONFICTION Needs new product, technical. Query. Pays expenses of writers on assignment.

TIPS "Write for the optical laboratory owner and manager."

$$$ MANAGED CARE

780 Township Line Rd., Yardley PA 19067. (267)685-2788. **Fax:** (267)685-2966. **E-mail:** pwehrwein@medimedia.com. **Website:** www.managedcaremag.com. **Contact:** Peter Wehrwein, editor. **75% freelance written.** Monthly magazine that delivers high-interest, full-length articles and shorter features on clinical and business aspects of the health care industry. Emphasizes practical, usable information that helps HMO medical directors and pharmacy directors cope with the options, challenges, and hazards in the rapidly changing health care industry. Estab. 1992. Circ. 60,000. Byline given. Pays on acceptance. Offers 20% kill fee. Publishes ms an average of 6 weeks after acceptance. Editorial lead time 3 months. Submit seasonal material 4 months in advance. Accepts queries by mail, e-mail, fax. Accepts simultaneous submissions. Responds in 3 weeks to queries. Responds in 2 months to mss. Sample copy free. Guidelines online.

NONFICTION Needs book excerpts, general interest, how-to, original research and review articles that examine the relationship between health care delivery and financing. Also considered occasionally are personal experience, opinion, interview/profile, and humor pieces, but these must have a strong managed care angle and draw upon the insights of (if they are not written by) a knowledgeable managed care professional. **Buys 40 mss/year.** Query with published clips. Length: 1,000-3,000 words. **Pays 75¢/word.** Pays expenses of writers on assignment.

PHOTOS State availability. Reviews contact sheets, negatives, transparencies, prints. Negotiates payment individually. Buys first-time rights.

TIPS "Know our audience (health plan executives) and their needs. Study our website to see what we cover."

$ $ PODIATRY MANAGEMENT

Kane Communications, Inc., P.O. Box 750129, Forest Hills NY 11375. (718)897-9700. **Fax:** (718)896-5747. **E-mail:** bblock@podiatrym.com. **Website:** www.podiatrym.com. Magazine published 9 times/year for practicing podiatrists. Aims to help the doctor of podiatric medicine to build a bigger, more successful practice, to conserve and invest his money, to keep him posted on the economic, legal, and sociological changes that affect him. Estab. 1982. Circ. 16,500. Byline given. Pays on publication. $75 kill fee. Submit seasonal material 4 months in advance. Accepts queries by e-mail. Accepts simultaneous submissions. Responds in 2 weeks to queries. Sample copy for $5 and 9x12 SAE. Guidelines for #10 SASE.

NONFICTION Buys 35 mss/year. Length: 1,500-3,000 words. **Pays $350-600.**

REPRINTS Send photocopy. Pays 33% of amount paid for an original article.

PHOTOS State availability. Pays $15 for b&w contact sheet. Buys one-time rights.

TIPS "Articles should be tailored to podiatrists, and preferably should contain quotes from podiatrists."

MUSIC TRADE

$ $ VENUES TODAY

4952 Warner Ave., Suite 201, Huntington Beach CA 92649. (714)378-5400. **Fax:** (714)378-0040. **E-mail:** linda@venuestoday.com; dave@venuestoday.com. **Website:** www.venuestoday.com. **Contact:** Linda Deckard, publisher and editor in chief. **70% freelance written.** Weekly magazine covering the live entertainment industry and the buildings that host shows and sports. Needs writers who can cover an exciting industry from the business side, not the consumer side. Readers are venue managers, concert promoters, those in the concert and sports business, not the audience for concerts and sports. Need business journalists who can cover the latest news and trends in the market. Estab. 2002. Byline given. Pays on publication. Publishes ms an average of 1 month after acceptance. Editorial lead time 1-2 months. Submit seasonal material 1-2 months in advance. Accepts queries by mail, e-mail, fax. Accepts simultaneous submissions. Responds in 1 week to queries. Sample copy online. Guidelines free.

NONFICTION Needs interview, photo feature, technical, travel. Does not want customer slant, marketing pieces. Query with published clips. Length: 500-1,500 words. **Pays $100-250.** Pays expenses of writers on assignment.

PHOTOS State availability. Captions, identification of subjects required. Reviews GIF/JPEG files. Negotiates payment individually. Buys one-time rights.

COLUMNS Venue News (new buildings, trend features, etc.); Bookings (show tours, business side); Marketing (of shows, sports, convention centers); Concessions (food, drink, merchandise). Length: 500-1,200 words. **Buys 250 mss/year. mss/year.** Query with published clips. **Pays $100-250.**

FILLERS Needs gags. **Buys 6 mss/year. Pays $100-300.**

PAPER

$ $ THE PAPER STOCK REPORT

McEntee Media Corp., 9815 Hazelwood Ave., Strongsville OH 44149. (440)238-6603. **Fax:** (440)238-6712. **E-mail:** ken@recycle.cc; psr@recycle.cc. **Website:** www.recycle.cc/psrpage.htm. **Contact:** Ken McEntee, editor/publisher. Bimonthly newsletter covering market trends and news in the paper recycling industry. Audience is interested in new innovative markets, applications for recovered scrap paper, as well as new laws and regulations impacting recycling. Estab. 1990. Circ. 2,000. Byline given. Pays on publication. No kill fee. Publishes ms an average of 1 month after acceptance. Editorial lead time 2 months. Submit seasonal material 2 months in advance. Accepts queries by mail, e-mail, fax, phone. Accepts simultaneous submissions. Responds in 1 month to queries. Sample copy for #10 SAE with 55¢ postage.

NONFICTION Needs book excerpts, essays, expose, general interest, historical, interview, new product, opinion, photo feature, technical, all related to paper recycling. **Buys 0-13 mss/year.** Send complete ms. Length: 250-1,000 words. **Pays $50-250 for assigned articles. Pays $25-250 for unsolicited articles.** Pays expenses of writers on assignment.

PHOTOS State availability. Identification of subjects required. Reviews contact sheets. Negotiates payment individually.

TIPS "Articles must be valuable to readers in terms of presenting new market opportunities or cost-saving measures."

PLUMBING, HEATING, AIR CONDITIONING & REFRIGERATION

♻$$ HPAC: HEATING PLUMBING AIR CONDITIONING

80 Valleybrook Dr., Toronto ON M3B 2S9 Canada. (416)510-5218. **Fax:** (416)510-5140. **E-mail:** smacisaac@hpacmag.com; kturner@hpacmag.com. **Website:** www.hpacmag.com. **Contact:** Sandy MacIsaac, art director; Kerry Turner, editor. **20% freelance written.** Monthly magazine. Estab. 1923. Circ. 19,500. Pays on publication. No kill fee. Publishes an average of 3 months after acceptance. Accepts queries by mail, e-mail. Accepts simultaneous submissions. Responds in 2 months to queries.

○ "We primarily want articles that show *HPAC* readers how they can increase their sales and business step-by-step based on specific examples of what others have done."

NONFICTION Needs how-to, technical. Length: 1,000-1,500 words. **Pays 50¢/word.** Pays expenses of writers on assignment.

REPRINTS Send tearsheet or photocopy with rights for sale noted and information about when and where the material previously appeared.

PHOTOS Prefers JPEGs or hi-res PDFs. Photos purchased with ms.

TIPS "Topics must relate directly to the day-to-day activities of *HPAC* readers in Canada. Must be detailed, with specific examples, quotes from specific people or authorities—show depth. We specifically want material from other parts of Canada besides southern Ontario. U.S. material must relate to Canadian readers' concerns."

$$ SNIPS MAGAZINE

BNP Media, 2401 W. Big Beaver Rd., Suite 700, Troy MI 48084. (248)244-6416. **Fax:** (248)362-0317. **E-mail:** mcconnellm@bnpmedia.com. **Website:** www.snipsmag.com. **Contact:** Michael McConnell, editor.

2% freelance written. Monthly magazine for sheet metal, heating, ventilation, air conditioning, and metal roofing contractors. Estab. 1932. No kill fee. Publishes ms an average of 3 months after acceptance. Accepts queries by mail, e-mail, fax, phone. Accepts simultaneous submissions. Call for writer's guidelines.

NONFICTION Length: under 1,000 words unless on special assignment. **Pays $200-300.** Pays expenses of writers on assignment.

PRINTING

$$ IN-PLANT GRAPHICS

NAPCO Media, 1500 Spring Garden St., 12th Floor, Philadelphia PA 19130. (215)238-5321. **Fax:** (215)238-5457. **E-mail:** bobneubauer@napco.com. **Website:** www.inplantgraphics.com. **Contact:** Bob Neubauer, editor. **40% freelance written.** *In-Plant Graphics* features articles designed to help in-house printing departments increase productivity, save money, and stay competitive. *IPG* features advances in graphic arts technology and shows in-plants how to put this technology to use. Audience consists of print shop managers working for (nonprint related) corporations (i.e., hospitals, insurance companies, publishers, nonprofits), universities, and government departments. They often oversee graphic design, prepress, printing, bindery, and mailing departments. Estab. 1951. Circ. 23,100. Byline given. Pays on publication. No kill fee. Publishes ms an average of 3 months after acceptance. Editorial lead time 2 months. Submit seasonal material 3 months in advance. Accepts queries by e-mail. Accepts simultaneous submissions. Guidelines online.

NONFICTION Needs interview, new product, technical. Special issues: See editorial calendar online. No articles on desktop publishing software or design software. No Internet publishing articles. **Buys 5 mss/ year.** Query with published clips. Length: 800-1,500 words. **Pays $350-500.** Pays expenses of writers on assignment.

PHOTOS Photos should be at least 266 dpi. State availability. Captions, identification of subjects required. Reviews transparencies, prints. Negotiates payment individually. Buys one-time rights.

COLUMNS Query with published clips.

TIPS "To get published in *IPG*, writers must contact the editor with an idea in the form of a query letter that includes published writing samples. Writers who have covered the graphic arts in the past may be assigned stories for an agreed-upon fee. We don't want stories that tout only 1 vendor's products and serve as glorified commercials. All profiles must be well balanced, covering a variety of issues. If you can tell us about an in-house printing operation doing innovative things, we will be interested."

⚙️⑤ SCREEN PRINTING

ST Media Group International, 11262 Cornell Park Dr., Cincinnati OH 45242. (513)421-2050, ext. 331. **Fax:** (513)421-5144. **E-mail:** ben.rosenfield@stmediagroup.com. **Website:** www.screenweb.com. **Contact:** Ben Rosenfield, managing editor. **30% freelance written.** Monthly magazine for the screen printing industry, including screen printers (commercial, industrial, and captive shops), suppliers and manufacturers, ad agencies, and allied profession. Estab. 1953. Circ. 17,500. Byline given. Pays on publication. No kill fee. Publishes ms an average of 3 months after acceptance. Accepts queries by mail, e-mail, fax. Accepts simultaneous submissions. Sample copy available. Guidelines for #10 SASE.

○ Works with a small number of new/unpublished writers each year.

NONFICTION Buys 10-15 mss/year. Query. Unsolicited mss not returned. Length: 2,000-3,000 words. **Pays $300-500 for major features.** Pays expenses of writers on assignment.

PHOTOS Cover photos negotiable; b&w or color. Published material becomes the property of the magazine.

TIPS "Be an expert in the screen-printing industry with supreme or special knowledge of a particular screen-printing process, or have special knowledge of a field or issue of particular interest to screen-printers. If the author has a working knowledge of screen printing, assignments are more readily available. General management articles are rarely used."

PROFESSIONAL PHOTOGRAPHY

⚙️⑤ THE PHOTO REVIEW

200 E. Maple Ave., Suite 200, Langhorne PA 19047. (215)891-0214. **Fax:** (215)891-9358. **E-mail:** info@photoreview.org. **Website:** www.photoreview.org. **50% freelance written.** Quarterly magazine covering art

photography and criticism. "*The Photo Review* publishes critical reviews of photography exhibitions and books, critical essays, and interviews. We do not publish how-to or technical articles." Estab. 1976. Circ. 2,000. Byline given. Pays on publication. No kill fee. Publishes ms an average of 9-12 months after acceptance. Editorial lead time 3 months. Submit seasonal material 6 months in advance. Accepts queries by mail. Accepts simultaneous submissions. Responds in 2 months to queries. Responds in 3 months to mss. Sample copy for $7. E-mail for guidelines.

NONFICTION Needs interview, photography essay, critical review. No how-to articles. **Buys 20 mss/year.** Send complete ms. 2-20 typed pages by e-mail **Pays $10-250.** Pays expenses of writers on assignment.

REPRINTS "Send tearsheet, photocopy, or typed ms with rights for sale noted and information about when and where the material previously appeared." Payment varies.

PHOTOS Send photos. Captions required. Reviews electronic images. Offers no additional payment for photos accepted with ms. Buys all rights.

REAL ESTATE

ⓒ⑨⑤⑤ CANADIAN PROPERTY MANAGEMENT

Media Edge, 5255 Yonge St., Suite 1000, Toronto ON M2N 2P4 Canada. (416)512-8186. **E-mail:** barbc@mediaedge.ca. **Website:** www.reminetwork.com/canadian-property-management/home/. **Contact:** Barbara Carss, editor in chief. **10% freelance written.** Magazine published 8 times/year covering Canadian commercial, industrial, institutional (medical and educational), and residential properties. *Canadian Property Management* is a trade journal supplying building owners and property managers with Canadian industry news, case law reviews, technical updates for building operations, and events listings. Building and professional profile articles are regular features. Estab. 1985. Circ. 12,500. Byline given. Pays on publication. No kill fee. Publishes ms an average of 3 months after acceptance. Editorial lead time 2 months. Submit seasonal material 2 months in advance. Accepts queries by mail, e-mail, phone. Accepts simultaneous submissions. Responds in 3 weeks to queries; in 2 months to mss. Sample copy: $5, subject to availability. Guidelines free.

NONFICTION Needs interview, technical. No promotional articles (i.e., marketing a product or service geared to this industry). Query with published clips. Length: 700-1,200 words. **Pays 35¢/word.** Pays expenses of writers on assignment.

PHOTOS State availability. Captions, identification of subjects, model releases required. Reviews transparencies, 3x5 prints, digital (at least 300 dpi). Offers no additional payment for photos accepted with ms.

TIPS "We do not accept promotional articles serving companies or their products. Freelance articles that are strong and information-based and that serve the interests and needs of property managers and building owners stand a better chance of being published. Proposals and inquiries with article ideas are appreciated the most. A good understanding of the real estate industry (management structure) is also helpful for the writer."

JOURNAL OF PROPERTY MANAGEMENT

Institute of Real Estate Management, 430 N. Michigan Ave., Chicago IL 60611. **Website:** www.irem.org. **Contact:** Mariana Toscas, MFA, managing editor. **30% freelance written.** Bimonthly magazine covering real estate management. The *Journal* has a feature/information slant designed to educate readers in the application of new techniques and to keep them abreast of current industry trends. Circ. 20,000. Byline given. Pays on acceptance. No kill fee. Publishes mss an average of 3 months after acceptance. Accepts queries by mail, e-mail. Accepts simultaneous submissions. Responds in 6 weeks to queries; in 1 month to mss. Sample copy free. Guidelines online.

NONFICTION Needs how-to, interview, technical. No non-real-estate subjects, personality, or company humor. **Buys 8-12 mss/year.** Query with published clips. Length: 750-1,500 words. Pays expenses of writers on assignment.

REPRINTS Send tearsheet, photocopy, or typed ms. Pays 35% of amount paid for an original article.

PHOTOS State availability. Identification of subjects, model releases required. Reviews contact sheets. May offer additional payment for photos accepted with ms. Buys one-time rights.

COLUMNS Insurance; Tax Issues; Technology; Maintentance; Personal Development; Legal Issues. Length: 500 words. **Buys 6-8 mss/year.** Query.

OFFICE BUILDINGS MAGAZINE

Yale Robbins, Inc., 205 Lexington Ave., 12th Fl., New York NY 10016. (212)683-5700. **Fax:** (212)497-0017.

E-mail: mrosupport@mrofficespace.com. **Website:** marketing.yrpubs.com/officebuildings. **15% freelance written.** Annual magazine published in 12 separate editions covering market statistics, trends, and thinking of area professionals on the current and future state of the real estate market. Estab. 1987. Circ. 10,500. Byline sometimes given. Pays 1 month after publication. Offers kill fee. Editorial lead time 2 months. Accepts queries by mail, e-mail. Accepts simultaneous submissions. Sample copy and writer's guidelines free.

NONFICTION Buys 15-20 mss/year. Query with published clips. Length: 1,500-2,000 words. **Pays $600-700.** Pays expenses of writers on assignment.

REM

2255B Queen St. E., Suite #1178, Toronto ON M4E 1G3 Canada. (416)425-3504. **E-mail:** jim@remonline.com. **Website:** www.remonline.com. **Contact:** Jim Adair, managing editor. **35% freelance written.** Monthly Canadian trade journal covering real estate. "*REM* provides Canadian real estate agents and brokers with news and opinions they can't get anywhere else. It is an independent publication and not affiliated with any real estate board, association, or company." Estab. 1989. Circ. 28,000. Byline given. Pays on acceptance. Offers 25% kill fee. Publishes ms an average of 2 months after acceptance. Editorial lead time 3 months. Submit seasonal material 3 months in advance. Accepts queries by mail, e-mail. Accepts simultaneous submissions. Responds in 2 weeks. Sample copy free.

NONFICTION Needs book excerpts, expose, inspirational, interview, new product, personal experience. "No articles geared to consumers about market conditions or how to choose a realtor. Must have Canadian content." Buys 60 mss/year. Query. Length: 500-1,500 words. **Pays $200-400.**

PHOTOS Send photos. Captions, identification of subjects required. Reviews transparencies, prints, GIF/JPEG files. Offers $25/photo. Buys one-time rights plus rights to place on REM websites.

TIPS "Stories must be of interest or practical use for Canadian realtors. Check out our website to see the types of stories we require."

ZONING PRACTICE

American Planning Association, 205 N. Michigan Ave., Suite 1200, Chicago IL 60601. (312)431-9100. **Fax:** (312)786-6700. **E-mail:** zoningpractice@planning.org. **Website:** www.planning.org/zoningpractice/index.htm. **90% freelance written.** Monthly newsletter covering land-use regulations including zoning. Publication is aimed at practicing urban planners and those involved in land-use decisions, such as zoning administrators and officials, planning commissioners, zoning boards of adjustment, land-use attorneys, developers, and others interested in this field. The material published comes from writers knowledgeable about zoning and subdivision regulations, preferably with practical experience in the field. Anything published needs to be of practical value to our audience in their everyday work. Estab. 1984. Circ. 2,000. Byline given. Pays on publication. Offers 50% kill fee. Publishes ms an average of 3 months after acceptance. Editorial lead time 6 months. Accepts queries by mail, e-mail, fax, phone. Accepts simultaneous submissions. Responds in 2 weeks to queries. Responds in 1 month to mss. Single copy: $10. Guidelines available at www.planning.org/zoningpractice/guidelines.htm.

NONFICTION Needs technical. See description. We do not need general or consumer-interest articles about zoning because this publication is aimed at practitioners. **Buys 12 mss/year.** Query. Length: 3,000-5,000 words. **Pays $300 minimum for assigned articles.** Pays expenses of writers on assignment.

PHOTOS State availability. Captions required. Reviews GIF/JPEG files. Negotiates payment individually. Buys all rights.

TIPS "Breaking in is easy if you know the subject matter and can write in plain English for practicing planners. We are always interested in finding new authors. We generally expect authors will earn another $200 premium for participating in an online forum called Ask the Author, in which they respond to questions from readers about their article. This requires a deep practical sense of how to make things work with regard to your topic."

RESOURCES & WASTE REDUCTION

$ $ WATER WELL JOURNAL

National Ground Water Association, 601 Dempsey Rd., Westerville OH 43081. **Fax:** (614)898-7786. **E-mail:** tplumley@ngwa.org. **Website:** www.waterwelljournal.org. **Contact:** Thad Plumley, director of publications/editor; Mike Price, senior editor. Each month the *Water Well Journal* covers the topics of

drilling, rigs and heavy equipment, pumping systems, water quality, business management, water supply, on-site waste water treatment, and diversification opportunities, including geothermal installations, environmental remediation, irrigation, dewatering, and foundation installation. It also offers updates on regulatory issues that impact the ground water industry. Circ. 24,000. Byline given. Pays on publication. Publishes ms an average of 3 months after acceptance. Editorial lead time 6 weeks. Submit seasonal material 3 months in advance. Accepts queries by mail. Accepts simultaneous submissions. Responds in 2 weeks to queries. Responds in 1 month to mss. Guidelines free.

NONFICTION Needs essays, historical, how-to, interview, new product, personal experience, photo feature, technical, business management. No company profiles or extended product releases. **Buys up to 30 mss/year.** Query with published clips. Length: 1,000-3,000 words. **Pays $150-400.** Pays expenses of writers on assignment.

PHOTOS State availability. Captions, identification of subjects required. Offers $50-250/photo.

TIPS "Some previous experience or knowledge in groundwater/drilling/construction industry helpful. Published clips are a must."

SELLING & MERCHANDISING

$ THE AMERICAN SALESMAN

National Research Bureau, 320 Valley St., Burlington IA 52601. (319)752-5415. **Fax:** (319)752-3421. **E-mail:** contact@salestrainingandtechniques.com. **E-mail:** articles@salestrainingandtechniques.com. **Website:** www.salestrainingandtechniques.com. **80% freelance written.** Monthly magazine covering sales and marketing. *The American Salesman Magazine* is designed for sales professionals. Its primary objective is to provide informative articles that develop the attitudes, skills, and personal and professional qualities of sales representatives, allowing them to use more of their potential to increase productivity and achieve goals. Byline given. Publishes ms an average of 1 month after acceptance. Editorial lead time 1 month. Submit seasonal material 2 months in advance. Accepts queries by e-mail. Accepts simultaneous submissions. Sample copy free. Guidelines by e-mail.

NONFICTION Needs personal experience. **Buys 24 mss/year.** Send complete ms. Length: 500-1,000 words. **Pays 4¢/word.** Pays expenses of writers on assignment.

😊 💲 BALLOONS & PARTIES MAGAZINE

PartiLife Publications, LLC, 65 Sussex St., Hackensack NJ 07601. (201)441-4224. Fax: (201)342-8118. E-mail: info@balloonsandparties.com. **Website:** www.balloonsandparties.com. **Contact:** Mark Zettler, publisher. **10% freelance written.** International trade journal published bi-monthly for professional party decorators and gift delivery businesses. *BALLOONS & Parties Magazine* is published 6 times/year by PartiLife Publications, LLC, for the balloon, party, and event fields. New product data, letters, mss, and photographs should be sent as "Attention: Editor" and should include sender's full name, address, and telephone number. SASE required on all editorial submissions. All submissions considered for publication unless otherwise noted. Unsolicited materials are submitted at sender's risk and *BALLOONS & Parties*/PartiLife Publications, LLC, assumes no responsibility for unsolicited materials. Estab. 1986. Circ. 7,000. Byline given. Pays on publication. No kill fee. Publishes ms an average of 3 months after acceptance. Submit seasonal material 6 months in advance. Accepts queries by mail, e-mail, fax, phone. Accepts simultaneous submissions. Responds in 6 weeks to queries. Sample copy for SAE with 9x12 envelope.

NONFICTION Needs essays, how-to, interview, new product, personal experience, photo feature, technical, craft. **Buys 12 mss/year.** Send complete ms. Length: 500-1,500 words. **Pays $100-300 for assigned articles. Pays $50-200 for unsolicited articles.** Pays expenses of writers on assignment.

REPRINTS Send typed ms with rights for sale noted and information about when and where the material previously appeared. Length: up to 2,500 words. Pays 10¢/word.

PHOTOS Send photos. Captions, identification of subjects, model releases required. Reviews 2x2 transparencies, 3x5 prints. Buys all rights.

COLUMNS Problem Solver (small business issues); Recipes That Cook (centerpiece ideas with detailed how-to); 400-1,000 words. Send complete ms with photos.

TIPS "Show unusual, lavish, and outstanding examples of balloon sculpture, design and decorating, and other craft projects. Offer specific how-to information. Be positive and motivational in style."

➍ C&I RETAILING

C&I Media, a Division of the Intermedia Group, 41 Bridge Rd., Glebe NSW 2037 Australia. (61)(2)8586-6172. **Fax:** (61)(2)9660-4419. **E-mail:** magazine@c-store.com.au. **Website:** www.c-store.com.au. Bi-monthly magazine covering retail store layout, consumer packaged goods, forecourt, impulse retailing as well as convenience food. Circ. 27,000. Accepts simultaneous submissions.

NONFICTION Needs general interest, how-to, new product, industry news. Query. Pays expenses of writers on assignment.

ENLIGHTENMENT

Bravo Integrated Media, 620 W. Germantown Pike, Suite 440, Plymouth Meeting PA 19462. (800)774-9861. **Website:** www.enlightenmentmag.com. **Contact:** Linda Longo, editorial director. **25% freelance written. Prefers to work with published/established writers.** Monthly magazine for lighting showrooms/department stores. Estab. 1923. Circ. 10,000. Pays on publication. No kill fee. Publishes ms an average of 6 months after acceptance. Submit seasonal material 6 months in advance. Accepts queries by mail, e-mail. Accepts simultaneous submissions. Responds in 2 months to queries. Sample copy for SAE with 9x12 envelope and 4 first-class stamps.

NONFICTION Needs interview, personal experience, technical, profile (of a successful lighting retailer/lamp buyer). **Buys less than 10 mss/year.** Query. Pays expenses of writers on assignment.

REPRINTS Send tearsheet and information about when and where the material previously appeared.

PHOTOS State availability. Captions required.

TIPS "Have a unique perspective on retailing lamps and lighting fixtures. We often use freelancers located in a part of the country where we'd like to profile a specific business or person. Anyone who has published an article dealing with any aspect of home furnishings will have high priority."

😊 💲 GIFTWARE NEWS

704 N. Wells St., Chicago IL 60654. (312)849-2220. **Fax:** (312)849-2174. **E-mail:** giftwarenews@talcott.com. **E-mail:** cjohnson@talcott.com. **Contact:** Claire Johnson, managing editor. **20% freelance written.** Monthly magazine covering gifts, collect-

ibles, and tabletops for giftware retailers. *"Giftware News* is designed and written for those professionals involved in the retail giftware industry. *Giftware News* serves gift stores, stationary stores, department stores, as well as other retail outlets selling giftware, stationary, party and paper, tabletop, and decorative accessories. *Giftware News* is unique in the industry with an abundance of information, a wealth of product photography, outstanding graphic design, and high-quality printing that all combine with *Giftware News'* digital products to result in a package that is unmatched by any other giftware publication." Estab. 1976. Circ. 21,000. Byline given. Pays on publication. No kill fee. Publishes ms an average of 2 months after acceptance. Submit seasonal material 6 months in advance. Accepts queries by mail, e-mail. Accepts simultaneous submissions. Responds in 2 months to mss. Sample copy: $8.

NONFICTION Needs how-to, new product. **Buys 20 mss/year.** Send complete ms. Length: 1,500-2,000 words. **Pays $400-500 for assigned articles. Pays $200-300 for unsolicited articles.** Pays expenses of writers on assignment.

PHOTOS Send photos. Identification of subjects required. Reviews 4x5 transparencies, 5x7 prints, electronic images. Offers no additional payment for photos accepted with ms.

COLUMNS Stationery, giftbaskets, collectibles, holiday, merchandise, tabletop, wedding market and display—all for the gift retailer. Length: 1,500-2,500 words. **Buys 10 mss/year.** Send complete ms. **Pays $100-250.**

TIPS "We are not looking so much for general journalists but rather experts in particular fields who can also write."

🄢🄢 NICHE

The Rosen Group, 3000 Chestnut Ave., Suite 112, Baltimore MD 21211. (410)889-3093, ext. 231. **Fax:** (410)243-7089. **E-mail:** hoped@rosengrp.com. **Website:** www.nichemagazine.com. **Contact:** Hope Daniels, editorial director. **50% freelance written.** Quarterly trade magazine for the progressive craft gallery retailer. Each issue includes retail gallery profiles, store design trends, management techniques, financial information, and merchandising strategies for small business owners, as well as articles about craft artists and craft mediums. Estab. 1988. Circ. 15,000. Byline given. Pays on publication. No kill fee. Publish-

es ms an average of 6-9 months after acceptance. Editorial lead time 9 months. Submit queries for seasonal material 1 year in advance. Accepts queries by e-mail. Accepts simultaneous submissions. Responds in 4-6 weeks to queries; 3 months to mss. Sample copy for $3.

NONFICTION Needs interview. **Buys 15-20 mss/year.** Query with published clips. **Pays $150-300.**

PHOTOS Send photos. Captions required. Reviews e-images only. Negotiates payment individually.

COLUMNS Retail Details (short items at the front of the book, general retail information); Artist Profiles (short biographies of American Craft Artists); Retail Resources (including book/video/seminar reviews and educational opportunities pertaining to retailers). Query with published clips. **Pays $25-100 per item.**

🄢 O&A MARKETING NEWS

KAL Publications, Inc., 559 S. Harbor Blvd., Suite A, Anaheim CA 92805-4525. (714)563-9300. **Fax:** (714)563-9310. **E-mail:** kathy@kalpub.com. **Website:** www.kalpub.com. **3% freelance written.** Bimonthly tabloid. *O&A Marketing News* is editorially directed to people engaged in the distribution, merchandising, installation, and servicing of gasoline, oil, TBA, quick lube, carwash, convenience store, alternative fuel, and automotive aftermarket products in the 13 Western states. Estab. 1966. Circ. 7,500. Byline sometimes given. Pays on publication. No kill fee. Publishes ms an average of 2 months after acceptance. Editorial lead time 1 month. Submit seasonal material 1 month in advance. Accepts queries by mail, e-mail, fax. Accepts simultaneous submissions. Responds in 2 months. Sample copy for SASE with 9x13 envelope and 10 first-class stamps.

NONFICTION Needs interview, photo feature, industry news. Does not want anything that doesn't pertain to the petroleum marketing industry in the 13 Western states. **Buys 35 mss/year.** Send complete ms. Length: 100-500 words. **Pays $1.25/column inch.**

PHOTOS State availability of or send photos. Captions, identification of subjects required. Reviews contact sheets, 4x6 prints, digital images. Offers $5/photo. Buys electronic rights.

COLUMNS Nevada News (petroleum marketing news in state of Nevada). **Buys 7 mss/year.** Send complete ms. **Pays $1.25/column inch.**

FILLERS Needs gags, short humor. **Buys 7 mss/year.** Length: 1-200 words. **Pays per column inch.**

TIPS "Seeking Western industry news pertaining to the petroleum marketing industry. It can be something simple—like a new gas station or quick lube opening. News from 'outlying' states such as Montana, Idaho, Wyoming, New Mexico, and Hawaii is always needed—but any timely, topical news-oriented stories will also be considered."

💲💲 PRODUCE RETAILER

Vance Publishing Corp., 10901 W. 84th Ter., Suite 200, Lenexa KS 66214. (913)438-0603; (512)906-0733. **E-mail:** PamelaR@produceretailer.com; treyes@produceretailer.com. **Website:** produceretailer.com. **Contact:** Pamela Riemenschneider, editor; Tony Reyes, art director. **10% freelance written.** Monthly magazine. "*Produce Merchandising* is the only monthly journal on the market that is dedicated solely to produce merchandising information for retailers. Our purpose is to provide information about promotions, merchandising, and operations in the form of ideas and examples." Estab. 1988. Circ. 12,000. Byline given. Pays on acceptance. No kill fee. Publishes ms an average of 3 months after acceptance. Editorial lead time 3 months. Accepts queries by mail. Accepts simultaneous submissions. Responds in 2 weeks to queries. Sample copy free.

NONFICTION Needs how-to, interview, new product, photo feature, technical. **Buys 48 mss/year.** Query with published clips. Length: 1,000-1,500 words. **Pays $200-600.** Pays expenses of writers on assignment.

PHOTOS State availability of or send photos. Captions, identification of subjects, model releases required. Reviews color slides and 3x5 or larger prints. Offers no additional payment for photos accepted with ms. Buys all rights.

COLUMNS Contact: Contact editor for a specific assignment. **Buys 30 mss/year.** Query with published clips. **Pays $200-450.**

TIPS Send in clips and contact the editor with specific story ideas. Story topics are typically outlined up to a year in advance.

💲💲 SMART RETAILER

Emmis Communications, P.O. Box 5000, N7528 Aanstad Rd., Iola WI 54945. (800)331-0038. **Fax:** (715)445-4053. **E-mail:** stephanieh@jonespublishing.com. **Website:** www.smart-retailer.com. **Contact:** Stephanie Hintz, editor. **50% freelance written.** Magazine published 7 times/year covering independent retail, gift, and home decor. *Smart Retailer* is a trade publication for independent retailers of gifts and home accents. Estab. 1993. Circ. 32,000. Byline given. Pays 1 month after acceptance of final ms. Offers $50 kill fee. Publishes ms an average of 4-6 months after acceptance. Editorial lead time 4-6 months. Submit seasonal material 8-10 months in advance. Accepts queries by mail, e-mail, fax. Accepts simultaneous submissions. Usually responds in 4-6 weeks (only if accepted). Sample articles are available on website. Guidelines by e-mail.

NONFICTION Needs how-to, interview, new product, finance, legal, marketing, small business. No fiction, poetry, fillers, photos, artwork, or profiles of businesses, unless queried and first assigned. **Buys 20 mss/year.** Send complete ms, with résumé and published clips to: Writers Query, *Smart Retailer*. Length: 1,000-2,500 words. **Pays $275-500 for assigned articles. Pays $200-350 for unsolicited articles.** Pays expenses of writers on assignment. Limit agreed upon in advance.

COLUMNS Display & Design (store design and product display), 1,500 words; Retailer Profile (profile of retailer, assigned only), 1,800 words; Vendor Profile (profile of manufacturer, assigned only), 1,200 words; Technology (Internet, computer-related articles as applies to small retailers), 1,500 words; Marketing (marketing ideas and advice as applies to small retailers), 1,500 words; Finance (financial tips and advice as applies to small retailers), 1,500 words; Legal (legal tips and advice as applies to small retailers), 1,500 words; Employees (tips and advice on hiring, firing, and working with employees as applies to small retailers), 1,500 words. **Buys 15 mss/year.** Query with published clips or send complete ms. **Pays $250-350.**

💲💲 TRAVEL GOODS SHOWCASE

Travel Goods Association, 301 North Harrison St., #412, Princeton NJ 08540. (877)842-1938. **Fax:** (877)842-1938. **E-mail:** info@travel-goods.org; cathy@travel-goods.org. **Website:** www.travel-goods.org. **Contact:** Cathy Hays. **5-10% freelance written.** Magazine published quarterly. *Travel Goods Showcase*, the largest trade magazine devoted to travel products, contains articles for retailers, dealers, manufacturers, and suppliers about luggage, business cases, personal leather goods, handbags, and accessories. Special articles report on trends in fashion, promotions, selling and marketing techniques, industry statistics, and other educational and promotional improvements and advancements. Estab. 1975. Circ. 21,000. Byline given. Pays on acceptance. Offers $50 kill fee. Publishes ms an average of 2 months after acceptance. Editorial lead time 3 months. Submit seasonal material 2 months in advance. Accepts queries by mail, e-mail. Accepts simultaneous submissions. Responds in 2 weeks to queries; 1 month to mss. Sample copy and writer's guidelines free.

NONFICTION Needs interview, new product, technical, travel, retailer profiles with photos. No manufacturer profiles. **Buys 3 mss/year.** Query with published clips. Length: 1,200-1,600 words. **Pays $200-400.** Pays expenses of writers on assignment.

❸❸❸ VM+SD

ST Media Group International, 11262 Cornell Park Dr., Cincinnati OH 45242. (513)421-2050. **Fax:** (513)421-5144. **E-mail:** carly.hagedon@stmediagroup.com; kaileigh.peyton@stmediagroup.com. **Website:** www.vmsd.com. **Contact:** Carly Hagedon, managing editor; Kaileigh Peyton, associate editor. **10% freelance written.** Monthly magazine covering retailing store design, store planning, visual merchandising, brand marketing. Estab. 1872. Circ. 20,000. Byline given. Pays on acceptance. Offers $100 kill fee. Publishes ms an average of 1-2 months after acceptance. Editorial lead time 2-3 months. Submit seasonal material 3-4 months in advance. Accepts queries by e-mail. Accepts simultaneous submissions. Sample copy free. Guidelines available online and by e-mail.

○ Articles need to get behind the story, tell not only what retailers did when building a new store, renovating an existing store, mounting a new in-store merchandise campaign, but also why they did what they did: specific goals, objectives, strategic initiatives, problems to solve, target markets to reach, etc.

NONFICTION **Buys 2-3 mss/year.** Query with details of project, including a press release if available, high-resolution, professional photos, the date the store opened, and any other information available. Length: 500-1,000 words. **Pays $400-1,000.** Pays expenses of writers on assignment.

PHOTOS Send photos. Reviews GIF/JPEG files. Negotiates payment individually. Buys one-time rights.

COLUMNS Editorial calendar available online. **Buys 5-6 mss/year.** Query. **Pays $500-750.**

TIPS "We need to see a demonstrated understanding of our industry, its issues and major players; strong reporting and interviewing skills are also important. Merely facile writing is not enough for us."

SPORT TRADE

❸❸ GOLF COURSE MANAGEMENT

Golf Course Superintendents Association of America (GCSAA), 1421 Research Park Dr., Lawrence KS 66049. (785)832-4456. **Fax:** (785)832-3665. **E-mail:** shollister@gcsaa.org; mhirt@gcsaa.org; tcarson@gcsaa.org. **Website:** www.gcsaa.org. **Contact:** Scott Hollister, editor in chief; Megan Hirt, managing editor; Teresa Carson, science editor. **50% freelance written.** Monthly magazine covering the golf course superintendent. *GCM* helps the golf course superintendent become more efficient in all aspects of their job. Estab. 1924. Circ. 40,000. Byline given. Pays on acceptance. No kill fee. Publishes ms an average of 6 months after acceptance. Editorial lead time 6 months. Submit seasonal material 6 months in advance. Accepts queries by e-mail. Accepts simultaneous submissions. Responds in 3 weeks to queries; in 1 month to mss. Sample copy free. Guidelines online.

NONFICTION Needs how-to, interview. No articles about playing golf. **Buys 40 mss/year.** Query for either feature, research, or superintendent article. Submit electronically, preferably as e-mail attachment. Send one-page synopsis or query for feature article to Scott Hollister. For research articles, submit to Teresa Carson. If you are a superintendent, contact Megan Hirt. Length: 1,500-2,500 words. **Pays $400-600.** Pays expenses of writers on assignment.

PHOTOS Send photos. Identification of subjects required. Offers no additional payment for photos accepted with ms. Buys all rights.

TIPS "Writers should have prior knowledge of golf course maintenance, agronomy and turfgrass science, and the overall profession of the golf course superintendent."

IDEA FITNESS JOURNAL

IDEA Health & Fitness Association, Inc., 10455 Pacific Center Court, San Diego CA 92121. (858)535-8979. **Fax:** (858)535-8234. **E-mail:** swebster@ideafit.com. **Website:** www.ideafit.com. **70% freelance written.** Magazine published 10 times/year for fitness professionals—personal trainers, group fitness instructors, and studio and health club owners—covering topics such as exercise science, nutrition, injury prevention, entrepreneurship in fitness, fitness-oriented research, and program design. Estab. 1984. Circ. 20,000. Byline given. Pays within 60 days of final acceptance. No kill fee. Publishes ms an average of 4 months after acceptance. Accepts queries by e-mail. Accepts simultaneous submissions. Responds in 2 months to queries. Sample copy: $5. Guidelines online.

NONFICTION Needs how-to, technical. Articles must not be published elsewhere. No general information on fitness; our readers are pros who need detailed information. **Buys 15 mss/year.** Query. Length: 3,000-3,500 words. **Payment varies.** Pays expenses of writers on assignment.

PHOTOS State availability. Model releases required. Offers no additional payment for photos with ms. Buys all rights.

COLUMNS Exercise Rx (geared to the intermediate/advanced trainer who is familiar with training variables and needs information on how to manipulate them); Profit Center (marketing a personal training business, retaining clients, payment schemes, finance and administration, and career options); Trainer-Entrepreneur (provides insight to personal trainer business owners on how to leverage their talents and other business concepts for added business success); Tricks of the Trade (Q&A format covering diverse areas of a personal trainer's career); Nutrition (focuses on a particular nutrient or food category, or describes eating behaviors, dietary plans, or nutrition myths); Group Exercise Skills & Drills (supports the growth of all group fitness professionals through targeted teaching skills topics such as cuing techniques, management styles, tips and tricks for interacting with members, and career enrichment); Buzz (a short list of progressive classes and formats from around the world); Class Take Out (a choreographed class format, complete with diagrams, music suggestions, counts, injury prevention, etc.); Ignite/Ebb/Core (offers practical and effective ideas for the different sections of a group exercise class: the warm-up, cool-down, and core sections); Inner IDEA (addresses the wide array of science and programming that underpin mind-body focused techniques and philosophies); Senior Fitness (focuses on the special needs of older adults and includes communication, program design, exercise modifications, and business ideas for serving this burgeoning population well); all 1,200-1,400 words. **Buys 80 mss/year.** Query. **Payment varies.**

TIPS "We don't accept fitness information for the consumer audience on topics such as why exercise is good for you. Writers who have specific knowledge of, or experience working in, the fitness industry have an edge."

$$ REFEREE

Referee Enterprises, Inc., 2017 Lathrop Ave., Racine WI 53405. (800)733-6100. **Fax:** (262)632-5460. **E-mail:** submissions@referee.com. **Website:** www.referee.com. **Contact:** Julie Sternberg, managing editor. **75% freelance written.** Monthly magazine covering sports officiating. *Referee* is a magazine for and read by sports officials of all kinds with a focus on baseball, basketball, football, softball, and soccer officiating. Estab. 1976. Circ. 40,000. Byline given. Pays on acceptance. Offers kill fee. Kill fee negotiable. Publishes ms an average of 6 months after acceptance. Editorial lead time 6 months. Accepts queries by mail, e-mail. Accepts simultaneous submissions. Responds in 2 weeks to queries; 1 month to mss. Sample copy with #10 SASE. Guidelines online.

NONFICTION Needs book excerpts, essays, historical, how-to, humor, interview, opinion, photo feature, technical. "We don't want to see articles with themes not relating to sport officiating. General sports articles, although of interest to us, will not be published." **Buys 40 mss/year.** Query with published clips. Length: 500-3,500 words. **Pays $50-400.** Pays expenses of writers on assignment.

PHOTOS State availability. Identification of subjects required. Reviews photos mailed on CD or DVD. Offers $35-40 per photo. Purchase of rights negotiable.

TIPS "Query first and be persistent. We may not like your idea, but that doesn't mean we won't like your next one. Professionalism pays off."

STONE, QUARRY & MINING

🍁$$ CANADIAN MINING JOURNAL

Business Information Group, 38 Lesmill Rd., Unit 2, Toronto ON M3B 2T5 Canada. (416)510-6742. **E-mail:** rnoble@canadianminingjournal.com. **Website:** www.canadianminingjournal.com. **Contact:** Russell Noble, editor. **5% freelance written.** Magazine covering mining and mineral exploration by Canadian companies. *Canadian Mining Journal* provides articles and information of practical use to those who work in the technical, administrative, and supervisory aspects of exploration, mining, and processing in the Canadian mineral exploration and mining industry. Estab. 1882. Circ. 11,000. Byline given. Pays on publication. No kill fee. Publishes ms an average of 3 months after acceptance. Submit seasonal material 3 months in advance. Accepts queries by mail, e-mail, phone. Accepts simultaneous submissions. Responds in 1 week to queries; in 1 month to mss.

NONFICTION Needs opinion. **Buys 6 mss/year.** Query with published clips. Length: 500-1,400 words. **Pays $100-600.** Pays expenses of writers on assignment.

PHOTOS State availability. Photos require caption, identification of subjects. Reviews 4x6 prints or high-resolution files. Negotiates payment individually. Buys one-time rights.

COLUMNS Guest editorial (opinion on controversial subject related to mining industry), 600 words. **Buys 3 mss/year.** Query with published clips. **Pays $150.**

TIPS "We need articles about mine sites that would be expensive/difficult for me to reach. We also need to know the writer is competent to understand and describe the technology in an interesting way."

TOY, NOVELTY & HOBBY

💲💲 MODEL RETAILER

Kalmbach Publishing Co., 21027 Crossroads Circle, Waukesha WI 53187. (262)796-8776. **E-mail:** jreich@kalmbach.com. **E-mail:** editor@modelretailer.com. **Website:** www.modelretailer.com. Elizabeth Nash, associate editor

Elizabeth Nash, associate editor; Monica Freitag, editorial associate. **Contact:** Jeff Reich, editor. **30% freelance written.** Monthly magazine. *Model Retailer* covers the business of hobby retailing, from financial and store management issues to product and industry trends. Our goal is to provide owners and managers with the tools and information they need to be successful retailers. Estab. 1987. Circ. 6,000. Byline given. Pays on acceptance. 25% kill fee. Publishes ms an average of 2 months after acceptance. Editorial lead time 3 months. Submit seasonal material 6 months in advance. Accepts queries by e-mail. Accepts simultaneous submissions. Sample copy free. Guidelines online.

NONFICTION Needs book excerpts, essays, how-to, interview, new product, nostalgic, opinion, profile, reviews. No articles that do not have a strong hobby or small retail component. **Buys 30-40 mss/year.** Query

with published clips. "We welcome queries for feature articles and columns and the submission of articles sent on speculation. Queries and submissions accepted by e-mail only." Length: 800-1,600 words. **Pays $100-450.** Pays expenses of writers on assignment.

PHOTOS State availability. Captions, identification of subjects required. Reviews digital images. Negotiates payment individually. Buys one-time rights.

TRANSPORTATION

💲💲💲💲 RAILWAY TRACK AND STRUCTURES

Simmons-Boardman Publishing, 55 Broad St., 26th Floor, New York NY 10004. (212)620-7200. **Fax:** (212)633-1165. **E-mail:** Mischa@sbpub-chicago.com; Jnunez@sbpub-chicago.com. **Website:** www.rtands.com. **Contact:** Mischa Wanek-Libman, editor; Jennifer Nunez, assistant editor. **1% freelance written.** Monthly magazine covering railroad civil engineering. *RT&S* is a nuts-and-bolts journal to help railroad civil engineers do their jobs better. Estab. 1904. Circ. 9,500. Byline given. Pays on publication. Offers 90% kill fee. Publishes ms an average of 1 month after acceptance. Editorial lead time 2 months. Submit seasonal material 3 months in advance. Accepts queries by mail, fax, phone. Accepts simultaneous submissions. Responds in 1 month to queries and to mss. Sample copy online.

NONFICTION Needs how-to, new product, technical. Does not want nostalgia or "railroadiana." **Buys 1 mss/year.** Query. Length: 900-2,000 words. **Pays $500-1,000.** Pays expenses of writers on assignment.

PHOTOS State availability. Captions, identification of subjects, model releases required. Reviews GIF/JPEG files. Negotiates payment individually. Buys one-time rights.

TIPS "We prefer writers with a civil engineering background and railroad experience."

💲💲⊘ SCHOOL BUS FLEET

Bobit Business Media, 3520 Challenger St., Torrance CA 90503. (310)533-2400. **E-mail:** info@schoolbusfleet.com. **Website:** www.schoolbusfleet.com. Magazine covering school transportation of K-12 population. Most readers are school bus operators, public and private. Estab. 1956. Circ. 25,239. Byline given. Pays on acceptance. Offers 25% kill fee or $50. Publishes ms an average of 3 months after acceptance. Editorial lead time 3 months. Submit seasonal material 3 months in advance. Accepts queries by mail, e-mail. Accepts simultaneous submissions. Responds in 1 month to queries. Sample copy free. *Not currently accepting submissions.* Query first.

NONFICTION Pays expenses of writers on assignment.

🄢🄢 SCHOOL TRANSPORTATION NEWS

STN Media Co., P.O. Box 789, Redondo Beach CA 90277. (310)792-2226. **Fax:** (310)792-2231. **E-mail:** ryan@stnonline.com; sylvia@stonline.com. **Website:** www.stnonline.com. **Contact:** Ryan Gray, editor in chief; Sylvia Arroyo, managing editor. **20% freelance written.** Monthly magazine covering school bus and pupil transportation industries in North America. Contributors to *School Transportation News* must have a basic understanding of K-12 education and automotive fleets and specifically of school buses. Articles cover such topics as manufacturing, operations, maintenance and routing software, GPS, security and legislative affairs. A familiarity with these principles is preferred. Additional industry information is available on website. New writers must perform some research of the industry or exhibit core competencies in the subject matter. Estab. 1991. Circ. 24,000. Byline given. Pays on publication. No kill fee. Editorial lead time 1-2 months. Submit seasonal material 3 months in advance. Accepts queries by e-mail. Accepts simultaneous submissions. Sample copy free. Guidelines free.

NONFICTION Needs book excerpts, general interest, historical, humor, inspirational, interview, new product, personal experience, photo feature, technical. Does not want strictly localized editorial. Wants articles that put into perspective the issues of the day. Query with published clips. Length: 600-1,200 words. **Pays $150-300.** Pays expenses of writers on assignment.

PHOTOS Contact: Sylvia Arroyo, managing editor. Captions, model releases required. Reviews GIF/JPEG files. Offers $150-200/photo. Buys all rights.

COLUMNS Creative Special Report, Cover Story, Top Story; Book/Video Reviews (new programs/publications/training for pupil transporters), both 600 words. **Buys 40 mss/year.** Query with clips. **Pays $150.**

TRAVEL TRADE

⊘ LL&A MAGAZINE

Media Diversified, Inc., 96 Karma Rd., Markham ON L3R 4Y3 Canada. (905)944-0265. **Fax:** (416)296-0994. **E-mail:** tammy@mediadiversified.com. **E-mail:** carolyn@llanda.com. **Website:** www.llanda.com. Carolyn Camil-

leri. **5% freelance written.** Magazine published 3 times/year for the travel, business, and fashion accessory market. Established in 1966, this year represents the magazines 50th anniversary covering the travel, business, and fashion accessory market. Estab. 1966. Circ. 7,000. Byline given. Pays on publication. No kill fee. Editorial lead time 6 weeks. Accepts queries by e-mail. Accepts simultaneous submissions. Sample copy and guidelines free.

NONFICTION Needs general interest, how-to, new product, technical, trade. Pays expenses of writers on assignment.

🄢🄢 MIDWEST MEETINGS®

Hennen Publishing, 302 Sixth St. W., Suite A, Brookings SD 57006. (605)692-9559. **Fax:** (605)692-9031. **E-mail:** info@midwestmeetings.com; editor@midwestmeetings.com. **Website:** www.midwestmeetings.com. **Contact:** Randy Hennen. **20% freelance written.** Quarterly magazine covering meetings/conventions industry. "We provide information and resources to meeting/convention planners with a Midwest focus." Estab. 1996. Circ. 28,500. Byline given. Pays on acceptance. Publishes ms an average of 5 months after acceptance. Editorial lead time 3 months. Submit seasonal material 3 months in advance. Accepts queries by e-mail. Accepts simultaneous submissions. Sample copy free. Guidelines by e-mail.

NONFICTION Needs essays, general interest, historical, how-to, humor, interview, personal experience, travel. Does not want marketing pieces related to specific hotels/meeting facilities. **Buys 15-20 mss/year.** Send complete ms. Length: 500-1,000 words. **Pays 5-50¢/word.** Pays expenses of writers on assignment.

PHOTOS Send photos. Captions, identification of subjects and permission statements/photo releases required. Reviews JPEG/EPS/TIF files (300 dpi). Offers no additional payment for photos accepted with ms. Buys one time rights.

TIPS "If you were a meeting/event planner, what information would help you perform your job better? We like lots of quotes from industry experts, insider tips, personal experience stories, etc. If you're not sure, e-mail the editor."

🄢🄢🄢 RVBUSINESS

G&G Media Group, 2901 E. Bristol St., Suite B, Elkhart IN 46514. (574)266-7980, ext. 13. **Fax:** (574)266-7984. **E-mail:** bhampson@rvbusiness.com; bhampson@g-gmediagroup.com. **Website:** www.rvbusiness.com. **Contact:** Bruce Hampson, editor. **50% freelance written.** Bimonthly magazine. *RVBusiness* caters to a specific audience of people who manufacture, sell, market, insure, finance, service and supply, components for recreational vehicles. Estab. 1972. Circ. 21,000. Byline given. Pays on acceptance. Offers kill fee. Publishes ms an average of 2 months after acceptance. Editorial lead time 2 months. Accepts simultaneous submissions. Sample copy free.

NONFICTION Needs new product, photo feature, industry news and features. No general articles without specific application to market. **Buys 50 mss/year.** Query with published clips. Length: 125-2,200 words. **Pays $50-1,000.** Pays expenses of writers on assignment.

COLUMNS Top of the News (RV industry news), 75-400 words; Business Profiles, 400-500 words; Features (indepth industry features), 800-2,000 words. **Buys 50 mss/year.** Query. **Pays $50-1,000.**

🟡🟡 SPECIALTY TRAVEL INDEX

Alpine Hansen, P.O. Box 458, San Anselmo CA 94979. (415)455-1643. **E-mail:** info@specialtytravel.com. **Website:** www.specialtytravel.com. **90% freelance written.** Semiannual magazine covering adventure and special interest travel. Estab. 1980. Circ. 35,000. Byline given. Pays on receipt and acceptance of all materials. No kill fee. Editorial lead time 3 month. Submit seasonal material 3 months in advance. Accepts queries by mail, e-mail. Accepts simultaneous submissions. Writer's guidelines on request.

NONFICTION Needs how-to, personal experience, photo feature, travel. **Buys 15 mss/year.** Query. Length: 1,250 words. **Pays $300 minimum.** Pays expenses of writers on assignment.

REPRINTS Send tearsheet. Pays 100% of amount paid for an original article.

PHOTOS State availability. Captions, identification of subjects required. Reviews EPS/TIFF files. Negotiates payment individually.

VETERINARY

ANIMAL SHELTERING

P.O. Box 15276, North Hollywood CA 91615. (800)565-9226. **E-mail:** asm@humanesociety.org. **Website:** www.animalsheltering.org. **Contact:** Shevaun Brannigan, production/marketing manager; Carrie Allan, editor. **20% freelance written.** Magazine for animal care professionals and volunteers, dealing with animal welfare issues faced by animal shelters, animal control agencies, and rescue groups. Emphasis on news for the field and professional, hands-on work. Readers are shelter and animal control directors, kennel staff, field officers, humane investigators, animal control officers, animal rescuers, foster care volunteers, general volunteers, shelter veterinarians, and anyone concerned with local animal welfare issues. Estab. 1978. Circ. 6,000. Accepts simultaneous submissions. Sample copies are free; contact Shevaun Brannigan at sbrannigan@hsus.org. Guidelines available by e-mail.

NONFICTION Approximately 6-10 submissions published each year from non-staff writers; of those submissions, 50% are from writers new to the publication. **"Payment varies depending on length and complexity of piece. Longer features generally $400–600; short news pieces generally $200. We rarely take unsolicited work, so it's best to contact the editor with story ideas."** Pays expenses of writers on assignment.

REPRINTS "Aquires first publication rights. We also grant permission, with a credit to the magazine and writer, to readers who want to use the materials to educate their supporters, staff and volunteers. Contact asm@humanesociety.org for writers' guidelines."

PHOTOS Pays $150 for cover; $75 for inside.

🟡🟡 VETERINARY ECONOMICS

8033 Flint St., Lenexa KS 66214. (800)255-6864. **Fax:** (913)871-3808. **E-mail:** dvmnews@advanstar.com. **Website:** veterinarybusiness.dvm360.com. **20% freelance written.** Monthly magazine covering veterinary practice management. "We address the business concerns and management needs of practicing veterinarians." Estab. 1960. Circ. 54,000. Byline given. Pays on publication. No kill fee. Publishes ms an average of 6 months after acceptance. Editorial lead time 3 months. Submit seasonal material 3 months in advance. Accepts queries by mail, e-mail. Accepts simultaneous submissions. Responds in 3 months to queries. Sample copy free. Guidelines online.

NONFICTION Needs how-to, interview, personal experience. **Buys 24 mss/year.** Send complete ms. Length: 1,000-2,000 words. **Pays $40-350.** Pays expenses of writers on assignment.

PHOTOS Send photos. Captions, identification of subjects required. Reviews transparencies, prints. Offers no additional payment for photos accepted with ms. Buys one-time rights.

COLUMNS Practice Tips (easy, unique business tips), 250 words or fewer. Send complete ms. **Pays $40.**

CONTESTS & AWARDS

///

The contests and awards listed in this section are arranged by subject. Nonfiction writers can turn immediately to nonfiction awards listed alphabetically by the name of the contest or award. The same is true for fiction writers, poets, playwrights and screenwriters, journalists, children's writers, and translators. You'll also find general book awards, fellowships offered by arts councils and foundations, and multiple category contests.

New contests and awards are announced in various writer's publications nearly every day. However, many lose their funding or fold, and sponsoring magazines go out of business just as often. **Contact names, entry fees,** and **deadlines** have been highlighted and set in bold type for your convenience.

To make sure you have all the information you need about a particular contest, always send a SASE to the contact person in the listing before entering a contest or check their website. The listings in this section are brief, and many contests have lengthy, specific rules and requirements that we could not include in our limited space. Often a specific entry form must accompany your submission.

When you receive a set of guidelines, you'll see some contests are not applicable to all writers. The writer's age, previous publication, geographic location, and length of the work are common matters of eligibility. Read the requirements to ensure you don't enter a contest for which you're not qualified.

Winning a contest or award can launch a successful writing career. Take a professional approach by doing a little extra research. Find out who the previous winner of the award was by investing in a sample copy of the magazine in which the prize-winning article, poem, or short story appeared. Attend the staged reading of an award-winning play. Your extra effort will be to your advantage in competing with writers who simply submit blindly.

PLAYWRITING & SCRIPTWRITING

A+ PLAYWRITING CONTEST FOR TEACHERS

Pioneer Drama Service, Inc., P.O. Box 4267, Englewood CO 80155. (303)779-4035. **Fax:** (303)779-4315. **E-mail:** editors@pioneerdrama.com. **E-mail:** submissions@pioneerdrama.com. **Website:** www.pioneerdrama.com. **Contact:** Lori Conary, submissions editor. Playwright must be a current or retired faculty member at an accredited K-12 public or private school in the US or Canada. All plays submitted through this contest must have been produced within the last 2 years at the school where the playwright teaches. Rules and guidelines available online. Encourages the development of quality plays written specifically by teachers and other educators. All qualifying mss accepted for publication will be considered contest finalists. Deadline: Submissions will be accepted on an on-going basis with a June 30 cutoff each year. Prize: $500 royalty advance and a one-time $500 donation to the school theatre program where the play was first produced. Judged by editors.

ACCLAIM FILM AND TV SCRIPT CONTESTS

Acclaim Scripts, 300 Central Ave, Suite 501, St. Petersburg FL 33701. **E-mail:** info@acclaimscripts.com. **Website:** www.acclaimscripts.com. Annual contest for TV and film scripts. Open to all writers worldwide. Work must be original material of the author(s). Must not be sold or optioned at time of submission. Multiple entries may be submitted (include separate entry form for each submission). Two categories for TV: comedy and drama. Contests are ongoing and deadlines change; visit website to check for updated deadlines. Prize: TV: Winner of each category receives $500. Film: 1st Place: $1,000. All winners and finalists may receive consideration by established production companies and agencies.

THE ANNUAL CONTEST OF CONTEST WINNERS™ COMPETITION

ScriptDoctor.com, 3661 N. Campbell Ave., Suite 222, Tucson AZ 85719. **E-mail:** thedoc@scriptdoctor.com. **Website:** www.scriptdoctor.com. **Contact:** Howard Allen. Contest of Contest Winners ($_{TM}$) joins Sunscreen Film Festivals. There are only a few dozen prestigious, reputable competitions—but which screenplay from the winners of all of these quality competitions is the best of the best? No entry may have earned money or other consideration for more than $5,000. "Winners must have placed in a competition on our list or approved by us." Entrants qualify by having won or placed in a screenwriting competition during the past five years. With a decade of excellent industry response, a good showing in CCW proves your script stands out among the toughest competition. Provides industry-wide publicity. Deadline: Early: June 15 ($75); Late: July 15 ($85)/. Prize: Winners receive a free set of Story Notes from ScriptDoctor.com (rated No. 1 in national survey and valued at $1500), VIP Passes to the festival, along with discount lodging. Prizes given to the other Finalists:trophies at a presentation ceremony, Skype meeting with festival filmmakers, agents, and producers. Judged by working professionals, including ScriptDoctor Howard Allen, Chris Haughom, Victoria Lucas, and others.

APPALACHIAN FESTIVAL OF PLAYS & PLAYWRIGHTS

Barter Theatre, Box 867, c/o Barter Theatre, Abingdon VA 24212-0867. (276)619-3316. **Fax:** (276)619-3335. **E-mail:** apfestival@bartertheatre.com. **E-mail:** apfestival@bartertheatre.com. **Website:** www.bartertheatre.com. **Contact:** Nick Piper, Associate Artistic Director/Director, New Play Development. With the annual Appalachian Festival of New Plays & Playwrights, Barter Theatre wishes to celebrate new, previously unpublished/unproduced plays by playwrights from the Appalachian region. If the playwrights are not from Appalachia, the plays themselves must be about the region. Deadline: March 2. Prize: $250, a staged reading performed at Barter's Stage II theater, and some transportation compensation and housing during the time of the festival.

THE BLANK THEATRE COMPANY YOUNG PLAYWRIGHTS FESTIVAL

P.O. Box 38756, Hollywood CA 90038. (323)662-7734. **Fax:** (323)661-3903. **E-mail:** info@theblank.com. **E-mail:** submissions@youngplaywrights.com. **Website:** ypf.theblank.com. Purpose is to give young playwrights an opportunity to learn more about playwriting and to give them a chance to have their work mentored, developed, and presented by professional artists.

CALIFORNIA YOUNG PLAYWRIGHTS CONTEST

Playwrights Project, 3675 Ruffin Rd., Suite 330, San Diego CA 92123-1870 USA. (858)384-2970. **Fax:**

(858)384-2974. **E-mail:** write@playwrightsproject. org. **Website:** http://www.playwrightsproject.org/ programs/contest/. **Contact:** Cecelia Kouma, Executive Director. Annual contest open to Californians under age 19. Annual contest. "Our organization and the contest is designed to nurture promising young writers. We hope to develop playwrights and audiences for live theater. We also teach playwriting." Submissions are required to be unpublished and not produced professionally. Submissions made by the author. SASE for contest rules and entry form. Scripts must be a minimum of 10 standard typewritten pages; send 2 copies. Scripts will *not* be returned. If requested, entrants receive detailed evaluation letter. Guidelines available online. Deadline: June 1. Prize: Scripts will be produced in spring at a professional theatre in San Diego. Writers submitting scripts of 10 or more pages receive a detailed script evaluation letter upon request. Judged by professionals in the theater community, a committee of 5-7; changes somewhat each year.

DRURY UNIVERSITY ONE-ACT PLAY CONTEST

Drury University, 900 N. Benton Ave., Springfield MO 65802-3344. **E-mail:** msokol@drury.edu. **Contact:** Mick Sokol. Offered in even-numbered years for unpublished and professionally unproduced plays. One play per playwright. Guidelines for SASE or by e-mail. Deadline: December 1. Prize: 1st Place: $300; Honorable Mention: $150.

ESSENTIAL THEATRE PLAYWRITING AWARD

The Essential Theatre, 1414 Foxhall Ln., #10, Atlanta GA 30316. (404) 212-0815. **E-mail:** pmhardy@ aol.com. **Website:** www.essentialtheatre.com. **Contact:** Peter Hardy. Offered annually for unproduced, full-length plays by Georgia resident writers. No limitations as to style or subject matter. Submissions can be e-mailed in PDF or Word Documents, or sent by postal mail. See website for full guidelines. Deadline: April 23. Prize: $600 and full production.

SHUBERT FENDRICH MEMORIAL PLAYWRITING CONTEST

Pioneer Drama Service, Inc., P.O. Box 4267, Englewood CO 80155. (303)779-4035. **Fax:** (303)779-4315. **E-mail:** editors@pioneerdrama.com. **E-mail:** submissions@pioneerdrama.com. **Website:** www.pio-

neerdrama.com. **Contact:** Lori Conary, submissions editor. Annual competition that encourages the development of quality theatrical material for educational, community and children's theatre markets. Previously unpublished submissions only. Only considers mss with a running time between 20-90 minutes. Open to all writers not currently published by Pioneer Drama Service. Guidelines available online. No entry fee. Cover letter, SASE for return of ms, and proof of production or staged reading must accompany all submissions. Deadline: Ongoing contest; a winner is selected by June 1 each year from all submissions received the previous year. Prize: $1,000 royalty advance in addition to publication. Judged by editors.

FILMMAKERS INTERNATIONAL SCREENWRITING AWARDS

Beverly Hills CA 90210 USA. **E-mail:** info@filmmakers.com. **Website:** www.filmmakers.com/screenplay/. Early: Feb. 29; regular: April 30; late: June 30; Final Jul 31st. Grand Prize: $2500; 3 X Elite Prizes: $500 per category.

JOHN GASSNER MEMORIAL PLAYWRITING COMPETITION

New England Theatre Conference, 215 Knob Hill Dr., Hamden CT 06158. **Fax:** (203)288-5938. **E-mail:** mail@netconline.org. **Website:** www.netconline.org. Annually seeks unpublished full-length plays and scripts. Open to all. Playwrights living outside New England may participate. Deadline: April 15. Prize: 1st Place: $1,000; 2nd Place: $500.

THE MARILYN HALL AWARDS FOR YOUTH THEATRE

P.O. Box 148, Beverly Hills CA 90213. **Website:** www. beverlyhillstheatreguild.com. **Contact:** Candace Coster, competition coordinator. The Marilyn Hall Awards consist of 2 monetary prizes for plays suitable for grades 6-8 (middle school) or for plays suitable for grades 9-12 (high school). The 2 prizes will be awarded on the merits of the play scripts, which includes its suitability for the intended audience. The plays should be approximately 45-75 minutes in length. There is no production connected to any of the prizes, though a staged reading is optional at the discretion of the BHTG. Unpublished submissions only. Authors must be U.S. citizens or legal residents and must sign entry form personally. Deadline: The last day of February. Submission period begins January 15. Prize: 1st Prize: $700; 2nd Prize: $300.

AURAND HARRIS MEMORIAL PLAYWRITING AWARD

The New England Theatre Conference, Inc., 215 Knob Hill Dr., Hamden CT 06518. **Fax:** (203)288-5938. **E-mail:** mail@netconline.org. **Website:** www.netconline.org. Offered annually for an unpublished full-length play for young audiences. Guidelines available online or for SASE. Open to all. Deadline: May 1. Prize: 1st Place: $1,000; 2nd Place: $500

HRC SHOWCASE THEATRE PLAYWRITING CONTEST

P.O. Box 940, Hudson NY 12534. (518)851-7244. **E-mail:** hrcshowcaseplaycontest@gmail.com. **Website:** www.hrc-showcasetheatre.com. **Contact:** Jesse Waldinger, chair. HRC Showcase Theatre invites submissions of full-length plays to its annual contest from new, aspiring, or established playwrights. Each submitted play should be previously unpublished, run no more than 90 minutes, require no more than 6 actors, and be suitable for presentation as a staged reading by Equity actors. No musicals or children's plays. Deadline: February 1. Prize: $500. Four runner-ups will receive $100 each.

L.A. DESIGNERS' THEATRE-COMMISSIONS

L.A. Designers' Theatre, P.O. Box 1883, Studio City CA 91614. **E-mail:** ladesigners@gmail.com. **Contact:** Richard Niederberg, artistic director. "Quarterly contest to promote new work and push it through a Theatrical Production onto the conveyor belt to Filmed or Digital Origination entertainment. All submissions must be registered with the copyright office and be unpublished. Material will not be returned. Do not submit any proposal that will not fit in a #10 envelope. No rules, guidelines, fees, or entry forms. Just present an idea that can be commissioned into a full work. Proposals for as of yet uncompleted works are encouraged. Unpopular political, religious, social, or other themes are encouraged; 'street' language and nudity are acceptable. Open to any writer." Deadline: March 15, June 15, September 15, December 15. Prize: Production or publication of the work in the Los Angeles market. "We only want 'first refusal' for the Rights and a License that is clear of any legal, stated, unstated, or implied obligation to any other person or entity. You continue to *own* your work."

MARSH HAWK PRESS POETRY PRIZE

Marsh Hawk Press, P.O. Box 206, East Rockaway NY 11518-0206. **E-mail:** marshhawkpress1@aol.com.

Website: www.MarshHawkPress.org. **Contact:** Prize Director. The Marsh Hawk Press Poetry Prize offers $1,000, plus publication of a book-length ms. Additionally, The Robert Creeley Poetry Prize and The Rochelle Ratner Poetry Award, both cash prizes, go to the runners-up. Submissions must be unpublished as a collection, but individual poems may have been previously published elsewhere. Submit 48-70 pages of original poetry in any style in English, typed single-spaced, and paginated. (Longer mss will be considered if the press is queried before submission.) Contest mss may be submitted by electronic upload. See website for more information. If submitting via Post Office mail, the ms must be bound with a spring clip. Include 2 title pages: 1 with ms title, poet's name, and contact information only; 1 with ms title only (poet's name must not appear anywhere in the ms). Also include table of contents and acknowledgments page. Include SASE for results only; ms will not be returned. Guidelines available on website. Deadline: April 30. Judged by Mark Doty.

MOONDANCE INTERNATIONAL FILM FESTIVAL

970 Ninth St., Boulder CO 80302. 303-818-5771. **E-mail:** director@moondancefilmfestival.com; moondancefestival@gmail.com. **Website:** www.moondancefilmfestival.com; www.moondancefestival.com/blog. Written works submissions: feature screenplays, short screenplays, feature & short musical screenplays, feature & short screenplays for children, 1, 2 or 3-act stageplays, mini-series for TV, television movies of the week, television pilots, libretti, musical film scripts, short stories, radio plays & short stories for children. Submission service: www.withoutabox.com/login/1240. Accepts hard-copies of submissions, as well as digital submissions. Please include your full contact info on the cover page of your entry. Check out our submission guidelines on the website. Regular deadline: May 31; late deadline: June 30, extended deadline: July 15.

☻ NATIONAL ONE-ACT PLAYWRITING COMPETITION (CANADA)

Ottawa Little Theatre, 400 King Edward Ave., Ottawa ON K1N 7M7 Canada. (613)233-8948. **Fax:** (613)233-8027. **Website:** www.ottawalittletheatre.com. **Contact:** Lynn McGuigan, executive director. Encourages literary and dramatic talent in Canada. Guidelines available online. Deadline: October 15.

Prize: 1st Place: $1,000; 2nd Place: $750; 3rd Place: $500; Sybil Cooke Award for a Play Written for Children or Young People: $500. All winning plays will receive a public reading in April, and the winning playwrights will have a one-on-one meeting with a resident dramaturg. Judged by 3 adjudicators, including dramaturgs, directors who develop new work, and playwrights from across Canada.

THE PAGE INTERNATIONAL SCREENWRITING AWARDS

The PAGE Awards Committee, 7510 W. Sunset Blvd., #610, Hollywood CA 90046-3408 USA. **E-mail:** info@pageawards.com. **Website:** pageawards.com. **Contact:** Zoe Simmons, Contest Coordinator. Annual competition to discover the most talented new screenwriters from across the country and around the world. Each year, awards are presented to 31 screenwriters in 10 different genre categories: Action/Adventure, Comedy, Drama, Family Film, Historical Film, Science Fiction, Thriller/Horror, Short Film Script, TV Drama Pilot, and TV Comedy Pilot. Guidelines and entry forms are online. The contest is open to all writers 18 years of age and older who have not previously earned more than $25,000 writing for film and/or television. Please visit contest website for a complete list of rules and regulations. The PAGE Awards competition was founded to introduce the work of talented new screenwriters from around the world to people working in the Hollywood industry. Deadline: January 15 (early); February 15 (regular); March 15 (late); April 15 (last minute). Prizes: Over $50,000 in cash and prizes, including a $25,000 Grand Prize, plus Gold, Silver & Bronze prizes in all 10 genre categories. Most importantly, the award-winning writers receive extensive publicity and industry exposure for their scripts. As a result of winning the contest, many past PAGE Award Winners now have movies and television shows in production, on the air and in theaters. Judging is done entirely by Hollywood professionals, including industry script readers, consultants, agents, managers, producers, and development executives.

SCRIPTAPALOOZA SCREENPLAY & SHORTS COMPETITION

Endorsed by Write Brothers and Robert McKee, (310)801-5366. **E-mail:** info@scriptapalooza.com. **Website:** www.scriptapalooza.com. "From choosing our judges to creating opportunities, our top priority

has always been the writer. We surround ourselves with reputable and successful companies, including many producers, literary agents, and managers who read your scripts. Our past winners have won Emmy's, been signed by agents, managers, had their scripts optioned, and even made into movies. Scriptapalooza will promote, pitch and push the semifinalists and higher for a full year." Deadline: January 4, February 1, March 10, April 15, and April 29. Prize: 1st Place: $10,000; over $50,00 in prizes for the entire competition. The top 100 scripts will be considered by over 95 production companies. Judged by over 90 producers.

SCRIPTAPALOOZA TELEVISION WRITING COMPETITION

(310)801-5366. **E-mail:** info@scriptapalooza.com. **Website:** www.scriptapaloozatv.com. Bi-annual competition accepting entries in 4 categories: Reality shows, sitcoms, original pilots, and 1-hour dramas. There are more than 30 producers, agents, and managers reading the winning scripts. Two past winners won Emmys because of Scriptapalooza and 1 past entrant now writes for Comedy Central. Winners announced February 15 and August 30. For contest results, visit website. Length: Standard television format whether 1 hour, 1-half hour, or pilot. Open to any writer 18 or older. Guidelines available on website. Accepts inquiries by e-mail or phone. Deadline: October 15 and April 15. Prize: 1st Place: $500; 2nd Place: $200; 3rd Place: $100 (in each category); production company consideration. All the judging is done by over 25 producers.

TIPS Pilots should be fresh, new, and easy to visualize. Spec scripts should stay current with the shows, up-to-date story lines, characters, etc.

SCRIPT PIPELINE SCREENWRITING AND TV WRITING CONTESTS

2633 Lincoln Blvd. #701, Santa Monica CA 90405. (323) 424-4243. **E-mail:** entry@scriptpipeline.com. **Website:** scriptpipeline.com. **Contact:** Matt Misetich, director of development. Script Pipeline's 14th Annual Screenwriting and 9th Annual TV Writing Contests continue a long tradition of discovering up-and-coming talent and connecting them with top producers, agencies, and managers across studio and independent markets. This process has proven enormously successful, with numerous screenwriting contest alumni worldwide finding elite representation and gaining crucial introductions to otherwise impossible-to-reach industry execs. The result thus far is over $5 million in screenplays and TV pilots sold from competition finalists and "Recommend" writers since 2003. Last season, over 5,000 scripts were entered in the Screenwriting and TV Writing contests combined, making Script Pipeline one of the leading companies reviewing spec material. Purpose: to circulate exceptional material industry-wide, support writers long-term, and launch careers. Early deadline: March 1. Regular deadline: May 1. Late Deadline: May 15. Screenwriting Contest: $25,000 in cash for the winner and $1,500 in cash to the runner-up.

TV Writing Contest: $10,000 in cash for the winner and $1,000 in cash to the runner-up.

REVA SHINER COMEDY AWARD

Bloomington Playwrights Project, 107 W. 9th St., Bloomington IN 47404. **Website:** www.newplays. org. **Contact:** Susan Jones, Literary Manager. Annual award for unpublished/unproduced plays. The Bloomington Playwrights Project is a script-developing organization. Winning playwrights are expected to become part of the development process, working with the director in person or via long-distance. Check the website for more details. Deadline: October 31. Prize: $1,000, full production as a part of the Mainstage season. Judged by the literary committee of the BPP.

☻ SHRIEKFEST HORROR/SCI-FI FILM FESTIVAL & SCREENPLAY COMPETITION

P.O. Box 950921, Lake Mary FL 32795. **E-mail:** shriekfest@aol.com. **E-mail:** shriekfest@aol.com. **Website:** www.shriekfest.com. **Contact:** Denise Gossett. "Our awards are to help screenwriters move their script up the ladder and hopefully have it made into a film. Our winners take that win and parlay it into agents, film deals, and options. No, we don't use loglines anywhere; we keep your script private." "We accept award-winning screenplays. No restrictions as long as it's in the horror/thriller or sci-fi/fantasy genres. We accept shorts and features. No specific lengths." Deadline: May 1, July 1, July 10. Prize: Trophies, product awards, usually cash. "Our awards are updated all year long as sponsors step onboard." Judged by at least 20-30 judges who are all in different aspects of the entertainment industry, such as producers, directors, writers, actors, and agents.

SOUTHERN PLAYWRIGHTS COMPETITION

Jacksonville State University, Department of English, 700 Pelham Rd. N., Jacksonville AL 36265-1602. (256)782-5412. **Fax:** (256)782-5441. **E-mail:** jmaloney@jsu.edu. **E-mail:** jmaloney@jsu.edu. **Website:** www.jsu.edu/depart/english/southpla.htm. **Contact:** Joy Maloney. Competition for playwrights native to or a resident of Alabama, Arkansas, Florida, Georgia, Kentucky, Louisiana, Mississippi, North Carolina, South Carolina, Tennessee, Texas, Virginia, or West Virginia. Plays must deal with the Southern experience. Entries must be original, full-length plays. No musicals or adaptations will be accepted. The playwright may submit only one play. All entries must be typed, securely bound, and clearly identified. Synopsis of script must be included. No electronic entries accepted. Legal clearance of all materials not in the public domain will be the responsibility of the playwright. The Southern Playwrights Competition seeks to identify and encourage the best of Southern playwriting. Deadline: January 15. Prize: $1,000 and production of the play.

TELEVISION OUTREACH PROGRAM (TOP)

The Scriptwriters Network (SWN), P.O. Box 642806, Los Angeles CA 90064 USA. **E-mail:** top@scriptwritersnetwork.org. **E-mail:** top@scriptwritersnetwork.org. **Website:** www.scriptwritersnetwork.org. **Contact:** Lucas McCain, Director. The Television Outreach Program (TOP) is a Scriptwriters Network program to support undiscovered television writing talent. The program's objective is to help writers improve their craft so that they may achieve their goals of obtaining representation, script development, mentoring and career counseling services, landing writing assignments, and/or selling their work.

THEATRE CONSPIRACY ANNUAL NEW PLAY CONTEST

Theatre Conspiracy, 10091 McGregor Blvd., Ft. Myers FL 33919. (239)936-3239. **E-mail:** info@theatreconspiracy.org. **Website:** theatreconspiracy.org. **Contact:** Bill Taylor, producing artistic director. Offered annually for full-length plays that are unproduced. Work submitted to the contest must be a full length play with 7 actors or less and have simple to moderate technical demands. Plays having up to three previous productions are welcome. No musicals. Deadline: March 30. Prize: $700 and full production. Judged by a panel of qualified theatre teachers, directors, and performers.

☯ THEATRE IN THE RAW BIENNIAL ONE-ACT PLAY WRITING CONTEST

Theatre In the Raw, 3521 Marshall St., Vancouver BC V5N 4S2 Canada. (604)708-5448. **E-mail:** theatreintheraw@telus.net. **Website:** www.theatreintheraw.ca. Biennial contest for an original one-act play, presented in proper stage-play format, that is unpublished and unproduced. The play (with no more than 6 characters) cannot be longer than 25 double-spaced, typed pages equal to 30 minutes. Scripts must have page numbers. Scripts are to be mailed only & will not be accepted by e-mail. Deadline: December 31. Prize: 1st Place: $200, at least 1 dramatic reading or staging of the play at a Theatre In the Raw Cafe/Venue, or as part of a mini-tour program for the One-Act Play Series Nights; 2nd Place: $100; 3rd Place: $75. Winners announced June 30.

TVWRITER™ PEOPLE'S PILOT

TVWriter™, P.O. Box 65024, Port Ludlow WA 98365. (805)495-3659. **E-mail:** tvwriter@tvwriter.com. **E-mail:** tvwriter@tvwriter.com. **Website:** http://peoplespilot.com. **Contact:** Larry Brody. TVWriter.com helps to get TV pilot scripts read by those who can purchase them or hire writers. Deadline: November 1. Prize: $20,000+ worth of prizes in 3 categories. Free feedback for all entries. Judged by a team of television writing professionals.

JACKIE WHITE MEMORIAL NATIONAL CHILDREN'S PLAY WRITING CONTEST

1800 Nelwood Dr., Columbia MO 65202-1447. (573)874-5628. **E-mail:** jwmcontest@cectheatre.org. **Website:** www.cectheatre.org. **Contact:** Tom Phillips. Annual contest that encourages playwrights to write quality plays for family audiences. Previously unpublished submissions only. Submissions made by author. Play may be performed during the following season. All submissions will be read by at least 3 readers. Author will receive a written evaluation of the script. Guidelines available online. Deadline: June 1. Prize: $500 with production possible. Judging by current and past board members of CEC and by non-board members who direct plays at CEC.

WORLDFEST-HOUSTON INDEPENDENT INTERNATIONAL FILM FESTIVAL

WorldFest-Houston, 9898 Bissonnet St., Suite 650, Houston TX 77036. (713)965-9955. **Fax:** (713)965-9960. **E-mail:** entry@worldfest.org. **Website:** www.worldfest.org. mixed media art **Contact:** Entry Co-ordinator. WorldFest discovered Steven Spielberg, George Lucas, Ang Lee, Ridley Scott, the Coen Brothers, Francis Ford Coppola, John Lee Hancock, and David Lynch with their first awards. Screenplays must be submitted as actual printed scripts, 3-hole binders, no online reading. Competition for all genres of screenplays, plus 10 other competition categories of films and videos. Deadline: December 31; Final deadline is Jan 15. Prize: Cash, options, production deals, workshops, master classes, and seminars. Judged by a jury whose members are credentialed, experienced, award-winning writers, producers, and directors. No production assistants.

WRITE NOW

Indiana Repertory Theatre, 140 W. Washington St., Indianapolis IN 46204. 480-921-5770. **E-mail:** info@writenow.co. **Website:** www.writenow.co. The purpose of this biennial workshop is to encourage writers to create strikingly original scripts for young audiences. It provides a forum through which each playwright receives constructive criticism and the support of a development team consisting of a professional director and dramaturg. Finalists will spend approximately one week in workshop with their development team. At the end of the week, each play will be read as a part of the Write Now convening. Guidelines available online. Deadline: July 31.

YEAR END SERIES (YES) FESTIVAL OF NEW PLAYS

Theatre and Dance Program, School of the Arts, Nunn Dr., Northern Kentucky University, Highland Heights KY 41099-1007. 859.572.5648. **Fax:** (859)572-6057. **E-mail:** daniellyc1@nku.edu, or mking@nku.edu. **Website:** http://artscience.nku.edu/departments/theatre.html, https://artscience.nku.edu/content/dam/artscience/theatre/docs/16755YesFestivalFlyer.pdf. **Contact:** Michael King, co-project director; Corrie Danieley, co-project director. Receives submissions until September 30 in even-numbered years for the festivals which occur in April of odd-numbered years. Open to all writers. Flyers with submission guidelines and entry forms available on the website, or via e-mail. Deadline: September 30. Open to submissions on May 1. Prize: $250 and an expense-paid visit (travel and housing) to Northern Kentucky University to see the play produced.

ANNA ZORNIO MEMORIAL CHILDREN'S THEATRE PLAYWRITING COMPETITION

University of New Hampshire, Department of Theatre and Dance, PCAC, 30 Academic Way, Durham NH 03824. (603)862-3038. **Fax:** (603)862-0298. **E-mail:** mike.wood@unh.edu. **Website:** http://cola.unh.edu/theatre-dance/resource/zornio. **Contact:** Michael Wood. Offered every 4 years for unpublished well-written plays or musicals appropriate for young audiences with a maximum length of 60 minutes. May submit more than 1 play, but not more than 3. Honors the late Anna Zornio, an alumna of The University of New Hampshire, for dedication to and inspiration of playwriting for young people, K-12th grade. Deadline: March. Prize: $500.

ARTS COUNCILS & FELLOWSHIPS

$50,000 GIFT OF FREEDOM

A Room of Her Own Foundation, P.O. Box 778, Placitas NM 87043. **E-mail:** awards@aroho.org. **Website:** www.aroomofherownfoundation.org. **Contact:** Tracey Cravens-Gras, associate director. The publicly funded award provides very practical help—both materially and in professional guidance and moral support with mentors and advisory council—to assist women in making their creative contribution to the world. The Gift of Freedom competition will determine superior finalists from each of 3 genres: Creative nonfiction, fiction, and poetry. Open to female residents of the US. Award application cycle dates are yet to be determined. Visit website at www.aroho.org for more information about the next application window. Deadline: November 2. Prize: One genre finalist will be awarded the $50,000 Gift of Freedom grant, distributed over 2 years in support of the completion of a particular creative project. The 2 remaining genre finalists will each receive a $5,000 prize.

ALABAMA STATE COUNCIL ON THE ARTS INDIVIDUAL ARTIST FELLOWSHIP

201 Monroe St., Montgomery AL 36130. (334)242-4076, ext. 236. **Fax:** (334)240-3269. **E-mail:** anne.kimzey@arts.alabama.gov. **Website:** www.arts.state.al.us. **Contact:** Anne Kimzey, literature program manager. Must be a legal resident of Alabama who has lived in the state for 2 years prior to application. Competition receives 30+ submissions annually. Accepts inquiries by e-mail and phone. The following should be submitted: a résumé and a list of published works with reviews, if available; and a minimum of 10 pages of poetry or prose, with a maximum of 20 pages. Please label each page with title, artist's name, and date. If published, indicate where and the date of publication. Please do not submit bound material. Guidelines available in January on website. Recognizes the achievements and potential of Alabama writers. Deadline: March 1. Applications must be submitted online by eGRANT. Judged by independent peer panel. Winners notified by mail and announced on website in June.

ARROWHEAD REGIONAL ARTS COUNCIL INDIVIDUAL ARTIST CAREER DEVELOPMENT GRANT

Arrowhead Regional Arts Council, 600 E Superior St., Suite 404, Duluth MN 55802. (218)722-0952 or (800)569-8134. **E-mail:** info@aracouncil.org. **Website:** www.aracouncil.org. Award is to provide financial support to regional artists wishing to take advantage of impending, concrete opportunities that will advance their work or careers. Applicants must live in the 7-county region of Northeastern Minnesota. Deadline: October and April. Grant awards of up to $3,000. Candidates are reviewed by a panel of ARAC Board Members and Community Artists.

GEORGE BENNETT FELLOWSHIP

Phillips Exeter Academy, 20 Main Street, Exeter NH 03833. **E-mail:** teaching_opportunities@exeter.edu. **Website:** www.exeter.edu/bennettfellowship. Annual award for fellow and family to provide time and freedom from material considerations to a person seriously contemplating or pursuing a career as a writer. Applicants should have a ms in progress which they intend to complete during the fellowship period. Ms should be fiction, nonfiction, novel, short stories, or poetry. Duties: To be in residency at the Academy for the academic year; to make oneself available informally to students interested in writing. Committee favors writers who have not yet published a book with a major publisher. Deadline: November 30. A choice will be made, and all entrants notified in mid-April. Prize: Cash stipend (currently $14,933), room and board. Judged by committee of the English department.

DELAWARE DIVISION OF THE ARTS

820 N. French St., Wilmington DE 19801. (302)577-8278. **Fax:** (302)577-6561. **E-mail:** Roxanne.stanu-

lis@state.de.us. **Website:** www.artsdel.org. **Contact:** Roxanne Stanulis. Award to help further careers of emerging and established professional artists. For Delaware residents only. Guidelines available after May 1 on website. Accepts inquiries by e-mail, phone. Results announced in December. Winners notified by mail. Results available on website. Open to any Delaware writer over 18 years of ages and not in a degree-granting program. Deadline: August 1. Prize: $10,000 for masters; $6,000 for established professionals; $3,000 for emerging professionals. Judged by out-of-state, nationally recognized professionals in each artistic discipline.

TIPS "Follow all instructions and choose your best work sample."

✺✺✺✺ DOBIE PAISANO WRITER'S FELLOWSHIP

The Graduate School, The University of Texas at Austin, Attn: Dobie Paisano Program, 110 Inner Campus Drive Stop G0400, Austin TX 78712-0531. (512)232-3609. **Fax:** (512)471-7620. **E-mail:** gbarton@austin.utexas.edu. **Website:** www.utexas.edu/ogs/Paisano. **Contact:** Gwen Barton. Sponsored by the Graduate School at The University of Texas at Austin and the Texas Institute of Letters, the Dobie Paisano Fellowship Program provides solitude, time, and a comfortable place for Texas writers or writers who have written significantly about Texas through fiction, nonfiction, poetry, plays, or other mediums. The Dobie Paisano Ranch is a very rural and rustic setting, and applicants should read the guidelines closely to insure their ability to reside in this secluded environment. At the time of the application, the applicant must meet one of the following requirements: (1) be a native Texan, (2) have resided in Texas at least three years at some time, or (3) have published significant work with a Texas subject. Those who meet requirement 1 or 2 do not have to meet the Texas subject matter restriction. Deadline: January 15. Applications are accepted beginning December 1 and must be post-marked no later than January 15. The Ralph A. Johnston memorial Fellowship is for a period of 4 months with a stipend of $6,250 per month. It is aimed at writers who have already demonstrated some publishing and critical success. The Jesse H. Jones Writing Fellowship is for a period of approximately 6 months with a stipend of $3,000 per month. It is aimed at, but not limited to, writers who are early in their careers.

TIPS "Three sets of each complete application must be submitted. Electronic submissions are not allowed. Guidelines and application forms are on the website (http://www.utexas.edu/ogs/Paisano/info.html) or may be requested by sending a SASE (3-ounce postage) to the above address, attention of 'Dobie Paisano Fellowship Project.'"

FELLOWSHIPS FOR CREATIVE AND PERFORMING ARTISTS AND WRITERS

American Antiquarian Society, 185 Salisbury St., Worcester MA 01609-1634. (508)755-5221. **Fax:** (508)754-9069. **E-mail:** jmoran@mwa.org; library@americanantiquarian.org. **Website:** www.americanantiquarian.org. **Contact:** James David Moran. Annual fellowship for creative and performing artists, writers, filmmakers, journalists, and other persons whose goals are to produce imaginative, non-formulaic works dealing with pre-20th century American history. Application instructions available online. Website also lists potential fellowship projects. Deadline: October 5. Prize: The stipend will be $1,350 for fellows residing on campus (rent-free) in the society's scholars' housing, located next to the main library building. The stipend will be $1,850 for fellows residing off campus. Fellows will not be paid a travel allowance. Judged by AAS staff and outside reviewers.

TIPS "Successful applicants are those whose work is for the general public rather than for academic or educational audiences."

GUGGENHEIM FELLOWSHIPS

John Simon Guggenheim Memorial Foundation, 90 Park Ave., New York NY 10016. (212)687-4470. **E-mail:** fellowships@gf.org. **Website:** www.gf.org. Often characterized as "midcareer" awards, Guggenheim Fellowships are intended for men and women who have already demonstrated exceptional capacity for productive scholarship or exceptional creative ability in the arts. Fellowships are awarded through two annual competitions: one open to citizens and permanent residents of the United States and Canada, and the other open to citizens and permanent residents of Latin America and the Caribbean. Candidates must apply to the Guggenheim Foundation in order to be considered in either of these competitions. The Foundation receives between 3,500 and 4,000 applications each year. Although no one who applies is guaranteed success in the competition, there is no prescreening: all applications are reviewed. Approximately 200 Fellowships are awarded each year. Deadline: September 15.

MARILYN HOLLINSHEAD VISITING SCHOLARS FELLOWSHIP

University of Minnesota, 113 Anderson Library, 222 21st Ave. South, Minneapolis MN 55455. **Website:** http://www.lib.umn.edu/clrc/awards-grants-and-fellowships. Marilyn Hollinshead Visiting Scholars Fund for Travel to the Kerlan Collection is available for research study. Applicants may request up to $1,500. Send a letter with the proposed purpose and plan to use specific research materials (manuscripts and art), dates, and budget (including airfare and per diem). Travel and a written report on the project must be completed and submitted in the previous year. Deadline: June 1.

MCKNIGHT ARTIST FELLOWSHIPS FOR WRITERS, LOFT AWARD(S) IN CHILDREN'S LITERATURE/CREATIVE PROSE/POETRY

The Loft Literary Center, 1011 Washington Ave. S., Suite 200, Open Book, Minneapolis MN 55415. (612)215-2575. **Fax:** (612)215-2576. **E-mail:** loft@loft. org. **Website:** www.loft.org. **Contact:** Bao Phi. "The Loft administers the McKnight Artists Fellowships for Writers. Five $25,000 awards are presented annually to accomplished Minnesota writers and spoken word artists. Four awards alternate annually between creative prose (fiction and creative nonfiction) and poetry/spoken word. The fifth award is presented in children's literature and alternates annually for writing for ages 8 and under and writing for children older than 8." The awards provide the writers the opportunity to focus on their craft for the course of the fellowship year. Prize: $25,000.

TIPS "See guidelines and follow carefully and exactly."

MOONDANCER FELLOWSHIP FOR WRITING ABOUT NATURE AND THE OUTDOORS

The Writers' Colony at Dairy Hollow, 515 Spring St., Eureka Springs AR 72632. (479)253-7444. **Fax:** (479)253-9859. **E-mail:** director@writerscolony.org. **Website:** www.writerscolony.org. **Contact:** Linda Caldwell, Executive Director. "A two-week residency for writing in any genre about any aspect of nature and the outdoors. Works may be fiction or nonfiction. Supports writing of excellence which aspires to engage the mind, body and soul in the appreciation of nature. Applications accepted until May 31. "

NICKELODEON WRITING PROGRAM

Nickelodeon, Viacom, 231 W. Olive Ave., Burbank CA 91502. (818)736-3663. **E-mail:** info.writing@ nick.com. **Website:** www.nickwriting.com, www. facebook.com/nickwriting, twitter: @nickwriting. **Contact:** Karen Kirkland, Vice President. Offered annually for unpublished spec scripts. Must be 18 years or older to participate. Deadline: February 28. Prize: The Nickelodeon Writing Program offers aspiring television writers all over the globe, with diverse backgrounds and experiences, the opportunity to hone their skills while writing for our live action and animated shows. Participants will have hands-on interaction with executives writing spec scripts and pitching story ideas.

The Program, developed to broaden Nickelodeon's outreach efforts, provides a salaried position for up to six months (for International writers) and up to on

Application and submission guidelines are available on our website at www.nickwriting.com.

e year (for U.S. writers). Judged by experienced script analysts and Nickelodeon executives.

NORTH CAROLINA ARTS COUNCIL REGIONAL ARTIST PROJECT GRANTS

North Carolina Arts Council, Dept. of Cultural Resources, MSC #4632, Raleigh NC 27699-4634. (919)807-6512. **Fax:** (919)807-6532. **E-mail:** david. potorti@ncdcr.gov. **Website:** www.ncarts.org. **Contact:** David Potorti, literature director. See website for contact information for the local arts councils that distribute these grants. Open to any writer living in North Carolina. Deadline: Late summer/early fall. Prize: $500-3,000 awarded to writers to pursue projects that further their artistic development.

OREGON LITERARY FELLOWSHIPS

925 S.W. Washington, Portland OR 97205. (503)227-2583. **E-mail:** susan@literary-arts.org. **Website:** www.literary-arts.org. **Contact:** Susan Moore, Director of programs and events. Oregon Literary Fellowships are intended to help Oregon writers initiate, develop, or complete literary projects in poetry, fiction, literary nonfiction, drama, and young readers literature. Writers in the early stages of their career are encouraged to apply. The awards are merit-based. Guidelines available in February for SASE. Accepts inquiries by e-mail, phone. Oregon residents only. Recipients announced in January. Deadline: Last Friday in June. Prize: $3,000 minimum award, for

approximately 8 writers and 2 publishers. Judged by out-of-state writers

RHODE ISLAND ARTIST FELLOWSHIPS AND INDIVIDUAL PROJECT GRANTS

Rhode Island State Council on the Arts, State of Rhode Island, One Capitol Hill, 3rd Floor, Providence RI 02908. (401)222-3880. **Fax:** (401)222-3018. **E-mail:** Cristina.DiChiera@arts.ri.gov. **Website:** www.arts.ri.gov. **Contact:** Cristina DiChiera, director of individual artist programs. Annual fellowship competition is based upon panel review of poetry, fiction, and playwriting/screenwriting manuscripts. Project grants provide funds for community-based arts projects. Rhode Island artists who have lived in the state for at least 12 consecutive months may apply without a nonprofit sponsor. Applicants for all RSCA grant and award programs must be at least 18 years old and not currently enrolled in an arts-related degree program. Online application and guidelines can be found at www.arts.ri.gov/grants/guidelines/. Deadline: April 1 and October 1. Fellowship awards: $5,000 and $1,000. Grants range from $500-5,000, with an average of around $1,500. Judged by a rotating panel of artists.

SCREENPLAY FESTIVAL

15021 Ventura Blvd., #523, Sherman Oaks CA 91403. (424)248-9221. **Fax:** (866)770-2994. **E-mail:** info@screenplayfestival.com. **Website:** www.screenplayfestival.com. This festival is an opportunity to give all scriptwriters a chance to be noticed and have their work read by the power players. Entries in the feature-length competition must be more than 60 pages; entries in the short screenplay contest must be fewer than 60 pages. The Screenplay Festival was established to solve two major problems. One, it is simply too difficult for talented writers who have no "connections" to gain recognition and get their material read by legitimate agents, producers, directors and investors. Two, agents, producers, directors, and investors complain that they cannot find any great material, but they will generally not accept "unsolicited material." This means that unless the script comes from a source that is known to them, they will not read it. Screenplay Festival was established to help eliminate this "chicken and egg" problem. By accepting all submitted screenplays and judging them based upon their quality—not their source or their standardized formatting or the quality of the brads holding them

together—Screenplay Festival looks to give undiscovered screenwriters an opportunity to rise above the crowd. Deadline: September 1. Prize: $1,000 for feature film categories, $500 for television categories.

WALLACE E. STEGNER FELLOWSHIPS

Creative Writing Program, Stanford University, Stanford CA 94305-2087. (650)723-0011. **Fax:** (650)723-3679. **E-mail:** stegnerfellowship@stanford.edu. **Website:** www.stanford.edu/group/creativewriting/stegner. Offers 5 fellowships in poetry and 5 in fiction for promising writers who can benefit from 2 years of instruction and participation in the program. Online application preferred. "We do not require a degree for admission. No school of writing is favored over any other. Chronological age is not a consideration." Deadline: December 1. Open to submissions on September 1. Prize: Fellowships of $26,000, plus tuition of over $7,000/year.

TENNESSEE ARTS COMMISSION LITERARY FELLOWSHIP

Tennessee Arts Commission, 401 Charlotte Ave., Nashville TN 37243-0780. **Fax:** (615)741-8559. **E-mail:** lee.baird@state.tn.us. **Website:** tnartscommission.org. **Contact:** Lee Baird, director of literary programs. Awarded annually in recognition of professional Tennessee artists, i.e., individuals who have received financial compensation for their work as professional writers. Applicants must have a publication history other than vanity press. Three fellowships awarded annually to outstanding literary artists who live and work in Tennessee. Categories are in fiction, creative nonfiction, and poetry. Deadline: January 26. Prize: $5,000. Judged by an out-of-state adjudicator.

WISCONSIN INSTITUTE FOR CREATIVE WRITING FELLOWSHIP

6195B H.C. White Hall, 600 N. Park St., Madison WI 53706. **E-mail:** rfkuka@wisc.edu. **Website:** creativewriting.wisc.edu/fellowships.html. **Contact:** Sean Bishop, graduate coordinator. Fellowship provides time, space and an intellectual community for writers working on first books. Receives approximately 300 applicants a year for each genre. Judged by English Department faculty and current fellows. Candidates can have up to one published book in the genre for which they are applying. Open to any writer with either an M.F.A. or Ph.D. in creative writing. Please enclose a SASE for notification of results. Results announced on website by May 1. Applicants should submit up to 10 pages of poetry or one story or excerpt of up to 30 pages and a résumé or vita directly to the program during the month of February. See instructions on website for submitting online. An applicant's name must not appear on the writing sample (which must be in ms form) but rather on a separate sheet along with address, social security number, phone number, e-mail address and title(s) of submission(s). Candidates should also supply the names and phone numbers of two references. Accepts inquiries by e-mail and phone. **Deadline:** Last day of February. Open to submissions on December 15. **Prize:** $30,000 for a 9-month appointment.

TIPS "Send your best work. Stories seem to have a small advantage over novel excerpts."

FICTION

24-HOUR SHORT STORY CONTEST

WritersWeekly.com, 5726 Cortez Rd. W., #349, Bradenton FL 34210. 305-768-0261. **Fax:** 305-768-0261. **E-mail:** writersweekly@writersweekly.com. **Website:** www.writersweekly.com/misc/contest.php. **Contact:** Angela Hoy. Popular quarterly contest in which registered entrants receive a topic at start time (usually noon Central Time) and have 24 hours to write and submit a story on that topic. All submissions must be returned via e-mail. Each contest is limited to 500 people. Upon entry, entrant will receive guidelines and details on competition, including submission process. **Deadline:** Quarterly—see website for dates. **Prize:** 1st Place: $300; 2nd Place: $250; 3rd Place: $200. There are also 20 honorable mentions and 60 door prizes (randomly drawn from all participants). The top 3 winners' entries are posted on WritersWeekly. com (non-exclusive electronic rights only) and receive a Freelance Income Kit. Writers retain all rights to their work. See website for full details on prizes. Judged by Angela Hoy (publisher of WritersWeekly. com and Booklocker.com).

🌀 AEON AWARD

Albedo One/Aeon Press, Aeon Award, Albedo One, 2 Post Road, Lusk, Dublin Ireland. +353 1 8730177. **E-mail:** fraslaw@yahoo.co.uk. **Website:** www.albedo1.com. **Contact:** Frank Ludlow, event coordinator. Prestigious fiction writing competition for short stories in any speculative fiction genre, such as fantasy, science fiction, horror, or anything in-between or unclassifiable. Submit your story (which must be less than 10,000 words in length and previously unpublished) in the body of an e-mail with contact details and "Aeon Award Submission" as the subject. **Deadline:** November 30. Contest begins January 1. **Prize:** Grand Prize: €1,000; 2nd Prize: €200; and 3rd Prize: €100. The top three stories are guaranteed publication in *Albedo One*. Judged by Ian Watson, Eileen Gunn, Todd McCaffrey, and Michael Carroll.

🌀 AHWA FLASH & SHORT STORY COMPETITION

AHWA (Australian Horror Writers Association), **E-mail:** ahwacomps@australianhorror.com; ahwa@australianhorror.com. **E-mail:** ctrost@hotmail.com. **Website:** www.australianhorror.com. **Contact:** Cameron Trost, Competitions Officer. Competition/award for short stories and flash fiction. There are 2 categories: short stories (1,001 to 8,000 words) and flash fiction (less than 1,000 words). Writers may submit to one or both categories, but entry is limited to 1 story per author per category. Send submission as an attached rtf or doc. Mail submissions only accepted as a last resort. No previously published entries will be accepted—all tales must be an original work by the author. Stories can be as violent or as bloody as the storyline dictates, but those containing gratuitous sex or violence will not be considered. Please check entries for spelling and grammar mistakes and follow standard submission guidelines (e.g., 12 point font, Ariel, Times New Roman, or Courier New, one and a half spacing between lines, with title and page number on each page). Looking for horror stories, tales that frighten, yarns that unsettle readers in their comfortable homes. All themes in this genre will be accepted, from the well-used (zombies, vampires, ghosts etc) to the highly original, so long as the story is professional and well written. **Deadline:** May 31. **Prize:** The authors of the winning Flash Fiction and Short Story entries will each receive paid publication in *Midnight Echo*, the Magazine of the AHWA and an engraved plaque.

AMERICAN MARKETS NEWSLETTER SHORT STORY COMPETITION

1974 46th Ave., San Francisco CA 94116. **E-mail:** sheila.oconnor@juno.com. Award is to give short story writers more exposure. Contest offered biannually. Open to any writer. All kinds of fiction are considered. Especially looking for women's pieces—romance, with a twist in the tale—but all will be considered. Results announced within 3 months of deadlines. Winners notified by mail if they include SASE. Accepts fiction and nonfiction up to 2,000 words. Entries are eligible for cash prizes, and all entries are eligible for worldwide syndication whether they win or not. For guidelines, send SASE, fax or e-mail. Published and unpublished stories are actively encouraged. Add a note of where and when previously published. Send double-spaced mss with your story/article title, byline, word count, and address on the first page above your article/story's first paragraph (no need for separate cover page). There is no limit to the number of entries you may send. Deadline: June 30 and December 31. Prize: 1st Place: $300; 2nd Place: $100; 3rd Place: $50. Judged by a panel of independent judges.

SHERWOOD ANDERSON FICTION AWARD

Mid-American Review, Mid-American Review, Dept. of English, Box WM, BGSU, Bowling Green OH 43403. (419)372-2725. **Fax:** (419)372-4642. **E-mail:** mar@bgsu.edu. **Website:** www.bgsu.edu/midamericanreview. **Contact:** Abigail Cloud, editor-in-chief. Offered annually for unpublished mss (6,000 word limit). Contest is open to all writers not associated with a judge or *Mid-American Review*. Guidelines available online or for SASE. Deadline: November 1. Prize: $1,000, plus publication in the spring issue of *Mid-American Review*. Four Finalists: Notation, possible publication. Judged by editors and a well-known writer, i.e., Aimee Bender or Anthony Doerr.

THE SHERWOOD ANDERSON FOUNDATION FICTION AWARD

12330 Ashton Mill Terrace, Glen Allen VA 23059. **E-mail:** sherwoodandersonfoundation@gmail.com. **Website:** www.sherwoodandersonfoundation.org. **Contact:** Anna McKean, foundation president. Contest is to honor, preserve and celebrate the memory and literary work of Sherwood Anderson, American realist for the first half of the 20th century. Annual award supports developing writers of short stories and novels. Entrants must have published at least one book of fiction or have had several short stories published in major literary and/or commercial publication. Self-published stories do not qualify. Send a detailed résumé that includes a bibliography of your publications. Include a cover letter that provides a history of your writing experience and your plans for writing projects. Also, submit 2 or 3 examples of what you consider to be your best work. Do not send manuscripts by e-mail. Only mss in English will be accepted. Open to any writer who meets the qualifications listed above. Accepts inquiries by e-mail. Mail your application to the above address. No mss or publications will be returned. Deadline: April 1. Prize: $20,000 grant award.

AUTUMN HOUSE FICTION PRIZE

Autumn House Press, 87 ½ Westwood St., Pittsburgh PA 15211. **E-mail:** info@autumnhouse.org. **Website:** http://autumnhouse.org. Fiction submissions should be approximately 200-300 pages. All fiction sub-genres (short stories, short-shorts, novellas, or novels), or any combination of sub-genres, are eligible. All finalists will be considered for publication. Include SASE for results. Autumn House Press assumes no responsibility for lost or damaged manuscripts. All entries must be clearly marked "Fiction Prize" on the outside envelope. Enclose a $30 handling fee. Send manuscript and fee to: Autumn House Press: P.O. Box 60100, Pittsburgh, PA 15211. Deadline: June 30. Prize: Winners will receive book publication, $1,000 advance against royalties, and a $1,500 travel grant to participate in the Autumn House Master Authors Series in Pittsburgh. Judged by William Lychack (final judge).

BALCONES FICTION PRIZE

Austin Commmunity College, Department of Creative Writing, 1212 Rio Grande St., Austin TX 78701. (512)584-5045. **E-mail:** joconne@austincc.edu. **Website:** http://www.austincc.edu/crw/html/balconescenter.html. **Contact:** Joe O'Connell. Awarded to the best book of literary fiction published the previous year. Books of prose may be submitted by publisher or author. Send three copies. Deadline: January 31. Prize: $1,500, winner is flown to Austin for a campus reading.

THE BALTIMORE REVIEW CONTESTS

The Baltimore Review, 6514 Maplewood Rd., Baltimore MD 21212. **E-mail:** editor@baltimorereview.org. **Website:** www.baltimorereview.org. **Contact:** Barbara Westwood Diehl, senior editor. Each summer and winter issue includes a contest theme (see submissions guidelines for theme). Prizes are awarded for first, second, and third place among all categories—poetry, short stories, and creative nonfiction. All entries are considered for publication. Open to all writers. Only unpublished work will be considered.

Asks only for the right to publish the work for the first time. Deadline: May 31 and November 30. Prize: 1st Place: $500; 2nd Place: $200; 3rd Place: $100. All entries are considered for publication. Provides a small compensation to all contributors. Judged by the editors of *The Baltimore Review* and a guest, final judge.

BARD FICTION PRIZE

Bard College, P.O. Box 5000, Annandale-on-Hudson NY 12504-5000. (845)758-7087. **Fax:** (845)758-7917. **E-mail:** bfp@bard.edu. **Website:** www.bard.edu/bfp. **Contact:** Irene Zedlacher. The Bard Fiction Prize is awarded to a promising, emerging writer who is an American citizen aged 39 years or younger at the time of application. Cover letter should include name, address, phone, e-mail and name of publisher where book was previously published. Entries must be previously published. Open to U.S. citizens aged 39 and below. Guidelines available by SASE, fax, phone, e-mail, or on website. Results announced by October 15. Winners notified by phone. For contest results, e-mail, or visit website. The Bard Fiction Prize is intended to encourage and support young writers of fiction to pursue their creative goals and to provide an opportunity to work in a fertile and intellectual environment. Deadline: June 15. Prize: $30,000 and appointment as writer-in-residence at Bard College for 1 semester. Judged by a committee of 5 judges (authors associated with Bard College).

BELLEVUE LITERARY REVIEW GOLDENBERG PRIZE FOR FICTION

Bellevue Literary Review, NYU Dept of Medicine, 550 First Ave., OBV-A612, New York NY 10016. (212)263-3973. **E-mail:** info@blreview.org; stacy@blreview.org. **Website:** www.blreview.org. **Contact:** Stacy Bodziak, managing editor. The BLR prizes award outstanding writing related to themes of health, healing, illness, the mind and the body. Annual competition/award for short stories. Receives about 200-300 entries per category. Send credit card information or make checks payable to Bellevue Literary Review. Guidelines available in February. Accepts inquiries by e-mail, phone, mail. Submissions open in February. Results announced in December and made available to entrants with SASE, by e-mail, on website. Winners notified by mail, by e-mail. Entries should be unpublished. Anyone may enter contest. Length: No minimum; maximum of 5,000 words. Writers may submit own work. Deadline: July 1. Prize: $1,000 and

publication in *The Bellevue Literary Review.* Honorable mention winners receive $250 and publication. BLR editors select semi-finalists to be read by an independent judge who chooses the winner. Previous judges include Nathan Englander, Jane Smiley, Francine Prose, and Andre Dubus III.

BINGHAMTON UNIVERSITY JOHN GARDNER FICTION BOOK AWARD

Creative Writing Program, Binghamton University, Binghamton University, Department of English, General Literature, and Rhetoric, Library North Room 1149, P.O. Box 6000, Binghamton NY 13902-6000. (607)777-2713. **E-mail:** cwpro@binghamton.edu. **Website:** http://binghamton.edu/english/creative-writing/. **Contact:** Maria Mazziotti Gillan, director. Contest offered annually for a novel or collection of fiction published in previous year in a press run of 500 copies or more. Each book submitted must be accompanied by an application form. Publisher may submit more than 1 book for prize consideration. Send 2 copies of each book. Guidelines available on website. Author or publisher may submit. Deadline: March 1. Prize: $1,000. Judged by a professional writer not on Binghamton University faculty.

BOULEVARD SHORT FICTION CONTEST FOR EMERGING WRITERS

Boulevard Magazine, 6614 Clayton Rd., PMB #325, Richmond Heights MO 63117. (314)862-2643. **Website:** www.boulevardmagazine.org. **Contact:** Jessica Rogen, editor. Offered annually for unpublished short fiction to a writer who has not yet published a book of fiction, poetry, or creative nonfiction with a nationally distributed press. Holds first North American rights on anything not previously published. Open to any writer with no previous publication by a nationally known press. Guidelines for SASE or on website. Accepts works up to 8,000 words. Simultaneous submissions are allowed, but previously accepted or published work is ineligible. Entries will be judged by the editors of *Boulevard Magazine*. Submit online or via postal mail. Deadline: December 31. Prize: $1,500, and publication in 1 of the next year's issues.

⬤ THE CAINE PRIZE FOR AFRICAN WRITING

51 Southwark St., London SE1 1RU United Kingdom. **E-mail:** info@caineprize.com. **Website:** www.caine-prize.com. **Contact:** Lizzy Attree. Entries must have appeared for the first time in the 5 years prior to the

closing date for submissions, which is January 31 each year. Publishers should submit 6 copies of the published original with a brief cover note (no pro forma application). "Please indicate nationality or passport held." Submissions should be made by publishers only. Only one story per author will be considered in any one year. Only fiction work is eligible. Indicative length is between 3,000 and 10,000 words. See website for more details and rules. The Caine Prize is open to writers from anywhere in Africa for work published in English. Its focus is on the short story, reflecting the contemporary development of the African story-telling tradition. Deadline: January 31. Prize: £10,000.

JOHN W. CAMPBELL MEMORIAL AWARD FOR BEST SCIENCE FICTION NOVEL OF THE YEAR

English Department, University of Kansas, Lawrence KS 66045. (785)864-3380. **Fax:** (785)864-1159. **E-mail:** cmckit@ku.edu. **Website:** www.sfcenter.ku.edu/campbell.htm. **Contact:** Chris McKitterick. Honors the best science fiction novel of the year. Entries must be previously published. Open to any writer. Accepts inquiries by e-mail and fax. "Ordinarily publishers should submit work, but authors have done so when publishers would not. Send for list of jurors." Results announced in July. For contest results, send SASE. Deadline: Check website. Prize: Campbell Award trophy. Winners receive an expense-paid trip to the university to receive their award. Their names are also engraved on a permanent trophy. Judged by a jury.

☺ CANADIAN AUTHORS ASSOCIATION AWARD FOR FICTION

6 West St. N., Suite 203, Orilla ON L3X 5B8 Canada. **Website:** www.canadianauthors.org. **Contact:** Anita Purcell, executive director. Award for full-length, English language literature for adults by a Canadian author. Deadline: January 15. Prize: $1,000. Judging: Each year a trustee for each award appointed by the Canadian Authors Association selects up to 3 judges. Identities of the trustee and judges are confidential.

☺☺☺ CANADIAN TALES SHORT STORY COMPETITION

Red Tuque Books, Unit #6, 477 Martin St., Penticton BC V2A 5L2 Canada. (778)476-5750. **Fax:** (778)476-5750. **E-mail:** dave@redtuquebooks.ca. **Website:** www.redtuquebooks.ca. **Contact:** David Korinetz, contest director. Offered annually for unpublished works. Check the guidelines on the website. Purpose

of award is to promote Canada and Canadian publishing. Stories require a Canadian element. There are three ways to qualify. They can be written by a Canadian, written about Canadians, or take place somewhere in Canada. Deadline: December 31. Prize: 1st Place: $500; 2nd Place: $150; 3rd Place: $100; and 10 prizes of $25 will be given to honorable mentions. All 13 winners will be published in an anthology. They will each receive a complimentary copy. Judged by Canadian authors/publishers in the appropriate genre. Acquires first print rights. Contest open to anyone.

TIPS "The 2016 contest, 'Canadian Tales of the Fantastic,' will be looking for the fantastic (Sci-Fi/Fantasy/Horror). The 2017 contest, 'Canadian Tales of the Mysterious,' will be looking for stories that have an element of Mystery (Mystery/Detective/Ghost Story). The 2018 contest, 'Canadian Tales of the Heart,' will be looking for stories that elicit strong emotion (Romance/Humor/Contemporary). "

THE ALEXANDER CAPPON PRIZE FOR FICTION

New Letters, University of Missouri-Kansas City, *New Letters* Awards for Writers, UMKC, University House, 5101 Rockhill Rd., Kansas City MO 64110-2499. (816)235-1168. **Fax:** (816)235-2611. **E-mail:** newletters@umkc.edu. **Website:** http://www.newletters.org/writers-wanted/writing-contests. Offered annually for the best short story to discover and reward new and upcoming writers. Buys first North American serial rights. Open to any writer. Short story should not exceed 8,000 words. Deadline: May 18. Prize: 1st Place: $1,500 and publication in a volume of *New Letters*.

CASCADE WRITING CONTEST & AWARDS

Oregon Christian Writers, 1075 Willow Lake Road N., Keizer Oregon 97303. **E-mail:** cascade@oregonchristianwriters.org. **E-mail:** cascade@oregonchristianwriters.org. **Website:** http://oregonchristianwriters.org/. **Contact:** Marilyn Rhoads and Julie McDonald Zander. The Cascade Awards are presented at the annual Oregon Christian Writers Summer Conference (held at the Red Lion on the River in Portland, Oregon, each August) attended by national editors, agents, and professional authors. The contest is open for both published and unpublished works in the following categories: contemporary fiction book, historical fiction book, speculative fiction book, nonfiction book, memoir book, young adult/middle grade fiction book, young adult/middle grade nonfiction book, children's chapter book and picture book (fiction and nonfiction), poetry, devotional, article, column, story, or blog post. Two additional special Cascade Awards are presented each year: the Trailblazer Award to a writer who has distinguished him/herself in the field of Christian writing; and a Writer of Promise Award for a writer who demonstrates unusual promise in the field of Christian writing. For a full list of categories, entry rules, and scoring elements, visit website. Guidelines and rules available on the website. Entry forms will be available on the first day for entry. Annual multigenre competition to encourage both published and emerging writers in the field of Christian writing. Deadline: March 31. Submissions period begins February 14. Prize: Award certificate and pin presented at the Cascade Awards ceremony during the Oregon Christian Writers Annual Summer Conference. Finalists are listed in the conference notebook and winners are listed online. Cascade Trophies are awarded to the recipients of the Trailblazer and Writer of Promise Awards. Judged by published authors, editors, librarians, and retail book store owners and employees. Final judging by editors, agents, and published authors from the Christian publishing industry.

KAY CATTARULLA AWARD FOR BEST SHORT STORY

Texas Institute of Letters, P.O. Box 609, Round Rock TX 78680. **E-mail:** tilsecretary@yahoo.com. **Website:** www.texasinstituteofletters.org. Offered annually for work published January 1-December 31 of previous year to recognize the best short story. The story submitted must have appeared in print for the first time to be eligible. Writers must have been born in Texas, must have lived in Texas for at least 2 consecutive years, or the subject matter of the work must be associated with Texas. See website for guidelines. See website for details and instructions on entering the competition. Deadline: January 10. Prize: $1,000.

G. S. SHARAT CHANDRA PRIZE FOR SHORT FICTION

BkMk Press, University of Missouri-Kansas City, BkMk Press, University of Missouri-Kansas City, 5100 Rockhill Rd., Kansas City MO 64110-2499 USA. (816)235-2558. **Fax:** (816)235-2611. **E-mail:** bkmk@ umkc.edu; newletters@umkc.edu. **Website:** www.umkc.edu/bkmk. **Contact:** Ben Furnish. Offered annually for the best book-length ms collection (unpublished) of short fiction in English by a living author. Translations are not eligible. Initial judging is done by a network of published writers. Final judging is done by a writer of national reputation. Guidelines for SASE, by e-mail, or on website. Short fiction collections should be approximately 125 pages minimum, 300 pages maximum, double spaced. Deadline: January 15. Prize: $1,000, plus book publication by BkMk Press.

🌑 PEGGY CHAPMAN-ANDREWS FIRST NOVEL AWARD

P.O. Box 6910, Dorset DT6 9QB United Kingdom. **E-mail:** info@bridportprize.org.uk. **Website:** www.bridportprize.org.uk. **Contact:** Kate Wilson, Prize Administrator. Award to promote literary excellence and new writers. Enter first chapters of novel, up to 8,000 words (minimum 5,000 words) plus 300 word synopsis. Send SASE for entry form or enter online. Deadline: May 31. Prize: 1st Place: £1,000 plus mentoring & possible publication; Runner-Up: ££500. Judged by The Literary Consultancy & A.M. Heath Literary Agents.

🌑🌑🌑 *THE CHARITON REVIEW* SHORT FICTION PRIZE

Truman State University Press, 100 East Normal Ave., Kirksville MO 63501-4221. (660)785-7336. **Fax:** (660)785-4480. **E-mail:** chariton@truman.edu; tsup@truman.edu. **Website:** http://tsup.truman.edu. **Contact:** Barbara Smith-Mandell. An annual award for the best unpublished short fiction on any theme up to 5,000 words in English. Mss must be double-spaced on standard paper and bound only with a clip. Electronic submissions are not allowed. Include 2 title pages: 1 with the ms title and the author's contact information (name, address, phone, e-mail), and the other with only the ms title. (The author's name must not appear on or within the ms.) Enclose a SASE for notification when your ms is received. Mss will not be returned. Current Truman State University faculty, staff, or students are not eligible to compete. Deadline: September 30. Prize: $500 and publication in *The Chariton Review* for the winner. Two or three finalists will also be published and receive $200 each. The final judge will be announced after the finalists have been selected in January.

THE ARTHUR C. CLARKE AWARD

55 Burtt House, Fanshaw Street, London N1 6LE U.K.. **E-mail:** clarkeaward@gmail.com. **Website:** www.clarkeaward.com. **Contact:** Tom Hunter, award director. Annual award presented to the best science fiction novel, published between January 1 and December 31 of the year in question, receiving its first British publication during the calendar year. Deadline: 2nd week in December. Prize: £2,016 (rising by £1 each year), and an engraved bookend. Judged by representatives of the British Science Fiction Association, the Science Fiction Foundation, and Sci-Fi-London Film Festival

COPTALES CONTEST

Sponsored by Oak Tree Press, 1700 Dairy Avenue Apt #49, Corcoran CA 93212. **E-mail:** publisher@oaktreebooks.com. **E-mail:** CT-ContestAdmin@oaktreebooks.com. **Website:** www.oaktreebooks.com. **Contact:** Billie Johnson, publisher. Open to novels and true stories that feature a law enforcement main character. Word count should range from 60,000-80,000 words. Text must be typed in a clean, readable word document and double-spaced. Ms cover page must list author e-mail address and estimated word count. Guidelines and entry forms are available for SASE or online. The goal of the CopTales Contest is to discover and publish new authors, or authors shifting to a new genre. This annual contest is open to writers who have not published in the mystery genre in the past three years, as well as completely unpublished authors. Deadline: September 1. Prize: Publishing contract, book published in trade paperback and e-book formats with a professionally designed, four-color cover. See website for details. Judged by a select panel of editors and professional crime writers.

THE DANAHY FICTION PRIZE

Tampa Review, University of Tampa, 401 W. Kennedy Blvd., Tampa FL 33606. 813-253-6266. **E-mail:** utpress@ut.edu. **Website:** www.ut.edu/TampaReview. Annual award for the best previously unpublished short fiction. Deadline: November 30. Prize: $1,000, plus publication in *Tampa Review*.

DARK OAK MYSTERY CONTEST

Oak Tree Press, 1700 Dairy Avenue, # 49, Corcoran CA 93212. (217)824-6500. **E-mail:** publisher@oaktreebooks.com. **E-mail:** DO-ContestAdmin@oaktreebooks.com. **Website:** www.oaktreebooks.com. Offered annually for an unpublished mystery manuscript (between 60,00-80,000 words) of any sort from police procedurals to amateur sleuth novels. Acquires first North American, audio and film rights to winning entry. Open to authors not published in the past 3 years. Deadline: September 1. Prize: Publishing Agreement, and launch of the title. Judged by a select panel of editors and professional mystery writers.

THE DEADLY QUILL SHORT STORY WRITING CONTEST

Deadly Quill Magazine, **E-mail:** lorne@deadlyquill.com. **E-mail:** contest@deadlyquill.com. **Website:** www.deadlyquill.com. **Contact:** Lorne McMIllan. "We are hoping to give an outlet for short stories that follow the tradition of The Twilight Zone, Alfred Hitchcock, and The Outer Limits." Deadline: August 31. Prizes: $250 first place; $200 second place; $150 third place. Plus, more prizes described online. Author Edward Willett, Author Lorne McMillan, Author Colin Douglas

DEAD OF WINTER

E-mail: editors@toasted-cheese.com. **Website:** www.toasted-cheese.com. **Contact:** Stephanie Lenz, editor. The contest is a winter-themed horror fiction contest with a new topic/theme each year. Theme and word count parameters announced October 1. Entries must be unpublished. Accepts inquiries by e-mail. Cover letter should include name, address, e-mail, word count, and title. Word count parameters vary each year. Open to any writer. Guidelines available in October on website. Deadline: December 21. Results announced January 31. Winners notified by e-mail. List of winners on website. Prize: Amazon gift certificates and publication in *Toasted Cheese*. Also offers honorable mention. Judged by 2 *Toasted Cheese* editors who blind judge each contest. Each judge uses her own criteria to rate entries.

TIPS "Follow online submission guidelines."

WILLIAM F. DEECK MALICE DOMESTIC GRANTS FOR UNPUBLISHED WRITERS

Malice Domestic, P.O. Box 8007, Gaithersburg MD 20898-8007. 301-730-1675. **E-mail:** malicegrants@comcast.net. **Website:** www.malicedomestic.org. **Contact:** Harriette Sackler. Offered annually for unpublished work in the mystery field. Malice awards up to 2 grants to unpublished writers in the Malice Domestic genre at its annual convention in May. The competition is designed to help the next generation of Malice authors get their first work published and to foster quality Malice literature. Malice Domestic literature is loosely described as mystery stories of the Agatha Christie type, i.e., traditional mysteries. These works usually feature no excessive gore, gratuitous violence, or explicit sex. Writers who have been published previously in the mystery field, including publication of a mystery novel, short story, or dramatic work, are ineligible to apply. Members of the Malice Domestic Board of Directors and their families are ineligible to apply. Malice encourages applications from minority candidates. Guidelines online. Deadline: November 15. Prize: $1,500, plus a comprehensive registration to the following year's convention and two nights' lodging at the convention hotel.

☯☯☯☯ THE JACK DYER FICTION PRIZE

Crab Orchard Review, Department of English, Mail Code 4503, Faner Hall 2380, Southern Illinois University Carbondale, 1000 Faner Drive, Carbondale IL 62901. (618)453-6833. **Fax:** (618)453-8224. **E-mail:** jtribble@siu.edu. **Website:** www.craborchardreview.siu.edu. **Contact:** Jon C. Tribble, managing editor. Annual award for unpublished short fiction. Entries should consist of 1 story up to 6,000 words maximum in length. *Crab Orchard Review* acquires first North American serial rights to all submitted work. One winner and at least 2 finalists will be chosen. Length: 6,000 words maximum. All submissions must be made through Submittable. Submissions must be unpublished original work, written in English by a U.S. citizen, permanent resident, or person who has DACA/TPS status (current students and employees at Southern Illinois University Carbondale are not eligible). See Submittable guidelines online for complete formatting instructions. The author's name should not appear on any page of the entry. Results announced by end of August. Deadline: April 21. Submissions period begins February 21. Prize: $2,000, publication and 1-year subscription to *Crab Orchard Review*. Finalists are offered $500 and publication. Judged by editorial staff (pre-screening); winner chosen by genre editor.

TIPS "Carefully read directions for entering and follow them exactly. Send us your best work. Note that simultaneous submissions are accepted for this prize, but the winning entry must NOT be accepted elsewhere. All submissions should be made through Submittable: https://craborchardreview.submittable.com/submit."

☯ THE FAR HORIZONS AWARD FOR SHORT FICTION

The Malahat Review, University of Victoria, P.O. Box 1700, Stn CSC, Victoria BC V8W 2Y2 Canada. (250)721-8524. **Fax:** (250)472-5051. **E-mail:** malahat@uvic.ca. **E-mail:** horizons@uvic.ca. **Website:** www.malahatreview.ca. **Contact:** John Barton, editor. Submissions must be unpublished. No simultaneous submissions. Submit 1 piece of short fiction, 3,500 words maximum; no restrictions on subject matter or aesthetic approach. Include separate page with author's name, address, e-mail, and title; no identifying information on mss pages. E-mail submissions are accepted. Do not include SASE for results; mss will not be returned. Guidelines available on website. Winner and finalists contacted by e-mail. Open to "emerging short fiction writers from Canada, the US, and elsewhere" who have not yet published their fiction in a full-length book (48 pages or more). 2011 winner: Zoey Peterson; 2013 winner: Kerry-Lee Powell. Deadline: May 1. Prize: $1,000 CAD, publication in fall issue of *The Malahat Review* (see separate listing in Magazines/Journals). Announced in fall on website, Facebook page, and in quarterly e-newsletter, *Malahat Lite*.

FIRSTWRITER.COM INTERNATIONAL SHORT STORY CONTEST

firstwriter.com, United Kingdom. **Website:** https://www.firstwriter.com/competitions/short_story_contest/. **Contact:** J. Paul Dyson, managing editor. Accepts short stories up to 3,000 words on any subject and in any style. Deadline: April 1. The prize-money for first place is £200 (over $300). Ten special commendations will also be awarded, and all the winners will be published in firstwriter.magazine and receive a voucher that can be used to take out an annual subscription for free. Judged by firstwriter.magazine magazine editors.

☯ FISH PUBLISHING FLASH FICTION COMPETITION

Durrus, Bantry, County Cork Ireland. **E-mail:** info@fishpublishing.com. **Website:** www.fishpublishing.com. **Contact:** Clem Cairns. Annual prize awarding flash fiction. Max length: 300 words. You may enter as many times as you wish. See website for details and rules. "This is an opportunity to attempt what is one of the most difficult and rewarding tasks—to create, in a tiny fragment, a completely resolved and compelling story in 300 words or less." Deadline: February 28. First Prize: $1,200. The 10 published authors will receive 5 copies of the Anthology and will be invited to read at the launch during the West Cork Literary Festival in July. Judged by Nuala O'Connor.

THE GHOST STORY SUPERNATURAL FICTION AWARD

The Ghost Story, P.O. Box 601, Union ME 04862. E-mail: editor@theghoststory.com. Website: www.theghoststory.com. Contact: Paul Guernsey. Biannual contest for unpublished fiction. "Ghost stories are welcome, of course—but submissions may involve *any* paranormal or supernatural theme, as well as magic realism. What we're looking for is fine writing, fresh perspectives, and maybe a few surprises in the field of supernatural fiction." Guidelines available online. Length: 1,000-10,000 words. Deadline: April 30 and September 30. Winner receives $1,000 and publication in *The Ghost Story*. Honorable Mention wins $250 and publication, and Second Honorable Mention is awarded $100 and publication. Judged by the editors of *The Ghost Story*.

GIVAL PRESS NOVEL AWARD

Gival Press, LLC, P.O. Box 3812, Arlington VA 22203. (703)351-0079. E-mail: givalpress@yahoo.com. Website: www.givalpress.submittable.com. Contact: Robert L. Giron. Offered annually for a previously unpublished original novel (not a translation). Guidelines by phone, on website, via e-mail, or by mail with SASE. Results announced late fall of same year. Winners notified by phone. Results made available to entrants with SASE, by e-mail, on website. Open to any author who writes original work in English. Length: 30,000-100,000 words. Cover letter should include name, address, phone, e-mail, word count, novel title; include a short bio and short synopsis. Only the title and word count should appear on the actual ms. Writers may submit own work. Purpose is to award the best literary novel. Deadline: May 30. Prize: $3,000, plus publication of book with a standard contract and author's copies. Final judge is announced after winner is chosen. Entries read anonymously.

TIPS "Review the types of mss Gival Press has published. We stress literary works."

GIVAL PRESS SHORT STORY AWARD

Gival Press, P.O. Box 3812, Arlington VA 22203. (703)351-0079. E-mail: givalpress@yahoo.com. Web-site: www.givalpress.submittable.com. Contact: Robert L. Giron, publisher. Annual literary, short story contest. Entries must be unpublished. Open to anyone who writes original short stories, which are not a chapter of a novel, in English. Receives about 100-150 entries per category. Guidelines available online, via e-mail, or by mail. Results announced in the fall of the same year. Winners notified by phone. Results available with SASE, by e-mail, and on website. Length: 5,000-15,000 words. Include name, address, phone, e-mail, word count, title on cover letter; include short bio. Only the title and word count should be found on ms. Writers may submit their own fiction. Recognizes the best literary short story. Deadline: August 8. Prize: $1,000 and publication on website. Judged anonymously.

GLIMMER TRAIN'S FAMILY MATTERS CONTEST

Glimmer Train, P.O. Box 80430, Portland OR 97280. (503)221-0836. Fax: (503)221-0837. E-mail: eds@glimmertrain.org. Website: www.glimmertrain.org. Contact: Susan Burmeister-Brown. This contest is now held once a year, during the months of November and December. Winners are contacted on March 1. Submit online at www.glimmertrain.org. The word count for this contest generally ranges from 1,500 to 5,000 words, though up 12,000 words is fine. See complete guidelines online. Deadline: December 31. Prize: 1st Place: $2,500, publication in *Glimmer Train Stories*, and 10 copies of that issue; 2nd Place: $500 and consideration for publication; 3rd Place: $300 and consideration for publication. The editors judge.

TIPS "We are looking for stories about families of all configurations. It's fine to draw heavily on real life experiences, but the work must read like fiction and all stories accepted for publication will be presented as fiction."

GLIMMER TRAIN'S FICTION OPEN

Glimmer Train, Inc., Glimmer Train Press, Inc., P.O. Box 80430, Portland OR 97280. (503)221-0836. Fax: (503)221-0837. E-mail: eds@glimmertrain.org. Web-site: www.glimmertrain.org. Contact: Susan Burmeister-Brown. Submissions to this category generally range from 3,000-8,000 words, but up to 20,000 is fine. Held twice a year: March 1 - April 30 and July 1 - August 31. Submit online at www.glimmertrain.org. Winners will be called 2 months after the close of the contest. Deadline: April 30 and August 31. Prize:

1st Place: $3,000, publication in *Glimmer Train Stories*, and 10 copies of that issue; 2nd Place: $1,000 and consideration for publication; 3rd Place: $600 and consideration for publication. Judged by the editors.

TIPS This category is open to all writers and all themes. The prize was just increased in 2016.

GLIMMER TRAIN'S SHORT-STORY AWARD FOR NEW WRITERS

Glimmer Train Press, Inc., P.O. Box 80430, Portland OR 97280. (503)221-0836. **Fax:** (503)221-0837. **E-mail:** eds@glimmertrain.org. **Website:** www.glimmertrain.org. **Contact:** Susan Burmeister-Brown. Offered for any writer whose fiction hasn't appeared in a nationally distributed print publication with a circulation over 5,000. Submissions to this category generally range from 1,500–5,000 words, but up to 12,000 is fine. Held three times a year: January 1–February 29, May 1–June 30, September 1–October 31. Submit online at www.glimmertrain.org. Winners will be called 2 months after the close of the contest. Deadline: February 29, June 30, and October 31. Prize: 1st Place: $2,500, publication in *Glimmer Train Stories*, and 10 copies of that issue; 2nd Place: $500 and consideration for publication; 3rd Place: $300 and consideration for publication.

TIPS "In a recent edition of *Best American Short Stories*, of the top '100 Distinguished Short Stories,' 10 appeared in *Glimmer Train Stories*, more than any other publication in the country, including *The New Yorker*. Of those 10, 3 were those authors' first stories accepted for publication."

GLIMMER TRAIN'S VERY SHORT FICTION CONTEST

Glimmer Train Press, Inc., P.O. Box 80430, Portland OR 97280. (503)221-0836. **Fax:** (503)221-0837. **E-mail:** eds@glimmertrain.org. **Website:** www.glimmertrain.org. **Contact:** Susan Burmeister-Brown. Offered to encourage the art of the very short story. Word count: 3,000 maximum. Held twice a year: March 1–April 30 and July 1–August 31. Submit online at www.glimmertrain.org. Results announced 2 months after the close of the contest. To encourage the art of the very short story. Deadline: April 30 and August 31. Prize: 1st Place: $2,000, publication in *Glimmer Train Stories*, and 10 copies of that issue; 2nd Place: $500 and consideration for publication; 3rd Place: $300 and consideration for publication. Judged by the editors.

TIPS There is no minimum word count, though it is rare for a piece under 500 words to read as a full story.

THE GOVER PRIZE

Best New Writing, P.O. Box 11, Titusville NJ 08530. **Fax:** (609)968-1718. **E-mail:** submissions@bestnewwriting.com. **Website:** www.bestnewwriting.com/BNWgover.html. **Contact:** Christopher Klim, senior editor. The Gover Prize, named after groundbreaking author Robert Gover, awards an annual prize and publication in *Best New Writing* for the best short fiction and creative nonfiction. Open to all writers. Submissions must be previously unpublished. Guidelines available on website. Entries limited to 500 words or less. Deadline: January 10. Open to submissions on September 15. Prize: $250 grand prize; publication in *Best New Writing* for finalists (approximately 12), holds 6-month world exclusive rights. Judged by *Best New Writing* editorial staff.

⟲ LYNDALL HADOW/DONALD STUART SHORT STORY COMPETITION

Fellowship of Australian Writers (WA), P.O. Box 6180, Swanbourne WA 6910 Australia. (61)(8)9384-4771. **Fax:** (61)(8)9384-4854. **E-mail:** fellowshipaustralianwriterswa@gmail.com. **Website:** www.fawwa.org. Annual contest for unpublished short stories (maximum 3,000 words). Reserves the right to publish entries in a FAWWA publication or on website. Guidelines online or for SASE. Deadline: June 1. Submissions period begins April 1. Prize: 1st Place: $400; 2nd Place: $100; Highly Commended (2): $50.

HAMMETT PRIZE

International Association of Crime Writers, North American Branch, 243 Fifth Avenue, #537, New York NY 10016. **E-mail:** mfrisque@igc.org. **Website:** www.crimewritersna.org.. **Contact:** Mary A. Frisque, executive director, North American Branch. Award for crime novels, story collections, nonfiction by one author. "Our reading committee seeks suggestions from publishers and they also ask the membership for recommendations." Nominations announced in January; winners announced in fall. Winners notified by e-mail or mail and recognized at awards ceremony. For contest results, send SASE or e-mail. For guidelines, send SASE or e-mail. Accepts inquiries by e-mail. Entries must be previously published. To be eligible, the book must have been published in the US or Canada during the calendar year. The author must be a US or Canadian citizen or permanent resident. Award established to honor a work of literary excellence in the field of crime writing by a US or Canadian author.

Deadline: December 15. Prize: Trophy. Judged by a committee of members of the organization. The committee chooses 5 nominated books, which are then sent to 3 outside judges for a final selection. Judges are outside the crime writing field.

WILDA HEARNE FLASH FICTION CONTEST

Big Muddy: A Journal of the Mississippi River Valley, WHFF Contest, Southeast Missouri State University Press, One University Plaza, MS 2650, Cape Girardeau MO 63701. (573) 651-2044. **E-mail:** sswartwout@semo.edu. **Website:** www.semopress.com. **Contact:** Susan Swartwout, publisher. Annual competition for flash fiction, held by Southeast Missouri State University Press. Work must not be previously published. Send maximum of 500 words, double-spaced, with no identifying name on the pages, and a separate cover sheet with story title, author's name, address, and phone number. Send SASE for notification of results; all manuscripts will be recycled. Entries should be sent via postal mail. Deadline: October 1. Prize: $500 and publication in *Big Muddy: A Journal of the Mississippi River Valley*. Semi-finalists will be chosen by a team of published writers. The final manuscript will be chosen by Susan Swartwout, publisher of the Southeast Missouri State University Press.

DRUE HEINZ LITERATURE PRIZE

University of Pittsburgh Press, 7500 Thomas Blvd., Pittsburgh PA 15260. **Fax:** (412)383-2466. **E-mail:** info@upress.pitt.edu. **Website:** www.upress.pitt.edu. Offered annually to writers who have published a book-length collection of fiction or a minimum of 3 short stories or novellas in commercial magazines or literary journals of national distribution. Does not return mss. Deadline: June 30. Open to submissions on May 1. Prize: $15,000. Judged by anonymous nationally known writers such as Robert Penn Warren, Joyce Carol Oates, and Margaret Atwood.

LORIAN HEMINGWAY SHORT STORY COMPETITION

Hemingway Days Festival, P.O. Box 2011 c/o Cynthia. D. Higgs: Key West Editorial, Key West FL 33045. **E-mail:** shortstorykeywest@hushmail.com. **Website:** www.shortstorycompetition.com. **Contact:** Eva Eliot, editorial assistant. Offered annually for unpublished short stories up to 3,500 words. Guidelines available via mail, e-mail, or online. Accepts inquiries by e-mail, or visit website. Entries must be unpublished. Open to all writers whose work has not appeared in a nationally distributed publication with a circulation of 5,000 or more. Looking for excellence, pure and simple—no genre restrictions, no theme restrictions. We seek a writer's voice that cannot be ignored. All entrants will receive a letter from Lorian Hemingway and a list of winners, via mail or e-mail, by October 1. Results announced at the end of July during Hemingway Days festival. Winners notified by phone prior to announcement. Award to encourage literary excellence and the efforts of writers whose voices have yet to be heard. Deadline: May 15. Prizes: 1st Place: $1,500, plus publication of his or her winning story in *Cutthroat: A Journal of the Arts*; 2nd-3rd Place: $500; honorable mentions will also be awarded. Judged by a panel of writers, editors, and literary scholars selected by author Lorian Hemingway. (Lorian Hemingway is the competition's final judge.)

TONY HILLERMAN PRIZE

Wordharvest, 1063 Willow Way, Santa Fe NM 87507. (505)471-1565. **E-mail:** wordharvest@wordharvest.com. **Website:** www.wordharvest.com. **Contact:** Anne Hillerman and Jean Schaumberg, co-organizers. Awarded annually, and sponsored by St. Martin's Press, for the best first mystery set in the Southwest. Murder or another serious crime or crimes must be at the heart of the story, with the emphasis on the solution rather than the details of the crime. Multiple entries accepted. Accepts inquiries by e-mail, phone. Entries should be unpublished; self-published work is generally accepted. Length: no less than 220 type written pages, or approximately 60,000 words. Cover letter should include name, address, phone, e-mail, list of publishing credits. Please include SASE for response. Writers may submit their own work. Entries should be mailed to St. Martin's Press: St. Martin's Minotaur/THWC Competition, St. Martin's Minotaur, 175 Fifth Ave., New York, NY 10010. Honors the contributions made by Tony Hillerman to the art and craft of the mystery. Deadline: June 1. Prize: $10,000 advance and publication by St. Martin's Press. Nominees will be selected by judges chosen by the editorial staff of St. Martin's Press, with the assistance of independent judges selected by organizers of the Tony Hillerman Writers Conference (Wordharvest), and the winner will be chosen by St. Martin's editors.

INDIANA REVIEW POETRY CONTEST

Ballantine Hall 465, Indiana University, 1020 E. Kirkwood Ave., Bloomington IN 47405-7103. **E-mail:** inreview@indiana.edu. **Website:** http://indianareview.org. **Contact:** Peter Kispert, editor. Contest for poetry in any style and on any subject. Open to any writer. Mss will not be returned. No works forthcoming elsewhere, are eligible. Simultaneous submissions accepted, but in the event of entrant withdrawal, contest fee will not be refunded. Deadline: April 1. Submission period begins February 15. Prize: $1,000, publication in the *Indiana Review* and contributor's copies. Judged by Camille Rankine.

TIPS "We look for a command of language and structure, as well as a facility with compelling and unusual subject matter. It's a good idea to obtain copies of issues featuring past winners to get a more concrete idea of what we are looking for."

INK & INSIGHTS WRITING CONTEST

Critique My Novel, 2408 W. 8th, Amarillo TX 79106. **E-mail:** contest@InkandInsights.com. **Website:** http://InkandInsights.com. **Contact:** Catherine York, contest administrator. Ink & Insights is a writing contest geared toward strengthening the skills of independent writers by focusing on feedback. Each entry is assigned four judges who specialize in the genre of the manuscript. They read, score, and comment on specific aspects of the segment. The top three mss in the Master and Nonfiction categories move on to the Agent Round and receive a guaranteed read and feedback from a panel of agents. Send the first 10,000 words of your manuscript (unpublished, self-published, or published through a vanity/independent press). Include a cover sheet that contains the following information: novel title, genre, word count of full ms, e-mail address. Do not put name on submission. See website for full details and formatting guidelines. Deadline: April 30 (regular entry), June 30 (late entry). Prize: Prizes vary depending on category. Every novel receives personal feedback from 4 judges. Judges listed on website, including the agents who will be helping choose the top winners this year.

THE IOWA SHORT FICTION AWARD & JOHN SIMMONS SHORT FICTION AWARD

Iowa Writers' Workshop, 507 N. Clinton St., 102 Dey House, Iowa City IA 52242-1000. **Website:** www.uiowapress.org. **Contact:** James McCoy, director. Annual award to give exposure to promising writers who have not yet published a book of prose. Open to any writer. Current University of Iowa students are not eligible. No application forms are necessary. Announcement of winners made early in year following competition. Winners notified by phone. No application forms are necessary. Do not send original ms. Include SASE for return of ms. Entries must be unpublished, but stories previously published in periodicals are eligible for inclusion. The ms must be a collection of short stories of at least 150 word-processed, double-spaced pages. Deadline: September 30. Submission period begins August 1. Prize: Publication by University of Iowa Press. Judged by senior Iowa Writers' Workshop members who screen mss; published fiction author of note makes final selections.

🌑🌑🌑🌑 JESSE H. JONES AWARD FOR BEST WORK OF FICTION

P.O. Box 609, Round Rock TX 78680. **E-mail:** tilsecretary@yahoo.com. **Website:** http://texasinstituteofletters.org. Offered annually by Texas Institute of Letters for work published January 1-December 31 of year before award is given to recognize the writer of the best book of fiction entered in the competition. Writers must have been born in Texas, have lived in the state for at least 2 consecutive years at some time, or the subject matter of the work should be associated with the state. See website for details and information on submitting. Deadline: January 10. Prize: $6,000.

JAMES JONES FIRST NOVEL FELLOWSHIP

Wilkes University, Creative Writing Department, Wilkes University, 84 West South Street, Wilkes-Barre PA 18766. (570)408-4547. **Fax:** (570)408-3333. **E-mail:** jamesjonesfirstnovel@wilkes.edu. **Website:** www.wilkes.edu/. Offered annually for unpublished novels and novellas (must be works-in-progress). This competition is open to all American writers who have not previously published novels. Submit a 2-page (maximum) outline of the entire novel and the first 50 pages of the novel-in-progress are to be submitted. The ms must be typed and double-spaced; outline may be single-spaced. Entrants submitting via snail mail should include their name, address, telephone number, and e-mail address (if available) on the title page, but nowhere else on the manuscript. For those entrants submitting online, name, address, telephone number, and e-mail address should appear only on your cover letter. Cover letter should be dropped in the cover letter box and outline and ms should be attached as one document. The award is intended to honor the spirit of unblinking honesty, determination, and insight into modern culture exemplified by the late James Jones. Deadline: March 15. Submission period begins October 1. Prize: $10,000; 2 runners-up get $1,000 honorarium.

THE LAWRENCE FOUNDATION AWARD

Prairie Schooner, 123 Andrews Hall, University of Nebraska-Lincoln, Lincoln NE 68588-0334. (402)472-0911. **Fax:** (402)472-9771. **E-mail:** prairieschooner@unl.edu. **Website:** www.prairieschooner.unl.edu. Offered annually for the best short story published in Prairie Schooner in the previous year. Only work published in *Prairie Schooner* in the previous year is considered. Work is nominated by editorial staff. Results announced in the Spring issue. Winners notified by mail in February or March. Prize: $1,000. Judged by editorial staff of *Praire Schooner*.

LAWRENCE FOUNDATION PRIZE

Michigan Quarterly Review, 0576 Rackham Bldg., 915 E. Washington Street, Ann Arbor MI 48109-1070. (734)764-9265. **E-mail:** mqr@umich.edu. **Website:** www.michiganquarterlyreview.com. **Contact:** Vicki Lawrence, managing editor. This annual prize is awarded by the *Michigan Quarterly Review* editorial board to the author of the best short story published in *MQR* that year. The prize is sponsored by University of Michigan alumnus and fiction writer Leonard S. Bernstein, a trustee of the Lawrence Foundation of New York. Approximately 20 short stories are published in *MQR* each year. Guidelines available under submission guidelines on website. Prize: $1,000. Judged by editorial board.

LITERAL LATTÉ FICTION AWARD

Literal Latté, 200 E. 10th St., Suite 240, New York NY 10003. (212)260-5532. **E-mail:** litlatte@aol.com. **E-mail:** Link to submittable on www.literal-latte.com. **Website:** www.literal-latte.com. **Contact:** Edward Estlin, contributing editor. Award to provide talented writers with 3 essential tools for continued success: money, publication, and recognition. Offered annually for unpublished fiction (maximum 20,000 words). Guidelines online. Open to any writer. Deadline: January 15. Prize: 1st Place: $1,000 and publication in *Literal Latté*; 2nd Place: $300; 3rd Place: $200; also up to 7 honorable mentions. All winners published in *Literal Latté*.

LITERAL LATTE SHORT SHORTS CONTEST

Literal Latté, 200 E. 10th St., Suite 240, New York NY 10003. (212)260-5532. **E-mail:** litlatte@aol.com. E-mail: Link to submittable on www.literal-latte.com. **Website:** www.literal-latte.com. **Contact:** Jenine Gordon Bockman, editor. Annual contest. Send unpublished shorts, 2,000 words max. All styles welcome. Name, address, phone number, e-mail address (optional) on cover page only. Include SASE or e-mail address for reply. All entries considered for publication. Deadline: June 30. Prize: $500. Judged by the editors.

LITERARY FICTION CONTEST

The Writers' Workshop of Asheville, NC, Literary Fiction Contest, 387 Beaucatcher Rd., Asheville NC 28805. **E-mail:** writersw@gmail.com. **Website:** www.twwoa.org. Submit a short story or chapter of a novel of 5,000 words or less. Multiple entries are accepted. All work must be unpublished. Pages should be paper clipped, with your name, address, phone and title of work on a cover sheet. Double-space and use 12-point font. Deadline: August 30. Prize: 1st Place: Your choice of a 2 night stay at the Mountain Muse B&B in Asheville, 3 free online workshops, or 50 pages line-edited and revised by editorial staff; 2nd Place: 2 free workshops or 35 pages line-edited; 3rd Place: 1 free workshop or 25 pages line-edited; 10 Honorable Mentions.

THE MARY MACKEY SHORT STORY PRIZE CATEGORY

Soul-Making Keats Literary Competition, The Webhallow House, 1544 Sweetwood Dr., Broadmoor Village CA 94015. **E-mail:** SoulKeats@mail.com. **Website:** www.soulmakingcontest.us. **Contact:** Eileen Malone. Open annually to any writer. One story/entry, up to 5,000 words. All prose works must be typed, page numbered, and double-spaced. Identify only with 3x5 card. Deadline: November 30. Prize: Cash prizes.

✪$$ THE MALAHAT REVIEW NOVELLA PRIZE

The Malahat Review, University of Victoria, P.O. Box 1700 STN CSC, Victoria BC V8W 2Y2 Canada. (250)721-8524. **E-mail:** malahat@uvic.ca. **E-mail:** novella@uvic.ca. **Website:** malahatreview.ca. **Contact:** John Barton, editor. Held in alternate years with the Long Poem Prize. Submit novellas between 10,000 and 20,000 words in length. Include separate page with author's name, address, e-mail, and novella title; no identifying information on mss. pages. E-mail submissions are now accepted. Do not include SASE for results; mss will not be returned. Guidelines available on website. 2010 winner was Tony Tulathimutte, 2012 winner was Naben Ruthnum, and the 2014 winner was Dora Dueck. Winner and finalists contacted by e-mail. Offered to promote unpublished novellas. Obtains first world rights. After publication rights revert to the author. Open to any writer. Deadline: February 1 (even years). Prize: $1,500 CAD and one year's subscription Winner published in summer issue of *The Malahat Review* and announced on website, Facebook page, and in quarterly e-newsletter, *Malahat Lite*. Judges for the 2016 Novella Prize are Mark Anthony Jarman, Stephen Marche, and Joan Thomas. Their bios are on our website.

☻ THE MAN BOOKER PRIZE

Four Colman Getty PR, 20 St Thomas Street, London SE1 9BF United Kingdom. (44)(207)697 4200. **Website:** www.themanbookerprize.com. **Contact:** Four Colman Getty PR. Books are only accepted through UK publishers. However, publication outside the UK does not disqualify a book once it is published in the UK. Open to any full-length novel (published October 1-September 30). No novellas, collections of short stories, translations, or self-published books. Open to citizens of the Commonwealth or Republic of Ireland. Deadline: July. Prize: £50,000. Judges appointed by the Booker Prize Management Committee.

MARY MCCARTHY PRIZE IN SHORT FICTION

Sarabande Books, 2234 Dundee Rd., Suite 200, Louisville KY 40205. (502)458-4028. **Fax:** (502)458-4065. **E-mail:** info@sarabandebooks.org. **Website:** www.sarabandebooks.org. **Contact:** Sarah Gorham, Editor-in-Chief. Annual competition to honor a collection of short stories, novellas, or a short novel. All mss should be between 150 and 250 pages. All finalists considered for publication. Guidelines available online. Deadline: April 30. Submission period begins March 15. Prize: $2,000 and publication (standard royalty contract).

☻ MARJORIE GRABER MCINNIS SHORT STORY AWARD

ACT Writers Centre, Gorman House Arts Centre, Ainslie Ave., Braddon ACT 2612 Australia. (61)(2)6262-9191. **Fax:** (61)(2)6262-9191. **E-mail:** admin@actwriters.org.au. **Website:** www.actwriters.org.au. Open theme for a short story with 1,500-3,000 words. Guidelines available on website. Open only to unpub-

lished emerging writers residing within the ACT or region. Deadline: September 18. Submissions period begins in early September. Prize: $600 and publication. Five runners-up receive book prizes. All winners may be published in the ACT Writers Centre newsletter and on the ACT Writers Centre website.

MEMPHIS MAGAZINE FICTION CONTEST

Memphis Magazine, co-sponsored by booksellers of Laurelwood and Burke's Book Store, Fiction Contest, c/o *Memphis* magazine, P.O. Box 1738, Memphis TN 38101. (901)521-9000, ext. 451. **Fax:** (901)521-0129. **E-mail:** sadler@memphismagazine.com. **Website:** www.memphismagazine.com. **Contact:** Marilyn Sadler. Annual award for authors of short fiction living within 150 miles of Memphis. Each story should be between 3,000 and 4,500 words long. See website for guidelines and rules. Deadline: February 15. Prize: $1,000 grand prize, along with being published in the annual Cultural Issue; two honorable-mention awards of $500 each will be given if the quality of entries warrants.

DAVID NATHAN MEYERSON PRIZE FOR FICTION

Southwest Review, Southern Methodist University, P.O. Box 750374, Dallas TX 75275-0374. (214)768-1037. **Fax:** (214)768-1408. **E-mail:** swr@smu.edu. **Website:** www.smu.edu/southwestreview. **Contact:** Jennifer Cranfill, senior editor. Annual award given to a writer who has not published a first book of fiction, either a novel or collection of stories. All contest entrants will receive a copy of the issue in which the winning piece appears. Submissions must be no longer than 8,000 words. Work should be printed without the author's name. Name and address should appear only on the cover letter. Submissions will not be returned. Deadline: May 1 (postmarked). Prize: $1,000 and publication in the *Southwest Review*.

TIPS "A cover letter with name, address, and other relevant information may accompany the piece which must be printed without any identifying information. Get guidelines for SASE or online."

MILKWEED NATIONAL FICTION PRIZE

1011 Washington Ave. S., Suite 300, Minneapolis MN 55415. (612)332-3192. **Fax:** (612)215-2550. **E-mail:** editor@milkweed.org. **Website:** www.milkweed.org. **Contact:** Patrick Thoman, editor and program manager. Annual award for unpublished works. Mss should be one of the following: a novel, a collection of short stories, one or more novellas, or a combination of short stories and one or more novellas. Mss should be of high literary quality and between 150-400 pages in length. Work previously published as a book in the US is not eligible, but individual stories or novellas previously published in magazines or anthologies are eligible. Guidelines available online. Deadline: Rolling submissions. Check website for details of when they're accepting mss. Prize: Publication by Milkweed Editions and a cash advance of $5,000 against royalties, agreed upon in the contractual arrangement negotiated at the time of acceptance. Judged by the editors.

MONTANA PRIZE IN FICTION

Cutbank Literary Magazine, *CutBank*, University of Montana, English Dept., LA 133, Missoula MT 59812. **E-mail:** editor.cutbank@gmail.com. **Website:** www.cutbankonline.org. **Contact:** Allison Linville, editor-in-chief. The Montana Prize in Fiction seeks to highlight work that showcases an authentic voice, a boldness of form, and a rejection of functional fixedness. Accepts online submissions only. Send a single work, no more than 35 pages. Guidelines available online. Deadline: January 15. Submissions period begins November 9. Prize: $500 and featured in the magazine. Judged by a guest judge each year.

THE HOWARD FRANK MOSHER SHORT FICTION PRIZE

Vermont College, 36 College St., Montpelier VT 05602. (802)828-8517. **E-mail:** hungermtn@vcfa.edu. **Website:** www.hungermtn.org. **Contact:** Samantha Kolber, managing editor. The Howard Frank Mosher Short Fiction Prize is an annual contest for short fiction. Enter one original, unpublished story under 10,000 words. Do not put name or address on the story; entries are judged blind. Accepts submissions online or via postal mail. Deadline: March 1. Prize: One first place winner receives $1,000 and publication. Two honorable mentions receive $100 each, and are considered for publication. Judged by Janet Burroway in 2016 and Caitlyn Horrocks in 2017.

NATIONAL READERS' CHOICE AWARDS

Oklahoma Romance Writers of America (OKRWA), **E-mail:** nrca@okrwa.com. **Website:** www.okrwa.com. **Contact:** Kathy L Wheeler. "To provide writers of romance fiction with a competition where their published novels are judged by readers." See the website for categories and descriptions. Additional award for best first book. All entries must have an original copyright date during the current contest year. Entries will be accepted from authors, editors, publishers, agents, readers, whoever wants to fill out the entry form, pay the fee, and supply the books. No limit to the number of entries, but each title may be entered only in one category. Open to any writer published by an RWA approved non-vanity/non-subsidy press. For guidelines, send e-mail or visit website. Deadline: December 1st. Prize: Plaques and finalist certificates awarded at the awards banquet hosted at the Annual National Romance Writers Convention. Judged by readers.

NATIONAL WRITERS ASSOCIATION NOVEL WRITING CONTEST

The National Writers Association, 10940 S. Parker Rd. #508, Parker CO 80134. (303)841-0246. **E-mail:** natlwritersassn@hotmail.com. **Website:** www.nationalwriters.com. **Contact:** Sandy Whelchel, director. Open to any genre or category. Contest begins December 1. Open to any writer. Entries must be unpublished. Length: 20,000-100,000 words. Contest forms are available on the NWA website or an attachment will be sent upon request via e-mail or with an SASE. Annual contest to help develop creative skills, to recognize and reward outstanding ability, and to increase the opportunity for the marketing and subsequent publication of novel mss. Deadline: April 1. Prize: 1st Place: $500; 2nd Place: $250; 3rd Place: $150. Judged by editors and agents.

NATIONAL WRITERS ASSOCIATION SHORT STORY CONTEST

10940 S. Parker Rd., #508, Parker CO 80134. (303)841-0246. **E-mail:** natlwritersassn@hotmail.com. **Website:** www.nationalwriters.com. Any genre of short story manuscript may be entered. All entries must be postmarked by July 1. Contest opens April 1. Only unpublished works may be submitted. All manuscripts must be typed, double-spaced, in the English language. Maximum length is 5,000 words. Those unsure of proper manuscript format should request Research Report #35. The entry must be accompanied by an entry form (photocopies are acceptable) and return SASE if you wish the material and rating sheets returned. Submissions will be destroyed, otherwise. Receipt of entry will not be acknowledged without a return postcard. Author's name and address must appear on the first page. Entries remain the property of the author and may be submitted during the contest as long as they are not published before the final notification of winners. Final prizes will be awarded in June. The purpose of the National Writers Assn. Short Story Contest is to encourage the development of creative skills, recognize and reward outstanding ability in the area of short story writing. Prize: 1st Prize: $250; 2nd Prize: $100; 3rd Prize: $50; 4th-10th places will receive a book. 1st-3rd place winners may be asked to grant one-time rights for publication in *Authorship* magazine. Honorable Mentions receive a certificate. Judging will be based on originality, marketability, research, and reader interest. Copies of the judges evaluation sheets will be sent to entrants furnishing an SASE with their entry.

THE NELLIGAN PRIZE FOR SHORT FICTION

Colorado Review/Center for Literary Publishing, Colorado State University, 9105 Campus Delivery, Dept. of English, Colorado State University, Ft. Collins CO 80523-9105. (970)491-5449. **E-mail:** creview@colostate.edu. **Website:** http://nelliganprize.colostate.edu. **Contact:** Stephanie G'Schwind, editor. Annual competition/award for short stories. Receives approximately 900 stories. All entries are read blind by Colorado Review's editorial staff. Ten-to-fifteen entries are selected to be sent on to a final, outside judge. Stories must be unpublished and between 10 and 50 pages. "The Nelligan Prize for Short Fiction was established in memory of Liza Nelligan, a writer, editor, and friend of many in Colorado State University's English Department, where she received her master's degree in literature in 1992. By giving an award to the author of an outstanding short story each year, we hope to honor Liza Nelligan's life, her passion for writing, and her love of fiction." Deadline: March 14. Prize: $2,000 and publication of story in *Colorado Review*. Judged by a different writer each year.

🌑 SEAN O'FAOLAIN SHORT STORY COMPETITION

The Munster Literature Centre, Frank O'Connor House, 84 Douglas Street, Cork Ireland. +353-0214319255. **E-mail:** munsterlit@eircom.net. **Website:** www.munsterlit.ie. **Contact:** Patrick Cotter, artistic director. Entries should be unpublished. Anyone may enter contest. Length: 3,000 words max. Cover letter should include name, address, phone, e-mail, word count, novel/story title. Purpose is to reward writers of outstanding short stories. Deadline: July 31. Prize: 1st prize €2,000; 2nd prize €500. Four runners-up prizes of €100 (approx $146). All six stories to be published in *Southword Literary Journal*. First-Prize Winner offered week's residency in Anam Cara Artist's Retreat in Ireland.

FRANK O'CONNOR AWARD FOR SHORT FICTION

descant, Texas Christian University's literary journal, TCU Box 298300, Fort Worth TX 76129. (817)257-5907. **Fax:** (817)257-6239. **E-mail:** descant@tcu.edu. **Website:** www.descant.tcu.edu. **Contact:** Matthew Pitt, editor. Offered annually for an outstanding story accepted for publication in the current edition of the journal. Publication retains copyright but will transfer it to the author upon request. Deadline: September 1 - March 31. Prize: $500.

ON THE PREMISES CONTEST

On The Premises, LLC, 4323 Gingham Court, Alexandria VA 22310. **E-mail:** questions@onthepremises.com. **Website:** www.onthepremises.com. **Contact:** Tarl Kudrick or Bethany Granger, co-publishers. *On the Premises* aims to promote newer and/or relatively unknown writers who can write creative, compelling stories told in effective, uncluttered, and evocative prose. Each contest challenges writers to produce a great story based on a broad premise that the editors supply as part of the contest. Submissions are accepted only through web-based submissions system. Entries should be unpublished. Length: minimum 1,000 words; maximum 5,000. No name or contact info should be in ms. Writers may submit own work. Check website for details on the specific premise that writers should incorporate into their story. Results announced within 2 weeks of contest deadline. Winners notified via e-mail and with publication of *On the Premises*. Results made available to entrants on website and in publication. Deadline: Short story contests held twice a year; smaller mini-contests held four times a year; check website for exact dates. Prize: 1st Prize: $220; 2nd Prize: $160; 3rd Prize: $120; Honorable Mentions receive $60. All prize winners are published in *On the Premises* magazine in HTML and PDF format. Judged by a panel of judges with professional editing and writing experience.

TIPS "Write a compelling, creative and well-crafted short story that clearly uses the contest premise."

🕘🕘🕘 KENNETH PATCHEN AWARD FOR THE INNOVATIVE NOVEL

Eckhard Gerdes Publishing, 1110 Varsity Blvd., Apt. 221, DeKalb IL 60115. E-mail: egerdes@experimentalfiction.com. Website: www.experimentalfiction.com. Contact: Eckhard Gerdes. This award will honor the most innovative novel submitted during the previous calendar year. Kenneth Patchen is celebrated for being among the greatest innovators of American fiction, incorporating strategies of concretism, asemic writing, digression, and verbal juxtaposition into his writing long before such strategies were popularized during the height of American postmodernist experimentation in the 1970s. See guidelines and application form online at website. Deadline: All submissions must be postmarked between January 1 and July 31. Prize: $1,000 and 20 complimentary copies. Judged by novelist Dominic Ward.

🕘🕘🕘 THE PATERSON FICTION PRIZE

The Poetry Center at Passaic Community College, One College Blvd., Paterson NJ 07505. (973)684-6555. Fax: (973)523-6085. E-mail: mgillan@pccc.edu. Website: www.pccc.edu/poetry. Contact: Maria Mazziotti Gillan, executive director. Offered annually for a novel or collection of short fiction published the previous calendar year. For more information, visit the website or send SASE. Deadline: April 1. Prize: $1,000.

WILLIAM PEDEN PRIZE IN FICTION

The Missouri Review, 357 McReynolds Hall, Columbia MO 65211. (573)882-4474. Fax: (573)884-4671. E-mail: mutmrcontestquestion@moreview.com. Website: www.missourireview.com. Contact: Michael Nye, managing editor. Offered annually for the best story published in the past volume year of the magazine. All stories published in The Missouri Review are automatically considered. Guidelines online or for SASE. Prize: $1,000 and a reading/reception.

PEN/FAULKNER AWARDS FOR FICTION

PEN/Faulkner Foundation, 201 E. Capitol St. SE, Washington DC 20003. (202)898-9063. E-mail: awards@penfaulkner.org. Website: www.penfaulkner.org. Contact: Emma Snyder, executive director. Offered annually for best book-length work of fiction by an American citizen published in a calendar year. Deadline: October 31. Prize: $15,000 (one Winner); $5,000 (4 Finalists).

PHOEBE WINTER FICTION CONTEST

Phoebe, MSN 2D6, George Mason University, 4400 University Dr., Fairfax VA 22030. (703)993-2915. E-mail: phoebe@gmu.edu. Website: www.gmu.edu/pubs/phoebe. Offered annually for an unpublished story (25 pages maximum). Guidelines online or for SASE. First serial rights if work is accepted for publication. Purpose is to recognize new and exciting fiction. Deadline: March 21. Prize: $500 and publication in the Spring online issue. Judged by a recognized fiction writer, hired by Phoebe (changes each year). For 2016, the fiction judge will be Joshua Ferris.

TIPS Submit no more than 1 story/25 pages per entry.

EDGAR ALLAN POE AWARD

1140 Broadway, Suite 1507, New York NY 10001. (212)888-8171. E-mail: mwa@mysterywriters.org. Website: www.mysterywriters.org. Mystery Writers of America is the leading association for professional crime writers in the United States. Members of MWA include most major writers of crime fiction and nonfiction, as well as screenwriters, dramatists, editors, publishers, and other professionals in the field. Categories include: Best Novel, Best First Novel by an American Author, Best Paperback/E-Book Original, Best Fact Crime, Best Critical/Biographical, Best Short Story, Best Juvenile Mystery, Best Young Adult Myster, Best Television Series Episode Teleplay, and Mary Higgins Clark Award. Purpose of the award: Honor authors of distinguished works in the mystery field. Previously published submissions only. Submissions should be made by the publisher. Work must be published/produced the year of the contest. Deadline: November 30. Prize: Awards ceramic bust of "Edgar" for winner; certificates for all nominees. Judged by active status members of Mystery Writers of America (writers).

THE KATHERINE ANNE PORTER PRIZE FOR FICTION

Nimrod International Journal, The University of Tulsa, 800 S. Tucker Dr., Tulsa OK 74104. (918)631-3080. Fax: (918)631-3033. E-mail: nimrod@utulsa.edu. Website: www.utulsa.edu/nimrod. Contact: Eilis O'Neal. Submissions must be unpublished. Work must be in English or translated by original author. Author's name must not appear on ms. Include cover sheet with title, author's name, address, phone number, and e-mail address (author must have a US address by October of contest year to enter). Mark "Contest Entry" on submission envelop and cover sheet. Include SASE for results only; mss will not be returned. Guidelines available for #10 SASE or on website. 7,500-word maximum for short stories. Deadline: April 30. Prizes: 1st Place: $2,000 and publication; 2nd Place: $1,000 and publication. Judged by the *Nimrod* editors, who select the finalists and a recognized author, who selects the winners.

PRESS 53 AWARD FOR SHORT FICTION

Press 53, 560 N. Trade St., Suite 193, Winston-Salem NC 27101. (336)770-5353. **E-mail:** kevin@press53. com. **Website:** www.press53.com. **Contact:** Kevin Morgan Watson, Publisher. Awarded to an outstanding, unpublished collection of short stories. Details and guidelines available online. Deadline: December 31. Submission period begins September 1. Finalists announced March 1. Winner announced no later than May 1. Publication in October. Prize: Publication of winning short story collection, $1,000 cash advance, 1/4-page color ad in *Poets & Writers* magazine, plus 10 copies of the book. Judged by Press 53 publisher Kevin Morgan Watson.

◐ PRISM INTERNATIONAL ANNUAL SHORT FICTION CONTEST

Creative Writing Program, UBC, Buch. E462 - 1866 Main Mall, Vancouver BC V6T 1Z1 Canada. (604)822-2514. **Fax:** (604)822-3616. **Website:** http:// prismmagazine.ca/contests. **Contact:** Clara Kumagai, executive editor, promotions. Offered annually for unpublished work to award the best in contemporary fiction. Works of translation are eligible. Guidelines by SASE, by e-mail, or on website. Acquires first North American serial rights upon publication, and rights to publish online for promotional or archival purposes. Open to any writer except students and faculty in the Creative Writing Department at UBC, or people who have taken a creative writing course at UBC with the 2 years prior to the contest deadline. Deadline: February 1. Prize: 1st Place: $1,500; 1st Runner-up: $600; 2nd Runner-up: $400; winner is published.

◐ THOMAS H. RADDALL ATLANTIC FICTION AWARD

Writers' Federation of Nova Scotia, 1113 Marginal Rd., Halifax NS B3H 4P7 Canada. (902)423-8116. **Fax:** (902)422-0881. **E-mail:** director@writers.ns.ca. **Website:** www.writers.ns.ca. **Contact:** Nate Crawford, executive director. The Thomas Head Raddall Atlan-

tic Fiction Award is awarded for a novel or a book of short fiction by a full-time resident of Atlantic Canada. Detailed guidelines and eligibility criteria available online. Deadline: First Friday in December. Prize: Valued at $25,000 for winning title.

HAROLD U. RIBALOW PRIZE

Hadassah Magazine, Hadassah WZOA, 40 Wall Street 8th floor, New York NY 10005. (212) 451-6286. **Fax:** (212) 451-6257. **E-mail:** magtemp3@hadassah.org. **Website:** www.hadassahmagazine.org/. **Contact:** Deb Meisels, coordinator. Offered annually for English-language books of fiction (novel or short stories) on a Jewish theme published the previous year. Books should be submitted by the publisher. Administered annually by *Hadassah Magazine*. Deadline: April 1. Prize: $3,000. The official announcement of the winner will be made in the fall.

◐ THE ROGERS WRITERS' TRUST FICTION PRIZE

The Writers' Trust of Canada, 460 Richmond St. W., Suite 600, Toronto ON M5V 1Y1 Canada. (416)504-8222. **Fax:** (416)504-9090. **E-mail:** info@writerstrust.com. **Website:** www.writerstrust.com. **Contact:** Amanda Hopkins. Awarded annually to the best novel or short story collection published within the previous year. Presented at the Writers' Trust Awards event held in Toronto each fall. Open to Canadian citizens and permanent residents only. Deadline: July 27. Prize: $25,000 and $2,500 to 4 finalists.

THE SATURDAY EVENING POST GREAT AMERICAN FICTION CONTEST

The Saturday Evening Post Society, 1100 Waterway Blvd., Indianapolis IN 46202. **E-mail:** fictioncontest@saturdayeveningpost.com. **Website:** www.saturdayeveningpost.com/fiction-contest. "In its nearly 3 centuries of publication, *The Saturday Evening Post* has included fiction by a who's who of American authors, including F. Scott Fitzgerald, William Faulkner, Kurt Vonnegut, Ray Bradbury, Louis L'Amour, Sinclair Lewis, Jack London, and Edgar Allan Poe. The *Post's* fiction has not just entertained us; it has played a vital role in defining who we are as Americans. In launching this contest, we are seeking America's next great, unpublished voices." Entries must be character- or plot-driven stories in any genre of fiction that falls within the *Post's* broad range of interest. "We are looking for stories with universal appeal touching on shared experiences and themes that will resonate with readers from diverse backgrounds and experience." Stories must be submitted by the author and previously unpublished (excluding personal websites and blogs), and 1,500-5,000 words in length. No extreme profanity or graphic sex scenes. Submit story via the online at www.saturdayeveningpost.com/fiction-contest. All submissions must be made electronically in Microsoft Word format with the author's name, address, telephone number, and e-mail address on the first page. Do not submit hard copies via the mail; physical mss will not be read. "Due to staff limitations, we will not be able to update entrants on the status of their stories. We will inform winners or runners-up within 30 days of publication. We regret we will not be able to notify non-winning entrants." Deadline: July 1. The winning story will receive $500 and publication in the magazine and online. Five runners-up will be published online and receive $100 each.

JOANNA CATHERINE SCOTT NOVEL EXCERPT PRIZE CATEGORY

Soul-Making Keats Literary Competition Category, The Webhallow House, 1544 Sweetwood Dr., Broadmoor Village CA 94015-2029. **E-mail:** soulkeats@ mail.com. **Website:** www.soulmakingcontest.us. **Contact:** Eileen Malone. Open annually to any writer. Send first chapter or the first 20 pages, whichever comes first. Include a 1-page synopsis indicating category at top of page. Identify with 3x5 card only. Deadline: November 30. Prize: 1st Place: $100; 2nd Place: $50; 3rd Place: $25.

SCREAMINMAMAS MAGICAL FICTION CONTEST

1911 Cleveland St., Hollywood FL 33020. **E-mail:** screaminmamas@gmail.com. **Website:** www.screaminmamas.com/contests. **Contact:** Darlene Pistocchi, editor/managing director. This contest celebrates moms and the magical spirit of the holidays. If you had an opportunity to be anything you wanted to be, what would you be? Transport yourself! Become that character and write a short story around that character. Can be any genre. Length: 800-3,000 words. Open only to moms. Deadline: June 30. Prize: complementary subscription to magazine, plus publication.

⊕ SCREAMINMAMAS VALENTINE'S DAY CONTEST

1911 Cleveland St., Hollywood FL 33020. **E-mail:** screaminmamas@gmail.com. **Website:** www.screaminmamas.com/contests. **Contact:** Darlene Pistocchi,

editor/managing director. "Looking for light romantic comedy. Can be historical or contemporary—something to lift the spirits and celebrate the gift of innocent romance that might be found in the everyday life of a busy mom." Length: 800-2,000 words. Open only to moms. Deadline: June 30. Prize: Publication, complementary print copy.

SHEEHAN YA BOOK PRIZE

Elephant Rock Books, P.O. Box 119, Ashford CT 06278. **E-mail:** elephantrockbooksya@gmail.com. **Website:** elephantrockbooks.com/ya.html. **Contact:** Jotham Burrello and Amanda Hurley. Elephant Rock is a small independent publisher. Their first YA book, *The Carnival at Bray* by Jessie Ann Foley was a Morris Award Finalist, and Printz Honor Book. Runs contest every other year. Check website for details. Guidelines are available on the website: http://www. elephantrockbooks.com./about.html#submissions. "Elephant Rock Books' teen imprint is looking for a great story to follow our critically acclaimed novel, *The Carnival at Bray*. We're after quality stories with heart, guts, and a clear voice. We're especially interested in the quirky, the hopeful, and the real. We are not particularly interested in genre fiction and prefer standalone novels, unless you've got the next *Hunger Games*. We seek writers who believe in the transformative power of a great story, so show us what you've got." Deadline: July 1. Prize: $1,000 as an advance. Judges vary year-to-year.

MARY WOLLSTONECRAFT SHELLEY PRIZE FOR IMAGINATIVE FICTION

Rosebud, ROSEBUD MAGAZINE; ROSEBUD, INC., C/O Rosebud Magazine, N3310 Asje Rd., Cambridge WI 53523 USA. (608)423-9780. **E-mail:** jrodclark@ rsbd.net. **Website:** www.rsbd.net. **Contact:** J. Roderick Clark, editor. Publishes eclectic mix of poetry, fiction and nonfiction. Genres with a literary feel okay.

The Shelley Award is presented for any kind of unpublished imaginative fiction/short stories, 4,000 words or less. Entries are welcome any time. Acquires first rights. Open to any writer. Deadline: June 14 in even years. Prize: Grand Prize: $1,000. 4 runner-ups receive $100. All winners published in *Rosebud*. Judged by editor Rod Clark in 2016.

STONY BROOK SHORT FICTION PRIZE

Stony Brook Southampton, 239 Montauk Highway, Southampton NY 11968. **Website:** www.stonybrook. edu/fictionprize. "Only undergraduates enrolled full time in United States and Canadian universities and colleges for the current academic year are eligible. This prize has traditionally encouraged submissions from students with an Asian background, but we urge all students to enter." Submissions of no more than 7,500 words. All entries must be accompanied by proof of current undergraduate enrollment, such as a photocopy of a grade transcript, a class schedule or payment receipt showing your full time status. See website for full details. Deadline: March 15. Prize: $1,000.

STORYSOUTH MILLION WRITERS AWARD

E-mail: terry@storysouth.com. **Website:** www.storysouth.com. **Contact:** Terry Kennedy, editor. Annual award to honor and promote the best fiction published in online literary journals and magazines during the previous year. Anyone may nominate one story for the award. To be eligible for nomination, a story must be longer than 1,000 words. See website for details on how to nominate someone. Most literary prizes for short fiction have traditionally ignored web-published fiction. This award aims to show that world-class fiction is being published online and to promote to the larger reading and literary community. Deadline: August 15. Nominations of stories begins on March 15. Prize: Prize amounts subject to donation. Check website for details.

THREE CHEERS AND A TIGER

E-mail: editors@toasted-cheese.com. **Website:** www.toasted-cheese.com. **Contact:** Stephanie Lenz, editor. Contestants are to write a short story (following a specific theme) within 48 hours. Contests are held first weekend in spring (mystery) and first weekend in fall (science fiction/fantasy). Word limit announced at the start of the contest. Contest-specific information is announced 48 hours before the contest submission deadline. Results announced in April and October. Winners notified by e-mail. List of winners on website. Entries must be unpublished. Open to any writer. Accepts inquiries by e-mail. Cover letter should include name, address, e-mail, word count and title. Information should be in the body of the e-mail. It will be removed before the judging begins. Prize: Amazon gift certificates and publication. Blind-judged by 2 *Toasted Cheese* editors. Each judge uses his or her own criteria to choose entries.

THE THURBER PRIZE FOR AMERICAN HUMOR

77 Jefferson Ave., Columbus OH 43215. **Website:** www.thurberhouse.org. Entry fee: $65 per title. Published submissions or accepted for publication in U.S. for the first time. Primarily pictorial works such as cartoon collections are not considered. Word length: no requirement. See website for application form and guidelines. Results announced in September. Winners notified in person in New York City. For contest results, visit website. This award recognizes the art of humor writing. Deadline: April. Prize: $5,000 for the finalist, non-cash prizes awarded to two runners-up. Judged by well-known members of the national arts community.

$ TIMELESS LOVE/ROMANCE CONTEST

Sponsored by Oak Tree Press, 1700 Diary Avenue, #49, Corcoran CA 93217. **E-mail:** tl-contestadmin@oaktreebooks.com. **Website:** www.oaktreebooks.com. Annual contest for unpublished authors or authors shifting to a new genre. Accepts novels of all romance genres, from sweet to supernatural. Guidelines and entry forms are available for SASE. Deadline: July 31. Prize: Publication in both paper and e-book editions. Judged by publishing industry professionals who prescreen entries; publisher makes final selection.

TOM HOWARD/JOHN H. REID FICTION & ESSAY CONTEST

Winning Writers, 351 Pleasant Street, PMB 222, Northampton MA 01060-3961 USA. (866)946-9748. **Fax:** (413)280-0539. **E-mail:** adam@winningwriters.com. **Website:** www.winningwriters.com. **Contact:** Adam Cohen, President. Since 2001, Winning Writers has provided expert literary contest information to the public. We sponsor four contests. One of the "101 Best Websites for Writers" (*Writer's Digest*). See website for guidelines and to submit your entry. Prefers inquiries by e-mail. Length: 6,000 words max per entry. Writers may submit own work. Winners notified by e-mail. Results made available to entrants on website. Deadline: April 30. Prizes: Two 1st prizes of $1,500 will be awarded, plus 10 honorable mentions of $100 each. Top 12 entries published online. Judged by Arthur Powers, assisted by Lauren Singer.

TIPS Read past winning entries at https://winningwriters.com/our-contests/contest-archives. Read advice from the judge at https://winningwriters.com/resources/advice-from-arthur-powers-judge-tom-howard-fiction-essay-contest.

STEVEN TURNER AWARD FOR BEST FIRST WORK OF FICTION

6335 W. Northwest Hwy., #618, Dallas TX 75225. **Website:** www.texasinstituteofletters.org. Offered annually for work published January 1-December 31 for the best first book of fiction. Writers must have been born in Texas, have lived in the state for at least 2 consecutive years at some time, or the subject matter of the work should be associated with the state. Guidelines online. Deadline: normally first week in January; see website for specific date. Prize: $1,000.

WAASNODE SHORT FICTION PRIZE

Passages North, Department of English, Northern Michigan University, 1401 Presque Isle Ave., Marquette MI 49855. (906)227-1203. **Fax:** (906)227-1096. **E-mail:** passages@nmu.edu. **Website:** www.passagesnorth.com. **Contact:** Jennifer Howard. Offered every 2 years to publish new voices in literary fiction (maximum 10,000 words). Guidelines for SASE or online. Submissions accepted online. Deadline: April 15. Submission period begins February 15. Prize: $1,000 and publication for winner; 2 honorable mentions are also published; all entrants receive a copy of *Passages North*. Judged by Tiphanie Yanique in 2016.

WABASH PRIZE FOR FICTION

Sycamore Review, Department of English, 500 Oval Dr., Purdue University, West Lafayette IN 47907. **E-mail:** sycamore@purdue.edu; sycamorefiction@purdue.edu. **Website:** www.sycamorereview.com/contest/. **Contact:** Kara Krewer, editor-in-chief. Annual contest for unpublished fiction. For each submission, send one story (limit 7,500 words). Ms pages should be numbered and should include the title of the piece. All stories must be previously unpublished. See website for more guidelines. Submit via online submissions manager. Deadline: November 15. Prize: $1,000 and publication.

THE WASHINGTON WRITERS' PUBLISHING HOUSE FICTION PRIZE

Washington Writers' Publishing House, P.O. Box 15271, Washington DC 20003. **E-mail:** wwphpress@gmail.com. **Website:** www.washingtonwriters.org. Fiction writers living within 75 miles of the Capitol are invited to submit a ms of either a novel or a collection of short stories (no more than 350 pages, double-spaced). Author's name should not appear on the manuscript. The title page of each copy should contain the title only. Provide name, address, telephone number, e-mail address, and title on a separate cover sheet accompanying the submission. A separate page for acknowledgments may be included for stories or excerpts previously published in journals and anthologies. Send electronic copies to wwphpress@gmail.com or mail paper copies and/or reading fee (check to WWPH) with SASE to: Washington Writers' Publishing House Fiction Prize, c/o Elisavietta Ritchie, P.O. Box 298, Broomes Island, MD 20615. Deadline: November 15. Submission period begins July 1. Prize: $1,000 and 50 copies of the book.

WESTERN AUSTRALIAN PREMIER'S BOOK AWARDS

State Library of Western Australia, Perth Cultural Centre, 25 Francis St., Perth WA 6000 Australia. (61)(8)9427-3151. **E-mail:** premiersbookawards@slwa.wa.gov.au. **Website:** pba.slwa.wa.gov.au. **Contact:** Karen de San Miguel. Annual competition for Australian citizens or permanent residents of Australia, or writers whose work has Australia as its primary focus. Categories: children's books, digital narrative, fiction, nonfiction, poetry, scripts, writing for young adults, West Australian history, and Western Australian emerging writers. Submit 5 original copies of the work to be considered for the awards. All works must have been published between January 1 and December 31 of the prior year. See website for details and rules of entry. Deadline: January 31. Prize: Awards $25,000 for Premier's Prize; awards $15,000 each for the Children's Books, Digital Narrative, Fiction, and Nonfiction categories; awards $10,000 each for the Poetry, Scripts, Western Australian History, Western Australian Emerging Writers, and Writing for Young Adults; awards $5,000 for People's Choice Award.

THOMAS WOLFE PRIZE AND LECTURE

North Carolina Writers' Network, Thomas Wolfe Fiction Prize, Great Smokies Writing Program, Attn: Nancy Williams, CPO #1860, UNC, Asheville NC 28805. **Website:** englishcomplit.unc.edu/wolfe. The Thomas Wolfe Fiction Prize honors internationally celebrated North Carolina novelist Thomas Wolfe. The prize is administered by Tommy Hays and the Great Smokies Writing Program at the University of North Carolina at Asheville. Competition is open to all writers, regardless of geographical location or prior publication. Submit 2 copies of an unpublished fiction ms (short story or self-contained novel excerpt) not to exceed 12 double-spaced, single-sided pages. Deadline: January 30. Submissions period begins December 1. Prize: $1,000 and potential publication in *The Thomas Wolfe Review*.

TOBIAS WOLFF AWARD FOR FICTION

Bellingham Review, Mail Stop 9053, Western Washington University, Bellingham WA 98225. (360)650-4863. E-mail: bellingham.review@wwu.edu. Website: www.bhreview.org. Contact: Susanne Paola Antonetta, editor-in-chief; Louis McLaughlin, managing editor. Offered annually for unpublished work. Guidelines available on website, online submissions only. Categories: novel exceprts and short stories. Entries must be unpublished. Length: 6,000 words or less per story or chapter. Open to any writer. Electronic submissions only. Enter submissions through Submittable, a link to which is available on the website. Winner announced in August and notified by e-mail. Deadline: March 15. Submissions period begins December 1. Prize: $1,000, plus publication and subscription.

WORLD FANTASY AWARDS

P.O. Box 43, Mukilteo WA 98275. E-mail: sfexecsec@gmail.com. Website: www.worldfantasy.org. Contact: Peter Dennis Pautz, president. Offered annually for previously published work in several categories, including life achievement, novel, novella, short story, anthology, collection, artist, special award-pro and special award-nonpro. Works are recommended by attendees of current and previous 2 years' conventions and a panel of judges. Entries must be previously published. Published submissions from previous calendar year. Word length: 10,000-40,000 for novella, 10,000 for short story. All fantasy is eligible, from supernatural horror to Tolkien-esque to sword and sorcery to the occult, and beyond. Cover letter should include name, address, phone, e-mail, word count, title, and publications where submission was previously published, submitted to the address above and the panel of judges when they appear on the website. Results announced November 1 at annual convention. For contest results, visit website. Guidelines available in December for SASE or on website. Awards to recognize excellence in fantasy literature worldwide. Deadline: June 1. Prize: Trophy. Judged by panel.

WOW! WOMEN ON WRITING QUARTERLY FLASH FICTION CONTEST

WOW! Women on Writing, P.O. Box 41104, Long Beach CA 90853. E-mail: contestinfo@wow-womenonwriting.com. Website: www.wow-womenonwriting.com/contest.php. Contact: Angela Mackintosh, editor. Contest offered quarterly. Entries must be 250-750 words. "We are open to all themes and genres, although we do encourage writers to take a close look at our literary agent guest judge for the season if you are serious about winning." Deadline: August 31, November 30, February 28, May 31. Prize: 1st place: $350 cash prize, $25 Amazon gift certificate, story published on WOW! Women On Writing, interview on blog; 2nd place: $250 cash prize, $25 Amazon gift certificate, story published on WOW! Women On Writing, interview on blog; 3rd place: $150 cash prize, $25 Amazon gift certificate, story published on WOW! Women On Writing, interview on blog; 7 runners up: $25 Amazon gift certificate, story published on WOW! Women on Writing, interview on blog; 10 honorable mentions: $20 gift certificate from Amazon, story title and name published on WOW!Women On Writing. Judged by a different guest every season, who is either a literary agent, acquiring editor or publisher.

WRITER'S DIGEST SHORT SHORT STORY COMPETITION

Writer's Digest, 10151 Carver Road, Suite 200, Blue Ash OH 45242. (715)445-4612; ext. 13430. E-mail: WritersDigestShortShortStoryCompetition@fwmedia.com. Website: www.writersdigest.com. Contact: Nicole Howard. Looking for fiction that's bold, brilliant, and brief. Send your best in 1,500 words or fewer. All entries must be original, unpublished, and not submitted elsewhere at the time of submission. *Writer's Digest* reserves one-time publication rights to the 1st-25th winning entries. Winners will be notified by Feb. 28. Early bird deadline: November 17. Final deadline: December 15. Prize: 1st Place: $3,000 and a trip to the Writer's Digest Conference; 2nd Place: $1,500; 3rd Place: $500; 4th-10th Place: $100; 11th-25th Place: $50 gift certificate for writersdigestshop.com.

ZOETROPE SHORT STORY CONTEST

Zoetrope: All Story, Zoetrope: All-Story, Attn: Fiction Editor, 916 Kearny St., San Francisco CA 94133. (415)788-7500. E-mail: contests@all-story.com. Website: www.all-story.com. Annual short fiction contest. Considers submissions of short stories and one-act plays no longer than 7,000 words. Excerpts from larger works, screenplays, treatments, and poetry will be returned unread. For details, visit the website during the summer. Deadline: October 1. Submissions period begins July 1. Prizes: 1st place: $1,000 and publication on website; 2nd place: $500; 3rd place: $250.

ZONE 3 FICTION AWARD

Zone 3, Austin Peay State University, P.O. Box 4565, Clarksville TN 37044. (931)221-7031. **Fax:** (931)221-7149. **E-mail:** wallacess@apsu.edu. **Website:** www. apsu.edu/zone3/contests. **Contact:** Susan Wallace, Managing Editor. Annual contest for unpublished fiction. Open to any fiction writer. Accepts entries online and via postal mail. Deadline: April 1. Prize: $250 and publication.

NONFICTION

AMERICA & ME ESSAY CONTEST

Farm Bureau Insurance, P.O. Box 30400, Lansing MI 48909. **E-mail:** lfedewa@fbinsmi.com. **Website:** FarmBureauInsurance.com. **Contact:** Lisa Fedewa. Focuses on encouraging students to write about their personal Michigan heroes: someone who lives in the state and who has encouraged them, taught them important lessons, and helped them pursue their dreams. Open to Michigan eighth graders. Contest rules and entry form available on website. Encourages Michigan youth to recognize the heroes in their communities and their state. Deadline: November 18. Prize: $1,000, plaque, and medallion for top 10 winners.

ANNUAL MEMOIRS COMPETITION

The Writers' Workshop of Asheville, NC, Memoirs Contest, 387 Beaucatcher Rd., Asheville NC 28805. **E-mail:** writersw@gmail.com. **Website:** www.twwoa. org. **Contact:** Karen Ackerson. Submit a memoir of 5,000 words or less. Multiple entries are accepted. All work must be unpublished. Pages should be paper clipped, with your name, address, phone and title of work on a cover sheet. Double-space and use 12-point font. Deadline: November 30. Prize: 1st Place: A 2 night stay at the Mountain Muse B&B and 50 pages line-edited and revised by editorial staff; 2nd Place: A 2 night stay at the B&B and 50 pages line-edited; 3rd Place: 25 pages line-edited. Up to 10 Honorable Mentions. professional authors

THE DOROTHY CAPPON PRIZE FOR THE BEST ESSAY

New Letters, University of Missouri-Kansas City, *New Letters* Awards for Writers, UMKC, University House, 5101 Rockhill Rd., Kansas City MO 64110-2499. (816)235-1168. **Fax:** (816)235-2611. **E-mail:** newletters@umkc.edu. **Website:** www.newletters.org. **Contact:** Ashley Wann. Contest is offered annually for unpublished work to discover and reward emerging writers and to give experienced writers a place to try new genres. Acquires first North American serial rights. Open to any writer. Guidelines by SASE or online. Entries should not exceed 8,000 words. Deadline: May 18. Prize: 1st Place: $1,500 and publication in a volume of *New Letters*; runner-up will receive a copy of a recent book of poetry or fiction courtesy of BkMk Press. All entries will receive consideration for publication in future editions of *New Letters*.

MORTON N. COHEN AWARD

Modern Language Association of America, 85 Broad Street, suite 500, New York NY 10004-2434. (646)576-5141. **Fax:** (646)458-0030. **E-mail:** awards@mla.org. **Website:** www.mla.org. **Contact:** Coordinator of Book Prizes. Awarded in odd-numbered years for a distinguished collection of letters. At least 1 volume of the edition must have been published during the previous 2 years. Editors need not be members of the MLA. Under the terms of the award, the winning collection will be one that provides readers with a clear, accurate, and readable text; necessary background information; and succinct and eloquent introductory material and annotations. The edited collection should be in itself a work of literature. Deadline: May 1. Prize: A cash award and a certificate to be presented at the Modern Language Association's annual convention in January.

CARR P. COLLINS AWARD FOR NONFICTION

The Texas Institute of Letters, P.O. Box 609, Round Rock TX 78680. **E-mail:** tilsecretary@yahoo.com. **Website:** http://texasinstituteofletters.org/. Offered annually for work published January 1-December 31 of the previous year to recognize the best nonfiction book by a writer who was born in Texas, who has lived in the state for at least 2 consecutive years at one point, or a writer whose work has some notable connection with Texas. See website for guidelines and instructions on submitting. Deadline: January 10. Prize: $5,000.

✪ CREATIVE NONFICTION CONTEST

PRISM International, Creative Writing Program, UBC, Buch E462—1866 Main Mall, Vancouver BC V6T 1Z1 Canada. **E-mail:** promotions@prismmagazine.ca. **Website:** www.prismmagazine.ca. Offered annually for published and unpublished writers to promote and reward excellence in literary creative nonfiction. *PRISM* buys first North American serial rights upon publication. Also buys limited web rights for pieces selected for the website. Open to anyone except students and faculty of the Creative Writing Program at UBC or people who have taken a creative writing course at UBC in the 2 years prior to contest deadline. All entrants receive a 1-year subscription to *PRISM*. Entries are accepted via Submittable at http://prisminternational.submittable.com/submit or by mail. Deadline: November 30. Prize: $1,500 grand prize, $600 runner-up, and $400 second runner-up.

DIAGRAM ESSAY CONTEST

Department of English, University of Arizona, P.O. Box 210067, Tucson AZ 85721-0067. **E-mail:** nmp@thediagram.com; editor@thediagram.com. **Website:** www.thediagram.com/contest.html. **Contact:** Ander Monson, editor. Contest for essays up to 10,000 words. Deadline: End of November. Check website for more details. Prize: $1,000 and publication. Finalist essay also published. Judged by editors Ander Monson and Nicole Walker.

ANNIE DILLARD AWARD FOR CREATIVE NONFICTION

Bellingham Review, Mail Stop 9053, 516 High St., Western Washington University, Bellingham WA 98225. (360)650-4863. **E-mail:** bellingham.review@wwu.edu. **Website:** www.bhreview.org. **Contact:** Susanne Paola Antonetta, editor-in-chief; Louis McLaughlin, managing editor. Offered annually for unpublished essays on any subject and in any style. Guidelines available online. Deadline: March 15. Submission period begins December 1. Prize: $1,000, plus publication and copies. All finalists considered for publication. All entrants receive subscription.

TIPS "The *Bellingham Review* seeks literature of palpable quality: poems, stories, and essays so beguiling they invite us to come closer, look deeper, touch, sniff and taste their essence. We hunger for a kind of writing that nudges the limits of form or executes traditional forms exquisitely."

✪ THE DONNER PRIZE

The Award for Best Book on Public Policy by a Canadian, The Donner Canadian Foundation, 505 Danforth Avenue, Suite 201, Toronto ON M4K 1P5 Canada. (416)368-8253. **E-mail:** sherry@naylorandassociates.com. **Website:** www.donnerbookprize. com. **Contact:** Sherry Naylor. Annual award that rewards excellence and innovation in public policy writing by Canadians. Deadline: November 30. Prize: Winning book receives $50,000; shortlisted titles get $7,500 each.

THE ILA DINA FEITELSON RESEARCH AWARD

International Literacy Association, Division of Research & Policy, P.O. Box 8139, Newark DE 19714-8139. (302)731-1600, ext. 423. **Fax:** (302)731-1057. **E-mail:** research@reading.org. **Website:** http://www.literacyworldwide.org/about-us/awards-grants. **Contact:** Marcella Moore. This is an award for an exemplary work published in English in a refereed journal that reports on an empirical study investigating aspects of literacy acquisition, such as phonemic awareness, the alphabetic principle, bilingualism, or cross-cultural studies of beginning reading. Articles may be submitted for consideration by researchers, authors, et al. Copies of the applications and guidelines can be downloaded in PDF format from the website. Deadline: January 15. Prize: $500 award and recognition at the International Literacy Association's annual conference.

THE FOUNTAINHEAD ESSAY CONTEST

The Ayn Rand Institute, P.O. Box 57044, Irvine CA 92619-7044. (949) 222-6550. **Fax:** (949) 222-6558. **E-mail:** essays@aynrand.org. **Website:** https://www.aynrand.org/students/essay-contests. **Contact:** Anthony Loy. Competition for 11th and 12th grade students. Essays will be judged on whether the student is able to argue for and justify his or her view—not on whether the Institute agrees with the view the student expresses. Judges will look for writing that is clear, articulate and logically organized. Winning essays must demonstrate an outstanding grasp of the philosophic meaning of *The Fountainhead*. Deadline: April 29. Prizes: 1st Place: $10,000; 2nd Place: $2,000 (5 Winners); 3rd Place: $1,000 (10 Winners); Finalists: $100 (45 Winners); Semifinalists: $50 (175 Winners).

THE JOHN GUYON LITERARY NONFICTION PRIZE

Crab Orchard Review, Department of English, Faner Hall 2380 - Mail Code 4503, 1000 Faner Drive, Carbondale IL 62901. (618)453-6833. **Fax:** (618)453-8224. **E-mail:** jtribble@siu.edu. **Website:** www.craborchardreview.siu.edu. **Contact:** Jon C. Tribble, managing editor. Annual award for unpublished creative nonfiction. Not a prize for academic essays. Entries should consist of 1 creative nonfiction piece up to 6,500 words maximum in length. *Crab Orchard Review* acquires first North American serial rights to all submitted work. One winner and at least 2 finalists will be chosen. Length: 6,500 words maximum. All submissions must be made through Submittable. Submissions must be unpublished original work, written in English by a U.S. citizen, permanent resident, or person who has DACA/TPS status (current students and employees at Southern Illinois University Carbondale are not eligible). See Submittable guidelines online for complete formatting instructions. The author's name should not appear on any page of the entry. Results announced by end of August. Deadline: April 21. Submission period begins February 21. Prize: $2,000 and publication. Finalists are each offered $500 and publication.

TIPS "Carefully read directions for entering and follow them exactly. Send us your best work. Note that simultaneous submissions are accepted for this prize, but the winning entry must NOT be accepted elsewhere. All submissions should be made through Submittable: https://craborchardreview.submittable.com/submit."

HENDRICKS AWARD

The New Netherland Institute, Cultural Education Center, Room 10D45, 222 Madison Ave., Albany NY 12230. **Fax:** (518)473-0472. **E-mail:** nyslfnn@nysed.gov. **Website:** www.newnetherlandinstitute.org. Given annually to the best book or book-length ms relating to any aspect of New Netherland and its legacy. Two categories of submissions will be considered in alternate years: (1) recently completed dissertations and unpublished book-length manuscripts, and (2) recently published books. If there is no suitable winner in the designated category in any particular year, submissions from the alternate category will be considered. In addition, submissions from previous years will be reconsidered for the Award. Entries must be based on research completed or published within three years prior to the deadline for submission. Entries may deal with any aspect of New Netherland and its legacy. Biographies of individuals whose careers illuminate aspects of the history of New Netherland and its legacy are eligible, as are manuscripts dealing with literature and the arts, provided that the methodology is historical. Deadline: February 1. Prize:

$5,000 and a framed print of a painting by L.F. Tantillo. Judged by a 5-member panel of scholars.

⊕⊕ THOMAS J. HRUSKA MEMORIAL PRIZE IN NONFICTION

Passages North, Department of English, Northern Michigan University, 1401 Presque Isle Ave., Marquette MI 49855. (906) 227-1203. **Fax:** (906) 227-1096. **E-mail:** passages@nmu.edu. **Website:** www.passagesnorth.com. **Contact:** Kate Myers Hanson, acquisitions. Contest for nonfiction, held biennially. *Passages North* also offers poetry and fiction contests. Send SASE for announcement of winners. Author's name may appear anywhere on ms or cover letter. Manuscripts will not be returned. All entrants receive a contest issue. Honorable mentions will also be chosen for each contest and may or may not be published according to the needs of the editors. Deadline: April 15. Submissions open February 15. Prize: $1,000 and publication.

THE HUNGER MOUNTAIN CREATIVE NONFICTION PRIZE

Vermont College, 36 College St., Montpelier VT 05602. (802)828-8517. **E-mail:** hungermtn@vcfa.edu. **Website:** www.hungermtn.org. **Contact:** Samantha Kolber, Managing Editor. Annual contest for the best writing in creative nonfiction. Submit essays under 10,000 words. Guidelines available on website. Accepts entries online or via mail. Deadline: March 1. Prize: $1,000 and publication. Two honorable mentions receive $100 each. Judged by Robert Michael Pylein in 2016 and Joni Tevis in 2017.

ILA OUTSTANDING DISSERTATION OF THE YEAR AWARD

International Literacy Association, P.O. Box 8139, Newark DE 19714-8139. (302)731-1600. **Fax:** (302)731-1057. **E-mail:** research@reading.org. **Website:** http://www.literacyworldwide.org/about-us/awards-grants. **Contact:** Marcella Moore, project manager. Dissertations in reading or related fields are eligible for the competition. Studies using any research approach (ethnographic, experimental, historical, survey, etc.) are encouraged. Each study is assessed in the light of this approach, the scholarly qualification of its report, and its significant contributions to knowledge within the reading field. The application process is open to those who have completed dissertations in any aspect of the field of reading or literacy of the calendar year. A routine check is made with the home university of the applicant to protect all applicants, their universities, and the International Reading Association from false claims. Studies may use any research approach (ethnographic, experimental, historical, survey, etc.). Each study will be assessed in light of its approach, its scholarship, and its significant contributions to knowledge within the reading/literacy field. Deadline: January 15.

🚫 TILIA KLEBENOV JACOBS RELIGIOUS ESSAY PRIZE CATEGORY

Soul Making Keats Literary Competition, The Webhallow House, 1544 Sweetwood Dr., Broadmoor Village CA 94015-2029. **E-mail:** SoulKeats@mail.com. **Website:** www.soulmakingcontest.us. **Contact:** Eileen Malone. Call for thoughtful writings of up to 3,000 words. "No preaching, no proselytizing." Open annually to any writer. Previously published material is accepted. Indicate category on cover page and on identifying 3x5 card. Up to 3,000 words, double-spaced. See website for more details. Deadline: November 30. Prize: 1st Place: $100; 2nd Place: $50; 3rd Place: $25.

KATHERINE SINGER KOVACS PRIZE

Modern Language Association of America, 85 Broad Street, suite 500, New York NY 10004-2434. (646)576-5141. **Fax:** (646)458-0030. **E-mail:** awards@mla.org. **Website:** www.mla.org. **Contact:** Coordinator of Book Prizes. Offered annually for an outstanding book published in English or Spanish in the field of Latin American and Spanish literatures and cultures. Competing books should be broadly interpretive works that enhance understanding of the interrelations among literature, the other arts, and society. Books must have been published in the previous year. Authors need not be members of the MLA. Must send 6 copies of book. Deadline: May 1. Prize: A cash award and a certificate to be presented at the Modern Language Association's annual convention in January.

KATHERYN KROTZER LABORDE CREATIVE NONFICTION PRIZE CATEGORY

Soul-Making Keats Literary Competition, The Webhallow House, 1544 Sweetwood Dr., Broadmoor Village CA 94015-2029. **E-mail:** SoulKeats@mail.com. **Website:** www.soulmakingcontest.us. **Contact:** Eileen Malone. Creative nonfiction is the child of fiction and journalism. Unlike fiction, the characters and events are real, not imagined. Unlike journalism, the writer is part of the story she tells, if not as a par-

ticipant then as a thoughtful observer. Must be typed, page numbered, and double-spaced. Each entry up to 3,000 words. Identify only with 3x5 card. Open annually to any writer. Deadline: November 30. Prizes: First Place: $100; Second Place: $50; Third Place: $25.

TIPS "Looking for a strong voice, a solid sense of the story, and a clear sense of one's writing style. One last note: think about the STORY you are trying to tell and don't be a slave to the truth, the whole truth, and nothing but. This is art, not sworn testimony!"

🚫🚫🚫🚫 THE GILDER LEHRMAN LINCOLN PRIZE

Gettysburg College and Gilder Lehrman Institute of American History, 300 N. Washington St., Campus Box 435, Gettysburg PA 17325. (717)337-8255. **Fax:** (717)337-6596. **E-mail:** lincolnprize@gettysburg.edu. **Website:** www.gilderlehrman.org. The Gilder Lehrman Lincoln Prize, sponsored by the Gilder Lehrman Institute and Gettysburg College, is awarded annually for the finest scholarly work in English on Abraham Lincoln or the American Civil War era. Send 6 copies of the nominated work. Deadline: November 1. Prize: $50,000.

TIPS "This contest is for adults writers only."

LITERAL LATTÉ ESSAY AWARD

Literal Latté, 200 E. 10th St., Suite 240, New York NY 10003. (212)260-5532. **E-mail:** litlatte@aol.com. **E-mail:** Link to submittable on www.literal-latte.com. **Website:** www.literal-latte.com. **Contact:** Jenine Gordon Bockman. Open to any writer. Send previously unpublished personal essays, 20,000 words max. All topics accepted. Include e-mail address for reply. Acquires first rights. Visit website for guidelines and tastes. Deadline: September 30. Prize: 1st Place: $1,000; 2nd Place: $300; 3rd Place: $200. Judged by the editors.

JAMES RUSSELL LOWELL PRIZE

Modern Language Association of America, 85 Broad Street, suite 500, New York NY 10004-2434. (646)576-5141. **Fax:** (646)458-0030. **E-mail:** awards@mla.org. **Website:** www.mla.org. **Contact:** Coordinator of Book Prizes. For an outstanding literary or linguistic study, a critical edition of an important work, or a critical biography. Open to studies dealing with literary theory, media, cultural history, or interdisciplinary topics. Books must be published in the previous year. Authors must be current members of the MLA.

Send 6 copies of the book. Deadline: March 1. Prize: A cash award and a certificate to be presented at the Modern Language Association's annual convention in January.

RICHARD J. MARGOLIS AWARD

c/o Margolis & Bloom, LLP, 535 Boylston St., 8th Floor, Boston MA 02116. (617)267-9700, ext. 517. **Fax:** (617)267-3166. **E-mail:** hsm@margolis.com. **E-mail:** award@margolis.com. **Website:** www.margolisaward. org. **Contact:** Harry S. Margolis. Sponsored by the Blue Mountain Center, this annual award is given to a promising new journalist or essayist whose work combines warmth, humor, wisdom, and concern with social justice. Applicants should be aware that this award is for nonfiction reporting and commentary, not for creative nonfiction, fiction, or poetry. Applications should include at least 2 examples of your work (published or unpublished, 30 pages maximum) and a short biographical note including a description of your current and anticipated work. Also please indicate what you will work on while attending the Blue Mountain residency. Please send to award@margolis. com. Deadline: July 1. Prize: $5,000, plus a one month residency at the Blue Mountain Center.

HOWARD R. MARRARO PRIZE

Modern Language Association of America, 85 Broad Street, suite 500, New York NY 10004-2434. (646)576-5141. **Fax:** (646)458-0030. **E-mail:** awards@mla.org. **Website:** www.mla.org. **Contact:** Coordinator of Book Prizes. Offered in even-numbered years for an outstanding scholarly work on any phase of Italian literature or comparative literature involving Italian. Books must have been published in the previous year. Authors must be members of the MLA. Requires 4 copies of the book. Deadline: May 1. Prize: A cash award and a certificate to be presented at the Modern Language Association's annual convention in January.

KENNETH W. MILDENBERGER PRIZE

Modern Language Association of America, 85 Broad Street, suite 500, New York NY 10004-2434. (646)576-5141. **Fax:** (646)458-0030. **E-mail:** awards@mla.org. **Website:** www.mla.org. **Contact:** Coordinator of Book Prizes. Offered in odd-numbered years for a publication from the previous year in the field of language, culture, literacy, or literature with a strong application to the teaching of languages other than English. Author need not be a member of the MLA.

Books must have been published in the previous 2 years. Requires 4 copies of the book. Deadline: May 1. Prize: A cash award, and a certificate, to be presented at the Modern Language Association's annual convention in January, and a year's membership in the MLA.

C. WRIGHT MILLS AWARD

The Society for the Study of Social Problems, 901 McClung Tower, University of Tennessee, Knoxville TN 37996-0490. (865)689-1531. **Fax:** (865)689-1534. **E-mail:** mkoontz3@utk.edu. **Website:** www.sssp1.org. **Contact:** Michele Smith Koontz, Administrative Officer and Meeting Manager. Offered annually for a book published the previous year that most effectively critically addresses an issue of contemporary public importance; brings to the topic a fresh, imaginative perspective; advances social scientific understanding of the topic; displays a theoretically informed view and empirical orientation; evinces quality in style of writing; and explicitly or implicitly contains implications for courses of action. Self-nominations are acceptable. Edited volumes, textbooks, fiction, and self-published works are not eligible. Deadline: December 15. Prize: $500 stipend.

MLA PRIZE FOR A BIBLIOGRAPHY, ARCHIVE, OR DIGITAL PROJECT

Modern Language Association of America, 85 Broad Street, Suite 500, New York NY 10004-2434. (646)576-5141. **Fax:** (646)458-0030. **E-mail:** awards@mla.org. **Website:** www.mla.org. **Contact:** Coordinator of Book Prizes. Offered in even-numbered years for an outstanding enumerative or descriptive bibliography, archive, or digital project. Open to any writer or publisher. At least 1 volume must have been published in the previous 2 years. Editors need not be members of the MLA. Criteria for determining excellence include evidence of analytical rigor, meticulous scholarship, intellectual creativity, and subject range and depth. Deadline: May 1. Prize: A cash prize and a certificate to be presented at the Modern Language Association's annual convention in January.

MLA PRIZE FOR A FIRST BOOK

Modern Language Association of America, 85 Broad Street, Suite 500, New York NY 10004-2434. (646)576-5141. **Fax:** (646)458-0030. **E-mail:** awards@mla.org. **Website:** www.mla.org. **Contact:** Coordinator of Book Prizes. Offered annually for the first book-length scholarly publication by a current member of the association. To qualify, a book must be a literary or linguistic study, a critical edition of an important work, or a critical biography. Studies dealing with literary theory, media, cultural history, and interdisciplinary topics are eligible; books that are primarily translations will not be considered. See listing for James Russell Lowe Prize—prize offered for same criteria. Deadline: March 1. Prize: A cash award and a certificate to be presented at the Modern Language Association's annual convention in January.

MLA PRIZE FOR A SCHOLARLY EDITION

Modern Language Association of America, 85 Broad Street, suite 500, New York NY 10004-2434. (646)576-5141. **Fax:** (646)458-0030. **E-mail:** awards@mla.org. **Website:** www.mla.org. Offered in odd-numbered years for an outstanding scholarly edition. Editions may be in single or multiple volumes. At least one volume must have been published in the 2 years prior to the award deadline. Editors need not be members of the MLA. To qualify for the award, an edition should be based on an examination of all available relevant textual sources; the source texts and the edited text's deviations from them should be fully described; the edition should employ editorial principles appropriate to the materials edited, and those principles should be clearly articulated in the volume; the text should be accompanied by appropriate textual and other historical contextual information; the edition should exhibit the highest standards of accuracy in the presentation of its text and apparatus; and the text and apparatus should be presented as accessibly and elegantly as possible. Deadline: May 1. Prize: A cash award and a certificate to be presented at the Modern Language Association's annual convention in January.

MLA PRIZE FOR INDEPENDENT SCHOLARS

Modern Language Association of America, 85 Broad Street, Suite 500, New York NY 10004-2434. (646)576-5141. **Fax:** (646)458-0030. **E-mail:** awards@mla.org. **Website:** www.mla.org. Offered in even-numbered years for a scholarly book in the field of English or other modern languages and literatures. Book must have been published within the 2 years prior to prize deadline. At the time of publication of the book, author must not be enrolled in a program leading to an academic degree or hold a tenured, tenure-accruing, or tenure-track position in postsecondary education. Authors need not be members of the MLA. Requires 6 copies of the book and a completed application. Dead-

line: May 1. Prize: A cash award, a certificate, and a year's membership in the MLA.

MONTANA PRIZE IN CREATIVE NONFICTION

CutBank Literary Magazine, *CutBank*, University of Montana, English Dept., LA 133, Missoula MT 59812. **E-mail:** editor.cutbank@gmail.com. **Website:** www.cutbankonline.org. **Contact:** Allison Linville, editor-in-chief. The Montana Prize in Creative Nonfiction seeks to highlight work that showcases an authentic voice, a boldness of form, and a rejection of functional fixedness. Accepts online submissions only. Send a single work, no more than 35 pages. Guidelines available online. Deadline: January 15. Submissions period begins November 9. Prize: $500 and featured in the magazine. Judged by a guest judge each year.

LINDA JOY MYERS MEMOIR VIGNETTE PRIZE CATEGORY

Soul-Making Keats Literary Competition, Webhallow House, 1544 Sweetwood Dr., Broadmoor Village CA 94015-2029. **E-mail:** soulkeats@mail.com. **Website:** www.soulmakingcontest.us. **Contact:** Eileen Malone. Open annually to any writer. One memoir/entry, up to 1,500 words, double spaced. Previously published material is acceptable. Indicate category on first page. Identify only with 3x5 card. Deadline: November 30. Prize: 1st Place: $100; 2nd Place: $50; 3rd Place: $25.

☉ NATIONAL BUSINESS BOOK AWARD

PwC and BMO Financial Group, 121 Richmond St. W., Suite 605, Toronto ON M5H 2K1 Canada. (416)868-1500. **Fax:** (416)868-1502. **Website:** www.nbbaward.com. Offered annually for books published January 1-December 31 to recognize excellence in business writing in Canada. Publishers nominate books. Deadline: December 31. Prize: $20,000 (CAN).

NATIONAL WRITERS ASSOCIATION NONFICTION CONTEST

The National Writers Association, 10940 S. Parker Rd., #508, Parker CO 80134. (303)841-0246. **E-mail:** natl-writersassn@hotmail.com. **Website:** www.national-writers.com. Only unpublished works may be submitted. Judging of entries will not begin until the contest ends. Nonfiction in the following areas will be accepted: articles—submission should include query letter, 1st page of manuscript, separate sheet citing 5 possible markets; essay—the complete essay and 5 possible markets on separate sheet; nonfiction book proposal including query letter, chapter by chapter outline, first chapter, bio, and market analysis. Those unsure of proper manuscript format should request Research Report #35. The purpose of the National Writers Association Nonfiction Contest is to encourage the writing of nonfiction and recognize those who excel in this field. Deadline: December 31. Prize: 1st-5th place awards. Other winners will be notified by March 31st. 1st Prize: $200 and Clearinghouse representation if winner is book proposal; 2nd Prize: $100; 3rd Prize: $50; 4th-10th places will receive a book. Honorable Mentions receive a certificate. Judging will be based on originality, marketability, research, and reader interest. Copies of the judges evaluation sheets will be sent to entrants furnishing an SASE with their entry.

❂ NONFICTION AWARD

Saskatchewan Book Awards, Inc., P.O. Box 20025, Regina SK S4P 4J7 Canada. (306)569-1585. **E-mail:** director@bookawards.sk.ca. **Website:** www.bookawards.sk.ca. Offered annually. This award is presented to a Saskatchewan author for the best book of nonfiction, judged on the quality of writing. Deadline: November 1. Prize: $2,000 (CAD).

FRANK LAWRENCE AND HARRIET CHAPPELL OWSLEY AWARD

Southern Historical Association, Room 111 A, LeConte Hall, Athens GA 30602-1602. (706)542-8848. **Fax:** (706)542-2455. **E-mail:** sdendy@uga.edu. **Website:** sha.uga.edu. **Contact:** Dr. John B. Boles, Editor. Awarded for a distinguished book in Southern history published in even-numbered years. The decision of the Award Committee will be announced at the annual meeting in odd-numbered years. The award carries a cash payment to be fixed by the Council, a certificate for the author(s), and a certificate for the publisher. Deadline: March 1.

THE PHI BETA KAPPA AWARD IN SCIENCE

The Phi Beta Kappa Society, 1606 New Hampshire Ave. NW, Washington DC 20009. (202)265-3808. **Fax:** (202)986-1601. **E-mail:** awards@pbk.org. **Website:** www.pbk.org/bookawards. **Contact:** Awards Coordinator. Offered annually for outstanding contributions by scientists to the literature of science. To be eligible, biographies of scientists must have a substantial critical emphasis on their scientific research. Entries must have been published in the previous calendar year. Entries must be submitted by the publisher. Entries must be preceded by a letter certifying that the book(s) conforms to all the conditions of eligibility and stating the publication date of each entry. Two copies of the book must be sent with the nomination form. Books will not be entered officially in the competition until all copies and the letter of certification have been received. Open only to original works in English and authors of US residency and publication. The intent of the award is to encourage literate and scholarly interpretations of the physical and biological sciences and mathematics; monographs and compendiums are not eligible. Deadline: January 15. Prize: $10,000.

PRESERVATION FOUNDATION CONTESTS

The Preservation Foundation, Inc, 2313 Pennington Bend, Nashville TN 37214. (615)889-2968. **E-mail:** preserve@storyhouse.org. **E-mail:** preserve@storyhouse.org. **Website:** www.storyhouse.org. **Contact:** Richard Loller, publisher. Three contests offered annually for unpublished nonfiction. Biography/Autobiography (1,500-10,000 words)—a true story of an individual personally known to the author. Or a true story from the author's life, the whole or an episode. General nonfiction (1,500-10,000 words)—any appropriate nonfiction topic. Travel nonfiction (1,500-10,000 words)—must be the true story of trip by author or someone known personally by author. Open to any previously unpublished writer. Defined as having earned no more than $750 by creative writing in any previous year. Stories must be submitted by e-mail. No paper mss can be considered. No story may be entered in more than one contest. See website for contest details. Our purpose is to "Preserve the extraordinary works of "ordinary" people. Deadline: August 31. Prize: 1st Place: $100 in each category; certificates for finalists. Judged by a jury of three judges.

❂ EVELYN RICHARDSON MEMORIAL NONFICTION AWARD

Writers' Federation of Nova Scotia, 1113 Marginal Rd., Halifax NS B3H 4P7 Canada. (902)423-8116. **Fax:** (902)422-0881. **E-mail:** director@writers.ns.ca. **Website:** www.writers.ns.ca. The Evelyn Richardson Memorial Nonfiction Award is awarded for a book of creative nonfiction by a resident of Nova Scotia. Detailed guidelines and eligibility criteria available online. Deadline: First Friday in December. Prize: Valued at $2,000 for the winning title.

ALDO AND JEANNE SCAGLIONE PRIZE FOR COMPARATIVE LITERARY STUDIES

Modern Language Association of America, 85 Broad Street, Suite 500, New York NY 10004-2434. (646)576-5141. **Fax:** (646)458-0030. **E-mail:** awards@mla.org. **Website:** www.mla.org. **Contact:** Coordinator of Book Prizes. Offered annually for outstanding scholarly work in comparative literary studies involving at least 2 literatures. Works of literary history, literary criticism, philology, and literary theory are eligible, as are works dealing with literature and other arts and disciplines, including cinema; books that are primarily translations will not be considered. Books must have been published in the past calendar year. Authors must be current members of the MLA. Requires 4 copies of the book. Deadline: May 1. Prize: A cash award and a certificate to be presented at the Modern Language Association's annual convention in January.

ALDO AND JEANNE SCAGLIONE PRIZE FOR FRENCH AND FRANCOPHONE STUDIES

Modern Language Association of America, 85 Broad Street, Suite 500, New York NY 10004-2434. (646)576-5141. **Fax:** (646)458-0030. **E-mail:** awards@mla.org. **Website:** www.mla.org. Offered annually for an outstanding scholarly work in French or francophone linguistics or literary studies. Works of literary history, literary criticism, philology, and literary theory are eligible for consideration; books that are primarily translations will not be considered. Books must have been published in the previous year. Authors must be current members of the MLA. Requires 4 copies of the book. Deadline: May 1. Prize: A cash award and a certificate to be presented at the Modern Language Association's annual convention in January.

ALDO AND JEANNE SCAGLIONE PRIZE FOR ITALIAN STUDIES

Modern Language Association of America, 85 Broad Street, Suite 500, New York NY 10004-2434. (646)576-5141. **Fax:** (646)458-0030. **E-mail:** awards@mla.org. **Website:** www.mla.org. **Contact:** Coordinator of Book Prizes. Offered in odd-number years for an outstanding scholarly work on any phase of Italian literature or culture, or comparative literature involving Italian. This shall include works that study literary or cultural theory, science, history, art, music, society, politics, cinema, and linguistics, preferably but not necessarily relating other disciplines to literature.

Books must have been published in the previous year. Authors must be members of the MLA. Requires 4 copies of the book. Deadline: May 1. Prize: A cash award and a certificate to be presented at the Modern Language Association's annual convention in January.

ALDO AND JEANNE SCAGLIONE PRIZE FOR STUDIES IN GERMANIC LANGUAGES & LITERATURE

Modern Language Association of America, 85 Broad Street, Suite 500, New York NY 10004-2434. (646)576-5141. **Fax:** (646)458-0030. **E-mail:** awards@mla.org. **Website:** www.mla.org. Offered in even-numbered years for an outstanding scholarly work on the linguistics or literatures of any of the Germanic languages (Danish, Dutch, German, Norwegian, Swedish, Yiddish). Works of literary history, literary criticism, philology, and literary theory are eligible for consideration; books that are primarily translations will not be considered. Books must have been published in the previous 2 years. Authors must be members of the MLA. Requires 4 copies of the book. Deadline: May 1. Prize: A cash award, and a certificate to be presented at the Modern Language Association's annual convention in January.

ALDO AND JEANNE SCAGLIONE PUBLICATION AWARD FOR A MANUSCRIPT IN ITALIAN LITERARY STUDIES

Modern Language Association, 85 Broad Street, Suite 500, New York NY 10004-2434. (646)576-5141. **Fax:** (646)458-0030. **E-mail:** awards@mla.org. **Website:** www.mla.org. **Contact:** Coordinator of Book Prizes. Offered annually for an outstanding ms dealing with any aspect of the languages and literatures of Italy, including medieval Latin and comparative studies or intellectual history if the work's main thrust is clearly related to the humanities. Materials from ancient Rome are eligible if related to postclassical developments. Also eligible are translations of classical works of prose and poetry produced in Italy prior to 1900 in any language (e.g., neo-Latin, Greek) or in a dialect of Italian (e.g., Neapolitan, Roman, Sicilian). Eligible are book manuscripts in English or Italian that are ready for submission or already submitted to a press. Mss must be approved or ready for publication before award deadline. Authors must be current members of the MLA, residing in the United States or Canada. Requires 4 copies, plus contact and biographical information. Deadline: June 1. Prize: A cash award and a certificate to be presented at the Modern Language Association's annual convention in January.

WILLIAM SANDERS SCARBOROUGH PRIZE

Modern Language Association of America, 85 Broad Street, Suite 500, New York NY 10004-2434. (646)576-5141. **Fax:** (646)458-0030. **E-mail:** awards@mla.org. **Website:** www.mla.org. **Contact:** Coordinator of book prizes. Offered annually for an outstanding study of black American literature or culture. Books must have been published in the previous year. Authors need not be members of the MLA. Requires 4 copies of the book. Deadline: May 1. Prize: A cash award, and a certificate to be presented at the Modern Language Association's annual convention in January.

❂ SCHOLARLY WRITING AWARD

Saskatchewan Book Awards, Inc., P.O. Box 20025, Regina SK S4P 4J7 Canada. (306)569-1585. **E-mail:** director@bookawards.sk.ca. **Website:** www.bookawards.sk.ca. **Contact:** Courtney Bates-Hardy, Executive Director. Offered annually. This award is presented to a Saskatchewan author for the best contribution to scholarship. The work must recognize or draw on specific theoretical work within a community of scholars, and participate in the creation and transmission of scholarly knowledge. Prize: $2,000 (CAD).

SCREAMINMAMAS CREATIVE NONFICTION CONTEST

1911 Cleveland St., Hollywood FL 33020. **E-mail:** screaminmamas@gmail.com. **Website:** www.screaminmamas.com/contests. **Contact:** Darlene Pistocchi, editor/managing director. "Looking for stories that revolve around the kids and/or pets. Must be true! Take an incident or scene that is embedded in your brain and share it with us. Story can be dramatic or humorous, happy or sad. Looking for the real deal." Stories should be 600-1,000 words. Open only to moms. Deadline: March 31. Prize: Publication, complementary subscription.

❂ THE SHAUGHNESSY COHEN PRIZE FOR POLITICAL WRITING

The Writers' Trust of Canada, 460 Richmond St. W., Suite 600, Toronto ON M5V 1Y1 Canada. (416)504-8222. **Fax:** (416)504-9090. **E-mail:** info@writerstrust.com. **Website:** www.writerstrust.com. **Contact:** Amanda Hopkins. Awarded annually for a nonfiction book of outstanding literary merit that enlarges understanding of contemporary Canadian political and social issues. Presented at the Politics & the Pen event each spring in Ottawa. Open to Canadian citizens and permanent residents only. Prize: $25,000 and $2,500 to 4 finalists.

MINA P. SHAUGHNESSY PRIZE

Modern Language Association of America, 85 Broad Street, Suite 500, New York NY 10004-2434. (646)576-5141. **Fax:** (646)458-0030. **E-mail:** awards@mla.org. **Website:** www.mla.org. **Contact:** Coordinator of Book Prizes. Offered in even-numbered years for a work in the fields of language, culture, literacy, or literature with strong application to the teaching of English. Books must have been published in the previous 2 years. Authors need not be members of the MLA. Requires 4 copies of the book. Deadline: May 1. Prize: A cash prize, a certificate, to be presented at the Modern Language Association's annual convention in January, and a 1-year membership in the MLA.

CHARLES S. SYDNOR AWARD

Southern Historical Association, Rm. 111 A LeConte Hall, Athens GA 30602-1602. (706)542-8848. **Fax:** (706)542-2455. **E-mail:** sdendy@uga.edu. **Website:** sha.uga.edu/awards/syndor.htm. **Contact:** Southern Historical Association. Offered in even-numbered years for recognition of a distinguished book in Southern history published in odd-numbered years. Publishers usually submit books. Deadline: March 1.

◗ TONY LOTHIAN PRIZE

Under the auspices of the Biographers' Club, 79 Arlington Ave., London N1 7BA United Kingdom. (44) (20)7 359 7769. **E-mail:** ariane.bankes@gmail.com. **Website:** www.biographersclub.co.uk. **Contact:** Ariane Bankes, prize administrator. Entries should consist of a synopsis and 10 pages of a sample chapter for a proposed biography, plus CV, sources and a note on the market for the book: 20 pages maximum in all, unstapled. Open to any writer who has not previously been published or commissioned or written a biography. Deadline: July 28. Prize: £2,000. Judges have included Michael Holroyd, Victoria Glendinning, Selina Hastings, Frances Spalding, Lyndall Gordon, Anne de Courcy, Nigel Hamilton, Anthony Sampson, and Mary Lovell.

VFW VOICE OF DEMOCRACY

Veterans of Foreign Wars of the U.S., National Headquarters, 406 W. 34th St., Kansas City MO 64111.

(816)968-1117. **E-mail:** kharmer@vfw.org. **Website:** http://www.vfw.org/Community/Voice-of-Democracy/. The Voice of Democracy Program is open to students in grades 9-12 (on the Nov. 1 deadline), who are enrolled in a public, private or parochial high school or home study program in the United States and its territories. Contact your local VFW Post to enter (entry must not be mailed to the VFW National Headquarters, only to a local, participating VFW Post). Purpose is to give high school students the opportunity to voice their opinions about their responsibility to our country and to convey those opinions via the broadcast media to all of America. Deadline: November 1. Prize: Winners receive awards ranging from $1,000-30,000.

WABASH PRIZE FOR NONFICTION

Sycamore Review, Department of English, 500 Oval Dr., Purdue University, West Lafayette IN 47907. **E-mail:** sycamore@purdue.edu; sycamorenf@purdue.edu. **Website:** www.sycamorereview.com/contest/. **Contact:** Kara Krewer, editor-in-chief. Annual contest for unpublished nonfiction. For each submission, send one nonfiction piece (limit 7,500 words). Ms pages should be numbered and should include the title of the piece. All stories must be previously unpublished. See website for more guidelines. Submit via online submissions manager. Deadline: December 1. Prize: $1,000 and publication.

WESTERN WRITERS OF AMERICA

271CR 219, Encampment WY 82325. (307)329-8942. **Fax:** (307)327-5465 (call first). **E-mail:** wwa.moulton@gmail.com. **Website:** www.westernwriters.org. **Contact:** Candy Moulton, executive director. Seventeen Spur Award categories in various aspects of the American West. Send entry form with your published work. Accepts multiple submissions, each with its own entry form. The nonprofit Western Writers of America has promoted and honored the best in Western literature with the annual Spur Awards, selected by panels of judges. Awards, for material published last year, are given for works whose inspirations, image and literary excellence best represent the reality and spirit of the American West.

☀ THE HILARY WESTON WRITERS' TRUST PRIZE FOR NONFICTION

The Writers' Trust of Canada, 460 Richmond St. W., Suite 600, Toronto ON M5V 1Y1 Canada. (416)504-8222. **Fax:** (416)504-9090. **E-mail:** info@writerstrust.com. **Website:** www.writerstrust.com. **Contact:** Amanda Hopkins. Offered annually for a work of nonfiction published in the previous year. Award presented at the Writers' Trust Awards event held in Toronto each fall. Open to Canadian citizens and permanent residents only. Deadline: July 27. Prize: $60,000; $5,000 to 4 finalists.

THE ELIE WIESEL PRIZE IN ETHICS ESSAY CONTEST

The Elie Wiesel Foundation for Humanity, 555 Madison Ave., 20th Floor, New York NY 10022. **Fax:** (212)490-6006. **Website:** www.eliewieselfoundation.org. **Contact:** Leslie Meyers. This annual competition is intended to challenge undergraduate juniors and seniors in colleges and universities throughout the US to analyze ethical questions and concerns facing them in today's complex society. All students are encouraged to write thought-provoking, personal essays. Deadline: December 14. Prize: 1st Prize: $5,000; 2nd Prize: $2,500; 3rd Prize: $1,500; Honorable Mentions (2): $500. Judged by a distinguished panel of readers who evaluate all contest entries. A jury, including Elie Wiesel, chooses the winners.

WRITING CONFERENCE WRITING CONTESTS

P.O. Box 664, Ottawa KS 66067-0664. (785)242-2947. **Fax:** (785)242-2473. **E-mail:** jbushman@writingconference.com. **E-mail:** support@studentq.com. **Website:** www.writingconference.com. **Contact:** John H. Bushman, contest director. Unpublished submissions only. Submissions made by the author or teacher. Purpose of contest: To further writing by students with awards for narration, exposition and poetry at the elementary, middle school, and high school levels. Deadline: January 8. Prize: Awards plaque and publication of winning entry in The Writers' Slate online, April issue. Judged by a panel of teachers.

YEARBOOK EXCELLENCE CONTEST

100 Adler Journalism Building, Iowa City IA 52242-2004. (319)335-3457. **Fax:** (319)335-3989. **E-mail:** quill-scroll@uiowa.edu. **Website:** www.quillandscroll.org. **Contact:** Vanessa Shelton, executive director. High school students who are contributors to or staff members of a student yearbook at any public or private high school are invited to enter the competition. Awards will be made in each of the 18 divisions. There are two enrollment catego-

ries: Class A: more than 750 students; Class B: 749 or less. Winners will receive Quill and Scroll's National Award Gold Key and, if seniors, are eligible to apply for one of the Edward J. Nell Memorial or George and Ophelia Gallup scholarships. Open to students whose schools have Quill and Scroll charters. Previously published submissions only. Submissions made by the author or school yearbook adviser. Must be published in the 12-month span prior to contest deadline. Visit website for list of current and previous winners. Purpose is to recognize and reward student journalists for their work in yearbooks and to provide student winners an opportunity to apply for a scholarship to be used freshman year in college for students planning to major in journalism. **Deadline:** November 1.

LAMAR YORK PRIZE FOR FICTION AND NONFICTION CONTEST

The Chattahoochee Review, Georgia Perimeter College, 2101 Womack Rd., Dunwoody GA 30338-4497. (770)274-5479. **E-mail:** gpccr@gpc.edu. **Website:** thechattahoocheereview.gpc.edu. **Contact:** Anna Schachner, Editor. Offered annually for unpublished creative nonfiction and nonscholarly essays and fiction up to 5,000 words. *The Chattahoochee Review* buys first rights only for winning essay/ms for the purpose of publication in the summer issue. Entries should be submitted via Submittable. See website for details and guidelines. **Deadline:** January 31. Submission period begins October 1. **Prize:** 2 prizes of $1,000 each, plus publication. Judged by the editorial staff of *The Chattahoochee Review*.

ZONE 3 CREATIVE NONFICTION BOOK AWARD

Zone 3, Austin Peay State University, P.O. Box 4565, Clarksville TN 37044. (931)221-7031. **Fax:** (931)221-7149. **E-mail:** wallacess@apsu.edu. **Website:** www.apsu.edu/zone3/contests. **Contact:** Susan Wallace, Managing Editor. This competition is open to all authors writing original works in English. Looking for manuscripts that embrace creative nonfiction's potential by combining lyric exposition, researched reflection, travel dialogues, or creative criticism. Memoir, personal narrative, essay collections, and literary nonfiction are also invited. Submit one copy of ms of 150-300 pages. Accepts entries online and via postal mail. **Deadline:** April 1. **Prize:** $1,000 and publication.

WRITING FOR CHILDREN & YOUNG ADULTS

JANE ADDAMS CHILDREN'S BOOK AWARDS

Jane Addams Peace Association, 777 United Nations Plaza, 6th Floor, New York NY 10017. (212)652-8830. **E-mail:** info@janeaddamspeace.org. **Website:** www.janeaddamspeace.org. **Contact:** Heather Palmer, co-chair. The Jane Addams Children's Book Awards are given annually to the children's books published the preceding year that effectively promote the cause of peace, social justice, world community, and the equality of the sexes and all races as well as meeting conventional standards for excellence. Books eligible for this award may be fiction, poetry, or nonfiction. Books may be any length. Entries should be suitable for ages 2-12. See website for specific details on guidelines and required book themes. **Deadline:** December 31. Judged by a national committee of WILPF members concerned with children's books and their social values is responsible for making the changes each year.

AMERICAN ASSOCIATION OF UNIVERSITY WOMEN AWARD IN JUVENILE LITERATURE

4610 Mail Service Center, Raleigh NC 27699-4610. (919)807-7290. **E-mail:** michael.hill@ncdcr.gov. **Website:** www.ncdcr.gov. **Contact:** Michael Hill, awards coordinator. Annual award. Book must be published during the year ending June 30. Submissions made by author, author's agent or publisher. SASE for contest rules. Author must have maintained either legal residence or actual physical residence, or a combination of both, in the state of North Carolina for 3 years immediately preceding the close of the contest period. Only published work (books) eligible. Recognizes the year's best work of juvenile literature by a North Carolina resident. **Deadline:** July 15. **Prize:** Awards a cup to the winner and winner's name inscribed on a plaque displayed within the North Carolina Office of Archives and History. Judged by three-judge panel.

◐ HANS CHRISTIAN ANDERSEN AWARD

Nonnenweg 12, Postfach Basel CH-4009 Switzerland. **E-mail:** liz.page@ibby.org. **E-mail:** ibby@ibby.org. **Website:** www.ibby.org. **Contact:** Liz Page, director. The Hans Christian Andersen Award, awarded every two years by the International Board on Books for Young People (IBBY), is the highest international recognition given to an author and an illustrator of children's books. The Author's Award has been given since 1956, the Illustrator's Award since 1966. Her Majesty Queen Margrethe II of Denmark is the Patron of the Hans Christian Andersen Awards. The awards are presented at the biennial congresses of IBBY. Awarded to an author and to an illustrator, living at the time of the nomination, who by the outstanding value of their work are judged to have made a lasting contribution to literature for children and young people. The complete works of the author and of the illustrator will be taken into consideration in awarding the medal, which will be accompanied by a diploma. Candidates are nominated by National Sections of IBBY in good standing. Prize: Awards medals according to literary and artistic criteria. Judged by the Hans Christian Andersen Jury.

☼ MARILYN BAILLIE PICTURE BOOK AWARD

The Canadian Children's Book Centre, 40 Orchard View Blvd., Suite 217, Toronto ON M4R 1B9 Canada. (416)975-0010, ext. 222. **Fax:** (416)975-8970. **E-mail:** meghan@bookcentre.ca. **Website:** www.bookcentre. ca. **Contact:** Meghan Howe. The Marilyn Baillie Picture Book Award honors excellence in the illustrated picture book format. To be eligible, the book must be an original work in English, aimed at children ages 3-8, written and illustrated by Canadians and first published in Canada. Eligible genres include fiction, nonfiction and poetry. Books must be published between Jan. 1 and Dec. 31 of the previous calendar year. New editions or re-issues of previously published books are not eligible for submission. Send 5 copies of title along with a completed submission form. Deadline: mid-December annually. Prize: $20,000.

TIPS "Please visit website for submission guidelines and eligibility criteria."

MILDRED L. BATCHELDER AWARD

50 E. Huron St., Chicago IL 60611-2795. **Website:** http://www.ala.org/alsc/awardsgrants/. The Batchelder Award is given to the most outstanding children's book originally published in a language other than English in a country other than the United States, and subsequently translated into English for publication in the US. Visit website for terms and criteria of award. The purpose of the award, a citation to an American publisher, is to encourage international exchange of quality children's books by recognizing US publishers of such books in translation. Deadline: December 31.

JOHN AND PATRICIA BEATTY AWARD

2471 Flores St., San Mateo CA 94403. (650)376-0886. **Fax:** (650)539-2341. **E-mail:** sarahmae.harper@gmail. com. **Website:** www.cla-net.org. **Contact:** Sarah Mae Harper, award chair. The California Library Association's John and Patricia Beatty Award, sponsored by Baker & Taylor, honors the author of a distinguished book for children or young adults that best promotes an awareness of California and its people. Must be a children's or young adult books published in the previous year, set in California, and highlight California's cultural heritage or future. Send title suggestiosn to the committee members. Deadline: January 31. Prize: $500 and an engraved plaque. Judged by a committee of CLA members, who select the winning title from books published in the United States during the preceding year.

☼ THE GEOFFREY BILSON AWARD FOR HISTORICAL FICTION FOR YOUNG PEOPLE

The Canadian Children's Book Centre, 40 Orchard View Blvd., Suite 217, Toronto ON M4R 1B9 Canada. (416)975-0010, ext. 222. **Fax:** (416)975-8970. **Website:** www.bookcentre.ca. **Contact:** Meghan Howe. Awarded annually to reward excellence in the writing of an outstanding work of historical fiction for young readers, by a Canadian author, published in the previous calendar year. Open to Canadian citizens and residents of Canada for at least 2 years. Books must be published between January 1 and December 31 of the previous year. Books must be first foreign or first Canadian editions. Autobiographies are not eligible. Jury members will consider the following: historical setting and accuracy, strong character and plot development, well-told, original story, and stability of book for its intended age group. Send 5 copies of the title along with a completed submission form. Deadline: mid-December annaully. Prize: $5,000.

THE IRMA S. AND JAMES H. BLACK AWARD

Bank Street College of Education, 610 W. 112th St., New York NY 10025-1898. (212)875-4458. **Fax:** (212)875-4558. **E-mail:** kfreda@bankstreet.edu. **Website:** http://bankstreet.edu/center-childrens-literature/irma-black-award/. **Contact:** Kristin Freda. Award give to an outstanding book for young children—a book in which text and illustrations are inseparable, each enhancing and enlarging on the other to produce a singular whole. Entries must have been published during the previous calendar year. Publishers submit books. Submit only one copy of each book. Does not accept unpublished mss. Deadline: mid-December. Prize: A scroll with the recipient's name and a gold seal designed by Maurice Sendak. Judged by a committee of older children and children's literature professionals. Final judges are first-, second-, and third-grade classes at a number of cooperating schools.

BOSTON GLOBE-HORN BOOK AWARDS

The Boston Globe, Horn Book, Inc., 300 The Fenway, Palace Road Building, Suite P-311, Boston MA 02115. (617)278-0225. **Fax:** (617)278-6062. **E-mail:** info@hbook.com; khedeen@hbook.com. **Website:** hbook.com/bghb/. **Contact:** Katrina Hedeen. Offered annually for excellence in literature for children and young adults (published June 1-May 31). Categories: picture book, fiction and poetry, nonfiction. Judges may also name up to 2 honor books in each category. Books must be published in the US, but may be written or illustrated by citizens of any country. The Horn Book Magazine publishes speeches given at awards ceremonies. Guidelines for SASE or online. Submit a book directly to each of the judges. See website for details on submitting, as well as contest guidelines. Deadline: May 15. Prize: $500 and an engraved silver bowl; honor book recipients receive an engraved silver plate. Judged by a panel of 3 judges selected each year.

✪ ANN CONNOR BRIMER BOOK AWARD

The Ann Connor Brimer Award, P.O. Box 36036, Halifax NS B3J 3S9 Canada. (902)490-2742. **Website:** www.atlanticbookawards.ca/. **Contact:** Laura Carter, Atlantic Book Awards Festival Coordinator. In 1990, the Nova Scotia Library Association established the Ann Connor Brimer Award for writers residing in Atlantic Canada who have made an outstanding contribution to writing for Atlantic Candian young people. Author must be alive and residing in Atlantic Canada at time of nomination. Book intended for youth up to the age of 15. Book in print and readily available. Fiction or nonfiction (except textbooks). Book must have been published within the previous year. Prize: $2,000.

CHILDREN'S AFRICANA BOOK AWARD

Outreach Council of the African Studies Association, c/o Rutgers University -Livingston campus, 54 Joyce Kilmer Ave., Piscataway NJ 08854 USA. (703)549-8208; (301)585-9136. **E-mail:** africaaccess@aol.com. **E-mail:** Harriet@AfricaAccessReview.org. **Website:** www.africaaccessreview.org. **Contact:** Brenda Randolph, chairperson. The Children's Africana Book Awards are presented annually to the authors and illustrators of the best books on Africa for children and young people published or distributed in the U.S. The awards were created by the Outreach Council of the African Studies Association (ASA) to dispel stereotypes and encourage the publication and use of accurate, balanced children's materials about Africa. The awards are presented in 2 categories: Young Children and Older Readers. Entries must have been published in the calendar year previous to the award. Work submitted for awards must be suitable for children ages 4-18; a significant portion of books' content must be about Africa; must by copyrighted in the calendar year prior to award year; must be published or distributed in the US. Books should be suitable for children and young adults, ages 4-18. A significant portion of the book's content should be about Africa. Deadline: January 31 of the award year. Judged by African Studies and Children's Literature scholars. Nominated titles are read by committee members and reviewed by external African Studies scholars with specialized academic training.

CHILDREN'S BOOK GUILD AWARD FOR NONFICTION

E-mail: theguild@childrensbookguild.org. **Website:** www.childrensbookguild.org. Annual award. "One doesn't enter. One is selected. Our jury annually selects one author for the award." Honors an author or illustrator whose total work has contributed significantly to the quality of nonfiction for children. Prize: Cash and an engraved crystal paperweight. Judged by a jury of Children's Book Guild specialists, authors, and illustrators.

✪ CHILDREN'S LITERATURE AWARD

Saskatchewan Book Awards, Inc., Box 20025, Regina SK S4P 4J7 Canada. (306)569-1585. **Fax:** (306)569-4187. **E-mail:** director@bookawards.sk.ca. **E-mail:** info@bookawards.sk.ca. **Website:** www.bookawards.sk.ca. **Contact:** Courtney Bates-Hardy, Executive Director. Offered biennially. This award is presented to a Saskatchewan author or pair of authors, or to Saskatchewan author and a Saskatchewan illustrator, for the best book of children's literature, for ages 0-11, judged on the quality of the writing and illustration. Deadline: November 1. Prize: $2,000 (CAD).

⊕ CLA YOUNG ADULT BOOK AWARD

1150 Morrison Dr.,, Suite 400, Ottawa ON K2H 8S9 Canada. (613)232-9625. **Fax:** (613)563-9895. **E-mail:** cshea@cbvrsb.ca. **Website:** www.cla.ca. **Contact:** Carmelita Cechetto-Shea, chair. This award recognizes an author of an outstanding English language Canadian book which appeals to young adults between the ages of 13 and 18. To be eligible for consideration, the following must apply: it must be a work of fiction (novel, collection of short stories, or graphic novel), the title must be a Canadian publication in either hardcover or paperback, and the author must be a Canadian citizen or landed immigrant. The award is given annually, when merited, at the Canadian Library Association's annual conference. Deadline: December 31. Prize: $1,000.

MARGARET A. EDWARDS AWARD

50 East Huron St., Chicago IL 60611-2795. (312)280-4390 or (800)545-2433. **Fax:** (312)280-5276. **E-mail:** yalsa@ala.org. **Website:** www.ala.org/yalsa/edwards. **Contact:** Nichole O'Connor. Annual award administered by the Young Adult Library Services Association (YALSA) of the American Library Association (ALA) and sponsored by *School Library Journal* magazine. Awarded to an author whose book or books, over a period of time, have been accepted by young adults as an authentic voice that continues to illuminate their experiences and emotions, giving insight into their lives. The book or books should enable them to understand themselves, the world in which they live, and their relationship with others and with society. The book or books must be in print at the time of the nomination. Submissions must be previously published no less than 5 years prior to the first meeting of the current Margaret A. Edwards Award Committee at Midwinter Meeting. Nomination form is available on the YALSA website. Deadline: December 1. Prize: $2,000. Judged by members of the Young Adult Library Services Association.

DOROTHY CANFIELD FISHER CHILDREN'S BOOK AWARD

Midstate Library Service Center, 578 Paine Tpke. N., Berlin VT 05602. (802)828-6954. **E-mail:** grace. greene@state.vt.us. **Website:** www.dcfaward.org. **Contact:** Mary Linney, chair. Annual award to encourage Vermont children to become enthusiastic and discriminating readers by providing them with books of good quality by living American or Canadian authors published in the current year. E-mail for entry rules. Titles must be original work, published in the U.S., and be appropriate to children in grades 4-8. The book must be copyrighted in the current year. It must be written by an American author living in the U.S. or Canada, or a Canadian author living in Canada or the U.S. Deadline: December of year book was published. Prize: Awards a scroll presented to the winning author at an award ceremony. Judged by children, grades 4-8, who vote for their favorite book.

⊕ THE NORMA FLECK AWARD FOR CANADIAN CHILDREN'S NONFICTION

The Canadian Children's Book Centre, 40 Orchard View Blvd., Suite 217, Toronto ON M4R 1B9 Canada. (416)975-0010 ext. 222. **Fax:** (416)975-8970. **E-mail:** meghan@bookcentre.ca. **Website:** www.bookcentre. ca. **Contact:** Meghan Howe. The Norma Fleck Award was established by the Fleck Family Foundation to recognize and raise the profile of exceptional nonfiction books for children. Offered annually for books published between January 1 and December 31 of the previous calendar year. Open to Canadian citizens or landed immigrants. Books must be first foreign or first Canadian editions. Nonfiction books in the following categories are eligible: culture and the arts, science, biography, history, geography, reference, sports, activities, and pastimes. Deadline: mid-December annually. Prize: $10,000. The award will go to the author unless 40% or more of the text area is composed of original illustrations, in which case the award will be divided equally between author and illustrator.

FLICKER TALE CHILDREN'S BOOK AWARD

Morton Mandan Public Library, 609 W. Main St., Mandan ND 58554. **E-mail:** laustin@cdln.info. **Website:** www.ndla.info/flickertale. **Contact:** Linda Austin. Award gives children across the state of North Dakota a chance to vote for their book of choice from a nominated list of 20: 4 in the picture book category; 4 in the intermediate category; 4 in the juvenile category (for more advanced readers); 4 in the upper grade level nonfiction category. Also promotes awareness of quality literature for children. Previously published submissions only. Submissions nominated by librarians and teachers across the state of North Dakota. Deadline: April 1. Prize: A plaque from North Dakota

Library Association and banquet dinner. Judged by children in North Dakota.

THEODOR SEUSS GEISEL AWARD

Association for Library Service to Children, Division of the American Library Association, 50 E. Huron, Chicago IL 60611. (800)545-2433. **E-mail:** alscawards@ala.org. **Website:** www.ala.org. The Theodor Seuss Geisel Award is given annually to the author(s) and illustrator(s) of the most distinguished American book for beginning readers published in English in the United States during the preceding year. The award is to recognize the author(s) and illustrator(s) who demonstrate great creativity and imagination in his/her/their literary and artistic achievements to engage children in reading. Terms and criteria for the award are listed on the website. Entry will not be returned. Deadline: December 31. Prize: Medal, given at awards ceremony during the ALA Annual Conference.

GOLDEN KITE AWARDS

Society of Children's Book Writers and Illustrators (SCBWI), SCBWI Golden Kite Awards, 8271 Beverly Blvd., Los Angeles CA 90048-4515. (323)782-1010. **Fax:** (323)782-1892. **E-mail:** sararutenberg@scbwi.org. **Website:** www.scbwi.org. Given annually to recognize excellence in children's literature in 4 categories: fiction, nonfiction, picture book text, and picture book illustration. Books submitted must be published in the previous calendar year. Both individuals and publishers may submit. Submit 4 copies of book. Submit to one category only, except in the case of picture books. Must be a current member of the SCBWI. Deadline: December 1. Prize: One Golden Kite Award Winner and one Honor Book will be chosen per category. Winners and Honorees will receive a commemorative poster also sent to publishers, bookstores, libraries, and schools; a press release; an announcement on the SCBWI website; and on SCBWI Social Networks.

⊙ AMELIA FRANCES HOWARD-GIBBON ILLUSTRATOR'S AWARD

1150 Morrison Drie, Suite 400, Ottawa ON K 2H859 Canada. (613)232-9625. **Fax:** (613)563-9895. **Website:** www.cla.ca. **Contact:** Diana Cauthier. Annually awarded to an outstanding illustrator of a children's book published in Canada during the previous calendar year. The award is bestowed upon books that are suitable for children up to and including age 12.

To be eligible for the award, an illustrator must be a Canadian citizen or a permanent resident of Canada, and the text of the book must be worthy of the book's illustrations. Deadline: November 30. Prize: A plaque and a check for $1,000 (CAD).

CAROL OTIS HURST CHILDREN'S BOOK PRIZE

Westfield Athenaeum, 6 Elm St., Westfield MA 01085. (413)568-7833. **Fax:** (413)568-0988. **Website:** www. westath.org. **Contact:** Pamela Weingart. The Carol Otis Hurst Children's Book Prize honors outstanding works of fiction and nonfiction, including biography and memoir, written for children and young adults through the age of eighteen that exemplify the highest standards of research, analysis, and authorship in their portrayal of the New England Experience. The prize will be presented annually to an author whose book treats the region's history as broadly conceived to encompass one or more of the following elements: political experience, social development, fine and performing artistic expression, domestic life and arts, transportation and communication, changing technology, military experience at home and abroad, schooling, business and manufacturing, workers and the labor movement, agriculture and its transformation, racial and ethnic diversity, religious life and institutions, immigration and adjustment, sports at all levels, and the evolution of popular entertainment. The public presentation of the prize will be accompanied by a reading and/or talk by the recipient at a mutually agreed upon time during the spring immediately following the publication year. Books must have been copyrighted in their original format during the calendar year, January 1 to December 31, of the year preceding the year in which the prize is awarded. Any individual, publisher, or organization may nominate a book. See website for details and guidelines. Deadline: December 31. Prize: $500.

INTERNATIONAL READING ASSOCIATION CHILDREN'S AND YOUNG ADULT'S BOOK AWARDS

P.O. Box 8139, 800 Barksdale Rd., Newark DE 19714-8139. (302)731-1600, ext. 221. **E-mail:** kbaughman@reading.org; committees@reading.org. **Website:** www.reading.org. **Contact:** Kathy Baughman. The IRA Children's and Young Adults Book Awards are intended for newly published authors who show unusual promise in the children's and young adults' book field. Awards are given for fiction and nonfiction in each of three categories: primary, intermediate, and young adult. Books from all countries and published in English for the first time during the previous calendar year will be considered. See website for eligibility and criteria information. Entry should be the author's first or second book. Deadline: January 15. Prize: $1,000.

TIPS Provide believable and intriguing characters, truthful and authentic in its presentation of information and attitudes as they existed at the time and place which the story reflects.

◯ THE IODE JEAN THROOP BOOK AWARD

The Lillian H. Smith Children's Library, 239 College St., 4th St., Toronto ON M5T 1R5 Canada. (905)522-9537. **E-mail:** mcscott@torontopubliclibrary.ca; iodeontario@bellnet.ca. **Website:** www.iodeontario.ca. **Contact:** Martha Scott. Each year, the Municipal Chapter of Toronto IODE presents an award intended to encourage the publication of books for children between the ages of 6-12 years. The award-winner must be a Canadian citizen, resident in Toronto or the surrounding area, and the book must be published in Canada. Deadline: December 31. Prize: Award and cash prize of $2,000. Judged by a selected committee.

IRA SHORT STORY AWARD

International Reading Association, International Reading Association, 800 Barksdale Rd., P.O. Box 8139, Newark DE 19714-8139. (302)731-1600. **Fax:** (302)731-1057. **E-mail:** committees@reading.org. **Website:** www.reading.org. Offered to reward author of an original short story published for the first time in a periodical for children. (Periodicals should generally be aimed at readers around age 12.) Write for guidelines or download from website. Award is non-monetary. Both fiction and nonfiction stories are eligible; each will be rated according to the characteristics that are appropriate for the genre. The story should: create a believable world for the readers, be truthful and authentic in its presentation of information, serve as a reading and literary standard by which readers can measure other writing, and encourage young readers by providing them with an enjoyable reading experience. Deadline: November 15.

JEFFERSON CUP AWARD

P.O. Box 56312, Virginia Beach VA 23456. (757)689-0594. **Website:** www.vla.org. **Contact:** Susan M. Catlett, current chairperson. The Jefferson Cup honors a distinguished biography, historical fiction, or American history book for young people. The Jefferson Cup Committee's goal is to promote reading about America's past; to encourage the quality writing of United States history, biography, and historical fiction for young people; and to recognize authors in these disciplines. Deadline: January 31.

EZRA JACK KEATS/KERLAN MEMORIAL FELLOWSHIP

University of Minnesota Libraries, 113 Elmer L. Andersen Library, 222 21st Ave. S, Minneapolis MN 55455. **E-mail:** asc-clrc@umn.edu. **Website:** https://www.lib.umn.edu/clrc/awards-grants-and-fellowships. This fellowship from the Ezra Jack Keats Foundation will provide $1,500 to a talented writer and/or illustrator of children's books who wishes to use the Kerlan Collection for the furtherance of his or her artistic development. Special consideration will be given to someone who would find it difficult to finance a visit to the Kerlan Collection. The Ezra Jack Keats Fellowship recipient will receive transportation costs and a per diem allotment. See website for application deadline and for digital application materials. Winner will be notified in February. Study and written report must be completed within the calendar year. Deadline: January 30.

THE EZRA JACK KEATS NEW WRITER AND NEW ILLUSTRATOR AWARDS

450 14th St., Brooklyn NY 11215-5702. **E-mail:** foundation@ezra-jack-keats.org. **Website:** www.ezra-jack-keats.org. Annual award to recognize and encourage new authors and illustrators starting out in the field of children's books. Many past winners of the Ezra Jack Keats Book Award have gone on to distinguished careers, creating books beloved by parents, children, librarians, and teachers around the world. Writers and illustrators must have had no more than 3 books previously published. Prize: $1,000 honorarium for each winner. Judged by a distinguished selection committee of early childhood education specialists, librarians, illustrators and experts in children's literature.

KENTUCKY BLUEGRASS AWARD

Northern Kentucky University, 405 Steely Library, Nunn Drive, Highland Heights KY 41099. (859)572-6620. **E-mail:** smithjen@nku.edu. **Website:** kba.nku.edu. The Kentucky Bluegrass Award is a student choice program. The KBA promotes and encourages Kentucky students in kindergarten through grade 12 to read a variety of quality literature. Each year, a KBA committee for each grade category chooses the books for the four Master Lists (K-2, 3-5, 6-8 and 9-12). All Kentucky public and private schools, as well as public libraries, are welcome to participate in the program. To nominate a book, see the website for form and details. Deadline: March 1. Judged by students who read books and choose their favorite.

CORETTA SCOTT KING BOOK AWARDS

50 E. Huron St., Chicago IL 60611-2795. (800)545-2433. **E-mail:** olos@ala.org. **Website:** www.ala.org/csk. **Contact:** Office for Diversity, Literacy and Outreach Services. The Coretta Scott King Book Awards are given annually to outstanding African American authors and illustrators of books for children and young adults that demonstrate an appreciation of African American culture and universal human values. The award commemorates the life and work of Dr. Martin Luther King, Jr., and honors his wife, Mrs. Coretta Scott King, for her courage and determination to continue the work for peace and world brotherhood. Must be written for a youth audience in one of three categories: preschool-4th grade; 5th-8th grade; or 9th-12th grade. Book must be published in the year preceding the year the award is given, evidenced by the copyright date in the book. See website for full details, criteria, and eligibility concerns. Purpose is to encourage the artistic expression of the African American experience via literature and the graphic arts, including biographical, historical and social history treatments by African American authors and illustrators. Deadline: December 1. Judged by the Coretta Scott King Book Awards Committee.

☘ THE VICKY METCALF AWARD FOR LITERATURE FOR YOUNG PEOPLE

The Writers' Trust of Canada, 460 Richmond St. W., Suite 600, Toronto ON M5V 1Y1 Canada. (416)504-8222. **E-mail:** info@writerstrust.com. **Website:** www.writerstrust.com. **Contact:** Amanda Hopkins. The Vicky Metcalf Award is presented to a Canadian writer for a body of work in children's literature at The Writers' Trust Awards event held in Toronto each fall. Open to Canadian citizens and permanent residents only. Prize: $20,000.

MILKWEED PRIZE FOR CHILDREN'S LITERATURE

Milkweed Editions, 1011 Washington Ave. S., Suite 300, Minneapolis MN 55415. (612)332-3192. **Fax:**

(612)215-2550. **E-mail:** editor@milkweed.org. **Website:** www.milkweed.org. Milkweed Editions will award the Milkweed Prize for Children's Literature to the best mss for young readers that Milkweed accepts for publication during the calendar year by a writer not previously published by Milkweed. All mss for young readers submitted for publication by Milkweed are automatically entered into the competition. Seeking full-length fiction between 90-200 pages. Does not consider picture books or poetry collections for young readers. Recognizes an outstanding literary novel for readers ages 8-13 and encourage writers to turn their attention to readers in this age group. Prize: $10,000 cash prize in addition to a publishing contract negotiated at the time of acceptance. Judged by the editors of Milkweed Editions.

NATIONAL YOUNGARTS FOUNDATION

2100 Biscayne Blvd., Miami FL 33137. (305)377-1140. **Fax:** (305)377-1149. **E-mail:** info@nfaa.org; apply@youngarts.org. **Website:** www.youngarts.org. The National YoungArts Foundation (formerly known as the National Foundation for Advancement in the Arts) was established in 1981 by Lin and Ted Arison to identify and support the next generation of artists and to contribute to the cultural vitality of the nation by investing in the artistic development of talented young artists in the visual, literary, design and performing arts. Each year, there are approximately 11,000 applications submitted to YoungArts from 15-18 year old (or grades 10-12) artists, and from these, approximately 700 winners are selected who are eligible to participate in programs in Miami, New York, Los Angeles, and Washington D.C. (with Chicago and other regions in the works). YoungArts provides these emerging artists with life-changing experiences and validation by renowned mentors, access to significant scholarships, national recognition and other opportunities throughout their careers to help ensure that the nation's most outstanding emerging artists are encouraged to pursue careers in the arts. See website for details about applying. Prize: Cash awards up to $10,000.

JOHN NEWBERY MEDAL

Association for Library Service to Children, Division of the American Library Association, 50 E. Huron, Chicago IL 60611. (800)545-2433, ext. 2153. **Fax:** (312)280-5271. **E-mail:** alscawards@ala.org. **Website:** www.ala.org. The Newbery Medal is awarded annually by the American Library Association for the most distinguished contribution to American literature for children. Previously published submissions only; must be published prior to year award is given. SASE for award rules. Entries not returned. Medal awarded at Caldecott/Newbery banquet during ALA annual conference. Deadline: December 31. Judged by Newbery Award Selection Committee.

NEW VOICES AWARD

95 Madison Ave., Suite 1205, New York NY 10016. **Website:** www.leeandlow.com. Open to students. Annual award. Lee & Low Books is one of the few minority-owned publishing companies in the country and has published more than 100 first-time writers and illustrators. Winning titles include *The Blue Roses*, winner of a Patterson Prize for Books for Young People; *Janna and the Kings*, an IRA Children's Book Award Notable; and *Sixteen Years in Sixteen Seconds*, selected for the Texas Bluebonnet Award Masterlist. Submissions made by author. SASE for contest rules or visit website. Restrictions of media for illustrators: The author must be a writer of color who is a resident of the U.S. and who has not previously published a children's picture book. For additional information, send SASE or visit Lee & Low's website. Encourages writers of color to enter the world of children's books. Deadline: September 30. Prize: $1,000 and standard publication contract (regardless of whether or not writer has an agent) along with an advance against royalties; New Voices Honor Award: $500 prize. Judged by Lee & Low editors.

ORBIS PICTUS AWARD FOR OUTSTANDING NONFICTION FOR CHILDREN

1111 W. Kenyon Rd., Urbana IL 61801-1096. (217)328-3870. **Fax:** (217)328-0977. **E-mail:** elementary@ncte.org. **Website:** www.ncte.org/awards/orbispictus. The NCTE Orbis Pictus Award promotes and recognizes excellence in the writing of nonfiction for children. Orbis Pictus commemorates the work of Johannes Amos Comenius, *Orbis Pictus—The World in Pictures* (1657), considered to be the first book actually planned for children. Submissions should be made by an author, the author's agent, or by a person or group of people. Must be published in the calendar year of the competition. Deadline: November 1. Prize: A plaque given at the NCTE Elementary Section Luncheon at the NCTE Annual Convention in November. Up to 5 honor books awarded. Judged by members of the Orbis Pictus Committee.

THE ORIGINAL ART

128 E. 63rd St., New York NY 10065. (212)838-2560. **Fax:** (212)838-2561. **E-mail:** kim@societyillustrators.org; info@societyillustrators.org. **Website:** www.societyillustrators.org. **Contact:** Kate Feirtag, exhibition director. The Original Art is an annual exhibit created to showcase illustrations from the year's best children's books published in the US. For editors and art directors, it's an inspiration and a treasure trove of talent to draw upon. Previously published submissions only. Request "call for entries" to receive contest rules and entry forms. Works will be displayed at the Society of Illustrators Museum of American Illustration in New York City October-November annually. Deadline: July 18. Judged by 7 professional artists and editors.

HELEN KEATING OTT AWARD FOR OUTSTANDING CONTRIBUTION TO CHILDREN'S LITERATURE

CSLA, 10157 SW Barbur Blvd. #102C, Portland OR 97219. (503)244-6919. **Fax:** (503)977-3734. **E-mail:** sharper1@kent.edu. **Website:** www.cslainfo.org. **Contact:** S. Meghan Harper, awards chair. Annual award given to a person or organization that has made a significant contribution to promoting high moral and ethical values through children's literature. Recipient is honored in July during the conference. Awards certificate of recognition, the awards banquet, and one-night's stay in the hotel. A nomination for an award may be made by anyone. An application form is available online. Elements of creativity and innovation will be given high priority by the judges.

PATERSON PRIZE FOR BOOKS FOR YOUNG PEOPLE

The Poetry Center at Passaic County Community College, One College Blvd., Paterson NJ 07505. (973)684-6555. **Fax:** (973)523-6085. **E-mail:** mgillan@pccc.edu. **Website:** www.pccc.edu/poetry. **Contact:** Maria Mazziotti Gillan, executive director. Award for a book published in the previous year in each age category (Pre-K-Grade 3, Grades 4-6, Grades 7-12). Deadline: March 15. Prize: $500.

THE KATHERINE PATERSON PRIZE FOR YOUNG ADULT AND CHILDREN'S WRITING

Hunger Mountain, Vermont College of Fine Arts, 36 College St., Montpelier VT 05602. (802)828-8517. **E-mail:** hungermtn@vcfa.edu. **Website:** www.hungermtn.org. **Contact:** Samantha Kolber, Managing Editor. The annual Katherine Paterson Prize for Young

Adult and Children's Writing honors the best in young adult and children's literature. Submit young adult or middle grade mss, and writing for younger children, short stories, picture books, poetry, or novel excerpts, under 10,000 words. Guidelines available on website. Deadline: March 1. Prize: $1,000 and publication for the first place winner; $100 each and publication for the three category winners. Judged by a guest judge every year. The 2016 judge is Rita Williams-Garcia, author of Newbery Honor-winning novel, *One Crazy Summer*.

PENNSYLVANIA YOUNG READERS' CHOICE AWARDS PROGRAM

134 Bisbing Road, Henryville PA 18332. **Website:** www.psla.org. **Contact:** Alice L. Cyphers, co-coordinator. Submissions nominated by a person or group. Must be published within 5 years of the award—for example, books published in 2012 to present are eligible for the 2017-2018 award. Check the Program wiki at pyrca.wikispaces.com for submission information. View information at the Pennsylvania School Librarians' website or the Program wiki. Must be currently living in North America. The purpose of the Pennsylvania Young Reader's Choice Awards Program is to promote the reading of quality books by young people in the Commonwealth of Pennsylvania, to encourage teacher and librarian collaboration and involvement in children's literature, and to honor authors whose works have been recognized by the students of Pennsylvania. Deadline: September 15. Prize: Framed certificate to winning authors. Four awards are given, one for each of the following grade level divisions: K-3, 3-6, 6-8, YA. Judged by children of Pennsylvania (they vote).

PEN/PHYLLIS NAYLOR WORKING WRITER FELLOWSHIP

PEN America, PEN American Center, 588 Broadway, Suite 303, New York NY 10012. **E-mail:** awards@pen.org. **Website:** www.pen.org/awards. **Contact:** Arielle Anema, Literary Awards Coordinator. Offered annually to an author of children's or young-adult fiction. The Fellowship has been developed to help writers whose work is of high literary caliber but who have not yet attracted a broad readership. The Fellowship is designed to assist a writer at a crucial moment in his or her career to complete a book-length work-in-progress. Candidates have published at least one novel for children or young adults which have been received

warmly by literary critics, but have not generated sufficient income to support the author. Writers must be nominated by an editor or fellow author. See website for eligibility and nomination guidelines. Deadline: Submissions open during the summer of each year. Visit PEN.org/awards for up-to-date information on deadlines. Prize: $5,000.

PLEASE TOUCH MUSEUM BOOK AWARD

Memorial Hall in Fairmount Park, 4231 Avenue of the Republic, Philadelphia PA 19131. (215)578-5153. **Fax:** (215)578-5171. **E-mail:** hboyd@pleasetouchmuseum.org. **Website:** www.pleasetouchmuseum.org. **Contact:** Heather Boyd. This prestigious award has recognized and encouraged the publication of high quality books. The award was exclusively created to recognize and encourage the writing of publications that help young children enjoy the process of learning through books, while reflecting PTM's philosophy of learning through play. The awards to to books that are imaginative, exceptionally illustrated, and help foster a child's life-long love of reading. To be eligible for consideration, a book must be distinguished in text, illustration, and ability to explore and clarify an idea for young children (ages 7 and under). Deadline: October 1. Books for each cycle must be published within previous calendar year (September-August). Judged by a panel of volunteer educators, artists, booksellers, children's authors, and librarians in conjunction with museum staff.

POCKETS FICTION-WRITING CONTEST

P.O. Box 340004, Nashville TN 37203-0004. (615)340-7333. **Fax:** (615)340-7267. **E-mail:** pockets@upperroom.org. **Website:** www.pockets.upperroom.org. **Contact:** Lynn W. Gilliam, senior editor. Designed for 6- to 12-year-olds, *Pockets* magazine offers wholesome devotional readings that teach about God's love and presence in life. The content includes fiction, scripture stories, puzzles and games, poems, recipes, colorful pictures, activities, and scripture readings. Freelance submissions of stories, poems, recipes, puzzles and games, and activities are welcome. Stories should be 750-1,000 words. Multiple submissions are permitted. Past winners are ineligible. The primary purpose of *Pockets* is to help children grow in their relationship with God and to claim the good news of the gospel of Jesus Christ by applying it to their daily lives. *Pockets* espouses respect for all human beings and for God's creation. It regards a child's faith journey as an integral part of all of life and sees prayer as undergirding that journey. Deadline: August 15. Submission period begins March 15. Prize: $500 and publication in magazine.

MICHAEL L. PRINTZ AWARD

Young Adult Library Services Association, Division of the American Library Association, 50 E. Huron, Chicago IL 60611. (800)545-2433. **Fax:** (312)280-5276. **E-mail:** yalsa@ala.org. **Website:** www.ala.org/yalsa/printz. **Contact:** Nichole O'Connor, program officer for events and conferences. The Michael L. Printz Award annually honors the best book written for teens, based entirely on its literary merit, each year. In addition, the Printz Committee names up to 4 honor books, which also represent the best writing in young adult literature. The award-winning book can be fiction, nonfiction, poetry or an anthology, and can be a work of joint authorship or editorship. The books must be published between January 1 and December 31 of the preceding year and be designated by its publisher as being either a young adult book or one published for the age range that YALSA defines as young adult, e.g. ages 12 through 18. Deadline: December 1. Judged by an award committee.

PURPLE DRAGONFLY BOOK AWARDS

4696 W. Tyson St., Chandler AZ 85226-2903. (480)940-8182. **Fax:** (480)940-8787. **E-mail:** cristy@fivestarpublications.com; fivestarpublications@gmail.com. **Website:** www.purpledragonflybookawards.com; www.fivestarpublications.com; www.fivestar-bookawards.com. **Contact:** Cristy Bertini, contest coordinator. The Purple Dragonfly Book Awards are designed with children in mind. Awards are divided into 43 distinct subject categories, ranging from books on the environment and cooking to sports and family issues. The Purple Dragonfly Book Awards are geared toward stories that appeal to children of all ages. The awards are open to books published in any calendar year and in any country that are available for purchase. Books entered must be printed in English. Traditionally published, partnership published and self-published books are permitted, as long as they fit the above criteria. Submit materials to: Cristy Bertini, Attn: Five Star Book Awards, 1271 Turkey St., Ware, MA 01082. Deadline: May 1. Prize: Grand Prize winner will receive a $300 cash prize, 100 foil award seals (more can be ordered for an extra charge), 1 hour of marketing consultation from Five Star Publications, and $100 worth of Five Star Publications' titles, as well as publicity on Five Star Publications' websites and inclusion in a winners' news release sent to a comprehensive list of media outlets. The Grand Prize winner will also be placed in the Five Star Dragonfly Book Awards virtual bookstore with a thumbnail of the book's cover, price, 1-sentence description and link to Amazon.com for purchasing purposes, if applicable. 1st Place: All first-place winners of categories will be put into a drawing for a $100 prize. In addition, each first-place winner in each category receives a certificate commemorating their accomplishment, 25 foil award seals (more can be ordered for an extra charge) and mention on Five Star Publications' websites. Judged by industry experts with specific knowledge about the categories over which they preside.

QUILL AND SCROLL WRITING, PHOTO AND MULTIMEDIA CONTEST AND BLOGGING COMPETITION

School of Journalism, Univ. of Iowa, 100 Adler Journalism Bldg., Iowa City IA 52242-2004. (319)335-3457. **Fax:** (319)335-3989. **E-mail:** quill-scroll@uiowa.edu. **E-mail:** vanessa-shelton@uiowa.edu. **Website:** quillandscroll.org. **Contact:** Vanessa Shelton, contest director. Entries must have been published in a high school or profesional newspaper or website during the previous year, and must be the work of a currently enrolled high school student, when published. Open to students. Annual contest. Previously published submissions only. Submissions made by the author or school media adviser. Deadline: February 5. Prize: Winners will receive *Quill and Scroll*'s National Award Gold Key and, if seniors, are eligible to apply for one of the scholarships offered by *Quill and Scroll*. All winning entries are automatically eligible for the International Writing and Photo Sweepstakes Awards. Engraved plaque awarded to sweepstakes winners.

⬤ THE RED HOUSE CHILDREN'S BOOK AWARD

Red House Children's Book Award, 123 Frederick Road, Cheam, Sutton, Surrey SM1 2HT United Kingdom. **E-mail:** info@rhcba.co.uk. **Website:** www.redhouse-childrensbookaward.co.uk. **Contact:** Sinead Kromer, national coordinator. The Red House Children's Book Award is the only national book award that is entirely voted for by children. A shortlist is drawn up from children's nominations and any child can then vote for the winner of the three categories: Books for Younger Children, Books for Younger Readers and Books for Older Readers. The book with the most votes is then crowned the winner of the Red House Children's Book Award. Deadline: December 31.

TOMÁS RIVERA MEXICAN AMERICAN CHILDREN'S BOOK AWARD

Dr. Jesse Gainer, Texas State University, 601 University Drive, San Marcos TX 78666-4613. (512)245-2357. **E-mail:** riverabookaward@txstate.edu. **Website:** www.riverabookaward.org. **Contact:** Dr. Jesse Gainer, award director. Texas State University College of Education developed the Tomas Rivera Mexican American Children's Book Award to honor authors and illustrators who create literature that depicts the Mexican American experience. The award was established in 1995 and was named in honor of Dr. Tomas Rivera, a distinguished alumnus of Texas State University. The book will be written for younger children, ages pre-K to 5th grade (awarded in even years), or older children, ages 6th grade to 12 grade (awarded in odd years). The text and illustrations will be of highest quality. The portrayal/representations of Mexican Americans will be accurate and engaging, avoid stereotypes, and reflect rich characterization. The book may be fiction or non- fiction. See website for more details and directions. Deadline: November 1.

✪ ROCKY MOUNTAIN BOOK AWARD: ALBERTA CHILDREN'S CHOICE BOOK AWARD

Box 42, Lethbridge AB T1J 3Y3 Canada. (403)381-0855. **Website:** http://www.rmba.info. **Contact:** Michelle Dimnik, contest director. Annual contest open to Alberta students. No entry fee. Awards: Gold medal and author tour of selected Alberta schools. Judging by students. Canadian authors and/or illustrators only. Submit entries to Richard Chase. Previously unpublished submissions only. Submissions made by author's agent or nominated by a person or group. Must be published within the 3 years prior to that year's award. Register before January 20th to take part in the Rocky Mountain Book Award. SASE for contest rules and entry forms. Purpose of contest: "Reading motivation for students, promotion of Canadian authors, illustrators and publishers."

SCBWI MAGAZINE MERIT AWARDS

4727 Wilshire Blvd., Suite 301, Los Angeles CA 90010. (323)782-1010. **Fax:** (323)782-1892. **E-mail:** grants@scbwi.org. **Website:** www.scbwi.org. **Contact:** Stepha-nie Gordon, award coordinator. The SCBWI is a professional organization of writers and illustrators and others interested in children's literature. Membership is open to the general public at large. All magazine work for young people by an SCBWI member—writer, artist or photographer—is eligible during the year of original publication. In the case of co-authored work, both authors must be SCBWI members. Members must submit their own work. Requirements for entrants: 4 copies each of the published work and proof of publication (may be contents page) showing the name of the magazine and the date of issue. Previously published submissions only. For rules and procedures see website. Must be a SCBWI member. Recognizes outstanding original magazine work for young people published during that year, and having been written or illustrated by members of SCBWI. Deadline: December 15 of the year of publication. Submission period begins January 1. Prize: Awards plaques and honor certificates for each of 4 categories (fiction, nonfiction, illustration and poetry). Judged by a magazine editor and two "full" SCBWI members.

SCBWI WORK-IN-PROGRESS GRANTS

8271 Beverly Blvd., Los Angeles CA 90048. (323)782-1010. **Fax:** (323)782-1892. **E-mail:** grants@scbwi.org. **E-mail:** wipgrant@scbwi.org. **Website:** www.scbwi.org. The SCBWI Work-in-Progress Grants have been established to assist children's book writers in the completion of a specific project. Five categories: Picture Book Text, Chapter Books/Early Readers, Middle Grade, Young Adult Fiction, Nonfiction, and Multi-Cultural Fiction or Nonfiction. SASE for applications for grants. The grants are available to both full and associate members of the SCBWI. They are not available for projects on which there are already contracts. Previous recipients not eligible to apply. Deadline: March 31. Submission period begins March 1.

SYDNEY TAYLOR BOOK AWARD

Association of Jewish Libraries, P.O. Box 1118, Teaneck NJ 07666. (212)725-5359. **E-mail:** chair@sydneytaylorbookaward.org; Ellen.tilman@gmail.com. **Website:** www.sydneytaylorbookaward.org. **Contact:** Ellen Tilman, chair. The Sydney Taylor Book Award is presented annually to outstanding books for children and teens that authentically portray the Jewish experience. Deadline: November 30. Cannot guarantee that books received after November 30 will be considered. Prize: Gold medals are presented in 3 categories: younger readers, older readers, and teen readers. Honor books are awarded in silver medals, and notable books are named in each category.

SYDNEY TAYLOR MANUSCRIPT COMPETITION

Association of Jewish Libraries, Sydney Taylor Manuscript Award Competition, 204 Park St., Montclair NJ 07042-2903. **E-mail:** stmacajl@aol.com. **Website:** www.jewishlibraries.org/main/Awards/SydneyTaylorManuscriptAward.aspx. **Contact:** Aileen Grossberg. This competition is for unpublished writers of fiction. Material should be for readers ages 8-13, with universal appeal that will serve to deepen the understanding of Judaism for all children, revealing positive aspects of Jewish life. Download rules and forms from website. Must be an unpublished fiction writer or a student; also, books must range from 64-200 pages in length. "AJL assumes no responsibility for publication, but hopes this cash incentive will serve to encourage new writers of children's stories with Jewish themes for all children." To encourage new fiction of Jewish interest for readers ages 8-13. Deadline: September 30. Prize: $1,000. Judging by qualified judges from within the Association of Jewish Libraries.

◷ TD CANADIAN CHILDREN'S LITERATURE AWARD

The Canadian Children's Book Centre, 40 Orchard View Blvd., Suite 217, Toronto ON M4R 1B9 Canada. (416)975-0010, ext. 222. **Fax:** (416)975-8970. **E-mail:** meghan@bookcentre.ca. **Website:** www.bookcentre.ca. **Contact:** Meghan Howe. The TD Canadian Children's Literature Award is for the most distinguished book of the year. All books, in any genre, written and illustrated by Canadians and for children ages 1-12 are eligible. Only books first published in Canada are eligible for submission. Books must be published between January 1 and December 31 of the previous calendar year. Open to Canadian citizens and/or permanent residents of Canada. Deadline: mid-December. Prizes: Two prizes of $30,000, 1 for English, 1 for French. $20,000 will be divided among the Honour Book English titles and Honour Book French titles, to a maximum of 4; $2,500 shall go to each of the publishers of the English and French grand-prize winning books for promotion and publicity.

VEGETARIAN ESSAY CONTEST

The Vegetarian Resource Group, P.O. Box 1463, Baltimore MD 21203. (410)366-VEGE. **Fax:** (410)366-8804. **E-mail:** vrg@vrg.org. **Website:** www.vrg.org. Write a 2-3 page essay on any aspect of vegetarianism. Entrants should base their paper on interviewing, research, and/or personal opinion. You need not be a vegetarian to enter. Three different entry categories: age 14-18; age 9-13; and age 8 and under. Prize: $50.

LAURA INGALLS WILDER MEDAL

50 E. Huron, Chicago IL 60611. (800)545-2433. **E-mail:** alscawards@ala.org. **Website:** www.ala.org/alsc/awardsgrants/bookmedia/wildermedal. Award offered every 2 years. The Wilder Award honors an author or illustrator whose books, published in the US, have made, over a period of years, a substantial and lasting contribution to literature for children. The candidates must be nominated by ALSC members. Medal presented at Newbery/Caldecott banquet during annual conference. Judging by Wilder Award Selection Committee.

RITA WILLIAMS YOUNG ADULT PROSE PRIZE CATEGORY

Soul-Making Keats Literary Competition, The Webhallow House, 1544 Sweetwood Drive, Broadmoor Village CA 94015-2029. **E-mail:** SoulKeats@mail.com. **Website:** www.soulmakingcontest.us. **Contact:** Eileen Malone. For writers in grades 9-12 or equivalent age. Up to 3,000 words in prose form of choice. Complete rules and guidelines available online. Deadline: November 30 (postmarked). Prize: $100 for first place; $50 for second place; $25 for third place. Judged (and sponsored) by Rita Wiliams, an Emmy-award winning investigative reporter with KTVU-TV in Oakland, California.

TIPS "This contest is for young adult writers, high school age writers; no adults writing for children."

PAUL A. WITTY OUTSTANDING LITERATURE AWARD

P.O. Box 8139, Newark DE 19714-8139. (800)336-7323. **Fax:** (302)731-1057. **Website:** www.reading.org. **Contact:** Marcie Craig Post, executive director. This award recognizes excellence in original poetry or prose written by students. Elementary and secondary students whose work is selected will receive an award. Deadline: February 2. Prize: Not less than $25 and a citation of merit.

WORK-IN-PROGRESS GRANT

Society of Children's Book Writers and Illustrators (SCBWI), 8271 Beverly Blvd., Los Angeles CA 90048. (323)782-1010. **E-mail:** grants@scbwi.org; wipgrant@scbwi.org. **Website:** www.scbwi.org. Four grants—

one designated specifically for a contemporary novel for young people, one for nonfiction, one for an unpublished writer, one general fiction—to assist SCBWI members in the completion of a specific project. Open to SCBWI members only. Deadline: March 31. Open to submissions on March 1.

THE YOUNG ADULT FICTION PRIZE

Victorian Premier's Literary Awards, State Government of Victoria, The Wheeler Centre, 176 Little Lonsdale Street, Melbourne VIC 3000 Australia. (61)(3)90947800. **E-mail:** vpla@wheelercentre.com. **Website:** http://www.wheelercentre.com/projects/victorian-premier-s-literary-awards-2016/about-the-awards. **Contact:** Project Officer. Prize: $25,000.

YOUNG READER'S CHOICE AWARD

Paxson Elementary School, 101 Evans, Missoula MT 59801. **E-mail:** hbray@missoula.lib.mt.us. **Website:** www.pnla.org. **Contact:** Honore Bray, president. The Pacific Northwest Library Association's Young Reader's Choice Award is the oldest children's choice award in the U.S. and Canada. Nominations are taken only from children, teachers, parents and librarians in the Pacific Northwest: Alaska, Alberta, British Columbia, Idaho, Montana and Washington. Nominations will not be accepted from publishers. Nominations may include fiction, nonfiction, graphic novels, anime, and manga. Nominated titles are those published 3 years prior to the award year. Deadline: February 1. Books will be judged on popularity with readers. Age appropriateness will be considered when choosing which of the three divisions a book is placed. Other considerations may include reading enjoyment; reading level; interest level; genre representation; gender representation; racial diversity; diversity of social, political, economic, or religions viewpoints; regional consideration; effectiveness of expression; and imagination. The Pacific Northwest Library Association is committed to intellectual freedom and diversity of ideas. No title will be excluded because of race, nationality, religion, gender, sexual orientation, political or social view of either the author or the material.

GENERAL

ALCUIN SOCIETY BOOK DESIGN AWARDS

P.O. Box 3216, Vancouver BC V6B 3X8 Canada. (604)732-5403. **E-mail:** awards@alcuinsociety.com; info@alcuinsociety.com. **Website:** www.alcuinsociety.com. **Contact:** Leah Gordon. The Alcuin Society Awards for Excellence in Book Design in Canada is the only national competition for book design in Canada. Winners are selected from books designed and published in Canada. Awards are presented annually at appropriate ceremonies held in each year. Winning books are exhibited nationally and internationally at the Tokyo, Frankfurt, and Leipzig Book Fairs, and are Canada's entries in the international competition in Leipzig, "Book Design from all over the World" in the following spring. Submit previously published material from the year before the award's call for entries. Submissions made by the publisher, author or designer (Canadian). Deadline: March 1. Prizes: 1st, 2nd, and 3rd in each category (at the discretion of the judges). Judged by professionals and those experienced in the field of book design.

AUSTRALIAN CHRISTIAN BOOK OF THE YEAR AWARD

SparkLit, PO Box 198, Forest Hill Victoria 3131 Australia. **E-mail:** admin@sparklit.org. **E-mail:** admin@sparklit.org. **Website:** www.sparklit.org. **Contact:** The Awards Coordinator. SparkLit advances God's kingdom by empowering Christian writers and publishers. (Formerly the Society for Promoting Christian Knowledge Australia and the Australian Christian Literature Society.) The Australian Christian Book of the Year Award is given annually to an original book written by an Australian citizen normally resident in Australia. A short list is released in July. The results are announced and prizes are presented in August. The award recognizes and encourages excellence in Australian Christian writing. Deadline: March 31. Prize: $3,000 (AUD), a framed certificate and extensive promotion.

JAMIE CAT CALLAN HUMOR PRIZE

Category in the Soul-Making Keats Literary Competition, The Webhallow House, 1544 Sweetwood Dr., Broadmoor Village CA 94015-2029. **E-mail:** SoulKeats@mail.com. **Website:** www.soulmakingcontest.us. **Contact:** Eileen Malone. Any form, 2,500 words or less. One piece per entry. Previously published material is accepted. Open annually to any writer. Deadline: November 30. Prize: First Place: $100; Second Place: $50; Third Place: $25. Judged by Jamie Cat Callan.

DON FREEMAN ILLUSTRATOR GRANTS

4727 Wilshire Blvd Suite 301, Los Angeles CA 90010. (323)782-1010. **Fax:** (323)782-1892. **E-mail:** grants@scbwi.org; sarahbaker@scbwi.org. **Website:** www.scbwi.org. **Contact:** Sarah Baker. The grant-in-aid is available to both full and associate members of the SCBWI who, as artists, seriously intend to make picture books their chief contribution to the field of children's literature. Applications and prepared materials are available in October. Grant awarded and announced in August. SASE for award rules and entry forms. SASE for return of entries. Enables picture book artists to further their understanding, training, and work in the picture book genre. Deadline: March 31. Submission period begins March 1. Prize: Two grants of $1,000 each awarded annually. One grant to a published illustrator and one to a pre-published illustrator.

THE GLENNA LUSCHEI PRAIRIE SCHOONER AWARDS

Prairie Schooner, 123 Andrews Hall, P.O. Box 880334, Lincoln NE 68588-0334. (402)472-0911. **Fax:** (402)472-1817. **E-mail:** prairieschooner@unl.edu; psbookprize@unl.edu. **Website:** http://prairieschooner.unl.edu/. **Contact:** Kwame Dawes. Annual awards for work published in *Prairie Schooner* in the previous year. Offers one large prize and 10 smaller awards. See website for more details. Contact *Prairie Schooner* for further information. Prize: One award of $1,500 and 10 awards of $250 each.

◎ INSCRIBE CONTESTS

InScribe Christian Writers' Fellowship, PO Box 99509, Edmonton AB T5B 0E1 Canada. **E-mail:** fellowscripteditor@gmail.com. **Website:** www.inscribe.org. **Contact:** Contest Director. Check Website www.inscribe.org for updated details. Contest details are included in *Fellowscipt* magazine. Deadline: Contests offered twice per year. See website for details. Prize: 1st Place: $100; 2nd Place: $50; 3rd Place: $30. InScribe reserves the right to publish winning entries in its magazine, *FellowScript*, and/or on its website Judged by a different judge for each category. All judging is blind.

DOROTHEA LANGE–PAUL TAYLOR PRIZE

Center for Documentary Studies, 1317 W. Pettigrew St., Duke University, Durham NC 27705. (919)660-3685. **Fax:** (919)681-7600. **E-mail:** caitlin.johnson@duke.edu; docstudies@duke.edu. **Website:** http://documentarystudies.duke.edu/awards/dorothea-lange-paul-taylor-prize. **Contact:** Caitlin Johnson. Award from the Center for Documentary Studies at Duke University, supporting documentary artists, working alone or in teams, who are involved in extended, on-going fieldwork projects that rely on and exploit the interplay of words and images. More information available at documentarystudies.duke.edu/awards. First announced a year after the Center for Documentary Studies' founding at Duke University, the prize was created to encourage a collaboration between documentary writers and photographers in the tradition of the acclaimed photographer Dorothea Lange and writer and social scientist Paul Taylor. Deadline: May 9. Submissions accepted starting in February. Prize: The winner receives $10,000, features in Center for Documentary Studies' print and digital publications, and inclusion in the Archive of Documentary Arts at Rubenstein Library, Duke University.

MCLAREN MEMORIAL COMEDY PLAY WRITING COMPETITION

Midland Community Theatre, 2000 W. Wadley, Midland TX 79705. (432)682-2544. **Fax:** (432)682-6136. **Website:** www.mctmidland.org. **Contact:** McLaren Chair. The McLaren Memorial Comedy Play Writing Competition was established to honor long-time MCT volunteer Mike McLaren who loved a good comedy, whether he was on stage or in the front row. Open to students. Annual contest. Unpublished submissions only. Submissions made by author. Rights to winning material acquired or purchased. First right of production or refusal is acquired by MCT. The contest is open to any playwright, but the play submitted must be unpublished and never produced in a for-profit setting. One previous production in a nonprofit theatre is acceptable. "Readings" do not count as productions. Deadline: January 31. Prize: $400. Judged by the audience present at the McLaren Festival when the staged readings are performed.

MLA PRIZE IN UNITED STATES LATINA & LATINO AND CHICANA & CHICANO LITERARY AND CULTURAL STUDIES

Modern Language Association of America, 85 Broad Street, suite 500, New York NY 10004-2434. (646)576-5141. **Fax:** (646)458-0030. **E-mail:** awards@mla.org. **Website:** www.mla.org. **Contact:** Coordinator of Book Prizes. Offered in odd-numbered years for an outstanding scholarly study in any language of United States Latina and Latino or Chicana and Chicano literature or culture. Books must have been published in the two previous years before the award. Authors must be current members of the MLA. Requires 4 copies of the book. Deadline: May 1. Prize: A cash award, and a certificate to be presented at the Modern Language Association's annual convention in January.

NACUSA YOUNG COMPOSERS' COMPETITION

Box 49256 Barrington Station, Los Angeles CA 90049. (541)765-2406. **E-mail:** nacusa@music-usa.org; membership@mail.music-usa.org. **Website:** http://music-usa.org. **Contact:** John Winsor webmaster@music-usa.org. Applications online. Must be a paid member of NACUSA. The competition is open to all NACUSA members who are American citizens or residents, who have reached their 18th birthday but have not yet reached there 32nd birthday by the submission deadline. Encourages the composition of new American concert hall music. Deadline: December 15. Prize: All prizes come with a possible performance on a NACUSA National concert. First Prize is $400; Second Prize is $300; Third Prize is $200.

NORTH AMERICAN INTERNATIONAL AUTO SHOW HIGH SCHOOL POSTER CONTEST

Detroit Auto Dealers Association, 1900 W. Big Beaver Rd., Troy MI 48084-3531 USA. (248)643-0250. **Fax:** (248)283-5148. **E-mail:** sherp@dada.org. **Website:** www.naias.com. **Contact:** Sandy Herp. Open to students. Annual contest. Submissions made by the author and illustrator. Entrants must be Michigan high school students enrolled in grades 10-12. Winning posters may be displayed at the NAIAS and reproduced in the official NAIAS program, which is available to the public, international media, corporate executives and automotive suppliers. Winning posters may also be displayed on the official NAIAS website at the sole discretion of the NAIAS. Contact Detroit Auto Dealers Association (DADA) for contest rules and entry forms or retrieve rules from website. Deadline: November. Prize: Chairman's Award: $1,000; State Farm Insurance Award: $1,000; Designer's Best of Show (Digital and Traditional): $500; Best Theme: $250; Best Use of Color: $250; Most Creative: $250. A winner will be chosen in each category from grades 10, 11 and 12. Prizes: 1st place in 10, 11, 12: $500; 2nd place: $250; 3rd place: $100. Judged by an independent panel of recognized representatives of the art community.

OHIOANA WALTER RUMSEY MARVIN GRANT

Ohioana Library Association, 274 E. First Ave., Suite 300, Columbus OH 43201. (614)466-3831. **Fax:** (614)728-6974. **E-mail:** ohioana@ohioana.org. **Website:** www.ohioana.org. **Contact:** David Weaver, executive director. Open to unpublished authors born in Ohio or who have lived in Ohio for a minimum of 5 years. Must be 30 years of age or younger. Guidelines for SASE or on website. Winner notified in early summer. Up to 6 pieces of prose may be submitted; maximum 60 pages, minimum 10 pages double-spaced, 12-point type. Entries must be unpublished. Award to encourage young, unpublished writers 30 years of age or younger. Competition for short stories or novels in progress. Deadline: January 31. Prize: $1,000.

DAVID RAFFELOCK AWARD FOR PUBLISHING EXCELLENCE

National Writers Association, 10940 S. Parker Rd., #508, Parker CO 80134. (303)841-0246. **E-mail:** natlwritersassn@hotmail.com. **Website:** www.nationalwriters.com. **Contact:** Sandy Whelchel. Contest is offered annually for books published the previous year. Published works only. Open to any writer. Guidelines for SASE, by e-mail, or on website. Winners will be notified by mail or phone. List of winners available for SASE or visit website. Purpose is to assist published authors in marketing their works and to reward outstanding published works. Deadline: May 15. Prize: Publicity tour, including airfare, valued at $5,000.

RAMIREZ FAMILY AWARD FOR MOST SIGNIFICANT SCHOLARLY BOOK

The Texas Institute of Letters, P.O. Box 609, Round Rock TX 78680. **E-mail:** tilsecretary@yahoo.com. **Website:** http://texasinstituteofletters.org. Offered annually for submissions published January 1-December 31 of previous year to recognize the writer of the book making the most important contribution to knowledge. Writer must have been born in Texas, have lived in the state at least 2 consecutive years at some time, or the subject matter of the book should be associated with the state. See website for guidelines. Deadline: Visit website for exact date. Prize: $2,500.

THE SCARS EDITOR'S CHOICE AWARDS

E-mail: editor@scars.tv. **Website:** http://scars.tv. **Contact:** Janet Kuypers, editor/publisher (whom all reading fee checks need to be made out to). Award to showcase good writing in an annual book. Categories: short stories, poetry. Entries may be unpublished or previously published, as long as you retain the rights to your work. Open to any writer. For guidelines, visit website. Accepts inquiries by e-mail. E-mail is always preferred for inquiries and submissions. ("If you have access to e-mail, we will request that you e-mail your contest submission, and we will hold it until we receive the reading fee payment for the submission.") Length: "We appreciate shorter works. Shorter stories, more vivid and more real storylines in writing have a good chance." Results announced at book publication, online. Winners notified by mail when book is printed. For contest results, send SASE or e-mail or look at the contest page at website. Prize: Publication of story/essay and 1 copy of the book.

BYRON CALDWELL SMITH BOOK AWARD

The University of Kansas, Hall Center for the Humanities, 900 Sunnyside Ave., Lawrence KS 66045. (785)864-4798. **E-mail:** vbailey@ku.edu. **Website:** www.hallcenter.ku.edu. **Contact:** Victor Bailey, director. Offered in odd years. To qualify, applicants must live or be employed in Kansas and have written an outstanding book published within the previous 2 calendar years. Translations are eligible. Guidelines for SASE or online. Deadline: March 1. Prize: $1,500.

❁❁ FRED WHITEHEAD AWARD FOR DESIGN OF A TRADE BOOK

Texas Institute of Letters, P.O. Box 609, Round Rock TX 78680. **E-mail:** tilsecretary@yahoo.com. **Website:** www.texasinstituteofletters.org. Offered annually for the best design for a trade book. Open to Texas residents or those who have lived in Texas for 2 consecutive years. See website for guidelines. Deadline: early January; see website for exact date. Prize: $750.

❂ THE WRITERS' TRUST ENGEL/FINDLEY AWARD

The Writers' Trust of Canada, 460 Richmond St. W., Suite 600, Toronto ON M5V 1Y1 Canada. (416)504-8222. **Fax:** (416)504-9090. **E-mail:** info@writerstrust.com. **Website:** www.writerstrust.com. **Contact:** Amanda Hopkins. The Writers' Trust Engel/Findley Award is presented annually at The Writers' Trust Awards Event, held in Toronto each fall, to a Canadian writer for a body of work in hope of continued contribution to the richness of Canadian literature. Open to Canadian citizens and permanent residents only. Prize: $25,000.

JOURNALISM

AAAS KAVLI SCIENCE JOURNALISM AWARDS

American Association for the Advancement of Science, AAAS Office of Public Programs, 1200 New York Ave. NW, Washington DC 20005. **E-mail:** sja@aaas.org. **Website:** www.aaas.org/SJAwards. **Contact:** Awards Coordinator. The AAAS Kavli Science Journalism Awards represent the pinnacle of achievement for professional journalists in the science writing field. The awards recognize outstanding reporting worldwide for a general audience and honor individuals (rather than institutions, publishers or employers) for their coverage of the sciences, engineering, and mathematics. Entries are submitted online only at https://sjawards.aaas.org. See website for guidelines and details. Deadline: August 1. Prize: $5,000 and $3,000 awards in each category; award includes travel expenses to AAAS Annual Meeting for awards ceremony. Judged by committees of reporters and editors.

THE AMERICAN LEGION FOURTH ESTATE AWARD

The American Legion, The American Legion, 700 N. Pennsylvania St., Indianapolis IN 46204. (317)630-1253. **E-mail:** pr@legion.org. **Website:** www.legion.org/presscenter/fourthestate. Offered annually for journalistic works published the previous calendar year. Subject matter must deal with a topic or issue of national interest or concern. Entry must include cover letter explaining entry, and any documentation or evidence of the entry's impact on the community, state, or nation. No printed entry form. Guidelines available by SASE or online. Deadline: March 31. Prize: $2,000 stipend to defray expenses of recipient accepting the award at The American Legion National Convention in August/September. Judged by members of the Media & Communications Commission of The American Legion.

❂ ATLANTIC JOURNALISM AWARDS

46 Swanton Dr., Dartmouth NS B2W2C5 Canada. (902)478-6026. **Fax:** (902)462-1892. **E-mail:** office@

ajas.ca. **Website:** ajas.ca. **Contact:** Bill Skerrett, executive director. Offered annually to recognize excellence and achievement by journalists in print and electronic news media in Atlantic Canada. Guidelines and entry forms available via mail request, or website (download entry form). Entries are usually nominated by editors, news directors, etc. Freelancers are eligible to enter. The competition is open to any journalist living in Atlantic Canada whose entry was originally published or broadcast during the previous year in Atlantic Canada. Deadline: January 31. Prize: A plaque presented at an awards dinner.

INVESTIGATIVE JOURNALISM GRANT

Fund For Investigative Journalism, Fund for Investigative Journalism, 529 14th Street NW, 13th Floor, Washington DC 20045. (202)662-7564. **E-mail:** fundfij@gmail.com. **Website:** www.fij.org. **Contact:** Sandy Bergo, executive director. Offered 3 times/year for original investigative print, online, radio, and TV stories and books. Guidelines online. See website for details on applying for a grant. Deadlines: Vary. Check website. Grants of $500-10,000. (Typical grant: $5,000.)

FRANK LUTHER MOTT-KAPPA TAU ALPHA RESEARCH AWARD IN JOURNALISM

University of Missouri School of Journalism, 76 Gannett Hall, Columbia MO 65211-1200. (573)882-7685. **E-mail:** umcjourkta@missouri.edu. **Website:** www.kappataualpha.org. **Contact:** Dr. Keith Sanders, exec. dir., Kappa Tau Alpha. Offered annually for best researched book in mass communication. Submit 6 copies; no forms required. Deadline: December 9. Prize: $1,000. Judged by a panel of university professors of journalism and mass communication and national officers of Kappa Tau Alpha.

☼ NATIONAL MAGAZINE AWARDS

National Magazine Awards Foundation, 2300 Yonge St., Suite 1600, Toronto ON M4P 1E4 Canada. (416) 939-6200. **E-mail:** staff@magazine-awards.com. **E-mail:** staff@magazine-awards.com. **Website:** www.magazine-awards.com. **Contact:** Barbara Gould. The National Magazine Awards Foundation is a bilingual, not-for-profit institution whose mission is to recognize and promote excellence in the content and creation of Canadian print and digital publications through an annual program of awards and national publicity efforts. Deadline: January 15. Cash prizes

for winners. Certificates and seals for all finalists and winners. Judged by 200+ peer judges from the Canadian magazine industry.

☼ SANOFI PASTEUR MEDAL FOR EXCELLENCE IN HEALTH RESEARCH JOURNALISM

Canadians for Health Research, P.O. Box 126, Westmount QC H3Z 2T1 Canada. (514)398-7478. **Fax:** (514)398-8361. **E-mail:** info@chrcrm.org. **Website:** www.chrcrm.org. Offered annually for work published the previous calendar year in Canadian newspapers or magazines. Applicants must have demonstrated an interest and effort in reporting health research issues within Canada. Guidelines available on website. Deadline: April 1 (postmarked). Prize: $2,500 bursary and a medal.

SCIENCE IN SOCIETY AWARDS

National Association of Science Writers, Inc., P.O. Box 7905, Berkeley CA 94707. (510)647-9500. **E-mail:** director@nasw.org. **Website:** www.nasw.org. **Contact:** Tinsley Davis. Offered annually for investigative or interpretive reporting about the sciences and their impact on society. Categories: books, commentary and opinions, science reporting, longform science reporting, and science reporting for a local or regional market. Material may be a single article or broadcast, or a series. Works must have been first published or broadcast in North America between January 1 and December 31 of the previous year. Deadline: February 1. Prize: $2,500, and a certificate of recognition in each category.

☼ SOVEREIGN AWARD

The Jockey Club of Canada, P.O. Box 66, Station B, Etobicoke ON M9W 5K9 Canada. (416)675-7756. **Fax:** (416)675-6378. **E-mail:** jockeyclub@bellnet.ca. **Website:** www.jockeyclubcanada.com. **Contact:** Stacie Roberts, exec. dir.. The Jockey Club of Canada was founded in 1973 by E.P. Taylor to serve as the international representative of the Canadian Thoroughbred industry and to promote improvements to Thoroughbred racing and breeding, both in Canada and internationally. Submissions for these media awards must be of Canadian Thoroughbred racing or breeding content. They must have appeared in a media outlet recognized by The Jockey Club of Canada. See website for eligibility details and guidelines. Deadline: December 31.

TRANSLATION

AMERICAN-SCANDINAVIAN FOUNDATION TRANSLATION PRIZE

The American-Scandinavian Foundation, 58 Park Ave., New York NY 10016. (212)779-3587. **E-mail:** grants@amscan.org; info@amscan.org. **Website:** www.amscan.org. **Contact:** Matthew Walters, director of fellowships & grants. The annual ASF translation competition is awarded for the most outstanding translations of poetry, fiction, drama, or literary prose written by a Scandinavian author born after 1800. Accepts inquiries by e-mail, or through online application. Instructions an application available online. Entries must be unpublished. Length: No more than 50 pages for drama and fiction; no more than 25 pages for poetry. Open to any writer. Results announced in November. Winners notified by e-mail. Results available on the ASF website. Guidelines available online. Deadline: June 1. Prize: The Nadia Christensen Prize includes a $2,500 award, publication of an excerpt in *Scandinavian Review*, and a commemorative bronze medallion; The Leif and Inger Sjöberg Award, given to an individual whose literature translations have not previously been published, includes a $2,000 award, publication of an excerpt in *Scandinavian Review*, and a commemorative bronze medallion.

DER-HOVANESSIAN PRIZE

New England Poetry Club, 376 School St., Watertown MA 02472. **E-mail:** contests@nepoetryclub.org. **Website:** www.nepoetryclub.org. **Contact:** Audrey Kalajin. For a translation from any language into English. Send a copy of the original. Funded by John Mahtesian. Contest open to members and nonmembers. Poems should be typed and submitted in duplicate with author's name, address, phone, and e-mail address of writer on only 1 copy. Label poems with contest name. Entries should be sent by regular mail only. Entries should be original, unpublished poems in English. No poem should be entered in more than 1 contest, nor have won a previous contest. Deadline: May 31. Prize: $200. Judges are well-known poets and sometimes winners of previous NEPC contests.

SOEURETTE DIEHL FRASER AWARD FOR BEST TRANSLATION OF A BOOK

P.O. Box 609, Round Rock TX 78680. **E-mail:** tilsecretary@yahoo.com. **Website:** http://texasinstituteoflet-ters.org. Offered every 2 years to recognize the best translation of a literary book into English. Translator must have been born in Texas or have lived in the state for at least 2 consecutive years at some time. Check website for guidelines and instructions on submitting. Deadline: January 10. Prize: $1,000.

JOHN GLASSCO TRANSLATION PRIZE

Literary Translators' Association of Canada, 615-01 Concordia University, 1455 boul. de Maisonneuve Ouest, Montréal QC H3G 1M8 Canada. (514)848-2424, ext. 8702. **E-mail:** info@attlc-ltac.org. **Website:** http://attlc-ltac.org/john-glassco-translation-prize. **Contact:** Glassco Prize Committee. Offered annually for a translator's first book-length literary translation into French or English, published in Canada during the previous calendar year. The translator must be a Canadian citizen or permanent resident. Eligible genres include fiction, creative nonfiction, poetry, and children's books. Deadline: July 31. Prize: $1,000.

THE HAROLD MORTON LANDON TRANSLATION AWARD

Academy of American Poets, 75 Maiden Lane, Suite 901, New York NY 10038. (212)274-0343. **Fax:** (212)274-9427. **E-mail:** awards@poets.org. **Website:** www.poets.org. **Contact:** Awards Coordinator. This annual award recognizes a poetry collection translated from any language into English and published in the previous calendar year. A noted translator chooses the winning book. Deadline: February 15. Prize: $1,000.

FENIA AND YAAKOV LEVIANT MEMORIAL PRIZE IN YIDDISH STUDIES

Modern Language Association of America, 85 Broad Street, suite 500, New York NY 10004-2434. (646)576-5141. **Fax:** (646)458-0030. **E-mail:** awards@mla.org. **Website:** www.mla.org. **Contact:** Coordinator of book prizes. Offered in even-numbered years for an outstanding English translation of a Yiddish literary work or the publication of a scholarly work. Cultural studies, critical biographies, or edited works in the field of Yiddish folklore or linguistic studies are eligible to compete. See website for details on which they are accepting. Books must have been published within the past 4 years. Authors need not be members of the MLA. Requires 4 copies of the book. Deadline: May 1. Prize: A cash prize, and a certificate, to be presented at the Modern Language Association's annual convention in January.

🐟 MARSH AWARD FOR CHILDREN'S LITERATURE IN TRANSLATION

The English-Speaking Union, Dartmouth House, 37 Charles St., London En W1J 5ED United Kingdom. 020 7529 1590. **E-mail:** emma.coffey@esu.org. **Website:** www.marshchristiantrust.org; www.esu.org. **Contact:** Emma Coffey, education officer. The Marsh Award for Children's Literature in Translation, awarded biennially, was founded to celebrate the best translation of a children's book from a foreign language into English and published in the UK. It aims to spotlight the high quality and diversity of translated fiction for young readers. The Award is administered by the ESU on behalf of the Marsh Christian Trust. Submissions will be accepted from publishers for books produced for readers from 5 to 16 years of age. Guidelines and eligibility criteria available online.

PEN AWARD FOR POETRY IN TRANSLATION

PEN America, 588 Broadway, Suite 303, New York NY 10012. **E-mail:** awards@pen.org. **Website:** www.pen.org/awards. **Contact:** Arielle Anema. This award recognizes book-length translations of poetry from any language into English, published during the current calendar year. All books must have been published in the US. Translators may be of any nationality. US residency/citizenship not required. Submissions must be made publishers or literary agents. Self-published books are not eligible. Books with more than 2 translators are not eligible. Re-translations are ineligible, unless the work can be said to provide a significant revision of the original translation. Deadline: Submissions are accepted during the summer of each year. Visit PEN.org/awards for updated on deadline dates. Prize: $3,000. Judged by a single translator of poetry appointed by the PEN Translation Committee.

PEN TRANSLATION PRIZE

PEN America, 588 Broadway, Suite 303, New York NY 10012. **E-mail:** awards@pen.org. **Contact:** Arielle Anema, Literary Awards Coordinator. *PEN will only accept submissions from publishers or literary agents.* This award is offered for book-length translations from any language into English, published during the current calendar year. No technical, scientific, or bibliographic translations. Self-published books are not eligible. Although all eligible books must have been published in the United States, translators may be of any nationality; US residency or citizenship is not required. PEN will only accept submissions from publishers or literary agents. Deadline: Submissions will be accepted during the summer of each year. Visit PEN.org/awards for up-to-date information on deadlines. Prize: $3,000. Judged by three to five translators and/or writers selected by the PEN Translation Committee.

LOIS ROTH AWARD

Modern Language Association, 85 Broad Street, suite 500, New York NY 10004-2434. (646)576-5141. **Fax:** (646)458-0030. **E-mail:** awards@mla.org. **Website:** www.mla.org. Offered in odd-numbered years for an outstanding translation into English of a book-length literary work. Translators need not be members of the MLA. Translations must have been published in the previous calendar year. Requires 6 copies, plus 12-15 pages of text in the original language. Deadline: April 1. Prize: A cash award and a certificate to be presented at the Modern Language Association's annual convention in January.

ALDO AND JEANNE SCAGLIONE PRIZE FOR A TRANSLATION OF A LITERARY WORK

Modern Language Association, 85 Broad Street, suite 500, New York NY 10004-2434. (646)576-5141. **Fax:** (646)458-0030. **E-mail:** awards@mla.org. **Website:** www.mla.org. **Contact:** Coordinator of Book Prizes. Offered in even-numbered years for an outstanding translation into English of a book-length literary work. Translations must have been published in the previous calendar year. Translators need not be members of the MLA. Requires 6 copies of the book, plus 12-15 pages of text in the original language. Deadline: April 1. Prize: A cash award and a certificate to be presented at the Modern Language Association's annual convention in January.

ALDO AND JEANNE SCAGLIONE PRIZE FOR A TRANSLATION OF A SCHOLARLY STUDY OF LITERATURE

Modern Language Association of America, 85 Broad Street, Suite 500, New York NY 10004-2434. (646)576-5141. **Fax:** (646)458-0030. **E-mail:** awards@mla.org. **Website:** www.mla.org. **Contact:** Coordinator of Book Prizes. Offered in odd-numbered years for an outstanding translation into English of a book-length work of literary history, literary criticism, philology, or literary theory. Translators need not be members of the MLA. Books must have been published in the previous 2 years. Requires 4 copies of the book. Deadline: May 1. Prize: A cash award and a certificate to be presented at the Modern Language Association's annual convention in January.

ALDO AND JEANNE SCAGLIONE PRIZE FOR STUDIES IN SLAVIC LANGUAGES AND LITERATURES

Modern Language Association of America, 85 Broad Street, Suite 500, New York NY 10004-2434. (646)576-5141. **Fax:** (646)458-0030. **E-mail:** awards@mla.org. **Website:** www.mla.org. **Contact:** Coordinator of Book Prizes. Offered in odd-numbered years for an outstanding work on the linguistics or literatures of the Slavic languages. Books must have been published in the previous 2 years. Requires 4 copies of the book. Authors need not be members of the MLA. Deadline: May 1. Prize: A cash award and a certificate to be presented at the Modern Language Association's annual convention in January.

POETRY

49TH PARALLEL AWARD FOR POETRY

Western Washington University, Mail Stop 9053, Bellingham WA 98225. (360)650-4863. **E-mail:** bellingham.review@wwu.edu. **Website:** www.bhreview.org. **Contact:** Susanne Paola Antonetta, editor-in-chief; Louis McLaughlin, managing editor. Annual poetry contest, supported by the *Bellingham Review*, given for a poem or group of poems of any style or length. Upload entries via Submittable online. Up to 3 poems per entry. Deadline: March 15. Submissions period begins December 1. Prize: $1,000.

⊙ J.M. ABRAHAM POETRY PRIZE

Writers' Federation of Nova Scotia, 1113 Marginal Rd., Halifax NS B3H 4P7 Canada. (902)423-8116. **Fax:** (902)422-0881. **E-mail:** director@writers.ns.ca. **Website:** www.writers.ns.ca. The J.M. Abraham Poetry Prize is an annual award designed to honor the best book of poetry by a resident of Atlantic Canada. Formerly known as the Atlantic Poetry Prize. Detailed guidelines and eligibility criteria available online. Deadline: First Friday in December. Prize: Valued at $2,000 for the winning title.

AKRON POETRY PRIZE

The University of Akron Press, 120 E. Mill St., Suite 415, Akron OH 44308. **E-mail:** uapress@uakron.edu. **Website:** www.uakron.edu/uapress/akron-poetry-prize/. **Contact:** Mary Biddinger, editor/award director. Submissions must be unpublished. Considers simultaneous submissions (with notification of acceptance elsewhere). Submit at least 48 pages and no longer than 90 pages, typed, single-spaced. See website for complete guidelines. Manuscripts will be accepted via Submittable.com between April 15 and June 15 each year. Competition receives 500+ entries. 2015 winner was Sandra Simonds for *Further Problems With Pleasure*. Winner posted on website by September 30. Intimate friends, relatives, current and former students of the final judge (students in an academic, degree-conferring program or its equivalent), and current faculty, staff, students, and alumni of the University of Akron or the Northeast Ohio MFA Program (NEOMFA) are not eligible to enter the Akron Poetry Prize competition. Deadline: April 15-June 15. Prize: $1,500, plus publication of a book-length ms.

THE AMERICAN POETRY JOURNAL BOOK PRIZE

P.O. Box 2080, Aptos CA 95001-2080. **E-mail:** dreamhorsepress@yahoo.com. **Website:** www.dreamhorsepress.com. Both free and formal verse styles are welcome. Multiple submissions are acceptable. Submit 50-65 paginated pages of poetry, table of contents, acknowledgments, bio, and e-mail address (for results). No SASE required; mss will be recycled. Guidelines available on website. Deadline: Last day in February for snail mail postmarks, five days later for electronic submissions. Prize: $1,000, publication and 20 copies. All entries will be considered for publication.

ANABIOSIS PRESS CHAPBOOK CONTEST

2 South New St., Bradford MA 01835. (978)469-7085. **E-mail:** rsmyth@anabiosispress.org. **Website:** www.anabiosispress.org. **Contact:** Richard Smyth, editor. Submit 16-20 pages of poetry on any subject. Include separate pages with a biography, table of contents, and acknowledgments for any previous publications. Include SASE with correct postage for return of ms or notification of winner. All entrants receive a copy of the winning chapbook). Winners announced by September 30. Deadline: June 30 (postmarked). Prize: $100, plus publication of the winning chapbook, and 100 copies of the first run.

THE ANHINGA PRESS-ROBERT DANA PRIZE FOR POETRY

Anhinga Press, P.O. Box 3665, Tallahassee FL 32315. **E-mail:** info@anhinga.org. **Website:** www.anhinga.

org. **Contact:** Kristine Snodgrass, poetry editor. Offered annually for a book-length collection of poetry by an author writing in English. Guidelines on website. Past winners include Frank X. Gaspar, Earl S. Braggs, Julia Levine, Keith Ratzlaff, Lynn Aarti Chandhok, and Rhett Iseman Trull. Mss must be 48-80 pages, excluding front matter. Deadline: Submissions will be accepted from February 15-May 15. Prize: $2,000, a reading tour of selected Florida colleges and universities, and the winning ms will be published. Past judges include Jan Beatty, Richard Blaco, Denise Duhamel, Donald Hall, Joy Harjo, Robert Dana, Mark Jarman, and Tony Hoagland.

ANNUAL GIVAL PRESS OSCAR WILDE AWARD

Gival Press, LLC, P.O. Box 3812, Arlington VA 22203. (703)351-0079. **E-mail:** givalpress@yahoo.com. **Website:** www.givalpress.com. **Contact:** Robert L. Giron. Award given to the best previously unpublished original poem—written in English of any length, in any style, typed, double-spaced on 1 side only—which best relates gay/lesbian/bisexual/transgendered (GLBTQ) life, by a poet who is 18 years or older. Entrants are asked to submit their poems without any kind of identification (with the exception of titles) and with a separate cover page with the following information: name, address (street, city, and state with zip code), telephone number, e-mail address (if available), and a list of poems by title. Checks drawn on American banks should be made out to Gival Press, LLC. May submit via portal: www.givalpress.submittable.com. Deadline: June 27 (postmarked). Prize: $100 and the poem, along with information about the poet, will be published on the Gival Press website. Judged by the previous winner, who reads the poems anonymously.

⊘ ANNUAL WORLD HAIKU COMPETITION & ANNUAL WORLD TANKA CONTEST

P.O. Box 17331, Arlington VA 22216. **E-mail:** LPEzineSubmissions@gmail.com. **Website:** http://lyrical-passionpoetry.yolasite.com. **Contact:** Raquel D. Bailey. Contest is now closed. Requires first rights for all previously unpublished works. Only e-mail entries accepted for contests. Promotes Japanese short form poetry. Deadline: See website for details. Prize: Monetary compensation and publication. Judged by experienced editors and award-winning writers from the contemporary writing community.

ART AFFAIR POETRY CONTEST

Art Affair Annual Literary Contests, P.O. Box 54302, Oklahoma City OK 73154 USA. **E-mail:** okpoets@aol.com. **Website:** www.shadetreecreations.com. **Contact:** Barbara Shepherd, contest chair. The annual Art Affair Poetry Contest is open to any poet. Multiple entries accepted with entry fee for each and may be mailed in the same packet. Guidelines available on website. Winners' list will be published on the Art Affair website in December. Poems must be unpublished. Submit original poems on any subject, in any style, no more than 60 lines (put line count in the upper right-hand corner of first page). Include cover page with poet's name, address, phone number, and title of poem. Do not include SASE; poem mss will not be returned. Deadline: October 1. Prizes: 1st Prize: $40 and certificate; 2nd Prize: $25 and certificate; and 3rd Prize: $15 and certificate. Honorable Mention certificates will be awarded at the discretion of the judges.

ATLANTIS AWARD

The Poet's Billow, 245 N. Collingwood, Syracuse NY 13206. **E-mail:** thepoetsbillow@gmail.com. **Website:** http://thepoetsbillow.org. **Contact:** Robert Evory. Annual award open to any writer to recognize one outstanding poem from its entries. Finalists with strong work will also be published. Submissions must be previously unpublished. Deadline: October 1. Submissions open July 1. Prize: $200 and winning poet will be featured in an interview on The Poet's Billow website. Poem will be published and displayed in The Poet's Billow Literary Art Gallery and nominated for a Pushcart Prize. If the poet qualifies, the poem will also be submitted to The Best New Poets anthology. Judged by the editors, and, occasionally, a guest judge.

BARROW STREET PRESS BOOK CONTEST

P.O. Box 1558, Kingston RI 02881. **Website:** www.barrowstreet.org. The Barrow Street Press Book Contest award will be given for the best previously unpublished ms of poetry in English. Submit a 50-70 page unpublished ms of original poetry in English. Please number the pages of your ms and include a table of contents and an acknowledgments page for any previously published poems. Include two title pages. The author's name, address, and telephone number should appear on the first title page only and should not appear anywhere else in the ms. The second title page should contain only the ms title. Deadline: June 30. Prize: $1,000. Judged by Denise Duhamel.

💲💲 ELINOR BENEDICT POETRY PRIZE

Passages North, Northern Michigan University, 1401 Presque Isle Ave., Marquette MI 49855. **E-mail:** passages@nmu.edu. **Website:** passagesnorth.com/contests/. **Contact:** Jennifer A. Howard, Editor-in-Chief. Prize given biennially for a poem or a group of poems. Check website to see if award is currently being offered this year. Deadline: April 15. Submission period begins February 15. Prize: $1,000 and publication for winner; 2 honorable mentions are also published; all entrants receive a copy of *Passages North*.

BERMUDA TRIANGLE PRIZE

The Poet's Billow, 6135 Avon St., Portage MI 49024. **E-mail:** thepoetsbillow@gmail.com. **Website:** http://thepoetsbillow.org. **Contact:** Robert Evory. Annual award open to any writer to recognize three poems that address a theme set by the editors. Finalists with strong work will also be published. Submissions must be previously unpublished. Please submit online. Deadline: March 15. Submission period begins November 15. Prize: $50 each to three poems. The winning poems will be published and displayed in The Poet's Billow Literary Art Gallery and nominated for a Pushcart Prize. If the poet qualifies, the poem will also be submitted to The Best New Poets anthology. Judged by the editors, and, occasionally, a guest judge.

THE PATRICIA BIBBY FIRST BOOK AWARD

Patricia Bibby Award, Tebot Bach, P.O. Box 7887, Huntington Beach CA 92615-7887. **E-mail:** mifanwy@tebotbach.org; info@tebotbach.org. **Website:** www.tebotbach.org. **Contact:** Mifanwy Kaiser. Annual competition open to all poets writing in English who have not committed to publishing collections of poetry of 36 poems or more in editions of over 400 copies. Offers award and publication of a book-length poetry ms by Tebot Bach. Complete guidelines available by e-mail or on website. Deadline: November 30. Prize: $500 and book publication. Judges for each year's competition announced online.

BINGHAMTON UNIVERSITY MILT KESSLER POETRY BOOK AWARD

Binghamton University Creative Writing Program, Department of English, General Literature, and Rhetoric, Library North Room 1149, Vestal Parkway East, P.O. Box 6000, Binghamton NY 13902-6000. (607)777-2713. **Fax:** (607)777-2408. **E-mail:** cwpro@binghamton.edu. **Website:** www2.binghamton.edu/english/creative-writing/binghamton-center-for-writers. **Contact:** Maria Mazziotti Gillan, creative writing program director. Annual award for a book of poems written in English, 48 pages or more in length, selected by judges as the strongest collection of poems published in that year. Print on demand is acceptable but no self-published or vanity press work will be considered. Each book submitted must be accompanied by an application form available online. Poet or publisher may submit more than 1 book for prize consideration. Send 2 copies of each book. Deadline: March 1. Prize: $1,000.

THE BITTER OLEANDER PRESS LIBRARY OF POETRY AWARD

The Bitter Oleander Press, 4983 Tall Oaks Dr., Fayetteville NY 13066-9776. (315)637-3047. **E-mail:** info@bitteroleander.com. **Website:** www.bitteroleander.com. **Contact:** Paul B. Roth. The Bitter Oleander Press Library of Poetry Book Award replaces the 15-year long run of the Frances Locke Memorial Poetry Award. Guidelines available on website. Entrants must not be friends or employees of The Bitter Oleander Press. Deadline: June 15 (postmarked). Open to submissions on May 1. Early or late entries will be disqualified. Prize: $1,000, plus book publication of the winning ms.

BLUE LIGHT POETRY PRIZE AND CHAPBOOK CONTEST

1563 - 45th Avenue, San Francisco CA 94122. **E-mail:** bluelightpress@aol.com. **E-mail:** bluelightpress@aol.com. **Website:** www.bluelightpress.com. **Contact:** Diane Frank, Chief Editor. The Blue Light Poetry Prize and Chapbook Contest offers a cash prize and publication by Blue Light Press (see separate listing in Book/Chapbook Publishers). Deadline: June 15. The winner will be published by Blue Light Press, with 20 copies the author's book. We have a group of poets who read manuscripts. Some years, we publish more than one winner.

BLUE MOUNTAIN ARTS/SPS STUDIOS POETRY CARD CONTEST

P.O. Box 1007, Boulder CO 80306. (303)449-0536. **Fax:** (303)447-0939. **E-mail:** poetrycontest@sps.com; editorial@sps.com. **Website:** www.sps.com. **Contact:** Becky Milanski. Biannual poetry card contest. All entries must be the original creation of the submitting author. Looking for original poetry that's non-rhyming, although rhyming poetry may be considered. Poems may also be considered for possible publication on greeting cards or in book anthologies. Guidelines available online. Deadline: December 31 and June 30. Prize: 1st Place: $300; 2nd Place: $150; 3rd Place: $50. Judged by the Blue Mountain Arts editorial staff.

⊘ THE FREDERICK BOCK PRIZE

Poetry, 61 W. Superior St., Chicago IL 60654. (312)787-7070. **Fax:** (312)787-6650. **E-mail:** editors@ poetrymagazine.org. **Website:** www.poetryfoundation.org. Several prizes are awarded annually for the best work printed in *Poetry* during the preceding year. Only poems already published in the magazine are eligible for consideration, and no formal application is necessary. The winners are announced in the November issue. Upon acceptance, *Poetry* licenses exclusive worldwide first serial rights, including electronic rights, for publication, as well as non-exclusive rights to reprint, reuse, and archive the work, in any format, in perpetuity. Copyright reverts to author upon first publication. Any writer may submit poems to *Poetry*. Prize: $500.

THE BOSTON REVIEW ANNUAL POETRY CONTEST

Poetry Contest, Boston Review, P.O. Box 425786, Cambridge MA 02142. (617)324-1360. **Fax:** (617)452-3356. **E-mail:** review@bostonreview.net. **Website:** www.bostonreview.net. Offers $1,500 and publication in *Boston Review* (see separate listing in Magazines/Journals). Any poet writing in English is eligible, unless he or she is a current student, former student, or close personal friend of the judge. Submissions must be unpublished. Submit up to 5 poems, no more than 10 pages total, via online contest entry manager. Include cover sheet with poet's name, address, and phone number; no identifying information on the poems themselves. No cover note is necessary for online submissions. No mss will be returned. Guidelines available for SASE or on website. Deadline: June 1. Winner announced in early November on website. Prize: $1,500 and publication.

BOULEVARD POETRY CONTEST FOR EMERGING POETS

PMB 325, 6614 Clayton Rd., Richmond Heights MO 63117. **E-mail:** editors@boulevardmagazine.org. **Website:** www.boulevardmagazine.org. **Contact:** Jessica Rogen, editor. Annual Emerging Poets Contest offers $1,000 and publication in *Boulevard* (see separate

listing in Magazines/Journals) for the best group of 3 poems by a poet who has not yet published a book of poetry with a nationally distributed press. All entries will be considered for publication and payment at regular rates. Submissions must be unpublished. Considers simultaneous submissions. Submit 3 poems, typed; may be a sequence or unrelated. On page one of first poem type poet's name, address, phone number, and titles of the 3 poems. Deadline: June 1. Prize: $1,000 and publication.

$ $ BARBARA BRADLEY PRIZE

New England Poetry Club, 376 School St., Watertown MA 02472. **E-mail:** contests@nepoetryclub.org. **Website:** www.nepoetryclub.org. **Contact:** Audrey Kalajin. For a lyric poem under 20 lines, written by a woman. Contest open to members and nonmembers. Poems should be typed and submitted in duplicate with author's name, address, phone, and e-mail address of writer on only 1 copy. (Judges receive copies without names.) Copy only. Label poems with contest name. Entries should be sent by regular mail only. Special delivery or signature required mail will be returned by the post office. Entries should be original, unpublished poems in English. No poem should be entered in more than 1 contest, nor have won a previous contest. No entries will be returned. NEPC will not engage in correspondence regarding poems or contest decisions. Deadline: May 31. Prize: $200. Judged by well-known poets and sometimes winners of previous NEPC contests.

BRICK ROAD POETRY BOOK CONTEST

Brick Road Poetry Press, Inc., 513 Broadway, Columbus GA 31901. (706) 649-3080. **Fax:** (706) 649-3094. **E-mail:** kbadowski@brickroadpoetrypress.com. **Website:** www.brickroadpoetrypress.com. **Contact:** Ron Self and Keith Badowski, co-editors/founders. Annual competition for an original collection of 50-100 pages of poetry. Book-length poetry mss only. Simultaneous submissions accepted. Single sided, single spaced only. No more than one poem per page. Electronic submissions are accepted, see website for details. Include a cover letter with poetry publication/ recognition highlights. Deadline: November 1. Submission period begins August 1. Prize: $1,000, publication in both print and e-book formats, and 25 copies of the book. May also offer publication contracts to the top finalists. Judged by Keith Badowski & Ron Self, Brick Road poetry editors.

BRIGHT HILL PRESS POETRY CHAPBOOK COMPETITION

Bright Press Hill & Literary Center, 94 Church St., Treadwell NY 13846. (607)829-5055. **E-mail:** brighthillpress@stny.rr.com; wordthur@stny.rr.com. **Website:** www.brighthillpress.org. The annual Bright Hill Press Chapbook Award recognizes an outstanding collection of poetry. Guidelines available for SASE, by e-mail, or on website. Collection of original poetry, 48-64 pages, single spaced, one poem to a page (no name) with table of contents. Ms must be submitted in Times New Roman, 12 pt. type only. No illustrations, no cover suggestions. Bio and acknowledgments of poems that have been previously published should be included in a separate document, or in comments box if submitting online. See website for more details, and information on submitting a hard copy. Deadline: November 30. Prize: A publication contract with Bright Hill Press and $1,000, publication in print format, and 30 copies of the printed book. Judged by a nationally-known poet.

BRITTINGHAM PRIZE IN POETRY

University of Wisconsin Press, 1930 Monroe Street, 3rd Floor, Madison WI 5311-2059. (608)263-1110. **Fax:** (608)263-1132. **E-mail:** rwallace@wisc.edu. **E-mail:** uwiscpress@uwpress.wisc.edu. **Website:** www.wisc.edu/wisconsinpress/poetryguide.html. **Contact:** Ronald Wallace, contest director. The annual Brittingham Prize in Poetry is 1 of 2 prizes awarded by The University of Wisconsin Press (see separate listing for the Felix Pollak Prize in Poetry in this section). Submissions must be unpublished as a collection, but individual poems may have been published elsewhere (publication must be acknowledged). Considers simultaneous submissions if notified of selection elsewhere. Submit 60-90 unbound ms pages, typed single-spaced (with double spaces between stanzas). Clean photocopies are acceptable. Include 1 title page with poet's name, address, and telephone number and 1 with title only. No translations. Strongly encourages electronic submissions via web page. SASE required for postal submissions. Will return results only; mss will not be returned. Guidelines available on website. The Brittingham Prize in Poetry is awarded annually to the best book-length manuscript of original poetry submitted in an open competition. The award is administered by the University of Wisconsin–Madison English Department, and the winner is chosen by a nationally recognized poet.

The resulting book is published by the University of Wisconsin Press. Deadline: Submit August 15-September 15. Prize: Offers $1,000, plus publication. Judged by a distinguished poet who will remain anonymous until the winners are announced in mid-February.

BOB BUSH MEMORIAL AWARD FOR FIRST BOOK OF POETRY

Texas Institute of Letters, P.O. Box 609, Round Rock TX 78680. **E-mail:** tilsecretary@yahoo.com. **Website:** www.texasinstituteofletters.org. Offered annually for best first book of poetry published in previous year. Writer must have been born in Texas, have lived in the state at least 2 consecutive years at some time, or the subject matter should be associated with the state. Deadline: See website for exact date. Prize: $1,000.

GERALD CABLE BOOK AWARD

Silverfish Review Press, P.O. Box 3541, Eugene OR 97403. (541)344-5060. **E-mail:** sfrpress@earthlink.net. **Website:** www.silverfishreviewpress.com. **Contact:** Rodger Moody, editor. Awarded annually to a book-length ms of original poetry by an author who has not yet published a full-length collection. There are no restrictions on the kind of poetry or subject matter; translations are not acceptable. Mss should be at least 48 pages in length. Clean photo copies are acceptable. The poet's name should not appear on the ms. Include a separate title page with name, address, and phone number. Poems may have appeared in periodicals, chapbooks, or anthologies, but should not be acknowledged. Simultaneous submissions are accepted. Accepts e-mail submissions. See website for more details and guidelines. Deadline: October 15. Prize: $1,000, publication, and 25 copies of the book. The winner will be announced in March.

CAKETRAIN COMPETITION

P.O. Box 82588, Pittsburgh PA 15218. **E-mail:** editors@caketrain.org. **Website:** www.caketrain.org. **Contact:** Amanda Raczkowski, editor; Joseph Reed, editor. Annual contest for full length works of fiction and poetry chapbooks sponsored by *Caketrain* literary journal. Can submit by mail with SASE or by e-mail. See website for guidelines. Deadline: October 1. Prize: $250 cash and 25 copies of their book.

CAROLINA WREN PRESS POETRY SERIES CONTEST

120 Morris St., Durham NC 27701. (919)560-2738. **Fax:** (919)560-2759. **E-mail:** carolinawrenpress@

earthlink.net. **Website:** www.carolinawrenpress.org. **Contact:** Andrea Selch, Poetry Editor. Carolina Wren Press is a nonprofit organization whose mission is to publish quality writing, especially by writers historically neglected by mainstream publishing, and to develop diverse and vital audiences through publishing, outreach, and educational programs. Submit a copy of a 48-72 page manuscript. Manuscript should be single-spaced and paginated. Please include a table of contents. Title page should not include author information–no name, address, etc. Within the manuscript, do include a page acknowledging individual poems that have been previously published. Open only to poets who have had no more than one full-length book published. Deadline: June 15 of odd-numbered years. Prize: $1,000 and publication.

THE CENTER FOR BOOK ARTS POETRY CHAPBOOK COMPETITION

The Center for Book Arts, 28 W. 27th St., 3rd Floor, New York NY 10001. (212)481-0295. **Fax:** (866)708-8994. **E-mail:** info@centerforbookarts.org. **Website:** http://centerforbookarts.org/opportunities/for-writers/. Annual competition for unpublished collections of poetry. Individual poems may have been previously published. Collection must not exceed 500 lines or 24 pages (does not include cover page, title pages, table of contents, or acknowledgements pages). Copies of winning chapbooks available through website. The cover page should contain, on a single detachable page, the ms title and author's name, along with address, phone number, and e-mail. The author's name should not appear anywhere else. A second title page should be provided without the author's name or other identification. Please provide a table of contents and a separate acknowledgements page containing prior magazine or anthology publication of individual poems. Mss should be bound with a simple spring clip. Poems may have appeared in journals or anthologies but not as part of a book-length collection. Competition is open to all poets writing in English who have published no more than 2 full-length books. Poets may not have studied with either judge in a degree-granting program for the last 5 years. Deadline: December 15. Prize: $500 award, $500 honorarium for a reading, publication, and 10 copies of chapbook.

JOHN CIARDI PRIZE FOR POETRY

BkMk Press, University of Missouri-Kansas City, 5101 Rockhill Rd., Kansas City MO 64110. (816)235-2558.

E-mail: bkmk@umkc.edu. **Website:** www.newletters.org. Offered annually for the best book-length collection (unpublished) of poetry in English by a living author. Translations are not eligible. Guidelines for SASE, by e-mail, or on website. Poetry mss should be approximately 50-110 pages, single-spaced. Deadline: January 15. Prize: $1,000, plus book publication by BkMk Press. Judged by a network of published writers. Final judging is done by a writer of national reputation.

CIDER PRESS REVIEW BOOK AWARD

P.O. Box 33384, San Diego CA 92163. **E-mail:** editor@ciderpressreview.com. **Website:** http://ciderpressreview.com/. Annual award from *Cider Press Review*. Submissions must be unpublished as a collection, but individual poems may have been previously published elsewhere. Submit book-length ms of 48-80 pages. Submissions can be made online using the submission form on the website or by mail. If sending by mail, include 2 cover sheets—1 with title, author's name, and complete contact information; and 1 with title only, all bound with a spring clip. Does not require SASE; notification via e-mail and on the website, only. Mss cannot be returned. Online submissions must be in Word for PC or PDF format, and should not include title page with author's name. The editors strongly urge contestants to use online delivery if possible. Review the complete submission guidelines and learn more online at website. Deadline: November 30. Open to submissions on September 1. Prize: $1,500, publication, and 25 author's copies of a book length collection of poetry. Author receives a standard publishing contract. Initial print run is not less than 1,000 copies. CPR acquires first publication rights. Judged by Jeffrey Harrison in 2014. Previous judge was Charles Harper Webb.

CLEVELAND STATE UNIVERSITY POETRY CENTER PRIZES

Cleveland State University Poetry Center, Cleveland State University Poetry Center, 2121 Euclid Avenue, Rhodes Tower, Room 1841, Cleveland OH 44115-2214. (216)687-3986. **Fax:** (216)687-6943. **E-mail:** poetrycenter@csuohio.edu. **Website:** www.csuohio.edu/poetrycenter. **Contact:** Caryl Pagel. Manuscript should contain a minimum of 48 and a maximum of 100 pages of poetry. See website for specific details and rules. Offered annually to identify, reward, and publish the best unpublished book-length poetry ms (minimum 48 pages) in 2 categories: First Book Award and Open Competition (for poets who have published at least one collection with a press run of 500). Deadline: March 31. Submissions open on January 1. Prize: First Book and Open Book Competitions awards publication and a $1,000 advance against royalties for an original manuscript of poetry in each category. Judged by Emily Kendal Frey, Siwar Masannat, Jon Woodward, Daniel Borzutzky, and Chris Kraus.

CLOCKWISE CHAPBOOK COMPETITION

Tebot Bach, Tebot Bach, Clockwise, P.O. Box 7887, Huntington Beach CA 92615. (714)968-0905. **Fax:** (714)968-4677. **E-mail:** mifanwy@tebotbach.org. **Website:** www.tebotbach.org/clockwise.html. Annual competition for a collection of poetry. Submit 24-32 pages of original poetry in English. Must be previously unpublished poetry for the full collection; individual poems may have been published. Full guidelines, including submission info, available online. Deadline: July 15. Prize: $500 and a book publication in Perfect Bound Editions. Winner announced in September with publication January. Judged by Gail Wronsky.

✎ TOM COLLINS POETRY PRIZE

Fellowship of Australian Writers (WA), P.O. Box 6180, Swanbourne WA 6910 Australia. (61)(8)9384-4771. **Fax:** (61)(8)9384-4854. **E-mail:** fellowshipaustralianwriterswa@gmail.com. **Website:** www.fawwa. org. Annual contest for unpublished poems, maximum 60 lines. Reserves the right to publish entries in a FAWWA publication or on its website. Guidelines online or for SASE. See website for details, guidelines, and entry form. Deadline: December 15. Submission period begins September 1. Prize: 1st Place: $1,000; 2nd Place; $400; 4 Highly Commended: $150 each.

THE COLORADO PRIZE FOR POETRY

Colorado Review/Center for Literary Publishing, Department of English, Colorado State University, 9105 Campus Delivery, Ft. Collins CO 80523. (970)491-5449. **E-mail:** creview@colostate.edu. **Website:** http://coloradoprize.colostate.edu. **Contact:** Stephanie G'Schwind, editor. Submission must be unpublished as a collection, but individual poems may have been published elsewhere. Submit mss of 48-100 pages of poetry on any subject, in any form, double- or single-spaced. Include 2 titles pages: 1 with ms title only, the other with ms title and poet's name, address, and phone number. Enclose SASP for notification of re-

ceipt and SASE for results; mss will not be returned. Guidelines available for SASE or by e-mail. Guidelines available for SASE or online at website. Poets can also submit online via online submission manager through website. Deadline: January 14. Prize: $2,000 and publication of a book-length ms. Judged by Tyrone Williams in 2016 (final round).

CONCRETE WOLF POETRY CHAPBOOK CONTEST

P.O. Box 1808, Kingston WA 98346. **E-mail:** concretewolf@yahoo.com. **Website:** http://concretewolf. com. Prefers chapbooks that have a theme, either obvious (i.e., chapbook about a divorce) or understated (i.e., all the poems mention the color blue). Likes a collection that feels more like a whole than a sampling of work. No preference as to formal or free verse. Slightly favors lyric and narrative poetry to language and concrete, but excellent examples of any style will grab their attention. Considers simultaneous submissions if notified of acceptance elsewhere. Submit up to 28 pages of poetry, paginated. Include table of contents and acknowledgments page. Include 2 cover sheets: 1 with ms title, poet's name, address, phone number, and e-mail; 1 without poet's identification. Include SASE for results; mss will not be returned. Send 10x12 envelope stamped with $3.50 for copy of winning chapbook. Guidelines available on website. Deadline: November 30. Prize: Publication and 100 author copies of a perfectly-bound chapbook.

THE CONNECTICUT RIVER REVIEW POETRY CONTEST

P.O. Box 270554, W. Hartford CT 06127. **E-mail:** connpoetry@comcast.net. **Website:** ctpoetry.net. Send up to 3 unpublished poems, any form, 80-line limit. Include 2 copies of each poem: 1 with complete contact informatoin and 1 with no contact information. Include a SASE. Deadline: September 30. Open to submissions on August 1. 1st Place: $400; 2nd Place: $100; 3rd Place: $50.

CPR EDITOR'S PRIZE

P.O. Box 33384, San Diego CA 92163. **E-mail:** editor@ ciderpressreview.com. **Website:** http://ciderpressreview.com/bookaward. Annual award from *Cider Press Review*. Submissions must be unpublished as a collection, but individual poems may have been previously published elsewhere. Submit book-length ms of 48-80 pages of original poetry. Submissions can be made online using the submission form on the website or by mail. If sending by mail, include 2 cover sheets—1 with title, author's name, and complete contact information; and 1 with title only, all bound with a spring clip. Check website for change of address coming in the future. Include SASE for results only if no e-mail address included; notification via e-mail and on the website; manuscripts cannot be returned. Online submissions must be in Word for PC or PDF format, and should not include title page with author's name. The editors strongly urge contestants to use online delivery if possible. Review the complete submission guidelines and learn more online at website. Deadline: submit between April 1-June 30. Prize: $1,000, publication, and 25 author's copies of a book length collection of poetry. Author receives a standard publishing contract. Initial print run is not less than 1,000 copies. CPR acquires first publication rights. Judged by *Cider Press Review* editors.

CRAB ORCHARD SERIES IN POETRY FIRST BOOK AWARD

First Book Award, Dept. of English, Mail Code 4503, Southern Illinois University Carbondale, 1000 Faner Drive, Carbondale IL 62901. (618)453-6833. **Fax:** (618)453-8224. **E-mail:** jtribble@siu.edu. **Website:** www.craborchardreview.siu.edu. **Contact:** Jon Tribble, series editor. Annual award that selects a first book of poems for publication from an open competition of manuscripts, in English, by a U.S. citizen, permanent resident, or person who has DACA/TPS status who has neither published, who has neither published, nor committed to publish, a volume of poetry 48 pages or more in length in an edition of over 500 copies (individual poems may have been previously published; for the purposes of the Crab Orchard Series in Poetry, a ms which was in whole or in part submitted as a thesis or dissertation as a requirement for the completion of a degree is considered unpublished and is eligible). Current or former students, colleagues, and close friends of the final judge, and current and former students and employees of Southern Illinois University Carbondale and authors who have published a book with Southern Illinois University Press or have a book under contract with Southern Illinois University Press are not eligible. See website for complete formatting instructions and guidelines. Accepts submissions only through Submittable, online. Mss are recommended to be a minimum of 50 pages to a recommended maximum of 75 pages of original

poetry, but no manuscript will be rejected solely because of length. Considers simultaneous submissions, but series editor must be informed immediately upon acceptance. Author's name should appear nowhere in manuscript. Do not include acknowledgments page. Deadline: July 8. Submission period begins May 15. Prize: The winner will be awarded a publication contract with Southern Illinois University Press, a $2,500 prize, and a $1,500 as an honorarium for a reading at Southern Illinois University Carbondale. The reading will follow the publication of the poet's collection. Judged by a published poet. Check website for current judge.

CRAB ORCHARD SERIES IN POETRY OPEN COMPETITION AWARDS

Department of English, Mail Code 4503, Faner Hall 2380, Southern Illinois University Carbondale, Carbondale IL 62901. (618)453-6833. **Fax:** (618)453-8224. **E-mail:** jtribble@siu.edu. **Website:** www.craborchardreview.siu.edu. **Contact:** Jon Tribble, series editor. Annual competition to award unpublished, original collections of poems written in English by United States citizens, permanent residents, or persons who have DACA/TPS status (individual poems may have been previously published; for the purposes of the Crab Orchard Series in Poetry, a ms which was in whole or in part submitted as a thesis or dissertation as a requirement for the completion of a degree is considered unpublished and is eligible). Two volumes of poems will be selected from the open competition of mss. Current or former students, colleagues, and close friends of the final judge, and current and former students and employees of Southern Illinois University Carbondale and authors who have published a book with Southern Illinois University Press or have a book under contract with Southern Illinois University Press are not eligible. See website for complete formatting instructions and guidelines. Accepts submissions only through Submittable, online. Mss are recommended to be a minimum of 50 pages to a recommended maximum of 80 pages of original poetry, but no manuscript will be rejected solely because of length. Considers simultaneous submissions, but series editor must be informed immediately upon acceptance. Deadline: November 22. Submission period begins October 1. Prize: Both winners will be awarded a publication contract with Southern Illinois University Press, a $2,500 prize, and a $1,500 as an honorarium for a reading at Southern Illinois University Carbondale. Both readings will follow the publication of the poets' collections. Judged by a published poet. Check website for current judge.

THE CRAZYHORSE PRIZE IN POETRY

Crazyhorse, Department of English, College of Charleston, 66 George St., Charleston SC 29424. (843)953-4470. **E-mail:** crazyhorse@cofc.edu. **Website:** http://crazyhorse.cofc.edu. **Contact:** Prize Director. The *Crazyhorse* Prize in Poetry is for a single poem. All entries will be considered for publication. Submissions must be unpublished. Submit online or by mail up to 3 original poems (no more than 10 pages). Include cover page (placed on top of ms) with poet's name, address, e-mail, and telephone number; no identifying information on mss (blind judging). Accepts multiple submissions with separate fee for each. Include SASP for notification of receipt of ms and SASE for results only; mss will not be returned. Guidelines available for SASE or on website. Deadline: January 31. Submissions period begins January 1. Prize: $2,000 and publication in *Crazyhorse*. Judged by genre judges for first round, guest judge for second round. Judges change on a yearly basis.

DANCING POETRY CONTEST

AEI Contest Chair, Judy Cheung, 704 Brigham Ave., Santa Rosa CA 95404-5245. (707)528-0912. **E-mail:** jhcheung@comcast.net. **Website:** www.dancingpoetry.com. **Contact:** Judy Cheung, contest chair. Line Limit: 40 lines maximum each poem. No limit on number of entries. Send 2 typed, clear copies of each entry. Show name, address, telephone number, e-mail and how you heard about the contest on one copy only. Poems must be in English or include English translation. Deadline: May 15. Prizes: Three Grand Prizes will receive $100 each plus the poems will be danced and videotaped at this year's Dancing Poetry Festival; six First Prizes will receive $50 each; twelve Second Prizes will receive $25 each; and thirty Third Prizes will receive $10 each.

DREAM HORSE PRESS NATIONAL POETRY CHAPBOOK PRIZE

P.O. Box 2080, Aptos CA 95001-2080. **E-mail:** dreamhorsepress@yahoo.com. **Website:** www.dreamhorsepress.com. **Contact:** J.P. Dancing Bear, Editor/Publisher. All entries will be considered for publication. Submissions may be previously published in magazines/journals but not in books or chapbooks. Considers simultaneous submissions with notification. Submit 20-28 pages of poetry in a readable font with table of contents, acknowledgments, bio, e-mail address for results, and entry fee. Poet's name should not appear anywhere on the manuscript. Accepts multiple submissions (with separate fee for each entry). Manuscripts will be recycled after judging. Guidelines available on website. Make checks/money orders made payable to Dream Horse Press. Recent previous winners include M.R.B. Chelko, Cynthia Arrieu-King, and Ariana-Sophia Kartsonis. Deadline: June 30. Prize: $500, publication, and 25 copies of a handsomely printed chapbook. Judged by C.J. Sage.

T.S. ELIOT PRIZE FOR POETRY

Truman State University Press, 100 E. Normal Ave., Kirksville MO 63501. (660)785-7336. **Fax:** (660)785-4480. **E-mail:** tsup@truman.edu. **Website:** tsup.truman.edu. **Contact:** Barbara Smith-Mandell, Editor-in-Chief. The ms may include individual poems previously published in journals or anthologies, but may not include more than 1/3 of the total poems from a published chapbook or self-published book. Submit 60-100 pages. Include 2 title pages: 1 with poet's name, address, e-mail address, phone number, and ms title; the other with ms title only. Include SASE for acknowledgment of ms receipt only; mss will not be returned. Guidelines available for SASE or on website. Deadline: October 31. Prize: $2,000 and publication. Judge announced after close of competition.

⚛ FAR HORIZONS AWARD FOR POETRY

The Malahat Review, University of Victoria, P.O. Box 1700, Stn CSC, Victoria BC V8W 2Y2 Canada. (250)721-8524. **Fax:** (250)472-5051. **E-mail:** malahat@uvic.ca. **Website:** www.malahatreview.ca. **Contact:** John Barton, editor. The biennial Far Horizons Award for Poetry offers $1,000 CAD and publication in *The Malahat Review* (see separate listing in Magazines/Journals). 2010 winner: Darren Bifford; 2012 winner: Kayla Czaga. 2014 winner: Laura Ritland. Winner and finalists contacted by e-mail. Winner published in fall in *The Malahat Review* and announced on website, Facebook page, and in quarterly e-newsletter, *Malahat lite*. Submissions must be unpublished. No simultaneous submissions. Submit up to 3 poems per entry, each poem not to exceed 60 lines; no restrictions on subject matter or aesthetic approach. Include separate page with poet's name, address, e-mail, and poem title(s); no identifying information on mss pages. E-mail submissions are acceptable: please send to horizons@uvic.ca. Do not include SASE for results; mss will not be returned. Full guidelines available on website. Open to "emerging poets from Canada, the United States, and elsewhere" who have not yet published a full-length book (48 pages or more). Deadline: May 1 (even-numbered years). Prize: $1,000. Judged by Steven Heighton in 2016.

JANICE FARRELL POETRY PRIZE CATEGORY

Soul-Making Keats Literary Competition, The Webhallow House, 1544 Sweetwood Dr., Broadmoor Village CA 94015. **E-mail:** SoulKeats@mail.com. **Website:** www.soulmakingcontest.us. **Contact:** Eileen Malone. Previously published okay. Poetry may be double- or single-spaced. One-page poems only, and only 1 poem/page. All poems must be titled. Three poems/entry. Identify with 3x5 card only. Open to all writers. Deadline: November 30. Prizes: First: $100, Second: $50, Third: $25. Judged by a local San Francisco Bay Area successfully published poet.

THE JEAN FELDMAN POETRY PRIZE

Washington Writers' Publishing House, 4640 23rd Rd. N., Arlington VA 22207. **E-mail:** wwphpress@gmail.com. **Website:** www.washingtonwriters.org. **Contact:** Holly Karapetkova. Poets living within 75 miles of the Capitol are invited to submit a ms of either a novel or a collection of short stories. Ms should be 50-70 pages, single spaced. Author's name should not appear on the manuscript. The title page of each copy should contain the title only. Provide name, address, telephone number, e-mail address, and title on a separate cover sheet accompanying the submission. A separate page for acknowledgments may be included for stories or excerpts previously published in journals and anthologies. E-mail electronic copies to wwphpress@gmail.com or mail paper copies and/or reading fee (check to WWPH) with SASE to: The Jean Feldman Poetry Prize, WWPH, c/o Holly Karapetkova, 4640 23rd Rd. N., Arlington, VA 22207. Deadline: November 1. Submission period begins July 1. Prize: $1,000 and 50 copies of the book.

FIELD POETRY PRIZE

Oberlin College Press/FIELD, 50 N. Professor St., Oberlin OH 44074-1095. (440)775-8408. **Fax:** (440)775-8124. **E-mail:** oc.press@oberlin.edu. **Website:** www.oberlin.edu/ocpress/prize.htm. **Contact:** Marco Wilkinson, managing editor. Offered annually

for an unpublished book-length collection of poetry (mss of 50-80 pages). Contest seeks to encourage the finest in contemporary poetry writing. Open to any writer. Deadline: Submit in May only. Prize: $1,000 and a standard royalty contract.

FIRST BOOK AWARD FOR POETRY

Zone 3, Austin Peay State University, Austin Peay State University, PO Box 4565, Clarksville TN 37044. (931)221-7031. **Fax:** (931)221-7149. **E-mail:** zone3@apsu.edu. **Website:** www.apsu.edu/zone3/. **Contact:** Andrea Spofford, poetry editor; Susan Wallace, managing editor. Annual poetry award for anyone who has not published a full-length collection of poems (48 pages or more). Accepts entries via postal mail or online. Separate instructions for both, see website for guidelines and details. Deadline: April 1. Prize: $1,000 and publication.

❂ FISH POETRY PRIZE

Durrus, Bantry Co. Cork Ireland. **E-mail:** info@fishpublishing.com. **Website:** www.fishpublishing.com. For poems up to 300 words. Age Range: Adult. The best 10 will be published in the Fish Anthology, launched in July at the West Cork Literary Festival. Entries must not have been published before. Enter online or by post. See website for full details of competitions, and information on the Fish Editorial and Critique Services, and the Fish Online Writing Courses. Do not put your name or address or any other details on the poem, use a separate sheet. Receipt of entry will be acknowleged by e-mail. Poems will not be returned. Word count: 300 max for each poem. You may enter as many as you wish, provided there is an entry fee for each one. Full details and rules are online. Entry is deemed to be acceptance of these rules. Publishing rights of the 10 winning poems are held by Fish Publishing for one year after the publication of the Anthology. The aim of the competition is to discover and publish new writers. Deadline: March 31. Prize: $1,000. Results announced May 15. Judged by Dave Lordan in 2016.

FIVE POINTS JAMES DICKEY PRIZE FOR POETRY

Five Points, Georgia State University, P.O. Box 3999, Atlanta GA 30302-3999. (404)413-5812. **Website:** five-points.gsu.edu. Offered annually for unpublished poetry. Enter on website or send 3 unpublished poems, no longer than 50 lines each, name and address on each poem, SASE for receipt and notification of winner. Winner announced in Spring issue. Deadline: December 1. Prize: $1,000, plus publication.

FOOD VERSE CONTEST

Literal Latte, 200 East 10th St., Suite 240, New York NY 10003. (212)260-5532. **E-mail:** litlatte@aol.com. **E-mail:** See link to submittable on www.literal-latte. com. **Website:** www.literal-latte.com. **Contact:** Jenine Gordon Bockman, editor. Open to any writer. Poems should have food as an ingredient. Submissions required to be unpublished. Guidelines online at website. Literal Latté acquires first rights. Annual contest to give support and exposure to great writing. Deadline: March 15. Prize: $500. Judged by the editors.

FOUR WAY BOOKS INTRO PRIZE IN POETRY

Four Way Books, Box 535, Village Station, New York NY 10014. (212)334-5430. **Fax:** (212)334-5435. **E-mail:** editors@fourwaybooks.com. **Website:** www. fourwaybooks.com. **Contact:** Ryan Murphy, Assoc. Director. The Four Way Books Intro Prize in Poetry, offered biennially in even-numbered years, offers publication by Four Way Books (see separate listing in Book Publishers), honorarium, and a reading at one or more participating series In New York City. Open to any poet writing in English who has not published a book-length collection of poetry. Entry form and guidelines available on website at www.fourwaybooks. com. Deadline: March 31 (postmark or online submission). Winner announced by e-mail and on website. Prize: Publication and $1,000. Copies of winning books available through Four Way Books online and at bookstores (to the trade through University Press of New England).

GERTRUDE PRESS POETRY CHAPBOOK CONTEST

P.O. Box 28281, Portland OR 97228. **E-mail:** editor@ gertrudepress.org; poetry@gertrudepress.org. **Website:** www.gertrudepress.org. Annual chapbook contest for 25-30 pages of poetry. Individual poems may have been previously published; unpublished poems are welcome. Poetry may be of any subject matter, and writers from all backgrounds are encouraged to submit. Include list of acknowledgments and cover letter indicating how poet learned of the contest. Include 1 title page with identifying information and 1 without. Guidelines available in *Gertrude* (see separate listing in Magazines/Journals), for SASE, by e-mail, or on

website. Deadline: May 15. Submission period begins September 15. Prize: $175, publication, 50 complimentary copies of the chapbook, and 2 e-book files.

ALLEN GINSBERG POETRY AWARDS

The Poetry Center at Passaic County Community College, One College Blvd., Paterson NJ 07505. (973)684-6555. **Fax:** (973)523-6085. **E-mail:** mgillan@pccc. edu. **Website:** www.pccc.edu/poetry. **Contact:** Maria Mazziotti Gillan, executive director. All winning poems, honorable mentions, and editor's choice poems will be published in *The Paterson Literary Review*. Winners will be asked to participate in a reading that will be held in the Paterson Historic District. Submissions must be unpublished. Submit up to 5 poems (no poem more than 2 pages long). Send 4 copies of each poem entered. Include cover sheet with poet's name, address, phone number, e-mail address and poem titles. Poet's name should not appear on poems. Include SASE for results only; poems will not be returned. Guidelines available for SASE or on website. Deadline: April 1 (postmark). Prize: 1st Prize: $1,000; 2nd Prize: $200; 3rd Prize: $100.

GIVAL PRESS POETRY AWARD

Gival Press, LLC, P.O. Box 3812, Arlington VA 22203. (703)351-0079. **E-mail:** givalpress@yahoo.com. **Website:** www.givalpress.submittable.com. **Contact:** Robert L. Giron, editor. Offered annually for a previously unpublished poetry collection as a complete ms, which may include previously published poems; previously published poems must be acknowledged, and poet must hold rights. Guidelines for SASE, by e-mail, or online. Open to any writer, as long as the work is original, not a translation, and is written in English. The copyright remains in the author's name; certain rights fall to the publisher per the contract. Must be at least 45 typed pages of poetry, on one side only. Entrants are asked to submit their poems without any kind of identification (with the exception of the titles) and with a separate cover page with the following information: Name, address (street, city, state, and zip code), telephone number, e-mail address (if available), short bio, and a list of the poems by title. Checks drawn on American banks should be made out to Gival Press, LLC. The competition seeks to award well-written, origional poetry in English on any topic, in any style. Deadline: December 15 (postmarked). Prize: $1,000, publication, and 20 copies of the publication. The editor narrows entries to the top

10; previous winner selects top 5 and chooses the winner—all done anonymously.

PATRICIA GOEDICKE PRIZE IN POETRY

CutBank Literary Magazine, *CutBank*, University of Montana, English Dept., LA 133, Missoula MT 59812. **E-mail:** editor.cutbank@gmail.com. **Website:** www.cutbankonline.org. **Contact:** Billy Wallace, editor-in-chief. The Patricia Goedicke Prize in Poetry seeks to highlight work that showcases an authentic voice, a boldness of form, and a rejection of functional fixedness. Accepts online submissions only. Submit up to 5 poems. Guidelines available online. Deadline: January 15. Submissions period begins November 1. Prize: $500 and featured in the magazine. Judged by a guest judge each year.

GOLDEN ROSE AWARD

New England Poetry Club, 654 Green St., No. 2, Cambridge MA 02139. **E-mail:** contests@nepoetryclub.org; info@nepoetryclub.org. **Website:** www.nepoetryclub.org. **Contact:** NEPC contest coordinator. Given annually to the poet, who by their poetry and inspiration to and encouragement of other writers, has made a significant mark on American poetry. Traditionally given to a poet with some ties to New England so that a public reading may take place. Contest open to members and nonmembers. Poems should be typed and submitted in duplicate with author's name, address, phone, and e-mail address of writer on only 1 copy. (Judges receive copies without names.) Copy only. Label poems with contest name. Entries should be sent by regular mail only. Special delivery or signature required mail will be returned by the post office. Entries should be original, unpublished poems in English. No poem should be entered in more than 1 contest, nor have won a previous contest. No entries will be returned. NEPC will not engage in correspondence regarding poems or contest decisions. Deadline: May 31. Judged by well-known poets and sometimes winners of previous NEPC contests.

THE GREEN ROSE PRIZE IN POETRY

New Issues Poetry & Prose, Deptartment of English, Western Michigan University, 1903 W. Michigan Ave., Kalamazoo MI 49008-5463. **E-mail:** new-issues@wmich.edu. **Website:** www.wmich.edu/newissues. Offered annually for unpublished poetry. The university will publish a book of poems by a poet writing in English who has published 1 or more full-length

collections of poetry. *New Issues* may publish as many as 3 additional mss from this competition. Guidelines for SASE or online. *New Issues Poetry & Prose* obtains rights for first publication. Book is copyrighted in the author's name. Considers simultaneous submissions, but *New Issues* must be notified of acceptance elsewhere. Submit a ms of at least 48 pages, typed; single-spaced preferred. Clean photocopies acceptable. Do not bind; use manila folder or metal clasp. Include cover page with poet's name, address, phone number, and title of the ms. Also include brief bio, table of contents, and acknowledgments page. Submissions are also welcome through the online submission manager: www.newissuespoetryprose.submittable.com. For hardcopy manuscripts only, you may include SASP for notification of receipt of ms and SASE for results only; mss will be recycled. Guidelines available for SASE, by fax, e-mail, or on website. Winner is announced in January or February on website. The winning manuscript will be published in spring of following year. 2014 winner was Kathleen Halme (*My Multiverse*). Deadline: Submit May 1-September 30. Winner is announced in January or February on website. Prize: $2,000 and publication of a book of poems.

◐ THE GRIFFIN POETRY PRIZE

The Griffin Trust for Excellence in Poetry, 363 Parkridge Crescent, Oakville ON L6M 1A8 Canada. (905)618-0420. **E-mail:** info@griffinpoetryprize.com. **Website:** www.griffinpoetryprize.com. **Contact:** Ruth Smith. The Griffin Poetry Prize is one of the world's most generous poetry awards. The awards go to one Canadian and one international poet for a first collection written in, or translated into, English. Submissions must come from publishers. A book of poetry must be a first-edition collection. Books should have been published in the previous calendar year. Deadline: December 31. Prize: Two $65,000 (CAD) prizes. An additional $10,000 (CAD) goes to each shortlisted poet for their participation in the Shortlist Readings. Judges are chosen annually by the Trustees of The Griffin Trust For Excellence in Poetry.

GREG GRUMMER POETRY AWARD

Phoebe, MSN 2C5, George Mason University, 4400 University Dr., Fairfax VA 22030. **E-mail:** phoebe@gmu.edu. **Website:** www.phoebejournal.com. **Contact:** Q Wang & Doug Luman, poetry editors. Offered annually for unpublished work. Submit up to 4 poems, no more than 10 pages total. Guidelines online. Requests first serial rights, if work is to be published, and $500 first prize. Judge will be Jericho Brown. The purpose of the award is to recognize new and exciting poetry. Deadline: March 31. Prize: $500 and publication in the *Phoebe*. Judged by poet Jericho Brown.

THE HILARY THAM CAPITAL COLLECTION

The Word Works, Nancy White, c/o SUNY Adiorndack, 640 Bay Rd., Queensbury NY 12804. **E-mail:** editor@wordworksbooks.org. **Website:** www.word-worksbooks.org. **Contact:** Nancy White, editor. The Hilary Tham Capital Collection publishes only poets who volunteer for literary nonprofits. Every nominated poet is invited to submit; authors have until May 1 to send their ms via online submissions at website, or to Nancy White. Details available online. Deadline: April 15 to send nomination. Judged by Eduardo Corral in 2016. Past judges include Denise Duhamel, Kimiko Hahn, and Michael Klein.

THE BESS HOKIN PRIZE

Poetry, 61 W. Superior St., Chicago IL 60654. (312)787-7070. **Fax:** (312)787-6650. **E-mail:** editors@poetry-magazine.org. **Website:** www.poetrymagazine.org. Offered annually for poems published in *Poetry* during the preceding year (October-September). Upon acceptance, *Poetry* licenses exclusive worldwide first serial rights, including electronic rights, for publication, as well as non-exclusive rights to reprint, reuse, and archive the work, in any format, in perpetuity. Copyright reverts to author upon first publication. "Established in 1947 through the generosity of our late friend and guarantor, Mrs. David Hokin, and is given annually in her memory." Prize: $1,000.

INDIANA REVIEW POETRY PRIZE

Indiana Review, Poetry Prize, Indiana Review, Ballantine Hall 529, 1020 E. Kirkwood Ave., Bloomington IN 47405-7103. **E-mail:** inreview@indiana.edu. **Website:** www.indianareview.org. Offered annually for unpublished work. Open to any writer. Guidelines available on website. All entries are considered for publication. Send no more than 3 poems per entry, 8 pages maximum. Each fee entitles entrant to a 1-year subscription. No longer accepts hard-copy submissions. Deadline: April 1. Submission period begins February 1. Prize: $1,000 and publication. Judged by Camille Rankine in 2016. Different judge every year.

IOWA POETRY PRIZE

University of Iowa Press, 119 West Park Rd., 100 Kuhl House, Iowa City IA 52242. (319)335-2000. **Fax:** (319)335-2055. **E-mail:** uipress@uiowa.edu. **Website:** www.uiowapress.org. Offered annually to encourage poets and their work. Submissions must be postmarked during the month of April; put name on title page only. This page will be removed before ms is judged. Open to writers of English (US citizens or not). Mss will not be returned. Previous winners are not eligible. Mss should be 50-150 pages in length. Poems included in the collection may have appeared in journals or anthologies; poems from a poet's previous collections may be included only in manuscripts of new and selected poems. Deadline: April 30. Prize: Publication under standard royalty agreement.

ALICE JAMES AWARD

Alice James Books, 114 Prescott Street, Farmington ME 04938. (207)778-7071. **Fax:** (207)778-7766. **E-mail:** ajb@alicejamesbooks.org. **Website:** www.alice-jamesbooks.org. **Contact:** Alyssa Neptune, Managing Editor. For complete contest guidelines, visit website or send a SASE. Open to anyone residing in the United States. Offered annually for unpublished, full-length poetry collection. Deadline: October 1. Prize: $2,000 and publication.

ALICE JAMES AWARD

Alice James Books, University of Maine at Farmington, 114 Prescott St., Farmington ME 04938. (207)778-7071. **Fax:** (207)778-7766. **E-mail:** ajb@alicejames-books.org; info@alice jamesbooks.org. **Website:** www. alicejamesbooks.org. **Contact:** Alyssa Neptune, managing editor. Offered annually for unpublished, full-length poetry collections. Emerging and established poets are welcome. Submit 48-80 pages of poetry. Guidelines for submissions available online. Deadline: October 1. Prize: $2,000, publication, and distribution through Consortium.

RANDALL JARRELL POETRY COMPETITION

North Carolina Writers' Network, Terry L. Kennedy, MFA Writing Program, 3302 MHRA Building, UNC Greensboro, Greensboro NC 27402-6170. **E-mail:** tlkenned@uncg.edu. **Website:** www.ncwriters.org. **Contact:** Terry L. Kennedy, associate director. Offered annually for unpublished work to honor Randall Jarrell and his life at UNC Greensboro, by recognizing the best poetry submitted. The competition is open to any writer who is a legal resident of North Carolina or a member of the North Carolina Writers' Network. Submissions should be one poem only (40-line limit). Poem must be typed (single-spaced) and stapled in the left-hand corner. Author's name should not appear on the poem. Instead, include a separate cover sheet with author's name, address, e-mail address, phone number, and poem title. Poem will not be returned. Include a self-addressed stamped envelope for a list of winner and finalists. The winner and finalists will be announced in May. Deadline: March 1. Prize: $200 and publication at *storySouth* (www.storysouth.com).

JUNIPER PRIZE FOR FICTION

University of Massachusetts Press, East Experiment Station, 671 North Pleasant St., Amherst MA 01003. (413)545-2217. **Fax:** (413)545-1226. **E-mail:** info@umpress.umass.edu; kfisk@umpress.umass.edu. **E-mail:** fiction@umpress.umass.edu. **Website:** www.umass.edu/umpress. **Contact:** Karen Fisk, competition coordinator. Award to honor and publish outstanding works of literary fiction. Competition open to all writers in English. Novels, novellas, and collections of stories are all eligible. Work that has previously appeared in magazines, in whole or in part, may be included, but should be so identified on the cover sheet. Mss must be at least 150 pages and no longer than 350 pages. Guidelines available on website. Deadline: September 30. Submissions period begins August 1. Winners announced online in April on the press website. Prize: $1,000 cash and publication.

JUNIPER PRIZE FOR POETRY

University of Massachusetts Press, East Experiment Station, 671 North Pleasant St., Amherst MA 01003. (413)545-2217. **Fax:** (413)545-1226. **E-mail:** info@umpress.umass.edu; kfisk@umpress.umass.edu. **E-mail:** poetry@umpress.umass.edu. **Website:** www.umass.edu/umpress. **Contact:** Karen Fisk, competition coordinator. The University of Massachusetts Press offers the annual Juniper Prize for Poetry, awarded in alternate years for the first and subsequent books. Considers simultaneous submissions, but if accepted for publication elsewhere, please notify immediately. Mss by more than 1 author, entries of more than 1 mss simultaneously or within the same year, and translations are not eligible. Submit paginated ms of 50-70 pages of poetry, with paginated contents page, credits page, and information on previously published books. Include 2 cover sheets: 1 with contract information, 1

without. Mss will not be returned. Guidelilnes available for SASE or on website. Deadline: September 30. Submissions period begins August 1. Winners announced online in April on the press website. Prize: Publication and $1,000 in addition to royalties.

BARBARA MANDIGO KELLY PEACE POETRY AWARDS

Nuclear Age Peace Foundation, PMB 121, 1187 Coast Village Rd., Suite 1, Santa Barbara CA 93108-2794. (805)965-3443. **Fax:** (805)568-0466. **E-mail:** cwarner@napf.org. **Website:** www.wagingpeace.org; www.peacecontests.org. **Contact:** Carol Warner, poetry award coordinator. The Barbara Mandigo Kelly Peace Poetry Contest was created to encourage poets to explore and illuminate positive visions of peace and the human spirit. The annual contest honors the late Barbara Kelly, a Santa Barbara poet and long-time supporter of peace issues. Awards are given in 3 categories: adult (over 18 years), youth between 12 and 18 years, and youth under 12. All submitted poems should be unpublished. Deadline: April 1 (postmarked) or e-mailed (cwarner@napf.org). Prize: Adult: $1,000; Youth (13-18): $200; Youth (12 and under): $200. Honorable Mentions may also be awarded. Judged by a committee of poets selected by the Nuclear Age Peace Foundation. The foundation reserves the right to publish and distribute the award-winning poems, including honorable mentions.

LEVIS READING PRIZE

Virginia Commonwealth University, Department of English, Levis Reading Prize, VCU Department of English, 900 Park Avenue, Hibbs Hall, Room 306, P.O. Box 842005, Richmond VA 23284-2005. (804)828-1329. **Fax:** (804)828-8684. **E-mail:** bloomquistjmp@mymail.vcu.edu. **Website:** www.english.vcu.edu/mfa/levis. **Contact:** John-Michael Bloomquist. Offered annually for books of poetry published in the previous year to encourage poets early in their careers. The entry must be the writer's first or second published book of poetry. Previously published books in other genres, or previously published chapbooks or self-published material, do not count as books for this purpose. Entries may be submitted by either author or publisher, and must include three copies of the book (48 pages or more), a cover letter, and a brief biography of the author including previous publications. (Entries from vanity presses are not eligible.) The book must have been published in the previous calendar year. Entrants wishing acknowledgment of receipt must include a self-addressed stamped postcard. Deadline: February 1. Prize: $5,000 and an expense-paid trip to Richmond to present a public reading.

THE RUTH LILLY POETRY PRIZE

Poetry, 61 W. Superior St., Chicago IL 60654. (312)787-7070. **Fax:** (312)787-6650. **E-mail:** editors@poetry-magazine.org. **Website:** www.poetrymagazine.org. Awarded annually, the $100,000 Ruth Lilly Poetry Prize honors a living U.S. poet whose lifetime accomplishments warrant extraordinary recognition. Established in 1986 by Ruth Lilly, the Prize is one of the most prestigious awards given to American poets and is one of the largest literary honors for work in the English language. Deadline: No submissions or nominations considered. Prize: $100,000.

LITERAL LATTÉ POETRY AWARD

Literal Latté, 200 E. 10th St., Suite 240, New York NY 10003. (212)260-5532. **E-mail:** LitLatte@aol.com. **Website:** www.literal-latte.com. **Contact:** Jenine Gordon Bockman, editor. Offered annually to any writer for unpublished poetry (maximum 2,000 words per poem). All styles welcome. Winners published in *Literal Latté*. Acquires first rights. Deadline: Postmark by July 15. Prizes: 1st Place: $1,000; 2nd Place: $300; 3rd Place: $200. Judged by the editors.

LUMINA POETRY CONTEST

Sarah Lawrence College, Sarah Lawrence College Slonim House 1 Mead Way, Bronxville NY 10708. **Website:** www.luminajournal.com. Annual poetry competition held by the Sarah Lawrence College's graduate literary journal. Submit online. Include a 100-word bio at the bottom of cover letter. Submit up to 3 poems, 60 lines maximum per poem. Does not accept previously published material or simultaneous submissions. Deadline: October 15. Prize: 1st Place: $500 and publication; 2nd Place: $250 and publication; 3rd Place: $100 and online publication.

THE MACGUFFIN'S NATIONAL POET HUNT CONTEST

The MacGuffin, The MacGuffin, Schoolcraft College, 18600 Haggerty Rd., Livonia MI 48152. (734)462-4400, ext. 5327. **Fax:** (734)462-4679. **E-mail:** macguffin@schoolcraft.edu. **E-mail:** macguffin@schoolcraft.edu. **Website:** www.schoolcraft. edu/a-z-index/the-macguffin. **Contact:** Gordon Krupsky, managing editor. *The MacGuffin* is a na-

tional literary magazine from Schoolcraft College in Livonia, Michigan. An entry consists of three poems. Poems must not be previously published, and must be the original work of the contestant. See website for additional details. The mission of *The MacGuffin* is to encourage, support, and enhance the literary arts in the Schoolcraft College community, the region, the state, and the nation. Deadline: June 3. Submissions period begins April 1. Prize: $500. Judged by Li-Young Lee.

NAOMI LONG MADGETT POETRY AWARD

Lotus Press, Inc., 8300 East Jefferson Ave., #504, Detroit MI 48214. (313)736-5338. **E-mail:** broadsidelotus@gmail.com. **Website:** www.lotuspress.org. **Contact:** Gloria House. Offered annually to recognize an unpublished book-length poetry ms by an African American. Guidelines available online. Poems in the ms should total *approximately* 60-90 pages, exclusive of a table of contents or other optional introductory material. Poems that have been published individually in periodicals or anthologies are acceptable. Will not consider an entire collection that has been previously published. Deadline: March 1. Submission period begins January 2. Prize: $500 and publication by Lotus Press.

MAIN STREET RAG'S ANNUAL POETRY BOOK AWARD

Main Street Rag Publishing Company, P.O. Box 690100, Charlotte NC 28227-7001. (704)573-2516. **E-mail:** editor@mainstreetrag.com. **Website:** www. mainstreetrag.com. **Contact:** M. Scott Douglass, publisher/managing editor. Submit 48-84 pages of poetry, no more than 1 poem/page (individual poems may be longer than 1 page). Guidelines available on website. The purpose of this contest is to select manuscripts for publication and offer prize money to the manuscript we feel best represents our label. Deadline: January 31. Prize: 1st Place: $1,200 and 50 copies of book; runners-up are also be offered publication. Judged by 1 panel that consists of *MSR* editors, associated editors and college-level instructors, and previous contest winners.

✪ THE MALAHAT REVIEW LONG POEM PRIZE

The Malahat Review, Box 1700 STN CSC, Victoria BC V8W 2Y2 Canada. **E-mail:** malahat@uvic.ca. **Website:** www.malahatreview.ca. **Contact:** John Barton, editor. Long Poem Prize offered in alternate years with the Novella Contest. Open to any writer. Offers 2 awards of $1,000 CAD each for a long poem or cycle (10-20 printed pages). Includes publication in *The Malahat Review* and a 1-year subscription. Open to entries from Canadian, American, and overseas authors. Obtains first world rights. Publication rights after revert to the author. Submissions must be unpublished. No simultaneous submissions. Submit a single poem or cycle of poems, 10-20 published pages (a published page equals 32 lines or less, including breaks between stanzas); no restrictions on subject matter or aesthetic approach. Include separate page with poet's name, address, e-mail, and title; no identifying information on mss pages. Do not include SASE for results; mss will not be returned. Guidelines available on website. Deadline: February 1 (odd-numbered years). Prize: Two $1,000 prizes. Winners published in the summer issue of *The Malahat Review*, announced in summer on website, Facebook page, and in quarterly e-newsletter *Malahat lite*. Judged by 3 recognized poets. Preliminary readings by editorial board.

THE MORTON MARR POETRY PRIZE

Southwest Review, Southern Methodist University, P.O. Box 750374, Dallas TX 75275-0374. (214)768-1037. **Fax:** (214)768-1408. **E-mail:** swr@mail.smu.edu. **Website:** www.smu.edu/southwestreview. **Contact:** Prize coordinator. Annual award for poem(s) by a writer who has not yet published a book of poetry. Submit no more than 6 poems in a "traditional" form (e.g., sonnet, sestine, villanelle, rhymed stanzas, blank verse, et al.). Submissions will not be returned. All entrants will receive a copy of the issue in which the winning poems appear. Deadline: September 30. Prizes: $1,000 for 1st place; $500 for 2nd place; plus publication in the *Southwest Review*.

KATHLEEN MCCLUNG SONNET PRIZE CATEGORY

Soul-Making Keats Literary Competition, The Webhallow House, 1544 Sweetwood Dr., Broadmoor Village CA 94015-2029. **E-mail:** soulkeats@mail.com. **Website:** www.soulmakingcontest.us. **Contact:** Eileen Malone. Call for Shakespearean and Petrarchan sonnets on the theme of the "beloved." Previously published material is accepted. Indicate category on cover page and on identifying 3x5 card. Open annually to any writer. Deadline: November 30. Prize:1st Place: $100; 2nd Place: $50; 3rd Place: $25.

THE KATHRYN A. MORTON PRIZE IN POETRY

Sarabande Books, Inc., 2234 Dundee Rd., Suite 200, Louisville KY 40205. (502)458-4028. **E-mail:** info@sarabandebooks.org. **Website:** www.sarabandebooks.org. **Contact:** Sarah Gorham, editor-in-chief. The Kathryn A. Morton Prize in Poetry is awarded annually to a book-length ms (at least 48 pages). All finalists are considered for publication. Competition receives approximately 1,400 entries. Guidelines available online. Mss can be submitted online or via postal mail. Deadline: April 30. Submissions period begins March 15. Prize: $2,000, publication, and a standard royalty contract.

SHEILA MARGARET MOTTON PRIZE

New England Poetry Club, 2 Farrar St., Cambridge MA 02138. (617)744-6034. **E-mail:** info@nepoetryclub.org. **Website:** www.nepoetryclub.org. **Contact:** Audrey Kalajin. Awarded for a book of poems published in the last 2 years. Send 2 copies of book. Deadline: May 31. Prize: $500. Judged by well-known poets and sometimes winners of previous NEPC contests.

ERIKA MUMFORD PRIZE

New England Poetry Club, 376 School St., Watertown MA 02472. **E-mail:** contests@nepoetryclub.org. **Website:** www.nepoetryclub.org/contests.htm. **Contact:** Audrey Kalajin. Offered annually for a poem in any form about foreign culture or travel. Funded by Erika Mumford's family and friends. Contest open to members and nonmembers. Deadline: May 31. Prize: $250. Judged by well-known poets and sometimes winners of previous NEPC contests.

⊜ NATIONAL POETRY COMPETITION

The Poetry Society, 22 Betterton St., London WC2H 9BX United Kingdom. 020 7420 9880. **E-mail:** info@poetrysociety.org.uk. **Website:** www.poetrysociety.org.uk. **Contact:** Competition organizer. The Poetry Society was founded in 1909 to promote "a more general recognition and appreciation of poetry". Since then, it has grown into one of Britain's most dynamic arts organizations, representing British poetry both nationally and internationally. Today it has nearly 4000 members worldwide and publishes *The Poetry Review*. With innovative education and commissioning programs and a packed calendar of performances, readings and competitions, The Poetry Society champions poetry for all ages. Open to anyone aged

17 or over. Submissions must be unpublished (poems posted on websites are considered published). Submit original poems in English, on any subject, no more than 40 lines/poem, typed on 1 side only of A4 paper, double- or single-spaced. Each poem must be titled. No identifying information on poems. Do not staple pages. Accepts online submissions; full details available on the National Poetry Competition pages on the Poetry Society website. Entry form (required) available for A5 SAE (1 entry form covers multiple entries, may be photocopied). Include stamped SAE for notification of receipt of postal entries (confirmation of online entries will be e-mailed at time of submission); poems will not be returned. Guidelines available on website. Deadline: October 31. 1st Prize: £5,000; 2nd Prize: £2,000; 3rd Prize: £1,000; plus 7 commendations of £200 each. Winners will be published in *The Poetry Review*, and on the Poetry Society website; the top 3 winners will receive a year's free membership of The Poetry Society.

THE NATIONAL POETRY REVIEW BOOK PRIZE

The National Poetry Review, P.O. Box 2080, Aptos CA 95001-2080. **E-mail:** editor@nationalpoetryreview. com. **Website:** www.nationalpoetryreview.com. **Contact:** C.J. Sage, editor. Submit 45-80 pages of poetry via e-mail and PayPal (strongly preferred) or via mail. Include cover letter with bio and acknowledgments page. Include e-mail address (no SASE; mss will be recycled). Guidelines available on website. Deadline: June 30 (postmark). Prize: $1,000 plus publication and 15 copies of the book.

NATIONAL WRITERS ASSOCIATION POETRY CONTEST

The National Writers Association, 10940 S. Parker Rd. #508, Parker CO 80134. (303)841-0246. **E-mail:** natlwritersassn@hotmail.com. **Website:** www.nationalwriters.com. **Contact:** Sandy Whelchel, director. Annual contest to encourage the writing of poetry, an important form of individual expression but with a limited commercial market. Deadline: October 1. Prize: 1st Place: $100; 2nd Place: $50; 3rd Place: $25.

THE PABLO NERUDA PRIZE FOR POETRY

Nimrod International Journal, 800 S. Tucker Dr., Tulsa OK 74104. (918)631-3080. **Fax:** (918)631-3033. **E-mail:** nimrod@utulsa.edu. **Website:** www.utulsa. edu/nimrod. **Contact:** Eilis O'Neal. Annual award to discover new writers of vigor and talent. Open to

US residents only. Submissions must be unpublished. Work must be in English or translated by original author. Submit 3-10 pages of poetry (1 long poem or several short poems). Poet's name must not appear on ms. Include cover sheet with poem title(s), poet's name, address, phone and fax numbers, and e-mail address (poet must have a US address by October of contest year to enter). Mark "Contest Entry" on submission envelope and cover sheet. Include SASE for results only; mss will not be returned. Guidelines available for #10 SASE or on website. Deadline: April 30. Prizes: 1st Place: $2,000 and publication; 2nd Place: $1,000 and publication. Judged by the *Nimrod* editors (finalists). A recognized author selects the winners.

THE NEW ISSUES POETRY PRIZE

New Issues Poetry & Prose, New Issues Poetry & Prose, Department of English, Western Michigan University, 1903 W. Michigan Ave., Kalamazoo MI 49008-5331. **E-mail:** new-issues@wmich.edu. **Website:** www.wmich.edu/newissues. Offered annually for publication of a first book of poems by a poet writing in English who has not previously published a full-length collection of poems in an edition of 500 or more copies. *New Issues Poetry & Prose* obtains rights for first publication. Book is copyrighted in author's name. Guidelines for SASE or online. Additional mss will be considered from those submitted to the competition for publication. Considers simultaneous submissions, but *New Issues* must be notified of acceptance elsewhere. Submit ms of at least 40 pages, typed, single-spaced preferred. Clean photocopies acceptable. Do not bind; use manila folder or metal clasp. Include cover page with poet's name, address, phone number, and title of the ms. Also include brief bio and acknowledgments page. Submissions are also welcome through the online submission manager: www.newissuespoetryprose.submittable.com. For hardcopy submissions only, you may include SASP for notification of receipt of ms and SASE for results only; no mss will be returned. Winning manuscript will be named in May and published in the next spring. Deadline: November 30. Prize: $2,000, plus publication of a book-length ms. A national judge selects the prize winner and recommends other manuscripts. The editors decide on the other books considering the judge's recommendation, but are not bound by it. 2016 judge: Mary Szybist.

NEW LETTERS PRIZE FOR POETRY

New Letters Awards for Writers, UMKC, University House, 5101 Rockhill Rd., Kansas City MO 64110-2499. 816-235-1168. **E-mail:** newletters@umkc.edu. **Website:** www.newletters.org. The annual New Letters Poetry Prize awards $1,500 and publication in *New Letters* (see separate listing in Magazines/Journals) to the best group of 3-6 poems. All entries will be considered for publication in *New Letters*. Submissions must be unpublished. Considers simultaneous submissions with notification upon acceptance elsewhere. Accepts multiple entries with separate fee for each. Submit up to 6 poems (need not be related). Include 2 cover sheets: 1 with poet's name, address, e-mail, phone number, prize category (poetry), and poem title(s); the second with category and poem title(s) only. No identifying information on ms pages. Accepts electronic submissions. Include SASE for notification of receipt of ms and entry number, and SASE for results only (send only 1 envelope if submitting multiple entries); mss will not be returned. Guidelines available by SASE or on website. Current students and employees of the University of Missouri-Kansas City, and current volunteer members of the *New Letters* and BkMk Press staffs, are not eligible. Deadline: May 18 (postmarked). Prize: $1,500 and publication.

NFSPS POETRY CONVENTION MADNESS CONTEST

2029 103rd Ave. NW, Coon Rapids MN 55433. **E-mail:** pwilliamstein@yahoo.com; schambersmediator@yahoo.com. **Website:** www.mnpoets.com. **Contact:** Peter Stein; Sue Chambers. Enter to win your way to the NFSPS National Poetry Convention in Chaska, MN June 9th-13th. For more details about the event, visit www.nfspsconvention.com. Must be original work of the contestant. Deadline: January 31. Prizes: 1st Place: Hotel Lodging at Oak Ridge Convention Center for four nights, June 9th-12th. 2nd Place: Meals payed for during the course of the convention. 3rd Place: Registration to the Convention. 1st-3rd Honorable Mentions: Subscription to Poem by Post for one year.

THE ORPHIC PRIZE FOR POETRY

Dream Horse Press, P.O. Box 2080, Aptos CA 95001-2080. **E-mail:** dreamhorsepress@yahoo.com. **Website:** www.dreamhorsepress.com. **Contact:** J.P. Dancing Bear, Editor/Publisher. The Orphic Prize for Poetry is an annual award offered by Dream Horse Press. All entries will be considered for publication. Both free verse and formal verse styles are welcome. Submissions may be entered in other contests, "but if your manuscript is accepted for publication elsewhere, you must notify Dream Horse Press immediately." Submit 48-80 pages of poetry, paginated, with table of contents, acknowledgments, and bio. Include separate cover letter with poet's name, biographical information, and e-mail address (when available). Poet's name should not appear anywhere on the ms. Manuscripts will be recycled after judging. Guidelines available on website. Recent winners include: Sheila Black and Ash Bowen. Deadline: October 31. Five day extended deadline for electronic submissions. Prize: $1,000 and publication of a book-length ms by Dream Horse Press. Judging is anonymous.

PANGAEA PRIZE

The Poet's Billow, 6135 Avon St, Portage MI 49024. **E-mail:** thepoetsbillow@gmail.com. **Website:** http://thepoetsbillow.org. **Contact:** Robert Evory. Annual award open to any writer to recognize the best series of poems, ranging between two and up to seven poems in a group. Finalists with strong work will also be published. Submissions must be previously unpublished. Please submit online. Deadline: May 1. Prize: $100. The winning poem will be published and displayed in The Poet's Billow Literary Art Gallery and nominated for a Pushcart Prize. If the poet qualifies, the poem will also be submitted to The Best New Poets anthology. Judged by the editors, and, occasionally, a guest judge.

THE PATERSON POETRY PRIZE

The Poetry Center at Passaic County Community College, One College Blvd., Paterson NJ 07505. (973)684-6555. **Fax:** (973)523-6085. **E-mail:** mgillan@pccc.edu. **Website:** www.pccc.edu/poetry. **Contact:** Maria Mazziotti Gillan, executive director. The Paterson Poetry Prize offers an annual award for the strongest book of poems (48 or more pages) published in the previous year. The winner will be asked to participate in an awards ceremony and to give a reading at The Poetry Center. Minimum press run: 500 copies. Publishers may submit more than 1 title for prize consideration; 3 copies of each book must be submitted. Include SASE for results; books will not be returned (all entries will be donated to The Poetry Center Library). Guidelines and application form (required) available for SASE or on website. Deadline: February 1. Prize: $1,000.

PAUMANOK POETRY AWARD

English Department, Farmingdale State College, Knapp Hall, Farmingdale State College of New York, 2350 Broadhollow Rd., Route 110, Farmingdale NY 11735. **E-mail:** brownml@farmingdale.edu. **Website:** www.farmingdale.edu. **Contact:** Margery L. Brown, director, Visiting Writers Program. "Offered annually for published or unpublished poems. Send cover letter, 1-paragraph bio, 3-5 poems (name and address on each poem). Include SASE for notification of winners. (Send photocopies only; mss will *not* be returned.)" Deadline: September 15, postmark. Prize: 1st Place: $1,500, plus expenses for a reading in series; Runners-up (2): $750, plus expenses for a reading in series.

PAVEMENT SAW PRESS CHAPBOOK AWARD

321 Empire St., Montpelier OH 43543-1301. **E-mail:** info@pavementsaw.org. **E-mail:** editor@pavement-saw.org. **Website:** www.pavementsaw.org. **Contact:** David Baratier, editor. Pavement Saw Press has been publishing steadily since the fall of 1993. Each year since 1999, they have published at least 4 full-length paperback poetry collections, with some printed in library edition hard covers, 1 chapbook, and a yearly literary journal anthology. They specialize in finding authors who have been widely published in literary journals but have not published a chapbook or full-length book. Submit up to 32 pages of poetry. Include signed cover letter with poet's name, address, phone number, e-mail, publication credits, a brief biography, and ms title. Also include 2 cover sheets: 1 with poet's contact information and ms title, 1 with the ms title only. Do not put name on mss pages except for first title page. No mss will be returned. Deadline: December 31 (postmark). Prize: Chapbook Award offers $500, publication, and 50 author copies.

JEAN PEDRICK PRIZE

New England Poetry Club, 2 Farrar St., Cambridge MA 02138. **E-mail:** contests@nepoetryclub.org. **Website:** www.nepoetryclub.org. **Contact:** Audrey Kalajin. Prize for a chapbook of poems published in the last two years. Send 2 copies of the chapbook. Deadline: May 31. Prize: $100. Judged by well-known poets and sometimes winners of previous NEPC contests.

PEN/JOYCE OSTERWEIL AWARD FOR POETRY

PEN America, 588 Broadway, Suite 303, New York NY 10012. **E-mail:** awards@pen.org. **Website:** www.pen. org/awards. **Contact:** Arielle Anema, Literary Awards Coordinator. *Candidates may only be nominated by members of PEN.* This award recognizes the high literary character of the published work to date of a new and emerging American poet of any age, and the promise of further literary achievement. Nominated writer may not have published more than 1 book of poetry. Offered in odd-numbered years and alternates with the PEN/Voelcker Award for Poetry. Electronic letters of nomination will be requested during open submissions season. Submissions will be accepted during the summer of even-numbered year. Visit PEN. org/awards for up-to-date information on deadlines. Prize: $5,000. Judged by a panel of 3 judges selected by the PEN Awards Committee.

PEN/VOELCKER AWARD FOR POETRY

PEN America, 588 Broadway, Suite 303, New York NY 10012. **E-mail:** awards@pen.org. **Website:** www. pen.org/awards. **Contact:** Arielle Anema, Literary Awards Coordinator. The PEN/Voelcker Award for Poetry, established by a bequest from Hunce Voelcker, this award is given to a poet whose distinguished and growing body of work to date represents a notable and accomplished presence in American literature. The poet honored by the award is one for whom the exceptional promise seen in earlier work has been fulfilled, and who continues to mature with each successive volume of poetry. The award is given in even-numbered years and carries a stipend of $5,000. Please note that submissions will only be accepted from Professional Members of PEN and that it is understood that all nominations made for the PEN/Voelcker Award supplement internal nominations made by the panel of judges. PEN Members are asked to submit a letter of nomination through an online submissions form. Deadline: Nominations from PEN Members will be accepted during the summer of each odd-numbered year. Visit PEN.org/awards for up-to-date information on deadlines. Prize: $5,000. Judged by a panel of 3 poets or other writers chosen by the PEN Literary Awards Committee.

PERUGIA PRESS PRIZE

Perugia Press, P.O. Box 60364, Florence MA 01062. **Website:** www.perugiapress.com. **Contact:** Susan Kan. Submissions must be unpublished as a collection, but individual poems may have been previously published in journals, chapbooks, and anthologies. Considers simultaneous submissions if notified of acceptance elsewhere. Follow online guidelines carefully. Electronic submissions available through website. No translations or self-published books. Multiple submissions accepted if accompanied by separate entry fee for each. Use USPS or electronic submission, not FedEx or UPS. Winner announced by April 1 by e-mail or SASE (if included with entry). The Perugia Press Prize is for a first or second poetry book by a woman. Poet must have no more than 1 previously published book of poems (chapbooks don't count). Deadline: November 15. Open to submissions on August 1. Prize: $1,000 and publication. Judged by panel of Perugia authors, booksellers, scholars, etc.

THE RICHARD PETERSON POETRY PRIZE

Crab Orchard Review, Dept. of English, Mail Code 4503, Faner Hall 2380, Southern Illinois University at Carbondale, 1000 Faner Drive, Carbondale IL 62901. (618)453-6833. **Fax:** (618)453-8224. **E-mail:** jtribble@siu.edu. **Website:** www.craborchardreview.siu.edu. **Contact:** Jon Tribble, managing editor. Annual award for unpublished poetry. Entries should consist of 1 poem up to 5 pages in length. *Crab Orchard Review* acquires first North American serial rights to all submitted work. One winner and at least 2 finalists will be chosen. Entries should consist of 1 poem up to 5 pages in length. All submissions must be made through Submittable. Submissions must be unpublished original work, written in English by a U.S. citizen, permanent resident, or person who has DACA/TPS status (current students and employees at Southern Illinois University Carbondale are not eligible). See Submittable guidelines online for complete formatting instructions. The author's name should not appear on any page of the entry. Results announced by end of August. Deadline: April 21. Submission period begins February 21. Prize: $2,000 plus publication. At least 2 finalists will be chosen and offered $500 each plus publication. Judged by the editors of *Crab Orchard Review.*

⊘ POETS & PATRONS ANNUAL CHICAGOLAND POETRY CONTEST

Sponsored by Poets & Patrons of Chicago, 416 Gierz St., Downers Grove IL 60515. **E-mail:** eatonb1016@aol.com. **Website:** www.poetsandpatrons.net. **Contact:** Barbara Eaton, director. Annual contest for unpublished poetry. Guidelines available for self-addressed, stamped envelope. The purpose of the contest is to encourage the crafting of poetry. Deadline: September 1. Prize: 1st Place: $45; 2nd Place: $20; 3rd Place: $10 cash. Poet retains rights. Judged by out-of-state professionals.

POETS OUT LOUD PRIZE

Poets Out Loud, Fordham University at Lincoln Center, 113 W. 60th St., Room 924-I, New York NY 10023. (212)636-6792. **Fax:** (212)636-7153. **E-mail:** pol@fordham.edu. **Website:** www.fordham.edu/pol. Annual competition for an unpublished, full-length poetry ms (50-80 pages). Deadline: November 1. Prize: $1,000, book publication, and book launch in POL reading series.

A. POULIN, JR. POETRY PRIZE

BOA Editions, Ltd., BOA Editions, Ltd., P.O. Box 30971, Rochester NY 14603. **E-mail:** fisher@boaeditions.org. **Website:** www.boaeditions.org. The A. Poulin, Jr. Poetry Prize is awarded to honor a poet's first book, while also honoring the late founder of BOA Editions, Ltd., a not-for-profit publishing house of poetry, poetry in translation, and short fiction. Published books in other genres do not disqualify contestants from entering this contest. Send by first class or priority mail (recommended). Entrants must be a citizen or legal resident of the US. Poets who are at least 18 years of age, and who have yet to publish a full-length book collection of poetry, are eligible. Translations are not eligible. Individual poems may have been previously published in magazines, journals, anthologies, chapbooks of 32 pages or less, or self-published books of 46 pages or less, but must be submitted in ms form. Submit 48-100 pages of poetry, paginated consecutively, typed or computer-generated in 11 point font. Bind with spring clip (no paperclips). Include cover/title page with poet's name, address, telephone number, and e-mail address. Also include the table of contents, list of acknowledgments, and entry form (available for download on website). Multiple entries accepted with separate entry fee for each. No e-mail submissions. Deadline: November 30. Open to submissions on August 1. Prize: Awards $1,500 honorarium and book publication in the A. Poulin, Jr. New Poets of America Series.

PRESS 53 AWARD FOR POETRY

Press 53, 560 N. Trade St., Suite 103, Winston-Salem NC 27101. (336)770-5353. **E-mail:** kevin@press53.com. **Website:** www.press53.com. **Contact:** Kevin Morgan Watson, publisher. Awarded to an outstanding, unpublished collection of poetry. Details and guidelines available online. Deadline: July 31. Submission period begins April 1. Winner and finalists announced on by November 1. Publication in April. Prize: Publication of winning poetry collection as a Tom Lombardo Poetry Selection, $1,000 cash advance, 1/4-page color ad in Poets & Writers magazine, and 10 copies of the book. Judged by Press 53 poetry series editor Tom Lombardo.

RATTLE POETRY PRIZE

RATTLE, 12411 Ventura Blvd., Studio City CA 91604. (818) 505-6777. **E-mail:** tim@rattle.com. **Website:** www.rattle.com. **Contact:** Timothy Green, editor. *Rattle*'s mission is to promote the practice of poetry. To enter, purchase a one-year subscription to *Rattle* at the regular $20 rate. Open to writers, worldwide; poems must be written in English. No previously published works, or works accepted for publication elsewhere. No simultaneous submissions are allowed. Send up to 4 poems per entry. "More than anything, our goal is to promote a community of active poets." Deadline: July 15. Prize: One $10,000 winner and ten $200 finalists will be selected in a blind review by the editors of *Rattle* and printed in the Winter issue; one $1,000 Readers' Choice Award will then be chosen from among the finalists by subscriber and entrant vote. Judged by the editors of *Rattle*.

RHINO FOUNDERS' PRIZE

RHINO, The Poetry Forum, P.O. Box 591, Evanston IL 60204. **E-mail:** editors@rhinopoetry.org. **Website:** rhinopoetry.org. **Contact:** Editors. Send best unpublished poetry (3-5 pages). Visit website for previous winners and more information. Submit online or by mail. Include a cover letter listing your name, address, e-mail, and/or telephone number, titles of poems, how you learned about RHINO, and fee. Mss will not be returned. Deadline: October 31. Open to submissions on September 1. Prize: $500, publication, featured on website, and nominated for a Pushcart Prize. Two runners-ups will receive $50, publication, and will be featured on website. Occasionally nominates runner-up for a Pushcart Prize.

ROANOKE-CHOWAN POETRY AWARD

The North Carolina Literary & Historical Assoc., 4610 Mail Service Center, Raleigh NC 27699-4610. (919)807-7290. **Fax:** (919)733-8807. **E-mail:** michael. hill@ncdcr.gov. **Website:** litandhist.ncdcr.gov. **Contact:** Michael Hill, awards coordinator. Offers annual award for an original volume of poetry published during the 12 months ending June 30 of the year for which the award is given. Open to authors who have maintained legal or physical residence, or a combination of both, in North Carolina for the 3 years preceding the close of the contest period. Submit 3 copies of each entry. Guidelines available for SASE or by fax or e-mail. Winner announced October 15. Deadline: July 15.

VERN RUTSALA POETRY PRIZE

P.O. Box 610, Corvallis OR 97339. (541)752-0075. **E-mail:** michael@cloudbankbooks.com. **Contact:** Michael Malan. For contest submissions, the writer's name, address, e-mail, and the titles of the poems pieces being submitted should be typed on a cover sheet only, not on the pages of poems. No electronic submissions. Deadline: January 2. Prize: $1,000 plus publication of full-length ms. Judged by Dennis Schmitz.

MAY SARTON AWARD

New England Poetry Club, 654 Green St., No. 2, Cambridge MA 02139. (617)744-6034. **E-mail:** contests@nepoetryclub.org. **Website:** www.nepoetryclub.org. **Contact:** NEPC contest coordinator. "Given intermittently to a poet whose work is an inspiration to other poets. Recipients are chosen by the board." "Contest open to members and nonmembers. Poems should be typed and submitted in duplicate with author's name, address, phone, and e-mail address of writer on only 1 copy. (Judges receive copies without names.) Copy only. Label poems with contest name. Entries should be sent by regular mail only. Special delivery or signature required mail will be returned by the post office. Entries should be original, unpublished poems in English. No poem should be entered in more than 1 contest, nor have won a previous contest. No entries will be returned. NEPC will not engage in correspondence regarding poems or contest decisions." To recognize emerging poets of exceptional promise and distinguished achievement. Established to honor the memory of longtime Academy Fellow May Sarton, a poet, novelist, and teacher who during her career encouraged the work of young poets. Deadline: May 31. Prize: $250. Judges are well-known poets and sometimes winners of previous NEPC contests.

SCREAMINMAMAS MOTHER'S DAY POETRY CONTEST

1911 Cleveland St., Hollywood FL 33020. **E-mail:** screaminmamas@gmail.com. **Website:** www.scream-inmamas.com/contests. **Contact:** Darlene Pistocchi, editor/managing director. "What does it mean to be a mom? There is so much to being a mom—get deep, get creative! We challenge you to explore different types of poetry: descriptive, reflective, narrative, lyric, sonnet, ballad, limerick.. you can even go epic!" Open only to moms. Deadline: December 31. Prize: complementary subscription to magazine, publication.

☺ SHORT GRAIN CONTEST

P.O. Box 3986, Regina SK S4P 3R9 Canada. (306)791-7749. **E-mail:** grainmag@skwriter.com. **Website:** www.grainmagazine.ca/short-grain-contest. **Contact:** Jordan Morris, business administrator (inquiries only). The annual Short Grain Contest includes a category for poetry of any style up to 100 lines and fiction of any style up to 2,500 words, offering 3 prizes. Each entry must be original, unpublished, not submitted elsewhere for publication or broadcast, nor accepted elsewhere for publication or broadcast, nor entered simultaneously in any other contest or competition for which it is also eligible to win a prize. Entries must be typed on 8½x11 paper. It must be legible. No simultaneous submissions. A separate covering page must be attached to the text of your entry, and must provide the following information: Author's name, complete mailing address, telephone number, e-mail address, entry title, category name, and line count. Online submissions are accepted, see website for details. An absolutely accurate word or line count is required. No identifying information on the text pages. Entries will not be returned. Names of the winners and titles of the winning entries will be posted on the *Grain Magazine* website in August; only the winners will be notified. Deadline: April 1. Prize: $1,000, plus publication in *Grain Magazine*; 2nd Place: $750; 3rd Place: $500.

SLAPERING HOL PRESS CHAPBOOK COMPETITION

The Hudson Valley Writers' Center, 300 Riverside Dr., Sleepy Hollow NY 10591. (914)332-5953. **Fax:** (914)332-4825. **E-mail:** info@writerscenter.org. **Website:** www.writerscenter.org. **Contact:** Margo Stever, editor. The annual competition is open to poets who have not published a book or chapbook, though individual poems may have already appeared. Manu-scripts may be either a collection of poems or one long poem and should be a minimum of 16 pages and a maximum of 20 pages (not including the title page or table of contents). Purpose is to provide publishing opportunities for emerging poets. Deadline: May 15. Prize: $1,000, publication of chapbook, 20 copies of chapbook, and a reading at The Hudson Valley Writers' Center.

SLIPSTREAM ANNUAL POETRY CHAPBOOK CONTEST

Slipstream, Slipstream Poetry Contest, Dept. W-1, P.O. Box 2071, Niagara Falls NY 14301. **E-mail:** editors@slipstreampress.org. **Website:** www.slipstreampress.org. **Contact:** Dan Sicoli, co-editor. *Slipstream Magazine* is a yearly anthology of some of the best poetry you'll find today in the American small press. Send up to 40 pages of poetry: any style, format, or theme (or no theme). Send only copies of your poems, not originals. Manuscripts will no longer be returned. See website for specific details. Offered annually to help promote a poet whose work is often overlooked or ignored. Open to any writer. Deadline: December 1. Prize: $1,000, plus 50 professionally-printed copies of your book.

HELEN C. SMITH MEMORIAL AWARD FOR BEST BOOK OF POETRY

The Texas Institute of Letters, P.O. Box 609, Round Rock TX 78680. **E-mail:** tilsecretary@yahoo.com. **Website:** http://texasinstituteofletters.org/. Offered annually for the best book of poems published January 1-December 31 of previous year. Poet must have been born in Texas, have lived in the state at some time for at least 2 consecutive years, or the subject matter must be associated with the state. See website for submission details and information. Deadline: January 10. Prize: $1,200.

THE RICHARD SNYDER MEMORIAL PUBLICATION PRIZE

Ashland Poetry Press, 401 College Ave., Ashland University, Ashland OH 44805. **E-mail:** app@ashland.edu. **Website:** www.ashlandpoetrypress.com. **Contact:** Cassandra Brown, managing editor. Submissions must be unpublished in book form. Considers simultaneous submissions. Submit 50-96 pages of poetry. Competition receives 400+ entries/year. Winners will be announced in *Writer's Chronicle* and *Poets & Writers*. Copies of winning books available from Small Press Distribution and directly from the Ashland University Bookstore online. The Ashland Poetry Press publishes 2-4 books of poetry/year. Deadline: April 1. Prize: $1,000 plus book publication. Judged by Andrew Hudgins in 2016.

SOCIETY OF CLASSICAL POETS POETRY COMPETITION

The Society of Classical Poets, 11 Heather Ln., Mount Hope NY 10940. **E-mail:** submissions@classicalpoets.org. **Website:** www.classicalpoets.org. **Contact:** Evan Mantyk, president. Annual competition for a group of poems that address one or more of the following themes: beauty, Falun Dafa, great culture, or humor. Poems must incorporate meter and rhyme. All entries are considered for publication. Submit 3-5 poems of up to 50 lines each. Deadline: December 31. Prize: $500. Judged by Evan Mantyk, the society's president.

THE SOW'S EAR CHAPBOOK COMPETITION

The Sow's Ear Review, 1748 Cave Ridge Rd., Mount Jackson VA 22842. (540)955-3955. **E-mail:** sepoetryreview@gmail.com. **Website:** www.sows-ear.kitenet.net. **Contact:** Sarah Kohrs, managing editor. The Sow's Ear Poetry Review sponsors an annual chapbook competition. Open to adults. Open to adults. Send 22-26 pages of poetry plus a title page and a table of contents, all without your name. On a separate sheet list chapbook title, your name, address, phone number, e-mail address if available, and publication credits for submitted poems, if any. No length limit on poems, but no more than one poem on a page. Simultaneous submission is allowed, but if your chapbook is accepted elsewhere, you must withdraw promptly from our competition. Poems previously published are acceptable if you hold publication rights. Send SASE or e-mail address for notification. Entries will not be returned. Deadline: May 1 (postmark). Prize: Offers $1,000, publication as the spring issue of the magazine, 25 author's copies, and distribution to subscribers.

THE SOW'S EAR POETRY COMPETITION

The Sow's Ear Poetry Review, 1748 Cave Ridge Road, Mount Jackson VA 22842. **E-mail:** rglesman@gmail.com. **Website:** www.sowsearpoetry.org. **Contact:** Sarah Kohrs, managing editor. Open to adults. Send unpublished poems to the address above. Please do not put your name on poems. Include a separate sheet with poem titles, name, address, phone, and e-mail address if available, or a SASE for notification of results. No length limit on poems. Simultaneous

submission acceptable (checks with finalists before sending to final judge). Send poems in September or October. Deadline: November 1. Prize: $1,000, publication, and the option of publication for approximately 20 finalists.

THE EDWARD STANLEY AWARD

Prairie Schooner, 123 Andrews Hall, P.O. Box 880334, Lincoln NE 68588-0334. (402)472-0911. **Fax:** (402)472-9771. **E-mail:** prairieschooner@unl.edu. **Website:** www.prairieschooner.unl.edu. **Contact:** Editor in Chief. Offered annually for poetry published in Prairie Schooner in the previous year. Prize: $1,000.

STEVENS POETRY MANUSCRIPT CONTEST

NFSPS Stevens Poetry Manuscript Competition, 499 Falcon Ridge Way, Bolingbrook IL 60440. **E-mail:** stevens.nfsps@gmail.com. **Website:** www.nfsps.org. **Contact:** Wilda Morris, Chair. National Federation of State Poetry Societies (NFSPS) offers annual award of $1,000, publication of ms, and 50 author's copies for the winning poetry manuscript by a single author. Submit 48-70 pages of poetry by a single author, typewritten, or computer printed. No illustrations. No author identification in the manuscript. No more than one poem per page. May include previously published poems (acknowledgements on separate sheet). Simultaenous and multiple submissions permitted. Deadline: October 1. Submissions open September 1. Prize: $1,000, publication and 50 copies of the book.

THE RUTH STONE POETRY PRIZE

Vermont College, 36 College St., Montpelier VT 05602. (802)828-8517. **E-mail:** hungermtn@vcfa.edu. **Website:** www.hungermtn.org. **Contact:** Samantha Kolber, managing editor. The Ruth Stone Poetry Prize is an annual poetry contest. Enter up to 3 original, unpublished poems. Do not include name or address on submissions; entries are read blind. Accepts submissions online or via postal mail. Deadline: March 1. Prize: One first place winner receives $1,000 and publication on Hunger Mountain online. Two honorable mentions receive $100 and publication on Hunger Mountain online. Judged by Lee Upton in 2016.

THE ELIZABETH MATCHETT STOVER MEMORIAL AWARD

Southwest Review, Southern Methodist University, P.O. Box 750374, Dallas TX 75275-0374. (214)768-1037. **Fax:** (214)768-1408. **E-mail:** swr@mail.smu.edu. **Website:** www.smu.edu/southwestreview. **Con-

tact: Jennifer Cranfill, senior editor, and Willard Spiegelman, editor-in-chief. Offered annually to the best works of poetry that have appeared in the magazine in the previous year. Please note that mss are submitted for publication, not for the prizes themselves. Guidelines for SASE and online. Prize: $300. Judged by Jennifer Cranfill and Willard Spiegelman.

STROKESTOWN INTERNATIONAL POETRY COMPETITION

Strokestown International Poetry Festival, Strokestown Poetry Festival Office, Strokestown, County Roscommon Ireland. (+353) 71 9633759. **E-mail:** director@strokestownpoetry.org. **Website:** www.strokestownpoetry.org. **Contact:** Martin Dyar, Director. Poem cannot exceed 70 lines. Ten short-listed poets will be invited to Strokestown for the festival. This annual competition was established to promote excellence in poetry and participation in the reading and writing of it. Acquires first publication rights. Deadline: January. Prize: 1st Place: €1,500; 2nd Place: €500; 3rd Place: €300; 3 shortlisted prizes of €100 each.

THE TAMPA REVIEW PRIZE FOR POETRY

University of Tampa, 401 W. Kennedy Blvd., Tampa FL 33606. 813-253-6266. **E-mail:** utpress@ut.edu. **Website:** www.ut.edu/tampareview. Annual award for the best previously unpublished collection of poetry (at least 48 pages, though preferably 60-100). Deadline: December 31. Prize: $2,000, plus publication.

THE TENTH GATE PRIZE

E-mail: editor@wordworksbooks.org. **Website:** www.wordworksbooks.org. **Contact:** Leslie McGrath, Series Editor; Nancy White, Editor. Publication and cash prize awarded annually by The Word Works to a full-length ms by a poet who has already published at least 2 full-length collections. Submit 48-80 pages. Include acknowledgments and past book publications in the "NOTES" section of the online submissions manager. Submit via online submissions manager: wordworksbooks.org/submissions. Founded in honor of Jane Hirshfield, The Tenth Gate Prize supports the work of mid-career poets. Deadline: July 15. Open to submissions on June 1. Prize: $1,000 and publication. Judged by the editors.

TOM HOWARD/MARGARET REID POETRY CONTEST

Winning Writers, Winning Writers, 351 Pleasant St., PMB 222, Northampton MA 01060-3961 USA. (866)946-9748. **Fax:** (413)280-0539. **E-mail:** adam@winningwriters.com. **Website:** www.winningwriters.com. **Contact:** Adam Cohen. Winning Writers provides expert literary contest information to the public. It is one of the "101 Best Websites for Writers" (*Writer's Digest*). Submissions maybe published or unpublished, may have won prizes elsewhere, and may be entered in other contests. Length limit: 250 lines per poem. Deadline: September 30. Submission period begins April 15. Prizes: Two top awards of $1,500 each, with 10 Honorable Mentions of $100 each (any style). All entries that win cash prizes will be published on the Winning Writers website. Judged by Soma Mei Sheng Frazier.

TOR HOUSE PRIZE FOR POETRY

Robinson Jeffers Tor House Foundation, Poetry Prize Coordinator, Tor House Foundation, Box 223240, Carmel CA 93922. (831)624-1813. **Fax:** (831)624-3696. **E-mail:** thf@torhouse.org. **Website:** www.torhouse.org. **Contact:** Eliot Ruchowitz-Roberts, Poetry Prize Coordinator. The annual Prize for Poetry is a living memorial to American poet Robinson Jeffers (1887-1962). Open to well-crafted poetry in all styles, ranging from experimental work to traditional forms, including short narrative poems. Poems must be original and unpublished. Each poem should be typed on 8 1/2" by 11" paper, and no longer than three pages. On a cover sheet only, include: name, mailing address, telephone number and e-mail; titles of poems; bio optional. Multiple and simultaneous submissions welcome. Deadline: March 14. Prize: $1,000 honorarium for award-winning poem; $200 Honorable Mention.

KINGSLEY & KATE TUFTS POETRY AWARDS

Claremont Graduate University, Claremont Graduate University, 160 E. Tenth St., Harper East B7, Claremont CA 91711-6165. (909)621-8974. **E-mail:** tufts@cgu.edu. **Website:** www.cgu.edu/tufts. The $100,000 Kingsley Tufts Poetry Award was created to both honor the poet and provide the resources that allow artists to continue working towards the pinnacle of their craft; the Kingsley Tufts Awards goes to a book published by a mid-career poet. The $10,000 Kate Tufts Award is presented annually for a first book by a poet of genuine promise. "Any poet will tell you that the only thing more rare than meaningful recognition is a meaningful payday. For two outstanding poets each year, the Kingsley and Kate Tufts awards represent both." Deadline: July 1, for books published in the preceding year. Prize: $100,000 for the Kingsley Tufts Poetry Award and $10,000 for the Kate Tufts Discovery Award. Please see website for current judges.

⟳ UTMOST CHRISTIAN POETRY CONTEST

Utmost Christian Writers Foundation, 121 Morin Maze, Edmonton Alberta T6K 1V1 Canada, (780)265-4650. **E-mail:** nnharms@telusplanet.net. **Website:** www.utmostchristianwriters.com. **Contact:** Nathan Harms, executive director. Utmost is founded on—and supported by—the dreams, interests and aspirations of individual people. Contest is only open to Christians. Poems may be rhymed or free verse, up to 60 lines, but must not have been published previously or have won any prize in any previous competition of any kind. Submit up to 5 poems. Deadline: February 28. Prizes: 1st Place: $1,000; 2nd Place: $500; 10 prizes of $100 are offered for honorable mention; $300 for best rhyming poem; and $200 for an honorable mention rhyming poem. Judged by a committee of the Directors of Utmost Christian Writers Foundation (who work under the direction of Barbara Mitchell, chief judge).

DANIEL VAROUJAN AWARD

New England Poetry Club, 376 School St., Watertown MA 02472. **E-mail:** contests@nepoetryclub.org. **Website:** www.nepoetryclub.org. **Contact:** Audrey Kalajin. For an unpublished poem (not a translation) worthy of Daniel Varoujan, a poet killed by the Turks in the genocide which destroyed three-fourths of the Armenian population. Previous winners may not enter again. Send entry in duplicate, one without name and address of writer. Deadline: May 31. Prize: $1,000. Judged by well-known poets and sometimes winners of previous NEPC contests.

VASSAR MILLER PRIZE IN POETRY

University of North Texas Press, 1155 Union Circle, #311336, Denton TX 76203. (940)565-2142. **Fax:** (940)565-4590. **Website:** http://untpress.unt.edu. **Contact:** John Poch. Annual prize awarded to a collection of poetry. No limitations to entrants. In years when the judge is announced, it is asked that students of the judge not enter to avoid a perceived conflict. All entries should contain identifying material only on the one cover sheet. Entries are read anonymously. Deadline: Mss may be submitted between 9 A.M. on September 1 and 5 P.M. on October

31, through online submissions manager only. Prize: $1,000 and publication by University of North Texas Press. Judged by a different eminent writer selected each year. Some prefer to remain anonymous until the end of the contest.

⟳ 16TH ANNUAL VENTURA COUNTY WRITERS CLUB POETRY CONTEST

Ventura County Writers Club Poetry Contest, P.O. Box 3373, Thousand Oaks CA 91362. **E-mail:** poetrycontest@venturacountywriters.com. **Website:** www.venturacountywriters.com. **Contact:** Poetry Contest Chair. Annual poetry contest for youth and adult poets. Youth division for poets under 18: Division A is open to entrants ages 13-18; and, Division B is open to poets ages 12 and under. Adult division for poets 18 and older. Club membership not required to enter and entries accepted worldwide as long as fees are paid, poem is unpublished and in English. Enter through website. Deadline: February 14. Entries accepted beginning January 1. Prize: The adult winners will be awarded $100 for first place, $75 for second and $50 for third place. The two youth categories will receive $50 for first place, $35 for second and $25 for third place.

MARICA AND JAN VILCEK PRIZE FOR POETRY

Bellevue Literary Review, New York University School of Medicine, OBV-A612, 550 First Ave., New York NY 10016. (212)263-3973. **E-mail:** info@BLReview.org. **Website:** www.BLReview.org. **Contact:** Stacy Bodziak. The annual Marica and Jan Vilcek Prize for Poetry recognizes outstanding writing related to themes of health, healing, illness, the mind, and the body. All entries will be considered for publication. No previously published poems (including Internet publication). Submit up to 3 poems (5 pages maximum). Electronic (online) submissions only; combine all poems into 1 document and use first poem as document title. See guidelines for additional submission details. Guidelines available for SASE or on website. Deadline: July 1. Prize: $1,000 for best poem and publication in *Bellevue Literary Review*. Previous judges include Mark Doty, Cornelius Eady, Naomi Shihab Nye, and Tony Hoagland.

WABASH PRIZE FOR POETRY

Sycamore Review, Department of English, 500 Oval Dr., Purdue University, West Lafayette IN 47907. **E-mail:** sycamore@purdue.edu; sycamorepoetry@

purdue.edu. **Website:** www.sycamorereview.com/contest/. **Contact:** Anthony Sutton, editor-in-chief. Annual contest for unpublished poetry. For each submission, send up to 3 poems (no more than 6 total pages). Ms pages should be numbered and should include the title of each poem. See website for more guidelines. Submit online via Submittable. Deadline: December 1. Prize: $1,000 and publication.

THE WASHINGTON PRIZE

The Word Works, Dearlove Hall, SUNY Adirondack, 640 Bay Rd., Queensbury NY 12804. **E-mail:** editor@wordworksbooks.org. **Website:** www.wordworksbooks.org. **Contact:** Rebecca Kutzer-Rice, Washington Prize administrator. In addition to its general poetry book publications, The Word Works runs four imprints: The Washington Prize, The Tenth Gate Prize, International Editions, and the Hilary Tham Capital Collection. Selections announced in late summer. Book publication planned for spring of the following year. Submit a poetry ms of 48-80 pages. Submit online with no identifying information appearing within the manuscript; or, if on paper, include 2 title pages, 1 with and 1 without author information, including an acknowledgments page, a table of contents and a brief bio. Electronic submissions are accepted at www.wordworksbooks.org/submissions. The Washington Prize allows poets from all stages of their careers to compete on a level playing field for publication and national recognition. Deadline: Submit January 15-March 15 (postmark). Prize: $1,500 and publication of a book-length ms of original poetry in English by a living US or Canadian citizen. Judged by two tiers of readers, followed by five final judges working as a panel.

WERGLE FLOMP HUMOR POETRY CONTEST

Winning Writers, 351 Pleasant St., PMB 222, Northampton MA 01060 USA. (866)946-9748. **Fax:** (413)280-0539. **E-mail:** adam@winningwriters.com. **Website:** www.winningwriters.com. **Contact:** Adam Cohen. Winning Writers provides expert literary contest information to the public. It is one of the "101 Best Websites for Writers" (*Writer's Digest*). Submit one humor poem online. Length limit: 250 lines. The poem should be in English. Inspired gibberish is also accepted. Submissions may be previously published and may be entered in other contests. Deadline: April 1. Prize: 1st prize of $1,000; 2nd prize of $250; 10 honor-

able mentions of $100 each. All winners of cash prizes published on website. Judged by Jendi Reiter, assisted by Lauren Singer.

WHITE PINE PRESS POETRY PRIZE

White Pine Press, P.O. Box 236, Buffalo NY 14201. **E-mail:** wpine@whitepine.org. **Website:** www.whitepine.org. **Contact:** Dennis Maloney, editor. Offered annually for previously published or unpublished poets. Manuscript: 60-80 pages of original work; translations are not eligible. Poems may have appeared in magazines or limited-edition chapbooks. Open to any US citizen. Deadline: November 30 (postmarked). Prize: $1,000 and publication. Final judge is a poet of national reputation. All entries are screened by the editorial staff of White Pine Press.

STAN AND TOM WICK POETRY PRIZE

Wick Poetry Center, P.O. Box 5190, Kent OH 44240. (330)672-2067. **E-mail:** wickpoetry@kent.edu. **Website:** www.kent.edu/wick/stan-and-tom-wick-poetry-prize. **Contact:** David Hassler, director. Offered annually to a poet who has not previously published a full-length collection of poetry (a volume of 50 or more pages published in an edition of 500 or more copies). Submissions must consist of 50-70 pages of poetry, typed on one side only, with no more than one poem included on a single page. Also accepts submissions online through Submittable. See website for details and guidelines. Deadline: May 1. Submissions period begins February 1. Prize: $2,500 and publication of full-length book of poetry by Kent State University Press.

J. HOWARD AND BARBARA M.J. WOOD PRIZE

Poetry, 61 W. Superior St., Chicago IL 60654. (312)787-7070. **Fax:** (312)787-6650. **E-mail:** editors@poetrymagazine.org. **Website:** www.poetrymagazine.org. Offered annually for poems published in *Poetry* during the preceding year (October-September). Upon acceptance, *Poetry* licenses exclusive worldwide first serial rights, including electronic rights, for publication, as well as non-exclusive rights to reprint, reuse, and archive the work, in any format, in perpetuity. Copyright reverts to author upon first publication. Prize: $5,000.

WORKING PEOPLE'S POETRY COMPETITION

Blue Collar Review, P.O. Box 11417, Norfolk VA 23517. **E-mail:** red-ink@earthlink.net. **Website:** www.partisanpress.org. Poetry should be typed as you would like to see it published, with your name and address on each page. Include cover letter with entry. Guidelines available on website. Deadline: May 15. Prize: $100, 1-year subscription to *Blue Collar Review* (see separate listing in Magazines/Journals) and 1-year posting of winning poem to website.

JAMES WRIGHT POETRY AWARD

Mid-American Review, Dept. of English, Bowling Green State University, Bowling Green OH 43403. (419)372-2725. **Fax:** (419)372-4642. **E-mail:** clouda@bgsu.edu. **Website:** www.bgsu.edu/midamericanreview. **Contact:** Abigail Cloud, poetry editor. Offered annually for unpublished poetry. Open to all writers not associated with *Mid-American Review* or judge. Guidelines available online or for SASE. Deadline: November 1. Prize: $1,000 and publication in spring issue of *Mid-American Review*. Judged by editors and a well known poet, i.e., Kathy Fagan, Bob Hicok, Michelle Boisseau. Judged by Maggie Smith in 2016.

THE YALE SERIES OF YOUNGER POETS

Yale University Press, P.O. Box 209040, New Haven CT 06520-9040. **Website:** youngerpoets.yupnet.org. The Yale Series of Younger Poets champions the most promising new American poets. The Yale Younger Poets prize is the oldest annual literary award in the United States. Open to U.S. citizens under age 40 at the time of entry who have not published a volume of poetry; poets may have published a limited edition chapbook of 300 copies or less. Poems may have been previously published in newspapers and periodicals and used in the book ms if so identified. No translations. Submit 48-64 pages of poetry, paginated, with each new poem starting on a new page. Accepts hard copy and electronic submissions. Deadline: November 15. Submissions period begins October 1.

THE YEMASSEE POETRY CONTEST

Yemassee, Department of English, University of South Carolina, Columbia SC 29208. **E-mail:** editor@yemasseejournal.com. **Website:** http://yemasseejournal.com. **Contact:** Contest Coordinator. The annual Yemassee Poetry Contest offers a $1000 prize and publication in *Yemassee*. Submissions must be unpublished. Considers simultaneous submissions with notice of acceptance elsewhere. Submit 3-5 poems via Submittable page: https://yemassee.submittable.com/submit. Include cover letter with poet's name, contact information, and poem title(s); no identifying information on ms pages except poem title (which should appear on every page). Deadline: January 15.

ZONE 3 FIRST BOOK AWARD FOR POETRY

Zone 3, Austin Peay State University, Austin Peay State University, PO Box 4565, Clarksville TN 37044. (931)221-7031. **Fax:** (931)221-7149. **E-mail:** spofforda@apsu.edu; wallacess@apsu.edu. **Website:** www.apsu.edu/zone3/. **Contact:** Andrea Spofford, poetry editor; Susan Wallace, managing editor. Offered annually for anyone who has not published a full-length collection of poems (48 pages or more). Submit a ms of 48-80 pages. Deadline: April 15. Prize: $1,000 and publication.

MULTIPLE WRITING AREAS

🌐💲💲 AESTHETICA ART PRIZE

Aesthetica Magazine, P.O. Box 371, York YO23 1WL United Kingdom. **E-mail:** info@aestheticamagazine.com; artprize@aestheticamagazine.com. **Website:** www.aestheticamagazine.com. The Aesthetica Art Prize is a celebration of excellence in art from across the world and offers artists the opportunity to showcase their work to wider audiences and further their involvement in the international art world. There are 4 categories: Photograpic & Digital Art, Three Dimensional Design & Sculpture, Painting & Drawing, Video Installation & Performance. See guidelines at Artwork & Photography, Fiction, and Poetry. See guidelines at www.aestheticamagazine.com. The Aesthetica Art Prize is a celebration of excellence in art from across the world and offers artists the opportunity to showcase their work to wider audiences and further their involvement in the international art world. There are 4 categories: Photograpic & Digital Art, Three-Dimensional Design & Sculpture, Painting & Drawing, Video Installation & Performance. See guidelines at Artwork & Photography, Fiction, and Poetry. See guidelines at www.aestheticamagazine.com. Works should be completed in English Deadline: August 31. Prizes include: £5,000 main prize courtesy of Hiscox, £1,000 Student Prize courtesy of Hiscox, group exhibition and publication in the Aesthetica Art Prize Anthology. Entry is £15 and permits submission of two works in one category.

MARIE ALEXANDER POETRY SERIES

English Department, 2801 S. University Ave., Little Rock AR 72204. **E-mail:** editor@mariealexanderseries.com. **Website:** mariealexanderseries.com. **Contact:** Nickole Brown. Annual contest for a collection of previously unpublished prose poems or flash fiction by a U.S. writer. Deadline: July 31. Open to submissions on July 1. Prize: $1,000, plus publication.

ALLIGATOR JUNIPER AWARD

Alligator Juniper/Prescott College, 220 Grove Ave., Prescott AZ 86301. (928)350-2012. **Fax:** (928)776-5102. **E-mail:** alligatorjuniper@prescott.edu. **Website:** www.prescott.edu/alligatorjuniper/national-contest/index.html. **Contact:** Skye Anicca, managing editor. Annual contest for unpublished fiction, creative nonfiction, and poetry. Open to all age levels. Each entrant receives a personal letter from staff regarding the status of their submission, as well as minor feedback on the piece. Accepts simultaneous submissions, but inform on cover letter and contact immediately, should work be selected elsewhere. Maximum length: 30 pages or 5 poems. Deadline: October 1. Prize: $1,000 plus publication in all three categories. Finalists in each genre are recognized as such, published, and paid in copies. Judged by the distinguished writers in each genre and Prescott College writing students enrolled in the Literary Journal Practicum course.

AMERICAS AWARD

Consortium of Latin American Studies Program, Stone Center for Latin American Studies, Tulane University, 100 Jones Hall, New Orleans LA 70118-5698. **Website:** http://claspprograms.org/americasaward. **Contact:** Denise Woltering. The Américas Award encourages and commends authors, illustrators, and publishers who produce quality children's and young adult books that portray Latin America, the Caribbean, or Latinos in the United States. Up to 2 awards (for primary and secondary reading levels) are given in recognition of US published works of fiction, poetry, folklore, or selected nonfiction (from picture books to works for young adults). The award winners and commended titles are selected for their (1) distinctive literary quality; (2) cultural contextualization; (3) exceptional integration of text, illustration and design; and (4) potential for classroom use. To nominate a copyright title from the previous year, publishers are invited to submit review copies to the committee members listed on the website. Publishers should send 8 copies of the nominated book. Deadline: January 4. Prize: $500, plaque and a formal presentation at the Library of Congress, Washington DC.

THE AMERICAN GEM LITERARY FESTIVAL

FilmMakers Magazine / Write Brothers, FilmMakers Magazine (filmmakers.com), **E-mail:** info@filmmakers.com. **Website:** http://filmmakers.com/contests/short_story/. **Contact:** Jennifer Brooks. Worldwide contest to recognize excellent short screenplays and short stories. Ms submissions must be between 3-45 pages (there is an extra fee for anything between 46-65 pages) and up to industry standards. See website for more details. Must not have been previously optioned or sold to market or to a film producer. Preferable that the ms has not yet been adapted to a screenplay. Short stories should be no more than 50 pages, double-spaced, to a maximum of 12,500 words. Must not have been previously published. Deadlines: Early: Feb 29; Regular: April 30; Late: June 30; Final: July 31. Prize: Short Script: 1st Place: $1,000. Other cash and prizes to top 5.

AMERICAN LITERARY REVIEW CONTESTS

American Literary Review, P.O. Box 311307, University of North Texas, Denton TX 76203-1307. (940)565-2755. **E-mail:** americanliteraryreview@gmail.com. **Website:** www.americanliteraryreview.com. Contest to award excellence in short fiction, creative nonfiction, and poetry. Multiple entries are acceptable, but each entry must be accompanied with a reading fee. Do not put any identifying information in the file itself; include the author's name, title(s), address, e-mail address, and phone number in the boxes provided in the online submissions manager. Short fiction: Limit 8,000 words per work. Creative nonfiction: Limit 6,500 words per work. Deadline: October 1. Submission period begins June 1. Prize: $1,000 prize for each category, along with publication in the Spring online issue of the *American Literary Review*.

ARIZONA LITERARY CONTEST & BOOK AWARDS

Arizona Authors' Association, 6939 East Chaparral Road, Paradise Valley AZ 85253-7000 USA. (602) 554-8101. **E-mail:** AzAuthors@gmail.com. **E-mail:** AzAuthors@gmail.com. **Website:** www.azauthors.com. **Contact:** Lisa Aquilina, President. Arizona Authors' Association sponsors annual literary competition in poetry, short story, essay, unpublished novels, and published books (fiction, nonfiction, and children's literature) and Arizona Book of the Year. Cash prizes awarded ($500 Book of the Year) from Green Pieces Press and 1st, 2nd, and 3rd place in seven categories ($150, $75 and $30, respectively) from Vignetta Syndicate LLC. New category in 2016, New Drama Writing, with a grand prize of $250. All category winners are published in the *Arizona Literary Magazine*. Poetry, short story, essay, and new drama writing submissions must be unpublished. Work must have been published in the current or immediate past calendar year. Considers simultaneous submissions. Entry form and guidelines available on website or upon request after submitting an SASE. Deadline: July 1. Begins accepting submissions January 1. Finalists notified by Labor Day weekend. Prizes: Grand Prize, Arizona Book of the Year Award: $500. All categories except new drama writing: 1st Prize: $150 and publication; 2nd Prize: $75 and publication; 3rd Prize: $30 and publication. New drama writing grand prize $250 and publication. Features in *Arizona Literary Magazine* can be taken instead of money and publication. 1st and 2nd prize winners in poetry, essay, and short story are nominated for the Pushcart Prize. Judged by nationwide published authors, editors, literary agents, and reviewers. Winners announced at an awards dinner and ceremony held the first Saturday in November.

ART AFFAIR SHORT STORY AND WESTERN SHORT STORY CONTESTS

Art Affair - Contest, P.O. Box 54302, Oklahoma City OK 73154 USA. **E-mail:** artaffair@aol.com. **Website:** www.shadetreecreations.com. The annual Art Affair Writing Contests include (General) Short Story and Western Short Story categories. See separate listing for Poetry contest. Open to any writer. All short stories must be unpublished. Multiple entries accepted in both categories with separate entry fees for each. Submit original stories on any subject and timeframe for general Short Story category, and submit original western stories for Western Short Story—word limit for all entries is 5,000 words. Guidelines available on website. Put word count in the upper right-hand corner of first page; mark "Western" on western short stories. All ms must be double-spaced on 8.5x11 white paper. Type title of story on first page and headers (with page numbers) on following pages. Include cover page with writer's name, address, phone number, and manuscript title. Deadline: October 1. Prize (in both categories): 1st Place: $50; 2nd Place: $25; 3rd Place: $15.

ARTIST TRUST FELLOWSHIP AWARD

1835 12th Ave., Seattle WA 98122. (209)467-8734, ext. 11. **Fax:** (866)218-7878. **E-mail:** info@artisttrust.org. **Website:** www.artisttrust.org. **Contact:** Miguel Guillen, program manager. Fellowships award $7,500 to practicing professional artists of exceptional talent and demonstrated ability. The Fellowship is a merit-based, not a project-based award. Recipients present a Meet the Artist Event to a community in Washington state that has little or no access to the artist and their work. Awards 14 fellowships of $7,500 and 2 residencies with $1,000 stipends at the Millay Colony. Artist Trust Fellowships are awarded in two-year cycles. Applicants must be 18 years of age or older, Washington State residents at the time of application and payment, and generative artists. Deadline: January 13. Applications available December 3. Prize: $7,500.

ARTS & LETTERS PRIZES

Arts & Letters Journal of Contemporary Culture, Campus Box 89, GC&SU, Milledgeville GA 31061. (478)445-1289. **E-mail:** al.journal@gcsu.edu. **Website:** al.gcsu.edu. **Contact:** The Editors. Offered annually for unpublished work. Deadline: March 31. Prize: $1,000 prize for each of the four major genres. Fiction, poetry, and creative nonfiction winners are published in Fall or Spring issue. The prize-winning one-act play is produced at the Georgia College campus (usually in March). Judged by the editors (initial screening); see website for final judges and further details about submitting work.

THE ATHENAEUM LITERARY AWARD

The Athenaeum of Philadelphia, 219 S. 6th St., Philadelphia PA 19106-3794. (215)925-2688. **Fax:** (215)925-3755. **E-mail:** jilly@PhilaAthenaeum.org. **Website:** www.PhilaAthenaeum.org. **Contact:** Jill Lee, Librarian. The Athenaeum Literary Award was established to recognize and encourage literary achievement among authors who are bona fide residents of Philadelphia or Pennsylvania living within a radius of 30 miles of City Hall at the time their book was written or published. Any volume of general literature is eligible; technical, scientific, and juvenile books are not included. Nominated works are reviewed on the basis of their significance and importance to the general public as well as for literary excellence. Deadline: December 31.

ATLANTIC WRITING COMPETITION FOR UNPUBLISHED MANUSCRIPTS

Writers' Federation of Nova Scotia, 1113 Marginal Rd., Halifax NS B3H 4P7. (902)423-8116. **Fax:** (902)422-0881. **E-mail:** programs@writers.ns.ca. **Website:** www.writers.ns.ca. **Contact:** Robin Spittal, communications and development officer. Annual program designed to honor work by unpublished writers in all 4 Atlantic Provinces. Entry is open to writers unpublished in the category of writing they wish to enter. Prizes are presented in the fall of each year. Categories include: novel, writing for children, poetry, short story, juvenile/young adult novel, creative nonfiction, and play. Judges return written comments when competition is concluded. Page lengths and rules vary based on categories. See website for details. Anyone resident in the Atlantic Provinces since September 1st immediately prior to the deadline date is eligible to enter. Only one entry per category is allowed. Each entry requires its own entry form and registration fee. Deadline: January 7. Prizes vary based on categories. See website for details.

AUTUMN HOUSE POETRY, FICTION, AND NONFICTION PRIZES

P.O. Box 60100, Pittsburgh PA 15211. (412)381-4261. **E-mail:** gcerto@autumnhouse.org; info@autumnhouse.org. **E-mail:** https://autumnhousepress.submittable.com/submit. **Website:** http://autumnhouse.org. **Contact:** Christine Stroud, senior editor. Offers annual prize and publication of book-length ms with national promotion. Submission must be unpublished as a collection, but individual poems, stories, and essays may have been previously published elsewhere. Considers simultaneous submissions. "Autumn House is a nonprofit corporation with the mission of publishing and promoting poetry and other fine literature. We have published books by Chana Bloch, Ellery Akers, Gerald Stern, Ruth L. Schwartz, Ed Ochester, Andrea Hollander, George Bilgere, Ada Limon, and many others." Submit 50-80 pages of poetry or 200-300 pages of prose (include 2 cover sheets requested). Guidelines available for SASE, by e-mail, or on website. Competition receives 1,500 entries/year. Winners announced through mailings, website, and ads in *Poets & Writers*, *American Poetry Review*, and *Writer's Chronicle* (extensive publicity for winner). Copies of winning books available from Amazon.com, Barnes & Noble, and other retailers. Deadline: June 30. Prize:

The winner (in each of three categories) will receive book publication, $1,000 advance against royalties, and a $1,500 travel/publicity grant to promote his or her book. Judged by David St. John(poetry), William Lychack (fiction), and Michael Martone (nonfiction).

AWP AWARD SERIES

Association of Writers & Writing Programs, George Mason University, 4400 University Drive, MSN 1E3, Fairfax VA 22030. **E-mail:** supriya@awpwriter.org. **Website:** www.awpwriter.org. **Contact:** Supriya Bhatnagar, director of publications. AWP sponsors the Award Series, an annual competition for the publication of excellent new book-length works. The competition is open to all authors writing in English regardless of nationality or residence, and is available to published and unpublished authors alike. Guidelines on website. Entries must be unpublished. Open to any writer. Entries are not accepted via postal mail. Offered annually to foster new literary talent. Deadline: Postmarked between January 1 and February 28. Prize: AWP Prize for the Novel: $2,500 and publication by New Issues Press; Donald Hall Prize for Poetry: $5,500 and publication by the University of Pittsburgh Press; Grace Paley Prize in Short Fiction: $5,500 and publication by the University of Massachusetts Press; and AWP Prize for Creative Nonfiction: $2,500 and publication by the University of Georgia Press.

THE BASKERVILLE PUBLISHERS POETRY AWARD & THE BETSY COLQUITT POETRY AWARD

descant, Texas Christian University's literary journal, TCU, Box 297270, Fort Worth TX 76129. **Fax:** (817)257-6239. **Website:** www.descant.tcu.edu. **Contact:** Matthew Pitt, Editor. Annual award for an outstanding poem published in the latest issue of *descant*. Deadline: September-April. Prize: $250 for Baskerville Award; $500 for Betsy Colquitt Award. Publication retains copyright, but will transfer it to the author upon request.

THE BLACK RIVER CHAPBOOK COMPETITION

Black Lawrence Press, 326 Bingham St., Pittsburgh PA 15211. **E-mail:** editors@blacklawrencepress.com. **Website:** www.blacklawrence.com. **Contact:** Kit Frick, senior editor. Twice each year Black Lawrence Press will run the Black River Chapbook Competition for an unpublished chapbook of poems or short fiction between 16-36 pages in length. Submit through Submittable. Spring deadline: May 31. Fall deadline: October 31. Prize: $500, publication, and 10 copies. Judged by a revolving panel of judges, in addition to the Chapbook Editor and other members of the *BLP* editorial staff.

☯ JAMES TAIT BLACK MEMORIAL PRIZES

University of Edinburgh, School of Literatures, Languages, and Cultures, 50 George Square, Edinburgh EH8 9LH Scotland. (44-13)1650-3619. **E-mail:** s.strathdee@ed.ac.uk. **Website:** http://www.ed.ac.uk/news/events/tait-black. Open to any writer. Entries must be previously published. Winners notified by phone, via publisher. Contact department of English Literature for list of winners or check website. Accepts inquiries by e-mail or phone. Eligible works must be written in English and first published or co-published in Britain in the year of the award. Works should be submitted by publishers. Deadline: December 1. Prize: Two prizes each of £10,000 are awarded: one for the best work of fiction, one for the best biography or work of that nature, published during the calendar year January 1 to December 31. Judged by professors of English Literature with the assistance of teams of postgraduate readers.

☯ THE BOARDMAN TASKER PRIZE FOR MOUNTAIN LITERATURE

The Boardman Tasker Charitable Trust, 8 Bank View Rd., Darley Abbey Derby DE22 1EJ UK. 01332 342246. **E-mail:** steve@people-matter.co.uk. **Website:** www.boardmantasker.com. **Contact:** Steve Dean. Offered annually to reward a work with a mountain theme, whether fiction, nonfiction, drama, or poetry, written in the English language (initially or in translation). Subject must be concerned with a mountain environment. Previous winners have been books on expeditions, climbing experiences, a biography of a mountaineer, novels. Guidelines available in January by e-mail or on website. Entries must be previously published. Open to any writer. Writers may obtain information, but entry is by publishers only (includes self-publishing). Awarded for a work published or distributed for the first time in the United Kingdom during the previous year. Not an anthology. The award is to honor Peter Boardman and Joe Tasker, who disappeared on Everest in 1982. Deadline: August 1. Prize: £3,000 Judged by a panel of 3 judges elected by trustees.

☯ BOOK OF THE YEAR AWARD

Saskatchewan Book Awards, Inc., P.O. Box 20025, Regina SK S4P 4J7 Canada. (306)569-1585. **E-mail:** director@bookawards.sk.ca. **Website:** www.bookawards.sk.ca. Offered annually. This award is presented to a Saskatchewan author for the best book, judged on the quality of writing. Books from the following categories will be considered: children's; drama; fiction (short fiction by a single author, novellas, novels); nonfiction (all categories of nonfiction writing except cookbooks, directories, how-to books, or bibliographies of minimal critical content); poetry. Visit website for more details. Deadline: November 1. Prize: $3,000 (CAD).

☯ BOROONDARA LITERARY AWARDS

City of Boroondara, 340 Camberwell Rd., Camberwell VIC 3124 Australia. **E-mail:** bla@boroondara.vic.gov.au. **Website:** www.boroondara.vic.gov.au/literary-awards. Contest for unpublished work in 2 categories: Young Writers: 5th-6th grade (Junior), 7th-9th grade (Middle), and 10th-12th grade (Senior), prose and poetry on any theme; and Open Short Story (1,500-3,000 words). Deadline: 5pm on August 28. Prizes: Young Writers, Junior: 1st Place: $150; 2nd Place: $100; 3rd Place: $50. Young Writers, Middle and Senior: 1st Place: $600; 2nd Place: $400; 3rd Place: $200. Open Short Story: 1st Place: $1,500; 2ndPlace: $1000; 3rd Place $500.

THE BOSTON AUTHORS CLUB BOOK AWARDS

The Boston Authors Club, 33 Brayton Road, Brighton MA 02135. (617)783-1357. **E-mail:** alan.lawson@bc.edu. **Website:** www.bostonauthorsclub.org. **Contact:** Alan Lawson, president. Julia Ward Howe Prize offered annually in the spring for books published the previous year. Two awards are given: one for adult books of fiction, nonfiction, or poetry, and one for children's books, middle grade and young adult novels, nonfiction, or poetry. No picture books or subsidized publishers. There must be two copies of each book submitted. Authors must live within 100 miles of Boston the year their book is published. Deadline: January 15. Prize: $1,000 in each category. Several books will also be cited with no cash awards as Finalists or Highly Recommended.

THE BRIAR CLIFF REVIEW FICTION, POETRY, AND CREATIVE NONFICTION COMPETITION

The Briar Cliff Review, Briar Cliff University, 3303 Rebecca St., Sioux City IA 51104-0100. **E-mail:** tricia.

currans-sheehan@briarcliff.edu (editor); jeanne.emmons@briarcliff.edu (poetry). **Website:** www.bcreview.org. **Contact:** Tricia Currans-Sheehan, editor. *The Briar Cliff Review* sponsors an annual contest offering $1,000 and publication to each 1st Prize winner in fiction, poetry, and creative nonfiction. Previous year's winner and former students of editors ineligible. Winning pieces accepted for publication on the basis of first-time rights. Considers simultaneous submissions, "but notify us immediately upon acceptance elsewhere. We guarantee a considerate reading." No mss returned. Word limit for short story/creative nonfiction is 5,000. For poetry, no more than one poem per page. Award to reward good writers and showcase quality writing. Deadline: November 1. Prize: $1,000 and publication to each 1st Prize winner in fiction, poetry, and creative nonfiction. Judged by *Briar Cliff Review* editors.

THE BRIDPORT PRIZE

P.O. Box 6910, Dorset DT6 9QB United Kingdom. **E-mail:** info@bridportprize.org.uk; kate@bridportprize.org.uk. **Website:** www.bridportprize.org.uk. **Contact:** Kate Wilson, Bridport Prize administrator. Award to promote literary excellence, discover new talent. Categories: Short stories, poetry, flash fiction, first novel. Entries must be unpublished. Length: 5,000 maximum for short stories; 42 lines for poetry, 250 words for flash fiction and 8,000 words max for opening chapters of a novel. Deadline: May 31 each year. Open for submissions starting November 15. Prize: £5,000; £1,000; £500; various runners-up prizes and publication of approximately 13 best stories and 13 best poems in anthology; plus 6 best flash fiction stories. 1st Prize of £1,000 for the best short, short story of under 250 words. £1,000 plus up to a year's mentoring for winner of Peggy Chapman-Andrews Award for a first novel. Judged by 1 judge for short stories (in 2016, Tessa Hadley), 1 judge for poetry (in 2016, Patience Agbabi) and 1 judge for flash fiction (in 2016, Tim Stevenson). The Novel award is judged by a group comprising representatives from The Literary Consultancy, A.M. Heath Literary Agents, and (in 2016) judge Kerry Young.

BRITISH CZECH AND SLOVAK ASSOCIATION WRITING COMPETITION

24 Ferndale, Tunbridge Wells Kent TN2 3NS England. **E-mail:** prize@bcsa.co.uk. **Website:** www.bcsa.co.uk/specials.html. Annual contest for original writing (entries should be 1,500-2,000 words) in English on the links between Britain and the Czech/Slovak Republics, or describing society in transition in the Republics since 1989. Entries can be fact or fiction. Topics can include history, politics, the sciences, economics, the arts, or literature. Deadline: June 30. Winners announced in November. Prize: 1st Place: £300; 2nd Place: £100.

THE RBC BRONWEN WALLACE AWARD FOR EMERGING WRITERS

The Writers' Trust of Canada, 460 Richmond St. W., Suite 600, Toronto ON M5C 1P1 Canada. (416)504-8222. **Fax:** (416)504-9090. **E-mail:** info@writerstrust.com. **Website:** www.writerstrust.com. **Contact:** Amanda Hopkins. Presented annually to a Canadian writer under the age of 35 who is not yet published in book form. The award, which alternates each year between poetry and short fiction, was established in memory of Bronwen Wallace. Deadline: March 7. Prize: $5,000. Two finalists receive $1,000 each.

BURNABY WRITERS' SOCIETY CONTEST

E-mail: info@bws.ca. **Website:** www.bws.ca; www.burnabywritersnews.blogspot.com. **Contact:** Contest Committee. Offered annually for unpublished work. Open to all residents of British Columbia. Categories vary from year to year. Send SASE for current rules. For complete guidelines see website or burnabywritersnews.blogspot.com. Purpose is to encourage talented writers in all genres. Deadline: May 31. Prizes: 1st Place: $200; 2nd Place: $100; 3rd Place: $50; and public reading.

CALIFORNIA BOOK AWARDS

Commonwealth Club of California, 555 Post Street, San Francisco CA 94102 USA. (415) 597-6700. **Fax:** (415)597-6729. **E-mail:** bookawards@commonwealthclub.org. **Website:** www.commonwealthclub.org/. **Contact:** Renee Miguel. Offered annually to recognize California's best writers and illuminate the wealth and diversity of California-based literature. Award is for published submissions appearing in print during the previous calendar year. Can be nominated by publisher or author. Open to California residents (or residents at time of publication). Submit at least 6 copies of each book entered with an official entry form. Open to books, published during the year prior to the contest, whose author must have been a legal resident of California at the time the manuscript was submitted for publication. Entry form and guidelines available for SASE or on website. Deadline: December 22. Prize: Medals and cash prizes to be awarded at publicized event. Judged by 12-15 California professionals with a diverse range of views, backgrounds, and literary experience.

CANADIAN AUTHORS ASSOCIATION EMERGING WRITER AWARD

6 West St. N., Suite 203, Orilla ON L3X 5B8 Canada. **Website:** www.canadianauthors.org. **Contact:** Anita Purcell, executive director. Annual award for a writer under 30 years of age deemed to show exceptional promise in the field of literary creation. Deadline: January 15. Prize: $500. Judging: Each year a trustee for each award appointed by the Canadian Authors Association selects up to 3 judges. Identities of the trustee and judges are confidential.

CBC LITERARY PRIZES/PRIX LITTÉRAIRES RADIO-CANADA

CBC Radio/Radio Canada, Canada Council for the Arts, *enRoute* magazine, P.O. Box 6000, Montreal QC H3C 3A8 Canada. (877)888-6788. **E-mail:** canadawrites@cbc.ca. **Website:** www.cbc.ca/canadawrites. **Contact:** Daphné Santos-Vieira, coordinator. The CBC Literary Prizes Competitions are the only literary competitions that celebrate original, unpublished works in Canada's 2 official languages. There are 3 categories: short story, poetry, and creative nonfiction. Submissions to the short story and creative nonfiction must be 1,200-1,500 words; poetry submissions must be 400-600 words. Poetry submissions can take the form of a long narrative poem, a sequence of connected poems, or a group of unconnected poems. Canadian citizens, living in Canada or abroad, and permanent residents of Canada are eligible to enter. Deadline: October 31 for short story; February 29 for creative nonfiction; May 30 for poetry. See website for when each competition is accepting entries. Prize: For each category, in both English and French: 1st Prize: $6,000; 2nd Prize: $1,000. In addition, winning entries are published in Air Canada's *enRoute* magazine and broadcast on CBC radio. Winning authors also get a 10 days residency at the Banff Centre. First publication rights are granted by winners to *enRoute* magazine and broadcast rights are given to CBC radio. Submissions are judged blind by a jury of qualified writers and editors from around the country. Each category has 3 jurors.

CHRISTIAN BOOK AWARDS

Evangelical Christian Publishers Association, 9633 S. 48th St., Suite 140, Phoenix AZ 85044. (480)966-3998. **Fax:** (480)966-1944. **E-mail:** info@ecpa.org. **Website:** www.ecpa.org. **Contact:** Stan Jantz, ED. The Evangelical Christian Publishers Association (ECPA) recognizes quality and encourages excellence by presenting the ECPA Christian Book Awards® (formerly known as Gold Medallion) each year. Categories include Fiction, Nonfiction, Children, Inspiration, Bibles, Bible Reference, and New Author. All entries must be evangelical in nature and submitted through an ECPA member publisher. Books must have been published in the calendar year prior to the award. Publishing companies submitting entries must be ECPA members in good standing. See website for details. The Christian Book Awards® recognize the highest quality in Christian books and is among the oldest and most prestigious awards program in Christian publishing. Deadline: September 30. Submission period begins September 1. Judged by ECPA members, who are experts, authors and retailers with years of experience in their field.

THE CITY OF VANCOUVER BOOK AWARD

Cultural Services Dept., Woodward's Heritage Building, 111 W. Hastings St., Suite 501, Vancouver BC V6B 1H4 Canada. (604) 829-2007. **Fax:** (604)871-6005. **E-mail:** marnie.rice@vancouver.ca; culture@vancouver.ca. **Website:** https://vancouver.ca/people-programs/city-of-vancouver-book-award.aspx. The annual City of Vancouver Book Award recognizes authors of excellence of any genre who contribute to the appreciation and understanding of Vancouver's history, unique character, or the achievements of its residents. The book must exhibit excellence in one or more of the following areas: content, illustration, design, format. The book must not be copyrighted prior to the previous year. Submit four copies of book. See website for details and guidelines. Deadline: May 18. Prize: $3,000. Judged by an independent jury.

COLORADO BOOK AWARDS

Colorado Humanities & Center for the Book, 7935 E. Prentice Ave., Suite 450, Greenwood Village CO 80111. (303)894-7951. **Fax:** (303)864-9361. **E-mail:**

lansdown@coloradohumanities.org. **Website:** www. coloradohumanities.org. **Contact:** Marnie Lansdown. An annual program that celebrates the accomplishments of Colorado's outstanding authors, editors, illustrators, and photographers. Awards are presented in at least ten categories including anthology/collection, biography, children's, creative nonfiction, fiction, history, nonfiction, pictorial, poetry, and young adult. To be eligible for a Colorado Book Award, a primary contributor to the book must be a Colorado writer, editor, illustrator, or photographer. Current Colorado residents are eligible, as are individuals engaged in ongoing literary work in the state and authors whose personal history, identity, or literary work reflect a strong Colorado influence. Authors not currently Colorado residents who feel their work is inspired by or connected to Colorado should submit a letter with his/her entry describing the connection. Deadline: January 8.

THE CUTBANK CHAPBOOK CONTEST

CutBank Literary Magazine, *CutBank*, University of Montana, English Dept., LA 133, Missoula MT 59812. **E-mail:** editor.cutbank@gmail.com. **Website:** www. cutbankonline.org. **Contact:** Allison Linville, editor-in-chief. This competition is open to original English language mss in the genres of poetry, fiction, and creative nonfiction. While previously published stand-alone pieces or excerpts may be included in a ms, the ms as a whole must be an unpublished work. Looking for startling, compelling, and beautiful original work. "We're looking for a fresh, powerful manuscript. Maybe it will overtake us quietly; gracefully defy genres; satisfyingly subvert our expectations; punch us in the mouth page in and page out. We're interested in both prose and poetry—and particularly work that straddles the lines between genres." Accepts online submissions only. Submit up to 25-40 pages of poetry or prose. Guidelines available online. Deadline: March 31. Submissions period begins January1. Prize: $1,000 and 25 contributor copies. Judged by a guest judge each year.

CWW ANNUAL WISCONSIN WRITERS AWARDS

Council for Wisconsin Writers, 6973 Heron Way, De Forest WI 53532. **E-mail:** karlahuston@gmail.com. **Website:** www.wiswriters.org. **Contact:** Geoff Gilpin, president and annual awards co-chair; Karla Huston, secretary and annual awards co-chair; Jennifer Morales, annual awards co-chair; Edward Schultz,

annual awards co-chair. Offered annually for work published by Wisconsin writers during the previous calendar year. Nine awards: Major Achievement (presented in alternate years); short fiction; short non-fiction; nonfiction book; poetry book; fiction book; children's literature; Lorine Niedecker Poetry Award; Christopher Latham Sholes Award for Outstanding Service to Wisconsin Writers p(resented in alternate years); Essay Award for Young Writers. Open to Wisconsin residents. Entries may be submitted via postal mail only. See website for guidelines and entry forms. Deadline: February 1. Submissions open on November 1. Prizes: First place prizes: $500. Honorable mentions: $50.

DANA AWARDS IN THE NOVEL, SHORT FICTION, AND POETRY

200 Fosseway Dr., Greensboro NC 27445. (336)644-8028. **E-mail:** danaawards@gmail.com. **Website:** www.danaawards.com. **Contact:** Mary Elizabeth Parker, chair. Three awards offered annually for unpublished work written in English. Works previously published online are not eligible. The Dana Awards are re-vamping. The Novel Award is now increased to $2,000, based on a new partnership with Blue Mary Books: Blue Mary has agreed to consider for possible publication not only the Novel Award winning manuscript, but the top 9 other Novel finalists, as well as the 30 top Novel semifinalists. The Short Fiction and Poetry Awards offer the traditional $1,000 awards each and do not offer a publishing option (currently, Blue Mary publishes only novels). See website for further updates. Categories: Novel: For the first 40 pages of a novel completed or in progress; Fiction: Short fiction (no memoirs) up to 10,000 words; Poetry: For best group of 5 poems based on excellence of all 5 (no light verse, no single poem over 100 lines). Purpose is monetary award for work that has not been previously published or received monetary award, but will accept work published simply for friends and family. Deadline: October 31 (postmarked). Prizes: $2,000 for the Novel Award; $1,000 each for the Short Fiction and Poetry awards awards.

DIAGRAM/NEW MICHIGAN PRESS CHAPBOOK CONTEST

New Michigan Press, P.O. Box 210067, English, ML 424, University of Arizona, Tucson AZ 85721. **E-mail:** nmp@thediagram.com. **Website:** www.thediagram. com. **Contact:** Ander Monson, editor. The annual *DI-*

AGRAM/New Michigan Press Chapbook Contest offers $1,000, plus publication and author's copies, with discount on additional copies. Submit 18-44 pages of poetry, fiction, mixed-genre, or genre-bending work. Do not send originals of anything. Include SASE. Guidelines available on website. Deadline: April 29. Prize: $1,000, plus publication. Finalist chapbooks also considered for publication.

EATON LITERARY AGENCY'S ANNUAL AWARDS PROGRAM

Eaton Literary Agency, P.O. Box 49795, Sarasota FL 34230-6795. (941)366-6589. **Fax:** (941)365-4679. **E-mail:** eatonlit@aol.com. **Website:** www.eatonliterary. com. **Contact:** Richard Lawrence, V.P.. Offered biannually for unpublished mss. Entries must be unpublished. Open to any writer. Guidelines available for SASE, by fax, e-mail, or on website. Accepts inquiries by fax, phone, and e-mail. Results announced in April and September. Winners notified by mail. For contest results, send SASE, fax, e-mail, or visit website. Deadline: March 31 (short story); August 31 (book-length). Prize: $2,500 (book-length); $500 (short story). Judged by an independent agency in conjunction with some members of Eaton's staff.

THE VIRGINIA FAULKNER AWARD FOR EXCELLENCE IN WRITING

Prairie Schooner, 123 Andrews Hall, University of Nebraska-Lincoln, Lincoln NE 68588-0334. (402)472-0911. **Fax:** (402)472-1817. **E-mail:** PrairieSchooner@unl.edu. **Website:** www.prairieschooner.unl. edu. **Contact:** Kwame Dawes. Offered annually for work published in *Prairie Schooner* in the previous year. Categories: short stories, essays, novel excerpts, and translations. Accepts inquiries by fax and e-mail. Reads unsolicited mss between May 1 and September 1. Winning entry must have been published in *Prairie Schooner* in the year preceding the award. Results announced in the Spring issue. Winners notified by mail in February or March. Prize: $1,000. Judged by editorial board.

FINELINE COMPETITION FOR PROSE POEMS, SHORT SHORTS, AND ANYTHING IN BETWEEN

Mid-American Review, Dept. of English, Bowling Green State University, Bowling Green OH 43403. (419)372-2725. **E-mail:** mar@bgsu.edu. **Website:** www.bgsu.edu/midamericanreview. **Contact:** Abigail Cloud, editor-in-chief. Offered annually for previously unpublished submissions. Contest open to all writers not associated with current judge or *Mid-American Review*. Deadline: June 1. Prize: $1,000, plus publication in fall issue of *Mid-American Review*; 10 finalists receive notation plus possible publication. 2015 judge: Michael Czyzniejewski.

FISH SHORT MEMOIR PRIZE

Fish Publishing, Durrus, Bantry Co. Cork Ireland. **E-mail:** info@fishpublishing.com. **Website:** www. fishpublishing.com. Annual worldwide contest to recognize the best memoirs submitted to Fish Publishing. Submissions must not have been previously published. Enter online or via postal mail. See website for full details. Word limit: 4,000. Deadline: January 31. Prize: 1st Prize: $1,200. The 10 best memoirs will be published in the Fish Anthology, launched in July at the West Cork Literary Festival.

FREEFALL SHORT PROSE AND POETRY CONTEST

Freefall Literary Society of Calgary, 922 9th Ave. SE, Calgary AB T2G 0S4 Canada. **E-mail:** editors@freefallmagazine.ca. **Website:** www.freefallmagazine.ca. **Contact:** Ryan Stromquist, managing editor. Offered annually for unpublished work in the categories of poetry (5 poems/entry) and prose (3,000 words or less). Recognizes writers and offers publication credits in a literary magazine format. Contest rules and entry form online. Acquires first Canadian serial rights; ownership reverts to author after one-time publication. Deadline: December 31. Prize: 1st Place: $500 (CAD); 2nd Place: $250 (CAD); 3rd Place: $75; Honorable Mention: $25. All prizes include publication in the spring edition of *FreeFall Magazine*. Winners will also be invited to read at the launch of that issue, if such a launch takes place. Honorable mentions in each category will be published and may be asked to read. Travel expenses not included. Judged by current guest editor for issue (who are also published authors in Canada).

GOVERNOR GENERAL'S LITERARY AWARDS

Canada Council for the Arts, 150 Elgin St., P.O. Box 1047, Ottawa ON K1P 5V8 Canada. 1-800-263-5588, ext. 5573. **Website:** www.canadacouncil.ca. The Canada Council for the Arts provides a wide range of grants and services to professional Canadian artists and art organizations in dance, media arts, music, theatre, writing, publishing, and the visual arts. Books must be first edition literary trade books written, translated, or illustrated by Canadian citizens or permanent residents of Canada and published in Canada or abroad in the previous year. In the case of translation, the original work must also be a Canadian-authored title. For complete eligibility criteria, deadlines, and submission procedures, please visit the website at www.canadacouncil.ca. The Governor General's Literary Awards are given annually for the best English-language and French-language work in each of 7 categories, including fiction, nonfiction, poetry, drama, children's literature (text), children's literature (illustrated books), and translation. Deadline: Depends on the book's publication date. See website for details. Prize: Each GG winner receives $25,000. Non-winning finalists receive $1,000. Publishers of the winning titles receive a $3,000 grant for promotional purposes. Evaluated by fellow authors, translators, and illustrators. For each category, a jury makes the final selection.

GREAT LAKES COLLEGES ASSOCIATION NEW WRITERS AWARD

The Great Lakes Colleges Association, 535 W. William, Suite 301, Ann Arbor MI 48103. (734)661-2350. **Fax:** (734)661-2349. **E-mail:** wegner@glca.org. **Website:** www.glca.org. **Contact:** Gregory R. Wegner, Director of Program Development. The Great Lakes Colleges Association (GLCA) is a consortium of 13 independent liberal arts colleges in Ohio, Michigan, Indiana, and Pennsylvania. Nominations should be made by the publisher and should emphasize literary excellence. Deadline: July 25. Prize: Honorarium of at least $500 for winning writers who are invited to give a reading at a member college campus. Each award winner receives invitations from several of the 13 colleges of the GLCA to visit campus. At these campus events an author will give readings, meet students and faculty, and occasionally lead discussions or classes. In addition to an honorarium for each campus visit, travel costs to colleges are paid by GLCA and its member colleges. Judged by professors of literature and writers in residence at GLCA colleges.

HACKNEY LITERARY AWARDS

4650 Old Looney Mill Rd, Birmingham AL 35243. **E-mail:** info@hackneyliteraryawards.org. **Website:** www.hackneyliteraryawards.org. **Contact:** Myra Crawford, PhD, executive director. Offered annu-

ally for unpublished novels, short stories (maximum 5,000 words), and poetry (50 line limit). Guidelines on website. Deadline: September 30 (novels), November 30 (short stories and poetry). Prize: $5,000 in annual prizes for poetry and short fiction ($2,500 national and $2,500 state level). 1st Place: $600; 2nd Place: $400; 3rd Place: $250; plus $5,000 for an unpublished novel. Competition winners will be announced on the website each March.

THE JULIA WARD HOWE/BOSTON AUTHORS AWARD

The Boston Authors Club, The Boston Authors Club, 36 Sunhill Lane, Newton Center MA 02459. **E-mail:** bostonauthors@aol.com;. **Website:** www.bostonauthorsclub.org. **Contact:** Alan Lawson. This annual award honors Julia Ward Howe and her literary friends who founded the Boston Authors Club in 1900. It also honors the membership over 110 years, consisting of novelists, biographers, historians, governors, senators, philosophers, poets, playwrights, and other luminaries. There are 2 categories: trade books and books for young readers (beginning with chapter books through young adult books). Authors must live or have lived (college counts) within a hundred 100-mile radius of Boston within the last 5 years. Subsidized books, cook books and picture books are not eligible. Deadline: January 15. Prize: $1,000. Judged by the members.

HENRY HOYNS & POE/FAULKNER FELLOWSHIPS

Creative Writing Program, 219 Bryan Hall, P.O. Box 400121, University of Virginia, Charlottesville VA 22904-4121. (434)924-6675. **Fax:** (434)924-1478. **E-mail:** creativewriting@virginia.edu. **Website:** creativewriting.virginia.edu. **Contact:** Jeb Livingood, associate director. Two-year MFA program in poetry and fiction; all students receive fellowships and teaching stipends that total $18,000 in both years of study. Sample poems/prose required with application. Deadline: December 15.

INDIANA REVIEW ½ K PRIZE

Indiana Review, Ballantine Hall 465, 1020 E. Kirkwood Ave., Indiana University, Bloomington IN 47405-7103. (812)855-3439. **Fax:** (812)855-9535. **E-mail:** inreview@indiana.edu. **Website:** http://indianareview.org. **Contact:** Katie Moulton, consulting editor. Offered annually for unpublished work. Maximum story/poem length is 500 words. Guidelines available in March for SASE, by phone, e-mail, on website, or in publication. Open to any writer. Cover letter should include name, address, phone, e-mail, word count and title. No identifying information on ms. "We look for command of language and form." Results announced in August. Winners notified by mail. For contest results, send SASE or visit website. Deadline: August 15. Submission period begins July 1. Prize: $1,000, plus publication, contributor's copies, and a year's subscription to *Indiana Review*.

INSIGHT WRITING CONTEST

Insight Magazine, 55 W. Oak Ridge Dr., Hagerstown MD 21740-7390. **Fax:** (301)393-4055. **E-mail:** insight@rhpa.org. **Website:** www.insightmagazine.org. **Contact:** Omar Miranda, editor. Annual contest for writers in the categories of student short story, general short story, and student poetry. Unpublished submissions only. General category is open to all writers; student categories must be age 22 and younger. Deadline: July 31. Prizes: Student Short and General Short Story: 1st Prize: $250; 2nd Prize: $200; 3rd Prize: $150. Student Poetry: 1st Prize: $100; 2nd Prize: $75; 3rd Prize: $50.

THE IOWA REVIEW AWARD IN POETRY, FICTION, AND NONFICTION

308 EPB, University of Iowa, Iowa City IA 52242. **E-mail:** iowa-review@uiowa.edu. **Website:** www.iowareview.org. *The Iowa Review* Award in Poetry, Fiction, and Nonfiction presents $1,500 to each winner in each genre and $750 to runners-up. Winners and runners-up published in *The Iowa Review*. Submissions must be unpublished. Considers simultaneous submissions (with notification of acceptance elsewhere). Submit up to 25 pages of prose, (double-spaced) or 10 pages of poetry (1 poem or several, but no more than 1 poem per page). Submit online. Include cover page with writer's name, address, e-mail and/or phone number, and title of each work submitted. Personal identification must not appear on ms pages. Guidelines available on website. Deadline: January 31. Submission period begins January 1. Judged by Brenda Shaughnessy, Kelly Link, and Eula Biss in 2016.

JAPAN-U.S. FRIENDSHIP COMMISSION PRIZE FOR THE TRANSLATION OF JAPANESE LITERATURE

Japanese Literary Translation Prize, Donald Keene Center of Japanese Culture, Columbia University, 507 Kent Hall 1140 Amsterdam Ave., New York NY 10027.

Website: http://www.keenecenter.org/. **Contact:** Yoshiko Niiya, Program Coordinator. The Donald Keene Center of Japanese Culture at Columbia University annually awards Japan-U.S. Friendship Commission Prizes for the Translation of Japanese Literature. A prize is given for the best translation of a modern work or a classical work, or the prize is divided between equally distinguished translations. Translators must be citizens or permanent residents of the United States. Deadline: June 1. Prize: $6,000.

LEAGUE OF UTAH WRITERS CONTEST

The League of Utah Writers, The League of Utah Writers, P.O. Box 64, Lewiston UT 84320. (435)755-7609. **E-mail:** luwcontest@gmail.com; luwriters@gmail.com. **Website:** www.luwriters.org. Open to any writer, the LUW Contest provides authors an opportunity to get their work read and critiqued. Multiple categories are offered; see website for details. Entries must be the original and unpublished work of the author. Winners are announced at the Annual Writers Round-Up in September. Those not present will be notified by e-mail. Deadline: June 15. Submissions period begins March 15. Prize: Cash prizes are awarded. Judged by professional authors and editors from outside the League.

LES FIGUES PRESS NOS BOOK CONTEST

P.O. Box 7736, Los Angeles CA 90007. (323)734-4732. **E-mail:** info@lesfigues.com. **Website:** www.lesfigues.com. **Contact:** Teresa Carmody, director. Les Figues Press creates aesthetic conversations between writers/artists and readers, especially those interested in innovative/experimental/avant-garde work. The Press intends in the most premeditated fashion to champion the trinity of Beauty, Belief, and Bawdry. Submit a 64-250 page unpublished manuscript through electronic submissions manager. Eligible submissions include: poetry, novellas, innovative novels, anti-novels, short story collections, lyric essays, hybrids, and all forms *not otherwise specified*. Guidelines available online. Deadline: September 15. Prize: $1,000, plus publication by Les Figues Press. Each entry receives LFP book.

THE HUGH J. LUKE AWARD

Prairie Schooner, 123 Andrews Hall, University of Nebraska-Lincoln, Lincoln NE 68588-0334. (402)472-0911. **Fax:** (402)472-1817. **E-mail:** prairieschooner@unl.edu. **Website:** www.prairieschooner.unl.edu. **Contact:** Kwame Dawes. Offered annually for work published in *Prairie Schooner* in the previous year. Results announced in the Spring issue. Winners notified by mail in February or March. Prize: $250. Judged by editorial staff of *Prairie Schooner*.

⊘ MANITOBA BOOK AWARDS

c/o Manitoba Writers' Guild, 218-100 Arthur St., Winnipeg MB R3B 1H3 Canada. (204)944-8013. **E-mail:** events@mbwriter.mb.ca. **Website:** www.manitobabookawards.com. **Contact:** Anita Daher. Offered annually: The McNally Robinson Book of Year Award (adult); The McNally Robinson Book for Young People Awards (8 and under and 9 and older); The John Hirsch Award for Most Promising Manitoba Writer; The Mary Scorer Award for Best Book by a Manitoba Publisher; The Carol Shields Winnipeg Book Award; The Eileen McTavish Sykes Award for Best First Book; The Margaret Laurence Award for Fiction; The Alexander Kennedy Isbister Award for Nonfiction; The Manuela Dias Book Design of the Year Award; The Best Illustrated Book of the Year Award; the biennial Le Prix Littéraire Rue-Deschambault; The Beatrice Mosionier Aboriginal Writer of the Year Award; and The Chris Johnson Award for Best Play by a Manitoba Playwright. Guidelines and submission forms available online. Open to Manitoba writers only. Deadline: October 31 and December 31. See website for specific details on book eligibility at deadlines. Prize: Several prizes up to $5,000 (Canadian).

⊘ THE MCGINNIS-RITCHIE MEMORIAL AWARD

Southwest Review, Southern Methodist University, P.O. Box 750374, Dallas TX 75275-0374. (214)768-1037. **Fax:** (214)768-1408. **E-mail:** swr@mail.smu.edu. **Website:** www.smu.edu/southwestreview. **Contact:** Jennifer Cranfill, senior editor. The McGinnis-Ritchie Memorial Award is given annually to the best works of fiction and nonfiction that appeared in the magazine in the previous year. Mss are submitted for publication, not for the prizes themselves. Guidelines for SASE or online. Prize: $500. Judged by Jennifer Cranfill and Willard Spiegelman.

TIPS "Not an open contest. Annual prize in which winners are chosen from published pieces during the preceding year."

MINNESOTA BOOK AWARDS

325 Cedar Street, Suite 555, St. Paul MN 55101. (651)222-3242. **Fax:** (651)222-1988. **E-mail:** mnboo-kawards@thefriends.org; friends@thefriends.org; info@thefriends.org. **Website:** www.mnbookawards.org. A year-round program celebrating and honoring Minnesota's best books, culminating in an annual awards ceremony. Recognizes and honors achievement by members of Minnesota's book and book arts community. All books must be the work of a Minnesota author or primary artistic creator (current Minnesota resident who maintains a year-round residence in Minnesota). All books must be published within the calendar year prior to the Awards presentation. Deadline: Nomination should be submitted by 5:00 p.m. on the first Friday in December.

MISSISSIPPI REVIEW PRIZE

Mississippi Review, 118 College Dr., #5144, Hattiesburg MS 39406-0001. (601)266-4321. **Fax:** (601)266-5757. **E-mail:** msreview@usm.edu. **Website:** www.mississippireview.com. Annual contest starting August 1 and running until January 1. Winners and finalists will make up next spring's print issue of the national literary magazine *Mississippi Review*. Each entrant will receive a copy of the prize issue. Contest is open to all writers in English except current or former students or employees of The University of Southern Mississippi. Fiction entries should be 1,000-8,000 words, poetry entries should be 3-5 poems totaling 10 pages or less. There is no limit on the number of entries you may submit. Online submissions must be submitted through Submittable site: mississippireview.submittable.com/submit. No mss will be returned. Previously published work is ineligible. Winners will be announced in March and publication is scheduled for June of following year. Entries should have "MR Prize," author name, address, phone, e-mail and title of work on page 1. Deadline: January 1. Prize: $1,000 in fiction and poetry. Judged by Andrew Malan Milward in fiction, and Angela Ball in poetry.

MOUNTAINS & PLAINS INDEPENDENT BOOKSELLERS ASSOCIATION READING THE WEST BOOK AWARDS

Mountains & Plains Independent Booksellers Association, 3278 Big Spruce Way, Park City UT 84098 USA. **E-mail:** Submission is via an online form, posted on the website (www.mountainsplains.org) in the spring of each year. **Website:** http://www.mountainsplains.org/reading-the-west-book-awards/. **Contact:** Laura P Burnett. Mountains & Plains Independent Booksellers Association is a professional trade organization with the primary mission of supporting independent bookseller members in a 12-state region in the West. Also welcomes as members colleagues in the book industry including authors, publishers, sales representatives, and others. The purpose of these annual awards is to honor outstanding books published in the previous calendar year which are set in the region (Arizona, Colorado, Kansas, Montana, Nebraska, Nevada, New Mexico, Oklahoma, South Dakota, Texas, Utah, and Wyoming) or that evoke the spirit of the region. The author's place of residence is immaterial for these awards. Deadline: Nomination period October 1-December 31 for books published in the previous calendar year. Prize: All nominated titles are listed on the website (www.mountainsplains.org). Shortlist and winning titles are recognized via a press release, e-announcement, and on the website. Winners are recognized at a Reading the West luncheon at the Fall Discovery Show and in promotional materials. Judged by 2 panels of judges, 1 for adult titles and 1 for children's titles. Other categories/panels may be convened at the Association's discretion.

NATIONAL BOOK AWARDS

The National Book Foundation, 90 Broad St., Suite 604, New York NY 10004. (212)685-0261. **E-mail:** nationalbook@nationalbook.org; agall@nationalbook.org. **Website:** www.nationalbook.org. **Contact:** Amy Gall. The National Book Foundation and the National Book Awards celebrate the best of American literature, expand its audience, and enhance the cultural value of great writing in America. The contest offers prizes in 4 categories: fiction, nonfiction, poetry, and young people's literature. Books should be published between December 1 and November 30 of the past year. Submissions must be previously published and must be entered by the publisher. General guidelines available on website. Interested publishes should phone or e-mail the Foundation. Deadline: Submit entry form, payment, and a copy of the book by July 1. Prize: $10,000 in each category. Finalists will each receive a prize of $1,000. Judged by a category specific panel of 5 judges for each category.

NATIONAL OUTDOOR BOOK AWARDS

921 S. 8th Ave., Stop 8128, Pocatello ID 83209. (208)282-3912. **E-mail:** wattron@isu.edu. **Website:** www.noba-web.org. **Contact:** Ron Watters. Nine categories: History/biography, outdoor literature, instructional texts, outdoor adventure guides, nature guides, children's books, design/artistic merit, natural history literature, and nature and the environment. Additionally, a special award, the Outdoor Classic Award, is given annually to books which, over a period of time, have proven to be exceptionally valuable works in the outdoor field. Application forms and eligibility requirements are available online. Applications for the Awards program become available in early June. Deadline: August 25. Prize: Winning books are promoted nationally and are entitled to display the National Outdoor Book Award (NOBA) medallion.

THE NEUTRINO SHORT-SHORT CONTEST

Passages North, Dept. of English, Northern Michigan University, 1401 Presque Isle Ave., Marquette MI 49855. (906)227-1203. **Fax:** (906)227-1096. **E-mail:** passages@nmu.edu. **Website:** www.passagesnorth.com. **Contact:** Jennifer Howard. Offered every 2 years to publish new voices in literary fiction, nonfiction, hybrid-essays and prose poems (maximum 1,000 words). Guidelines available for SASE or online. Deadline: April 15. Submission period begins February 15. Prize: $1,000, and publication for the winner; 2 honorable mentions also published; all entrants receive a copy of *Passages North*. Judged by Lindsay Hunter in 2016.

NEW ENGLAND BOOK AWARDS

1955 Massachusetts Ave., #2, Cambridge MA 02140. (617)547-3642. **Fax:** (617)547-3759. **E-mail:** nan@neba.org. **Website:** http://www.newenglandbooks.org/BookAwards. **Contact:** Nan Sorenson, administrative coordinator. Annual award. Previously published submissions only. Submissions made by New England booksellers; publishers. Submit written nominations only; actual books should not be sent. Member bookstores receive materials to display winners' books. Award is given to a specific title, fiction, nonfiction, children's. The titles must be either about New England, set in New England or by an author residing in the New England. The titles must be hardcover, paperback original or reissue that was published between September 1 and August 31. Entries must be still in print and available. Deadline: June 10. Prize: Winners will receive $250 for literacy to a charity of their choice. Judged by NEIBA membership.

NEW LETTERS LITERARY AWARDS

New Letters, University of Missouri-Kansas City, 5101 Rockhill Rd., Kansas City MO 64110-2499 USA.

(816)235-1168. **Fax:** (816)235-2611. **Website:** http://www.newletters.org/writers-wanted/writing-contests. Award has 3 categories (fiction, poetry, and creative nonfiction) with 1 winner in each. Offered annually for previously unpublished work. For guidelines, send an SASE to *New Letters*, or visit http://www.newletters.org/writers-wanted/writing-contests. Deadline: May 18. Prize: 1st place: $1,500, plus publication. Judged by regional writers of prominence and experience. Final judging by someone of national repute. Previous judges include Maxine Kumin, Albert Goldbarth, Charles Simic, and Janet Burroway.

NEW MILLENNIUM AWARDS FOR FICTION, POETRY, AND NONFICTION

New Millennium Writings, 4021 Garden Dr., Knoxville TN 37918. (865)254-4880. **Website:** www.newmillenniumwritings.org. **Contact:** Alexis Williams, Editor and Publisher. No restrictions as to style, content or number of submissions. Previously published pieces acceptable if online or under 5,000 print circulation. Simultaneous and multiple submissions welcome. Each fiction or nonfiction piece is a separate entry and should total no more than 6,000 words, except for the Short-Short Fiction Award, which should total no more than 1,000 words. (Nonfiction includes essays, profiles, memoirs, interviews, creative nonfiction, travel, humor, etc.) Each poetry entry may include up to 3 poems, not to exceed 5 pages total. All 20 poetry finalists will be published. Include name, phone, address, e-mail, and category on cover page only. Apply online via submissions manager. Send SASE or IRC for list of winners or await your book. Deadline: Postmarked on or before January 31 for the Winter Awards and July 31 for the Summer Awards. Prize: $1,000 for Best Poem; $1,000 for Best Fiction; $1,000 for Best Nonfiction; $1,000 for Best Short-Short Fiction.

NEW SOUTH WRITING CONTEST

English Department, Georgia State University, P.O. Box 3970, Atlanta GA 30302-3970. **E-mail:** newsouth@gsu.edu. **Website:** newsouthjournal.com/contest. **Contact:** Stephanie Devine, editor-in-chief. Offered annually to publish the most promising work of up-and-coming writers of poetry (up to 3 poems) and fiction (9,000 word limit). Rights revert to writer upon publication. Guidelines online. Deadline: April 15. Prize: 1st Place: $1,000 in each category; 2nd Place: $250; and publication to winners. Judged by Anya Silver in poetry and Matthew Salesses in prose.

NORTHERN CALIFORNIA BOOK AWARDS

Northern California Book Reviewers Association, c/o Poetry Flash, 1450 Fourth St. #4, Berkeley CA 94710. (510)525-5476. **E-mail:** ncbr@poetryflash.org; editor@poetryflash.org. **Website:** www.poetryflash.org. **Contact:** Joyce Jenkins, executive director. Annual Northern California Book Award for outstanding book in literature, open to books published in the current calendar year by Northern California authors. NCBR presents annual awards to Bay Area (northern California) authors annually in fiction, nonfiction, poetry and children's literature. Previously published books only. Must be published the calendar year prior to spring awards ceremony. Submissions nominated by publishers; author or agent could also nominate published work. Send 3 copies of the book to attention: NCBR. Encourages writers and stimulates interest in books and reading. Deadline: December 28. Prize: $100 honorarium and award certificate. Judging by voting members of the Northern California Book Reviewers.

OHIOANA BOOK AWARDS

Ohioana Library Association, 274 E. First Ave., Suite 300, Columbus OH 43201-3673. (614)466-3831. **Fax:** (614)728-6974. **E-mail:** ohioana@ohioana.org. **Website:** www.ohioana.org. **Contact:** David Weaver, executive director. Writers must have been born in Ohio or lived in Ohio for at least 5 years, but books about Ohio or an Ohioan need not be written by an Ohioan. Finalists announced in May and winners in July. Winners notified by mail in early summer. Offered annually to bring national attention to Ohio authors and their books, published in the last year. (Books can only be considered once.) Categories: Fiction, nonfiction, juvenile, poetry, and books about Ohio or an Ohioan. Deadline: December 31. Prize: $1,000 cash prize, certificate, and glass sculpture. Judged by a jury selected by librarians, book reviewers, writers and other knowledgeable people.

OKLAHOMA BOOK AWARDS

200 NE 18th St., Oklahoma City OK 73105. (405)521-2502. **Fax:** (405)525-7804. **E-mail:** connie.armstrong@libraries.ok.gov. **Website:** www.odl.state.ok.us/ocb. **Contact:** Connie Armstrong, executive director. This award honors Oklahoma writers and books about Oklahoma. Awards are presented to best books in fiction, nonfiction, children's, design and illustration, and poetry books about Oklahoma

or books written by an author who was born, is living or has lived in Oklahoma. SASE for award rules and entry forms. Winner will be announced at banquet in Oklahoma City. The Arrell Gibson Lifetime Achievement Award is also presented each year for a body of work. Previously published submissions only. Submissions made by the author, author's agent, or entered by a person or group of people, including the publisher. Must be published during the calendar year preceding the award. Deadline: January 10. Prize: Awards a medal. Judging by a panel of 5 people for each category, generally a librarian, a working writer in the genre, booksellers, editors, etc.

☾ OPEN SEASON AWARDS

The Malahat Review, University of Victoria, P.O. Box 1700, Stn CSC, Victoria BC V8V 2Y2 Canada. (250)721-8524. **Fax:** (250)472-5051. **E-mail:** malahat@uvic.ca. **Website:** www.malahatreview.ca. **Contact:** John Barton, editor. The Open Season Awards accepts entries of poetry, fiction, and creative nonfiction. Winners published in spring issue of *Malahat Review* announced in winter on website, facebook page, and in quarterly e-newsletter, *Malahat lite*. Submissions must be unpublished. No simultaneous submissions. Submit up to 3 poems of 100 lines or less; 1 piece of fiction 2,500 words maximum; or 1 piece of creative nonfiction, 2,500 words maximum. No restrictions on subject matter or aesthetic approach. Include separate page with writer's name, address, e-mail, and title(s); no identifying information on mss pages. E-mail submissions now accepted: season@uvic.ca. Do not include SASE for results; mss will not be returned. Guidelines available on website. Winners and finalists will be contacted by e-mail. Deadline: November 1. Prize: $1,000 CAD and publication in *The Malahat Review* in each category.

OREGON BOOK AWARDS

925 SW Washington St., Portland OR 97205. (503)227-2583. **Fax:** (503)241-4256. **E-mail:** la@literary-arts.org. **Website:** www.literary-arts.org. **Contact:** Susan Denning, director of programs and events. The annual Oregon Book Awards celebrate Oregon authors in the areas of poetry, fiction, nonfiction, drama and young readers' literature published between August 1 and July 31 of the previous calendar year. Awards are available for every category. See website for details. Entry fee determined by initial print run; see website for details. Entries must be previously published. Or-

egon residents only. Accepts inquiries by phone and e-mail. Finalists announced in January. Winners announced at an awards ceremony in November. List of winners available in April. Deadline: August 29. Prize: Grant of $2,500. (Grant money could vary.) Judged by writers who are selected from outside Oregon for their expertise in a genre. Past judges include Mark Doty, Colson Whitehead and Kim Barnes.

JUDITH SIEGEL PEARSON AWARD

Judith Siegel Pearson Award, c/o Department of English, Wayne State University, Attn: Royanne Smith, 5057 Woodward Ave, Ste. 9408, Detroit MI 48202. **E-mail:** fm8146@wayne.edu. **Website:** https://wsu-writingawards.submittable.com/submit. **Contact:** Donovan Hohn. Offers an annual award for the best creative or scholarly work on a subject concerning women. The type of work accepted rotates each year: drama in 2016, poetry in 2017; nonfiction in 2018; fiction in 2019. Open to all interested writers and scholars. Only submit the appropriate genre in each year. Submit electronically on the web site listed here. Deadline: February 22. Prize: $500. Judged by members of the writing faculty of the Wayne State University English Department.

PEN CENTER USA LITERARY AWARDS

PEN Center USA, P.O. Box 6037, Beverly Hills CA 90212. (323)424-4939. **E-mail:** awards@penusa.org. **E-mail:** awards@penusa.org. **Website:** www.penusa.org. Offered for work published or produced in the previous calendar year. Open to writers living west of the Mississippi River. Award categories: fiction, poetry, research nonfiction, creative nonfiction, translation, children's/young adult, graphic literature, drama, screenplay, teleplay, journalism. Guidelines and submission form available on website. No anthologies, publish-on-demand, or self-published work. Deadline for book categories: 4 copies must be postmarked by December 31. Deadline for non-book categories: 4 copies must be postmarked by February 28. Prize: $1,000.

PENGUIN RANDOM HOUSE CREATIVE WRITING AWARDS

One Scholarship Way, P.O. Box 297, St. Peter MN 56082. (212)782-9348. **Fax:** (212) 782-5157. **E-mail:** creativewriting@penguinrandomhouse.com. **Website:** www.penguinrandomhouse.com/creativewriting. **Contact:** Melanie Fallon Hauska, director. Offered annually for unpublished work to NYC public high school seniors. 72 awards given in literary and nonliterary categories. Four categories: poetry, fiction/drama, personal essay, and graphic novel. Applicants must be seniors (under age 21) at a New York high school. No college essays or class assignments will be accepted. Word length: 2,500 words or less. Applicants must be seniors (under age 21) at a New York high school. Results announced mid-May. Winners notified by mail and phone. For contest results, send SASE, fax, e-mail or visit website. Deadline: February 5 for all categories. Graphic Novel extended deadline: March 1st. Prize: Awards range from $500-10,000. The program usually awards just under $100,000 in scholarships.

THE PINCH LITERARY AWARDS

Literary Awards, The Pinch, Department of English, The University of Memphis, Memphis TN 38152-6176. (901)678-4591. **E-mail:** editor@thepinchjournal.com. **Website:** www.thepinchjournal.com. Offered annually for unpublished short stories of 5,000 words maximum or up to three poems. Guidelines on website. Cost: $20, which is put toward one issue of *The Pinch*. Deadline: March 15. Prize: 1st place Fiction: $1,500 and publication; 1st place Poetry: $1,000 and publication. Offered annually for unpublished short stories and prose of up to 5,000 words and 1-3 poems. Deadline: March 15. Open to submissions on December 15. Prizes: $1,000 for 1st place in each category.

PNWA LITERARY CONTEST

Pacifc Northwest Writers Association, PMB 2717, 1420 NW Gilman Blvd., Suite 2, Issaquah WA 98027. (452)673-2665. **Fax:** (452)961-0768. **E-mail:** pnwa@pnwa.org. **Website:** www.pnwa.org. Annual literary contest with 12 different categories. See website for details and specific guidelines. Each entry receives 2 critiques. Winners announced at the PNWA Summer Conference, held annually in mid-July. Deadline: February 20. Prize: 1st Place: $600; 2nd Place: $300; 3rd Place: $100. Judged by an agent or editor attending the conference.

PRAIRIE SCHOONER BOOK PRIZE

Prairie Schooner and the University of Nebraska Press, Prairie Schooner Prize Series, 123 Andrews Hall, Lincoln NE 68588-0334. (402)472-0911. **E-mail:** PSBookPrize@unl.edu. **Website:** prairieschooner.unl.edu. **Contact:** Kwame Dawes, editor. Annual competition/award for story collections. The Prairie

Schooner Book Prize Series welcomes manuscripts from all living writers, including non-US citizens, writing in English. Both unpublished and published writers are welcome to submit manuscripts. Writers may enter both contests. Simultaneous submissions are accepted, but we ask that you notify us immediately if your manuscript is accepted for publication somewhere else. No past or present paid employee of Prairie Schooner or the University of Nebraska Press or current faculty or student at the University of Nebraska will be eligible for the prizes. Deadline: March 15. Prize: $3,000 and publication through the University of Nebraska Press.

THE PRESIDIO LA BAHIA AWARD

Sons of the Republic of Texas, 1717 Eighth St., Bay City TX 77414-5033. (979)245-6644. **Fax:** (979)244-3819. **E-mail:** srttexas@srttexas.org. **Website:** www.srttexas.org. **Contact:** Scott Dunbar, chairman. "Material may be submitted concerning the influence on Texas culture of our Spanish Colonial heritage in laws, customs, language, religion, architecture, art, and other related fields." Offered annually to promote suitable preservation of relics, appropriate dissemination of data, and research into Texas heritage, with particular attention to the Spanish Colonial period. Deadline: September 30. Prizes: $2,000 available annually for winning participants; 1st Place: Minimum of $1,200; 2nd and 3rd prizes at the discretion of the judges. Judged by members of the Sons of the Republic of Texas on the Presidio La Bahia Award Committee.

PRIME NUMBER MAGAZINE AWARDS

Press 53, 560 N. Trade St., Suite 103, Winston-Salem NC 27101. (336)770-5353. **Fax:** N/A. **E-mail:** kevin@press53.com. **Website:** www.press53.com. **Contact:** Kevin Morgan Watson, Publisher. Awards $1,000 in poetry and short fiction. Details and guidelines available online. Deadline: April 15. Submission period begins January 1. Finalists announced June 1. Winner announced on August 1. Prize: $1,000 cash. All winners receive publication in Prime Number Magazine online. Judged by industry professionals to be named when the contest begins.

☉ PRISM INTERNATIONAL ANNUAL SHORT FICTION, POETRY, AND CREATIVE NONFICTION CONTESTS

PRISM International, Creative Writing Program, UBC, Buch. E462, 1866 Main Mall, Vancouver BC V6T 1Z1 Canada. **E-mail:** promotions@prismmagazine.ca. **Website:** www.prismmagazine.ca. **Contact:** Claire Matthews. Offered annually for unpublished work to award the best in contemporary fiction, poetry, drama, translation, and nonfiction. Works of translation are eligible. Guidelines are available on website. Acquires first North American serial rights upon publication, and limited web rights for pieces selected for website. Open to any writer except students and faculty in the Creative Writing Department at UBC, or people who have taken a creative writing course at UBC within 2 years of the contest deadline. Entry includes subscription. Deadlines: Creative Nonfiction: November 20; Fiction and Poetry: January 15. Prize: All grand prizes are $1,500, $600 for first runner up, and $400 for second runner up. Winners are published.

SUMMERFIELD G. ROBERTS AWARD

Sons of the Republic of Texas, 1717 Eighth St., Bay City TX 77414-5033. (979)245-6644. **Fax:** (979)244-3819. **E-mail:** aa-srt@son-rep-texas.net. **Website:** www.srttexas.org. **Contact:** David Hanover, chairman. The manuscripts must be written or published during the calendar year for which the award is given. No entry may be submitted more than one time. There is no word limit on the material submitted for the award. The manuscripts may be fiction, nonfiction, poems, essays, plays, short stories, novels, or biographies. The competition is open to all writers everywhere; they need not reside in Texas nor must the publishers be in Texas. Judges each year are winners of the award in the last three years. The purpose of this award is to encourage literary effort and research about historical events and personalities during the days of the Republic of Texas,1836-1846, and to stimulate interest in this period. Deadline: January 15. Prize: $2,500.

ROYAL DRAGONFLY BOOK AWARDS

Five Star Publications, Inc., 4696 W. Tyson St., Chandler AZ 85226. (480)940-8182. **Fax:** (480)940-8787. **E-mail:** cristy@fivestarpublications.com; fivestarpublications@gmail.com. **E-mail:** cristy@fivestarpublications.com. **Website:** www.fivestarpublications.com; www.fivestarbookawards.com; www.royaldragonflybookawards.com. **Contact:** Cristy Bertini. Offered annually for any previously published work to honor authors for writing excellence of all types of literature—fiction and nonfiction—in 62 categories, appealing to a wide range of ages and comprehensive

list of genres. Open to any title published in English. Entry forms are downloadable at www.royaldragonflybookawards.com. Guidelines available online. Send submissions to Cristy Bertini, Attn.: Five Star Book Awards, 1271 Turkey St., Ware, MA 01082. Deadline: October 1. Prize: Grand Prize winner receives $300, while another entrant will be the lucky winner of a $100 drawing. All first-place winners receive foil award seals and are included in a publicity campaign announcing winners. All first- and second-place winners and honorable mentions receive certificates.

ERNEST SANDEEN PRIZE IN POETRY AND RICHARD SULLIVAN PRIZE IN SHORT FICTION

University of Notre Dame, Dept. of English, 356 O'Shaughnessy Hall, Notre Dame IN 46556-5639. (574)631-7526. **Fax:** (574)631-4795. **E-mail:** creative-writing@nd.edu. **Website:** http://english.nd.edu/creative-writing/publications/sandeen-sullivan-prizes. **Contact:** Director of Creative Writing. The Sandeen & Sullivan Prizes in Poetry and Short Fiction is awarded to the author who has published at least one volume of short fiction or one volume of poetry. Awarded biannually, but judged quadrennially. Though the Sandeen Prize is open to any author, with the exception of graduates of the University of Notre Dame, who has published at least one volume of short stories (Sullivan) or one collection of poetry (Sandeen), judges pay special attention to second volumes. Please include a vita and/or a biographical statement which includes your publishing history. Will also see a selection of reviews of the earlier collection. Please submit two copies of mss and inform if the mss is available on computer disk. Include an SASE for acknowledgment of receipt of your submission. If you would like your manuscript returned, please send an SASE. Manuscripts will not otherwise be returned. Submissions Period: May 1 - September 1. Prize: $1,000, a $500 award and a $500 advance against royalties from the Notre Dame Press.

SANTA FE WRITERS PROJECT LITERARY AWARDS PROGRAM

Santa Fe Writers Project, 369 Montezuma Ave., #350, Santa Fe NM 87501. **E-mail:** info@sfwp.com. **Website:** www.sfwp.com. **Contact:** Andrew Gifford. Annual contest seeking fiction and nonfiction of any genre. The Literary Awards Program was founded by a group of authors to offer recognition for excellence in writing in a time of declining support for writers and the craft of literature. Past judges have included Richard Currey, Jayne Anne Phillips, Chris Offutt, Lee Gutkind, and David Morrell. Deadline: December 15. Prize: $3,500 and publication.

THE MONA SCHREIBER PRIZE FOR HUMOROUS FICTION & NONFICTION

3940 Laurel Canyon Blvd., #566, Studio City CA 91604. **E-mail:** brad.schreiber@att.net. **Website:** www.bradschreiber.com. **Contact:** Brad Schreiber. No SASEs. Non-US entries should enclose US currency or checks written in US dollars. Include e-mail address. No previously published work. The purpose of the contest is to award the most creative humor writing, in any form less than 750 words, in either fiction or nonfiction, including but not limited to stories, articles, essays, speeches, shopping lists, diary entries, and anything else writers dream up. Complete rules and previous winning entries on website. Deadline: December 1. Prize: 1st Place: $500; 2nd Place: $250; 3rd Place: $100. Judged by Brad Schreiber, author, journalist, consultant, and instructor.

SKIPPING STONES BOOK AWARDS

Skipping Stones, P.O. Box 3939, Eugene OR 97403-0939 USA. **E-mail:** editor@SkippingStones.org. **Website:** www.skippingstones.org. **Contact:** Arun N. Toke', Exec. Editor. Open to published books, publications/magazines, educational videos, and DVDs. Annual awards. Submissions made by the author or publishers and/or producers. Send request for contest rules and entry forms or visit website. Many educational publications announce the winners of our book awards. The winning books and educational videos/DVDs are announced in the July-September issue of *Skipping Stones* and also on the website. In addition to announcements on social media pages, the reviews of winning titles are posted on website. *Skipping Stones* multicultural magazine has been published for over 25 years. Recognizes exceptional, literary and artistic contributions to juvenile/children's literature, as well as teaching resources and educational audio/video resources in the areas of multicultural awareness, nature and ecology, social issues, peace, and nonviolence. Deadline: February 28. Prize: Winners receive gold honor award seals, attractive honor certificates, and publicity via multiple outlets. Judged by a multicultural selection committee of editors, students, parents, teachers, and librarians.

THE BERNICE SLOTE AWARD

Prairie Schooner, 123 Andrews Hall, PO Box 880334, Lincoln NE 68588-0334. (402)472-0911. **Fax:** (402)472-1817. **E-mail:** PrairieSchooner@unl. edu. **Website:** www.prairieschooner.unl.edu. **Contact:** Kwame Dawes. Categories: short stories, essays and poetry. For guidelines, send SASE or visit website. Only work published in the journal during the previous year will be considered. Work is nominated by the editorial staff. Offered annually for the best work by a beginning writer published in *Prairie Schooner* in the previous year. Celebrates the best and finest writing that they have published for the year. Prize: $500. Judged by editorial staff of *Prairie Schooner*.

JEFFREY E. SMITH EDITORS' PRIZE IN FICTION, ESSAY AND POETRY

The Missouri Review, 357 McReynolds Hall, UMC, Columbia MO 65211. (573)882-4474. **Fax:** (573)884-4671. **E-mail:** contest_question@moreview.com. **Website:** www.missourireview.com. **Contact:** Editor. Offered annually for unpublished work in 3 categories: fiction, essay, and poetry. Guidelines online or for SASE. Deadline: October 15. Prize: $5,000 and publication for each category winner.

KAY SNOW WRITING CONTEST

Willamette Writers, Willamette Writers, 2108 Buck St., West Linn OR 97068. (503)305-6729. **Fax:** (503)344-6174. **E-mail:** reg@willamettewriters.com. **Website:** www.willamettewriters.com. Willamette Writers is the largest writers' organization in Oregon and one of the largest writers' organizations in the United States. It is a non-profit, tax-exempt Oregon corporation led by volunteers. Elected officials and directors administer an active program of monthly meetings, special seminars, workshops, and an annual writing conference. Continuing with established programs and starting new ones is only made possible by strong volunteer support. See website for specific details and rules. There are six different categories writers can enter: Adult Fiction, Adult Nonfiction, Poetry, Juvenile Short Story, Screenwriting, and Student Writer. The purpose of this annual writing contest, named in honor of Willamette Writer's founder, Kay Snow, is to help writers reach professional goals in writing in a broad array of categories and to encourage student writers. Deadline: April 23. Submission deadline begins January 15. Prize: One first prize of

$300, one second place prize of $150, and a third place prize of $50 per winning entry in each of the six categories. Student first prize is $50, $20 for second place, $10 for third.

SOCIETY OF MIDLAND AUTHORS AWARD

Society of Midland Authors, Society of Midland Authors, P.O. Box 10419, Chicago IL 60610-0419. **E-mail:** marlenetbrill@comcast.net. **Website:** www.midlandauthors.com. **Contact:** Marlene Targ Brill, awards chair. Since 1957, the Society has presented annual awards for the best books written by Midwestern authors. The contest is open to any title published within the year prior to the contest year. Open to adult and children's authors/poets who reside in, were born in, or have strong ties to a Midland state, which includes Illinois, Indiana, Iowa, Kansas, Michigan, Minnesota, Missouri, Nebraska, North Dakota, South Dakota, Ohio, and Wisconsin. The Society of Midland Authors (SMA) Award is presented to one title in each of six categories: adult nonfiction, adult fiction, adult biography and memoir, children's nonfiction, children's fiction, and poetry. Books and entry forms must be mailed to the 3 judges in each category; for a list of judges and the entry form, visit the website. Do not mail books to the society's P.O. box. The fee can be sent to the SMA P.P. box or paid via Paypal. Deadline: January 7. Prize: $500 and a plaque that is awarded at the SMA banquet in May in Chicago. Honorary winners receive a plaque.

SOUL-MAKING KEATS LITERARY COMPETITION

The Webhallow House, 1544 Sweetwood Dr., Broadmoor Village CA 94015-2029. **E-mail:** SoulKeats@mail.com. **Website:** www.soulmakingcontest.us. **Contact:** Eileen Malone, award director. Annual open contest offers cash prizes in each of 13 literary categories. Competition receives 600 entries/year. Names of winners and judges are posted on website. Winners announced in January by SASE and on website. Winners are invited to read at the Koret Auditorium, San Francisco. Event is televised. Submissions in some categories may be previously published. No names or other identifying information on mss; include 3x5 card with poet's name, address, phone, fax, e-mail, title(s) of work, and category entered. Include SASE for results only; mss will not be returned. Guidelines available on website. Deadline: November 30. Prizes: 1st Prize: $100; 2nd Prize: $50; 3rd Prize: $25.

○ SUBTERRAIN MAGAZINE'S ANNUAL LITERARY AWARDS COMPETITION: THE LUSH SUBTERRAIN MAGAZINE'S ANNUAL LUSH TRIUMPHANT LITERARY AWARDS COMPETITION

P.O. Box 3008 MPO, Vancouver BC V6B 3X5 Canada. (604)876-8710. **Fax:** (604)879-2667. **E-mail:** subter@portal.ca. **Website:** www.subterrain.ca. Entrants may submit as many entries in as many categories as they like. Fiction: Max of 3,000 words. Poetry: A suite of 5 related poems (max of 15 pages). Creative Nonfiction (based on fact, adorned with fiction): Max of 4,000 words. All entries must be previously unpublished material and not currently under consideration in any other contest or competition. Deadline: May 15. Prize: Winners in each category will receive $1,000 cash (plus payment for publication) and publication in the Winter issue. First runner-up in each category will be published in the Spring issue of *subTerrain*.

THE TEXAS INSTITUTE OF LETTERS LITERARY AWARDS

E-mail: Betwx@aol.com. **Website:** www.texasinstituteofletters.org. The Texas Institute of Letters gives annual awards for books by Texas authors and writers who have produced books about Texas, including Best Books of Poetry, Fiction, and Nonfiction. Awards are also given for best Short Story, Magazine or Newspaper Article, Essay, and best Books for Children and Young Adults. Work submitted must have been published in the year stipulated, and entries may be made by authors or by their publishers. Complete guidelines and award information is available on the Texas Institute of Letters website.

○ TORONTO BOOK AWARDS

City of Toronto c/o Toronto Arts & Culture, Cultural Partnerships, City Hall, 9E, 100 Queen St. W., Toronto ON M5H 2N2 Canada. **E-mail:** shan@toronto.ca. **Website:** www.toronto.ca/book_awards. The Toronto Book Awards honor authors of books of literary or artistic merit that are evocative of Toronto. There are no separate categories; all books are judged together. Any fiction or nonfiction book published in English for adults and/or children that are evocative of Toronto are eligible. To be eligible, books must be published between January 1 and December 31 of previous year. Deadline: April 30. Prize: Each finalist receives $1,000 and the winning author receives the remaining prize money ($14,000 total in prize money available).

THE ROBERT WATSON LITERARY PRIZE IN FICTION AND POETRY

The Robert Watson Literary Prizes, *The Greensboro Review*, MFA Writing Program, 3302 MHRA Building, Greensboro NC 27402-6170. (336)334-5459. **E-mail:** jlclark@uncg.edu. **Website:** www.greensbororeview.org. **Contact:** Jim Clark, editor. Offered annually for fiction (up to 25 double-spaced pages) and poetry (up to 10 pages). Entries must be unpublished. Open to any writer. Guidelines available online. Submit online: https://greensbororeview.submittable.com/submit. Deadline: September 15. Prize: $1,000 each for best short story and poem. Judged by editors of *The Greensboro Review*.

WESTERN HERITAGE AWARDS

National Cowboy & Western Heritage Museum, 1700 NE 63rd St., Oklahoma City OK 73111-7997. (405)478-2250. **Fax:** (405)478-4714. **Website:** www.nationalcowboymuseum.org. **Contact:** Jessica Limestall. The National Cowboy & Western Heritage Museum Western Heritage Awards were established to honor and encourage the legacy of those whose works in literature, music, film, and television reflect the significant stories of the American West. Accepted categories for literary entries: western novel, nonfiction book, art book, photography book, juvenile book, magazine article, or poetry book. Previously published submissions only; must be published the calendar year before the awards are presented. Requirements for entrants: The material must pertain to the development or preservation of the West, either from a historical or contemporary viewpoint. Literary entries must have been published between December 1 and November 30 of calendar year. Five copies of each published work must be furnished for judging with each entry, along with the completed entry form. Works recognized during special awards ceremonies held annually at the museum. There is an autograph party preceding the awards. Awards ceremonies are sometimes broadcast. The WHA are presented annually to encourage the accurate and artistic telling of great stories of the West through 16 categories of western literature, television, film and music; including fiction, nonfiction, children's books and poetry. See website for details and category definitions. Deadline: November 30. Prize: Awards a Wrangler bronze sculpture designed by famed western artist, John Free. Judged by a panel of judges selected each year with distinction in various fields of western art and heritage.

WESTMORELAND POETRY & SHORT STORY CONTEST

Westmoreland Arts & Heritage Festival, 252 Twin Lakes Road, Latrobe PA 15650-9415. (724)834-7474. **Fax:** (724)850-7474. **E-mail:** info@artsandheritage.com. **Website:** www.artsandheritage.com. **Contact:** Diane Shrader. Offered annually for unpublished work. Two categories: Poem and Short Story. Short story entries no longer than 4,000 words. Family-oriented festival and contest. Deadline: February 16. Prizes: Award: $200; 1st Place: $125; 2nd Place: $100; 3rd Place: $75.

WILLA LITERARY AWARD

Women Writing the West, 8547 East Arapaho Rd., #J-541, Greenwood Village CO 80112-1436. **E-mail:** Anneschroederauthor@gmail.com. **Website:** www.womenwritingthewest.org. **Contact:** Anne Schroeder. The WILLA Literary Award honors the year's best in published literature featuring women's or girls' stories set in the West. Women Writing the West (WWW), a nonprofit association of writers and other professionals writing and promoting the Women's West, underwrites and presents the nationally recognized award annually (for work published between January 1 and December 31). The award is named in honor of Pulitzer Prize winner Willa Cather, one of the country's foremost novelists. The award is given in 7 categories: historical fiction, contemporary fiction, original softcover fiction, creative nonfiction, scholarly nonfiction, poetry, and children's/young adult fiction/nonfiction. Entry forms available on the website. Deadline: November 1–February 1. Prize: $100 and a trophy. Finalist receives a plaque. Both receive digital and sticker award emblems for book covers. Notice of Winning and Finalist titles mailed to more than 4,000 booksellers, libraries, and others. Award announcement is in early August, and awards are presented to the winners and finalists at the annual WWW Fall Conference. Judged by professional librarians not affiliated with WWW.

TENNESSEE WILLIAMS/NEW ORLEANS LITERARY FESTIVAL CONTESTS

Tennessee Williams/New Orleans Literary Festival, 938 Lafayette St., Suite 514, New Orleans LA 70113. (504)581-1144. **E-mail:** info@tennesseewilliams.net. **Website:** www.tennesseewilliams.net/

contests. **Contact:** Paul J. Willis. Annual contests for: Unpublished One Act, Unpublished Short Fiction, and Unpublished Poem. Plays should run no more than one hour in length. Unlimited entries per person. Production criteria include scripts requiring minimal technical support for a 100-seat theater. Cast of characters must be small. See website for additional guidelines and entry form. Fiction must not exceed 7,000 words. Poetry submissions should be 2-4 poems not exceeding 400 lines total. "Our competitions provide playwrights an opportunity to see their work fully produced before a large audience during one of the largest literary festivals in the nation, and for the festival to showcase the undiscovered talents of poetry and fiction writers." Deadline: November 1 (One Act); November 15 (Poetry); December 1 (Fiction). Prize: One Act: $1,500, staged read at the next festival, full production at the festival the following year, VIP All-Access Festival pass for two years ($1,000 value), and publication in Bayou. Poetry: $1,500, public reading at next festival, publication in Louisiana Cultural Vistas Magazine. Fiction: $1,500, public reading at next festival, publication in Louisiana Literature. Judged by an anonymous expert panel for One Act contest. Judged by special guest judges, who change every year, for fiction and poetry.

☼ THE WORD AWARDS

The Word Guild, The Word Guild, Suite # 226, 245 King George Rd, Brantford ON N3R 7N7 Canada. 800-969-9010 x 1. **E-mail:** info@thewordguild.com. **E-mail:** info@thewordguild.com. **Website:** www.thewordguild.com. **Contact:** Karen deBlieck. The Word Guild is an organization of Canadian writers and editors who are Christian, and who are committed to encouraging one another and to fostering standards of excellence in the art, craft, practice and ministry of writing. Memberships available for various experience levels. Yearly conference Write Canada (please see website for information) and features keynote speakers, continuing classes and workshops. Editors and agents on site. The Word Awards is for work published in the past year, in almost 30 categories including books, articles, essays, fiction, nonfiction, novels, short stories, songs, and poetry. Please see website for more information. Deadline: January 15. Prize $50 CAD for article and short pieces; $100 CAD for book entries. Finalists book entries are eli-

gible for the $5,000 Grace Irwin prize. Judged by industry leaders and professionals.

WORLD'S BEST SHORT-SHORT STORY CONTEST, NARRATIVE NONFICTION CONTEST & SOUTHEAST REVIEW POETRY CONTEST

The Southeast Review, Florida State University, English Department, Tallahassee FL 32306. **E-mail:** southeastreview@gmail.com. **Website:** www.southeastreview.org. **Contact:** Erin Hoover, editor. Annual award for unpublished short-short stories (500 words or less), poetry, and narrative nonfiction (6,000 words or less). Visit website for details. Deadline: March 15. Prize: $500 per category. Winners and finalists will be published in *The Southeast Review*.

WRITER'S DIGEST SELF-PUBLISHED BOOK AWARDS

Writer's Digest, 10151 Carver Road, Suite #200, Blue Ash OH 45242. (715)445-4612, ext. 13430. **E-mail:** WritersDigestSelfPublishingCompetition@fwmedia.com. **Website:** www.writersdigest.com. **Contact:** Nicole Howard. Contest open to all English-language, self-published books for which the authors have paid the full cost of publication, or the cost of printing has been paid for by a grant or as part of a prize. Categories include: Mainstream/Literary Fiction, Genre Fiction, Nonfiction, Inspirational (spiritual/new age), Life Stories (biographies/autobiographies/family histories/memoirs), Children's Books, Reference Books (directories/encyclopedias/guide books), Poetry, and Middle-Grade/Young Adult Books. Judges reserve the right to re-categorize entries. Judges reserve the right to withhold prizes in any category. All winners will be notified in October. Entrants must send a printed and bound book. Entries will be evaluated on content, writing quality, and overall quality of production and appearance. No handwritten books are accepted. Books must have been published within the past 5 years from the competition deadline. Books which have previously won awards from *Writer's Digest* are not eligible. Early bird deadline: April 1; Deadline: May 2. Prizes: Grand Prize: $8,000, a trip to the Writer's Digest Conference, promotion in *Writer's Digest*, 10 copies of the book will be sent to major review houses, and a guaranteed review in *Midwest Book Review*; 1st Place (9 winners): $1,000 and promotion in *Writer's Digest*; Honorable Mentions: $50 worth of Writer's Digest Books and promotion on writersdigest.com. All entrants will receive a brief commentary from one of the judges.

WRITER'S DIGEST SELF-PUBLISHED E-BOOK AWARDS

Writer's Digest, 10151 Carver Road, Suite #200, Blue Ash OH 45242. (715)445-4612, ext. 13430. **E-mail:** WritersDigestSelfPublishingCompetition@fwmedia. com. **Website:** www.writersdigest.com. **Contact:** Nicole Howard. Contest open to all English-language, self-published e-books for which the authors have paid the full cost of publication, or the cost of publication has been paid for by a grant or as part of a prize. Categories include: Mainstream/Literary Fiction, Genre Fiction, Nonfiction (includes reference books), Inspirational (spiritual/new age), Life Stories (biographies/autobiographies/family histories/memoirs), Children's Books, Poetry, and Middle-Grade/ Young Adult Books. Judges reserve the right to re-categorize entries. Judges reserve the right to withhold prizes in any category. All winners will be notified by December 31. Entrants must enter online. Entrants may provide a file of the book or submit entry by the Amazon gifting process. Acceptable file types include: .epub, .mobi, .ipa. Word processing documents will not be accepted. Entries will be evaluated on content, writing quality, and overall quality of production and appearance. Books must have been published within the past 5 years from the competition deadline. Books which have previously won awards from *Writer's Digest* are not eligible. Early bird deadline: August 1; Deadline: September 19. Prizes: Grand Prize: $3,000, promotion in *Writer's Digest*, a full 250-word (minimum) editorial review, $200 worth of Writer's Digest Books, and more; 1st Place (9 winners): $1,000 and promotion in *Writer's Digest*; Honorable Mentions: $50 worth of Writer's Digest Books and promotion on writersdigest.com. All entrants will receive a brief commentary from one of the judges.

WRITERS-EDITORS NETWORK INTERNATIONAL WRITING COMPETITION

CNW Publishing, P.O. Box A, North Stratford NH 03590-0167. **E-mail:** contestentry@writers-editors. com. **E-mail:** info@writers-editors.com. **Website:** www.writers-editors.com. **Contact:** Dana K. Cassell, executive director. Annual award to recognize publishable talent. New categories and awards for 2016: Nonfiction (unpublished or self-published; may be an article, blog post, essay/opinion piece, column, non-

fiction book chapter, children's article or book chapter); fiction (unpublished or self-published; may be a short story, novel chapter, Young Adult [YA] or children's story or book chapter); poetry (unpublished or self-published; may be traditional or free verse poetry or children's verse). Guidelines available online. Open to any writer. Maximum length: 4,000 words. Accepts inquiries by e-mail, phone and mail. Entry form online. Results announced May 31. Winners notified by mail and posted on website. Results available for SASE or visit website. Deadline: March 15. Prize: 1st Place: $150 plus one year Writers-Editors membership; 2nd Place: $100; 3rd Place: $75. All winners and Honorable Mentions will receive certificates as warranted. Most Promising entry in each category will receive a free critique by a contest judge. Judged by editors, librarians, and writers.

◎ WRITERS' GUILD OF ALBERTA AWARDS

Writers' Guild of Alberta, Percy Page Centre, 11759 Groat Rd., Edmonton AB T5M 3K6 Canada. (780)422-8174. **Fax:** (780)422-2663. **E-mail:** mail@ writersguild.ca. **Website:** writersguild.ca. **Contact:** Executive Director. Offers the following awards: Wilfrid Eggleston Award for Nonfiction; Georges Bugnet Award for Fiction; Howard O'Hagan Award for Short Story; Stephan G. Stephansson Award for Poetry; R. Ross Annett Award for Children's Literature; Gwen Pharis Ringwood Award for Drama; Jon Whyte Memorial Essay Award; James H. Gray Award for Short Nonfiction. Eligible entries will have been published anywhere in the world between January 1 and December 31 of the current year. The authors must have been residents of Alberta for at least 12 of the 18 months prior to December 31. Unpublished mss, except in the drama and essay categories, are not eligible. Anthologies are not eligible. Works may be submitted by authors, publishers, or any interested parties. Deadline: December 31. Prize: Winning authors receive $1,500; short piece prize winners receive $700.

WRITERS' LEAGUE OF TEXAS BOOK AWARDS

Writers' League of Texas, 611 S. Congress Ave., Suite 200A-3, Austin TX 78704. (512)499-8914. **Fax:** (512)499-0441. **E-mail:** sara@writersleague.org. **E-mail:** sara@writersleague.org. **Website:** www.writersleague.org. Open to Texas authors of books published the previous year. Authors are required to show proof of Texas residency (current or past), but are not required to be members of the Writers' League of Texas. Deadline: Open to submissions from October 1 to January 15. Prize: $1,000 and a commemorative award.

THE YOUTH HONOR AWARDS

Skipping Stones Youth Honor Awards, Skipping Stones Magazine, Skipping Stones Magazine, P.O. Box 3939, Eugene OR 97403 USA. (541)342-4956. **E-mail:** info@skippingstones.org. **E-mail:** editor@skipping-stones.org. **Website:** www.skippingstones.org. **Contact:** Arun N. Toke, Editor and Publisher. *Skipping Stones* is an international, literary, and multicultural, children's magazine that encourages cooperation, creativity, and celebration of cultural and linguistic diversity. It explores stewardship of the ecological and social webs that nurture us. It offers a forum for communication among children from different lands and backgrounds. *Skipping Stones* expands horizons in a playful, creative way. This is a non-commercial, non-profit magazine with no advertisements. In its 28th year. Original writing and art from youth, ages 7 to 17, should be typed or neatly handwritten. The entries should be appropriate for ages 7 to 17. Prose under 1,000 words; poems under 30 lines. Word limit: 1,000. Poetry: 30 lines. Non-English and bilingual writings are welcome. To promote multicultural, international and nature awareness. Deadline: June 25. Prize: An Honor Award Certificate, a subscription to Skipping Stones and five nature and/or multicultural books. They are also invited to join the Student Review Board. Everyone who enters the contest receives the autumn issue featuring the ten winners and other noteworthy entries. Editors and interns at the *Skipping Stones* magazine

☯ SASKATCHEWAN BOOK AWARDS

Saskatchewan Book Awards, Inc., 315-1102 8th Ave., Regina SK S4R 1C9 Canada. 306-569-1585. **E-mail:** director@bookawards.sk.ca. **Website:** www.bookawards.sk.ca. **Contact:** Courtney Bates-Hardy, Administrative Director. Saskatchewan Book Awards celebrates, promotes and rewards Saskatchewan authors and publishers worthy of recognition through 14 awards, granted on an annual or semi-annual basis. Awards: Fiction, Nonfiction, Poetry, Scholarly, First Book, Prix du livre français, Regina, Saskatoon, Aboriginal Peoples' Writing, Aboriginal Peoples' Publishing, Publishing in Education, Publishing, Children's Literature/Young Adult Literature, Book of the Year.

Saskatchewan Book Awards is the only provincially-focused book award program in Saskatchewan and a principal ambassador for Saskatchewan's literary community. Its solid reputation for celebrating artistic excellence in style is recognized nationally. Deadline: Early November. Prize: $2,000 (CAD) for all awards except Book of the Year, which is $3,000 (CAD). Juries are made up of writing and publishing professionals from outside of Saskatchewan.

PROFESSIONAL ORGANIZATIONS

AGENTS' ORGANIZATIONS

ASSOCIATION OF AUTHORS' AGENTS (AAA), 5-8 Lower John St., Golden Square, London W1F 9HA. E-mail: anthonygoff@davidhigham.co.uk. Website: www.agentsassoc.co.uk.

ASSOCIATION OF AUTHORS' REPRESENTATIVES (AAR). E-mail: info@aar-online.org. Website: www.aar-online.org.

ASSOCIATION OF TALENT AGENTS (ATA), 9255 Sunset Blvd., Suite 930, Los Angeles CA 90069. (310)274-0628. E-mail: shellie@agentassociation.com. Website: www.agentassociation.com.

WRITERS' ORGANIZATIONS

ACADEMY OF AMERICAN POETS 584 Broadway, Suite 604, New York NY 10012. E-mail: academy@poets.org. Website: www.poets.org.

AMERICAN CRIME WRITERS LEAGUE (ACWL), 17367 Hilltop Ridge Dr., Eureka MO 63205. Website: www.acwl.org.

AMERICAN INDEPENDENT WRITERS (AIW), 1001 Connecticut Ave. NW, Suite 701, Washington DC 20036. E-mail: info@aiwriters.org. Website: americanindependentwriters.org.

AMERICAN MEDICAL WRITERS ASSOCIATION (AMWA), 30 West Gude Dr., Suite 525, Rockville MD 20850-4347. E-mail: amwa@amwa.org. Website: www.amwa.org.

AMERICAN SCREENWRITERS ASSOCIATION (ASA), 269 S. Beverly Dr., Suite 2600, Beverly Hills CA 90212. (866)265-9091. E-mail: asa@goasa.com. Website: www.asascreenwriters.com.

AMERICAN TRANSLATORS ASSOCIATION (ATA), 225 Reinekers Ln., Suite 590, Alexandria VA 22314. (703)683-6100. E-mail: ata@atanet.org. Website: www.atanet.org.

EDUCATION WRITERS ASSOCIATION (EWA), 2122 P St., NW Suite 201, Washington DC 20037. E-mail: ewa@ewa.org. Website: ewa.org.

HORROR WRITERS ASSOCIATION (HWA), 244 5th Ave., Suite 2767, New York NY 10001. E-mail: hwa@horror.org. Website: www.horror.org.

THE INTERNATIONAL WOMEN'S WRITING GUILD (IWWG), P.O. Box 810, Gracie Station, New York NY 10028. Website: www.iwwg.com.

MYSTERY WRITERS OF AMERICA (MWA), 1140 Broadway, Suite 1507, New York NY 10001. (212)888-8171. E-mail: mwa@mysterywriters.org. Website: www.mysterywriters.org.

NATIONAL ASSOCIATION OF SCIENCE WRITERS (NASW), P.O. Box 7905, Berkeley, CA 94707. (510)647-9500. E-mail: lfriedmann@nasw.org. Website: www.nasw.org.

NATIONAL ASSOCIATION OF WOMEN WRITERS (NAWW), 24165 IH-10 W., Suite 217-637, San Antonio TX 78257. Phone/Fax: (866)821-5829. Website: www.naww.org.

ORGANIZATION OF BLACK SCREENWRITERS (OBS). 1999 W. Adams Blvd., Mezzanine, Los Angeles CA 90018. Website: www.obswriter.com.

OUTDOOR WRITERS ASSOCIATION OF AMERICA (OWAA), 121 Hickory St., Suite 1, Missoula MT 59801. E-mail: krhoades@owaa.org. Website: www.owaa.org.

POETRY SOCIETY OF AMERICA (PSA), 15 Gramercy Park, New York NY 10003. Website: www.poetrysociety.org.

POETS & WRITERS, 90 Broad St., Suite 2100, New York NY 10004. (212)226-3586. Fax: (212)226-3963. Website: www.pw.org.

ROMANCE WRITERS OF AMERICA (RWA), 114615 Benfer Rd., Houston TX 77069. (832)717-5200. Fax: (832)717-5201. E-mail: info@rwanational.org. Website: www.rwanational.org.

SCIENCE FICTION AND FANTASY WRITERS OF AMERICA (SFWA), P.O. Box 877, Chestertown MD 21620. E-mail: execdir@sfwa.org. Website: www.sfwa.org.

SOCIETY OF AMERICAN BUSINESS EDITORS & WRITERS (SABEW), University of Missouri, School of Journalism, 30 Neff Annex, Columbia MO 65211. (602) 496-7862. E-mail: sabew@sabew.org. Website: www.sabew.org.

SOCIETY OF AMERICAN TRAVEL WRITERS (SATW), 7044 S. 13 St., Oak Creek WI 53154. E-mail: satw@satw.org. Website: www.satw.org.

SOCIETY OF CHILDREN'S BOOK WRITERS & ILLUSTRATORS (SCBWI), 8271 Beverly Blvd., Los Angeles CA 90048. E-mail: scbwi@scbwi.org. Website: www.scbwi.org.

WESTERN WRITERS OF AMERICA (WWA). E-mail: spiritfire@kc.rr.com. Website: www.westernwriters.org.

INDUSTRY ORGANIZATIONS

AMERICAN BOOKSELLERS ASSOCIATION (ABA), 200 White Plains Rd., Suite 600, Tarrytown NY 10591. (914)591-2665. E-mail:

info@bookweb.org. Website: www.bookweb.org.

AMERICAN SOCIETY OF JOURNALISTS & AUTHORS (ASJA), 1501 Broadway, Suite 302, New York NY 10036. (212)997-0947. E-mail: director@asja.org. Website: www.asja.org.

ASSOCIATION FOR WOMEN IN COMMUNICATIONS (AWC), 3337 Duke St., Alexandria VA 22314. (703)370-7436. E-mail: info@womcom.org. Website: www.womcom.org.

ASSOCIATION OF AMERICAN PUBLISHERS (AAP), 71 5th Ave., 2nd Floor, New York NY 10003. Website: www.publishers.org.

THE ASSOCIATION OF WRITERS & WRITING PROGRAMS (AWP), Mail Stop 1E3, George Mason University, Fairfax VA 22030. Website: www.awpwriter.org.

THE AUTHORS GUILD, INC., 31 E. 32nd St., 7th Floor, New York NY 10016. E-mail: staff@authorsguild.org. Website: authorsguild.org.

CANADIAN AUTHORS ASSOCIATION (CAA), P.O. Box 581, Stn. Main Orilla ON L3V 6K5 Canada. Website: www.canauthors.org.

CHRISTIAN BOOKSELLERS ASSOCIATION (CBA), P.O. Box 62000, Colorado Springs CO 80962. Website: www.cbaonline.org.

THE DRAMATISTS GUILD OF AMERICA, 1501 Broadway, Suite 701, New York NY 10036. Website: www.dramatistsguild.com.

NATIONAL LEAGUE OF AMERICAN PEN WOMEN (NLAPW), 1300 17th St. NW, Washington DC 20036-1973. Website: www.americanpenwomen.org.

NATIONAL WRITERS ASSOCIATION (NWA), 10940 S. Parker Rd., #508, Parker CO 80134. Website: www.nationalwriters.com

NATIONAL WRITERS UNION (NWU), 256 West 38th St., Suite 703, New York, NY 10018. E-mail: nwu@nwu.org. Website: www.nwu.org.

PEN AMERICAN CENTER, 588 Broadway, Suite 303, New York NY 10012-3225. E-mail: pen@pen.org. Website: www.pen.org.

THE PLAYWRIGHTS GUILD OF CANADA (PGC), 215 Spadina Ave., Suite #210, Toronto ON M5T 2C7 Canada. E-mail: info@playwrightsguild.ca. Website: www.playwrightsguild.com.

VOLUNTEER LAWYERS FOR THE ARTS (VLA), One E. 53rd St., 6th Floor, New York NY 10022. (212)319-2787. Website: www.vlany.org.

WOMEN IN FILM (WIF), 6100 Wilshire Blvd., Suite 710, Los Angeles CA 90048. E-mail: info@wif.org. Website: www.wif.org.

WOMEN'S NATIONAL BOOK ASSOCIATION (WNBA), P.O. Box 237, FDR Station, New York NY 10150. E-mail: publicity@bookbuzz.com. Website: www.wnba-books.org.

WRITERS GUILD OF ALBERTA (WGA), 11759 Groat Rd., Edmonton AB T5M 3K6 Canada. E-mail: mail@writersguild.ab.ca. Website: writersguild.ab.ca.

WRITERS GUILD OF AMERICA-EAST (WGA),
555 W. 57th St., Suite 1230, New York NY
10019. E-mail: info@wgaeast.org. Website:
www.wgaeast.org.

WRITERS GUILD OF AMERICA-WEST (WGA),
7000 W. Third St., Los Angeles CA 90048.
Website: www.wga.org.

WRITERS UNION OF CANADA (TWUC), 90
Richmond St. E., Suite 200, Toronto ON M5C
1P1 Canada. E-mail: info@writersunion.ca.
Website: www.writersunion.ca.

GLOSSARY

#10 ENVELOPE. A standard, business-size envelope.

ADVANCE. A sum of money a publisher pays a writer prior to the publication of a book. It is usually paid in installments, such as one-half on signing contract; one-half on delivery of complete and satisfactory manuscript.

AGENT. A liaison between a writer and editor or publisher. An agent shops a manuscript around, receiving a commission when the manuscript is accepted. Agents usually take a 10-15% fee from the advance and royalties.

ARC. Advance reader copy.

ASSIGNMENT. Editor asks a writer to produce a specific article for an agreed-upon fee.

AUCTION. Publishers sometimes bid for the acquisition of a book manuscript that has excellent sales prospects. The bids are for the amount of the author's advance, advertising and promotional expenses, royalty percentage, etc. Auctions are conducted by agents.

AVANT-GARDE. Writing that is innovative in form, style, or subject.

BACKLIST. A publisher's list of its books that were not published during the current season, but that are still in print.

BIMONTHLY. Every two months.

BIO. A sentence or brief paragraph about the writer; can include education and work experience.

BIWEEKLY. Every two weeks.

BLOG. Short for weblog. Used by writers to build platform by posting regular commentary, observations, poems, tips, etc.

BLURB. The copy on paperback book covers or hard cover book dust jackets, either promoting the book and the author or featuring testimonials from book reviewers or well-known people in the book's field. Also called flap copy or jacket copy.

BOILERPLATE. A standardized contract.

BOUND GALLEYS. Prepublication edition of book, usually photocopies of final galley proofs; also known as "bound proofs."

BYLINE. Name of the author appearing with the published piece.

CATEGORY FICTION. A term used to include all types of fiction.

CHAPBOOK. A small booklet usually paperback of poetry, ballads, or tales.

CIRCULATION. The number of subscribers to a magazine.

CLIPS. Samples, usually from newspapers or magazines, of a writer's published work.

COFFEE-TABLE BOOK. A heavily illustrated oversize book.

COMMERCIAL NOVELS. Novels designed to appeal to a broad audience. These are often broken down into categories such as western, mystery and romance. See also genre.

CONTRIBUTOR'S COPIES. Copies of the issues of magazines sent to the author in which the author's work appears.

CO-PUBLISHING. Arrangement where author and publisher share publications costs and profits of a book. Also known as cooperative publishing.

COPYEDITING. Editing a manuscript for grammar, punctuation, printing style, and factual accuracy.

COPYRIGHT. A means to protect an author's work.

COVER LETTER. A brief letter that accompanies the manuscript being sent to an agent or editor.

CREATIVE NONFICTION. Nonfictional writing that uses an innovative approach to the subject and creative language.

CRITIQUING SERVICE. An editing service in which writers pay a fee for comments on the salability or other qualities of their manuscript. Fees vary, as do the quality of the critiques.

CV. Curriculum vita. A brief listing of qualifications and career accomplishments.

ELECTRONIC RIGHTS. Secondary or subsidiary rights dealing with electronic/multimedia formats (i.e., the Internet, CD-ROMs, electronic magazines).

ELECTRONIC SUBMISSION. A submission made by modem or on computer disk.

EROTICA. Fiction that is sexually oriented.

EVALUATION FEES. Fees an agent may charge to evaluate material. The extent and quality of this evaluation varies, but comments usually concern salability of the manuscript.

FAIR USE. A provision of the copyright law that says short passages from copyrighted material may be used without infringing on the owner's rights.

FEATURE. An article giving the reader information of human interest rather than news.

FILLER. A short item used by an editor to "fill" out a newspaper column or magazine page. It could be a joke, an anecdote, etc.

FILM RIGHTS. Rights sold or optioned by the agent/author to a person in the film industry, enabling the book to be made into a movie.

FOREIGN RIGHTS. Translation or reprint rights to be sold abroad.

FRONTLIST. A publisher's list of books that are new to the current season.

GALLEYS. First typeset version of manuscript that has not yet been divided into pages.

GENRE. Refers either to a general classification of writing, such as the novel or the poem, or to the categories within those classifications, such as the problem novel or the sonnet.

GHOSTWRITER. Writer who puts into literary form an article, speech, story, or book based on another person's ideas or knowledge.

GRAPHIC NOVEL. A story in graphic form, long comic strip, or heavily illustrated story; of 40 pages or more.

HI-LO. A type of fiction that offers a high level of interest for readers at a low reading level.

HIGH CONCEPT. A story idea easily expressed in a quick, one-line description.

HONORARIUM. Token payment.

HOOK. Aspect of the work that sets it apart from others and draws in the reader/viewer.

HOW-TO. Books and magazine articles offering a combination of information and advice in describing how something can be accomplished.

IMPRINT. Name applied to a publisher's specific line of books.

JOINT CONTRACT. A legal agreement between a publisher and two or more authors, establishing provisions for the division of royalties the book generates.

KILL FEE. Fee for a complete article that was assigned and then cancelled.

LEAD TIME. The time between the acquisition of a manuscript by an editor and its actual publication.

LITERARY FICTION. The general category of serious, non-formulaic, intelligent fiction.

MAINSTREAM FICTION. Fiction that transcends popular novel categories such as mystery, romance and science fiction.

MARKETING FEE. Fee charged by some agents to cover marketing expenses. It may be used to cover postage, telephone calls, faxes, photocopying or any other expense incurred in marketing a manuscript.

MASS MARKET. Non-specialized books of wide appeal directed toward a large audience.

MEMOIR. A narrative recounting a writer's (or fictional narrator's) personal or family history; specifics may be altered, though essentially considered nonfiction.

MIDDLE GRADE OR MID-GRADE. The general classification of books written for readers approximately ages 9-11. Also called middle readers.

MIDLIST. Those titles on a publisher's list that are not expected to be big sellers, but are expected to have limited/modest sales.

MODEL RELEASE. A paper signed by the subject of a photograph giving the photographer permission to use the photograph.

MULTIPLE CONTRACT. Book contract with an agreement for a future book(s).

MULTIPLE SUBMISSIONS. Sending more than one book or article idea to a publisher at the same time.

NARRATIVE NONFICTION. A narrative presentation of actual events.

NET ROYALTY. A royalty payment based on the amount of money a book publisher receives on the sale of a book after booksellers' discounts, special sales discounts and returns.

NOVELLA. A short novel, or a long short story; approximately 7,000 to 15,000 words.

ON SPEC. An editor expresses an interest in a proposed article idea and agrees to consider the finished piece for publication "on speculation." The editor is under no obligation to buy the finished manuscript.

ONE-TIME RIGHTS. Rights allowing a manuscript to be published one time. The work can be sold again by the writer without violating the contract.

OPTION CLAUSE. A contract clause giving a publisher the right to publish an author's next book.

PAYMENT ON ACCEPTANCE. The editor sends you a check for your article, story or poem as soon as he decides to publish it.

PAYMENT ON PUBLICATION. The editor doesn't send you a check for your material until it is published.

PEN NAME. The use of a name other than your legal name on articles, stories or books. Also called a pseudonym.

PHOTO FEATURE. Feature in which the emphasis is on the photographs rather than on accompanying written material.

PICTURE BOOK. A type of book aimed at preschoolers to 8-year-olds that tells a story using a combination of text and artwork, or artwork only.

PLATFORM. A writer's speaking experience, interview skills, website and other abilities which help form a following of potential buyers for that author's book.

POD. Print on demand.

PROOFREADING. Close reading and correction of a manuscript's typographical errors.

PROPOSAL. A summary of a proposed book submitted to a publisher, particularly used for nonfiction manuscripts. A proposal often contains an individualized cover letter, one-page overview of the book, marketing information, competitive books, author information, chapter-by-chapter outline, and two to three sample chapters.

QUERY. A letter that sells an idea to an editor or agent. Usually a query is brief (no more than one page) and uses attention-getting prose.

REMAINDERS. Copies of a book that are slow to sell and can be purchased from the publisher at a reduced price.

REPORTING TIME. The time it takes for an editor to report to the author on his/her query or manuscript.

REPRINT RIGHTS. The rights to republish a book after its initial printing.

ROYALTIES, STANDARD HARDCOVER BOOK. 10 percent of the retail price on the first 5,000 copies sold; 12 percent on the next 5,000; 15 percent thereafter.

ROYALTIES, STANDARD MASS PAPERBACK BOOK. 4-8 percent of the retail price on the first 150,000 copies sold.

ROYALTIES, STANDARD TRADE PAPERBACK BOOK. No less than 6 percent of list price on the first 20,000 copies; 7½ percent thereafter.

SASE. Self-addressed, stamped envelope; should be included with all correspondence.

SELF-PUBLISHING. In this arrangement the author pays for manufacturing, production and marketing of his book and keeps all income derived from the book sales.

SEMIMONTHLY. Twice per month.

SEMIWEEKLY. Twice per week.

SERIAL. Published periodically, such as a newspaper or magazine.

SERIAL FICTION. Fiction published in a magazine in installments, often broken off at a suspenseful spot.

SERIAL RIGHTS. The right for a newspaper or magazine to publish sections of a manuscript.

SHORT-SHORT. A complete short story of 1,500 words.

SIDEBAR. A feature presented as a companion to a straight news report (or main magazine article) giving sidelights on human-interest aspects or sometimes elucidating just one aspect of the story.

SIMULTANEOUS SUBMISSIONS. Sending the same article, story or poem to several publishers at the same time. Some publishers refuse to consider such submissions.

SLANT. The approach or style of a story or article that will appeal to readers of a specific magazine.

SLICE-OF-LIFE VIGNETTE. A short fiction piece intended to realistically depict an interesting moment of everyday living.

SLUSH PILE. The stack of unsolicited or misdirected manuscripts received by an editor or book publisher.

SOCIAL NETWORKS. Websites that connect users: sometimes generally, other times around specific interests. Four popular ones at the moment are Facebook, Twitter, Instagram and LinkedIn.

SUBAGENT. An agent handling certain subsidiary rights, usually working in conjuction with the agent who handled the book rights. The percentage paid the book agent is increased to pay the subagent.

SUBSIDIARY RIGHTS. All rights other than book publishing rights included in a book publishing contract, such as paperback rights, book club rights and movie rights. Part of an agent's job is to negotiate those rights and advise you on which to sell and which to keep.

SUBSIDY PUBLISHER. A book publisher who charges the author for the cost to typeset and print his book, the jacket, etc., as opposed to a royalty publisher who pays the author.

SYNOPSIS. A brief summary of a story, novel or play. As part of a book proposal, it is a comprehensive summary condensed in a page or page and a half, single-spaced.

TABLOID. Newspaper format publication on about half the size of the regular newspaper page.

TEARSHEET. Page from a magazine or newspaper containing your printed story, article, poem or ad.

TOC. Table of Contents.

TRADE BOOK. Either a hardcover or softcover book; subject matter frequently concerns a special interest for a general audience; sold mainly in bookstores.

TRADE PAPERBACK. A soft-bound volume published and designed for the general public; available mainly in bookstores.

TRANSLATION RIGHTS. Sold to a foreign agent or foreign publisher.

UNSOLICITED MANUSCRIPT. A story, article, poem or book that an editor did not specifically ask to see.

YA. Young adult books

BOOK PUBLISHERS SUBJECT INDEX

///

FICTION

ADVENTURE

HORROR

HUMOR

MAINSTREAM

OCCULT

PICTURE BOOKS

TRANSLATION

WAR

WESTERN

YOUNG ADULT

NONFICTION

AGRICULTURE

DANCE

ECONOMICS

EDUCATION

HOBBIES

MARINE SUBJECTS

MEDICINE

LITERATURE

MEMOIRS

RELIGION

SCIENCE

YOUNG ADULT

GENERAL INDEX

C